2015 EDITION

Best Colleges

HOW TO ORDER: Additional copies of U.S.News & World Report's Best Colleges 2015 guidebook are available for purchase at www.usnews.com/college2015 or by calling (800) 836-6397.

To order custom reprints, please call (877) 652-5295 or email usnews@wrightsmedia.com.

For permission to republish articles, data or other content from this book, email permissions@usnews.com.

Copyright © 2014 by U.S.News & World Report L.P., 1050 Thomas Jefferson Street, N.W., Washington, D.C. 20007-3837, ISBN 978-1-931469-65-4. All rights reserved. Published by U.S.News & World Report L.P., Washington, D.C. Printed in the U.S.A. on mostly recycled paper.

Bryn Mawr College in Pennsylvania
BRETT ZIEGLER FOR USN&WR

Contents

⌕ Chapter One
Study the Schools

Chapter Two
Take a Road Trip

60
At Clemson in South Carolina

BRETT ZIEGLER FOR USN&WR

NORTHERN ARIZONA UNIVERSITY

Introducing
Personalized Learning

The First Competency-Based, Online Bachelor's Degrees Offered by a Public University

Designed for motivated adults, Northern Arizona University's competency-based Personalized Learning program makes earning a respected degree accessible and affordable with six months of unlimited online lessons for just $2,500.

- Fully Accredited
- Entirely Online
- 100% Self-Paced
- Remarkably Affordable

Download your free information kit:

nau.edu/personalized

66
James Madison University

BEST COLLEGES U.S.News *& WORLD REPORT* **RANKINGS** | **30th** *Edition*

Bonus Section

Online Programs

BRETT ZIEGLER FOR USN&WR

Find your place in the world

Academically rigorous. Amazingly affordable. Truly global.

With more than 170 undergraduate and graduate programs, Queens College opens doors to careers in the arts & humanities, business, education, the sciences, and social sciences.

- An accessible, award-winning faculty dedicated to scholarship and research

- Ranked eighth among Top Public Regional Universities in the North by *U.S. News & World Report's Best Colleges* 2014

- A beautiful, green 80-acre campus in the world's most exciting city

www.qc.cuny.edu

152

Eric Tims is attending
Bowdoin College
in Maine

Chapter Four
NEWS YOU CAN USE

🔒 Getting In

Chapter Five
NEWS YOU CAN USE

💲 Finding the Money

BRETT ZIEGLER FOR USN&WR

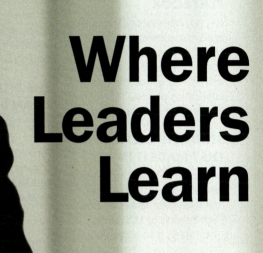

Where Leaders Learn

Annick Routhier-Labadie
Rhodes Scholar
Seton Hall Class of 2007

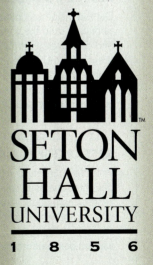

SETON
HALL
UNIVERSITY
1 8 5 6

www.shu.edu

@usnews.com

BEST COLLEGES
U.S.News
& WORLD REPORT
2015

GETTING IN

COLLEGE ADMISSIONS PLAYBOOK

Get tips from Varsity Tutors, an academic tutoring and test prep provider. This blog offers advice on mastering the SAT and ACT as well as the college application process.

usnews.com/collegeplaybook

STUDENTS ON HOW THEY MADE IT IN

Seniors from high schools across the country – including several that have been ranked as Best High Schools by U.S. News – talk about their admissions experiences and offer advice to students getting ready to apply to college.

usnews.com/studentprofiles

COLLEGE VISITS

TAKE A ROAD TRIP

We've gone on numerous trips to visit campuses in case you can't. Check out our compendium of more than 20 different trips to 90-plus schools.

usnews.com/roadtrips

RANKINGS INSIGHT

MORSE CODE BLOG

Get the inside scoop on the rankings – and the commentary and controversy surrounding them – from U.S. News' Bob Morse, the mastermind behind our education rankings projects.

usnews.com/morsecode

PAYING FOR COLLEGE

RESEARCHING AID

Visit our guide to all your possible sources of college funds. Learn about your savings options and which schools meet students' full need.

usnews.com/payforcollege

SCHOLARSHIP COACH

Get the latest advice from Scholarship America bloggers on how to find great scholarships, apply for them successfully and more.

usnews.com/scholarshipcoach

THE STUDENT LOAN RANGER

Don't fall into the trap of taking on too much debt. Bloggers from American Student Assistance provide guidance if you must turn to loans to pay for college.

usnews.com/studentloanranger

IN-DEPTH DATA

COLLEGE COMPASS

Gain access to the U.S. News College Compass, which offers comprehensive searchable data and tools for high school students starting down the path to campus. To get a 25 percent discount, subscribe at:

usnews.com/compassoffer

DISTANCE LEARNING

ONLINE EDUCATION

Do you need to balance school with work or other obligations? Consult our rankings of the best online degree programs for leads on how to get your diploma without leaving home.

usnews.com/online

FOR SCHOOLS ONLY

ACADEMIC INSIGHTS

U.S. News Academic Insights is an analytics dashboard intended for use by institutions that comprises all of the undergraduate and graduate historical rankings data we've collected. The dashboard allows for peer group comparisons and includes easy-to-understand visualizations.

ai.usnews.com

Executive Committee Chairman and Editor-in-Chief Mortimer B. Zuckerman
Editor and Chief Content Officer Brian Kelly
Executive Editors Margaret Mannix, Tim Smart

BEST COLLEGES

Managing Editor Anne McGrath
Chief Data Strategist Robert J. Morse
Director of Data Projects Diane Tolis
Senior Data Analyst Samuel Flanigan
Art Director Rebecca Pajak
Director of Photography Avijit Gupta
Photography Editor Brett Ziegler
Designer Michelle Rock
News Editor Elizabeth Whitehead
Contributors Cathie Gandel, Christopher J. Gearon, Katherine Hobson, Beth Howard, Ned Johnson, Darcy Lewis, Margaret Loftus, Michael Morella, Courtney Rubin, Arlene Weintraub
Research Manager Myke Freeman
Directory Janie S. Price

USNEWS.COM/EDUCATION
Vice President, Education Chris DiCosmo
Education Editor Anita Narayan
Assistant Education Editor Allison Gualtieri
Reporters/Writers Devon Haynie, Alexandra Pannoni, Delece Smith-Barrow, Susannah Snider
Web Producers Briana Boyington, Travis Mitchell
Product/Project Managers Matthew Monks, Erica Ryan

ACADEMIC INSIGHTS
Director Evan Jones
Account Manager Cale Gosnell
Product Marketing Specialist Taylor Suggs

INFORMATION SERVICES
Vice President, Data and Information Strategy Stephanie Salmon
Data Analysts Eric Brooks, Melinda Foster, Matthew Mason
Data Collection Geneva Dampare, Alexandra Harris, Catherine Piacente

INFORMATION TECHNOLOGY
Vice President, Information Technology Yingjie Shu
Director of Engineering Matt Kupferman
Senior Systems Manager Cathy Cacho
Primary Developers Bethany Morin, José Velazquez, Brian Stewart, Kate Burgett, Will Ferguson, Max McBride, Alan Weinstein
Digital Production Michael A. Brooks, Manager; Michael Fingerhuth

President and Chief Executive Officer William Holiber

ADVERTISING
Publisher and Chief Advertising Officer Kerry Dyer
National Sales Director Ed Hannigan
Director of Strategy and Sales Planning Alexandra Kalaf
Marketing Director Mary Catherine Bain
Health Care Manager Colin Hamilton
Senior Account Executives Steve Hiel, Heather Levine, Shannon Tkach
Corporate Advocacy Manager Fred Kuhn
Director of Event Sales Peter Bowes
Account Executives Gregg Barton, Laura Gabriel, Courtney Ramsdell, Christine Savino
Senior Manager, Sales Strategy Joe Hayden
Digital Strategy Manager Rachel Wulfow
Account Managers Katie Harper, Dana Jelen, Ivy Zenati
Sales Planners Rachel Halasz, Michael Machado, Melissa Tacchi
Sales Development Coordinator Kelly Cohen
Marketing Coordinator Riki Smolen
Executive Assistant to the President Judy David
Executive Assistant to the Publisher Anny Lasso
Sales Administration Coordinator Carmen Caraballo

ADVERTISING OPERATIONS
Director of Advertising Services Phyllis A. Panza
Senior Advertising Operations Manager Cory Nesser
Advertising Operations Manager Clay Lynch
Advertising Operations Coordinator Karolee Jarnecki

Vice President, Manufacturing and Specialty Marketing Mark W. White
Director of Specialty Marketing Abbe Weintraub

Chief Financial Officer Thomas H. Peck
Senior Vice President, Operations Karen S. Chevalier
Senior Vice President, Strategic Development and General Counsel Peter Dwoskin
Senior Vice President, Human Resources Jeff Zomper
Vice President, Finance Neil Maheshwari

Additional copies of the 2015 edition of **U.S.News & World Report's Best Colleges** guidebook are available for purchase at (800) 836-6397 or online at usnews.com/college2015. To order custom reprints, please call (877) 652-5295 or email usnews@wrightsmedia.com. For all other permissions, email permissions@usnews.com.

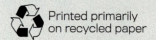

Printed primarily on recycled paper

The Jesuits were brave enough to shape our city.

Our students are bold enough to create A BETTER WORLD.

This is at the very heart of what it means to receive a Jesuit education at Loyola.

Please visit apply.loyno.edu or call us at 1.800.4.LOYOLA.

LOYOLA
UNIVERSITY
NEW ORLEANS

Helping students take the next step toward college

$670,000 in Scholarships

10 $25,000 National Winners

42 $10,000 State Winners

$24 million awarded to more than **5,600** students

ONLINE APPLICATION
Deadline to apply: December 15, 2014

Follow us

Are you active in your community? Have you led or initiated a project that benefits others? Have you overcome personal challenges or difficulties to achieve your goals?

If the answer to any of these questions is **"Yes"** then you **may already be an AXA Achiever.**

Find out what it takes to win an **AXA Achievement℠ Scholarship.** If you're headed for college, you could be one of 52 high school seniors nationwide who qualify.

To learn more and apply, visit
www.axa-achievement.com

AXA Achievement℠ The Official Scholarship of the U.S. News America's Best Colleges Guidebook

The AXA Achievement℠ Scholarship, in association with U.S. News & World Report, is a program of AXA Achievement – a philanthropic program dedicated to providing resources that help make college possible through access and advice. AXA Achievement is funded by the AXA Foundation, the philanthropic arm of AXA Equitable.

Paying for college is one of the biggest risks families face – AXA Achievement℠ can help.

TAB STICKERS

Use these stickers to tab your college choices inside this issue.

Next steps toward college

Taking the right small steps today can help eliminate the risk of not being able to afford a college education

Filling out the FAFSA helps you minimize borrowing. It's a misconception that filling out the Free Application for Federal Student Aid (FAFSA) is the fast track to student loan debt. You risk losing need-based grants and scholarships from the university. The reason? The universities you selected on the FAFSA to receive your information use it to evaluate your financial aid eligibility.

To avoid losing need-based aid for which you are eligible:

1. Fill out the FAFSA as early as possible. Some need-based aid is limited in numbers and available on a first come first serve basis for those who qualify. For instance, a university could have a limited amount of grant aid. Applying late could cost you that money.

2. Select schools. Always select schools that are being considered on the form. Otherwise, the information won't arrive to the colleges who need it. Amend the FAFSA form online if school choices change.

3. Fill out the special circumstances forms when needed. Whether you're applying for next year or are already in college, you need to fill out a special circumstances form if your income changes due to a number of reasons including a medical situation, a layoff, or a salary reduction.

4. Practice filling out the FAFSA on the FAFSA4caster site from the department of education as early as middle school. It's designed to roughly estimate financial aid years in advance.

5. Teens should follow up with schools to make sure information is received and to check on financial aid availability. Bonus: you may find out about a scholarship you previously didn't know about during the phone call.

Choosing universities with the lowest listed tuition prices sometimes can cost you more money. A private school with a "sticker price" that is four times more than that of a state school may offer scholarships and grants that make it the cheaper alternative. How do you find out which schools offer the best financial aid packages before applying for college? Net price calculators available on most college websites are one way to estimate what you would pay based on individual circumstances.

To better understand the relative costs of higher education:

1. Narrow college choices down to ten by factors such as majors, campus size and internship placement. Teens should visit with their high school counselor to start the process of college selection and career exploration.

2. Students should request information from each school on what's important to them. For instance, they can and should call the career center to ask about graduate employment rates.

3. Visit the websites of your top 10 college choices and enter information such as family income and number of children in college. To find the net price calculator on a university website, enter net price calculator into the search box on the school's homepage.

4. Call financial aid offices at the top 5 choices to see if there are any changes in grant awards for the year the student will be attending. Available funds change, so you want to make sure you factor in the most recent information into your family's application decisions.

5. Use the Net price calculator as a baseline. Teens could also qualify for merit-based educational assistance.

To learn more and apply, visit www.axa-achievement.com

AXA Achievement℠ is proud to partner with Scholarship America®, one of the nation's largest nonprofit private sector scholarship and educational support organizations. This program is administered by Scholarship Management Services℠, a program of Scholarship America. www.scholarshipamerica.org.

"AXA Achievement℠" is a service mark of the AXA Foundation. The "AXA Achievement℠ Scholarship" program is not associated with the National Merit Scholarship Corporation's "Achievement Scholarship®" program.

By **BRIAN KELLY** *and* **ROBERT J. MORSE**

Brian Kelly
*Editor and Chief
Content Officer*

Robert J. Morse
Chief Data Strategist

This college search thing can be a little intimidating, especially if you're going through it for the first time. This is our 30th go-round at U.S. News, so we feel like we've got some experience worth sharing.

We're proud of the fact that the U.S. News Best Colleges rankings have now been published 30 times, starting in 1983. Over the years, we've improved our information and sharpened our focus, with our primary objective being to help students and their parents make one of life's major decisions. There was a big void in that kind of information when we started this project. Colleges, like a lot of institutions, are not always eager to share facts, especially when doing so opens them up to comparisons with their competitors. In the early days, many schools did not want to cooperate with us. Some education experts said we were making the college evaluation process too simple. We disagreed, and the positive response from our readers assured us that we were on the right track. We've played a key role in the years since in making all college information more standard, more reliable, and more useful.

U.S. News started the rankings for the same reason we do them today: A college education is one of the most important – and most costly – investments that people ever make. Prospective students and their parents need objective measures that allow them

to evaluate and compare schools; the rankings are one tool to help them make choices. This perspective is more relevant than ever with some private colleges now costing around $250,000 for a bachelor's degree. At the same time, many public high schools have greatly reduced their college counseling resources, leaving students and parents to educate themselves about the admission process.

Of course, we have changed our ranking methodology formula over the years to reflect changes in the world of higher education. We make it clear that we are not doing peer reviewed social science research, though we do maintain very high survey and data standards. We have always been open and transparent. We have always said that the rankings are evolving and not perfect. The first were based solely on schools' academic reputation among leaders at peer institutions; in the late

1980s, we developed a ranking methodology in which reputation accounted for 25 percent of a school's score and important quantitative measures such as graduation and retention rates, average class size and student-faculty ratios, for 75 percent. Over time, we have shifted weight from inputs (indicators of the quality of students and resources) to outputs (success in graduating students). We operate under this guiding principle: The methodology is altered only if a change will better help our readers and web audience compare schools as they're making decisions about where to apply and enroll.

It has helped us a great deal to have these principles to focus on as we have faced the inevitable and continuous criticisms from academia about our rankings and their growing influence. One main critique remains: that it is impossible to reduce the complexities

of any given college's offerings and attributes to one rank number. Indeed, it's important to keep in mind that our information is a starting point. The next steps in a college search should include detailed research on a smaller list of choices, campus visits and conversations with students, faculty and alumni wherever you can find them. This feedback from academia has helped improve the rankings over time. We constantly meet with our critics, listen to their points of view, debate them on the merits of what we do and make appropriate changes.

U.S. News is keenly aware that the higher education community is also a major audience for and consumer of our rankings. We understand how seriously academics, college presidents, top administrators, trustees and governing boards take our rankings and data. They study, analyze and use them in various ways, including benchmarking against peers, alumni fundraising and advertising to attract students.

A trusted source. What does all of this mean in today's global information marketplace? U.S. News has become a trusted, respected, unbiased source that higher education administrators and policymakers and the collegebound public in the U.S. and worldwide turn to for reliable guidance. In the process of helping consumers, U.S. News provides colleges a great deal of free exposure to potential applicants; our Internet traffic for education nears 10 mil-

Students hit the books, and their laptops, at Drexel University in Philadelphia.

lion visitors a month, with more than 10 percent coming from foreign countries. U.S. News is on balance helping, not hurting, colleges. And the Best Colleges rankings are a part of the still-evolving higher education accountability movement. Universities are increasingly being held responsible for their educational policies, how their funds are spent, the level of student engagement and how much graduates have learned. The U.S. News rankings have become the annual public benchmark to measure the academic performance of the country's colleges and universities.

We know our role has limits. The rankings should only be used as one factor in the college search process and not as the sole basis upon which to choose one school over another. We've long said that there is no single "best college." There is only the best college for you or, more likely, a handful of schools that make sense, one of which will turn out to be the right fit. Besides the rankings, we can help collegebound high school students and their parents with a great deal of information on all aspects of the application process, from getting in to getting financial aid. Our website, usnews.com, has thousands of pages of rankings, research, sortable data, photos, videos and a personalized tool called College Compass.

We've been doing this for 30 years, so we know the process is not simple. But our experience tells us the hard work is worth it in the end. ●

BRETT ZIEGLER FOR USN&WR

THE CURE FOR CANCER MAY HAVE BEEN IN OUR LAPS THIS WHOLE TIME.

The search to find a cure for cancer has spanned decades in hospitals and research labs all over the globe. But at Texas A&M University, we're looking for a cure in a brand-new place: man's best friend. As one of the leading veterinary schools in the country, we know all too well about treating animals with cancer. And what we have discovered is that dogs experience this disease much like humans do. So as we treat these dogs for cancer, we are working to develop new therapies that could also work on us. Today the world faces countless challenges, but we don't hesitate. At Texas A&M, we step up.

To see more, visit tamu.edu.

Study

the Schools

Viewing books from the
Italian Renaissance, at the
University of Pennsylvania

BRETT ZIEGLER FOR USN&WR

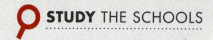

YOUR GOAL:

Four Fabulous Years

AS YOU SEARCH FOR A GOOD FIT, LOOK FOR PROGRAMS THAT AIM TO ENGAGE AND BOND STUDENTS

By **CHRISTOPHER J. GEARON**

Consider this shocking stat as you shop for a college: Fully one-third of freshmen don't return for sophomore year. And only 61 percent of undergraduates get a degree within six years.

So your guidance counselor isn't kidding when she says your job is to find the right college, one that's a great fit for you. Not your parents, not your friends – you. But you also might want to check out what each of your

Service learning

A University of Maryland–Baltimore County summer education practicum includes service experience in a local school. Students also meet to discuss what they're learning; below, they hear from psych major Monique Brewer.

BRETT ZIEGLER FOR USN&WR

schools of interest is doing to make itself "sticky." The goal "is to get students connected," says Martha McCaughey, a sociology professor and faculty coordinator of the required first-year seminar at Appalachian State University in North Carolina. The semesterlong discussion-based class pairs small groups of freshmen with faculty members teaching a topic they are passionate about.

"It boosted my excitement to learn more," says Eguono Akpoduado, a 2014 graduate in psychology from Raleigh who picked a course that explored the science, psychology and philosophy of consciousness from among 100-plus topics. The seminar format emphasizes communication and writing skills and introduces students to research tools and methods they'll need to be successful scholars. ASU's first-year retention rate is 88 percent.

The reasons students drop out or transfer run the gamut, of course – from family issues and money problems to loneliness and academic struggles. Some can't be overcome. But research has made it pretty clear that creating bonds "both academically and socially" is key to success in college, says Alexander McCormick, director of the annual National Survey

6
Fully ONE-THIRD of freshmen DON'T RETURN for sophomore year.'

of Student Engagement and associate professor in the department of education leadership and policy studies at Indiana University–Bloomington. Schools of all types are adding "high-impact practices" shown to get students pumped up about their studies and help them connect with peers and professors, from service-learning classes that incorporate volunteer work to internships to undergraduate research (Page 26). These practices, along with a move to make advising "intrusive" (read: unavoidable), are worth looking for in your college search.

Last year's NSSE survey of nearly 335,000 freshmen and seniors at 568 schools, designed to find out if students are getting the learning experiences that research shows matter, revealed that freshmen who participated in at least one high-impact practice were more satisfied with their college experience and more likely to say they'd choose the same school again. Better yet, "experience at least two," McCormick says, one when you're a freshman and one in your major.

Retention and graduation rates certainly merit comparison. Columbia University, the University of Chicago and Yale University can

Close community
A dorm room on Elon's living-learning arts floor

KIM WALKER – ELON UNIVERSITY

Just in case you've been looking for us,

We've added some *new* addresses recently.

Prato, Italy
A new campus nested serenely in the cradle of the Renaissance

Old Lyme, CT
A fine-arts College that adds a new dimension to our art program

Orange, CT
A new corporate-style graduate campus for the College of Business

San Francisco, CA
A whole new approach to training engineers for the 21st century

Ras Laffan, Qatar
Fire Science Engineering in one of the most rapidly growing economies in the world

 University of New Haven

300 Boston Post Road | West Haven, CT 06516 | admissions@newhaven.edu | **www.newhaven.edu/growth**

all boast that 99 percent of their first-year students come back, and all but a few of them graduate. But the rates at many places run much lower. "More than half our students aren't ready for college and only half our students graduate within six years," says Ken O'Donnell, senior director of student engagement and academic initiatives and partnerships for the California State University System, where retention rates range from 92 percent at California Polytechnic State University–San Luis Obispo to 71 percent at Cal State–Bakersfield. The 23-school system is raising its investment in high-impact practices by 40 percent this school year, to $12 million.

If schools on your shortlist have a low freshman retention or graduation rate, it's smart to ask the admissions office why. And ask for details about programs aimed at bringing the rates up. Many schools can say they've added these practices, but "the quality varies a lot," cautions Debra Humphreys, vice president for policy and public engagement at the Association of American Colleges and Universities.

The homesickness and rocky adjustment to college-level work many freshmen face can be eased by "first-year experiences" like the seminars at ASU and others that regularly mix small groups of students and faculty to engage in critical inquiry, writing and collaborative learning. Some institutions, including Ohio State, Syracuse University in New York, Elon University in North Carolina and Vanderbilt in Tennessee, emphasize "learning communities" for freshmen (older students, too), in which groups of students who share an interest take two or more linked classes together and get to know one another and their professors well. The idea: to keep the discussions going after class ends.

Living and learning together

Many of these schools stretch the concept into "living-learning communities," so that classmates who study together live together, too, and those conversations can carry over into the dorm. The University of Maryland offers 25 to 30 such residential options, for example, focused around themes ranging from social change to globalization and women in engineering; about half of the 4,000 freshmen join one. Members live on the same floor or in the same dorm for their first two years. The communities provide themed experiences (the global issues community might take a field trip to the World Bank or an embassy in

INSIDE SCOOP

DEBRA SHAVER
Dean of Admission, Smith College

WHY CONSIDER A WOMEN'S COLLEGE?

There are incredible role models at women's colleges. At Smith, over half the faculty are women, and every leadership position is filled by a woman. Leadership becomes a habit at a women's college. This is an unbelievable network of women invested in other women and in their success in all sorts of ways. The bonds among graduates, I think, are really strong in terms of making sure that their sisters have every opportunity in career paths or life paths.

nearby Washington, D.C., for example, or hold a session on international internships), and students take a class related to the theme each semester.

"We bonded almost immediately," says Beena Raghavendran, a Maryland Honors College senior from Mason, Ohio, double-majoring in journalism and government and politics. She chose the "Design, Cultures and Creativity" community, an interdisciplinary program focused on exploring the digital world and emerging technologies. Maryland boasts nearly a 95 percent retention rate, while 97 percent of those in the Honors College return.

Building community service into the coursework is another method a whole range of schools, including Brown University in Rhode Island, the University of Michigan and James Madison University in Virginia, are using to engage students. A sociology class might operate a food pantry, for example; an architecture class might design a green community center. By supplementing material covered in class with a team effort to actually solve problems in the community, service-learning courses help make "what's happening in the textbooks come alive," says Richard Guarasci, president of Wagner College in New York City, a liberal arts school considered a leader in the practice.

The class discussion, in turn, adds meaning to the fieldwork. University of Maryland–Baltimore County senior Monique Brewer is a psychology and education major who took a service-learning practicum over the summer that involved assisting at a local elementary school with enrichment activities in reading and other subjects. The meetings of practicum members, she notes, offered them all the chance to "actively reflect on their service" and better "guide their own learning."

Wagner College tees up service learning from the get-go, combining it with first-year learning communities. Students choose a community and take courses that combine two seemingly disparate topics, such as introductory environmental biology and introductory economics, and consider them in an integrated manner – focusing on environmental sustainability, for example. The service component for that class gets students interacting with families and local officials and chemical company representatives in an area impacted by high cancer rates, researching how to improve community health, developing policy papers and taking ideas to members of Congress.

"I fell in love with the community and fell in love with teaching English and Spanish," says Kellie Griffith, a 2014

JIM GIPE

World Renowned, Nationally Ranked

At the University of Memphis, Real-World Experience Is…Real.

Memphis has a way of changing the world. Whether it's the birth of rock 'n' roll, the advent of overnight package delivery at FedEx® or the lifesaving treatments continually being developed at St. Jude Children's Research Hospital, Memphis is a place where innovation thrives.

The University of Memphis is part of that innovation. We offer several programs that are nationally ranked by *U.S. News & World Report*, including one of the nation's most successful internship programs.

Our faculty, students and alumni are known as *Dreamers. Thinkers. Doers.*, and they're changing the world every single day.

U.S. News & World Report has ranked the University of Memphis nationally for the following:

- Internship Programs — Ranked Top 10 for percentage of students with internships (Feb. 2013)

- Online MBA Programs for Veterans — #24

- Elementary and Secondary Education: NCTQ Teacher Prep Honor Roll — Ranked #27 and #28 out of 800

- Audiology — #12

- Speech-Language Pathology — #15

- Rehabilitation Counseling — #17

us.memphis.edu

A Tennessee Board of Regents Institution · An Equal Opportunity/Affirmative Action University

THE UNIVERSITY OF **MEMPHIS**®

Dreamers. Thinkers. Doers.

Wagner grad from Long Island who spent time working in the Port Richmond community near campus. As part of her first-year learning community combining courses in Spanish and philosophy, she studied contemporary moral ethics and wrestled with immigration issues in class, then saw firsthand how existing policies affect the lives of area immigrants by volunteering at an immigrant advocacy center.

Academic frustration can certainly derail the best-laid plans, so many schools are greatly strengthening their advisory systems and revamping remedial education. It's become common for faculty members teaching first-year seminars to also take on advisory duties for students in the class, for example. At Arizona State, eAdvisor, an online system, maps the route to a degree and sends out an alert if a student loses his or her way. Challenging core classes

At Wagner. Kellie Griffith's first-year experience involved volunteering at an immigrant center.

are required sooner rather than later – an electrical engineering major must take calculus in the first term, for example – to minimize the odds of changing majors too late to finish college on time. Anyone who gets off track for any reason can't enroll for classes before meeting with his or her adviser, who also gets an alert to meet with the student.

Traditional remedial programs, which require noncredit refresher work in the basics before allowing on-level classes, are in some cases being replaced with "corequisite" remediation that provides extra instruction along with the regular coursework. At Austin Peay State University in Tennessee, for example, enhanced sections of college-level algebra have been subbed for two remedial courses. One-time remedial students enroll in a regular course, along with a linked workshop that provides added instruction on key concepts and in areas of weakness flagged by an initial assessment. Students are succeeding at twice the rate of peers in traditional remedial courses. "It can be as simple as math that takes place five

times a week instead of three," says Tom Sugar, senior vice president of Complete College America, which advocates corequisite remediation as one way to boost college completion and close attainment gaps. Another innovation: Summer bridge programs that include four to six weeks of intensive coursework and tutoring, and give incoming students the added boost of a comfort level with dorm life and some friendships.

Beyond the first year

Practices that benefit older students, both because they make the educational experience more interesting and because they burnish the bona fides needed to land a job, include study abroad, the opportunity to conduct undergraduate research, an internship program and a capstone program that asks students to integrate and apply what they've learned in a culminating project. It was "a stressful process at times, but 100 percent worth it," says Zoë Zwegat, a 2014 grad of the College of Wooster in anthropology, of her project: a 100-plus page thesis on historical Japanese woodblock prints and their impact on gender roles and national identity.

The Ohio college requires all students to seal their undergrad careers with Independent Study at Wooster, which carries through all of senior year and includes weekly advising sessions with a faculty mentor. President Grant Cornwell thinks the program has a lot to do with the fact that more than 90 percent of Wooster grads get a job or go on for more education within six months of graduation. Clemson University in South Carolina, Portland State University in Oregon and Princeton University in New Jersey are a few other schools with capstone programs.

For many students, of course, it's a budget crisis that throws them off track. Cord Speck, who just completed his bachelor's in exercise science at Georgia State, thought last summer that he might not make it, since money was tight. But then the school gave him $2,000, which "helped out big time." Georgia State had been dropping 1,000-plus students for nonpayment each semester, including many seniors. "We realized that in many cases the balances they owed were less than $300," says Vice Provost Timothy Renick. "They just needed a helping hand to cover the gap."

In 2011, officials began calling students minutes after they'd been dropped from a class to let them know that the gap in funding had been covered. Last year, the school awarded 2,600 Panther Retention Grants averaging about $900 each. And some 700 students collected a diploma who otherwise would have missed graduation. ●

FEEL RIGHT AT HOME

RICHMOND
THE AMERICAN INTERNATIONAL
UNIVERSITY
IN LONDON

DISCOVER SOMETHING TYPICALLY AMERICAN IN A VERY BRITISH SETTING

The American Liberal Arts Curriculum of Richmond, the American International University in London

Wide range of merit scholarships and need-based grants available

Degrees accredited in the US and validated in the UK

Small class sizes taught by faculty

Students of over 100 different nationalities

Campuses in two of the most exclusive areas of London

Internships in London and worldwide

t: 617 450 5617
e: usadmissions@richmond.ac.uk
www.richmond.ac.uk/choices

A Focus on Student

Some colleges and universities are much more determined than others to provide freshmen and all undergrads with the best possible educational experience, recognizing that certain enriched offerings, from learning communities and internships to study abroad and senior capstone projects, are linked to student success. Here, U.S. News highlights schools with outstanding examples of eight programs that education experts, including staff members of the Association of American Colleges and Universities, agree are key.

College presidents, chief academic officers and deans of admissions were invited in the spring of 2014 to nominate up to 10 institutions with stellar examples of each, from a list of all bachelor's-granting regionally accredited colleges. Schools that were named the most times in each area are listed in alphabetical order.

(*Public)

First-Year Experience

Orientation can go only so far in making freshmen feel connected. Many schools now build into the curriculum first-year seminars or other academic programs that bring small groups of students together with faculty or staff on a regular basis.

Alverno College (WI)
Appalachian State University (NC)*
Butler University (IN)
Columbia University (NY)
Elon University (NC)
Evergreen State College (WA)*
Indiana U.-Purdue U.-Indianapolis*
Ohio State University-Columbus*
Stanford University (CA)
Univ. of Maryland-College Park*
University of Michigan-Ann Arbor*
U. of North Carolina-Chapel Hill*
Univ. of South Carolina*
University of Virginia*
Wagner College (NY)

Internships

Schools nominated in this category require or encourage students to apply what they're learning in the classroom to work in the real world through closely supervised internships or practicums, or through cooperative education, in which one period of study typically alternates with one of work.

Belmont University (TN)
Berea College (KY)

Butler University (IN)
Cornell University (NY)
Drexel University (PA)
Elon University (NC)
Georgia Institute of Technology*
Northeastern University (MA)
Purdue Univ.-West Lafayette (IN)*
Rochester Inst. of Technology (NY)
University of Cincinnati*
Univ. of Southern California
Wagner College (NY)

Learning Communities

In these communities, students typically take two or more linked courses as a group and get to know one another and their professors well. Some learning communities are also residential.

Elon University (NC)
Evergreen State College (WA)*
Indiana U.-Purdue U.-Indianapolis*
Ohio State University-Columbus*
Syracuse University (NY)
Univ. of Maryland-College Park*
University of Michigan-Ann Arbor*
Univ. of Missouri*
Univ. of South Carolina*
Univ. of Wisconsin-Madison*
Wagner College (NY)
Yale University (CT)

Senior Capstone

Whether they're called a senior capstone or go by some other name, these culminating experiences ask students nearing the end of their college years to create a project that integrates and

synthesizes what they've learned. The project might be a thesis, a performance or an exhibit of artwork.

Brown University (RI)
Carleton College (MN)
College of Wooster (OH)
Elon University (NC)
Kalamazoo College (MI)
Northeastern University (MA)
Portland State University (OR)*
Princeton University (NJ)
Stanford University (CA)
Yale University (CT)

Service Learning

Required (or for-credit) volunteer work in the community is an instructional strategy in these programs. What's learned in the field bolsters what happens in class, and vice versa.

Berea College (KY)
Brown University (RI)
Butler University (IN)
College of the Ozarks (MO)
Duke University (NC)
Elon University (NC)
Georgetown University (DC)
James Madison University (VA)*
John Carroll University (OH)
Loyola University Maryland
Michigan State University*
Northeastern University (MA)
Portland State University (OR)*
Stanford University (CA)
Tulane University (LA)
University of Michigan-Ann Arbor*
U. of North Carolina-Chapel Hill*
University of Pennsylvania

Success

Wagner College (NY)
Warren Wilson College (NC)

Study Abroad

Programs at these schools involve substantial academic work abroad for credit – a year, a semester or an intensive experience equal to a course – and considerable interaction with the local culture.

American University (DC)
Arcadia University (PA)
Beloit College (WI)
Boston University
Butler University (IN)
Carleton College (MN)
Centre College (KY)
College of St. Benedict (MN)
Dartmouth College (NH)
Dickinson College (PA)
Elon University (NC)
Goucher College (MD)
Kalamazoo College (MI)
Lee University (TN)
Lewis & Clark College (OR)
Macalester College (MN)
Michigan State University*
Middlebury College (VT)

New York University
Northeastern University (MA)
Oberlin College (OH)
Stanford University (CA)
St. John's University (MN)
St. Olaf College (MN)
Syracuse University (NY)
University of Chicago
University of Evansville (IN)
Univ. of Minnesota-Twin Cities*
University of Texas-Austin*
Webster University (MO)

Undergraduate Research/Creative Projects

Independently or in small teams, and mentored by a faculty member, students do intensive and self-directed research or creative work that results in an original scholarly paper or product that can be formally presented on or off campus.

Butler University (IN)
California Institute of Technology
Calvin College (MI)
Carleton College (MN)
Carnegie Mellon University (PA)

College of Wooster (OH)
Creighton University (NE)
Dartmouth College (NH)
Duke University (NC)
Elon University (NC)
Furman University (SC)
Grinnell College (IA)
Harvard University (MA)
Hope College (MI)
James Madison University (VA)*
Johns Hopkins University (MD)
Massachusetts Inst. of Technology
Oberlin College (OH)
Ohio State University-Columbus*
Princeton University (NJ)
Rice University (TX)
Stanford University (CA)
Trinity University (TX)
Truman State University (MO)*
University of California-Berkeley*
Univ. of California-Los Angeles*
Univ. of Maryland-Baltimore County*
University of Michigan-Ann Arbor*
U. of North Carolina-Chapel Hill*
University of Washington*
Williams College (MA)
Yale University (CT)

Writing in the Disciplines

These colleges typically make writing a priority at all levels of instruction and across the curriculum. Students are encouraged to produce and refine various forms of writing for a range of audiences in different disciplines.

Brown University (RI)
Carleton College (MN)
Clemson University (SC)*
Cornell University (NY)
Duke University (NC)
George Mason University (VA)*
Hamilton College (NY)
Harvard University (MA)
Princeton University (NJ)
University of California-Davis*
Washington State University*

BRETT ZIEGLER FOR USN&WR

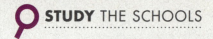
Companies Come to Class

EMPLOYERS IN NEED OF SKILLED HIGH-TECH HIRES ARE TEAMING UP WITH COLLEGES TO TRAIN THEM

By **CATHIE GANDEL**

Tom Hubschman adjusts his safety glasses as sparks fly from the computer-controlled plasma torch slicing through a piece of metal. This spring day, the Boston University mechanical engineering major from Andover, Massachusetts, is working on his senior design project in the school's high-tech Engineering Product Innovation Center. At his disposal are hardware and software for computer-assisted design and 3D prototyping, a machine shop, an automated robotic manufacturing line, a metals foundry and a carpentry shop. These riches are the result of a collaboration with four big partners – General Electric Aviation, Schlumberger, Procter & Gamble and technology company PTC – plus a substantial investment by the university.

Any BU student interested in taking a product from design to manufacturing is welcome at 9-month-old EPIC, although the chief beneficiaries are the future engineers. These days, having access to cutting-edge technologies while in college can lower the odds of making costly and time-consuming mistakes later – when the task is to design parts for a jet engine, for example – and thus be a big advantage in the job search. For engineers in training, "EPIC is a savior," Hubschman says. "They can say, 'Oh yes, I know that machine, and not from a book. I've worked with it. I've had my hands on it.'"

Businesses expect to reap the rewards in the form of experienced hires. Employers are struggling to find talent in engineering, data analytics, cybersecurity, health care and environmental sciences; a recent Gallup poll reported that only about 1 in 10 business leaders "strongly agree" that American higher education is graduating students with the competencies necessary in their workforce. "Industry is not getting either the quality or quantity of employees they need," says Anthony P. Carnevale, director of Georgetown University's Center on Education and the Workforce. "So they are having to get involved. It's a new era."

What does this new era look like? Besides EPIC's four principal partners, companies like Stanley Black and Decker and GibbsCAM have donated money, equipment or software as well as expertise in the form of seminars, curriculum development and mentoring. Parsons, an engineering management firm in Pasadena, California, is providing scholarships to undergrads in a cybersecurity honors program at the University of Maryland–College Park. At schools like North Carolina State University in Raleigh and New York's Fordham University, IBM provides access to case study projects and analytics software to give business and computer science students experience with data mining, predictive analytics and interactive marketing. IBM data scientists also visit campus as guest lecturers.

A payoff in real-world practice

The hoped-for result: "What's going to come out of EPIC is that perfect mesh of highly motivated, very talented engineers who have had hands-on experience," predicts Greg Morris, head of the additive technologies group at GE Aviation in Cincinnati and a member of EPIC's Industrial Advisory Board. "And those students will be very attractive to companies like GE." Among them is Tom Hubschman, who upon graduation is joining the Lynn, Massachusetts, office of GE Aviation in an entry-level program that will rotate him through departments such as design, systems engineering and aircraft electrical systems.

For students, the payoff is in practical experience and contacts. Hubschman's design problem at the moment, for

ELLEN WEBBER FOR USN&WR

Tom Hubschman's senior project is a task for an energy company.

example, is hardly theoretical. He's working on a project for electronics firm Schneider Electric. "We're pretesting a new generation of HVAC controllers and will report back to Schneider where the failures are and how to improve the design," he says.

Many Fridays at the University of Tennessee-Knoxville, an executive from FedEx, JPMorgan Chase or the Kroger Co., among other companies, sits down with undergrads in the business analytics program. "The students have an opportunity to get up close and personal with someone who is using data analytics every day," says Frank Guess, a professor in the department. At industry partner Pershing, Yoakley & Associates Analytics in Knoxville, students hired as interns "work directly with clients at all levels of the analytics lifecycle," from project planning to selection of appropriate mathematical models to imple-

> STUDENTS CAN SAY, "OH, YES, I KNOW THAT MACHINE, AND NOT FROM A BOOK. I'VE WORKED WITH IT."

mentation and delivery, says Blair Christian, a data scientist at the firm who spends 30 percent of his time at the university teaching business analytics.

Students also benefit from one-on-one interaction with executives by acting as hosts when they come to speak on campus. "He became my mentor," says Camille Crumpton, a 2013 grad now getting her master's in business analytics at UT, of her pairing with an executive from American Express. She still talks to him when she needs advice.

Some of these developing partnerships take an especially local focus, which has long been the particular province of

COMMUNITY COLLEGES

Tricks of the Transfer

When a community college is the economical first step toward a bachelor's degree, an articulation agreement is often the key to getting to Step 2. These agreements, which spell out what it takes to transfer to four-year institutions in the same area, are often complicated and murky. Some states, including Florida, California, Massachusetts, Pennsylvania and Virginia, guarantee that anyone who earns an associate degree in the state will also earn admission as a junior to a state university. Many students are on their own, however. And they all too often find that courses do not transfer or will not apply toward a major, slowing down the march toward a degree and adding to its cost. The National Center for Education Statistics reported in 2011 that 37 percent of community college students plan to complete a bachelor's, but only 12 percent actually do.

"The ladder between two-year and four-year schools is often very weak," says Anthony P. Carnevale, director of Georgetown University's Center on Education and the Workforce. He advises anyone who plans to use community college as a steppingstone to a particular university to first find out from the four-year college which schools it has articulation agreements with. Ask, too, if other students have climbed that particular ladder. If the answer is "two in the last 10 years," go find another community college, Carnevale says.

The fine print. It's also vital to read any agreement carefully, says Anthony Ervin, an academic advisor in the Biomanufacturing Research Institute and Technology Enterprise program at North Carolina Central University in Durham. His advice: Don't assume anything – ask upfront. What classes will transfer for full credit? The content of the coursework needs to measure up. It's entirely possible, says Ervin, to take general chemistry in community college only to find that the class does not fulfill the general chemistry requirement at your chosen four-year school. And most public universities require a minimum grade of "C" to transfer credits. In 2012, the College Board's Initiative on Transfer Policy and Practice recommended that four-year colleges create more transparent transfer policies and establish a presence on the community college campus to help guide transfers.

Meantime, FinAid.org, a website that offers comprehensive information about financial aid, also lists articulation agreements by state. And many states have created their own websites that provide background on articulation agreements and the transfer process.

Some universities also publicize the information. At Central Michigan University's site, for example, you can see which courses meet its requirements both by community college and by degree program. Someone attending Henry Ford Community College in the biomedical sciences who wants to transfer to CMU later, for example, can see that Bio 251, a microbiology course, will count as CMU's Bio 208. If community college is a moneysaving move, such research upfront on a planned transfer is apt to be a worthwhile investment. –*C.G.*

MCGUIRE CENTER
FOR ENTREPRENEURSHIP
30 Years of Excellence in Entrepreneurship Education

One of the first

UNIVERSITY ENTREPRENEURSHIP CENTERS

in the world and still one of
the best.

entrepreneurship.eller.arizona.edu   mcguireexperience.com

community colleges. While more than one-third of community college students intend to transfer on for a bachelor's degree (box, Page 30), many are using these tailored programs to slip directly into their area's technical workforce. Since 2008, for example, Pacific Gas & Electric has worked closely with California community colleges to train workers for PG&E and other utility companies. Des Moines Area Community College in Iowa has teamed up with Accumold, a manufacturer of micromolded parts for cell phones and medical devices. Students learn everything from tool- and die-making to robotics and automation.

Scaling up these sorts of local programs is a major goal

Milwaukee, the University of Wisconsin–Whitewater, Marquette University and Gateway Technical College all offer courses that explore the scientific, legal, social, economic and ecological facets of water.

If cybersecurity is your thing, chances are you might head to Baltimore or Washington. Last year, Northrop Grumman Corp., a leading global security company, joined the University of Maryland–College Park in launching the Advanced Cybersecurity Experience for Students, a pioneering undergraduate cybersecurity honors program. Participants, who might be majoring in math, engineering, computer science, business or criminology, live and study together. Technical skills are part of the curriculum, but "they will be out of date in five, six, 10 years," says Michel Cukier, director of ACES. "It's much more important to learn to identify the right problem to solve." To do that, students study cybersecurity policy, economics, ethics, history and psychology along with the technology. Northrop Grumman is providing feedback on the curriculum, internship opportunities and advisers who will help students with professional development.

Sydnee Shannon (center) lives and studies with her peers in Maryland's cybersecurity honors program.

Sydnee Shannon, a sophomore from Ellicott City, Maryland, says the ACES program is "a perfect way to connect my math major with cryptography," and that she is particularly enjoying seeing "how students with different backgrounds approach the same problem." She applied for and landed a summer internship at Northrop Grumman as a software engineer.

of the Business-Higher Education Forum, which last year launched a six-year effort to work with business leaders in various regions "to identify their specific needs, and then get them together with local universities to align education with those needs," says Brian Fitzgerald, the group's CEO. A number of projects are in various stages of development, with additional collaborations expected in the future.

Northeast Natural Energy of Charleston, West Virginia, is working with West Virginia University in Morgantown to create a curriculum in the emerging field of shale energy research. Case Western Reserve University in Cleveland has partnered with Sherwin Williams and power management company Eaton to develop a program on materials and polymer science. The Milwaukee region, home to over 150 water technology companies like Badger Meter, A. O. Smith Corp. and Kohler Co., has become a "global water technology center," says Dean Amhaus, president of the area Water Council, comprised of schools, local governments, nongovernmental organizations and corporations. "We have students coming here for an undergraduate degree because they want to be in the water network we have," he says. The University of Wisconsin–

Softer skills, too

Beyond honing their technical chops in the real world, the aim is that students gain exposure to the soft skills they're going to need, too: the ability to work on a team, to think critically, to synthesize data, to ask the right question and to communicate with others about problems and challenges. Knowing how to make sense of data, and also how to translate it for nontechnical audiences, is a characteristic of "the real gems" his company is looking for in hiring, says Sean Groer, managing director of customer analytics at consulting firm KPMG in Atlanta, which has a partnership with the University of Tennessee.

The advantages work the other way, too, says GE Aviation's Morris. Management and marketing students, say, can take advantage of EPIC to get a background in manufacturing, adding the ability to talk technology with customers and suppliers. That added ease, he says, makes them "just that much more valuable" to potential employers. ●

BRETT ZIEGLER FOR USN&WR

THIS IS A SMART CHOICE.

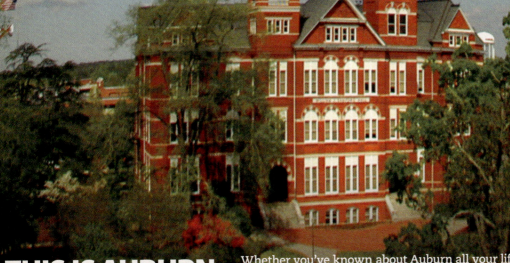

THIS IS AUBURN.

Whether you've known about Auburn all your life or are just learning about this university, we invite you to discover the real Auburn.

This is a university whose alumni include the CEO of Apple, the founders of Habitat for Humanity and Wikipedia, an Oscar-winning actor, sports legends, and astronauts. Graduates are recruited by top companies around the globe.

This is a university where you will make friends for a lifetime with a 250,000-strong, worldwide network of alumni who will think of you as family.

This is a university that will surprise you, impress you, and propel you to success as it has for generations before you. **auburn.edu**

AUBURN
UNIVERSITY

Gee-Whiz

GYMS

DUSTIN CHAMBERS FOR USN&WR

YOUR COLLEGE'S REC CENTER COULD BE THE FANCIEST HEALTH CLUB YOU EVER JOIN

By **COURTNEY RUBIN**

There are eight basketball courts, a 1/3-mile cork-screw track suspended high above the ground floor, a 20-foot climbing wall rising out of an outdoor pool, a PGA golf simulator and a hot tub that seats 50 people. Atop the "fitness tower," five stories of cardio equipment and exercise rooms, sits a yoga studio whose enormous windows open up to the sky like garage doors.

A five-star spa? A billionaire's vacation home? Actually, this is the new student recreation center at Auburn University in Alabama, $72 million worth of exercise opportunities.

Auburn is hardly alone in offering up fitness facilities "that you can't match once you leave," says Patricia Ketcham, president of the American College Health Association. Eastern Washington University boasts an indoor climbing wall with 33 routes, including one that simulates ice-climbing. Virginia Commonwealth University has a water slide, 18,000 square feet of fitness and weight lifting equipment, and a gym with artificial turf for indoor soccer games. The University of Missouri–Columbia's website describes a "resort quality" beach club, complete with waterfalls, whirlpools and a "lazy river" for floating. "It's always Spring Break in the Tiger Grotto," adds the website.

The University of North Carolina–Greensboro has broken ground on a $91 million recreation center; a $78 million expansion at Louisiana State University will include a suspended track and an indoor rock climbing wall. James Madison University in Virginia is spending $57 million to double its recreation facilities, adding, among other things, a batting cage, a water volleyball court and an additional indoor running track. According to a survey released in 2013 by NIRSA: Leaders in Collegiate Recreation, 92 institutions reported plans for construction or renovation, for a total of more than $1.7 billion in capital projects.

What's driving the boom? "Students are a lot more in-

One highlight of Auburn University's new rec center is a "corkscrew" track suspended above ground level.

terested in health and wellness these days," says Brad Cardinal, a professor of exercise and sports science at Oregon State University who has studied student fitness. Cardinal recently surveyed international students within their first five years in America and found that "they all noticed how prominent student health is relative to the culture they'd come from," he says.

Often, in fact, the push to build comes directly from students, who vote to tax themselves to pay for facilities that won't even be open until nearly all have graduated. Auburn University's project, for example, got its start in 2008, when the student government president ran on a platform to overhaul student recreation. During her term, more than 70 percent of students voted in favor of gradually raising their activity fee from $7.50 to $200 to help fund the building.

And the move toward bigger, shinier rec centers is coinciding

with society's growing focus on preventing disease, as well as accumulating evidence that physical activity and academic success appear to go hand in hand. As Donna Shalala, former Health and Human Services secretary and current president of the University of Miami noted in March during a discussion about the role of colleges at a Partnership for a Healthier America summit, "We have a captive audience, and campuses are good places to learn healthy habits."

Many schools are wasting no time. Stanford University recently launched a Student Wellness Passport Program, which awards students stamps for 12 health-related "trips" such as attending a group fitness class, getting a physical and wearing a bike helmet. Students who complete nine of

The University of Missouri's swimming facilities include a lazy river, waterfalls and whirlpools.

the 12 are entered in a drawing to win a prize. At the University of Miami, students are encouraged to take classes on meditation, healthy cooking and smoking cessation, as well as to attend play sessions that include finger painting, board games and hula hooping. "It takes more than daily physical activity to maintain good health," notes the wellness center's website. Indeed, many of these new gyms – actually, they're more apt to be called "recreation and wellness centers" – are designed with sofas, meeting rooms and courtyards as places to de-stress, socialize and study as well as sweat.

"It's easy to criticize these amenities as overdone, and say it's just administrators saying, 'We need to have the best and the biggest,'" says Don Stenta, director of student life's recreational sports department at Ohio State University. "We need to help students be successful academically and then successful after graduation, and there's a lot of research about how important a positive recreation experience is."

Maybe it's just that overachievers are more likely to hit the gym: A 2009 study published in the journal Medicine & Science in Sports & Exercise found that the more hours a student spent studying, the more likely he or she was to also show up for some exercise. On the other hand, a 2010 study at Saginaw Valley State University in Michigan found that even controlling for study time, students who regularly participated in vigorous exercise had higher GPAs. Whatever the explanation, a Purdue University analysis of student behavior has linked gym time and GPA, too. Students who worked out 16 times a month earned a GPA of 3.1 or higher, while students who used the gym at least seven times had an average GPA of 3.06. Students

MATT SLABY – LUCEO FOR USN&WR

who didn't use the gym at all: 2.82. Purdue's fitness facilities recently underwent a $98 million makeover.

The ever-increasing range of activities available isn't just for show – it's to draw students in for one thing, and intrigue them enough to come back for others. It gets much harder to form an exercise habit, Ketcham notes, once students graduate and land a job. At Ohio State University, for example, a Hogwarts Express spin class invited participants to wear Harry Potter costumes. Stenta says the class drew people who'd never been inside the rec center or tried a cycling class – his goal.

Auburn University's old facility drew about 900 students a day. The new one generally draws 3,500 and has even topped 5,000 on occasion. Colorado State University in 2011 spent $32 million renovating its recreation center. An additional $3.3 million was spent on converting a virtually unused lap pool into a leisure pool, complete with a climbing wall, lights and speakers for a grotto effect. There was a 77 percent jump in aquatic facility traffic from fall 2011 to fall 2013.

The increasingly luxe facilities can be potent recruiting tools, some observers say. "I can't tell you how many tours I start with prospective students where I say, 'Hey, are you thinking of coming here?' And the kid is like, 'Eh, I don't know,'" says David Frock, Clemson University's director of student recreation. "But by the time you leave the rec center, they're like, 'Oh, I want to come here.'" A 2013 study released by the National Bureau of Economic Research suggests that fancy amenities matter less at elite colleges and universities, where prospective students tend to be more focused on the quality of instruction.

Growing up in a working-class neighborhood of Portland, Oregon, Tram Hoang, the first member of her family to get a four-year degree, had never worked out at a gym – and in fact had only seen cardio equipment on TV. Hoang, who graduated from Oregon State University in the spring, was drawn to the rec center first to play volleyball, and gradually got up the nerve to ask for help using the machines. By senior year, she practically lived there, she says. "During a weekend where it snowed, the campus was closed for three days, but the rec facilities were open. Everyone was there, renting snowshoes, working out and studying," she says. "I don't think people realize how important recreation is until they get here." ●

Good News on Gluten

Never mind the beer and pizza. From salad dressings to French fries, most processed foods are a no-go for students who suffer from celiac disease and sensitivity to gluten. Until recently, the limited options available for gluten-free students left them little choice but to eat in their rooms, convince a cafeteria worker to make them a plain chicken breast on a grill not used for buns, or throw caution to the wind, sometimes ending up too sick for class.

"We had students with celiac disease who were having to drop out, or were selecting colleges and universities based on where they can eat," says Beckee Moreland, director of a gluten-free kitchens education program at the National Foundation for Celiac Awareness. The advocacy group a couple years ago began offering university dining services workers a two-hour online or onsite seminar on gluten-free meal prep. So far, about 700 have taken the course, Moreland says.

The spur to action. One reason dining halls are rapidly changing their practices: A 2013 Justice Department settlement with Lesley University in Massachusetts, requiring the school to "continually provide" gluten-free options, after a complaint that the school was in violation of the Americans With Disabilities Act by requiring students to live on campus and buy meal plans, but not accommodating the gluten-free diners. Lesley now labels meals "made without gluten" and stores and prepares them in a separate area in the kitchen. There are separate toaster ovens and microwaves for students heating meals.

At Boston College, those who head for the dining hall's "Plain & Simple" line also get food made in an isolated preparation station. And a campus deli offers sandwiches on gluten-free bread, prepared on dedicated cutting boards. North Carolina State University has set up a "worry-free" station with a dedicated toaster and gluten-free breads, bagels and muffins. "Secret shoppers" occasionally go to the dining halls to watch preparation and buy menu items – and write up reports highlighting any problems.

"Now when there's Mexican food I can get corn tortillas instead of flour," says Matthew Schneider, a senior at Michigan State who was diagnosed with celiac disease in sixth grade. "And sometimes they even have gluten-free dessert." There's also a locked refrigerator – students must ask for a key – stocked with safe options for the taking. –*C.R.*

ISTOCKPHOTO

The heart of Wake Forest has been re-engineered for fun.

Taking On
STRESS

COLLEGES ARE FINDING NEW WAYS TO PROMOTE STUDENTS' SOCIAL AND EMOTIONAL WELLBEING

By **BETH HOWARD**

The quad at Wake Forest University in North Carolina once existed to showcase the handsome brick Georgian buildings; the broad lawns were even cordoned off to student traffic. Now, students gather here at café tables, sit and play the outdoor piano, grab a Frisbee or a football from a pile of equipment for some impromptu play, and read magazines from an al fresco library while sipping coffee from a nearby cart.

Engineered by Dan Biederman, the man who revitalized New York City's once drug-ridden Bryant Park, the campus redo was executed expressly to help harried students take some down time and mingle – and breathe. "You used to see students checking emails on their smartphones when they walked from one part of campus to another," says Elizabeth Law, a May grad in communications. "This encourages you to unplug a little bit. More people are making eye contact and stopping to actually talk to each other."

The Wake Forest project is one example of the myriad ways colleges and universities are working to relieve student stress and to prevent or tackle anxiety and depression, lately at record highs. According to the 2013 National College Health Assessment, almost a third of college students said they felt so depressed during the previous year that it was difficult to function, and more than half had experienced overwhelming anxiety. Almost 8 percent seriously considered suicide. "Mental health

ANDY McMILLAN FOR USN&WR

disorders are the most common health problems on college campuses outside of colds and allergies," says Jerald Kay, chair of the department of psychiatry at Wright State University in Ohio and co-author of "Mental Health Care in the College Community." While suicide rates have not been rising, Kay says, that is small comfort: Suicide is still the second-leading cause of death among college students, after vehicle accidents. The University of Pennsylvania, shaken by three suicides in four months this past year, has convened a task force to confront the vexing problem.

To nip stress before it leads to bigger problems, a growing number of schools, including New York University, Harvard, and the University of Missouri, are offering training in meditation and mindfulness to quiet the tendency to worry about all sorts of potential catastrophes; after students at Santa Clara University in California took an eight-week meditation class, they reported greater reductions in stress than those who did not take the class. During finals, staff, faculty and alumni of Macalester College in Minnesota bring their pooches to campus for cuddling breaks and camaraderie. Says senior Kenzie Ellis, a Russian studies major: "There's that look you get from other students that says, 'Hey, we're both freaking out about finals right now, but at least we're petting dogs, isn't this great?'" Kent State University in Ohio has a similar program.

Wake Forest students stop to play a solar-powered piano.

Besides the prevention efforts, counseling departments are trying innovative approaches to meet the growing demand for their services. "More schools have walk-in hours so that students don't get wait-listed," says Josh Gunn, director of counseling and psychological services at Kennesaw State University near Atlanta and president of the American College Counseling Association. With budgets stretched thin, he notes, students at some colleges have to wait days or weeks to see a counselor. Many schools, including Kennesaw and Wake Forest, have added the option of group therapy to that of private sessions. The University of Florida offers a seven-week anxiety education class to give students tools for taming their tension. Schools are also experimenting with technology, using web-based resources to teach students how to cope, for instance.

Going to college has always involved the stress of making new friends and learning to regulate one's sleeping, eating, studying and partying. Yet today's students face a unique set of emotional challenges in the still-sputtering economy. "There's tremendous pressure to succeed," says Victor Schwartz, medical director of The JED Foundation, a nonprofit that promotes emotional health on campus founded by Phil and Donna Satow after their son took his own life in 1999 as a sophomore at the University of Arizona. "Students anticipate stiff competition when it comes to getting a job after graduation, and, with soaring tuitions, there's more financial pressure on them."

The result, he says: A need to "work the résumé and do well at every endeavor." And when you compare yourself "to everyone else's highlight reels," it's easy to feel "like you're not measuring up," says Kaitlin Gladney, a recent Duke University grad who has experienced anxiety and depression and received counseling on campus. The Duke Endowment is funding a four-year Student Resiliency Project at Duke and several other schools that will investigate ways colleges can foster an ability to bounce back from reversals.

Ironically, hovering "helicopter" parents seeking only to help their college kids, by mediating disputes between roommates and calling professors about grades, say, may be making matters worse. A new study in the Journal of Child and Family Studies shows that children with overinvolved parents were more prone to depressive symptoms. Helicopter parenting undermines students' sense of competence, explains study author Holly Schiffrin, a psychology professor at the University of Mary Washington in Virginia. "It tells students that parents don't think they're capable of handling problems, and it prevents students from practicing the very skills they need to feel confident."

Other relatively new factors colleges face include the growing population of students with conditions such as schizophrenia and bipolar disorder who can attend school thanks to improved therapies, and an expected wave of veterans, many of whom will be bringing issues to campus that colleges are not accustomed to seeing, such as post-traumatic stress disorder and traumatic brain injury. More than a million vets have tapped the GI bill to attend college since 2009. Being older, soldiers are less likely to find social support on campus. "The vet population is one of our biggest challenges now," Kay says.

Families have a big role to play in safeguarding their

students' mental health. At the college research stage, it's possible to find out what resources are offered by talking to admissions officers and checking out school websites. "School programs vary tremendously, from comprehensive and robust to having next-to-nothing," Schwartz says. One measure: participation in the JED Campus Seal program,

ANDY MCMILLAN FOR USN&WR

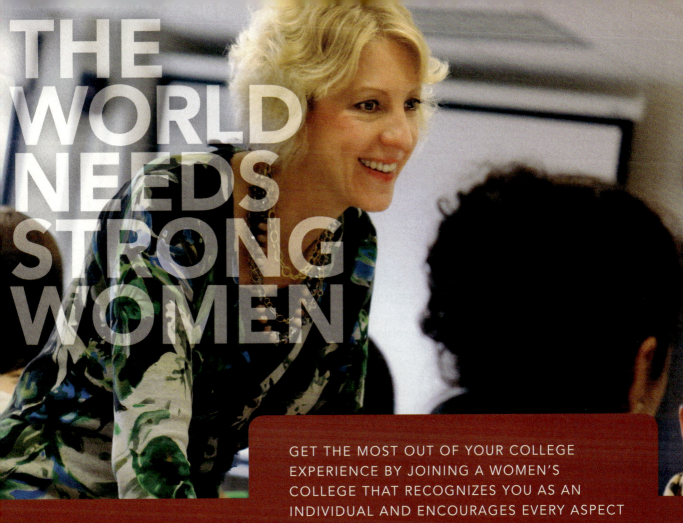

THE WORLD NEEDS STRONG WOMEN

GET THE MOST OUT OF YOUR COLLEGE EXPERIENCE BY JOINING A WOMEN'S COLLEGE THAT RECOGNIZES YOU AS AN INDIVIDUAL AND ENCOURAGES EVERY ASPECT OF YOUR DEVELOPMENT.

A college where large **lecture halls are replaced with smart classrooms**, so you get the most out of collaborative learning. Where **professors know you by name** – and are often on speed dial – to ensure their vital role in your college experience. Where standardized tests are replaced with in-depth, semester-long projects, so you **dive deeper into the learning process** and make learning your own.

Alverno is **world-renowned** for bridging classroom learning to real-world work experience, so **you graduate with the precise career-ready** skills employers are seeking.

If this sounds like the place for you, then **YOU BELONG** at Alverno!

94%
of Alverno grads are employed within six months of graduation*

60 areas of study

10:1
student to faculty ratio

[w] alverno.edu/usnews
[e] admissions@alverno.edu
[p] 800-933-3401

ALVERNO COLLEGE
ESTABLISHED 1887
MILWAUKEE WISCONSIN

*Rolling 3-year average. ± 4% margin for error.

which signifies comprehensive mental health and suicide prevention programming.

So far, 30 schools, including Cornell, Columbia and Alfred University in New York; Pennsylvania State University in Altoona and Emory University in Georgia have the JED Seal. Anyone who has struggled or is taking a psychiatric medication can let the school know without repercussions once accepted – and should, experts say. Work out a plan if you decide to transition care to campus, and at the very least make sure someone there is keeping the student "on the school's radar," Schwartz advises.

Starting well before college, parents should be conscious of

promoting their child's independence and autonomy, experts advise. Instead of jumping in to take care of everyday issues, Schiffrin says, offer support by, for example, role-playing tricky conversations a student might need to have with a high school teacher, professor or peer: "'What would you say when X?' and 'And how would you respond if Y?'"

But do keep the lines of communication to campus open, experts advise. "No one knows a child better than a parent," says Penny Rue, vice president for campus life at Wake Forest. "Look for a change in their energy levels and listen for changes in vocal modulation. Probe a little about their sleep and nutrition habits. Both too much and too little sleep are signs of depression."

Students can inoculate themselves in a couple of ways. One good step is to seek out a niche from the start where you feel you fit in, perhaps by choosing to live in a learning community (story, Page 18) or by joining an organization that suits your interests. Another healthful measure: Get some exercise. Charlie Shuford, a sophomore studying music and art at Appalachian State University in North Carolina who has battled depression, keeps symptoms at bay by competing on the cycling team. A 2013 University of Minnesota study showed that students who engaged in vigorous exercise for 20 minutes at least three times a week were less likely to report poor mental health and stress. Shuford is cautious about loading his schedule, too: "I'm thinking of going to college for five years instead of four so I don't allow myself to get too stressed out."

Beyond the anti-anxiety and meditation workshops, many students who feel vulnerable swear by support groups such as those sponsored by Active Minds, an advocacy group on 453 college campuses. At Duke, Gladney started a chapter of the national nonprofit To Write Love on Her Arms, aimed at supporting people coping with depression, addiction and self-injury. It's not therapy. But "students have told me that it's created a safe space where they're comfortable discussing the topic, free from fear of rejection or stigma," Gladney says.

When a student experiences a bout of depression or another issue, it's important to reach out for counseling services. There are people on most campuses whose sincere wish it is "to make sure you are emotionally well and socially adjusted," says Gunn. Don't wait, he cautions, until you feel hopeless. ●

NASHVILLE, TENNESSEE

...Fisk University

Lamar Allen, '16

I wanted to attend a historically black institution that would culturally nurture and academically challenge me. Fisk pulled me in with its rich history, family-oriented environment and its reputation for academic achievement.

As a business administration major concentrating in accounting, I have been able to develop my quantitative and financial skills with the help of the small class sizes and my professors, who have given me the personal attention I desired. Fisk's Exceptional Confidence In Emerging Leaders program has further en-

Why

abled me to refine my professional skills, build my "brand," and strategically set goals as I pursue a career in corporate America. As part of the EXCEL program, Fisk has given me the opportunity to interact and build relationships with associates of top investing firms such as Goldman Sachs and Morgan Stanley.

Fisk is located in Nashville, and one can find plenty to do in the Music City, whether it's grabbing a bite to eat on the West End or enjoying a great day at Centennial Park. I have been enriched by the legacy and history of this institution and am truly thankful for the support of my Fisk family. ●

CLOCKWISE FROM TOP LEFT: COURTESY OF FISK UNIVERSITY;
BO BOTELLI – UC DAVIS; COURTESY OF MICHAEL GALLAGHER; ISTOCKPHOTO

DAVIS

...University of California-Davis

Carly Sandstrom, '14

The first time I visited Davis I fell in love with this university – the trees, arboretum, a picturesque downtown that seems straight out of a movie, and the smiles of people as you pass by. There was an instant comfort here that I hadn't felt at other universities. UC-Davis gave me a chance to attend a school that's both strong academically and encourages service. As a double major in international relations and economics, I worked, for example, with the provost's staff to oversee the Education Abroad Center (which coordinates international study opportunities), and I had an eye-opening internship with Gov. Jerry Brown's Let's Get Healthy California task force that devised a comprehensive plan to make residents healthier by encouraging everything from increased immunizations to better eating habits.

A favorite memory: One day freshman year, I was biking through campus with the student body president (a position I took over my third year) and another student. The president saw members of the student ministry doing some landscaping in their front yard. He got off his bike and urged us to pitch in and help. That is UC Davis – spontaneous and giving. ●

I Picked...

COLORADO

...U.S. Air Force Academy

Michael Gallagher, '14

Since I was 6 years old, I've wanted to be an Air Force pilot, so the academy was the obvious choice for me after high school. The experience has been both rigorous and rewarding. During the week, cadets study everything from the military strategy of Operation Iraqi Freedom to the rocket propulsion needed to transfer from low Earth to high Earth orbit. Training continues on weekends, when we learn skills like land navigation and marksmanship. Instructors are constantly available, even on weekends, for cadets needing help with class work or coping with the stresses of training. I have participated in specialized training like the Unmanned Aerial Systems program, while also studying cyberwarfare and space operations to expose myself to the many different career paths in the Air Force. The academy demands mastery and will ensure you get extra instruction, if necessary, till you achieve it. Though we work hard, cadets still manage to have fun doing everything from seeing movies to applying woodland tactics with the Airsoft Club to learning blues dancing. Beyond just preparing me well for my future in the Air Force, the academy has enabled me to form close friendships with fellow cadets. They are my brothers and sisters in arms whom I would trust with my car – or my life. ●

Cheering on the
Clemson Tigers

BRETT ZIEGLER FOR USN&WR

TAKE A Road Trip

Missouri

A student at work in the Olin Library at Washington University in St. Louis

University
of Missouri

Washington
University
in St. Louis

Missouri University
of Science and
Technology

College of the Ozarks

By **DELECE SMITH-BARROW**

Take a break and enjoy the ride as U.S. News hits the road for you through the college towns of Missouri. The trip begins in St. Louis, at Wash U, then heads to Rolla and the Missouri University of Science & Technology, drops down to the College of the Ozarks in Point Lookout, and ends up in Columbia at Mizzou.

Photography by **MATT SLABY** *– Luceo for USN&WR*

Washington University in St. Louis

R ohan Puthanangady, a Wash U sophomore from Massachusetts, was drawn to the medium-sized university at the heart of the country by the school's academic strength; compared to his high school curriculum, says the business major, "the workload is way more here." He's come to love just about everything about the place: the food (from locally grown vegetarian to Indian and kosher fare), the faculty (even deans invite students over for dinner), the residence halls (which come with peer and faculty mentors) and a collegial atmosphere that makes it easier to get through long nights of studying. "The people here are incredibly down to earth and friendly," observes Puthanangady. "There's no sense of competitiveness."

That feeling of support and togetherness is a common theme on the sprawling green campus located west of downtown St. Louis, about 10 miles from the iconic Gateway Arch and adjacent to Forest Park's acres of bike and running trails; golf and tennis facilities; and art, history and science museums and zoo. Two upperclass "student associates" are assigned to each freshman floor to help newcomers make a happy transition to college; peer mentors who live in the residential colleges are available for

group or one-on-one academic assistance. You can study, sleep and still have a social life, says Vera Schulte, a sophomore from Seattle who likes to do some of her work curled up by the fireplace in Danforth University Center, near all the hubbub of the adjacent dining area. Schulte, who is majoring in philosophy,

UNDERGRADUATES
Full-time: 6,587

TOTAL COST*
$60,844

U.S. NEWS RANKING
National Universities
#14

*Tuition, fees and room & board

one of the 10 residential colleges specially designed to foster community. In gardens and other gathering spaces, undergrads and faculty fellows can continue conversations started in class or simply

people together on campus for several days of fun and fundraising for charity; in the fall, a widely attended event inspired by the Hindu Festival of Lights known as Diwali is hosted by Ashoka, the South Asian student association, as a way to celebrate those cultures. Students can join any of several hundred interest groups, from one dedicated to collegiate jugglers to a society for people who like to churn butter the "olde-fashioned way." They can also join a Greek organization or play one of 33 club sports.

If campus activities

The university's architecture was inspired by that of Oxford and Cambridge.

neuroscience and psychology – that's one major – as a premed student, relies on a team of advisers to keep her on track academically: a four-year adviser, a major adviser, a residential adviser and her premed adviser.

Outside of class hours, freshmen and sophomores might well be found hanging out in the South 40, in

socialize. Students often play Frisbee on the large field affectionately known as The Swamp, grab a bite at Bear's Den, or stop in at the fitness center or several student-run businesses, such as Bears Bikes or Wash-U-Wash.

In the spring, Thurtene, a popular student-run carnival complete with rides, brings students and towns-

don't offer enough excitement, St. Louis serves up plenty, too, from Cardinals games at Busch Stadium to the nightlife of the Delmar Loop. In this popular section of the city, students can dine at Blueberry Hill, catch a show at Tivoli Theatre, browse through the art galleries and check out some live music. ●

In the design center, future engineers can work on projects around the clock.

Missouri University of Science and Technology

Rolla

A message painted outside of the library at Missouri University of Science and Technology one day last fall read "121 daze" – a countdown to the much-anticipated 10-day extravaganza every March that sweeps campus and the city of Rolla in honor of St. Patrick's Day. S&T, as the school is commonly known, does not have a religious affiliation, but St. Patrick is the patron saint of engineers, and there are plenty of those here. "It's pretty much like Rolla's homecoming," says

UNDERGRADUATES
Full-time: **5,472**

TOTAL COST*
In-state: **$19,077**
Out-of-state: **$34,944**

U.S. NEWS RANKING
National Universities
#138

*Tuition, fees and room & board

Steve Ludwig, a senior mechanical engineering major from St. Louis and a member of the board of the festivities, which include parties, a parade and a leprechaun look-alike contest. Even the mayor has been known to attend. As early as November, the booth selling green S&T sweatshirts is set up and in business.

Engineering is indeed one of the university's strongest departments; undergraduates interested in the field can select from 15 majors, from aerospace and ceramic to metallurgical and nuclear. All told, more than 90 percent of the student body majors in a science, technology, engineering or math – STEM – discipline. The rest choose from among the select few other pathways, which include business, economics, psychology, English and history.

The engineering bent is evident on a stroll around campus. There's the windmill that contributes to wind turbine research, and the student-built "smart" bridge spanning a creekbed that is made of material often used in advanced aircraft; sensors feed instrumentation that measures strain on the bridge. You'll pass Solar Village, where four solar homes students built over the years provide housing and a self-sustaining electrical power grid. S&T is the kind of school where students spend their free time in the advanced computer labs of the 24/7 design center, working in teams to develop everything from solar cars and hydrogen fuel cells to concrete canoes and off-road vehicles.

When they aren't studying, many students are active in the vibrant 28-chapter Greek system. To fight the common association of Greek life with partying, anyone

DUCKS HAPPEN HERE

Deep in the woods of the Pacific Northwest there is a premier public research university
—a place where innovators gather, and green is a way of life. There, nestled in a valley
between the blue Pacific and the mighty Cascade Range, you'll find a curious sort … those
that boldly advance the pursuit of excellence, and do the deeds that change the world.
They flock together in a proud space that is inclusive, supportive, and reminds you of home.
This is the Rubicon of the new frontier, out West—where you'll find the Ducks … in flight.

UNIVERSITY OF OREGON

1-800-BE-A-DUCK
uoregon.edu

An equal-opportunity, affirmative-action institution committed to cultural diversity and compliance with the Americans with Disabilities Act.

who wants to participate is strongly encouraged to get involved in other aspects of campus life as well; some fraternities and sororities even require three other extracurricular activities. It forces you to "structure your day," says Pi Kappa Alpha member Raheel Hassan, a senior majoring in biology who has also been active in the Industrial Designers Society of America and the spring break community service program.

Life lessons. Women say they learn some valuable life lessons, like how to make your voice heard when you're one of only a few women in the room. (The student body is about 75 percent male.) Shelby McNeil, a senior applied mathematics major from Republic, Missouri, says that she sometimes has felt not taken seriously – when, for example, students needing help in math class bypass her, a math major, to ask a guy who is not a major for assistance.

Victoria Willcut, a junior environmental engineering student from Puxico, Missouri, has noticed that women may have to speak up to make sure they get the desirable roles in group projects. But male classmates generally treat her fine, she says, and she has no doubt the campus community wants her to succeed.

Faculty describe students as both hardworking and welcoming. "They're very career-oriented," says Jerri Arnold-Cook, director of leadership and cultural programs. At the same time, those who come to S&T really like "how friendly we are." ●

College of the Ozarks
Point Lookout

A 1973 Wall Street Journal article dubbed College of the Ozarks "Hard Work U." More than 40 years later, students and faculty at this unique Christian college still embrace the name. Banners shout it out from every corner of campus. You can even see it inscribed on the white coats of nursing students.

The moniker is more than a catchy slogan. From freshman year on, full-time students are assigned to some 15 hours a week (plus two 40-hour workweeks) at one of more than 75 job stations, as part of the college's required work education program. Some butcher or milk cows on one of the campus's three farms, while others pre-

UNDERGRADUATES
Full-time: 1,498

TOTAL COST*
$6,630

U.S. NEWS RANKING
Regional Colleges,
Midwest
#4

*Fees, room & board. Tuition
($18,100) is covered by work and aid.

pare food in the cafeteria or write press releases in the public relations office.

"Our students are crucial to the operation of this place," says Chris Larsen, the dean of work education. Students learn initiative, responsibility, communication and other skills through their campus jobs, he says.

While figuring out how

to balance work with study and other activities can be challenging for incoming students, there's a big payoff: no out-of-pocket tuition. The work education program (which some students participate in during the summer, too), federal grants and College of the Ozarks scholarships cover tuition for all full-time students; very few students graduate with debt. Fees and room and board run a bit over $6,500 a year.

"I have a lot of friends at home that are up to their eyeballs in debt," says Kelsea Inson, a senior from Warrenton, Virginia. College of the Ozarks is the only four-year institution she applied to after attending community college. She's majoring in graphic design, one of 44 majors

Taking a break in the Plaster Business Building, also home to criminal justice and computer science

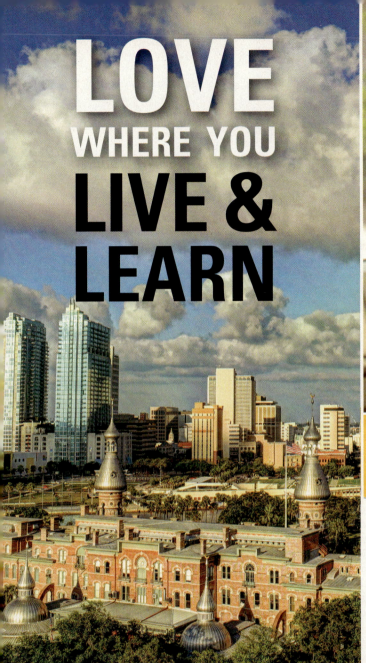

LOVE
WHERE YOU
LIVE &
LEARN

THE UNIVERSITY OF TAMPA offers students the best of it all: academic excellence, abundant internships, big-city living and beautiful weather. With more than 160 areas of study, UT is committed to preparing students for success through experiential learning. Ranked as one of the top universities in the south by *U.S. News & World Report*, UT produces outstanding graduates who are ready to compete in the global marketplace.

www.ut.edu/explore

THE UNIVERSITY OF TAMPA

offered; the others, along with general liberal arts options, include business, nursing and education.

Inson is one of the fraction of students – some 20 percent of the 1,500 population – who hail from outside the Ozarks region; most slots go to students within the area, which encompasses parts of Missouri, Arkansas, Illinois, Oklahoma and Kansas. The hilly landscape provides a bucolic backdrop for the manicured grounds, some 1,000 acres of lawns and flower beds. Besides the farms, students heading to class might pass the farmer's market during the fall months and Edwards Mill, a grist mill where they can grind whole grain into flour and weave textiles.

For fun. Ozarks students have a sizable menu of activities to choose from for the hours when they're not studying or working, from the College Republicans club and student government to the basketball, baseball and volleyball teams to jazz band and the Ozarks Fisheries and Wildlife Club. Popular campuswide yearly events include the bluegrass-

heavy Sadie Hawkins dance and Mudfest, which involves a fiercely fought tug-of-war contest over a pit of mud.

There's a strong interest in spirituality here. "I wanted to go somewhere where I would enhance my faith," says Michaela Moore, a sophomore nursing major from Waynesville, Missouri. Moore is a Southern Baptist who participates in the Fellowship of Christian Athletes and plans to get involved with the Nurses Christian Fellowship. At noon, activity in the dining hall pauses for a moment of prayer, and students are required to attend at least five chapel services each semester.

Everyone is encouraged to pursue an experience abroad, although the school doesn't offer any semesterlong options; past opportunities have included study trips to China and Belize. Through the Patriotic Education Travel program, students travel with veterans to battlegrounds where they have served to get an understanding of the history and an appreciation for what it was like to be on the front lines. ●

Among the college's 75 work stations are three farms.

University of Missouri
Columbia

One landmark you're sure to notice as you walk around the University of Missouri is the set of six pillars called The Columns that symbolize the beginning and the end of a student's time at the school. Before fall classes begin, freshmen run through the columns toward the heart of campus as part of "Tiger Walk," an event that marks the start of their college careers. Graduating students pass through in the opposite direction during "Senior Sendoff."

In between, the 27,000 undergraduates at Mizzou, which prides itself in being both a land-grant institu-

tion with a public service mission and a research university, find plenty to do. More than 280 degree programs are offered through 13 colleges and schools. Many undergrads participate in research projects, investigating everything from how plants defend themselves against bacterial infections to highway safety, either independently or with faculty mentors. The university emphasizes experiential learning in other ways as well; about 18 percent of undergraduates each year receive credit through courses that intersperse classwork with community service.

And budding reporters and editors in the univer-

would at any paper.

"The journalism school was a huge draw for me," says Madalyne Bird, a senior from Kansas City who is focusing on multiplatform design. "It's so rewarding, but it's also a huge time commitment."

In general, the 1,262-acre campus – which also happens to be a registered botanic garden, a "living museum" of some 42,000 plants and trees – has the

UNDERGRADUATES
Full-time: **25,258**

TOTAL COST*
In-state: **$18,819**
Out-of-state: **$33,846**

U.S. NEWS RANKING
National Universities
#99

*Tuition, fees and room & board

students may find a tight community within the Honors College, which offers small classes and a book club, among other activities. Much of the bonding happens within the 750-plus student organizations, which range from UNICEF Mizzou to the chess club to the Quarter Scale Tractor Pulling Team.

Anyone who is into playing sports has more than 45 club options to choose from. Fans can also cheer on some 20 teams that compete for the university in the Southeastern Conference; the football team recently added 2014 AT&T Cotton Bowl champions to its list of accolades. The women's volleyball team also celebrated a big victory last November when it won the Southeastern Conference championship.

The tiger spirit is on full display during the week-long Homecoming spectacular, one of the most unifying campus events. Homecoming is also an opportunity each year to embrace the university's multicultural identity – its varied student body, alumni, faculty and staff – by hosting events such as the Black Family Reunion.

Columbia is a college "town" of just over 113,000 residents that welcomes and caters to the school community, and students regularly head off campus to its coffee shops, music venues and many restaurants. Shakespeare's Pizza and Lakota Coffee on South 9th Street are some of the more popular dining spots, while The Blue Note and Missouri Theatre are a safe bet for finding some live entertainment. ●

Practicing at Mizzou's pool (top), and studying and socializing at the university center

sity's renowned School of Journalism are trained using the hands-on Missouri Method; to complement their classwork, they get intensive practice at one of several publications, radio stations or advertising agencies. Students guided by faculty put out the local Columbia Missourian newspaper, for example, which publishes five days a week and is updated online 24/7. Students discuss how stories are told during budget meetings, as they feel of a "big small place," says Nick Droege, a 2014 grad from St. Louis and former president of the Missouri Students Association. "There are so many opportunities here to make it smaller."

For example, some

Pennsylvania

By **MICHAEL MORELLA**

The Keystone State is home to about 100 colleges and universities, and the Philadelphia metro area alone claims several hundred thousand college students. U.S. News spent a few days in and around the City of Brotherly Love, touring Drexel and the University of Pennsylvania downtown before stopping by the suburban liberal arts enclaves of Haverford and Bryn Mawr.

PA

Bryn Mawr College
Haverford College
Drexel University
University of Pennsylvania
PHILADELPHIA

Photography by **BRETT ZIEGLER** *for USN&WR*

Drexel University

Philadelphia

Almost a century ago, engineering students at what was then the Drexel Institute of Art, Science and Industry near Center City Philadelphia began alternating periods of classroom instruction with hands-on work experience. Today, more than 75 majors offer such co-operative education programs; by the time they graduate, some 90 percent of Drexel undergrads will have had at least one (full-time) six-month co-op job at one of 1,600-plus employers, including the Children's Hospital of Philadelphia, Merck, the Philadelphia Housing Authority and the Philadelphia Museum of Art.

"They throw you right in when you get here," says international business major Sandra Petri, class of 2016. Petri, from Mount Royal, New Jersey, has completed co-ops at Comcast and the nonprofit World Trade Center of Greater Philadelphia. The average six-month salary is a little more than $16,000, though some positions are not paid. And roughly half of each graduating class is offered a job with a co-op employer, notes Peter Franks, vice provost for career education.

The career development center helps facilitate the co-op process, but students must be proactive in securing their positions. Most complete their degrees in five years with up to three co-ops, though some choose a four-year, single-placement program. Classes are arranged in 10-week quarters, which students say tend to be fast-paced and require careful time management. "Drexel has this kind of motif of initiative," says senior Christopher Gray, a business administration and entrepreneurship major from Birmingham, Alabama, who has had a co-op at Fannie Mae and a self-guided one with other students that involved designing a mobile app for finding college scholarships.

The co-op program attracted Ethan Collik, a

UNDERGRADUATES
Full-time: 11,480

TOTAL COST*
$61,418

U.S. NEWS RANKING
National Universities
#95

*Tuition, fees and room & board

Scaling the rec center climbing wall (above). A draping class in Drexel's fashion design program

recent accounting and legal studies grad from Cherry Hill, New Jersey, "but there were so many other things keeping me here," he says. Undergrads can choose from among 300 organizations, including the Campus Activities Board, The Triangle campus newspaper, and the Drexel football team, an improv comedy group. (The university doesn't have an athletic football team, though the Dragons do compete in 18 Division I sports.) About 10 percent of students join fraternities and sororities.

Urban vibe. Drexel's 126 acres in the University City neighborhood have an "urban college town" feel, notes recent mechanical engineering grad Graham Donaldson of Woodcliff Lake, New Jersey. The campus can feel crowded, students say, though most welcome the chance to explore the nearby music, art, sports, culture and other attractions. Popular hangouts on campus include the Creese Student Center with lounges, a theater and Drexel's underground main dining center; the recreation center; and Buckley field and green, home to frequent pickup sports games.

Classes average about 18 undergraduates, and the student-faculty ratio is 9-to-1. First-year students live in one of several mostly high-rise dorms clustered around the north end of campus, and they may apply to live in learning communities based on field of study. (Engineering, business and health professions are popular.) Some upperclassmen reside on campus, but most find places around Philly. ●

University of Pennsylvania
Philadelphia

Upon founding what would become the University of Pennsylvania, Benjamin Franklin stressed the importance of students learning all that is "most useful and most ornamental." Today, cultivating "Renaissance students" remains a major part of Penn's DNA, says Chicago native and recent communication grad Ernest Owens. More than 9,000 undergraduates attend the Ivy League school, situated on about 300 acres in the heart of Philadelphia, just west of downtown and the Schuylkill River.

One of the oldest and most selective institutions in the country, Penn accepted around 12 percent of its 31,200-plus applicants for fall 2013; 94 percent of those admitted came from the top 10 percent of their high school classes. "People are competitive," notes Yadavan Mahendraraj, a spring grad in management and marketing from Allendale, New Jersey, but "it's not cutthroat."

Undergrads can select from 91 different majors – or create their own – at the schools of arts and sciences, engineering, nursing and the storied Wharton business school. (The 11,000 graduate students can enroll at eight additional schools.) Students often

Members of the Onda Latina dance club practice between classes (top). In a forensic anthropology lab class (above), students examine skulls.

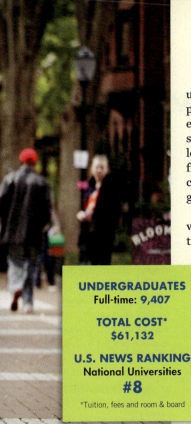

UNDERGRADUATES
Full-time: 9,407

TOTAL COST*
$61,132

U.S. NEWS RANKING
National Universities
#8

*Tuition, fees and room & board

undergrads live on campus, which spans about eight blocks and includes several museums and galleries, La Casa Latina and five other cultural resource centers and no shortage of green spaces.

Students can keep busy with more than 400 activities, and about a third join fraternities and sororities. The Netter Center for Community Partnerships coordinates volunteer and civic engagement programs, as well as a range of service-learning courses that, for example, examine urban education in underserved West Philadelphia schools. Penn also boasts 11 undergraduate research journals and more than 100 research centers through which student scholars can earn grants for their own projects or join faculty efforts. And at least 4 out of 5 undergrads participate in internships.

"I can barely wrap my head around how there's so much to do," notes senior Jacob Meiner, of New Rochelle, New York, who is studying Near Eastern languages and civilizations and marketing and operations management.

Some undergrads say the university can feel decentralized and that school spirit can be lacking at Quaker athletic events. But Penn pride shows at gatherings like Spring Fling, billed as one of the biggest college festivals on the East Coast, and Hey Day, when juniors don straw hats and red shirts and march around campus with canes to celebrate their soon-to-be seniority. ●

marvel at "how much individual attention you can get at such a large school," says sophomore nursing major Maci McCravy, from Tulsa, Oklahoma. A low 6-to-1 student-faculty ratio helps, as do opportunities like Wharton's Lunch & Learn program, through which the university pays for undergrads to take faculty members out for meals.

The small-school-within-a-large-university feel owes much to the system of College Houses. All freshmen reside in these 11 living-learning communities, along with a number of faculty members (and sometimes their families) and have access to in-house advising and tutoring, house-based social and educational events and research opportunities, as well as more than 40 themed programs focused on music and social change, for instance, or international studies and business. Over half of

Haverford College
Haverford

'There are no closed doors" at Haverford, says junior Alana Thurston, a Boston-area native majoring in chemistry, of the academic, social and other opportunities available to undergraduates. Many students attribute that pervasive feeling of openness to a highly influential honor code, rooted in the Quaker traditions of the college's founders, that

(where trees outnumber students), complete with a duck pond and bounded by a 2 ¼-mile nature trail. Virtually everybody lives on campus, as do 60 percent of professors (most in faculty housing), so the Haverford community is close-knit. Classes average 15 students, and – count on it – "the professor will know your name," says Chloe Wang, a sophomore interested

Students in class at Quaker-founded Haverford

aims to promote integrity and mutual respect. Set along Philadelphia's historic Main Line, about 8 miles from the city center, the liberal arts college's campus is an arboretum

UNDERGRADUATES
Full-time: 1,187

TOTAL COST*
$61,564

U.S. NEWS RANKING
National Liberal Arts Colleges
#8

*Tuition, fees and room & board

in chemistry from Dobbs Ferry, New York.

There's widespread agreement that the honor code really works. No resident assistants are needed to police the dorms (though students have access to upperclassmen and administrative support), and it's standard practice to take exams without proctors and to leave laptops unattended and bikes unlocked around campus. Haverfordians come together each semester for Plenary to discuss issues on campus and to make changes to policies as needed. "Really, at its core, every student is invested in making this a healthy community that's inclusive," says Dylan Reichman, a junior majoring in political science from Maplewood, New Jersey.

In keeping with Haverford's liberal arts mission, at least 19 of the 32 courses required to complete a degree must be outside one's major. Nearly all undergrads complete a thesis in their chosen field. About half study abroad.

In their residence halls, first-year students join a

make the effort to get off campus," notes Rosalie Samide, a spring psychology grad from Latrobe, Pennsylvania. One option is to take classes or eat at sister school Bryn Mawr (story, at right), with whom many activities are shared. Haverfordians can also take classes at the University of Pennsylvania and local rival Swarthmore College.

Moreover, given the proximity to Philadelphia, Haverford isn't "kind of stuck in the woods like

Hard at work in a cell and molecular biology "super lab"

"customs group," a community of peers and upperclass students who can offer advice on academics, programs on campus, and other topics. Older students can opt to live in housing built around a theme, in which residents often host events for all students. Examples: Nerd House, a community where residents have regular board game nights and murder mystery parties, and Culinary House, where they hold dinners and cooking classes.

While some students acknowledge the school can seem a bit insular, "it doesn't feel small if you

a lot of similarly sized schools," says Phil Drexler, a recent grad in physics from Wilmington, Delaware. Many students take advantage of the city's museums, shows, dining and sports teams. Especially popular are events organized by the student-run group Fords Against Boredom, such as Ben & Jerry's bingo and midnight cheesesteak runs. On campus, students cheer on the Division III Fords, hang out in the Coop or the student-run Lunt Café, and enjoy frequent a capella concerts and events like the winter SnowBall and spring festival. ●

Bryn Mawr College
Bryn Mawr

Ivy Gray-Klein was working on her thesis and venting her stress on her blog when she received a surprise in the mail: a care package of snacks and study-break reading material from a 2001 Bryn Mawr alumna, a loyal reader she had never met. "We all kind of have each other's backs," says Gray-Klein, a Chicago native who graduated in May with a degree in art history.

Surrounded by trees, elegant lawns and castle-like Gothic architecture, some 1,300 women attend the suburban Philadelphia institution, the smallest of the Northeast's elite women's colleges once collectively known as the Seven Sisters. Students credit much of the family atmosphere to the honor code, under which they can safely leave belongings around campus, schedule their own exams (and take them without proctors) and typically avoid discussing grades. They also value the school's self-governance system, within which students decide policies.

Close partner. Bryn Mawr enjoys a partnership with neighboring Haverford College (Page 57); students at each have access to the other's facilities, organizations, social activities and classes, and even can complete majors at the other institution. Bryn Mawr offers majors in archaeology and geology, for instance, while Haverford has religion, music and fine arts.

Whatever their intended major, all first-year students must complete the Emily Balch Seminar, an intensive writing course centered on a broad subject like humanity and technology. Popular among older students are 360-degree course clusters, interdisciplinary cohorts of classes that often involve off-campus experiences and are taught by faculty

UNDERGRADUATES
Full-time: **1,315**

TOTAL COST*
$59,890

U.S. NEWS RANKING
National Liberal Arts Colleges
#27

*Tuition, fees and room & board

from a range of fields; the eco-literacy cluster, for example, blends economics, education and literature.

Campus dining earns rave reviews – it's not uncommon to see Haverford students in line – as do the residence halls, where many rooms contain comfy touches like fireplaces and window seats. Most Mawrters share the view that attending a women's college is empowering, and praise the school's diversity; undergraduates hail from 43 states and 62 countries, and more than half are from abroad or students of color. "There is no one set Bryn Mawr woman," says senior economics major Mfon-ido Akpan, who is from Nigeria. Classes are typically small, and the student-

A quiet moment (above) and a class at the smallest of the original Seven Sisters

popular), and social activities include teas hosted by campus clubs or academic departments, and performances at the cathedral-like Goodhart Hall. Cherished traditions include Lantern Night, when sophomores present freshmen with lanterns in a gesture of passing on "the light of knowledge," and leaving food and other tokens at the statue of Athena, the college's patron goddess, for luck. "It's not a typical college experience," says recent math and computer science grad Natalie Kato of Los Angeles. "But that doesn't mean it's not wonderful." ●

faculty ratio is just 8-to-1. Professors "care about your well-being," says Lindsey Crowe, a 2014 grad in English from Los Angeles.

On the other hand, students say that the college can feel small. But town is just a short walk away, and downtown Philly is about a 20-minute train ride. There are 100-plus organizations and clubs (Ultimate Frisbee with Haverford is especially

South

Furman University
Clemson University
University of South Carolina
College of Charleston

By **MARGARET LOFTUS**

Come along with U.S. News on a tour of South Carolina, as we check out a range of college options for you. The trip begins in the historic heart of Charleston, then heads north to the home of the Carolina Gamecocks and on to Tigers country, and ends in Greenville, at Furman University.

College of Charleston

Ask College of Charleston students what it was about their campus visit that drew them to the school, and you might hear something like, "They had me at the Cistern." Hollywood couldn't conjure a more storybook backdrop for a southern college than this grand grassy yard (named for the oval cistern at its center), shaded by majestic oaks draped with Spanish moss and fronted by 19th-century Randall Hall, a national historic landmark and one of the oldest academic buildings still in use in the country.

Outside the yard's stone walls, campus is concentrated in 20-odd blocks of historic downtown Charleston, its buildings ranging from the sleek and corporate-looking Beatty Center, which houses the business school, to rehabbed "singles," the narrow, deep homes characteristic of the city that house some academic departments. Students consider the city their turf, says Jimmie Foster, assistant vice president for admissions and enrollment management. "King Street is an extension of campus," he says of the historic main thoroughfare and shopping district. Some 30 percent of the college population (and 90 percent of freshmen) live on campus, which, like the city itself, is easily negotiated on foot or by using the school's bike share program. Students who want to explore more widely can hop on the city's CARTA bus system for free.

Of 57 majors, the most popular coincide with the region's strong suits. Those pursuing the health sciences conduct undergraduate research at the Medical University of South Carolina a few blocks away; tourism and hospitality students feed into the city's booming hotel industry. Marine biology students benefit from the coastal location and from the recent purchase of Dixie Plantation along the nearby Stono River, whose wetlands, pine forest and tidal marshes will be used for

UNDERGRADUATES
Full-time: 9,708

TOTAL COST*
In-state: $22,145
Out-of-state: $39,135

U.S. NEWS RANKING
Regional Universities, South
#13

*Tuition, fees and room & board

Photography by **BRETT ZIEGLER** *for USN&WR*

Carolina

Art students tackle welding at the College of Charleston. Below, the choir rehearses.

research. The college also boasts strong programs in studio art, dance and theater. And the School of Languages, Culture and World Affairs offers one of the most extensive foreign language programs in the region, ranging from ancient Greek to Japanese.

The Honors College enrolls some 700 students, who take 30 percent of their courses – small seminars – through the program and have special opportunities like a semester in Washington and priority access to funds for undergraduate research. They also have the option of living with other honors students in a living-learning community.

Student stats. Two-thirds of Charleston undergrads come from the Palmetto State, and the rest are largely from the East Coast. There are more women (64 percent) than men, and minorities now stand at 15 percent of the total population, a figure the school's new president has pledged to increase.

Students rally around Cougars basketball, and enjoy the nearby beaches in warm weather and a thriving nightlife scene on King Street. Many stick around after graduation, says Justin Lyons (class of 2014), a Spanish major from Fort Mill, South Carolina, who plans to find work and stay on for at least a year. "Why," he wonders, "would you want to leave?" ●

University of South Carolina

Columbia

The change of classes at the University of South Carolina is a sea of garnet sweatshirts and baseball caps, moving in waves along the brick paths that crisscross campus. USC students are fanatics about their sports teams, which are named after the Carolina Gamecock, a moniker the British gave to South Carolina planter and revolutionary war hero Thomas Sumter for his fierce fighting tactics. "Sports are a huge part of the culture," says Katy Hallman, a junior public health major from Greenville, South Carolina. So much so that the fight song is played every morning at 9:00. "It puts some pep in your step to make those early classes," she says.

The school was founded in 1801 as part of a movement spurred by Thomas Jefferson to establish public colleges in the South. During the Civil War, its gracious federal-style buildings served as hospitals for both sides, and thus were spared when General William Tecumseh Sherman torched much of Columbia. Today, the university is anchored by the oak-lined lawn known as the horseshoe, flanked by the original buildings that now house honors student apartments, the president's quarters and

UNDERGRADUATES
Full-time: 22,533

TOTAL COST*
In-state: **$19,725**
Out-of-state: **$37,437**

U.S. NEWS RANKING
National Universities
#113

*Tuition, fees and room & board

the country's oldest freestanding college library.

While the campus spans some 480 acres, its historic heart feels more like a leafy liberal arts college than the center of a large public university in a city of 132,000. Yes, there's sometimes too much bureaucracy, students say, and occasional lectures with 100-plus attendees. But they also remark on how small the school can seem. "It doesn't feel like 30,000 people are here until you're in the stadium," says Erik Telford of Columbia, who recently graduated with a management major. Some 400 student organizations, from the Clarinet Association to the skydiving club, provide newcomers access to others with similar interests.

Family feel. "If you find the right place, [it's] going to feel like a family," says Lauren Harper, a sophomore public relations major from Fort Mill, South Carolina. More than a fifth of students belong to a fraternity or sorority, but "if you're not Greek, you're not going to feel left out," says senior broadcast journalism major Sydney Patterson, from Lancaster, an hour or so from campus.

Like a lot of universities, USC boasts multiple living-learning communities – niche housing designed to bring like-minded students together, both in class and socially. Administrators also tout the University 101 class, a semesterlong course to help smooth the transition to college by introducing resources and teaching study skills. "The whole focus is to take a large group and make it a small group," says Jerry Brewer, associate vice president for student life and development. An honors college gives students the opportunity to design their own course of study, take small

Studying together in the USC library, and pausing for a break in the lounge (at top)

Clemson University
Clemson

L est visitors lose their way to Clemson University, a trail of tiger paw prints painted on the highway leads to campus – advance notice of the fervent school spirit at this institution in the foothills of the Blue Ridge. Once you're here, the tiger paw logo and the color orange are ubiquitous. As mechanical engineering senior Chris Hapstack puts it, "our blood runs orange."

Clemson stands on what was once the estate of 19th-century politician John Calhoun, whose son-in-law, Thomas Green Clemson, willed the land and the bulk of his fortune to the state

UNDERGRADUATES
Full-time: **16,050**

TOTAL COST*
In-state: **$21,524**
Out-of-state: **$38,958**

U.S. NEWS RANKING
National Universities
#62

*Tuition, fees and room & board

discussion-based classes and live in a tight-knit community while enjoying access to the facilities of a large university. Roughly 65 percent of the population hails from South Carolina, with most of the out-of-staters coming from the East Coast.

A city that often is defined in terms of its proximity to the beach and mountains (both two hours away), Columbia is becoming a destination in its own right, with a revitalized downtown, a world-class art museum, Riverbanks Zoo and year-round festivals. Nonetheless, the action comes to a halt on the fall Saturdays when the Gamecocks play at home. ●

to establish a college. Opened in 1893 as an all-male military college, the school went coed and civilian in 1955; the old family home, Fort Hill, still anchors Clemson's 17,000 acres, which are bordered on the west by Hartwell Lake, a hub of

At Clemson University's equine center, members of the equestrian team prepare to head out for a ride.

student recreation.

Despite the size, the main part of campus is walkable, with residential halls encircling the library and academic buildings. The tiny town of Clemson is also within walking distance, and nearby Greenville and Anderson are reachable by a free bus service. While approximately 60 percent of the some 20,000 students are from South Carolina, Director of Admission Robert Barkley says the school has seen an uptick in popularity outside the region. "Thirty years ago we were this sleepy little university in the hills. [Now] it's big-time opportunities with a small-school feel."

Strong in science. As a land grant university, the school is particularly strong in the sciences. Engineering is by far the most popular major, pursued by a full third of the freshman class, with business coming in second. The university also boasts a nursing program and the only architectural school in the state.

With faculty members engaged in ongoing studies of everything from computational modeling to the behavior of wild Brazilian monkeys or people using social media, Clemson offers undergraduates ample opportunities to assist professors in their research projects. Two cutting-edge social media "listening centers" feature arrays of large screens that display streams of data from online communities and social media sources and feed research on sentiment and trending topics, for instance. Students can also conduct their own studies through the Creative Inquiry program, in a team effort that can span up to four semesters.

The Calhoun Honors College offers qualified students smaller, more intimate classes, from a 15-person section of Chemistry 101 to a course on "Harry Potter," as well as the chance to reside together in a living-learning community. Each year, the honors college awards travel grants to support the pursuit of internships, volunteer work and study elsewhere during winter and summer breaks.

Several years ago, Clemson launched a transfer program that invites a select group of students whose applications aren't quite strong enough for admission to come to town and attend community college freshman year. The program provides housing off campus, academic advising and access to university facilities and activities to participating students, three-quarters of whom make the transfer to Clemson for sophomore year.

With few distractions outside of campus besides a handful of bars in town and the Smokin' Pig for an occasional barbecue fix, social activities revolve around football, Greek life (23 percent of students are in sororities or frats) and intramural sports. More than 400 clubs are active, too, from the Fellowship of Christian Athletes and the Darfur Awareness Club to the Model Railroaders. ●

Furman University

Greenville

With a spring-fed lake, golf course and miles of paved woodland trails, Furman University has a peaceful gated-community feel – conducive, administrators hope, to what they and students both describe as a rigorous academic experience. "It's hard. Get ready to work. But it's worth it," says student body president Brian Boda, a senior from Marietta, Georgia, majoring in political science.

A student-faculty ratio of 11-to-1 keeps average class size to 19 and fosters close relationships between students and professors, students say. "There's no handholding," says Boda, but professors are supportive. He was especially impressed that one of his political science professors spent hours helping him hone a personal statement for a grad school application last semester. Health sci-

UNDERGRADUATES
Full-time: **2,675**

TOTAL COST*
$55,872

U.S. NEWS RANKING
National Liberal Arts Colleges
#51

*Tuition, fees and room & board

portunities with faculty abound. Undergrads are "the primary collaborators," says Brad Pochard, associate vice president for admission. "When they leave here, they have grad-level research experience." Six years ago, the school launched an annual "engage day," during which students present research across campus, with topics ranging from population control policies of China and India to the significance of the millennial vote. Internships are strongly encouraged: Some 68 percent of students now complete at least one at partnering institutions such as Greenville Hospital System, the accounting

A lakeside study session outside Furman's student center, and hanging out over lunch (below)

students are from South Carolina; two-thirds are from the Southeast. Pochard says that 15 to 18 percent of the population is considered "nonwhite," including international students; but to some, at least, the campus seems too homogenous and affluent. "I wish it was more diverse," says health sciences major Melanie Brannon, a junior from Roswell, Georgia. A taste of the wider world is provided by the location on the edge of Greenville, a city of 61,000 noted for its lively downtown and arts and music scene. Thanks to the nearby North American headquarters of French tire manufacturer Michelin and German carmaker BMW, the former textile hub has a thriving international community.

Outdoor action. Furman fields 20 NCAA Division I teams, and club teams in rugby and cycling are known for being extremely competitive. The region is rich in outdoor recreation, including kayaking, skiing, rock climbing and biking (as the home of former professional cyclist George Hincapie, Greenville is a cycling hub). More than 150 organizations offer the possibility to get active, the most popular of which is the Heller Service Corps, a volunteer organization that involves some 1,800 students a year with 50 partners; they do everything from host a Valentine's dance for adults with special needs to volunteer at animal shelters. A big attraction, says programming director Deanna Heine, a senior from Carrollton, Georgia, is that volunteering gets students "out of the Furman bubble." ●

ences, political science and business administration are the most popular of 45 majors, and the music program is particularly well-regarded; among its

alumni is Boston Pops conductor Keith Lockhart.
   Though Furman has only two graduate programs, in education and chemistry, research op-

firm KPMG in Atlanta, and the U.S. Trade and Development Agency in Washington, D.C. The goal is 100 percent.
   About a quarter of

The U.S. NEW RANKI

James Madison
University in Virginia

BRETT ZIEGLER FOR USN&WR

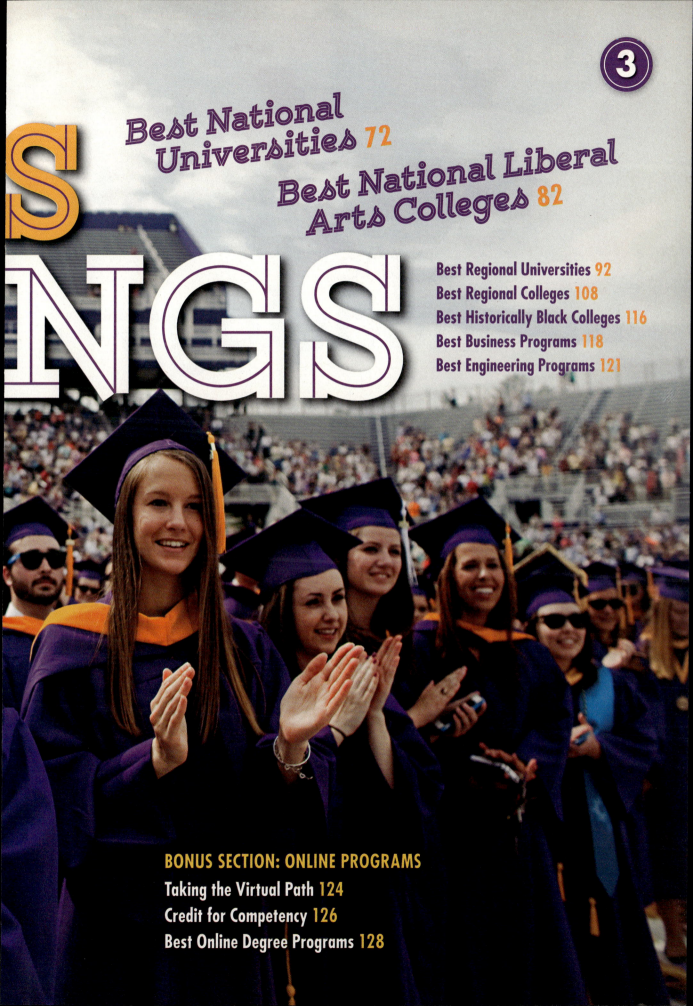

RANKINGS

3

A Close Look at the Methodology

HOW COLLEGEBOUND STUDENTS CAN MAKE THE MOST OF OUR STATISTICS

By **ROBERT J. MORSE AND SAMUEL FLANIGAN**

The host of intangibles that make up the college experience can't be measured by a series of data points. But for families concerned with finding the best academic value for their money, the U.S. News Best Colleges rankings, now in their 30th year, provide an excellent starting point for the search. They allow you to compare at a glance the relative quality of institutions based on such widely accepted indicators of excellence as freshman retention and graduation rates and the strength of the faculty. And as you check out the data for colleges already on your short list, you may discover unfamiliar schools with similar metrics, and thus broaden your options.

Yes, many factors other than those spotlighted here will figure in your decision, including location and the feel of campus life; the range of academic offerings, activities and sports; and the cost and availability of financial aid. But

BRETT ZIEGLER FOR USN&WR

The University of Pennsylvania

More @ usnews.com/bestcolleges

if you combine the information in this book with campus visits, interviews and your own intuition, our rankings can be a powerful tool in your quest for the right college.

How does the methodology work? The U.S. News ranking system rests on two pillars. The formula uses quantitative measures that education experts have proposed as reliable indicators of academic quality, and it's based on our researched view of what matters in education. First, schools are categorized by their mission, which is derived from the breakdown of types of higher education institutions developed by the Carnegie Foundation for the Advancement of Teaching. The Carnegie classification has been the basis of the Best Colleges ranking category system since our first ranking was published three decades ago, given that it is used extensively by higher education researchers. The U.S. Department of Education and many higher education associations use the system to organize their data and to determine colleges' eligibility for grant money, for example.

In short, the Carnegie categories are the accepted standard. The category names we use are our own – National Universities, National Liberal Arts Colleges, Regional Universities and Regional Colleges – but the definitions of each rely on the Carnegie principles.

The national universities (Page 72) offer a full range of undergraduate majors, plus master's and Ph.D. programs, and emphasize faculty research. The national liberal arts colleges (Page 82) focus almost exclusively on undergraduate education. They award at least 50 percent of their degrees in the arts and sciences.

The regional universities (Page 92) offer a broad scope of undergraduate degrees and some master's degree programs but few, if any, doctoral programs. The regional colleges (Page 108) focus on undergraduate education but grant fewer than 50 percent of their degrees in liberal arts disciplines; this category also includes schools that have small bachelor's degree programs but primarily grant two-year associate degrees. The regional universities and regional colleges are further divided and ranked in four geographical groups: North, South, Midwest and West.

Next, we gather data from each college on up to 16 indicators of academic excellence. Each factor is assigned a weight that reflects our judgment about how much a measure matters. Finally, the colleges and universities in

each category are ranked against their peers, based on their composite weighted score.

Some schools are not ranked and thus do not appear in the tables. The main reason a school falls into this group is that SAT or ACT test scores are not used in admissions decisions for first-time, first-year, degree-seeking applicants. In a few cases, colleges were ineligible because they received too few ratings in the peer assessment survey to be reliably ranked or had a total enrollment of fewer than 200 students, a large proportion of nontraditional students, or no first-year students (as is the situation at so-called upper-division schools).

As a result of these eligibility standards, many of the for-profit institutions are not ranked; their bachelor's degree candidates are largely nontraditional students in degree completion programs, for example, or they don't use test scores in making admissions decisions. We also did not rank a number of highly specialized schools in the arts, business and engineering.

Most of the data come from the colleges themselves, via the U.S. News statistical survey. This year, 91.5 percent of the 1,365 ranked colleges and universities returned their statistical information during our spring and summer data collection period.

For colleges that were eligible to be ranked but declined to fill out our survey, we made extensive use of the data those institutions reported to the U.S. Department of Education's National Center for Education Statistics and other organizations. We obtained missing data on faculty salaries from the American Association of University Professors, for example, information on graduation rates from the National Collegiate Athletic Association and data on alumni giving from the Council for Aid to Education. The National Center for Education Statistics is a rich source on SAT and ACT scores, acceptance rates, retention and graduation rates, student-faculty ratios, and information on financial resources and faculty.

Data that did not come from this year's survey are footnoted, and schools are identified as nonresponders. Estimates may be used in the calculations when schools fail to report data points that are not available from other sources, but estimates are not displayed in the tables. Missing data are reported as N/A.

The indicators we use to capture academic quality fall into a number of categories: assessment by administrators at peer institutions (and, for national universities and

Measuring What's Important

The U.S. News rankings are based on several key measures of quality, listed below. Scores for each measure are weighted as shown to arrive at a final overall score. In the case of the national universities and national liberal arts colleges, the assessment figure represents input from both academic peers (15 percent) and high school guidance counselors (7.5 percent); for regional universities and colleges, it reflects peer opinion only.

The Scoring Breakdown

Graduation and retention rates	22.5%
Assessment of excellence	22.5%
Faculty resources	20%
Student selectivity	12.5%
Financial resources	10%
Graduation rate performance*	7.5%
Alumni giving	5%

*The difference between actual and predicted graduation rates.

liberal arts colleges, by high school guidance counselors as well), how well schools perform at retaining and graduating students, the quality of and investment in the faculty, student selectivity, financial resources and the state of alumni giving. The indicators include input measures that reflect a school's student body, its faculty and its resources, along with outcome measures that signal how well the institution does its job of educating students.

An explanation of the measures and their weightings in the ranking formula follows; more detail on the methodology can be found at usnews.com/collegemeth.

Assessment by peers and counselors

(22.5 percent). The ranking formula gives significant weight to the opinions of those in a position to judge a school's undergraduate academic excellence. The academic peer assessment survey allows presidents, provosts and deans of admissions to account for intangibles at peer institutions such as faculty dedication to teaching. For their views on the

are judged based on the peer assessment only.

In order to reduce the impact of strategic voting by respondents, we eliminated the two highest and two lowest scores each school received before calculating the average score. Ipsos Public Affairs collected the data in the spring of 2014; of the 4,533 academics who were sent questionnaires, 42 percent responded. The counselors' response rate this past spring was 9 percent.

Retention (22.5 percent). The higher the proportion of freshmen who return to campus for sophomore year and eventually graduate, the better a school most likely is at offering the classes and services that students need to succeed. This measure has two components: six-year graduation rate (80 percent of the retention score) and freshman retention rate (20 percent).

The graduation rate indicates the average proportion of a graduating class earning a degree in six years or less. We consider freshman classes that started from fall 2004 through fall

> # THE RANKINGS provide a launching pad
> ## for more research – not an easy answer.'

national universities and the national liberal arts colleges, we also surveyed 2,152 counselors at public high schools that appeared in the 2013 U.S. News ranking of Best High Schools and 400 college counselors at the largest independent schools.

Each person surveyed was asked to rate schools' academic programs on a 5-point scale from 1 (marginal) to 5 (distinguished). Those who didn't know enough about a school to evaluate it fairly were asked to mark "don't know." The score used in the rankings is the average of these scores; "don't knows" are not counted.

In the case of the national universities and national liberal arts colleges, the academic peer assessment accounts for 15 percentage points of the weighting, and 7.5 percentage points go to the counselors' ratings. The two most recent years' results were averaged to compute the high school counselor score, a way of reducing year-to-year volatility in the average. The academic peer assessment score continues to be based only on the most recent year's results. (For the full results of the high school counselors' ratings of the colleges, visit usnews.com/counselors.) The regional universities and the regional colleges

2007. Freshman retention indicates the average proportion of freshmen who entered the school in the fall of 2009 through fall 2012 and returned the following fall.

Faculty resources (20 percent). Research shows that the more satisfied students are about their contact with professors, the more they will learn and the more likely they are to graduate. We use six factors from the 2013-2014 academic year to assess a school's commitment to instruction.

Class size has two components, the proportion of classes with fewer than 20 students (30 percent of the faculty resources score) and the proportion with 50 or more students (10 percent of the score). Faculty salary (35 percent) is the average faculty pay, plus benefits, during the 2012-13 and 2013-14 academic years, adjusted for regional differences in the cost of living using indexes from the consulting firm Runzheimer International.

We also weigh the proportion of professors with the highest degree in their field (15 percent), the student-faculty ratio (5 percent) and the proportion of faculty who are full time (5 percent).

Student selectivity (12.5 percent). A school's academic atmosphere is determined in part by the abilities and ambitions of the students. We factor in the admissions test scores for all enrollees who took the critical reading and math portions of the SAT and the composite ACT score (65 percent of the selectivity score); the proportion of enrolled freshmen at national universities and national liberal arts colleges who graduated in the top 10 percent of their high school classes or in the top quarter at regional universities and regional colleges (25 percent); and the acceptance rate, or the ratio of students admitted to applicants (10 percent). The data are all for the fall

Haverford College

2013 entering class. While the ranking calculation takes account of both the SAT and ACT scores of all entering students, the table displays the score range for whichever test was taken by most students.

For the second year, we're using footnotes to more clearly indicate schools that did not report fall 2013 SAT and ACT test scores for all new students for whom they had scores (including athletes, international students, minority students, legacies, those admitted by special arrangement, and those who started in the summer of 2013) or schools that declined to tell us whether all students with scores were represented. We have long discounted the value of such schools' reported scores in the ranking model since the effect of leaving students out could be that lower scores are omitted.

Financial resources (10 percent). Generous per-student spending indicates that a college can offer a wide variety of programs and services. U.S. News measures financial resources by using the average spending per student on instruction, research, student services and related educational expenditures in the 2012 and 2013 fiscal years. Spending on sports, dorms and hospitals doesn't count.

Graduation rate performance (7.5 percent). For the second year, the graduation rate performance indicator has been applied in all of the Best Colleges ranking categories. This indicator shows the effect of programs and policies on the graduation rate after controlling for spending and student characteristics such as test scores and the proportion receiving Pell grants.

We measure the difference between a school's six-year graduation rate for the class that entered in 2007 and the rate we predicted for the class. If the actual graduation rate is higher than the predicted rate, then the college is enhancing achievement.

Alumni giving rate (5 percent). This reflects the average percentage of living alumni with bachelor's degrees who gave to their school during 2011-12 and 2012-13, an indirect measure of student satisfaction.

To arrive at a school's rank, we calculated the weighted sum of its scores. The final scores were rescaled so that the top college or university in each category received a value of 100, and the other schools' weighted scores were calculated as a proportion of that top score. Final scores were rounded to the nearest whole number and ranked in descending order. Schools that are tied appear in alphabetical order.

Be sure to check out usnews.com regularly over the coming year, since we may add content to the Best Colleges pages as we obtain additional information. And as you mine the tables that follow for insights (a sense of which schools might be impressed enough by your SAT or ACT scores to offer some merit aid, for example, or where you will be apt to get the most attention from professors), keep in mind that the rankings provide a launching pad for more research – not an easy answer. ●

BRETT ZIEGLER FOR USN&WR

Best National Univer[sities]

Rank	School (State) (*Public)	Overall score	Peer assessment score (5.0=highest)	High school counselor assessment score	Graduation and retention rank	Average freshman retention rate	2013 graduation rate Predicted	Actual	Over-performance(+) Under-performance(-)	Facu resou ran
1.	Princeton University (NJ)	100	4.8	4.9	2	98%	94%	97%	+3	5
2.	Harvard University (MA)	99	4.9	4.9	2	97%	95%	97%	+2	3
3.	Yale University (CT)	98	4.8	4.9	1	99%	95%	98%	+3	8
4.	Columbia University (NY)	95	4.6	4.9	5	99%	94%	96%	+2	4
4.	Stanford University (CA)	95	4.9	4.9	5	98%	94%	96%	+2	10
4.	University of Chicago	95	4.6	4.7	10	99%	93%	93%	None	1
7.	Massachusetts Inst. of Technology	93	4.9	4.9	15	98%	95%	93%	-2	12
8.	Duke University (NC)	92	4.4	4.8	10	97%	94%	94%	None	1
8.	University of Pennsylvania	92	4.4	4.8	2	98%	94%	96%	+2	6
10.	California Institute of Technology	91	4.6	4.8	22	97%	95%	93%	-2	11
11.	Dartmouth College (NH)	90	4.2	4.8	5	98%	93%	95%	+2	15
12.	Johns Hopkins University (MD)	89	4.6	4.8	18	97%	93%	93%	None	18
13.	Northwestern University (IL)	88	4.3	4.7	10	97%	94%	94%	None	6
14.	Washington University in St. Louis	86	4.0	4.6	10	97%	95%	94%	-1	12
15.	Cornell University (NY)	85	4.5	4.8	15	97%	92%	93%	+1	20
16.	Brown University (RI)	84	4.4	4.8	5	98%	93%	94%	+1	17
16.	University of Notre Dame (IN)	84	3.9	4.7	5	98%	92%	95%	+3	16
16.	Vanderbilt University (TN)	84	4.1	4.6	18	97%	92%	93%	+1	12
19.	Rice University (TX)	82	4.0	4.5	18	97%	92%	91%	-1	9
20.	University of California–Berkeley*	79	4.7	4.7	22	97%	87%	91%	+4	32
21.	Emory University (GA)	77	4.0	4.5	29	95%	92%	91%	-1	24
21.	Georgetown University (DC)	77	4.0	4.8	15	96%	92%	92%	None	44
23.	Univ. of California–Los Angeles*	76	4.2	4.5	22	97%	86%	90%	+4	32
23.	University of Virginia*	76	4.3	4.5	10	97%	88%	93%	+5	32
25.	Carnegie Mellon University (PA)	75	4.2	4.7	32	95%	91%	88%	-3	20
25.	Univ. of Southern California	75	3.9	4.3	27	97%	91%	91%	None	38
27.	Tufts University (MA)	73	3.6	4.5	18	97%	92%	92%	None	31
27.	Wake Forest University (NC)	73	3.5	4.4	33	94%	89%	86%	-3	28
29.	University of Michigan–Ann Arbor*	72	4.4	4.4	22	97%	89%	90%	+1	68
30.	U. of North Carolina–Chapel Hill*	71	4.1	4.5	29	97%	87%	90%	+3	68
31.	Boston College	69	3.6	4.4	22	95%	90%	91%	+1	53
32.	New York University	68	3.8	4.5	40	92%	89%	84%	-5	20
33.	College of William and Mary (VA)*	67	3.7	4.4	27	96%	89%	90%	+1	55
33.	University of Rochester (NY)	67	3.4	4.1	37	96%	90%	85%	-5	23
35.	Brandeis University (MA)	66	3.5	4.1	29	93%	91%	90%	-1	49
35.	Georgia Institute of Technology*	66	4.2	4.4	50	95%	87%	82%	-5	110
37.	Univ. of California–San Diego*	65	3.8	4.1	35	95%	84%	86%	+2	99
38.	Case Western Reserve Univ. (OH)	64	3.5	4.3	62	93%	88%	80%	-8	32
38.	University of California–Davis*	64	3.8	4.2	48	93%	80%	84%	+4	55
40.	Lehigh University (PA)	63	3.3	4.1	33	94%	91%	86%	-5	41
40.	Univ. of California–Santa Barbara*	63	3.5	3.9	50	92%	81%	86%	+5	28
42.	Boston University	62	3.5	4.2	40	92%	84%	84%	None	32
42.	Northeastern University (MA)	62	3.2	4.2	56	95%	79%	83%	+4	24
42.	Rensselaer Polytechnic Inst. (NY)	62	3.4	4.2	45	93%	89%	85%	-4	41
42.	University of California–Irvine*	62	3.6	4.0	37	94%	82%	86%	+4	38
42.	U. of Illinois–Urbana-Champaign*	62	3.9	4.1	40	94%	83%	84%	+1	55
47.	Univ. of Wisconsin–Madison*	61	4.1	4.1	40	95%	85%	84%	-1	91
48.	Pennsylvania State U.–Univ. Park*	60	3.6	4.1	37	92%	76%	85%	+9	90
48.	University of Florida*	60	3.6	3.8	35	96%	83%	87%	+4	99
48.	University of Miami (FL)	60	3.2	4.0	62	91%	86%	82%	-4	44
48.	University of Washington*	60	3.8	4.0	56	93%	80%	82%	+2	144
48.	Yeshiva University (NY)	60	2.8	3.4	40	91%	83%	89%	+6	24

Note: Key to footnotes, Page 80.

% of classes under 20 ('13)	% of classes of 50 or more ('13)	Student/faculty ratio ('13)	Selectivity rank	SAT/ACT 25th-75th percentile ('13)	Freshmen in top 10% of HS class ('13)	Acceptance rate ('13)	Financial resources rank	Alumni giving rank	Average alumni giving rate
71%	11%	6/1	5	1410-1600	95%[5]	7%	10	1	63%
76%	10%	7/1	5	1410-1600	95%[5]	6%	5	10	35%
77%	7%	6/1	3	1420-1590	95%[5]	7%	1	7	36%
82%	9%	6/1	5	1400-1570	93%[5]	7%	11	13	34%
69%	12%	5/1	5	1380-1570	96%[5]	6%	8	7	36%
76%	5%	6/1	3	1440-1590	98%	9%	6	4	40%
69%	12%	8/1	1	1430-1570	99%[5]	8%	7	6	37%
71%	6%	7/1	14	1360-1550	90%[5]	12%	14	10	35%
68%	10%	6/1	10	1360-1540	94%[5]	12%	11	15	34%
63%	10%	3/1	1	1490-1600	99%[5]	11%	1	30	23%
62%	9%	8/1	10	1360-1560	90%[5]	10%	16	2	48%
72%	10%	10/1	18	1340-1520	84%[5]	17%	3	12	34%
75%	7%	7/1	10	1390-1550	91%[5]	14%	11	24	26%
65%	12%	8/1	5	32-34	95%[5]	16%	4	19	27%
56%	18%	9/1	20	1320-1520	87%[5]	16%	17	16	30%
69%	10%	8/1	39	1330-1540[3]	94%[5]	9%	24	5	38%
60%	9%	10/1	15	32-34	90%[5]	22%	29	3	42%
65%	9%	8/1	10	32-34	88%[5]	13%	15	27	26%
68%	10%	6/1	15	1370-1550	87%	17%	23	17	29%
60%	16%	17/1	20	1250-1500	98%	18%	38	98	13%
59%	8%	8/1	29	1260-1470	76%[5]	27%	18	18	28%
60%	7%	11/1	18	1320-1500	92%[5]	17%	29	19	26%
50%	22%	17/1	25	1190-1450	97%	20%	20	104	12%
55%	16%	16/1	24	1250-1460	92%[5]	30%	59	32	22%
67%	11%	13/1	22	1340-1530	80%[5]	25%	29	54	17%
57%	13%	9/1	22	1280-1480	88%[5]	20%	26	13	34%
68%	8%	9/1	15	1370-1520	91%[5]	19%	29	37	20%
57%	1%	11/1	32	1230-1420[2]	76%[5]	35%	9	24	26%
47%	18%	15/1	39	28-32	65%[4]	33%	41	46	19%
39%	13%	13/1	32	1200-1410	78%	27%	34	42	20%
51%	7%	13/1	25	1270-1450	81%[5]	32%	71	24	26%
62%	9%	10/1	45	1260-1460	63%[5]	32%	34	147	9%
48%	8%	12/1	25	1270-1460	80%[5]	33%	110	29	24%
70%	13%	10/1	30	1250-1450[2]	75%[5]	36%	21	52	18%
60%	10%	10/1	42	1230-1470	65%[5]	37%	52	19	27%
39%	25%	18/1	28	1290-1480	81%[5]	41%	43	19	27%
40%	35%	19/1	30	1180-1400	100%	37%	21	166	8%
64%	11%	10/1	32	1270-1480	67%[5]	42%	26	42	20%
40%	23%	17/1	50	1080-1340	100%	41%	28	156	8%
48%	11%	10/1	43	1220-1410	60%[5]	31%	55	30	23%
49%	18%	17/1	39	1130-1370	100%	40%	69	60	16%
62%	12%	13/1	50	1190-1390	58%[5]	37%	47	132	9%
66%	7%	13/1	32	1300-1480	64%[5]	32%	82	104	12%
51%	13%	15/1	36	1290-1488	72%[5]	41%	43	98	12%
50%	20%	19/1	64	1040-1290	96%	41%	46	196	6%
42%	20%	18/1	50	26-31	55%[5]	62%	64	127	10%
46%	19%	17/1	54	26-30	51%	51%	59	132	9%
42%	13%	17/1	107	1070-1280	36%[5]	55%	52	65	15%
47%	16%	21/1	45	1170-1360	77%	47%	47	72	15%
50%	8%	12/1	36	1230-1420	72%[5]	40%	25	65	15%
34%	22%	11/1	54	1100-1360	92%[5]	55%	34	75	14%
64%	1%	6/1	88	1100-1370	45%	82%	18	48	18%

What Is a National University?

To assess nearly 1,600 of the country's four-year colleges and universities, U.S. News first assigns each to a group of its peers, based on the categories of higher education institutions developed in 2010 by the Carnegie Foundation for the Advancement of Teaching. The National Universities category consists of the 280 institutions (173 public, 100 private and seven for-profit) that offer a wide range of undergraduate majors as well as master's and doctoral degrees; some emphasize research. A list of the top 30 public national universities appears on Page 80.

Data on up to 16 indicators of academic quality are gathered from each institution and tabulated. Schools are ranked by their total weighted score; those receiving the same rank are tied and listed in alphabetical order. For a description of the methodology, see Page 68, and for more on a college, turn to the directory at the back of the book.

Rank	School (State) (*Public)	Overall score	Peer assessment score (5.0=highest)	High school counselor assessment score	Average freshman retention rate	2013 graduation rate Predicted	2013 graduation rate Actual	% of classes under 20 ('13)	% of classes of 50 or more ('13)	SAT/ACT 25th-75th percentile ('13)	Freshmen in top 10% of HS class ('13)	Accept-ance rate ('13)	Average alumni giving rate
53.	University of Texas–Austin*	59	4.0	4.2	93%	82%	79%	35%	26%	1140-1380	75%	40%	12%
54.	George Washington University (DC)	58	3.5	4.3	93%	87%	81%	56%	9%	1200-1390	50%[5]	34%	9%
54.	Ohio State University–Columbus*	58	3.7	4.1	93%	80%	83%	30%	23%	27-31	58%	56%	14%
54.	Pepperdine University (CA)	58	3.2	4.3	91%	78%	80%	68%	3%	1130-1340	47%[5]	37%	9%
54.	Tulane University (LA)	58	3.4	4.2	90%	82%	76%	64%	6%	29-32[3]	58%[5]	26%	18%
58.	Fordham University (NY)	57	3.2	4.1	89%	78%	80%	51%	1%	1160-1350	47%[5]	47%	20%
58.	Southern Methodist University (TX)	57	3.0	3.9	90%	77%	79%	59%	7%	27-31	48%[5]	51%	21%
58.	Syracuse University (NY)	57	3.3	4.0	92%	75%	81%	63%	9%	1040-1270	39%[5]	49%	16%
58.	University of Connecticut*	57	3.1	4.0	93%	76%	83%	47%	17%	1130-1330	45%[5]	54%	17%
62.	Brigham Young Univ.–Provo (UT)	56	3.0	4.0	87%	78%	77%	57%	14%	26-31	54%	49%	14%
62.	Clemson University (SC)*	56	3.1	4.0	91%	77%	82%	51%	14%	1150-1340	56%	57%	24%
62.	Purdue Univ.–West Lafayette (IN)*	56	3.6	4.2	90%	68%	71%	38%	18%	1080-1320	47%[5]	60%	20%
62.	University of Georgia*	56	3.4	4.0	94%	81%	83%	40%	11%	1150-1330	53%	55%	11%
62.	Univ. of Maryland–College Park*	56	3.6	4.0	95%	84%	84%	44%	17%	1200-1420	71%	47%	8%
62.	University of Pittsburgh*	56	3.4	3.9	92%	78%	80%	41%	19%	1180-1360	53%	54%	11%
68.	Texas A&M Univ.–College Station*	55	3.6	4.1	92%	75%	81%	21%	25%	1070-1290	53%	69%	22%
68.	Worcester Polytechnic Inst. (MA)	55	2.9	4.0	96%	84%	81%	65%	11%	1220-1410[2]	64%	52%	14%
70.	Rutgers, St. U. of N.J.–New Brunswick*	53	3.4	4.0	92%	75%	79%	35%	21%	1090-1330	38%[5]	60%	8%
71.	American University (DC)	52	3.1	4.0	90%	83%	80%	47%	2%	1160-1350[2]	47%[5]	43%	9%
71.	Baylor University (TX)	52	3.2	4.1	86%	77%	75%	51%	10%	24-29	42%	57%	15%
71.	University of Iowa*	52	3.5	3.8	86%	65%	70%	55%	12%	23-28	24%	80%	9%
71.	Univ. of Minnesota–Twin Cities*	52	3.6	3.9	90%	78%	75%	39%	20%	26-30	45%	44%	10%
71.	Virginia Tech*	52	3.4	4.0	92%[8]	78%	83%	27%	20%	1120-1320	41%	70%	13%
76.	Clark University (MA)	50	2.8	3.8	90%	76%	81%	58%	5%	1110-1320[2]	38%[5]	62%	16%
76.	Indiana University–Bloomington*	50	3.6	4.0	89%	70%	77%	36%	17%	1060-1290	35%[5]	72%	14%
76.	Marquette University (WI)	50	3.0	3.9	89%	73%	78%	41%	13%	25-29	36%[5]	57%	15%
76.	Miami University–Oxford (OH)*	50	3.1	3.9	89%	73%	81%	30%	12%	25-30	39%[5]	67%	19%
76.	Stevens Institute of Technology (NJ)	50	2.7	3.8	94%	82%	79%	38%	9%	1210-1390	68%[5]	38%	15%
76.	SUNY Col. of Envir. Sci. and Forestry*	50	2.8	3.7	86%	63%	72%	66%	9%	1080-1260	27%	51%	22%
76.	Texas Christian University	50	2.8	3.9	88%	71%	76%	41%	7%	25-29	42%[5]	47%	22%
76.	University of Delaware*	50	3.1	3.8	92%	77%	82%	33%	16%	1090-1300	37%[5]	63%	10%
76.	Univ. of Massachusetts–Amherst*	50	3.2	4.0	89%	65%	73%	44%	19%	1110-1310	28%[5]	63%	10%
85.	Michigan State University*	49	3.5	3.9	91%	70%	78%	25%	22%	23-28[3]	28%[5]	69%	12%
85.	Univ. of California–Santa Cruz*	49	3.0	3.8	90%	78%	76%	46%	25%	1000-1280	96%	52%	6%
85.	University of Vermont*	49	2.9	3.7	86%	68%	76%	52%	14%	1080-1290	33%[5]	78%	11%
88.	Binghamton University–SUNY*	48	2.9	3.8	91%	79%	81%	45%	14%	1203-1385	52%[5]	42%	7%
88.	Colorado School of Mines*	48	3.3	4.1	90%	80%	70%	24%	17%	28-32	66%	36%	18%
88.	Stony Brook–SUNY*	48	3.2	3.6	90%	70%	66%	43%	21%	1150-1350	47%[5]	39%	9%
88.	University of Alabama*	48	3.0	3.7	86%	65%	67%	43%	18%	22-30	41%	57%	36%
88.	University of Colorado–Boulder*	48	3.5	3.8	85%	68%	70%	47%	16%	24-29	27%	88%	8%
88.	University of Denver	48	2.8	3.6	87%	73%	78%	50%	6%	25-30	45%[5]	77%	9%
88.	University of Tulsa (OK)	48	2.6	3.6	88%	81%	69%	62%	2%	25-32	74%[5]	41%	21%
95.	Drexel University (PA)	47	3.0	4.0	85%	73%	70%	57%	7%	1070-1310	33%[5]	82%	9%
95.	Florida State University*	47	3.0	3.6	92%	69%	77%	34%	15%	25-29	42%	57%	18%
95.	North Carolina State U.–Raleigh*	47	3.1	3.8	92%	74%	74%	28%	17%	1150-1320	50%	47%	13%
95.	University of San Diego	47	2.8	3.9	89%	76%	75%	39%	0.3%	1110-1320	45%	49%	12%
99.	St. Louis University	46	2.9	3.9	86%	74%	70%	54%	8%	25-30	41%[5]	64%	13%
99.	Univ. of Missouri*	46	3.3	3.7	84%	66%	70%	42%	16%	23-28	27%	79%	16%
99.	Univ. of Nebraska–Lincoln*	46	3.1	3.8	84%	64%	67%	41%	15%	22-28	26%	64%	21%
99.	University of New Hampshire*	46	2.8	3.7	87%	65%	80%	44%	16%	1000-1210	20%	78%	8%
103.	Auburn University (AL)*	45	3.1	3.9	89%	67%	68%	30%	16%	24-30	29%	83%	11%
103.	University at Buffalo–SUNY*	45	3.0	3.7	88%	65%	72%	33%	21%	1050-1290	28%[5]	57%	8%
103.	University of Dayton (OH)	45	2.6	3.5	88%	67%	77%	35%	4%	24-29	24%[5]	52%	15%
106.	Iowa State University*	44	3.2	3.8	87%	66%	68%	30%	23%	22-28	25%	85%	14%
106.	Loyola University Chicago	44	2.9	4.0	86%	73%	71%	38%	7%	24-29	37%[5]	91%	11%
106.	University of Kansas*	44	3.3	3.8	80%	67%	62%	45%	12%	22-28	26%	88%	16%
106.	University of Oklahoma*	44	3.0	3.8	84%	69%	66%	41%	11%	23-29	33%	80%	19%
106.	University of Oregon*	44	3.3	3.9	86%	62%	67%	38%	21%	990-1240	25%[5]	74%	10%
106.	University of San Francisco	44	2.8	3.8	86%	64%	69%	52%	3%	1070-1270	33%[5]	61%	9%
106.	University of Tennessee*	44	3.1	3.8	86%	72%	68%	29%	15%	24-29	52%[5]	72%	10%
113.	Univ. of California–Riverside*	43	3.1	3.8	88%	70%	69%	28%	30%	990-1210	94%	60%	4%
113.	Univ. of South Carolina*	43	2.9	3.8	87%	70%	73%	33%	16%	1110-1300	30%	64%	18%
113.	University of St. Thomas (MN)	43	2.5	3.6	88%	66%	75%	41%	2%	23-28[3]	22%	86%	18%
116.	Catholic University of America (DC)	42	2.7	3.7	82%	62%	69%	61%	5%	1010-1220	N/A	60%	8%

Note: Key to footnotes, Page 80.

HIGHER EDUCATION AT THE
HIGHEST PROVEN VALUE

TOP 40 BESTVALUE IN PUBLIC COLLEGES
KIPLINGER

We get it — higher education is an expensive investment. So we're increasing scholarships. Managing costs. And doing everything we can to increase the long-term value of a Purdue degree. Because when we say that big ideas are at the core of higher education — we mean it. Which is why we're forging the way in STEM leadership by investing in our students. And changing the world as a result.

purdue.edu/purduemoves

WE ARE PURDUE. WHAT WE MAKE MOVES THE WORLD FORWARD.

EA/EOU

Rank	School (State) (*Public)	Overall score	Peer assessment score (5.0=highest)	High school counselor assessment score	Average freshman retention rate	2013 graduation rate Predicted	2013 graduation rate Actual	% of classes under 20 ('13)	% of classes of 50 or more ('13)	SAT/ACT 25th-75th percentile ('13)	Freshmen in top 10% of HS class ('13)	Accept-ance rate ('13)	Average alumni giving rate
116.	Duquesne University (PA)	42	2.6	3.7	87%	65%	76%	44%	8%	1050-1220[2]	27%	74%	8%
116.	Illinois Institute of Technology	42	2.7	3.7	93%	80%	63%	59%	7%	25-30	45%[5]	57%	9%
116.	Michigan Technological University*	42	2.7	3.9	82%	69%	66%	47%	13%	24-29	30%	78%	13%
116.	University of the Pacific (CA)	42	2.6	3.7	86%	73%	63%	52%	5%	1030-1320	36%	73%	11%
121.	Clarkson University (NY)	41	2.7	3.6	87%	73%	75%	35%	24%	1090-1290	40%	64%	14%
121.	Colorado State University*	41	2.9	3.6	85%	60%	64%	37%	19%	22-27	22%	77%	9%
121.	DePaul University (IL)	41	2.8	3.7	86%	61%	70%	41%	1%	23-28[2]	25%[5]	60%	6%
121.	Temple University (PA)*	41	2.9	3.8	88%	58%	66%	38%	7%	1010-1230[2]	20%	64%	7%
121.	University of Arizona*	41	3.5	3.7	79%	65%	61%	37%	16%	970-1220[2]	31%	78%	6%
126.	Rutgers, The State U. of N.J.–Newark*	40	2.7	3.8	85%	55%	67%	29%	18%	960-1158	22%	54%	5%
126.	Seton Hall University (NJ)	40	2.7	3.8	82%	59%	64%	47%	3%	1020-1220	35%	79%	7%
126.	University at Albany–SUNY*	40	2.8	3.6	84%	58%	66%	23%	20%	1010-1180	19%	56%	7%
129.	Arizona State University–Tempe*	39	3.2	3.6	83%	56%	59%	43%	18%	1020-1270[2]	31%	80%	8%
129.	Louisiana State Univ.–Baton Rouge*	39	2.8	3.5	84%	65%	69%	36%	20%	23-28	25%	75%	11%
129.	Ohio University*	39	2.9	3.7	80%	52%	67%	35%	16%	22-26	17%	73%	7%
129.	University of Cincinnati*	39	2.7	3.5	85%	58%	64%	42%	13%	22-28	22%	73%	13%
129.	University of Kentucky*	39	2.9	3.7	82%	61%	60%	30%	17%	22-28	31%	69%	17%
129.	University of Utah*	39	3.0	3.5	87%	60%	60%	35%	22%	21-27	21%[5]	82%	11%
135.	Hofstra University (NY)	38	2.8	3.7	78%	68%	62%	50%	4%	1050-1230[2]	24%[5]	59%	10%
135.	New School (NY)	38	2.7	3.9	82%	64%	65%	89%	1%	990-1240[2]	15%[4]	67%	3%
135.	University of Arkansas*	38	2.8	3.4	82%	68%	60%	44%	18%	23-28	28%	59%	27%
138.	George Mason University (VA)*	37	3.0	3.9	87%	62%	67%	29%	15%	1050-1250[2]	20%[5]	62%	5%
138.	Missouri Univ. of Science & Tech.*	37	2.7	3.6	84%	72%	63%	30%	20%	25-31	41%	82%	16%
138.	Oregon State University*	37	2.9	3.7	83%	53%	61%	28%	23%	970-1220	25%	79%	12%
138.	Washington State University*	37	3.0	3.5	82%	62%	65%	37%	20%	910-1150	30%	82%	14%
142.	Illinois State University*	36	2.4	3.5	84%	55%	72%	34%	11%	22-26[3]	N/A	69%	7%
142.	Kansas State University*	36	2.9	3.7	81%	64%	60%	41%	13%	21-27[2]	22%	96%	22%
142.	St. John Fisher College (NY)	36	2.2	3.2	83%	60%	73%	45%	0.3%	990-1170	26%	63%	15%
145.	Howard University (DC)	35	2.8	3.9	82%	57%	61%	42%	10%	980-1190[3]	23%	57%	5%
145.	Oklahoma State University*	35	2.7	3.5	79%	64%	61%	36%	12%	22-28	28%	76%	14%
145.	St. John's University (NY)	35	2.7	3.8	78%	52%	55%	38%	6%	990-1210	17%[4]	53%	5%
145.	University of Texas–Dallas*	35	2.7	3.8	86%	74%	63%	25%	27%	1150-1370	38%	59%	3%
149.	Adelphi University (NY)	34	2.2	3.3	82%	58%	63%	52%	2%	1020-1220[9]	26%[5]	68%	7%
149.	New Jersey Inst. of Technology*	34	2.6	3.5	83%	64%	58%	28%	8%	1030-1250	27%[5]	65%	9%
149.	San Diego State University*	34	2.8	3.6	88%	52%	67%	26%	26%	1000-1200	27%	37%	5%
149.	University of Alabama–Birmingham*	34	2.7	3.4	80%	62%	53%	42%	15%	22-28	30%	87%	12%
149.	University of Illinois–Chicago*	34	3.0	3.7	80%	63%	57%	38%	19%	22-26[3]	24%	71%	4%
149.	Univ. of Maryland–Baltimore County*	34	2.8	3.6	86%	68%	65%	39%	12%	1110-1310	25%	63%	4%
149.	University of Mississippi*	34	2.7	3.5	83%	55%	58%	42%	17%	21-27[2]	24%	59%	14%
156.	Maryville Univ. of St. Louis	32	1.9	3.3	85%	63%	67%	69%	0.2%	23-27	27%	76%	7%
156.	Mississippi State University*	32	2.5	3.4	81%	60%	59%[6]	37%	14%	20-28	28%	71%	16%
156.	Texas Tech University*	32	2.8	3.6	82%	58%	59%	24%	20%	1010-1210	22%	66%	13%
156.	Univ. of Massachusetts–Lowell*	32	2.4	3.6	81%	55%	54%	50%	5%	1030-1230	22%[5]	64%	11%
156.	Virginia Commonwealth University*	32	2.8	3.7	86%	54%	57%	31%	17%	1000-1210	20%	64%	5%
161.	Biola University (CA)	31	1.9	3.5	86%	62%	69%	47%	6%	1000-1240	33%[5]	75%	11%
161.	University of Louisville (KY)*	31	2.7	3.6	78%	60%	53%	31%	10%	22-28[3]	20%[4]	71%	14%
161.	University of Rhode Island*	31	2.7	3.5	81%	60%	60%	34%	11%	1000-1210[3]	19%	76%	6%
161.	University of South Florida*	31	2.7	3.3	89%	65%	63%	28%	14%	1080-1260	36%	45%	13%
161.	University of Wyoming*	31	2.6	3.4	74%	60%	54%	43%	10%	22-27	23%	96%	9%[4]
166.	University of Idaho*	30	2.6	3.5	79%	54%	54%	49%	11%	910-1170	16%	65%	9%
166.	University of La Verne (CA)	30	1.9	3.2	85%	52%	59%	62%	1%	950-1130	23%	34%	6%
168.	Andrews University (MI)	29	1.7	3.3	79%	54%	60%	67%	8%	20-27	22%[5]	39%	6%
168.	University of Hawaii–Manoa*	29	2.7	3.1	78%	63%	57%	50%	13%	970-1200[3]	27%	80%	7%
168.	University of North Dakota*	29	2.5	3.6	76%	54%	55%	41%	9%	21-26[3]	15%	71%	12%
168.	University of South Dakota*	29	2.4	3.6	76%	51%	56%	50%	6%	21-26	15%	88%	8%
168.	West Virginia University*	29	2.6	3.2	78%	55%	57%	36%	19%	21-26	20%[5]	85%	13%
173.	Azusa Pacific University (CA)	28	1.9	3.4	85%	62%	65%	59%	3%	980-1190	27%	82%	7%[4]
173.	Ball State University (IN)*	28	2.5	3.4	79%	53%	60%	33%	9%	980-1170[2]	19%	61%	11%
173.	Bowling Green State University (OH)*	28	2.5	3.4	72%	47%	54%	46%	8%	20-25	12%	72%	7%
173.	Florida Institute of Technology	28	2.2	3.3	79%	66%	54%	53%	5%	1030-1260[3]	28%[5]	60%	20%
173.	Pace University (NY)	28	2.3	3.6	77%	56%	51%	51%	2%	940-1150	13%[5]	81%	5%
173.	University of Central Florida*	28	2.6	3.1	87%	71%	67%	29%	24%	1090-1270	30%	49%	10%
173.	University of Maine*	28	2.5	3.5	79%	58%	56%	45%	15%	950-1190	19%	83%	7%[4]
173.	Western Michigan University*	28	2.3	3.3	74%	47%	55%	39%	10%	19-25	12%	83%	6%

Note: Key to footnotes, Page 80.

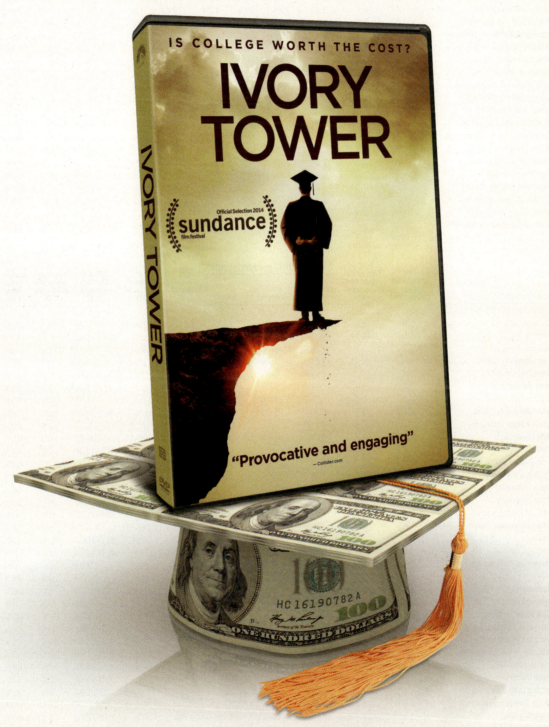

"I urge anyone dealing with the insanity of financing a college education to see this movie..."

— Robin Abcarian, *LOS ANGELES TIMES*

IS COLLEGE WORTH THE COST?

IVORY TOWER

IVORY TOWER

Official Selection 2014
sundance
film festival

"Provocative and engaging"
— Collider.com

**OWN IT NOW ON DIGITAL HD
ON DVD SEPTEMBER 30**

PG-13 SOME SUGGESTIVE AND PARTYING IMAGES

 CNN FILMS

© 2014 CABLE NEWS NETWORK INC. ALL RIGHTS RESERVED. TAKEPART.COM/IVORYTOWER

 participant MEDIA

Rank	School (State) (*Public)	Overall score	Peer assessment score (5.0=highest)	High school counselor assessment score	Average freshman retention rate	2013 graduation rate Predicted	2013 graduation rate Actual	% of classes under 20 ('13)	% of classes of 50 or more ('13)	SAT/ACT 25th-75th percentile ('13)	Freshmen in top 10% of HS class ('13)	Acceptance rate ('13)	Average alumni giving rate
181.	Edgewood College (WI)	27	1.7	3.1	80%	50%	57%	78%	0%	20-25	15%	77%	11%
181.	Immaculata University (PA)	27	1.9	3.0	82%	42%	48%	86%	0.2%	830-1060	N/A	82%	12%
181.	North Dakota State University*	27	2.4	3.7	78%	53%	53%	30%	20%	21-26[3]	16%	84%	11%
181.	South Dakota State University*	27	2.3	3.6	75%	52%	57%	32%	15%	20-25	13%	92%	14%
181.	Spalding University[1] (KY)	27	1.7	3.4	73%[8]	29%	42%[6]	79%[4]	1%[4]	18-22[4]	N/A	29%[4]	4%[4]
181.	St. Mary's Univ. of Minnesota	27	2.0	3.5	77%	55%	55%	72%	0%	20-26	18%[5]	75%	13%
181.	University of Alabama–Huntsville*	27	2.4	3.6	79%	61%	48%	41%	11%	23-29	28%[5]	81%	2%
181.	U. of North Carolina–Greensboro*	27	2.5	3.5	76%	52%	55%	45%	13%	950-1120	22%	58%	5%[7]
189.	Southern Illinois U.–Carbondale*	26	2.5	3.2	65%	46%	44%	56%	5%	19-25	11%	79%	6%
189.	University of Houston*	26	2.5	3.4	83%	55%	48%	31%	22%	1030-1250	34%	58%	13%
189.	Univ. of Missouri–Kansas City*	26	2.5	3.3	73%	63%	51%	57%	10%	21-27	26%	65%	8%
189.	University of New Mexico*	26	2.7	3.6	77%	54%	48%	39%	15%	19-25	N/A	57%	4%
189.	Widener University (PA)	26	2.0	3.2	73%	50%	56%	58%	2%	920-1130[3]	15%	67%	3%
194.	Central Michigan University*	25	2.2	3.3	77%	50%	59%	33%	8%	20-24	15%	63%	6%
194.	Indiana U.–Purdue U.–Indianapolis*	25	2.8	3.9	72%	48%	42%	37%	10%	890-1120	15%	70%	9%
194.	Kent State University (OH)*	25	2.4	3.3	77%	45%	51%	52%	8%	20-25	14%	83%	4%
194.	Northern Illinois University*	25	2.3	3.2	70%	48%	51%	48%	11%	19-24	12%	52%	5%
194.	University of Montana*	25	2.6	3.4	73%	49%	48%	47%	11%	21-26	18%	96%	7%
194.	University of Nevada–Reno*	25	2.4	3.2	79%	56%	51%	35%	19%	960-1190	23%	84%	9%
194.	Utah State University*	25	2.5	3.4	70%	56%	51%	41%	16%	20-26	19%	98%	6%
201.	Louisiana Tech University*	24	2.3	3.3	77%	54%	50%	49%	8%	21-26	24%	67%	12%
201.	U. of North Carolina–Charlotte*	24	2.6	3.6	78%	54%	54%	25%	23%	1000-1170	19%	63%	4%

School (State) (*Public)	Peer assessment score (5.0=highest)	High school counselor assessment score	Average freshman retention rate	2013 graduation rate Predicted	2013 graduation rate Actual	% of classes under 20 ('13)	% of classes of 50 or more ('13)	SAT/ACT 25th-75th percentile ('13)	Freshmen in top 10% of HS class ('13)	Acceptance rate ('13)	Average alumni giving rate
SECOND TIER (SCHOOLS RANKED 203 THROUGH 268 ARE LISTED HERE ALPHABETICALLY)											
Ashland University (OH)	1.8	3.2	72%	58%	56%	68%	0.1%	20-25	19%	72%	5%
Barry University (FL)	1.9	3.1	60%[8]	43%	37%	68%	1%	833-1040	N/A	47%	4%
Benedictine University (IL)	2.0	3.5	77%[8]	56%	52%	72%	0.3%	20-26[3]	21%	70%	5%
Bowie State University (MD)*	1.8	3.2	72%	30%	38%[6]	45%	1%	810-960[3]	N/A	52%	6%
Cardinal Stritch University[1] (WI)	1.7	3.2	69%[8]	48%	50%[6]	93%[4]	0%[4]	1067-1084[4]	9%[4]	42%[4]	3%[4]
Clark Atlanta University	2.2	3.4	64%	34%	39%	45%	3%	770-940[3]	9%[4]	57%	3%[7]
Cleveland State University*	2.1	3.0	66%	38%	32%	36%	11%	19-25[3]	14%	63%	3%
East Carolina University (NC)*	2.2	3.3	80%	53%	57%	31%	14%	960-1170[3]	15%	73%	4%
East Tennessee State University[1]*	2.0	3.2	69%[8]	50%	41%[8]	42%[4]	7%[4]	19-25[4]	19%[4]	89%[4]	4%[4]
Florida A&M University*	2.1	3.3	81%	43%	41%	32%	12%	18-22	16%[5]	45%	6%
Florida Atlantic University*	2.2	3.0	78%	48%	41%	24%	16%	960-1130	11%	48%	3%
Florida International University*	2.2	3.3	83%	62%	52%	21%	22%	1070-1230	23%[5]	43%	7%
Georgia Southern University*	2.2	3.2	79%	53%	50%	25%	10%	1040-1180	19%[5]	57%	8%
Georgia State University*	2.6	3.5	83%	57%	53%	19%	15%	960-1170	N/A	54%	6%
Indiana State University*	2.4	3.4	62%	39%	42%	29%	11%	800-1020	8%	83%	6%
Indiana Univ. of Pennsylvania*	2.0	3.1	75%	41%	51%	29%	14%	880-1070[3]	8%	90%	7%
Jackson State University[1] (MS)*	1.8	2.9	73%[8]	33%	42%[6]	N/A	N/A	17-21[9]	N/A	65%	4%[7]
Lamar University (TX)*	2.0	3.0	59%	39%	34%	48%	6%	870-1080	15%	77%	2%
Lynn University (FL)	1.8	2.8	65%	32%	41%	38%	0.3%	820-1050	1%[5]	78%	8%
Middle Tennessee State Univ.*	2.1	3.2	71%	48%	47%	40%	8%	19-24[3]	16%	70%	5%
Montana State University*	2.5	3.5	75%	55%	49%	40%	16%	21-27[3]	19%	85%	8%
Morgan State University (MD)*	1.9	3.1	72%	36%	35%	42%	0.1%	820-980[2]	3%	56%	14%
National-Louis University (IL)	1.7	2.8	72%[8]	47%	30%[6]	N/A	N/A	N/A[2]	N/A	N/A	N/A
New Mexico State University*	2.4	3.4	72%	44%	43%	48%	10%	18-24	21%	85%	7%
North Carolina A&T State Univ.*	2.0	3.2	73%[8]	32%	42%	34%	7%	830-990	10%	57%	8%
Northern Arizona University*	2.4	3.3	73%	52%	49%	33%	12%	940-1160[2]	21%	91%	4%
Nova Southeastern University (FL)	1.8	2.6	71%	55%	41%	81%	0.1%	950-1190	24%	57%	2%
Oakland University (MI)*	2.1	3.2	74%	54%	43%	37%	14%	20-26	17%	66%	4%
Old Dominion University (VA)*	2.6	3.6	80%	53%	51%	34%	11%	930-1130	10%	77%	6%
Our Lady of the Lake University (TX)	1.6	3.4	62%	43%	32%	68%	0%	870-960	12%	23%	14%
Portland State University[1] (OR)*	2.5	3.6	72%[8]	51%	39%[6]	N/A	N/A	19-26[4]	N/A	N/A	3%[4]
Regent University (VA)	1.8	3.4	74%	56%	54%	49%	0%	940-1170	14%	85%	4%
Sam Houston State University (TX)*	2.0	3.3	75%	48%	51%	24%	13%	880-1090[3]	14%	74%	9%
South Carolina State University*	2.1	3.3	63%	24%	36%	53%	3%	720-870	2%	92%	N/A
Tennessee State University*	2.0	3.2	62%[8]	31%	29%	54%	1%	16-20[3]	N/A	53%	4%[4]

Note: Key to footnotes, Page 80.

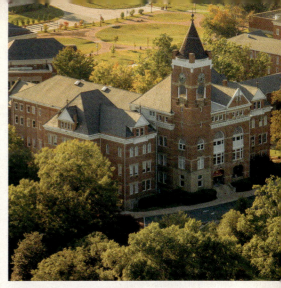

WINTHROP
U N I V E R S I T Y

THE
Winthrop
Experience

IN THE HEART OF THE CAROLINAS

- Contemporary university in a traditional setting of exceptional beauty

- Graduates prepared for successful careers and grounded in strong values

- Nationally accredited academic programs; student-faculty ratio of 15:1; more than 100 undergraduate and 40 graduate programs

- Emphasis on undergraduate research, global learning, community service and diversity

- Nationally competitive Division I intercollegiate athletics

- Located 20 miles south of Charlotte in Rock Hill, South Carolina

Learn More

www.winthrop.edu/usnews
www.facebook.com/winthrop.university
www.twitter.com/winthropu
800/WINTHROP (946-8476)

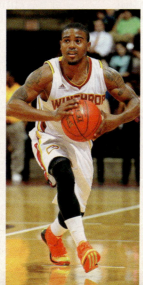

School (State) (*Public)	Peer assessment score (5.0=highest)	High school counselor assessment score	Average freshman retention rate	2013 graduation rate		% of classes under 20 ('13)	% of classes of 50 or more ('13)	SAT/ACT 25th-75th percentile ('13)	Freshmen in top 10% of HS class ('13)	Accept-ance rate ('13)	Average alumni giving rate
				Predicted	Actual						
SECOND TIER (SCHOOLS RANKED 203 THROUGH 268 ARE LISTED HERE ALPHABETICALLY)											
Texas A&M University–Commerce*	2.1	3.8	68%[8]	42%	45%	46%	4%	880-1090	16%	68%	3%
Texas A&M Univ.–Corpus Christi*	2.1	3.8	61%	38%	35%	18%	19%	870-1060[3]	10%	87%	2%[4]
Texas A&M Univ.–Kingsville*	2.0	3.7	60%	30%	34%	37%	5%	16-21	9%	88%	N/A
Texas Southern University*	2.0	3.3	60%	14%	16%	38%	11%	750-920	5%	45%	2%
Texas Woman's University*	2.2	3.4	69%	47%	42%	44%	13%	840-1070[2]	16%	86%	1%
Trevecca Nazarene University (TN)	1.6	3.4	74%	55%	47%	75%	2%	21-26[3]	N/A	68%	7%
Trinity International Univ. (IL)	1.7	3.2	71%[8]	56%	45%	71%	0.4%	25-29	17%	94%	7%
University of Akron (OH)*	2.3	3.2	69%	40%	40%	38%	7%	18-25	13%	96%	14%
University of Alaska–Fairbanks*	2.4	3.2	76%	56%	38%	65%	4%	18-25	18%	80%	5%
Univ. of Arkansas–Little Rock*	2.1	3.1	70%[8]	38%	24%	60%	3%	22	N/A	69%	2%
University of Colorado–Denver*	2.7	3.6	74%	55%	41%	35%	11%	20-25[3]	21%	69%	3%
University of Louisiana–Lafayette*	2.2	3.2	74%	49%	45%	33%	8%	21-25	17%	59%	7%
Univ. of Massachusetts–Boston*	2.5	3.6	77%	55%	44%	32%	6%	950-1160[3]	N/A	70%	5%
University of Memphis*	2.4	3.3	77%	50%	44%	44%	11%	20-26	16%	73%	6%
Univ. of Missouri–St. Louis*	2.4	3.3	76%	53%	46%	47%	9%	21-26	30%	74%	6%
University of Nebraska–Omaha*	2.5	3.5	73%	50%	42%	35%	11%	20-26	15%	71%	5%
University of Nevada–Las Vegas*	2.4	3.2	77%	54%	43%	26%	18%	890-1110	21%	85%	5%
University of New Orleans*	2.0	3.3	66%	46%	32%	31%[4]	16%[4]	21-25	16%	50%	1%
University of Northern Colorado*	2.2	3.3	69%[8]	48%	46%	25%	13%	20-24[2]	12%	70%	5%[7]
University of North Texas*	2.4	3.3	77%	56%	46%	26%	24%	1000-1210[3]	20%	61%	3%
University of South Alabama*	2.0	2.8	66%	53%	33%	46%	9%	20-26[2]	N/A	86%	2%[7]
Univ. of Southern Mississippi*	2.2	3.3	74%	51%	45%	45%	9%	19-25	6%[5]	66%	9%
University of Texas–Arlington*	2.5	3.6	74%	58%	44%	28%	26%	960-1200	28%	60%	3%
University of Texas–El Paso*	2.2	3.3	73%[8]	36%	37%[8]	33%[4]	12%[4]	17-22[4]	17%[4]	100%[4]	5%[7]
University of Texas–San Antonio*	2.3	3.5	62%	42%	30%	20%	26%	950-1180	19%	62%	5%
University of Toledo (OH)*	2.3	3.2	65%	49%	46%	27%	16%	19-25	17%	91%	5%
University of West Florida*	2.0	3.0	72%	54%	42%	32%	11%	21-25[3]	12%	48%	15%
Univ. of Wisconsin–Milwaukee*	2.7	3.6	71%	43%	41%	43%	10%	19-24[3]	9%	88%	3%
Wayne State University (MI)*	2.5	3.4	77%	49%	32%	49%	9%	19-26	23%	76%	5%
Wichita State University (KS)*	2.4	3.2	72%	53%	46%	41%	11%	21-26[2]	23%	96%	7%
Wright State University (OH)*	2.3	3.2	63%	43%	41%	44%	13%	19-25	15%	96%	4%

▶ The Top 30 Public National Universities

Rank School (State)

1. University of California–Berkeley
2. Univ. of California–Los Angeles
2. University of Virginia
4. University of Michigan–Ann Arbor
5. U. of North Carolina–Chapel Hill
6. College of William and Mary (VA)
7. Georgia Institute of Technology
8. Univ. of California–San Diego
9. University of California–Davis

Rank School (State)

10. Univ. of California–Santa Barbara
11. University of California–Irvine
11. U. of Illinois–Urbana-Champaign
13. Univ. of Wisconsin–Madison
14. Pennsylvania State U.–Univ. Park
14. University of Florida
14. University of Washington
17. University of Texas–Austin
18. Ohio State University–Columbus

Rank School (State)

19. University of Connecticut
20. Clemson University (SC)
20. Purdue Univ.–West Lafayette (IN)
20. University of Georgia
20. Univ. of Maryland–College Park
20. University of Pittsburgh
25. Texas A&M Univ.–College Station
26. Rutgers, St. U. of N.J.–New Brunswick

Rank School (State)

27. University of Iowa
27. Univ. of Minnesota–Twin Cities
27. Virginia Tech
30. Indiana University–Bloomington
30. Miami University–Oxford (OH)
30. SUNY Col. of Envir. Sci. and Forestry
30. University of Delaware
30. Univ. of Massachusetts–Amherst

Footnotes:

1. School refused to fill out U.S. News statistical survey. Data that appear are from school in previous years or from another source such as the National Center for Education Statistics.
2. SAT and/or ACT not required by school for some or all applicants.
3. In reporting SAT/ACT scores, the school did not include all students for whom it had scores or refused to tell U.S. News whether all students with scores had been included.
4. Data reported to U.S. News in previous years.
5. Data based on fewer than 51 percent of enrolled freshmen.
6. Some or all data reported to the NCAA and/or the National Center for Education Statistics.
7. Data reported to the Council for Aid to Education.

8. Average graduation or freshman retention rates, normally based on four years of data, are given here for less than four years because school didn't report rates for the most recent year or years to U.S. News.
9. SAT and/or ACT may not be required by school for some or all applicants, and in reporting SAT/ACT scores, the school did not include all students for whom it had scores, or refused to tell U.S. News whether all students with scores had been included.

N/A means not available.

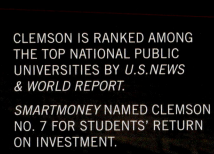

CLEMSON IS RANKED AMONG THE TOP NATIONAL PUBLIC UNIVERSITIES BY *U.S.NEWS & WORLD REPORT.*

SMARTMONEY NAMED CLEMSON NO. 7 FOR STUDENTS' RETURN ON INVESTMENT.

CLEMSON IS RANKED NO.12 FOR HAPPIEST STUDENTS BY *THE PRINCETON REVIEW.*

LEADERS AHEAD

U.S.News & World Report ranks Clemson University as one of the nation's top public universities.

Recognized as one of the country's most spirited campuses, Clemson attracts students who are gifted academically, crave challenge and are determined to make a difference.

Offering 80-plus undergraduate majors and a number of cross-cultural opportunities, Clemson prepares students to be leaders in their professions and through their service to others.

Turning heads, advancing forward. Clemson University.

Learn more about our programs and check out Clemson's campus at *clemson.edu/visit.*

CLEMSON
UNIVERSITY

Best National Liberal

Rank	School (State) (*Public)	Overall score	Peer assessment score (5.0=highest)	High school counselor assessment score	Graduation and retention rank	Average freshman retention rate	2013 graduation rate Predicted	2013 graduation rate Actual	Over-performance(+) Under-performance(-)	Faculty resource rank
1.	Williams College (MA)	100	4.7	4.7	3	97%	94%	95%	+1	3
2.	Amherst College (MA)	96	4.6	4.6	1	98%	93%	96%	+3	16
3.	Swarthmore College (PA)	94	4.5	4.5	4	96%	95%	93%	-2	10
4.	Wellesley College (MA)	93	4.4	4.6	12	96%	91%	91%	None	9
5.	Bowdoin College (ME)	92	4.3	4.5	4	96%	93%	93%	None	14
5.	Pomona College (CA)	92	4.3	4.5	1	98%	94%	96%	+2	25
7.	Middlebury College (VT)	91	4.3	4.4	4	96%	93%	94%	+1	33
8.	Carleton College (MN)	90	4.3	4.4	4	97%	91%	92%	+1	16
8.	Claremont McKenna College (CA)	90	4.1	4.5	12	96%	93%	93%	None	5
8.	Haverford College (PA)	90	4.0	4.3	4	97%	94%	93%	-1	5
11.	Davidson College (NC)	88	4.2	4.3	9	96%	93%	92%	-1	4
11.	Vassar College (NY)	88	4.2	4.6	9	96%	90%	94%	+4	22
13.	United States Naval Academy (MD)*	87	4.1	4.8	20	97%	79%	88%	+9	52
14.	Washington and Lee University (VA)	86	3.7	4.2	15	95%	93%	90%	-3	2
15.	Colby College (ME)	85	4.0	4.3	15	94%	87%	93%	+6	20
15.	Hamilton College (NY)	85	3.8	4.3	15	95%	90%	93%	+3	10
15.	Harvey Mudd College (CA)	85	4.3	4.6	23	98%	95%	91%	-4	57
15.	Wesleyan University (CT)	85	4.1	4.5	9	96%	90%	92%	+2	40
19.	Bates College (ME)	84	4.0	4.3	20	93%	86%	93%	+7	45
19.	Grinnell College (IA)	84	4.2	4.3	28	94%	88%	86%	-2	20
19.	Smith College (MA)	84	4.2	4.5	35	93%	82%	86%	+4	29
22.	Colgate University (NY)	83	3.9	4.3	20	94%	87%	91%	+4	22
23.	Oberlin College (OH)	82	4.1	4.3	31	93%	88%	88%	None	22
24.	Macalester College (MN)	81	4.0	4.3	28	95%	88%	87%	-1	29
24.	Scripps College (CA)	81	3.7	4.4	33	93%	89%	84%	-5	19
24.	United States Military Academy (NY)*	81	4.1	4.8	41	95%	78%	84%	+6	81
27.	Bryn Mawr College (PA)	80	4.0	4.3	50	91%	85%	84%	-1	25
27.	Colorado College	80	3.8	4.1	23	96%	85%	87%	+2	10
27.	United States Air Force Acad. (CO)*	80	4.0	4.7	50	90%	80%	85%	+5	57
30.	Kenyon College (OH)	79	3.8	4.2	28	94%	90%	89%	-1	33
30.	University of Richmond (VA)	79	3.7	4.1	41	94%	86%	85%	-1	7
32.	Barnard College (NY)	78	3.9	4.4	15	96%	87%	90%	+3	91
32.	Bucknell University (PA)	78	3.8	4.3	15	94%	88%	91%	+3	76
34.	College of the Holy Cross (MA)	76	3.5	4.0	12	95%	86%	91%	+5	52
35.	Lafayette College (PA)	75	3.4	4.0	23	94%	87%	88%	+1	45
35.	Pitzer College (CA)	75	3.5	4.3	48	92%	76%	82%	+6	33
37.	Dickinson College (PA)	74	3.6	4.1	48	90%	81%	85%	+4	25
37.	Franklin and Marshall College (PA)	74	3.6	4.0	35	93%	85%	87%	+2	49
37.	Skidmore College (NY)	74	3.5	4.2	35	94%	78%	86%	+8	40
37.	Whitman College (WA)	74	3.4	4.1	31	94%	85%	88%	+3	40
41.	Mount Holyoke College (MA)	73	4.0	4.2	50	91%	83%	82%	-1	76
41.	Soka University of America (CA)	73	2.3	3.0	23	96%	76%	84%	+8	1
41.	Union College (NY)	73	3.2	4.0	35	93%	83%	88%	+5	16
44.	Occidental College (CA)	72	3.7	4.0	35	93%	83%	88%	+5	81
45.	Bard College (NY)	71	3.4	4.0	77	88%	88%	74%	-14	15
45.	Centre College (KY)	71	3.4	4.1	44	91%	81%	82%	+1	84
45.	Connecticut College	71	3.5	4.1	44	90%	84%	84%	None	73
45.	Sewanee–University of the South (TN)	71	3.5	4.1	61	88%	80%	78%	-2	36
45.	Trinity College (CT)	71	3.5	4.1	41	91%	81%	86%	+5	91
50.	Gettysburg College (PA)	70	3.4	3.9	44	90%	86%	84%	-2	52

Note: Key to footnotes, Page 89.

Arts Colleges

% of classes under 20 ('13)	% of classes of 50 or more ('13)	Student/faculty ratio ('13)	Selectivity rank	SAT/ACT 25th-75th percentile ('13)	Freshmen in top 10% of HS class ('13)	Acceptance rate ('13)	Financial resources rank	Alumni giving rank	Average alumni giving rate
75%	3%	7/1	5	1330-1540	88%[5]	18%	4	2	58%
71%	3%	8/1	5	1350-1530	86%[5]	14%	10	6	53%
75%	2%	8/1	3	1350-1530	89%[5]	14%	8	16	43%
73%	0.4%	7/1	8	1310-1510	83%[5]	29%	8	11	47%
71%	2%	9/1	5	1360-1510[2]	83%[5]	15%	13	5	53%
68%	2%	8/1	2	1380-1540	92%[5]	14%	7	25	38%
62%	3%	9/1	12	1280-1490	74%[5]	18%	3	6	53%
66%	1%	9/1	8	1340-1520	79%[5]	21%	25	4	54%
85%	1%	9/1	11	1320-1500	74%[5]	12%	13	16	43%
82%	0.3%	9/1	3	1310-1490	95%[5]	23%	12	13	45%
72%	0%	10/1	33	1230-1440[3]	81%[5]	26%	27	3	55%
64%	1%	8/1	17	1310-1480	66%	24%	13	47	32%
68%	0%	9/1	24	1180-1380	54%	7%	2	123	20%
73%	0.2%	8/1	8	30-33	80%[5]	18%	25	15	44%
71%	2%	10/1	19	1260-1430[2]	64%[5]	26%	27	22	39%
74%	1%	9/1	14	1300-1470	72%[5]	27%	21	18	42%
60%	5%	9/1	1	1400-1560	97%	19%	17	59	29%
72%	5%	9/1	14	1310-1490	67%[5]	20%	45	13	45%
68%	3%	10/1	24	1260-1430[2]	56%[5]	24%	34	6	53%
68%	0%	9/1	21	28-32	63%[5]	35%	22	31	37%
68%	5%	9/1	31	1220-1450[2]	62%[5]	43%	19	36	35%
66%	2%	9/1	13	1270-1450	76%[5]	27%	38	21	40%
77%	2%	9/1	21	1270-1455	62%[5]	30%	31	37	34%
71%	1%	10/1	21	1240-1460	64%[5]	34%	45	25	38%
84%	1%	10/1	17	1280-1453	75%[5]	36%	22	19	41%
92%	0%	7/1	52	1180-1385[3]	46%	9%	4	63	29%
75%	3%	8/1	28	1210-1470	65%[5]	40%	19	25	38%
64%	0%	10/1	19	1220-1430[2]	66%[5]	22%	31	131	19%
75%	0%	8/1	24	29-32	55%	15%	4	177	12%
67%	0%	10/1	24	1230-1410	65%[5]	38%	34	31	36%
67%	0%	8/1	28	1210-1410	64%[5]	31%	22	75	26%
73%	10%	10/1	14	1240-1440	77%[5]	21%	56	75	25%
58%	3%	9/1	28	1200-1400	62%[5]	30%	42	51	31%
65%	2%	10/1	52	1220-1390[2]	57%[5]	33%	50	9	51%
60%	1%	10/1	33	1180-1370	62%[5]	34%	31	40	34%
71%	0%	10/1	47	1210-1400[2]	55%[5]	15%	27	40	33%
76%	0%	9/1	43	1190-1365[2]	46%[5]	45%	59	65	28%
63%	0.4%	9/1	33	1220-1410[2]	56%[5]	36%	42	65	27%
73%	1%	9/1	45	1130-1350	45%[5]	35%	47	73	26%
66%	1%	9/1	36	1220-1422	61%	57%	62	35	36%
66%	4%	10/1	60	1220-1430[2]	57%[5]	47%	38	48	31%
98%	0%	8/1	52	1080-1340	50%[5]	43%	1	131	19%
72%	0%	10/1	46	1220-1400[2]	64%[5]	37%	50	43	33%
58%	0.2%	10/1	38	1210-1400	51%[5]	42%	62	86	25%
77%	1%	10/1	63	1170-1380[2]	58%[5]	38%	13	22	39%
60%	0%	10/1	42	26-31	52%	69%	71	10	50%
67%	2%	9/1	60	1240-1410[2]	52%[5]	37%	42	51	31%
61%	1%	11/1	47	26-30[2]	42%[5]	60%	56	25	38%
60%	2%	9/1	66	1150-1330	23%[5]	32%	27	43	33%
68%	0.3%	10/1	32	1200-1370[2]	69%[5]	42%	61	92	24%

What Is a National Liberal Arts College?

The country's 249 liberal arts colleges emphasize undergraduate education and award at least half of their degrees in the arts and sciences, which include such disciplines as English, the biological and physical sciences, history, foreign languages and the visual and performing arts but exclude professional disciplines such as business, education and nursing. There are 221 private and 27 public liberal arts colleges; one is for-profit. The top 10 public colleges appear below.

The Top 10 Public Colleges

Rank School (State)

1. United States Naval Academy (MD)
2. United States Military Academy (NY)
3. United States Air Force Acad. (CO)
4. Virginia Military Institute
5. New College of Florida
6. St. Mary's College of Maryland
7. University of Minnesota–Morris
8. U. of North Carolina–Asheville
9. Massachusetts Col. of Liberal Arts
10. Purchase College–SUNY

Rank	School (State) (*Public)	Overall score	Peer assessment score (5.0=highest)	High school counselor assessment score	Average freshman retention rate	2013 graduation rate		% of classes under 20 ('13)	% of classes of 50 or more ('13)	SAT/ACT 25th-75th percentile ('13)	Freshmen in top 10% of HS class ('13)	Accept-ance rate ('13)	Average alumni giving rate
						Predicted	Actual						
51.	Denison University (OH)	68	3.3	3.9	90%	82%	81%	73%	0%	27-31[2]	45%	46%	29%
51.	DePauw University (IN)	68	3.4	3.9	91%	79%	79%	65%	0%	25-29	49%[5]	61%	30%
51.	Furman University (SC)	68	3.4	3.9	89%	84%	84%	53%	0.2%	1130-1340[2]	48%[5]	64%	26%
54.	Rhodes College (TN)	67	3.4	4.1	91%	82%	79%	68%	0%	27-31	50%[5]	58%	36%
54.	St. Olaf College (MN)	67	3.6	4.0	94%	82%	87%	54%	3%	26-31	54%[5]	59%	23%
56.	St. John's College (MD)	65	3.4	3.9	86%	75%	65%	97%	1%	1140-1410[2]	19%[5]	87%	21%
56.	St. Lawrence University (NY)	65	3.2	3.7	91%	74%	80%	64%	1%	1120-1310[2]	34%[5]	46%	27%
56.	Wheaton College (IL)	65	3.3	3.9	95%	84%	87%	57%	5%	27-32	58%[5]	70%	26%
59.	Lawrence University (WI)	64	3.1	3.9	89%	79%	82%	76%	2%	26-31[2]	42%[5]	73%	33%
59.	Sarah Lawrence College (NY)	64	3.4	4.2	87%	76%	69%	93%	1%	1150-1350[2]	35%[5]	77%	19%
61.	Beloit College (WI)	63	3.2	3.8	89%	75%	78%	74%	0%	24-30[2]	29%	68%	25%
61.	Hobart & William Smith Colleges (NY)	63	3.2	3.8	88%	74%	79%	65%	0.4%	1120-1290[2]	36%[5]	50%	29%
61.	Wabash College (IN)	63	3.3	3.8	86%	73%	69%	73%	2%	1028-1250	33%	70%	38%
64.	Gustavus Adolphus College (MN)	62	3.2	3.7	92%	73%	82%	60%	1%	24-30[2]	33%	63%	27%
64.	Kalamazoo College (MI)	62	3.3	3.9	92%	80%	77%	60%	2%	25-30	38%[5]	67%	29%
64.	Muhlenberg College (PA)	62	2.8	3.5	92%	79%	86%	71%	1%	1140-1340[2]	45%[5]	46%	18%
64.	Virginia Military Institute*	62	3.1	3.8	84%	60%	76%	64%	0.2%	1050-1250	16%	48%	31%
64.	Willamette University (OR)	62	3.2	3.8	88%	78%	78%	63%	0%	1080-1310	41%	58%	17%
69.	Berea College (KY)	61	3.3	3.4	80%	47%	62%	70%	0%	22-26	25%	34%	18%
69.	College of Wooster (OH)	61	3.1	3.7	89%	74%	75%	71%	1%	25-30	40%[5]	56%	26%
69.	Hillsdale College (MI)	61	2.5	3.5	97%	80%	81%	72%	1%	27-31	56%[5]	50%	21%
69.	Wheaton College (MA)	61	3.4	4.0	86%	82%	76%	69%	2%	1110-1340[2]	37%[5]	74%	25%
73.	Agnes Scott College (GA)	60	3.1	3.7	82%	72%	72%	71%	0%	1010-1310[2]	40%	67%	41%
73.	Earlham College (IN)	60	3.3	3.9	85%	73%	71%	73%	3%	1150-1340[2]	29%[5]	64%	25%
73.	Illinois Wesleyan University	60	3.0	3.6	90%	79%	78%	66%	1%	25-30	45%	58%	20%
73.	St. John's University (MN)	60	3.2	3.7	90%	71%	79%	57%	1%	23-28	22%	75%	27%
77.	Lewis & Clark College (OR)	59	3.3	3.8	86%	81%	74%	69%	1%	1180-1370[2]	39%[5]	63%	20%
77.	Reed College[1] (OR)	59	3.7	4.4	92%[8]	86%	78%[6]	N/A	N/A	1280-1470[9]	N/A	49%	26%[7]

BRETT ZIEGLER FOR USN&WR

Pomona College in California, tied at No. 5

Note: Key to footnotes, Page 89.

HELPING HERE

CAN HELP YOU HERE

HELP YOUR NEIGHBORS

ATTEND COLLEGE FULL-TIME

SERVE PART-TIME

EXTRA PAYCHECK

GI BILL

OTHER BENEFITS

CAREER TRAINING

BE PART OF A TEAM

College doesn't have to mean debt. Earn the money you need to pay your way by serving part-time in your community and state. Check out the Guard online. Help is on the way.

NATIONALGUARD.com

Programs and benefits subject to change.

Rank	School (State) (*Public)	Overall score	Peer assessment score (5.0=highest)	High school counselor assessment score	Average freshman retention rate	2013 graduation rate Predicted	2013 graduation rate Actual	% of classes under 20 ('13)	% of classes of 50 or more ('13)	SAT/ACT 25th-75th percentile ('13)	Freshmen in top 10% of HS class ('13)	Acceptance rate ('13)	Average alumni giving rate
77.	Thomas Aquinas College (CA)	59	2.7	3.0	87%	80%	80%	100%	0%	1160-1340	29%[5]	81%	61%
77.	Wofford College (SC)	59	2.9	3.6	89%	80%	82%	58%	0.2%	1080-1260	42%	69%	32%
81.	Allegheny College (PA)	58	3.0	3.5	87%	76%	79%	64%	1%	1070-1290	41%	65%	24%
81.	Hendrix College (AR)	58	3.3	3.9	85%	77%	68%	66%	0.3%	26-32	46%	80%	25%
81.	Knox College (IL)	58	3.0	3.5	88%	77%	79%	75%	1%	25-30[2]	26%	75%	33%
81.	Spelman College (GA)	58	3.4	3.8	89%	64%	68%	63%	3%	850-1215	31%	41%	34%
81.	Transylvania University (KY)	58	2.8	3.3	87%	75%	72%	74%	0%	24-30	39%	83%	37%
81.	University of Puget Sound (WA)	58	3.2	3.7	87%[8]	77%	78%	57%	0.3%	1120-1330[3]	26%[5]	85%	16%
87.	New College of Florida*	57	3.0	3.9	83%	74%	66%	77%	1%	1190-1380	41%	69%	21%
87.	Southwestern University (TX)	57	3.1	3.6	86%	79%	70%	71%	1%	1055-1280	37%	52%	21%
89.	Austin College (TX)	56	3.1	3.7	82%	74%	72%	66%	1%	1100-1330[3]	35%	59%	12%[7]
89.	Bennington College (VT)	56	2.8	3.7	85%	72%	67%	89%	0.4%	1180-1380[2]	44%[5]	65%	25%
89.	College of St. Benedict (MN)	56	3.1	3.4	89%	75%	82%	57%	1%	23-28	33%	76%	19%
89.	Luther College (IA)	56	3.1	3.5	87%	69%	76%	56%	1%	23-29	32%	72%	25%
89.	Millsaps College (MS)	56	3.0	3.6	80%	74%	64%	84%	0%	23-28	31%	47%	20%
89.	St. John's College (NM)‡	56	3.1	4.1	74%	74%	57%	95%	0%	1160-1450[2]	25%[5]	93%	14%
89.	St. Mary's College of Maryland*	56	2.9	3.6	88%	70%	79%	65%	1%	1070-1310[3]	28%[5]	73%	11%
96.	St. Mary's College (IN)	55	3.0	3.9	87%	71%	71%	57%	1%	23-28[3]	27%[5]	86%	30%
96.	Washington and Jefferson Col. (PA)	55	2.8	3.5	83%[8]	71%	77%	65%	0%	1050-1230[2]	37%	40%	17%
96.	Westmont College (CA)	55	2.9	3.2	87%	77%	76%	59%	3%	1060-1310	29%	70%	24%
99.	Albion College (MI)	54	2.8	3.4	79%	70%	74%	70%	1%	22-28	21%	56%	23%
99.	College of the Atlantic (ME)	54	2.7	3.3	85%	70%	69%	93%	0%	1110-1330[2]	10%	73%	39%
99.	Drew University (NJ)	54	2.9	3.4	79%	71%	69%	73%	0.3%	990-1220	31%[5]	77%	21%
99.	Hope College (MI)	54	3.1	3.6	89%	73%	78%	54%	2%	24-29	34%	70%	23%
99.	Ohio Wesleyan University	54	3.0	3.7	83%	71%	69%	68%	0%	22-27[2]	32%[5]	75%	23%
99.	St. Michael's College (VT)	54	2.8	3.4	89%	68%	75%	56%	1%	1060-1290[2]	26%	75%	17%
105.	Augustana College (IL)	53	2.9	3.4	86%	71%	78%	64%	1%	22-27[9]	24%	59%	27%
105.	Cornell College (IA)	53	2.9	3.8	82%	69%	68%	71%	0%	23-29	39%	59%	23%
105.	Goucher College (MD)	53	3.1	3.7	84%	70%	68%	77%	1%	1010-1280[2]	31%[5]	72%	18%
105.	Hampden-Sydney College (VA)	53	2.8	3.3	79%	66%	62%	73%	0%	1005-1215	13%	55%	32%
105.	Juniata College (PA)	53	2.7	3.5	87%	71%	75%	69%	2%	1040-1260[9]	34%	74%	28%
105.	Stonehill College (MA)	53	2.8	3.5	88%	77%	85%	55%	1%	1030-1240[2]	31%	71%	15%
105.	Washington College (MD)	53	2.8	3.7	83%	72%	68%	62%	1%	1050-1280[2]	33%[5]	66%	21%
112.	Hollins University (VA)	52	2.6	3.5	70%	63%	60%	90%	0%	970-1220	24%	69%	31%
113.	Hanover College (IN)	51	2.7	3.4	81%	73%	72%	74%	0%	1000-1200	32%	67%	22%
113.	Ripon College (WI)	51	2.6	3.2	85%	64%	74%	73%	2%	21-28	23%	75%	31%
113.	Siena College (NY)	51	2.8	3.3	87%	65%	80%	44%	0%	1000-1200[3]	24%	58%	17%
116.	Calvin College (MI)	50	2.9	3.4	87%	71%	73%	35%	2%	23-29[2]	30%	70%	25%
116.	Susquehanna University (PA)	50	2.8	3.1	84%	70%	75%	55%	0%	1020-1230[2]	26%	72%	15%
116.	Sweet Briar College (VA)	50	2.6	3.4	74%	68%	57%	88%	0%	938-1210	30%	84%	33%
116.	Westminster College (PA)	50	2.6	3.2	86%	61%	77%	70%	1%	920-1150	17%	73%	20%
120.	Coe College (IA)	49	2.8	3.3	80%	69%	67%	72%	1%	23-28	31%	62%	21%
120.	Lake Forest College (IL)	49	2.9	3.6	84%	72%	64%	60%	1%	23-28[2]	27%[5]	57%	24%
120.	St. Anselm College (NH)	49	2.7	3.1	86%	68%	74%	60%	3%	1060-1230[2]	22%	74%	20%
123.	St. Norbert College (WI)	48	2.7	3.4	83%	67%	74%	45%	1%	22-27	27%	82%	18%
124.	Birmingham-Southern Col. (AL)	47	2.8	3.3	81%[8]	72%	62%	62%	1%	23-27	24%	64%	28%
124.	Eckerd College (FL)	47	2.9	3.6	81%	64%	66%	45%	1%	1030-1220	N/A	72%	N/A
124.	Linfield College (OR)	47	2.7	3.4	83%	67%	68%	64%	1%	980-1200	34%[4]	92%	15%
124.	Presbyterian College (SC)	47	2.6	3.4	82%	70%	68%	62%	0%	1000-1210[2]	35%	66%	16%
124.	Randolph-Macon College (VA)	47	2.7	3.4	78%	64%	61%	72%	0%	970-1180	14%	64%	36%
129.	Berry College (GA)	46	2.8	3.5	78%	71%	60%	50%	0.2%	24-29	32%	60%	20%
129.	Concordia College–Moorhead (MN)	46	2.8	3.4	84%	69%	71%	50%	1%	22-28	30%	78%	19%
129.	Goshen College (IN)	46	2.6	3.3	79%	67%	70%	67%	1%	950-1250	25%	55%	25%
129.	McDaniel College (MD)	46	2.7	3.4	83%	69%	72%	63%	0%	1000-1210[3]	26%	76%	16%
133.	Moravian College (PA)	45	2.4	3.0	78%	67%	74%	67%	1%	940-1170[2]	19%	80%	16%
133.	Morehouse College (GA)	45	3.2	3.8	82%	55%	54%	48%	2%	900-1110	21%	67%	23%
133.	Randolph College (VA)	45	2.5	3.2	77%	67%	52%	84%	0%	970-1200	17%	83%	21%
133.	Roanoke College (VA)	45	2.8	3.3	80%	65%	64%	57%	1%	980-1190	18%	73%	20%
133.	Wesleyan College (GA)	45	2.7	3.5	79%	62%	64%	85%	0.3%	880-1130	N/A	43%	27%
133.	Whittier College (CA)	45	3.0	3.4	83%	67%	66%	55%	1%	930-1150[3]	23%	63%	21%
139.	Alma College (MI)	44	2.6	3.2	80%	65%	61%	71%	2%	22-27[3]	27%	69%	22%
139.	Central College (IA)	44	2.6	3.2	81%	65%	65%	60%	0.3%	21-26	21%	66%	18%
139.	Gordon College (MA)	44	2.6	3.3	82%	71%	72%	67%	3%	1015-1292[3]	34%[5]	43%	8%
139.	Grove City College (PA)	44	2.4	3.0	90%	81%	82%	46%	5%	1079-1334	41%	81%	21%

Note: Key to footnotes, Page 89.

Rank	School (State) (*Public)	Overall score	Peer assessment score (5.0=highest)	High school counselor assessment score	Average freshman retention rate	2013 graduation rate		% of classes under 20 ('13)	% of classes of 50 or more ('13)	SAT/ACT 25th-75th percentile ('13)	Freshmen in top 10% of HS class ('13)	Acceptance rate ('13)	Average alumni giving rate
						Predicted	Actual						
139.	Houghton College (NY)	44	2.4	3.0	87%	67%	73%	73%	2%	980-1235	35%	91%	18%
139.	Principia College (IL)	44	2.2	2.9	80%[8]	76%	82%	N/A	N/A	918-1223	26%[5]	84%	N/A
139.	Simpson College (IA)	44	2.6	3.2	80%	63%	65%	72%	1%	21-27	29%	88%	16%
139.	University of Minnesota–Morris*	44	2.8	3.6	82%	59%	63%	55%	4%	23-28[3]	31%	58%	13%
139.	Wittenberg University (OH)	44	2.5	3.7	77%	67%	63%	54%	1%	23-28[2]	22%	89%	12%
148.	Centenary College of Louisiana	43	2.3	3.2	71%	70%	59%	83%	0.4%	22-28	25%	66%	13%
148.	Hiram College (OH)	43	2.4	3.4	76%	60%	66%	78%	0%	19-25	12%	57%	14%
148.	Nebraska Wesleyan University	43	2.6	3.4	79%	63%	68%	65%	2%	22-26	23%	77%	15%
148.	Oglethorpe University (GA)	43	2.7	3.4	78%	63%	62%	84%	0%	1030-1240	20%	56%	14%
148.	Salem College (NC)	43	2.4	3.1	77%	63%	64%	90%	0%	1000-1200	39%	58%	23%
148.	St. Vincent College (PA)	43	2.4	2.9	83%	64%	70%	55%	0%	910-1150	20%	69%	20%
148.	Wells College (NY)	43	2.7	3.6	73%[8]	63%	58%	89%	0%	930-1070[2]	32%	60%	23%
155.	Carthage College (WI)	42	2.5	3.4	76%	63%	65%	64%	0.1%	21-27	21%	70%	14%
155.	Georgetown College (KY)	42	2.5	3.6	75%	67%	57%	79%	0%	20-25	20%	86%	14%
155.	Illinois College	42	2.5	2.8	81%	62%	64%	70%	1%	19-25[2]	22%	61%	25%
155.	William Jewell College (MO)	42	2.5	3.4	75%	69%	59%	72%	0%	22-28[2]	23%	58%	11%
159.	College of Idaho	41	2.6	3.1	85%	67%	67%	60%	1%	21-27	26%	68%	34%
159.	Lycoming College (PA)	41	2.5	3.2	81%	60%	64%	62%	1%	930-1150[2]	19%	72%	19%
159.	U. of North Carolina–Asheville*	41	2.9	3.4	80%	58%	60%	50%	2%	1100-1290	22%	69%	8%
159.	Wartburg College (IA)	41	2.6	3.4	79%	66%	63%	50%	2%	21-26[3]	26%	78%	23%
159.	Westminster College (MO)	41	2.5	3.2	79%	65%	68%	65%	0%	21-27	28%	69%	16%
164.	Doane College (NE)	40	2.2	3.1	76%	53%	61%	74%	1%	21-26[3]	20%	72%	21%
165.	Fisk University (TN)	39	2.6	3.4	N/A	54%	52%	68%	1%	17-23	N/A	21%	24%
165.	Hartwick College (NY)	39	2.6	3.4	74%	63%	58%	62%	0.2%	1010-1230[2]	20%	84%	16%
165.	Lyon College (AR)	39	2.6	3.1	67%	65%	50%	68%	1%	23-28	29%	59%	17%
165.	Massachusetts Col. of Liberal Arts*	39	2.5	3.3	75%	49%	57%	72%	0.2%	910-1150[3]	25%[5]	67%	10%

100%
of our students will have
Real-World Experience
before graduation

Cradles to Crayons

experience360
PROGRAM

Experience360 prepares Delaware Valley College students for the real world. One of the few colleges in the country that requires an experiential learning component, DelVal combines professional development, problem-based learning and a wide variety of experiences that make up a co-curricular transcript — making our students more qualified for the challenges of the 21st century.

DELAWARE VALLEY COLLEGE

700 E. Butler Ave. | Doylestown, PA 18901 | P. 215.345.1500

LEARN MORE AT
delval.edu/e360

Rank	School (State) (*Public)	Overall score	Peer assessment score (5.0=highest)	High school counselor assessment score	Average freshman retention rate	2013 graduation rate		% of classes under 20 ('13)	% of classes of 50 or more ('13)	SAT/ACT 25th-75th percentile ('13)	Freshmen in top 10% of HS class ('13)	Acceptance rate ('13)	Average alumni giving rate
						Predicted	Actual						
165.	Monmouth College (IL)	39	2.6	2.9	75%	58%	59%	67%	0.3%	20-25	15%	64%	20%
165.	Warren Wilson College (NC)	39	2.6	3.3	68%	68%	51%	84%	0%	1010-1250	22%	70%	11%
171.	Purchase College–SUNY*	38	2.4	3.3	82%	48%	60%	77%	1%	980-1180[3]	13%[5]	33%	4%
172.	Eastern Mennonite University (VA)	37	2.4	3.0	78%	62%	63%	69%	2%	863-1128	16%	65%	23%
172.	Emory and Henry College (VA)	37	2.5	3.1	73%	55%	48%	74%	0%	880-1120[3]	26%[4]	66%	30%[4]
172.	Guilford College (NC)	37	2.8	3.2	74%	58%	57%	55%	0%	970-1220[2]	11%	68%	13%
172.	Northland College (WI)	37	2.3	3.0	71%	61%	58%	70%	0%	21-27	18%	59%	11%
176.	Ouachita Baptist University (AR)	36	2.2	3.2	79%	65%	60%	54%	1%	21-27	29%	70%	18%
177.	Albright College (PA)	34	2.5	3.1	74%	58%	54%	63%	1%	930-1130[2]	20%	62%	11%
178.	Bridgewater College (VA)	33	2.4	3.0	75%	57%	60%	43%	0%	930-1130	20%	55%	18%
178.	Erskine College (SC)	33	2.3	3.3	68%[8]	65%	58%	79%	0.3%	910-1110	N/A	70%	16%
178.	Wisconsin Lutheran College	33	2.1	2.7	78%	66%	64%	68%	1%	21-27	19%	64%	16%
178.	Xavier University of Louisiana	33	2.7	3.4	68%	51%	46%	51%	6%	20-26	28%	54%	12%

School (State) (*Public)	Peer assessment score (5.0=highest)	High school counselor assessment score	Average freshman retention rate	2013 graduation rate		% of classes under 20 ('13)	% of classes of 50 or more ('13)	SAT/ACT 25th-75th percentile ('13)	Freshmen in top 10% of HS class ('13)	Acceptance rate ('13)	Average alumni giving rate
				Predicted	Actual						
SECOND TIER (SCHOOLS RANKED 182 THROUGH 236 ARE LISTED HERE ALPHABETICALLY)											
Allen University (SC)	1.7	2.2	46%	35%	23%	N/A	N/A	16[2]	N/A	50%	N/A
American Jewish University (CA)	2.2	2.8	70%	69%	53%[6]	N/A	N/A	780-1240[9]	N/A	42%	N/A
Amridge University (AL)	1.4	2.0	N/A	46%	23%[6]	N/A	N/A	N/A[2]	N/A	N/A	N/A
Ave Maria University[1] (FL)	2.1	2.6	70%[8]	68%	43%[6]	N/A	N/A	20-27[4]	N/A	61%[4]	N/A
Bay Path University (MA)	2.2	2.4	74%	50%	55%	78%	0%	840-1090[2]	14%	58%	5%

MATT SLABY – LUCEO FOR USN&WR

Washington and Lee in Virginia, No. 14

School (State) (*Public)	Peer assessment score (5.0=highest)	High school counselor assessment score	Average freshman retention rate	2013 graduation rate		% of classes under 20 ('13)	% of classes of 50 or more ('13)	SAT/ACT 25th-75th percentile ('13)	Freshmen in top 10% of HS class ('13)	Acceptance rate ('13)	Average alumni giving rate
				Predicted	Actual						
SECOND TIER (SCHOOLS RANKED 182 THROUGH 236 ARE LISTED HERE ALPHABETICALLY)											
Bennett College[1] (NC)	2.2	2.1	68%[8]	32%	41%[6]	74%[4]	0.4%[4]	15-20[4]	5%[4]	69%[4]	N/A
Bethany College (WV)	2.4	3.0	60%	53%	48%	80%	0%	770-1040	12%	49%	18%
Bethany Lutheran College (MN)	2.1	2.7	72%	59%	49%	75%	0.4%	20-26	14%	75%	15%
Bloomfield College (NJ)	2.0	2.5	67%	31%	37%	71%	1%	770-930	6%	59%	4%
Brevard College (NC)	2.3	3.0	58%	49%	43%	74%	0%	850-1050	5%	45%	6%
Bryn Athyn Col. of New Church (PA)	1.8	2.5	64%	62%	50%	81%[4]	0%[4]	920-1130[3]	N/A	52%	N/A
Burlington College (VT)	2.3	3.2	62%[8]	39%	17%	97%[4]	0%[4]	820-1130[9]	5%[5]	83%	9%
Castleton State College (VT)*	2.0	2.4	71%	41%	51%	73%	2%	850-1060[3]	8%[5]	79%	9%
Claflin University (SC)	2.1	2.4	73%	38%	44%	63%	1%	710-960	13%	61%	47%
Clearwater Christian College (FL)	1.8	2.4	66%	53%	54%	75%	2%	19-25	10%[5]	70%	3%
Col. of Sts. John Fisher & Thomas More[1] (TX)	2.3	2.4	N/A	65%	33%[6]	N/A	N/A	N/A[2]	N/A	N/A	N/A
Colorado Mesa University*	2.0	2.9	65%	37%	33%	50%	7%	18-23	10%	82%	2%
Dillard University (LA)	2.1	3.0	64%[8]	34%	48%	63%	1%	17-20	14%[5]	35%	4%
Eastern Nazarene College (MA)	2.2	2.5	68%	55%	58%	80%	5%	820-1090[3]	9%	51%	N/A
Fort Lewis College (CO)*	2.5	2.9	64%	44%	37%	46%	3%	20-25[3]	10%	88%	2%
Green Mountain College (VT)	2.1	2.8	70%[8]	55%	40%	61%	0%	920-1200[9]	N/A	76%	7%
Harrisburg Univ. of Science and Tech. (PA)	1.9	3.0	62%[8]	N/A	24%	76%	0%	830-1050[9]	N/A	47%[4]	N/A
Holy Cross College[1] (IN)	2.6	3.6	55%[8]	45%	21%[6]	66%[4]	1%[4]	19-24[4]	N/A	81%[4]	5%[4]
Huston-Tillotson University[1] (TX)	2.0	2.7	57%[8]	25%	23%[6]	N/A	N/A	700-900[9]	N/A	46%	N/A
Johnson C. Smith University (NC)	2.1	2.5	68%	36%	44%	75%	0.2%	733-920	8%	37%	15%
Judson College[1] (AL)	2.2	2.8	71%[8]	53%	38%[6]	N/A	N/A	19-24[9]	N/A	74%	20%[7]
Kentucky State University*	2.0	3.3	51%	28%	18%	53%	0.2%	16-20	N/A	38%	4%
The King's College (NY)	2.2	2.7	64%	58%	61%	35%	0%	1050-1230	15%[5]	71%	14%
Lane College[1] (TN)	1.9	2.1	55%[8]	18%	33%[6]	50%[4]	0%[4]	14-17[4]	3%[4]	33%[4]	1%
Life University (GA)	1.6	2.6	70%	50%	22%	68%	1%	19[3]	N/A	41%	1%
Louisiana State University–Alexandria*	2.0	3.1	57%	22%	20%	50%	4%	18-22	13%	61%	3%
Marymount Manhattan College (NY)	2.2	3.2	66%	60%	44%	57%	1%	930-1153	N/A	75%	7%
Maryville College (TN)	2.4	2.6	72%	64%	56%	45%	0.4%	21-26	14%[5]	73%	25%
Pacific Union College (CA)	2.4	3.1	76%	55%	37%	60%	5%	890-1150	N/A	51%	7%
Pine Manor College (MA)	2.0	2.5	59%	29%	36%	88%	0%	660-860[3]	N/A	64%	6%
Rust College (MS)	2.1	2.6	60%	19%	20%	N/A	N/A	13-14	N/A	14%	N/A
San Diego Christian College[1]	1.9	2.9	59%[8]	47%	44%[8]	80%[4]	1%[4]	18-22[4]	5%[4]	43%[4]	N/A
Savannah State University (GA)*	2.0	2.8	70%[8]	23%	29%	30%	1%	770-910	N/A	83%	N/A
Shawnee State University (OH)*	2.0	2.5	52%	35%	24%	44%	3%	17-23[2]	12%	83%	1%
Shorter University[1] (GA)	2.0	2.7	54%[8]	51%	49%[6]	N/A	N/A	820-1060[9]	N/A	68%	4%
Simpson University (CA)	2.4	3.2	71%	50%	49%	71%	5%	910-1150	23%	56%	4%
Stillman College[1] (AL)	2.4	3.1	60%[8]	32%	28%[8]	65%[4]	1%[4]	16-19[4]	5%[4]	41%[4]	5%[4]
SUNY College–Old Westbury*	2.4	3.0	77%	32%	37%	38%	1%	920-1080[3]	N/A	58%	1%
Tougaloo College (MS)	2.1	2.1	74%	46%	50%	70%	0.3%	15-21	19%	34%	13%
University of Hawaii–Hilo*	2.5	3.2	70%[8]	44%	36%	47%	4%	823-1050[3]	18%	75%	N/A
University of Maine–Machias*	2.2	2.8	66%	38%	31%	77%	0%	820-1050	N/A	85%	0.1%
University of Pikeville (KY)	1.7	3.3	52%	45%	29%	48%	3%	17-22	15%	100%	5%
Univ. of Science and Arts of Okla.*	2.5	3.2	67%	43%	37%[6]	75%	2%	19-24	29%	62%	7%
University of Virginia–Wise*	2.5	3.4	69%	40%	42%	67%	1%	860-1050[3]	15%	75%	10%
Univ. of Wisconsin–Parkside*	2.1	2.9	65%	41%	31%	45%	9%	19-23[2]	10%	69%	1%
Virginia Intermont College[1]	1.5	2.7	63%[8]	44%	25%[6]	95%[4]	0.3%[4]	18-23[4]	9%[4]	99%[4]	4%[4]
Virginia Wesleyan College	2.5	3.0	65%	53%	44%	81%	0%	907-1142[9]	14%	93%	8%
Western State Colorado University*	2.1	3.1	64%	45%	42%	56%	0.4%	19-24	6%	92%	N/A
West Virginia State University*	2.1	3.1	53%	29%	17%	53%	2%	18-22	N/A	45%	2%
William Peace University[1] (NC)	2.0	2.7	68%[8]	46%	38%[6]	55%[4]	1%[4]	16-24[4]	6%[4]	61%[4]	2%[4]

Footnotes:

1. School refused to fill out U.S. News statistical survey. Data that appear are from school in previous years or from another source such as the National Center for Education Statistics.
2. SAT and/or ACT not required by school for some or all applicants.
3. In reporting SAT/ACT scores, the school did not include all students for whom it had scores, or refused to tell U.S. News whether all students with scores had been included.
4. Data reported to U.S. News in previous years.
5. Data based on fewer than 51 percent of enrolled freshmen.
6. Some or all data reported to the NCAA and/or the National Center for Education Statistics.
7. Data reported to the Council for Aid to Education.

8. Average graduation or freshman retention rates, normally based on four years of data, are given here for less than four years because school didn't report rates for the most recent year or years to U.S. News.
9. SAT and/or ACT may not be required by school for some or all applicants, and in reporting SAT/ACT scores, the school did not include all students for whom it had scores, or refused to tell U.S. News whether all students with scores had been included.
† School appeared in a different U.S. News ranking category last year.

N/A means not available.

ATHENS

...University of Georgia

Tia Samrawit Ayele, '14

I chose UGA because of its affordability, excellent academic reputation and strong sense of community. After completing my first year, I realized that it was the best decision I had ever made. As an Honors student, I have the best of both worlds: I attend a large land-grant university but still get a tightknit community feel from the Honors college. As an international affairs major, I've been able to pursue undergraduate research

Why I

TUCSON

...University of Arizona

Daniel Fried, '14

I chose UA for its rich, research-driven academic environment and opportunities for student involvement. As a computer science, information science and mathematics major, I took advantage of research opportunities in artificial intelligence and data visualization beginning my freshman year. I was impressed by the freedom and support that the school gives students to pursue their passions. My interests have led me outside the campus borders: UA's study abroad program allowed me to spend a summer in Germany doing machine learning research, and I also had the opportunity to do a semesterlong research internship in Japan working in computational linguistics.

UA students have strikingly diverse backgrounds and extracurricular interests. They help guide NASA rovers on Mars, launch award-winning businesses, and participate in over 600 student organizations on campus. Tucson's idyllic weather and nearby mountains allow year-round hiking, cycling and rock climbing, and the city has a thriving art and cultural scene. My time at UA has shaped my personal development and opened doors for my future that I never anticipated. ●

with renowned experts on Middle Eastern Studies, intern at a leading economic policy think tank, and develop other areas of interest – from women's issues to the Arabic language. UGA really encourages students to gain experience outside the classroom. With the enthusiastic support of school administrators, I received a prestigious 11-month grant to intern abroad in Ethiopia. And through UGA's School of Public and International Affairs, I received a public policy fellowship that afforded me another internship opportunity, this time in the Washington, D.C., office of Georgia Sen. Johnny Isakson. My entire experience at UGA has given me outstanding contacts and policy exposure, which will be invaluable as I pursue a career in foreign affairs. ●

Picked...

BOSTON

...Northeastern University

Rachael Tompa, '14

When I originally applied to Northeastern, I was excited because it was located in a vibrant city – Boston – and because it put such a strong emphasis on practical learning. I knew I wanted a career in aerospace and defense, so when I visited campus, I was happy not only to be shown the usual sights like dorms, classrooms and the beautiful rec center, but also to be taken on faculty-led tours of the university's state-of-the art electrical, mechanical and civil engineering labs. I was impressed, too, by Northeastern's outstanding co-op program, which enables students to rotate classroom work with on-the-job experience at major companies. Over the last few years, this has al-

lowed me to work on real-world projects in the fields I am particularly interested in. I got tremendous experience as I spent six-month rotations working in operations at Raytheon Company, flight testing at Sikorsky Aircraft, and in thermal engineering at NASA's Jet Propulsion Laboratory. These rotations, along with relationships I formed with professors, have helped me grow and have made it possible for me to be accepted to graduate school, where I will be studying aeronautics and astronautics. ●

CLOCKWISE FROM TOP: PAUL EFLAND – UNIVERSITY OF GEORGIA; MARIAH TAUGER – NORTHEASTERN UNIVERSITY; BEATRIZ VERDUGO – UNIVERSITY OF ARIZONA; ISTOCKPHOTO

Best Regional Universities

What Is a Regional University?

Like the national universities, the institutions that appear here provide a full range of undergraduate majors and master's programs; the difference is that they offer few, if any, doctoral programs. The 620 universities in this category are not ranked nationally but rather against their peer group in one of four regions – North, South, Midwest and West – because, in general, they tend to draw students most heavily from surrounding states.

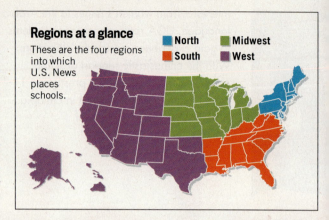

Regions at a glance
These are the four regions into which U.S. News places schools.

- North
- Midwest
- South
- West

NORTH ▶

Rank School (State) (*Public)	Overall score	Peer assessment score (5.0=highest)	Average freshman retention rate	2013 graduation rate Predicted	2013 graduation rate Actual	% of classes under 20 ('13)	% of classes of 50 or more ('13)	Student/ faculty ratio ('13)	SAT/ACT 25th-75th percentile ('13)	Freshmen in top 25% of HS class ('13)	Accept- ance rate ('13)	Average alumni giving rate
1. Villanova University (PA)	100	4.3	94%	89%	90%	48%	2%	12/1	1210-1400	88%[5]	49%	23%
2. Providence College (RI)	83	3.7	91%	78%	85%	48%	3%	12/1	1050-1260[2]	67%[5]	60%	19%
3. College of New Jersey*	80	3.5	94%	81%	85%	39%	0.2%	13/1	1130-1340	89%	43%	6%
3. Fairfield University (CT)	80	3.5	88%	79%	82%	53%	0.4%	11/1	1090-1250[2]	64%[4]	70%	16%
3. Loyola University Maryland	80	3.6	88%	81%	84%	38%	1%	12/1	1100-1268[2]	67%[5]	58%	14%
6. Bentley University (MA)	78	3.4	94%	82%	87%	29%	0.3%	14/1	1140-1310[3]	75%[5]	44%	7%
7. University of Scranton (PA)	76	3.4	89%	68%	82%	49%	0.1%	11/1	1030-1210	59%[5]	75%	15%
8. Rochester Inst. of Technology (NY)	74	4.0	88%	72%	66%	43%	5%	14/1	1110-1320	64%	60%	7%
9. Ithaca College (NY)	72	3.5	84%[8]	73%	76%	59%	4%	11/1	1080-1270[2]	63%[5]	67%	9%
9. Quinnipiac University (CT)	72	3.4	87%	73%	76%	47%	1%	11/1	1000-1190	66%	67%	10%
11. Bryant University (RI)	70	3.0	88%	72%	82%	25%	0%	16/1	1050-1220[2]	50%[5]	77%	8%
11. Marist College (NY)	70	3.3	90%	73%	80%	48%	0%	16/1	1090-1260[9]	64%[5]	37%	15%
11. St. Joseph's University (PA)	70	3.3	89%	73%	79%	34%	1%	14/1	1020-1200[2]	52%[5]	79%	11%
14. Emerson College (MA)	69	3.2	88%	82%	81%	63%	2%	13/1	1140-1320	68%[5]	48%	7%
14. SUNY–Geneseo*	69	3.6	91%	80%	78%	33%	9%	19/1	1178-1360	84%[5]	53%	10%
16. Simmons College (MA)	66	3.1	85%	69%	71%	69%	4%	10/1	1040-1250[3]	61%[5]	49%	17%
17. Gallaudet University (DC)	64	3.2	72%	47%	48%	94%	0%	8/1	15-20	N/A	65%	N/A
18. Manhattan College (NY)	63	3.0	85%	66%	74%	47%	0%	12/1	970-1190	52%[5]	66%	15%
19. Le Moyne College (NY)	61	3.0	85%	59%	74%	40%	2%	13/1	980-1170[3]	51%	62%	16%
19. Mount St. Mary's University (MD)	61	3.1	80%	63%	66%	46%	1%	13/1	990-1180	35%	67%	23%
19. Pratt Institute (NY)	61	3.3	83%	67%	62%	71%	1%	10/1	1070-1300	N/A	67%	N/A
19. Rowan University (NJ)*	61	3.1	86%	58%	70%	45%	1%	13/1	1000-1230	63%[4]	60%	4%
23. Rider University (NJ)	60	2.9	80%	55%	65%	51%	1%	12/1	930-1150	38%	69%	10%
24. St. Bonaventure University (NY)	59	3.0	81%	57%	67%	62%	0%	11/1	930-1180	45%[5]	80%	20%
25. CUNY–Baruch College*	58	3.1	90%	54%	67%	20%	15%	16/1	1130-1330	70%	27%	6%
25. SUNY–New Paltz*	58	3.0	88%	56%	70%	40%	3%	15/1	1030-1220	70%[5]	44%	7%
27. Canisius College (NY)	57	2.8	83%	64%	67%	49%	0.3%	12/1	980-1200	53%	73%	12%
28. Ramapo College of New Jersey*	56	2.8	88%	69%	73%	37%	0%	17/1	990-1200	52%[5]	55%	13%
28. Rutgers, The State U. of N.J.–Camden*	56	3.1	82%	50%	55%	37%	8%	11/1	930-1140[3]	43%	59%	3%
28. Wagner College (NY)	56	3.0	82%	71%	62%	63%	1%	14/1	1050-1270[2]	73%	70%	11%
31. Assumption College (MA)	55	2.7	83%	59%	73%	40%	0%	12/1	1020-1215[2]	40%	74%	13%
31. CUNY–Queens College*	55	2.8	87%	42%	56%	41%	5%	14/1	1030-1220	65%	37%	20%
31. Hood College (MD)	55	2.9	77%	62%	66%	72%	0.3%	12/1	910-1160[2]	45%[5]	81%	19%
31. La Salle University (PA)	55	3.1	81%	59%	65%	44%	2%	13/1	880-1100	38%	80%	11%
31. Nazareth College (NY)	55	2.6	81%	70%	68%	62%	0%	10/1	1020-1180[2]	65%	68%	12%
31. Springfield College (MA)	55	2.8	85%	51%	69%	52%	2%	13/1	920-1130	35%	70%	12%
37. Monmouth University (NJ)	54	2.9	80%	59%	61%	44%	0%	14/1	970-1150	49%[5]	78%	5%
38. Alfred University (NY)	53	2.9	74%	60%	62%	59%	3%	12/1	1000-1200	43%	70%	15%

▶ More @ usnews.com/bestcolleges

Note: Key to footnotes, Page 106.

Check our Rankings!

www.newpaltz.edu

#2 in the Top 50 affordable colleges nationally with a high return on investment. — *Affordable Colleges Online*

#5 of the Top 50 public colleges/universities nationally for best lifetime degree value. — *The College Database*

#6 among the best public regional universities in the North. — *U.S. News & World Report's Best Colleges 2014*

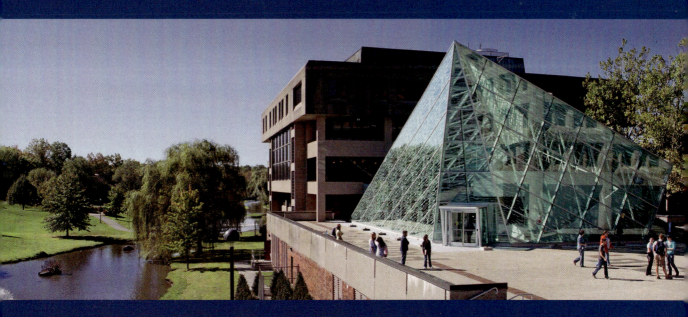

New Paltz

STATE UNIVERSITY OF NEW YORK

NORTH ▶

Rank	School (State) (*Public)	Overall score	Peer assessment score (5.0=highest)	Average freshman retention rate	2013 graduation rate Predicted	2013 graduation rate Actual	% of classes under 20 ('13)	% of classes of 50 or more ('13)	Student/ faculty ratio ('13)	SAT/ACT 25th-75th percentile ('13)	Freshmen in top 25% of HS class ('13)	Accept- ance rate ('13)	Average alumni giving rate
38.	Marywood University (PA)	53	2.6	83%	56%	65%	62%	1%	11/1	950-1150	47%	70%	16%
38.	Sacred Heart University (CT)	53	2.9	79%	63%	70%	42%	1%	14/1	1020-1170[2]	39%[5]	61%	7%
41.	Arcadia University (PA)	52	2.8	80%	64%	61%	75%	4%	12/1	1000-1178	62%	60%	14%
41.	College of St. Rose (NY)	52	2.6	79%	59%	66%	65%	0.1%	13/1	940-1150[9]	44%	78%	19%
41.	King's College (PA)	52	2.6	78%	54%	66%	59%	0%	13/1	940-1150[2]	38%	72%	13%
41.	Misericordia University (PA)	52	2.6	84%	55%	69%	48%	0%	13/1	970-1140[3]	56%	65%	21%
41.	Molloy College (NY)	52	2.3	89%	54%	66%	69%	0%	10/1	970-1140	56%[5]	73%	10%
41.	Richard Stockton Col. of N.J.*	52	2.8	86%	55%	65%	24%	2%	17/1	980-1170	60%	62%	3%
41.	Roger Williams University (RI)	52	2.9	80%	63%	62%	46%	1%	14/1	1020-1200[9]	37%[5]	81%	7%
41.	SUNY College–Oneonta*	52	2.9	85%	59%	68%	38%	4%	18/1	1020-1180	58%[5]	43%	7%
41.	SUNY–Fredonia*	52	2.8	81%	52%	65%	62%	5%	15/1	950-1140	39%	52%	6%
50.	CUNY–Hunter College*	51	3.2	86%	49%	50%	38%	7%	14/1	1070-1270	56%	31%	11%
50.	Montclair State University (NJ)*	51	3.0	83%	52%	63%	34%	2%	17/1	880-1060	35%	65%	4%
50.	New York Inst. of Technology	51	2.8	75%	60%	47%	62%	1%	11/1	1020-1220	52%[5]	74%	14%
50.	Niagara University (NY)	51	2.8	80%	54%	65%	51%	1%	12/1	930-1120[3]	41%	66%	12%
50.	Notre Dame of Maryland University	51	2.8	73%	56%	53%	88%	0%	12/1	930-1150	61%	50%	11%
50.	Salve Regina University (RI)	51	2.7	81%	65%	64%	39%	0%	13/1	1020-1190[2]	45%	67%	16%
56.	Chatham University (PA)	50	2.6	74%	61%	50%	83%	0%	10/1	950-1190[2]	65%	61%	22%
56.	Mercyhurst University (PA)	50	2.6	80%	54%	61%	52%	1%	14/1	940-1160	29%	75%	15%
56.	St. Francis University (PA)	50	2.5	82%	59%	70%	55%	2%	14/1	930-1160	42%	76%	15%
56.	SUNY–Oswego*	50	3.0	80%	51%	58%	56%	6%	18/1	1040-1180[3]	55%	49%	8%
60.	College at Brockport–SUNY*	49	2.7	83%	51%	67%	36%	6%	19/1	960-1150	39%	48%	5%
60.	Emmanuel College (MA)	49	2.6	82%	56%	58%	44%	0%	14/1	1000-1180[2]	54%[5]	60%	18%
60.	Gannon University (PA)	49	2.7	79%	58%	64%	54%	1%	14/1	930-1150	54%	80%	10%
60.	Suffolk University (MA)	49	2.9	75%	57%	55%	37%	1%	11/1	890-1130	42%[5]	83%	5%
60.	Towson University (MD)*	49	3.1	85%	57%	65%	30%	2%	17/1	990-1170	49%	60%	4%
65.	CUNY–City College*	48	3.0	84%	55%	42%	44%	0.4%	14/1	970-1090[3]	44%[5]	34%	23%
65.	Johnson & Wales University (RI)	48	2.9	76%	37%	54%	44%	0.1%	24/1	N/A[2]	N/A	76%	N/A
65.	Salisbury University (MD)*	48	2.9	82%	62%	67%	34%	4%	16/1	1080-1230[9]	59%[5]	55%	13%
65.	West Chester Univ. of Pennsylvania*	48	2.8	86%	55%	69%	22%	7%	20/1	1020-1190	45%	52%	6%
65.	Western New England Univ. (MA)	48	2.6	75%	59%	59%	51%	0%	13/1	960-1180	44%[5]	82%	6%
70.	CUNY–Brooklyn College*	47	3.0	84%	45%	51%	33%	3%	16/1	980-1170	50%[5]	34%	6%
70.	DeSales University (PA)	47	2.5	83%	60%	70%	44%	2%	14/1	930-1190	47%[5]	76%	9%
70.	St. Joseph's College New York	47	2.5	85%	56%	72%	66%	0%	14/1	950-1150	N/A	75%	5%
70.	SUNY College–Cortland*	47	2.7	83%	52%	70%	25%	8%	17/1	980-1130[2]	61%[4]	47%	7%
74.	Endicott College (MA)	46	2.5	83%	59%	70%	51%	0%	14/1	980-1160	39%[5]	72%	16%
74.	Iona College (NY)	46	2.8	82%	62%	63%	38%	0.1%	15/1	900-1110	31%[5]	92%	9%
74.	Keene State College (NH)*	46	2.8	77%	48%	63%	55%	1%	16/1	860-1080[3]	19%	82%	7%
74.	Norwich University (VT)	46	2.7	79%	59%	57%	57%	1%	13/1	950-1160[3]	33%	63%	14%
74.	SUNY–Plattsburgh*	46	2.7	81%	50%	60%	45%	5%	16/1	930-1120[3]	45%	46%	7%
79.	Fairleigh Dickinson Univ. (NJ)	45	3.0	73%	55%	51%	67%	1%	14/1	900-1100	43%	53%	4%
79.	Philadelphia University	45	2.6	76%	61%	58%	61%	1%	12/1	960-1160	45%	63%	7%
79.	University of New England (ME)	45	2.8	76%	62%	58%	50%	6%	13/1	950-1150	58%[4]	86%	10%
79.	Wheelock College (MA)	45	2.6	71%	53%	54%	60%	0%	12/1	890-1090	38%[5]	73%	15%
83.	Manhattanville College (NY)	44	2.6	73%	63%	58%	71%	0%	12/1	970-1180[2]	N/A	77%	13%
83.	Slippery Rock U. of Pennsylvania*	44	2.7	82%	47%	63%	17%	8%	20/1	910-1090	36%	67%	9%
83.	University of Hartford (CT)	44	2.8	72%	60%	58%	62%	1%	10/1	950-1150[3]	N/A	65%	4%
83.	Wilkes University (PA)	44	2.5	80%	59%	58%	52%	6%	14/1	930-1150	53%	80%	14%
87.	College of St. Elizabeth (NJ)	43	2.3	69%	47%	56%	87%	0%	10/1	748-960	10%	48%	15%
87.	Millersville U. of Pennsylvania*	43	2.7	81%	54%	61%	23%	7%	22/1	920-1110	34%	65%	6%
87.	Roberts Wesleyan College (NY)	43	2.5	81%	56%	61%	64%	2%	12/1	920-1170	52%	73%	12%
87.	The Sage Colleges (NY)	43	2.4	76%	40%	58%	59%	0%	11/1	840-1090[2]	43%	57%	11%
87.	Shippensburg U. of Pennsylvania*	43	2.8	71%	48%	55%	26%	3%	19/1	890-1080	26%	83%	13%
87.	SUNY College–Potsdam*	43	2.7	76%	46%	51%	68%	2%	13/1	930-1170[2]	23%[5]	68%	9%
87.	Univ. of Massachusetts–Dartmouth*	43	3.0	73%	55%	49%	38%	12%	18/1	980-1180	46%	75%	6%
87.	University of St. Joseph (CT)	43	2.6	77%[8]	55%	52%	73%	1%	10/1	880-1040	41%	64%	14%
87.	York College of Pennsylvania	43	2.5	76%	55%	58%	44%	0.3%	16/1	950-1138	40%	74%	8%
96.	Robert Morris University (PA)	42	2.6	78%	51%	56%	43%	5%	15/1	940-1140	42%	80%	5%
96.	Rosemont College (PA)	42	2.2	71%	51%	68%	85%	0%	10/1	800-1040	49%[5]	58%	14%
98.	Bloomsburg U. of Pennsylvania*	41	2.7	80%	49%	62%	19%	7%	21/1	890-1070	26%	89%	8%
98.	Eastern University (PA)	41	2.3	79%	56%	55%	85%	0.2%	13/1	920-1160	51%	75%	11%

Note: Key to footnotes, Page 106.

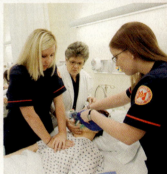

Go beyond.

Florida Southern College's programs are infused with experiences that take you beyond the classroom to immerse you fully in your field. Science students conduct collaborative research with faculty and publish in national journals. Performance majors take the stage alongside world-renowned artists. Business students intern at international Fortune 500 companies. Small classes and a commitment to engaged learning that includes guaranteed internships and study-abroad experiences ensure that *your program* is tailored to *your goals*. Go beyond the ordinary.

FLORIDA SOUTHERN COLLEGE®

FLSOUTHERN.EDU • LAKELAND, FLORIDA

NORTH ▶

Rank	School (State) (*Public)	Overall score	Peer assessment score (5.0=highest)	Average freshman retention rate	2013 graduation rate Predicted	2013 graduation rate Actual	% of classes under 20 ('13)	% of classes of 50 or more ('13)	Student/ faculty ratio ('13)	SAT/ACT 25th-75th percentile ('13)	Freshmen in top 25% of HS class ('13)	Accept-ance rate ('13)	Average alumni giving rate
98.	Stevenson University (MD)	41	2.7	74%	55%	56%	65%	0%	13/1	890-1100[3]	31%	60%	4%
98.	St. Peter's University (NJ)	41	2.5	74%	46%	53%	67%	0%	13/1	830-1000	38%	54%	13%
98.	University of New Haven (CT)	41	2.6	75%	55%	55%	38%	3%	16/1	930-1130	41%[5]	74%	9%
103.	Eastern Connecticut State Univ.*	40	2.6	77%	50%	51%	37%	1%	16/1	930-1100	31%	65%	8%
103.	Plymouth State University (NH)*	40	2.7	74%	45%	56%	53%	2%	16/1	860-1070	20%	78%	6%
103.	William Paterson Univ. of N.J.*	40	2.6	77%	47%	49%	52%	0.4%	15/1	920-1100	N/A	68%	5%
106.	SUNY Buffalo State*	39	2.7	75%	42%	50%	46%	7%	15/1	890-1060	32%[5]	49%	4%[4]
106.	SUNY Institute of Tech.–Utica/Rome*	39	2.4	75%	52%	48%	64%	1%	18/1	1010-1160	45%	48%	4%
106.	Waynesburg University (PA)	39	2.4	80%	51%	54%	68%	1%	14/1	890-1110	47%	83%	7%
109.	Gwynedd Mercy University (PA)	38	2.4	80%	49%	67%	70%	3%	14/1	850-1050	21%	66%	6%
109.	Mount St. Mary College (NY)	38	2.4	70%	48%	52%	48%	0.2%	14/1	910-1093	38%	86%	11%
111.	Alvernia University (PA)	37	2.5	73%	44%	51%	64%	1%	12/1	890-1070[3]	33%	78%	9%
111.	Cairn University	37	2.1	76%[8]	52%	60%[6]	68%	1%	13/1	900-1170[3]	49%[5]	68%	14%
111.	Central Connecticut State Univ.*	37	2.6	78%	50%	52%	42%	2%	16/1	910-1100	21%	64%	5%
111.	Lesley University (MA)	37	2.5	76%[8]	57%	48%[6]	73%[4]	0%[4]	28/1[4]	970-1180[4]	40%[4]	64%[4]	N/A
115.	Albertus Magnus College (CT)	36	2.4	80%[8]	42%	43%	98%	0%	14/1	820-930	26%[5]	71%	18%
115.	Caldwell University (NJ)	36	2.2	75%	46%	55%	70%	0%	11/1	830-1070	25%[5]	66%	14%
115.	CUNY–College of Staten Island*	36	2.7	83%	38%	50%	30%	3%	15/1	920-1100	N/A	100%	2%
115.	University of Baltimore[1] (MD)*	36	2.7	77%[8]	N/A	N/A	30%[4]	0%[4]	19/1[4]	17-21[4]	N/A	64%[4]	8%[4]
115.	Westfield State University (MA)*	36	2.5	80%	49%	59%	35%	1%	17/1	910-1090	22%	75%	4%
120.	College of Mount St. Vincent (NY)	35	2.3	71%	47%	52%	53%	0%	13/1	810-990[4]	26%	91%	16%
120.	Utica College (NY)	35	2.5	66%	46%	47%	66%	0%	11/1	830-1050[9]	28%	85%	9%
122.	CUNY–John Jay Col. of Crim. Justice*	34	3.0	78%	42%	43%	31%	1%	18/1[4]	840-1030	N/A	53%	1%
122.	Point Park University (PA)	34	2.3	76%	46%	50%	75%	1%	13/1	870-1100	31%[5]	74%	3%
122.	Rhode Island College*	34	2.8	76%	47%	43%	50%	1%	14/1	820-1030[3]	40%	72%	6%
125.	CUNY–Lehman College*	33	2.7	80%[8]	33%	36%	46%	1%	15/1	890-1050	N/A	25%	4%[7]
125.	Frostburg State University (MD)*	33	2.7	74%	46%	47%	50%	2%	16/1	860-1070	27%	59%	5%
125.	Georgian Court University (NJ)	33	2.1	71%	48%	51%	73%	0%	12/1	790-1010[3]	30%	78%	10%
125.	Holy Family University (PA)	33	2.0	77%	49%	55%	63%	0.2%	12/1	850-1020	35%	78%	5%
125.	Keuka College (NY)	33	2.4	71%	42%	48%	63%	1%	14/1	860-1050[3]	27%	88%	11%
125.	Kutztown Univ. of Pennsylvania*	33	2.6	75%	47%	55%	23%	12%	20/1	870-1050	20%	75%	6%
125.	St. Thomas Aquinas College (NY)	33	2.5	77%[8]	46%	53%	50%	13%	20/1	830-1050[3]	30%[5]	82%	14%
125.	Worcester State University (MA)*	33	2.6	78%	50%	49%	69%	0.2%	18/1	920-1110	N/A	61%	7%
133.	Cabrini College (PA)	32	2.3	72%	50%	46%	76%	0%	12/1	780-1000[3]	21%	74%	7%
133.	East Stroudsburg Univ. of Pa.*	32	2.5	73%[8]	47%	56%	28%	11%	22/1	880-1010[3]	10%[5]	78%	5%[7]
135.	Delaware State University*	31	2.5	66%	36%	37%	50%	3%	16/1	820-970	26%	45%	6%
135.	Edinboro Univ. of Pennsylvania*	31	2.5	72%	38%	46%	30%	9%	19/1	820-1040	24%	87%	5%
135.	Mansfield Univ. of Pennsylvania*	31	2.3	71%	44%	50%	35%	6%	17/1	850-1070	29%	92%	8%
135.	Western Connecticut State Univ.*	31	2.5	73%	51%	44%	36%	2%	15/1	890-1080	28%	65%	N/A

School (State) (*Public)	Peer assessment score (5.0=highest)	Average freshman retention rate	2013 graduation rate Predicted	2013 graduation rate Actual	% of classes under 20 ('13)	% of classes of 50 or more ('13)	Student/ faculty ratio ('13)	SAT/ACT 25th-75th percentile ('13)	Freshmen in top 25% of HS class ('13)	Accept-ance rate ('13)	Average alumni giving rate
SECOND TIER (SCHOOLS RANKED 139 THROUGH 181 ARE LISTED HERE ALPHABETICALLY)											
American International College (MA)	2.0	64%	45%	45%	54%	3%	14/1	836-869	N/A	68%	8%
Anna Maria College (MA)	1.9	61%[8]	41%	47%	77%	1%	10/1	765-975[4]	N/A	78%	9%
Bridgewater State University (MA)*	2.5	81%[8]	50%	58%	44%	1%	19/1	890-1090[3]	N/A	79%	5%
California U. of Pennsylvania*	2.4	76%	46%	54%	22%	15%	20/1	850-1040	25%	90%	5%
Carlow University[1] (PA)	2.2	70%[8]	46%	53%[6]	N/A	N/A	11/1[4]	855-1035[9]	N/A	95%	N/A
Centenary College (NJ)	2.1	76%	46%	57%	82%	0%	17/1	820-1090	28%[5]	91%	6%
Chestnut Hill College (PA)	2.3	72%	48%	41%	82%	0%	10/1	850-1060	29%	57%	18%
Cheyney U. of Pennsylvania*	1.8	55%	25%	25%	47%	10%	16/1	670-850[3]	9%[5]	88%	4%
Clarion U. of Pennsylvania*	2.3	70%[8]	39%	53%	21%	7%	20/1	840-1030	9%	93%	6%
College of New Rochelle[1] (NY)	2.2	56%[8]	27%	29%[6]	N/A	N/A	14/1[4]	900-1055[9]	N/A	57%	N/A
College of St. Joseph (VT)	2.3	53%	35%	21%	97%	0%	7/1	705-985[3]	20%[4]	73%	4%
Coppin State University[1] (MD)*	2.2	66%[8]	29%	16%[6]	N/A	N/A	14/1[4]	810-950[4]	N/A	36%[4]	6%[7]
Curry College (MA)	2.1	68%	47%	45%	61%	0%	11/1	840-1030[2]	20%[5]	87%	4%
Daemen College (NY)	2.2	78%	55%	49%	57%	2%	14/1	920-1140[2]	51%	49%	5%
Dominican College (NY)	2.1	68%	43%	36%	61%	1%	15/1	810-1000	N/A	72%	N/A
Dowling College (NY)	1.9	64%	43%	34%	75%	1%	15/1	N/A[2]	N/A	74%	N/A

Note: Key to footnotes, Page 106.

1

FLORIDA'S FIRST AND FINEST REGIONAL UNIVERSITY

NO. 1 IN FLORIDA *"America's Top Colleges" by Forbes* (2011)

NO. 1 IN FLORIDA AND NO. 9 IN THE NATION FOR PART-TIME MBA *Bloomberg Businessweek* (2013)

NO. 1 MBA IN FLORIDA *Forbes* 2005–2013

MOST BEAUTIFUL CAMPUSES *The Best Colleges* 2011-2013

Winter Park · Orlando, FL | rollins.edu

ROLLINS

NORTH ▶

School (State) (*Public)	Peer assessment score (5.0=highest)	Average freshman retention rate	2013 graduation rate		% of classes under 20 ('13)	% of classes of 50 or more ('13)	Student/ faculty ratio ('13)	SAT/ACT 25th-75th percentile ('13)	Freshmen in top 25% of HS class ('13)	Accept-ance rate ('13)	Average alumni giving rate
			Predicted	Actual							
SECOND TIER CONTINUED (SCHOOLS RANKED 139 THROUGH 181 ARE LISTED HERE ALPHABETICALLY)											
D'Youville College (NY)	2.1	74%	50%	41%	63%	3%	11/1	950-1140	47%[5]	79%	18%
Felician College (NJ)	2.1	70%	43%	46%	85%	0%	12/1	780-980[3]	24%	88%	5%
Fitchburg State University (MA)*	2.5	76%	50%	50%	38%	1%	15/1	900-1090	N/A	74%	5%
Framingham State University (MA)*	2.5	74%	53%	51%	41%	1%	16/1	930-1100	28%[5]	56%	5%
Franklin Pierce University (NH)	2.4	65%	50%	44%	67%	2%	12/1	860-1060	20%	93%	5%
Husson University (ME)	2.2	70%	39%	44%	57%	0.4%	15/1	850-1080	59%	80%	5%
Johnson State College (VT)*	2.2	N/A	38%	33%[6]	N/A	N/A	N/A	N/A[2]	N/A	N/A	N/A
Kean University (NJ)*	2.4	77%	44%	46%	31%	0%	17/1	810-1000[3]	26%	80%	2%
Lincoln University (PA)*	2.3	66%	33%	40%	49%	1%	17/1	770-960	28%	61%	8%
LIU Post (NY)	2.4	71%	52%	39%	62%	2%	11/1	880-1060	N/A	81%	2%
Lock Haven U. of Pennsylvania*	2.3	70%[8]	42%	50%	30%	12%	21/1	840-1050	30%	86%	6%
Medaille College (NY)	1.9	67%[8]	48%	53%[6]	52%	1%	18/1	760-970[3]	N/A	54%	N/A
Monroe College (NY)	2.0	75%	N/A	71%	46%	0%	15/1	N/A[2]	N/A	44%	1%
Neumann University (PA)	2.3	72%	48%	50%	51%	1%	14/1	770-950	N/A	94%	10%
New England College (NH)	2.4	60%	44%	40%	80%	1%	14/1	810-1020[2]	12%[5]	90%	6%
New Jersey City University*	2.3	70%	39%	32%	55%	0%	15/1	820-1012	37%[5]	41%	4%
Nyack College[1] (NY)	2.1	66%[8]	44%	41%[6]	N/A	N/A	13/1[4]	770-1055[9]	N/A	97%	N/A
Rivier University (NH)	2.1	77%[8]	50%	59%	N/A	N/A	17/1	860-1020[9]	N/A	N/A	N/A
Salem State University (MA)*	2.5	77%	46%	46%	47%	1%	15/1	890-1080[3]	N/A	72%	5%
Southern Connecticut State Univ.*	2.6	76%	47%	49%	41%	1%	14/1	820-1020	21%	75%	3%[7]
St. Joseph's College[1] (ME)	2.5	75%[8]	52%	55%[6]	N/A	N/A	15/1[4]	870-1050[9]	N/A	78%	N/A
Touro College (NY)	1.9	83%[8]	63%	50%	87%	1%	16/1	1040-1260[2]	N/A	65%	1%
Trinity University[1] (DC)	2.7	64%[8]	46%	37%[6]	N/A	N/A	12/1[4]	N/A[2]	N/A	52%	N/A
University of Bridgeport (CT)	2.1	58%	44%	27%	62%	1%	17/1	830-1010	30%[5]	64%	2%
Univ. of Maryland–Eastern Shore*	2.6	68%	35%	32%	57%	4%	14/1	790-960[3]	N/A	55%	3%
University of Southern Maine*	2.7	67%	49%	32%	43%	3%	14/1	870-1100[3]	34%	82%	3%[7]
Univ. of the District of Columbia*	1.9	50%[8]	44%	14%[6]	N/A	N/A	N/A	N/A[2]	N/A	43%[4]	N/A

SOUTH ▶

Rank	School (State) (*Public)	Overall score	Peer assessment score (5.0=highest)	Average freshman retention rate	2013 graduation rate		% of classes under 20 ('13)	% of classes of 50 or more ('13)	Student/ faculty ratio ('13)	SAT/ACT 25th-75th percentile ('13)	Freshmen in top 25% of HS class ('13)	Accept-ance rate ('13)	Average alumni giving rate
					Predicted	Actual							
1.	Elon University (NC)	100	4.0	90%	79%	82%	49%	0.2%	12/1	1120-1320	63%[5]	54%	20%
2.	Rollins College (FL)	98	3.8	83%	75%	68%	69%	0%	10/1	1100-1290[2]	67%[5]	47%	15%
3.	Samford University (AL)	89	3.8	86%	72%	69%	67%	2%	12/1	23-28	59%[5]	77%	11%
4.	The Citadel (SC)*	88	3.9	83%	59%	69%	37%	3%	14/1	970-1190[3]	34%	76%	27%
5.	Belmont University (TN)	85	3.8	82%	71%	68%	43%	0.1%	13/1	24-29	61%	80%	25%
6.	James Madison University (VA)*	84	3.9	91%	69%	81%	33%	13%	16/1	1050-1240	45%	61%	7%
6.	Stetson University (FL)	84	3.5	78%	69%	64%	57%	1%	12/1	1070-1270[2]	61%	59%	11%
8.	Mercer University (GA)	82	3.7	82%	72%	59%	64%	2%	12/1	1080-1270	72%	69%	10%
9.	Appalachian State University (NC)*	78	3.6	88%	61%	68%	38%	9%	16/1	1050-1220	58%	66%	9%
10.	Embry-Riddle Aeronautical U. (FL)	77	3.6	75%	61%	56%	25%	1%	14/1	980-1230[2]	52%[5]	74%	2%
11.	Loyola University New Orleans	76	3.6	78%	70%	55%	50%	2%	11/1	22-28	43%[5]	87%	9%
12.	Union University (TN)	74	3.2	91%	67%	64%	70%	1%	11/1	22-29[3]	62%	74%	12%[4]
13.	Bellarmine University (KY)	72	3.2	81%	64%	66%	52%	1%	12/1	22-27	54%[5]	95%	16%
13.	College of Charleston (SC)*	72	3.6	83%	68%	64%	37%	5%	16/1	1070-1250[3]	60%	72%	7%
13.	Univ. of Mary Washington (VA)*	72	3.3	83%	69%	74%	50%	3%	14/1	1010-1210	50%	81%	16%
16.	Univ. of North Carolina–Wilmington*	70	3.2	86%	65%	71%	34%	7%	17/1	1110-1270	64%	57%	6%
17.	Christopher Newport Univ. (VA)*	69	3.2	84%	66%	66%	47%	4%	16/1	1070-1250[2]	53%	59%	13%
18.	Hampton University (VA)	67	3.0	77%	53%	68%	55%	4%	10/1	920-1090[2]	45%	36%	12%
18.	Lipscomb University (TN)	67	3.0	74%	66%	64%	54%	7%	12/1	22-28	55%[5]	53%	14%
18.	Queens University of Charlotte (NC)	67	3.0	70%	54%	52%	68%	0%	12/1	940-1140	42%	77%	27%
18.	Spring Hill College (AL)	67	3.0	76%	63%	56%	56%	0%	13/1	21-27	45%	44%	19%
22.	Harding University (AR)	65	3.1	81%	60%	62%	54%	7%	15/1	22-28	50%	76%	11%
23.	Converse College (SC)	64	2.7	70%[8]	63%	62%	83%	0%	11/1	960-1160[3]	43%	52%	23%[4]
24.	University of Tampa (FL)	63	3.1	73%	58%	60%	41%	1%	17/1	980-1150	46%[5]	52%	18%
25.	Winthrop University (SC)*	61	3.2	72%	51%	56%	49%	2%	14/1	920-1140	51%	72%	6%
26.	Christian Brothers University (TN)	60	2.8	76%	58%	55%	76%	0%	10/1	21-27	60%	51%	12%
26.	Murray State University (KY)*	60	3.0	71%	56%	53%	55%	5%	16/1	20-26	43%	82%	22%
28.	Georgia College & State Univ.*	58	3.0	85%	60%	61%	39%	6%	17/1	1050-1230	N/A	68%	5%

Note: Key to footnotes, Page 106.

SOUTH ▶

Rank	School (State) (*Public)	Overall score	Peer assessment score (5.0=highest)	Average freshman retention rate	2013 graduation rate		% of classes under 20 ('13)	% of classes of 50 or more ('13)	Student/ faculty ratio ('13)	SAT/ACT 25th-75th percentile ('13)	Freshmen in top 25% of HS class ('13)	Accept-ance rate ('13)	Average alumni giving rate
					Predicted	Actual							
29.	Mississippi College	57	3.1	72%	57%	53%	60%	1%	15/1	21-27	42%	67%	6%
30.	Longwood University (VA)*	56	2.8	79%	54%	63%	48%	1%	18/1	920-1090	33%	81%	11%
31.	Campbell University (NC)	54	3.0	75%	67%	49%	59%	7%	16/1	820-1290[3]	54%	70%	12%
31.	Western Kentucky University*	54	2.9	73%	45%	50%	49%	6%	18/1	19-25	50%[5]	92%	11%
33.	Lynchburg College (VA)	53	2.6	74%	55%	56%	60%	0.1%	11/1	890-1110	37%[4]	64%	13%
34.	Gardner-Webb University (NC)	52	2.7	71%	50%	56%	69%	0%	13/1	900-1120	55%	48%	9%
34.	Radford University (VA)*	52	3.0	76%	48%	59%	34%	7%	18/1	900-1080	22%	78%	5%
34.	Tennessee Technological Univ.*	52	3.0	73%	56%	51%	37%	11%	20/1	20-26	55%	93%	9%
37.	Columbia College (SC)	51	2.7	64%	49%	42%	75%	0%	11/1	920-1130	63%	64%	13%
37.	Columbia International Univ. (SC)	51	2.4	82%	59%	65%	66%	7%	16/1	940-1200[3]	37%	63%	6%
37.	Marymount University (VA)	51	2.8	70%	56%	58%	49%	0.2%	13/1	930-1130	44%[5]	83%	7%
37.	University of Montevallo (AL)*	51	3.0	75%	51%	45%	48%	1%	16/1	20-26	N/A	67%	15%
37.	Western Carolina University (NC)*	51	3.0	75%	50%	51%	26%	6%	16/1	940-1120	38%	39%	5%
37.	William Carey University (MS)	51	2.5	76%	44%	62%	69%	1%	14/1	21-28[3]	59%	50%	5%
43.	Brenau University (GA)	50	2.8	69%	39%	46%	82%	0.4%	12/1	890-1070	N/A	78%	6%
43.	Freed-Hardeman University (TN)	50	2.5	74%	58%	52%	51%	1%	13/1	21-27	55%	92%	13%
43.	Wingate University (NC)	50	2.8	74%	54%	53%	42%	1%	16/1	910-1120	50%	79%	14%
46.	Marshall University (WV)*	49	3.2	70%	49%	45%	42%	4%	19/1	20-24	N/A	79%	6%
47.	Mississippi Univ. for Women*	48	3.0	76%	43%	39%	67%	2%	13/1	18-24	59%	43%	5%
47.	Shenandoah University (VA)	48	2.7	76%	55%	45%	71%	1%	10/1	850-1090	36%	84%	7%
49.	Mary Baldwin College (VA)	47	2.9	62%	51%	39%	54%	1%	10/1	830-1060	46%	93%	18%
49.	Thomas More College (KY)	47	2.6	66%	54%	57%	79%	0%	13/1	20-25	27%	88%	18%
51.	Palm Beach Atlantic University (FL)	46	2.7	69%	57%	48%	64%	2%	13/1	925-1180	N/A	84%	5%
51.	University of North Florida*	46	2.8	83%	56%	50%	25%	12%	20/1	1080-1230	56%	53%	8%
53.	Arkansas State University*	44	2.9	71%	40%	36%	48%	5%	18/1	21-26	47%	76%	9%
53.	Lincoln Memorial University (TN)	44	2.3	68%	45%	48%	82%	1%	13/1	19-27[3]	N/A	70%	5%
53.	Morehead State University (KY)*	44	2.7	69%	42%	45%	55%	4%	18/1	19-25	46%	83%	8%
53.	University of Tennessee–Martin*	44	2.7	73%	50%	46%	54%	7%	17/1	20-25[3]	59%[5]	77%	6%
57.	Coastal Carolina University (SC)*	43	2.8	63%	50%	46%	36%	3%	17/1	910-1090	33%	64%	5%
57.	Lee University (TN)	43	2.7	73%	53%	52%	52%	7%	18/1	21-27[3]	49%	92%	9%
57.	Univ. of Tennessee–Chattanooga*	43	3.1	68%	51%	37%	39%	9%	18/1	21-25	45%	78%	5%
60.	University of North Georgia*	42	2.8	79%	57%	52%[8]	30%	3%	22/1	1010-1190	70%[5]	60%	8%
60.	Winston-Salem State Univ.[1] (NC)*	42	2.5	78%[8]	32%	39%[6]	47%[4]	1%[4]	13/1[4]	16-19[4]	35%[4]	56%[4]	7%[4]
62.	Austin Peay State University (TN)*	40	3.0	68%	41%	38%	53%	5%	19/1[4]	19-24[9]	37%	86%	5%
62.	Eastern Kentucky University*	40	2.8	66%	43%	39%	56%	4%	16/1	19-25	N/A	74%	N/A
62.	Pfeiffer University (NC)	40	2.5	68%	49%	48%	75%	0%	12/1	870-1080	35%	98%	12%
65.	Belhaven University (MS)	39	2.7	67%	51%	39%	77%	0.3%	12/1	19-25	26%	56%	9%
65.	North Carolina Central Univ.*	39	2.4	71%	32%	40%	40%	5%	15/1	800-950	22%	39%	11%
65.	St. Leo University (FL)	39	2.6	70%	45%	46%	52%	0%	14/1	910-1093[2]	29%	77%	5%
65.	St. Thomas University (FL)	39	2.5	67%	45%	40%	60%	0%	14/1	785-990	11%[5]	42%	1%
65.	University of Central Arkansas*	39	2.7	71%	50%	42%	45%	3%	17/1	20-26	43%	92%	7%
70.	Kennesaw State University (GA)*	38	3.0	77%	54%	43%	25%	16%	21/1	990-1170	53%[5]	55%	5%
70.	Northern Kentucky University*	38	2.7	67%	46%	38%	34%	3%	19/1	20-25	32%	59%	8%
70.	Piedmont College (GA)	38	2.3	73%	53%	46%	74%	0.2%	14/1	920-1150	47%	60%	5%
73.	Alcorn State University (MS)*	37	2.5	68%	29%	35%	51%	5%	16/1	16-19	N/A	83%	5%[4]
73.	Jacksonville University (FL)	37	2.6	63%	52%	38%	67%	0.3%	14/1	910-1110[3]	N/A	47%	5%
75.	Valdosta State University (GA)*	36	2.7	68%	44%	40%	46%	4%	20/1	950-1120	N/A	55%	3%
76.	Albany State University (GA)*	35	2.4	69%	30%	43%	52%	1%	20/1	820-950	27%[5]	24%	4%
76.	Auburn University–Montgomery (AL)*	35	3.0	58%	43%	33%	52%	1%	16/1	18-23	38%	72%	N/A
76.	Francis Marion University (SC)*	35	2.5	67%	43%	41%	44%	6%	15/1	830-1060	42%	57%	3%
76.	Troy University (AL)*	35	2.8	68%	41%	34%	45%	4%	19/1	18-25	52%[5]	67%	9%
80.	Liberty University (VA)	34	2.5	77%	46%	50%	42%	5%	18/1	900-1150	38%	21%	2%
81.	Campbellsville University (KY)	33	2.5	69%[8]	46%	41%	59%	0.2%	13/1	18-24	N/A	68%	10%
81.	Union College (KY)	33	2.3	56%	38%	34%	78%	0%	13/1	19-24	N/A	75%	17%
81.	University of Louisiana–Monroe*	33	2.7	71%	44%	40%	38%	14%	21/1	20-25	50%	77%	5%
81.	University of North Alabama*	33	2.8	69%	48%	32%	45%	3%	21/1	19-25	N/A	73%	7%
85.	King University (TN)	32	2.3	70%	53%	47%	71%	0.2%	12/1	20-25[3]	40%	64%	12%
85.	Southern Polytechnic State U. (GA)*	32	2.7	75%[8]	55%	38%	42%[4]	3%[4]	19/1[4]	21-26[4]	42%[4]	79%[4]	2%[4]
87.	Florida Gulf Coast University*	31	2.7	75%[8]	54%	44%	19%	16%	23/1	940-1100[3]	36%	66%	N/A
87.	McNeese State University (LA)*	31	2.6	69%	39%	37%	36%	9%	22/1	20-24	41%	60%	7%
87.	Nicholls State University (LA)*	31	2.5	70%[8]	43%	42%	40%	11%	20/1	20-24	40%	87%	7%

SOUTH ▶

Rank	School (State) (*Public)	Overall score	Peer assessment score (5.0=highest)	Average freshman retention rate	2013 graduation rate Predicted	2013 graduation rate Actual	% of classes under 20 ('13)	% of classes of 50 or more ('13)	Student/ faculty ratio ('13)	SAT/ACT 25th-75th percentile ('13)	Freshmen in top 25% of HS class ('13)	Accept- ance rate ('13)	Average alumni giving rate
87.	Northwestern State U. of La.*	31	2.4	70%	38%	42%	45%	10%	19/1	19-24	44%	58%	3%
87.	U. of North Carolina–Pembroke*	31	2.5	67%	36%	33%	44%	2%	15/1	840-1010	35%	71%	3%
92.	Arkansas Tech University*	30	2.6	69%	42%	41%	42%	6%	20/1	18-25	33%	85%	4%
92.	Delta State University (MS)*	30	2.5	63%	43%	35%	68%	1%	19/1	18-22	40%	89%	N/A
92.	U. of South Florida–St. Petersburg[1]*	30	2.7	67%[8]	N/A	31%[6]	21%[4]	14%[4]	21/1[4]	21-24[4]	56%[4]	46%[4]	6%[4]
92.	University of the Cumberlands (KY)	30	2.3	58%	50%	43%	59%	2%	14/1	19-25	38%	71%	17%
92.	University of West Georgia*	30	2.8	72%	44%	42%	28%	10%	19/1	870-1030[3]	N/A	54%	4%
92.	Virginia State University*	30	2.5	65%[8]	32%	42%[6]	N/A	N/A	16/1	730-910[3]	17%	54%	N/A

School (State) (*Public)	Peer assessment score (5.0=highest)	Average freshman retention rate	2013 graduation rate Predicted	2013 graduation rate Actual	% of classes under 20 ('13)	% of classes of 50 or more ('13)	Student/ faculty ratio ('13)	SAT/ACT 25th-75th percentile ('13)	Freshmen in top 25% of HS class ('13)	Accept- ance rate ('13)	Average alumni giving rate
SECOND TIER (SCHOOLS RANKED 98 THROUGH 126 ARE LISTED HERE ALPHABETICALLY)											
Alabama A&M University*	2.3	69%	31%	29%	48%	4%	18/1	15-19	N/A	90%	6%
Alabama State University*	2.5	61%	24%	26%	N/A	N/A	17/1	15-20[3]	1%	54%	N/A
Armstrong State University (GA)*	2.3	68%	43%	34%	39%	5%	19/1	920-1090	N/A	68%	5%
Bethel University (TN)	2.2	62%[8]	36%	34%	70%	1%	13/1	17-23[9]	N/A	62%	3%
Charleston Southern University (SC)	2.6	64%[8]	46%	36%	56%	4%	15/1	870-1080[3]	37%[4]	69%	4%
Columbus State University (GA)*	2.5	68%	41%	31%	42%	7%	17/1	880-1100	38%[5]	56%	5%
Cumberland University (TN)	2.5	67%	47%	37%	59%	3%	14/1	19-23	29%	47%	5%
Fairmont State University (WV)*	2.2	65%	35%	34%	46%	5%	17/1	18-23	39%	66%	1%
Fayetteville State University (NC)*	2.2	72%	27%	32%	38%	1%	17/1	770-910[3]	17%	61%	2%
Florida Memorial University[1]	1.9	70%[8]	30%	40%[6]	N/A	N/A	17/1[4]	N/A[2]	N/A	42%	N/A
Georgia Southwestern State University*	2.4	65%	41%	36%	52%	2%	17/1	860-1050	36%	68%	1%
Grambling State University (LA)*	2.4	N/A	25%	31%	40%	10%	23/1	16-20[3]	22%	44%	2%[7]
Henderson State University (AR)*	2.6	60%	43%	29%	59%	2%	15/1	19-24	26%	62%	3%
Jacksonville State University (AL)*	2.7	69%	40%	31%	38%	6%	17/1	19-26[3]	39%	83%	7%
Lindsey Wilson College (KY)	2.4	56%	34%	29%	61%	0%	14/1	19-24[2]	33%	72%	12%
Louisiana State U.–Shreveport*	2.7	67%	44%	31%	56%	6%	21/1[4]	20-24[3]	N/A	89%	N/A
Mississippi Valley State Univ.[1]*	2.2	61%[8]	21%	24%[6]	N/A	N/A	13/1[4]	15-19[9]	N/A	23%	N/A
Montreat College[1] (NC)	2.1	51%[8]	46%	39%[6]	N/A	N/A	13/1[4]	820-1080[9]	N/A	54%	N/A
Norfolk State University (VA)*	2.4	N/A	34%	33%	51%[4]	4%[4]	18/1	770-948[3]	26%[4]	65%	3%[4]
Our Lady of Holy Cross College[1] (LA)	2.7	77%[8]	36%	24%[6]	N/A	N/A	12/1[4]	N/A[2]	N/A	48%	N/A
Shepherd University (WV)*	2.5	67%[8]	46%	38%	53%	1%	17/1	900-1080[3]	N/A	94%	7%
Southeastern Louisiana University*	2.4	67%	39%	36%	31%	8%	22/1	20-24	30%	89%	4%
Southern Arkansas University*	2.2	62%	36%	31%	47%	3%	15/1	18-24	42%	61%	4%
Southern Univ. and A&M College (LA)*	2.3	69%	30%	32%	N/A	N/A	25/1	17-20[3]	23%	N/A	N/A
Southern University–New Orleans[1]*	2.3	61%[8]	26%	11%[6]	N/A	N/A	19/1[4]	840-1290[4]	N/A	49%[4]	N/A
Southern Wesleyan University[1] (SC)	2.3	63%[8]	42%	47%[6]	N/A	N/A	21/1[4]	810-1050[9]	N/A	94%	N/A
South University[1] (GA)	1.9	30%[8]	N/A	18%[6]	N/A	N/A	10/1[4]	N/A[2]	N/A	52%	N/A
Tusculum College[1] (TN)	2.4	57%[8]	45%	34%[6]	N/A	N/A	17/1[4]	840-1040[4]	N/A	72%[4]	5%[7]
University of West Alabama*	2.4	56%[8]	36%	31%	57%	3%	15/1	18-22	N/A	61%	4%
Warner University[1] (FL)	2.3	59%[8]	36%	38%[6]	58%[4]	1%[4]	17/1[4]	16-21[4]	21%[4]	50%[4]	1%[4]

MIDWEST ▶

Rank	School (State) (*Public)	Overall score	Peer assessment score (5.0=highest)	Average freshman retention rate	2013 graduation rate Predicted	2013 graduation rate Actual	% of classes under 20 ('13)	% of classes of 50 or more ('13)	Student/ faculty ratio ('13)	SAT/ACT 25th-75th percentile ('13)	Freshmen in top 25% of HS class ('13)	Accept- ance rate ('13)	Average alumni giving rate
1.	Creighton University (NE)	100	4.0	89%	82%	76%	49%	4%	11/1	24-30	68%	77%	16%
2.	Butler University (IN)	96	3.9	90%	79%	74%	55%	4%	11/1	25-30	81%	66%	23%
3.	Drake University (IA)	92	3.8	87%	75%	73%	52%	6%	11/1	25-30	73%	66%	12%
4.	Bradley University (IL)	90	3.6	87%	69%	76%	55%	3%	12/1	23-28	64%	67%	12%
5.	Valparaiso University (IN)	89	3.8	84%	69%	70%	52%	4%	14/1	23-29	68%	80%	15%
5.	Xavier University (OH)	89	3.6	83%	73%	76%	43%	2%	12/1	23-27	54%[5]	70%	17%
7.	John Carroll University (OH)	83	3.4	88%	64%	75%	44%	0.1%	13/1	22-27	51%[5]	83%	15%
8.	Drury University (MO)	80	3.0	83%	44%	64%	71%	1%	11/1	22-28	59%	73%	15%
9.	Truman State University (MO)*	77	3.6	87%	76%	72%	45%	2%	17/1	25-30	80%	72%	9%
9.	University of Evansville (IN)	77	3.3	84%	69%	63%	64%	1%	13/1	23-29	66%	84%	15%
11.	Elmhurst College (IL)	75	3.2	78%	63%	74%	64%	0.3%	13/1	21-26	47%	72%	9%
12.	Hamline University (MN)	71	3.2	81%	65%	66%	52%	5%	13/1	21-27	47%	66%	15%

Note: Key to footnotes, Page 106.

Rank	School (State) (*Public)	Overall score	Peer assessment score (5.0=highest)	Average freshman retention rate	2013 graduation rate		% of classes under 20 ('13)	% of classes of 50 or more ('13)	Student/faculty ratio ('13)	SAT/ACT 25th-75th percentile ('13)	Freshmen in top 25% of HS class ('13)	Accept-ance rate ('13)	Average alumni giving rate
					Predicted	Actual							
13.	St. Catherine University (MN)	69	3.1	83%	57%	61%	65%	2%	12/1	22-26	52%	59%	15%
14.	Baldwin Wallace University (OH)	68	2.9	81%	64%	71%	60%	1%	13/1	21-27[2]	50%	64%	12%
14.	Milwaukee School of Engineering	68	3.4	80%	69%	56%	40%	0%	14/1	25-30	N/A	68%	9%
14.	North Central College (IL)	68	3.0	80%	67%	64%	36%	0%	16/1	22-27	57%	64%	20%
14.	Rockhurst University (MO)	68	3.0	84%	67%	69%	41%	1%	11/1	23-28	53%	75%	15%
18.	University of Northern Iowa*	67	3.1	82%	57%	66%	47%	6%	16/1	20-24[3]	45%	83%	10%
19.	Dominican University (IL)	65	2.8	82%	60%	63%	61%	0.2%	11/1	20-24	48%	60%	19%
20.	Bethel University (MN)	64	2.6	85%	67%	71%	52%	2%	12/1	22-28	60%	95%	12%
20.	Kettering University (MI)	64	2.6	91%	74%	61%	62%	1%	13/1	25-30	66%	65%	7%
20.	Otterbein University (OH)	64	3.0	76%	59%	59%	70%	0.3%	12/1	22-27[3]	54%	74%	15%
23.	Augsburg College (MN)	63	3.0	81%	54%	64%	67%	2%	13/1	20-24[3]	43%	74%	11%
23.	College of St. Scholastica (MN)	63	2.8	82%	59%	68%	60%	2%	15/1	21-26	55%	73%	11%
23.	Lewis University (IL)	63	2.7	81%	54%	63%	66%	0.2%	13/1	21-26	47%	56%	7%
26.	Grand Valley State University (MI)*	62	3.1	83%[8]	60%	66%	25%	7%	17/1	21-26	50%	83%	5%
26.	Indiana Wesleyan University	62	2.5	75%	55%	71%	63%	2%	14/1	21-27	57%	97%	9%
26.	University of Indianapolis	62	3.2	74%	57%	57%	62%	0.2%	12/1	910-1120	56%	81%	13%
26.	Webster University (MO)	62	2.7	80%	66%	59%	85%	0%	9/1	20-27	42%	57%	5%
30.	Franciscan Univ. of Steubenville (OH)	61	2.3	86%	65%	71%	50%	2%	14/1	23-28	52%[5]	76%	14%
31.	Eastern Illinois University*	59	2.7	79%	48%	60%	45%	3%	14/1	19-24	32%	62%	5%
31.	Univ. of Wisconsin–La Crosse*	59	3.0	86%	69%	69%	28%	10%	20/1	23-27	69%	77%	5%
33.	Univ. of Wisconsin–Eau Claire*	58	3.0	83%	63%	68%	29%	11%	21/1	22-26	51%	80%	9%
34.	St. Ambrose University (IA)	57	2.7	79%	54%	61%	65%	0.1%	10/1	20-25	36%	71%	8%
35.	University of Michigan–Dearborn*	56	2.8	83%	56%	52%	34%	6%	14/1	22-27	57%	63%	8%
36.	Capital University (OH)	55	2.5	75%	59%	58%	59%	2%	12/1	21-27[3]	45%	76%	8%
36.	Univ. of Illinois–Springfield*	55	2.7	74%	55%	43%	54%	2%	13/1	20-27	44%	60%	5%
36.	University of Minnesota–Duluth*	55	2.9	76%	53%	59%	37%	13%	19/1	22-26	44%	78%	9%
39.	University of St. Francis (IL)	53	2.4	80%	57%	57%	65%	0%	12/1	21-25	46%	51%	6%
39.	Western Illinois University*	53	2.7	69%	46%	56%	49%	4%	15/1	18-23	28%	59%	5%
41.	Anderson University (IN)	52	2.5	74%	57%	57%	69%	2%	13/1	940-1140	52%	55%	8%
41.	Carroll University (WI)	52	2.7	77%	58%	57%	58%	3%	16/1	21-26	58%	81%	11%
41.	University of Detroit Mercy	52	2.5	81%	63%	57%	59%	3%	13/1	21-26[3]	55%	62%	10%
44.	Aquinas College (MI)	51	2.6	76%	57%	58%	60%	1%	12/1	21-26	45%	71%	12%
44.	Baker University (KS)	51	2.4	78%	60%	52%	69%	1%	12/1	21-26	42%	88%	16%
44.	Concordia University (NE)	51	2.4	77%	60%	64%	51%	1%	14/1	21-27	43%	72%	22%
47.	Southern Illinois U.–Edwardsville*	50	2.8	71%	56%	50%	37%	11%	18/1	20-25	39%	84%	5%
48.	Univ. of Wisconsin–Whitewater*	49	2.8	78%	50%	55%	34%	6%	21/1	20-24	30%	70%	10%
49.	Heidelberg University (OH)	48	2.6	62%	52%	51%	61%	1%	15/1	19-25	33%[4]	74%	20%
49.	Olivet Nazarene University (IL)	48	2.6	75%	60%	57%	42%	8%	17/1	20-26	48%	79%	16%
49.	Spring Arbor University (MI)	48	2.4	74%	51%	57%	69%	1%	15/1	20-26	48%	65%	12%
49.	St. Xavier University (IL)	48	2.7	72%	52%	47%	38%	2%	13/1	19-24[3]	54%	79%	8%
49.	University of Findlay (OH)	48	2.6	77%	60%	56%	57%	3%	14/1	20-25[3]	44%	66%	8%
54.	Ferris State University (MI)*	47	2.8	73%	47%	54%	34%	7%	16/1	19-24[3]	N/A	76%	3%
54.	Lawrence Technological Univ. (MI)	47	2.6	78%	61%	44%	72%	0.3%	11/1	22-29	52%	58%	4%
54.	Malone University (OH)	47	2.2	69%	54%	59%	59%	1%	13/1	19-26	42%	72%	12%
54.	North Park University (IL)	47	2.6	74%	56%	56%	57%	3%	11/1	19-25	N/A	52%	10%
54.	Univ. of Nebraska–Kearney*	47	2.7	79%	47%	53%	44%	4%	16/1	20-25	41%	85%	9%
54.	Univ. of Wisconsin–Stevens Point*	47	2.7	81%	55%	58%	26%	12%	20/1	21-25	45%	80%	5%
54.	Ursuline College (OH)	47	2.2	68%	45%	50%	84%	0%	9/1	19-24	38%	58%	17%
61.	Concordia University Wisconsin	46	2.5	75%	50%	56%	53%	2%	12/1	20-25[3]	43%	70%	5%
61.	Mount St. Joseph University (OH)	46	2.3	71%	48%	57%	56%	0.3%	11/1	19-24	29%	88%	12%
61.	Muskingum University (OH)	46	2.4	69%	54%	48%	68%	1%	14/1	18-24	43%	76%	18%
61.	Winona State University (MN)*	46	2.9	78%	53%	56%	28%	11%	20/1	21-25	31%	61%	8%
65.	University of Wisconsin–Stout*	45	2.7	72%	47%	54%	36%	2%	18/1	20-24	28%	82%	5%
65.	Walsh University (OH)	45	2.2	75%	51%	55%	66%	0.3%	13/1	20-25[3]	46%	77%	12%
67.	Missouri State Univ.*	44	2.7	75%	55%	53%	27%	10%	20/1	21-26	53%	85%	7%
67.	Mount Vernon Nazarene U. (OH)	44	2.1	74%	54%	60%	71%	1%	13/1	20-26	49%	64%	7%
69.	Alverno College (WI)	43	2.8	71%	40%	39%	69%	0%	10/1	17-23	35%	79%	13%
69.	College of St. Mary (NE)	43	2.3	68%	38%	42%	74%	0%	8/1	20-26	51%	54%	27%
69.	McKendree University (IL)	43	2.4	78%	58%	48%	71%	0%	14/1	20-25	43%	63%	8%
69.	Minnesota State Univ.–Mankato*	43	2.8	74%	48%	49%	35%	8%	25/1	20-24	23%	66%	6%
69.	Quincy University (IL)	43	2.5	71%	51%	50%	70%	0.3%	14/1	20-25	40%	89%	13%

MIDWEST ▶

Rank	School (State) (*Public)	Overall score	Peer assessment score (5.0=highest)	Average freshman retention rate	2013 graduation rate		% of classes under 20 ('13)	% of classes of 50 or more ('13)	Student/ faculty ratio ('13)	SAT/ACT 25th-75th percentile ('13)	Freshmen in top 25% of HS class ('13)	Acceptance rate ('13)	Average alumni giving rate
					Predicted	Actual							
69.	University of St. Francis (IN)	43	2.5	71%	46%	57%	54%	1%	12/1	890-1060	38%	97%	7%
69.	Univ. of Wisconsin–Oshkosh*	43	2.8	76%	51%	54%	38%	9%	22/1	20-24[3]	33%	67%	5%
69.	Univ. of Wisconsin–River Falls*	43	2.7	72%	51%	52%	46%	4%	21/1	20-24	32%	73%	7%[7]
77.	Concordia University Chicago	41	2.4	66%	60%	53%	66%	0.2%	12/1	20-24	18%[4]	54%	9%
77.	Eastern Michigan University*	41	2.7	75%	47%	38%	41%	4%	18/1	19-25	40%	61%	3%
77.	Univ. of Wisconsin–Green Bay*	41	2.8	73%	53%	46%	35%	10%	21/1	21-25	N/A	66%	5%
80.	Dakota State University (SD)*	40	2.4	65%	46%	49%	61%	1%	18/1	19-24	23%	83%	12%
80.	Northwest Missouri State Univ.*	40	2.7	67%[8]	50%	48%	45%	7%	22/1	20-25	40%	73%	4%
80.	Robert Morris University (IL)	40	2.3	49%	27%	46%[8]	63%	0.4%	18/1	15-21[3]	14%	21%	2%
80.	Univ. of Wisconsin–Platteville*	40	2.8	76%[8]	50%	52%	29%	7%	23/1	21-26[3]	36%	79%	N/A
84.	Madonna University (MI)	39	2.2	82%	50%	56%	70%	4%	12/1	19-25	40%	62%	3%
84.	Ohio Dominican University	39	2.5	65%[8]	41%	42%	59%	0%	14/1	20-24	46%	49%	8%
84.	Pittsburg State University (KS)*	39	2.5	72%	46%	46%	37%	10%	19/1	19-24	38%	79%	9%
84.	Rockford University (IL)	39	2.3	64%[8]	50%	50%	79%	0%	10/1	19-25	N/A	41%	9%
84.	Southwestern College (KS)	39	1.9	63%	50%	53%	81%	1%	10/1	20-25	49%	90%	7%
84.	University of Central Missouri*	39	2.6	68%[8]	49%	53%	41%	5%	16/1	19-24[3]	32%	81%	3%[7]
84.	Wayne State College (NE)*	39	2.4	67%	43%	46%	48%	1%	20/1	19-24[2]	29%	100%	13%
91.	Mount Mary University (WI)	38	2.2	67%	42%	41%	89%	0%	10/1	17-23	53%	54%	15%
91.	Northern Michigan University[1]*	38	2.8	72%[8]	50%	49%[6]	31%[4]	11%[4]	22/1[4]	19-24[4]	35%[4]	68%[4]	6%[4]
91.	Roosevelt University (IL)	38	2.4	60%[8]	48%	42%	60%	1%	11/1	19-25	11%	79%	5%[4]
91.	Washburn University (KS)*	38	2.6	65%	46%	37%	45%	2%	14/1	19-25	38%	98%	9%
95.	Lindenwood University (MO)	37	1.9	72%	40%	45%	62%	0.1%	15/1	20-25	33%	66%	38%
95.	Marian University (WI)	37	2.1	68%	45%	49%	73%	1%	11/1	18-22	32%	76%	8%
95.	Southeast Missouri State Univ.*	37	2.4	72%	48%	49%	36%	3%	21/1	20-25	43%	88%	6%
95.	William Woods University (MO)	37	2.2	73%	53%	56%	82%	1%	10/1	19-25	37%	78%	10%
99.	Bemidji State University (MN)*	36	2.5	69%	46%	48%	45%	6%	26/1	19-23	23%	67%	5%
99.	St. Cloud State University (MN)*	36	2.7	71%[8]	45%	47%	38%	4%	19/1	18-24	24%	82%	3%
99.	University of Michigan–Flint*	36	2.7	74%	47%	38%	44%	5%	16/1	18-24	42%	78%	N/A
99.	Univ. of Wisconsin–Superior*	36	2.5	69%	48%	41%	58%	2%	13/1	19-24	17%	66%	3%
103.	Emporia State University (KS)*	35	2.5	71%	48%	41%	48%	4%	18/1	19-25[3]	36%	61%	8%
103.	Graceland University (IA)	35	2.0	68%	46%	47%	63%	3%	15/1	18-24	34%	50%	17%
105.	Oakland City University (IN)	34	1.9	75%	46%	52%	84%[4]	0%[4]	15/1	870-1070[9]	N/A	73%	N/A
106.	Concordia University–St. Paul (MN)	33	2.5	69%	49%	46%	60%	0%	16/1	18-24[3]	22%	53%	3%
106.	Minnesota State Univ.–Moorhead*	33	2.6	67%	46%	46%	40%	6%	17/1	20-25	30%	89%	2%[7]
106.	Minot State University (ND)*	33	2.4	67%	42%	37%	65%	1%	13/1	19-24	22%	57%	4%
109.	Fontbonne University (MO)	32	2.4	71%[8]	45%	41%	N/A	N/A	10/1	21-25	N/A	65%	N/A
109.	Upper Iowa University	32	2.1	64%	35%	40%	82%	0.1%	17/1	19-25	32%	58%	4%
109.	Viterbo University[1] (WI)	32	2.5	76%[8]	53%	51%[6]	N/A	N/A	12/1[4]	21-26[9]	N/A	71%	N/A

School (State) (*Public)	Peer assessment score (5.0=highest)	Average freshman retention rate	2013 graduation rate		% of classes under 20 ('13)	% of classes of 50 or more ('13)	Student/ faculty ratio ('13)	SAT/ACT 25th-75th percentile ('13)	Freshmen in top 25% of HS class ('13)	Acceptance rate ('13)	Average alumni giving rate
			Predicted	Actual							
SECOND TIER (SCHOOLS RANKED 112 THROUGH 146 ARE LISTED HERE ALPHABETICALLY)											
Aurora University[1] (IL)	2.2	70%[8]	52%	50%[6]	N/A	N/A	17/1[4]	19-24[9]	N/A	76%	3%[7]
Avila University[1] (MO)	2.2	66%[8]	54%	45%[6]	N/A	N/A	15/1[4]	20-24[9]	N/A	61%	N/A
Black Hills State University[1] (SD)*	2.5	61%[8]	43%	32%[6]	N/A	N/A	19/1[4]	19-23[9]	N/A	89%	N/A
Calumet College of St. Joseph (IN)	2.0	57%	36%	34%	72%	2%	12/1	780-940[9]	14%	40%	2%
Chicago State University*	1.8	55%	29%	21%	60%	0.1%	12/1	17-20	N/A	29%	N/A
Columbia College Chicago[1] (IL)	2.6	63%[8]	54%	41%[6]	N/A	N/A	10/1[4]	N/A[2]	N/A	91%	N/A
Cornerstone University (MI)	2.0	76%	54%	43%	52%	3%	24/1	21-26[3]	49%	68%	8%
Davenport University (MI)	1.8	79%[8]	30%	42%	72%	0.1%	14/1[4]	N/A[2]	N/A	92%	N/A
DeVry University (IL)	1.7	N/A	N/A	31%	N/A	N/A	19/1	N/A[2]	N/A	N/A	N/A
Fort Hays State University (KS)*	2.3	68%[8]	45%	40%[6]	43%	3%	18/1	740-1230[4]	31%	89%	N/A
Friends University[1] (KS)	2.1	60%[8]	46%	29%[6]	N/A	N/A	9/1[4]	18-24[9]	N/A	59%	N/A
Indiana University Northwest*	2.1	67%	33%	24%	32%	8%	17/1	780-1020	32%	76%	7%
Indiana U.–Purdue U.–Fort Wayne*	2.6	62%	41%	25%	48%	4%	17/1	890-1090	38%	83%	4%
Indiana University–South Bend*	2.3	64%	37%	26%	47%	2%	13/1	860-1060	29%	70%	8%
Indiana University Southeast*	2.2	62%	39%	30%	38%	1%	15/1	850-1050	34%	79%	9%
Lake Erie College (OH)	1.8	67%	46%	46%	66%	0%	14/1	19-23[3]	28%	56%	8%
Lakeland College[1] (WI)	2.0	71%[8]	44%	44%[6]	N/A	N/A	15/1[4]	19-24[3]	N/A	66%	N/A

Note: Key to footnotes, Page 106.

MIDWEST ▶

SECOND TIER (SCHOOLS RANKED 112 THROUGH 146 ARE LISTED HERE ALPHABETICALLY)

School (State) (*Public)	Peer assessment score (5.0=highest)	Average freshman retention rate	2013 graduation rate		% of classes under 20 ('13)	% of classes of 50 or more ('13)	Student/faculty ratio ('13)	SAT/ACT 25th-75th percentile ('13)	Freshmen in top 25% of HS class ('13)	Acceptance rate ('13)	Average alumni giving rate
			Predicted	Actual							
Marygrove College (MI)	2.0	67%[8]	40%	29%	N/A	N/A	11/1	14-18[9]	N/A	94%	N/A
Metropolitan State University[1] (MN)*	2.4	69%[8]	42%	30%[6]	N/A	N/A	16/1[4]	N/A[2]	N/A	100%	3%[7]
MidAmerica Nazarene University[1] (KS)	2.1	74%[8]	54%	48%[6]	N/A	N/A	7/1[4]	19-21[9]	N/A	72%	4%[7]
Missouri Baptist University[1]	2.0	65%[8]	46%	34%[6]	N/A	N/A	19/1[4]	830-1120[4]	N/A	58%[4]	N/A
Newman University (KS)	2.1	71%	53%	52%	66%	1%	15/1	20-27[2]	51%	44%	6%
Northeastern Illinois University*	2.3	64%	36%	20%	38%	2%	16/1	16-21[3]	16%	60%	2%
Park University[1] (MO)	2.1	67%[8]	41%	39%[8]	80%[4]	0%[4]	11/1[4]	17-23[4]	37%[4]	69%[4]	1%[4]
Purdue University–Calumet (IN)*	2.5	69%	36%	30%	26%	7%	19/1	870-1080	36%	76%	5%
Saginaw Valley State Univ. (MI)*	2.4	69%[8]	46%	42%	33%	3%	20/1	19-24	39%	79%	5%
Siena Heights University (MI)	2.2	64%	43%	43%	79%	0.2%	12/1	19-23	33%	68%	5%
Southwest Baptist University[1] (MO)	2.2	67%[8]	50%	48%[6]	N/A	N/A	16/1[4]	20-26[9]	N/A	90%	N/A
Southwest Minnesota State University*	2.3	68%	43%	43%	43%	3%	16/1	19-24[3]	27%	65%	11%
Tiffin University (OH)	2.3	66%	39%	43%	61%	0%	18/1	18-23[9]	N/A	59%	12%
University of Dubuque (IA)	2.5	69%[8]	45%	40%[6]	65%[4]	1%[4]	13/1[4]	17-22[3]	17%[4]	77%	9%[4]
University of Mary[1] (ND)	2.4	71%[8]	51%	48%[6]	N/A	N/A	17/1[4]	20-25[9]	N/A	83%	N/A
University of Southern Indiana*	2.4	68%	42%	37%	44%	4%	16/1	890-1110	36%	69%	4%
University of St. Mary (KS)	2.1	60%	53%	53%	72%	0%	10/1	19-24[3]	3%	47%	N/A
Youngstown State University (OH)*	2.1	68%	37%	33%	39%	7%	17/1	17-23	17%	86%	4%

WEST ▶

Rank	School (State) (*Public)	Overall score	Peer assessment score (5.0=highest)	Average freshman retention rate	2013 graduation rate		% of classes under 20 ('13)	% of classes of 50 or more ('13)	Student/faculty ratio ('13)	SAT/ACT 25th-75th percentile ('13)	Freshmen in top 25% of HS class ('13)	Acceptance rate ('13)	Average alumni giving rate
					Predicted	Actual							
1.	Trinity University (TX)	100	4.1	89%	92%	82%	64%	1%	9/1	1150-1370	73%	64%	14%
2.	Santa Clara University (CA)	98	3.9	94%	82%	84%	40%	2%	12/1	1190-1380	80%[5]	50%	22%
3.	Gonzaga University (WA)	89	3.9	93%	76%	82%	41%	2%	12/1	1100-1290	68%	68%	18%
3.	Loyola Marymount University (CA)	89	3.8	90%	74%	76%	47%	2%	11/1	1090-1300	57%[5]	54%	20%
5.	Seattle University	82	3.6	87%	71%	77%	58%	1%	12/1	1050-1260	62%[5]	73%	10%
6.	Mills College (CA)	81	3.5	79%	71%	62%	75%	0.3%	10/1	1040-1250	71%	68%	21%

JIM LO SCALZO FOR USN&WR

Mills College in California, No. 6 in the West

WEST ▶

Rank	School (State) (*Public)	Overall score	Peer assessment score (5.0=highest)	Average freshman retention rate	2013 graduation rate		% of classes under 20 ('13)	% of classes of 50 or more ('13)	Student/faculty ratio ('13)	SAT/ACT 25th-75th percentile ('13)	Freshmen in top 25% of HS class ('13)	Acceptance rate ('13)	Average alumni giving rate
					Predicted	Actual							
7.	Chapman University (CA)	79	3.5	92%	80%	76%	42%	2%	14/1	1120-1300	93%[5]	45%	9%
8.	University of Portland (OR)	75	3.6	90%	75%	75%	35%	1%	13/1	1090-1300	70%	67%	11%
9.	Whitworth University (WA)	74	3.5	86%	75%	74%	58%	2%	11/1	1090-1290[2]	N/A	78%	18%
10.	Cal. Poly. State U.–San Luis Obispo*	73	3.9	93%	72%	72%	16%	13%	19/1	1130-1320[3]	83%[5]	35%	5%
11.	St. Mary's College of California	72	3.4	88%	62%	60%	50%	0.2%	12/1	1010-1210	64%[5]	69%	12%
12.	University of Redlands (CA)	71	3.2	88%	70%	73%	58%	1%	14/1	1030-1230	65%	67%	13%
13.	St. Edward's University (TX)	67	3.3	82%	60%	69%	55%	0.1%	13/1	1020-1220	54%	79%	7%
13.	University of Dallas	67	3.2	80%	74%	66%	63%	3%	11/1	1090-1330	68%[5]	90%	21%
15.	California Lutheran University	66	3.3	84%	68%	70%	55%	1%	15/1	1010-1203	68%[5]	48%	15%
16.	Point Loma Nazarene University (CA)	65	3.1	85%	71%	72%	45%	4%	14/1	1040-1260	67%	67%	9%
17.	Abilene Christian University (TX)	64	3.4	75%	59%	57%	48%	8%	14/1	21-27	57%	49%	10%
17.	Pacific Lutheran University (WA)	64	3.2	82%	66%	70%	46%	3%	14/1	980-1220[3]	70%[5]	77%	11%
19.	Seattle Pacific University	63	3.2	86%	69%	69%	44%	5%	15/1	1030-1250	57%	83%	6%[7]
20.	Westminster College (UT)	61	3.0	78%	64%	60%	67%	0%	9/1	22-28	55%	75%	15%
21.	St. Mary's Univ. of San Antonio (TX)	57	3.0	73%	60%	56%	53%	0%	12/1	950-1150	57%	58%	7%
21.	Western Washington University*	57	3.2	84%	61%	69%	36%	16%	20/1	990-1220	50%	84%	5%
23.	Mount St. Mary's College (CA)	56	3.1	82%	42%	66%	54%	1%	12/1	830-1020	46%[5]	91%	12%
23.	N.M. Inst. of Mining and Tech.*	56	3.3	74%	78%	44%	56%	6%	13/1	23-29	67%	32%	N/A
25.	Oklahoma City University	54	3.1	77%[8]	70%	59%	72%	1%	11/1	23-29	61%	70%	5%
25.	Pacific University (OR)	54	3.0	79%	71%	62%	67%	3%	10/1	990-1210	N/A	86%	9%
27.	LeTourneau University (TX)	52	2.8	76%	59%	52%	63%	2%	13/1	1030-1300[2]	67%	41%	8%
27.	University of St. Thomas (TX)	52	3.1	78%	62%	51%	70%	0%	10/1	1000-1210	54%	77%	8%
29.	Regis University (CO)	51	3.1	84%	61%	58%	71%	1%	14/1	22-27[3]	56%	92%	6%
30.	George Fox University (OR)	50	2.9	82%	61%	62%	55%	4%	14/1	940-1200	57%	75%	5%
31.	Calif. State Poly. Univ.–Pomona*	49	3.5	90%	43%	53%	16%	12%	28/1	930-1190[3]	N/A	53%	3%
31.	Evergreen State College (WA)*	49	3.2	73%	50%	57%	38%	8%	23/1	950-1210	23%[5]	97%	6%
33.	California State U.–Long Beach*	48	3.2	88%	58%	60%	22%	11%	22/1	940-1160	84%[4]	35%	5%
33.	Dominican University of California	48	2.8	84%	54%	53%	60%[4]	1%[4]	10/1	960-1160[3]	54%[4]	78%	7%[4]
35.	California State Univ.–Chico*	45	2.9	86%	55%	56%	28%	13%	24/1	910-1110	76%[5]	67%	5%
35.	Dallas Baptist University	45	2.8	73%	55%	55%	68%	2%	14/1	18-27	46%	42%	1%
35.	Hardin-Simmons University (TX)	45	2.7	65%	52%	51%	71%	0.2%	12/1	20-25	56%	38%	7%
38.	California Baptist University	44	2.9	77%	55%	58%	55%	5%	18/1	850-1110	43%	79%	3%
38.	San Jose State University (CA)*	44	3.1	86%	45%	48%	20%	15%	29/1	880-1160	N/A	64%	2%
40.	California State U.–Fullerton*	43	3.1	87%	47%	53%	22%	10%	26/1	920-1120	61%	48%	2%
40.	Fresno Pacific University (CA)	43	2.9	78%	51%	54%	68%	3%	13/1	880-1100	66%	78%	N/A
40.	Oklahoma Christian U.	43	3.0	75%	57%	46%	56%	5%	16/1	22-28	58%	63%	11%
43.	Northwest Nazarene University (ID)	42	2.7	74%[8]	58%	53%[6]	63%	4%	17/1	920-1160	57%	29%	14%[4]
43.	Sonoma State University (CA)*	42	3.0	81%	51%	54%	40%	9%	25/1	880-1090[3]	N/A	90%	1%
43.	Univ. of Mary Hardin-Baylor (TX)	42	3.0	64%	50%	47%	49%	2%	16/1	940-1140	51%	85%	6%
46.	California State Univ.–Fresno*	41	2.9	85%	36%	49%	17%	11%	22/1	800-1020	80%	60%	4%
46.	Oral Roberts University (OK)	41	2.6	81%	53%	53%	61%	5%	15/1	20-25[3]	46%[4]	44%	8%
46.	St. Martin's University (WA)	41	2.8	76%	51%	48%	64%	4%	12/1	950-1190[3]	52%	88%	7%
49.	Texas Wesleyan University	40	2.8	65%	48%	42%	75%	0.2%	15/1	940-1090	30%	46%	5%
50.	Texas State University*	39	2.8	78%	54%	57%	26%	17%	20/1	940-1130	49%	74%	4%
51.	Central Washington University*	38	2.8	76%	44%	51%	45%	5%	17/1	880-1100[3]	N/A	82%	2%
51.	Concordia University (CA)	38	2.8	75%	59%	63%	50%	1%	20/1	903-1110	40%[5]	67%	5%
51.	Notre Dame de Namur University[1] (CA)	38	2.8	77%[8]	51%	49%[6]	65%[4]	0%[4]	12/1[4]	18-22[4]	29%[4]	75%[4]	7%[4]
51.	Univ. of Colo.–Colorado Springs*	38	3.1	69%	52%	46%	37%	7%	17/1	21-25	36%	91%	3%
55.	California State U.–Stanislaus*	37	2.7	86%	41%	53%	19%	11%	21/1	810-1020[2]	N/A	74%	1%
56.	La Sierra University (CA)	36	2.4	76%	50%	59%	67%	4%	14/1	810-1040[3]	41%	47%	5%
56.	Woodbury University (CA)	36	2.5	77%	43%	45%	80%	0%	10/1	880-1110	N/A	57%	3%
58.	California State U.–Sacramento*	35	3.1	81%	41%	42%	20%	17%	28/1	830-1060[2]	N/A	71%	2%[7]
58.	Humboldt State University (CA)*	35	2.8	75%	48%	42%	31%	14%	23/1	870-1110[2]	39%	76%	7%
58.	San Francisco State University*	35	3.1	80%	46%	45%	25%	20%	22/1	880-1110	N/A	60%	2%
58.	Southern Utah University*	35	2.8	65%	47%	41%	43%	7%	20/1	20-26	42%	57%	3%
58.	Walla Walla University (WA)	35	2.7	79%	53%	44%	N/A	N/A	13/1	930-1190[9]	N/A	94%	15%[4]
63.	Boise State University (ID)*	34	3.1	70%	45%	38%	35%	11%	20/1	920-1150	38%	78%	8%
63.	Texas A&M International University*	34	2.6	72%	36%	44%	33%	14%	22/1	800-1010	53%	49%	10%
63.	Univ. of the Incarnate Word (TX)	34	2.7	74%	43%	40%	56%	1%	14/1	870-1060	43%	93%	6%
66.	Calif. State U.–San Bernardino*	33	2.7	88%	36%	44%	21%	20%	27/1	790-990[2]	N/A	55%	2%

Note: Key to footnotes, Page 106.

| Rank | School (State) (*Public) | Overall score | Peer assessment score (5.0=highest) | Average freshman retention rate | 2013 graduation rate | | % of classes under 20 ('13) | % of classes of 50 or more ('13) | Student/faculty ratio ('13) | SAT/ACT 25th-75th percentile ('13) | Freshmen in top 25% of HS class ('13) | Accept-ance rate ('13) | Average alumni giving rate |
					Predicted	Actual							
66.	Eastern Washington University*	33	2.7	75%	42%	45%	37%	12%	21/1	870-1090	N/A	78%	4%
68.	California State U.–Monterey Bay*	32	2.8	79%	46%	38%	17%	6%	28/1	870-1090	46%	45%	2%
68.	California State U.–Northridge*	32	3.1	76%	37%	46%	11%	18%	27/1	800-1040[3]	N/A	61%	1%[7]
68.	Holy Names University (CA)	32	2.6	72%	51%	35%	76%	0%	10/1	820-1000	N/A	57%	11%
68.	Houston Baptist University	32	2.6	65%	54%	43%	60%	2%	16/1	960-1170	53%	36%	4%
68.	University of Alaska–Anchorage*	32	3.0	71%	42%	28%	53%	4%	12/1	880-1080[2]	31%	80%	5%
68.	University of Texas–Tyler*	32	2.8	65%	49%	44%	31%	13%	17/1	960-1158	44%[5]	82%	1%[7]
68.	Weber State University (UT)*	32	2.9	72%	44%	43%	45%	7%	21/1	18-24[2]	N/A	100%	2%
75.	Alaska Pacific University	31	2.5	69%[8]	62%	39%	96%	0%	8/1	915-1085[3]	35%[4]	37%	N/A
75.	California State U.–Channel Islands[1]*	31	2.7	84%[8]	N/A	53%[6]	N/A	N/A	21/1[4]	850-1060[4]	N/A	64%[4]	1%[7]
75.	Prescott College (AZ)	31	2.6	67%	52%	37%	99%	1%	9/1	910-1260	28%[4]	73%	3%[4]
75.	University of Central Oklahoma*	31	3.1	66%	42%	36%	32%	2%	21/1	20-24	37%	80%	1%
79.	Southern Oregon University*	29	2.8	69%	48%	38%	46%	4%	19/1	890-1120	N/A	93%	2%
80.	California State Univ.–Bakersfield[1]*	28	2.7	72%[8]	36%	41%[6]	N/A	N/A	28/1[4]	790-1020[4]	N/A	66%[4]	1%[7]
80.	Concordia University[1] (OR)	28	2.6	70%[8]	49%	47%[6]	58%[4]	1%[4]	23/1[4]	880-1120[4]	44%[4]	54%[4]	1%[4]
80.	Hawaii Pacific University	28	2.7	69%	53%	41%	46%	1%	15/1	870-1110	53%	64%	2%
80.	West Texas A&M University*	28	2.7	64%	48%	43%	42%	8%	19/1	19-24	42%	74%	3%
84.	California State U.–Los Angeles*	27	2.9	82%	33%	36%	27%	8%	27/1	770-990[2]	3%	63%	2%
84.	California State Univ.–San Marcos*	27	2.6	80%[4]	45%	48%	15%	10%	25/1[4]	850-1050[9]	N/A	67%	1%[7]
84.	Lubbock Christian University (TX)	27	2.5	64%	43%	41%	67%	3%	12/1	19-24[3]	39%	95%	5%
84.	Northeastern State University (OK)*	27	2.7	65%	34%	30%	58%	4%	19/1	18-23	43%	73%	3%
84.	Southern Nazarene University (OK)	27	2.6	57%[8]	51%	46%	70%	2%	15/1	19-24[4]	49%[5]	N/A	4%[7]
84.	Stephen F. Austin State Univ. (TX)*	27	2.7	65%	45%	43%	30%	11%	19/1	890-1090	41%	57%	3%
84.	Western Oregon University*	27	2.7	70%[8]	46%	44%	55%	3%	16/1	840-1070	32%	91%	N/A

Gain the Experience to Move the World.

Move the World.

IONA COLLEGE

Located just 20 miles from Midtown Manhattan in suburban New Rochelle, N.Y., Iona College is an ideal place to discover and develop your place in the world. It's here that you will begin to test your character and challenge your limits inside and outside of the classroom. The experiences, knowledge, connections and confidence that you'll gain at Iona will prepare you to move the world and your career forward.

CONTACT US TO VISIT OR TO APPLY: IONA.EDU/USNEWS   ADMISSIONS@IONA.EDU   800.231.IONA

WEST ▶

SECOND TIER (SCHOOLS RANKED 91 THROUGH 120 ARE LISTED HERE ALPHABETICALLY)

School (State) (*Public)	Peer assessment score (5.0=highest)	Average freshman retention rate	2013 graduation rate Predicted	2013 graduation rate Actual	% of classes under 20 ('13)	% of classes of 50 or more ('13)	Student/faculty ratio ('13)	SAT/ACT 25th-75th percentile ('13)	Freshmen in top 25% of HS class ('13)	Acceptance rate ('13)	Average alumni giving rate
Adams State University[1] (CO)*	2.6	59%[8]	31%	25%[6]	N/A	N/A	16/1[4]	17-22[9]	N/A	53%	N/A
Angelo State University (TX)*	2.4	60%	41%	28%	31%	9%	18/1	18-23[3]	35%	80%	2%
California State U.–Dominguez Hills*	2.4	76%	30%	29%	18%	12%	27/1	760-940[2]	N/A	80%	2%
California State Univ.–East Bay*	2.5	76%	41%	38%	17%	19%	27/1	800-1010[9]	N/A	68%	1%[7]
Cameron University (OK)*	2.4	56%	36%	20%	45%	1%	20/1	16-21[2]	15%	100%	3%
Chaminade Univ. of Honolulu	2.6	70%	46%	38%	59%	0%	11/1	870-1060	6%	84%	5%
Colorado Christian University[1]	2.5	69%[8]	51%	42%[6]	N/A	N/A	13/1[4]	N/A[2]	N/A	98%[4]	N/A
Colorado State University–Pueblo*	2.7	63%	33%	33%	45%	7%	15/1	18-23[3]	34%	95%	2%
Concordia University Texas[1]	2.6	56%[8]	50%	34%[6]	63%[4]	0%[4]	10/1[4]	900-1130[4]	45%[4]	95%[4]	N/A
East Central University[1] (OK)*	2.4	59%[8]	39%	33%[6]	N/A	N/A	19/1[4]	18-23[9]	N/A	98%	N/A
Eastern New Mexico University[1]*	2.4	63%[8]	42%	26%[6]	N/A	N/A	19/1[4]	17-22[9]	N/A	63%	N/A
Eastern Oregon University[1]*	2.4	68%[8]	38%	32%[6]	64%[4]	3%[4]	23/1[4]	820-1050[4]	36%[4]	67%[4]	2%[4]
Grand Canyon University[1] (AZ)	2.0	42%[8]	N/A	30%[6]	34%[4]	19%[4]	16/1[4]	20[4]	N/A	41%[4]	N/A
Midwestern State University (TX)*	2.4	70%	44%	44%	37%	12%	17/1	900-1090[3]	36%	72%	5%
Montana State Univ.–Billings*	2.9	57%	42%	27%	51%	3%	18/1	18-23	31%	99%	6%
Northwestern Oklahoma State U.*	2.4	62%	40%	35%	47%	4%	17/1	18-22	28%	66%	3%
Prairie View A&M University (TX)*	2.2	67%	34%	34%[6]	22%	10%	18/1	750-940	14%	85%	N/A
Sierra Nevada College (NV)	2.1	68%	56%	45%	81%	0%	11/1	870-1070[3]	20%	87%	4%
Southeastern Oklahoma State U.*	2.4	56%	42%	31%	56%	4%	17/1	18-22	38%	80%	11%
Southwestern Assemblies of God University (TX)	2.4	66%	35%	38%[6]	N/A	N/A	18/1	19-24[4]	N/A	30%	1%
Southwestern Oklahoma State U.*	2.4	65%	42%	30%	45%	7%	18/1	18-24	43%	90%	1%
Sul Ross State University (TX)*	2.2	N/A	29%	30%	60%	4%	16/1	14-19[3]	16%	N/A	N/A
Tarleton State University (TX)*	2.4	67%	42%	43%	28%	9%	19/1	870-1060[3]	24%	77%	2%[7]
Texas A&M University–Texarkana*	2.5	44%[8]	N/A	N/A	N/A	N/A	N/A	19-24[3]	39%	36%	N/A
University of Houston–Clear Lake*	2.7	N/A	N/A	N/A	30%	5%	16/1	N/A	N/A	N/A	3%
University of Houston–Victoria*	2.5	N/A	N/A	N/A	30%	2%	19/1	810-1005[9]	23%	52%	1%[7]
University of Texas–Brownsville*	2.4	58%	22%	26%	38%	10%	19/1	810-1000	43%	87%	0.4%[7]
U. of Texas of the Permian Basin*	2.5	63%	43%	27%	41%	9%	20/1	910-1122	60%	82%	6%
University of Texas–Pan American*	2.6	75%	33%	39%	16%	24%	22/1	18-22	53%	69%	5%[4]
Wayland Baptist University (TX)	2.1	52%	30%	33%	86%	0.1%	10/1	17-23	28%	99%	1%

The Top Public Regional Universities ▶

NORTH
Rank School (State)

1. College of New Jersey
2. SUNY–Geneseo
3. Rowan University (NJ)
4. CUNY–Baruch College
4. SUNY–New Paltz
6. Ramapo College of New Jersey
6. Rutgers, The State U. of New Jersey–Camden
8. CUNY–Queens College
9. Richard Stockton Col. of N.J.
9. SUNY College–Oneonta
9. SUNY–Fredonia
12. CUNY–Hunter College
12. Montclair State University (NJ)
14. SUNY–Oswego
15. College at Brockport–SUNY
15. Towson University (MD)

SOUTH
Rank School (State)

1. The Citadel (SC)
2. James Madison University (VA)
3. Appalachian State University (NC)
4. College of Charleston (SC)
4. Univ. of Mary Washington (VA)
6. Univ. of North Carolina–Wilmington
7. Christopher Newport Univ. (VA)
8. Winthrop University (SC)
9. Murray State University (KY)
10. Georgia College & State Univ.
11. Longwood University (VA)
12. Western Kentucky University
13. Radford University (VA)
13. Tennessee Technological Univ.
15. University of Montevallo (AL)
15. Western Carolina University (NC)

MIDWEST
Rank School (State)

1. Truman State University (MO)
2. University of Northern Iowa
3. Grand Valley State University (MI)
4. Eastern Illinois University
4. Univ. of Wisconsin–La Crosse
6. Univ. of Wisconsin–Eau Claire
7. University of Michigan–Dearborn
8. Univ. of Illinois–Springfield
8. University of Minnesota–Duluth
10. Western Illinois University
11. Southern Illinois U.–Edwardsville
12. Univ. of Wisconsin–Whitewater
13. Ferris State University (MI)
13. Univ. of Nebraska–Kearney
13. Univ. of Wisconsin–Stevens Point

WEST
Rank School (State)

1. Cal. Poly. State U.–San Luis Obispo
2. Western Washington University
3. N.M. Inst. of Mining and Tech.
4. Calif. State Poly. Univ.–Pomona
4. Evergreen State College (WA)
6. California State U.–Long Beach
7. California State Univ.–Chico
8. San Jose State University (CA)
9. California State U.–Fullerton
10. Sonoma State University (CA)
11. California State Univ.–Fresno
12. Texas State University
13. Central Washington University
13. Univ. of Colo.–Colorado Springs
15. California State U.–Stanislaus

Footnotes:
1. School refused to fill out U.S. News statistical survey. Data that appear are from school in previous years or from another source such as the National Center for Education Statistics.
2. SAT and/or ACT not required by school for some or all applicants.
3. In reporting SAT/ACT scores, the school did not include all students for whom it had scores, or refused to tell U.S. News whether all students with scores had been included.
4. Data reported to U.S. News in previous years.
5. Data based on fewer than 51 percent of enrolled freshmen.
6. Some or all data reported to the NCAA and/or the National Center for Education Statistics.

7. Data reported to the Council for Aid to Education.
8. Average graduation or freshman retention rates, normally based on four years of data, are given here for less than four years because school didn't report rates for the most recent year or years to U.S. News.
9. SAT and/or ACT may not be required by school for some or all applicants, and in reporting SAT/ACT scores, the school did not include all students for whom it had scores, or refused to tell U.S. News whether all students with scores had been included.

N/A means not available.

SCOOT SUCHMAN – LOYOLA UNIVERSITY MARYLAND

Loyola University Maryland,
tied at No. 3 in the North

Best Regional Colleges

What Is a Regional College?

According to the Carnegie Classification of Institutions of Higher Education, these schools focus almost entirely on the undergraduate experience and offer a broad range of programs in the liberal arts (which account for fewer than half of all bachelor's degrees granted) and in fields such as business, nursing and education. They grant few graduate degrees. Because most of the 364 colleges in the category draw heavily from nearby states, they are ranked by region.

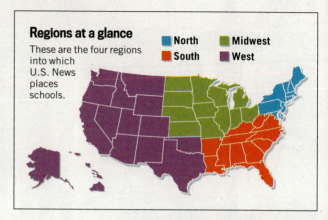

Regions at a glance
These are the four regions into which U.S. News places schools.

- North
- South
- Midwest
- West

NORTH ▶

Rank	School (State) (*Public)	Overall score	Peer assessment score (5.0=highest)	Average freshman retention rate	2013 graduation rate Predicted	2013 graduation rate Actual	% of classes under 20 ('13)	% of classes of 50 or more ('13)	Student/ faculty ratio ('13)	SAT/ACT 25th-75th percentile ('13)	Freshmen in top 25% of HS class ('13)	Accept- ance rate ('13)	Average alumni giving rate
1.	U. S. Coast Guard Acad. (CT)*	100	4.1	91%	83%	91%	71%	0.3%	7/1	1190-1360[3]	80%	16%	31%
2.	Cooper Union (NY)	96	4.1	94%	83%	82%	64%	2%	7/1	1220-1490	95%[5]	8%	25%
3.	U.S. Merchant Marine Acad. (NY)*	76	3.7	86%[8]	73%	74%	70%	3%	13/1	1183-1351	57%	18%	N/A
4.	Elizabethtown College (PA)	71	3.4	85%	65%	77%	65%	1%	12/1	1000-1230	65%	70%	23%
5.	Messiah College (PA)	68	3.5	86%	67%	76%	46%	3%	13/1	1030-1260	68%	66%	15%
6.	Lebanon Valley College (PA)	63	3.2	85%	64%	73%	57%	1%	12/1	1000-1220[2]	74%	67%	18%
7.	Massachusetts Maritime Academy*	60	3.4	88%	56%	67%	50%	0%	15/1	980-1170	N/A	59%	9%
8.	Maine Maritime Academy*	59	3.3	80%[8]	49%	65%	50%	1%	11/1	920-1130	32%	65%	15%
9.	Elmira College (NY)	54	3.1	73%	63%	62%	63%	0%	10/1	940-1160	58%	80%	21%
9.	Merrimack College (MA)	54	3.4	82%	61%	60%	42%	0%	13/1	920-1130[2]	34%	79%	13%
11.	Seton Hill University (PA)	52	3.2	76%[8]	54%	62%	59%	0%	14/1	900-1150[2]	47%	65%	18%
12.	Bard College at Simon's Rock (MA)	50	3.3	75%	76%	28%	99%	0%	6/1	1290-1460[2]	67%[5]	92%	14%
12.	Wentworth Inst. of Technology (MA)	50	3.3	80%	54%	61%	36%	1%	17/1	1010-1210	40%	57%	5%
14.	Champlain College (VT)	48	3.0	78%	54%	57%	61%	0%	14/1	990-1240[3]	39%[5]	71%	6%
14.	Geneva College (PA)	48	2.8	77%	53%	67%	63%	4%	14/1	950-1190	45%	69%	11%
16.	Cedar Crest College (PA)	46	2.7	71%	54%	60%	79%	2%	9/1	840-1050	43%	59%	11%
17.	Wilson College (PA)	45	2.4	61%	49%	56%	88%	0%	8/1	860-1120[2]	53%	53%	24%
18.	University of Maine–Farmington*	44	2.8	73%	43%	55%	62%	1%	13/1	880-1150[2]	43%	84%	4%
19.	Delaware Valley College (PA)	43	2.9	72%	55%	57%	57%	3%	13/1	880-1123	41%	68%	8%
20.	St. Francis College (NY)	42	2.9	79%	40%	52%	47%	1%	18/1	850-1030	N/A	64%	10%
20.	SUNY Maritime College*	42	3.0	79%	53%	50%	37%	3%	15/1	930-1170	30%[5]	64%	5%
22.	SUNY College of Technology–Alfred*	41	2.8	82%[8]	34%	52%	56%	5%	18/1	840-1070[2]	N/A	55%	6%[4]
22.	Vaughn Col. of Aeron. and Tech. (NY)	41	2.6	80%	38%	56%	64%	0%	15/1	885-1093	N/A	77%	2%
24.	Cazenovia College (NY)	40	2.6	67%	48%	59%	70%	0%	12/1	860-1070[2]	40%	78%	14%
24.	College of Our Lady of the Elms (MA)	40	2.3	81%	44%	68%	67%	1%	13/1	820-1040[3]	35%[4]	75%	17%
26.	Dean College (MA)	36	2.7	69%[8]	42%	62%	63%	0%	16/1	750-950	11%[5]	68%	N/A
27.	Lasell College (MA)	35	2.6	70%	47%	53%	64%	0%	14/1	880-1070	N/A	76%	12%
28.	Farmingdale State College–SUNY*	33	2.6	82%	38%	43%	24%	1%	19/1	950-1110	36%[5]	51%	2%
28.	Pennsylvania College of Technology*	33	2.9	67%	44%	55%	62%	0%	17/1	N/A[2]	N/A	90%	N/A
28.	SUNY College of A&T–Cobleskill*	33	2.7	75%	32%	44%	33%	6%	18/1	760-1000[2]	22%	73%	5%
31.	Concordia College[1] (NY)	32	2.7	69%[8]	47%	48%[6]	60%[4]	0%[4]	13/1[4]	18-24[4]	25%[4]	72%[4]	8%[4]
31.	Unity College (ME)	32	2.5	75%	50%	51%	66%	0%	11/1	910-1110[2]	29%	89%	3%
33.	La Roche College (PA)	30	2.4	71%	44%	46%	70%	0%	13/1	800-1040	26%[5]	56%	4%
33.	SUNY College of Technology–Delhi*	30	2.7	70%	30%	35%	48%	4%	18/1	808-983[2]	14%[5]	59%	4%
33.	Thiel College (PA)	30	2.6	63%	45%	34%	62%	2%	14/1	870-1060[3]	34%	66%	18%
36.	Vermont Technical College*	29	2.3	70%	47%	40%[6]	74%	0.2%	10/1	810-1040[9]	27%[5]	67%	N/A

NORTH ▶

Rank	School (State) (*Public)	Overall score	Peer assessment score (5.0=highest)	Average freshman retention rate	2013 graduation rate		% of classes under 20 ('13)	% of classes of 50 or more ('13)	Student/ faculty ratio ('13)	SAT/ACT 25th-75th percentile ('13)	Freshmen in top 25% of HS class ('13)	Accept- ance rate ('13)	Average alumni giving rate
					Predicted	Actual							
37.	University of Maine–Fort Kent*	27	2.4	62%	37%	44%	71%	1%	14/1	818-1000[2]	10%	63%	7%
38.	Keystone College (PA)	26	2.4	67%	35%	39%	80%	0%	11/1	800-1000	N/A	72%	7%[4]
38.	Mount Aloysius College (PA)	26	2.8	63%[8]	36%	35%[8]	66%	0%	13/1	830-1030[3]	N/A	71%	N/A
40.	Mount Ida College (MA)	25	2.3	61%	41%	39%	79%	0%	14/1	790-980	N/A	68%	2%
40.	Nichols College (MA)	25	2.5	63%	45%	46%	34%	0%	17/1	840-1030[2]	16%[5]	82%	10%
40.	Paul Smith's College[1] (NY)	25	2.7	76%[8]	49%	42%[6]	N/A	N/A	15/1[4]	880-1060[9]	N/A	75%	N/A
43.	Morrisville State College (NY)*	24	2.5	60%	N/A	29%	47%	3%	16/1	840-1030[2]	16%	59%	4%
44.	Thomas College (ME)	22	2.3	65%[8]	37%	45%	53%	0%	22/1	790-1010	34%	73%	5%
44.	Valley Forge Christian College[1] (PA)	22	2.2	75%[8]	46%	52%[6]	N/A	N/A	17/1[4]	890-1040[9]	N/A	66%	N/A
46.	Univ. of Maine–Presque Isle*	21	2.4	63%	36%	30%	71%	0%	14/1	N/A[2]	25%[5]	78%	2%
46.	Washington Adventist Univ. (MD)	21	2.2	70%	41%	34%	78%	0%	10/1	720-960	N/A	53%	3%

School (State) (*Public)	Peer assessment score (5.0=highest)	Average freshman retention rate	2013 graduation rate		% of classes under 20 ('13)	% of classes of 50 or more ('13)	Student/ faculty ratio ('13)	SAT/ACT 25th-75th percentile ('13)	Freshmen in top 25% of HS class ('13)	Accept- ance rate ('13)	Average alumni giving rate
			Predicted	Actual							
SECOND TIER (SCHOOLS RANKED 48 THROUGH 61 ARE LISTED HERE ALPHABETICALLY)											
Bay State College (MA)	2.1	N/A	N/A	17%[6]	N/A	N/A	18/1	N/A[2]	N/A	59%	N/A
Becker College (MA)	2.5	64%[8]	38%	24%	59%	1%	17/1	890-1120	26%[5]	63%	N/A
CUNY–Medgar Evers College*	2.2	53%[8]	39%	13%	25%	0.1%	18/1	690-860[9]	N/A	100%	N/A
CUNY–New York City Col. of Tech.*	2.7	76%	33%	25%	29%	0%	19/1	N/A[2]	N/A	71%	1%[4]
CUNY–York College*	2.4	76%	24%	24%	20%	43%	21/1	871[4]	N/A	65%	N/A
Daniel Webster College[1] (NH)	2.4	61%[8]	52%	42%[6]	N/A	N/A	13/1[4]	830-1100[3]	N/A	60%	N/A
Fisher College (MA)	2.4	63%	26%	35%	26%[4]	0%[4]	16/1	730-920[2]	N/A	65%	N/A
Five Towns College (NY)	2.2	N/A	N/A	38%[6]	51%	1%	15/1	770-1000	36%[5]	55%	N/A
Lyndon State College[1] (VT)*	2.5	65%[8]	37%	34%[6]	N/A	N/A	14/1[4]	810-1050[9]	N/A	99%	N/A
Post University (CT)	2.4	47%	37%	35%	59%	0%	19/1	760-960	20%[5]	64%	N/A
Southern Vermont College	2.4	63%[8]	39%	31%[6]	N/A	N/A	N/A	N/A[2]	N/A	N/A	N/A
SUNY College of Technology–Canton*	2.5	73%[8]	35%	29%	44%	3%	19/1	820-1020[2]	15%	78%	3%
University of Maine–Augusta*	2.6	53%	11%	12%	72%	0.3%	17/1	760-1010[9]	9%	95%	0.2%
Wesley College (DE)	2.7	46%	45%	22%	78%[4]	0%[4]	16/1	750-940[3]	23%	63%[4]	8%[4]

SOUTH ▶

Rank	School (State) (*Public)	Overall score	Peer assessment score (5.0=highest)	Average freshman retention rate	2013 graduation rate		% of classes under 20 ('13)	% of classes of 50 or more ('13)	Student/ faculty ratio ('13)	SAT/ACT 25th-75th percentile ('13)	Freshmen in top 25% of HS class ('13)	Accept- ance rate ('13)	Average alumni giving rate
					Predicted	Actual							
1.	Asbury University (KY)	100	3.3	80%	63%	64%	62%	0%	13/1	21-27	54%	66%	18%
1.	High Point University (NC)	100	3.5	77%	50%	62%	57%	1%	14/1	980-1170	51%[5]	84%	7%
1.	John Brown University (AR)	100	3.2	80%	62%	65%	50%	0%	15/1	23-29	65%	70%	18%
4.	University of the Ozarks (AR)	94	3.3	63%[8]	56%	48%	84%	0%	10/1	20-26	44%	61%	15%
5.	Florida Southern College	92	3.2	76%	55%	58%	58%	0%	13/1	1010-1180	56%[4]	50%	14%
6.	Covenant College (GA)	91	3.0	83%	59%	58%	54%	1%	14/1	1060-1280	55%[5]	57%	15%
6.	Meredith College (NC)	91	3.1	76%[8]	57%	62%	N/A	N/A	12/1	930-1140[2]	52%	62%	19%
8.	Flagler College (FL)	88	3.3	72%	54%	63%	42%	0%	17/1	930-1130[3]	31%	50%	20%
9.	Milligan College (TN)	86	2.9	82%	61%	52%	70%[4]	1%[4]	12/1	22-26	65%[4]	68%	23%
9.	Tuskegee University (AL)	86	3.1	76%	48%	42%	56%	9%	12/1	18-23[3]	60%	41%	24%
11.	Wheeling Jesuit University (WV)	85	3.0	74%	58%	54%	61%	0%	12/1	20-24	43%	67%	15%
12.	West Virginia Wesleyan College	83	3.0	67%	56%	60%	59%	0.3%	13/1	20-25	56%	77%	17%
13.	LaGrange College (GA)	82	3.0	62%	50%	38%	75%	2%	11/1	910-1090	36%	58%	13%
14.	Aquinas College (TN)	80	2.8	75%	44%	67%	85%	8%	9/1	23-27	43%[5]	52%	N/A
15.	Carson-Newman University (TN)	79	3.1	65%	42%	50%	63%	0%	12/1	20-26[3]	47%[4]	67%	9%
16.	Catawba College (NC)	77	2.9	69%	54%	52%	68%	0%	14/1	850-1090[2]	22%	41%	17%
16.	Coker College (SC)	77	2.8	74%[8]	34%	43%	72%	0%	12/1	870-1050	21%	53%	12%
18.	Univ. of South Carolina–Aiken*	75	3.3	69%	43%	42%	52%	1%	15/1	860-1070	36%	70%	7%
19.	University of Charleston (WV)	74	3.2	67%	56%	46%	59%	2%	14/1	19-24	70%[4]	69%	7%
20.	Lenoir-Rhyne University (NC)	73	3.0	65%	54%	49%	46%	1%	13/1	880-1080[3]	44%	68%	20%
21.	Anderson University (SC)	72	3.2	73%	48%	41%	47%	3%	16/1	960-1180	64%	65%	8%
22.	Bryan College (TN)	71	2.8	71%	54%	62%	68%	1%	15/1	20-25	51%[4]	38%	11%

SOUTH ▶

Rank	School (State) (*Public)	Overall score	Peer assessment score (5.0=highest)	Average freshman retention rate	2013 graduation rate Predicted	2013 graduation rate Actual	% of classes under 20 ('13)	% of classes of 50 or more ('13)	Student/faculty ratio ('13)	SAT/ACT 25th-75th percentile ('13)	Freshmen in top 25% of HS class ('13)	Acceptance rate ('13)	Average alumni giving rate
23.	Blue Mountain College (MS)	70	2.7	77%	46%	51%	71%	0%	13/1	18-23	38%	51%	7%
23.	Huntingdon College (AL)	70	2.8	59%	52%	43%	63%	0%	14/1	19-24	40%	63%	24%
25.	Averett University (VA)	69	2.9	59%	35%	33%	76%	0%	12/1	840-1030	30%	88%	5%
25.	Barton College (NC)	69	2.7	68%	42%	48%	65%	0%	11/1	840-1020	38%	42%	9%
25.	North Greenville University (SC)	69	2.8	71%	43%	55%	71%	0%	14/1	920-1340	39%	58%	5%
25.	University of Mobile (AL)	69	3.1	74%	49%	49%	59%	1%	12/1	20-25	50%	71%	1%
29.	Alice Lloyd College (KY)	67	3.0	58%	43%	32%	51%	2%	17/1	18-23	51%	9%	42%
29.	Elizabeth City State Univ. (NC)*	67	2.5	75%	28%	42%	66%	1%	16/1	780-945[3]	5%	52%	10%
31.	Kentucky Wesleyan College	66	2.7	60%	45%	38%	84%	0.4%	11/1	19-25	39%	67%	15%
32.	U. of South Carolina–Upstate*	64	3.1	67%	41%	40%	53%	1%	16/1	870-1038[3]	40%	57%	2%
33.	Newberry College (SC)	63	2.7	66%	46%	44%	64%	0%	12/1	830-1060	16%	59%	14%
34.	Southern Adventist University[1] (TN)	62	2.8	74%[8]	52%	44%	57%[4]	7%[4]	14/1[4]	20-25[3]	N/A	45%[4]	7%[7]
35.	Bethune-Cookman University (FL)	61	2.8	66%	26%	55%	44%	2%	18/1	15-18	12%	67%	4%
35.	Toccoa Falls College (GA)	61	2.6	69%	46%	46%	61%	1%	14/1	880-1130[2]	44%	54%	3%
37.	Alderson Broaddus University (WV)	60	2.6	64%	48%	45%	70%	5%	15/1	19-24	36%	43%	14%
37.	Belmont Abbey College (NC)	60	2.9	65%	49%	38%	63%	0%	17/1	868-1070[2]	26%	68%	9%
37.	Mars Hill University (NC)	60	2.9	57%	41%	38%	72%	0%	12/1	830-1040	26%	64%	10%
40.	Keiser University (FL)	59	2.2	76%	N/A	68%	81%	0%	12/1	N/A[2]	N/A	N/A	N/A
41.	Southeastern University (FL)	58	2.8	66%	44%	39%	64%	5%	20/1	850-1080[3]	N/A	59%	3%
41.	Tennessee Wesleyan College	58	2.6	63%	48%	44%	71%	4%	12/1	19-24	20%[5]	71%	12%
43.	Brescia University (KY)	57	2.8	58%	47%	30%	88%	0%	13/1	19-24	N/A	45%	14%
43.	Philander Smith College (AR)	57	2.2	63%	27%	44%	83%	0%	10/1	16-22	44%	42%	13%
43.	Univ. of Arkansas–Pine Bluff*	57	2.8	56%	23%	26%	55%	4%	15/1	15-20	27%	28%	11%
46.	Oakwood University[1] (AL)	56	2.9	71%[8]	40%	38%[6]	N/A	N/A	N/A	17-22[4]	N/A	34%[4]	N/A
47.	Emmanuel College (GA)	55	2.4	62%	33%	46%	68%	0%	13/1	830-1030	N/A	48%	8%
47.	Faulkner University[1] (AL)	55	2.7	53%[8]	36%	34%[6]	72%[4]	2%[4]	15/1[4]	18-23[4]	22%[4]	60%[4]	3%[4]
47.	Ferrum College (VA)	55	3.0	54%	38%	32%	56%	0%	16/1	780-990	15%[5]	74%	9%
50.	Concord University (WV)*	53	2.8	63%	37%	35%	57%	2%	17/1	18-24[3]	44%	45%	4%
50.	Davis and Elkins College[1] (WV)	53	2.7	55%[8]	44%	51%[6]	N/A	N/A	14/1[4]	17-23[9]	N/A	57%	N/A
52.	Welch College (TN)	52	2.3	65%	42%	37%	84%	3%	10/1	18-25	42%	52%	14%
52.	West Liberty University (WV)*	52	2.6	70%	36%	41%	67%	0.4%	14/1	18-24[3]	37%	71%	N/A
54.	Bluefield College (VA)	51	2.5	53%	41%	45%	77%	0%	14/1	800-1010	27%	57%	8%
54.	Lees-McRae College (NC)	51	2.7	60%	47%	38%	72%	0%	15/1	840-1080[2]	29%	66%	9%
56.	Kentucky Christian University	50	2.5	61%	39%	39%	67%	1%	12/1	18-23	32%	51%	3%
56.	Ohio Valley University (WV)	50	2.2	59%	46%	40%	86%	0%	10/1	19-23	29%	38%	5%
56.	University of Mount Olive (NC)	50	2.4	64%	34%	37%	70%[4]	0%[4]	14/1	833-1060[9]	N/A	48%	4%[7]
59.	Univ. of South Carolina–Beaufort*	49	2.9	53%	40%	27%	59%	1%	17/1	830-1010	24%	68%	4%
59.	Williams Baptist College (AR)	49	2.6	N/A	43%	39%	58%	0%	13/1	20-25[3]	N/A	68%	4%
61.	Midway College[1] (KY)	48	2.4	72%[8]	37%	48%[6]	N/A	N/A	14/1[4]	19-25[9]	N/A	54%	N/A
62.	Clayton State University (GA)*	47	2.8	67%	35%	29%	44%	4%	18/1	860-1030	40%[4]	46%	4%
62.	Methodist University[1] (NC)	47	2.9	55%[8]	47%	40%[6]	N/A	N/A	12/1[4]	860-1060[4]	N/A	61%[4]	N/A
64.	Indian River State College (FL)*	45	2.9	60%[8]	N/A	N/A	39%	2%	23/1	N/A[2]	N/A	100%	1%[7]
64.	Lander University[1] (SC)*	45	2.6	61%[8]	42%	40%[6]	N/A	N/A	16/1[4]	833-1050[4]	N/A	42%[4]	N/A
64.	Limestone College (SC)	45	2.4	59%	44%	37%	63%	0%	13/1	930-1090[3]	19%	54%	5%
64.	Reinhardt University (GA)	45	2.6	64%[8]	46%	28%	79%	0%	14/1	860-1120[3]	30%	60%	5%
68.	Virginia Union University	43	2.7	54%[8]	27%	35%	48%	1%	14/1	670-840	18%	83%	9%
69.	Central Baptist College (AR)	42	2.2	59%	34%	38%	85%	0%	12/1	19-23[3]	38%	55%	9%
70.	Everglades University[1] (FL)	41	2.2	66%[8]	N/A	62%[6]	N/A	N/A	8/1[4]	N/A[2]	N/A	91%[4]	N/A
71.	Fort Valley State University (GA)*	40	2.4	61%	36%	28%	47%	5%	19/1	15-18	23%[5]	31%	16%
71.	Glenville State College (WV)*	40	2.4	64%	30%	30%	65%	0.4%	16/1	16-21	20%	67%	6%
71.	North Carolina Wesleyan College	40	2.5	55%	36%	33%	74%	0%	13/1	760-970[2]	14%	47%	3%
74.	Louisiana College[1]	38	2.5	64%[8]	51%	39%[6]	N/A	N/A	16/1[4]	18-23[9]	N/A	74%	N/A
74.	Point University (GA)	38	2.2	59%	40%	48%	N/A	N/A	19/1	18-22	34%[5]	54%	6%[4]

Note: Key to footnotes, Page 114.

SOUTH ▶

School (State) (*Public)	Peer assessment score (5.0=highest)	Average freshman retention rate	2013 graduation rate Predicted	2013 graduation rate Actual	% of classes under 20 ('13)	% of classes of 50 or more ('13)	Student/ faculty ratio ('13)	SAT/ACT 25th-75th percentile ('13)	Freshmen in top 25% of HS class ('13)	Accept-ance rate ('13)	Average alumni giving rate
Abraham Baldwin Agricultural College (GA)*	2.7	59%[8]	N/A	N/A	N/A	N/A	22/1	810-990[3]	N/A	71%	N/A
Bluefield State College (WV)*	2.4	57%	28%	22%	75%	0.3%	15/1	16-21	N/A	41%	4%
Brewton-Parker College[1] (GA)	2.3	42%[8]	31%	21%[6]	N/A	N/A	15/1[4]	810-990[9]	N/A	51%	N/A
Chipola College[1] (FL)*	2.6	N/A	N/A	N/A	N/A	N/A	19/1[4]	N/A[2]	N/A	N/A	N/A
Chowan University (NC)	2.3	44%	33%	24%	34%	2%	17/1	700-870	11%	62%	10%
Edward Waters College[1] (FL)	1.9	54%[8]	30%	19%[6]	N/A	N/A	17/1[4]	15-18[9]	N/A	27%	N/A
Florida College	2.6	N/A	55%	11%[6]	67%	6%	11/1	20-26[3]	N/A	74%	65%
Georgia Gwinnett College*	2.7	67%[8]	N/A	27%	24%	0%	19/1	820-1055[2]	15%	90%	9%
Gordon State College[1] (GA)*	2.5	N/A	N/A	N/A	N/A	N/A	21/1[4]	750-950[9]	N/A	45%	N/A
Greensboro College[1] (NC)	2.6	47%[8]	45%	40%[6]	N/A	N/A	11/1[4]	790-1020[9]	N/A	78%	N/A
LeMoyne-Owen College (TN)	2.6	54%[8]	25%	15%[6]	95%	0%	13/1	N/A	N/A	27%	N/A
Livingstone College (NC)	2.0	52%	17%	20%	46%	1%	15/1	11-16[3]	6%	72%	36%
Mid-Continent University[1] (KY)	1.6	65%[8]	31%	23%[6]	88%[4]	0%[4]	21/1[4]	N/A[2]	26%[4]	87%[4]	N/A
Middle Georgia State College[1]*	2.7	68%[8]	15%	20%[6]	N/A	N/A	19/1[4]	810-1020[4]	N/A	47%[4]	N/A
Paine College (GA)	2.3	61%	26%	21%	65%	0%	13/1	14-18	15%[5]	44%	13%
Shaw University[1] (NC)	2.2	52%[8]	20%	27%[8]	66%[4]	1%[4]	15/1[4]	13-16[4]	5%[4]	54%[4]	N/A
St. Augustine's University (NC)	2.1	52%	25%	38%	N/A	N/A	13/1	665-858[3]	N/A	67%	5%
Thomas University (GA)	2.2	47%[8]	29%	27%	N/A	N/A	10/1	810-1060[2]	N/A	69%	N/A
Truett McConnell College (GA)	2.5	65%	40%	16%	62%	4%	16/1	840-1050	32%	81%	9%
University of Arkansas–Fort Smith[1]*	2.8	63%[8]	35%	23%[6]	N/A	N/A	18/1[4]	19-25[9]	N/A	57%	N/A
Victory University[1] (TN)	1.8	64%[8]	31%	13%[6]	N/A	N/A	24/1[4]	N/A[2]	N/A	95%[4]	N/A
Voorhees College[1] (SC)	2.1	46%[8]	26%	30%[6]	N/A	N/A	13/1[4]	N/A[2]	N/A	51%	N/A
Webber International University (FL)	2.4	48%	36%	32%	42%	0%	24/1	17-21	22%	64%	0.3%[4]

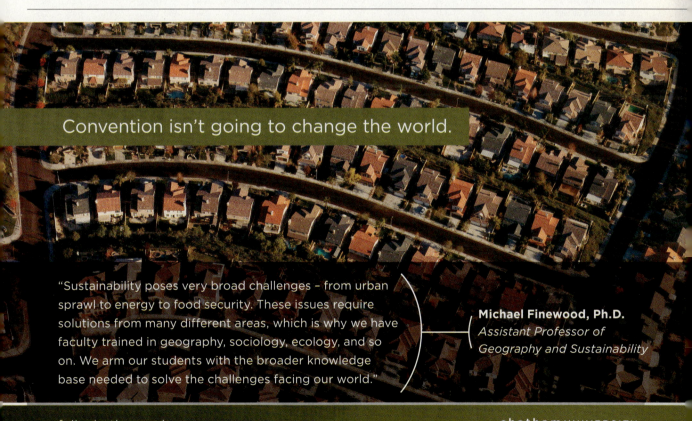

Convention isn't going to change the world.

"Sustainability poses very broad challenges – from urban sprawl to energy to food security. These issues require solutions from many different areas, which is why we have faculty trained in geography, sociology, ecology, and so on. We arm our students with the broader knowledge base needed to solve the challenges facing our world."

Michael Finewood, Ph.D.
Assistant Professor of Geography and Sustainability

falk.chatham.edu

chatham UNIVERSITY
FALK SCHOOL OF SUSTAINABILITY

Eden Hall Campus | Bachelor of Sustainability | Master of Sustainability | Master of Arts in Food Studies

MIDWEST ▶

Rank	School (State) (*Public)	Overall score	Peer assessment score (5.0=highest)	Average freshman retention rate	2013 graduation rate		% of classes under 20 ('13)	% of classes of 50 or more ('13)	Student/faculty ratio ('13)	SAT/ACT 25th-75th percentile ('13)	Freshmen in top 25% of HS class ('13)	Accept-ance rate ('13)	Average alumni giving rate
					Predicted	Actual							
1.	Taylor University (IN)	100	3.8	88%	67%	74%	63%	5%	13/1	24-31	67%[5]	88%	22%
2.	Ohio Northern University	93	3.5	86%	67%	69%	64%	1%	12/1	23-29	69%	68%	15%
3.	Augustana College (SD)	87	3.5	83%	62%	66%	53%	1%	12/1	23-28	63%	68%	18%
4.	College of the Ozarks (MO)	83	3.6	87%	51%	65%	50%	2%	15/1	20-25[3]	50%	12%	19%
5.	Dordt College (IA)	80	3.4	79%	59%	62%	59%	5%	12/1	21-28	44%	76%	26%
6.	Cedarville University (OH)	79	3.2	85%	67%	73%	65%	6%	13/1	24-29	61%	74%	11%
6.	Franklin College[1] (IN)	79	3.2	77%[8]	55%	59%[6]	79%[4]	0%[4]	12/1[4]	19-24[4]	46%[4]	65%[4]	27%[4]
6.	Marietta College (OH)	79	3.2	78%[8]	58%	55%	78%	0%	11/1	21-27[3]	59%	64%	20%
6.	Northwestern College (IA)	79	3.3	78%	60%	63%	68%	0.3%	11/1	22-27	49%	76%	22%
10.	Univ. of Northwestern–St. Paul (MN)	75	3.0	78%[8]	58%	66%[6]	61%[4]	3%[4]	14/1[4]	22-27[4]	50%	59%[4]	17%[4]
11.	Buena Vista University (IA)	74	3.1	73%	53%	53%	75%	1%	9/1	20-25	42%	70%	7%
11.	Loras College (IA)	74	3.2	79%	55%	61%	55%	1%	12/1	21-26	39%[5]	69%	20%
11.	University of Mount Union (OH)	74	3.1	74%	52%	63%	53%	0.4%	13/1	20-25[3]	34%	71%	21%
14.	Huntington University (IN)	73	3.1	77%	59%	62%	71%	1%	13/1	880-1130	53%	97%	18%
14.	Millikin University (IL)	73	3.4	77%	55%	60%	60%	1%	11/1	21-26	41%	55%	13%
16.	St. Mary-of-the-Woods College (IN)	72	3.0	73%	43%	60%	92%	0%	8/1	780-1020	41%	98%	24%
17.	Clarke University (IA)	71	2.8	78%	51%	70%	75%	2%	10/1	20-25[3]	46%	78%	19%
18.	Hastings College (NE)	70	3.0	71%	56%	61%	67%	0%	13/1	21-26	40%	74%	22%
19.	Bethel College (IN)	68	3.0	80%	50%	62%	77%	1%	13/1	900-1130	51%	72%	8%
20.	Benedictine College (KS)	67	3.3	79%	48%	59%	55%	2%	14/1	22-28[3]	46%	97%	24%
21.	Mount Mercy University (IA)	66	2.7	79%	51%	73%	60%	1%	14/1	20-24	41%	68%	14%
22.	Adrian College (MI)	64	3.2	66%	55%	54%	72%	1%	13/1	19-24	41%[4]	56%	16%
23.	Morningside College (IA)	63	3.0	72%	53%	58%	53%	0.4%	13/1	20-25	46%	53%	23%
23.	Stephens College (MO)	63	2.8	68%	53%	57%	79%	0%	10/1	19-26	39%[5]	68%	12%
25.	Bethel College (KS)	62	3.0	73%	55%	53%	68%	2%	10/1	19-26	21%	64%	23%
25.	Marian University (IN)	62	3.0	71%	47%	53%	63%	5%	12/1	19-25	43%	58%	15%
27.	Manchester University (IN)	60	3.2	69%	55%	48%	54%	1%	15/1	890-1130	48%	71%	18%
28.	Bluffton University (OH)	59	2.8	65%	54%	60%	64%	0.4%	14/1	19-25	36%	53%	16%
28.	St. Joseph's College (IN)	59	3.0	68%	50%	45%	79%	2%	14/1	890-1080	35%	64%	20%
28.	Trinity Christian College (IL)	59	2.8	78%	53%	58%	56%	0.4%	11/1	20-25	27%	79%	13%
31.	Eureka College (IL)	58	2.6	65%	55%	61%	73%	0%	12/1	19-25	39%	66%	20%
32.	Trine University (IN)	55	2.9	73%	52%	51%	61%	0%	15/1	980-1190[3]	57%	75%	10%
33.	Greenville College (IL)	53	2.7	72%[8]	50%	50%	66%	4%	15/1	18-25	40%	61%	17%
34.	Culver-Stockton College (MO)	52	3.0	68%	48%	45%	64%	0%	13/1	18-23	25%	59%	18%
35.	Blackburn College (IL)	51	2.6	67%	47%	45%	80%	0%	11/1	19-26	41%	68%	18%
36.	Judson University (IL)	50	2.7	71%	55%	50%	63%	2%	10/1	19-25[3]	29%	93%	7%
37.	University of Jamestown (ND)	49	2.8	67%	49%	52%	62%	2%	12/1	21-24[3]	36%	57%	22%
38.	Briar Cliff University (IA)	48	2.6	65%	44%	45%	66%	0.4%	12/1	19-25	32%	54%	16%
38.	University of Sioux Falls (SD)	48	2.8	69%	50%	47%	60%	1%	14/1	20-26	46%	97%	5%
40.	Central Methodist University (MO)	45	2.7	65%	42%	43%	66%	1%	13/1	19-24[3]	43%	65%	10%
40.	Defiance College (OH)	45	2.6	60%	48%	46%	79%	0%	11/1	18-23	25%	72%	10%
40.	Martin Luther College[1] (MN)	45	2.2	84%[8]	61%	72%[6]	N/A	N/A	13/1[4]	22-27[9]	N/A	96%	N/A
40.	University of Minnesota–Crookston*	45	2.6	71%	43%	44%	65%	1%	18/1	19-24	28%	69%	7%
44.	Valley City State University (ND)*	44	2.5	60%	43%	46%	71%	0.3%	11/1	18-23	21%	83%	12%
45.	Mount Marty College (SD)	43	2.3	68%	45%	52%	80%	0%	10/1	19-24[4]	44%	72%	5%
46.	Grace College and Seminary (IN)	42	2.5	80%	57%	60%	51%	5%	25/1	910-1150[3]	47%	78%	15%
47.	Northern State University (SD)*	40	2.5	69%	45%	53%	64%	3%	19/1	19-25	26%	93%	13%
47.	Olivet College (MI)	40	2.7	67%	37%	43%	63%	1%	18/1	17-22	N/A	51%	11%
49.	Evangel University (MO)	39	2.5	73%[8]	51%	49%[6]	65%[4]	3%[4]	16/1	19-26[3]	40%[4]	67%[4]	N/A
49.	Tabor College (KS)	39	2.4	63%	50%	54%	64%	2%	15/1	19-25	20%	74%	13%
49.	Union College (NE)	39	2.2	70%	51%	35%	72%	3%	11/1	19-26	28%[5]	52%	24%
52.	MacMurray College (IL)	37	2.4	60%	38%	38%	75%	0%	12/1	19-22	33%	75%	20%
52.	McPherson College (KS)	37	2.2	60%	51%	49%	70%	0%	14/1	19-24[3]	N/A	63%	N/A
54.	Crown College[1] (MN)	36	2.4	71%[8]	45%	52%[6]	N/A	N/A	N/A	863-1098[4]	N/A	56%[4]	N/A
54.	Dakota Wesleyan University (SD)	36	2.6	67%[8]	45%	38%	70%	0%	11/1	19-27	26%	73%[4]	N/A
54.	Grand View University[1] (IA)	36	2.6	69%[8]	46%	45%[8]	65%[4]	0.2%[4]	14/1[4]	810-1060[4]	40%[4]	92%[4]	5%[4]
54.	Kansas Wesleyan University	36	2.4	57%	46%	43%	72%	1%	12/1	20-24	43%	54%	12%
58.	Wilmington College (OH)	34	2.8	N/A	46%	46%[6]	N/A	N/A	15/1	N/A[2]	N/A	N/A	9%[7]
59.	Notre Dame College of Ohio[1]	32	2.7	66%[8]	40%	42%[8]	55%[4]	0%[4]	14/1[4]	18-22[4]	15%[4]	88%[4]	12%[4]
59.	Ottawa University (KS)	32	2.3	58%	48%	34%	70%	0%	16/1	19-25	38%	99%	6%
61.	Rochester College (MI)	31	2.4	60%	46%	44%	85%	0.3%	11/1	18-24[9]	N/A	66%	N/A
62.	Dickinson State University (ND)*	30	2.3	55%[8]	38%	38%	80%	0.2%	11/1	18-23[3]	N/A	49%	N/A
62.	Maranatha Baptist University (WI)	30	1.5	75%[8]	44%	57%	75%	4%	16/1	20-26	N/A	64%	N/A
64.	Dunwoody College of Tech. (MN)	29	2.3	N/A	N/A	N/A	92%	0%	9/1	N/A[2]	1%	76%	5%

Note: Key to footnotes, Page 114.

Rank	School (State) (*Public)	Overall score	Peer assessment score (5.0=highest)	Average freshman retention rate	2013 graduation rate Predicted	Actual	% of classes under 20 ('13)	% of classes of 50 or more ('13)	Student/ faculty ratio ('13)	SAT/ACT 25th-75th percentile ('13)	Freshmen in top 25% of HS class ('13)	Accept-ance rate ('13)	Average alumni giving rate
64.	Kuyper College[1] (MI)	29	2.5	76%[8]	51%	48%[6]	N/A	N/A	13/1[4]	18-25[9]	N/A	68%	N/A
66.	North Central University (MN)	28	2.6	68%	45%	41%	N/A	N/A	16/1[4]	19-26	40%	79%	4%
67.	Sterling College (KS)	27	2.2	63%	44%	42%	70%	1%	13/1	19-25	29%	44%	N/A
68.	Bethany College (KS)	26	2.3	64%[8]	50%	39%	75%	1%	12/1	18-23	20%	59%	13%
69.	Bismarck State College (ND)*	24	2.4	N/A	N/A	N/A	66%	0.3%	15/1	17-23[2]	N/A	100%	N/A
69.	Lake Superior State University (MI)*	24	2.6	69%[8]	42%	40%	53%	7%	15/1	20-25[4]	40%	90%	3%[4]
69.	Midland University[1] (NE)	24	2.1	63%[8]	45%	48%[6]	44%[4]	5%[4]	10/1[4]	19-24[4]	28%[4]	98%[4]	11%[4]

School (State) (*Public)	Peer assessment score (5.0=highest)	Average freshman retention rate	2013 graduation rate Predicted	Actual	% of classes under 20 ('13)	% of classes of 50 or more ('13)	Student/ faculty ratio ('13)	SAT/ACT 25th-75th percentile ('13)	Freshmen in top 25% of HS class ('13)	Accept-ance rate ('13)	Average alumni giving rate
SECOND TIER (SCHOOLS RANKED 72 THROUGH 95 ARE LISTED HERE ALPHABETICALLY)											
Central Christian College[1] (KS)	1.7	60%[8]	39%	36%[6]	N/A	N/A	12/1[4]	18-24[9]	N/A	50%	N/A
Central State University (OH)*	1.9	49%	26%	25%	53%	0.4%	13/1	15-19	18%	33%	15%
Finlandia University[1] (MI)	2.3	49%[8]	38%	41%[6]	N/A	N/A	10/1[4]	17-22[9]	N/A	59%	N/A
Grace Bible College[1] (MI)	1.9	62%[8]	47%	30%[6]	N/A	N/A	12/1[4]	N/A[2]	N/A	75%	N/A
Grace University[1] (NE)	2.0	79%[8]	49%	36%[6]	N/A	N/A	8/1[4]	19-24[9]	N/A	58%	N/A
Hannibal-LaGrange University (MO)	2.0	60%	48%	48%[6]	76%	1%	13/1[4]	19-25[3]	N/A	68%	5%
Herzing University[1] (WI)	1.6	35%[8]	N/A	38%[6]	N/A	N/A	14/1[4]	N/A[2]	N/A	81%[4]	N/A
Indiana University East*	2.5	66%	31%	24%	63%	3%	15/1	820-1030	29%	54%	8%
Indiana University–Kokomo*	2.4	62%	36%	28%	45%	2%	16/1	850-1040	29%	74%	9%
Iowa Wesleyan College[1]	2.0	43%[8]	36%	31%[6]	N/A	N/A	9/1[4]	19-24[9]	N/A	60%	5%[7]
Kendall College[1] (IL)	2.3	55%[8]	49%	39%[8]	60%[4]	1%[4]	15/1[4]	15-19[4]	N/A	99%[4]	N/A
Lincoln College[1] (IL)	2.0	53%[8]	N/A	N/A	N/A	N/A	N/A	15-19[4]	N/A	N/A	1%[7]
Mayville State University (ND)*	2.0	53%	40%	36%	72%	1%	14/1	17-21	34%	51%	9%
Missouri Southern State University*	2.4	62%	42%	36%	49%	0.2%	19/1	18-24[3]	33%	97%	4%
Missouri Valley College[1]	1.9	49%[8]	33%	28%[6]	N/A	N/A	14/1[4]	18-21[9]	N/A	22%	N/A
Missouri Western State University*	2.1	61%	33%	33%	50%	6%	18/1	17-23[2]	28%	100%	7%
Ohio Christian University[1]	2.1	53%[8]	32%	40%[6]	N/A	N/A	8/1[4]	17-23[9]	N/A	97%	N/A
Presentation College[1] (SD)	2.1	50%[8]	36%	45%[6]	N/A	N/A	10/1[4]	18-22[9]	N/A	66%	N/A
Purdue Univ.–North Central (IN)*	3.0	57%[8]	32%	22%	52%	3%	17/1	860-1050[2]	25%	73%	N/A
Silver Lake College[1] (WI)	2.0	74%[8]	45%	40%[6]	N/A	N/A	5/1[4]	17-23[9]	N/A	60%	N/A
Waldorf College[1] (IA)	1.9	48%[8]	51%	41%[6]	N/A	N/A	21/1[4]	19-23[9]	N/A	51%	N/A
Wilberforce University[1] (OH)	2.1	78%[8]	36%	30%[6]	N/A	N/A	12/1[4]	N/A[2]	N/A	58%	N/A
William Penn University[1] (IA)	2.0	57%[8]	29%	28%[6]	N/A	N/A	17/1[4]	17-22[9]	N/A	58%	N/A
York College (NE)	2.0	66%[8]	50%	36%	80%	0%	13/1	17-22	24%	49%	13%[4]

Augustana College in South Dakota, No. 3 in the Midwest

MATT ADDINGTON – AUGUSTANA COLLEGE

WEST ▶

Rank School (State) (*Public)	Overall score	Peer assessment score (5.0=highest)	Average freshman retention rate	2013 graduation rate		% of classes under 20 ('13)	% of classes of 50 or more ('13)	Student/ faculty ratio ('13)	SAT/ACT 25th-75th percentile ('13)	Freshmen in top 25% of HS class ('13)	Accept- ance rate ('13)	Average alumni giving rate
				Predicted	Actual							
1. Carroll College (MT)	100	3.7	82%	57%	67%	66%	2%	12/1	22-27	61%	53%	15%
2. Texas Lutheran University	95	3.8	70%	54%	52%	65%	0%	14/1	930-1140	53%	51%	15%
3. California Maritime Academy*	92	3.5	81%	56%	60%	N/A	N/A	14/1	990-1200[3]	N/A	63%	7%[4]
4. Oklahoma Baptist University	84	3.6	75%	57%	55%	70%	2%	16/1	21-27	58%	56%	7%
5. Master's Col. and Seminary (CA)	83	3.4	81%	62%	54%	74%	6%	10/1	940-1200	55%[5]	78%	7%
6. Oklahoma Wesleyan University	81	3.7	59%	45%	56%	77%	1%	15/1	18-24	N/A	24%	7%[4]
7. Corban University (OR)	80	3.4	75%	55%	54%	53%	2%	13/1	950-1180[3]	63%	34%	13%
7. Menlo College (CA)	75	3.2	75%	50%	60%	53%	0%	14/1	882-1097[3]	N/A	40%	5%
8. Oregon Inst. of Technology*	75	3.7	73%	44%	43%	57%	3%	13/1	880-1140[3]	59%	71%	2%
8. Warner Pacific College (OR)	75	3.4	69%	44%	32%	73%	1%	11/1	830-1100	25%	53%	5%
11. Brigham Young University–Idaho[1]	71	4.0	72%[8]	46%	53%[6]	N/A	N/A	24/1[4]	20-25[9]	N/A	100%	N/A
12. Vanguard Univ. of Southern California	67	3.0	74%	49%	52%	62%	4%	15/1	850-1073	41%	70%	6%
13. East Texas Baptist University	65	3.5	58%	44%	33%	62%	0.3%	13/1	18-22	40%	74%	7%
13. Rocky Mountain College (MT)	65	3.0	68%	51%	40%	68%	1%	12/1	19-25	35%	67%	8%
15. Howard Payne University (TX)	64	3.2	62%	44%	40%	71%	0.3%	10/1	860-1050	24%	54%	6%
16. Brigham Young University–Hawaii[1]	63	3.7	61%[8]	58%	52%[6]	N/A	N/A	16/1[4]	21-26[9]	N/A	36%	N/A
16. Northwest University (WA)	63	3.2	77%	48%	43%	68%	4%	11/1	950-1170[3]	N/A	86%	N/A
18. McMurry University (TX)	62	3.1	58%	42%	38%	71%	1%	12/1	860-1090	37%	59%	6%
19. Hope International University (CA)	58	3.3	69%	50%	44%	70%	0%	10/1	860-1090	13%[5]	47%	7%
20. Northwest Christian University (OR)	52	2.8	68%[8]	46%	45%	82%	1%	12/1	885-1065	N/A	70%	N/A
21. Lewis-Clark State College (ID)*	49	3.6	54%[8]	36%	29%	63%	1%	16/1[4]	820-1030[9]	12%	100%	N/A
22. University of Great Falls (MT)	43	3.1	62%	37%	24%[6]	67%	0%	14/1	840-1090[4]	N/A	84%[4]	N/A
23. Southwestern Christian Univ.[1] (OK)	37	3.1	64%[8]	30%	21%[6]	82%[4]	0%[4]	20/1[4]	860-1180[4]	N/A	88%[4]	3%[4]
24. Okla. State U. Inst. of Tech.–Okmulgee*	36	3.3	55%	34%	26%	81%	0%	19/1	16-21[3]	18%	54%	2%
25. St. Gregory's University (OK)	35	3.1	N/A	38%	28%	N/A	N/A	N/A	N/A[2]	N/A	57%	N/A

School (State) (*Public)		Peer assessment score (5.0=highest)	Average freshman retention rate	2013 graduation rate		% of classes under 20 ('13)	% of classes of 50 or more ('13)	Student/ faculty ratio ('13)	SAT/ACT 25th-75th percentile ('13)	Freshmen in top 25% of HS class ('13)	Accept- ance rate ('13)	Average alumni giving rate
				Predicted	Actual							
SECOND TIER (SCHOOLS RANKED 26 THROUGH 33 ARE LISTED HERE ALPHABETICALLY)												
Bacone College[1] (OK)		2.0	47%[8]	22%	11%[6]	N/A	N/A	15/1[4]	15-19[9]	N/A	72%	N/A
Jarvis Christian College (TX)		2.5	52%	27%	9%	58%	7%	18/1	13-18	8%	100%	5%
Metropolitan State Univ. of Denver[1]*		3.2	65%[8]	30%	22%[8]	34%[4]	1%[4]	20/1[4]	18-23[4]	22%[4]	71%[4]	N/A
Nevada State College[1]*		2.4	63%[8]	N/A	18%[6]	N/A	N/A	19/1[4]	N/A[2]	N/A	50%	N/A
Oklahoma Panhandle State Univ.[1]*		2.7	55%[8]	33%	32%[8]	N/A	N/A	N/A	710-950[4]	N/A	61%[4]	N/A
Patten University[1] (CA)		2.2	N/A	42%	27%[6]	N/A	N/A	N/A	N/A[2]	N/A	N/A	N/A
Rogers State University (OK)*		2.8	58%	30%	20%	50%	1%	19/1	17-23[3]	20%	54%	3%[4]
Wiley College (TX)		2.8	52%	22%	19%	58%	2%	17/1	14-18[2]	8%	94%	4%

The Top Public Regional Colleges ▶

NORTH

Rank School (State)

1. U. S. Coast Guard Acad. (CT)
2. U.S. Merchant Marine Acad. (NY)
3. Massachusetts Maritime Academy
4. Maine Maritime Academy
5. University of Maine–Farmington

SOUTH

Rank School (State)

1. Univ. of South Carolina–Aiken
2. Elizabeth City State Univ. (NC)
3. U. of South Carolina–Upstate
4. Univ. of Arkansas–Pine Bluff
5. Concord University (WV)

MIDWEST

Rank School (State)

1. University of Minnesota–Crookston
2. Valley City State University (ND)
3. Northern State University (SD)
4. Dickinson State University (ND)
5. Bismarck State College (ND)
5. Lake Superior State University (MI)

WEST

Rank School (State)

1. California Maritime Academy
2. Oregon Inst. of Technology
3. Lewis-Clark State College (ID)
4. Oklahoma State University Institute of Technology–Okmulgee

Footnotes:
1. School refused to fill out U.S. News statistical survey. Data that appear are from school in previous years or from another source such as the National Center for Education Statistics.
2. SAT and/or ACT not required by school for some or all applicants.
3. In reporting SAT/ACT scores, the school did not include all students for whom it had scores or refused to tell U.S. News whether all students with scores had been included.
4. Data reported to U.S. News in previous years.
5. Data based on fewer than 51 percent of enrolled freshmen.
6. Some or all data reported to the NCAA and/or the National Center for Education Statistics.
7. Data reported to the Council for Aid to Education.

8. Average graduation or freshman retention rates, normally based on four years of data, are given here for less than four years because school didn't report rates for the most recent year or years to U.S. News.
9. SAT and/or ACT may not be required by school for some or all applicants, and in reporting SAT/ACT scores, the school did not include all students for whom it had scores, or refused to tell U.S. News whether all students with scores had been included.

N/A means not available.

CHRISTOPHER NEWPORT
UNIVERSITY

Meet Linda Oh, a biology major in CNU's pre-dentistry program. As a Bonner Service Scholar she completes more than 300 hours of service each year working to inspire local youth and helping them overcome challenges.

LEADERSHIP. SERVICE. HONOR.
LEARN TO LEAD A LIFE OF SIGNIFICANCE

At Christopher Newport University our outstanding liberal arts and sciences programs shape hearts and minds for a lifetime of service. Your journey begins in the classroom, where you will study with accomplished scholars of outstanding quality.

Outside the classroom you will join students like Linda in fine-tuning your leadership skills by collaborating closely with fellow CNU Captains and professors, to make a lasting impact on campus, in the community and around the globe. From mentoring inner-city youth and playing the cello in the University Orchestra, like Linda, to ground-breaking research, CNU prepares you to do the work that shapes, defines and enriches the world.

Learn today how you will serve the greater good.

Find out what it means to be a Captain.

#GreaterGood   1 Avenue of the Arts • Newport News, VA 23606   www.cnu.edu

Best
Historically Black Colleges

Increasingly, the nation's top historically black colleges and universities are an appealing option for applicants of all races; many HBCUs, in fact, now actively recruit Hispanic, international and white students in addition to the African-American high school grads heading to college in record numbers. Which schools offer the best undergraduate education? In the spring of 2014, U.S. News conducted the annual separate peer survey of administrators at the HBCUs, asking the president, provost and admissions dean at each to rate the academic quality of all other HBCUs with which they are familiar. In addition to the peer survey results, the rankings below are based on nearly all the same ranking indicators (although weighted slightly differently) as those used in ranking the regional universities (box, right). These include retention and gradua-tion rates, high school class standing, admission test scores and the strength of the faculty, among others.

To be part of the universe, a school has to be designated by the Department of Education as an HBCU. The college must also be a baccalaureate-granting institution that enrolls primarily first-year, first-time students and have been part of this year's Best Colleges survey and ranking process. If an HBCU is unranked in the 2015 Best Colleges rankings, it is also unranked here; reasons that schools are not ranked vary, but include a school's policy not to use SAT or ACT test scores in admissions decisions. There are 80 HBCUs; 69 were ranked. HBCUs in the top three-quarters are numerically ranked, and those in the bottom quarter are listed alphabetically. For more detail on the HBCU rankings and methodology, visit usnews.com/hbcu.

Graduation and retention rates	27.5%
Peer assessment	25%
Faculty resources	20%
Student selectivity	12.5%
Financial resources	10%
Alumni giving	5%

Rank	School (State) (*Public)	Overall score	Peer assessment score (5.0=highest)	Average freshman retention rate	Average graduation rate	% of classes under 20 ('13)	% of classes of 50 or more ('13)	Student/faculty ratio ('13)	% of faculty who are full time ('13)	SAT/ACT 25th-75th percentile ('13)	Freshmen in top 25% of HS class ('13)	Acceptance rate ('13)	Average alumni giving rate
1.	Spelman College (GA)	100	4.7	89%	73%	63%	3%	10/1	88%	850-1215	66%	41%	34%
2.	Howard University (DC)	80	4.3	82%	64%[6]	42%	10%	8/1	90%	980-1190[3]	54%	57%	5%
3.	Morehouse College (GA)	78	4.4	82%	56%[6]	48%	2%	12/1	91%	900-1110	41%	67%	23%
4.	Hampton University (VA)	75	4.4	77%	59%[6]	55%	4%	10/1	91%	920-1090[2]	45%	36%	12%
5.	Tuskegee University (AL)	68	4.1	76%	44%[6]	56%	9%	12/1	95%	18-23[3]	60%	41%	24%
6.	Xavier University of Louisiana	64	4.1	68%	46%[6]	51%	6%	13/1	96%	20-26	56%	54%	12%
7.	Fisk University (TN)	61	3.5	N/A	53%[6]	68%	1%	11/1	83%	17-23	N/A	21%	24%
8.	Florida A&M University*	55	3.9	81%	41%	32%	12%	17/1	90%	18-22	46%[5]	45%	6%
9.	Claflin University (SC)	54	3.5	73%	44%	63%	1%	14/1	87%	710-960	35%	61%	47%
10.	North Carolina A&T State Univ.*	52	4.0	73%[8]	41%[6]	34%	7%	16/1	89%	830-990	31%	57%	8%
11.	North Carolina Central Univ.*	47	3.7	71%	40%	40%	5%	15/1	89%	800-950	22%	39%	11%
12.	Tougaloo College (MS)	46	3.0	74%	47%[6]	70%	0.3%	10/1	94%	15-21	25%	34%	13%
13.	Delaware State University*	45	3.5	66%	36%	50%	3%	16/1	84%	820-970	26%	45%	6%
13.	Dillard University (LA)	45	3.5	64%[8]	33%[6]	63%	1%	14/1	69%	17-20	31%[5]	35%	4%
15.	Morgan State University (MD)*	44	3.7	72%	31%[6]	42%	0.1%	17/1	94%	820-980[2]	9%	56%	14%
15.	Winston-Salem State Univ.[1] (NC)*	44	3.4	78%[8]	39%[6]	47%[4]	1%[4]	13/1[4]	90%[4]	16-19[4]	35%[4]	56%[4]	7%[4]
17.	Johnson C. Smith University (NC)	43	3.1	68%	41%	75%	0.2%	11/1	85%	733-920	25%	37%	15%
18.	Clark Atlanta University	42	3.6	64%	40%[6]	45%	3%	16/1	81%	770-940[3]	31%[4]	57%	3%[7]
19.	Jackson State University[1] (MS)*	41	3.7	73%[8]	42%[6]	N/A	N/A	18/1[4]	89%[4]	17-21[9]	N/A	65%	4%[7]
20.	Elizabeth City State Univ. (NC)*	40	2.9	75%	40%[6]	66%	1%	16/1	86%	780-945[3]	5%	52%	10%
21.	Lincoln University (PA)*	39	3.1	66%	38%[6]	49%	1%	17/1	79%	770-960	28%	61%	8%
21.	Tennessee State University*	39	3.5	62%[8]	32%[6]	54%	1%	15/1	86%	16-20[3]	N/A	53%	4%[4]
23.	Alabama A&M University*	38	3.5	69%	32%[6]	48%	4%	18/1	91%	15-19	N/A	90%	6%
23.	Univ. of Maryland–Eastern Shore*	38	3.5	68%	32%[6]	57%	4%	14/1	81%	790-960[3]	N/A	55%	3%
25.	Bennett College[1] (NC)	35	3.2	68%[8]	41%[6]	74%[4]	0.4%[4]	10/1[4]	87%[4]	15-20[4]	21%[4]	69%[4]	N/A
25.	Bowie State University (MD)*	35	3.3	72%	38%[6]	45%	1%	16/1	77%	810-960[3]	N/A	52%	6%
27.	Alcorn State University (MS)*	34	3.1	68%	35%[6]	51%	5%	16/1	91%	16-19	N/A	83%	5%[4]
28.	Albany State University (GA)*	33	3.1	69%	42%	52%	1%	20/1	84%	820-950	27%[5]	24%	4%
28.	Fayetteville State University (NC)*	33	3.2	72%	33%[6]	38%	1%	17/1	93%	770-910[3]	17%	61%	.2%
30.	South Carolina State University*	32	2.7	63%	38%[6]	53%	3%	14/1	90%	720-870	30%	92%	N/A
31.	Bethune-Cookman University (FL)	31	3.4	66%	42%[6]	44%	2%	18/1	88%	15-18	12%	67%	4%
32.	Virginia State University*	30	3.1	65%[8]	42%[6]	N/A	N/A	16/1	86%	730-910[3]	17%	54%	N/A
33.	Oakwood University (AL)	29	3.1	71%[8]	38%[6]	N/A	N/A	N/A	100%[4]	17-22[4]	N/A	34%[4]	N/A
34.	Norfolk State University (VA)*	28	3.3	N/A	35%[6]	51%[4]	4%[4]	18/1	N/A	770-948[3]	26%[4]	65%	3%[4]
35.	Philander Smith College (AR)	27	2.7	63%	31%	83%	0%	10/1	91%	16-22	44%	42%	13%
35.	Univ. of Arkansas–Pine Bluff*	27	2.9	56%	25%	55%	4%	15/1	93%	15-20	27%	28%	11%
37.	Prairie View A&M University (TX)*	26	3.2	67%	34%[6]	22%	10%	18/1	93%	750-940	14%	85%	N/A
38.	Fort Valley State University (GA)*	25	2.9	61%	32%[6]	47%	5%	19/1	89%	15-18	23%[5]	31%	16%

Note: Key to footnotes, Page 106.

Rank	School (State) (*Public)	Overall score	Peer assessment score (5.0=highest)	Average freshman retention rate	Average graduation rate	% of classes under 20 ('13)	% of classes of 50 or more ('13)	Student/faculty ratio ('13)	% of faculty who are full time ('13)	SAT/ACT 25th-75th percentile ('13)	Freshmen in top 25% of HS class ('13)	Acceptance rate ('13)	Average alumni giving rate
38.	Kentucky State University*	25	3.1	51%	20%[6]	53%	0.2%	14/1	91%	16-20	N/A	38%	4%
40.	Stillman College[1] (AL)	24	2.7	60%[8]	28%[8]	65%[4]	1%[4]	16/1[4]	95%[4]	16-19[4]	25%[4]	41%[4]	5%[4]
41.	Alabama State University*	23	3.1	61%	26%	N/A	N/A	17/1	86%	15-20[3]	1%	54%	N/A
41.	Central State University (OH)*	23	2.8	49%	24%[6]	53%	0.4%	13/1	74%	15-19	18%	33%	15%
41.	West Virginia State University*	23	3.0	53%	22%[6]	53%	2%	15/1	84%	18-22	N/A	45%	2%
44.	Cheyney U. of Pennsylvania*	22	2.9	55%	25%[6]	47%	10%	16/1	90%	670-850[3]	9%[5]	88%	4%
45.	Paine College (GA)	20	2.8	61%	24%	65%	0%	13/1	86%	14-18	15%[5]	44%	13%
45.	Southern U. and A&M College (LA)*	20	3.1	69%	27%[6]	N/A	N/A	25/1	83%	17-20[3]	23%	N/A	N/A
47.	Savannah State University (GA)*	19	3.1	70%[8]	32%[6]	30%	1%	23/1	92%	770-910	N/A	83%	N/A
48.	Livingstone College (NC)	18	2.6	52%	27%	46%	1%	15/1	98%	11-16[3]	6%	72%	36%
49.	Texas Southern University*	17	3.0	60%	13%[6]	38%	11%	19/1	80%	750-920	20%	45%	2%
50.	Bluefield State College (WV)*	16	2.7	57%	26%[6]	75%	0.3%	15/1	77%	16-21	N/A	41%	4%
50.	Florida Memorial University[1]	16	2.7	70%[8]	40%[6]	N/A	N/A	17/1[4]	84%[4]	N/A[2]	N/A	42%	N/A
50.	Grambling State University (LA)*	16	2.9	N/A	29%[6]	40%	10%	23/1	96%	16-20[3]	22%	44%	2%[7]
50.	Mississippi Valley State Univ.[1]*	16	2.8	61%[8]	24%[6]	N/A	N/A	13/1[4]	93%[4]	15-19[9]	N/A	23%	N/A

School (State) (*Public)	Peer assessment score (5.0=highest)	Average freshman retention rate	Average graduation rate	% of classes under 20 ('13)	% of classes of 50 or more ('13)	Student/faculty ratio ('13)	% of faculty who are full time ('13)	SAT/ACT 25th-75th percentile ('13)	Freshmen in top 25% of HS class ('13)	Acceptance rate ('13)	Average alumni giving rate
SECOND TIER (SCHOOLS RANKED 54 THROUGH 69 ARE LISTED HERE ALPHABETICALLY)											
Allen University (SC)	2.5	46%	15%[6]	N/A	N/A	15/1	98%	16[9]	N/A	50%	N/A
Coppin State University (MD)*	2.8	66%[8]	16%[6]	N/A	N/A	14/1[4]	75%[4]	810-950[4]	N/A	36%[4]	6%[7]
Edward Waters College (FL)	2.2	54%[8]	19%[6]	N/A	N/A	17/1[4]	100%[4]	15-18[9]	N/A	27%	N/A
Huston-Tillotson University[1] (TX)	2.9	57%[8]	23%[6]	N/A	N/A	13/1[4]	84%[4]	700-900[9]	N/A	46%	N/A
Jarvis Christian College (TX)	2.4	52%	16%[6]	58%	7%	18/1	81%	13-18	8%	100%	5%
Lane College[1] (TN)	2.7	55%[8]	33%[6]	50%[4]	0%[4]	16/1[4]	98%[4]	14-17[4]	12%[4]	33%[4]	N/A
LeMoyne-Owen College (TN)	2.4	54%[8]	15%[6]	95%	0%	13/1	N/A	N/A	N/A	27%	N/A
Rust College (MS)	2.7	60%	27%[6]	N/A	N/A	18/1	97%	13-14	N/A	14%	N/A
Shaw University (NC)	2.7	52%[8]	27%[8]	66%[4]	1%[4]	15/1[4]	81%[4]	13-16[4]	5%[4]	54%[4]	N/A
Southern University–New Orleans[1]*	2.7	61%[8]	11%[6]	N/A	N/A	19/1[4]	100%[4]	840-1290[4]	N/A	49%[4]	N/A
St. Augustine's University (NC)	2.5	52%	25%[6]	N/A	N/A	13/1	80%	665-858[3]	N/A	67%	5%
Univ. of the District of Columbia*	2.4	50%[8]	14%[6]	N/A	N/A	N/A	N/A[4]	N/A[2]	N/A	43%[4]	N/A
Virginia Union University	2.8	54%[8]	32%	48%	1%	14/1	84%	670-840	18%	83%	9%
Voorhees College (SC)	2.5	46%[8]	30%[6]	N/A	N/A	13/1[4]	80%[4]	N/A[2]	N/A	51%	N/A
Wilberforce University (OH)	2.7	78%[8]	30%[6]	N/A	N/A	12/1[4]	64%[4]	N/A[2]	N/A	58%	N/A
Wiley College (TX)	2.8	52%	18%[6]	58%	2%	17/1	83%	14-18[9]	8%	94%	4%

Sources: Statistical data from the schools. Peer assessment data collected by Ipsos Public Affairs.

JIM LO SCLAZO FOR USN&WR

Morehouse College in Atlanta, No. 3

Best Business Programs

In the spring of 2014, U.S. News surveyed deans and senior faculty at all undergraduate business programs accredited by the Association to Advance Collegiate Schools of Business. Participants were asked to rate the quality of programs with which they're familiar on a scale of 1 (marginal) to 5 (distinguished); 38 percent of those surveyed responded. The undergrad business rankings are based solely on this peer survey. Deans and faculty, two per school, also were asked to nominate the 10 best programs in a number of specialty areas; the five schools receiving the most mentions in each appear.

Top Programs ▶

Rank	School (State) (*Public)	Peer assessment score (5.0=highest)
1.	University of Pennsylvania (Wharton)	4.8
2.	Massachusetts Inst. of Technology (Sloan)	4.6
2.	University of California–Berkeley (Haas)	4.6
4.	University of Michigan–Ann Arbor (Ross)*	4.5
5.	New York University (Stern)	4.4
6.	U. of N. Carolina–Chapel Hill (Kenan-Flagler)*	4.3
6.	University of Virginia (McIntire)*	4.3
8.	Carnegie Mellon University (Tepper) (PA)	4.2
8.	Indiana University–Bloomington (Kelley)*	4.2
8.	University of Texas–Austin (McCombs)*	4.2
11.	Cornell University (Dyson) (NY)	4.1
11.	University of Notre Dame (IN)	4.1
11.	Univ. of Southern California (Marshall)	4.1
14.	Washington University in St. Louis (Olin)	4.0
15.	Emory University (Goizueta) (GA)	3.9
15.	Georgetown University (McDonough) (DC)	3.9
15.	U. of Illinois–Urbana-Champaign*	3.9
15.	Univ. of Minnesota–Twin Cities (Carlson)*	3.9
15.	Univ. of Wisconsin–Madison*	3.9
20.	Ohio State University–Columbus (Fisher)*	3.8
21.	Boston College (Carroll)	3.7
21.	Michigan State University (Broad)*	3.7
21.	Pennsylvania State U.–Univ. Park (Smeal)*	3.7
21.	Purdue U.–West Lafayette (Krannert) (IN)*	3.7
21.	University of Arizona (Eller)*	3.7
21.	University of Georgia (Terry)*	3.7
21.	Univ. of Maryland–College Park (Smith)*	3.7
21.	University of Washington*	3.7
29.	Arizona State University–Tempe (Carey)*	3.6
29.	Babson College (MA)	3.6
29.	Georgia Institute of Technology*	3.6
29.	Texas A&M Univ.–College Station (Mays)*	3.6
29.	University of Florida (Warrington)*	3.6
34.	Brigham Young Univ.–Provo (Marriott) (UT)	3.5
34.	Case Western Reserve U. (Weatherhead) (OH)	3.5
34.	University of Colorado–Boulder*	3.5
34.	University of Iowa (Tippie)*	3.5
34.	Wake Forest University (Calloway) (NC)	3.5
39.	Boston University	3.4
39.	College of William and Mary (VA)*	3.4
39.	University of California–Irvine*†	3.4
39.	University of Pittsburgh*	3.4
39.	Univ. of South Carolina (Moore)*	3.4
39.	Virginia Tech (Pamplin)*	3.4
45.	George Washington University (DC)	3.3
45.	Georgia State University (Robinson)*	3.3
45.	Southern Methodist University (Cox) (TX)	3.3
45.	Syracuse University (Whitman) (NY)	3.3
45.	Tulane University (Freeman) (LA)	3.3
45.	University of Arkansas (Walton)*	3.3
51.	Auburn University (AL)*	3.2
51.	Bentley University (MA)	3.2
51.	Pepperdine University (Graziadio) (CA)	3.2
51.	University of Connecticut*	3.2
51.	University of Kansas*	3.2
51.	Univ. of Massachusetts–Amherst (Isenberg)*	3.2
51.	Univ. of Missouri (Trulaske)*	3.2
51.	Univ. of Nebraska–Lincoln*	3.2
51.	University of Oregon (Lundquist)*	3.2
51.	University of Tennessee*	3.2
51.	University of Utah (Eccles)*	3.2
62.	Baylor University (Hankamer) (TX)	3.1
62.	CUNY–Baruch College (Zicklin)*	3.1
62.	Florida State University*	3.1
62.	George Mason University (VA)*	3.1
62.	Miami University–Oxford (Farmer) (OH)*	3.1
62.	Northeastern University (MA)	3.1
62.	Rensselaer Polytechnic Inst. (Lally) (NY)	3.1
62.	Santa Clara University (Leavey) (CA)	3.1
62.	Temple University (Fox) (PA)*	3.1
62.	United States Air Force Acad. (CO)*	3.1
62.	University of Alabama (Culverhouse)*	3.1
62.	Univ. of California–San Diego*	3.1
62.	University of Kentucky (Gatton)*	3.1
62.	University of Miami (FL)	3.1
62.	University of Oklahoma (Price)*	3.1
62.	University of Richmond (Robins) (VA)	3.1
62.	Villanova University (PA)	3.1
79.	American University (Kogod) (DC)	3.0
79.	Clemson University (SC)*	3.0
79.	Fordham University (NY)	3.0
79.	Iowa State University*	3.0
79.	Louisiana State Univ.–Baton Rouge (Ourso)*	3.0
79.	Loyola University Chicago	3.0
79.	St. Louis University	3.0
79.	Texas Christian University (Neeley)	3.0
79.	University at Buffalo–SUNY*	3.0
79.	Univ. of California–Riverside*	3.0
79.	University of Delaware*	3.0
79.	University of Denver (Daniels)	3.0
79.	University of Illinois–Chicago*	3.0
79.	University of Louisville (KY)*	3.0
93.	Brandeis University (MA)	2.9
93.	Colorado State University*	2.9
93.	Creighton University (NE)	2.9
93.	DePaul University (IL)	2.9
93.	Drexel University (LeBow) (PA)	2.9
93.	Lehigh University (PA)	2.9
93.	Loyola Marymount University (CA)	2.9
93.	Marquette University (WI)	2.9
93.	North Carolina State U.–Raleigh*	2.9
93.	Oklahoma State University*	2.9
93.	Rochester Inst. of Technology (NY)	2.9
93.	Rutgers, St. U. of N.J.–New Brunswick*	2.9
93.	San Diego State University*	2.9
93.	Seattle University (Albers)	2.9
93.	Texas Tech University (Rawls)*	2.9
93.	University of Colorado–Denver*	2.9
93.	University of Houston (Bauer)*	2.9
93.	University of Mississippi*	2.9
93.	University of Texas–Dallas*	2.9
93.	Washington State University*	2.9
113.	Binghamton University–SUNY*	2.8
113.	Gonzaga University (WA)	2.8
113.	James Madison University (VA)*	2.8
113.	Kansas State University*	2.8
113.	Ohio University*	2.8
113.	Oregon State University*	2.8
113.	Rollins College (FL)	2.8
113.	Rutgers, The State U. of N.J.–Newark*	2.8
113.	Seton Hall University (Stillman) (NJ)	2.8
113.	St. Joseph's University (Haub) (PA)	2.8
113.	University at Albany–SUNY*	2.8
113.	University of Alabama–Birmingham*	2.8
113.	University of Cincinnati*	2.8
113.	Univ. of Colo.–Colorado Springs*	2.8
113.	University of Memphis (Fogelman)*	2.8
113.	Univ. of Missouri–St. Louis*	2.8
113.	U. of North Carolina–Charlotte (Belk)*	2.8
113.	University of San Francisco (McLaren)	2.8
113.	Univ. of Wisconsin–Milwaukee*	2.8
113.	Virginia Commonwealth University*	2.8

Note: Peer assessment survey conducted by Ipsos Public Affairs. To be ranked in a specialty, an undergraduate business school may have either a program or course offerings in that subject area. Extended undergraduate business rankings can be found at usnews.com/bestcolleges. †University of California–Irvine was inadvertently omitted from the ranking originally published in this guidebook.

HOUSTON
WE ARE
BAUER

YOUR CAREER STARTS HERE

The need for prepared young professionals in Houston — one of the country's fastest growing economies —
is unquestioned. At the C. T. Bauer College of Business at the University of Houston, we're answering the call
by designing degree programs that prepare our students not only to get hired upon graduation but to find a career.
With undergraduate courses that focus on energy, entrepreneurship, startups, sales and more, Bauer students
have the opportunity not just to learn about business but to experience it firsthand.

BAUER
COLLEGE OF BUSINESS
UNIVERSITY of HOUSTON

The University of Houston is an EEO/AA institution.

bauer.uh.edu

C. T. Bauer College of Business is an
AACSB accredited business school.

BEST BUSINESS PROGRAMS

Best in the Specialties ▶

(*Public)

ACCOUNTING**
1. University of Texas–Austin (McCombs)*
2. U. of Illinois–Urbana-Champaign*
3. Brigham Young Univ.–Provo (Marriott) (UT)
4. University of Notre Dame (IN)
5. University of Pennsylvania (Wharton)
5. Univ. of Southern California (Marshall)

ENTREPRENEURSHIP**
1. Babson College (MA)
2. Massachusetts Inst. of Technology (Sloan)
3. Univ. of Southern California (Marshall)
4. Indiana University–Bloomington (Kelley)*
4. University of Pennsylvania (Wharton)

FINANCE**
1. University of Pennsylvania (Wharton)
2. New York University (Stern)
3. University of Michigan–Ann Arbor (Ross)*
4. Massachusetts Inst. of Technology (Sloan)
5. University of California–Berkeley (Haas)*
5. University of Texas–Austin (McCombs)*

INSURANCE/RISK MANAGEMENT
1. University of Georgia (Terry)*
2. University of Pennsylvania (Wharton)
3. Univ. of Wisconsin–Madison*
4. Temple University (Fox) (PA)*
5. Georgia State University (Robinson)*

INTERNATIONAL BUSINESS
1. Univ. of South Carolina (Moore)*
2. New York University (Stern)
3. University of Pennsylvania (Wharton)
4. Univ. of Southern California (Marshall)
5. University of Michigan–Ann Arbor (Ross)*

MANAGEMENT
1. University of Michigan–Ann Arbor (Ross)*
1. University of Pennsylvania (Wharton)
3. University of Virginia (McIntire)*
4. University of California–Berkeley (Haas)*
5. U. of North Carolina–Chapel Hill (Kenan-Flagler)*

MANAGEMENT INFORMATION SYSTEMS
1. Massachusetts Inst. of Technology (Sloan)
2. Carnegie Mellon University (Tepper) (PA)
3. Univ. of Minnesota–Twin Cities (Carlson)*
4. University of Texas–Austin (McCombs)*
5. University of Arizona (Eller)*

MARKETING
1. University of Michigan–Ann Arbor (Ross)*
1. University of Pennsylvania (Wharton)
3. University of Texas–Austin (McCombs)*
4. Indiana University–Bloomington (Kelley)*
5. University of California–Berkeley (Haas)*

**The ranking originally published in this guidebook was incorrect and has been revised here.

PRODUCTION/OPERATIONS MANAGEMENT
1. Massachusetts Inst. of Technology (Sloan)
2. Carnegie Mellon University (Tepper) (PA)
3. Purdue Univ.–West Lafayette (Krannert) (IN)*
4. University of Pennsylvania (Wharton)
5. University of Michigan–Ann Arbor (Ross)*

QUANTITATIVE ANALYSIS/METHODS
1. Massachusetts Inst. of Technology (Sloan)
2. Carnegie Mellon University (Tepper) (PA)
3. University of Pennsylvania (Wharton)
4. Purdue Univ.–West Lafayette (Krannert) (IN)*
5. Georgia Institute of Technology*
5. University of California–Berkeley (Haas)*

REAL ESTATE
1. University of Pennsylvania (Wharton)
2. Univ. of Wisconsin–Madison*
3. University of California–Berkeley (Haas)*
4. University of Georgia (Terry)*
5. Univ. of Southern California (Marshall)

SUPPLY CHAIN MANAGEMENT/LOGISTICS
1. Michigan State University (Broad)*
2. Massachusetts Inst. of Technology (Sloan)
3. Arizona State University–Tempe (Carey)*
4. University of Tennessee*
5. Ohio State University–Columbus (Fisher)*
5. Pennsylvania State U.–Univ. Park (Smeal)*

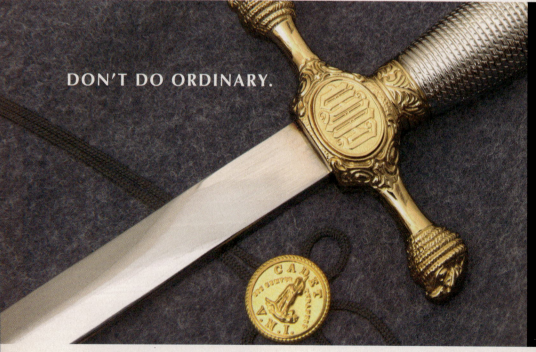

DON'T DO ORDINARY.

- ◆ Science
- ◆ Technology
- ◆ Engineering
- ◆ Math
- ◆ Liberal Arts
- ◆ Small Class Sizes
- ◆ Civilian & Military Career Paths

VMI.EDU
800-767-4207

Virginia Military Institute

NO ORDINARY COLLEGE.   NO ORDINARY LIFE.

In the top four public liberal arts colleges in the nation for 12 years. – *U.S. News and World Report*

Best Engineering Programs

O n these pages, U.S. News ranks undergraduate engineering programs accredited by ABET (formerly the Accreditation Board for Engineering and Technology). The rankings are based solely on a survey of engineering deans and senior faculty at accredited programs, conducted during the spring of 2014. Surveys sent to the dean and a faculty member at each program asked them to rate programs with which they're familiar on a scale from 1 (marginal) to 5 (distinguished). Students who prefer an engineering program that focuses on its undergrads can use the list below of top institutions whose terminal engineering degree is a bachelor's or master's; universities that grant doctorates in engineering, whose programs are ranked separately on the next page, may boast a wider range of offerings at the undergraduate level. Thirty-four percent of those surveyed returned ratings of the group below; 52 percent did so for the doctorate group. Respondents were also asked to name 10 top programs in specialty areas; those mentioned most often appear here.

Top Programs ▶ AT ENGINEERING SCHOOLS WHOSE HIGHEST DEGREE IS A BACHELOR'S OR MASTER'S

Rank	School (State) (*Public)	Peer assessment score (5.0=highest)
1.	Harvey Mudd College (CA)	4.4
1.	Rose-Hulman Inst. of Tech. (IN)	4.4
3.	Franklin W. Olin Col. of Engineering (MA)	4.1
3.	United States Military Academy (NY)*	4.1
5.	United States Air Force Acad. (CO)*	4.0
6.	United States Naval Academy (MD)*	3.9
7.	Cal. Poly. State U.–San Luis Obispo*	3.8
8.	Bucknell University (PA)	3.7
8.	Cooper Union (NY)	3.7
8.	Embry-Riddle Aeronautical U. (FL)	3.7
11.	Villanova University (PA)	3.5
12.	Baylor University (TX)	3.4
12.	U. S. Coast Guard Acad. (CT)*	3.4
14.	Embry-Riddle Aeronautical U.–Prescott (AZ)	3.3
14.	Kettering University (MI)	3.3
14.	Lafayette College (PA)	3.3
14.	Milwaukee School of Engineering	3.3
14.	Santa Clara University (CA)	3.3
14.	Swarthmore College (PA)	3.3
14.	Union College (NY)	3.3
14.	Univ. of Colo.–Colorado Springs*	3.3

Rank	School (State) (*Public)	Peer assessment score (5.0=highest)
14.	University of San Diego	3.3
23.	Calif. State Poly. Univ.–Pomona*	3.2
23.	The Citadel (SC)*	3.2
23.	Lawrence Technological Univ. (MI)	3.2
23.	San Jose State University (CA)*	3.2
23.	Trinity University (TX)	3.2
23.	Virginia Military Institute*	3.2
29.	Gonzaga University (WA)	3.1
29.	Miami University–Oxford (OH)*	3.1
29.	Smith College (MA)	3.1
29.	U.S. Merchant Marine Acad. (NY)*	3.1
29.	Valparaiso University (IN)	3.1
34.	Bradley University (IL)	3.0
34.	Loyola Marymount University (CA)	3.0
34.	Mercer University (GA)	3.0
34.	Rowan University (NJ)*	3.0
34.	Seattle University	3.0
34.	University of Michigan–Dearborn*	3.0
34.	University of St. Thomas (MN)	3.0
41.	Boise State University (ID)*	2.9
41.	California State U.–Los Angeles*	2.9

Rank	School (State) (*Public)	Peer assessment score (5.0=highest)
41.	LeTourneau University (TX)	2.9
41.	Northern Illinois University*	2.9
41.	Ohio Northern University	2.9
41.	Univ. of Arkansas–Little Rock*	2.9
47.	Brigham Young University–Idaho	2.8
47.	California State U.–Long Beach*	2.8
47.	California State U.–Northridge*	2.8
47.	Grand Valley State University (MI)*	2.8
47.	Hofstra University (NY)	2.8
47.	Loyola University Maryland	2.8
47.	Maine Maritime Academy*	2.8
47.	Manhattan College (NY)	2.8
47.	Penn State Univ.–Erie, Behrend Col.*	2.8
47.	Texas Christian University	2.8
47.	Trinity College (CT)	2.8
47.	Univ. of Massachusetts–Dartmouth*	2.8
47.	University of Minnesota–Duluth*	2.8
47.	University of North Texas*	2.8
47.	University of Portland (OR)	2.8
47.	Univ. of Wisconsin–Platteville*	2.8

Best in the Specialties ▶

(*Public)

AEROSPACE/AERONAUTICAL/ASTRONAUTICAL
1. Embry-Riddle Aeronautical U. (FL)
2. United States Air Force Acad. (CO)*
3. Embry-Riddle Aeronautical U.–Prescott (AZ)
4. Cal. Poly. State U.–San Luis Obispo*

CHEMICAL
1. Rose-Hulman Inst. of Tech. (IN)
2. Bucknell University (PA)

CIVIL
1. Rose-Hulman Inst. of Tech. (IN)
2. United States Military Academy (NY)*
3. Cal. Poly. State U.–San Luis Obispo*

4. Bucknell University (PA)
5. Harvey Mudd College (CA)

COMPUTER ENGINEERING
1. Rose-Hulman Inst. of Tech. (IN)
2. San Jose State University (CA)*
2. United States Air Force Acad. (CO)*
4. Cal. Poly. State U.–San Luis Obispo*
4. Harvey Mudd College (CA)

ELECTRICAL/ELECTRONIC/COMMUNICATIONS
1. Rose-Hulman Inst. of Tech. (IN)
2. Cal. Poly. State U.–San Luis Obispo*

3. United States Air Force Acad. (CO)*
4. Harvey Mudd College (CA)
5. Bucknell University (PA)
5. Cooper Union (NY)

INDUSTRIAL/MANUFACTURING
1. Cal. Poly. State U.–San Luis Obispo*

MECHANICAL
1. Rose-Hulman Inst. of Tech. (IN)
2. Cal. Poly. State U.–San Luis Obispo*
3. United States Military Academy (NY)*
4. Harvey Mudd College (CA)
4. Kettering University (MI)

Note: Peer assessment survey conducted by Ipsos Public Affairs. To be ranked in a specialty, a school may have either a program or course offerings in that subject area; ABET accreditation of that program is not needed. Based on a recommendation by the American Society for Engineering Education, a few schools with small doctoral programs are part of the bachelor's and master's category. Extended rankings can be found at usnews.com/bestcolleges.

BEST ENGINEERING PROGRAMS

Top Programs ▶ AT ENGINEERING SCHOOLS WHOSE HIGHEST DEGREE IS A DOCTORATE

Rank	School (State) (*Public)	Peer assessment score (5.0=highest)
1.	Massachusetts Inst. of Technology	4.8
2.	Stanford University (CA)	4.7
3.	University of California–Berkeley*	4.6
4.	California Institute of Technology	4.5
4.	Georgia Institute of Technology*	4.5
6.	U. of Illinois–Urbana-Champaign*	4.4
7.	Carnegie Mellon University (PA)	4.3
7.	University of Michigan–Ann Arbor*	4.3
9.	Purdue Univ.–West Lafayette (IN)*	4.2
10.	Cornell University (NY)	4.1
10.	Princeton University (NJ)	4.1
10.	University of Texas–Austin*	4.1
13.	Northwestern University (IL)	4.0
14.	Univ. of Wisconsin–Madison*	3.9
15.	Johns Hopkins University (MD)	3.8
15.	Texas A&M Univ.–College Station*	3.8
15.	Virginia Tech*	3.8
18.	Duke University (NC)	3.7
18.	Pennsylvania State U.–Univ. Park*	3.7
18.	Rice University (TX)	3.7
18.	Univ. of California–Los Angeles*	3.7
22.	Columbia University (NY)	3.6
22.	Univ. of Maryland–College Park*	3.6
22.	Univ. of Minnesota–Twin Cities*	3.6

Rank	School (State) (*Public)	Peer assessment score (5.0=highest)
22.	University of Washington*	3.6
26.	Harvard University (MA)	3.5
26.	Ohio State University–Columbus*	3.5
26.	Univ. of California–San Diego*	3.5
26.	University of Pennsylvania	3.5
26.	Univ. of Southern California	3.5
31.	North Carolina State U.–Raleigh*	3.4
31.	Rensselaer Polytechnic Inst. (NY)	3.4
31.	University of California–Davis*	3.4
31.	University of Virginia*	3.4
31.	Vanderbilt University (TN)	3.4
36.	Univ. of California–Santa Barbara*	3.3
36.	University of Colorado–Boulder*	3.3
36.	University of Florida*	3.3
36.	University of Notre Dame (IN)	3.3
36.	Yale University (CT)	3.3
41.	Arizona State University–Tempe*	3.2
41.	Brown University (RI)	3.2
41.	Case Western Reserve Univ. (OH)	3.2
41.	Colorado School of Mines*	3.2
41.	Iowa State University*	3.2
41.	Lehigh University (PA)	3.2
41.	Washington University in St. Louis	3.2
48.	Dartmouth College (NH)	3.1

Rank	School (State) (*Public)	Peer assessment score (5.0=highest)
48.	Michigan State University*	3.1
48.	University of California–Irvine*	3.1
51.	Auburn University (AL)*	3.0
51.	Boston University	3.0
51.	Northeastern University (MA)	3.0
51.	Rutgers, St. U. of N.J.–New Brunswick*	3.0
51.	University of Arizona*	3.0
51.	University of Pittsburgh*	3.0
57.	Clemson University (SC)*	2.9
57.	Drexel University (PA)	2.9
57.	Tufts University (MA)	2.9
57.	University of Delaware*	2.9
57.	University of Iowa*	2.9
57.	Univ. of Massachusetts–Amherst*	2.9
57.	University of Tennessee*	2.9
57.	University of Utah*	2.9
65.	Illinois Institute of Technology	2.8
65.	Missouri Univ. of Science & Tech.*	2.8
65.	New York University	2.8
65.	Rochester Inst. of Technology (NY)	2.8
65.	University at Buffalo–SUNY*	2.8
65.	University of Rochester (NY)	2.8
65.	Washington State University*	2.8
65.	Worcester Polytechnic Inst. (MA)	2.8

SPECIAL OFFER $25 OFF
Initial Application Fee.
Apply at www.allsaintsuniversity.org
**Enter coupon code:
US2014**

ALL SAINTS UNIVERSITY
MEDICAL SCHOOL

WHY AN **ALL SAINTS MD**?

- Graduate in as little as 3 years & 4 months.
- Recognized by WHO, MCC, IMED, ECFMG.
- Small class size with student focused learning.
- 2 state of the art campuses on the islands of Dominica & St. Vincent.

- Affordable and competitive tuition. (compared to other medical schools)
- Academic scholarships up to 50% off your tuition.
- Residents in Canada, USA, Europe, Africa and the Middle East
- Diverse population of students.

APPLY ONLINE AT
www.allsaintsuniversity.org

Canada Office:
5145 Steeles Avenue West
Entrance C, Suite 223
Toronto, Ontario M9L 1R5, Canada
Tel: 416-743-9222

US Office:
1727 S. Indiana Ave.
Suite # 2
Chicago, IL 60616
Tel: 312-583-1034

STUDY MEDICINE IN THE CARIBBEAN

BECOME A DOC IN THE U.S.

4 Year MD Program
Financial Aid
Student Dorms
Modern Campus
Friendly Tuition ($5,900/semester)
U.S. Clinical Rotations
72% USMLE Passing Rate

RECEIVE $25 OFF
Initial application fee, Enter code: UNBCG
Visit us online cmumed.org

888 877 4268
info@cmumed.org
www.CMUMED.org

Best in the Specialties ▶ AT ENGINEERING SCHOOLS WHOSE HIGHEST DEGREE IS A DOCTORATE

(*Public)

AEROSPACE/AERONAUTICAL/ASTRONAUTICAL
1. Massachusetts Inst. of Technology
2. University of Michigan–Ann Arbor*
3. Georgia Institute of Technology*
4. California Institute of Technology
5. Purdue Univ.–West Lafayette (IN)*

BIOLOGICAL/AGRICULTURAL
1. Purdue Univ.–West Lafayette (IN)*
1. U. of Illinois–Urbana-Champaign*
3. Texas A&M Univ.–College Station*
4. Iowa State University*
5. University of Florida*

BIOMEDICAL/BIOMEDICAL ENGINEERING
1. Johns Hopkins University (MD)
2. Duke University (NC)
3. Massachusetts Inst. of Technology
4. Georgia Institute of Technology*
5. Rice University (TX)

CHEMICAL
1. Massachusetts Inst. of Technology
2. University of California–Berkeley*
3. Univ. of Minnesota–Twin Cities*
4. Stanford University (CA)
5. Univ. of Wisconsin–Madison*

CIVIL
1. U. of Illinois–Urbana-Champaign*
2. Georgia Institute of Technology*
3. University of California–Berkeley*
4. Purdue Univ.–West Lafayette (IN)*
5. Stanford University (CA)

COMPUTER ENGINEERING
1. Massachusetts Inst. of Technology
2. Stanford University (CA)
3. Carnegie Mellon University (PA)
4. University of California–Berkeley*
5. U. of Illinois–Urbana-Champaign*

ELECTRICAL/ELECTRONIC/COMMUNICATIONS
1. Massachusetts Inst. of Technology
2. Stanford University (CA)
3. University of California–Berkeley*
4. U. of Illinois–Urbana-Champaign*
5. University of Michigan–Ann Arbor*

ENGINEERING SCIENCE/ENGINEERING PHYSICS
1. U. of Illinois–Urbana-Champaign*
2. Massachusetts Inst. of Technology
2. Stanford University (CA)
2. University of California–Berkeley*
5. Harvard University (MA)
5. Virginia Tech*

ENVIRONMENTAL/ENVIRONMENTAL HEALTH
1. Stanford University (CA)
1. University of California–Berkeley*
3. Georgia Institute of Technology*
4. University of Michigan–Ann Arbor*
5. U. of Illinois–Urbana-Champaign*

INDUSTRIAL/MANUFACTURING
1. Georgia Institute of Technology*
2. University of Michigan–Ann Arbor*
3. University of California–Berkeley*
4. Purdue Univ.–West Lafayette (IN)*
5. Northwestern University (IL)

MATERIALS
1. Massachusetts Inst. of Technology
2. U. of Illinois–Urbana-Champaign*
3. University of California–Berkeley*
4. Stanford University (CA)
4. University of Michigan–Ann Arbor*

MECHANICAL
1. Massachusetts Inst. of Technology
2. Stanford University (CA)
3. University of Michigan–Ann Arbor*
4. University of California–Berkeley*
5. Georgia Institute of Technology*

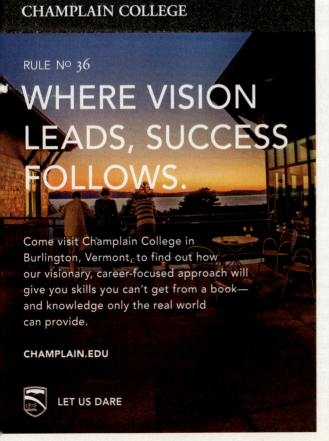

CHAMPLAIN COLLEGE

RULE No 36

WHERE VISION LEADS, SUCCESS FOLLOWS.

Come visit Champlain College in Burlington, Vermont, to find out how our visionary, career-focused approach will give you skills you can't get from a book—and knowledge only the real world can provide.

CHAMPLAIN.EDU

LET US DARE

THE SECRET TO SUCCESS?
CATCH THE BRAIN AT ITS MOST ADAPTABLE.

Before age 25, human brains are particularly malleable—it's a once-in-a-lifetime opportunity to help train young brains for future success.

From the *New York Times* bestselling **Change Your Brain, Change Your Life** series comes a new program designed to help teens and young adults:

- improve academic performance
- manage conditions like ADD, ADHD and depression
- enhance memory and sharpen attention

CHANGE YOUR BRAIN / CHANGE YOUR life BEFORE 25

Train the Developing Mind for a Lifetime of Success

Jesse Payne, Ed.D.
Foreword By **Daniel Amen, M.D.,** *New York Times* bestselling author of *Change Your Brain, Change Your Life*

GET IT TODAY!

HARLEQUIN

brain25.com

"This book is filled with practical wisdom to help boost the most important part of you, your developing brain."
—*New York Times* bestselling author Dr. Mark Hyman

The Virtual Path

GETTING YOUR DEGREE FROM A DISTANCE

By **ARLENE WEINTRAUB**

Cynthia Stebbins loved her first two years at Colorado State University in Fort Collins, but after she got married in May of 2013, she found herself in a bind. Her husband, Cody, who is in the Air Force, was transferred to Scott Air Force Base in Illinois. Stebbins, 21, didn't want to have a long-distance marriage, so she decided to finish her bachelor's the 21st-century way: online. She'll graduate next spring from CSU with a degree in psychology.

Although Stebbins sometimes misses the campus social life, she's confident she's getting just as rich an academic experience as when she was trekking from one classroom to another. All of the lectures she "attends" are prerecorded, so the work can be handled on her own time. But she still has to meet strict deadlines and must participate in online discussions with her classmates. One-on-one help from professors is easily available by phone or Skype conference. "The experience is similar to what it is on campus, and I appreciate that," she says. "I don't want my education to be different just because I've chosen this program."

Whether you're an undergrad like Stebbins who faces logistical challenges or a working student who wants a degree without giving up

that salary, attending class virtually is an increasingly viable and popular option. Some universities allow students to earn their degrees entirely online (ranking, Page 128); a growing number are dabbling by letting students earn a handful of credits virtually. Nearly 460 schools offered online bachelor's courses in 2013, according to the latest annual survey by Babson College in Massachusetts, which has been tracking the spread of online education for 11 years. And the proportion of all students, undergraduate and graduate, taking at least one online course hit a high of 33.5 percent in 2013, Babson reports.

A few bumps. Moving the lecture hall onto the Web isn't always a smooth process. In April, the high-profile pilot program Semester Online was discontinued; a consortium of 10 universities (Boston College, Northwestern University and Washington University in St. Louis among them) had tried offering for-credit virtual classes to their own students and to attendees of other colleges interested in transferring the credits. The organizer, Landover, Maryland-based 2U, declined to comment but said in a written statement that it found "significant challenges related to the complexities of a consortium structure." The firm contin-

ues to provide software solutions to individual schools developing online offerings, and in October will be working on its first online undergraduate degree program with Simmons College School of Nursing and Health Sciences in Boston.

But the end of Semester Online shouldn't be viewed as a sign that digitally enhanced learning is a bad idea, argues Elliott Visconsi, an English and law professor and chief academic digital officer at consortium member University of Notre Dame, which offered four undergrad courses online during the pilot. Instructors found the teaching "to be exciting and interesting, but new and unfamiliar," he says. While there were problems associated with students moving in and out of classes and seeking credits from other participating schools, he says, Notre Dame is now pursuing a variety of digital initiatives. "Our primary goal is to give our students a world-class

platforms as well as email. Traditional class members often are just not inclined to reach out to professors outside of class hours.

Some of Gilpin's students these days are military servicemen deployed to Afghanistan; indeed, online education is fast becoming a popular route to advancement for both active duty folks and veterans (Page 133). Some programs give veterans credit for time spent serving the country. "More often than not, veterans have had training and experience that could be equivalent to some of our introductory-level courses," says Christine Shakespeare, assistant vice president of continuing and professional education at Pace University. Those who apply to the Pace program submit information outlining their work and any courses they took in the military, which is then evaluated by faculty to determine how many credits they should receive.

A blend. The popularity of online study is starting to influence the in-class experience, inspiring a move to "blended learning," says Robert Lue, a professor and director of life sciences education at Harvard. Several professors there have adopted tools that were developed by HarvardX, the university's online-learning initiative that includes a collaboration with the Massachusetts Institute of Technology to offer non-credit massive open online courses, or MOOCs, from more than 30 colleges and universities, at no charge, to anyone interested.

These materials – a video that draws upon cooking techniques to teach basic physics concepts, for instance – are adapted to create what Lue calls the equivalent of "textbooks on steroids." Web-based videos might be interspersed with, say, quizzes or discussion questions that help students assess how well they're absorbing the material. What is becoming clear, says Lue, who is also the faculty director of HarvardX, is that "students find the digital media far more engaging. Time spent on tasks is greater. And the likelihood they'll actually do the preclass work is significantly greater."

Lately, interest has trickled down to collegebound high-schoolers, who are earning credits and even using free MOOCs to check out schools. ●

undergraduate experience," he says, "and certainly digital tools and strategies are part of that puzzle."

The best online courses are organized much like their offline counterparts, with video lectures and group projects accomplished via videoconference and shared documents, exams and opportunities to huddle with professors. When shopping for the best place to complete your bachelor's, check to make sure programs you're considering are fully accredited. You should also consider whether it's important to be able to do all your coursework on your own time – meaning the classes are "asynchronous" – or if you would enjoy synchronous classes that allow you to interact with professors and other students in real time.

And weigh your level of motivation. Most online learners agree that this mode of study is far from easy. You certainly have to be disciplined, particularly if you have a full-time day job. "It's

not like going to class a couple of times a week and then doing your homework," says Bettina Smith, 42, a financial services professional in Oakland, California, who entered Pace's online program in computer forensics in 2013 with the goal of finishing her bachelor's.

Arizona State University associate professor Dawn Gilpin, who teaches an online course in social media, says Web-based teaching platforms have become so sophisticated that students can easily be as engaged as they are in physical classes, if not more so.

"We have software that allows them to do a final presentation that's highly visual," with slides and narration, Gilpin says. They also are able to give and receive feedback from other students. And even though Gilpin typically has 200 students in each online class, she finds that she interacts individually with a larger percentage of those students than ones on campus, via Twitter chats and other social media

PHOTO ILLUSTRATION BY WILLIAM DUKE FOR USN&WR

The Measure of What You Know

A COMPETENCY-BASED PROGRAM LETS YOU ADVANCE WHEN YOU'RE READY

By **CATHIE GANDEL**

Craig Kilgo, 29, has a job as a project manager for the Department of Defense and a 6-month-old son. What he doesn't yet have is an undergrad degree. The obstacles: time and money. His solution? Sign up for a new breed of online bachelor's program that doesn't require regular class time and lets him move rapidly through material he already knows.

Kilgo, who lives in Arlington, Virginia, started out as a student at Cornell University after high school but found an Ivy League degree too costly. Now he's pursuing a bachelor's degree in Information Science and Technology in the "competency-based" Flexible Option offered by the University of Wisconsin–Milwaukee. A traditional college program requires the student to "sit in the classroom and go through the material in lock step with everybody else," says Aaron Brower, interim chancellor at the University of Wisconsin Extension, who is overseeing the Flexible Option. A regular online program allows you to go at your own pace, "but you still have to do A, B and C in sequence," he says.

In a competency-based program such as UW's, "you can skip A and B and go right to C, providing you can pass the assessments that show you have mastered the content of A and B," says Brower. And the assessments are not a matter of passing or failing. Instead, "You pass, or you haven't yet passed," he says. Students are assigned an academic success coach who, if they don't succeed the first time, can provide extra guidance and supplemental materials.

President Obama has encouraged innovation in competency-based education, arguing for the need to award credits based not on "seat time" but on mastering information. "If you're learning the material faster, you can finish faster," he said in a speech last year. Kilgo's experience on the job allowed him to breeze through a required Basics of Web Design course in just three weeks, for example, instead of the typical 16 weeks. The program is "perfect for me," he says. "I can leverage everything I've learned in my career while earning a degree from an accredited university."

And at less cost. At UW, students can take one course for $900 or choose the "all you can learn" option: as many courses as you care to squeeze in over a three-month "subscription" period for $2,250. Kilgo came into the program with about 63 credits from several schools under his belt. He completed five UW courses in each of his first two subscription periods and hopes to finish after two more three-month periods. Total cost: $9,000.

Besides the information science and technology bachelor's, UW offers Flex-

ISTOCKPHOTO

ible Option degrees in diagnostic imaging and nursing, a certificate in professional and technical communication, and an associate degree in arts and sciences. Other competency-based online degree programs include those at Western Governors University (business, teaching, information technology and health) and at Northern Arizona University (small business administration, computer information technology and liberal arts).

On campus, Purdue University in

West Lafayette, Indiana, is launching a competency-oriented grand experiment this fall known as the Purdue Polytechnic Institute, a collaboration between the colleges of technology, liberal arts, education and science. "Students will be immersed in project-based environments," says Jeffrey Evans, a professor and Purdue Poly-

> **SOME 300 STUDENTS ARE PARTICIPATING IN THE UW PROGRAM. BUT ALMOST 10,000 HAVE SHOWN INTEREST.**

technic faculty fellow. They will work on mastering a skill set or course material at their own pace, guided by a team of faculty mentors. Competencies will be demonstrated as they are acquired, rather than in a final exam, and will be documented by digital badges or certificates. "These can be stored and viewed by anyone given access, such as a potential employer," notes Evans, who says the belief at Purdue is that this model has the potential to be a game-changer in higher education.

Industry seems to be enthusiastic about the idea. At Southern New Hampshire University, for example,

employers such as McDonald's, Anthem BlueCross BlueShield and the city of Memphis have collaborated in creating the College for America, a program in which employees can learn marketable skills or a bachelor's degree in communications or healthcare management at their own pace for $2,500 per year. Some employers will reimburse the tuition. In the UW program, nurses who have families, are busy in the community and are working full-time can "seamlessly move forward in their careers while bringing new ideas to their workplace," says Mary Beth Kingston, executive vice president and chief nursing officer of Milwaukee-based Aurora Health Care. "It's win-win."

Demand for the UW Flexible Option has certainly been impressive, says Brower. While the university is getting it fully up to speed, nearly 300 students are participating in the program. But almost 10,000 people have so far shown interest. ●

THE RIGHT PEOPLE. THE RIGHT TOOLS. THE RIGHT PLACE. IT'S HOW WE MAKE HANDS-ON RESEARCH HAPPEN.*

*As early as your freshman year.

THIS IS SIU.

SIU Southern Illinois University
CARBONDALE

Best Online Degree Programs

When we surveyed colleges in 2013 about their online options, 283 schools reported having bachelor's programs that can be completed without showing up in person for class (though attendance may be required for testing, orientations or support services). These offerings, typically degree-completion programs aimed at working adults and community college grads, were evaluated on their success at engaging students, the credentials of their faculty and the services and technologies made available remotely. The table below features some of the most significant ranking factors, such as the prevalence of faculty holding a Ph.D., class size, the percentages of new entrants who stayed enrolled and later graduated, and the debt load of recent graduates. The top half of programs are listed here. Ranks are determined by the institutions' overall unrounded scores, which have been rounded below for display purposes. To see the rest of the ranked online bachelor's programs and to read the full methodology, visit usnews. com/online. You'll also find detail-rich profile pages for each of the schools and (in case you want to plan ahead) rankings of online graduate degree programs in business, engineering, nursing and more.

(*Public, **For profit)

Rank	School	Overall program score	Average peer assessment score (5.0=highest)	'13 total program enrollment	'13 - '14 tuition[1]	'13 full-time faculty with Ph.D.	'13 average class size	'13 retention rate	'13 graduation rate[2]	% graduates with debt ('13)	Average debt of graduates ('13)
1.	Central Michigan University*	100	3.0	1,346	$370	73%	19	80%	94%	47%	$9,757
1.	SUNY College of Technology–Delhi*	100	3.1	700	$245	45%	16	68%	49%	N/A	N/A
3.	Pace University (NY)	96	3.1	250	$570	82%	10	70%	45%	15%	$49,113
3.	Pennsylvania State University–World Campus*	96	4.0	3,845	$518	58%	26	70%	36%	N/A	N/A
5.	Embry-Riddle Aeronautical University (FL)	93	3.5	16,222	$325	45%	22	74%	21%	2%	$3,763
5.	University of Florida*	93	3.6	785	$812	89%	530	91%	63%	60%	$18,159
7.	Daytona State College (FL)*	92	2.8	1,560	$560	79%	18	79%	62%	33%	$25,500
7.	University of Alabama–Huntsville*	92	3.0	47	$427	100%	32	87%	89%	N/A	N/A
9.	Arizona State University*	91	3.7	7,437	$460	73%	46	80%	54%	72%	$22,087
9.	Indiana Univ.-Purdue Univ.–Fort Wayne*	91	3.5	359	$328	69%	N/A	60%	N/A	N/A	N/A
9.	University of Illinois–Chicago*	91	3.3	139	$572	36%	18	95%	84%	57%	$12,524
9.	University of Wisconsin–Superior*	91	3.8	484	$305	33%	10	62%	21%	N/A	N/A
13.	St. John's University (NY)	90	3.3	35	$1,215	88%	18	64%	15%	86%	$37,354
13.	University of Denver	90	3.2	50	$529	100%	11	91%	62%	33%	N/A
13.	University of La Verne (CA)	90	2.4	236	$570	94%	15	76%	53%	77%	$23,775
16.	Colorado State University–Global Campus*	89	3.1	5,776	$350	N/A	15	84%	46%	67%	$21,560
16.	Fort Hays State University (KS)*	89	2.9	7,165	$182	51%	23	73%[3]	65%	15%	$23,568
18.	Bellevue University (NE)	88	2.3	6,387	$375	44%	17	87%	58%	62%	$17,472
18.	Marist College (NY)	88	3.4	254	$600	77%	19	83%	71%	77%	$21,600
20.	University of Nebraska–Omaha*	86	3.4	2,529	$464	87%	20	57%	32%	59%	$31,152
21.	Palm Beach Atlantic University (FL)	85	2.8	80	$430	55%	10	82%	44%	75%	$27,654
21.	Regent University (VA)	85	3.0	2,612	$395	94%	16	60%	30%	72%	$35,435
21.	Washington State University*	85	3.3	2,114	$1,223	73%	22	62%	45%	73%	$25,441
21.	Wayne State University (MI)*	85	3.5	60	$884	100%	23	100%	N/A	N/A	N/A
25.	Savannah College of Art and Design (GA)	84	3.3	748	$732	32%	15	68%[3]	42%	90%	$51,044
25.	University of Wisconsin–Milwaukee*	84	3.7	285	$337	97%	23	65%	N/A	74%	$21,457
25.	University of Wisconsin–Platteville*	84	3.8	608	$370	71%	18	N/A	N/A	25%	N/A
28.	Loyola University Chicago	83	3.2	161	$615	56%	23	93%	N/A	55%	$17,168
29.	Ball State University (IN)*	82	3.7	284	$488	72%	N/A	41%	32%	70%	$29,679
29.	University of Bridgeport (CT)	82	2.2	127	$490	17%	14	81%	63%	N/A	N/A
31.	University of Illinois–Springfield*	81	3.6	920	$353	77%	N/A	68%	36%	N/A	N/A
32.	Loyola University New Orleans	80	1.9	43	$506	100%	16	90%[3]	78%	N/A	N/A
32.	Westfield State University (MA)*	80	1.9	176	$260	85%	20	88%	60%	75%	$14,500
34.	American Public University System (WV)**	79	3.1	61,776	$250	43%	16	52%	N/A	N/A	$6,267
34.	University of Missouri–St. Louis*	79	3.4	109	$445	50%	22	91%	68%	45%	$4,621
34.	Western Carolina University (NC)*	79	1.9	1,367	$468	76%	N/A	84%	58%	36%	$9,075
37.	California Baptist University	78	2.7	1,665	$495	72%	15	75%	N/A	72%	$35,211
37.	Drexel University (PA)	78	3.6	2,370	$707	59%	19	76%	26%	68%	$33,207
37.	McKendree University (IL)	78	1.9	81	$340	87%	11	N/A	N/A	60%	$2,500
37.	Norwich University (VT)	78	2.8	264	$350	100%	9	67%	17%[4]	0%	$0
41.	Brandman University (CA)	76	1.7	1,097	$500	100%	18	85%	52%	76%	$25,980
41.	California State University–Chico*	76	3.2	206	$619	73%	28	77%[3]	57%	N/A	N/A

Note: Key to footnotes, Page 133.

Discover where AP® can take you.

The Advanced Placement Program® helps students stand out in college admissions, earn college credit and placement, explore interests and discover new passions, and build the skills and knowledge they need to be successful in college.

Visit **exploreap.org**

© 2014 The College Board.
14b-9479

CollegeBoard

(*Public, **For profit)

Rank	School	Overall program score	Average peer assessment score (5.0=highest)	'13 total program enrollment	'13 - '14 tuition[1]	'13 full-time faculty with Ph.D.	'13 average class size	'13 retention rate	'13 graduation rate[2]	% graduates with debt ('13)	Average debt of graduates ('13)
41.	Sam Houston State University (TX)*	76	3.1	596	$195	94%	29	82%	N/A	60%	$27,028
41.	University of South Carolina–Aiken*	76	2.2	31	$768	44%	13	92%	67%	92%	$14,278
41.	Wright State University (OH)*	76	1.9	120	N/A	80%	25	75%	30%[4]	5%	$2,500
46.	City University of Seattle	75	2.2	766	$402	55%	12	81%[3]	33%	N/A	N/A
46.	Oregon State University*	75	1.9	2,492	$191	61%	25	72%	33%	75%	$26,584
48.	Charter Oak State College (CT)*	74	1.7	1,873	$339	N/A	11	85%	54%	N/A	N/A
48.	DePaul University (IL)	74	3.7	235	$550	87%	18	N/A	N/A	N/A	N/A
48.	Florida Institute of Technology	74	3.1	3,299	$495	71%	19	66%	10%	66%	$44,422
48.	Granite State College (NH)*	74	1.5	1,832	$305	33%	14	76%	47%	80%	$24,157
48.	University of Missouri*	74	3.4	811	$274	64%	15	N/A	N/A	N/A	N/A
48.	University of Northern Colorado*	74	2.9	314	$370	19%	17	100%	67%	N/A	N/A
48.	Utah State University*	74	3.7	1,584	$275	64%	60	N/A	N/A	32%	$23,439
48.	Wilmington University (DE)	74	1.9	4,380	$330	62%	15	74%	53%	52%	N/A
56.	Charleston Southern University (SC)	72	2.0	297	$490	47%	10	77%	46%[4]	N/A	$30,417
56.	Concordia University–St. Paul (MN)	72	2.6	722	$420	38%	N/A	80%[3]	63%	82%	$23,517
56.	George Washington University (DC)	72	3.6	233	$552	N/A	17	67%	55%	13%	$29,888
56.	Kaplan University (IA)**	72	2.0	35,372	$371	49%	20	65%	16%	88%	$31,915
56.	University of Arkansas*	72	1.9	202	$212	80%	12	N/A	61%	N/A	N/A
61.	St. Joseph's University (PA)	71	2.0	76	$500	90%	12	80%[3]	N/A	N/A	N/A
61.	University of Maine–Augusta*	71	2.0	3,253	$525	38%	20	78%	16%	76%	$23,339
61.	Upper Iowa University	71	2.6	1,424	$378	63%	13	56%	29%	N/A	N/A
61.	Western Illinois University*	71	2.3	754	$280	74%	35	61%[3]	47%	48%	$22,980
65.	Graceland University (IA)	70	1.4	143	$495	50%	15	78%	77%	65%	$29,864
65.	Lamar University (TX)*	70	2.1	1,151	$208	87%	30	75%	N/A	9%	$30,303
65.	Regis University (CO)	70	2.6	1,671	$460	6%	8	91%	34%	N/A	N/A
65.	Southeast Missouri State University*	70	2.7	565	$375	73%	24	76%	47%	N/A	N/A
69.	Columbia College (MO)	69	2.4	21,295	$245	67%	20	75%	45%	65%	$28,385
69.	Old Dominion University (VA)*	69	3.1	3,542	$285	83%	36	82%	50%	N/A	N/A
69.	University of Massachusetts–Dartmouth*	69	3.7	110	$304	N/A	13	73%	N/A	N/A	N/A
69.	University of Minnesota–Crookston*	69	2.8	1,048	$385	32%	24	72%	38%	72%	$21,682
69.	University of West Georgia*	69	1.6	419	$256	56%	35	90%	N/A	90%	$19,313
74.	Belhaven University (MS)	68	1.7	380	$375	54%	12	80%	42%	72%	$7,619
74.	Troy University (AL)*	68	3.1	6,900	$308	60%	28	62%	12%	N/A	N/A
74.	University of Nebraska–Lincoln*	68	3.6	34	$501	98%	40	N/A	N/A	50%	$32,500
77.	Eastern Kentucky University*	67	1.9	1,207	$395	67%	22	70%	9%	74%	$21,859
77.	Georgia College & State University*	67	2.7	22	$227	67%	15	N/A	N/A	N/A	N/A

MIKE ECKELKAMP FOR USN&WR

Bettina Smith is getting an online degree in computer forensics from No. 3 Pace.

Note: Key to footnotes, Page 133.

Shop the U.S. News Store

U.S. News
College Compass

- See complete U.S. News rankings
- Expanded data on nearly 1,800 schools
- Compare schools side-by-side
- Detailed financial aid information
- See entering student SAT scores and GPAs.

visit **usnews.com/store**

U.S. News publications also available on Kindle, iPad and Nook

(*Public, **For profit)

Rank	School	Overall program score	Average peer assessment score (5.0=highest)	'13 total program enrollment	'13 - '14 tuition[1]	'13 full-time faculty with Ph.D.	'13 average class size	'13 retention rate	'13 graduation rate[2]	% graduates with debt ('13)	Average debt of graduates ('13)
77.	John Brown University (AR)	67	1.6	99	$460	57%	14	68%	N/A	80%	$12,566
77.	Wheeling Jesuit University (WV)	67	1.9	106	$330	55%	20	81%	21%[4]	63%	$23,797
81.	Holy Apostles College and Seminary (CT)	66	1.9	N/A	$430	100%	10	N/A	N/A	N/A	N/A
81.	Lawrence Technological University (MI)	66	1.5	62	$944	N/A	12	90%	29%	N/A	N/A
81.	Malone University (OH)	66	1.4	114	$485	71%	16	N/A	61%	94%	$20,527
81.	North Carolina State University–Raleigh*	66	3.6	82	$408	100%	25	N/A	N/A	N/A	N/A
81.	Peirce College (PA)	66	1.1	1,343	$533	63%	17	68%	38%	85%	$22,784
81.	University of St. Francis (IL)	66	1.5	508	$585	50%	14	82%	45%	58%	$25,028
87.	California State University–Dominguez Hills*	65	2.8	814	N/A	90%	18	81%	29%	N/A	N/A
87.	Huntington University (IN)	65	1.5	30	$398	58%	6	N/A	100%	100%	$21,400
87.	National University (CA)	65	1.9	N/A	$336	64%	20	60%	37%	75%	$29,474
87.	University of Alabama–Birmingham*	65	3.1	146	$666	50%	34	N/A	N/A	N/A	N/A
87.	University of Cincinnati*	65	3.4	1,658	$396	N/A	N/A	70%	51%	72%	$29,521
87.	Western Kentucky University*	65	3.1	2,502	$445	N/A	22	N/A	N/A	67%	$17,613
93.	DeVry University (IL)**	64	2.2	27,263	$609	31%	27	81%	14%	81%	$42,576
93.	Duquesne University (PA)	64	3.3	N/A	$661	91%	16	N/A	N/A	N/A	N/A
93.	Limestone College (SC)	64	1.0	1,275	$376	66%	16	68%	35%	97%	$34,513
93.	St. Louis University	64	3.1	490	$610	65%	15	N/A	N/A	69%	$39,594
97.	Champlain College (VT)	63	1.7	1,052	$590	N/A	20	77%[3]	33%	N/A	N/A
97.	Concordia University Chicago	63	1.9	65	$475	67%	9	N/A	N/A	N/A	N/A
97.	Lee University (TN)	63	1.5	716	$175	100%	N/A	83%	N/A	71%	$2,614
97.	Linfield College (OR)	63	1.9	805	$435	60%	19	85%	61%	N/A	N/A
97.	Northern Arizona University*	63	3.5	3,100	$755	N/A	29	67%[3]	28%	67%	$22,208
102.	Benedictine University (IL)	62	1.9	56	$546	N/A	11	83%	36%[4]	82%	$30,045
102.	Florida State University*	62	3.5	494	$686	N/A	25	N/A	N/A	62%	$25,055
102.	Herzing University (WI)**	62	1.2	1,979	$500	29%	18	N/A	N/A	87%	$25,665
102.	Minot State University (ND)*	62	2.4	N/A	$201	57%	18	N/A	N/A	N/A	N/A
102.	University of Maine–Fort Kent*	62	1.8	198	$552	54%	20	71%	47%	48%	$13,948
102.	University of West Florida*	62	3.2	416	$552	N/A	23	67%[3]	12%	N/A	N/A
108.	Neumann University (PA)	61	1.9	N/A	$547	100%	N/A	83%	48%	N/A	N/A
108.	Northwestern State University of Louisiana*	61	1.2	3,890	$1,217	55%	29	67%	N/A	65%	$19,181
108.	Post University (CT)**	61	1.2	9,776	$550	50%	12	100%	30%	N/A	N/A
108.	University of Toledo (OH)*	61	1.9	1,324	$327	43%	15	56%[3]	36%	86%	$37,692
112.	Chatham University (PA)	60	1.9	122	$759	67%	14	30%	100%	73%	$16,163
112.	Madonna University (MI)	60	1.0	108	N/A	67%	N/A	97%	75%	N/A	N/A
112.	Monroe College (NY)**	60	1.9	498	$514	N/A	19	54%	45%	86%	$23,294
112.	Southwestern College (KS)	60	1.0	1,875	$411	55%	12	73%	45%	N/A	N/A
112.	University of Southern Indiana*	60	1.4	440	$318	67%	N/A	56%	51%	N/A	N/A

University of Florida, tied at No. 5

CHARLIE ARCHAMBAULT FOR USN&WR

Rank	School	Overall program score	Average peer assessment score (5.0=highest)	'13 total program enrollment	'13 - '14 tuition[1]	'13 full-time faculty with Ph.D.	'13 average class size	'13 retention rate	'13 graduation rate[2]	% graduates with debt ('13)	Average debt of graduates ('13)
117.	Bay State College (MA)	59	1.0	42	$375	40%	18	80%	N/A	N/A	N/A
117.	Rogers State University (OK)*	59	1.6	445	$333	70%	23	67%	28%	75%	N/A
117.	Toccoa Falls College (GA)	59	1.2	N/A	$285	59%	15	68%[3]	N/A	45%	$10,935
120.	Fitchburg State University (MA)*	58	1.9	86	N/A	67%	14	N/A	50%[4]	N/A	N/A
120.	Lynn University (FL)	58	1.6	183	$345	N/A	11	58%	49%	N/A	N/A
120.	New Mexico State University*	58	3.2	N/A	$764	81%	29	N/A	N/A	N/A	N/A
120.	University of West Alabama*	58	2.4	N/A	N/A	73%	20	N/A	N/A	N/A	N/A
124.	Florida International University*	57	3.0	N/A	$333	N/A	10	N/A	N/A	N/A	N/A
124.	Lindenwood University (MO)	57	1.7	N/A	$471	44%	15	N/A	N/A	N/A	N/A
124.	University of Tennessee–Martin*	57	3.3	605	N/A	74%	18	N/A	N/A	N/A	N/A
127.	Arkansas Tech University*	56	1.7	N/A	$398	61%	21	N/A	N/A	N/A	N/A
127.	Eastern University (PA)	56	1.9	N/A	$495	100%	8	N/A	50%	85%	$23,632
127.	Ohio State University–Columbus*	56	1.9	177	$387	27%	150	74%	99%	N/A	N/A
127.	Sacred Heart University (CT)	56	1.9	349	$515	N/A	12	N/A	N/A	36%	$10,371
131.	Baldwin Wallace University (OH)	55	1.2	13	$615	63%	N/A	N/A	N/A	N/A	N/A
131.	Bismarck State College (ND)*	55	1.2	321	$232	N/A	24	N/A	N/A	N/A	N/A
131.	Ferris State University (MI)*	55	2.0	811	$365	61%	20	N/A	N/A	N/A	N/A
131.	Montreat College (NC)	55	1.9	26	$395	100%	10	N/A	N/A	N/A	N/A
131.	Siena Heights University (MI)	55	1.2	1,059	$440	67%	19	N/A	84%	73%	$19,064
131.	University of Houston–Victoria*	55	1.7	N/A	$518	100%	48	N/A	N/A	N/A	N/A
131.	University of North Dakota*	55	3.5	N/A	$257	N/A	22	N/A	N/A	N/A	N/A
138.	Berkeley College (NY)**	54	1.6	1,383	$487	95%	22	79%	23%	92%	$33,131
138.	University of Texas of the Permian Basin*	54	1.8	484	$519	70%	N/A	N/A	N/A	N/A	N/A
138.	Valley City State University (ND)*	54	1.9	N/A	$430	24%	11	N/A	N/A	N/A	N/A
141.	Davenport University (MI)	53	1.8	1,796	$574	29%	18	N/A	N/A	N/A	N/A
141.	East Carolina University (NC)*	53	3.3	N/A	$611	N/A	17	N/A	N/A	N/A	N/A
141.	Liberty University (VA)	53	2.6	39,319	$340	N/A	21	60%	11%	74%	$27,300
141.	Nicholls State University (LA)*	53	1.9	122	$250	69%	N/A	N/A	N/A	N/A	N/A
141.	Our Lady of the Lake University (TX)	53	1.7	N/A	$290	100%	N/A	N/A	N/A	N/A	N/A
141.	Sullivan University (KY)**	53	1.2	268	$292	44%	19	N/A	N/A	76%	$22,508
141.	William Woods University (MO)	53	1.9	10	$200	50%	N/A	N/A	N/A	N/A	N/A

(*Public, **For profit)

► Best Online Bachelor's Programs For Veterans

Which programs offer military veterans and active-duty service members the best distance education? To ensure academic quality, all schools included in this ranking had to first qualify for a spot in the overall online ranking, above. They had to be housed in a regionally accredited institution and were judged on a multitude of factors, including program reputation, faculty credentials, high student graduation rate and low graduate debt load. Secondly, because veterans and active-duty members often wish to take full advantage of federal benefits designed to make their course credits more portable and less expensive, programs included in the veterans-focused rankings also had to offer at least one credit-granting course listed in the Defense Activity for Non-Traditional Education Support (DANTES) Nationally Accredited Distance Learning Programs Catalog. They had to belong to an institution that is a member of the Servicemembers Opportunity Colleges (SOC) Consortium, is certified for the GI Bill, and participates in the Yellow Ribbon Program or charges in-state tuition – that can be fully covered by the GI Bill – to all veterans applying from out of state. Programs that met all criteria were then numerically ranked in descending order based on their ranking in Best Online Bachelor's Programs.

Rank School (State)

1. Central Michigan University*
2. Embry-Riddle Aeronautical University–Worldwide (FL)
3. Arizona State University*
3. Indiana University-Purdue University–Fort Wayne*
5. Fort Hays State University (KS)*
6. Bellevue University (NE)
7. University of Nebraska–Omaha*

8. Regent University (VA)
8. Washington State University*
10. University of Wisconsin–Platteville*
11. Ball State University (IN)*
12. Western Carolina University (NC)*
13. California Baptist University
13. Drexel University (PA)
15. Brandman University (CA)
15. Sam Houston State University (TX)*

17. City University of Seattle
18. Charter Oak State College (CT)*
18. University of Missouri*
20. Kaplan University (IA)**
21. University of Maine–Augusta*
21. Upper Iowa University
21. Western Illinois University*
24. Regis University (CO)
25. Columbia College (MO)
25. Old Dominion University (VA)*

27. Belhaven University (MS)
27. Troy University (AL)*
27. University of Nebraska–Lincoln*
30. Eastern Kentucky University*
31. Peirce College (PA)
32. National University (CA)
32. University of Alabama–Birmingham*
32. University of Cincinnati*
32. Western Kentucky University*

N/A=Data were not provided by the school. **1.** Tuition is reported on a per-credit-hour basis. Out-of-state tuition is listed for public institutions. **2.** Displayed here for standardization are four-year graduation rates. **3.** 2012 retention rate is published in place of a 2013 rate when the latter was not reported by school. **4.** Three-year graduation rate is published when a four-year rate was not reported by school. Ranked online degree programs may be less than four years old.

Getting In

Haverford College in Pennsylvania

BRETT ZIEGLER FOR USN&WR

Education with purpose. An incredible array of academic choices. Small, engaging classes that provide real-world skills. Experiential opportunities to put those skills into practice. A campus life enriched by arts and athletics. A beautiful suburban campus just minutes from Boston. A close-knit community. **That's Merrimack College.**

Merrimack

North Andover, MA | www.merrimack.edu

National Liberal Arts Colleges ▶

School (State) (*Public)	SAT/ACT 25th-75th percentile ('13)	Average high school GPA ('13)	Freshmen in top 25% of class ('13)
Agnes Scott College (GA)	1010-1310[2]	3.6	67%
Albion College (MI)	22-28	3.5	52%
Allegheny College (PA)	1070-1290	3.7	70%
Alma College (MI)	22-27[3]	3.5	53%
Augustana College (IL)	22-27[9]	3.2	51%
Austin College (TX)	1100-1330[3]	3.5	74%
Beloit College (WI)	24-30[2]	3.4	61%
Berea College (KY)	22-26	3.4	73%
Berry College (GA)	24-29	3.7	65%
Birmingham-Southern College (AL)	23-27	3.5	56%
Calvin College (MI)	23-29[2]	3.7	55%
Carthage College (WI)	21-27	3.3	44%
Central College (IA)	21-26	3.5	53%
Coe College (IA)	23-28	3.6	61%
College of Idaho	21-27	3.6	55%
College of St. Benedict (MN)	23-28	3.7	70%
College of Wooster (OH)	25-30	3.7	73%[5]
College of the Atlantic (ME)	1110-1330[2]	3.6	69%
Concordia College–Moorhead (MN)	22-28	3.6	62%
Cornell College (IA)	23-29	3.5	69%
DePauw University (IN)	25-29	3.8	78%[5]
Doane College (NE)	21-26[3]	3.5	46%
Drew University (NJ)	990-1220	3.4	62%[5]
Earlham College (IN)	1150-1340[2]	3.5	60%[5]
Furman University (SC)	1130-1340[2]	N/A	76%[5]
Georgetown College (KY)	20-25	3.3	48%
Gordon College (MA)	1015-1292[3]	3.6	55%[5]
Goucher College (MD)	1010-1280[2]	3.2	58%[5]
Grove City College (PA)	1079-1334	3.7	65%
Gustavus Adolphus College (MN)	24-30[2]	3.6	67%
Hanover College (IN)	1000-1200	3.7	66%
Hobart and William Smith Colleges (NY)	1120-1290[2]	3.4	63%[5]
Hope College (MI)	24-29	3.7	64%
Houghton College (NY)	980-1235	3.5	61%
Illinois Wesleyan University	25-30	3.7	77%
Juniata College (PA)	1040-1260[9]	3.7	73%
Kalamazoo College (MI)	25-30	3.6	80%[5]
Knox College (IL)	25-30[2]	N/A	59%
Lake Forest College (IL)	23-28[2]	3.6	59%[5]
Linfield College (OR)	980-1200	3.7	72%[4]
Luther College (IA)	23-29	3.7	56%
McDaniel College (MD)	1000-1210[3]	3.5	52%
Millsaps College (MS)	23-28	3.6	59%
Muhlenberg College (PA)	1140-1340[2]	3.3	73%[5]
Nebraska Wesleyan University	22-26	3.7	50%
Oglethorpe University (GA)	1030-1240	3.5	55%
Ohio Wesleyan University	22-27[2]	3.4	55%[5]
Ouachita Baptist University (AR)	21-27	3.5	53%
Presbyterian College (SC)	1000-1210[2]	3.5	61%
Ripon College (WI)	21-28	3.4	53%
Roanoke College (VA)	980-1190	3.4	42%
Salem College (NC)	1000-1200	3.8	75%
Sarah Lawrence College (NY)	1150-1350[2]	3.6	66%[5]
Sewanee–University of the South (TN)	26-30[2]	3.6	72%[5]
Siena College (NY)	1000-1200[3]	3.4	58%
Simpson College (IA)	21-27	N/A	58%
Soka University of America (CA)	1080-1340	3.8	79%[5]
Southwestern University (TX)	1055-1280	N/A	72%
St. Anselm College (NH)	1060-1230[2]	3.2	58%

School (State) (*Public)	SAT/ACT 25th-75th percentile ('13)	Average high school GPA ('13)	Freshmen in top 25% of class ('13)
St. John's University (MN)	23-28	3.5	52%
St. Lawrence University (NY)	1120-1310[2]	3.5	71%[5]
St. Mary's College (IN)	23-28[3]	3.6	57%[5]
St. Mary's College of Maryland*	1070-1310[3]	N/A	64%[5]
St. Michael's College (VT)	1060-1290[2]	3.4	54%
St. Norbert College (WI)	22-27	3.5	56%
Stonehill College (MA)	1030-1230[2]	3.3	69%
Susquehanna University (PA)	1020-1230[2]	3.3	52%
Thomas Aquinas College (CA)	1160-1340	3.8	50%[5]
Transylvania University (KY)	24-30	3.7	75%
Trinity College (CT)	1150-1330	N/A	59%[5]
University of Minnesota–Morris*	23-28[3]	3.6	59%
University of North Carolina–Asheville*	1100-1290	3.4	54%
University of Puget Sound (WA)	1120-1330[3]	N/A	51%[5]
Virginia Military Institute*	1050-1250	3.6	48%
Wabash College (IN)	1028-1250	3.7	72%
Wartburg College (IA)	21-26[3]	3.5	55%
Washington College (MD)	1050-1280[2]	3.5	62%[5]
Washington and Jefferson College (PA)	1050-1230[2]	3.3	70%
Westminster College (MO)	21-27	3.4	50%
Westmont College (CA)	1060-1310	3.8	66%
Wheaton College (MA)	1110-1340[2]	3.3	70%[5]
Willamette University (OR)	1080-1310	3.7	75%
William Jewell College (MO)	22-28[2]	3.7	58%
Wisconsin Lutheran College	21-27	3.4	44%
Wittenberg University (OH)	23-28[2]	3.4	49%
Wofford College (SC)	1080-1260	3.5	77%

Regional Universities ▶

School (State) (*Public)	SAT/ACT 25th-75th percentile ('13)	Average high school GPA ('13)	Freshmen in top 25% of class ('13)
NORTH			
Arcadia University (PA)	1000-1178	3.6	62%
Assumption College (MA)	1020-1215[2]	3.3	40%
Bentley University (MA)	1140-1310[3]	N/A	75%[5]
Bryant University (RI)	1050-1220[2]	3.3	50%[5]
Canisius College (NY)	980-1200	3.5	53%
CUNY–Baruch College*	1130-1330	3.2	70%
CUNY–Brooklyn College*	980-1170	3.3	50%[5]
CUNY–Hunter College*	1070-1270	3.3	56%
CUNY–Queens College*	1030-1220	N/A	65%
Emerson College (MA)	1140-1320	3.6	68%[5]
Emmanuel College (MA)	1000-1180[2]	3.6	54%[5]
Ithaca College (NY)	1080-1270[2]	N/A	63%[5]
Le Moyne College (NY)	980-1170[3]	3.4	51%
Loyola University Maryland	1100-1268[2]	3.4	67%[5]
Marist College (NY)	1090-1260[9]	3.3	64%[5]
Nazareth College (NY)	1020-1180[2]	3.3	65%
New York Institute of Technology	1020-1220	3.5	52%[5]
Providence College (RI)	1050-1260[2]	3.4	67%[5]
Quinnipiac University (CT)	1000-1190	3.4	66%
Ramapo College of New Jersey*	990-1200	3.2	52%[5]
Richard Stockton Col. of New Jersey*	980-1170	N/A	60%
Rochester Institute of Technology (NY)	1110-1320	N/A	64%
Rowan University (NJ)*	1000-1230	3.5	63%[4]
Salisbury University (MD)*	1080-1230[9]	3.7	59%[5]
Salve Regina University (RI)	1020-1190[2]	3.0	45%
Simmons College (MA)	1040-1250[3]	3.4	61%[5]
St. Joseph's University (PA)	1020-1200[2]	3.5	52%[5]

Note: Key to footnotes, Page 80.

 **RESOURCES FOR EDUCATORS**

U.S. News offers resources that enable high school educators to help their students prepare for college!

 College-Planning Tools You Can Share With Your Students

 Special Offers For Students and Their Parents

 Bulk Order Discounts

Schools or organizations interested in purchasing our Best Colleges 2015 guidebooks inquire at:

1-800-836-6397 or email us at **booksales@usnews.com**

To learn more, visit www.usnews.com/school-resources

Regional Universities (continued)

School (State) (*Public)	SAT/ACT 25th–75th percentile ('13)	Average high school GPA ('13)	Freshmen in top 25% of class ('13)
SUNY College–Oneonta*	1020-1180	3.6	58%[5]
SUNY Institute of Tech.–Utica/Rome*	1010-1160	3.4	45%
SUNY–New Paltz*	1030-1220	3.6	70%[5]
SUNY–Oswego*	1040-1180[3]	3.5	55%
Towson University (MD)*	990-1170	3.6	49%
University of Scranton (PA)	1030-1210	3.4	59%[5]
Wagner College (NY)	1050-1270[2]	3.6	73%
West Chester Univ. of Pennsylvania*	1020-1190	3.5	45%
SOUTH			
Appalachian State University (NC)*	1050-1220	4.0	58%
Bellarmine University (KY)	22-27	3.5	54%[5]
Belmont University (TN)	24-29	3.6	61%
Christian Brothers University (TN)	21-27	3.7	60%

School (State) (*Public)	SAT/ACT 25th–75th percentile ('13)	Average high school GPA ('13)	Freshmen in top 25% of class ('13)
Christopher Newport University (VA)*	1070-1250[2]	3.7	53%
College of Charleston (SC)*	1070-1250[3]	3.9	60%
Elon University (NC)	1120-1320	3.9	63%[5]
Embry-Riddle Aeronautical Univ. (FL)	980-1230[2]	3.5	52%[5]
Harding University (AR)	22-28	3.6	50%
James Madison University (VA)*	1050-1240	N/A	45%
Kennesaw State University (GA)*	990-1170	3.2	53%[5]
Loyola University New Orleans	22-28	3.5	43%[5]
Mercer University (GA)	1080-1270	3.7	72%
Rollins College (FL)	1100-1290[2]	3.2	67%[5]
Samford University (AL)	23-28	3.7	59%[5]
Spring Hill College (AL)	21-27	3.4	45%
Stetson University (FL)	1070-1270[2]	3.9	61%
Union University (TN)	22-29[3]	3.7	62%
University of Mary Washington (VA)*	1010-1210	3.5	50%

JIM LO SCALZO FOR USN&WR

Purdue University in Indiana

School (State) (*Public)	SAT/ACT 25th-75th percentile ('13)	Average high school GPA ('13)	Freshmen in top 25% of class ('13)
Univ. of North Carolina–Wilmington*	1110-1270	4.0	64%
University of North Florida*	1080-1230	3.7	56%
University of North Georgia*	1010-1190	3.5	70%[5]
William Carey University (MS)	21-28[3]	N/A	59%
MIDWEST			
Aquinas College (MI)	21-26	3.5	45%
Augsburg College (MN)	20-24[3]	3.1	43%
Baker University (KS)	21-26	3.5	42%
Baldwin Wallace University (OH)	21-27[2]	3.5	50%
Bethel University (MN)	22-28	3.5	60%
Bradley University (IL)	23-28	3.7	64%
Capital University (OH)	21-27[3]	3.4	45%
Carroll University (WI)	21-26	N/A	58%
College of St. Scholastica (MN)	21-26	3.5	55%
Concordia University (NE)	21-27	3.6	43%
Concordia University Wisconsin	20-25[3]	N/A	43%
Creighton University (NE)	24-30	3.8	68%
Dominican University (IL)	20-24	3.6	48%
Drake University (IA)	25-30	3.7	73%
Drury University (MO)	22-28	3.7	59%
Elmhurst College (IL)	21-26	3.3	47%
Franciscan Univ. of Steubenville (OH)	23-28	3.7	52%[5]
Grand Valley State University (MI)*	21-26	3.5	50%
Hamline University (MN)	21-27	3.5	47%
Indiana Wesleyan University	21-27	3.6	57%
John Carroll University (OH)	22-27	3.5	51%[5]
Kettering University (MI)	25-30	3.7	66%
Lawrence Technological Univ. (MI)	22-29	3.4	52%
Lewis University (IL)	21-26	3.4	47%
McKendree University (IL)	20-25	3.4	43%
Missouri State University*	21-26	3.6	53%
North Central College (IL)	22-27	3.6	57%
Olivet Nazarene University (IL)	20-26	3.5	48%
Otterbein University (OH)	22-27[3]	3.5	54%
Rockhurst University (MO)	23-28	3.7	53%
St. Catherine University (MN)	22-26	3.6	52%
Truman State University (MO)*	25-30	3.8	80%
University of Detroit Mercy	21-26[3]	3.5	55%
University of Evansville (IN)	23-29	3.7	66%
University of Findlay (OH)	20-25[3]	3.3	44%
University of Michigan–Dearborn*	22-27	N/A	57%
University of Minnesota–Duluth*	22-26	3.4	44%
University of Nebraska–Kearney*	20-25	3.4	41%
University of Northern Iowa*	20-24[3]	3.4	45%
University of St. Francis (IL)	21-25	3.4	46%
University of Wisconsin–Eau Claire*	22-26	N/A	51%
University of Wisconsin–La Crosse*	23-27	N/A	69%
Univ. of Wisconsin–Stevens Point*	21-25	3.5	45%
Valparaiso University (IN)	23-29	3.7	68%
Walsh University (OH)	20-25[3]	3.3	46%
Webster University (MO)	20-27	3.4	42%
Xavier University (OH)	23-27	3.6	54%[5]
WEST			
Abilene Christian University (TX)	21-27	3.6	57%
California Lutheran University	1010-1203	3.7	68%[5]
Gonzaga University (WA)	1100-1290	3.7	68%
LeTourneau University (TX)	1030-1300[2]	3.6	67%
Loyola Marymount University (CA)	1090-1300	3.7	57%[5]
Mills College (CA)	1040-1250	3.6	71%
Oklahoma Christian University	22-28	3.5	58%
Oklahoma City University	23-29	3.6	61%

School (State) (*Public)	SAT/ACT 25th-75th percentile ('13)	Average high school GPA ('13)	Freshmen in top 25% of class ('13)
Pacific Lutheran University (WA)	980-1220[3]	3.7	70%[5]
Point Loma Nazarene University (CA)	1040-1260	3.8	67%
Regis University (CO)	22-27[3]	3.5	56%
Seattle Pacific University	1030-1250	3.5	57%
Seattle University	1050-1260	3.6	62%[5]
St. Edward's University (TX)	1020-1220	N/A	54%
St. Mary's College of California	1010-1210	3.6	64%[5]
University of Dallas	1090-1330	N/A	68%[5]
University of Portland (OR)	1090-1300	3.6	70%
University of Redlands (CA)	1030-1230	3.7	65%
University of St. Thomas (TX)	1000-1210	3.6	54%
Western Washington University*	990-1220	3.4	50%
Westminster College (UT)	22-28	3.5	55%

Regional Colleges ▶

School (State) (*Public)	SAT/ACT 25th-75th percentile ('13)	Average high school GPA ('13)	Freshmen in top 25% of class ('13)
NORTH			
Elizabethtown College (PA)	1000-1230	N/A	65%
Lebanon Valley College (PA)	1000-1220[2]	N/A	74%
Messiah College (PA)	1030-1260	3.7	68%
Wentworth Institute of Tech. (MA)	1010-1210	3.1	40%
SOUTH			
Aquinas College (TN)	23-27	3.5	43%[5]
Asbury University (KY)	21-27	N/A	54%
Covenant College (GA)	1060-1280	3.6	55%[5]
Florida Southern College	1010-1180	3.6	56%[4]
High Point University (NC)	980-1170	3.1	51%[5]
John Brown University (AR)	23-29	3.7	65%
MIDWEST			
Augustana College (SD)	23-28	3.7	63%
Benedictine College (KS)	22-28[3]	3.5	46%
Cedarville University (OH)	24-29	3.6	61%
Clarke University (IA)	20-25[3]	3.5	46%
College of the Ozarks (MO)	20-25[3]	3.6	50%
Dordt College (IA)	21-28	3.5	44%
Marietta College (OH)	21-27[3]	N/A	59%
Millikin University (IL)	21-26	3.3	41%
Mount Mercy University (IA)	20-24	3.3	41%
Northwestern College (IA)	22-27	3.5	49%
Ohio Northern University	23-29	3.7	69%
WEST			
Carroll College (MT)	22-27	3.6	61%
Oklahoma Baptist University	21-27	3.6	58%

Methodology: To be eligible, national universities, liberal arts colleges, regional universities and regional colleges all had to be listed among the top three-quarters of their peer groups in the 2015 Best Colleges rankings. They had to admit a meaningful proportion of non-A students, as indicated by fall 2013 admissions data on SAT Critical Reading and Math or Composite ACT scores and high school class standing. The cutoffs were: The 75th percentile for the SAT had to be less than or equal to 1,350; the 25th percentile, greater than or equal to 980. The ACT composite range: less than or equal to 30 and greater than or equal to 20. The proportion of freshmen from the top 10 percent of their high school class had to be less than or equal to 50 percent (for national universities and liberal arts colleges only); for all schools, the proportion of freshmen from the top 25 percent of their high school class had to be less than or equal to 80 percent, and greater than or equal to 40 percent. Average freshman retention rates for all schools had to be greater than or equal to 75 percent. Average high school GPA itself was not used in the calculations identifying the A-plus schools. N/A means not available.

The Value of a Gap Year

TAKING TIME OFF AND PUTTING IT TO GOOD USE CAN MAKE YOU A BETTER STUDENT

By **MARGARET LOFTUS**

While most of her high school friends were cracking the books and tailgating at college football games last year, Macon Bianucci of Charleston, South Carolina, was deep in the African bush, rescuing injured and snared wildlife and learning how to track game. College was in her plans – just not quite yet. After being accepted at several top-tier schools the previous fall, the graduate of Ashley Hall, a private all-girls school, decided to defer her admission to Northwestern University in Evanston, Illinois. "I wanted a break from studying," she says. She also wanted to try living in Africa and decided this "was a good time to do it."

Long a rite of passage for affluent Brits, the so-called gap year – time spent traveling, volunteering or working between high school and college – is now really catching on among U.S. students. A survey by the American Gap Association, a nonprofit that accredits companies that coordinate these stints, found that enrollment in respondents' programs climbed 27 percent from 2012 to 2013. "We had 50 percent more participants than we anticipated. It's exceeded our wildest expectations," says Jim Zambrano, the CEO of First Abroad, a Boston-based gap-year company launched in 2013 after a sister company in the U.K. noticed a surge in interest from Americans. And colleges say they're seeing more requests for deferments. At Tufts University, for instance, the number of incoming students asking to take a gap year doubled over the last year.

Many students, like Bianucci, handle their own planning and logistics. But these days,

Macon Bianucci (above right) helps sedate an elephant at the Victoria Wildlife Trust in Zimbabwe. At Northwestern, right.

FROM LEFT: COURTESY OF MACON BIANUCCI; ISTOCKPHOTO; PETER HOFFMAN FOR USN&WR

there's a whole industry bidding for gap-year business, from the Pioneer Project, through which students learn sustainable living skills like beekeeping and blacksmithing on a North Carolina farm to Art History Abroad, which offers six-week courses in Italy. Even colleges, including Tufts, Princeton and the University of North Carolina, have developed their own service-based gap-year offerings. "We aren't creating demand," says Alan Solomont, dean of Tufts' Tisch College of Citizenship and Public Service. "We're responding to appetite."

Burnout is one of the top reasons students take a break, according to an independent study of 280 gap-year participants by education policy experts Karl Haigler and Rae Nelson, authors of "Gap Year, American Style: Journeys Toward Learning, Serving, and Self-Discovery." That was true for Kenneth Hubbell, now a Princeton junior from Anchorage, Alaska, who pushed himself to excel in high school, was active on the debate team and volunteered regularly. "I poured so much energy into it. At the end of four years, I was tired of being that person," he says. He hadn't considered a year off until he received a brochure about Princeton's Bridge Year Program with his acceptance materials. He spent the next year living with a host family in Peru, taking Spanish lessons and working on service projects, including building a community park and assembling and distributing basic water filters, which reinforced his ambition to become a chemical engineer.

Time to explore. Subjects in the Haigler and Nelson study also cited a desire to find out more about themselves, a luxury in today's hypercompetitive culture, says Kim Oppelt, a former school counselor, now community relations manager at education solutions provider Hobsons in Arlington, Virginia. High school students used to have the time to sample a variety of electives, she notes, but they're "now under pressure to take advanced courses in every subject for all four years of high school. This gives them little time to explore their true interests."

That a trend in stepping off the

academic treadmill emerges in the wake of the Great Recession is no coincidence. Students and their families increasingly "are looking for value. They're thinking, 'if I'm spending this much on college, I want every year to count,'" says AGA Executive Director Ethan Knight.

Recent Cornell University grad Wes Cornell says his self-designed gap year doing scientific research around the world certainly matured him and shaped his academic focus. In Costa Rica, he researched the health care of workers at coffee farms through Duke University's Organization for Tropical Studies and did a program on sustainable development and tropical ecology with the environmental study abroad organization the School for Field Stud-

He cites Haigler and Nelson data showing that roughly 90 percent of those who opt for a gap year are back in school within a year of completing it. One of the goals of AGA, he says, is to figure out how to make federal financial aid available to students to use for gap years so the experience isn't available only to the affluent.

For the masses. Gap years don't have to cost a fortune, Zambrano says. First Abroad offers everything from bare-bones bus tours of Cambodia (starting at $879) to volunteering at a monkey rehab center in South Africa (from $1,059). While many high-end programs offer "a lot of hand-holding," he says, First Abroad's "give you the tools to head out there." For instance, the "Absolute Oz Jobs" package, which

tionately self-paying," says Solomont. "We want to make sure students who need financial assistance aren't precluded, so we'll provide aid."

Inspired by the Franklin Project, an initiative of the Aspen Institute that promotes national service for all Americans, the program will place participants in service organizations domestically and internationally. After the service year, they'll continue to interact with each other on campus through meetings, workshops and other events.

Counselors typically encourage students weighing a year off to apply to college anyway, while resources are easily accessible, and defer acceptance if they decide to go for it. On the other hand, students who are unsure of their college plans (or readiness) may benefit from putting off applying.

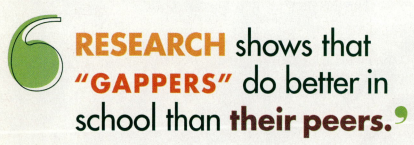

'RESEARCH shows that "GAPPERS" do better in school than their peers.'

ies. He interned with the Colombia Nature Conservancy in Cartagena, and did research on viral pathways at a summer camp program at the Weizmann Institute of Science in Israel. Once he got to Cornell, where he studied ecology and agriculture policy, he noticed a lot of classmates struggling to find themselves. "Having had time off, I was able to figure out what really interested me," he says.

Indeed, research has shown that "gappers" perform better in school than their peers. A 2011 study at Middlebury College conducted by its former dean of admissions Robert Clagett, now director of college counseling at a high school in Austin, Texas, found that students who had taken a year off had consistently higher GPAs than those who didn't. "A lot of our students say when they enter as freshman that they have a greater sense of purpose in their studies," says Princeton Bridge Year Director John Luria.

Still, parents often take some convincing. Many are "afraid of kids getting off the college path," says Knight.

costs around $1,000 (not including airfare or visa fees), features a weeklong orientation as a prelude to launching young people with a one-year visa into jobs in Australia.

Programs for pre-freshmen sponsored by colleges typically cover part or most of the expense. At UNC, participants in the Global Gap Year Fellowship are granted $7,500 to develop their own six-month service experience. Past fellows have taught English to high school students in China and worked in a medical clinic in Madagascar. Princeton's Bridge Year is a nine-month tuition-free program that places small groups at sites in five countries – Brazil, China, India, Peru and Senegal – to do service projects. "We give them a challenge that's going to push them outside their comfort zone but provides support," says Luria.

Kicking off in the fall of 2015, Tufts' 1+4 program is aimed at democratizing the gap experience. "When we looked at our own data in terms of students who have deferred admission to take a gap year on their own, they are dispropor-

"It may be the case that waiting to apply during the gap year could improve your chances of getting in the school of your choice," says Haigler, who once worked as a college counselor. "You might also find a school that is more suited to your evolving interest, the skills and knowledge you develop and what you learn about yourself." One student he and Nelson heard from in researching their book said that when she compared college application essays she wrote after a gap year to those she'd written in high school, "she didn't recognize herself" in the earlier essays.

Oppelt recommends that students who are serious about a year off talk to college counselors and teachers, as well as someone who works in the field they may be interested in, to develop a plan. Bianucci had a very clear idea of her goals and intended path from the outset. She arranged her gap year (funded by her parents) by combining three stints in Africa: a field guide course outside of Kruger National Park in South Africa, where she lived and trained to become a professional safari guide; an internship at a safari company in Arusha, Tanzania; and an internship at Victoria Falls Wildlife Trust in Zimbabwe. Her experiences, she says, strengthened her desire to major in environmental science and return to Africa one day. Meantime, she's really looking forward to school. ●

Meet the New SAT

HERE'S WHAT TO EXPECT FROM BOTH THE CURRENT VERSION AND THE OVERHAUL – ASSUMING YOU TAKE THE TEST

By **DARCY LEWIS**

f you're reading this book as a junior or senior, you're preparing to sit – or have already sat – for the familiar 2400-point SAT, complete with its fancy vocabulary words and mandatory essay. But members of the class of 2017 will begin prepping next year for a completely overhauled test. Last March, College Board President David Coleman announced major revisions to the fall 2015 PSAT and the 2016 SAT, saying the SAT had "become disconnected from the work of high schools."

The changes, which include going back to the old 1600-point composite score based on 800-point math and "evidence-based reading and writing" sections, and making the essay optional, are intended to better reflect the material

Jessa Stein (left), now a sophomore at Pitzer, opted to be judged on her other merits and held back her scores.

students are, or should be, learning in high school, as well as to improve the SAT's reliability as an indicator of how prepared applicants are to tackle college work. The current test is designed more to get at innate abilities; hence the "scholastic aptitude" of the SAT's original name. The new test "aligns with the Common Core curriculum standards," says Kasey Urquidez, dean of undergraduate admissions at the University of Arizona, who believes that the changes will be beneficial. Defenders of the current test think the change could weaken what they see as an effective tool to identify smart, capable students at academically weaker schools.

One big innovation is the way vocabulary will be handled; rather than test students' knowl-

DAVID WALTER BANKS FOR USN&WR

edge of obscure words out of context (like "cruciverbalist," "mellifluous," or "prestidigitation"), the focus will be on so-called high-utility words that appear in many disciplines, and they'll be used in a passage.

For example, after reading a selection about population density that uses the word "intense," test-takers might be asked which word has the closest meaning: "emotional," "concentrated," "brilliant" or "determined." Angel Perez, vice president and dean of admission at Pitzer College in Claremont, California, thinks this shift will let students from all backgrounds show what they really know, not just what they've memorized in prepping. Gary Gruber, who has written more than 40 test prep books, remains a fan of the way the current test gets students to tap their critical thinking skills and knowledge of Greek and Latin roots.

The new SAT will also require students to draw conclusions by

taking account of evidence, to revise and edit text, to analyze data and interpret graphs, and to solve the types of math problems most commonly seen in college courses and the workplace. It's no coincidence, observers say, that the new test will more closely resemble the ACT, which has been growing ever more popular. (The format of the ACT isn't changing, but the company plans to make the optional essay a more analytical exercise next year and break out new scores measuring job skills and proficiency in science, technology, engineering and math.) The redesigned SAT will last three hours, with an extra 50 minutes allotted for an optional essay in which students will analyze a passage and how the author builds an argument.

Another popular change is the elimination of the guessing penalty, the practice of subtracting points for wrong answers. "Being able to guess benefits those students who have some background knowledge," argues Rafael Figueroa, dean of college guidance at Albuquerque Academy in New Mexico.

Juniors and seniors, too, can take advantage of one much-heralded development that takes effect right away: the College Board's new partnership with the nonprofit Khan Academy to provide free online test prep materials. The idea is to start by taking a practice SAT, then master the material by watching in-depth explanatory videos and answering as many practice questions as you want. Starting with the 2015 PSAT, a personalized dashboard will allow students to track their progress.

Admissions deans and college counselors alike welcome the partnership as a possible step toward taming the over-

> **THE CHANGES ARE MEANT TO BETTER REFLECT WHAT STUDENTS ARE, OR SHOULD BE, LEARNING IN HIGH SCHOOL.**

wrought test prep culture that excludes many less savvy kids and those who are less affluent. "We want to assist students from all backgrounds – suburban, rural, inner city – so that they all have equal access to quality test prep materials, and now we can," says Mike Drish, director of admissions, recruitment and outreach at the University of Illinois at Urbana-Champaign.

Whichever test you take, devoting time to practice should increase your comfort level. But some experts advise against sitting for the real thing several times in an attempt to raise your score; some colleges may ask to see all your results – and they certainly want to see you engaged in more activities than test prep. Try to keep the testing in perspective, urges Stuart Schmill, dean of admissions at Massachusetts Institute of Technology. "There is some predictive value in SAT scores, but they are not determinative," he says. "Certainly there are students who get lower SAT scores who perform well here. And factors like persistence, resilience and organizational skills, which aren't measured on tests, also predict future academic success."

In fact, many fine colleges have concluded that they don't need test scores to make admissions decisions. Two that just joined the group this summer: Temple and Bryn Mawr in Pennsylvania. The National Center for Fair & Open Testing (fairtest.org) maintains a database of some 815 schools that are "test-optional" (applicants choose whether to submit scores) or that de-emphasize the tests. "I think taking standardized tests well is innate and doesn't necessarily show how well one will do in college or in life," says Jessa Stein of Denver, who chose not to send her SAT results of around 1800 to Pitzer College in California, her first choice. She wanted to be judged on her other strengths – teacher recommendations, essays and community service – and is now a sophomore at Pitzer.

Some test-optional schools later request scores for placement, merit aid consideration or internal research. "Many scores are extremely high and come accompanied by a note saying, 'I wanted you to judge me on what matters to me,'" says Martha Allman, dean of admissions at Wake Forest University, which asks freshmen to submit scores for research purposes only. That's "exactly what we like to hear." ●

The Rollout

● **Classes of 2015 and 2016:** Take current SAT; free Khan Academy prep materials available now at khanacademy.org/sat.

● **Class of 2017:** Take redesigned PSAT in October 2015 and redesigned SAT beginning in spring 2016; free Khan Academy prep materials available beginning in spring 2015.

Explore the U.S. News
Community College Directory

Search among nearly 950 schools across the U.S.

Visit: **usnews.com/education/community-colleges**

We Did It!

HOW EIGHT HIGH SCHOOL SENIORS MADE IT TO COLLEGE

By **CHRISTOPHER J. GEARON**

Want to know what the path to college acceptance will really be like? This past spring, U.S. News visited La Jolla High School in the San Diego Unified School District to ask several seniors who had recently gone through the process and were then weighing their options for lessons learned along the way – and their best tips for high school students just getting started.

Set in a postcard-perfect seaside community, La Jolla High is a comprehensive high school serving about 1,650 students. Because of the district's emphasis on school choice, students from an array of San Diego neighborhoods attend La Jolla. The school provides Advanced Placement courses in 21 curricular areas; 98 percent of students graduate, on average, and 70 percent go on to four-year colleges (about 22 percent go to a two-year school). White students comprise 56 percent of the student body, with Hispanics, Asians and African-Americans accounting for most of the rest.

Check out the varied routes that eight members of the class of 2014, now settling in for freshman year at a range of colleges nationwide, took to get there.

Photography by **BRETT ZEIGLER** *for USN&WR*

Eric Tims

▶ After applying to three dozen schools, Tims is attending Bowdoin College in Maine – and it wasn't even one of his original 35. A high school running back, Tims started with a list of 18 possibilities, a combination of Division I and III schools that included places where he would want to play football (Harvard, Brown, Dartmouth and Yale) and places he wouldn't (the University of Colorado-Boulder and the University of Oregon). But the calls just kept coming in from football coaches.

Tims got into half of the colleges he applied to (including Colorado, Oregon, George Fox University in Oregon, and the University of Redlands and the University of the Pacific in California), but no Ivies. Harvard's coach referred him to Bowdoin, and "after doing a lot of research, Bowdoin was a no-doubter," he says. He could see that it was a strong school academically and liked the sense of community: "It was like a big family." In addition to suiting up for the Polar Bears, Tims plans to major in computer science.

GPA: 3.3 unweighted
SAT/ACT scores: 620 math; 500 critical reading; 530 writing
Extracurrics: Football and working in customer service at an auto detailing firm
Essay: How he grew personally and as a student and focused on schoolwork while aiming for a possible college football career.
Big decision: He had an option to do a fifth-year program at a boarding school for another shot at the Ivies but wasn't interested.
Parental aid: "My parents helped me a lot." Mom kept him organized, and Dad talked to coaches.
Visits: He toured just three schools: Bowdoin, Redlands and Pomona. "Bowdoin looks classy," he says.
Do-over: After finding out that he was close to qualifying for an Ivy, he says he "would have worked harder" freshman and sophomore years.
Clincher: Some $46,000 of Bowdoin's annual $58,000 price tag is covered by grants and other financial aid.
Advice: Do research to find schools of interest, then reach out to faculty or coaches to establish relationships that can help you get in.

> **ESTABLISH RELATIONSHIPS WITH FACULTY OR COACHES.**
> –Eric Tims

Josephine Camacho

▶ Camacho grew up in "the projects of San Diego," she says, a 40-minute bus ride and a world away from La Jolla. A part of the history she shared with colleges was that she'd grown up in a community no stranger to "drugs, gangs and violence." Camacho wants to combine her love of working with older people and an interest in business. Determined to take advantage of all La Jolla had to offer, she pushed herself academically, concentrating on mastering English, Spanish and French and striving for good grades. And she resisted the temptation to transfer to a less rigorous school closer to home, as some kids who are bussed in from afar opt to do after a year or so.

For financial reasons, she applied to only California publics – eight Cal State campuses and the University of California schools at Berkeley, Santa Barbara and Santa Cruz. She got into seven and chose UC-Santa Cruz.

GPA: 3.4 unweighted

> **I PUT MY STORY OUT THERE ABOUT BEING FROM A TOUGH NEIGHBORHOOD.**
> –Josephine Camacho

SAT scores: 450 math; 400 critical reading; 410 writing

Extracurrics: Cheerleading; hostess and cashier at two restaurants, volunteer as a companion with the elderly, youth group leader and member of her church choir

Essay: "I put my story out there" about growing up in a tough neighborhood.

Incentive: She wants to finish what her mother, a Mexican university-trained accountant, had hoped to do – move out of the barrio and "achieve the American Dream."

Regret: Not studying for the SAT. "My classmates all had tutors and paid consultants." She didn't have the money or time.

The finances: The $34,000 in total costs will be covered by her father's unused GI Bill benefits and grants, some help from her parents and private scholarships.

Advice: It helped to keep separate folders on her laptop for each application, plus one quick-reference folder for PINs, passwords and usernames.

Luis Galvan

▶ Galvan is a first generation college student, headed to UC–Berkeley to study biochemistry in hopes of becoming a doctor. With money tight and his mother supporting seven, Galvan was greatly aided by a program called Reality Changers, a San Diego nonprofit that provides youth from disadvantaged backgrounds with academic support, leadership training and assistance with application costs. Galvan credits the program – which

also helped arrange an internship with a UC-San Diego researcher working on fortifying proteins against viruses – for his landing at Berkeley and becoming a Gates Millennium Scholar. The Gates program will cover tuition and living expenses for his undergrad degree and for graduate degrees in certain disciplines.

Galvan got into several California state schools but was turned down by Harvard, Yale, Princeton and the University of Pennsylvania.

GPA: 3.9 unweighted

SAT/ACT scores: 630 math; 570 critical reading; 510 writing/26 composite

Extracurrics: Fight Against Cancer Club; Reality Changers ambassador in the community, volunteer on community landscaping projects and at a soup kitchen

Essay: He drew an analogy between his internship and his performance as a student.

Big push: He figures he

> **WORK A LITTLE – ONE HOUR – EACH DAY ON YOUR ESSAYS.**
> –*Luis Galvan*

logged 350 hours applying to colleges and for the Gates program. With the help of Reality Changers, he reworked his Gates essay 20 times.

Regret: Putting the college essays off. Would have been better to "do a little – one hour – each day."

Heads-up: Found the College Scholarship Service Profile more challenging than the FAFSA.

Advice: Get involved in clubs freshman year so you can become an officer as a senior.

Emily Young

▶ An ACL injury led Young to become "fascinated" with biomedical engineering and biomechanics, she says. That interest led to an internship at a UC-San Diego biomechanics lab, where Young processed data and MRIs for research on rotator cuff problems. Young's interest,

internship and an early action application helped her get into the Massachusetts Institute of Technology, where she will study mechanical engineering with a concentration in biology and will also be playing lacrosse. She also got into Northeastern in Boston, and applied to UC–Berkeley, UCLA and

Georgetown but withdrew those applications once she heard from MIT. Young figures she put a solid month of work into the MIT application, including reading four years' worth of the university's admissions blogs, which offer advice and highlight accepted students.

GPA: 3.9 unweighted

ACT score: 33 composite

Extracurrics: Captain of field hockey and lacrosse teams, anti-bullying club; Girl Scouts, elementary-school lacrosse coach, internships in a biomechanics lab and as a pastry chef (which she suspects got admissions "to look at my application for a second longer")

Essay: She described the world she comes from, a family of "engineers, psychologists and doctors" who "inspire me to set high expectations for myself."

Smart start: Began considering schools at the end of her freshman year to improve her chances of being recruited for lacrosse.

Realization: "Coaches can't pull you through admissions" at schools like MIT.

Lesson: Her father, who hires fellows in his medical practice, showed her how little time it takes to screen an application (about 45 seconds).

Advice: It's better to focus on a couple of schools than to spread yourself thin by applying to 20. Also: "The first sentence of your essay needs to be incredible," and you need a strong finish.

Trevor Menders

▶ Menders got into his top choice, Columbia University, to major in dance (and perhaps in chemistry or math as well). He had great grades

THE FIRST SENTENCE OF YOUR ESSAY NEEDS TO BE INCREDIBLE.
–Emily Young

DOUBLE-CHECK AND TRIPLE-CHECK YOUR APPLICATION.
–Trevor Menders

FIND SCHOOLS THAT ARE A GOOD FIT INSTEAD OF FOCUSING ON REACHES.
–Hallie Bodenstab

SAT/ACT scores: 720 math; 730 critical reading; 720 writing
Extracurrics: Editor and writer on the school newspaper; city ballet preprofessional division and junior company, took classical voice lessons
Essay: Making good decisions after seeing friends making not-great ones
Noteworthy: He scored 2100 on the SAT after prepping with a $2 used study guide. The next time he worked math problems over a weekend before prom and scored 2170 the morning after it. "The prom helped me to relax."
Biggest surprise: Admissions officers are willing to work with you. "Reaching out to these people is scary, but it's really helpful."
Worked for him: Doing one application at a time, rather than completing a number simultaneously.
Campus visits: Showing up paid off. On the tours, he ruled out applying to Johns Hopkins University and Amherst College because he didn't get the right "vibes."
Advice: "Double- and triple-check your application." He had to amend his Columbia app after submitting it because he put links in the wrong place and one of seven essays under the wrong prompt.

and SAT scores, but "did very little community service, did not attend a multiweek overpriced SAT prep course, and did not destroy my junior year with all AP courses," he says. "Instead, I pursued what I wanted to do, took the courses I wanted to take at the appropriate level – and it all worked out."

He does have a clear passion for dance, though: He was a trainee with the City Ballet of San Diego for the season ending in May. Menders also got into Tulane University in New Orleans; Pomona College, UC–Berkeley and UC–Santa Barbara in California; and Vassar College and Skidmore College in New York, but not Harvard and Princeton. He was wait-listed at Duke and Vanderbilt.
GPA: 4.0 unweighted

Hallie Bodenstab

▶ Bodenstab's family hired an "expensive college counselor" to help guide the application process, leaving the budding engineer, who wants to go into sales, with mixed feelings. The counselor "kept me on track," which avoided fights with Mom and Dad, and helped her land a spot at her top choice – Lehigh University in Pennsylvania, where she is a third-generation legacy – by advising her to apply early decision.

But a downside, she feels, was that she ended up taking chemistry and AP English – a struggle – rather than regular senior English and an arts class; she loves and is active in the performing arts. She made sure she had applications ready to send to several other schools, including Lafayette College in Pennsylvania, the University of Puget Sound in Washington, and Carleton College in Minnesota, in case Lehigh said no.

In her application, she highlighted being a strong student with an interest in science balanced by a deep résumé in theater, music and art. She also pointed to a summer computer science internship at a local firm (an experience that dissuaded her from majoring in the subject).

GPA: 3.9 unweighted
ACT score: 32 composite
Extracurrics: Drama club; singing, kickboxing, working as a singing princess at kids' birthday parties ("It pays well, and I'm never bored.")
Essay: In response to a Lehigh prompt asking her to describe what her 1 million-hit YouTube video is about: "Using my voice against authority, and doing the right thing"
Helpful resource: "The Hidden Ivies" book. "A lot of good schools don't get enough credit."
Major selling point: She was attracted to Lehigh's "real engineering" program and

undergraduate research opportunities in the field.
Eye-opener: While several liberal arts schools tout their 3-2 programs – three years to get one bachelor's degree are followed by two years at a partner engineering school for a second bachelor's - it seemed too big a risk. Only

> **TRY LISTENING TO YOURSELF MORE THAN OTHERS.**
> –*Kurt Rustin*

the top students are likely to make the leap.
Stressor: Applying to one school while everybody else seems to be applying to 20.
Advice: Find schools that are a good fit instead of focusing your energy on reach schools.

Kurt Rustin

▶ Rustin is going to Northern Arizona University for mechanical engineering, hoping "to one day be an inventor" and hold his own patents. The track-and-field star and kayaker chose NAU for "its many labs that are about using your building skills, not just classroom smarts" because he considers himself to be more of a learn-by-doing kind of guy. "Learning on the job is definitely something I'm better at," he says.

Rustin didn't let ADHD and dyslexia hold him back, getting tutoring and extra help to succeed in AP and other challenging courses. He pursued his engineering interests by working as a hydroplane boat mechanical crew trainee and helping the Maritime Museum of San Diego build a full-scale replica of the Spanish galleon San Salvador. He also built La Jolla High's Latin de-

partment website. Rustin applied to 12 schools and got into almost all, including California Polytechnic State University, Purdue University in Indiana, Colorado School of Mines and the University of Colorado-Boulder; Bucknell University in Pennsylvania turned him down. He seriously considered CalPoly and Purdue, but had the impression they were

more classroom-based than "hands-on" NAU.
GPA: 3.8 unweighted
ACT score: 31 composite
Extracurrics: Track team captain, robotics team, La Jolla High garden club; flat water and ocean kayaking
Essay: Most of his schools didn't require an essay. Responding to one prompt asking what three items he would want with him if stranded in a foreign land, he explained why he would pick a machete, the American flag and a family photo album.
Research tip: On family road trips to areas he liked, he'd look up nearby colleges. "I'm a location guy" who thinks Flagstaff is beautiful.
Key realization: Learning shouldn't be a contest, so he didn't want to go to a school with "too much competition."
Great perk: While Rustin is an out-of-stater, he will pay tuition and fees of $14,000, about the halfway point between what in-state and out-of-state residents pay, thanks to being in one of the states in the Western Interstate Commission for Higher Education's Western Undergraduate Exchange.
Biggest surprise: "I only had to write two essays to apply to 12 colleges."
Advice: "Try to listen to yourself more than others."

Colleen Mellinger

▶ In hopes of becoming a university physics professor, Mellinger will study chemical physics at the University of California-San Diego. Although UCSD is close to home, Mellinger is still getting used to Southern California, having moved to La Jolla from Missouri before her senior year. She applied to schools where she would be able to do "a lot" of undergraduate research, beginning freshman year. "I also wanted to play college tennis," she says.

With interests ranging from sports to science competitions and community service, she highlighted herself as well-rounded in her applications. Mellinger also got into UC-Berkeley, Case Western Reserve in Cleveland and the University of Tulsa, and was wait-listed by Washington University in St. Louis, the University of Chicago and Johns Hopkins in Baltimore. She visited several colleges and "fell in love" with UCSD.

GPA: 3.9 unweighted

SAT/ACT scores: 760 math; 600 critical reading; 700 writing/30 composite

Extracurrics: Tennis team captain, archery team captain, Science Olympiad, technology club, academic team; volunteer with the Red Cross.

Essay: On being an inquisitive knowledge junkie: "Why? That's the question I always ask myself. Why do people

> ANYTHING YOU DO, WRITE IT DOWN, SO YOU REMEMBER LATER.
> *–Colleen Mellinger*

do what they do? Why do magnets stick together? Why does 'knife' start with a 'k'?"

Stressor: Applying to college at the same time she was getting adjusted to a new school and new part of the country.

Off the list: Stanford. After visiting, "I didn't think it would be a good fit for me. I wanted more balance between academics and social."

Do-over: Would have started earlier. "It all came so fast."

Need for structure: Applying to colleges is a lesson in organization. "I'm very much of a list person."

Notable step: She took the SAT four times and the ACT three times. Overkill? Her overall scores didn't rise by a lot, but she was pleased by her improvement in various sections.

Advice: Anything you do, write it down so you can remember later to reference it on applications. She had volunteered to help clean up in Joplin, Missouri, after a tornado hit, but nearly forgot to say so. ●

FIND THE BEST
ONLINE
PROGRAM
FOR YOU

Search nearly 1,000 online education programs to find one that best fits your needs.

Start your search today: **usnews.com/education/online-education**

Search for scholarships

🔒 **GETTING IN**

SAT prep 3:30

To-Do List
FOR YOUR COLLEGE SEARCH • By NED JOHNSON

✔ FRESHMAN YEAR

Get set for a great high school career. It's important to remember that what lies ahead is more than just a four-year audition for college. Still, it will help later to think now about what admissions staffers will look for three (short) years from now.

☐ **Seek advice and teacher feedback.**
Ask someone you trust to help you map out your classes. Grades are important in ninth grade. But rigor is key, too, so don't just go for easy A's. If you get a bad grade, accept it as constructive criticism, really read (or listen) to your teacher's comments and figure out how to do better.

☐ **Read voraciously.**
Books, newspapers, magazines, blogs – choose what engages you and remember to look up unfamiliar words.

☐ **Get involved.**
Not only will you develop talents and interests that will catch a college's eye, but also you'll find school is more fun when you have activities to look forward to.

✔ SOPHOMORE YEAR

Now that you're no longer a rookie, you'll want to focus on evolving as a learner. Besides studying the material, take note of what your teachers value and consider how you can learn more efficiently – and better.

Study!

☐ **Refine your route.**
Look ahead to which 11th and 12th grade courses you might be interested in taking and plan to work in any prerequisites.

☐ **Challenge yourself (wisely).**
Create a balanced schedule. You want to strive for the best possible grades, but overtaxing yourself is bound to be counterproductive.

Meet w/ guidance

☐ **Get some practice.**
Will you take the PSAT this year? You'll get a better sense of where you stand if you know what is on the test before you take it. Also, consider whether an SAT subject test makes sense in the spring. If you're enrolled in an AP or honors course now, the timing may be good. The College Board makes practice versions. Take at least one.

☐ **Put together a résumé.**
Start jotting down your hobbies, jobs and extracurricular activities. For now, it's just a way to keep track.

☐ **Make the most of your summer(s).**
Don't just hang out at the beach or pool. Work, volunteer, play sports or take a class. Find an activity that builds on a favorite subject or extracurricular interest.

✔ JUNIOR YEAR

Essays and testing and APs, oh my! Your grades, test scores and activities junior year constitute a big chunk of what colleges consider for admissions. Do your best in class and truly prepare for the tests you take. This can also be the time to step forward as a leader. Explore pursuits that interest you, not just because they'll look good on an application, but also because they'll help you grow as a person.

☐ **Ask for help.**
As Einstein allegedly put it, insanity is "doing the same thing over and over again and expecting different results." So if you feel stuck in your studies and in need of a breakthrough, ask teachers, parents or friends for help in finding a new approach.

☐ **Speak up in class.**
You will need to ask two junior-year teachers to write recommendations. They can't know you without hearing your thoughts, so make sure to contribute in class.

College list

DON'T GET  REJECTED

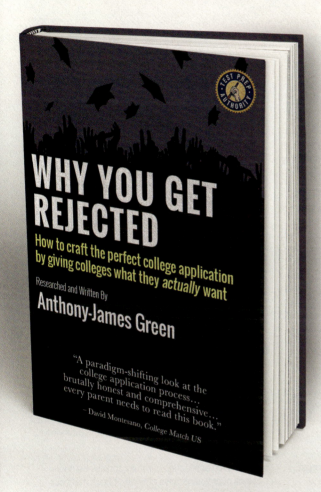

Why do colleges *actually* let you in?

Every year, droves of qualified applicants get rejected for failing to understand what colleges actually want.

Based on 10,000+ hours of experience with the world's most competitive applicants, this book will teach you:

- The 10 most-damning **college application mistakes**

- The 2 things every college <u>actually</u> wants from its applicants

- The step-by-step plan to make any admissions committee want you

- Over 115 tips, tricks, and strategies to perfect your application

"A 'no punches-pulled,' fast-paced guide through many of the realities, risks, and opportunities of the college application process."

- Eric Eisner,
Wall Street Journal's 2012 Education Innovator

From **Anthony-James Green**, the creator of:

TestPrepAuthority.com

DOWNLOAD A FREE COPY:
WhyYouGetRejected.com

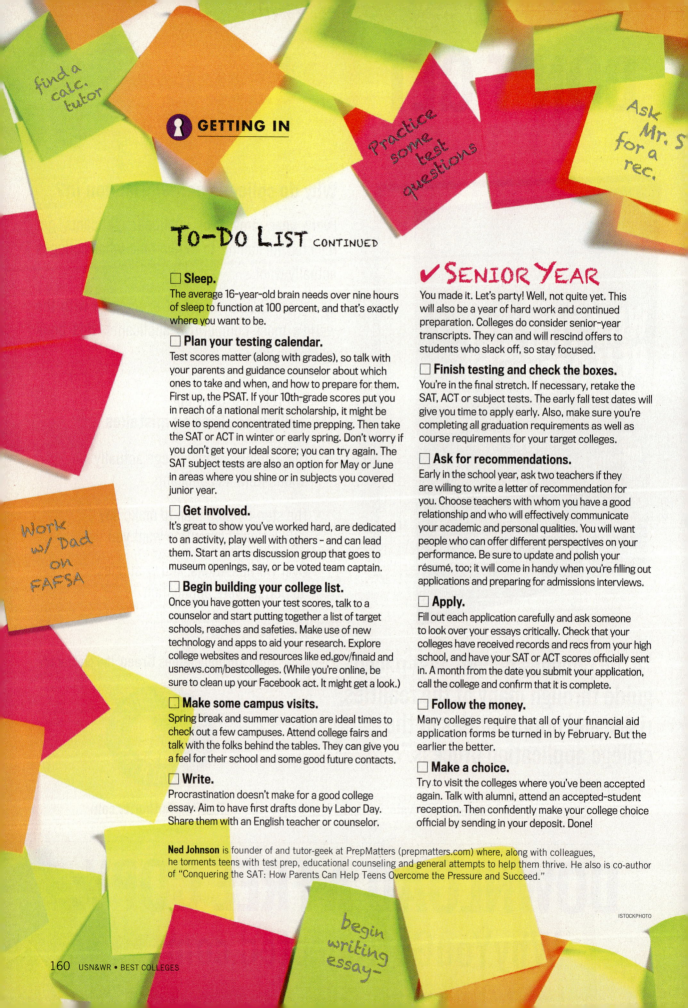

find a calc. tutor

Practice some test questions

Ask Mr. S for a rec.

TO-DO LIST CONTINUED

☐ Sleep.
The average 16-year-old brain needs over nine hours of sleep to function at 100 percent, and that's exactly where you want to be.

☐ Plan your testing calendar.
Test scores matter (along with grades), so talk with your parents and guidance counselor about which ones to take and when, and how to prepare for them. First up, the PSAT. If your 10th-grade scores put you in reach of a national merit scholarship, it might be wise to spend concentrated time prepping. Then take the SAT or ACT in winter or early spring. Don't worry if you don't get your ideal score; you can try again. The SAT subject tests are also an option for May or June in areas where you shine or in subjects you covered junior year.

☐ Get involved.
It's great to show you've worked hard, are dedicated to an activity, play well with others - and can lead them. Start an arts discussion group that goes to museum openings, say, or be voted team captain.

☐ Begin building your college list.
Once you have gotten your test scores, talk to a counselor and start putting together a list of target schools, reaches and safeties. Make use of new technology and apps to aid your research. Explore college websites and resources like ed.gov/finaid and usnews.com/bestcolleges. (While you're online, be sure to clean up your Facebook act. It might get a look.)

☐ Make some campus visits.
Spring break and summer vacation are ideal times to check out a few campuses. Attend college fairs and talk with the folks behind the tables. They can give you a feel for their school and some good future contacts.

☐ Write.
Procrastination doesn't make for a good college essay. Aim to have first drafts done by Labor Day. Share them with an English teacher or counselor.

Work w/ Dad on FAFSA

✔ SENIOR YEAR
You made it. Let's party! Well, not quite yet. This will also be a year of hard work and continued preparation. Colleges do consider senior-year transcripts. They can and will rescind offers to students who slack off, so stay focused.

☐ Finish testing and check the boxes.
You're in the final stretch. If necessary, retake the SAT, ACT or subject tests. The early fall test dates will give you time to apply early. Also, make sure you're completing all graduation requirements as well as course requirements for your target colleges.

☐ Ask for recommendations.
Early in the school year, ask two teachers if they are willing to write a letter of recommendation for you. Choose teachers with whom you have a good relationship and who will effectively communicate your academic and personal qualities. You will want people who can offer different perspectives on your performance. Be sure to update and polish your résumé, too; it will come in handy when you're filling out applications and preparing for admissions interviews.

☐ Apply.
Fill out each application carefully and ask someone to look over your essays critically. Check that your colleges have received records and recs from your high school, and have your SAT or ACT scores officially sent in. A month from the date you submit your application, call the college and confirm that it is complete.

☐ Follow the money.
Many colleges require that all of your financial aid application forms be turned in by February. But the earlier the better.

☐ Make a choice.
Try to visit the colleges where you've been accepted again. Talk with alumni, attend an accepted-student reception. Then confidently make your college choice official by sending in your deposit. Done!

Ned Johnson is founder of and tutor-geek at PrepMatters (prepmatters.com) where, along with colleagues, he torments teens with test prep, educational counseling and general attempts to help them thrive. He also is co-author of "Conquering the SAT: How Parents Can Help Teens Overcome the Pressure and Succeed."

begin writing essay-

ISTOCKPHOTO

Build Your Plan Online
Start Now at USNewsUniversityDirectory.com/Build

Connect
with more than
1,900 top colleges
and universities

Target
your search to the
schools that best
meet your needs

Access
the latest education
news from *U.S. News
& World Report*

Discover
how to get more
financial aid with our
free, expert guide

Get Free Assistance
With Your School Search:
855-237-2180

The #1 Authority on the Nation's Best Colleges

...Grinnell College

Jeremy Sanchez, '14

Grinnell fosters a sense of community among students and a desire to serve the "common good," which was obvious from my first visit to the school. A first-year student showed me around and, when I asked about the science facilities and professors, he found

Why I

...Barnard College

Gabrielle Davenport, '15

I first learned about Barnard when my older sister attended. Visiting campus, I was struck by how excited and confident the students seemed. When I applied, I felt this historic women's college would allow me to explore my varied interests and not press me to specialize too quickly,

as I worried might happen at other schools. The campus community itself feels small and personal. I've been able to pursue my interests in hip-hop, wellness and African diasporas.

Barnard encourages students to take initiative, and one of my most rewarding experiences was performing in – and helping organize – a conference celebrating the work of the noted black author Ntozake Shange, a Barnard alumna. The college's partnership with Columbia University gives us access to the resources of an Ivy League institution, while the incomparable New York City lies just outside our gates, offering me the chance to apply what I've learned to real-world situations. Over my years at Barnard, I have built warm relationships with faculty members and know that they will continue to be resources and mentors for me after I graduate. ●

CLOCKWISE FROM TOP: JUSTIN HAYWORTH – GRINNELL COLLEGE; COURTESY OF KENYON COLLEGE; BARNARD COLLEGE; ISTOCKPHOTO

friends who could answer my questions firsthand. The college offers many opportunities to apply what you learn in the classroom. For example, I performed enzyme kinetics research with a dedicated adviser in a biochemical lab and took advantage of the college's many service-learning and volunteer opportunities. For example, over several vacations I joined the student service organization, Alternative Break, on different trips, including one I led that involved working in a self-sustaining farming community that doubles as a home and workplace for people with special needs. Because of Grinnell's active study abroad program, I spent a semester in Marseille, France, where I became fluent in French. The college supported my successful application for a Fulbright scholarship, and after teaching for a year in Korea, I hope to go on to medical school. Grinnell opened doors for me that once seemed unimaginable to a first-generation Latino student. ●

Picked...

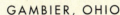

...Kenyon College

Rebecca Katzman, '14

Kenyon had the academic prestige of all of those East Coast liberal arts colleges I visited, but was the only school where I wrote down observations such as "comfortable feeling" and "happy people." It attracts students from all over the world, yet this beautiful middle-of-nowhere hilltop campus in the Midwest has a protective boarding school feel (earning it the name Kamp Kenyon), that is at once immersive and all-encompassing. Yet not far from campus, you'll find a rich agricultural landscape and people of vastly different political and socioeconomic backgrounds. As a sociology major and as the manager of Kenyon's Rural Life Center, I've met some of these people on projects ranging from an oral history of an Amish-run produce auction to a photo shoot involving local gun enthusiasts. I appreciate that Kenyon emphasizes writing throughout the curriculum and, as an English minor, I've been able to take classes with amazing professors like David Lynn, editor of the famous "Kenyon Review." I feel the college has prepared me for the future as I head off now to New York on a fellowship with a new media group. ●

Washington University in St. Louis

MATT SLABY - LUCEO FOR USN&WR

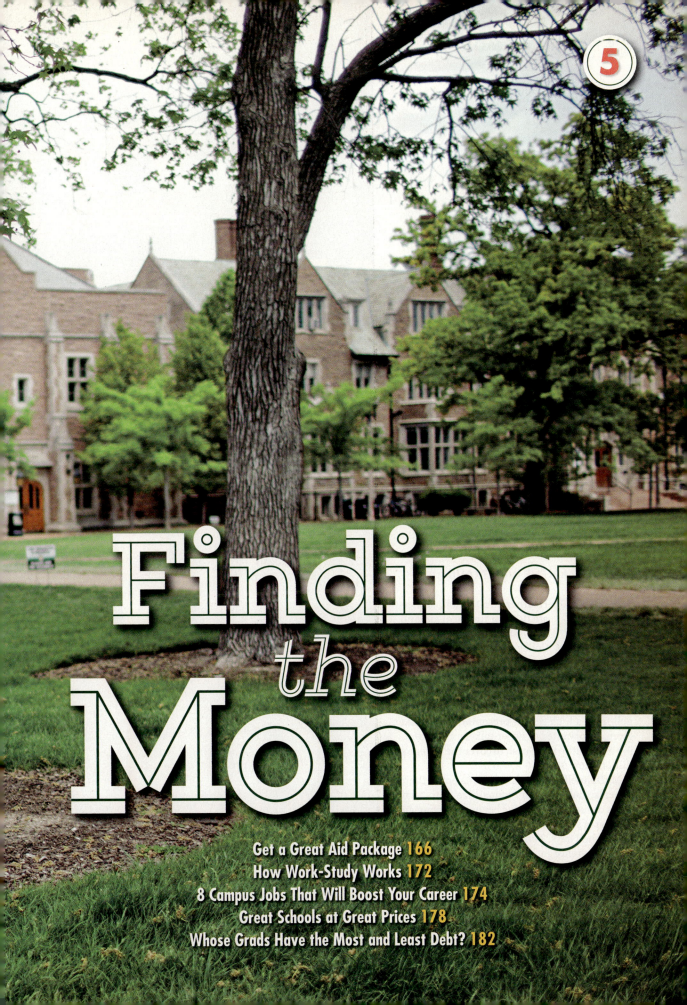

Finding the Money

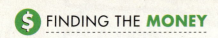
How to Nab a GREAT DEAL

HERE'S HOW YOU CAN NEGOTIATE THE FATTEST POSSIBLE AID PACKAGE

By **ARLENE WEINTRAUB**

NEWS YOU CAN USE

Heather McDonnell, associate dean of financial aid and admission at Sarah Lawrence College in Bronxville, New York, was shopping at the grocery story a few years ago when a man came up to her and appealed for mercy. It was a father who recognized McDonnell from a high school presentation she had given, who wanted to sweet-talk her into handing over a little more cash to cover the college's tuition (now $49,680 a year).

McDonnell prefers that parents email their appeals, but she can sympathize with that dad's desperation. "We've been witnessing an erosion of state and federal funding for years," McDonnell says. Ten years ago, for example, Sarah Lawrence got about $250,000 in Federal Supplemental Education Opportunity Grants for low-income students. By 2014, that figure had dropped to $137,728.

Sarah Lawrence is far from the only school feeling the financial-aid squeeze. The lingering effects of the recession and sputtering

University of Illinois students Nick and Alex Fregeau both snagged a scholarship for descendants of World War I veterans.

PETER HOFFMAN FOR USN&WR

economy have exacerbated family need even as they have hurt endowments, and last year, budget cuts hit federal financial-aid programs hard. The situation has improved only slightly this year.

Still, resourceful parents and students will find there's plenty of money out there for those who know where to look – and how to speak up when that fat welcome package announces a scrawnier-than-expected award.

Before you try to knock down the price

tag of your child's dream school, it's vital to understand the elements of the typical aid package. The first is federal need-based aid, which includes grants, funding for work-study jobs and subsidized Stafford loans (meaning the government pays the interest for you while you're in school). This aid is determined by your family's financial information on the Free Application for Federal Student Aid, or FAFSA. Families with exceptional need may also qualify for a federal Perkins loan. Then there are merit scholarships offered by the institutions themselves for academic achievements or talents.

Finally, there are federal loans that aren't subsidized, for people who don't qualify for that perk or who need more, and parent PLUS loans for Mom and Dad. An incoming freshman can borrow up to $5,500 in Stafford loans, of which no more than $3,500 can be subsidized. (The limits rise in later years and for students who are independent of their parents.) The interest rate on Staffords is now 4.66 percent.

Retired pharmaceutical executive David Goldman, of Flemington, New Jersey, learned the art of negotiating when the oldest of his four children got into two schools she liked. "We went to both colleges and showed each one the other college's offer," says Goldman. "We actually found they were very responsive. They might not like the word 'negotiation,' but clearly this was a negotiation." Using that tactic and others, such as nudging his kids toward well-funded private colleges likely to reward their academic achievements, Goldman estimates he has obtained over $200,000 in merit

INSIDE SCOOP

MARK KANTROWITZ
Senior vice president and publisher, Edvisors Network; financial aid expert

BEWARE, IF YOU BORROW

The idea is to minimize debt. Live like a student while you're in school so you don't have to live like a student after you graduate. A good rule of thumb: Your total student loan debt should be less than your starting salary. Borrow federal first because federal loans are cheaper; they're more available, and they have better repayment terms. Federal loans have fixed rates; most private student loans have variable rates. Parents shouldn't borrow more – for all their children – than their current annual income, and their goal should be to pay off the loans in 10 years or by retirement, whichever comes first.

aid unrelated to need for his kids, including his youngest, Michael, now a senior at Worcester Polytechnic Institute in Massachusetts. (His oldest ended up at Muhlenberg College in Pennsylvania, a choice that Goldman estimates saved $13,000 a year.)

It's important to know, too, that colleges that give you the same bottom line can get there different ways. Schools have plenty of leeway in how they give grants and loans; a much-desired viola player with perfect SAT scores might get 75 percent grants and 25 percent loans, say, while you're offered just the

opposite. You're clearly better off with the biggest possible handout.

But you can't assume you'll save by limiting your choices to public schools, warns Beth Walker, a financial planner at Strategic Wealth Associates in Colorado Springs. "The majority of what state schools have to offer is loans," she says. Well-endowed private colleges often "can give away more free money."

According to a survey released in 2013 by the National Association of College and University Business Officers, 65 percent of private colleges increased the amount by which they "discount" tuition via grants and scholarships for the 2011-2012 year. The average discount rate reached 45 percent in the fall of 2011.

Even if your child isn't a sought-after scholar, you may be able to successfully appeal for more funding after you receive your award letters. Linda Parker, director of financial aid at Union College in Schenectady, New York, says she often reconsiders aid packages when family circumstances have changed since the application arrived – a parent has lost a job or become ill, say. "If they document that," she says, "often students receive increased awards."

Or perhaps you face a challenge not accounted for on the FAFSA form. When Elizabeth Avery's daughter, Charlotte, was accepted by Union a year ago, she was thrilled, but there was a problem: Her father's take-home pay was going to fluctuate over the next few years because of an arrangement with a new employer. "We may look good on paper, but what we can afford is very different from what the government determined we can afford," says Avery, a relocation specialist in Pittsfield, Massachusetts. She sent an email to the aid office spelling out the family's circumstances. Charlotte received a $10,000 merit scholarship that renews every year.

It also can be worth your time to seek scholarships off the beaten path. By searching sites like Fastweb.com, Susan Fregeau, a certified public accountant in Westmont, Illinois, discovered the Laverne Noyes Foundation Scholarship, offered to descendants of people who served overseas in World War I. "I do genealogy, so I knew where Grandpa fought at that time," Fregeau

COURTESY OF MARK KANTROWITZ

Choose the Student Loan with No Origination Fees

Every family is different when it comes to saving, planning, and paying for higher education. When scholarships, grants, and federal student loans aren't enough to cover college expenses, consider a private student loan from Sallie Mae®.

Choose the Smart Option Student Loan® with:

• **Choice of interest rates,** variable or fixed

• **No fees** for origination

• **Flexible options** for repayment

• **Money-saving** benefits

• **Ability to apply for cosigner release** after graduation. For additional cosigner release eligibility criteria go to SallieMae.com/cosignerrelease

The Sallie Mae Smart Option Student Loan

Learn more at
SallieMae.com/USNews

Or call
1-866-425-2952

Encouraging Responsible Borrowing

Sallie Mae has helped more than 30 million Americans pay for college since 1972. We encourage students and families to supplement their savings by exploring grants, scholarships, federal and state student loans, and to consider the anticipated monthly payments on their total student loan debt and their expected future earnings before considering a private education loan.

This information is for degree-granting institutions only. Credit criteria and eligibility requirements apply.

WE RESERVE THE RIGHT TO MODIFY OR DISCONTINUE PRODUCTS, SERVICES, AND BENEFITS AT ANY TIME WITHOUT NOTICE. CHECK SALLIEMAE.COM FOR THE MOST UP-TO-DATE PRODUCT INFORMATION.

Smart Option Student Loans are made by Sallie Mae Bank or a lender partner. The Sallie Mae logo, Sallie Mae, and Smart Option Student Loan are service marks or registered service marks of Sallie Mae Bank or its subsidiaries. SLM Corporation and its subsidiaries, including Sallie Mae Bank, are not sponsored by or agencies of the United States of America. ©2014 Sallie Mae Bank. All rights reserved. SMSCH MKT9805 0814

says. Her oldest son, Nick, got $5,000 to help pay his four years of tuition at the University of Illinois. He graduated last spring and is starting law school there this fall. Younger brother Alex, now a junior at U of I, received $2,000 from Laverne Noyes for the 2013-2014 academic year.

To help families figure out what college is really going to cost, the Department of Education requires all schools to post "net price calculators" on their websites. The calculators use a family's financial information to estimate the final bill, accounting for the federal and state aid the student is likely to receive. College advisors warn parents not to take an estimate as gospel, though. The quality of the tool varies by school, and it may not collect all the information it needs to spit out a truly accurate figure.

"It's a great thing to examine, but all you're going to get is a ballpark," says William Wozniak, director of marketing at ISM College Planning, an Indianapolis nonprofit that counsels high school students on the application process. What's more, he says, many schools aren't diligent about updates. "Sometimes the calculator is really from the year before and doesn't include the new cost of attendance," he says.

If you've snatched up all the free money

you can find and need to fill in the gaps with loans, be aware of the long-term ramifications. Subsidized loans cost less over the long run because the government pays the interest while the student is in school. The government also covers it during the six months after graduation before repayment starts, and during any period of deferment for grad school or a period of unemployment, say. Congress in 2012 extended low student-loan interest rates but temporarily did away with the grace period after graduation, so students who received direct subsidized loans between July 1, 2012 and July 1, 2014, must either pay interest that accrues then or it will be added to their principal balance.

Patricia Seaman, a senior director at the National Endowment for Financial Education in Denver, suggests that families look at entry-level sala-

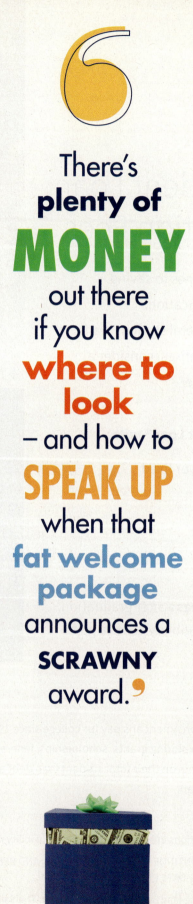

There's plenty of MONEY out there if you know where to look – and how to SPEAK UP when that fat welcome package announces a SCRAWNY award.

ries in the fields the student is considering, then calculate just how much of a burden repayment will be. "There's a huge difference between petroleum engineering, where salaries are really high, and social work, which is really low," Seaman says. "That social worker won't be able to buy a car off the bat and will be eating mac and cheese and ramen until she advances a bit."

And as you weigh whether to grab that parent PLUS loan the acceptance letter is offering, you may want to look into cheaper options. The interest rate on PLUS loans is currently fixed at 7.21 percent. Home equity loans are now being offered at an average interest rate of 6.1 percent, according to Bankrate.com, and the interest is deductible.

Seaman recommends knocking off some easy credits, such as electives, at lower-priced colleges, provided the credits will transfer. Her daughter, Katharine Rowan, took five courses one summer at a community college to fulfill elective requirements at the University of Wisconsin, where she's a senior studying electrical engineering. Seaman estimates she saved $6,000 in tuition and fees.

Guido Castellani III, who received about $200,000 in grants and scholarships to cover his four years at Sarah Lawrence, applied during the early decision round and was accepted, but knew there was "no way" he could afford it. So he scoured the Internet and discovered that as the son of a former marine officer, a Vietnam vet who passed away in 2003, he was eligible for certain scholarships and other funding. Castellani, who is originally from Scranton, Pennsylvania, was awarded $10,000 a year from the Marine Corps Scholarship Foundation plus about $950 a month in educational benefits from the U.S. Department of Veterans Affairs.

"I had to be persistent," says Castellani, who graduated in May. He negotiated with Sarah Lawrence's financial aid office to get additional aid junior year, and right before he graduated, he applied for – and won – a scholarship from the Children of Fallen Patriots Foundation to cover the $12,000 he'd accumulated in subsidized loans. His advice for incoming freshmen: "Do your research. The money is there." ●

NJIT
New Jersey Institute of Technology

Discover New Jersey Institute of Technology

Best College Value Nationally

- Over 125 undergraduate, master's and doctoral degree programs
- A student-faculty ratio of 16:1
- Ranked 8th among public colleges and universities for return on investment – *PayScale*

Six Colleges - One University

- Newark College of Engineering
- College of Computing Sciences
- College of Architecture and Design
- College of Science and Liberal Arts
- School of Management
- Albert Dorman Honors College

Cutting-Edge Research

- Over 25 specialized research centers and labs
- Ranked 5th among U.S. polytechnic institutions in research expenditures, topping $110 million
- Collaborative research with students and faculty to solve real-world problems

Internships, Co-ops, and High Tech Jobs

- Thousands of highly paid internship and co-op opportunities averaging $18 to $21 per hour
- Access to over 22,800 job opportunities posted through Career Development Services
- Ranked #1 nationally for alumni starting salary vs. annual tuition

ALWAYS **ON**

njit.edu/usn

NEW JERSEY INSTITUTE OF TECHNOLOGY • UNIVERSITY HEIGHTS, NEWARK, NJ 07102-1982

New Jersey's Science and Technology University

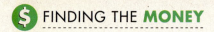
How Work-Study Works

IF A JOB IS PART OF YOUR AID AWARD, IT CAN PAY OFF IN SEVERAL WAYS

By **MICHAEL MORELLA**

Amber Bunnell had always wanted to work in a library. So when the option of holding down a work-study job was offered as part of her financial aid package from Macalester College in St. Paul, Minnesota, she stated that preference "in all capital letters" on her application for a position. Working about 10 hours per week at $7.25 an hour, the Savage, Minnesota, native started as a circulation aide, manning the front desk and sorting and shelving. The next year, she was promoted to help manage the staff of about 50 undergraduate employees, with a bump in pay. She added skills "that I can transfer into any career I choose," says Bunnell, who graduated in May with a degree in English and international studies and landed a job at another academic library in St. Paul.

Amber Bunnell's library job confirmed her desire to enter the field.

The basics. Hundreds of thousands of college students participate in the federal government's work-study program, part of its financial-aid superstructure for those who demonstrate need. The first step: Opt in when you're asked if you'd like to be considered for the program in question 31 of the Free Application for Federal Student Aid, or FAFSA. If you're eligible, and if you follow through by actually finding a position once you get to college, then you can expect to earn at least federal minimum wage – currently $7.25 an hour – or the state or local baseline, if higher. Most jobs are on campus, in the dining hall, bookstore or athletic department, say, though some might be with local employers. The government awarded a yearly average of nearly $1,700 per student at about 3,300 colleges in 2012-13, according to the latest Department of Education data.

Schools are required to kick in 25 percent of every student's funding, which means that annual awards often run around $2,000 or $2,500. You'll coordinate your own work schedule and may work as much as you like up to the ceiling imposed by the size of your award. (An award of slightly more than $1,000 per 14-week semester would work out to 10 hours a week at $7.25 per hour, for example.)

There are "a lot of different models out there" for actually securing a job, says Joe Weglarz, executive director of student financial services at Marist College in Poughkeepsie, New York. Marist holds a work-study job fair to introduce new students to prospective employers, and the student financial services office helps facilitate the job search. At Iowa State, students have access to a jobs portal of available positions, which they apply for on their own. Other schools, like Macalester, place students in positions based on their skills and academic interests.

Besides providing some tuition or spending money, work-study jobs can help you build a résumé, establish a network of mentors and potential references and learn useful skills. "If you want to be a physician or a pediatrician, it might not be a bad idea to work in a daycare center," suggests Cynthia Meekins, manager for student employment at Rutgers in New Brunswick, New Jersey. And research shows that students who work about 10 to 15 hours a week tend to perform better academically, adds Desiree Noah, who coordinates student employment at La Sierra University in Riverside, California, and is president-elect of the National Student Employment Association. One great perk of a work-study job is that your employer will probably give you a break when you're swamped at exam time and pulling all-nighters. ●

EMMA PULIDO

Some people will tell you to **study what you love.**

Some people will tell you to **study something practical.**

No matter what you study, AfterCollege will help you find scholarships, internships, and jobs based on your field of study.

It's never too early to start thinking about AfterCollege.

AfterCollege®
where your career begins

aftercollege.com

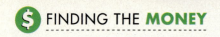
8 Great Campus Jobs That Will Turbocharge

YOUR CAREER

THE SKILLS AND EXPERIENCE YOU GAIN CAN BE WORTH AS MUCH AS THE PAYCHECK

By **COURTNEY RUBIN**

Want to boost your job prospects after graduation? Any part-time work during college can give you an edge, including a stint at McDonald's. "Balancing work and school shows you can manage your time," says Nicole van den Heuvel, director of the Center for Career Development at Rice University in Houston. "And jobs that aren't glamorous show that you're not a prima donna." But with a little strategizing, you can land a position that will really enhance your résumé.

First step: Go to the campus employment office during orientation. "You'll be on campus

Florida A&M student Charles Garner (center) attends a planning meeting for homecoming.

before the upperclassmen. Take advantage of that," suggests Michael Sciola, associate vice president for advancement and director of career services at Colgate University in New York. Here are some job ideas:

1. Social media coordinator

This job, which involves using Facebook, Twitter, YouTube and similar platforms to spread the college's or another employer's message, will enhance your communication skills and

is likely to make you savvy about the latest technologies. Experience could also include data analysis, looking at various metrics that measure viewer engagement, and strategizing how to improve those metrics.

Another perk is that you practice networking. "Twitter makes the world a lot smaller," says Charles Garner, who worked 11 hours a week as social media coordinator for the Office of Student Activities at Florida Agricultural & Mechanical University before graduating

in the spring and being commissioned as a naval officer. In promoting events like homecoming and Women's Week, he says, he used Twitter "to get in contact with celebrities, and to meet a lot of influential legislators and even the governor." Adds Garner, who wanted to burnish his credentials for an eventual career in public affairs: "Your network is your net worth."

2. Campus brand ambassador

The race to grab college students' attention and dollars has all sorts of companies, including General Mills, Google and Coca-Cola, hiring on-campus ambassadors to do everything from wear the brand's logo to tweet about the products.

Besides learning sales, marketing and strategy, you'll get a grounding in the products – and perhaps the inside track on a job after graduation. To stand out, you'll need creativity, but if you've got it, work as a brand ambassador often leads to sales and marketing trainee programs.

3. Help desk staffer or bookstore computer pro

You'll obviously pick up tech skills manning your school's help desk, but chances are you'll learn them working in the electronics section of the campus store, too. With many schools requiring laptops, this is typically where the machines are issued. You'll often install software and do minor troubleshooting, plus gain product knowledge.

After four years in the campus store at the University of North Carolina–Chapel Hill, Sam Hudson, who graduated in 2012, approached a representative at a job fair looking to fill positions at Lenovo. "I said, 'I've been giving out your computers for a couple of years,'" says Hudson. He's now an account coordinator for the company in North Carolina.

4. Assistant in the office of institutional research

This is the office that surveys students, alumni, professors and parents, which could involve quizzing the freshman class about the first-year experience, asking parents about their education financing plans, and gathering alumni perceptions of the school. So any job in this office will offer an opportunity to learn about collecting and analyzing data.

"I think that's one of the best tools any kid can have," says van den Heuvel. "To go into consulting, to go into investment banking, to do so many things."

5. Career center staffer

Any job in the career center teaches customer service and how to interact in a professional environment. "You'll learn how to greet people and how to make small talk," says Sciola. "All these little things are so important in getting a job."

Problem-solving and computer skills also will come into play as you help students and employers who are having trouble logging in to the career center's system or who want to

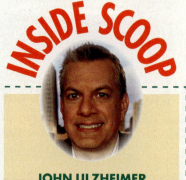

INSIDE SCOOP

JOHN ULZHEIMER
President, The Ulzheimer Group;
expert for CreditSesame.com

PARENTS, HERE'S A CREDIT CARD MOVE

No one under 21 can get a credit card without a job or a co-signer. If you want your kid to have a card, I suggest adding him or her as an authorized user on one of your accounts. If you fear wild spending sprees, most cards now offer text messages alerting you of transactions within seconds – and you can shut off your kid's access almost as quickly. Or request a low limit. Just because a card offers a $10,000 limit doesn't mean you have to take it. A debit card will keep your kid to a budget, but will do nothing to help him or her build a credit rating.

post a job. Plus, think of the job-search wisdom you'll soak up and the facetime you'll get with potential employers.

6. Child care provider

Many schools have an onsite daycare center, and it is probably looking for help. Besides teaching patience and responsibility, the position should allow you to get to know faculty and administrators outside the classroom. No matter how prominent, "they will always want to talk about their child," observes Mark Smith, associate vice chancellor and director of the career center at Washington University in St. Louis, who worked at the Harvard Yard child care center during his four years at Harvard – and then as an au pair while at Washington University School of Law. "These folks can help guide you," he says. As a bonus, you get "great training for possibly one of your most important future jobs, parent."

7. Student athletic trainer

You don't have to be interested in a health-related career for this job to be a résumé-enhancer. Assisting with treatments (learning to tape ankles or shoulders, say), helping set up for practices, and preparing for games teaches responsibility and teamwork, says van den Heuvel. And potential future employers will appreciate that you worked nights and weekends, in often stressful or high-pressure environments. Most of these jobs will lead to a certification in CPR, too.

8. Chief executive of your own startup

As a freshman at Syracuse University in New York, Courtnee Futch remembers working 20 hours a week at two different jobs and still having just $6.14 socked away in her bank account. "I thought, 'There has to be a better way to make money,'" says Futch, now a senior. She'd always loved to bake, so she whipped up a batch of bacon Rice Krispie treats with white chocolate and caramel drizzle, created a Facebook page for the business, which she named "ThunderCakes," and sold out in two hours. Currently, she has 15 unpaid interns, and this fall, as she prepares to ship her creations (bacon cheesecake brownies, vanilla chiffon cakes) all over New York state, she'll hire five employees.

"Running my own business has really taught me to focus, something I was never able to do before," she says. "I've learned a ton about bootstrapping, accountability and determination." ●

COURTESY OF JOHN ULZHEIMER

Need help finding the right school for you?

U.S. News
College Compass

#1 See complete U.S. News rankings

Expanded data on nearly 1,800 schools

Compare schools side-by-side

$ Detailed financial aid information

See entering student SAT scores and GPAs

PLUS, GET FREE ACCESS TO THE **MY FIT ENGINE**

The My Fit Engine helps you find out how schools measure up based on your preferences.

Buy today and save 25% off College Compass: usnews.com/compassoffer

Great Schools, Great Prices

Which colleges and universities offer students the best value? The calculation used here takes into account a school's academic quality, based on its U.S. News Best Colleges ranking, and the 2013-14 net cost of attendance for a student who received the average level of need-based financial aid. The higher the quality of the program and the lower the cost, the better the deal. Only schools in or near the top half of their U.S. News ranking categories are included because U.S. News considers the most significant values to be among colleges that perform well academically.

National Universities ▶

Rank	School (State) (*Public)	% receiving grants based on need ('13)	Average cost after receiving grants based on need ('13)	Average discount from total cost ('13)
1.	Harvard University (MA)	58%	$15,169	75%
2.	Princeton University (NJ)	59%	$17,994	68%
3.	Yale University (CT)	52%	$17,352	72%
4.	Stanford University (CA)	48%	$19,361	68%
5.	Massachusetts Inst. of Technology	57%	$21,363	64%
6.	Columbia University (NY)	48%	$21,906	66%
7.	Dartmouth College (NH)	49%	$22,503	65%
8.	California Institute of Technology	51%	$23,281	60%
9.	Rice University (TX)	41%	$19,976	63%
10.	University of Pennsylvania	47%	$23,542	62%
11.	Vanderbilt University (TN)	45%	$21,731	64%
12.	Brown University (RI)	44%	$22,162	64%
13.	Duke University (NC)	39%	$23,403	63%
14.	Brigham Young Univ.–Provo (UT)	37%	$12,798	27%
15.	Cornell University (NY)	48%	$23,936	61%
16.	University of Chicago	47%	$27,313	57%
17.	U. of North Carolina–Chapel Hill*	42%	$19,614	57%
18.	Emory University (GA)	44%	$23,604	61%
19.	Johns Hopkins University (MD)	43%	$27,666	56%
20.	Northwestern University (IL)	46%	$28,161	56%
21.	Univ. of California–Santa Cruz*	60%	$20,855	63%
22.	University of Notre Dame (IN)	47%	$29,428	51%
23.	Georgetown University (DC)	34%	$25,806	59%
24.	Pepperdine University (CA)	55%	$24,090	61%
25.	Clark University (MA)	62%	$22,395	54%
26.	University of California–Berkeley*	22%	$23,747	48%
27.	University of Virginia*	28%	$24,819	54%
28.	Tufts University (MA)	36%	$26,347	57%
29.	University of Rochester (NY)	52%	$28,024	54%
30.	Washington University in St. Louis	35%	$30,344	52%
31.	Texas A&M Univ.–College Station*	40%	$20,003	47%
32.	Brandeis University (MA)	51%	$28,248	54%
33.	Case Western Reserve Univ. (OH)	61%	$30,348	48%
34.	Lehigh University (PA)	41%	$25,285	56%
35.	Wake Forest University (NC)	37%	$28,126	53%
36.	Clarkson University (NY)	84%	$29,774	48%
37.	Boston College	37%	$28,248	53%
38.	Carnegie Mellon University (PA)	47%	$33,264	46%
39.	University of California–Irvine*	22%	$22,773	57%
40.	Rensselaer Polytechnic Inst. (NY)	65%	$35,187	43%
41.	Univ. of Southern California	37%	$31,530	49%
42.	Illinois Institute of Technology	63%	$26,134	52%
43.	Duquesne University (PA)	69%	$26,649	40%
44.	Yeshiva University (NY)	50%	$31,190	45%
45.	SUNY Col. of Envir. Sci. and Forestry*	64%	$26,312	20%
46.	North Carolina State U.–Raleigh*	43%	$21,769	39%
47.	Syracuse University (NY)	53%	$31,780	45%
48.	Univ. of California–Riverside*	45%	$23,743	57%
49.	Univ. of California–San Diego*	18%	$26,000	51%
50.	University of California–Davis*	27%	$28,040	50%

National Liberal Arts Colleges ▶

Rank	School (State) (*Public)	% receiving grants based on need ('13)	Average cost after receiving grants based on need ('13)	Average discount from total cost ('13)
1.	Amherst College (MA)	56%	$16,590	73%
2.	Williams College (MA)	52%	$18,977	69%
3.	Pomona College (CA)	56%	$19,040	68%
4.	Wellesley College (MA)	59%	$19,717	67%
5.	Soka University of America (CA)	90%	$18,602	56%
6.	Vassar College (NY)	58%	$20,211	67%
7.	Grinnell College (IA)	71%	$20,653	63%
8.	Bowdoin College (ME)	45%	$19,875	67%
9.	Washington and Lee University (VA)	41%	$18,725	68%
10.	Haverford College (PA)	49%	$20,977	66%
11.	Swarthmore College (PA)	50%	$21,969	64%
12.	Middlebury College (VT)	39%	$21,286	64%
13.	College of the Atlantic (ME)	86%	$18,149	64%
14.	Colby College (ME)	42%	$21,269	64%
15.	Macalester College (MN)	69%	$24,315	58%
16.	Colgate University (NY)	35%	$20,517	66%
17.	Claremont McKenna College (CA)	40%	$22,911	63%
18.	Smith College (MA)	59%	$24,306	60%
19.	Davidson College (NC)	45%	$23,741	59%
20.	Hamilton College (NY)	47%	$23,663	61%
21.	Agnes Scott College (GA)	77%	$20,733	56%
22.	Bates College (ME)	45%	$23,545	61%
23.	University of Richmond (VA)	39%	$21,438	63%
24.	Wesleyan University (CT)	44%	$24,358	62%
25.	Carleton College (MN)	55%	$27,084	55%
26.	Thomas Aquinas College (CA)	75%	$19,783	45%
27.	Bryn Mawr College (PA)	54%	$25,197	58%
28.	Mount Holyoke College (MA)	67%	$25,781	54%
29.	Cornell College (IA)	77%	$21,408	56%
30.	Ripon College (WI)	84%	$21,526	50%
31.	Centre College (KY)	59%	$23,722	51%
32.	Franklin and Marshall College (PA)	46%	$23,850	61%
33.	St. Olaf College (MN)	65%	$24,357	53%
34.	Trinity College (CT)	39%	$22,460	64%
35.	Transylvania University (KY)	68%	$21,493	51%
36.	Beloit College (WI)	69%	$24,005	52%
37.	Skidmore College (NY)	43%	$23,750	61%
38.	Wofford College (SC)	54%	$20,698	58%
39.	Knox College (IL)	75%	$23,894	52%
40.	Barnard College (NY)	39%	$24,376	60%

Methodology: The rankings were based on the following three variables: **1.** Ratio of quality to price: a school's overall score in the latest Best Colleges rankings divided by the net cost to a student receiving the average need-based scholarship or grant. The higher the ratio of rank to the discounted cost (tuition, fees, room and board and other expenses less average scholarship or grant), the better the value. **2.** Percentage of all undergrads receiving need-based scholarships or grants during the 2013-14 year. **3.** Average discount: percentage of a school's 2013-14 total costs covered by the average need-based scholarship or grant to undergrads. For public institutions, 2013-14 out-of-state tuition and percentage of out-of-state students receiving need-based scholarships or grants were used. Only those schools ranked in or near the top half of their U.S. News ranking categories were considered. Ranks were determined by standardizing scores achieved by every school in each of the three variables and weighting those scores. Ratio of quality to price accounted for 60 percent of the overall score; percentage of undergrads receiving need-based grants, for 25 percent; and average discount, for 15 percent. The school with the most total weighted points became No. 1 in its category.

ACADEMIC INSIGHTS
YOUR SCHOOL BY THE NUMBERS

Designed for schools, U.S. News Academic Insights provides instant access to a rich historical archive of undergraduate and graduate school rankings data.

Advanced Visualizations
Take complex data and turn it into six easily understandable and exportable views.

Download Center
Export large data sets from the new Download Center to create custom reports.

Dedicated Account Management
Have access to full analyst support for training, troubleshooting and advanced reporting.

Peer-Group Analysis
Flexibility to create your own peer groups to compare your intstitution on more than 350 metrics.

Historical Trending
Find out how institutions have performed over time based on more than 350 metrics.

To request a demo visit **AI.USNEWS.COM** or call **202.955.2181**

Regional Universities ▶

Rank School (State) (*Public)	% receiving grants based on need ('13)	Average cost after receiving grants based on need ('13)	Average discount from total cost ('13)
NORTH			
1. Villanova University (PA)	43%	$30,946	47%
2. Bentley University (MA)	44%	$27,905	51%
3. St. Bonaventure University (NY)	76%	$23,511	44%
4. Alfred University (NY)	87%	$22,315	48%
5. Rochester Inst. of Technology (NY)	70%	$29,127	39%
6. Le Moyne College (NY)	83%	$26,332	41%
7. Providence College (RI)	56%	$33,646	40%
8. Canisius College (NY)	77%	$26,359	45%
9. Gannon University (PA)	80%	$22,949	45%
10. Niagara University (NY)	75%	$23,513	44%
11. Simmons College (MA)	77%	$30,372	42%
12. University of Scranton (PA)	71%	$34,826	37%
13. Ithaca College (NY)	66%	$33,131	40%
14. Hood College (MD)	85%	$27,266	44%
15. Loyola University Maryland	50%	$34,970	38%
SOUTH			
1. Mercer University (GA)	73%	$24,314	50%
2. Harding University (AR)	56%	$17,827	33%
3. William Carey University (MS)	91%	$16,500	35%
4. Mississippi College	54%	$16,864	37%
5. Converse College (SC)	89%	$22,624	46%
6. Stetson University (FL)	75%	$28,529	47%
7. Christian Brothers University (TN)	82%	$21,156	44%
8. Rollins College (FL)	52%	$31,693	47%
9. Coastal Carolina University (SC)*	21%	$13,405	63%
10. Wingate University (NC)	72%	$18,370	51%
11. Elon University (NC)	31%	$29,959	31%
12. Samford University (AL)	42%	$27,649	32%
13. Columbia International Univ. (SC)	80%	$18,816	40%
14. Appalachian State University (NC)*	25%	$22,828	27%
15. The Citadel (SC)*	40%	$28,730	41%
MIDWEST			
1. Drury University (MO)	65%	$20,354	41%
2. Valparaiso University (IN)	72%	$24,509	47%
3. Creighton University (NE)	56%	$26,950	44%
4. University of Evansville (IN)	68%	$22,109	50%
5. Truman State University (MO)*	38%	$19,560	25%
6. John Carroll University (OH)	73%	$25,784	47%
7. Indiana Wesleyan University	78%	$19,610	43%
8. Dominican University (IL)	87%	$21,538	46%
9. Bradley University (IL)	72%	$27,024	36%
10. Elmhurst College (IL)	73%	$24,065	48%
11. Baldwin Wallace University (OH)	78%	$22,870	43%
12. Hamline University (MN)	84%	$25,350	46%
13. Drake University (IA)	59%	$28,575	36%
14. Butler University (IN)	64%	$30,932	37%
15. Aquinas College (MI)	85%	$19,548	47%
WEST			
1. Trinity University (TX)	47%	$24,820	49%
2. Gonzaga University (WA)	57%	$29,209	40%
3. Whitworth University (WA)	70%	$26,920	44%
4. Seattle Pacific University	73%	$23,960	50%
5. University of Redlands (CA)	78%	$29,779	49%
6. Abilene Christian University (TX)	67%	$25,084	40%
7. Seattle University	60%	$31,698	40%
8. University of Dallas	63%	$27,462	44%

Rank School (State) (*Public)	% receiving grants based on need ('13)	Average cost after receiving grants based on need ('13)	Average discount from total cost ('13)
9. Westminster College (UT)	58%	$24,509	42%
10. Pacific Lutheran University (WA)	75%	$28,452	41%
11. Mills College (CA)	82%	$37,381	35%
12. University of Portland (OR)	54%	$32,045	39%
13. LeTourneau University (TX)	72%	$24,031	38%
14. Santa Clara University (CA)	35%	$38,610	35%
15. Point Loma Nazarene University (CA)	66%	$29,348	34%

Regional Colleges ▶

Rank School (State) (*Public)	% receiving grants based on need ('13)	Average cost after receiving grants based on need ('13)	Average discount from total cost ('13)
NORTH			
1. Cooper Union (NY)	27%	$12,066	78%
2. Elizabethtown College (PA)	78%	$27,625	44%
3. Lebanon Valley College (PA)	83%	$26,515	45%
4. Elmira College (NY)	84%	$25,114	51%
5. Cedar Crest College (PA)	93%	$23,971	46%
6. Geneva College (PA)	81%	$21,212	42%
7. Seton Hill University (PA)	86%	$25,087	43%
8. Messiah College (PA)	72%	$27,114	37%
9. Bard College at Simon's Rock (MA)	72%	$24,528	59%
10. Wilson College (PA)	78%	$24,393	42%
SOUTH			
1. Alice Lloyd College (KY)	91%	$13,217	40%
2. Blue Mountain College (MS)	79%	$13,300	24%
3. John Brown University (AR)	66%	$20,844	40%
4. Milligan College (TN)	81%	$19,980	47%
5. University of the Ozarks (AR)	69%	$22,367	39%
6. Carson-Newman University (TN)	81%	$20,123	44%
7. Bryan College (TN)	74%	$17,920	42%
8. West Virginia Wesleyan College	80%	$21,952	46%
9. Meredith College (NC)	76%	$23,657	44%
10. Covenant College (GA)	61%	$22,560	44%
MIDWEST			
1. College of the Ozarks (MO)	94%	$13,292	52%
2. Augustana College (SD)	62%	$19,444	49%
3. Buena Vista University (IA)	85%	$21,145	48%
4. Manchester University (IN)	87%	$19,362	51%
5. Huntington University (IN)	76%	$20,503	42%
6. Loras College (IA)	73%	$21,112	47%
7. St. Joseph's College (IN)	83%	$18,892	50%
8. Taylor University (IN)	61%	$24,832	38%
9. Clarke University (IA)	87%	$23,027	44%
10. Culver-Stockton College (MO)	90%	$18,053	48%
WEST			
1. Texas Lutheran University	81%	$21,505	44%
2. Carroll College (MT)	63%	$25,560	37%
3. Corban University (OR)	83%	$23,974	40%
4. Howard Payne University (TX)	73%	$19,788	42%
5. Rocky Mountain College (MT)	75%	$20,447	42%
6. Northwest University (WA)	83%	$20,631	43%
7. Oklahoma Wesleyan University	70%	$24,238	29%
8. Master's Col. and Seminary (CA)	85%	$27,175	37%
9. Warner Pacific College (OR)	79%	$23,543	19%
10. Oklahoma Baptist University	63%	$26,493	21%

Two worlds.
One dream.

Singers and Scientists share more than might be expected. Whether it's a breakout melody or a breakthrough in research. When it comes together, everything fits. It can change lives forever. Stand Up To Cancer supports the collaboration, innovation and research that are turning discoveries into viable treatments and possibly, one day, a cure.

Stand up with us. Let your voice make a difference because when we work together, nothing is impossible.

Genentech
A Member of the Roche Group

Like, share and join SU2C.
Find out more at standup2cancer.org

Jennifer Hudson, Stand Up To Cancer Ambassador

Shiva Malek, Ph.D.

Stand Up To Cancer is a program of the Entertainment Industry Foundation (EIF), a 501(c)(3) charitable organization. Photo by Nigel Parry.

The Payback Picture

With tuition rising and financial aid budgets shrinking, many undergrads have to borrow their way to a degree. U.S. News has compiled a list of the schools whose class of 2013 graduated with the heaviest and lightest debt loads. The data include loans taken out by students from their colleges, from private financial institutions and from federal, state and local governments. Loans to parents are not included. The first data column indicates what percentage of the class graduated owing money and, by extrapolation, what percentage graduated debt free. "Average amount of debt" refers to the cumulative amount borrowed by students who incurred debt; it's not an average for all students.

MOST DEBT

National Universities ▶

School (State) (*Public)	% of grads with debt	Average amount of debt
Florida Institute of Technology	53%	$41,060
Rensselaer Polytechnic Inst. (NY)	67%	$40,584
Andrews University (MI)	65%	$39,010
Clarkson University (NY)	83%	$38,390
Texas Christian University	43%	$38,317
Texas Southern University*	84%	$37,915
Boston University	58%	$37,694
University of Dayton (OH)	63%	$37,551
University of St. Thomas (MN)	65%	$36,955
St. Louis University	63%	$36,808
Pace University (NY)	75%	$36,558
Southern Illinois U.–Carbondale*	70%	$36,172
University of New Hampshire*	77%	$36,064
Ashland University (OH)	87%	$36,058
Wake Forest University (NC)	47%	$35,902

National Liberal Arts Colleges ▶

School (State) (*Public)	% of grads with debt	Average amount of debt
St. Anselm College (NH)	80%	$42,196
Pacific Union College (CA)	64%	$42,153
Virginia Wesleyan College	81%	$40,804
College of St. Benedict (MN)	68%	$40,034
Wells College (NY)	78%	$39,965
Morehouse College (GA)	78%	$38,136
Gordon College (MA)	82%	$37,410
Albion College (MI)	67%	$37,191
Wartburg College (IA)	83%	$36,542
Siena College (NY)	79%	$35,569
Spelman College (GA)	60%	$35,516
Washington College (MD)	65%	$35,510
Johnson C. Smith University (NC)	99%	$35,505
St. John's University (MN)	66%	$35,349
St. Vincent College (PA)	84%	$35,200

Regional Universities ▶

School (State) (*Public)	% of grads with debt	Average amount of debt
NORTH		
St. Francis University (PA)	88%	$50,275
Anna Maria College (MA)	92%	$48,750
Quinnipiac University (CT)	71%	$44,552
Centenary College (NJ)	79%	$43,200
Alvernia University (PA)	85%	$42,552
SOUTH		
Florida Gulf Coast University*	49%	$56,208
The Citadel (SC)*	60%	$48,862
Freed-Hardeman University (TN)	75%	$36,434
Belmont University (TN)	58%	$36,003
Lynchburg College (VA)	79%	$35,330
MIDWEST		
Rockford University (IL)	89%	$45,577
College of St. Scholastica (MN)	76%	$43,113
College of St. Mary (NE)	79%	$40,026
St. Catherine University (MN)	88%	$39,312
Lawrence Technological Univ. (MI)	69%	$38,790
WEST		
LeTourneau University (TX)	77%	$44,584
Abilene Christian University (TX)	66%	$42,585
Trinity University (TX)	44%	$38,540
Walla Walla University (WA)	67%	$38,174
Hardin-Simmons University (TX)	72%	$38,032

Regional Colleges ▶

School (State) (*Public)	% of grads with debt	Average amount of debt
NORTH		
Mount Ida College (MA)	85%	$43,860
Maine Maritime Academy*	97%	$41,630
Delaware Valley College (PA)	77%	$41,036
Lasell College (MA)	86%	$40,709
Cedar Crest College (PA)	91%	$39,198
SOUTH		
Chowan University (NC)	91%	$40,839
Tuskegee University (AL)	62%	$39,250
Kentucky Christian University	79%	$37,413
Meredith College (NC)	64%	$35,425
Ferrum College (VA)	82%	$33,777
MIDWEST		
Adrian College (MI)	75%	$41,763
Buena Vista University (IA)	89%	$40,384
Mount Marty College (SD)	87%	$38,571
University of Jamestown (ND)	70%	$37,942
Marian University (IN)	84%	$37,865
WEST		
McMurry University (TX)	82%	$39,704
Texas Lutheran University	77%	$33,405
Menlo College (CA)	81%	$30,134
Oregon Inst. of Technology*	72%	$29,526
Hope International University (CA)	73%	$28,990

Note: Student debt load data are as of July 25, 2014.

LEAST DEBT

National Universities ▶

School (State) (*Public)	% of grads with debt	Average amount of debt
Princeton University (NJ)	24%	$5,558
Harvard University (MA)	26%	$12,560
Yale University (CT)	16%	$13,009
California Institute of Technology	40%	$15,010
Dartmouth College (NH)	56%	$15,660
Brigham Young Univ.–Provo (UT)	30%	$15,769
Stanford University (CA)	23%	$16,640
University at Buffalo–SUNY*	45%	$17,455
University of California–Berkeley*	43%	$17,468
U. of North Carolina–Chapel Hill*	39%	$17,602
Rice University (TX)	30%	$17,856
Massachusetts Inst. of Technology	41%	$17,891
Florida International University*	49%	$17,893
University of Nevada–Las Vegas*	44%	$17,930
San Diego State University*	48%	$18,100
University of Houston*	49%	$18,244
Duke University (NC)	37%	$18,456
Utah State University*	49%	$19,100
University of West Florida*	54%	$19,239
North Carolina State U.–Raleigh*	57%	$19,530
University of Pennsylvania	36%	$19,798
Florida Atlantic University*	48%	$19,898
University of New Orleans*	19%	$19,957
University of California–Davis*	58%	$19,970
SUNY Col. of Envir. Sci. and Forestry*	67%	$19,989

National Liberal Arts Colleges ▶

School (State) (*Public)	% of grads with debt	Average amount of debt
Berea College (KY)	67%	$6,652
Williams College (MA)	29%	$12,474
Louisiana State University–Alexandria*	58%	$12,547
University of Virginia–Wise*	62%	$12,772
Pomona College (CA)	33%	$13,441
Wellesley College (MA)	49%	$14,030
Haverford College (PA)	29%	$14,110
Amherst College (MA)	29%	$15,466
Thomas Aquinas College (CA)	89%	$15,521
Vassar College (NY)	51%	$16,365
Grinnell College (IA)	57%	$16,570
SUNY College–Old Westbury*	56%	$16,653
Whitman College (WA)	49%	$17,114
Soka University of America (CA)	71%	$17,439
Middlebury College (VT)	46%	$17,715
New College of Florida*	39%	$17,927
Carleton College (MN)	45%	$18,000
Pitzer College (CA)	44%	$18,030
Colgate University (NY)	34%	$18,719
Barnard College (NY)	45%	$18,815
Kenyon College (OH)	50%	$18,902
College of the Atlantic (ME)	61%	$19,285
Swarthmore College (PA)	36%	$19,338
Hamilton College (NY)	38%	$19,426
American Jewish University (CA)	61%	$20,000
Scripps College (CA)	48%	$20,125

Regional Universities ▶

School (State) (*Public)	% of grads with debt	Average amount of debt
NORTH		
CUNY–Brooklyn College*	46%	$11,000
CUNY–John Jay Col. of Crim. Justice*	20%	$11,246
CUNY–Hunter College*	72%	$13,000
CUNY–Lehman College*	24%	$15,075
SUNY College–Oneonta*	69%	$15,598
SOUTH		
Hampton University (VA)	80%	$9,878
University of North Georgia*	49%	$12,072
Lincoln Memorial University (TN)	60%	$12,187
William Carey University (MS)	87%	$16,500
Tennessee Technological Univ.*	53%	$17,023
MIDWEST		
Northeastern Illinois University*	18%	$13,213
William Woods University (MO)	63%	$15,581
Rockhurst University (MO)	73%	$16,817
Missouri State Univ.*	85%	$19,521
Univ. of Wisconsin–Eau Claire*	76%	$22,658
WEST		
California State U.–Fullerton*	42%	$12,962
California State U.–Long Beach*	43%	$13,386
California State U.–Channel Islands*	66%	$13,791
Southeastern Oklahoma State U.*	68%	$14,936
University of Texas–Pan American*	64%	$15,200

Regional Colleges ▶

School (State) (*Public)	% of grads with debt	Average amount of debt
NORTH		
U.S. Merchant Marine Acad. (NY)*	30%	$5,500
Dean College (MA)	70%	$11,678
Cooper Union (NY)	27%	$16,640
Fisher College (MA)	71%	$18,213
Farmingdale State College–SUNY*	46%	$18,515
SOUTH		
Alice Lloyd College (KY)	52%	$8,314
North Greenville University (SC)	70%	$15,000
Bryan College (TN)	88%	$16,494
High Point University (NC)	57%	$18,244
Newberry College (SC)	74%	$19,368
MIDWEST		
College of the Ozarks (MO)	13%	$6,424
Maranatha Baptist University (WI)	67%	$11,162
Bismarck State College (ND)*	61%	$12,377
Bethany College (KS)	82%	$16,300
Dunwoody College of Tech. (MN)	88%	$17,559
WEST		
Oklahoma State Univ. Institute of Tech.–Okmulgee*	75%	$8,675
Rogers State University (OK)*	58%	$17,153
Master's Col. and Seminary (CA)	71%	$18,961
Lewis-Clark State College (ID)*	64%	$20,021
California Maritime Academy*	65%	$20,665

20 15

SCHOOLS OF THE North

THE PROMISE OF
MANHATTAN COLLEGE

The promise of Manhattan College is rooted in Lasallian Catholic traditions of excellence in teaching, respect for human dignity and a commitment to social justice. For more than 160 years, Manhattan College has been delivering on this promise while educating tomorrow's leaders in arts, business, education and health, engineering and the sciences, all on a 22-acre residential campus only a subway ride on the 1 train away from midtown Manhattan.

Visit us at manhattan.edu to learn more about our inspiring academic offerings.

MANHATTAN COLLEGE

2015 SCHOOLS OF THE **South**

West Palm Beach, Florida

Palm Beach Atlantic University

Share the Spirit

At PBA, **we prepare you for the life you want to live**—professionally and spiritually—with our undergraduate, graduate and professional degree programs that interweave faith and knowledge.

Our academic excellence, spirituality and revitalizing atmosphere all come together to bring you an exceptional college experience like no other.

110,000

The number of **volunteer hours** students log each year in service to the community

$326 million

PBA's local economic impact

Recent campus speakers

have included Florida House Speaker **Will Weatherford**, Supreme Court Justice **Clarence Thomas**, Fox Business Channel investigative journalist **John Stossel**, columnist and neurosurgeon **Ben Carson** and former U.S. Attorney General **John Ashcroft**.

100%

The **pass rate** for education graduates on the Florida Teacher Certification Examination

94.44%

And for the second time, PBA pharmacy students earned the state's **top passing rate** on the licensure exam.

1 of the best universities in the South

according to *U.S. News & World Report,* and PrincetonReview.com includes PBA in *"Best Colleges: Region by Region."*

PALM BEACH ATLANTIC
U N I V E R S I T Y

To learn more, visit www.pba.edu

The digital magazine from the editors of U.S.News & World Report.

Become a political insider–get U.S.News Weekly today!

- ‣ The latest political news, insight, and analysis

- ‣ Exclusive Q&As with leading policymakers

- ‣ Hot gossip from Washington Whispers

- ‣ Commentary by Editor-in-Chief Mort Zuckerman

- ‣ Videos, quizzes, and polls

- ‣ News You Can Use, from Best Colleges to Best Cars

Get the U.S. News Weekly on your desktop by going to usnews.com/subscribe

App Store™ is a registered trademark of Apple Inc.

NOOK is a registered trademark of Barnes & Noble, Inc. NOOK Tablet is a trademark of Barnes & Noble, Inc.

Using the Directory

2015 EDITION

DIRECTORY OF COLLEGES AND UNIVERSITIES

INSIDE

The latest facts and figures on nearly 1,600 American colleges and universities, including schools' U.S. News rankings

New data on tuition, admissions, the makeup of the undergraduate student body, popular majors and financial aid

Statistical profiles of freshman classes, including entrance exam scores and high school class ranks

Using the Directory

How to interpret the statistics in the following entries on nearly 1,600 American colleges and universities - and how to get the most out of them

The snapshots of colleges and universities presented here, alphabetized by state, contain a wealth of helpful information on everything from the most popular majors offered to the stats on the freshman class that arrived in the fall of 2013. The statistics were collected in the spring and summer of 2014 and are as of Aug. 11, 2014; they are explained in detail below. A school whose name has been footnoted did not return the U.S. News statistical questionnaire, so limited data appear. If a college did not reply to a particular question, you'll see N/A, for "not available." By tapping our online directory at usnews.com/collegesearch, you can experiment with a customized search of our database that allows you to pick schools based on major, location and other criteria. To find a school of interest in the rankings tables, consult the index at the back of the book.

EXAMPLE

Fairfield University

Fairfield CT
1— (203) 254-4100
2— **U.S. News ranking:** Reg. U. (N), No. 3
3— **Website:** www.fairfield.edu
4— **Admissions email:** admis@fairfield.edu
5— **Private;** founded 1942 **Affiliation:** Roman Catholic (Jesuit)
6— **Freshman admissions:** more selective; 2013-2014: 9,582 applied, 6,742 accepted. Neither SAT nor ACT required. SAT 25/75 percentile: 1090-1250. High school rank: N/A
7— **Early decision deadline:** 11/15, notification date: 1/1 **Early action deadline:** 11/1, notification date: 1/1
8— **Application deadline (fall):** 1/15
9— **Undergraduate student body:** 3,546 full time, 327 part time; 40% male, 60% female; 0% American Indian, 2% Asian, 3% black, 8% Hispanic, 1% multiracial, 0% Pacific Islander, 72% white, 2% international; 31% from in state; 80% live on campus; 0% of students in fraternities, 0% in sororities
10— **Most popular majors:** 26% Business, Management, Marketing and Related Support Services, 10% Communication, Journalism and Related Programs, 13% Health Professions and Related Programs, 7% Psychology, 13% Social Sciences
11— **Expenses:** 2014-2015: $43,770; room/board: $13,190
12— **Financial aid:** (203) 254-4125; 51% of undergrads determined to have financial need; average aid package $29,726

---

1. TELEPHONE NUMBER
This number reaches the admissions office.

2. U.S. NEWS RANKING
The abbreviation indicates which category of institution the school falls into: National University (Nat. U.), National Liberal Arts College (Nat. Lib. Arts), Regional Universities (Reg. U.), or Regional Colleges (Reg. Coll.). The regional universities and regional colleges are further divided by region: North (N), South (S), Midwest (MidW), and West (W). "Business" refers to business specialty schools, and "Engineering" refers to engineering specialty schools. "Arts" refers to schools devoted to the fine and performing arts.

Next, you'll find the school's 2015 rank within its category. Colleges and universities falling in the top three-fourths of their categories are ranked numerically. Those ranked in the bottom 25 percent of their respective category are placed in the second tier, listed alphabetically. But remember: You cannot compare school ranks in different categories; U.S. News ranks schools only against their peers. Specialty schools that focus on business, engineering and the arts aren't ranked and are listed as unranked. Also unranked are schools with fewer than 200 students, a high percentage of older or part-time students, that don't use SAT or ACT test scores for admission decisions or that have received a very small number of peer assessment votes in a survey conducted in Spring 2014.

3. WEBSITE
Visit the school's website to research programs, take a virtual tour or submit an application. You can also find a link to each site at usnews.com.

4. ADMISSIONS EMAIL
You can use this email address to request information or to submit an application.

5. TYPE/AFFILIATION
Is the school public, private or for-profit? Affiliated with a religious denomination?

6. FRESHMAN ADMISSIONS
How competitive is the admissions process at this institution? Schools are designated "most selective," "more selective," "selective," "less selective" or "least selective." The more selective a school, the harder it will probably be to get in. All of the admissions statistics reported are for the class that entered in the fall of 2013. The 25/75 percentiles for the SAT Math and Critical Reading or ACT Composite show the range in which half the students scored: 25 percent of students scored at or below the lower end, and 75 percent scored at or below the upper end. If a school reported the averages and not the 25/75 percentiles, the average score is listed. The test score that is published represents the test that the greatest percentage of the entering students took.

7. EARLY DECISION/ EARLY ACTION DEADLINES
Applicants who plan to take the early decision route to fall 2015 enrollment will have to meet the deadline listed for the school. If the school offers an early action option, the application deadline and notification date are shown also.

8. APPLICATION DEADLINE
The date shown is the regular admission deadline for the academic year starting in the fall of 2015. "Rolling" means the school makes admissions decisions as applications come in until the class is filled.

9. UNDERGRADUATE STUDENT BODY
This section gives you the breakdown of full-time vs. part-time students, male and female enrollment, the ethnic makeup of the student body, in-state and out-of-state populations, the percentage of students living on campus, and the percentage in fraternities and sororities. All figures are for the 2013-14 academic year.

10. MOST POPULAR MAJORS
The five most popular majors appear, along with the percentage majoring in each among 2013 graduates with a bachelor's degree.

11. EXPENSES
The first figure represents tuition (including required fees); next is total room and board. Figures are for the 2014-15 academic year; if data are not available, we use figures for the 2013-14 academic year. For public schools, we list both in-state and out-of-state tuition.

12. FINANCIAL AID
The percentage of undergrads determined to have financial need and the amount of the average package (grants, loans and jobs) in 2013-14. We also provide the phone number of the financial aid office.

ALABAMA

Alabama Agricultural and Mechanical University

Normal AL
(256) 372-5245
U.S. News ranking: Reg. U. (S), second tier
Website: www.aamu.edu
Admissions email: admissions@aamu.edu
Public; founded 1875
Freshman admissions: less selective; 2013-2014: 6,142 applied, 5,521 accepted. ACT required. ACT 25/75 percentile: 15-19. High school rank: N/A
Early decision deadline: N/A, notification date: N/A
Early action deadline: N/A, notification date: N/A
Application deadline (fall): 7/15
Undergraduate student body: 3,802 full time, 253 part time; 49% male, 51% female; 0% American Indian, 1% Asian, 92% black, 1% Hispanic, 0% multiracial, 0% Pacific Islander, 5% white, 0% international; 76% from in state; 56% live on campus; 22% of students in fraternities, 25% in sororities
Most popular majors: Information not available
Expenses: 2014-2015: $8,298 in state, $15,798 out of state; room/board: $5,440
Financial aid: (256) 372-5400; 91% of undergrads determined to have financial need; average aid package $10,250

Alabama State University

Montgomery AL
(334) 229-4291
U.S. News ranking: Reg. U. (S), second tier
Website: www.alasu.edu
Admissions email: mpettway@alasu.edu
Public
Freshman admissions: least selective; 2013-2014: 7,446 applied, 4,036 accepted. Either SAT or ACT required. ACT 25/75 percentile: 15-20. High school rank: 1% in top tenth, 1% in top quarter, 42% in top half
Early decision deadline: N/A, notification date: N/A
Early action deadline: N/A, notification date: N/A
Undergraduate student body: 4,872 full time, 484 part time; 41% male, 59% female; 0% American Indian, 0% Asian, 93% black, 1% Hispanic, 1% multiracial, 0% Pacific Islander, 2% white, 2% international
Most popular majors: Information not available
Expenses: 2014-2015: $8,720 in state, $15,656 out of state; room/board: $5,422
Financial aid: (334) 229-4323; 96% of undergrads determined to have financial need; average aid package $18,859

Amridge University

Montgomery AL
(800) 351-4040
U.S. News ranking: Nat. Lib. Arts, second tier
Website: www.amridgeuniversity.edu/
Admissions email: admissions@amridgeuniversity.edu
Private; founded 1967
Affiliation: Church of Christ
Freshman admissions: selective; 2013-2014: N/A applied, N/A accepted. Neither SAT nor ACT required. ACT 25/75 percentile: N/A. High school rank: N/A
Early decision deadline: N/A, notification date: N/A
Early action deadline: N/A, notification date: N/A
Application deadline (fall): rolling
Undergraduate student body: 201 full time, 121 part time; 39% male, 61% female; 1% American Indian, 0% Asian, 42% black, 1% Hispanic, 0% multiracial, 0% Pacific Islander, 29% white, 0% international
Most popular majors: 3% Business, Management, Marketing, and Related Support Services, 1% Computer and Information Sciences and Support Services, 72% Liberal Arts and Sciences, General Studies and Humanities, 21% Theology and Religious Vocations
Expenses: 2014-2015: $10,305; room/board: N/A
Financial aid: (800) 351-4040

Athens State University

Athens AL
(256) 233-8217
U.S. News ranking: Reg. Coll. (S), unranked
Website: www.athens.edu/
Admissions email: N/A
Public; founded 1822
Freshman admissions: N/A; 2013-2014: N/A applied, N/A accepted. Neither SAT nor ACT required. ACT 25/75 percentile: N/A. High school rank: N/A
Early decision deadline: N/A, notification date: N/A
Early action deadline: N/A, notification date: N/A
Application deadline (fall): N/A
Undergraduate student body: 1,343 full time, 1,819 part time; 35% male, 65% female; 2% American Indian, 0% Asian, 11% black, 2% Hispanic, 1% multiracial, 0% Pacific Islander, 75% white, 0% international
Most popular majors: 12% Accounting, 14% Business Administration and Management, General, 14% Elementary Education and Teaching, 4% English Language and Literature, General, 5% Liberal Arts and Sciences/Liberal Studies
Expenses: 2014-2015: $6,120 in state, $11,490 out of state; room/board: N/A
Financial aid: (256) 233-8122; 69% of undergrads determined to have financial need; average aid package $7,820

Auburn University

Auburn University AL
(334) 844-6425
U.S. News ranking: Nat. U., No. 103
Website: www.auburn.edu
Admissions email: admissions@auburn.edu
Public; founded 1856
Freshman admissions: more selective; 2013-2014: 15,745 applied, 13,027 accepted. Either SAT or ACT required. ACT 25/75 percentile: 24-30. High school rank: 29% in top tenth, 60% in top quarter, 86% in top half
Early decision deadline: N/A, notification date: N/A
Early action deadline: 2/1, notification date: 10/15
Application deadline (fall): 6/1
Undergraduate student body: 18,011 full time, 1,788 part time; 51% male, 49% female; 1% American Indian, 2% Asian, 7% black, 3% Hispanic, 0% multiracial, 0% Pacific Islander, 85% white, 1% international; 63% from in state; 21% live on campus; 24% of students in fraternities, 38% in sororities
Most popular majors: 8% Biological and Biomedical Sciences, 19% Business, Management, Marketing, and Related Support Services, 6% Communication, Journalism, and Related Programs, 11% Education, 15% Engineering
Expenses: 2014-2015: $10,200 in state, $27,384 out of state; room/board: $12,178
Financial aid: (334) 844-4634; 38% of undergrads determined to have financial need; average aid package $10,820

Auburn University–Montgomery

Montgomery AL
(334) 244-3611
U.S. News ranking: Reg. U. (S), No. 76
Website: www.aum.edu
Admissions email: vsamuel@aum.edu
Public; founded 1967
Freshman admissions: selective; 2013-2014: 2,386 applied, 1,723 accepted. ACT required. ACT 25/75 percentile: 18-23. High school rank: 16% in top tenth, 38% in top quarter, 68% in top half
Early decision deadline: N/A, notification date: N/A
Early action deadline: N/A, notification date: N/A
Application deadline (fall): 8/1
Undergraduate student body: 2,997 full time, 1,337 part time; 38% male, 62% female; 0% American Indian, 5% Asian, 31% black, 1% Hispanic, 2% multiracial, 0% Pacific Islander, 55% white, 0% international; 92% from in state; 12% live on campus; 4% of students in fraternities, 9% in sororities
Most popular majors: 10% Biological and Biomedical Sciences, 24% Business, Management, Marketing, and Related Support Services, 14% Education, 18% Health Professions and Related Programs, 7% Homeland Security, Law Enforcement, Firefighting and Related Protective Services
Expenses: 2014-2015: $9,080 in state, $19,640 out of state; room/board: $5,390
Financial aid: (334) 244-3571; 66% of undergrads determined to have financial need; average aid package $10,944

Birmingham-Southern College

Birmingham AL
(205) 226-4696
U.S. News ranking: Nat. Lib. Arts, No. 124
Website: www.bsc.edu

Admissions email: admission@bsc.edu
Private; founded 1856
Affiliation: United Methodist
Freshman admissions: more selective; 2013-2014: 1,931 applied, 1,240 accepted. Either SAT or ACT required. ACT 25/75 percentile: 23-27. High school rank: 24% in top tenth, 56% in top quarter, 85% in top half
Early decision deadline: N/A, notification date: N/A
Early action deadline: 11/15, notification date: 12/15
Application deadline (fall): 7/15
Undergraduate student body: 1,167 full time, 21 part time; 54% male, 46% female; 1% American Indian, 4% Asian, 9% black, 3% Hispanic, 1% multiracial, 0% Pacific Islander, 81% white, 0% international; 45% from in state; 86% live on campus; 39% of students in fraternities, 54% in sororities
Most popular majors: 11% Biology/Biological Sciences, General, 22% Business Administration and Management, General, 7% English Language and Literature, General, 6% Psychology, General, 6% Teacher Education, Multiple Levels
Expenses: 2014-2015: $31,888; room/board: $10,990
Financial aid: (205) 226-4688; 56% of undergrads determined to have financial need; average aid package $26,237

Concordia College[1]

Selma AL
(334) 874-5700
U.S. News ranking: Reg. Coll. (S), unranked
Website: www.ccal.edu/
Admissions email: admission@ccal.edu
Private; founded 1922
Affiliation: Lutheran
Application deadline (fall): rolling
Undergraduate student body: N/A full time, N/A part time
Expenses: 2013-2014: $8,190; room/board: $4,340
Financial aid: (334) 874-5700

Faulkner University[1]

Montgomery AL
(334) 386-7200
U.S. News ranking: Reg. Coll. (S), No. 47
Website: www.faulkner.edu
Admissions email: admissions@faulkner.edu
Private; founded 1942
Affiliation: Church of Christ
Application deadline (fall): rolling
Undergraduate student body: N/A full time, N/A part time
Expenses: 2013-2014: $18,230; room/board: $6,780
Financial aid: (334) 386-7195

Huntingdon College

Montgomery AL
(334) 833-4497
U.S. News ranking: Reg. Coll. (S), No. 23
Website: www.huntingdon.edu
Admissions email: admiss@huntingdon.edu
Private; founded 1854
Affiliation: Methodist
Freshman admissions: selective; 2013-2014: 1,470 applied, 923 accepted. Either SAT or ACT required. ACT 25/75 percentile: 19-24. High school rank: 15% in top tenth, 40% in top quarter, 72% in top half
Early decision deadline: N/A, notification date: N/A
Early action deadline: N/A, notification date: N/A
Application deadline (fall): rolling
Undergraduate student body: 902 full time, 208 part time; 50% male, 50% female; 1% American Indian, 1% Asian, 19% black, 2% Hispanic, 3% multiracial, 0% Pacific Islander, 58% white, 0% international; 81% from in state; 59% live on campus; 22% of students in fraternities, 40% in sororities
Most popular majors: 9% Biological and Biomedical Sciences, 49% Business, Management, Marketing, and Related Support Services, 4% Communication, Journalism, and Related Programs, 5% Education, 6% Parks, Recreation, Leisure, and Fitness Studies
Expenses: 2014-2015: $24,550; room/board: $8,550
Financial aid: (334) 833-4519; 76% of undergrads determined to have financial need; average aid package $16,201

Jacksonville State University

Jacksonville AL
(256) 782-5268
U.S. News ranking: Reg. U. (S), second tier
Website: www.jsu.edu
Admissions email: info@jsu.edu
Public; founded 1883
Freshman admissions: selective; 2013-2014: 3,083 applied, 2,570 accepted. Either SAT or ACT required. ACT 25/75 percentile: 19-26. High school rank: 18% in top tenth, 39% in top quarter, 70% in top half
Early decision deadline: N/A, notification date: N/A
Early action deadline: N/A, notification date: N/A
Application deadline (fall): rolling
Undergraduate student body: 5,779 full time, 1,809 part time; 42% male, 58% female; 0% American Indian, 1% Asian, 28% black, 1% Hispanic, 0% multiracial, 0% Pacific Islander, 65% white, 2% international; 82% from in state; 25% live on campus; 14% of students in fraternities, 15% in sororities
Most popular majors: 13% Business Administration and Management, General, 5% Criminal Justice/Safety Studies, 7% Public Administration, 26% Registered Nursing/Registered Nurse, 13% Secondary Education and Teaching
Expenses: 2014-2015: $8,790 in state, $17,280 out of state; room/board: $6,985
Financial aid: (256) 782-5006; 86% of undergrads determined to have financial need; average aid package $9,094

Judson College[1]

Marion AL
(800) 447-9472
U.S. News ranking: Nat. Lib. Arts, second tier
Website: www.judson.edu/
Admissions email: admissions@judson.edu
Private

Application deadline (fall): N/A
Undergraduate student body: N/A
full time, N/A part time
Expenses: 2013-2014: $15,630;
room/board: $9,060
Financial aid: (334) 683-5170

Miles College[1]
Birmingham AL
(800) 445-0708
U.S. News ranking: Reg. Coll. (S),
unranked
Website: www.miles.edu
Admissions email: admissions@
mail.miles.edu
Private
Application deadline (fall): N/A
Undergraduate student body: N/A
full time, N/A part time
Expenses: 2013-2014: $11,454;
room/board: $6,896
Financial aid: (205) 929-1665

Oakwood University[1]
Huntsville AL
(256) 726-7356
U.S. News ranking: Reg. Coll. (S),
No. 46
Website: www.oakwood.edu
Admissions email: admissions@
oakwood.edu
Private; founded 1896
Affiliation: Seventh-day Adventist
Application deadline (fall): rolling
Undergraduate student body: N/A
full time, N/A part time
Expenses: 2013-2014: $16,234;
room/board: $9,700
Financial aid: (256) 726-7210

Samford University
Birmingham AL
(800) 888-7218
U.S. News ranking: Reg. U. (S),
No. 3
Website: www.samford.edu
Admissions email: admission@
samford.edu
Private; founded 1841
Affiliation: Baptist
Freshman admissions: more
selective; 2013-2014: 3,447
applied, 2,653 accepted. Either
SAT or ACT required. ACT 25/75
percentile: 23-28. High school
rank: 35% in top tenth, 59% in
top quarter, 82% in top half
Early decision deadline: N/A,
notification date: N/A
Early action deadline: N/A,
notification date: N/A
Application deadline (fall): 7/1
Undergraduate student body: 2,850
full time, 163 part time; 35%
male, 65% female; 0% American
Indian, 1% Asian, 7% black, 7%
Hispanic, 1% multiracial, 0%
Pacific Islander, 81% white, 3%
international; 37% from in state;
72% live on campus; 10% of
students in fraternities, 32% in
sororities
Most popular majors: 19%
Business, Management,
Marketing, and Related Support
Services, 9% Communication,
Journalism, and Related Programs,
7% Education, 15% Health
Professions and Related Programs,
7% Visual and Performing Arts
Expenses: 2014-2015: $27,324;
room/board: $9,736
Financial aid: (205) 726-2905;
44% of undergrads determined to
have financial need; average aid
package $17,036

Spring Hill College
Mobile AL
(251) 380-3030
U.S. News ranking: Reg. U. (S),
No. 18
Website: www.shc.edu
Admissions email: admit@shc.edu
Private; founded 1830
Affiliation: Catholic
Freshman admissions: more
selective; 2013-2014: 6,956
applied, 3,052 accepted. Either
SAT or ACT required. ACT 25/75
percentile: 21-27. High school
rank: 20% in top tenth, 45% in
top quarter, 75% in top half
Early decision deadline: N/A,
notification date: N/A
Early action deadline: N/A,
notification date: N/A
Application deadline (fall): 7/15
Undergraduate student body: 1,226
full time, 93 part time; 40%
male, 60% female; 1% American
Indian, 1% Asian, 16% black,
9% Hispanic, 2% multiracial,
0% Pacific Islander, 66% white,
1% international; 40% from in
state; 78% live on campus; N/A
of students in fraternities, N/A in
sororities
Most popular majors: 8% Biological
and Biomedical Sciences,
23% Business, Management,
and Related Support Services,
12% Education, 8%
Health Professions and Related
Programs, 10% Psychology
Expenses: 2014-2015: $32,468;
room/board: $11,696
Financial aid: (251) 380-3460;
70% of undergrads determined to
have financial need; average aid
package $30,311

Stillman College[1]
Tuscaloosa AL
(205) 366-8837
U.S. News ranking: Nat. Lib. Arts,
second tier
Website: www.stillman.edu
Admissions email: admissions@
stillman.edu
Private; founded 1876
Affiliation: Presbyterian Church
(USA)
Application deadline (fall): rolling
Undergraduate student body: N/A
full time, N/A part time
Expenses: 2013-2014: $14,910;
room/board: $7,056
Financial aid: (205) 366-8817

Talladega College[1]
Talladega AL
(256) 761-6235
U.S. News ranking: Nat. Lib. Arts,
unranked
Website: www.talladega.edu
Admissions email: admissions@
talladega.edu
Private
Application deadline (fall): N/A
Undergraduate student body: N/A
full time, N/A part time
Expenses: 2013-2014: $11,492;
room/board: $6,504
Financial aid: (256) 761-6341

Troy University
Troy AL
(334) 670-3179
U.S. News ranking: Reg. U. (S),
No. 76
Website: www.troy.edu/
Admissions email: admit@troy.edu
Public; founded 1887

Freshman admissions: selective;
2013-2014: 6,538 applied,
4,392 accepted. Either SAT
or ACT required. ACT 25/75
percentile: 18-25. High school
rank: N/A in top tenth, 52% in top
quarter, 84% in top half
Early decision deadline: N/A,
notification date: N/A
Early action deadline: N/A,
notification date: N/A
Application deadline (fall): rolling
Undergraduate student body: 9,141
full time, 7,175 part time; 38%
male, 62% female; 1% American
Indian, 1% Asian, 37% black,
3% Hispanic, 2% multiracial,
0% Pacific Islander, 49% white,
2% international; 66% from in
state; 35% live on campus; 13%
of students in fraternities, 15%
in sororities
Most popular majors: 46%
Business, Management,
Marketing, and Related Support
Services, 12% Foreign Languages,
Literatures, and Linguistics,
7% Homeland Security, Law
Enforcement, Firefighting and
Related Protective Services,
11% Psychology, 5% Public
Administration and Social Service
Professions
Expenses: 2013-2014: $9,416 in
state, $17,336 out of state; room/
board: $7,144
Financial aid: (334) 670-3186;
71% of undergrads determined to
have financial need; average aid
package $4,531

Tuskegee University
Tuskegee AL
(334) 727-8500
U.S. News ranking: Reg. Coll. (S),
No. 9
Website: www.tuskegee.edu
Admissions email:
admiweb@tusk.edu
Private; founded 1881
Freshman admissions: selective;
2013-2014: 8,894 applied,
3,679 accepted. Either SAT
or ACT required. ACT 25/75
percentile: 18-23. High school
rank: 20% in top tenth, 60% in
top quarter, 100% in top half
Early decision deadline: N/A,
notification date: N/A
Early action deadline: N/A,
notification date: N/A
Application deadline (fall): 3/15
Undergraduate student body: 2,468
full time, 116 part time; 42%
male, 58% female; 0% American
Indian, 0% Asian, 80% black,
0% Hispanic, 0% multiracial,
0% Pacific Islander, 0% white,
0% international; 37% from in
state; 74% live on campus; 1%
of students in fraternities, 2% in
sororities
Most popular majors: 11%
Agriculture, Agriculture
Operations, and Related Sciences,
7% Biology/Biological Sciences,
General, 20% Engineering,
10% Psychology, General, 5%
Registered Nursing, Nursing
Administration, Nursing Research
and Clinical Nursing
Expenses: 2014-2015: $20,025;
room/board: $9,104
Financial aid: (334) 727-8201;
87% of undergrads determined to
have financial need; average aid
package $17,250

University of Alabama
Tuscaloosa AL
(205) 348-5666
U.S. News ranking: Nat. U., No. 88
Website: www.ua.edu
Admissions email:
admissions@ua.edu
Public; founded 1831
Freshman admissions: more
selective; 2013-2014: 30,975
applied, 17,515 accepted. Either
SAT or ACT required. ACT 25/75
percentile: 22-30. High school
rank: 41% in top tenth, 60% in
top quarter, 83% in top half
Early decision deadline: N/A,
notification date: N/A
Early action deadline: N/A,
notification date: N/A
Application deadline (fall): rolling
Undergraduate student body:
26,548 full time, 2,892 part
time; 46% male, 54% female;
0% American Indian, 1% Asian,
11% black, 3% Hispanic, 2%
multiracial, 0% Pacific Islander,
79% white, 3% international;
55% from in state; 26% live
on campus; 24% of students in
fraternities, 35% in sororities
Most popular majors: 29%
Business, Management,
Marketing, and Related Support
Services, 10% Communication,
Journalism, and Related Programs,
8% Education, 7% Family and
Consumer Sciences/Human
Sciences, 9% Health Professions
and Related Programs
Expenses: 2014-2015: $9,826 in
state, $24,950 out of state; room/
board: $8,866
Financial aid: (205) 348-2976;
43% of undergrads determined to
have financial need; average aid
package $11,666

University of Alabama–Birmingham
Birmingham AL
(205) 934-8221
U.S. News ranking: Nat. U.,
No. 149
Website: www.uab.edu
Admissions email:
undergradadmit@uab.edu
Public; founded 1969
Freshman admissions: more
selective; 2013-2014: 5,689
applied, 4,934 accepted. Either
SAT or ACT required. ACT 25/75
percentile: 22-28. High school
rank: 30% in top tenth, 56% in
top quarter, 83% in top half
Early decision deadline: N/A,
notification date: N/A
Early action deadline: N/A,
notification date: N/A
Application deadline (fall): rolling
Undergraduate student body: 8,357
full time, 3,145 part time; 42%
male, 58% female; 0% American
Indian, 5% Asian, 26% black,
3% Hispanic, 3% multiracial,
0% Pacific Islander, 60% white,
1% international; 92% from in
state; 22% live on campus; 4%
of students in fraternities, 4% in
sororities
Most popular majors: 17%
Business, Management,
Marketing, and Related Support
Services, 9% Education, 6%
Engineering, 20% Health
Professions and Related Programs,
8% Psychology
Expenses: 2014-2015: $9,280 in
state, $21,220 out of state; room/
board: $10,112

Financial aid: (205) 934-8223;
61% of undergrads determined to
have financial need; average aid
package $8,941

University of Alabama–Huntsville
Huntsville AL
(256) 824-6070
U.S. News ranking: Nat. U.,
No. 181
Website: www.uah.edu
Admissions email:
admitme@uah.edu
Public; founded 1950
Freshman admissions: more
selective; 2013-2014: 2,054
applied, 1,656 accepted. Either
SAT or ACT required. ACT 25/75
percentile: 23-29. High school
rank: 28% in top tenth, 50% in
top quarter, 83% in top half
Early decision deadline: N/A,
notification date: N/A
Early action deadline: N/A,
notification date: N/A
Application deadline (fall): 8/20
Undergraduate student body: 4,237
full time, 1,459 part time; 56%
male, 44% female; 1% American
Indian, 4% Asian, 13% black,
3% Hispanic, 2% multiracial,
0% Pacific Islander, 70% white,
3% international; 90% from in
state; 20% live on campus; 6%
of students in fraternities, 7% in
sororities
Most popular majors: 8% Biological
and Biomedical Sciences,
22% Business, Management,
Marketing, and Related Support
Services, 25% Engineering,
17% Health Professions and
Related Programs, 3% Visual and
Performing Arts
Expenses: 2014-2015: $9,158 in
state, $21,232 out of state; room/
board: $8,433
Financial aid: (256) 824-6241;
54% of undergrads determined to
have financial need; average aid
package $9,419

University of Mobile
Mobile AL
(251) 442-2273
U.S. News ranking: Reg. Coll. (S),
No. 25
Website: www.umobile.edu
Admissions email: umadminfo@
umobile.edu
Private; founded 1961
Affiliation: Southern Baptist
Freshman admissions: selective;
2013-2014: 866 applied, 617
accepted. Either SAT or ACT
required. ACT 25/75 percentile:
20-25. High school rank: 18%
in top tenth, 50% in top quarter,
84% in top half
Early decision deadline: N/A,
notification date: N/A
Early action deadline: N/A,
notification date: N/A
Application deadline (fall): 8/1
Undergraduate student body: 1,257
full time, 224 part time; 33%
male, 67% female; 2% American
Indian, 1% Asian, 22% black,
1% Hispanic, 2% multiracial,
0% Pacific Islander, 65% white,
3% international; 78% from in
state; 44% live on campus; N/A
of students in fraternities, N/A in
sororities
Most popular majors: 19%
Business, Management,
Marketing, and Related Support
Services, 21% Education, 16%
Health Professions and Related

Programs, 10% Liberal Arts and Sciences, General Studies and Humanities, 5% Philosophy and Religious Studies
Expenses: 2014-2015: $19,700; room/board: $9,550
Financial aid: (251) 442-2385; 72% of undergrads determined to have financial need; average aid package $16,521

University of Montevallo

Montevallo AL
(205) 665-6030
U.S. News ranking: Reg. U. (S), No. 37
Website: www.montevallo.edu
Admissions email: admissions@um.montevallo.edu
Public; founded 1896
Freshman admissions: selective; 2013-2014: 1,545 applied, 1,032 accepted. Either SAT or ACT required. ACT 25/75 percentile: 20-26. High school rank: N/A
Early decision deadline: N/A, notification date: N/A
Early action deadline: N/A, notification date: N/A
Application deadline (fall): 8/1
Undergraduate student body: 2,350 full time, 270 part time; 34% male, 66% female; 1% American Indian, 1% Asian, 14% black, 2% Hispanic, 2% multiracial, 0% Pacific Islander, 74% white, 1% international; 95% from in state; 47% live on campus; 12% of students in fraternities, 17% in sororities
Most popular majors: 12% Business, Management, Marketing, and Related Support Services, 11% Education, 11% English Language and Literature/Letters, 8% Family and Consumer Sciences/Human Sciences, 15% Visual and Performing Arts
Expenses: 2014-2015: $10,660 in state, $21,220 out of state; room/board: $6,400
Financial aid: (205) 665-6050; 63% of undergrads determined to have financial need; average aid package $9,384

University of North Alabama

Florence AL
(256) 765-4608
U.S. News ranking: Reg. U. (S), No. 81
Website: www.una.edu
Admissions email: admissions@una.edu
Public; founded 1830
Freshman admissions: selective; 2013-2014: 2,816 applied, 2,057 accepted. Either SAT or ACT required. ACT 25/75 percentile: 19-25. High school rank: N/A
Early decision deadline: N/A, notification date: N/A
Early action deadline: N/A, notification date: N/A
Application deadline (fall): rolling
Undergraduate student body: 4,852 full time, 1,141 part time; 42% male, 58% female; 1% American Indian, 0% Asian, 14% black, 2% Hispanic, 2% multiracial, 0% Pacific Islander, 72% white, 5% international; 84% from in state; 23% live on campus; 11% of students in fraternities, 11% in sororities

Most popular majors: 16% Business, Management, Marketing, and Related Support Services, 7% Communication, Journalism, and Related Programs, 12% Education, 17% Health Professions and Related Programs, 8% Social Sciences
Expenses: 2014-2015: $9,073 in state, $16,393 out of state; room/board: $6,327
Financial aid: (256) 765-4278; 81% of undergrads determined to have financial need; average aid package $7,104

University of South Alabama

Mobile AL
(251) 460-6141
U.S. News ranking: Nat. U., second tier
Website: www.southalabama.edu
Admissions email: admiss@usouthal.edu
Public; founded 1963
Freshman admissions: selective; 2013-2014: 4,814 applied, 4,142 accepted. Neither SAT nor ACT required. ACT 25/75 percentile: 20-26. High school rank: N/A
Early decision deadline: N/A, notification date: N/A
Early action deadline: N/A, notification date: N/A
Application deadline (fall): 7/15
Undergraduate student body: 8,767 full time, 2,540 part time; 43% male, 57% female; 1% American Indian, 3% Asian, 23% black, 2% Hispanic, 2% multiracial, 0% Pacific Islander, 64% white, 3% international; 81% from in state; 27% live on campus; N/A of students in fraternities, N/A in sororities
Most popular majors: 4% Biomedical Sciences, General, 5% Elementary Education and Teaching, 5% Multi-/Interdisciplinary Studies, General, 18% Registered Nursing/Registered Nurse, 5% Speech Communication and Rhetoric
Expenses: 2013-2014: $6,948 in state, $13,596 out of state; room/board: $7,260
Financial aid: (251) 460-6231

University of West Alabama

Livingston AL
(205) 652-3578
U.S. News ranking: Reg. U. (S), second tier
Website: www.uwa.edu
Admissions email: admissions@uwa.edu
Public; founded 1835
Freshman admissions: selective; 2013-2014: 1,363 applied, 831 accepted. Either SAT or ACT required. ACT 25/75 percentile: 18-22. High school rank: N/A
Early decision deadline: N/A, notification date: N/A
Early action deadline: N/A, notification date: N/A
Application deadline (fall): rolling
Undergraduate student body: 1,696 full time, 303 part time; 43% male, 57% female; 0% American Indian, 1% Asian, 42% black, 2% Hispanic, 1% multiracial, 0% Pacific Islander, 43% white, 5% international; 80% from in state; 45% live on campus; 5% of students in fraternities, 6% in sororities

Most popular majors: 10% Accounting, 10% Finance, General, 13% Physical Education Teaching and Coaching, 6% Sociology, 12% Teacher Education, Multiple Levels
Expenses: 2013-2014: $7,660 in state, $14,170 out of state; room/board: $6,618
Financial aid: (205) 652-3576

ALASKA

Alaska Pacific University

Anchorage AK
(800) 252-7528
U.S. News ranking: Reg. U. (W), No. 75
Website: www.alaskapacific.edu
Admissions email: admissions@alaskapacific.edu
Private; founded 1957
Affiliation: United Methodist
Freshman admissions: selective; 2013-2014: 494 applied, 184 accepted. Either SAT or ACT required. SAT 25/75 percentile: 915-1085. High school rank: N/A
Early decision deadline: N/A, notification date: N/A
Early action deadline: N/A, notification date: N/A
Application deadline (fall): rolling
Undergraduate student body: 245 full time, 142 part time; 34% male, 66% female; 18% American Indian, 2% Asian, 3% black, 3% Hispanic, 9% multiracial, 1% Pacific Islander, 55% white, 0% international
Most popular majors: 19% Business Administration and Management, General, 10% Counseling Psychology, 14% Education, General, 9% Human Services, General, 19% Marine Biology and Biological Oceanography
Expenses: 2014-2015: $19,680; room/board: $7,000
Financial aid: (907) 564-8341; 72% of undergrads determined to have financial need; average aid package $10,310

University of Alaska–Anchorage

Anchorage AK
(907) 786-1480
U.S. News ranking: Reg. U. (W), No. 68
Website: www.uaa.alaska.edu
Admissions email: enroll@uaa.alaska.edu
Public; founded 1954
Freshman admissions: selective; 2013-2014: 3,913 applied, 3,117 accepted. Neither SAT nor ACT required. SAT 25/75 percentile: 880-1080. High school rank: 11% in top tenth, 31% in top quarter, 62% in top half
Early decision deadline: N/A, notification date: N/A
Early action deadline: N/A, notification date: N/A
Application deadline (fall): 7/1
Undergraduate student body: 7,683 full time, 8,894 part time; 41% male, 59% female; 7% American Indian, 7% Asian, 4% black, 7% Hispanic, 10% multiracial, 1% Pacific Islander, 58% white, 2% international; 91% from in state; N/A live on campus; N/A of students in fraternities, N/A in sororities

Most popular majors: 20% Business, Management, Marketing, and Related Support Services, 8% Engineering, 16% Health Professions and Related Programs, 8% Psychology, 5% Social Sciences
Expenses: 2014-2015: $6,002 in state, $19,322 out of state; room/board: $8,680
Financial aid: (907) 786-1586; 53% of undergrads determined to have financial need; average aid package $8,933

University of Alaska–Fairbanks

Fairbanks AK
(800) 478-1823
U.S. News ranking: Nat. U., second tier
Website: www.uaf.edu
Admissions email: fyapply@uaf.edu
Public; founded 1917
Freshman admissions: selective; 2013-2014: 1,529 applied, 1,221 accepted. Either SAT or ACT required. ACT 25/75 percentile: 18-25. High school rank: 18% in top tenth, 39% in top quarter, 67% in top half
Early decision deadline: N/A, notification date: N/A
Early action deadline: N/A, notification date: N/A
Application deadline (fall): 6/15
Undergraduate student body: 3,654 full time, 4,424 part time; 43% male, 57% female; 14% American Indian, 1% Asian, 2% black, 5% Hispanic, 4% multiracial, 0% Pacific Islander, 45% white, 1% international; 87% from in state; 27% live on campus; N/A of students in fraternities, N/A in sororities
Most popular majors: 8% Biological and Biomedical Sciences, 9% Business, Management, Marketing, and Related Support Services, 13% Engineering, 8% Social Sciences, 6% Visual and Performing Arts
Expenses: 2014-2015: $6,752 in state, $20,072 out of state; room/board: $7,450
Financial aid: (907) 474-7256; 54% of undergrads determined to have financial need; average aid package $10,058

University of Alaska–Southeast[1]

Juneau AK
(907) 465-6350
U.S. News ranking: Reg. U. (W), unranked
Website: www.uas.alaska.edu
Admissions email: admissions@uas.alaska.edu
Public
Application deadline (fall): N/A
Undergraduate student body: N/A full time, N/A part time
Expenses: 2013-2014: $5,693 in state, $16,269 out of state; room/board: $9,829
Financial aid: (907) 796-6255

ARIZONA

American Indian College of the Assemblies of God[1]

Phoenix AZ
(800) 933-3828
U.S. News ranking: Reg. Coll. (W), unranked
Website: www.aicag.edu
Admissions email: aicadm@aicag.edu
Private
Application deadline (fall): N/A
Undergraduate student body: N/A full time, N/A part time
Expenses: 2013-2014: $12,000; room/board: $6,202
Financial aid: (800) 933-3828

Arizona State University–Tempe

Tempe AZ
(480) 965-7788
U.S. News ranking: Nat. U., No. 129
Website: www.asu.edu
Admissions email: admissions@asu.edu
Public; founded 1885
Freshman admissions: more selective; 2013-2014: 21,770 applied, 17,465 accepted. Neither SAT nor ACT required. SAT 25/75 percentile: 1020-1270. High school rank: 31% in top tenth, 63% in top quarter, 90% in top half
Early decision deadline: N/A, notification date: N/A
Early action deadline: N/A, notification date: N/A
Undergraduate student body: 34,989 full time, 3,746 part time; 56% male, 44% female; 1% American Indian, 7% Asian, 4% black, 19% Hispanic, 4% multiracial, 0% Pacific Islander, 58% white, 7% international; 77% from in state; 23% live on campus; 8% of students in fraternities, 13% in sororities
Most popular majors: 8% Biological and Biomedical Sciences, 20% Business, Management, Marketing, and Related Support Services, 7% Engineering, 10% Social Sciences, 8% Visual and Performing Arts
Expenses: 2014-2015: $9,811 in state, $23,312 out of state; room/board: $9,440
Financial aid: (480) 965-3355; 58% of undergrads determined to have financial need; average aid package $13,786

Everest College–Phoenix[1]

Phoenix AZ
(888) 523-3117
U.S. News ranking: Reg. Coll. (W), unranked
Website: www.everestcollegephoenix.edu
Admissions email: N/A
For-profit
Application deadline (fall): N/A
Undergraduate student body: N/A full time, N/A part time
Expenses: 2013-2014: $12,960; room/board: N/A
Financial aid: N/A

Frank Lloyd Wright School of Architecture

Scottsdale AZ
(608) 588-4770
U.S. News ranking: Arts, unranked
Website: www.taliesin.edu/
Admissions email: N/A
Private
Freshman admissions: N/A; 2013-2014: N/A applied, N/A accepted. Neither SAT nor ACT required. SAT 25/75 percentile: N/A. High school rank: N/A
Early decision deadline: N/A, notification date: N/A
Early action deadline: N/A, notification date: N/A
Application deadline (fall): 4/1
Undergraduate student body: 2 full time, N/A part time; 100% male, 0% female; N/A American Indian, N/A Asian, N/A black, N/A Hispanic, N/A multiracial, N/A Pacific Islander, N/A white, N/A international
Most popular majors: Information not available
Expenses: 2014-2015 tuition/fees/room/board: $30,300
Financial aid: N/A; 0% of undergrads determined to have financial need; average aid package $4,500

Grand Canyon University[1]

Phoenix AZ
(800) 800-9776
U.S. News ranking: Reg. U. (W), second tier
Website: apply.gcu.edu
Admissions email: golopes@gcu.edu
For-profit; founded 1949
Application deadline (fall): rolling
Undergraduate student body: N/A full time, N/A part time
Expenses: 2013-2014: $18,600; room/board: $7,400
Financial aid: (602) 639-6600

Northcentral University

Prescott Valley AZ
(888) 327-2877
U.S. News ranking: Nat. U., unranked
Website: www.ncu.edu
Admissions email: admissions@ncu.edu
For-profit; founded 1996
Freshman admissions: N/A; 2013-2014: N/A applied, N/A accepted. Neither SAT nor ACT required. ACT 25/75 percentile: N/A. High school rank: N/A
Early decision deadline: N/A, notification date: N/A
Early action deadline: N/A, notification date: N/A
Application deadline (fall): rolling
Undergraduate student body: 195 full time, 241 part time; 35% male, 65% female; 0% American Indian, 1% Asian, 11% black, 5% Hispanic, 1% multiracial, 0% Pacific Islander, 33% white, 0% international
Most popular majors: 10% Accounting and Business/Management, 59% Business Administration and Management, General, 8% Computer Science, 10% Criminal Justice/Law Enforcement Administration, 6% Homeland Security
Expenses: N/A
Financial aid: (928) 541-7777

Northern Arizona University

Flagstaff AZ
(928) 523-5511
U.S. News ranking: Nat. U., second tier
Website: www.nau.edu
Admissions email: undergraduate.admissions@nau.edu
Public; founded 1899
Freshman admissions: selective; 2013-2014: 33,989 applied, 31,057 accepted. Neither SAT nor ACT required. SAT 25/75 percentile: 940-1160. High school rank: 21% in top tenth, 47% in top quarter, 80% in top half
Early decision deadline: N/A, notification date: N/A
Early action deadline: N/A, notification date: N/A
Application deadline (fall): rolling
Undergraduate student body: 18,769 full time, 3,901 part time; 42% male, 58% female; 3% American Indian, 2% Asian, 3% black, 19% Hispanic, 5% multiracial, 0% Pacific Islander, 63% white, 4% international; 72% from in state; 32% live on campus; N/A of students in fraternities; N/A in sororities
Most popular majors: 18% Business, Management, Marketing, and Related Support Services, 13% Education, 8% Health Professions and Related Programs, 11% Liberal Arts and Sciences, General Studies and Humanities, 8% Social Sciences
Expenses: 2014-2015: $10,030 in state, $22,510 out of state; room/board: N/A
Financial aid: (928) 523-4951

Prescott College

Prescott AZ
(877) 350-2100
U.S. News ranking: Reg. U. (W), No. 75
Website: www.prescott.edu/
Admissions email: admissions@prescott.edu
Private; founded 1966
Freshman admissions: selective; 2013-2014: 399 applied, 291 accepted. Either SAT or ACT required. SAT 25/75 percentile: 910-1260. High school rank: N/A
Early decision deadline: 12/1, notification date: 12/15
Early action deadline: N/A, notification date: N/A
Application deadline (fall): 8/15
Undergraduate student body: 444 full time, 101 part time; 45% male, 55% female; 2% American Indian, 1% Asian, 1% black, 6% Hispanic, 4% multiracial, 0% Pacific Islander, 73% white, 1% international; 11% from in state; 16% live on campus; 0% of students in fraternities, 0% in sororities
Most popular majors: 18% Education, 9% Multi/Interdisciplinary Studies, 9% Natural Resources and Conservation, 9% Parks, Recreation, Leisure, and Fitness Studies, 20% Psychology
Expenses: 2014-2015: $25,640; room/board: $8,266
Financial aid: (928) 350-1111; 67% of undergrads determined to have financial need; average aid package $19,706

Southwest University of Visual Arts[1]

Tucson AZ
(800) 825-8753
U.S. News ranking: Arts, unranked
Website: suva.edu/
Admissions email: N/A
For-profit
Application deadline (fall): N/A
Undergraduate student body: N/A full time, N/A part time
Expenses: 2013-2014: $34,541; room/board: N/A
Financial aid: N/A

University of Advancing Technology[1]

Tempe AZ
(602) 383-8228
U.S. News ranking: Reg. Coll. (W), unranked
Website: www.uat.edu
Admissions email: admissions@uat.edu
For-profit
Application deadline (fall): N/A
Undergraduate student body: N/A full time, N/A part time
Expenses: 2013-2014: $19,700; room/board: $10,568
Financial aid: (800) 658-5744

University of Arizona

Tucson AZ
(520) 621-3237
U.S. News ranking: Nat. U., No. 121
Website: www.arizona.edu
Admissions email: admissions@arizona.edu
Public; founded 1885
Freshman admissions: selective; 2013-2014: 26,481 applied, 20,546 accepted. Neither SAT nor ACT required. SAT 25/75 percentile: 970-1220. High school rank: 31% in top tenth, 60% in top quarter, 88% in top half
Early decision deadline: N/A, notification date: N/A
Early action deadline: N/A, notification date: N/A
Application deadline (fall): 5/1
Undergraduate student body: 28,401 full time, 3,269 part time; 48% male, 52% female; 1% American Indian, 6% Asian, 3% black, 24% Hispanic, 4% multiracial, 0% Pacific Islander, 55% white, 6% international; 74% from in state; 20% live on campus; N/A of students in fraternities, N/A in sororities
Most popular majors: 10% Biological and Biomedical Sciences, 17% Business, Management, Marketing, and Related Support Services, 5% Multi/Interdisciplinary Studies, 8% Psychology, 9% Social Sciences
Expenses: 2014-2015: $10,581 in state, $28,379 out of state; room/board: $9,700
Financial aid: (520) 621-5200; 55% of undergrads determined to have financial need; average aid package $12,495

University of Phoenix[1]

Phoenix AZ
(866) 766-0766
U.S. News ranking: Nat. U., unranked
Website: www.phoenix.edu
Admissions email: N/A
For-profit
Application deadline (fall): N/A

Undergraduate student body: N/A full time, N/A part time
Expenses: N/A
Financial aid: N/A

Western International University

Tempe AZ
(602) 943-2311
U.S. News ranking: Reg. U. (W), unranked
Website: www.west.edu/
Admissions email: N/A
For-profit; founded 1978
Freshman admissions: N/A; 2013-2014: 2 applied, 2 accepted. Neither SAT nor ACT required. ACT 25/75 percentile: N/A. High school rank: N/A
Early decision deadline: N/A, notification date: N/A
Early action deadline: N/A, notification date: N/A
Application deadline (fall): rolling
Undergraduate student body: 1,495 full time, 0 part time; 35% male, 65% female; 2% American Indian, 0% Asian, 15% black, 15% Hispanic, 4% multiracial, 1% Pacific Islander, 49% white, 1% international
Most popular majors: 11% Accounting, 15% Behavioral Sciences, 10% Business Administration and Management, General, 43% Business/Commerce, General, 4% Information Technology
Expenses: 2013-2014: $6,000; room/board: N/A
Financial aid: (602) 943-2311

ARKANSAS

Arkansas Baptist College[1]

Little Rock AR
(501) 244-5104
U.S. News ranking: Reg. Coll. (S), unranked
Website: www.arkansasbaptist.edu
Admissions email: jocelyn.spriggs@arkansasbaptist.edu
Private
Application deadline (fall): N/A
Undergraduate student body: N/A full time, N/A part time
Expenses: 2013-2014: $8,040; room/board: $8,040
Financial aid: (501) 374-0804

Arkansas State University

State University AR
(870) 972-3024
U.S. News ranking: Reg. U. (S), No. 53
Website: www.astate.edu
Admissions email: admissions@astate.edu
Public; founded 1909
Freshman admissions: selective; 2013-2014: 4,838 applied, 3,653 accepted. Either SAT or ACT required. ACT 25/75 percentile: 21-26. High school rank: 25% in top tenth, 47% in top quarter, 72% in top half
Early decision deadline: N/A, notification date: N/A
Early action deadline: N/A, notification date: N/A
Application deadline (fall): 8/18
Undergraduate student body: 7,645 full time, 2,453 part time; 42% male, 58% female; 0% American Indian, 1% Asian, 15% black, 2% Hispanic, 2% multiracial, 0% Pacific Islander, 73% white, 6% international; 90% from in state; 31% live on campus; 12% of students in fraternities, 10% in sororities
Most popular majors: 14% Business, Management, Marketing, and Related Support Services, 17% Education, 13% Health Professions and Related Programs, 10% Liberal Arts and Sciences, General Studies and Humanities, 8% Social Sciences
Expenses: 2014-2015: $7,720 in state, $13,480 out of state; room/board: $7,750
Financial aid: (870) 972-2310; 83% of undergrads determined to have financial need; average aid package $10,500

Arkansas Tech University

Russellville AR
(479) 968-0343
U.S. News ranking: Reg. U. (S), No. 92
Website: www.atu.edu
Admissions email: tech.enroll@atu.edu
Public; founded 1909
Freshman admissions: selective; 2013-2014: 3,849 applied, 3,272 accepted. Either SAT or ACT required. ACT 25/75 percentile: 18-25. High school rank: 13% in top tenth, 33% in top quarter, 62% in top half
Early decision deadline: N/A, notification date: N/A
Early action deadline: N/A, notification date: N/A
Application deadline (fall): rolling
Undergraduate student body: 7,063 full time, 3,419 part time; 46% male, 54% female; 1% American Indian, 1% Asian, 8% black, 5% Hispanic, 2% multiracial, 0% Pacific Islander, 79% white, 3% international; 96% from in state; 30% live on campus; 5% of students in fraternities, 7% in sororities
Most popular majors: 6% Business Administration and Management, General, 8% Early Childhood Education and Teaching, 18% Multi-/Interdisciplinary Studies, Other, 5% Psychology, General, 9% Registered Nursing/Registered Nurse
Expenses: 2014-2015: $7,248 in state, $13,518 out of state; room/board: $6,734
Financial aid: (479) 968-0399; 69% of undergrads determined to have financial need; average aid package $9,028

Central Baptist College

Conway AR
(501) 329-6873
U.S. News ranking: Reg. Coll. (S), No. 69
Website: www.cbc.edu
Admissions email: admissions@cbc.edu
Private; founded 1952
Affiliation: Baptist Missionary Association of America
Freshman admissions: selective; 2013-2014: 386 applied, 212 accepted. Either SAT or ACT required. ACT 25/75 percentile: 19-23. High school rank: 18% in top tenth, 38% in top quarter, 64% in top half

Early decision deadline: N/A, notification date: N/A
Early action deadline: N/A, notification date: N/A
Application deadline (fall): rolling
Undergraduate student body: 650 full time, 177 part time; 51% male, 49% female; 1% American Indian, 0% Asian, 22% black, 2% Hispanic, 1% multiracial, 0% Pacific Islander, 70% white, 3% international; 90% from in state; 18% live on campus; 0% of students in fraternities, 0% in sororities
Most popular majors: 21% Bible/ Biblical Studies, 5% Business, Management, Marketing, and Related Support Services, Other, 11% General Studies, 6% Management Information Systems, General, 21% Organizational Behavior Studies
Expenses: 2014-2015: $13,800; room/board: $7,500
Financial aid: (501) 329-6872; 76% of undergrads determined to have financial need; average aid package $11,885

Harding University

Searcy AR
(800) 477-4407
U.S. News ranking: Reg. U. (S), No. 22
Website: www.harding.edu
Admissions email: admissions@ harding.edu
Private; founded 1924
Affiliation: Church of Christ
Freshman admissions: more selective; 2013-2014: 2,180 applied, 1,663 accepted. Either SAT or ACT required. ACT 25/75 percentile: 22-28. High school rank: 27% in top tenth, 50% in top quarter, 77% in top half
Early decision deadline: N/A, notification date: N/A
Early action deadline: 11/15, notification date: N/A
Application deadline (fall): rolling
Undergraduate student body: 4,105 full time, 323 part time; 46% male, 54% female; 1% American Indian, 1% Asian, 4% black, 3% Hispanic, 1% multiracial, 0% Pacific Islander, 83% white, 7% international; 28% from in state; 69% live on campus; 55% of students in fraternities, 54% in sororities
Most popular majors: 17% Business, Management, Marketing, and Related Support Services, 14% Education, 12% Health Professions and Related Programs, 8% Liberal Arts and Sciences, General Studies and Humanities, 6% Parks, Recreation, Leisure, and Fitness Studies
Expenses: 2014-2015: $17,040; room/board: $6,516
Financial aid: (501) 279-5278; 61% of undergrads determined to have financial need; average aid package $16,825

Henderson State University

Arkadelphia AR
(870) 230-5028
U.S. News ranking: Reg. U. (S), second tier
Website: www.hsu.edu/admissions
Admissions email: admissions@hsu.edu
Public; founded 1890
Freshman admissions: selective;

2013-2014: 3,388 applied, 2,106 accepted. Either SAT or ACT required. ACT 25/75 percentile: 19-24. High school rank: 12% in top tenth, 26% in top quarter, 52% in top half
Early decision deadline: N/A, notification date: N/A
Early action deadline: N/A, notification date: N/A
Application deadline (fall): rolling
Undergraduate student body: 2,878 full time, 321 part time; 44% male, 56% female; 0% American Indian, 1% Asian, 24% black, 3% Hispanic, 5% multiracial, 0% Pacific Islander, 66% white, 1% international; 85% from in state; 42% live on campus; 16% of students in fraternities, 13% in sororities
Most popular majors: 14% Business, Management, Marketing, and Related Support Services, 22% Education, 6% Health Professions and Related Programs, 13% Liberal Arts and Sciences, General Studies and Humanities, 8% Psychology
Expenses: 2014-2015: $7,561 in state, $13,921 out of state; room/ board: $6,500
Financial aid: (870) 230-5148; 82% of undergrads determined to have financial need; average aid package $12,619

Hendrix College

Conway AR
(800) 277-9017
U.S. News ranking: Nat. Lib. Arts, No. 81
Website: www.hendrix.edu
Admissions email: adm@hendrix.edu
Private; founded 1876
Affiliation: United Methodist
Freshman admissions: more selective; 2013-2014: 1,926 applied, 1,548 accepted. Either SAT or ACT required. ACT 25/75 percentile: 26-32. High school rank: 46% in top tenth, 74% in top quarter, 95% in top half
Early decision deadline: N/A, notification date: N/A
Early action deadline: 11/15, notification date: 12/15
Application deadline (fall): 6/1
Undergraduate student body: 1,409 full time, 7 part time; 45% male, 55% female; 2% American Indian, 5% Asian, 5% black, 5% Hispanic, 2% multiracial, 0% Pacific Islander, 71% white, 4% international; 49% from in state; 92% live on campus; 0% of students in fraternities, 0% in sororities
Most popular majors: 17% Biology/ Biological Sciences, General, 5% Drama and Dramatics/ Theatre Arts, General, 4% Multi-/ Interdisciplinary Studies, Other, 16% Psychology, General, 17% Sociology
Expenses: 2014-2015: $39,290; room/board: $10,912
Financial aid: (501) 450-1368; 63% of undergrads determined to have financial need; average aid package $29,590

John Brown University

Siloam Springs AR
(877) 528-4636
U.S. News ranking: Reg. Coll. (S), No. 1
Website: www.jbu.edu
Admissions email: jbuinfo@jbu.edu
Private; founded 1919
Affiliation: Interdenominational
Freshman admissions: more selective; 2013-2014: 1,143 applied, 798 accepted. Either SAT or ACT required. ACT 25/75 percentile: 23-29. High school rank: 30% in top tenth, 65% in top quarter, 86% in top half
Early decision deadline: N/A, notification date: N/A
Early action deadline: N/A, notification date: N/A
Application deadline (fall): rolling
Undergraduate student body: 1,571 full time, 510 part time; 44% male, 56% female; 1% American Indian, 1% Asian, 2% black, 5% Hispanic, 3% multiracial, 0% Pacific Islander, 80% white, 7% international; 40% from in state; 69% live on campus; 0% of students in fraternities, 0% in sororities
Most popular majors: 46% Business, Management, Marketing, and Related Support Services, 6% Communication, Journalism, and Related Programs, 10% Education, 6% Family and Consumer Sciences/ Human Sciences, 7% Visual and Performing Arts
Expenses: 2014-2015: $23,588; room/board: $8,468
Financial aid: (479) 524-7115; 72% of undergrads determined to have financial need; average aid package $18,422

Lyon College

Batesville AR
(800) 423-2542
U.S. News ranking: Nat. Lib. Arts, No. 165
Website: www.lyon.edu
Admissions email: admissions@ lyon.edu
Private; founded 1872
Affiliation: Presbyterian
Freshman admissions: more selective; 2013-2014: 1,308 applied, 769 accepted. Either SAT or ACT required. ACT 25/75 percentile: 23-28. High school rank: 29% in top tenth, 55% in top quarter, 87% in top half
Early decision deadline: N/A, notification date: N/A
Early action deadline: 10/31, notification date: 11/15
Application deadline (fall): rolling
Undergraduate student body: 562 full time, 30 part time; 46% male, 54% female; 2% American Indian, 1% Asian, 4% black, 4% Hispanic, 0% multiracial, 0% Pacific Islander, 78% white, 3% international; 80% from in state; 72% live on campus; 39% of students in fraternities, 29% in sororities
Most popular majors: 19% Biology/ Biological Sciences, General, 8% Business Administration and Management, General, 12% English Language and Literature, General, 8% Mathematics, General, 18% Psychology, General
Expenses: 2014-2015: $24,300; room/board: $7,790
Financial aid: (870) 698-4257; 78% of undergrads determined to have financial need; average aid package $21,772

Ouachita Baptist University

Arkadelphia AR
(870) 245-5110
U.S. News ranking: Nat. Lib. Arts, No. 176
Website: www.obu.edu
Admissions email: admissions@obu.edu
Private; founded 1886
Affiliation: Arkansas Baptist State Convention
Freshman admissions: more selective; 2013-2014: 1,740 applied, 1,220 accepted. Either SAT or ACT required. ACT 25/75 percentile: 21-27. High school rank: 29% in top tenth, 53% in top quarter, 80% in top half
Early decision deadline: N/A, notification date: N/A
Early action deadline: N/A, notification date: N/A
Application deadline (fall): rolling
Undergraduate student body: 1,507 full time, 36 part time; 47% male, 53% female; 1% American Indian, 1% Asian, 8% black, 4% Hispanic, 0% multiracial, 0% Pacific Islander, 84% white, 2% international; 61% from in state; 95% live on campus; 20% of students in fraternities, 30% in sororities
Most popular majors: 12% Biological and Biomedical Sciences, 15% Business, Management, Marketing, and Related Support Services, 9% Communication, Journalism, and Related Programs, 11% Theology and Religious Vocations, 13% Visual and Performing Arts
Expenses: 2014-2015: $23,320; room/board: $6,900
Financial aid: (870) 245-5570; 60% of undergrads determined to have financial need; average aid package $22,141

Philander Smith College

Little Rock AR
(501) 370-5221
U.S. News ranking: Reg. Coll. (S), No. 43
Website: www.philander.edu
Admissions email: admissions@ philander.edu
Private; founded 1877
Affiliation: United Methodist
Freshman admissions: selective; 2013-2014: 5,181 applied, 2,151 accepted. Either SAT or ACT required. ACT 25/75 percentile: 16-22. High school rank: 16% in top tenth, 44% in top quarter, 64% in top half
Early decision deadline: N/A, notification date: N/A
Early action deadline: N/A, notification date: N/A
Application deadline (fall): 7/1
Undergraduate student body: 523 full time, 33 part time; 34% male, 66% female; 0% American Indian, 0% Asian, 90% black, 0% Hispanic, 1% multiracial, 0% Pacific Islander, 1% white, 8% international; 50% from in state; 40% live on campus; 4% of students in fraternities, 2% in sororities
Most popular majors: 10% Biological and Biomedical Sciences, 30% Business, Management, Marketing, and Related Support Services, 9% Parks, Recreation, Leisure, and Fitness Studies, 9% Public

Administration and Social Service Professions, 19% Social Sciences
Expenses: 2014-2015: $10,490; room/board: $8,104
Financial aid: (501) 370-5350

Southern Arkansas University

Magnolia AR
(870) 235-4040
U.S. News ranking: Reg. U. (S), second tier
Website: www.saumag.edu
Admissions email: muleriders@saumag.edu
Public; founded 1909
Freshman admissions: selective; 2013-2014: 2,720 applied, 1,654 accepted. Either SAT or ACT required. ACT 25/75 percentile: 18-24. High school rank: 20% in top tenth, 42% in top quarter, 74% in top half
Early decision deadline: N/A, notification date: N/A
Early action deadline: N/A, notification date: N/A
Application deadline (fall): 8/27
Undergraduate student body: 2,497 full time, 463 part time; 42% male, 58% female; 1% American Indian, 1% Asian, 28% black, 2% Hispanic, 0% multiracial, 1% Pacific Islander, 65% white, 3% international; 77% from in state; 45% live on campus; 2% of students in fraternities, 9% in sororities
Most popular majors: 22% Business, Management, Marketing, and Related Support Services, 13% Education, 8% Health Professions and Related Programs, 7% Homeland Security, Law Enforcement, Firefighting and Related Protective Services, 10% Liberal Arts and Sciences, General Studies and Humanities
Expenses: 2013-2014: $7,466 in state, $10,616 out of state; room/ board: $5,740
Financial aid: (870) 235-4023

University of Arkansas

Fayetteville AR
(800) 377-8632
U.S. News ranking: Nat. U., No. 135
Website: www.uark.edu
Admissions email: uofa@uark.edu
Public; founded 1871
Freshman admissions: more selective; 2013-2014: 18,908 applied, 11,076 accepted. Either SAT or ACT required. ACT 25/75 percentile: 23-28. High school rank: 28% in top tenth, 57% in top quarter, 88% in top half
Early decision deadline: N/A, notification date: N/A
Early action deadline: 11/1, notification date: 12/15
Application deadline (fall): 8/1
Undergraduate student body: 18,565 full time, 2,444 part time; 49% male, 51% female; 1% American Indian, 2% Asian, 5% black, 6% Hispanic, 3% multiracial, 0% Pacific Islander, 79% white, 3% international; 63% from in state; 29% live on campus; 22% of students in fraternities, 36% in sororities
Most popular majors: 22% Business, Management, Marketing, and Related Support Services, 9% Engineering, 6% Health Professions and Related Programs, 6% Parks, Recreation,

Leisure, and Fitness Studies, 9% Social Sciences
Expenses: 2014-2015: $8,210 in state, $20,300 out of state; room/board: $9,454
Financial aid: (479) 575-3806; 46% of undergrads determined to have financial need; average aid package $9,386

University of Arkansas–Fort Smith[1]
Fort Smith AR
(479) 788-7120
U.S. News ranking: Reg. Coll. (S), second tier
Website: www.uafortsmith.edu/Home/Index
Admissions email: N/A
Public
Application deadline (fall): N/A
Undergraduate student body: N/A full time, N/A part time
Expenses: 2013-2014: $4,528 in state, $10,072 out of state; room/board: $7,920
Financial aid: (479) 788-7090

University of Arkansas–Little Rock
Little Rock AR
(501) 569-3127
U.S. News ranking: Nat. U., second tier
Website: www.ualr.edu/
Admissions email: admissions@ualr.edu
Public; founded 1927
Freshman admissions: selective; 2013-2014: 997 applied, 685 accepted. Either SAT or ACT required. Average composite ACT score: 22. High school rank: N/A
Early decision deadline: N/A, notification date: N/A
Early action deadline: N/A, notification date: N/A
Application deadline (fall): 8/1
Undergraduate student body: 5,552 full time, 4,418 part time; 41% male, 59% female; 0% American Indian, 2% Asian, 26% black, 6% Hispanic, 6% multiracial, 0% Pacific Islander, 55% white, 3% international; 97% from in state; 10% live on campus; 3% of students in fraternities, 2% in sororities
Most popular majors: 18% Business, Management, Marketing, and Related Support Services, 16% Health Professions and Related Programs, 9% Homeland Security, Law Enforcement, Firefighting and Related Protective Services, 6% Liberal Arts and Sciences, General Studies and Humanities, 7% Psychology
Expenses: 2014-2015: $7,909 in state, $18,979 out of state; room/board: $8,540
Financial aid: (501) 569-3035; 73% of undergrads determined to have financial need; average aid package $11,080

University of Arkansas–Monticello[1]
Monticello AR
(870) 460-1026
U.S. News ranking: Reg. U. (S), unranked
Website: www.uamont.edu
Admissions email: admissions@uamont.edu
Public
Application deadline (fall): N/A

Undergraduate student body: N/A full time, N/A part time
Expenses: 2013-2014: $5,793 in state, $11,590 out of state; room/board: $5,834
Financial aid: (870) 460-1050

University of Arkansas–Pine Bluff
Pine Bluff AR
(870) 575-8492
U.S. News ranking: Reg. Coll. (S), No. 43
Website: www.uapb.edu/
Admissions email: jonesm@uapb.edu
Public; founded 1873
Freshman admissions: less selective; 2013-2014: 4,094 applied, 1,134 accepted. Either SAT or ACT required. ACT 25/75 percentile: 15-20. High school rank: 11% in top tenth, 27% in top quarter, 55% in top half
Early decision deadline: N/A, notification date: N/A
Early action deadline: N/A, notification date: N/A
Application deadline (fall): rolling
Undergraduate student body: 2,300 full time, 221 part time; 46% male, 54% female; 0% American Indian, 0% Asian, 93% black, 1% Hispanic, 0% multiracial, 0% Pacific Islander, 4% white, 1% international; 63% from in state; 43% live on campus; 4% of students in fraternities, 5% in sororities
Most popular majors: 8% Biology/Biological Sciences, General, 10% Business Administration and Management, General, 11% Criminal Justice/Safety Studies, 8% Family and Consumer Sciences/Human Sciences, General, 10% General Studies
Expenses: 2014-2015: $5,956 in state, $11,626 out of state; room/board: $7,400
Financial aid: (870) 575-8302; 90% of undergrads determined to have financial need; average aid package $10,960

University of Central Arkansas
Conway AR
(501) 450-3128
U.S. News ranking: Reg. U. (S), No. 65
Website: www.uca.edu
Admissions email: admissions@uca.edu
Public; founded 1907
Freshman admissions: selective; 2013-2014: 4,060 applied, 3,738 accepted. Either SAT or ACT required. ACT 25/75 percentile: 20-26. High school rank: 19% in top tenth, 43% in top quarter, 73% in top half
Early decision deadline: N/A, notification date: N/A
Early action deadline: N/A, notification date: N/A
Application deadline (fall): rolling
Undergraduate student body: 8,285 full time, 1,469 part time; 42% male, 58% female; 1% American Indian, 1% Asian, 19% black, 4% Hispanic, 3% multiracial, 0% Pacific Islander, 67% white, 3% international; 88% from in state; 36% live on campus; 23% of students in fraternities, 23% in sororities
Most popular majors: 5% Biology/Biological Sciences, General, 9% Health Professions and Related

Clinical Sciences, Other, 4% Kindergarten/Preschool Education and Teaching, 4% Psychology, General, 4% Registered Nursing/Registered Nurse
Expenses: 2014-2015: $7,889 in state, $13,806 out of state; room/board: $5,778
Financial aid: (501) 450-3140

University of the Ozarks
Clarksville AR
(479) 979-1227
U.S. News ranking: Reg. Coll. (S), No. 4
Website: www.ozarks.edu
Admissions email: admiss@ozarks.edu
Private; founded 1834
Affiliation: Presbyterian
Freshman admissions: selective; 2013-2014: 1,061 applied, 651 accepted. Either SAT or ACT required. ACT 25/75 percentile: 20-26. High school rank: 21% in top tenth, 44% in top quarter, 78% in top half
Early decision deadline: N/A, notification date: N/A
Early action deadline: N/A, notification date: N/A
Application deadline (fall): rolling
Undergraduate student body: 571 full time, 14 part time; 48% male, 52% female; 2% American Indian, 0% Asian, 8% black, 2% Hispanic, 0% multiracial, 0% Pacific Islander, 76% white, 12% international; 65% from in state; 76% live on campus; 0% of students in fraternities, 0% in sororities
Most popular majors: Information not available
Expenses: 2014-2015: $24,350; room/board: $7,000
Financial aid: (479) 979-1221; 72% of undergrads determined to have financial need; average aid package $29,788

Williams Baptist College
Walnut Ridge AR
(800) 722-4434
U.S. News ranking: Reg. Coll. (S), No. 59
Website: www.williamsbaptistcollege.com
Admissions email: admissions@wbcoll.edu
Private; founded 1941
Affiliation: Southern Baptist Convention
Freshman admissions: selective; 2013-2014: 531 applied, 361 accepted. Either SAT or ACT required. ACT 25/75 percentile: 20-25. High school rank: N/A
Early decision deadline: N/A, notification date: N/A
Early action deadline: N/A, notification date: N/A
Application deadline (fall): rolling
Undergraduate student body: 474 full time, 98 part time; 38% male, 62% female; 1% American Indian, 0% Asian, 7% black, 3% Hispanic, 0% multiracial, 0% Pacific Islander, 87% white, 3% international
Most popular majors: 9% Bible/Biblical Studies, 15% Elementary Education and Teaching, 14% Liberal Arts and Sciences/Liberal Studies, 9% Physical Education Teaching and Coaching, 21% Psychology, General

Expenses: 2014-2015: $14,360; room/board: $6,800
Financial aid: (870) 759-4112; 73% of undergrads determined to have financial need; average aid package $14,768

CALIFORNIA

Academy of Art University
San Francisco CA
(800) 544-2787
U.S. News ranking: Arts, unranked
Website: www.academyart.edu/
Admissions email: admissions@academyart.edu
For-profit; founded 1929
Freshman admissions: N/A; 2013-2014: 2,914 applied, 2,914 accepted. Neither SAT nor ACT required. SAT 25/75 percentile: N/A. High school rank: N/A
Early decision deadline: N/A, notification date: N/A
Early action deadline: N/A, notification date: N/A
Application deadline (fall): rolling
Undergraduate student body: 5,727 full time, 4,781 part time; 44% male, 56% female; 1% American Indian, 8% Asian, 7% black, 10% Hispanic, 3% multiracial, 0% Pacific Islander, 26% white, 22% international; 60% from in state; 13% live on campus; N/A of students in fraternities, N/A in sororities
Most popular majors: 15% Animation, Interactive Technology, Video Graphics and Special Effects, 11% Cinematography and Film/Video Production, 16% Fashion/Apparel Design, 8% Graphic Design, 11% Illustration
Expenses: 2014-2015: $24,600; room/board: $14,160
Financial aid: (415) 274-2223; 47% of undergrads determined to have financial need; average aid package $10,242

Alliant International University
San Diego CA
(858) 635-4772
U.S. News ranking: Nat. U., unranked
Website: www.alliant.edu
Admissions email: admissions@alliant.edu
Private; founded 1969
Freshman admissions: N/A; 2013-2014: N/A applied, N/A accepted. Neither SAT nor ACT required. ACT 25/75 percentile: N/A. High school rank: N/A
Early decision deadline: N/A, notification date: N/A
Early action deadline: N/A, notification date: N/A
Application deadline (fall): rolling
Undergraduate student body: 186 full time, 1,179 part time; 45% male, 55% female; 0% American Indian, 1% Asian, 4% black, 10% Hispanic, 1% multiracial, 0% Pacific Islander, 12% white, 69% international
Most popular majors: 76% Business Administration and Management, General, 24% Psychology, General
Expenses: 2014-2015: $19,930; room/board: $7,790
Financial aid: (858) 635-4700

American Jewish University
Bel-Air CA
(310) 440-1247
U.S. News ranking: Nat. Lib. Arts, second tier
Website: www.aju.edu
Admissions email: admissions@aju.edu
Private
Affiliation: Jewish
Freshman admissions: selective; 2013-2014: 98 applied, 41 accepted. Neither SAT nor ACT required. SAT 25/75 percentile: 780-1240. High school rank: N/A
Early decision deadline: N/A, notification date: N/A
Early action deadline: 11/15, notification date: 12/15
Application deadline (fall): rolling
Undergraduate student body: 108 full time, 4 part time; 50% male, 50% female; N/A American Indian, N/A Asian, N/A black, N/A Hispanic, N/A multiracial, N/A Pacific Islander, N/A white, N/A international
Most popular majors: Information not available
Expenses: 2014-2015: $29,132; room/board: $15,102
Financial aid: (310) 476-9777; 98% of undergrads determined to have financial need; average aid package $42,000

Argosy University[1]
Orange CA
(800) 377-0617
U.S. News ranking: Nat. U., unranked
Website: www.argosy.edu/
Admissions email: N/A
For-profit
Application deadline (fall): N/A
Undergraduate student body: N/A full time, N/A part time
Expenses: 2013-2014: $13,663; room/board: N/A
Financial aid: (714) 620-3687

Art Center College of Design
Pasadena CA
(626) 396-2373
U.S. News ranking: Arts, unranked
Website: www.artcenter.edu
Admissions email: admissions@artcenter.edu
Private; founded 1930
Freshman admissions: N/A; 2013-2014: 480 applied, 392 accepted. Neither SAT nor ACT required. SAT 25/75 percentile: N/A. High school rank: N/A
Early decision deadline: N/A, notification date: N/A
Early action deadline: N/A, notification date: N/A
Application deadline (fall): rolling
Undergraduate student body: 1,499 full time, 268 part time; 50% male, 50% female; 0% American Indian, 35% Asian, 1% black, 11% Hispanic, 4% multiracial, 0% Pacific Islander, 22% white, 24% international
Most popular majors: 6% Architecture and Related Services, 7% Communication, Journalism, and Related Programs, 2% Communications Technologies/Technicians and Support Services, 85% Visual and Performing Arts
Expenses: 2014-2015: $37,830; room/board: N/A
Financial aid: (626) 396-2215

Azusa Pacific University

Azusa CA
(800) 825-5278
U.S. News ranking: Nat. U., No. 173
Website: www.apu.edu
Admissions email: admissions@apu.edu
Private; founded 1899
Affiliation: Christian interdenominational
Freshman admissions: selective; 2013-2014: 5,105 applied, 4,201 accepted. Either SAT or ACT required. SAT 25/75 percentile: 980-1190. High school rank: 27% in top tenth, 62% in top quarter, 89% in top half
Early decision deadline: N/A, notification date: N/A
Early action deadline: 11/15, notification date: 1/15
Application deadline (fall): 6/1
Undergraduate student body: 5,683 full time, 860 part time; 36% male, 64% female; 0% American Indian, 8% Asian, 5% black, 23% Hispanic, 6% multiracial, 1% Pacific Islander, 50% white, 2% international; 83% from in state; 55% live on campus; 0% of students in fraternities, 0% in sororities
Most popular majors: 17% Business, Management, Marketing, and Related Support Services, 5% Communication, Journalism, and Related Programs, 14% Health Professions and Related Programs, 12% Liberal Arts and Sciences, General Studies and Humanities, 11% Psychology
Expenses: 2014-2015: $33,096; room/board: $8,990
Financial aid: (626) 815-6000

Biola University

La Mirada CA
(562) 903-4752
U.S. News ranking: Nat. U., No. 161
Website: www.biola.edu
Admissions email: admissions@biola.edu
Private; founded 1908
Affiliation: Christian, Interdenominational
Freshman admissions: selective; 2013-2014: 3,615 applied, 2,699 accepted. Either SAT or ACT required. SAT 25/75 percentile: 1000-1240. High school rank: 33% in top tenth, 63% in top quarter, 89% in top half
Early decision deadline: N/A, notification date: N/A
Early action deadline: 11/15, notification date: 12/15
Application deadline (fall): rolling
Undergraduate student body: 4,203 full time, 150 part time; 38% male, 62% female; 0% American Indian, 16% Asian, 2% black, 17% Hispanic, 6% multiracial, 0% Pacific Islander, 54% white, 2% international; 78% from in state; 42% live on campus; 0% of students in fraternities, 0% in sororities
Most popular majors: 15% Business, Management, Marketing, and Related Support Services, 9% Communication, Journalism, and Related Programs, 10% Psychology, 9% Theology and Religious Vocations, 14% Visual and Performing Arts

Expenses: 2014-2015: $33,322; room/board: $9,910
Financial aid: (562) 903-4742; 69% of undergrads determined to have financial need; average aid package $18,453

Brandman University

Irvine CA
(877) 516-4501
U.S. News ranking: Reg. U. (W), unranked
Website: www.brandman.edu
Admissions email: apply@brandman.edu
Private; founded 1958
Freshman admissions: N/A; 2013-2014: 74 applied, 55 accepted. Neither SAT nor ACT required. ACT 25/75 percentile: N/A. High school rank: N/A
Early decision deadline: N/A, notification date: N/A
Early action deadline: N/A, notification date: N/A
Application deadline (fall): rolling
Undergraduate student body: 1,552 full time, 2,333 part time; 38% male, 62% female; 1% American Indian, 3% Asian, 10% black, 27% Hispanic, 4% multiracial, 1% Pacific Islander, 46% white, 0% international; 83% from in state; 0% live on campus; 0% of students in fraternities, 0% in sororities
Most popular majors: 9% Business Administration and Management, General, 9% Developmental and Child Psychology, 14% Liberal Arts and Sciences/Liberal Studies, 16% Organizational Behavior Studies, 18% Psychology, General
Expenses: 2014-2015: $12,200; room/board: N/A
Financial aid: (415) 575-6122; 73% of undergrads determined to have financial need; average aid package $26,614

California Baptist University

Riverside CA
(877) 228-8866
U.S. News ranking: Reg. U. (W), No. 38
Website: www.calbaptist.edu
Admissions email: admissions@calbaptist.edu
Private; founded 1950
Affiliation: California Southern Baptist Convention
Freshman admissions: selective; 2013-2014: 3,853 applied, 3,036 accepted. Either SAT or ACT required. SAT 25/75 percentile: 850-1110. High school rank: 17% in top tenth, 43% in top quarter, 78% in top half
Early decision deadline: N/A, notification date: N/A
Early action deadline: 12/15, notification date: 1/31
Application deadline (fall): rolling
Undergraduate student body: 5,086 full time, 711 part time; 36% male, 64% female; 1% American Indian, 5% Asian, 8% black, 30% Hispanic, 3% multiracial, 1% Pacific Islander, 45% white, 2% international; 95% from in state; 40% live on campus; 0% of students in fraternities, 0% in sororities
Most popular majors: 10% Business/Commerce, General, 8% Kinesiology and Exercise Science, 6% Liberal Arts and Sciences/

Liberal Studies, 11% Psychology, General, 9% Registered Nursing/Registered Nurse
Expenses: 2014-2015: $29,422; room/board: $7,890
Financial aid: (951) 343-4236; 92% of undergrads determined to have financial need; average aid package $16,025

California College of the Arts

San Francisco CA
(800) 447-1278
U.S. News ranking: Arts, unranked
Website: www.cca.edu
Admissions email: enroll@cca.edu
Private; founded 1907
Freshman admissions: N/A; 2013-2014: 1,402 applied, 1,144 accepted. Neither SAT nor ACT required. SAT 25/75 percentile: N/A. High school rank: N/A
Early decision deadline: N/A, notification date: N/A
Early action deadline: N/A, notification date: N/A
Application deadline (fall): rolling
Undergraduate student body: 1,410 full time, 92 part time; 38% male, 62% female; 0% American Indian, 16% Asian, 4% black, 14% Hispanic, 0% multiracial, 1% Pacific Islander, 33% white, 22% international; 68% from in state; 20% live on campus; 1% of students in fraternities, 0% in sororities
Most popular majors: 15% Animation, Interactive Technology, Video Graphics and Special Effects, 16% Architecture, 27% Graphic Design, 17% Illustration, 13% Industrial and Product Design
Expenses: 2014-2015: $41,942; room/board: $8,200
Financial aid: (415) 703-9573; 61% of undergrads determined to have financial need; average aid package $27,449

California Institute of Integral Studies

San Francisco CA
(415) 575-6100
U.S. News ranking: Nat. U., unranked
Website: www.ciis.edu
Admissions email: N/A
Private
Freshman admissions: N/A; 2013-2014: 0 applied, 0 accepted. Neither SAT nor ACT required. ACT 25/75 percentile: N/A. High school rank: N/A
Early decision deadline: N/A, notification date: N/A
Early action deadline: N/A, notification date: N/A
Application deadline (fall): N/A
Undergraduate student body: 68 full time, 7 part time; 27% male, 73% female; 0% American Indian, 5% Asian, 8% black, 16% Hispanic, 5% multiracial, 1% Pacific Islander, 55% white, 4% international
Most popular majors: Information not available
Expenses: 2013-2014: $25,713; room/board: N/A
Financial aid: N/A

California Institute of Technology

Pasadena CA
(626) 395-6341
U.S. News ranking: Nat. U., No. 10
Website: www.caltech.edu
Admissions email: ugadmissions@caltech.edu
Private; founded 1891
Freshman admissions: most selective; 2013-2014: 5,535 applied, 584 accepted. Either SAT or ACT required. SAT 25/75 percentile: 1490-1600. High school rank: 99% in top tenth, 100% in top quarter, 100% in top half
Early decision deadline: N/A, notification date: N/A
Early action deadline: 11/1, notification date: 12/15
Application deadline (fall): 1/3
Undergraduate student body: 977 full time, 0 part time; 63% male, 37% female; 0% American Indian, 42% Asian, 2% black, 10% Hispanic, 6% multiracial, 0% Pacific Islander, 30% white, 9% international; 37% from in state; 84% live on campus; 0% of students in fraternities, 0% in sororities
Most popular majors: 12% Biological and Biomedical Sciences, 14% Computer and Information Sciences and Support Services, 43% Engineering, 13% Mathematics and Statistics, 18% Physical Sciences
Expenses: 2014-2015: $43,362; room/board: $12,918
Financial aid: (626) 395-6280; 51% of undergrads determined to have financial need; average aid package $39,813

California Institute of the Arts

Valencia CA
(661) 255-1050
U.S. News ranking: Arts, unranked
Website: www.calarts.edu
Admissions email: admiss@calarts.edu
Private; founded 1961
Freshman admissions: N/A; 2013-2014: N/A applied, N/A accepted. Neither SAT nor ACT required. SAT 25/75 percentile: N/A. High school rank: N/A
Early decision deadline: N/A, notification date: N/A
Early action deadline: N/A, notification date: N/A
Application deadline (fall): 1/5
Undergraduate student body: 973 full time, 13 part time; 47% male, 53% female; 1% American Indian, 11% Asian, 6% black, 11% Hispanic, 11% multiracial, 1% Pacific Islander, 44% white, 13% international
Most popular majors: 8% Acting, 6% Fine/Studio Arts, General, 8% Fine/Studio Arts, General, 8% Photography, 8% Technical Theatre/Theatre Design and Technology
Expenses: 2014-2015: $42,276; room/board: $13,000
Financial aid: (661) 253-7869; 74% of undergrads determined to have financial need; average aid package $35,705

California Lutheran University

Thousand Oaks CA
(877) 258-3678
U.S. News ranking: Reg. U. (W), No. 15
Website: www.callutheran.edu
Admissions email: admissions@callutheran.edu
Private; founded 1959
Affiliation: Lutheran
Freshman admissions: more selective; 2013-2014: 6,920 applied, 3,323 accepted. Either SAT or ACT required. SAT 25/75 percentile: 1010-1203. High school rank: 33% in top tenth, 68% in top quarter, 94% in top half
Early decision deadline: N/A, notification date: N/A
Early action deadline: 11/1, notification date: 1/15
Application deadline (fall): 3/15
Undergraduate student body: 2,717 full time, 171 part time; 45% male, 55% female; 1% American Indian, 6% Asian, 4% black, 25% Hispanic, 2% multiracial, 1% Pacific Islander, 52% white, 4% international; 88% from in state; 53% live on campus; 0% of students in fraternities, 0% in sororities
Most popular majors: 7% Biological and Biomedical Sciences, 25% Business, Management, Marketing, and Related Support Services, 13% Communication, Journalism, and Related Programs, 12% Psychology, 8% Social Sciences
Expenses: 2014-2015: $37,140; room/board: $12,400
Financial aid: (805) 493-3115; 68% of undergrads determined to have financial need; average aid package $24,570

California Maritime Academy

Vallejo CA
(707) 654-1330
U.S. News ranking: Reg. Coll. (W), No. 3
Website: www.csum.edu
Admissions email: admission@csum.edu
Public; founded 1929
Freshman admissions: selective; 2013-2014: 1,291 applied, 819 accepted. Either SAT or ACT required. SAT 25/75 percentile: 990-1200. High school rank: N/A
Early decision deadline: N/A, notification date: N/A
Early action deadline: N/A, notification date: N/A
Application deadline (fall): rolling
Undergraduate student body: 1,001 full time, 43 part time; 86% male, 14% female; 1% American Indian, 9% Asian, 4% black, 11% Hispanic, 8% multiracial, 2% Pacific Islander, 62% white, 0% international
Most popular majors: Information not available
Expenses: 2014-2015: $6,598 in state, $17,758 out of state; room/board: $11,610
Financial aid: (707) 654-1275; 60% of undergrads determined to have financial need; average aid package $17,560

California Polytechnic State University–San Luis Obispo

San Luis Obispo CA
(805) 756-2311
U.S. News ranking: Reg. U. (W), No. 10
Website: www.calpoly.edu
Admissions email: admissions@calpoly.edu
Public; founded 1901
Freshman admissions: more selective; 2013-2014: 40,402 applied, 13,953 accepted. Either SAT or ACT required. SAT 25/75 percentile: 1130-1320. High school rank: 49% in top tenth, 83% in top quarter, 98% in top half
Early decision deadline: 10/31, notification date: 12/15
Early action deadline: N/A, notification date: N/A
Application deadline (fall): 11/30
Undergraduate student body: 18,058 full time, 681 part time; 55% male, 45% female; 0% American Indian, 11% Asian, 1% black, 15% Hispanic, 7% multiracial, 0% Pacific Islander, 60% white, 1% international; 90% from in state; 38% live on campus; N/A of students in fraternities, N/A in sororities
Most popular majors: 12% Agriculture, Agriculture Operations, and Related Sciences, 6% Architecture and Related Services, 13% Business, Management, Marketing, and Related Support Services, 27% Engineering, 6% Social Sciences
Expenses: 2014-2015: $8,919 in state, $20,079 out of state; room/board: $11,447
Financial aid: (805) 756-2927; 43% of undergrads determined to have financial need; average aid package $10,129

California State Polytechnic University–Pomona

Pomona CA
(909) 869-3210
U.S. News ranking: Reg. U. (W), No. 31
Website: www.csupomona.edu
Admissions email: admissions@csupomona.edu
Public; founded 1938
Freshman admissions: less selective; 2013-2014: 31,465 applied, 16,636 accepted. Either SAT or ACT required. SAT 25/75 percentile: 930-1190. High school rank: N/A
Early decision deadline: N/A, notification date: N/A
Early action deadline: N/A, notification date: N/A
Application deadline (fall): 11/30
Undergraduate student body: 18,413 full time, 2,539 part time; 57% male, 43% female; 0% American Indian, 25% Asian, 3% black, 37% Hispanic, 4% multiracial, 0% Pacific Islander, 22% white, 4% international; 99% from in state; 12% live on campus; 2% of students in fraternities, 1% in sororities
Most popular majors: 24% Business Administration and Management, General, 6% Civil Engineering, General, 7% Hospitality Administration/Management, General, 4% Mechanical Engineering, 5% Psychology, General

Expenses: 2014-2015: $6,350 in state, $17,510 out of state; room/board: $12,111
Financial aid: (909) 869-3700; 67% of undergrads determined to have financial need; average aid package $11,558

California State University–Bakersfield[1]

Bakersfield CA
(661) 654-3036
U.S. News ranking: Reg. U. (W), No. 80
Website: www.csub.edu
Admissions email: admissions@csub.edu
Public
Application deadline (fall): N/A
Undergraduate student body: N/A full time, N/A part time
Expenses: 2013-2014: $6,775 in state, $17,935 out of state; room/board: $9,894
Financial aid: (661) 654-3016

California State University–Channel Islands[1]

Camarillo CA
(805) 437-8500
U.S. News ranking: Reg. U. (W), No. 75
Website: www.csuci.edu
Admissions email: N/A
Public
Application deadline (fall): N/A
Undergraduate student body: N/A full time, N/A part time
Expenses: 2013-2014: $6,471 in state, $17,631 out of state; room/board: $14,020
Financial aid: (805) 437-8530; 41% of undergrads determined to have financial need; average aid package $5,702

California State University–Chico

Chico CA
(800) 542-4426
U.S. News ranking: Reg. U. (W), No. 35
Website: www.csuchico.edu
Admissions email: info@csuchico.edu
Public; founded 1887
Freshman admissions: selective; 2013-2014: 19,217 applied, 12,905 accepted. Either SAT or ACT required. SAT 25/75 percentile: 910-1110. High school rank: 35% in top tenth, 76% in top quarter, 100% in top half
Early decision deadline: N/A, notification date: N/A
Early action deadline: N/A, notification date: N/A
Application deadline (fall): 11/30
Undergraduate student body: 14,209 full time, 1,083 part time; 48% male, 52% female; 1% American Indian, 6% Asian, 2% black, 23% Hispanic, 5% multiracial, 0% Pacific Islander, 52% white, 4% international; 99% from in state; 1% live on campus; 1% of students in fraternities, 1% in sororities
Most popular majors: 16% Business, Management, Marketing, and Related Support Services, 9% Health Professions and Related Programs, 8% Parks, Recreation, Leisure, and Fitness

Studies, 9% Social Sciences, 7% Visual and Performing Arts
Expenses: 2014-2015: $8,472 in state, $19,632 out of state; room/board: $10,480
Financial aid: (530) 898-6451; 58% of undergrads determined to have financial need; average aid package $15,927

California State University–Dominguez Hills

Carson CA
(310) 243-3300
U.S. News ranking: Reg. U. (W), second tier
Website: www.csudh.edu
Admissions email: info@csudh.edu
Public; founded 1960
Freshman admissions: less selective; 2013-2014: 9,719 applied, 7,766 accepted. Neither SAT nor ACT required. SAT 25/75 percentile: 760-940. High school rank: N/A
Early decision deadline: N/A, notification date: N/A
Early action deadline: N/A, notification date: N/A
Application deadline (fall): rolling
Undergraduate student body: 8,565 full time, 3,858 part time; 36% male, 64% female; 0% American Indian, 9% Asian, 17% black, 54% Hispanic, 3% multiracial, 0% Pacific Islander, 9% white, 2% international; 100% from in state; 5% live on campus; 1% of students in fraternities, 1% in sororities
Most popular majors: 20% Business, Management, Marketing, and Related Support Services, 12% Health Professions and Related Programs, 8% Liberal Arts and Sciences, General Studies and Humanities, 10% Psychology, 10% Social Sciences
Expenses: 2014-2015: $6,099 in state, $15,027 out of state; room/board: $12,358
Financial aid: (310) 243-3691; 73% of undergrads determined to have financial need; average aid package $6,328

California State University–East Bay

Hayward CA
(510) 885-2784
U.S. News ranking: Reg. U. (W), second tier
Website: www.csueastbay.edu
Admissions email: admissions@csueastbay.edu
Public; founded 1957
Freshman admissions: less selective; 2013-2014: 14,128 applied, 9,637 accepted. Neither SAT nor ACT required. SAT 25/75 percentile: 800-1010. High school rank: N/A
Early decision deadline: N/A, notification date: N/A
Early action deadline: N/A, notification date: N/A
Application deadline (fall): 11/30
Undergraduate student body: 10,505 full time, 1,555 part time; 39% male, 61% female; 0% American Indian, 24% Asian, 11% black, 26% Hispanic, 6% multiracial, 1% Pacific Islander, 21% white, 6% international; 99% from in state; N/A live on campus; N/A of students in fraternities, N/A in sororities

Most popular majors: 27% Business Administration and Management, General, 14% Health Services/Allied Health/Health Sciences, General, 7% Psychology, General, 6% Public Administration, 9% Social Sciences, General
Expenses: 2013-2014: $6,550 in state, $17,710 out of state; room/board: $11,742
Financial aid: (510) 885-2784; average aid package $11,366

California State University–Fresno

Fresno CA
(559) 278-2191
U.S. News ranking: Reg. U. (W), No. 46
Website: www.csufresno.edu
Admissions email: tinab@csufresno.edu
Public; founded 1911
Freshman admissions: selective; 2013-2014: 17,578 applied, 10,523 accepted. Either SAT or ACT required. SAT 25/75 percentile: 800-1020. High school rank: 15% in top tenth, 80% in top quarter, 100% in top half
Early decision deadline: N/A, notification date: N/A
Early action deadline: N/A, notification date: N/A
Application deadline (fall): 11/30
Undergraduate student body: 17,571 full time, 2,724 part time; 43% male, 57% female; 0% American Indian, 16% Asian, 4% black, 43% Hispanic, 3% multiracial, 0% Pacific Islander, 25% white, 3% international; 99% from in state; 5% live on campus; 6% of students in fraternities, 6% in sororities
Most popular majors: 14% Business, Management, Marketing, and Related Support Services, 13% Health Professions and Related Programs, 7% Homeland Security, Law Enforcement, Firefighting and Related Protective Services, 8% Liberal Arts and Sciences, General Studies and Humanities, 7% Psychology
Expenses: 2014-2015: $6,298 in state, $17,458 out of state; room/board: $10,604
Financial aid: (559) 278-2182; 74% of undergrads determined to have financial need; average aid package $10,717

California State University–Fullerton

Fullerton CA
(657) 278-7788
U.S. News ranking: Reg. U. (W), No. 40
Website: www.fullerton.edu
Admissions email: admissions@fullerton.edu
Public; founded 1957
Freshman admissions: selective; 2013-2014: 41,013 applied, 19,668 accepted. SAT required. SAT 25/75 percentile: 920-1120. High school rank: 20% in top tenth, 61% in top quarter, 95% in top half
Early decision deadline: N/A, notification date: N/A
Early action deadline: N/A, notification date: N/A
Application deadline (fall): 11/30
Undergraduate student body: 26,682 full time, 6,434 part time; 45% male, 55% female;

0% American Indian, 22% Asian, 2% black, 38% Hispanic, 4% multiracial, 0% Pacific Islander, 26% white, 4% international; 99% from in state; 6% live on campus; 2% of students in fraternities, 2% in sororities
Most popular majors: 24% Business, Management, Marketing, and Related Support Services, 13% Communication, Journalism, and Related Programs, 8% Health Professions and Related Programs, 7% Psychology, 6% Social Sciences
Expenses: 2014-2015: $6,316 in state, $17,476 out of state; room/board: $13,510
Financial aid: (714) 278-3128; 59% of undergrads determined to have financial need; average aid package $12,298

California State University–Long Beach

Long Beach CA
(562) 985-5471
U.S. News ranking: Reg. U. (W), No. 33
Website: www.csulb.edu
Admissions email: N/A
Public; founded 1949
Freshman admissions: selective; 2013-2014: 55,896 applied, 19,681 accepted. Either SAT or ACT required. SAT 25/75 percentile: 940-1160. High school rank: N/A
Early decision deadline: N/A, notification date: N/A
Early action deadline: N/A, notification date: N/A
Application deadline (fall): 11/30
Undergraduate student body: 25,756 full time, 4,718 part time; 43% male, 57% female; 1% American Indian, 22% Asian, 4% black, 37% Hispanic, 4% multiracial, 1% Pacific Islander, 21% white, 6% international; 99% from in state; 9% live on campus; 2% of students in fraternities, 2% in sororities
Most popular majors: 15% Business, Management, Marketing, and Related Support Services, 10% Communication, Journalism, and Related Programs, 10% Health Professions and Related Programs, 10% Social Sciences, 10% Visual and Performing Arts
Expenses: 2014-2015: $6,420 in state, $12,108 out of state; room/board: $11,300
Financial aid: (562) 985-8403; 70% of undergrads determined to have financial need; average aid package $13,877

California State University–Los Angeles

Los Angeles CA
(323) 343-3901
U.S. News ranking: Reg. U. (W), No. 84
Website: www.calstatela.edu
Admissions email: admission@calstatela.edu
Public; founded 1947
Freshman admissions: least selective; 2013-2014: 28,506 applied, 17,816 accepted. Neither SAT nor ACT required. SAT 25/75 percentile: 770-990. High school rank: N/A in top tenth, 3% in top quarter, 100% in top half

Early decision deadline: N/A, notification date: N/A
Early action deadline: N/A, notification date: N/A
Application deadline (fall): 11/30
Undergraduate student body: 16,276 full time, 3,298 part time; 41% male, 59% female; 0% American Indian, 16% Asian, 5% black, 59% Hispanic, 2% multiracial, 0% Pacific Islander, 8% white, 5% international; 99% from in state; 5% live on campus; 1% of students in fraternities, 1% in sororities
Most popular majors: 21% Business, Management, Marketing, and Related Support Services, 9% Health Professions and Related Programs, 7% Homeland Security, Law Enforcement, Firefighting and Related Protective Services, 7% Psychology, 9% Social Sciences
Expenses: 2013-2014: $6,335 in state, $15,263 out of state; room/board: $10,851
Financial aid: (323) 343-1784; 81% of undergrads determined to have financial need; average aid package $12,724

California State University–Monterey Bay

Seaside CA
(831) 582-3738
U.S. News ranking: Reg. U. (W), No. 68
Website: www.csumb.edu
Admissions email: admissions@csumb.edu
Public; founded 1994
Freshman admissions: selective; 2013-2014: 13,803 applied, 6,161 accepted. Either SAT or ACT required. SAT 25/75 percentile: 870-1090. High school rank: 12% in top tenth, 46% in top quarter, 87% in top half
Early decision deadline: N/A, notification date: N/A
Early action deadline: N/A, notification date: N/A
Application deadline (fall): 11/30
Undergraduate student body: 4,954 full time, 354 part time; 38% male, 62% female; 1% American Indian, 5% Asian, 7% black, 34% Hispanic, 7% multiracial, 1% Pacific Islander, 38% white, 2% international; 98% from in state; 44% live on campus; 6% of students in fraternities, 4% in sororities
Most popular majors: 17% Business, Management, Marketing, and Related Support Services, 17% Liberal Arts and Sciences, General Studies and Humanities, 9% Parks, Recreation, Leisure, and Fitness Studies, 12% Psychology, 9% Social Sciences
Expenses: 2013-2014: $5,963 in state, $17,123 out of state; room/board: $9,748
Financial aid: (831) 582-5100

California State University–Northridge

Northridge CA
(818) 677-3700
U.S. News ranking: Reg. U. (W), No. 68
Website: www.csun.edu
Admissions email: admissions.records@csun.edu
Public; founded 1958

Freshman admissions: less selective; 2013-2014: 30,903 applied, 18,947 accepted. Either SAT or ACT required. SAT 25/75 percentile: 800-1040. High school rank: N/A
Early decision deadline: N/A, notification date: N/A
Early action deadline: N/A, notification date: N/A
Application deadline (fall): 11/30
Undergraduate student body: 27,993 full time, 5,405 part time; 45% male, 55% female; 0% American Indian, 11% Asian, 6% black, 40% Hispanic, 3% multiracial, 0% Pacific Islander, 26% white, 7% international; 97% from in state; N/A live on campus; N/A of students in fraternities, N/A in sororities
Most popular majors: 20% Business, Management, Marketing, and Related Support Services, 8% Communication, Journalism, and Related Programs, 7% English Language and Literature/Letters, 6% Liberal Arts and Sciences, General Studies and Humanities, 14% Social Sciences
Expenses: 2014-2015: $6,296 in state, $17,716 out of state; room/board: $12,404
Financial aid: (818) 677-4085

California State University–Sacramento

Sacramento CA
(916) 278-3901
U.S. News ranking: Reg. U. (W), No. 58
Website: www.csus.edu
Admissions email: admissions@csus.edu
Public; founded 1947
Freshman admissions: less selective; 2013-2014: 20,803 applied, 14,696 accepted. Neither SAT nor ACT required. SAT 25/75 percentile: 830-1060. High school rank: N/A
Early decision deadline: N/A, notification date: N/A
Early action deadline: 11/30, notification date: N/A
Application deadline (fall): 11/30
Undergraduate student body: 21,034 full time, 4,978 part time; 44% male, 56% female; 1% American Indian, 22% Asian, 6% black, 21% Hispanic, 5% multiracial, 1% Pacific Islander, 37% white, 1% international; 99% from in state; 4% live on campus; 7% of students in fraternities, 5% in sororities
Most popular majors: 20% Business, Management, Marketing, and Related Support Services, 7% Communication, Journalism, and Related Programs, 8% Homeland Security, Law Enforcement, Firefighting and Related Protective Services, 6% Psychology, 9% Social Sciences
Expenses: 2014-2015: $6,648 in state, $17,808 out of state; room/board: N/A
Financial aid: (916) 278-6554; 75% of undergrads determined to have financial need; average aid package $10,690

California State University–San Bernardino

San Bernardino CA
(909) 537-5188
U.S. News ranking: Reg. U. (W), No. 66
Website: www.csusb.edu
Admissions email: moreinfo@csusb.edu
Public; founded 1962
Freshman admissions: less selective; 2013-2014: 13,062 applied, 7,147 accepted. Neither SAT nor ACT required. SAT 25/75 percentile: 790-990. High school rank: N/A
Early decision deadline: N/A, notification date: N/A
Early action deadline: N/A, notification date: 5/1
Application deadline (fall): rolling
Undergraduate student body: 14,246 full time, 1,837 part time; 39% male, 61% female; 0% American Indian, 6% Asian, 7% black, 55% Hispanic, 3% multiracial, 0% Pacific Islander, 17% white, 6% international; 99% from in state; 8% live on campus; 4% of students in fraternities, 4% in sororities
Most popular majors: 21% Business Administration and Management, General, 8% Criminal Justice/Law Enforcement Administration, 8% Liberal Arts and Sciences/Liberal Studies, 13% Psychology, General, 5% Sociology
Expenses: 2014-2015: $6,549 in state, $17,709 out of state; room/board: $9,933
Financial aid: (909) 537-7800; 82% of undergrads determined to have financial need; average aid package $8,834

California State University–San Marcos

San Marcos CA
(760) 750-4848
U.S. News ranking: Reg. U. (W), No. 84
Website: www.csusm.edu
Admissions email: apply@csusm.edu
Public; founded 1989
Freshman admissions: less selective; 2013-2014: 11,402 applied, 7,604 accepted. Neither SAT nor ACT required. SAT 25/75 percentile: 850-1050. High school rank: N/A
Early decision deadline: N/A, notification date: N/A
Early action deadline: N/A, notification date: N/A
Undergraduate student body: 8,819 full time, 1,856 part time; 40% male, 60% female; 0% American Indian, 10% Asian, 3% black, 34% Hispanic, 5% multiracial, 0% Pacific Islander, 37% white, 2% international; 98% from in state; N/A live on campus; N/A of students in fraternities, N/A in sororities
Most popular majors: Information not available
Expenses: 2014-2015: $7,704 in state, $24,336 out of state; room/board: N/A
Financial aid: (760) 750-4850

California State University–Stanislaus

Turlock CA
(209) 667-3152
U.S. News ranking: Reg. U. (W), No. 55
Website: www.csustan.edu
Admissions email: Outreach_Help_Desk@csustan.edu
Public; founded 1957
Freshman admissions: less selective; 2013-2014: 5,804 applied, 4,280 accepted. Neither SAT nor ACT required. SAT 25/75 percentile: 810-1020. High school rank: N/A
Early decision deadline: N/A, notification date: N/A
Early action deadline: N/A, notification date: N/A
Application deadline (fall): 11/30
Undergraduate student body: 6,547 full time, 1,207 part time; 36% male, 64% female; 0% American Indian, 11% Asian, 3% black, 45% Hispanic, 4% multiracial, 1% Pacific Islander, 28% white, 2% international; 100% from in state; 7% live on campus; 7% of students in fraternities, 6% in sororities
Most popular majors: 19% Business Administration and Management, General, 9% Liberal Arts and Sciences/Liberal Studies, 11% Psychology, General, 12% Social Sciences, General
Expenses: 2014-2015: $6,491 in state, $17,651 out of state; room/board: $8,546
Financial aid: (209) 667-3336; 68% of undergrads determined to have financial need; average aid package $10,840

Chapman University

Orange CA
(888) 282-7759
U.S. News ranking: Reg. U. (W), No. 7
Website: www.chapman.edu
Admissions email: admit@chapman.edu
Private; founded 1861
Affiliation: Christian Church (Disciples of Christ)
Freshman admissions: more selective; 2013-2014: 11,750 applied, 5,253 accepted. Either SAT or ACT required. SAT 25/75 percentile: 1120-1300. High school rank: 48% in top tenth, 93% in top quarter, 98% in top half
Early decision deadline: N/A, notification date: N/A
Early action deadline: 11/1, notification date: 1/10
Application deadline (fall): 1/15
Undergraduate student body: 5,753 full time, 252 part time; 41% male, 59% female; 0% American Indian, 10% Asian, 2% black, 14% Hispanic, 6% multiracial, 0% Pacific Islander, 60% white, 4% international; 74% from in state; 32% live on campus; 28% of students in fraternities, 38% in sororities
Most popular majors: 15% Business Administration and Management, General, 14% Cinematography and Film/Video Production, 6% Psychology, General, 6% Public Relations/Image Management, 9% Speech Communication and Rhetoric
Expenses: 2014-2015: $45,393; room/board: $12,954

Financial aid: (714) 997-6741; 60% of undergrads determined to have financial need; average aid package $31,182

Claremont McKenna College

Claremont CA
(909) 621-8088
U.S. News ranking: Nat. Lib. Arts, No. 8
Website: www.claremontmckenna.edu
Admissions email: admission@cmc.edu
Private; founded 1946
Freshman admissions: most selective; 2013-2014: 5,518 applied, 647 accepted. Either SAT or ACT required. SAT 25/75 percentile: 1320-1500. High school rank: 74% in top tenth, 96% in top quarter, 100% in top half
Early decision deadline: 11/1, notification date: 12/15
Early action deadline: N/A, notification date: N/A
Application deadline (fall): 1/1
Undergraduate student body: 1,312 full time, 4 part time; 52% male, 48% female; 0% American Indian, 11% Asian, 4% black, 11% Hispanic, 8% multiracial, 0% Pacific Islander, 44% white, 14% international; 46% from in state; 94% live on campus; 0% of students in fraternities, 0% in sororities
Most popular majors: 14% Accounting, 25% Economics, General, 12% International Relations and Affairs, 21% Political Science and Government, General, 8% Psychology, General
Expenses: 2014-2015: $47,395; room/board: $14,820
Financial aid: (909) 621-8356; 40% of undergrads determined to have financial need; average aid package $40,677

Cogswell Polytechnical College

Sunnyvale CA
(408) 541-0100
U.S. News ranking: Reg. Coll. (W), unranked
Website: www.cogswell.edu
Admissions email: info@cogswell.edu
Private; founded 1887
Freshman admissions: N/A; 2013-2014: 194 applied, 151 accepted. Neither SAT nor ACT required. SAT 25/75 percentile: 1000-1360. High school rank: N/A
Early decision deadline: N/A, notification date: N/A
Early action deadline: N/A, notification date: N/A
Application deadline (fall): rolling
Undergraduate student body: 315 full time, 147 part time; 76% male, 24% female; 0% American Indian, 12% Asian, 4% black, 15% Hispanic, 12% multiracial, 3% Pacific Islander, 42% white, 1% international; 89% from in state; N/A live on campus; N/A of students in fraternities, N/A in sororities
Most popular majors: 44% Animation, Interactive Technology, Video Graphics and Special Effects

Expenses: 2014-2015: $16,160; room/board: $7,200
Financial aid: (408) 541-0100

Concordia University

Irvine CA
(949) 214-3010
U.S. News ranking: Reg. U. (W), No. 51
Website: www.cui.edu
Admissions email: admission@cui.edu
Private; founded 1972
Affiliation: Lutheran Church-Missouri Synod
Freshman admissions: selective; 2013-2014: 2,768 applied, 1,850 accepted. Either SAT or ACT required. SAT 25/75 percentile: 903-1110. High school rank: 20% in top tenth, 40% in top quarter, 79% in top half
Early decision deadline: N/A, notification date: N/A
Early action deadline: 12/1, notification date: 12/15
Application deadline (fall): rolling
Undergraduate student body: 1,746 full time, 198 part time; 38% male, 62% female; 0% American Indian, 6% Asian, 3% black, 18% Hispanic, 4% multiracial, 0% Pacific Islander, 49% white, 3% international; 88% from in state; 47% live on campus; N/A of students in fraternities, N/A in sororities
Most popular majors: 23% Business Administration and Management, General, 7% Communication, General, 11% Liberal Arts and Sciences/Liberal Studies, 8% Psychology, General, 16% Registered Nursing/Registered Nurse
Expenses: 2014-2015: $30,640; room/board: $9,270
Financial aid: (949) 854-8002; 72% of undergrads determined to have financial need; average aid package $18,553

Dominican University of California

San Rafael CA
(415) 485-3204
U.S. News ranking: Reg. U. (W), No. 33
Website: www.dominican.edu
Admissions email: enroll@dominican.edu
Private; founded 1890
Freshman admissions: selective; 2013-2014: 2,322 applied, 1,800 accepted. Either SAT or ACT required. SAT 25/75 percentile: 960-1160. High school rank: N/A
Early decision deadline: N/A, notification date: N/A
Early action deadline: N/A, notification date: N/A
Application deadline (fall): rolling
Undergraduate student body: 1,298 full time, 305 part time; 26% male, 74% female; 1% American Indian, 17% Asian, 4% black, 23% Hispanic, 3% multiracial, 1% Pacific Islander, 33% white, 2% international
Most popular majors: Information not available
Expenses: 2014-2015: $41,730; room/board: $13,940
Financial aid: (415) 257-1321; 80% of undergrads determined to have financial need; average aid package $27,587

Fashion Institute of Design & Merchandising

Los Angeles CA
(800) 624-1200
U.S. News ranking: Arts, unranked
Website: fidm.edu/
Admissions email: admissions@fidm.edu
Private
Freshman admissions: N/A; 2013-2014: 2,431 applied, 1,278 accepted. Neither SAT nor ACT required. SAT 25/75 percentile: N/A. High school rank: N/A
Early decision deadline: N/A, notification date: N/A
Early action deadline: N/A, notification date: N/A
Application deadline (fall): rolling
Undergraduate student body: 4,008 full time, 471 part time; 10% male, 90% female; 1% American Indian, 13% Asian, 6% black, 23% Hispanic, 3% multiracial, 1% Pacific Islander, 36% white, 11% international
Most popular majors: Information not available
Expenses: 2013-2014: $28,920; room/board: N/A
Financial aid: N/A

Fresno Pacific University

Fresno CA
(559) 453-2039
U.S. News ranking: Reg. U. (W), No. 40
Website: www.fresno.edu
Admissions email: ugadmis@fresno.edu
Private; founded 1944
Affiliation: Mennonite Brethren
Freshman admissions: selective; 2013-2014: 705 applied, 553 accepted. Either SAT or ACT required. SAT 25/75 percentile: 880-1100. High school rank: 31% in top tenth, 66% in top quarter, 94% in top half
Early decision deadline: N/A, notification date: N/A
Early action deadline: N/A, notification date: N/A
Application deadline (fall): 7/31
Undergraduate student body: 2,158 full time, 254 part time; 31% male, 69% female; 1% American Indian, 4% Asian, 6% black, 41% Hispanic, 2% multiracial, 0% Pacific Islander, 38% white, 2% international; 95% from in state; 26% live on campus; 0% of students in fraternities, 0% in sororities
Most popular majors: 25% Business, Management, Marketing, and Related Support Services, 25% Education, 5% Health Professions and Related Programs, 16% Liberal Arts and Sciences, General Studies and Humanities, 6% Social Sciences
Expenses: 2014-2015: $26,638; room/board: $7,360
Financial aid: (559) 453-2027; 86% of undergrads determined to have financial need; average aid package $19,359

Golden Gate University

San Francisco CA
(415) 442-7800
U.S. News ranking: Reg. U. (W), unranked
Website: www.ggu.edu
Admissions email: info@ggu.edu
Private; founded 1901
Freshman admissions: N/A; 2013-2014: N/A applied, N/A accepted. Neither SAT nor ACT required. ACT 25/75 percentile: N/A. High school rank: N/A
Early decision deadline: N/A, notification date: N/A
Early action deadline: N/A, notification date: N/A
Application deadline (fall): rolling
Undergraduate student body: 104 full time, 371 part time; 46% male, 54% female; 0% American Indian, 18% Asian, 11% black, 17% Hispanic, 4% multiracial, 2% Pacific Islander, 29% white, 2% international
Most popular majors: Information not available
Expenses: 2013-2014: $14,400; room/board: N/A
Financial aid: (415) 442-7270

Harvey Mudd College

Claremont CA
(909) 621-8011
U.S. News ranking: Nat. Lib. Arts, No. 15
Website: www.hmc.edu
Admissions email: admission@hmc.edu
Private; founded 1955
Freshman admissions: most selective; 2013-2014: 3,375 applied, 643 accepted. Either SAT or ACT required. SAT 25/75 percentile: 1400-1560. High school rank: 97% in top tenth, 100% in top quarter, 100% in top half
Early decision deadline: 11/15, notification date: 12/15
Early action deadline: N/A, notification date: N/A
Application deadline (fall): 1/2
Undergraduate student body: 805 full time, 2 part time; 54% male, 46% female; 0% American Indian, 22% Asian, 1% black, 9% Hispanic, 4% multiracial, 0% Pacific Islander, 47% white, 11% international; 42% from in state; 99% live on campus; 0% of students in fraternities, 0% in sororities
Most popular majors: 1% Biological and Biomedical Sciences, 27% Computer and Information Sciences and Support Services, 33% Engineering, 14% Mathematics and Statistics, 19% Physical Sciences
Expenses: 2014-2015: $48,594; room/board: $15,833
Financial aid: (909) 621-8055; 50% of undergrads determined to have financial need; average aid package $39,799

Holy Names University

Oakland CA
(510) 436-1351
U.S. News ranking: Reg. U. (W), No. 68
Website: www.hnu.edu
Admissions email: admissions@hnu.edu
Private; founded 1868

Affiliation: Roman Catholic
Freshman admissions: less selective; 2013-2014: 561 applied, 318 accepted. Either SAT or ACT required. SAT 25/75 percentile: 820-1000. High school rank: N/A
Early decision deadline: N/A, notification date: N/A
Early action deadline: N/A, notification date: N/A
Application deadline (fall): rolling
Undergraduate student body: 677 full time, 211 part time; 31% male, 69% female; 1% American Indian, 17% Asian, 21% black, 28% Hispanic, 4% multiracial, 4% Pacific Islander, 18% white, 2% international; 92% from in state; 44% live on campus; N/A of students in fraternities, N/A in sororities
Most popular majors: 30% Business, Management, Marketing, and Related Support Services, 14% Health Professions and Related Programs, 9% Liberal Arts and Sciences, General Studies and Humanities, 18% Psychology, 12% Social Sciences
Expenses: 2014-2015: $34,488; room/board: $11,608
Financial aid: (510) 436-1327; 89% of undergrads determined to have financial need; average aid package $25,551

Hope International University

Fullerton CA
(714) 879-3901
U.S. News ranking: Reg. Coll. (W), No. 19
Website: www.hiu.edu
Admissions email: admissions@hiu.edu
Private; founded 1928
Affiliation: Christian Churches/Churches of Christ
Freshman admissions: less selective; 2013-2014: 376 applied, 178 accepted. Either SAT or ACT required. SAT 25/75 percentile: 860-1090. High school rank: 2% in top tenth, 13% in top quarter, 40% in top half
Early decision deadline: N/A, notification date: N/A
Early action deadline: N/A, notification date: N/A
Application deadline (fall): rolling
Undergraduate student body: 672 full time, 249 part time; 45% male, 55% female; 0% American Indian, 3% Asian, 8% black, 17% Hispanic, 14% multiracial, 1% Pacific Islander, 44% white, 1% international; 76% from in state; 60% live on campus; N/A of students in fraternities, N/A in sororities
Most popular majors: 18% Business Administration and Management, General, 16% Human Development and Family Studies, General, 16% Psychology, General, 9% Social Sciences, General, 27% Theological and Ministerial Studies, Other
Expenses: 2014-2015: $27,130; room/board: $8,750
Financial aid: (714) 879-3901; 78% of undergrads determined to have financial need; average aid package $15,152

Humboldt State University

Arcata CA
(707) 826-4402
U.S. News ranking: Reg. U. (W), No. 58
Website: www.humboldt.edu
Admissions email: hsuinfo@humboldt.edu
Public; founded 1913
Freshman admissions: selective; 2013-2014: 11,261 applied, 8,514 accepted. Neither SAT nor ACT required. SAT 25/75 percentile: 870-1110. High school rank: 9% in top tenth, 39% in top quarter, 76% in top half
Early decision deadline: N/A, notification date: N/A
Early action deadline: N/A, notification date: N/A
Application deadline (fall): 11/30
Undergraduate student body: 7,255 full time, 498 part time; 47% male, 53% female; 1% American Indian, 3% Asian, 4% black, 27% Hispanic, 6% multiracial, 0% Pacific Islander, 50% white, 1% international; 93% from in state; 25% live on campus; 1% of students in fraternities, 1% in sororities
Most popular majors: 10% Biological and Biomedical Sciences, 8% Liberal Arts and Sciences, General Studies and Humanities, 14% Natural Resources and Conservation, 11% Social Sciences, 10% Visual and Performing Arts
Expenses: 2014-2015: $7,154 in state, $18,314 out of state; room/board: $11,678
Financial aid: (707) 826-4321; 76% of undergrads determined to have financial need; average aid package $13,368

Humphreys College[1]

Stockton CA
(209) 478-0800
U.S. News ranking: Reg. Coll. (W), unranked
Website: www.humphreys.edu
Admissions email: ugadmission@humphreys.edu
Private
Application deadline (fall): N/A
Undergraduate student body: N/A full time, N/A part time
Expenses: 2013-2014: $11,277; room/board: N/A
Financial aid: (209) 478-0800

John F. Kennedy University[1]

Pleasant Hill CA
(925) 969-3330
U.S. News ranking: Reg. U. (W), unranked
Website: www.jfku.edu
Admissions email: proginfo@jfku.edu
Private
Application deadline (fall): N/A
Undergraduate student body: N/A full time, N/A part time
Expenses: N/A
Financial aid: (925) 969-3385

Laguna College of Art and Design

Laguna Beach CA
(949) 376-6000
U.S. News ranking: Arts, unranked
Website: www.lcad.edu/
Admissions email: admissions@lcad.edu

Private
Freshman admissions: N/A; 2013-2014: 818 applied, 346 accepted. Neither SAT nor ACT required. SAT 25/75 percentile: N/A. High school rank: N/A
Early decision deadline: N/A, notification date: N/A
Early action deadline: N/A, notification date: N/A
Application deadline (fall): 8/1
Undergraduate student body: 466 full time, 48 part time; 40% male, 60% female; 2% American Indian, 15% Asian, 2% black, 16% Hispanic, 0% multiracial, 1% Pacific Islander, 48% white, 4% international
Most popular majors: Information not available
Expenses: 2014-2015: $27,300; room/board: N/A
Financial aid: (949) 376-6000

La Sierra University

Riverside CA
(951) 785-2176
U.S. News ranking: Reg. U. (W), No. 56
Website: www.lasierra.edu
Admissions email: admissions@lasierra.edu
Private; founded 1922
Affiliation: Seventh-day Adventist
Freshman admissions: less selective; 2013-2014: 3,479 applied, 1,627 accepted. Either SAT or ACT required. SAT 25/75 percentile: 810-1040. High school rank: 10% in top tenth, 41% in top quarter, 63% in top half
Early decision deadline: N/A, notification date: N/A
Early action deadline: N/A, notification date: N/A
Application deadline (fall): 7/1
Undergraduate student body: 1,912 full time, 193 part time; 42% male, 58% female; 0% American Indian, 15% Asian, 7% black, 41% Hispanic, 4% multiracial, 2% Pacific Islander, 16% white, 13% international; 93% from in state; 35% live on campus; 0% of students in fraternities, 0% in sororities
Most popular majors: 11% Biology/Biological Sciences, General, 25% Business Administration and Management, General, 9% Health and Physical Education/Fitness, General, 7% History, General, 8% Psychology, General
Expenses: 2014-2015: $29,895; room/board: $7,650
Financial aid: (909) 785-2175; 78% of undergrads determined to have financial need; average aid package $22,673

Loyola Marymount University

Los Angeles CA
(310) 338-2750
U.S. News ranking: Reg. U. (W), No. 3
Website: www.lmu.edu
Admissions email: admissions@lmu.edu
Private; founded 1911
Affiliation: Roman Catholic
Freshman admissions: more selective; 2013-2014: 11,472 applied, 6,209 accepted. Either SAT or ACT required. SAT 25/75 percentile: 1090-1300. High school rank: 29% in top tenth, 57% in top quarter, 89% in top half

Early decision deadline: N/A, notification date: N/A
Early action deadline: 11/1, notification date: 12/20
Application deadline (fall): 1/15
Undergraduate student body: 5,935 full time, 270 part time; 43% male, 57% female; 0% American Indian, 10% Asian, 6% black, 22% Hispanic, 7% multiracial, 0% Pacific Islander, 49% white, 5% international; 78% from in state; 52% live on campus; 19% of students in fraternities, 34% in sororities
Most popular majors: 23% Business/Commerce, General, 6% English Language and Literature, General, 12% Social Sciences, General, 11% Speech Communication and Rhetoric, 15% Visual and Performing Arts, General
Expenses: 2014-2015: $41,372; room/board: $14,395
Financial aid: (310) 338-2753; 59% of undergrads determined to have financial need; average aid package $27,339

Master's College and Seminary

Santa Clarita CA
(800) 568-6248
U.S. News ranking: Reg. Coll. (W), No. 5
Website: www.masters.edu
Admissions email: admissions@masters.edu
Private; founded 1927
Affiliation: Evangelical
Freshman admissions: selective; 2013-2014: 556 applied, 433 accepted. Either SAT or ACT required. SAT 25/75 percentile: 940-1200. High school rank: 28% in top tenth, 55% in top quarter, 82% in top half
Early decision deadline: N/A, notification date: N/A
Early action deadline: 11/15, notification date: 12/22
Application deadline (fall): rolling
Undergraduate student body: 967 full time, 131 part time; 52% male, 48% female; 1% American Indian, 6% Asian, 3% black, 9% Hispanic, 6% multiracial, 1% Pacific Islander, 66% white, 5% international; 73% from in state; 82% live on campus; N/A of students in fraternities, N/A in sororities
Most popular majors: 29% Bible/Biblical Studies, 8% Biology/Biological Sciences, General, 13% Business, Management, Marketing, and Related Support Services, 9% Communication, Journalism, and Related Programs, 11% Liberal Arts and Sciences, General Studies and Humanities
Expenses: 2014-2015: $29,860; room/board: $9,720
Financial aid: (661) 259-3540; 88% of undergrads determined to have financial need; average aid package $19,982

Menlo College

Atherton CA
(800) 556-3656
U.S. News ranking: Reg. Coll. (W), No. 8
Website: www.menlo.edu
Admissions email: admissions@menlo.edu
Private; founded 1927

Freshman admissions: less selective; 2013-2014: 3,752 applied, 1,519 accepted. Either SAT or ACT required. SAT 25/75 percentile: 882-1097. High school rank: N/A
Early decision deadline: N/A, notification date: N/A
Early action deadline: 11/15, notification date: 1/15
Application deadline (fall): 4/1
Undergraduate student body: 704 full time, 9 part time; 62% male, 38% female; 0% American Indian, 7% Asian, 5% black, 21% Hispanic, 8% multiracial, 2% Pacific Islander, 35% white, 13% international; 83% from in state; 61% live on campus; 0% of students in fraternities, 0% in sororities
Most popular majors: 8% Accounting, 9% Finance, General, 20% Marketing/Marketing Management, General, 8% Psychology, General
Expenses: 2014-2015: $37,520; room/board: $12,260
Financial aid: (650) 543-3880; 64% of undergrads determined to have financial need; average aid package $28,231

Mills College

Oakland CA
(510) 430-2135
U.S. News ranking: Reg. U. (W), No. 6
Website: www.mills.edu
Admissions email: admission@mills.edu
Private; founded 1852
Freshman admissions: more selective; 2013-2014: 1,827 applied, 1,242 accepted. Either SAT or ACT required. SAT 25/75 percentile: 1040-1250. High school rank: 41% in top tenth, 71% in top quarter, 97% in top half
Early decision deadline: N/A, notification date: N/A
Early action deadline: 11/15, notification date: 12/15
Application deadline (fall): 3/1
Undergraduate student body: 922 full time, 63 part time; 0% male, 100% female; 1% American Indian, 12% Asian, 6% black, 22% Hispanic, 9% multiracial, 1% Pacific Islander, 47% white, 1% international; 82% from in state; 58% live on campus; 0% of students in fraternities, 0% in sororities
Most popular majors: 10% Biological and Biomedical Sciences, 16% English Language and Literature/Letters, 10% Psychology, General, 24% Social Sciences, 13% Visual and Performing Arts
Expenses: 2014-2015: $42,918; room/board: $12,914
Financial aid: (510) 430-2000; 85% of undergrads determined to have financial need; average aid package $37,766

Mount St. Mary's College

Los Angeles CA
(310) 954-4250
U.S. News ranking: Reg. U. (W), No. 23
Website: www.msmc.la.edu
Admissions email: admissions@msmc.la.edu
Private; founded 1925
Affiliation: Roman Catholic

Freshman admissions: less selective; 2013-2014: 1,886 applied, 1,716 accepted. Either SAT or ACT required. SAT 25/75 percentile: 830-1020. High school rank: 17% in top tenth, 46% in top quarter, 91% in top half
Early decision deadline: N/A, notification date: N/A
Early action deadline: 12/1, notification date: 1/30
Application deadline (fall): 8/1
Undergraduate student body: 2,092 full time, 533 part time; 6% male, 94% female; 0% American Indian, 16% Asian, 7% black, 58% Hispanic, 2% multiracial, 1% Pacific Islander, 10% white, 1% international; 99% from in state; 20% live on campus; 0% of students in fraternities, 2% in sororities
Most popular majors: 5% Biological and Biomedical Sciences, 12% Business, Management, Marketing, and Related Support Services, 37% Health Professions and Related Programs, 9% Psychology, 11% Social Sciences
Expenses: 2014-2015: $34,826; room/board: $10,793
Financial aid: (310) 954-4191; 91% of undergrads determined to have financial need; average aid package $28,423

National Hispanic University[1]

San Jose CA
(408) 254-2772
U.S. News ranking: Nat. Lib. Arts, unranked
Website: www.nhu.edu
Admissions email: university@nhu.edu
For-profit
Application deadline (fall): N/A
Undergraduate student body: N/A full time, N/A part time
Expenses: 2013-2014: $8,196; room/board: N/A
Financial aid: (408) 254-2708

National University[1]

La Jolla CA
(800) 628-8648
U.S. News ranking: Reg. U. (W), unranked
Website: www.nu.edu
Admissions email: advisor@nu.edu
Private; founded 1971
Application deadline (fall): rolling
Undergraduate student body: N/A full time, N/A part time
Expenses: 2013-2014: $11,796; room/board: N/A
Financial aid: (858) 642-8500

NewSchool of Architecture and Design[1]

San Diego CA
(800) 490-7081
U.S. News ranking: Arts, unranked
Website: newschoolarch.edu/
Admissions email: N/A
For-profit
Application deadline (fall): N/A
Undergraduate student body: N/A full time, N/A part time
Expenses: 2013-2014: $24,536; room/board: N/A
Financial aid: N/A

Notre Dame de Namur University[1]

Belmont CA
(650) 508-3600
U.S. News ranking: Reg. U. (W), No. 51
Website: www.ndnu.edu
Admissions email: admissions@ndnu.edu
Private; founded 1851
Affiliation: Catholic
Application deadline (fall): rolling
Undergraduate student body: N/A full time, N/A part time
Expenses: 2013-2014: $31,206; room/board: $12,152
Financial aid: (650) 508-3600

Occidental College

Los Angeles CA
(800) 825-5262
U.S. News ranking: Nat. Lib. Arts, No. 44
Website: www.oxy.edu
Admissions email: admission@oxy.edu
Private; founded 1887
Freshman admissions: more selective; 2013-2014: 6,072 applied, 2,574 accepted. Either SAT or ACT required. SAT 25/75 percentile: 1210-1400. High school rank: 51% in top tenth, 83% in top quarter, 100% in top half
Early decision deadline: 11/15, notification date: 12/15
Early action deadline: N/A, notification date: N/A
Application deadline (fall): 1/10
Undergraduate student body: 2,113 full time, 15 part time; 44% male, 56% female; 0% American Indian, 13% Asian, 4% black, 16% Hispanic, 9% multiracial, 0% Pacific Islander, 51% white, 4% international; 51% from in state; 80% live on campus; 9% of students in fraternities, 14% in sororities
Most popular majors: 10% Biology/Biological Sciences, General, 14% Economics, General, 6% English Language and Literature/Letters, Other, 11% International Relations and Affairs, 8% Psychology, General
Expenses: 2014-2015: $47,522; room/board: $13,450
Financial aid: (323) 259-2548; 58% of undergrads determined to have financial need; average aid package $41,535

Otis College of Art and Design

Los Angeles CA
(310) 665-6820
U.S. News ranking: Arts, unranked
Website: www.otis.edu
Admissions email: admissions@otis.edu
Private; founded 1918
Freshman admissions: N/A; 2013-2014: 1,584 applied, 733 accepted. Either SAT or ACT required. SAT 25/75 percentile: N/A. High school rank: N/A
Early decision deadline: N/A, notification date: N/A
Early action deadline: N/A, notification date: N/A
Application deadline (fall): rolling
Undergraduate student body: 1,018 full time, 14 part time; 35% male, 65% female; 1% American Indian, 32% Asian, 3% black,

13% Hispanic, 6% multiracial, 0% Pacific Islander, 22% white, 18% international
Most popular majors: Information not available
Expenses: 2014-2015: $40,490; room/board: $11,800
Financial aid: (310) 665-6880; 69% of undergrads determined to have financial need; average aid package $24,527

Pacific Union College
Angwin CA
(707) 965-6425
U.S. News ranking: Nat. Lib. Arts, second tier
Website: www.puc.edu
Admissions email: enroll@puc.edu
Private; founded 1882
Affiliation: Seventh-day Adventist
Freshman admissions: selective; 2013-2014: 2,103 applied, 1,063 accepted. Either SAT or ACT required. SAT 25/75 percentile: 890-1150. High school rank: N/A
Early decision deadline: N/A, notification date: N/A
Early action deadline: N/A, notification date: N/A
Application deadline (fall): rolling
Undergraduate student body: 1,454 full time, 191 part time; 44% male, 56% female; 0% American Indian, 18% Asian, 8% black, 27% Hispanic, 7% multiracial, 2% Pacific Islander, 27% white, 2% international
Most popular majors: 19% Biological and Biomedical Sciences, 13% Business, Management, Marketing, and Related Support Services, 7% Education, 23% Health Professions and Related Programs, 7% Visual and Performing Arts
Expenses: 2014-2015: $28,131; room/board: $7,485
Financial aid: (707) 965-7200; 79% of undergrads determined to have financial need; average aid package $22,489

Patten University[1]
Oakland CA
(877) 472-8836
U.S. News ranking: Reg. Coll. (W), second tier
Website: www.patten.edu/
Admissions email: Admissions@patten.edu
Private
Application deadline (fall): N/A
Undergraduate student body: N/A full time, N/A part time
Expenses: N/A
Financial aid: (510) 261-8500

Pepperdine University
Malibu CA
(310) 506-4392
U.S. News ranking: Nat. U., No. 54
Website: www.pepperdine.edu
Admissions email: admission-seaver@pepperdine.edu
Private; founded 1937
Affiliation: Church of Christ
Freshman admissions: more selective; 2013-2014: 9,721 applied, 3,630 accepted. Either SAT or ACT required. SAT 25/75 percentile: 1130-1340. High school rank: 47% in top tenth, 83% in top quarter, 96% in top half
Early decision deadline: N/A, notification date: N/A

Early action deadline: N/A, notification date: N/A
Application deadline (fall): 1/5
Undergraduate student body: 3,172 full time, 366 part time; 41% male, 59% female; 0% American Indian, 14% Asian, 7% black, 16% Hispanic, 6% multiracial, 0% Pacific Islander, 42% white, 9% international; 85% from in state; 58% live on campus; 18% of students in fraternities, 31% in sororities
Most popular majors: 29% Business, Management, Marketing, and Related Support Services, 18% Communication, Journalism, and Related Programs, 6% Multi/Interdisciplinary Studies, 8% Psychology, 11% Social Sciences
Expenses: 2014-2015: $46,692; room/board: $13,390
Financial aid: (310) 506-4301; 57% of undergrads determined to have financial need; average aid package $40,616

Pitzer College
Claremont CA
(909) 621-8129
U.S. News ranking: Nat. Lib. Arts, No. 35
Website: www.pitzer.edu
Admissions email: admission@pitzer.edu
Private; founded 1963
Freshman admissions: most selective; 2013-2014: 4,115 applied, 597 accepted. Neither SAT nor ACT required. SAT 25/75 percentile: 1210-1400. High school rank: 55% in top tenth, 96% in top quarter, 100% in top half
Early decision deadline: 11/15, notification date: 12/22
Early action deadline: N/A, notification date: N/A
Application deadline (fall): 1/1
Undergraduate student body: 1,044 full time, 37 part time; 40% male, 60% female; 0% American Indian, 6% Asian, 5% black, 15% Hispanic, 8% multiracial, 0% Pacific Islander, 49% white, 5% international; 48% from in state; 75% live on campus; 0% of students in fraternities, 0% in sororities
Most popular majors: 7% English Language and Literature, General, 10% Environmental Studies, 14% Multi-/Interdisciplinary Studies, Other, 7% Political Science and Government, 14% Psychology, General
Expenses: 2014-2015: $46,992; room/board: $14,758
Financial aid: (909) 621-8208; 33% of undergrads determined to have financial need; average aid package $40,635

Point Loma Nazarene University
San Diego CA
(619) 849-2273
U.S. News ranking: Reg. U. (W), No. 16
Website: www.pointloma.edu
Admissions email: admissions@pointloma.edu
Private; founded 1902
Affiliation: Church of the Nazarene
Freshman admissions: more selective; 2013-2014: 3,138 applied, 2,088 accepted. Either SAT or ACT required. SAT 25/75 percentile: 1040-1260. High

school rank: 30% in top tenth, 67% in top quarter, 89% in top half
Early decision deadline: N/A, notification date: N/A
Early action deadline: 11/15, notification date: 12/21
Application deadline (fall): 2/15
Undergraduate student body: 2,483 full time, 73 part time; 37% male, 63% female; 1% American Indian, 6% Asian, 3% black, 19% Hispanic, 5% multiracial, 1% Pacific Islander, 64% white, 0% international; 82% from in state; 67% live on campus; N/A of students in fraternities, N/A in sororities
Most popular majors: 7% Biological and Biomedical Sciences, 20% Business, Management, Marketing, and Related Support Services, 14% Health Professions and Related Programs, 7% Parks, Recreation, Leisure, and Fitness Studies, 10% Psychology
Expenses: 2014-2015: $31,406; room/board: $9,600
Financial aid: (619) 849-2538; 71% of undergrads determined to have financial need; average aid package $20,816

Pomona College
Claremont CA
(909) 621-8134
U.S. News ranking: Nat. Lib. Arts, No. 5
Website: www.pomona.edu
Admissions email: admissions@pomona.edu
Private; founded 1887
Freshman admissions: most selective; 2013-2014: 7,153 applied, 996 accepted. Either SAT or ACT required. SAT 25/75 percentile: 1380-1540. High school rank: 92% in top tenth, 99% in top quarter, 100% in top half
Early decision deadline: 11/1, notification date: 12/15
Early action deadline: N/A, notification date: N/A
Application deadline (fall): 1/1
Undergraduate student body: 1,596 full time, 16 part time; 48% male, 52% female; 0% American Indian, 12% Asian, 6% black, 15% Hispanic, 7% multiracial, 0% Pacific Islander, 45% white, 7% international; 33% from in state; 98% live on campus; 5% of students in fraternities, 0% in sororities
Most popular majors: 11% Economics, General, 9% Mathematics, General, 5% Molecular Biology, 8% Neuroscience, 5% Political Science and Government, General
Expenses: 2014-2015: $45,832; room/board: $14,700
Financial aid: (909) 621-8205; 56% of undergrads determined to have financial need; average aid package $43,665

San Diego Christian College[1]
El Cajon CA
(619) 588-7747
U.S. News ranking: Nat. Lib. Arts, second tier
Website: www.sdcc.edu/
Admissions email: admissions@sdcc.edu
Private; founded 1970
Application deadline (fall): rolling

Undergraduate student body: N/A full time, N/A part time
Expenses: 2013-2014: $25,888; room/board: $9,278
Financial aid: (619) 590-1786

San Diego State University
San Diego CA
(619) 594-6336
U.S. News ranking: Nat. U., No. 149
Website: www.sdsu.edu
Admissions email: admissions@sdsu.edu
Public; founded 1897
Freshman admissions: more selective; 2013-2014: 54,509 applied, 20,292 accepted. Either SAT or ACT required. SAT 25/75 percentile: 1000-1200. High school rank: 27% in top tenth, 71% in top quarter, 96% in top half
Early decision deadline: N/A, notification date: N/A
Early action deadline: N/A, notification date: N/A
Application deadline (fall): 11/30
Undergraduate student body: 24,431 full time, 3,378 part time; 45% male, 55% female; 0% American Indian, 7% Asian, 4% black, 31% Hispanic, 6% multiracial, 7% Pacific Islander, 36% white, 5% international; 93% from in state; 16% live on campus; 7% of students in fraternities, 8% in sororities
Most popular majors: 18% Business, Management, Marketing, and Related Support Services, 6% Health Professions and Related Programs, 6% Homeland Security, Law Enforcement, Firefighting and Related Protective Services, 9% Psychology, 13% Social Sciences
Expenses: 2014-2015: $6,866 in state, $18,026 out of state; room/board: $14,745
Financial aid: (619) 594-6323; 57% of undergrads determined to have financial need; average aid package $11,100

San Francisco Art Institute
San Francisco CA
(800) 345-7324
U.S. News ranking: Arts, unranked
Website: www.sfai.edu
Admissions email: admissions@sfai.edu
Private; founded 1871
Freshman admissions: N/A; 2013-2014: 415 applied, 344 accepted. Neither SAT nor ACT required. SAT 25/75 percentile: N/A. High school rank: N/A
Early decision deadline: N/A, notification date: N/A
Early action deadline: N/A, notification date: N/A
Application deadline (fall): rolling
Undergraduate student body: 444 full time, 34 part time; 43% male, 57% female; 1% American Indian, 4% Asian, 2% black, 16% Hispanic, 9% multiracial, 0% Pacific Islander, 48% white, 13% international; 61% from in state; 28% live on campus; 0% of students in fraternities, 0% in sororities

Most popular majors: 9% Cinematography and Film/Video Production, 7% Design and Visual Communications, General, 44% Painting, 17% Photography, 8% Printmaking
Expenses: 2014-2015: $40,096; room/board: $11,500
Financial aid: (415) 749-4520; 61% of undergrads determined to have financial need; average aid package $17,165

San Francisco Conservatory of Music
San Francisco CA
(800) 899-7326
U.S. News ranking: Arts, unranked
Website: www.sfcm.edu
Admissions email: admit@sfcm.edu
Private; founded 1917
Freshman admissions: N/A; 2013-2014: 296 applied, 118 accepted. Neither SAT nor ACT required. SAT 25/75 percentile: N/A. High school rank: N/A
Early decision deadline: N/A, notification date: N/A
Early action deadline: N/A, notification date: N/A
Application deadline (fall): 12/1
Undergraduate student body: 171 full time, 3 part time; 51% male, 49% female; 1% American Indian, 7% Asian, 3% black, 3% Hispanic, 15% multiracial, 0% Pacific Islander, 38% white, 26% international; 61% from in state; 13% live on campus; 0% of students in fraternities, 0% in sororities
Most popular majors: 7% Brass Instruments, 16% Keyboard Instruments, 11% Music Theory and Composition, 36% Stringed Instruments, 27% Voice and Opera
Expenses: 2014-2015: $40,992; room/board: N/A
Financial aid: (415) 759-3414; 88% of undergrads determined to have financial need; average aid package $24,016

San Francisco State University
San Francisco CA
(415) 338-6486
U.S. News ranking: Reg. U. (W), No. 58
Website: www.sfsu.edu
Admissions email: ugadmit@sfsu.edu
Public; founded 1899
Freshman admissions: selective; 2013-2014: 34,930 applied, 20,889 accepted. Either SAT or ACT required. SAT 25/75 percentile: 880-1110. High school rank: N/A
Early decision deadline: N/A, notification date: N/A
Early action deadline: N/A, notification date: N/A
Application deadline (fall): 11/30
Undergraduate student body: 22,111 full time, 4,045 part time; 43% male, 57% female; 0% American Indian, 29% Asian, 5% black, 24% Hispanic, 6% multiracial, 1% Pacific Islander, 24% white, 7% international; 99% from in state; 12% live on campus; 2% of students in fraternities, 5% in sororities
Most popular majors: 24% Business, Management, Marketing, and Related Support Services, 9% Communication, Journalism, and Related

Programs, 6% Health Professions and Related Programs, 10% Social Sciences, 9% Visual and Performing Arts
Expenses: 2014-2015: $6,468 in state, $17,628 out of state; room/board: $13,052
Financial aid: (415) 338-7000; 66% of undergrads determined to have financial need; average aid package $11,643

San Jose State University
San Jose CA
(408) 283-7500
U.S. News ranking: Reg. U. (W), No. 38
Website: www.sjsu.edu
Admissions email: admissions@sjsu.edu
Public; founded 1857
Freshman admissions: selective; 2013-2014: 27,679 applied, 17,733 accepted. Either SAT or ACT required. SAT 25/75 percentile: 880-1160. High school rank: N/A
Early decision deadline: N/A, notification date: N/A
Early action deadline: N/A, notification date: N/A
Application deadline (fall): 11/29
Undergraduate student body: 20,852 full time, 5,010 part time; 51% male, 49% female; 0% American Indian, 35% Asian, 3% black, 24% Hispanic, 5% multiracial, 1% Pacific Islander, 22% white, 5% international; 100% from in state; 14% live on campus; N/A of students in fraternities, N/A in sororities
Most popular majors: 26% Business, Management, Marketing, and Related Support Services, 8% Engineering, 9% Health Professions and Related Programs, 7% Psychology, 9% Visual and Performing Arts
Expenses: 2014-2015: $9,496 in state, $13,172 out of state; room/board: $13,350
Financial aid: (408) 283-7500; 71% of undergrads determined to have financial need; average aid package $14,956

Santa Clara University
Santa Clara CA
(408) 554-4700
U.S. News ranking: Reg. U. (W), No. 2
Website: www.scu.edu
Admissions email: Admission@scu.edu
Private; founded 1851
Affiliation: Catholic
Freshman admissions: more selective; 2013-2014: 14,980 applied, 7,456 accepted. Either SAT or ACT required. SAT 25/75 percentile: 1190-1380. High school rank: 50% in top tenth, 80% in top quarter, 97% in top half
Early decision deadline: 11/1, notification date: 12/23
Early action deadline: 11/1, notification date: 12/23
Application deadline (fall): 1/7
Undergraduate student body: 5,338 full time, 97 part time; 50% male, 50% female; 0% American Indian, 14% Asian, 3% black, 17% Hispanic, 7% multiracial, 0% Pacific Islander, 48% white, 3% international; 73% from in

state; 52% live on campus; N/A of students in fraternities, N/A in sororities
Most popular majors: 29% Business, Management, Marketing, and Related Support Services, 9% Communication, Journalism, and Related Programs, 11% Engineering, 7% Psychology, 13% Social Sciences
Expenses: 2014-2015: $43,812; room/board: $12,921
Financial aid: (408) 554-4505; 52% of undergrads determined to have financial need; average aid package $27,559

Scripps College
Claremont CA
(909) 621-8149
U.S. News ranking: Nat. Lib. Arts, No. 24
Website: www.scrippscollege.edu/
Admissions email: admission@scrippscollege.edu
Private; founded 1926
Freshman admissions: most selective; 2013-2014: 2,378 applied, 849 accepted. Either SAT or ACT required. SAT 25/75 percentile: 1280-1453. High school rank: 75% in top tenth, 99% in top quarter, 100% in top half
Early decision deadline: 11/15, notification date: 12/15
Early action deadline: N/A, notification date: N/A
Application deadline (fall): 1/1
Undergraduate student body: 979 full time, 11 part time; 0% male, 100% female; 0% American Indian, 17% Asian, 3% black, 8% Hispanic, 7% multiracial, 0% Pacific Islander, 51% white, 4% international; 51% from in state; 96% live on campus; 0% of students in fraternities, 0% in sororities
Most popular majors: 14% Area, Ethnic, Cultural, Gender, and Group Studies, 13% Biological and Biomedical Sciences, 8% Psychology, General, 19% Social Sciences, 9% Visual and Performing Arts
Expenses: 2014-2015: $47,378; room/board: $14,562
Financial aid: (909) 621-8275; 43% of undergrads determined to have financial need; average aid package $40,258

Simpson University
Redding CA
(530) 226-4606
U.S. News ranking: Nat. Lib. Arts, second tier
Website: www.simpsonu.edu
Admissions email: admissions@simpsonu.edu
Private; founded 1921
Affiliation: Christian and Missionary Alliance
Freshman admissions: selective; 2013-2014: 573 applied, 318 accepted. Either SAT or ACT required. SAT 25/75 percentile: 910-1150. High school rank: 23% in top tenth, 50% in top quarter, 88% in top half
Early decision deadline: N/A, notification date: N/A
Early action deadline: 8/31, notification date: N/A
Application deadline (fall): rolling
Undergraduate student body: 993 full time, 31 part time; 34% male, 66% female; 4% American Indian, 6% Asian, 3% black, 14% Hispanic, 0% multiracial,

0% Pacific Islander, 62% white, 0% international; 85% from in state; 61% live on campus; 0% of students in fraternities, 0% in sororities
Most popular majors: 29% Business/Commerce, General, 6% Communication and Media Studies, 23% Psychology, General, 12% Registered Nursing, Nursing Administration, Nursing Research and Clinical Nursing, 9% Theology and Religious Vocations, Other
Expenses: 2014-2015: $24,300; room/board: $7,700
Financial aid: (530) 226-4111; 89% of undergrads determined to have financial need; average aid package $20,435

Soka University of America
Aliso Viejo CA
(888) 600-Soka
U.S. News ranking: Nat. Lib. Arts, No. 41
Website: www.soka.edu
Admissions email: admission@soka.edu
Private; founded 1987
Freshman admissions: more selective; 2013-2014: 422 applied, 183 accepted. Either SAT or ACT required. SAT 25/75 percentile: 1080-1340. High school rank: 50% in top tenth, 79% in top quarter, 98% in top half
Early decision deadline: N/A, notification date: N/A
Early action deadline: 10/15, notification date: 12/1
Application deadline (fall): 1/15
Undergraduate student body: 412 full time, 0 part time; 36% male, 64% female; 1% American Indian, 19% Asian, 5% black, 8% Hispanic, 1% multiracial, 0% Pacific Islander, 20% white, 39% international; 60% from in state; 100% live on campus; 0% of students in fraternities, 0% in sororities
Most popular majors: 100% Liberal Arts and Sciences/Liberal Studies
Expenses: 2014-2015: $30,214; room/board: $11,134
Financial aid: N/A; 92% of undergrads determined to have financial need; average aid package $30,691

Sonoma State University
Rohnert Park CA
(707) 664-2778
U.S. News ranking: Reg. U. (W), No. 43
Website: www.sonoma.edu
Admissions email: student.outreach@sonoma.edu
Public; founded 1960
Freshman admissions: less selective; 2013-2014: 14,272 applied, 12,870 accepted. Either SAT or ACT required. SAT 25/75 percentile: 880-1090. High school rank: N/A
Early decision deadline: N/A, notification date: N/A
Early action deadline: N/A, notification date: N/A
Application deadline (fall): 11/30
Undergraduate student body: 7,652 full time, 699 part time; 39% male, 61% female; 1% American Indian, 5% Asian, 3% black, 19% Hispanic, 8% multiracial, 1% Pacific Islander, 60% white,

2% international; 99% from in state; 37% live on campus; 20% of students in fraternities, 13% in sororities
Most popular majors: 20% Business Administration and Management, General, 5% Health and Physical Education/Fitness, General, 6% Liberal Arts and Sciences/Liberal Studies, 8% Psychology, General, 7% Sociology
Expenses: 2014-2015: $7,276 in state, $18,436 out of state; room/board: $11,799
Financial aid: (707) 664-2287; 49% of undergrads determined to have financial need; average aid package $10,209

Southern California Institute of Architecture[1]
Los Angeles CA
(800) 774-7242
U.S. News ranking: Arts, unranked
Website: www.sciarc.edu
Admissions email: admissions@sciarc.edu
Private
Application deadline (fall): 1/15
Undergraduate student body: N/A full time, N/A part time
Expenses: 2013-2014: $37,300; room/board: N/A
Financial aid: (213) 613-2200

Stanford University
Stanford CA
(650) 723-2091
U.S. News ranking: Nat. U., No. 4
Website: www.stanford.edu
Admissions email: admission@stanford.edu
Private; founded 1885
Freshman admissions: most selective; 2013-2014: 38,828 applied, 2,208 accepted. Either SAT or ACT required. SAT 25/75 percentile: 1380-1570. High school rank: 96% in top tenth, 100% in top quarter, 100% in top half
Early decision deadline: N/A, notification date: N/A
Early action deadline: 11/1, notification date: 12/15
Application deadline (fall): 1/1
Undergraduate student body: 6,980 full time, 81 part time; 53% male, 47% female; 1% American Indian, 19% Asian, 6% black, 17% Hispanic, 11% multiracial, 0% Pacific Islander, 37% white, 8% international; 43% from in state; 91% live on campus; 24% of students in fraternities, 28% in sororities
Most popular majors: 6% Biological and Biomedical Sciences, 8% Computer and Information Sciences and Support Services, 15% Engineering, 16% Multi/Interdisciplinary Studies, 18% Social Sciences
Expenses: 2014-2015: $44,757; room/board: $13,631
Financial aid: (650) 723-3058; 50% of undergrads determined to have financial need; average aid package $43,900

St. Mary's College of California
Moraga CA
(925) 631-4224
U.S. News ranking: Reg. U. (W), No. 11
Website: www.stmarys-ca.edu
Admissions email: smcadmit@stmarys-ca.edu
Private; founded 1863
Affiliation: Roman Catholic
Freshman admissions: selective; 2013-2014: 4,864 applied, 3,379 accepted. Either SAT or ACT required. SAT 25/75 percentile: 1010-1210. High school rank: 31% in top tenth, 64% in top quarter, 92% in top half
Early decision deadline: N/A, notification date: N/A
Early action deadline: 11/15, notification date: 12/15
Application deadline (fall): 2/1
Undergraduate student body: 2,823 full time, 232 part time; 41% male, 59% female; 0% American Indian, 11% Asian, 4% black, 25% Hispanic, 6% multiracial, 1% Pacific Islander, 46% white, 2% international; 91% from in state; 55% live on campus; N/A of students in fraternities, N/A in sororities
Most popular majors: 23% Business, Management, Marketing, and Related Support Services, 11% Communication, Journalism, and Related Programs, 9% Liberal Arts and Sciences, General Studies and Humanities, 10% Psychology, 12% Social Sciences
Expenses: 2014-2015: $41,380; room/board: $14,400
Financial aid: (925) 631-4370; 75% of undergrads determined to have financial need; average aid package $26,434

Thomas Aquinas College
Santa Paula CA
(800) 634-9797
U.S. News ranking: Nat. Lib. Arts, No. 77
Website: www.thomasaquinas.edu
Admissions email: admissions@thomasaquinas.edu
Private; founded 1971
Affiliation: Catholic
Freshman admissions: selective; 2013-2014: 189 applied, 154 accepted. Either SAT or ACT required. SAT 25/75 percentile: 1160-1340. High school rank: 29% in top tenth, 50% in top quarter, 93% in top half
Early decision deadline: N/A, notification date: N/A
Early action deadline: N/A, notification date: N/A
Application deadline (fall): rolling
Undergraduate student body: 366 full time, 0 part time; 51% male, 49% female; 0% American Indian, 1% Asian, 0% black, 15% Hispanic, 5% multiracial, 0% Pacific Islander, 72% white, 4% international; 40% from in state; 99% live on campus; 0% of students in fraternities, 0% in sororities
Most popular majors: 100% Liberal Arts and Sciences, General Studies and Humanities
Expenses: 2014-2015: $24,500; room/board: $7,950

Financial aid: (805) 525-4417; 80% of undergrads determined to have financial need; average aid package $22,092

Trident University International[1]
Cypress CA
(800) 579-3170
U.S. News ranking: Nat. U., unranked
Website: www.trident.edu
Admissions email: N/A
For-profit
Application deadline (fall): rolling
Undergraduate student body: N/A full time, N/A part time
Expenses: 2013-2014: $6,600; room/board: N/A
Financial aid: (877) 835-9818

University of California–Berkeley
Berkeley CA
(510) 642-3175
U.S. News ranking: Nat. U., No. 20
Website: students.berkeley.edu/admissions/
Admissions email: N/A
Public; founded 1868
Freshman admissions: most selective; 2013-2014: 66,794 applied, 11,828 accepted. Either SAT or ACT required. SAT 25/75 percentile: 1250-1500. High school rank: 98% in top tenth, 100% in top quarter, 100% in top half
Early decision deadline: N/A, notification date: N/A
Early action deadline: N/A, notification date: N/A
Application deadline (fall): 11/30
Undergraduate student body: 25,220 full time, 731 part time; 48% male, 52% female; 0% American Indian, 35% Asian, 2% black, 13% Hispanic, 5% multiracial, 0% Pacific Islander, 29% white, 13% international
Most popular majors: Information not available
Expenses: 2014-2015: $13,844 in state, $25,064 out of state; room/board: $15,438
Financial aid: (510) 642-6442; 47% of undergrads determined to have financial need; average aid package $23,517

University of California–Davis
Davis CA
(530) 752-2971
U.S. News ranking: Nat. U., No. 38
Website: www.ucdavis.edu
Admissions email: undergraduateadmissions@ucdavis.edu
Public; founded 1905
Freshman admissions: most selective; 2013-2014: 55,833 applied, 23,049 accepted. Either SAT or ACT required. SAT 25/75 percentile: 1080-1340. High school rank: 100% in top tenth, 100% in top quarter, 100% in top half
Early decision deadline: N/A, notification date: N/A
Early action deadline: N/A, notification date: N/A
Application deadline (fall): 11/30
Undergraduate student body: 26,305 full time, 358 part time; 44% male, 56% female; 0% American Indian, 35% Asian, 2% black, 17% Hispanic, 5%

multiracial, 0% Pacific Islander, 31% white, 6% international; 97% from in state; 25% live on campus; N/A of students in fraternities, N/A in sororities
Most popular majors: 5% Biology/Biological Sciences, General, 4% Business/Managerial Economics, 6% Economics, General, 4% Political Science and Government, General, 10% Research and Experimental Psychology, Other
Expenses: 2014-2015: $13,896 in state, $36,774 out of state; room/board: $14,218
Financial aid: (530) 752-2396; 66% of undergrads determined to have financial need; average aid package $19,685

University of California–Irvine
Irvine CA
(949) 824-6703
U.S. News ranking: Nat. U., No. 42
Website: www.uci.edu
Admissions email: admissions@uci.edu
Public; founded 1965
Freshman admissions: more selective; 2013-2014: 60,690 applied, 24,931 accepted. Either SAT or ACT required. SAT 25/75 percentile: 1040-1290. High school rank: 96% in top tenth, 100% in top quarter, 100% in top half
Early decision deadline: N/A, notification date: N/A
Early action deadline: N/A, notification date: N/A
Application deadline (fall): 11/30
Undergraduate student body: 23,117 full time, 413 part time; 46% male, 54% female; 0% American Indian, 44% Asian, 2% black, 22% Hispanic, 4% multiracial, 0% Pacific Islander, 17% white, 9% international; 98% from in state; 43% live on campus; 9% of students in fraternities, 10% in sororities
Most popular majors: 13% Biology/Biological Sciences, General, 6% Business/Managerial Economics, 6% Political Science and Government, General, 5% Public Health, Other, 7% Social Psychology
Expenses: 2014-2015: $14,757 in state, $37,635 out of state; room/board: $12,638
Financial aid: (949) 824-5337; 69% of undergrads determined to have financial need; average aid package $21,592

University of California–Los Angeles
Los Angeles CA
(310) 825-3101
U.S. News ranking: Nat. U., No. 23
Website: www.ucla.edu/
Admissions email: ugadm@saonet.ucla.edu
Public; founded 1919
Freshman admissions: most selective; 2013-2014: 80,522 applied, 16,448 accepted. Either SAT or ACT required. SAT 25/75 percentile: 1190-1450. High school rank: 97% in top tenth, 100% in top quarter, 100% in top half
Early decision deadline: N/A, notification date: N/A
Early action deadline: N/A, notification date: N/A

Application deadline (fall): 11/30
Undergraduate student body: 28,084 full time, 590 part time; 45% male, 55% female; 0% American Indian, 31% Asian, 3% black, 18% Hispanic, 5% multiracial, 0% Pacific Islander, 29% white, 12% international; 92% from in state; 39% live on campus; 15% of students in fraternities, 15% in sororities
Most popular majors: Information not available
Expenses: 2014-2015: $12,702 in state, $35,580 out of state; room/board: $14,511
Financial aid: (310) 206-0400; 55% of undergrads determined to have financial need; average aid package $21,984

University of California–Riverside
Riverside CA
(951) 827-3411
U.S. News ranking: Nat. U., No. 113
Website: www.ucr.edu
Admissions email: admit@ucr.edu
Public; founded 1954
Freshman admissions: more selective; 2013-2014: 34,816 applied, 20,973 accepted. Either SAT or ACT required. SAT 25/75 percentile: 990-1210. High school rank: 94% in top tenth, 100% in top quarter, 100% in top half
Early decision deadline: N/A, notification date: N/A
Early action deadline: N/A, notification date: N/A
Application deadline (fall): 11/30
Undergraduate student body: 18,205 full time, 416 part time; 49% male, 51% female; 0% American Indian, 36% Asian, 5% black, 36% Hispanic, 4% multiracial, 0% Pacific Islander, 14% white, 3% international; 100% from in state; 31% live on campus; 5% of students in fraternities, 8% in sororities
Most popular majors: 13% Biological and Biomedical Sciences, 15% Business, Management, Marketing, and Related Support Services, 10% Psychology, 22% Social Sciences, 6% Visual and Performing Arts
Expenses: 2014-2015: $13,408 in state, $36,286 out of state; room/board: N/A
Financial aid: (951) 827-3878; 79% of undergrads determined to have financial need; average aid package $20,947

University of California–San Diego
La Jolla CA
(858) 534-4831
U.S. News ranking: Nat. U., No. 37
Website: www.ucsd.edu/
Admissions email: admissionsinfo@ucsd.edu
Public; founded 1960
Freshman admissions: most selective; 2013-2014: 67,400 applied, 24,832 accepted. Either SAT or ACT required. SAT 25/75 percentile: 1180-1400. High school rank: 100% in top tenth, 100% in top quarter, 100% in top half
Early decision deadline: N/A, notification date: N/A
Early action deadline: N/A, notification date: N/A
Application deadline (fall): 11/30

Undergraduate student body: 23,397 full time, 408 part time; 52% male, 48% female; 0% American Indian, 41% Asian, 2% black, 15% Hispanic, 0% multiracial, 0% Pacific Islander, 21% white, 17% international; 95% from in state; 45% live on campus; 10% of students in fraternities, 10% in sororities
Most popular majors: 20% Biology, General, 5% Communication and Media Studies, 13% Economics, 7% Political Science and Government, General, 8% Psychology, General
Expenses: 2013-2014: $13,302 in state, $36,180 out of state; room/board: $11,978
Financial aid: (858) 534-4480; 63% of undergrads determined to have financial need; average aid package $22,347

University of California–Santa Barbara
Santa Barbara CA
(805) 893-2485
U.S. News ranking: Nat. U., No. 40
Website: www.ucsb.edu
Admissions email: admissions@sa.ucsb.edu
Public; founded 1909
Freshman admissions: most selective; 2013-2014: 62,427 applied, 24,813 accepted. Either SAT or ACT required. SAT 25/75 percentile: 1130-1370. High school rank: 100% in top tenth, 100% in top quarter, 100% in top half
Early decision deadline: N/A, notification date: N/A
Early action deadline: N/A, notification date: N/A
Application deadline (fall): 11/30
Undergraduate student body: 19,076 full time, 286 part time; 48% male, 52% female; 1% American Indian, 24% Asian, 4% black, 24% Hispanic, 0% multiracial, 0% Pacific Islander, 40% white, 3% international; 96% from in state; 38% live on campus; 8% of students in fraternities, 12% in sororities
Most popular majors: 8% Biological and Biomedical Sciences, 6% Communication, Journalism, and Related Programs, 4% Physical Sciences, 10% Psychology, 23% Social Sciences
Expenses: 2014-2015: $13,746 in state, $36,624 out of state; room/board: $13,805
Financial aid: (805) 893-2432; 62% of undergrads determined to have financial need; average aid package $22,609

University of California–Santa Cruz
Santa Cruz CA
(831) 459-4008
U.S. News ranking: Nat. U., No. 85
Website: www.ucsc.edu
Admissions email: admissions@ucsc.edu
Public; founded 1965
Freshman admissions: more selective; 2013-2014: 38,640 applied, 20,039 accepted. Either SAT or ACT required. SAT 25/75 percentile: 1000-1280. High school rank: 96% in top tenth, 100% in top quarter, 100% in top half

Early decision deadline: N/A, notification date: N/A
Early action deadline: N/A, notification date: N/A
Application deadline (fall): 11/30
Undergraduate student body: 15,450 full time, 245 part time; 47% male, 53% female; 0% American Indian, 20% Asian, 2% black, 30% Hispanic, 7% multiracial, 0% Pacific Islander, 37% white, 1% international; 96% from in state; 48% live on campus; 1% of students in fraternities, 0% in sororities
Most popular majors: 6% Business/Managerial Economics, 5% English Language and Literature/Letters, Other, 5% Environmental Studies, 10% Psychology, General, 4% Sociology
Expenses: 2014-2015: $13,398 in state, $36,276 out of state; room/board: $14,730
Financial aid: (831) 459-2963; 71% of undergrads determined to have financial need; average aid package $22,938

University of La Verne
La Verne CA
(800) 876-4858
U.S. News ranking: Nat. U., No. 166
Website: www.laverne.edu
Admissions email: admission@laverne.edu
Private; founded 1891
Freshman admissions: selective; 2013-2014: 8,264 applied, 2,843 accepted. Either SAT or ACT required. SAT 25/75 percentile: 950-1130. High school rank: 23% in top tenth, 60% in top quarter, 89% in top half
Early decision deadline: N/A, notification date: N/A
Early action deadline: N/A, notification date: N/A
Application deadline (fall): rolling
Undergraduate student body: 2,595 full time, 87 part time; 41% male, 59% female; 0% American Indian, 7% Asian, 5% black, 51% Hispanic, 4% multiracial, 0% Pacific Islander, 26% white, 5% international; 96% from in state; 31% live on campus; 7% of students in fraternities, 16% in sororities
Most popular majors: 19% Business, Management, Marketing, and Related Support Services, 11% Education, 11% Liberal Arts and Sciences, General Studies and Humanities, 10% Psychology, 15% Social Sciences
Expenses: 2014-2015: $36,744; room/board: $12,200
Financial aid: (800) 649-0160; 83% of undergrads determined to have financial need; average aid package $28,603

University of Redlands
Redlands CA
(800) 455-5064
U.S. News ranking: Reg. U. (W), No. 12
Website: www.redlands.edu
Admissions email: admissions@redlands.edu
Private; founded 1907
Freshman admissions: more selective; 2013-2014: 4,668 applied, 3,137 accepted. Either SAT or ACT required. SAT 25/75 percentile: 1030-1230. High

school rank: 35% in top tenth, 65% in top quarter, 96% in top half
Early decision deadline: N/A, notification date: N/A
Early action deadline: 11/15, notification date: 12/31
Application deadline (fall): rolling
Undergraduate student body: 2,702 full time, 907 part time; 45% male, 55% female; 1% American Indian, 5% Asian, 5% black, 26% Hispanic, 4% multiracial, 1% Pacific Islander, 51% white, 1% international; 81% from in state; 59% live on campus; 13% of students in fraternities, 20% in sororities
Most popular majors: 42% Business, Management, Marketing, and Related Support Services, 6% Liberal Arts and Sciences, General Studies and Humanities, 6% Natural Resources and Conservation, 7% Psychology, 9% Social Sciences
Expenses: 2014-2015: $43,186; room/board: $12,710
Financial aid: (909) 335-4047; 78% of undergrads determined to have financial need; average aid package $34,707

University of San Diego
San Diego CA
(619) 260-4506
U.S. News ranking: Nat. U., No. 95
Website: www.SanDiego.edu
Admissions email: admissions@ SanDiego.edu
Private; founded 1949
Affiliation: Roman Catholic
Freshman admissions: more selective; 2013-2014: 14,693 applied, 7,178 accepted. Either SAT or ACT required. SAT 25/75 percentile: 1110-1320. High school rank: 45% in top tenth, 91% in top quarter, 95% in top half
Early decision deadline: N/A, notification date: N/A
Early action deadline: N/A, notification date: N/A
Application deadline (fall): 12/15
Undergraduate student body: 5,486 full time, 179 part time; 45% male, 55% female; 0% American Indian, 6% Asian, 3% black, 19% Hispanic, 6% multiracial, 0% Pacific Islander, 55% white, 6% international; 62% from in state; 44% live on campus; 21% of students in fraternities, 36% in sororities
Most popular majors: 6% Biological and Biomedical Sciences, 42% Business, Management, Marketing, and Related Support Services, 9% Communication, Journalism, and Related Programs, 7% Psychology, 13% Social Sciences
Expenses: 2014-2015: $42,908; room/board: $11,910
Financial aid: (619) 260-4514; 55% of undergrads determined to have financial need; average aid package $31,193

University of San Francisco
San Francisco CA
(415) 422-6563
U.S. News ranking: Nat. U., No. 106
Website: www.usfca.edu
Admissions email: admission@ usfca.edu

Private; founded 1855
Affiliation: Jesuit Catholic
Freshman admissions: more selective; 2013-2014: 14,844 applied, 9,076 accepted. Either SAT or ACT required. SAT 25/75 percentile: 1070-1270. High school rank: 33% in top tenth, 71% in top quarter, 94% in top half
Early decision deadline: 11/15, notification date: 1/1
Early action deadline: 11/15, notification date: 1/1
Application deadline (fall): rolling
Undergraduate student body: 6,111 full time, 281 part time; 38% male, 62% female; 0% American Indian, 19% Asian, 3% black, 19% Hispanic, 7% multiracial, 0% Pacific Islander, 31% white, 18% international; 79% from in state; 34% live on campus; 1% of students in fraternities, 1% in sororities
Most popular majors: 6% Business Administration and Management, General, 6% Finance, General, 5% Hematology Technology/ Technician, 9% Psychology, General, 10% Registered Nursing/ Registered Nurse
Expenses: 2014-2015: $41,450; room/board: $13,320
Financial aid: (415) 422-2620; 56% of undergrads determined to have financial need; average aid package $28,727

University of Southern California
Los Angeles CA
(213) 740-1111
U.S. News ranking: Nat. U., No. 25
Website: www.usc.edu/
Admissions email: admitusc@ usc.edu
Private; founded 1880
Freshman admissions: most selective; 2013-2014: 47,358 applied, 9,395 accepted. Either SAT or ACT required. SAT 25/75 percentile: 1280-1480. High school rank: 88% in top tenth, 97% in top quarter, 100% in top half
Early decision deadline: N/A, notification date: N/A
Early action deadline: N/A, notification date: N/A
Application deadline (fall): 1/10
Undergraduate student body: 17,729 full time, 716 part time; 50% male, 50% female; 0% American Indian, 23% Asian, 4% black, 14% Hispanic, 5% multiracial, 0% Pacific Islander, 38% white, 12% international; 69% from in state; 33% live on campus; 25% of students in fraternities, 19% in sororities
Most popular majors: 25% Business, Management, Marketing, and Related Support Services, 10% Communication, Journalism, and Related Programs, 10% Engineering, 13% Social Sciences, 12% Visual and Performing Arts
Expenses: 2014-2015: $48,280; room/board: $13,334
Financial aid: (213) 740-1111; 41% of undergrads determined to have financial need; average aid package $42,978

University of the Pacific
Stockton CA
(209) 946-2285
U.S. News ranking: Nat. U., No. 116
Website: www.pacific.edu
Admissions email: admissions@ pacific.edu
Private; founded 1851
Freshman admissions: more selective; 2013-2014: 14,222 applied, 10,332 accepted. Either SAT or ACT required. SAT 25/75 percentile: 1030-1320. High school rank: 36% in top tenth, 68% in top quarter, 90% in top half
Early decision deadline: N/A, notification date: N/A
Early action deadline: 11/15, notification date: 1/15
Application deadline (fall): 1/15
Undergraduate student body: 3,780 full time, 97 part time; 48% male, 52% female; 1% American Indian, 32% Asian, 3% black, 19% Hispanic, 4% multiracial, 0% Pacific Islander, 32% white, 5% international; 93% from in state; 46% live on campus; 15% of students in fraternities, 16% in sororities
Most popular majors: 14% Biology/ Biological Sciences, General, 15% Business Administration and Management, General, 7% Curriculum and Instruction, 8% Engineering, General, 7% Health and Physical Education/Fitness, General
Expenses: 2014-2015: $41,342; room/board: $12,582
Financial aid: (209) 946-2421; 73% of undergrads determined to have financial need; average aid package $29,290

University of the West[1]
Rosemead CA
(855) 469-3378
U.S. News ranking: Reg. Coll. (W), unranked
Website: www.uwest.edu
Admissions email: N/A
Private
Application deadline (fall): N/A
Undergraduate student body: N/A full time, N/A part time
Expenses: 2013-2014: $9,486; room/board: $6,070
Financial aid: (626) 571-8811

Vanguard University of Southern California
Costa Mesa CA
(800) 722-6279
U.S. News ranking: Reg. Coll. (W), No. 12
Website: www.vanguard.edu
Admissions email: admissions@ vanguard.edu
Private; founded 1920
Affiliation: Assemblies of God
Freshman admissions: selective; 2013-2014: 1,497 applied, 1,043 accepted. Either SAT or ACT required. SAT 25/75 percentile: 850-1073. High school rank: 16% in top tenth, 41% in top quarter, 76% in top half
Early decision deadline: N/A, notification date: N/A
Early action deadline: 12/1, notification date: 1/15
Application deadline (fall): rolling
Undergraduate student body: 1,576 full time, 559 part time; 32%

male, 68% female; 1% American Indian, 4% Asian, 4% black, 35% Hispanic, 5% multiracial, 1% Pacific Islander, 46% white, 1% international; 91% from in state; 46% live on campus; 0% of students in fraternities, 0% in sororities
Most popular majors: 20% Business, Management, Marketing, and Related Support Services, 9% Communication, Journalism, and Related Programs, 9% Health Professions and Related Programs, 20% Psychology, 9% Social Sciences
Expenses: 2014-2015: $30,050; room/board: $8,870
Financial aid: (714) 556-3610; 81% of undergrads determined to have financial need; average aid package $14,137

Westmont College
Santa Barbara CA
(800) 777-9011
U.S. News ranking: Nat. Lib. Arts, No. 96
Website: www.westmont.edu
Admissions email: admissions@ westmont.edu
Private; founded 1937
Affiliation: Christian nondenominational
Freshman admissions: more selective; 2013-2014: 2,145 applied, 1,505 accepted. Either SAT or ACT required. SAT 25/75 percentile: 1060-1310. High school rank: 29% in top tenth, 66% in top quarter, 94% in top half
Early decision deadline: N/A, notification date: N/A
Early action deadline: 11/15, notification date: 1/5
Application deadline (fall): 8/15
Undergraduate student body: 1,291 full time, 14 part time; 39% male, 61% female; 0% American Indian, 7% Asian, 1% black, 13% Hispanic, 7% multiracial, 0% Pacific Islander, 66% white, 1% international; 75% from in state; 84% live on campus; 0% of students in fraternities, 0% in sororities
Most popular majors: 9% Biology/ Biological Sciences, General, 14% Business/Managerial Economics, 9% English Language and Literature, General, 12% Kinesiology and Exercise Science, 11% Speech Communication and Rhetoric
Expenses: 2014-2015: $39,990; room/board: $12,580
Financial aid: (805) 565-6063; 65% of undergrads determined to have financial need; average aid package $28,681

Whittier College
Whittier CA
(562) 907-4238
U.S. News ranking: Nat. Lib. Arts, No. 133
Website: www.whittier.edu
Admissions email: admission@ whittier.edu
Private; founded 1887
Freshman admissions: selective; 2013-2014: 4,380 applied, 2,771 accepted. Either SAT or ACT required. SAT 25/75 percentile: 930-1150. High school rank: 23% in top tenth, 39% in top quarter, 89% in top half
Early decision deadline: N/A, notification date: N/A

Early action deadline: 12/1, notification date: 12/30
Application deadline (fall): rolling
Undergraduate student body: 1,668 full time, 27 part time; 44% male, 56% female; 1% American Indian, 11% Asian, 6% black, 38% Hispanic, 0% multiracial, 0% Pacific Islander, 36% white, 3% international; 81% from in state; 51% live on campus; 9% of students in fraternities, 13% in sororities
Most popular majors: 6% Biological and Biomedical Sciences, 14% Business, Management, Marketing, and Related Support Services, 9% Parks, Recreation, Leisure, and Fitness Studies, 10% Psychology, 19% Social Sciences
Expenses: 2014-2015: $41,711; room/board: $12,046
Financial aid: (562) 907-4285; 79% of undergrads determined to have financial need; average aid package $31,328

Woodbury University
Burbank CA
(818) 767-0888
U.S. News ranking: Reg. U. (W), No. 56
Website: www.woodbury.edu
Admissions email: info@woodbury.edu
Private; founded 1884
Freshman admissions: selective; 2013-2014: 858 applied, 486 accepted. Either SAT or ACT required. SAT 25/75 percentile: 880-1110. High school rank: N/A
Early decision deadline: N/A, notification date: N/A
Early action deadline: N/A, notification date: N/A
Application deadline (fall): rolling
Undergraduate student body: 1,172 full time, 185 part time; 49% male, 51% female; 0% American Indian, 10% Asian, 5% black, 29% Hispanic, 0% multiracial, 0% Pacific Islander, 38% white, 18% international; 97% from in state; 14% live on campus; 5% of students in fraternities, 7% in sororities
Most popular majors: 12% Accounting, 35% Architecture, 12% Business Administration and Management, General, 5% Film/Video and Photographic Arts, Other, 5% Psychology, General
Expenses: 2014-2015: $35,048; room/board: $10,522
Financial aid: (818) 767-0888; 87% of undergrads determined to have financial need; average aid package $21,758

COLORADO

Adams State University[1]
Alamosa CO
(800) 824-6494
U.S. News ranking: Reg. U. (W), second tier
Website: www.adams.edu
Admissions email: ascadmit@ adams.edu
Public
Application deadline (fall): N/A
Undergraduate student body: N/A full time, N/A part time
Expenses: 2013-2014: $7,449 in state, $18,081 out of state; room/ board: $8,282
Financial aid: (719) 587-7306

Art Institute of Colorado[1]

Denver CO
(800) 275-2420
U.S. News ranking: Arts, unranked
Website: www.
artinstitutes.edu/denver/
Admissions email: N/A
For-profit
Application deadline (fall): N/A
Undergraduate student body: N/A
full time, N/A part time
Expenses: 2013-2014: $17,632;
room/board: $10,287
Financial aid: (800) 275-2420

Colorado Christian University[1]

Lakewood CO
(303) 963-3200
U.S. News ranking: Reg. U. (W),
second tier
Website: www.ccu.edu
Admissions email:
admission@ccu.edu
Private
Application deadline (fall): N/A
Undergraduate student body: N/A
full time, N/A part time
Expenses: 2013-2014: $25,046;
room/board: $9,640
Financial aid: (303) 963-3230

Colorado College

Colorado Springs CO
(719) 389-6344
U.S. News ranking: Nat. Lib. Arts,
No. 27
Website: www.ColoradoCollege.edu
Admissions email: admission@
ColoradoCollege.edu
Private; founded 1874
Freshman admissions: most
selective; 2013-2014: 5,780
applied, 1,288 accepted. Neither
SAT nor ACT required. SAT
25/75 percentile: 1220-1430.
High school rank: 66% in top
tenth, 94% in top quarter, 99%
in top half
Early decision deadline: 11/15,
notification date: 12/15
Early action deadline: 11/15,
notification date: 12/20
Application deadline (fall): 1/15
Undergraduate student body: 2,025
full time, 15 part time; 45%
male, 55% female; 0% American
Indian, 4% Asian, 2% black,
9% Hispanic, 8% multiracial,
0% Pacific Islander, 70% white,
6% international; 19% from in
state; 76% live on campus; 9%
of students in fraternities, 11%
in sororities
Most popular majors: 6% Biology/
Biological Sciences, General,
6% Economics, General, 6%
Environmental Science, 5%
Fine/Studio Arts, General, 7%
Sociology
Expenses: 2014-2015: $46,410;
room/board: $10,752
Financial aid: (719) 389-6651;
38% of undergrads determined to
have financial need; average aid
package $39,513

Colorado Mesa University

Grand Junction CO
(800) 982-6372
U.S. News ranking: Nat. Lib. Arts,
second tier
Website: www.coloradomesa.edu/
Admissions email: admissions@
coloradomesa.edu
Public; founded 1925

Freshman admissions: selective;
2013-2014: 6,420 applied,
5,265 accepted. Either SAT
or ACT required. ACT 25/75
percentile: 18-23. High school
rank: 10% in top tenth, 24% in
top quarter, 52% in top half
Early decision deadline: N/A,
notification date: N/A
Early action deadline: N/A,
notification date: N/A
Application deadline (fall): rolling
Undergraduate student body: 7,267
full time, 2,308 part time; 45%
male, 55% female; 1% American
Indian, 1% Asian, 3% black,
15% Hispanic, 4% multiracial,
1% Pacific Islander, 72% white,
0% international; 88% from in
state; 23% live on campus; 0%
of students in fraternities, 0% in
sororities
Most popular majors: 6% Biology/
Biological Sciences, General, 26%
Business/Commerce, General, 8%
Kinesiology and Exercise Science,
7% Psychology, General, 12%
Registered Nursing/Registered
Nurse
Expenses: 2014-2015: $7,625 in
state, $18,985 out of state; room/
board: $10,065
Financial aid: (970) 248-1396;
70% of undergrads determined to
have financial need; average aid
package $7,859

Colorado School of Mines

Golden CO
(303) 273-3220
U.S. News ranking: Nat. U., No. 88
Website: www.mines.edu
Admissions email:
admit@mines.edu
Public; founded 1874
Freshman admissions: most
selective; 2013-2014: 12,169
applied, 4,434 accepted. Either
SAT or ACT required. ACT 25/75
percentile: 28-32. High school
rank: 66% in top tenth, 93% in
top quarter, 100% in top half
Early decision deadline: N/A,
notification date: N/A
Early action deadline: N/A,
notification date: N/A
Application deadline (fall): 4/1
Undergraduate student body: 4,082
full time, 211 part time; 73%
male, 27% female; 0% American
Indian, 5% Asian, 1% black, 8%
Hispanic, 4% multiracial, 0%
Pacific Islander, 75% white, 4%
international; 68% from in state;
40% live on campus; 10% of
students in fraternities, 16% in
sororities
Most popular majors: 1% Computer
and Information Sciences
and Support Services, 88%
Engineering, 6% Mathematics and
Statistics, 3% Physical Sciences,
2% Social Sciences
Expenses: 2014-2015: $16,918
in state, $33,598 out of state;
room/board: $10,484
Financial aid: (303) 273-3220;
54% of undergrads determined to
have financial need; average aid
package $11,887

Colorado State University

Fort Collins CO
(970) 491-6909
U.S. News ranking: Nat. U.,
No. 121
Website: www.colostate.edu
Admissions email: admissions@
colostate.edu
Public; founded 1870
Freshman admissions: more
selective; 2013-2014: 17,970
applied, 13,914 accepted. Either
SAT or ACT required. ACT 25/75
percentile: 22-27. High school
rank: 22% in top tenth, 52% in
top quarter, 88% in top half
Early decision deadline: N/A,
notification date: N/A
Early action deadline: 12/1,
notification date: 2/1
Application deadline (fall): 2/1
Undergraduate student body:
21,283 full time, 2,515 part
time; 49% male, 51% female;
0% American Indian, 2% Asian,
2% black, 10% Hispanic, 3%
multiracial, 0% Pacific Islander,
74% white, 3% international;
81% from in state; 25% live
on campus; 7% of students in
fraternities, 9% in sororities
Most popular majors: 9% Biological
and Biomedical Sciences,
14% Business, Management,
Marketing, and Related Support
Services, 10% Family and
Consumer Sciences/Human
Sciences, 7% Parks, Recreation,
Leisure, and Fitness Studies, 10%
Social Sciences
Expenses: 2014-2015: $9,897 in
state, $26,077 out of state; room/
board: $10,488
Financial aid: (970) 491-6321;
57% of undergrads determined to
have financial need; average aid
package $11,806

Colorado State University–Pueblo

Pueblo CO
(719) 549-2461
U.S. News ranking: Reg. U. (W),
second tier
Website:
www.colostate-pueblo.edu
Admissions email:
info@colostate-pueblo.edu
Public; founded 1933
Freshman admissions: less
selective; 2013-2014: 3,038
applied, 2,897 accepted. Either
SAT or ACT required. ACT 25/75
percentile: 18-23. High school
rank: 11% in top tenth, 34% in
top quarter, 67% in top half
Early decision deadline: N/A,
notification date: N/A
Early action deadline: N/A,
notification date: N/A
Application deadline (fall): 8/1
Undergraduate student body: 3,742
full time, 1,465 part time; 44%
male, 56% female; 1% American
Indian, 2% Asian, 8% black,
31% Hispanic, 3% multiracial,
0% Pacific Islander, 51% white,
1% international; 93% from in
state; 19% live on campus; 2%
of students in fraternities, 2% in
sororities
Most popular majors: 12%
Business/Commerce, General, 9%
Kinesiology and Exercise Science,
7% Mass Communication/Media
Studies, 10% Registered Nursing/
Registered Nurse, 13% Sociology
Expenses: 2013-2014: $7,327 in
state, $17,649 out of state; room/
board: $8,856

Financial aid: (719) 549-2753;
77% of undergrads determined to
have financial need; average aid
package $9,424

Colorado Technical University[1]

Colorado Springs CO
(888) 897-6555
U.S. News ranking: Nat. U.,
unranked
Website: www.coloradotech.edu
Admissions email:
info@ctuonline.edu
For-profit
Application deadline (fall): N/A
Undergraduate student body: N/A
full time, N/A part time
Expenses: 2013-2014: $11,300;
room/board: N/A
Financial aid: (719) 598-2900

Fort Lewis College

Durango CO
(970) 247-7184
U.S. News ranking: Nat. Lib. Arts,
second tier
Website: www.fortlewis.edu
Admissions email: admission@
fortlewis.edu
Public; founded 1911
Freshman admissions: selective;
2013-2014: 2,560 applied,
2,240 accepted. Either SAT
or ACT required. ACT 25/75
percentile: 20-25. High school
rank: 10% in top tenth, 32% in
top quarter, 65% in top half
Early decision deadline: N/A,
notification date: N/A
Early action deadline: 1/15,
notification date: 3/15
Application deadline (fall): 8/1
Undergraduate student body: 3,698
full time, 330 part time; 51%
male, 49% female; 22% American
Indian, 1% Asian, 1% black,
10% Hispanic, 6% multiracial,
0% Pacific Islander, 58% white,
1% international; 57% from in
state; 38% live on campus; 0%
of students in fraternities, 0% in
sororities
Most popular majors: 21%
Business, Management,
Marketing, and Related Support
Services, 8% Physical Sciences,
8% Psychology, 10% Social
Sciences
Expenses: 2014-2015: $7,252 in
state, $17,780 out of state; room/
board: $10,346
Financial aid: (970) 247-7142;
70% of undergrads determined to
have financial need; average aid
package $13,241

Jones International University

Centennial CO
(800) 811-5663
U.S. News ranking: Reg. U. (W),
unranked
Website:
www.jonesinternational.edu/
Admissions email: info@
jonesinternational.edu
For-profit; founded 1995
Freshman admissions: N/A; 2013-
2014: N/A applied, N/A accepted.
Neither SAT nor ACT required.
ACT 25/75 percentile: N/A. High
school rank: N/A
Early decision deadline: N/A,
notification date: N/A
Early action deadline: N/A,
notification date: N/A

Application deadline (fall): rolling
Undergraduate student body: 758
full time, 833 part time; 33%
male, 67% female; 1% American
Indian, 1% Asian, 33% black, 3%
Hispanic, 10% multiracial, 0%
Pacific Islander, 26% white, 0%
international
Most popular majors: 78%
Business Administration
and Management, General,
22% Business/Corporate
Communications
Expenses: 2013-2014: $12,720;
room/board: N/A
Financial aid: (800) 811-5663

Metropolitan State University of Denver[1]

Denver CO
(303) 556-3058
U.S. News ranking: Reg. Coll. (W),
second tier
Website: www.mscd.edu
Admissions email: askmetro@
mscd.edu
Public; founded 1963
Application deadline (fall): 4/30
Undergraduate student body: N/A
full time, N/A part time
Expenses: 2013-2014: $5,744 in
state, $17,837 out of state; room/
board: N/A
Financial aid: (303) 556-4741

Naropa University

Boulder CO
(303) 546-3572
U.S. News ranking: Reg. U. (W),
unranked
Website: www.naropa.edu
Admissions email: admissions@
naropa.edu
Private; founded 1974
Freshman admissions: N/A; 2013-
2014: 79 applied, 63 accepted.
Neither SAT nor ACT required.
ACT 25/75 percentile: N/A. High
school rank: N/A
Early decision deadline: N/A,
notification date: N/A
Early action deadline: N/A,
notification date: N/A
Application deadline (fall): rolling
Undergraduate student body: 359
full time, 24 part time; 36%
male, 64% female; 0% American
Indian, 1% Asian, 1% black,
8% Hispanic, 8% multiracial,
0% Pacific Islander, 65% white,
3% international; 37% from in
state; 19% live on campus; N/A
of students in fraternities, N/A in
sororities
Most popular majors: 9% English
Language and Literature, General,
7% Environmental Studies, 9%
Health and Physical Education/
Fitness, Other, 22% Multi-/
Interdisciplinary Studies, Other,
29% Psychology, General
Expenses: 2014-2015: $29,970;
room/board: $9,072
Financial aid: (303) 546-3565;
67% of undergrads determined to
have financial need; average aid
package $37,824

Regis University

Denver CO
(303) 458-4900
U.S. News ranking: Reg. U. (W),
No. 29
Website: www.regis.edu
Admissions email:
regisadm@regis.edu
Private; founded 1877
Affiliation: Roman Catholic (Jesuit)

Freshman admissions: selective; 2013-2014: 2,298 applied, 2,122 accepted. Either SAT or ACT required. ACT 25/75 percentile: 22-27. High school rank: 27% in top tenth, 56% in top quarter, 85% in top half **Early decision deadline:** N/A, notification date: N/A **Early action deadline:** N/A, notification date: N/A **Application deadline (fall):** 8/1 **Undergraduate student body:** 2,508 full time, 2,664 part time; 37% male, 63% female; 1% American Indian, 4% Asian, 5% black, 18% Hispanic, 2% multiracial, 0% Pacific Islander, 62% white, 1% international; 69% from in state; 48% live on campus; 0% of students in fraternities, 0% in sororities **Most popular majors:** 26% Business, Management, Marketing, and Related Support Services, 5% Computer and Information Sciences and Support Services, 35% Health Professions and Related Programs, 7% Liberal Arts and Sciences, General Studies and Humanities, 5% Social Sciences **Expenses:** 2014-2015: $33,060; room/board: $9,500 **Financial aid:** (303) 458-4066; 71% of undergrads determined to have financial need; average aid package $27,538

Rocky Mountain College of Art and Design

Lakewood CO
(303) 225-8576
U.S. News ranking: Arts, unranked
Website: www.rmcad.edu/
Admissions email: admissions@rmcad.edu
For-profit; founded 1963
Freshman admissions: N/A; 2013-2014: 279 applied, 190 accepted. Neither SAT nor ACT required. SAT 25/75 percentile: N/A. High school rank: N/A **Early decision deadline:** N/A, notification date: N/A **Early action deadline:** N/A, notification date: N/A **Application deadline (fall):** rolling **Undergraduate student body:** 554 full time, 185 part time; 37% male, 63% female; 1% American Indian, 3% Asian, 6% black, 10% Hispanic, 2% multiracial, 0% Pacific Islander, 62% white, 0% international; 59% from in state; 0% live on campus; 0% of students in fraternities, 0% in sororities **Most popular majors:** 10% Animation, Interactive Technology, Video Graphics and Special Effects, 17% Computer Graphics, 20% Fine/Studio Arts, General, 26% Illustration, 11% Interior Design **Expenses:** 2014-2015: $22,470; room/board: N/A **Financial aid:** (303) 753-6046; 78% of undergrads determined to have financial need; average aid package $19,249

United States Air Force Academy

USAF Academy CO
(800) 443-9266
U.S. News ranking: Nat. Lib. Arts, No. 27
Website: academyadmissions.com
Admissions email: rr_webmail@usafa.edu
Public; founded 1954
Freshman admissions: most selective; 2013-2014: 9,634 applied, 1,486 accepted. Either SAT or ACT required. ACT 25/75 percentile: 29-32. High school rank: 55% in top tenth, 85% in top quarter, 97% in top half **Early decision deadline:** N/A, notification date: N/A **Early action deadline:** N/A, notification date: N/A **Application deadline (fall):** 12/31 **Undergraduate student body:** 3,993 full time, 0 part time; 78% male, 22% female; 0% American Indian, 5% Asian, 6% black, 9% Hispanic, 7% multiracial, 1% Pacific Islander, 67% white, 1% international; 8% from in state; 100% live on campus; 0% of students in fraternities, 0% in sororities **Most popular majors:** 7% Biological and Biomedical Sciences, 11% Business, Management, Marketing, and Related Support Services, 40% Engineering, 11% Multi/Interdisciplinary Studies, 15% Social Sciences **Expenses:** N/A **Financial aid:** (719) 333-3160

University of Colorado–Boulder

Boulder CO
(303) 492-6301
U.S. News ranking: Nat. U., No. 88
Admissions email: apply@colorado.edu
Public; founded 1876
Freshman admissions: more selective; 2013-2014: 22,473 applied, 19,710 accepted. Either SAT or ACT required. ACT 25/75 percentile: 24-29. High school rank: 27% in top tenth, 56% in top quarter, 88% in top half **Early decision deadline:** N/A, notification date: N/A **Early action deadline:** 11/15, notification date: 2/1 **Application deadline (fall):** 1/15 **Undergraduate student body:** 23,853 full time, 2,128 part time; 55% male, 45% female; 0% American Indian, 5% Asian, 2% black, 10% Hispanic, 4% multiracial, 0% Pacific Islander, 74% white, 4% international; 63% from in state; 28% live on campus; 11% of students in fraternities, 17% in sororities **Most popular majors:** 10% Biological and Biomedical Sciences, 11% Business, Management, Marketing, and Related Support Services, 9% Communication, Journalism, and Related Programs, 10% Psychology, 15% Social Sciences **Expenses:** 2014-2015: $10,789 in state, $33,151 out of state; room/board: $12,810 **Financial aid:** (303) 492-5091; 40% of undergrads determined to have financial need; average aid package $16,054

University of Colorado– Colorado Springs

Colorado Springs CO
(719) 255-3383
U.S. News ranking: Reg. U. (W), No. 51
Website: www.uccs.edu
Admissions email: admrecor@uccs.edu
Public; founded 1965
Freshman admissions: selective; 2013-2014: 7,034 applied, 6,401 accepted. Either SAT or ACT required. ACT 25/75 percentile: 21-25. High school rank: 13% in top tenth, 36% in top quarter, 70% in top half **Early decision deadline:** N/A, notification date: N/A **Early action deadline:** N/A, notification date: N/A **Application deadline (fall):** rolling **Undergraduate student body:** 6,940 full time, 2,111 part time; 47% male, 53% female; 1% American Indian, 3% Asian, 4% black, 14% Hispanic, 6% multiracial, 0% Pacific Islander, 69% white, 1% international; 89% from in state; 13% live on campus; 1% of students in fraternities, 3% in sororities **Most popular majors:** 8% Biological and Biomedical Sciences, 21% Business Administration, Management and Operations, 12% Health Professions and Related Programs, 8% Psychology, 11% Social Sciences **Expenses:** 2014-2015: $16,212 in state, $21,522 out of state; room/board: N/A **Financial aid:** (719) 262-3460; 57% of undergrads determined to have financial need; average aid package $6,759

University of Colorado–Denver

Denver CO
(303) 556-2704
U.S. News ranking: Nat. U., second tier
Website: www.ucdenver.edu
Admissions email: admissions@ucdenver.edu
Public; founded 1912
Freshman admissions: selective; 2013-2014: 4,370 applied, 3,029 accepted. Either SAT or ACT required. ACT 25/75 percentile: 20-25. High school rank: 21% in top tenth, 50% in top quarter, 81% in top half **Early decision deadline:** N/A, notification date: N/A **Early action deadline:** N/A, notification date: N/A **Application deadline (fall):** rolling **Undergraduate student body:** 7,782 full time, 5,228 part time; 47% male, 53% female; 0% American Indian, 10% Asian, 5% black, 15% Hispanic, 3% multiracial, 0% Pacific Islander, 52% white, 10% international; 93% from in state; 5% live on campus; N/A of students in fraternities, N/A in sororities **Most popular majors:** 9% Biology/Biological Sciences, General, 16% Business Administration and Management, General, 6% Psychology, General, 11% Registered Nursing/Registered Nurse, 6% Speech Communication and Rhetoric

Expenses: 2013-2014: $9,625 in state, $26,105 out of state; room/board: $10,790 **Financial aid:** (303) 556-2886; 60% of undergrads determined to have financial need; average aid package $9,061

University of Denver

Denver CO
(303) 871-2036
U.S. News ranking: Nat. U., No. 88
Website: www.du.edu
Admissions email: admission@du.edu
Private; founded 1864
Freshman admissions: more selective; 2013-2014: 13,735 applied, 10,539 accepted. Either SAT or ACT required. ACT 25/75 percentile: 25-30. High school rank: 45% in top tenth, 76% in top quarter, 95% in top half **Early decision deadline:** N/A, notification date: N/A **Early action deadline:** 11/1, notification date: 1/15 **Application deadline (fall):** 1/15 **Undergraduate student body:** 5,129 full time, 388 part time; 45% male, 55% female; 1% American Indian, 4% Asian, 3% black, 9% Hispanic, 3% multiracial, 0% Pacific Islander, 68% white, 9% international; 46% from in state; 45% live on campus; 24% of students in fraternities, 28% in sororities **Most popular majors:** 7% Biological and Biomedical Sciences, 35% Business, Management, Marketing, and Related Support Services, 7% Communication, Journalism, and Related Programs, 17% Social Sciences, 8% Visual and Performing Arts **Expenses:** 2014-2015: $42,090; room/board: $11,307 **Financial aid:** (303) 871-4020; 42% of undergrads determined to have financial need; average aid package $32,462

University of Northern Colorado

Greeley CO
(970) 351-2881
U.S. News ranking: Nat. U., second tier
Website: www.unco.edu
Admissions email: admissions.help@unco.edu
Public; founded 1890
Freshman admissions: selective; 2013-2014: 7,602 applied, 5,289 accepted. Neither SAT nor ACT required. ACT 25/75 percentile: 20-24. High school rank: 12% in top tenth, 38% in top quarter, 73% in top half **Early decision deadline:** N/A, notification date: N/A **Early action deadline:** N/A, notification date: N/A **Undergraduate student body:** 8,723 full time, 987 part time; 37% male, 63% female; 0% American Indian, 2% Asian, 4% black, 16% Hispanic, 3% multiracial, 0% Pacific Islander, 58% white, 1% international; 87% from in state; 32% live on campus; 3% of students in fraternities, 5% in sororities **Most popular majors:** 9% Business, Management, Marketing, and Related Support Services, Other, 14% Health Professions and Related Clinical Sciences, Other, 17% Multi-/Interdisciplinary

Studies, General, 8% Parks, Recreation, Leisure, and Fitness Studies, Other, 7% Psychology, Other **Expenses:** 2014-2015: $7,573 in state, $18,817 out of state; room/board: $10,360 **Financial aid:** (970) 351-2502; 72% of undergrads determined to have financial need; average aid package $6,416

Western State Colorado University

Gunnison CO
(800) 876-5309
U.S. News ranking: Nat. Lib. Arts, second tier
Website: www.western.edu
Admissions email: discover@western.edu
Public; founded 1901
Freshman admissions: selective; 2013-2014: 1,523 applied, 1,406 accepted. Either SAT or ACT required. ACT 25/75 percentile: 19-24. High school rank: 6% in top tenth, 25% in top quarter, 62% in top half **Early decision deadline:** N/A, notification date: N/A **Early action deadline:** N/A, notification date: N/A **Application deadline (fall):** rolling **Undergraduate student body:** 1,869 full time, 323 part time; 58% male, 42% female; 0% American Indian, 1% Asian, 2% black, 9% Hispanic, 3% multiracial, 0% Pacific Islander, 75% white, 1% international; 74% from in state; 45% live on campus; 0% of students in fraternities, 0% in sororities **Most popular majors:** 9% Biological and Biomedical Sciences, 24% Business, Management, Marketing, and Related Support Services, 18% Parks, Recreation, Leisure, and Fitness Studies, 9% Psychology, 9% Social Sciences **Expenses:** 2014-2015: $7,874 in state, $18,319 out of state; room/board: $9,050 **Financial aid:** (970) 943-3085; 60% of undergrads determined to have financial need; average aid package $11,909

CONNECTICUT

Albertus Magnus College

New Haven CT
(800) 578-9160
U.S. News ranking: Reg. U. (N), No. 115
Website: www.albertus.edu
Admissions email: admissions@albertus.edu
Private; founded 1925
Affiliation: Roman Catholic
Freshman admissions: least selective; 2013-2014: 698 applied, 496 accepted. Either SAT or ACT required. SAT 25/75 percentile: 820-930. High school rank: 5% in top tenth, 26% in top quarter, 69% in top half **Early decision deadline:** N/A, notification date: N/A **Early action deadline:** N/A, notification date: N/A **Application deadline (fall):** 8/15 **Undergraduate student body:** 1,199 full time, 79 part time; 35% male, 65% female; 0% American Indian, 1% Asian, 28% black, 14% Hispanic, 2% multiracial,

0% Pacific Islander, 45% white, 0% international; 93% from in state; N/A live on campus; N/A of students in fraternities, N/A in sororities
Most popular majors: Information not available
Expenses: 2014-2015: $28,930; room/board: $12,960
Financial aid: (203) 773-8508; 83% of undergrads determined to have financial need; average aid package $15,988

Central Connecticut State University

New Britain CT
(860) 832-2278
U.S. News ranking: Reg. U. (N), No. 111
Website: www.ccsu.edu
Admissions email: admissions@ ccsu.edu
Public; founded 1849
Freshman admissions: selective; 2013-2014: 5,551 applied, 3,560 accepted. Either SAT or ACT required. SAT 25/75 percentile: 910-1100. High school rank: 10% in top tenth, 21% in top quarter, 71% in top half
Early decision deadline: N/A, notification date: N/A
Early action deadline: N/A, notification date: N/A
Application deadline (fall): 5/1
Undergraduate student body: 7,624 full time, 2,147 part time; 52% male, 48% female; 0% American Indian, 3% Asian, 11% black, 12% Hispanic, 2% multiracial, 0% Pacific Islander, 68% white, 1% international; 97% from in state; 21% live on campus; 0% of students in fraternities, 0% in sororities
Most popular majors: 25% Business, Management, Marketing, and Related Support Services, 7% Communication, Journalism, and Related Programs, 8% Education, 5% Engineering Technologies and Engineering-Related Fields, 16% Social Sciences
Expenses: 2014-2015: $8,877 in state, $19,163 out of state; room/board: $10,872
Financial aid: (860) 832-2200; 74% of undergrads determined to have financial need; average aid package $8,113

Charter Oak State College

New Britain CT
(860) 832-3855
U.S. News ranking: Nat. Lib. Arts, unranked
Website: www.charteroak.edu
Admissions email: info@charteroak.edu
Public
Freshman admissions: N/A; 2013-2014: N/A applied, N/A accepted. Neither SAT nor ACT required. ACT 25/75 percentile: N/A. High school rank: N/A
Early decision deadline: N/A, notification date: N/A
Early action deadline: N/A, notification date: N/A
Application deadline (fall): rolling
Undergraduate student body: 301 full time, 1,280 part time; 34% male, 66% female; 0% American Indian, 2% Asian, 17% black, 11% Hispanic, 1% multiracial, 0% Pacific Islander, 64% white, 1% international; 73% from in

state; 0% live on campus; 0% of students in fraternities, 0% in sororities
Most popular majors: Information not available
Expenses: 2014-2015: $8,592 in state, $11,082 out of state; room/ board: N/A
Financial aid: N/A; 69% of undergrads determined to have financial need; average aid package $7,618

Connecticut College

New London CT
(860) 439-2200
U.S. News ranking: Nat. Lib. Arts, No. 45
Website: www.conncoll.edu
Admissions email: admission@ conncoll.edu
Private; founded 1911
Freshman admissions: more selective; 2013-2014: 4,701 applied, 1,726 accepted. Neither SAT nor ACT required. SAT 25/75 percentile: 1240-1410. High school rank: 52% in top tenth, 90% in top quarter, 100% in top half
Early decision deadline: 11/15, notification date: 12/15
Early action deadline: N/A, notification date: N/A
Application deadline (fall): 1/1
Undergraduate student body: 1,877 full time, 38 part time; 39% male, 61% female; 0% American Indian, 3% Asian, 4% black, 9% Hispanic, 3% multiracial, 0% Pacific Islander, 70% white, 5% international; 19% from in state; 99% live on campus; 0% of students in fraternities, 0% in sororities
Most popular majors: 10% Biology, General, 14% Economics, 7% International Relations and National Security Studies, 7% Political Science and Government, 10% Psychology, General
Expenses: 2014-2015: $47,740; room/board: $13,155
Financial aid: (860) 439-2058; 52% of undergrads determined to have financial need; average aid package $37,372

Eastern Connecticut State University

Willimantic CT
(860) 465-5286
U.S. News ranking: Reg. U. (N), No. 103
Website: www.easternct.edu
Admissions email: admissions@ easternct.edu
Public; founded 1889
Freshman admissions: selective; 2013-2014: 5,111 applied, 3,299 accepted. Either SAT or ACT required. SAT 25/75 percentile: 930-1100. High school rank: 9% in top tenth, 31% in top quarter, 72% in top half
Early decision deadline: N/A, notification date: N/A
Early action deadline: N/A, notification date: N/A
Application deadline (fall): rolling
Undergraduate student body: 4,395 full time, 784 part time; 46% male, 54% female; 0% American Indian, 2% Asian, 6% black, 9% Hispanic, 2% multiracial, 0% Pacific Islander, 70% white, 1% international; 96% from in state; 53% live on campus; N/A of students in fraternities, N/A in sororities

Most popular majors: 15% Business, Management, Marketing, and Related Support Services, 9% Communication, Journalism, and Related Programs, 13% Liberal Arts and Sciences, General Studies and Humanities, 12% Psychology, 12% Social Sciences
Expenses: 2014-2015: $9,560 in state, $19,846 out of state; room/board: $11,610
Financial aid: (860) 465-5205; 68% of undergrads determined to have financial need; average aid package $8,245

Fairfield University

Fairfield CT
(203) 254-4100
U.S. News ranking: Reg. U. (N), No. 3
Website: www.fairfield.edu
Admissions email: admis@fairfield.edu
Private; founded 1942
Affiliation: Roman Catholic (Jesuit)
Freshman admissions: more selective; 2013-2014: 9,582 applied, 6,742 accepted. Neither SAT nor ACT required. SAT 25/75 percentile: 1090-1250. High school rank: N/A
Early decision deadline: 11/15, notification date: 1/1
Early action deadline: 11/1, notification date: 1/1
Application deadline (fall): 1/15
Undergraduate student body: 3,546 full time, 327 part time; 40% male, 60% female; 0% American Indian, 2% Asian, 3% black, 8% Hispanic, 1% multiracial, 0% Pacific Islander, 72% white, 2% international; 31% from in state; 80% live on campus; 0% of students in fraternities, 0% in sororities
Most popular majors: 26% Business, Management, Marketing, and Related Support Services, 10% Communication, Journalism, and Related Programs, 13% Health Professions and Related Programs, 7% Psychology, 13% Social Sciences
Expenses: 2014-2015: $43,770; room/board: $13,190
Financial aid: (203) 254-4125; 51% of undergrads determined to have financial need; average aid package $29,726

Lyme Academy College of Fine Arts

Old Lyme CT
(860) 434-5232
U.S. News ranking: Arts, unranked
Website: www.lymeacademy.edu
Admissions email: admissions@ lymeacademy.edu
Private
Freshman admissions: N/A; 2013-2014: N/A applied, N/A accepted. Neither SAT nor ACT required. SAT 25/75 percentile: N/A. High school rank: N/A
Early decision deadline: N/A, notification date: N/A
Early action deadline: N/A, notification date: N/A
Application deadline (fall): N/A
Undergraduate student body: N/A full time, N/A part time; N/A male, N/A female; N/A American Indian, N/A Asian, N/A black, N/A Hispanic, N/A multiracial, N/A Pacific Islander, N/A white, N/A international

Most popular majors: Information not available
Expenses: 2013-2014: $29,616; room/board: N/A
Financial aid: (860) 434-5232

Mitchell College[1]

New London CT
(800) 443-2811
U.S. News ranking: Reg. Coll. (N), unranked
Website: www.mitchell.edu
Admissions email: admissions@ mitchell.edu
Private
Application deadline (fall): N/A
Undergraduate student body: N/A full time, N/A part time
Expenses: 2013-2014: $29,458; room/board: $12,492
Financial aid: (860) 701-5061

Post University

Waterbury CT
(203) 596-4520
U.S. News ranking: Reg. Coll. (N), second tier
Website: www.post.edu
Admissions email: admissions@post.edu
For-profit; founded 1890
Freshman admissions: less selective; 2013-2014: 5,923 applied, 3,762 accepted. Either SAT or ACT required. SAT 25/75 percentile: 760-960. High school rank: 5% in top tenth, 20% in top quarter, 50% in top half
Early decision deadline: N/A, notification date: N/A
Early action deadline: N/A, notification date: N/A
Application deadline (fall): rolling
Undergraduate student body: 2,903 full time, 4,468 part time; 41% male, 59% female; 0% American Indian, 1% Asian, 16% black, 6% Hispanic, 2% multiracial, 0% Pacific Islander, 30% white, 1% international; 49% from in state; 11% live on campus; 0% of students in fraternities, 0% in sororities
Most popular majors: 14% Accounting, 50% Business Administration and Management, General, 5% Child Development, 14% Criminal Justice/Safety Studies, 17% Human Services, General
Expenses: 2013-2014: $27,450; room/board: $10,430
Financial aid: (203) 596-4526

Quinnipiac University

Hamden CT
(800) 462-1944
U.S. News ranking: Reg. U. (N), No. 9
Website: www.quinnipiac.edu
Admissions email: admissions@ quinnipiac.edu
Private; founded 1929
Freshman admissions: selective; 2013-2014: 20,693 applied, 13,912 accepted. Either SAT or ACT required. SAT 25/75 percentile: 1000-1190. High school rank: 25% in top tenth, 66% in top quarter, 93% in top half
Early decision deadline: 11/1, notification date: 12/1
Early action deadline: N/A, notification date: N/A
Application deadline (fall): 2/1

Undergraduate student body: 6,307 full time, 235 part time; 38% male, 62% female; 0% American Indian, 2% Asian, 4% black, 8% Hispanic, 2% multiracial, 0% Pacific Islander, 78% white, 2% international; 25% from in state; 75% live on campus; 14% of students in fraternities, 15% in sororities
Most popular majors: 21% Business, Management, Marketing, and Related Support Services, 19% Communication, Journalism, and Related Programs, 30% Health Professions and Related Programs, 6% Psychology, 6% Social Sciences
Expenses: 2014-2015: $40,670; room/board: $14,490
Financial aid: (203) 582-8750; 63% of undergrads determined to have financial need; average aid package $24,214

Sacred Heart University

Fairfield CT
(203) 371-7880
U.S. News ranking: Reg. U. (N), No. 38
Website: www.sacredheart.edu
Admissions email: enroll@ sacredheart.edu
Private; founded 1963
Affiliation: Roman Catholic
Freshman admissions: selective; 2013-2014: 7,908 applied, 4,800 accepted. Neither SAT nor ACT required. SAT 25/75 percentile: 1020-1170. High school rank: 14% in top tenth, 39% in top quarter, 80% in top half
Early decision deadline: 12/1, notification date: 12/15
Early action deadline: N/A, notification date: N/A
Application deadline (fall): rolling
Undergraduate student body: 3,773 full time, 722 part time; 36% male, 64% female; 0% American Indian, 2% Asian, 3% black, 6% Hispanic, 0% multiracial, 0% Pacific Islander, 66% white, 1% international; 41% from in state; 54% live on campus; 6% of students in fraternities, 14% in sororities
Most popular majors: 4% Biological and Biomedical Sciences, 31% Business, Management, Marketing, and Related Support Services, Other, 18% Health Professions and Related Clinical Sciences, Other, 5% Homeland Security, Law Enforcement, Firefighting and Related Protective Services, 10% Psychology
Expenses: 2014-2015: $35,750; room/board: $13,514
Financial aid: (203) 371-7980; 72% of undergrads determined to have financial need; average aid package $19,511

Southern Connecticut State University

New Haven CT
(203) 392-5656
U.S. News ranking: Reg. U. (N), second tier
Website: www.southernct.edu/
Admissions email: information@ southernct.edu
Public; founded 1893
Freshman admissions: less selective; 2013-2014: 4,870 applied, 3,673 accepted. Either SAT or ACT required. SAT 25/75

percentile: 820-1020. High school rank: 5% in top tenth, 21% in top quarter, 59% in top half
Early decision deadline: N/A, notification date: N/A
Early action deadline: N/A, notification date: N/A
Application deadline (fall): rolling
Undergraduate student body: 7,016 full time, 1,241 part time; 39% male, 61% female; 0% American Indian, 2% Asian, 15% black, 11% Hispanic, 2% multiracial, 0% Pacific Islander, 60% white, 0% international; 96% from in state; 32% live on campus; 1% of students in fraternities, 1% in sororities
Most popular majors: 12% Business/Commerce, General, 10% Education, General, 15% Health and Wellness, General, 14% Liberal Arts and Sciences/Liberal Studies, 10% Psychology, General
Expenses: 2014-2015: $9,156 in state, $19,442 out of state; room/board: $11,334
Financial aid: (203) 392-5222; 69% of undergrads determined to have financial need; average aid package $13,685

Trinity College
Hartford CT
(860) 297-2180
U.S. News ranking: Nat. Lib. Arts, No. 45
Website: www.trincoll.edu
Admissions email: admissions.office@trincoll.edu
Private; founded 1823
Freshman admissions: more selective; 2013-2014: 7,652 applied, 2,432 accepted. Either SAT or ACT required. SAT 25/75 percentile: 1150-1330. High school rank: 23% in top tenth, 59% in top quarter, 99% in top half
Early decision deadline: 11/15, notification date: 12/15
Early action deadline: N/A, notification date: N/A
Application deadline (fall): 1/1
Undergraduate student body: 2,214 full time, 117 part time; 52% male, 48% female; 0% American Indian, 5% Asian, 6% black, 7% Hispanic, 3% multiracial, 0% Pacific Islander, 65% white, 8% international; 18% from in state; 89% live on campus; 20% of students in fraternities, 16% in sororities
Most popular majors: 19% Economics, General, 5% English Language and Literature, General, 5% History, General, 12% Political Science and Government, General, 5% Psychology, General
Expenses: 2014-2015: $49,056; room/board: $12,700
Financial aid: (860) 297-2046; 42% of undergrads determined to have financial need; average aid package $42,585

United States Coast Guard Academy
New London CT
(800) 883-8724
U.S. News ranking: Reg. Coll. (N), No. 1
Website: www.uscga.edu
Admissions email: admissions@uscga.edu
Public; founded 1931

Freshman admissions: more selective; 2013-2014: 1,992 applied, 328 accepted. Either SAT or ACT required. SAT 25/75 percentile: 1190-1360. High school rank: 47% in top tenth, 80% in top quarter, 94% in top half
Early decision deadline: N/A, notification date: N/A
Early action deadline: 11/15, notification date: N/A
Application deadline (fall): 2/1
Undergraduate student body: 902 full time, N/A part time; 66% male, 34% female; 1% American Indian, 5% Asian, 2% black, 13% Hispanic, 7% multiracial, 1% Pacific Islander, 68% white, 3% international; 6% from in state; 100% live on campus; 0% of students in fraternities, 0% in sororities
Most popular majors: 18% Business Administration and Management, General, 31% Engineering, 19% Marine Biology and Biological Oceanography, 14% Mathematics and Statistics, Other, 18% Political Science and Government, General
Expenses: N/A
Financial aid: N/A; 0% of undergrads determined to have financial need; average aid package $0

University of Bridgeport
Bridgeport CT
(203) 576-4552
U.S. News ranking: Reg. U. (N), second tier
Website: www.bridgeport.edu
Admissions email: admit@bridgeport.edu
Private; founded 1927
Freshman admissions: less selective; 2013-2014: 5,248 applied, 3,351 accepted. Either SAT or ACT required. SAT 25/75 percentile: 830-1010. High school rank: 8% in top tenth, 30% in top quarter, 70% in top half
Early decision deadline: N/A, notification date: N/A
Early action deadline: N/A, notification date: N/A
Application deadline (fall): rolling
Undergraduate student body: 2,035 full time, 800 part time; 34% male, 66% female; 1% American Indian, 3% Asian, 35% black, 18% Hispanic, 2% multiracial, 0% Pacific Islander, 27% white, 14% international; 62% from in state; 44% live on campus; 5% of students in fraternities, 5% in sororities
Most popular majors: 6% Business/Commerce, General, 11% Dental Hygiene/Hygienist, 15% General Studies, 12% Human Services, General, 28% Psychology, General
Expenses: 2014-2015: $29,910; room/board: $12,710
Financial aid: (203) 576-4568; 81% of undergrads determined to have financial need; average aid package $24,745

University of Connecticut
Storrs CT
(860) 486-3137
U.S. News ranking: Nat. U., No. 58
Website: www.uconn.edu
Admissions email: beahusky@uconn.edu
Public; founded 1881

Freshman admissions: more selective; 2013-2014: 27,479 applied, 14,745 accepted. Either SAT or ACT required. SAT 25/75 percentile: 1130-1330. High school rank: 45% in top tenth, 82% in top quarter, 97% in top half
Early decision deadline: N/A, notification date: N/A
Early action deadline: N/A, notification date: N/A
Application deadline (fall): 1/15
Undergraduate student body: 17,219 full time, 813 part time; 51% male, 49% female; 0% American Indian, 9% Asian, 5% black, 8% Hispanic, 3% multiracial, 0% Pacific Islander, 63% white, 3% international; 79% from in state; 72% live on campus; 11% of students in fraternities, 15% in sororities
Most popular majors: 12% Business, Management, Marketing, and Related Support Services, 9% Engineering, 13% Health Professions and Related Programs, 8% Psychology, 12% Social Sciences
Expenses: 2014-2015: $12,700 in state, $32,880 out of state; room/board: $12,074
Financial aid: (860) 486-2819; 58% of undergrads determined to have financial need; average aid package $12,917

University of Hartford
West Hartford CT
(860) 768-4296
U.S. News ranking: Reg. U. (N), No. 83
Website: www.hartford.edu
Admissions email: admission@hartford.edu
Private; founded 1877
Freshman admissions: less selective; 2013-2014: 16,481 applied, 10,750 accepted. Either SAT or ACT required. SAT 25/75 percentile: 950-1150. High school rank: N/A
Early decision deadline: N/A, notification date: N/A
Early action deadline: 11/15, notification date: 12/1
Application deadline (fall): rolling
Undergraduate student body: 4,495 full time, 692 part time; 50% male, 50% female; 1% American Indian, 3% Asian, 15% black, 9% Hispanic, 2% multiracial, 0% Pacific Islander, 60% white, 5% international; 44% from in state; 68% live on campus; N/A of students in fraternities, N/A in sororities
Most popular majors: 14% Business, Management, Marketing, and Related Support Services, Other, 7% Education, Other, 8% Engineering, Other, 15% Health Professions and Related Clinical Sciences, Other, 15% Visual and Performing Arts, Other
Expenses: 2014-2015: $35,444; room/board: $11,518
Financial aid: (860) 768-4296; 75% of undergrads determined to have financial need; average aid package $23,729

University of New Haven
West Haven CT
(203) 932-7319
U.S. News ranking: Reg. U. (N), No. 98
Website: www.newhaven.edu
Admissions email: adminfo@newhaven.edu
Private; founded 1920
Freshman admissions: selective; 2013-2014: 10,169 applied, 7,567 accepted. Either SAT or ACT required. SAT 25/75 percentile: 930-1130. High school rank: 14% in top tenth, 41% in top quarter, 76% in top half
Early decision deadline: N/A, notification date: N/A
Early action deadline: 12/1, notification date: 1/15
Application deadline (fall): rolling
Undergraduate student body: 4,407 full time, 457 part time; 51% male, 49% female; 0% American Indian, 2% Asian, 8% black, 8% Hispanic, 1% multiracial, 0% Pacific Islander, 53% white, 8% international; 43% from in state; 52% live on campus; N/A of students in fraternities, N/A in sororities
Most popular majors: 7% Biological and Biomedical Sciences, 12% Business, Management, Marketing, and Related Support Services, 6% Engineering, 43% Homeland Security, Law Enforcement, Firefighting and Related Protective Services, 7% Visual and Performing Arts
Expenses: 2014-2015: $34,630; room/board: $14,410
Financial aid: (203) 932-7315; 78% of undergrads determined to have financial need; average aid package $20,633

University of St. Joseph
West Hartford CT
(860) 231-5216
U.S. News ranking: Reg. U. (N), No. 87
Website: www.usj.edu
Admissions email: admissions@usj.edu
Private; founded 1932
Affiliation: Roman Catholic
Freshman admissions: less selective; 2013-2014: 1,153 applied, 737 accepted. Either SAT or ACT required. SAT 25/75 percentile: 880-1040. High school rank: 1% in top tenth, 41% in top quarter, 83% in top half
Early decision deadline: N/A, notification date: N/A
Early action deadline: N/A, notification date: N/A
Application deadline (fall): rolling
Undergraduate student body: 794 full time, 255 part time; 2% male, 98% female; 0% American Indian, 3% Asian, 13% black, 13% Hispanic, 2% multiracial, 0% Pacific Islander, 57% white, 0% international; 93% from in state; 41% live on campus; N/A of students in fraternities, N/A in sororities
Most popular majors: 9% Business, Management, Marketing, and Related Support Services, 10% Family and Consumer Sciences/Human Sciences, 28% Health Professions and Related Programs, 13% Psychology, 13% Public Administration and Social Service Professions

Expenses: 2014-2015: $34,755; room/board: $14,426
Financial aid: (860) 231-5223; 89% of undergrads determined to have financial need; average aid package $22,299

Wesleyan University
Middletown CT
(860) 685-3000
U.S. News ranking: Nat. Lib. Arts, No. 15
Website: www.wesleyan.edu
Admissions email: admissions@wesleyan.edu
Private; founded 1831
Freshman admissions: most selective; 2013-2014: 10,690 applied, 2,181 accepted. Either SAT or ACT required. SAT 25/75 percentile: 1310-1490. High school rank: 67% in top tenth, 91% in top quarter, 99% in top half
Early decision deadline: 11/15, notification date: 12/15
Early action deadline: N/A, notification date: N/A
Application deadline (fall): 1/1
Undergraduate student body: 2,899 full time, 7 part time; 48% male, 52% female; 0% American Indian, 8% Asian, 7% black, 10% Hispanic, 6% multiracial, 0% Pacific Islander, 53% white, 8% international; 8% from in state; 99% live on campus; 4% of students in fraternities, 1% in sororities
Most popular majors: 6% Economics, General, 7% English Language and Literature, General, 6% Physiological Psychology/Psychobiology, 6% Political Science and Government, General, 9% Psychology, General
Expenses: 2014-2015: $47,972; room/board: $13,226
Financial aid: (860) 685-2800; 47% of undergrads determined to have financial need; average aid package $43,670

Western Connecticut State University
Danbury CT
(203) 837-9000
U.S. News ranking: Reg. U. (N), No. 135
Website: www.wcsu.edu
Admissions email: admissions@wcsu.edu
Public; founded 1903
Freshman admissions: selective; 2013-2014: 3,613 applied, 2,366 accepted. Either SAT or ACT required. SAT 25/75 percentile: 890-1080. High school rank: 10% in top tenth, 28% in top quarter, 69% in top half
Early decision deadline: N/A, notification date: N/A
Early action deadline: N/A, notification date: N/A
Application deadline (fall): rolling
Undergraduate student body: 4,394 full time, 1,098 part time; 47% male, 53% female; 0% American Indian, 3% Asian, 11% black, 15% Hispanic, 1% multiracial, 0% Pacific Islander, 68% white, 0% international; 93% from in state; 26% live on campus; N/A of students in fraternities, N/A in sororities
Most popular majors: 31% Business, Management, Marketing, and Related Support Services, 10% Education, 11% Health Professions and Related

Programs, 10% Homeland Security, Law Enforcement, Firefighting and Related Protective Services, 8% Psychology
Expenses: 2014-2015: $9,077 in state, $19,363 out of state; room/board: $11,311
Financial aid: (203) 837-8580; 70% of undergrads determined to have financial need; average aid package $8,566

Yale University
New Haven CT
(203) 432-9300
U.S. News ranking: Nat. U., No. 3
Website: www.yale.edu/
Admissions email: student.questions@yale.edu
Private; founded 1701
Freshman admissions: most selective; 2013-2014: 29,610 applied, 2,031 accepted. Either SAT or ACT required. SAT 25/75 percentile: 1420-1590. High school rank: 95% in top tenth, 99% in top quarter, 100% in top half
Early decision deadline: N/A, notification date: N/A
Early action deadline: 11/1, notification date: 12/15
Application deadline (fall): 1/1
Undergraduate student body: 5,424 full time, 6 part time; 51% male, 49% female; 1% American Indian, 16% Asian, 7% black, 10% Hispanic, 6% multiracial, 0% Pacific Islander, 47% white, 11% international; 6% from in state; 87% live on campus; N/A of students in fraternities, N/A in sororities
Most popular majors: 7% Biology/Biological Sciences, General, 11% Economics, General, 7% History, General, 10% Political Science and Government, General, 7% Psychology, General
Expenses: 2014-2015: $45,800; room/board: $14,000
Financial aid: (203) 432-2700; 52% of undergrads determined to have financial need; average aid package $46,844

DELAWARE

Delaware State University
Dover DE
(302) 857-6353
U.S. News ranking: Reg. U. (N), No. 135
Website: www.desu.edu
Admissions email: admissions@desu.edu
Public; founded 1891
Freshman admissions: less selective; 2013-2014: 7,700 applied, 3,428 accepted. Either SAT or ACT required. SAT 25/75 percentile: 820-970. High school rank: 10% in top tenth, 26% in top quarter, 62% in top half
Early decision deadline: N/A, notification date: N/A
Early action deadline: N/A, notification date: N/A
Application deadline (fall): rolling
Undergraduate student body: 3,579 full time, 313 part time; 38% male, 62% female; 0% American Indian, 1% Asian, 75% black, 6% Hispanic, 4% multiracial, 0% Pacific Islander, 11% white, 2% international; 46% from in state;

59% live on campus; 4% of students in fraternities, 7% in sororities
Most popular majors: 12% Business, Management, Marketing, and Related Support Services, 11% Communication, Journalism, and Related Programs, 11% Health Professions and Related Programs, 10% Psychology, 9% Social Sciences
Expenses: 2014-2015: $7,336 in state, $15,692 out of state; room/board: $10,708
Financial aid: (302) 857-6250; 82% of undergrads determined to have financial need; average aid package $11,479

Goldey-Beacom College[1]
Wilmington DE
(302) 225-6248
U.S. News ranking: Business, unranked
Website: gbc.edu
Admissions email: admissions@gbc.edu
Private; founded 1886
Application deadline (fall): rolling
Undergraduate student body: N/A full time, N/A part time
Expenses: 2013-2014: $22,140; room/board: $5,353
Financial aid: (302) 225-6265

University of Delaware
Newark DE
(302) 831-8123
U.S. News ranking: Nat. U., No. 76
Website: www.udel.edu/
Admissions email: admissions@udel.edu
Public; founded 1743
Freshman admissions: more selective; 2013-2014: 24,657 applied, 15,621 accepted. Either SAT or ACT required. SAT 25/75 percentile: 1090-1300. High school rank: 37% in top tenth, 72% in top quarter, 96% in top half
Early decision deadline: N/A, notification date: N/A
Early action deadline: N/A, notification date: N/A
Application deadline (fall): 1/15
Undergraduate student body: 16,037 full time, 1,592 part time; 43% male, 57% female; 0% American Indian, 4% Asian, 5% black, 7% Hispanic, 3% multiracial, 0% Pacific Islander, 76% white, 4% international; 40% from in state; 44% live on campus; 17% of students in fraternities, 19% in sororities
Most popular majors: 20% Business, Management, Marketing, and Related Support Services, 8% Education, 8% Engineering, 9% Health Professions and Related Programs, 12% Social Sciences
Expenses: 2014-2015: $12,342 in state, $30,692 out of state; room/board: $11,868
Financial aid: (302) 831-8761; 51% of undergrads determined to have financial need; average aid package $15,357

Wesley College
Dover DE
(302) 736-2400
U.S. News ranking: Reg. Coll. (N), second tier
Website: www.wesley.edu
Admissions email: admissions@wesley.edu
Private; founded 1873
Affiliation: United Methodist
Freshman admissions: least selective; 2013-2014: N/A applied, N/A accepted. SAT required. SAT 25/75 percentile: 750-940. High school rank: 5% in top tenth, 23% in top quarter, 58% in top half
Early decision deadline: 11/1, notification date: 11/15
Early action deadline: N/A, notification date: N/A
Application deadline (fall): 4/30
Undergraduate student body: 1,416 full time, 184 part time; 48% male, 52% female; 0% American Indian, 1% Asian, 42% black, 5% Hispanic, 3% multiracial, 0% Pacific Islander, 45% white, 0% international
Most popular majors: Information not available
Expenses: 2014-2015: $24,100; room/board: $10,890
Financial aid: (302) 736-2321

Wilmington University
New Castle DE
(302) 328-9407
U.S. News ranking: Nat. U., unranked
Website: www.wilmu.edu
Admissions email: undergradadmissions@wilmu.edu
Private; founded 1967
Freshman admissions: N/A; 2013-2014: 1,075 applied, 1,070 accepted. Neither SAT nor ACT required. ACT 25/75 percentile: N/A. High school rank: N/A
Early decision deadline: N/A, notification date: N/A
Early action deadline: N/A, notification date: N/A
Application deadline (fall): rolling
Undergraduate student body: 3,509 full time, 5,102 part time; 35% male, 65% female; 1% American Indian, 2% Asian, 23% black, 3% Hispanic, 1% multiracial, 0% Pacific Islander, 48% white, 3% international
Most popular majors: Information not available
Expenses: 2014-2015: $10,190; room/board: N/A
Financial aid: (302) 328-9437

DISTRICT OF COLUMBIA

American University
Washington DC
(202) 885-6000
U.S. News ranking: Nat. U., No. 71
Website: www.american.edu
Admissions email: admissions@american.edu
Private; founded 1893
Affiliation: United Methodist
Freshman admissions: more selective; 2013-2014: 17,545 applied, 7,565 accepted. Neither SAT nor ACT required. SAT 25/75 percentile: 1160-1350. High school rank: 47% in top tenth, 78% in top quarter, 96% in top half
Early decision deadline: 11/15, notification date: 12/31
Early action deadline: N/A, notification date: N/A

Application deadline (fall): 1/15
Undergraduate student body: 6,986 full time, 355 part time; 39% male, 61% female; 0% American Indian, 6% Asian, 6% black, 10% Hispanic, 5% multiracial, 0% Pacific Islander, 57% white, 7% international; 19% from in state; N/A live on campus; 21% of students in fraternities, 19% in sororities
Most popular majors: 14% Business Administration and Management, General, 5% Criminal Justice/Safety Studies, 25% International Relations and Affairs, 6% Mass Communication/Media Studies, 9% Political Science and Government, General
Expenses: 2014-2015: $41,833; room/board: $14,408
Financial aid: (202) 885-6100; 54% of undergrads determined to have financial need; average aid package $27,414

The Catholic University of America
Washington DC
(800) 673-2772
U.S. News ranking: Nat. U., No. 116
Website: www.cua.edu
Admissions email: cua-admissions@cua.edu
Private; founded 1887
Affiliation: Roman Catholic
Freshman admissions: selective; 2013-2014: 6,298 applied, 3,783 accepted. Either SAT or ACT required. SAT 25/75 percentile: 1010-1220. High school rank: N/A
Early decision deadline: N/A, notification date: N/A
Early action deadline: 11/15, notification date: 12/15
Application deadline (fall): 2/15
Undergraduate student body: 3,456 full time, 257 part time; 46% male, 54% female; 0% American Indian, 3% Asian, 5% black, 11% Hispanic, 3% multiracial, 0% Pacific Islander, 63% white, 5% international; 4% from in state; 59% live on campus; 1% of students in fraternities, 1% in sororities
Most popular majors: 11% Architecture, 5% Mass Communication/Media Studies, 12% Political Science and Government, General, 8% Psychology, General, 11% Registered Nursing/Registered Nurse
Expenses: 2014-2015: $39,726; room/board: $14,518
Financial aid: (202) 319-5307; 60% of undergrads determined to have financial need; average aid package $24,381

Corcoran College of Art and Design[1]
Washington DC
(202) 639-1814
U.S. News ranking: Arts, unranked
Website: www.corcoran.edu
Admissions email: admissions@corcoran.org
Private; founded 1890
Application deadline (fall): rolling
Undergraduate student body: N/A full time, N/A part time
Expenses: 2013-2014: $31,130; room/board: N/A
Financial aid: (202) 639-1818

Gallaudet University
Washington DC
(202) 651-5750
U.S. News ranking: Reg. U. (N), No. 17
Website: www.gallaudet.edu
Admissions email: admissions.office@gallaudet.edu
Private; founded 1864
Freshman admissions: less selective; 2013-2014: 521 applied, 341 accepted. Either SAT or ACT required. ACT 25/75 percentile: 15-20. High school rank: N/A
Early decision deadline: N/A, notification date: N/A
Early action deadline: N/A, notification date: N/A
Application deadline (fall): rolling
Undergraduate student body: 1,006 full time, 71 part time; 46% male, 54% female; 0% American Indian, 4% Asian, 11% black, 14% Hispanic, 3% multiracial, 0% Pacific Islander, 60% white, 7% international; 3% from in state; 75% live on campus; 18% of students in fraternities, 10% in sororities
Most popular majors: 9% Business, Management, Marketing, and Related Support Services, 8% Communication, Journalism, and Related Programs, 8% Parks, Recreation, Leisure, and Fitness Studies, 8% Psychology, 9% Visual and Performing Arts
Expenses: 2013-2014: $13,800; room/board: $11,580
Financial aid: (202) 651-5290

Georgetown University
Washington DC
(202) 687-3600
U.S. News ranking: Nat. U., No. 21
Website: www.georgetown.edu
Admissions email: guadmiss@georgetown.edu
Private; founded 1789
Affiliation: Roman Catholic (Jesuit)
Freshman admissions: most selective; 2013-2014: 19,885 applied, 3,397 accepted. Either SAT or ACT required. SAT 25/75 percentile: 1320-1500. High school rank: 92% in top tenth, 98% in top quarter, 100% in top half
Early decision deadline: N/A, notification date: N/A
Early action deadline: 11/1, notification date: 12/15
Application deadline (fall): 1/10
Undergraduate student body: 7,300 full time, 336 part time; 45% male, 55% female; 0% American Indian, 9% Asian, 6% black, 8% Hispanic, 4% multiracial, 0% Pacific Islander, 59% white, 11% international; 3% from in state; 64% live on campus; 0% of students in fraternities, 0% in sororities
Most popular majors: 22% Business, Management, Marketing, and Related Support Services, 7% English Language and Literature/Letters, 6% Foreign Languages, Literatures, and Linguistics, 7% Health Professions and Related Programs, 33% Social Sciences
Expenses: 2014-2015: $46,744; room/board: $14,348
Financial aid: (202) 687-4547; 37% of undergrads determined to have financial need; average aid package $39,305

George Washington University
Washington DC
(202) 994-6040
U.S. News ranking: Nat. U., No. 54
Website: www.gwu.edu
Admissions email:
gwadm@gwu.edu
Private; founded 1821
Freshman admissions: more
selective; 2013-2014: 21,789
applied, 7,493 accepted. Either
SAT or ACT required. SAT 25/75
percentile: 1200-1390. High
school rank: 50% in top tenth,
84% in top quarter, 98% in
top half
Early decision deadline: 11/1,
notification date: 12/15
Early action deadline: N/A,
notification date: N/A
Application deadline (fall): 1/15
Undergraduate student body: 9,609
full time, 748 part time; 45%
male, 55% female; 0% American
Indian, 9% Asian, 7% black, 7%
Hispanic, 3% multiracial, 0%
Pacific Islander, 60% white, 9%
international; 2% from in state;
66% live on campus; 23% of
students in fraternities, 23% in
sororities
Most popular majors: 17%
Business, Management,
Marketing, and Related Support
Services, 5% Communication,
Journalism, and Related Programs,
6% Health Professions and
Related Programs, 6% Psychology,
37% Social Sciences
Expenses: 2014-2015: $48,760;
room/board: $11,700
Financial aid: (202) 994-6620;
47% of undergrads determined to
have financial need; average aid
package $42,335

Howard University
Washington DC
(202) 806-2700
U.S. News ranking: Nat. U.,
No. 145
Website: www.howard.edu
Admissions email: admission@
howard.edu
Private; founded 1867
Freshman admissions: selective;
2013-2014: 11,599 applied,
6,612 accepted. Either SAT
or ACT required. SAT 25/75
percentile: 980-1190. High school
rank: 23% in top tenth, 54% in
top quarter, 85% in top half
Early decision deadline: N/A,
notification date: N/A
Early action deadline: 11/1,
notification date: 12/20
Application deadline (fall): 2/15
Undergraduate student body: 6,495
full time, 479 part time; 33%
male, 67% female; 2% American
Indian, 1% Asian, 91% black,
0% Hispanic, 0% multiracial,
0% Pacific Islander, 1% white,
3% international; 5% from in
state; 56% live on campus; 3%
of students in fraternities, 5% in
sororities
Most popular majors: 7% Biological
and Biomedical Sciences,
18% Business, Management,
Marketing, and Related Support
Services, 16% Communication,
Journalism, and Related Programs,
22% Health Professions and
Related Programs, 6% Social
Sciences
Expenses: 2014-2015: $23,970;
room/board: $13,646

Financial aid: (202) 806-2762;
85% of undergrads determined to
have financial need; average aid
package $17,178

Strayer University[1]
Washington DC
(202) 408-2400
U.S. News ranking: Reg. U. (N),
unranked
Website: www.strayer.edu
Admissions email:
mzm@strayer.edu
For-profit
Application deadline (fall): N/A
Undergraduate student body: N/A
full time, N/A part time
Expenses: 2013-2014: $15,495;
room/board: N/A
Financial aid: (888) 311-0355

Trinity University[1]
Washington DC
(202) 884-9400
U.S. News ranking: Reg. U. (N),
second tier
Website: www.trinitydc.edu
Admissions email:
admissions@trinitydc.edu
Private
Application deadline (fall): N/A
Undergraduate student body: N/A
full time, N/A part time
Expenses: 2013-2014: $21,630;
room/board: $9,660
Financial aid: (202) 884-9530

University of the District of Columbia
Washington DC
(202) 274-5010
U.S. News ranking: Reg. U. (N),
second tier
Website: www.udc.edu/
Admissions email: N/A
Public; founded 1976
Freshman admissions: less
selective; 2013-2014: N/A
applied, N/A accepted. Neither
SAT nor ACT required. ACT 25/75
percentile: N/A. High school
rank: N/A
Early decision deadline: N/A,
notification date: N/A
Early action deadline: N/A,
notification date: N/A
Application deadline (fall): 6/15
Undergraduate student body: 1,986
full time, 2,726 part time; 37%
male, 63% female; N/A American
Indian, N/A Asian, N/A black, N/A
Hispanic, N/A multiracial, N/A
Pacific Islander, N/A white, N/A
international
Most popular majors: Information
not available
Expenses: 2014-2015: $7,255 in
state, $14,535 out of state; room/
board: N/A
Financial aid: (202) 274-5060;
70% of undergrads determined to
have financial need; average aid
package $8,990

University of the Potomac
Washington DC
(202) 686-0876
U.S. News ranking: Business,
unranked
Website: www.potomac.edu
Admissions email: admissions@
potomac.edu
For-profit; founded 1989
Freshman admissions: least
selective; 2013-2014: N/A
applied, N/A accepted. Neither

SAT nor ACT required. ACT 25/75
percentile: N/A. High school
rank: N/A
Early decision deadline: N/A,
notification date: N/A
Early action deadline: N/A,
notification date: N/A
Application deadline (fall): rolling
Undergraduate student body: 277
full time, 24 part time; 52%
male, 48% female; 1% American
Indian, 2% Asian, 58% black,
6% Hispanic, 3% multiracial, 0%
Pacific Islander, 23% white, 0%
international
Most popular majors: Information
not available
Expenses: 2013-2014: $13,434;
room/board: N/A
Financial aid: (888) 635-1121

FLORIDA

Ave Maria University[1]
Ave Maria FL
(877) 283-8648
U.S. News ranking: Nat. Lib. Arts,
second tier
Website: www.avemaria.edu
Admissions email: N/A
Private; founded 2003
Affiliation: Catholic
Application deadline (fall): rolling
Undergraduate student body: N/A
full time, N/A part time
Expenses: 2013-2014: $23,000;
room/board: $9,286
Financial aid: N/A

Barry University
Miami Shores FL
(305) 899-3100
U.S. News ranking: Nat. U.,
second tier
Website: www.barry.edu
Admissions email: admissions@
mail.barry.edu
Private; founded 1940
Affiliation: Roman Catholic
Freshman admissions: selective;
2013-2014: 7,845 applied,
3,670 accepted. Either SAT
or ACT required. SAT 25/75
percentile: 833-1040. High
school rank: N/A
Early decision deadline: N/A,
notification date: N/A
Early action deadline: N/A,
notification date: N/A
Application deadline (fall): rolling
Undergraduate student body: 3,619
full time, 722 part time; 38%
male, 62% female; 0% American
Indian, 1% Asian, 32% black,
29% Hispanic, 1% multiracial,
0% Pacific Islander, 20% white,
7% international
Most popular majors: Information
not available
Expenses: 2014-2015: $28,160;
room/board: $10,200
Financial aid: (800) 899-3673;
82% of undergrads determined to
have financial need; average aid
package $19,214

Beacon College
Leesburg FL
(706) 323-5364
U.S. News ranking: Nat. Lib. Arts,
unranked
Website: www.beaconcollege.edu/
Admissions email: admissions@
beaconcollege.edu
Private; founded 1989
Freshman admissions: N/A; 2013-
2014: 139 applied, 90 accepted.

Neither SAT nor ACT required.
ACT 25/75 percentile: N/A. High
school rank: N/A
Early decision deadline: N/A,
notification date: N/A
Early action deadline: N/A,
notification date: N/A
Application deadline (fall): rolling
Undergraduate student body:
188 full time, 2 part time; 69%
male, 31% female; 1% American
Indian, 4% Asian, 15% black,
5% Hispanic, 3% multiracial, 0%
Pacific Islander, 70% white, 3%
international
Most popular majors: 54%
Human Services, General, 31%
Information Science/Studies, 15%
Liberal Arts and Sciences, General
Studies and Humanities
Expenses: 2013-2014: $31,496;
room/board: $8,862
Financial aid: (352) 787-7660

Bethune-Cookman University
Daytona Beach FL
(800) 448-0228
U.S. News ranking: Reg. Coll. (S),
No. 35
Website:
www.bethune.cookman.edu
Admissions email: admissions@
cookman.edu
Private; founded 1904
Affiliation: Methodist
Freshman admissions: least
selective; 2013-2014: 7,420
applied, 4,943 accepted. Either
SAT or ACT required. ACT 25/75
percentile: 15-18. High school
rank: 4% in top tenth, 12% in top
quarter, 47% in top half
Early decision deadline: N/A,
notification date: N/A
Early action deadline: N/A,
notification date: N/A
Application deadline (fall): rolling
Undergraduate student body: 3,608
full time, 116 part time; 41%
male, 59% female; 0% American
Indian, 0% Asian, 90% black,
3% Hispanic, 2% multiracial,
0% Pacific Islander, 2% white,
2% international; 67% from in
state; 49% live on campus; 3%
of students in fraternities, 5% in
sororities
Most popular majors: 9% Business
Administration and Management,
General, 14% Corrections and
Criminal Justice, Other, 9% Mass
Communication/Media Studies,
10% Psychology, General, 12%
Registered Nursing/Registered
Nurse
Expenses: 2013-2014: $14,410;
room/board: $8,548
Financial aid: (386) 481-2620

Chipola College[1]
Marianna FL
(850) 718-2211
U.S. News ranking: Reg. Coll. (S),
second tier
Website: www.chipola.edu
Admissions email: N/A
Public
Application deadline (fall): N/A
Undergraduate student body: N/A
full time, N/A part time
Expenses: 2013-2014: $3,120 in
state, $8,950 out of state; room/
board: $4,560
Financial aid: (800) 433-3243

Clearwater Christian College
Clearwater FL
(800) 348-4463
U.S. News ranking: Nat. Lib. Arts,
second tier
Website: www.clearwater.edu
Admissions email: admissions@
clearwater.edu
Private; founded 1966
Affiliation: Christian
nondenominational
Freshman admissions: selective;
2013-2014: 468 applied, 328
accepted. Either SAT or ACT
required. ACT 25/75 percentile:
19-25. High school rank: 10%
in top tenth, 32% in top quarter,
65% in top half
Early decision deadline: N/A,
notification date: N/A
Early action deadline: N/A,
notification date: N/A
Application deadline (fall): rolling
Undergraduate student body: 475
full time, 20 part time; 52%
male, 48% female; 0% American
Indian, 2% Asian, 4% black,
12% Hispanic, 1% multiracial,
0% Pacific Islander, 79% white,
1% international; 43% from in
state; 68% live on campus; 0%
of students in fraternities, 0% in
sororities
Most popular majors: 13%
Biological and Biomedical
Sciences, 15% Business,
Management, Marketing, and
Related Support Services, 19%
Education, 12% Liberal Arts and
Sciences, General Studies and
Humanities
Expenses: 2014-2015: $17,765;
room/board: $8,300
Financial aid: (727) 726-1153;
80% of undergrads determined to
have financial need; average aid
package $13,050

Daytona State College[1]
Daytona Beach FL
(386) 506-3059
U.S. News ranking: Reg. Coll. (S),
unranked
Website: www.daytonastate.edu
Admissions email: N/A
Public; founded 1957
Application deadline (fall): rolling
Undergraduate student body: N/A
full time, N/A part time
Expenses: 2013-2014: $3,134 in
state, $12,421 out of state; room/
board: N/A
Financial aid: (386) 506-3015

Eckerd College
St. Petersburg FL
(727) 864-8331
U.S. News ranking: Nat. Lib. Arts,
No. 124
Website: www.eckerd.edu
Admissions email: admissions@
eckerd.edu
Private; founded 1958
Affiliation: Presbyterian
Freshman admissions: selective;
2013-2014: 3,509 applied,
2,534 accepted. Either SAT
or ACT required. SAT 25/75
percentile: 1030-1220. High
school rank: N/A
Early decision deadline: N/A,
notification date: N/A
Early action deadline: 11/15,
notification date: 12/15
Application deadline (fall): rolling

Undergraduate student body: 1,780 full time, 41 part time; 40% male, 60% female; 1% American Indian, 1% Asian, 2% black, 8% Hispanic, 3% multiracial, 0% Pacific Islander, 79% white, 5% international; 21% from in state; 85% live on campus; N/A of students in fraternities, N/A in sororities
Most popular majors: 9% Biology, General, 8% Communication and Media Studies, 14% Environmental Studies, 13% Marine Sciences, 10% Psychology, General
Expenses: 2014-2015: $38,668; room/board: $10,550
Financial aid: (727) 864-8334; 59% of undergrads determined to have financial need; average aid package $30,880

Edison State College
Fort Myers FL
(800) 749-2322
U.S. News ranking: Reg. Coll. (S), unranked
Website: www.edison.edu
Admissions email: N/A
Public
Freshman admissions: N/A; 2013-2014: 4,759 applied, 3,768 accepted. Neither SAT nor ACT required. SAT 25/75 percentile: 850-1030. High school rank: N/A
Early decision deadline: N/A, notification date: N/A
Early action deadline: N/A, notification date: N/A
Application deadline (fall): 8/20
Undergraduate student body: 5,354 full time, 10,446 part time; 40% male, 60% female; 0% American Indian, 2% Asian, 11% black, 25% Hispanic, 1% multiracial, 0% Pacific Islander, 55% white, 2% international
Most popular majors: 34% Business, Management, Marketing, and Related Support Services, 29% Education, 25% Health Professions and Related Programs
Expenses: 2013-2014: $3,281 in state, $12,979 out of state; room/board: $7,626
Financial aid: (239) 489-9127

Edward Waters College[1]
Jacksonville FL
(904) 470-8200
U.S. News ranking: Reg. Coll. (S), second tier
Website: www.ewc.edu
Admissions email: admissions@ewc.edu
Private
Application deadline (fall): N/A
Undergraduate student body: N/A full time, N/A part time
Expenses: 2013-2014: $11,525; room/board: $7,156
Financial aid: (904) 470-8192

Embry-Riddle Aeronautical University
Daytona Beach FL
(800) 862-2416
U.S. News ranking: Reg. U. (S), No. 10
Website: www.embryriddle.edu
Admissions email: dbadmit@erau.edu
Private; founded 1926

Freshman admissions: selective; 2013-2014: 4,074 applied, 3,017 accepted. Neither SAT nor ACT required. SAT 25/75 percentile: 980-1230. High school rank: 23% in top tenth, 52% in top quarter, 80% in top half
Early decision deadline: N/A, notification date: N/A
Early action deadline: N/A, notification date: N/A
Application deadline (fall): rolling
Undergraduate student body: 4,359 full time, 320 part time; 83% male, 17% female; 0% American Indian, 5% Asian, 6% black, 7% Hispanic, 4% multiracial, 0% Pacific Islander, 53% white, 16% international; 35% from in state; 36% live on campus; N/A of students in fraternities, N/A in sororities
Most popular majors: 33% Aeronautics/Aviation/Aerospace Science and Technology, General, 24% Aerospace, Aeronautical and Astronautical/Space Engineering, 10% Air Traffic Controller, 6% Business Administration, Management and Operations, Other, 5% Homeland Security
Expenses: 2014-2015: $31,948; room/board: $9,850
Financial aid: (800) 943-6279; 66% of undergrads determined to have financial need; average aid package $14,099

Everglades University[1]
Boca Raton FL
(888) 772-6077
U.S. News ranking: Reg. Coll. (S), No. 70
Website: www. evergladesuniversity.edu
Admissions email: N/A
Private
Application deadline (fall): N/A
Undergraduate student body: N/A full time, N/A part time
Expenses: 2013-2014: $15,400; room/board: N/A
Financial aid: (888) 772-6077

Flagler College
St. Augustine FL
(800) 304-4208
U.S. News ranking: Reg. Coll. (S), No. 8
Website: www.flagler.edu
Admissions email: admiss@flagler.edu
Private; founded 1968
Freshman admissions: selective; 2013-2014: 5,396 applied, 2,691 accepted. Either SAT or ACT required. SAT 25/75 percentile: 930-1130. High school rank: 9% in top tenth, 31% in top quarter, 67% in top half
Early decision deadline: 12/1, notification date: 12/15
Early action deadline: N/A, notification date: N/A
Application deadline (fall): 3/1
Undergraduate student body: 2,746 full time, 93 part time; 41% male, 59% female; 0% American Indian, 1% Asian, 4% black, 8% Hispanic, 3% multiracial, 0% Pacific Islander, 76% white, 3% international; 62% from in state; 34% live on campus; N/A of students in fraternities, N/A in sororities
Most popular majors: 15% Business, Management, Marketing, and Related Support Services, 13% Communication,

Journalism, and Related Programs, 11% Psychology, 12% Visual and Performing Arts
Expenses: 2014-2015: $16,180; room/board: $9,000
Financial aid: (904) 819-6225; 64% of undergrads determined to have financial need; average aid package $11,619

Florida A&M University
Tallahassee FL
(850) 599-3796
U.S. News ranking: Nat. U., second tier
Website: www.famu.edu
Admissions email: ugradmissions@famu.edu
Public; founded 1887
Freshman admissions: selective; 2013-2014: 5,029 applied, 2,263 accepted. Either SAT or ACT required. ACT 25/75 percentile: 18-22. High school rank: 16% in top tenth, 46% in top quarter, 84% in top half
Early decision deadline: N/A, notification date: N/A
Early action deadline: N/A, notification date: N/A
Application deadline (fall): 5/15
Undergraduate student body: 8,024 full time, 906 part time; 39% male, 61% female; 0% American Indian, 1% Asian, 94% black, 1% Hispanic, 0% multiracial, 0% Pacific Islander, 3% white, 1% international; 84% from in state; 27% live on campus; 2% of students in fraternities, 2% in sororities
Most popular majors: 12% Business, Management, Marketing, and Related Support Services, 6% Communication, Journalism, and Related Programs, 20% Health Professions and Related Programs, 7% Psychology, 8% Social Sciences
Expenses: 2013-2014: $5,785 in state, $17,725 out of state; room/board: $9,356
Financial aid: (850) 412-7927; 85% of undergrads determined to have financial need; average aid package $13,039

Florida Atlantic University
Boca Raton FL
(561) 297-3040
U.S. News ranking: Nat. U., second tier
Website: www.fau.edu
Admissions email: Admissions@fau.edu
Public; founded 1961
Freshman admissions: selective; 2013-2014: 24,889 applied, 11,880 accepted. Either SAT or ACT required. SAT 25/75 percentile: 960-1130. High school rank: 11% in top tenth, 37% in top quarter, 77% in top half
Early decision deadline: N/A, notification date: N/A
Early action deadline: N/A, notification date: N/A
Application deadline (fall): 5/1
Undergraduate student body: 15,891 full time, 9,899 part time; 44% male, 56% female; 0% American Indian, 4% Asian, 17% black, 24% Hispanic, 3% multiracial, 0% Pacific Islander, 48% white, 2% international; 96% from in state; 6% live on campus; 2% of students in fraternities, 3% in sororities

Most popular majors: Information not available
Expenses: 2014-2015: $6,039 in state, $21,575 out of state; room/board: $11,847
Financial aid: (561) 297-3530; 66% of undergrads determined to have financial need; average aid package $10,405

Florida College
Temple Terrace FL
(800) 326-7655
U.S. News ranking: Reg. Coll. (S), second tier
Website: www.floridacollege.edu/
Admissions email: N/A
Private
Freshman admissions: selective; 2013-2014: 344 applied, 255 accepted. Either SAT or ACT required. ACT 25/75 percentile: 20-26. High school rank: N/A
Early decision deadline: N/A, notification date: N/A
Early action deadline: N/A, notification date: N/A
Application deadline (fall): 8/1
Undergraduate student body: 533 full time, 25 part time; 50% male, 50% female; 1% American Indian, 1% Asian, 6% black, 5% Hispanic, 5% multiracial, 0% Pacific Islander, 81% white, 1% international
Most popular majors: Information not available
Expenses: 2013-2014: $14,490; room/board: $7,760
Financial aid: N/A

Florida Gulf Coast University
Fort Myers FL
(239) 590-7878
U.S. News ranking: Reg. U. (S), No. 87
Website: www.fgcu.edu
Admissions email: admissions@fgcu.edu
Public; founded 1991
Freshman admissions: selective; 2013-2014: 10,804 applied, 7,108 accepted. Either SAT or ACT required. SAT 25/75 percentile: 940-1100. High school rank: 11% in top tenth, 36% in top quarter, 77% in top half
Early decision deadline: N/A, notification date: N/A
Early action deadline: N/A, notification date: N/A
Application deadline (fall): rolling
Undergraduate student body: 10,138 full time, 2,723 part time; 44% male, 56% female; 0% American Indian, 2% Asian, 7% black, 19% Hispanic, 2% multiracial, 0% Pacific Islander, 67% white, 2% international; 93% from in state; 33% live on campus; N/A of students in fraternities, N/A in sororities
Most popular majors: 27% Business, Management, Marketing, and Related Support Services, 10% Communication, Journalism, and Related Programs, 10% Education, 9% Health Professions and Related Programs
Expenses: 2013-2014: $6,118 in state, $24,255 out of state; room/board: $8,359
Financial aid: (239) 590-7920; 54% of undergrads determined to have financial need; average aid package $9,083

Florida Institute of Technology
Melbourne FL
(800) 888-4348
U.S. News ranking: Nat. U., No. 173
Website: www.fit.edu
Admissions email: admission@fit.edu
Private; founded 1958
Freshman admissions: selective; 2013-2014: 7,820 applied, 4,727 accepted. Either SAT or ACT required. SAT 25/75 percentile: 1030-1260. High school rank: 28% in top tenth, 55% in top quarter, 89% in top half
Early decision deadline: N/A, notification date: N/A
Early action deadline: N/A, notification date: N/A
Application deadline (fall): rolling
Undergraduate student body: 3,068 full time, 190 part time; 73% male, 27% female; 0% American Indian, 2% Asian, 5% black, 6% Hispanic, 2% multiracial, 0% Pacific Islander, 43% white, 30% international; 55% from in state; 50% live on campus; 14% of students in fraternities, 16% in sororities
Most popular majors: 8% Aerospace, Aeronautical and Astronautical/Space Engineering, 5% Aviation/Airway Management and Operations, 7% Electrical and Electronics Engineering, 5% Marine Biology and Biological Oceanography, 9% Mechanical Engineering
Expenses: 2014-2015: $37,990; room/board: $13,110
Financial aid: (321) 674-8070; 54% of undergrads determined to have financial need; average aid package $32,854

Florida International University
Miami FL
(305) 348-2363
U.S. News ranking: Nat. U., second tier
Website: www.fiu.edu
Admissions email: admiss@fiu.edu
Public; founded 1972
Freshman admissions: more selective; 2013-2014: 16,549 applied, 7,122 accepted. Either SAT or ACT required. SAT 25/75 percentile: 1070-1230. High school rank: 23% in top tenth, 51% in top quarter, 79% in top half
Early decision deadline: N/A, notification date: N/A
Early action deadline: N/A, notification date: N/A
Application deadline (fall): 5/1
Undergraduate student body: 25,938 full time, 13,107 part time; 45% male, 55% female; 0% American Indian, 3% Asian, 12% black, 67% Hispanic, 2% multiracial, 0% Pacific Islander, 10% white, 5% international; 97% from in state; 8% live on campus; N/A of students in fraternities, N/A in sororities
Most popular majors: 5% Biological and Biomedical Sciences, 35% Business, Management, Marketing, and Related Support Services, 6% Homeland Security, Law Enforcement, Firefighting and Related Protective Services, 10% Psychology, 9% Social Sciences

Expenses: 2014-2015: $6,496 in state, $18,895 out of state; room/board: $10,702
Financial aid: (305) 348-2431; 74% of undergrads determined to have financial need; average aid package $7,964

Florida Memorial University[1]
Miami FL
(305) 626-3750
U.S. News ranking: Reg. U. (S), second tier
Website: www.fmuniv.edu/
Admissions email: admit@fmuniv.edu
Private
Application deadline (fall): N/A
Undergraduate student body: N/A full time, N/A part time
Expenses: 2013-2014: $14,776; room/board: $6,112
Financial aid: (305) 626-3745

Florida Southern College
Lakeland FL
(863) 680-4131
U.S. News ranking: Reg. Coll. (S), No. 5
Website: www.flsouthern.edu
Admissions email: fscadm@flsouthern.edu
Private; founded 1883
Affiliation: United Methodist
Freshman admissions: selective; 2013-2014: 4,963 applied, 2,476 accepted. Either SAT or ACT required. SAT 25/75 percentile: 1010-1180. High school rank: 20% in top tenth, 56% in top quarter, 81% in top half
Early decision deadline: 12/1, notification date: 12/15
Early action deadline: N/A, notification date: N/A
Application deadline (fall): rolling
Undergraduate student body: 2,120 full time, 72 part time; 41% male, 59% female; 0% American Indian, 2% Asian, 6% black, 9% Hispanic, 4% multiracial, 0% Pacific Islander, 73% white, 6% international; 64% from in state; 79% live on campus; 37% of students in fraternities, 32% in sororities
Most popular majors: 26% Business, Management, Marketing, and Related Support Services, 8% Communication, Journalism, and Related Programs, 10% Education, 11% Health Professions and Related Programs, 9% Visual and Performing Arts
Expenses: 2014-2015: $29,990; room/board: $10,000
Financial aid: (863) 680-4140; 73% of undergrads determined to have financial need; average aid package $23,599

Florida State College–Jacksonville[1]
Jacksonville FL
(877) 633-5950
U.S. News ranking: Reg. Coll. (S), unranked
Website: www.fscj.edu
Admissions email: N/A
Public
Application deadline (fall): N/A
Undergraduate student body: N/A full time, N/A part time

Expenses: 2013-2014: $2,830 in state, $9,944 out of state; room/board: N/A
Financial aid: (904) 359-5433

Florida State University
Tallahassee FL
(850) 644-6200
U.S. News ranking: Nat. U., No. 95
Website: www.fsu.edu
Admissions email: admissions@admin.fsu.edu
Public; founded 1851
Freshman admissions: more selective; 2013-2014: 29,579 applied, 16,803 accepted. Either SAT or ACT required. ACT 25/75 percentile: 25-29. High school rank: 42% in top tenth, 77% in top quarter, 97% in top half
Early decision deadline: N/A, notification date: N/A
Early action deadline: N/A, notification date: N/A
Application deadline (fall): 1/15
Undergraduate student body: 28,910 full time, 3,618 part time; 45% male, 55% female; 0% American Indian, 3% Asian, 8% black, 17% Hispanic, 2% multiracial, 0% Pacific Islander, 67% white, 1% international; 90% from in state; 20% live on campus; 16% of students in fraternities, 22% in sororities
Most popular majors: 5% Criminal Justice/Safety Studies, 6% English Language and Literature, General, 5% Finance, General, 5% International Relations and Affairs, 6% Psychology, General
Expenses: 2014-2015: $6,507 in state, $21,673 out of state; room/board: $10,208
Financial aid: (850) 644-1993; 56% of undergrads determined to have financial need; average aid package $9,033

Hodges University
Naples FL
(239) 513-1122
U.S. News ranking: Reg. U. (S), unranked
Website: www.hodges.edu
Admissions email: admit@hodges.edu
Private; founded 1990
Freshman admissions: N/A; 2013-2014: 204 applied, 195 accepted. Neither SAT nor ACT required. ACT 25/75 percentile: N/A. High school rank: N/A
Early decision deadline: N/A, notification date: N/A
Early action deadline: N/A, notification date: N/A
Application deadline (fall): rolling
Undergraduate student body: 1,303 full time, 576 part time; 36% male, 64% female; 1% American Indian, 2% Asian, 16% black, 35% Hispanic, 1% multiracial, 0% Pacific Islander, 44% white, 0% international
Most popular majors: Information not available
Expenses: 2013-2014: $12,740; room/board: N/A
Financial aid: (239) 513-1122

Indian River State College
Fort Pierce FL
(772) 462-7460
U.S. News ranking: Reg. Coll. (S), No. 64
Website: www.irsc.edu
Admissions email: N/A
Public
Freshman admissions: least selective; 2013-2014: 1,725 applied, 1,725 accepted. Neither SAT·nor ACT required. ACT 25/75 percentile: N/A. High school rank: N/A
Early decision deadline: N/A, notification date: N/A
Early action deadline: N/A, notification date: N/A
Application deadline (fall): rolling
Undergraduate student body: 5,939 full time, 11,308 part time; 40% male, 60% female; 0% American Indian, 1% Asian, 18% black, 17% Hispanic, 2% multiracial, 0% Pacific Islander, 57% white, 1% international
Most popular majors: Information not available
Expenses: 2013-2014: $2,764 in state, $10,201 out of state; room/board: N/A
Financial aid: (772) 462-7450

Jacksonville University
Jacksonville FL
(800) 225-2027
U.S. News ranking: Reg. U. (S), No. 73
Website: www.jacksonville.edu
Admissions email: admissions@ju.edu
Private; founded 1934
Freshman admissions: selective; 2013-2014: 3,498 applied, 1,657 accepted. Either SAT or ACT required. SAT 25/75 percentile: 910-1110. High school rank: N/A
Early decision deadline: N/A, notification date: N/A
Early action deadline: N/A, notification date: N/A
Application deadline (fall): rolling
Undergraduate student body: 2,201 full time, 1,224 part time; 38% male, 62% female; 1% American Indian, 3% Asian, 16% black, 7% Hispanic, 0% multiracial, 0% Pacific Islander, 49% white, 3% international; 61% from in state; 29% live on campus; 8% of students in fraternities, 7% in sororities
Most popular majors: 13% Business, Management, Marketing, and Related Support Services, 52% Health Professions and Related Programs, 4% Parks, Recreation, Leisure, and Fitness Studies, 5% Social Sciences, 5% Visual and Performing Arts
Expenses: 2014-2015: $31,370; room/board: $10,820
Financial aid: (904) 256-7060; 72% of undergrads determined to have financial need; average aid package $22,702

Keiser University
Ft. Lauderdale FL
(954) 776-4456
U.S. News ranking: Reg. Coll. (S), No. 40
Website: www.keiseruniversity.edu
Admissions email: N/A
Private; founded 1977

Freshman admissions: less selective; 2013-2014: N/A applied, N/A accepted. Neither SAT nor ACT required. ACT 25/75 percentile: N/A. High school rank: N/A
Early decision deadline: N/A, notification date: N/A
Early action deadline: N/A, notification date: N/A
Application deadline (fall): rolling
Undergraduate student body: 12,007 full time, 4,032 part time; 32% male, 68% female; 0% American Indian, 2% Asian, 20% black, 31% Hispanic, 4% multiracial, 0% Pacific Islander, 40% white, 0% international; 89% from in state; 0% live on campus; N/A of students in fraternities, N/A in sororities
Most popular majors: 21% Business Administration and Management, General, 20% Criminal Justice/Safety Studies, 13% Health Services Administration, 10% Health Services/Allied Health/Health Sciences, General, 10% Multi-/Interdisciplinary Studies, General
Expenses: 2013-2014: $16,284; room/board: N/A
Financial aid: (954) 351-4456

Lynn University
Boca Raton FL
(800) 888-5966
U.S. News ranking: Nat. U., second tier
Website: www.lynn.edu
Admissions email: admission@lynn.edu
Private; founded 1962
Freshman admissions: less selective; 2013-2014: 2,698 applied, 2,094 accepted. Either SAT or ACT required. SAT 25/75 percentile: 820-1050. High school rank: 1% in top tenth, 9% in top quarter, 41% in top half
Early decision deadline: N/A, notification date: N/A
Early action deadline: 11/15, notification date: 12/15
Application deadline (fall): rolling
Undergraduate student body: 1,634 full time, 151 part time; 53% male, 47% female; 1% American Indian, 2% Asian, 10% black, 13% Hispanic, 0% multiracial, 0% Pacific Islander, 39% white, 24% international; 44% from in state; 50% live on campus; 5% of students in fraternities, 8% in sororities
Most popular majors: 48% Business, Management, Marketing, and Related Support Services, 10% Communication, Journalism, and Related Programs, 6% Homeland Security, Law Enforcement, Firefighting and Related Protective Services, 9% Psychology, 8% Visual and Performing Arts
Expenses: 2014-2015: $34,550; room/board: $10,900
Financial aid: (561) 237-7186; 43% of undergrads determined to have financial need; average aid package $20,042

Miami Dade College[1]
Miami FL
(305) 237-8888
U.S. News ranking: Reg. Coll. (S), unranked
Website: www.mdc.edu/
Admissions email: mdcinfo@mdc.edu
Public

Application deadline (fall): N/A
Undergraduate student body: N/A full time, N/A part time
Expenses: 2013-2014: $3,426 in state, $11,955 out of state; room/board: N/A
Financial aid: (305) 237-6040

Miami International University of Art & Design[1]
Miami FL
(305) 428-5700
U.S. News ranking: Arts, unranked
Website: www.aimiu.aii.edu/
Admissions email: N/A
For-profit
Application deadline (fall): N/A
Undergraduate student body: N/A full time, N/A part time
Expenses: 2013-2014: $17,704; room/board: $10,350
Financial aid: N/A

New College of Florida
Sarasota FL
(941) 487-5000
U.S. News ranking: Nat, Lib. Arts, No. 87
Website: www.ncf.edu
Admissions email: admissions@ncf.edu
Public; founded 2001
Freshman admissions: more selective; 2013-2014: 1,205 applied, 834 accepted. Either SAT or ACT required. SAT 25/75 percentile: 1190-1380. High school rank: 41% in top tenth, 75% in top quarter, 94% in top half
Early decision deadline: N/A, notification date: N/A
Early action deadline: N/A, notification date: N/A
Application deadline (fall): 4/15
Undergraduate student body: 793 full time, 0 part time; 43% male, 57% female; 0% American Indian, 3% Asian, 3% black, 14% Hispanic, 4% multiracial, 0% Pacific Islander, 74% white, 1% international; 82% from in state; 80% live on campus; 0% of students in fraternities, 0% in sororities
Most popular majors: 100% Liberal Arts and Sciences, General Studies and Humanities, Other
Expenses: 2014-2015: $6,872 in state, $29,900 out of state; room/board: $8,856
Financial aid: (941) 359-4255; 57% of undergrads determined to have financial need; average aid package $13,005

Northwest Florida State College[1]
Niceville FL
(850) 729-6922
U.S. News ranking: Reg. Coll. (S), unranked
Website: www.owcc.cc.fl.us/
Admissions email: N/A
Public
Application deadline (fall): N/A
Undergraduate student body: N/A full time, N/A part time
Expenses: 2013-2014: $3,064 in state, $11,373 out of state; room/board: N/A
Financial aid: (850) 729-5370

Nova Southeastern University

Ft. Lauderdale FL
(954) 262-8000
U.S. News ranking: Nat. U., second tier
Website: www.nova.edu
Admissions email: admissions@nova.edu
Private; founded 1964
Freshman admissions: selective; 2013-2014: 4,328 applied, 2,487 accepted. Either SAT or ACT required. SAT 25/75 percentile: 950-1190. High school rank: 24% in top tenth, 53% in top quarter, 85% in top half
Early decision deadline: N/A, notification date: N/A
Early action deadline: N/A, notification date: N/A
Application deadline (fall): rolling
Undergraduate student body: 3,452 full time, 1,704 part time; 29% male, 71% female; 0% American Indian, 7% Asian, 21% black, 31% Hispanic, 2% multiracial, 0% Pacific Islander, 31% white, 5% international; 83% from in state; 18% live on campus; 2% of students in fraternities, 4% in sororities
Most popular majors: 21% Biological and Biomedical Sciences, 20% Business, Management, Marketing, and Related Support Services, 5% Education, 31% Health Professions and Related Programs, 8% Psychology
Expenses: 2014-2015: $26,700; room/board: $10,580
Financial aid: (954) 262-3380; 77% of undergrads determined to have financial need; average aid package $25,035

Palm Beach Atlantic University

West Palm Beach FL
(888) 468-6722
U.S. News ranking: Reg. U. (S), No. 51
Website: www.pba.edu
Admissions email: admit@pba.edu
Private; founded 1968
Affiliation: Christian Interdenominational
Freshman admissions: selective; 2013-2014: 1,618 applied, 1,361 accepted. Either SAT or ACT required. SAT 25/75 percentile: 925-1180. High school rank: N/A
Early decision deadline: N/A, notification date: N/A
Early action deadline: 3/31, notification date: 4/15
Application deadline (fall): rolling
Undergraduate student body: 2,358 full time, 529 part time; 37% male, 63% female; 0% American Indian, 1% Asian, 14% black, 13% Hispanic, 2% multiracial, 0% Pacific Islander, 61% white, 4% international; 68% from in state; 47% live on campus; N/A of students in fraternities, N/A in sororities
Most popular majors: 30% Business, Management, Marketing, and Related Support Services, 11% Health Professions and Related Programs, 11% Psychology, 11% Theology and Religious Vocations, 11% Visual and Performing Arts
Expenses: 2014-2015: $26,274; room/board: $8,600

Financial aid: (561) 803-2000; 76% of undergrads determined to have financial need; average aid package $17,424

Ringling College of Art and Design

Sarasota FL
(800) 255-7695
U.S. News ranking: Arts, unranked
Website: www.ringling.edu
Admissions email: admissions@ringling.edu
Private; founded 1931
Freshman admissions: N/A; 2013-2014: 1,225 applied, 898 accepted. Neither SAT nor ACT required. SAT 25/75 percentile: N/A. High school rank: N/A
Early decision deadline: N/A, notification date: N/A
Early action deadline: N/A, notification date: N/A
Application deadline (fall): rolling
Undergraduate student body: 1,212 full time, 41 part time; 39% male, 61% female; 1% American Indian, 8% Asian, 3% black, 16% Hispanic, 2% multiracial, 0% Pacific Islander, 58% white, 13% international; 59% from in state; 63% live on campus; 0% of students in fraternities, 0% in sororities
Most popular majors: 22% Animation, Interactive Technology, Video Graphics and Special Effects, 7% Game and Interactive Media Design, 11% Graphic Design, 31% Illustration, 7% Photography
Expenses: 2014-2015: $40,040; room/board: $13,580
Financial aid: (941) 351-5100; 81% of undergrads determined to have financial need; average aid package $18,218

Rollins College

Winter Park FL
(407) 646-2161
U.S. News ranking: Reg. U. (S), No. 2
Website: www.rollins.edu
Admissions email: admission@rollins.edu
Private; founded 1885
Freshman admissions: more selective; 2013-2014: 4,729 applied, 2,233 accepted. Neither SAT nor ACT required. SAT 25/75 percentile: 1100-1290. High school rank: 34% in top tenth, 67% in top quarter, 90% in top half
Early decision deadline: 11/15, notification date: 12/15
Early action deadline: N/A, notification date: N/A
Application deadline (fall): 2/15
Undergraduate student body: 1,890 full time, N/A part time; 42% male, 58% female; 0% American Indian, 3% Asian, 3% black, 13% Hispanic, 3% multiracial, 0% Pacific Islander, 68% white, 7% international; 51% from in state; 62% live on campus; 24% of students in fraternities, 33% in sororities
Most popular majors: 11% Business, Management, Marketing, and Related Support Services, 11% Communication, Journalism, and Related Programs, 10% Psychology, 27% Social Sciences, 12% Visual and Performing Arts
Expenses: 2014-2015: $43,080; room/board: $13,470

Financial aid: (407) 646-2395; 54% of undergrads determined to have financial need; average aid package $34,014

Southeastern University

Lakeland FL
(800) 500-8760
U.S. News ranking: Reg. Coll. (S), No. 41
Website: www.seu.edu
Admissions email: admission@seu.edu
Private; founded 1935
Affiliation: Assemblies of God
Freshman admissions: less selective; 2013-2014: 2,124 applied, 1,260 accepted. Either SAT or ACT required. SAT 25/75 percentile: 850-1080. High school rank: N/A
Early decision deadline: N/A, notification date: N/A
Early action deadline: N/A, notification date: N/A
Application deadline (fall): 5/1
Undergraduate student body: 2,473 full time, 610 part time; 45% male, 55% female; 0% American Indian, 1% Asian, 14% black, 16% Hispanic, 1% multiracial, 0% Pacific Islander, 62% white, 1% international; 69% from in state; 47% live on campus; N/A of students in fraternities, N/A in sororities
Most popular majors: 16% Business, Management, Marketing, and Related Support Services, 10% Communication, Journalism, and Related Programs, 11% Education, 12% Public Administration and Social Service Professions, 23% Theology and Religious Vocations
Expenses: 2014-2015: $22,202; room/board: $9,298
Financial aid: (863) 667-5026; 84% of undergrads determined to have financial need; average aid package $12,967

Stetson University

DeLand FL
(800) 688-0101
U.S. News ranking: Reg. U. (S), No. 6
Website: www.stetson.edu
Admissions email: admissions@stetson.edu
Private; founded 1883
Freshman admissions: more selective; 2013-2014: 10,509 applied, 6,227 accepted. Neither SAT nor ACT required. SAT 25/75 percentile: 1070-1270. High school rank: 26% in top tenth, 61% in top quarter, 89% in top half
Early decision deadline: N/A, notification date: N/A
Early action deadline: N/A, notification date: N/A
Application deadline (fall): rolling
Undergraduate student body: 2,692 full time, 37 part time; 43% male, 57% female; 0% American Indian, 2% Asian, 8% black, 14% Hispanic, 4% multiracial, 0% Pacific Islander, 66% white, 4% international; 74% from in state; 68% live on campus; 28% of students in fraternities, 27% in sororities
Most popular majors: 6% Biological and Biomedical Sciences, 25% Business, Management, Marketing, and Related Support

Services, 9% Psychology, 9% Social Sciences, 11% Visual and Performing Arts
Expenses: 2014-2015: $40,040; room/board: $11,476
Financial aid: (386) 822-7120; 75% of undergrads determined to have financial need; average aid package $31,980

St. Leo University

Saint Leo FL
(800) 334-5532
U.S. News ranking: Reg. U. (S), No. 65
Website: www.saintleo.edu
Admissions email: admission@saintleo.edu
Private; founded 1889
Affiliation: Roman Catholic
Freshman admissions: less selective; 2013-2014: 3,178 applied, 2,435 accepted. Neither SAT nor ACT required. SAT 25/75 percentile: 910-1093. High school rank: 9% in top tenth, 29% in top quarter, 66% in top half
Early decision deadline: N/A, notification date: N/A
Early action deadline: N/A, notification date: N/A
Application deadline (fall): rolling
Undergraduate student body: 2,163 full time, 71 part time; 48% male, 52% female; 0% American Indian, 1% Asian, 11% black, 17% Hispanic, 3% multiracial, 0% Pacific Islander, 47% white, 13% international; 71% from in state; 61% live on campus; 20% of students in fraternities, 23% in sororities
Most popular majors: 32% Business, Management, Marketing, and Related Support Services, 7% Education, 11% Homeland Security, Law Enforcement, Firefighting and Related Protective Services, 9% Parks, Recreation, Leisure, and Fitness Studies, 10% Psychology
Expenses: 2014-2015: $20,110; room/board: $9,920
Financial aid: (352) 588-8270; 72% of undergrads determined to have financial need; average aid package $19,072

St. Petersburg College[1]

St. Petersburg FL
(727) 341-4772
U.S. News ranking: Reg. Coll. (S), unranked
Website: www.spcollege.edu/
Admissions email: information@spcollege.edu
Public
Application deadline (fall): N/A
Undergraduate student body: N/A full time, N/A part time
Expenses: 2013-2014: $3,232 in state, $11,477 out of state; room/board: N/A
Financial aid: (727) 791-2442

St. Thomas University

Miami Gardens FL
(305) 628-6546
U.S. News ranking: Reg. U. (S), No. 65
Website: www.stu.edu
Admissions email: signup@stu.edu
Private; founded 1961
Affiliation: Roman Catholic
Freshman admissions: less selective; 2013-2014: 817 applied, 347 accepted. Either SAT or ACT required. SAT 25/75

percentile: 785-990. High school rank: 6% in top tenth, 11% in top quarter, 46% in top half
Early decision deadline: N/A, notification date: N/A
Early action deadline: N/A, notification date: N/A
Application deadline (fall): rolling
Undergraduate student body: 963 full time, 72 part time; 45% male, 55% female; 0% American Indian, 0% Asian, 24% black, 43% Hispanic, 1% multiracial, 0% Pacific Islander, 8% white, 19% international; 89% from in state; 30% live on campus; N/A of students in fraternities, N/A in sororities
Most popular majors: 52% Business, Management, Marketing, and Related Support Services, 4% Education, 13% Homeland Security, Law Enforcement, Firefighting and Related Protective Services, 10% Psychology, 5% Social Sciences
Expenses: 2014-2015: $27,150; room/board: $7,720
Financial aid: (305) 474-6960; 72% of undergrads determined to have financial need

University of Central Florida

Orlando FL
(407) 823-3000
U.S. News ranking: Nat. U., No. 173
Website: www.ucf.edu
Admissions email: admission@ucf.edu
Public; founded 1963
Freshman admissions: more selective; 2013-2014: 31,820 applied, 15,572 accepted. Either SAT or ACT required. SAT 25/75 percentile: 1090-1270. High school rank: 30% in top tenth, 71% in top quarter, 97% in top half
Early decision deadline: N/A, notification date: N/A
Early action deadline: N/A, notification date: N/A
Application deadline (fall): 5/1
Undergraduate student body: 36,160 full time, 15,109 part time; 45% male, 55% female; 0% American Indian, 6% Asian, 11% black, 22% Hispanic, 3% multiracial, 0% Pacific Islander, 57% white, 1% international; 95% from in state; 18% live on campus; 6% of students in fraternities, 7% in sororities
Most popular majors: 22% Business, Management, Marketing, and Related Support Services, 8% Education, 6% Engineering, 14% Health Professions and Related Programs, 10% Psychology
Expenses: 2014-2015: $6,368 in state, $22,467 out of state; room/board: $9,300
Financial aid: (407) 823-2827; 66% of undergrads determined to have financial need; average aid package $7,998

University of Florida

Gainesville FL
(352) 392-1365
U.S. News ranking: Nat. U., No. 48
Website: www.ufl.edu
Admissions email: N/A
Public; founded 1853

Freshman admissions: more selective; 2013-2014: 27,107 applied, 12,618 accepted. Either SAT or ACT required. SAT 25/75 percentile: 1170-1360. High school rank: 77% in top tenth, 97% in top quarter, 100% in top half
Early decision deadline: N/A, notification date: N/A
Early action deadline: N/A, notification date: N/A
Application deadline (fall): 11/1
Undergraduate student body: 30,314 full time, 2,854 part time; 45% male, 55% female; 0% American Indian, 8% Asian, 7% black, 19% Hispanic, 3% multiracial, 1% Pacific Islander, 58% white, 1% international; 97% from in state, 23% live on campus; 20% of students in fraternities, 21% in sororities
Most popular majors: 10% Biological and Biomedical Sciences, 10% Business, Management, Marketing, and Related Support Services, 8% Communication, Journalism, and Related Programs, 13% Engineering, 13% Social Sciences
Expenses: 2014-2015: $6,313 in state, $28,591 out of state; room/board: $9,630
Financial aid: (352) 392-1271; 56% of undergrads determined to have financial need; average aid package $11,745

University of Miami
Coral Gables FL
(305) 284-4323
U.S. News ranking: Nat. U., No. 48
Website: www.miami.edu
Admissions email: admission@miami.edu
Private; founded 1925
Freshman admissions: most selective; 2013-2014: 28,902 applied, 11,691 accepted. Either SAT or ACT required. SAT 25/75 percentile: 1230-1420. High school rank: 72% in top tenth, 92% in top quarter, 98% in top half
Early decision deadline: 11/1, notification date: 12/20
Early action deadline: 11/1, notification date: 2/1
Application deadline (fall): 1/1
Undergraduate student body: 10,637 full time, 743 part time; 49% male, 51% female; 0% American Indian, 5% Asian, 7% black, 22% Hispanic, 3% multiracial, 0% Pacific Islander, 43% white, 14% international; 46% from in state; 38% live on campus; 14% of students in fraternities, 17% in sororities
Most popular majors: 14% Biological and Biomedical Sciences, 16% Business, Management, Marketing, and Related Support Services, 9% Communication, Journalism, and Related Programs, 11% Health Professions and Related Programs, 12% Social Sciences
Expenses: 2014-2015: $44,350; room/board: $12,684
Financial aid: (305) 284-5212; 46% of undergrads determined to have financial need; average aid package $32,813

University of North Florida
Jacksonville FL
(904) 620-2624
U.S. News ranking: Reg. U. (S), No. 51
Website: www.unf.edu
Admissions email: admissions@unf.edu
Public; founded 1965
Freshman admissions: more selective; 2013-2014: 10,635 applied, 5,682 accepted. Either SAT or ACT required. SAT 25/75 percentile: 1080-1230. High school rank: 24% in top tenth, 56% in top quarter, 87% in top half
Early decision deadline: N/A, notification date: N/A
Early action deadline: N/A, notification date: N/A
Application deadline (fall): rolling
Undergraduate student body: 10,088 full time, 4,175 part time; 45% male, 55% female; 0% American Indian, 4% Asian, 10% black, 9% Hispanic, 5% multiracial, 0% Pacific Islander, 70% white, 1% international; 97% from in state; 21% live on campus; N/A of students in fraternities, N/A in sororities
Most popular majors: 20% Business, Management, Marketing, and Related Support Services, 9% Communication, Journalism, and Related Programs, 8% Education, 15% Health Professions and Related Programs, 10% Psychology
Expenses: 2014-2015: $6,385 in state, $20,103 out of state; room/board: $9,484
Financial aid: (904) 620-2604; 59% of undergrads determined to have financial need; average aid package $8,042

University of South Florida
Tampa FL
(813) 974-3350
U.S. News ranking: Nat. U., No. 161
Website: www.usf.edu
Admissions email: admission@admin.usf.edu
Public; founded 1956
Freshman admissions: more selective; 2013-2014: 28,512 applied, 12,900 accepted. Either SAT or ACT required. SAT 25/75 percentile: 1080-1260. High school rank: 36% in top tenth, 65% in top quarter, 76% in top half
Early decision deadline: N/A, notification date: N/A
Early action deadline: N/A, notification date: N/A
Application deadline (fall): 3/1
Undergraduate student body: 23,734 full time, 7,366 part time; 45% male, 55% female; 0% American Indian, 6% Asian, 11% black, 20% Hispanic, 3% multiracial, 0% Pacific Islander, 55% white, 3% international; 93% from in state; 24% live on campus; 7% of students in fraternities, 8% in sororities
Most popular majors: 15% Criminology, 17% Finance, General, 9% Medical Microbiology and Bacteriology, 9% Psychology, General, 10% Registered Nursing/Registered Nurse
Expenses: 2014-2015: $6,410 in state, $17,325 out of state; room/board: $9,400

Financial aid: (813) 974-4700; 74% of undergrads determined to have financial need; average aid package $9,376

University of South Florida–St. Petersburg[1]
St. Petersburg FL
(727) 873-4142
U.S. News ranking: Reg. U. (S), No. 92
Website: www.usfsp.edu
Admissions email: admissions@usfsp.edu
Public; founded 1965
Application deadline (fall): 4/15
Undergraduate student body: N/A full time, N/A part time
Expenses: 2013-2014: $5,716 in state, $15,638 out of state; room/board: $9,190
Financial aid: (727) 873-4128

University of Tampa
Tampa FL
(888) 646-2738
U.S. News ranking: Reg. U. (S), No. 24
Website: www.ut.edu
Admissions email: admissions@ut.edu
Private; founded 1931
Freshman admissions: selective; 2013-2014: 15,345 applied, 8,011 accepted. Either SAT or ACT required. SAT 25/75 percentile: 980-1150. High school rank: 18% in top tenth, 46% in top quarter, 84% in top half
Early decision deadline: N/A, notification date: N/A
Early action deadline: 11/15, notification date: 12/15
Application deadline (fall): rolling
Undergraduate student body: 6,188 full time, 311 part time; 45% male, 55% female; 0% American Indian, 1% Asian, 6% black, 12% Hispanic, 2% multiracial, 0% Pacific Islander, 59% white, 10% international; 40% from in state; 63% live on campus; 10% of students in fraternities, 23% in sororities
Most popular majors: 7% Biological and Biomedical Sciences, 26% Business, Management, Marketing, and Related Support Services, 12% Communication, Journalism, and Related Programs, 10% Parks, Recreation, Leisure, and Fitness Studies, 12% Social Sciences
Expenses: 2014-2015: $26,330; room/board: $9,624
Financial aid: (813) 253-6219; 60% of undergrads determined to have financial need; average aid package $16,113

University of West Florida
Pensacola FL
(850) 474-2230
U.S. News ranking: Nat. U., second tier
Website: uwf.edu
Admissions email: admissions@uwf.edu
Public; founded 1963
Freshman admissions: selective; 2013-2014: 12,347 applied, 5,937 accepted. Either SAT or ACT required. ACT 25/75 percentile: 21-25. High school rank: 12% in top tenth, 36% in top quarter, 75% in top half

Early decision deadline: N/A, notification date: N/A
Early action deadline: N/A, notification date: N/A
Application deadline (fall): 6/30
Undergraduate student body: 7,581 full time, 2,577 part time; 43% male, 57% female; 1% American Indian, 3% Asian, 13% black, 9% Hispanic, 4% multiracial, 0% Pacific Islander, 67% white, 2% international; 90% from in state; 19% live on campus; N/A of students in fraternities, N/A in sororities
Most popular majors: 15% Business Administration and Management, General, 13% Health Services/Allied Health/Health Sciences, General, 7% Mass Communication/Media Studies, 7% Social Sciences, General, 8% Special Education and Teaching, General
Expenses: 2014-2015: $8,942 in state, $21,824 out of state; room/board: $9,323
Financial aid: (850) 474-3127; 67% of undergrads determined to have financial need; average aid package $8,412

Warner University[1]
Lake Wales FL
(800) 309-9563
U.S. News ranking: Reg. U. (S), second tier
Website: www.warner.edu
Admissions email: admissions@warner.edu
Private
Affiliation: Church of God, Anderson IN
Application deadline (fall): rolling
Undergraduate student body: N/A full time, N/A part time
Expenses: 2013-2014: $18,430; room/board: $7,649
Financial aid: (863) 638-7202

Webber International University
Babson Park FL
(800) 741-1844
U.S. News ranking: Reg. Coll. (S), second tier
Website: www.webber.edu
Admissions email: admissions@webber.edu
Private; founded 1927
Freshman admissions: less selective; 2013-2014: 944 applied, 602 accepted. Either SAT or ACT required. ACT 25/75 percentile: 17-21. High school rank: 6% in top tenth, 22% in top quarter, 53% in top half
Early decision deadline: N/A, notification date: N/A
Early action deadline: N/A, notification date: N/A
Application deadline (fall): 8/1
Undergraduate student body: 633 full time, 34 part time; 69% male, 31% female; 0% American Indian, 2% Asian, 22% black, 16% Hispanic, 3% multiracial, 0% Pacific Islander, 48% white, 8% international; 90% from in state; 52% live on campus; N/A of students in fraternities, N/A in sororities
Most popular majors: 67% Business, Management, Marketing, and Related Support Services, 5% Computer and Information Sciences and Support Services, 4% Homeland Security, Law Enforcement, Firefighting and

Related Protective Services, 4% Legal Professions and Studies, 17% Parks, Recreation, Leisure, and Fitness Studies
Expenses: 2014-2015: $24,034; room/board: $8,462
Financial aid: (863) 638-2930; 69% of undergrads determined to have financial need; average aid package $19,481

GEORGIA

Abraham Baldwin Agricultural College
Tifton GA
(800) 733-3653
U.S. News ranking: Reg. Coll. (S), second tier
Website: www.abac.edu/
Admissions email: N/A
Public; founded 1908
Freshman admissions: least selective; 2013-2014: 1,567 applied, 1,111 accepted. Either SAT or ACT required. SAT 25/75 percentile: 810-990. High school rank: N/A
Early decision deadline: N/A, notification date: N/A
Early action deadline: N/A, notification date: N/A
Application deadline (fall): 8/1
Undergraduate student body: 2,350 full time, 1,044 part time; 46% male, 54% female; 0% American Indian, 1% Asian, 12% black, 6% Hispanic, 1% multiracial, 0% Pacific Islander, 78% white, 2% international
Most popular majors: Information not available
Expenses: 2013-2014: $4,281 in state, $10,415 out of state; room/board: N/A
Financial aid: (229) 391-4910

Agnes Scott College
Decatur GA
(800) 868-8602
U.S. News ranking: Nat. Lib. Arts, No. 73
Website: www.agnesscott.edu
Admissions email: admission@agnesscott.edu
Private; founded 1889
Affiliation: Presbyterian Church (USA)
Freshman admissions: more selective; 2013-2014: 1,340 applied, 896 accepted. Neither SAT nor ACT required. SAT 25/75 percentile: 1010-1310. High school rank: 40% in top tenth, 67% in top quarter, 91% in top half
Early decision deadline: N/A, notification date: N/A
Early action deadline: N/A, notification date: N/A
Application deadline (fall): 5/1
Undergraduate student body: 897 full time, 18 part time; 1% male, 99% female; 0% American Indian, 5% Asian, 35% black, 9% Hispanic, 6% multiracial, 0% Pacific Islander, 31% white, 10% international; 63% from in state; 82% live on campus; N/A of students in fraternities, N/A in sororities
Most popular majors: 13% Biological and Biomedical Sciences, 11% English Language and Literature/Letters, 17% Psychology, 20% Social Sciences, 8% Visual and Performing Arts

Expenses: 2014-2015: $35,982; room/board: $10,850
Financial aid: (404) 471-6395; 77% of undergrads determined to have financial need; average aid package $32,875

Albany State University
Albany GA
(229) 430-4646
U.S. News ranking: Reg. U. (S), No. 76
Website: www.asurams.edu/
Admissions email: admissions@asurams.edu
Public; founded 1903
Freshman admissions: less selective; 2013-2014: 6,393 applied, 1,537 accepted. Either SAT or ACT required. SAT 25/75 percentile: 820-950. High school rank: 7% in top tenth, 27% in top quarter, 66% in top half
Early decision deadline: N/A, notification date: N/A
Early action deadline: N/A, notification date: N/A
Application deadline (fall): 6/1
Undergraduate student body: 3,019 full time, 641 part time; 34% male, 66% female; 0% American Indian, 0% Asian, 92% black, 1% Hispanic, 0% multiracial, 0% Pacific Islander, 4% white, 0% international; 98% from in state; 42% live on campus; 6% of students in fraternities, 10% in sororities
Most popular majors: 8% Biology/Biological Sciences, General, 11% Business Administration and Management, General, 11% Criminal Justice/Safety Studies, 8% Early Childhood Education and Teaching, 9% Psychology, General
Expenses: 2014-2015: $6,024 in state, $18,226 out of state; room/board: $7,646
Financial aid: (229) 430-4650; 94% of undergrads determined to have financial need; average aid package $4,977

Armstrong State University
Savannah GA
(912) 344-2503
U.S. News ranking: Reg. U. (S), second tier
Website: www.armstrong.edu
Admissions email: adm-info@mail.armstrong.edu
Public; founded 1935
Freshman admissions: selective; 2013-2014: 2,497 applied, 1,692 accepted. Either SAT or ACT required. SAT 25/75 percentile: 920-1090. High school rank: N/A
Early decision deadline: N/A, notification date: N/A
Early action deadline: N/A, notification date: N/A
Application deadline (fall): 7/15
Undergraduate student body: 4,699 full time, 1,678 part time; 33% male, 67% female; 0% American Indian, 4% Asian, 24% black, 7% Hispanic, 4% multiracial, 0% Pacific Islander, 60% white, 2% international; 93% from in state; 49% live on campus; N/A of students in fraternities, N/A in sororities
Most popular majors: 42% Health Services/Allied Health/Health Sciences, General

Expenses: 2014-2015: $5,934 in state, $17,700 out of state; room/board: $8,946
Financial aid: (912) 921-5990; 66% of undergrads determined to have financial need; average aid package $9,145

Art Institute of Atlanta[1]
Atlanta GA
(770) 394-8300
U.S. News ranking: Arts, unranked
Website: www.artinstitutes.edu/atlanta/
Admissions email: aiaadm@aii.edu
For-profit
Application deadline (fall): N/A
Undergraduate student body: N/A full time, N/A part time
Expenses: 2013-2014: $17,596; room/board: $11,268
Financial aid: (770) 394-8300

Bauder College[1]
Atlanta GA
(800) 241-3797
U.S. News ranking: Reg. Coll. (S), unranked
Website: www.bauder.edu
Admissions email: N/A
For-profit
Application deadline (fall): N/A
Undergraduate student body: N/A full time, N/A part time
Expenses: 2013-2014: $13,089; room/board: N/A
Financial aid: N/A

Berry College
Mount Berry GA
(706) 236-2215
U.S. News ranking: Nat. Lib. Arts, No. 129
Website: www.berry.edu
Admissions email: admissions@berry.edu
Private; founded 1902
Freshman admissions: more selective; 2013-2014: 3,901 applied, 2,353 accepted. Either SAT or ACT required. ACT 25/75 percentile: 24-29. High school rank: 32% in top tenth, 65% in top quarter, 92% in top half
Early decision deadline: N/A, notification date: N/A
Early action deadline: N/A, notification date: N/A
Application deadline (fall): 7/25
Undergraduate student body: 2,107 full time, 34 part time; 38% male, 62% female; 0% American Indian, 1% Asian, 4% black, 6% Hispanic, 3% multiracial, 0% Pacific Islander, 84% white, 1% international; 69% from in state; 86% live on campus; N/A of students in fraternities, N/A in sororities
Most popular majors: 10% Agriculture, Agriculture Operations, and Related Sciences, 13% Biological and Biomedical Sciences, 13% Business, Management, Marketing, and Related Support Services, 10% Psychology, 9% Social Sciences
Expenses: 2014-2015: $30,530; room/board: $10,660
Financial aid: (706) 236-1714; 74% of undergrads determined to have financial need; average aid package $24,002

Brenau University
Gainesville GA
(770) 534-6100
U.S. News ranking: Reg. U. (S), No. 43
Website: www.brenau.edu
Admissions email: admissions@brenau.edu
Private; founded 1878
Freshman admissions: less selective; 2013-2014: 2,160 applied, 1,691 accepted. Either SAT or ACT required. SAT 25/75 percentile: 890-1070. High school rank: N/A
Early decision deadline: N/A, notification date: N/A
Early action deadline: N/A, notification date: N/A
Application deadline (fall): rolling
Undergraduate student body: 1,074 full time, 626 part time; 11% male, 89% female; 0% American Indian, 2% Asian, 31% black, 6% Hispanic, 3% multiracial, 0% Pacific Islander, 51% white, 3% international; 95% from in state; 23% live on campus; 0% of students in fraternities, 24% in sororities
Most popular majors: 31% Business, Management, Marketing, and Related Support Services, 10% Education, 32% Health Professions and Related Programs, 6% Liberal Arts and Sciences, General Studies and Humanities, 8% Visual and Performing Arts
Expenses: 2014-2015: $24,780; room/board: $11,998
Financial aid: (770) 534-6176; 84% of undergrads determined to have financial need; average aid package $16,844

Brewton-Parker College[1]
Mount Vernon GA
(912) 583-3265
U.S. News ranking: Reg. Coll. (S), second tier
Website: www.bpc.edu
Admissions email: admissions@bpc.edu
Private
Application deadline (fall): N/A
Undergraduate student body: N/A full time, N/A part time
Expenses: 2013-2014: $13,560; room/board: $6,926
Financial aid: (912) 583-3215

Clark Atlanta University
Atlanta GA
(800) 688-3228
U.S. News ranking: Nat. U., second tier
Website: www.cau.edu
Admissions email: cauadmissions@cau.edu
Private; founded 1988
Affiliation: Methodist
Freshman admissions: less selective; 2013-2014: 5,873 applied, 3,336 accepted. Either SAT or ACT required. SAT 25/75 percentile: 770-940. High school rank: 9% in top tenth, 31% in top quarter, 65% in top half
Early decision deadline: N/A, notification date: N/A
Early action deadline: N/A, notification date: N/A
Application deadline (fall): 6/1

Undergraduate student body: 2,514 full time, 115 part time; 25% male, 75% female; 0% American Indian, 0% Asian, 87% black, 1% Hispanic, 0% multiracial, 0% Pacific Islander, 0% white, 1% international; 36% from in state; 62% live on campus; 2% of students in fraternities, 3% in sororities
Most popular majors: 7% Biological and Biomedical Sciences, 23% Business, Management, Marketing, and Related Support Services, 23% Communication, Journalism, and Related Programs, 12% Psychology, 10% Visual and Performing Arts
Expenses: 2014-2015: $21,334; room/board: $10,262
Financial aid: (404) 880-8111; 95% of undergrads determined to have financial need; average aid package $7,879

Clayton State University
Morrow GA
(678) 466-4115
U.S. News ranking: Reg. Coll. (S), No. 62
Website: www.clayton.edu
Admissions email: ccsu-info@mail.clayton.edu
Public; founded 1969
Freshman admissions: selective; 2013-2014: 2,048 applied, 949 accepted. Either SAT or ACT required. SAT 25/75 percentile: 860-1030. High school rank: N/A
Early decision deadline: N/A, notification date: N/A
Early action deadline: N/A, notification date: N/A
Application deadline (fall): 7/1
Undergraduate student body: 3,939 full time, 2,954 part time; 30% male, 70% female; 0% American Indian, 4% Asian, 65% black, 1% Hispanic, 0% multiracial, 3% Pacific Islander, 21% white, 1% international; 88% from in state; 5% live on campus; 8% of students in fraternities, 8% in sororities
Most popular majors: 5% Business Administration and Management, General, 13% Community Psychology, 11% Hospital and Health Care Facilities Administration/Management, 12% Liberal Arts and Sciences/Liberal Studies, 13% Registered Nursing/Registered Nurse
Expenses: 2014-2015: $6,194 in state, $18,700 out of state; room/board: $9,692
Financial aid: (678) 466-4185; 87% of undergrads determined to have financial need; average aid package $8,842

Columbus State University
Columbus GA
(706) 507-8800
U.S. News ranking: Reg. U. (S), second tier
Website: www.columbusstate.edu
Admissions email: admissions@columbusstate.edu
Public; founded 1958
Freshman admissions: selective; 2013-2014: 3,172 applied, 1,775 accepted. Either SAT or ACT required. SAT 25/75 percentile: 880-1100. High school rank: 17% in top tenth, 38% in top quarter, 67% in top half

Early decision deadline: N/A, notification date: N/A
Early action deadline: N/A, notification date: N/A
Application deadline (fall): 6/30
Undergraduate student body: 4,979 full time, 2,042 part time; 40% male, 60% female; 1% American Indian, 2% Asian, 36% black, 5% Hispanic, 3% multiracial, 0% Pacific Islander, 52% white, 1% international; 83% from in state; 19% live on campus; 4% of students in fraternities, 4% in sororities
Most popular majors: Information not available
Expenses: 2014-2015: $6,898 in state, $19,794 out of state; room/board: $9,684
Financial aid: (706) 568-2036; 72% of undergrads determined to have financial need; average aid package $9,124

Covenant College
Lookout Mountain GA
(706) 820-2398
U.S. News ranking: Reg. Coll. (S), No. 6
Website: www.covenant.edu
Admissions email: admissions@covenant.edu
Private; founded 1955
Affiliation: Presbyterian Church in America
Freshman admissions: more selective; 2013-2014: 1,109 applied, 629 accepted. Either SAT or ACT required. SAT 25/75 percentile: 1060-1280. High school rank: 24% in top tenth, 55% in top quarter, 88% in top half
Early decision deadline: N/A, notification date: N/A
Early action deadline: N/A, notification date: N/A
Application deadline (fall): rolling
Undergraduate student body: 1,050 full time, 54 part time; 44% male, 56% female; 1% American Indian, 2% Asian, 3% black, 2% Hispanic, 2% multiracial, 0% Pacific Islander, 88% white, 2% international; 24% from in state; 83% live on campus; 0% of students in fraternities, 0% in sororities
Most popular majors: 12% Business, Management, Marketing, and Related Support Services, 20% Education, 10% English Language and Literature/Letters, 10% Psychology, 11% Social Sciences
Expenses: 2014-2015: $30,160; room/board: $8,830
Financial aid: (706) 419-1126; 62% of undergrads determined to have financial need; average aid package $24,354

Dalton State College[1]
Dalton GA
(706) 272-4436
U.S. News ranking: Reg. Coll. (S), unranked
Website: www.daltonstate.edu/
Admissions email: N/A
Public
Application deadline (fall): N/A
Undergraduate student body: N/A full time, N/A part time
Expenses: 2013-2014: $3,910 in state, $11,768 out of state; room/board: $6,590
Financial aid: (706) 272-4545

Emmanuel College

Franklin Springs GA
(800) 860-8800
U.S. News ranking: Reg. Coll. (S),
No. 47
Website: www.ec.edu
Admissions email: admissions@
ec.edu
Private; founded 1919
Affiliation: International
Pentecostal Holiness
Freshman admissions: less
selective; 2013-2014: 876
applied, 419 accepted. Either
SAT or ACT required. SAT 25/75
percentile: 830-1030. High
school rank: N/A
Early decision deadline: N/A,
notification date: N/A
Early action deadline: N/A,
notification date: N/A
Application deadline (fall): 8/1
Undergraduate student body: 702
full time, 104 part time; 49%
male, 51% female; 0% American
Indian, 1% Asian, 19% black,
4% Hispanic, 2% multiracial,
0% Pacific Islander, 68% white,
5% international; 76% from in
state; 59% live on campus; 0%
of students in fraternities, 0% in
sororities
Most popular majors: 8% Biological
and Biomedical Sciences, 18%
Health and Physical Education/
Fitness, 19% Teacher Education
and Professional Development,
Specific Levels and Methods, 17%
Theology and Religious Vocations
Expenses: 2014-2015: $18,170;
room/board: $7,200
Financial aid: (706) 245-2843;
80% of undergrads determined to
have financial need; average aid
package $15,077

Emory University

Atlanta GA
(404) 727-6036
U.S. News ranking: Nat. U., No. 21
Website: www.emory.edu
Admissions email: admission@
emory.edu
Private; founded 1836
Affiliation: Methodist
Freshman admissions: most
selective; 2013-2014: 17,681
applied, 4,685 accepted. Either
SAT or ACT required. SAT 25/75
percentile: 1260-1470. High
school rank: 76% in top tenth,
95% in top quarter, 99% in
top half
Early decision deadline: 11/1,
notification date: 12/15
Early action deadline: N/A,
notification date: N/A
Application deadline (fall): 1/15
Undergraduate student body: 7,676
full time, 160 part time; 43%
male, 57% female; 0% American
Indian, 22% Asian, 9% black,
6% Hispanic, 3% multiracial,
0% Pacific Islander, 40% white,
15% international; 27% from in
state; 67% live on campus; 30%
of students in fraternities, 31%
in sororities
Most popular majors: 9% Biology/
Biological Sciences, General,
14% Business Administration
and Management, General,
9% Economics, General, 6%
Psychology, General, 6%
Registered Nursing/Registered
Nurse
Expenses: 2014-2015: $45,008;
room/board: $12,760

Financial aid: (404) 727-6039;
48% of undergrads determined to
have financial need; average aid
package $38,978

Fort Valley State University

Fort Valley GA
(478) 825-6307
U.S. News ranking: Reg. Coll. (S),
No. 71
Website: www.fvsu.edu
Admissions email: admissap@
mail.fvsu.edu
Public; founded 1895
Freshman admissions: less
selective; 2013-2014: 3,465
applied, 1,069 accepted. Either
SAT or ACT required. ACT 25/75
percentile: 15-18. High school
rank: 5% in top tenth, 23% in top
quarter, 47% in top half
Early decision deadline: N/A,
notification date: N/A
Early action deadline: N/A,
notification date: N/A
Application deadline (fall): 7/19
Undergraduate student body: 2,570
full time, 288 part time; 43%
male, 57% female; 0% American
Indian, 0% Asian, 97% black,
0% Hispanic, 0% multiracial,
0% Pacific Islander, 2% white,
0% international; 98% from in
state; 43% live on campus; N/A
of students in fraternities, N/A in
sororities
Most popular majors: 19%
Biology, General, 14% Business
Administration, Management and
Operations, 14% Criminal Justice
and Corrections, 9% Human
Development, Family Studies,
and Related Services, 19%
Psychology, General
Expenses: 2014-2015: $6,448 in
state, $19,364 out of state; room/
board: $7,920
Financial aid: (478) 825-6351;
93% of undergrads determined to
have financial need; average aid
package $14,962

Georgia College & State University

Milledgeville GA
(478) 445-1283
U.S. News ranking: Reg. U. (S),
No. 28
Website: www.gcsu.edu
Admissions email: info@gcsu.edu
Public; founded 1889
Freshman admissions: selective;
2013-2014: 4,051 applied,
2,754 accepted. Either SAT
or ACT required. SAT 25/75
percentile: 1050-1230. High
school rank: N/A
Early decision deadline: N/A,
notification date: N/A
Early action deadline: 11/1,
notification date: 12/15
Application deadline (fall): 4/1
Undergraduate student body: 5,264
full time, 465 part time; 40%
male, 60% female; 0% American
Indian, 1% Asian, 5% black,
5% Hispanic, 2% multiracial,
0% Pacific Islander, 85% white,
1% international; 99% from in
state; 35% live on campus; 3%
of students in fraternities, 15%
in sororities
Most popular majors: 11%
Business Administration and
Management, General, 7%
Community Health and Preventive

Medicine, 6% Marketing/
Marketing Management, General,
9% Psychology, General, 10%
Registered Nursing/Registered
Nurse
Expenses: 2014-2015: $8,960 in
state, $27,308 out of state; room/
board: $9,940
Financial aid: (478) 445-5149;
56% of undergrads determined to
have financial need; average aid
package $9,398

Georgia Gwinnett College

Lawrenceville GA
(877) 704-4422
U.S. News ranking: Reg. Coll. (S),
second tier
Website: www.ggc.edu
Admissions email: N/A
Public; founded 2005
Freshman admissions: less
selective; 2013-2014: 3,454
applied, 3,111 accepted. Neither
SAT nor ACT required. SAT 25/75
percentile: 820-1055. High
school rank: 4% in top tenth, 15%
in top quarter, 42% in top half
Early decision deadline: N/A,
notification date: N/A
Early action deadline: N/A,
notification date: N/A
Application deadline (fall): 6/1
Undergraduate student body: 6,832
full time, 2,887 part time; 46%
male, 54% female; 0% American
Indian, 8% Asian, 36% black,
17% Hispanic, 4% multiracial,
0% Pacific Islander, 33% white,
1% international; 99% from in
state; 7% live on campus; N/A
of students in fraternities, N/A in
sororities
Most popular majors: 14%
Biological and Biomedical
Sciences, 38% Business,
Management, Marketing, and
Related Support Services, 6%
Computer and Information
Sciences and Support Services,
14% Education, 10% Psychology
Expenses: 2014-2015: $5,352 in
state, $15,048 out of state; room/
board: $11,890
Financial aid: N/A; 78% of
undergrads determined to have
financial need; average aid
package $7,613

Georgia Institute of Technology

Atlanta GA
(404) 894-4154
U.S. News ranking: Nat. U.,
No. 35
Website: admission.gatech.edu/
information/
Admissions email: admission@
gatech.edu
Public; founded 1885
Freshman admissions: most
selective; 2013-2014: 17,669
applied, 7,265 accepted. Either
SAT or ACT required. SAT 25/75
percentile: 1290-1480. High
school rank: 81% in top tenth,
95% in top quarter, 99% in
top half
Early decision deadline: N/A,
notification date: N/A
Early action deadline: 10/21,
notification date: 1/4
Application deadline (fall): 1/10
Undergraduate student body:
13,291 full time, 1,267 part
time; 67% male, 33% female; 0%
American Indian, 17% Asian,

6% black, 7% Hispanic, 3%
multiracial, 0% Pacific Islander,
55% white, 10% international;
71% from in state; 52% live
on campus; 23% of students in
fraternities, 29% in sororities
Most popular majors: 6% Biological
and Biomedical Sciences,
14% Business, Management,
Marketing, and Related Support
Services, 7% Computer and
Information Sciences and Support
Services, 58% Engineering, 3%
Multi/Interdisciplinary Studies
Expenses: 2014-2015: $11,394
in state, $30,698 out of state;
room/board: $12,840
Financial aid: (404) 894-4582;
45% of undergrads determined to
have financial need; average aid
package $11,347

Georgia Southern University

Statesboro GA
(912) 478-5391
U.S. News ranking: Nat. U.,
second tier
Website:
www.georgiasouthern.edu/
Admissions email: admissions@
georgiasouthern.edu
Public; founded 1906
Freshman admissions: selective;
2013-2014: 10,134 applied,
5,759 accepted. Either SAT
or ACT required. SAT 25/75
percentile: 1040-1180. High
school rank: 19% in top tenth,
45% in top quarter, 76% in
top half
Early decision deadline: N/A,
notification date: N/A
Early action deadline: N/A,
notification date: N/A
Application deadline (fall): 5/1
Undergraduate student body:
15,762 full time, 2,142 part
time; 50% male, 50% female;
0% American Indian, 1% Asian,
26% black, 4% Hispanic, 2%
multiracial, 0% Pacific Islander,
63% white, 1% international;
96% from in state; 29% live
on campus; 12% of students in
fraternities, 15% in sororities
Most popular majors: 20%
Business, Management,
Marketing, and Related Support
Services, 8% Education, 7%
Health Professions and Related
Programs, 8% Liberal Arts
and Sciences, General Studies
and Humanities, 7% Parks,
Recreation, Leisure, and Fitness
Studies
Expenses: 2014-2015: $7,190 in
state, $20,086 out of state; room/
board: $9,752
Financial aid: (912) 681-5413;
69% of undergrads determined to
have financial need; average aid
package $9,393

Georgia Southwestern State University

Americus GA
(229) 928-1273
U.S. News ranking: Reg. U. (S),
second tier
Website: www.gsw.edu
Admissions email: admissions@
gsw.edu
Public; founded 1906
Freshman admissions: selective;
2013-2014: 1,245 applied, 847
accepted. Either SAT or ACT
required. SAT 25/75 percentile:

860-1050. High school rank:
16% in top tenth, 36% in top
quarter, 68% in top half
Early decision deadline: 12/15,
notification date: 1/15
Early action deadline: N/A,
notification date: N/A
Application deadline (fall): 7/21
Undergraduate student body: 1,870
full time, 797 part time; 36%
male, 64% female; 0% American
Indian, 1% Asian, 30% black,
3% Hispanic, 1% multiracial,
0% Pacific Islander, 61% white,
2% international; 99% from in
state; 28% live on campus; 8%
of students in fraternities, 8% in
sororities
Most popular majors: 14%
Accounting, 20% Business
Administration and Management,
General, 9% Elementary
Education and Teaching, 8%
Psychology, General, 18%
Registered Nursing/Registered
Nurse
Expenses: 2014-2015: $6,106 in
state, $18,612 out of state; room/
board: $7,140
Financial aid: (229) 928-1378;
77% of undergrads determined to
have financial need; average aid
package $8,929

Georgia State University

Atlanta GA
(404) 413-2500
U.S. News ranking: Nat. U.,
second tier
Website: www.gsu.edu
Admissions email: admissions@
gsu.edu
Public; founded 1913
Freshman admissions: selective;
2013-2014: 13,489 applied,
7,269 accepted. Either SAT
or ACT required. SAT 25/75
percentile: 960-1170. High
school rank: N/A
Early decision deadline: N/A,
notification date: N/A
Early action deadline: 11/15,
notification date: 1/30
Application deadline (fall): 3/1
Undergraduate student body:
18,429 full time, 6,436 part
time; 42% male, 58% female;
0% American Indian, 11% Asian,
40% black, 9% Hispanic, 4%
multiracial, 0% Pacific Islander,
31% white, 2% international;
97% from in state; 17% live
on campus; N/A of students in
fraternities, N/A in sororities
Most popular majors: 27%
Business, Management,
Marketing, and Related Support
Services, 8% Education, 9%
Psychology, 12% Social Sciences,
7% Visual and Performing Arts
Expenses: 2014-2015: $10,240
in state, $28,450 out of state;
room/board: $13,342
Financial aid: (404) 651-2227;
78% of undergrads determined to
have financial need; average aid
package $9,292

Gordon State College[1]

Barnesville GA
(678) 359-5021
U.S. News ranking: Reg. Coll. (S),
second tier
Website: www.gordonstate.edu/
Admissions email: N/A
Public
Application deadline (fall): N/A

Undergraduate student body: N/A full time, N/A part time
Expenses: 2013-2014: $3,408 in state, $9,695 out of state; room/board: $6,357
Financial aid: N/A

Kennesaw State University

Kennesaw GA
(770) 423-6300
U.S. News ranking: Reg. U. (S), No. 70
Website: www.kennesaw.edu
Admissions email: ksuadmit@kennesaw.edu
Public; founded 1963
Freshman admissions: selective; 2013-2014: 10,058 applied, 5,572 accepted. Either SAT or ACT required. SAT 25/75 percentile: 990-1170. High school rank: 21% in top tenth, 53% in top quarter, 81% in top half
Early decision deadline: N/A, notification date: N/A
Early action deadline: N/A, notification date: N/A
Application deadline (fall): 5/9
Undergraduate student body: 16,869 full time, 5,752 part time; 42% male, 58% female; 0% American Indian, 3% Asian, 17% black, 7% Hispanic, 4% multiracial, 0% Pacific Islander, 62% white, 2% international; 94% from in state; 14% live on campus; 4% of students in fraternities, 5% in sororities
Most popular majors: 23% Business, Management, Marketing, and Related Support Services, 8% Communication, Journalism, and Related Programs, 15% Education, 5% Health Professions and Related Programs, 8% Social Sciences
Expenses: 2014-2015: $6,932 in state, $19,828 out of state; room/board: $6,014
Financial aid: (770) 423-6074; 70% of undergrads determined to have financial need; average aid package $7,590

LaGrange College

LaGrange GA
(706) 880-8005
U.S. News ranking: Reg. Coll. (S), No. 13
Website: www.lagrange.edu
Admissions email: admission@lagrange.edu
Private; founded 1831
Affiliation: United Methodist
Freshman admissions: selective; 2013-2014: 1,664 applied, 966 accepted. Either SAT or ACT required. SAT 25/75 percentile: 910-1090. High school rank: 16% in top tenth, 36% in top quarter, 69% in top half
Early decision deadline: N/A, notification date: N/A
Early action deadline: N/A, notification date: N/A
Application deadline (fall): rolling
Undergraduate student body: 786 full time, 70 part time; 46% male, 54% female; 1% American Indian, 1% Asian, 23% black, 2% Hispanic, 2% multiracial, 0% Pacific Islander, 70% white, 1% international; 85% from in state; 56% live on campus; 22% of students in fraternities, 28% in sororities

Most popular majors: 10% Biology/Biological Sciences, General, 8% Business Administration and Management, General, 9% Psychology, General, 19% Registered Nursing/Registered Nurse, 8% Visual and Performing Arts, General
Expenses: 2014-2015: $26,590; room/board: $11,050
Financial aid: (706) 880-8229; 87% of undergrads determined to have financial need; average aid package $23,456

Life University

Marietta GA
(770) 426-2884
U.S. News ranking: Nat. Lib. Arts, second tier
Website: www.life.edu
Admissions email: admissions@life.edu
Private; founded 1974
Freshman admissions: selective; 2013-2014: 269 applied, 110 accepted. Either SAT or ACT required. Average composite ACT score: 19. High school rank: N/A
Early decision deadline: N/A, notification date: N/A
Early action deadline: N/A, notification date: N/A
Application deadline (fall): 9/1
Undergraduate student body: 556 full time, 255 part time; 52% male, 48% female; 1% American Indian, 2% Asian, 25% black, 8% Hispanic, 0% multiracial, 0% Pacific Islander, 33% white, 3% international
Most popular majors: 28% Biology/Biological Sciences, General, 11% Business Administration and Management, General, 9% Dietetics/Dietitian, 19% Kinesiology and Exercise Science, 11% Psychology, General
Expenses: 2013-2014: $9,747; room/board: N/A
Financial aid: (770) 426-2901; 82% of undergrads determined to have financial need; average aid package $10,600

Mercer University

Macon GA
(478) 301-2650
U.S. News ranking: Reg. U. (S), No. 8
Website: www.mercer.edu
Admissions email: admissions@mercer.edu
Private; founded 1833
Freshman admissions: more selective; 2013-2014: 3,864 applied, 2,666 accepted. Either SAT or ACT required. SAT 25/75 percentile: 1080-1270. High school rank: 41% in top tenth, 72% in top quarter, 92% in top half
Early decision deadline: N/A, notification date: N/A
Early action deadline: 11/1, notification date: 11/15
Application deadline (fall): 7/1
Undergraduate student body: 3,659 full time, 760 part time; 37% male, 63% female; 0% American Indian, 5% Asian, 33% black, 4% Hispanic, 2% multiracial, 0% Pacific Islander, 47% white, 3% international; 83% from in state; 72% live on campus; 24% of students in fraternities, 24% in sororities

Most popular majors: 12% Biological and Biomedical Sciences, 18% Business, Management, Marketing, and Related Support Services, 10% Engineering, 10% Psychology, 9% Social Sciences
Expenses: 2014-2015: $33,780; room/board: $11,271
Financial aid: (478) 301-2670; 73% of undergrads determined to have financial need; average aid package $32,951

Middle Georgia State College[1]

Macon GA
(800) 272-7619
U.S. News ranking: Reg. Coll. (S), second tier
Website: www.mga.edu
Admissions email: N/A
Public
Application deadline (fall): rolling
Undergraduate student body: N/A full time, N/A part time
Expenses: 2013-2014: $3,326 in state, $9,613 out of state; room/board: $8,270
Financial aid: (800) 272-7619

Morehouse College

Atlanta GA
(404) 215-2632
U.S. News ranking: Nat. Lib. Arts, No. 133
Website: www.morehouse.edu
Admissions email: admissions@morehouse.edu
Private; founded 1867
Freshman admissions: selective; 2013-2014: 2,689 applied, 1,797 accepted. Either SAT or ACT required. SAT 25/75 percentile: 900-1110. High school rank: 21% in top tenth, 41% in top quarter, 73% in top half
Early decision deadline: 11/1, notification date: 12/15
Early action deadline: 11/1, notification date: 12/15
Application deadline (fall): 2/15
Undergraduate student body: 2,017 full time, 172 part time; 100% male, 0% female; 0% American Indian, 0% Asian, 95% black, 0% Hispanic, 0% multiracial, 0% Pacific Islander, 0% white, 2% international; 32% from in state; 66% live on campus; 19% of students in fraternities, N/A in sororities
Most popular majors: 9% Biology/Biological Sciences, General, 23% Business Administration and Management, General, 8% Kinesiology and Exercise Science, 11% Political Science and Government, General, 7% Psychology, General
Expenses: 2014-2015: $26,090; room/board: $13,322
Financial aid: (404) 681-2800; 84% of undergrads determined to have financial need; average aid package $19,258

Oglethorpe University

Atlanta GA
(404) 364-8307
U.S. News ranking: Nat. Lib. Arts, No. 148
Website: www.oglethorpe.edu
Admissions email: admission@oglethorpe.edu
Private; founded 1835

Freshman admissions: selective; 2013-2014: 4,403 applied, 2,455 accepted. Either SAT or ACT required. SAT 25/75 percentile: 1030-1240. High school rank: 20% in top tenth, 55% in top quarter, 86% in top half
Early decision deadline: N/A, notification date: N/A
Early action deadline: 11/15, notification date: 12/5
Application deadline (fall): rolling
Undergraduate student body: 992 full time, 81 part time; 43% male, 57% female; 0% American Indian, 4% Asian, 18% black, 10% Hispanic, 2% multiracial, 0% Pacific Islander, 35% white, 5% international; 69% from in state; 58% live on campus; 12% of students in fraternities, 13% in sororities
Most popular majors: 18% Business, Management, Marketing, and Related Support Services, 26% English Language and Literature/Letters, 14% Social Sciences, 11% Visual and Performing Arts
Expenses: 2014-2015: $32,500; room/board: $11,700
Financial aid: (404) 364-8356; 71% of undergrads determined to have financial need; average aid package $25,722

Paine College

Augusta GA
(706) 821-8320
U.S. News ranking: Reg. Coll. (S), second tier
Website: www.paine.edu
Admissions email: admissions@paine.edu
Private; founded 1882
Affiliation: Christian Methodist Episcopal and United Methodist Churches
Freshman admissions: less selective; 2013-2014: 2,771 applied, 1,213 accepted. Either SAT or ACT required. ACT 25/75 percentile: 14-18. High school rank: 5% in top tenth, 15% in top quarter, 42% in top half
Early decision deadline: N/A, notification date: N/A
Early action deadline: N/A, notification date: N/A
Application deadline (fall): 7/15
Undergraduate student body: 838 full time, 86 part time; 51% male, 49% female; 0% American Indian, 0% Asian, 91% black, 2% Hispanic, 1% multiracial, 0% Pacific Islander, 2% white, 1% international; 71% from in state; 53% live on campus; 9% of students in fraternities, 3% in sororities
Most popular majors: 23% Business Administration and Management, General, 10% Communication, General, 8% History, General, 11% Psychology, General, 18% Sociology
Expenses: 2013-2014: $13,332; room/board: $6,494
Financial aid: (706) 821-8262

Piedmont College

Demorest GA
(800) 277-7020
U.S. News ranking: Reg. U. (S), No. 70
Website: www.piedmont.edu
Admissions email: ugrad@piedmont.edu
Private; founded 1897

Affiliation: Nat. Assoc. of Congreg. Christ. Churches & United Church of Christ
Freshman admissions: selective; 2013-2014: 920 applied, 553 accepted. Either SAT or ACT required. SAT 25/75 percentile: 920-1150. High school rank: 22% in top tenth, 47% in top quarter, 83% in top half
Early decision deadline: N/A, notification date: N/A
Early action deadline: N/A, notification date: N/A
Application deadline (fall): 7/1
Undergraduate student body: 1,131 full time, 150 part time; 35% male, 65% female; 1% American Indian, 1% Asian, 9% black, 3% Hispanic, 2% multiracial, 0% Pacific Islander, 78% white, 0% international; 92% from in state; 45% live on campus; 0% of students in fraternities, 0% in sororities
Most popular majors: 21% Business, Management, Marketing, and Related Support Services, 24% Education, General, 15% Health Professions and Related Programs, 22% Social Sciences, 7% Visual and Performing Arts
Expenses: 2014-2015: $21,350; room/board: $8,786
Financial aid: (706) 776-0114; 84% of undergrads determined to have financial need; average aid package $17,457

Point University

West Point GA
(706) 385-1202
U.S. News ranking: Reg. Coll. (S), No. 74
Website: www.point.edu
Admissions email: admissions@point.edu
Private; founded 1937
Affiliation: Christian Churches/Churches of Christ
Freshman admissions: selective; 2013-2014: 934 applied, 500 accepted. Either SAT or ACT required. ACT 25/75 percentile: 18-22. High school rank: 12% in top tenth, 34% in top quarter, 66% in top half
Early decision deadline: N/A, notification date: N/A
Early action deadline: N/A, notification date: N/A
Application deadline (fall): 8/5
Undergraduate student body: 1,293 full time, 146 part time; 44% male, 56% female; 0% American Indian, 0% Asian, 41% black, 4% Hispanic, 3% multiracial, 0% Pacific Islander, 36% white, 1% international; 74% from in state; 77% live on campus; N/A of students in fraternities, N/A in sororities
Most popular majors: 5% Biological and Biomedical Sciences, 15% Business, Management, Marketing, and Related Support Services, 10% Education, 25% Philosophy and Religious Studies, 35% Social Sciences
Expenses: 2014-2015: $17,650; room/board: $6,350
Financial aid: (800) 766-1222; 79% of undergrads determined to have financial need; average aid package $20,000

Reinhardt University
Waleska GA
(770) 720-5526
U.S. News ranking: Reg. Coll. (S), No. 64
Website: www.reinhardt.edu/
Admissions email: admissions@reinhardt.edu
Private
Affiliation: United Methodist
Freshman admissions: less selective; 2013-2014: 1,731 applied, 1,032 accepted. Either SAT or ACT required. SAT 25/75 percentile: 860-1120. High school rank: 8% in top tenth, 30% in top quarter, 61% in top half
Early decision deadline: N/A, notification date: N/A
Early action deadline: N/A, notification date: N/A
Application deadline (fall): 8/15
Undergraduate student body: 1,148 full time, 76 part time; 50% male, 50% female; N/A American Indian, N/A Asian, N/A black, N/A Hispanic, N/A multiracial, N/A Pacific Islander, N/A white, N/A international
Most popular majors: 11% Business/Commerce, General, 18% Elementary Education and Teaching, 8% Music Teacher Education, 8% Music, General, 19% Organizational Leadership
Expenses: 2014-2015: $19,166; room/board: $7,276
Financial aid: (770) 720-5667; 80% of undergrads determined to have financial need; average aid package $13,546

Savannah College of Art and Design
Savannah GA
(912) 525-5100
U.S. News ranking: Arts, unranked
Website: www.scad.edu
Admissions email: admission@scad.edu
Private; founded 1978
Freshman admissions: N/A; 2013-2014: 8,626 applied, 5,611 accepted. Either SAT or ACT required. SAT 25/75 percentile: N/A. High school rank: 16% in top tenth, 42% in top quarter, 76% in top half
Early decision deadline: N/A, notification date: N/A
Early action deadline: N/A, notification date: N/A
Application deadline (fall): rolling
Undergraduate student body: 7,739 full time, 1,593 part time; 36% male, 64% female; 1% American Indian, 7% Asian, 10% black, 8% Hispanic, 0% multiracial, 0% Pacific Islander, 54% white, 12% international; 23% from in state; 41% live on campus; N/A of students in fraternities, N/A in sororities
Most popular majors: 10% Animation, Interactive Technology, Video Graphics and Special Effects, 7% Cinematography and Film/Video Production, 6% Fashion/Apparel Design, 9% Graphic Design, 12% Illustration
Expenses: 2014-2015: $34,295; room/board: $13,710
Financial aid: (912) 525-6104; 56% of undergrads determined to have financial need; average aid package $26,987

Savannah State University
Savannah GA
(912) 356-2181
U.S. News ranking: Nat. Lib. Arts, second tier
Website: www.savannahstate.edu
Admissions email: admissions@savannahstate.edu
Public; founded 1890
Freshman admissions: less selective; 2013-2014: 2,786 applied, 2,309 accepted. Either SAT or ACT required. SAT 25/75 percentile: 770-910. High school rank: N/A
Early decision deadline: N/A, notification date: N/A
Early action deadline: N/A, notification date: N/A
Application deadline (fall): 8/1
Undergraduate student body: 4,098 full time, 504 part time; 45% male, 55% female; 0% American Indian, 0% Asian, 89% black, 2% Hispanic, 3% multiracial, 0% Pacific Islander, 4% white, 0% international; 92% from in state; 55% live on campus; N/A of students in fraternities, N/A in sororities
Most popular majors: 7% Biological and Biomedical Sciences, 9% Business, Management, Marketing, and Related Support Services, 7% Homeland Security, Law Enforcement, Firefighting and Related Protective Services, 6% Psychology, 7% Public Administration and Social Service Professions
Expenses: 2013-2014: $5,415 in state, $15,176 out of state; room/board: $7,154
Financial aid: (912) 356-2253

Shorter University[1]
Rome GA
(800) 868-6980
U.S. News ranking: Nat. Lib. Arts, second tier
Website: www.shorter.edu
Admissions email: admissions@shorter.edu
Private
Application deadline (fall): N/A
Undergraduate student body: N/A full time, N/A part time
Expenses: 2013-2014: $19,670; room/board: $10,200
Financial aid: (706) 233-7227

Southern Polytechnic State University
Marietta GA
(678) 915-4188
U.S. News ranking: Reg. U. (S), No. 85
Website: www.spsu.edu/
Admissions email: admiss@spsu.edu
Public; founded 1948
Freshman admissions: selective; 2013-2014: N/A applied, N/A accepted. Either SAT or ACT required. ACT 25/75 percentile: 21-26. High school rank: N/A
Early decision deadline: N/A, notification date: N/A
Early action deadline: N/A, notification date: N/A
Application deadline (fall): 7/1
Undergraduate student body: 4,142 full time, 1,590 part time; 81% male, 19% female; 0% American Indian, 7% Asian, 18% black, 8% Hispanic, 4% multiracial, 0% Pacific Islander, 57% white, 3% international

Most popular majors: Information not available
Expenses: 2013-2014: $6,810 in state, $20,594 out of state; room/board: $7,650
Financial aid: (678) 915-7290

South University[1]
Savannah GA
(912) 201-8000
U.S. News ranking: Reg. U. (S), second tier
Website: www.southuniversity.edu
Admissions email: cshall@southuniversity.edu
Private
Application deadline (fall): N/A
Undergraduate student body: N/A full time, N/A part time
Expenses: 2013-2014: $16,360; room/board: $9,105
Financial aid: (912) 201-8000

Spelman College
Atlanta GA
(800) 982-2411
U.S. News ranking: Nat. Lib. Arts, No. 81
Website: www.spelman.edu
Admissions email: admiss@spelman.edu
Private; founded 1881
Freshman admissions: selective; 2013-2014: 5,701 applied, 2,325 accepted. Either SAT or ACT required. SAT 25/75 percentile: 850-1215. High school rank: 31% in top tenth, 66% in top quarter, 90% in top half
Early decision deadline: 11/1, notification date: 12/15
Early action deadline: 11/15, notification date: 12/31
Application deadline (fall): 2/1
Undergraduate student body: 2,061 full time, 68 part time; 0% male, 100% female; 0% American Indian, 0% Asian, 84% black, 0% Hispanic, 3% multiracial, 0% Pacific Islander, 0% white, 1% international; 27% from in state; 71% live on campus; 0% of students in fraternities, 10% in sororities
Most popular majors: 13% Biology/Biological Sciences, General, 6% Economics, General, 9% English Language and Literature, General, 12% Political Science and Government, General, 24% Psychology, General
Expenses: 2014-2015: $25,496; room/board: $11,945
Financial aid: (404) 270-5212; 84% of undergrads determined to have financial need; average aid package $18,184

Thomas University
Thomasville GA
(229) 227-6934
U.S. News ranking: Reg. Coll. (S), second tier
Website: www.thomasu.edu
Admissions email: rgagliano@thomasu.edu
Private; founded 1950
Freshman admissions: less selective; 2013-2014: 153 applied, 105 accepted. Neither SAT nor ACT required. SAT 25/75 percentile: 810-1060. High school rank: N/A
Early decision deadline: N/A, notification date: N/A
Early action deadline: N/A, notification date: N/A
Application deadline (fall): rolling

Undergraduate student body: 506 full time, 380 part time; 46% male, 54% female; 0% American Indian, 1% Asian, 25% black, 5% Hispanic, 0% multiracial, 0% Pacific Islander, 52% white, 4% international
Most popular majors: 14% Business Administration and Management, General, 15% Criminal Justice/Law Enforcement Administration, 21% Registered Nursing, Nursing Administration, Nursing Research and Clinical Nursing, Other, 10% Social Work, 12% Vocational Rehabilitation Counseling/Counselor
Expenses: 2014-2015: $15,750; room/board: $5,050
Financial aid: (229) 227-6925

Toccoa Falls College
Toccoa Falls GA
(888) 785-5624
U.S. News ranking: Reg. Coll. (S), No. 35
Website: www.tfc.edu
Admissions email: admissions@tfc.edu
Private; founded 1907
Affiliation: Christian and Missionary Alliance
Freshman admissions: selective; 2013-2014: 1,128 applied, 609 accepted. Neither SAT nor ACT required. SAT 25/75 percentile: 880-1130. High school rank: 18% in top tenth, 44% in top quarter, 75% in top half
Early decision deadline: N/A, notification date: N/A
Early action deadline: N/A, notification date: N/A
Application deadline (fall): rolling
Undergraduate student body: 777 full time, 93 part time; 47% male, 53% female; 1% American Indian, 8% Asian, 6% black, 2% Hispanic, 0% multiracial, 0% Pacific Islander, 81% white, 1% international; 61% from in state; 69% live on campus; 0% of students in fraternities, 0% in sororities
Most popular majors: 7% Bible/Biblical Studies, 6% Business Administration and Management, General, 21% Counseling Psychology, 14% Missions/Missionary Studies and Missiology, 6% Youth Ministry
Expenses: 2014-2015: $19,700; room/board: $7,020
Financial aid: (706) 886-6831; 88% of undergrads determined to have financial need; average aid package $15,725

Truett McConnell College
Cleveland GA
(706) 865-2134
U.S. News ranking: Reg. Coll. (S), second tier
Website: www.truett.edu
Admissions email: admissions@truett.edu
Private; founded 1946
Affiliation: Southern Baptist
Freshman admissions: less selective; 2013-2014: 470 applied, 379 accepted. Either SAT or ACT required. SAT 25/75 percentile: 840-1050. High school rank: 11% in top tenth, 32% in top quarter, 62% in top half
Early decision deadline: N/A, notification date: N/A

Early action deadline: N/A, notification date: N/A
Application deadline (fall): 8/1
Undergraduate student body: 691 full time, 915 part time; 43% male, 57% female; 0% American Indian, 0% Asian, 7% black, 4% Hispanic, 0% multiracial, 0% Pacific Islander, 82% white, 3% international; 93% from in state; 68% live on campus; N/A of students in fraternities, N/A in sororities
Most popular majors: 17% Business, Management, Marketing, and Related Support Services, 16% Education, 29% Philosophy and Religious Studies, 9% Psychology, 7% Visual and Performing Arts
Expenses: 2014-2015: $17,300; room/board: $6,820
Financial aid: (800) 226-8621; 84% of undergrads determined to have financial need; average aid package $13,444

University of Georgia
Athens GA
(706) 542-8776
U.S. News ranking: Nat. U., No. 62
Website: www.admissions.uga.edu
Admissions email: adm-info@uga.edu
Public; founded 1785
Freshman admissions: more selective; 2013-2014: 20,045 applied, 10,962 accepted. Either SAT or ACT required. SAT 25/75 percentile: 1150-1330. High school rank: 53% in top tenth, 91% in top quarter, 99% in top half
Early decision deadline: N/A, notification date: N/A
Early action deadline: 10/15, notification date: 12/1
Application deadline (fall): 1/15
Undergraduate student body: 24,746 full time, 1,532 part time; 43% male, 57% female; 0% American Indian, 9% Asian, 7% black, 5% Hispanic, 3% multiracial, 0% Pacific Islander, 73% white, 1% international; 92% from in state; 28% live on campus; 22% of students in fraternities, 29% in sororities
Most popular majors: 6% Biology/Biological Sciences, General, 5% Finance, General, 3% International Relations and Affairs, 4% Marketing/Marketing Management, General, 7% Psychology, General
Expenses: 2014-2015: $10,836 in state, $29,046 out of state; room/board: $9,246
Financial aid: (706) 542-6147; 40% of undergrads determined to have financial need; average aid package $11,169

University of North Georgia
Dahlonega GA
(706) 864-1800
U.S. News ranking: Reg. U. (S), No. 60
Website: ung.edu/
Admissions email: bacheloradmissions@ung.edu
Public; founded 1873
Freshman admissions: more selective; 2013-2014: 3,711 applied, 2,236 accepted. Either

SAT or ACT required. SAT 25/75 percentile: 1010-1190. High school rank: 28% in top tenth, 70% in top quarter, 97% in top half
Early decision deadline: N/A, notification date: N/A
Early action deadline: N/A, notification date: N/A
Application deadline (fall): 7/1
Undergraduate student body: 10,022 full time, 4,829 part time; 44% male, 56% female; 0% American Indian, 3% Asian, 4% black, 9% Hispanic, 1% multiracial, 0% Pacific Islander, 62% white, 1% international; 97% from in state; 17% live on campus; 2% of students in fraternities, 3% in sororities
Most popular majors: 7% Business Administration and Management, General, 7% Criminal Justice/Safety Studies, 8% Early Childhood Education and Teaching, 6% Elementary Education and Teaching, 7% Special Education and Teaching, General
Expenses: 2014-2015: $6,816 in state, $19,712 out of state; room/board: $9,162
Financial aid: (706) 864-1412; 61% of undergrads determined to have financial need; average aid package $12,752

University of West Georgia

Carrollton GA
(678) 839-5600
U.S. News ranking: Reg. U. (S), No. 92
Website: www.westga.edu
Admissions email: admiss@westga.edu
Public; founded 1906
Freshman admissions: less selective; 2013-2014: 7,266 applied, 3,913 accepted. Either SAT or ACT required. SAT 25/75 percentile: 870-1030. High school rank: N/A
Early decision deadline: N/A, notification date: N/A
Early action deadline: N/A, notification date: N/A
Application deadline (fall): 6/1
Undergraduate student body: 8,369 full time, 1,590 part time; 37% male, 63% female; 0% American Indian, 1% Asian, 34% black, 4% Hispanic, 3% multiracial, 0% Pacific Islander, 53% white, 1% international; 97% from in state; 31% live on campus; 3% of students in fraternities, 4% in sororities
Most popular majors: 21% Business, Management, Marketing, and Related Support Services, 16% Education, 15% Health Professions and Related Programs, 6% Psychology, 14% Social Sciences
Expenses: 2014-2015: $6,956 in state, $19,852 out of state; room/board: $8,532
Financial aid: (678) 839-6421; 77% of undergrads determined to have financial need; average aid package $7,209

Valdosta State University

Valdosta GA
(229) 333-5791
U.S. News ranking: Reg. U. (S), No. 75
Website: www.valdosta.edu
Admissions email: admissions@valdosta.edu
Public; founded 1906
Freshman admissions: selective; 2013-2014: 5,701 applied, 3,148 accepted. Either SAT or ACT required. SAT 25/75 percentile: 950-1120. High school rank: N/A
Early decision deadline: N/A, notification date: N/A
Early action deadline: N/A, notification date: N/A
Application deadline (fall): 6/15
Undergraduate student body: 8,277 full time, 1,441 part time; 41% male, 59% female; 0% American Indian, 1% Asian, 36% black, 4% Hispanic, 3% multiracial, 0% Pacific Islander, 52% white, 2% international; 95% from in state; 33% live on campus; 4% of students in fraternities, 3% in sororities
Most popular majors: 21% Business, Management, Marketing, and Related Support Services, 15% Education, 8% English Language and Literature/Letters, 10% Health Professions and Related Programs, 6% Homeland Security, Law Enforcement, Firefighting and Related Protective Services
Expenses: 2014-2015: $7,162 in state, $20,058 out of state; room/board: $7,992
Financial aid: (229) 333-5935; 78% of undergrads determined to have financial need; average aid package $13,406

Wesleyan College

Macon GA
(800) 447-6610
U.S. News ranking: Nat. Lib. Arts, No. 133
Website: www.wesleyancollege.edu
Admissions email: admissions@wesleyancollege.edu
Private; founded 1836
Affiliation: United Methodist
Freshman admissions: selective; 2013-2014: 779 applied, 338 accepted. Either SAT or ACT required. SAT 25/75 percentile: 880-1130. High school rank: N/A
Early decision deadline: 11/15, notification date: 12/15
Early action deadline: 1/15, notification date: 3/15
Application deadline (fall): rolling
Undergraduate student body: 469 full time, 179 part time; 0% male, 100% female; 0% American Indian, 1% Asian, 29% black, 4% Hispanic, 3% multiracial, 0% Pacific Islander, 41% white, 21% international; 92% from in state; 85% live on campus; N/A of students in fraternities, N/A in sororities
Most popular majors: 9% Biology/Biological Sciences, General, 24% Business Administration, Management and Operations, Other, 8% Communication and Media Studies, 9% Psychology, General, 8% Social Sciences, General
Expenses: 2014-2015: $19,900; room/board: $8,800

HAWAII

Brigham Young University–Hawaii[1]

Laie Oahu HI
(808) 293-3738
U.S. News ranking: Reg. Coll. (W), No. 16
Website: www.byuh.edu
Admissions email: admissions@byuh.edu
Private
Application deadline (fall): N/A
Undergraduate student body: N/A full time, N/A part time
Expenses: 2013-2014: $4,770; room/board: $5,240
Financial aid: (808) 293-3530

Chaminade University of Honolulu

Honolulu HI
(808) 735-4735
U.S. News ranking: Reg. U. (W), second tier
Website: www.chaminade.edu
Admissions email: admissions@chaminade.edu
Private; founded 1955
Affiliation: Roman Catholic
Freshman admissions: less selective; 2013-2014: 914 applied, 764 accepted. Either SAT or ACT required. SAT 25/75 percentile: 870-1060. High school rank: 3% in top tenth, 6% in top quarter, 23% in top half
Early decision deadline: N/A, notification date: N/A
Early action deadline: N/A, notification date: N/A
Application deadline (fall): rolling
Undergraduate student body: 1,286 full time, 40 part time; 32% male, 68% female; 0% American Indian, 38% Asian, 3% black, 5% Hispanic, 18% multiracial, 15% Pacific Islander, 16% white, 2% international; 76% from in state; 27% live on campus; 0% of students in fraternities, 0% in sororities
Most popular majors: 11% Business Administration and Management, General, 21% Criminal Justice/Safety Studies, 6% Elementary Education and Teaching, 10% History, Other, 16% Psychology, General
Expenses: 2014-2015: $21,084; room/board: $11,640
Financial aid: (808) 735-4780; 71% of undergrads determined to have financial need; average aid package $17,742

Hawaii Pacific University

Honolulu HI
(808) 544-0238
U.S. News ranking: Reg. U. (W), No. 80
Website: www.hpu.edu
Admissions email: admissions@hpu.edu
Private; founded 1965
Freshman admissions: selective; 2013-2014: 4,206 applied, 2,697 accepted. Either SAT or ACT required. SAT 25/75

Financial aid: (888) 665-5723; 65% of undergrads determined to have financial need; average aid package $19,206

percentile: 870-1110. High school rank: 25% in top tenth, 53% in top quarter, 85% in top half
Early decision deadline: N/A, notification date: N/A
Early action deadline: N/A, notification date: N/A
Application deadline (fall): rolling
Undergraduate student body: 3,719 full time, 1,863 part time; 44% male, 56% female; 0% American Indian, 18% Asian, 5% black, 14% Hispanic, 19% multiracial, 3% Pacific Islander, 30% white, 7% international; 68% from in state; 4% live on campus; N/A of students in fraternities, N/A in sororities
Most popular majors: 23% Business, Management, Marketing, and Related Support Services, 8% Communication, Journalism, and Related Programs, 6% Computer and Information Sciences and Support Services, 23% Health Professions and Related Programs, 7% Psychology
Expenses: 2014-2015: $21,130; room/board: $13,330
Financial aid: (808) 544-0253; 53% of undergrads determined to have financial need; average aid package $16,906

University of Hawaii–Hilo

Hilo HI
(800) 897-4456
U.S. News ranking: Nat. Lib. Arts, second tier
Website: www.uhh.hawaii.edu
Admissions email: uhhadm@hawaii.edu
Public
Freshman admissions: less selective; 2013-2014: 1,676 applied, 1,257 accepted. Either SAT or ACT required. SAT 25/75 percentile: 823-1050. High school rank: 18% in top tenth, 53% in top quarter, 85% in top half
Early decision deadline: N/A, notification date: N/A
Early action deadline: N/A, notification date: N/A
Application deadline (fall): 7/1
Undergraduate student body: 2,766 full time, 691 part time; 41% male, 59% female; 1% American Indian, 19% Asian, 1% black, 2% Hispanic, 14% multiracial, 32% Pacific Islander, 26% white, 5% international; 69% from in state; N/A live on campus; N/A of students in fraternities, N/A in sororities
Most popular majors: 10% Biological and Biomedical Sciences, 9% Business, Management, Marketing, and Related Support Services, 11% Health Professions and Related Programs, 12% Psychology, 15% Social Sciences
Expenses: 2014-2015: $7,036 in state, $19,036 out of state; room/board: $9,382
Financial aid: (808) 974-7323; 65% of undergrads determined to have financial need; average aid package $12,761

University of Hawaii–Manoa

Honolulu HI
(808) 956-8975
U.S. News ranking: Nat. U., No. 168
Website: www.manoa.hawaii.edu/
Admissions email: ar-info@hawaii.edu
Public; founded 1907
Freshman admissions: selective; 2013-2014: 7,361 applied, 5,869 accepted. Either SAT or ACT required. SAT 25/75 percentile: 970-1200. High school rank: 27% in top tenth, 58% in top quarter, 89% in top half
Early decision deadline: N/A, notification date: N/A
Early action deadline: N/A, notification date: N/A
Application deadline (fall): 3/1
Undergraduate student body: 12,064 full time, 2,435 part time; 45% male, 55% female; 0% American Indian, 41% Asian, 1% black, 2% Hispanic, 15% multiracial, 17% Pacific Islander, 20% white, 2% international; 73% from in state; 23% live on campus; 1% of students in fraternities, 1% in sororities
Most popular majors: 19% Business, Management, Marketing, and Related Support Services, 7% Education, 6% Engineering, 6% Psychology, 12% Social Sciences
Expenses: 2014-2015: $10,620 in state, $29,412 out of state; room/board: $13,284
Financial aid: (808) 956-7251; 55% of undergrads determined to have financial need; average aid package $11,649

University of Hawaii–Maui College[1]

Kahului HI
(800) 479-6692
U.S. News ranking: Reg. Coll. (W), unranked
Website: maui.hawaii.edu/
Admissions email: N/A
Public
Application deadline (fall): N/A
Undergraduate student body: N/A full time, N/A part time
Expenses: 2013-2014: $2,670 in state, $7,422 out of state; room/board: N/A
Financial aid: (808) 984-3277

University of Hawaii–West Oahu[1]

Kapolei HI
(808) 689-2900
U.S. News ranking: Reg. Coll. (W), unranked
Website: www.uhwo.hawaii.edu
Admissions email: uhwo.admissions@hawaii.edu
Public; founded 1976
Application deadline (fall): 8/1
Undergraduate student body: N/A full time, N/A part time
Expenses: 2013-2014: $6,296 in state, $17,816 out of state; room/board: N/A
Financial aid: (808) 689-2900

IDAHO

Boise State University
Boise ID
(208) 426-1156
U.S. News ranking: Reg. U. (W), No. 63
Website: www.BoiseState.edu
Admissions email: bsuinfo@boisestate.edu
Public; founded 1932
Freshman admissions: selective; 2013-2014: 7,822 applied, 6,078 accepted. Either SAT or ACT required. SAT 25/75 percentile: 920-1150. High school rank: 14% in top tenth, 38% in top quarter, 74% in top half
Early decision deadline: N/A, notification date: N/A
Early action deadline: N/A, notification date: N/A
Application deadline (fall): 5/15
Undergraduate student body: 12,452 full time, 6,574 part time; 46% male, 54% female; 1% American Indian, 2% Asian, 2% black, 9% Hispanic, 3% multiracial, 0% Pacific Islander, 76% white, 4% international; 80% from in state; 6% live on campus; 2% of students in fraternities, 2% in sororities
Most popular majors: 5% Accounting, 5% Business/Commerce, General, 5% Psychology, General, 9% Registered Nursing/Registered Nurse, 7% Speech Communication and Rhetoric
Expenses: 2014-2015: $6,292 in state, $18,892 out of state; room/board: $7,540
Financial aid: (208) 426-1540; 59% of undergrads determined to have financial need; average aid package $10,072

Brigham Young University–Idaho[1]
Rexburg ID
(208) 496-1036
U.S. News ranking: Reg. Coll. (W), No. 11
Website: www.byui.edu
Admissions email: admissions@byui.edu
Private
Application deadline (fall): N/A
Undergraduate student body: N/A full time, N/A part time
Expenses: 2013-2014: $3,850; room/board: $4,000
Financial aid: (208) 496-1600

College of Idaho
Caldwell ID
(800) 224-3246
U.S. News ranking: Nat. Lib. Arts, No. 159
Website: www.collegeofidaho.edu
Admissions email: admission@collegeofidaho.edu
Private; founded 1891
Freshman admissions: more selective; 2013-2014: 1,302 applied, 889 accepted. Either SAT or ACT required. ACT 25/75 percentile: 21-27. High school rank: 26% in top tenth, 55% in top quarter, 87% in top half
Early decision deadline: N/A, notification date: N/A
Early action deadline: 11/15, notification date: 12/15
Application deadline (fall): 7/15

Undergraduate student body: 1,055 full time, 40 part time; 45% male, 55% female; 1% American Indian, 3% Asian, 1% black, 15% Hispanic, 1% multiracial, 0% Pacific Islander, 62% white, 8% international; 83% from in state; 65% live on campus; 18% of students in fraternities, 17% in sororities
Most popular majors: 9% Biological and Biomedical Sciences, 13% Business, Management, Marketing, and Related Support Services, 12% Psychology, 9% Social Sciences, 9% Visual and Performing Arts
Expenses: 2014-2015: $24,625; room/board: $8,764
Financial aid: (208) 459-5307; 73% of undergrads determined to have financial need; average aid package $24,550

Idaho State University[1]
Pocatello ID
(208) 282-2475
U.S. News ranking: Nat. U., unranked
Website: www.isu.edu
Admissions email: info@isu.edu
Public
Application deadline (fall): N/A
Undergraduate student body: N/A full time, N/A part time
Expenses: 2013-2014: $6,344 in state, $18,676 out of state; room/board: $8,280
Financial aid: (208) 282-2756

Lewis-Clark State College
Lewiston ID
(208) 792-2210
U.S. News ranking: Reg. Coll. (W), No. 21
Website: www.lcsc.edu
Admissions email: admissions@lcsc.edu
Public; founded 1893
Freshman admissions: least selective; 2013-2014: 861 applied, 859 accepted. Neither SAT nor ACT required. SAT 25/75 percentile: 820-1030. High school rank: 3% in top tenth, 12% in top quarter, 44% in top half
Early decision deadline: N/A, notification date: N/A
Early action deadline: N/A, notification date: N/A
Application deadline (fall): 8/8
Undergraduate student body: 2,443 full time, 1,861 part time; 39% male, 61% female; 2% American Indian, 1% Asian, 1% black, 5% Hispanic, 3% multiracial, 0% Pacific Islander, 83% white, 3% international; 80% from in state; N/A live on campus; 0% of students in fraternities, 0% in sororities
Most popular majors: 29% Business, Management, Marketing, and Related Support Services, 10% Education, 18% Health Professions and Related Programs, 6% Parks, Recreation, Leisure, and Fitness Studies, 8% Public Administration and Social Service Professions
Expenses: 2014-2015: $5,900 in state, $16,418 out of state; room/board: $6,570
Financial aid: (208) 792-2224; 78% of undergrads determined to have financial need; average aid package $8,160

Northwest Nazarene University
Nampa ID
(208) 467-8000
U.S. News ranking: Reg. U. (W), No. 43
Website: www.nnu.edu
Admissions email: Admissions@nnu.edu
Private; founded 1913
Affiliation: Church of the Nazarene
Freshman admissions: selective; 2013-2014: 1,227 applied, 357 accepted. Either SAT or ACT required. SAT 25/75 percentile: 920-1160. High school rank: 27% in top tenth, 57% in top quarter, 82% in top half
Early decision deadline: N/A, notification date: N/A
Early action deadline: 12/15, notification date: 1/15
Application deadline (fall): 8/15
Undergraduate student body: 1,136 full time, 352 part time; 44% male, 56% female; 0% American Indian, 2% Asian, 2% black, 8% Hispanic, 2% multiracial, 0% Pacific Islander, 73% white, 2% international; 57% from in state; 70% live on campus; N/A of students in fraternities, N/A in sororities
Most popular majors: 7% Biological and Biomedical Sciences, 21% Business, Management, Marketing, and Related Support Services, 13% Education, 15% Health Professions and Related Programs, 6% Liberal Arts and Sciences, General Studies and Humanities
Expenses: 2014-2015: $27,340; room/board: $6,400
Financial aid: (208) 467-8347; 83% of undergrads determined to have financial need; average aid package $18,967

University of Idaho
Moscow ID
(888) 884-3246
U.S. News ranking: Nat. U., No. 166
Website: www.uidaho.edu/admissions
Admissions email: admissions@uidaho.edu
Public; founded 1889
Freshman admissions: selective; 2013-2014: 7,994 applied, 5,173 accepted. Either SAT or ACT required. SAT 25/75 percentile: 910-1170. High school rank: 16% in top tenth, 42% in top quarter, 73% in top half
Early decision deadline: N/A, notification date: N/A
Early action deadline: N/A, notification date: N/A
Application deadline (fall): 8/1
Undergraduate student body: 7,927 full time, 1,529 part time; 53% male, 47% female; 1% American Indian, 1% Asian, 1% black, 8% Hispanic, 3% multiracial, 0% Pacific Islander, 80% white, 3% international; 76% from in state; 19% live on campus; 20% of students in fraternities, 20% in sororities
Most popular majors: 3% Elementary Education and Teaching, 5% General Studies, 3% Human Resources Management/Personnel Administration, General, 9% Psychology, General, 3% Sociology

Expenses: 2014-2015: $6,784 in state, $20,314 out of state; room/board: $8,022
Financial aid: (208) 885-6312; 66% of undergrads determined to have financial need; average aid package $13,202

ILLINOIS

American Academy of Art[1]
Chicago IL
(312) 461-0600
U.S. News ranking: Arts, unranked
Website: www.aaart.edu
Admissions email: N/A
For-profit
Application deadline (fall): N/A
Undergraduate student body: N/A full time, N/A part time
Expenses: 2013-2014: $29,020; room/board: N/A
Financial aid: N/A

American InterContinental University[1]
Hoffman Estates IL
(855) 377-1888
U.S. News ranking: Reg. U. (Mid. W), unranked
Website: www.aiuniv.edu
Admissions email: N/A
For-profit
Application deadline (fall): N/A
Undergraduate student body: N/A full time, N/A part time
Expenses: N/A
Financial aid: N/A

Augustana College
Rock Island IL
(800) 798-8100
U.S. News ranking: Nat. Lib. Arts, No. 105
Website: www.augustana.edu
Admissions email: admissions@augustana.edu
Private; founded 1860
Affiliation: Evangelical Lutheran Church in America
Freshman admissions: selective; 2013-2014: 5,831 applied, 3,421 accepted. Neither SAT nor ACT required. ACT 25/75 percentile: 22-27. High school rank: 24% in top tenth, 51% in top quarter, 84% in top half
Early decision deadline: N/A, notification date: N/A
Early action deadline: N/A, notification date: N/A
Application deadline (fall): rolling
Undergraduate student body: 2,509 full time, 15 part time; 43% male, 57% female; 0% American Indian, 2% Asian, 4% black, 9% Hispanic, 3% multiracial, 0% Pacific Islander, 78% white, 2% international; 85% from in state; 68% live on campus; 23% of students in fraternities, 37% in sororities
Most popular majors: 20% Biological and Biomedical Sciences, 18% Business, Management, Marketing, and Related Support Services, 7% Education, 9% Psychology, 9% Social Sciences
Expenses: 2014-2015: $37,236; room/board: $9,435
Financial aid: (309) 794-7207; 78% of undergrads determined to have financial need; average aid package $26,018

Aurora University[1]
Aurora IL
(800) 742-5281
U.S. News ranking: Reg. U. (Mid. W), second tier
Website: www.aurora.edu
Admissions email: admission@aurora.edu
Private
Application deadline (fall): N/A
Undergraduate student body: N/A full time, N/A part time
Expenses: 2013-2014: $20,720; room/board: $8,636
Financial aid: (630) 844-5533

Benedictine University
Lisle IL
(630) 829-6300
U.S. News ranking: Nat. U., second tier
Website: www.ben.edu
Admissions email: admissions@ben.edu
Private; founded 1887
Affiliation: Roman Catholic
Freshman admissions: selective; 2013-2014: 2,108 applied, 1,465 accepted. Either SAT or ACT required. ACT 25/75 percentile: 20-26. High school rank: 21% in top tenth, 48% in top quarter, 79% in top half
Early decision deadline: N/A, notification date: N/A
Early action deadline: N/A, notification date: N/A
Application deadline (fall): rolling
Undergraduate student body: 2,431 full time, 529 part time; 42% male, 58% female; 0% American Indian, 18% Asian, 8% black, 10% Hispanic, 0% multiracial, 0% Pacific Islander, 44% white, 1% international; 92% from in state; 22% live on campus; N/A of students in fraternities, N/A in sororities
Most popular majors: 10% Biology/Biological Sciences, General, 7% Educational Leadership and Administration, General, 19% Health Services/Allied Health/Health Sciences, General, 39% Marketing/Marketing Management, General, 8% Psychology, General
Expenses: 2014-2015: $26,950; room/board: $8,280
Financial aid: (630) 829-6108; 78% of undergrads determined to have financial need; average aid package $18,064

Blackburn College
Carlinville IL
(800) 233-3550
U.S. News ranking: Reg. Coll. (Mid. W), No. 35
Website: www.blackburn.edu
Admissions email: admit@mail.blackburn.edu
Private; founded 1837
Affiliation: Presbyterian
Freshman admissions: selective; 2013-2014: 528 applied, 359 accepted. Either SAT or ACT required. ACT 25/75 percentile: 19-26. High school rank: 15% in top tenth, 41% in top quarter, 72% in top half
Early decision deadline: N/A, notification date: N/A
Early action deadline: N/A, notification date: N/A
Application deadline (fall): rolling

Undergraduate student body: 523 full time, 20 part time; 42% male, 58% female; 1% American Indian, 0% Asian, 9% black, 1% Hispanic, 1% multiracial, 0% Pacific Islander, 87% white, 0% international; 89% from in state; 71% live on campus; 0% of students in fraternities, 0% in sororities
Most popular majors: 11% Biology/Biological Sciences, General, 9% Business Administration, Management and Operations, Other, 9% Criminal Justice/Safety Studies, 13% Psychology, General, 9% Sport and Fitness Administration/Management
Expenses: 2014-2015: $19,560; room/board: $6,750
Financial aid: (800) 233-3550; 82% of undergrads determined to have financial need; average aid package $16,445

Bradley University
Peoria IL
(800) 447-6460
U.S. News ranking: Reg. U. (Mid. W), No. 4
Website: www.bradley.edu
Admissions email: admissions@bradley.edu
Private; founded 1897
Freshman admissions: more selective; 2013-2014: 8,969 applied, 6,004 accepted. Either SAT or ACT required. ACT 25/75 percentile: 23-28. High school rank: 30% in top tenth, 64% in top quarter, 91% in top half
Early decision deadline: N/A, notification date: N/A
Early action deadline: N/A, notification date: N/A
Application deadline (fall): rolling
Undergraduate student body: 4,620 full time, 235 part time; 48% male, 52% female; 1% American Indian, 4% Asian, 7% black, 6% Hispanic, 0% multiracial, 0% Pacific Islander, 74% white, 1% international; 87% from in state; 68% live on campus; 31% of students in fraternities, 31% in sororities
Most popular majors: 4% Civil Engineering, General, 5% Elementary Education and Teaching, 6% Mechanical Engineering, 6% Psychology, General, 6% Registered Nursing/Registered Nurse
Expenses: 2014-2015: $30,844; room/board: $9,420
Financial aid: (309) 677-3089; 75% of undergrads determined to have financial need; average aid package $19,802

Chicago State University
Chicago IL
(773) 995-2513
U.S. News ranking: Reg. U. (Mid. W), second tier
Website: www.csu.edu
Admissions email: ug-admissions@csu.edu
Public; founded 1867
Freshman admissions: less selective; 2013-2014: 5,219 applied, 1,495 accepted. ACT required. ACT 25/75 percentile: 17-20. High school rank: N/A
Early decision deadline: N/A, notification date: N/A
Early action deadline: N/A, notification date: N/A

Application deadline (fall): rolling
Undergraduate student body: 2,852 full time, 1,488 part time; 29% male, 71% female; 0% American Indian, 1% Asian, 78% black, 6% Hispanic, 0% multiracial, 0% Pacific Islander, 2% white, 0% international
Most popular majors: 12% Business Administration and Management, General, 8% Criminal Justice/Safety Studies, 11% General Studies, 18% Liberal Arts and Sciences/Liberal Studies, 13% Psychology, General
Expenses: 2014-2015: $11,396 in state, $20,096 out of state; room/board: $8,724
Financial aid: (773) 995-2304; 97% of undergrads determined to have financial need; average aid package $11,693

Columbia College Chicago[1]
Chicago IL
(312) 344-7130
U.S. News ranking: Reg. U. (Mid. W), second tier
Website: www.colum.edu
Admissions email: admissions@colum.edu
Private
Application deadline (fall): N/A
Undergraduate student body: N/A full time, N/A part time
Expenses: 2013-2014: $22,792; room/board: $12,375
Financial aid: (312) 344-7054

Concordia University Chicago
River Forest IL
(877) 282-4422
U.S. News ranking: Reg. U. (Mid. W), No. 77
Website: www.cuchicago.edu/
Admissions email: admission@cuchicago.edu
Private; founded 1864
Affiliation: Lutheran
Freshman admissions: selective; 2013-2014: 3,692 applied, 2,009 accepted. Either SAT or ACT required. ACT 25/75 percentile: 20-24. High school rank: 9% in top tenth, 18% in top quarter, 82% in top half
Early decision deadline: N/A, notification date: N/A
Early action deadline: N/A, notification date: N/A
Application deadline (fall): rolling
Undergraduate student body: 1,489 full time, 115 part time; 40% male, 60% female; 0% American Indian, 2% Asian, 14% black, 23% Hispanic, 3% multiracial, 0% Pacific Islander, 56% white, 1% international; 74% from in state; 41% live on campus; 0% of students in fraternities, 0% in sororities
Most popular majors: 21% Business, Management, Marketing, and Related Support Services, 24% Education, 8% Parks, Recreation, Leisure, and Fitness Studies, 10% Psychology, 7% Social Sciences
Expenses: 2014-2015: $28,908; room/board: $8,992
Financial aid: (708) 209-3113; 86% of undergrads determined to have financial need; average aid package $19,291

DePaul University
Chicago IL
(312) 362-8300
U.S. News ranking: Nat. U., No. 121
Website: www.depaul.edu
Admissions email: admission@depaul.edu
Private; founded 1898
Affiliation: Roman Catholic
Freshman admissions: more selective; 2013-2014: 19,957 applied, 11,948 accepted. Neither SAT nor ACT required. ACT 25/75 percentile: 23-28. High school rank: 25% in top tenth, 57% in top quarter, 89% in top half
Early decision deadline: N/A, notification date: N/A
Early action deadline: 11/15, notification date: 1/15
Application deadline (fall): 2/1
Undergraduate student body: 13,594 full time, 2,826 part time; 46% male, 54% female; 0% American Indian, 7% Asian, 8% black, 17% Hispanic, 4% multiracial, 0% Pacific Islander, 56% white, 3% international; 80% from in state; 16% live on campus; 6% of students in fraternities, 9% in sororities
Most popular majors: 28% Business/Commerce, General, 11% Liberal Arts and Sciences/Liberal Studies, 7% Psychology, General, 9% Social Sciences, General, 13% Speech Communication and Rhetoric
Expenses: 2014-2015: $35,071; room/board: $12,552
Financial aid: (312) 362-8091; 70% of undergrads determined to have financial need; average aid package $20,634

DeVry University
Downers Grove IL
(866) 338-7940
U.S. News ranking: Reg. U. (Mid. W), second tier
Website: www.devry.edu
Admissions email: N/A
For-profit; founded 1931
Freshman admissions: less selective; 2013-2014: N/A applied, N/A accepted. Neither SAT nor ACT required. ACT 25/75 percentile: N/A. High school rank: N/A
Early decision deadline: N/A, notification date: N/A
Early action deadline: N/A, notification date: N/A
Application deadline (fall): rolling
Undergraduate student body: 19,414 full time, 29,368 part time; 55% male, 45% female; 1% American Indian, 4% Asian, 21% black, 16% Hispanic, 1% multiracial, 1% Pacific Islander, 39% white, 1% international
Most popular majors: 21% Business Administration and Management, General, 46% Business Administration, Management and Operations, Other, 10% Computer Systems Analysis/Analyst, 8% Computer Systems Networking and Telecommunications, 4% Electrical, Electronic and Communications Engineering Technology/Technician
Expenses: 2014-2015: $17,132; room/board: N/A
Financial aid: N/A

Dominican University
River Forest IL
(708) 524-6800
U.S. News ranking: Reg. U. (Mid. W), No. 19
Website: public.dom.edu/
Admissions email: domadmis@dom.edu
Private; founded 1901
Affiliation: Roman Catholic
Freshman admissions: selective; 2013-2014: 3,502 applied, 2,100 accepted. Either SAT or ACT required. ACT 25/75 percentile: 20-24. High school rank: 22% in top tenth, 48% in top quarter, 85% in top half
Early decision deadline: N/A, notification date: N/A
Early action deadline: N/A, notification date: N/A
Application deadline (fall): 7/1
Undergraduate student body: 1,907 full time, 162 part time; 34% male, 66% female; 0% American Indian, 3% Asian, 7% black, 40% Hispanic, 1% multiracial, 0% Pacific Islander, 44% white, 3% international; 91% from in state; 29% live on campus; 0% of students in fraternities, 0% in sororities
Most popular majors: 23% Business, Management, Marketing, and Related Support Services, 14% Health Professions and Related Programs, 8% Multi/Interdisciplinary Studies, 12% Social Sciences, 8% Visual and Performing Arts
Expenses: 2014-2015: $29,770; room/board: $9,100
Financial aid: (708) 524-6809; 91% of undergrads determined to have financial need; average aid package $21,837

Eastern Illinois University
Charleston IL
(877) 581-2348
U.S. News ranking: Reg. U. (Mid. W), No. 31
Website: www.eiu.edu
Admissions email: admissions@eiu.edu
Public; founded 1895
Freshman admissions: selective; 2013-2014: 7,881 applied, 4,879 accepted. Either SAT or ACT required. ACT 25/75 percentile: 19-24. High school rank: 10% in top tenth, 32% in top quarter, 67% in top half
Early decision deadline: N/A, notification date: N/A
Early action deadline: N/A, notification date: N/A
Application deadline (fall): 8/15
Undergraduate student body: 7,327 full time, 1,020 part time; 40% male, 60% female; 0% American Indian, 1% Asian, 18% black, 5% Hispanic, 2% multiracial, 0% Pacific Islander, 71% white, 1% international; 97% from in state; 37% live on campus; 21% of students in fraternities, 18% in sororities
Most popular majors: 12% Business, Management, Marketing, and Related Support Services, 23% Education, 8% Liberal Arts and Sciences, General Studies and Humanities, 9% Parks, Recreation, Leisure, and Fitness Studies, 6% Social Sciences

Expenses: 2014-2015: $11,108 in state, $28,088 out of state; room/board: $9,358
Financial aid: (217) 581-3713; 68% of undergrads determined to have financial need; average aid package $10,588

East-West University[1]
Chicago IL
(312) 939-0111
U.S. News ranking: Nat. Lib. Arts, unranked
Website: www.eastwest.edu
Admissions email: seeyou@eastwest.edu
Private; founded 1980
Application deadline (fall): rolling
Undergraduate student body: N/A full time, N/A part time
Expenses: 2013-2014: $18,795; room/board: $8,541
Financial aid: (312) 939-0111

Elmhurst College
Elmhurst IL
(630) 617-3400
U.S. News ranking: Reg. U. (Mid. W), No. 11
Website: www.elmhurst.edu
Admissions email: admit@elmhurst.edu
Private; founded 1871
Affiliation: United Church of Christ
Freshman admissions: selective; 2013-2014: 2,702 applied, 1,940 accepted. Either SAT or ACT required. ACT 25/75 percentile: 21-26. High school rank: 20% in top tenth, 47% in top quarter, 78% in top half
Early decision deadline: N/A, notification date: N/A
Early action deadline: N/A, notification date: N/A
Application deadline (fall): 7/15
Undergraduate student body: 2,736 full time, 164 part time; 40% male, 60% female; 0% American Indian, 5% Asian, 5% black, 13% Hispanic, 3% multiracial, 0% Pacific Islander, 73% white, 0% international; 90% from in state; 37% live on campus; 10% of students in fraternities, 16% in sororities
Most popular majors: 20% Business, Management, Marketing, and Related Support Services, 12% Education, 13% Health Professions and Related Programs, 9% Psychology, 9% Social Sciences
Expenses: 2014-2015: $33,950; room/board: $9,386
Financial aid: (630) 617-3075; 73% of undergrads determined to have financial need; average aid package $26,127

Eureka College
Eureka IL
(309) 467-6350
U.S. News ranking: Reg. Coll. (Mid. W), No. 31
Website: www.eureka.edu
Admissions email: admissions@eureka.edu
Private; founded 1855
Affiliation: Christian Church (Disciples of Christ)
Freshman admissions: selective; 2013-2014: 884 applied, 586 accepted. Either SAT or ACT required. ACT 25/75 percentile: 19-25. High school rank: 17% in top tenth, 39% in top quarter, 68% in top half

Early decision deadline: N/A, notification date: N/A
Early action deadline: N/A, notification date: N/A
Application deadline (fall): 8/1
Undergraduate student body: 641 full time, 51 part time; 41% male, 59% female; 0% American Indian, 1% Asian, 4% black, 3% Hispanic, 2% multiracial, 0% Pacific Islander, 86% white, 0% international; 95% from in state; 52% live on campus; 23% of students in fraternities, 19% in sororities
Most popular majors: 19% Business Administration and Management, General, 7% Corrections and Criminal Justice, Other, 14% Elementary Education and Teaching, 8% History, Other, 9% Speech Communication and Rhetoric
Expenses: 2014-2015: $20,060; room/board: $8,500
Financial aid: (309) 467-6311; 79% of undergrads determined to have financial need; average aid package $13,993

Governors State University[1]
University Park IL
(708) 534-4490
U.S. News ranking: Reg. U. (Mid. W), unranked
Website: www.govst.edu/
Admissions email: N/A
Public
Application deadline (fall): N/A
Undergraduate student body: N/A full time, N/A part time
Expenses: N/A
Financial aid: (708) 534-4480

Greenville College
Greenville IL
(618) 664-7100
U.S. News ranking: Reg. Coll. (Mid. W), No. 33
Website: www.greenville.edu
Admissions email: admissions@greenville.edu
Private; founded 1892
Affiliation: Free Methodist
Freshman admissions: selective; 2013-2014: 1,851 applied, 1,132 accepted. Either SAT or ACT required. ACT 25/75 percentile: 18-25. High school rank: 14% in top tenth, 40% in top quarter, 79% in top half
Early decision deadline: N/A, notification date: N/A
Early action deadline: N/A, notification date: N/A
Application deadline (fall): rolling
Undergraduate student body: 1,090 full time, 39 part time; 52% male, 48% female; 0% American Indian, 1% Asian, 8% black, 4% Hispanic, 2% multiracial, 0% Pacific Islander, 76% white, 3% international; 64% from in state; 81% live on campus; 0% of students in fraternities, 0% in sororities
Most popular majors: 6% Biological and Biomedical Sciences, 26% Business, Management, Marketing, and Related Support Services, 5% Communication, Journalism, and Related Programs, 19% Education, 12% Visual and Performing Arts
Expenses: 2014-2015: $24,360; room/board: $8,044

Financial aid: (618) 664-7110; 86% of undergrads determined to have financial need; average aid package $19,350

Harrington College of Design[1]
Chicago IL
(866) 590-4423
U.S. News ranking: Arts, unranked
Website: www.harrington.edu/
Admissions email: N/A
For-profit
Application deadline (fall): N/A
Undergraduate student body: N/A full time, N/A part time
Expenses: 2013-2014: $19,305; room/board: N/A
Financial aid: N/A

Illinois College
Jacksonville IL
(217) 245-3030
U.S. News ranking: Nat. Lib. Arts, No. 155
Website: www.ic.edu
Admissions email: admissions@ic.edu
Private; founded 1829
Affiliation: Presbyterian Church (USA) and United Church of Christ
Freshman admissions: selective; 2013-2014: 2,560 applied, 1,569 accepted. Neither SAT nor ACT required. ACT 25/75 percentile: 19-25. High school rank: 22% in top tenth, 56% in top quarter, 88% in top half
Early decision deadline: N/A, notification date: N/A
Early action deadline: 12/15, notification date: 12/23
Application deadline (fall): rolling
Undergraduate student body: 981 full time, 29 part time; 50% male, 50% female; 0% American Indian, 1% Asian, 12% black, 7% Hispanic, 3% multiracial, 0% Pacific Islander, 73% white, 3% international; 87% from in state; 81% live on campus; 0% of students in fraternities, 0% in sororities
Most popular majors: 25% Biological and Biomedical Sciences, 10% English Language and Literature/Letters, 13% Multi/Interdisciplinary Studies, 9% Psychology
Expenses: 2014-2015: $29,210; room/board: $9,190
Financial aid: (217) 245-3035; 84% of undergrads determined to have financial need; average aid package $25,220

Illinois Institute of Art at Chicago[1]
Chicago IL
(800) 351-3450
U.S. News ranking: Arts, unranked
Website: www.artinstitutes.edu/chicago/
Admissions email: N/A
For-profit
Application deadline (fall): N/A
Undergraduate student body: N/A full time, N/A part time
Expenses: 2013-2014: $17,488; room/board: $12,897
Financial aid: N/A

Illinois Institute of Technology
Chicago IL
(800) 448-2329
U.S. News ranking: Nat. U., No. 116
Website: iit.edu/undergrad_admission/
Admissions email: admission@iit.edu
Private; founded 1890
Freshman admissions: more selective; 2013-2014: 2,840 applied, 1,618 accepted. Either SAT or ACT required. ACT 25/75 percentile: 25-30. High school rank: 45% in top tenth, 74% in top quarter, 96% in top half
Early decision deadline: N/A, notification date: N/A
Early action deadline: 12/1, notification date: N/A
Application deadline (fall): 8/1
Undergraduate student body: 2,712 full time, 214 part time; 70% male, 30% female; 0% American Indian, 11% Asian, 7% black, 15% Hispanic, 0% multiracial, 0% Pacific Islander, 37% white, 25% international; 86% from in state; 59% live on campus; 10% of students in fraternities, 14% in sororities
Most popular majors: 20% Architecture and Related Services, 4% Business, Management, Marketing, and Related Support Services, 12% Computer and Information Sciences and Support Services, 45% Engineering, 3% Mathematics and Statistics
Expenses: 2014-2015: $41,335; room/board: $10,900
Financial aid: (312) 567-7219; 63% of undergrads determined to have financial need; average aid package $33,658

Illinois State University
Normal IL
(309) 438-2181
U.S. News ranking: Nat. U., No. 142
Website: www.ilstu.edu
Admissions email: admissions@ilstu.edu
Public; founded 1857
Freshman admissions: selective; 2013-2014: 15,354 applied, 10,582 accepted. Either SAT or ACT required. ACT 25/75 percentile: 22-26. High school rank: N/A
Early decision deadline: N/A, notification date: N/A
Early action deadline: N/A, notification date: N/A
Application deadline (fall): 5/1
Undergraduate student body: 16,683 full time, 1,066 part time; 45% male, 55% female; 0% American Indian, 2% Asian, 7% black, 8% Hispanic, 2% multiracial, 0% Pacific Islander, 80% white, 0% international; 97% from in state; 33% live on campus; 8% of students in fraternities, 11% in sororities
Most popular majors: 22% Business, Management, Marketing, and Related Support Services, 6% Communication, Journalism, and Related Programs, 17% Education, 6% Social Sciences, 6% Visual and Performing Arts
Expenses: 2014-2015: $12,830 in state, $20,420 out of state; room/board: $9,970

Financial aid: (309) 438-2231; 65% of undergrads determined to have financial need; average aid package $10,074

Illinois Wesleyan University
Bloomington IL
(800) 332-2498
U.S. News ranking: Nat. Lib. Arts, No. 73
Website: www.iwu.edu
Admissions email: iwuadmit@iwu.edu
Private; founded 1850
Freshman admissions: more selective; 2013-2014: 3,556 applied, 2,076 accepted. Either SAT or ACT required. ACT 25/75 percentile: 25-30. High school rank: 45% in top tenth, 77% in top quarter, 96% in top half
Early decision deadline: N/A, notification date: N/A
Early action deadline: 11/15, notification date: 1/15
Application deadline (fall): rolling
Undergraduate student body: 2,001 full time, 8 part time; 44% male, 56% female; 0% American Indian, 5% Asian, 5% black, 6% Hispanic, 1% multiracial, 0% Pacific Islander, 74% white, 5% international; 88% from in state; 71% live on campus; 31% of students in fraternities, 33% in sororities
Most popular majors: 7% Accounting, 8% Biological and Biomedical Sciences, 14% Business/Commerce, General, 8% Psychology, General, 7% Registered Nursing/Registered Nurse
Expenses: 2014-2015: $40,844; room/board: $9,446
Financial aid: (309) 556-3096; 63% of undergrads determined to have financial need; average aid package $28,729

Judson University
Elgin IL
(800) 879-5376
U.S. News ranking: Reg. Coll. (Mid. W), No. 36
Website: www.judsonu.edu
Admissions email: admissions@judsonu.edu
Private; founded 1913
Affiliation: American Baptist
Freshman admissions: selective; 2013-2014: 556 applied, 519 accepted. Either SAT or ACT required. ACT 25/75 percentile: 19-25. High school rank: 8% in top tenth, 29% in top quarter, 76% in top half
Early decision deadline: N/A, notification date: N/A
Early action deadline: N/A, notification date: N/A
Application deadline (fall): rolling
Undergraduate student body: 783 full time, 283 part time; 44% male, 56% female; 0% American Indian, 2% Asian, 6% black, 9% Hispanic, 2% multiracial, 0% Pacific Islander, 60% white, 4% international; 74% from in state; 65% live on campus; 0% of students in fraternities, 0% in sororities
Most popular majors: 13% Architecture and Related Services, 36% Business, Management, Marketing, and Related Support Services, 7% Communication,

Journalism, and Related Programs, 7% Education, 10% Public Administration and Social Service Professions
Expenses: 2013-2014: $27,530; room/board: $8,990
Financial aid: (847) 628-2532

Kendall College[1]
Chicago IL
(877) 588-8860
U.S. News ranking: Reg. Coll. (Mid. W), second tier
Website: www.kendall.edu
Admissions email: admissions@kendall.edu
For-profit; founded 1934
Application deadline (fall): rolling
Undergraduate student body: N/A full time, N/A part time
Expenses: 2013-2014: $24,396; room/board: $11,700
Financial aid: (312) 752-2028

Knox College
Galesburg IL
(800) 678-5669
U.S. News ranking: Nat. Lib. Arts, No. 81
Website: www.knox.edu
Admissions email: admission@knox.edu
Private; founded 1837
Freshman admissions: more selective; 2013-2014: 2,660 applied, 1,994 accepted. Neither SAT nor ACT required. ACT 25/75 percentile: 25-30. High school rank: 26% in top tenth, 59% in top quarter, 91% in top half
Early decision deadline: N/A, notification date: N/A
Early action deadline: 12/1, notification date: 12/31
Application deadline (fall): 2/1
Undergraduate student body: 1,399 full time, 25 part time; 43% male, 57% female; 0% American Indian, 5% Asian, 7% black, 10% Hispanic, 4% multiracial, 0% Pacific Islander, 58% white, 12% international; 58% from in state; 86% live on campus; 26% of students in fraternities, 16% in sororities
Most popular majors: 5% Biology/Biological Sciences, General, 10% Creative Writing, 6% Economics, General, 6% Psychology, General, 5% Social Sciences, Other
Expenses: 2014-2015: $40,497; room/board: $8,724
Financial aid: (309) 341-7130; 77% of undergrads determined to have financial need; average aid package $31,441

Lake Forest College
Lake Forest IL
(847) 735-5000
U.S. News ranking: Nat. Lib. Arts, No. 120
Website: www.lakeforest.edu
Admissions email: admissions@lakeforest.edu
Private; founded 1857
Freshman admissions: more selective; 2013-2014: 3,684 applied, 2,110 accepted. Neither SAT nor ACT required. ACT 25/75 percentile: 23-28. High school rank: 27% in top tenth, 59% in top quarter, 90% in top half
Early decision deadline: 11/15, notification date: 12/13
Early action deadline: 11/15, notification date: 12/13

Application deadline (fall): 2/15
Undergraduate student body: 1,575 full time, 19 part time; 42% male, 58% female; 0% American Indian, 5% Asian, 6% black, 15% Hispanic, 3% multiracial, 0% Pacific Islander, 58% white, 10% international; 66% from in state; 75% live on campus; 11% of students in fraternities, 17% in sororities
Most popular majors: 7% Biology, General, 12% Communication and Media Studies, 6% Economics, 7% English Language and Literature, General, 8% Psychology, General
Expenses: 2013-2014: $39,842; room/board: $9,292
Financial aid: (847) 735-5104

Lewis University

Romeoville IL
(800) 897-9000
U.S. News ranking: Reg. U. (Mid. W), No. 23
Website: www.lewisu.edu
Admissions email: admissions@lewisu.edu
Private; founded 1932
Affiliation: Roman Catholic
Freshman admissions: selective; 2013-2014: 5,432 applied, 3,035 accepted. Either SAT or ACT required. ACT 25/75 percentile: 21-26. High school rank: 18% in top tenth, 47% in top quarter, 81% in top half
Early decision deadline: N/A, notification date: N/A
Early action deadline: N/A, notification date: N/A
Application deadline (fall): rolling
Undergraduate student body: 3,723 full time, 890 part time; 44% male, 56% female; 0% American Indian, 3% Asian, 8% black, 17% Hispanic, 2% multiracial, 0% Pacific Islander, 65% white, 1% international; 94% from in state; 26% live on campus; 3% of students in fraternities, 3% in sororities
Most popular majors: 4% Aviation/Airway Management and Operations, 8% Business Administration and Management, General, 10% Criminal Justice/Safety Studies, 8% Psychology, General, 18% Registered Nursing/Registered Nurse
Expenses: 2014-2015: $27,830; room/board: $9,750
Financial aid: (815) 836-5263; 77% of undergrads determined to have financial need; average aid package $19,415

Lexington College

Chicago IL
(312) 226-6294
U.S. News ranking: Business, unranked
Website: www.lexingtoncollege.edu
Admissions email: admissions@lexingtoncollege.edu
Private
Affiliation: Roman Catholic
Freshman admissions: least selective; 2013-2014: N/A applied, N/A accepted. Neither SAT nor ACT required. ACT 25/75 percentile: N/A. High school rank: N/A
Early decision deadline: N/A, notification date: N/A
Early action deadline: N/A, notification date: N/A
Application deadline (fall): N/A

Undergraduate student body: 46 full time, 13 part time; 0% male, 100% female; N/A American Indian, N/A Asian, N/A black, N/A Hispanic, N/A multiracial, N/A Pacific Islander, N/A white, N/A international
Most popular majors: Information not available
Expenses: 2013-2014: $25,800; room/board: N/A
Financial aid: (312) 226-6294

Lincoln College[1]

Lincoln IL
(800) 569-0556
U.S. News ranking: Reg. Coll. (Mid. W), second tier
Website: www.lincolncollege.edu
Admissions email: admission@lincolncollege.edu
Private; founded 1865
Application deadline (fall): rolling
Undergraduate student body: N/A full time, N/A part time
Expenses: 2013-2014: $17,500; room/board: $7,000
Financial aid: (309) 452-0500

Loyola University Chicago

Chicago IL
(312) 915-6500
U.S. News ranking: Nat. U., No. 106
Website: www.luc.edu
Admissions email: admission@luc.edu
Private; founded 1870
Affiliation: Roman Catholic
Freshman admissions: more selective; 2013-2014: 14,355 applied, 13,121 accepted. Either SAT or ACT required. ACT 25/75 percentile: 24-29. High school rank: 37% in top tenth, 68% in top quarter, 92% in top half
Early decision deadline: N/A, notification date: N/A
Early action deadline: N/A, notification date: N/A
Application deadline (fall): rolling
Undergraduate student body: 9,339 full time, 829 part time; 36% male, 64% female; 0% American Indian, 11% Asian, 4% black, 13% Hispanic, 6% multiracial, 0% Pacific Islander, 61% white, 3% international; 67% from in state; 44% live on campus; 9% of students in fraternities, 12% in sororities
Most popular majors: 12% Biological and Biomedical Sciences, 21% Business, Management, Marketing, and Related Support Services, 10% Health Professions and Related Programs, 11% Psychology, 11% Social Sciences
Expenses: 2014-2015: $37,412; room/board: $13,110
Financial aid: (773) 508-3155; 71% of undergrads determined to have financial need; average aid package $30,280

MacMurray College

Jacksonville IL
(217) 479-7056
U.S. News ranking: Reg. Coll. (Mid. W), No. 52
Website: www.mac.edu
Admissions email: admissions@mac.edu
Private; founded 1846
Affiliation: United Methodist

Freshman admissions: selective; 2013-2014: 1,027 applied, 769 accepted. Either SAT or ACT required. ACT 25/75 percentile: 19-22. High school rank: 7% in top tenth, 33% in top quarter, 74% in top half
Early decision deadline: N/A, notification date: N/A
Early action deadline: N/A, notification date: N/A
Application deadline (fall): 8/25
Undergraduate student body: 517 full time, 54 part time; 44% male, 56% female; 1% American Indian, 1% Asian, 13% black, 5% Hispanic, 2% multiracial, 0% Pacific Islander, 75% white, 0% international; 83% from in state; 49% live on campus; N/A of students in fraternities, N/A in sororities
Most popular majors: Information not available
Expenses: 2014-2015: $23,600; room/board: $8,000
Financial aid: (217) 479-7041; 90% of undergrads determined to have financial need; average aid package $20,237

McKendree University

Lebanon IL
(618) 537-6831
U.S. News ranking: Reg. U. (Mid. W), No. 69
Website: www.mckendree.edu
Admissions email: inquiry@mckendree.edu
Private; founded 1828
Affiliation: Methodist
Freshman admissions: selective; 2013-2014: 1,617 applied, 1,017 accepted. Either SAT or ACT required. ACT 25/75 percentile: 20-25. High school rank: 13% in top tenth, 43% in top quarter, 75% in top half
Early decision deadline: N/A, notification date: N/A
Early action deadline: N/A, notification date: N/A
Application deadline (fall): rolling
Undergraduate student body: 1,777 full time, 581 part time; 44% male, 56% female; 1% American Indian, 1% Asian, 15% black, 4% Hispanic, 1% multiracial, 0% Pacific Islander, 70% white, 1% international; 85% from in state; 63% live on campus; 1% of students in fraternities, 14% in sororities
Most popular majors: 15% Business Administration and Management, General, 6% Elementary Education and Teaching, 8% Human Resources Management/Personnel Administration, General, 7% Psychology, General, 19% Registered Nursing/Registered Nurse
Expenses: 2014-2015: $26,900; room/board: $8,920
Financial aid: (618) 537-6828; 87% of undergrads determined to have financial need; average aid package $19,908

Midstate College[1]

Peoria IL
(309) 692-4092
U.S. News ranking: Reg. Coll. (Mid. W), unranked
Website: www.midstate.edu/
Admissions email: jauer@midstate.edu
For-profit
Application deadline (fall): rolling

Undergraduate student body: N/A full time, N/A part time
Expenses: 2013-2014: $16,230; room/board: N/A
Financial aid: (309) 692-4092

Millikin University

Decatur IL
(217) 424-6210
U.S. News ranking: Reg. Coll. (Mid. W), No. 14
Website: www.millikin.edu
Admissions email: admis@millikin.edu
Private; founded 1901
Affiliation: Presbyterian
Freshman admissions: selective; 2013-2014: 3,906 applied, 2,153 accepted. Either SAT or ACT required. ACT 25/75 percentile: 21-26. High school rank: 19% in top tenth, 41% in top quarter, 71% in top half
Early decision deadline: N/A, notification date: N/A
Early action deadline: N/A, notification date: N/A
Application deadline (fall): rolling
Undergraduate student body: 2,044 full time, 110 part time; 41% male, 59% female; 0% American Indian, 1% Asian, 12% black, 6% Hispanic, 4% multiracial, 0% Pacific Islander, 76% white, 1% international; 89% from in state; 64% live on campus; 16% of students in fraternities, 18% in sororities
Most popular majors: 18% Business, Management, Marketing, and Related Support Services, 6% Communication, Journalism, and Related Programs, 14% Education, 12% Health Professions and Related Programs, 22% Visual and Performing Arts
Expenses: 2014-2015: $29,620; room/board: $9,240
Financial aid: (217) 424-6343; 82% of undergrads determined to have financial need; average aid package $22,862

Monmouth College

Monmouth IL
(800) 747-2687
U.S. News ranking: Nat. Lib. Arts, No. 165
Website: www.monmouthcollege.edu/admissions
Admissions email: admissions@monmouthcollege.edu
Private; founded 1853
Affiliation: Presbyterian USA
Freshman admissions: selective; 2013-2014: 2,973 applied, 1,912 accepted. Either SAT or ACT required. ACT 25/75 percentile: 20-25. High school rank: 15% in top tenth, 37% in top quarter, 72% in top half
Early decision deadline: N/A, notification date: N/A
Early action deadline: N/A, notification date: N/A
Application deadline (fall): rolling
Undergraduate student body: 1,243 full time, 13 part time; 45% male, 55% female; 1% American Indian, 1% Asian, 13% black, 9% Hispanic, 1% multiracial, 0% Pacific Islander, 68% white, 2% international; 92% from in state; 92% live on campus; 26% of students in fraternities, 23% in sororities

Undergraduate student body: N/A full time, N/A part time
Expenses: 2013-2014: $16,230; room/board: N/A
Financial aid: (309) 692-4092

Most popular majors: 20% Business, Management, Marketing, and Related Support Services, 14% Communication, Journalism, and Related Programs, 15% Education, 6% History, 7% Psychology
Expenses: 2014-2015: $33,200; room/board: $7,650
Financial aid: (309) 457-2129; 86% of undergrads determined to have financial need; average aid package $28,809

National-Louis University

Chicago IL
(888) 658-8632
U.S. News ranking: Nat. U., second tier
Website: www.nl.edu
Admissions email: nluinfo@nl.edu
Private
Freshman admissions: selective; 2013-2014: N/A applied, N/A accepted. Neither SAT nor ACT required. ACT 25/75 percentile: N/A. High school rank: N/A
Early decision deadline: N/A, notification date: N/A
Early action deadline: N/A, notification date: N/A
Application deadline (fall): rolling
Undergraduate student body: 784 full time, 643 part time; 23% male, 77% female; 0% American Indian, 2% Asian, 41% black, 25% Hispanic, 1% multiracial, 1% Pacific Islander, 24% white, 1% international
Most popular majors: 9% Elementary Education and Teaching, 6% Management Information Systems, General, 31% Management Science, 30% Multi-/Interdisciplinary Studies, Other, 5% Public Administration and Social Service Professions, Other
Expenses: 2013-2014: $15,915; room/board: N/A
Financial aid: (847) 465-5350

North Central College

Naperville IL
(630) 637-5800
U.S. News ranking: Reg. U. (Mid. W), No. 14
Website: www.noctrl.edu
Admissions email: ncadm@noctrl.edu
Private; founded 1861
Affiliation: United Methodist
Freshman admissions: more selective; 2013-2014: 4,082 applied, 2,598 accepted. Either SAT or ACT required. ACT 25/75 percentile: 22-27. High school rank: 20% in top tenth, 57% in top quarter, 86% in top half
Early decision deadline: N/A, notification date: N/A
Early action deadline: N/A, notification date: N/A
Application deadline (fall): rolling
Undergraduate student body: 2,592 full time, 205 part time; 45% male, 55% female; 0% American Indian, 2% Asian, 3% black, 8% Hispanic, 3% multiracial, 0% Pacific Islander, 78% white, 1% international; 94% from in state; 55% live on campus; N/A of students in fraternities, N/A in sororities
Most popular majors: 6% Business Administration and Management, General, 6% Elementary Education and Teaching, 4%

Graphic Design, 5% Marketing/ Marketing Management, General, 8% Psychology, General
Expenses: 2014-2015: $34,230; room/board: $9,795
Financial aid: (630) 637-5600; 76% of undergrads determined to have financial need; average aid package $23,286

Northeastern Illinois University

Chicago IL
(773) 442-4000
U.S. News ranking: Reg. U. (Mid. W), second tier
Website: www.neiu.edu
Admissions email: admrec@neiu.edu
Public; founded 1867
Freshman admissions: less selective; 2013-2014: 5,291 applied, 3,181 accepted. Either SAT or ACT required. ACT 25/75 percentile: 16-21. High school rank: 3% in top tenth, 16% in top quarter, 61% in top half
Early decision deadline: N/A, notification date: N/A
Early action deadline: N/A, notification date: N/A
Application deadline (fall): 7/1
Undergraduate student body: 5,068 full time, 3,882 part time; 45% male, 55% female; 0% American Indian, 9% Asian, 10% black, 35% Hispanic, 2% multiracial, 0% Pacific Islander, 37% white, 4% international; 99% from in state; 0% live on campus; 1% of students in fraternities, 1% in sororities
Most popular majors: 16% Business, Management, Marketing, and Related Support Services, 12% Education, 10% Liberal Arts and Sciences, General Studies and Humanities, 9% Public Administration and Social Service Professions, 9% Social Sciences
Expenses: 2014-2015: $10,764 in state, $19,884 out of state; room/board: N/A
Financial aid: (773) 442-5000; 71% of undergrads determined to have financial need; average aid package $8,085

Northern Illinois University

DeKalb IL
(815) 753-0446
U.S. News ranking: Nat. U., No. 194
Website: www.niu.edu/
Admissions email: admission@ niu.edu
Public; founded 1895
Freshman admissions: selective; 2013-2014: 19,763 applied, 10,278 accepted. Either SAT or ACT required. ACT 25/75 percentile: 19-24. High school rank: 12% in top tenth, 34% in top quarter, 70% in top half
Early decision deadline: N/A, notification date: N/A
Early action deadline: N/A, notification date: N/A
Application deadline (fall): 8/1
Undergraduate student body: 13,821 full time, 1,993 part time; 50% male, 50% female; 0% American Indian, 5% Asian, 17% black, 13% Hispanic, 3% multiracial, 0% Pacific Islander, 59% white, 1% international;

98% from in state; 28% live on campus; 9% of students in fraternities, 7% in sororities
Most popular majors: 4% Accounting, 4% Health/Medical Preparatory Programs, Other, 6% Psychology, General, 6% Registered Nursing/ Registered Nurse, 6% Speech Communication and Rhetoric
Expenses: 2014-2015: $13,636 in state, $22,914 out of state; room/board: $10,756
Financial aid: (815) 753-1300; 74% of undergrads determined to have financial need; average aid package $12,919

North Park University

Chicago IL
(773) 244-5500
U.S. News ranking: Reg. U. (Mid. W), No. 54
Website: www.northpark.edu
Admissions email: admissions@ northpark.edu
Private; founded 1891
Affiliation: Evangelical Covenant Church
Freshman admissions: selective; 2013-2014: 3,961 applied, 2,073 accepted. Either SAT or ACT required. ACT 25/75 percentile: 19-25. High school rank: N/A
Early decision deadline: N/A, notification date: N/A
Early action deadline: N/A, notification date: N/A
Application deadline (fall): 7/1
Undergraduate student body: 1,861 full time, 343 part time; 37% male, 63% female; 0% American Indian, 5% Asian, 9% black, 18% Hispanic, 3% multiracial, 0% Pacific Islander, 52% white, 4% international; 73% from in state; 46% live on campus; 0% of students in fraternities, 0% in sororities
Most popular majors: 7% Biology/ Biological Sciences, General, 18% Business Administration and Management, General, 6% Criminal Justice/Safety Studies, 5% Elementary Education and Teaching, 19% Registered Nursing/Registered Nurse
Expenses: 2014-2015: $24,540; room/board: $8,660
Financial aid: (773) 244-5526

Northwestern University

Evanston IL
(847) 491-7271
U.S. News ranking: Nat. U., No. 13
Website: www.northwestern.edu
Admissions email: ug-admission@ northwestern.edu
Private; founded 1851
Freshman admissions: most selective; 2013-2014: 32,796 applied, 4,598 accepted. Either SAT or ACT required. SAT 25/75 percentile: 1390-1550. High school rank: 91% in top tenth, 99% in top quarter, 99% in top half
Early decision deadline: 11/1, notification date: 12/15
Early action deadline: N/A, notification date: N/A
Application deadline (fall): 1/1
Undergraduate student body: 8,423 full time, 265 part time; 49% male, 51% female; 0% American

Indian, 17% Asian, 5% black, 10% Hispanic, 5% multiracial, 0% Pacific Islander, 54% white, 7% international; 28% from in state; 65% live on campus; 38% of students in fraternities, 42% in sororities
Most popular majors: 6% Biology/Biological Sciences, General, 12% Economics, General, 8% Journalism, 7% Psychology, General, 6% Speech Communication and Rhetoric
Expenses: 2014-2015: $47,251; room/board: $14,389
Financial aid: (847) 491-7400; 47% of undergrads determined to have financial need; average aid package $38,798

Olivet Nazarene University

Bourbonnais IL
(815) 939-5011
U.S. News ranking: Reg. U. (Mid. W), No. 49
Website: www.olivet.edu
Admissions email: admissions@ olivet.edu
Private; founded 1907
Affiliation: Church of the Nazarene
Freshman admissions: selective; 2013-2014: 3,775 applied, 2,975 accepted. Either SAT or ACT required. ACT 25/75 percentile: 20-26. High school rank: 21% in top tenth, 48% in top quarter, 79% in top half
Early decision deadline: N/A, notification date: N/A
Early action deadline: N/A, notification date: N/A
Application deadline (fall): 8/1
Undergraduate student body: 2,905 full time, 430 part time; 37% male, 63% female; 0% American Indian, 2% Asian, 10% black, 5% Hispanic, 1% multiracial, 0% Pacific Islander, 80% white, 1% international; 67% from in state; 82% live on campus; 0% of students in fraternities, 0% in sororities
Most popular majors: 4% Biology/ Biological Sciences, General, 4% Business Administration and Management, General, 9% Elementary Education and Teaching, 24% Registered Nursing/Registered Nurse, 4% Social Work
Expenses: 2014-2015: $31,390; room/board: $7,900
Financial aid: (815) 939-5249; 81% of undergrads determined to have financial need; average aid package $23,598

Principia College

Elsah IL
(618) 374-5181
U.S. News ranking: Nat. Lib. Arts, No. 139
Website: www.principiacollege.edu
Admissions email: collegeadmissions@principia.edu
Private; founded 1910
Affiliation: Christian Science
Freshman admissions: selective; 2013-2014: 189 applied, 159 accepted. Either SAT or ACT required. SAT 25/75 percentile: 918-1223. High school rank: 26% in top tenth, 50% in top quarter, 83% in top half
Early decision deadline: N/A, notification date: N/A
Early action deadline: N/A, notification date: N/A

Application deadline (fall): rolling
Undergraduate student body: 480 full time, N/A part time; 46% male, 54% female; 0% American Indian, 0% Asian, 1% black, 3% Hispanic, 3% multiracial, 0% Pacific Islander, 69% white, 18% international; 12% from in state; 99% live on campus; 0% of students in fraternities, 0% in sororities
Most popular majors: Information not available
Expenses: 2014-2015: $26,850; room/board: $10,650
Financial aid: (618) 374-5186; 68% of undergrads determined to have financial need; average aid package $28,291

Quincy University

Quincy IL
(217) 228-5210
U.S. News ranking: Reg. U. (Mid. W), No. 69
Website: www.quincy.edu
Admissions email: admissions@ quincy.edu
Private; founded 1860
Affiliation: Catholic
Freshman admissions: selective; 2013-2014: 1,078 applied, 955 accepted. Either SAT or ACT required. ACT 25/75 percentile: 20-25. High school rank: 16% in top tenth, 40% in top quarter, 71% in top half
Early decision deadline: N/A, notification date: N/A
Early action deadline: N/A, notification date: N/A
Application deadline (fall): rolling
Undergraduate student body: 1,082 full time, 114 part time; 44% male, 56% female; 1% American Indian, 1% Asian, 11% black, 4% Hispanic, 2% multiracial, 0% Pacific Islander, 71% white, 0% international; 72% from in state; 57% live on campus; 6% of students in fraternities, 8% in sororities
Most popular majors: 11% Biological and Biomedical Sciences, 23% Business, Management, Marketing, and Related Support Services, 10% Education, 10% Health Professions and Related Programs, 9% Liberal Arts and Sciences, General Studies and Humanities
Expenses: 2014-2015: $26,572; room/board: $9,968
Financial aid: (217) 228-5260; 87% of undergrads determined to have financial need; average aid package $23,232

Robert Morris University

Chicago IL
(312) 935-4400
U.S. News ranking: Reg. U. (Mid. W), No. 80
Website: www.robertmorris.edu/
Admissions email: enroll@ robertmorris.edu
Private; founded 1913
Freshman admissions: less selective; 2013-2014: 4,080 applied, 857 accepted. Either SAT or ACT required. ACT 25/75 percentile: 15-21. High school rank: 3% in top tenth, 14% in top quarter, 38% in top half
Early decision deadline: N/A, notification date: N/A
Early action deadline: N/A, notification date: N/A

Application deadline (fall): rolling
Undergraduate student body: 2,649 full time, 132 part time; 49% male, 51% female; 0% American Indian, 3% Asian, 28% black, 27% Hispanic, 1% multiracial, 0% Pacific Islander, 38% white, 1% international; 92% from in state; 8% live on campus; N/A of students in fraternities, N/A in sororities
Most popular majors: 64% Business, Management, Marketing, and Related Support Services, 10% Computer and Information Sciences and Support Services, 19% Multi/ Interdisciplinary Studies, 7% Visual and Performing Arts
Expenses: 2014-2015: $23,700; room/board: $11,649
Financial aid: (312) 935-4408; 93% of undergrads determined to have financial need; average aid package $15,243

Rockford University

Rockford IL
(815) 226-4050
U.S. News ranking: Reg. U. (Mid. W), No. 84
Website: www.rockford.edu
Admissions email: rcadmissions@ rockford.edu
Private; founded 1847
Freshman admissions: selective; 2013-2014: 1,074 applied, 440 accepted. Either SAT or ACT required. ACT 25/75 percentile: 19-25. High school rank: N/A
Early decision deadline: N/A, notification date: N/A
Early action deadline: N/A, notification date: N/A
Application deadline (fall): rolling
Undergraduate student body: 838 full time, 143 part time; 36% male, 64% female; 0% American Indian, 2% Asian, 7% black, 5% Hispanic, 9% multiracial, 0% Pacific Islander, 67% white, 1% international; 87% from in state; 32% live on campus; 0% of students in fraternities, N/A in sororities
Most popular majors: Information not available
Expenses: 2014-2015: $27,500; room/board: $7,710
Financial aid: (815) 226-3396; 92% of undergrads determined to have financial need; average aid package $19,056

Roosevelt University

Chicago IL
(877) 277-5978
U.S. News ranking: Reg. U. (Mid. W), No. 91
Website: www.roosevelt.edu
Admissions email: admission@ roosevelt.edu
Private; founded 1945
Freshman admissions: selective; 2013-2014: 3,370 applied, 2,655 accepted. Either SAT or ACT required. ACT 25/75 percentile: 19-25. High school rank: 2% in top tenth, 11% in top quarter, 39% in top half
Early decision deadline: N/A, notification date: N/A
Early action deadline: N/A, notification date: N/A
Application deadline (fall): rolling
Undergraduate student body: 2,731 full time, 927 part time; 38% male, 62% female; 0% American Indian, 5% Asian, 20% black,

19% Hispanic, 3% multiracial, 0% Pacific Islander, 47% white, 3% international; 85% from in state; 25% live on campus; 0% of students in fraternities, 2% in sororities
Most popular majors: 29% Business, Management, Marketing, and Related Support Services, 7% Education, 16% Psychology, 7% Social Sciences, 7% Visual and Performing Arts
Expenses: 2014-2015: $26,900; room/board: $12,532
Financial aid: (312) 341-3565; 82% of undergrads determined to have financial need; average aid package $23,001

School of the Art Institute of Chicago

Chicago IL
(312) 629-6100
U.S. News ranking: Arts, unranked
Website: www.saic.edu
Admissions email: admiss@saic.edu
Private; founded 1866
Freshman admissions: N/A; 2013-2014: 3,704 applied, 2,655 accepted. Either SAT or ACT required. SAT 25/75 percentile: N/A. High school rank: N/A
Early decision deadline: N/A, notification date: N/A
Early action deadline: 1/3, notification date: 9/1
Application deadline (fall): 6/1
Undergraduate student body: 2,469 full time, 245 part time; 30% male, 70% female; 0% American Indian, 13% Asian, 3% black, 6% Hispanic, 3% multiracial, 0% Pacific Islander, 45% white, 27% international; 30% from in state; 17% live on campus; 0% of students in fraternities, 0% in sororities
Most popular majors: 5% Art History, Criticism and Conservation, 3% Art Teacher Education, 3% Art Therapy/Therapist, 4% Creative Writing, 72% Fine/Studio Arts, General
Expenses: 2014-2015: $42,230; room/board: $15,230
Financial aid: (312) 629-6600; 50% of undergrads determined to have financial need; average aid package $31,525

Shimer College[1]

Chicago IL
(312) 235-3500
U.S. News ranking: Nat. Lib. Arts, unranked
Website: www.shimer.edu
Admissions email: admission@shimer.edu
Private
Application deadline (fall): N/A
Undergraduate student body: N/A full time, N/A part time
Expenses: 2013-2014: $31,527; room/board: N/A
Financial aid: (847) 249-7180

Southern Illinois University–Carbondale

Carbondale IL
(618) 536-4405
U.S. News ranking: Nat. U., No. 189
Website: www.siu.edu
Admissions email: admissions@siu.edu

Public; founded 1869
Freshman admissions: selective; 2013-2014: 11,573 applied, 9,176 accepted. Either SAT or ACT required. ACT 25/75 percentile: 19-25. High school rank: 11% in top tenth, 31% in top quarter, 61% in top half
Early decision deadline: N/A, notification date: N/A
Early action deadline: N/A, notification date: N/A
Application deadline (fall): 5/1
Undergraduate student body: 11,844 full time, 1,507 part time; 55% male, 45% female; 0% American Indian, 2% Asian, 20% black, 7% Hispanic, 3% multiracial, 0% Pacific Islander, 64% white, 3% international; 87% from in state; 31% live on campus; 4% of students in fraternities, 2% in sororities
Most popular majors: 9% Business, Management, Marketing, and Related Support Services, 17% Education, 7% Engineering Technologies and Engineering-Related Fields, 8% Health Professions and Related Programs, 6% Social Sciences
Expenses: 2014-2015: $12,251 in state, $24,874 out of state; room/board: $9,694
Financial aid: (618) 453-4334; 71% of undergrads determined to have financial need; average aid package $13,707

Southern Illinois University–Edwardsville

Edwardsville IL
(618) 650-3705
U.S. News ranking: Reg. U. (Mid. W), No. 47
Website: www.siue.edu
Admissions email: admissions@siue.edu
Public; founded 1957
Freshman admissions: selective; 2013-2014: 7,646 applied, 6,437 accepted. Either SAT or ACT required. ACT 25/75 percentile: 20-25. High school rank: 16% in top tenth, 39% in top quarter, 73% in top half
Early decision deadline: N/A, notification date: N/A
Early action deadline: N/A, notification date: N/A
Application deadline (fall): 5/1
Undergraduate student body: 9,556 full time, 1,673 part time; 47% male, 53% female; 0% American Indian, 2% Asian, 15% black, 4% Hispanic, 3% multiracial, 0% Pacific Islander, 75% white, 1% international; N/A from in state; N/A live on campus; 8% of students in fraternities, 9% in sororities
Most popular majors: 9% Biology/Biological Sciences, General, 9% Business Administration and Management, General, 4% Elementary Education and Teaching, 7% Psychology, General, 10% Registered Nursing/Registered Nurse
Expenses: 2014-2015: $9,738 in state, $20,682 out of state; room/board: $8,750
Financial aid: (618) 650-3839; 70% of undergrads determined to have financial need; average aid package $11,179

St. Augustine College[1]

Chicago IL
(773) 878-3656
U.S. News ranking: Reg. Coll. (Mid. W),* unranked
Website: www.staugustinecollege.edu/index.asp
Admissions email: info@staugustine.edu
Private
Application deadline (fall): N/A
Undergraduate student body: N/A full time, N/A part time
Expenses: 2013-2014: $9,120; room/board: N/A
Financial aid: (773) 878-3813

St. Xavier University

Chicago IL
(773) 298-3050
U.S. News ranking: Reg. U. (Mid. W), No. 49
Website: www.sxu.edu
Admissions email: admission@sxu.edu
Private; founded 1846
Affiliation: Roman Catholic
Freshman admissions: selective; 2013-2014: 6,693 applied, 5,307 accepted. Either SAT or ACT required. ACT 25/75 percentile: 19-24. High school rank: 25% in top tenth, 54% in top quarter, 84% in top half
Early decision deadline: N/A, notification date: N/A
Early action deadline: N/A, notification date: N/A
Application deadline (fall): rolling
Undergraduate student body: 2,452 full time, 468 part time; 33% male, 67% female; 0% American Indian, 3% Asian, 16% black, 23% Hispanic, 2% multiracial, 0% Pacific Islander, 50% white, 0% international; 95% from in state; 22% live on campus; 0% of students in fraternities, 0% in sororities
Most popular majors: 16% Business, Management, Marketing, and Related Support Services, 12% Education, 24% Health Professions and Related Programs, 11% Liberal Arts and Sciences, General Studies and Humanities, 12% Psychology
Expenses: 2014-2015: $30,100; room/board: $10,320
Financial aid: (773) 298-3070; 89% of undergrads determined to have financial need; average aid package $23,096

Trinity Christian College

Palos Heights IL
(800) 748-0085
U.S. News ranking: Reg. Coll. (Mid. W), No. 28
Website: www.trnty.edu
Admissions email: admissions@trnty.edu
Private; founded 1959
Affiliation: Reformed
Freshman admissions: selective; 2013-2014: 670 applied, 526 accepted. Either SAT or ACT required. ACT 25/75 percentile: 20-25. High school rank: 13% in top tenth, 27% in top quarter, 56% in top half
Early decision deadline: N/A, notification date: N/A
Early action deadline: N/A, notification date: N/A
Application deadline (fall): rolling

Undergraduate student body: 1,106 full time, 227 part time; 35% male, 65% female; 1% American Indian, 2% Asian, 9% black, 11% Hispanic, 2% multiracial, 0% Pacific Islander, 72% white, 3% international; 71% from in state; 45% live on campus; N/A of students in fraternities, N/A in sororities
Most popular majors: 18% Business, Management, Marketing, and Related Support Services, 33% Education, 13% Health Professions and Related Programs, 6% Psychology, 6% Public Administration and Social Service Professions
Expenses: 2014-2015: $25,290; room/board: $9,390
Financial aid: (708) 239-4706; 80% of undergrads determined to have financial need; average aid package $16,080

Trinity International University

Deerfield IL
(800) 822-3225
U.S. News ranking: Nat. U., second tier
Website: www.tiu.edu
Admissions email: tcadmissions@tiu.edu
Private; founded 1897
Affiliation: Evangelical Free Church of America
Freshman admissions: selective; 2013-2014: 439 applied, 412 accepted. Either SAT or ACT required. ACT 25/75 percentile: 25-29. High school rank: 17% in top tenth, 34% in top quarter, 74% in top half
Early decision deadline: N/A, notification date: N/A
Early action deadline: N/A, notification date: N/A
Application deadline (fall): rolling
Undergraduate student body: 850 full time, 313 part time; 47% male, 53% female; 0% American Indian, 2% Asian, 20% black, 20% Hispanic, 2% multiracial, 1% Pacific Islander, 45% white, 1% international
Most popular majors: Information not available
Expenses: 2014-2015: $27,360; room/board: $8,710
Financial aid: (847) 317-8060; 82% of undergrads determined to have financial need; average aid package $22,707

University of Chicago

Chicago IL
(773) 702-8650
U.S. News ranking: Nat. U., No. 4
Website: www.uchicago.edu
Admissions email: collegeadmissions@uchicago.edu
Private; founded 1890
Freshman admissions: most selective; 2013-2014: 30,271 applied, 2,670 accepted. Either SAT or ACT required. SAT 25/75 percentile: 1440-1590. High school rank: 98% in top tenth, 100% in top quarter, 100% in top half
Early decision deadline: N/A, notification date: N/A
Early action deadline: 11/8, notification date: 12/16
Application deadline (fall): 1/1

Undergraduate student body: 5,585 full time, 74 part time; 53% male, 47% female; 0% American Indian, 18% Asian, 5% black, 9% Hispanic, 4% multiracial, 0% Pacific Islander, 45% white, 9% international; 18% from in state; 53% live on campus; N/A of students in fraternities, N/A in sororities
Most popular majors: 10% Biological and Biomedical Sciences, 5% English Language and Literature/Letters, 8% Mathematics and Statistics, 5% Public Administration and Social Service Professions, 26% Social Sciences
Expenses: 2014-2015: $48,253; room/board: $14,205
Financial aid: (773) 702-8666; 48% of undergrads determined to have financial need; average aid package $38,808

University of Illinois–Chicago

Chicago IL
(312) 996-4350
U.S. News ranking: Nat. U., No. 149
Website: www.uic.edu
Admissions email: uicadmit@uic.edu
Public; founded 1965
Freshman admissions: selective; 2013-2014: 14,653 applied, 10,427 accepted. Either SAT or ACT required. ACT 25/75 percentile: 22-26. High school rank: 24% in top tenth, 63% in top quarter, 92% in top half
Early decision deadline: N/A, notification date: N/A
Early action deadline: N/A, notification date: N/A
Application deadline (fall): 1/15
Undergraduate student body: 15,402 full time, 1,258 part time; 50% male, 50% female; 0% American Indian, 23% Asian, 8% black, 25% Hispanic, 2% multiracial, 0% Pacific Islander, 38% white, 2% international; 98% from in state; 17% live on campus; 1% of students in fraternities, 1% in sororities
Most popular majors: 5% Accounting, 12% Biology/Biological Sciences, General, 5% Finance, General, 15% Psychology, General, 5% Registered Nursing/Registered Nurse
Expenses: 2014-2015: $13,640 in state, $26,030 out of state; room/board: $10,882
Financial aid: (312) 996-3126; 76% of undergrads determined to have financial need; average aid package $14,130

University of Illinois–Springfield

Springfield IL
(217) 206-4847
U.S. News ranking: Reg. U. (Mid. W), No. 36
Website: www.uis.edu
Admissions email: admissions@uis.edu
Public; founded 1969
Freshman admissions: selective; 2013-2014: 1,469 applied, 878 accepted. Either SAT or ACT required. ACT 25/75 percentile: 20-27. High school rank: 21% in top tenth, 44% in top quarter, 80% in top half

Early decision deadline: N/A, notification date: N/A
Early action deadline: N/A, notification date: N/A
Application deadline (fall): rolling
Undergraduate student body: 1,969 full time, 1,070 part time; 49% male, 51% female; 0% American Indian, 4% Asian, 13% black, 6% Hispanic, 2% multiracial, 0% Pacific Islander, 68% white, 3% international; 87% from in state; 30% live on campus; 0% of students in fraternities, 0% in sororities
Most popular majors: 16% Business Administration and Management, General, 7% Communication, General, 8% Computer Science, 7% Criminal Justice/Safety Studies, 10% Psychology, General
Expenses: 2014-2015: $11,367 in state, $20,517 out of state; room/board: $9,600
Financial aid: (217) 206-6724; 70% of undergrads determined to have financial need; average aid package $12,257

University of Illinois– Urbana-Champaign

Champaign IL
(217) 333-0302
U.S. News ranking: Nat. U., No. 42
Website: www.illinois.edu
Admissions email: ugradadmissions@illinois.edu
Public; founded 1867
Freshman admissions: more selective; 2013-2014: 33,203 applied, 20,716 accepted. Either SAT or ACT required. ACT 25/75 percentile: 26-31. High school rank: 55% in top tenth, 87% in top quarter, 99% in top half
Early decision deadline: N/A, notification date: N/A
Early action deadline: N/A, notification date: N/A
Application deadline (fall): 1/2
Undergraduate student body: 31,516 full time, 1,179 part time; 56% male, 44% female; 0% American Indian, 15% Asian, 6% black, 8% Hispanic, 3% multiracial, 0% Pacific Islander, 53% white, 15% international; 89% from in state; 50% live on campus; 21% of students in fraternities, 21% in sororities
Most popular majors: 8% Biological and Biomedical Sciences, 14% Business, Management, Marketing, and Related Support Services, 9% Communication, Journalism, and Related Programs, 17% Engineering, 9% Social Sciences
Expenses: 2014-2015: $15,602 in state, $30,228 out of state; room/board $10,848
Financial aid: (217) 333-0100; 46% of undergrads determined to have financial need; average aid package $15,312

University of St. Francis

Joliet IL
(800) 735-7500
U.S. News ranking: Reg. U. (Mid. W), No. 39
Website: www.stfrancis.edu
Admissions email: admissions@stfrancis.edu
Private; founded 1920
Affiliation: Roman Catholic

Freshman admissions: selective; 2013-2014: 1,706 applied, 877 accepted. Either SAT or ACT required. ACT 25/75 percentile: 21-25. High school rank: 20% in top tenth, 46% in top quarter, 84% in top half
Early decision deadline: N/A, notification date: N/A
Early action deadline: N/A, notification date: N/A
Application deadline (fall): 8/1
Undergraduate student body: 1,364 full time, 58 part time; 35% male, 65% female; 0% American Indian, 2% Asian, 7% black, 15% Hispanic, 2% multiracial, 0% Pacific Islander, 71% white, 1% international; 95% from in state; 26% live on campus; 0% of students in fraternities, 0% in sororities
Most popular majors: 6% Biology/Biological Sciences, General, 14% Business, Management, Marketing, and Related Support Services, 11% Education, 6% Homeland Security, Law Enforcement, Firefighting and Related Protective Services, 31% Registered Nursing/Registered Nurse
Expenses: 2014-2015: $28,790; room/board: $8,770
Financial aid: (815) 740-3403; 86% of undergrads determined to have financial need; average aid package $22,137

VanderCook College of Music

Chicago IL
(800) 448-2655
U.S. News ranking: Arts, unranked
Website: www.vandercook.edu
Admissions email: admissions@vandercook.edu
Private; founded 1909
Freshman admissions: N/A; 2013-2014: 123 applied, 46 accepted. Neither SAT nor ACT required. SAT 25/75 percentile: N/A. High school rank: 0% in top tenth, 77% in top quarter, 92% in top half
Early decision deadline: N/A, notification date: N/A
Early action deadline: N/A, notification date: N/A
Application deadline (fall): rolling
Undergraduate student body: 99 full time, 34 part time; 52% male, 48% female; 0% American Indian, 1% Asian, 6% black, 21% Hispanic, 3% multiracial, 0% Pacific Islander, 66% white, 3% international; 77% from in state; 8% live on campus; N/A of students in fraternities, N/A in sororities
Most popular majors: 100% Music Teacher Education
Expenses: 2014-2015: $25,690; room/board: $8,820
Financial aid: (312) 225-6288; 89% of undergrads determined to have financial need; average aid package $16,599

Western Illinois University

Macomb IL
(309) 298-3157
U.S. News ranking: Reg. U. (Mid. W), No. 39
Website: www.wiu.edu
Admissions email: admissions@wiu.edu
Public; founded 1899

Freshman admissions: selective; 2013-2014: 10,554 applied, 6,260 accepted. Either SAT or ACT required. ACT 25/75 percentile: 18-23. High school rank: 9% in top tenth, 28% in top quarter, 61% in top half
Early decision deadline: N/A, notification date: N/A
Early action deadline: N/A, notification date: N/A
Application deadline (fall): 5/15
Undergraduate student body: 8,805 full time, 1,068 part time; 51% male, 49% female; 0% American Indian, 1% Asian, 17% black, 8% Hispanic, 2% multiracial, 0% Pacific Islander, 67% white, 2% international; 89% from in state; 42% live on campus; 6% of students in fraternities, 6% in sororities
Most popular majors: 12% Business Administration and Management, General, 16% Criminal Justice/Law Enforcement Administration, 8% Elementary Education and Teaching, 13% General Studies, 7% Parks, Recreation and Leisure Facilities Management, General
Expenses: 2014-2015: $11,283 in state, $15,599 out of state; room/board: $9,450
Financial aid: (309) 298-2446; 74% of undergrads determined to have financial need; average aid package $10,450

Wheaton College

Wheaton IL
(630) 752-5005
U.S. News ranking: Nat. Lib. Arts, No. 56
Website: www.wheaton.edu
Admissions email: admissions@wheaton.edu
Private; founded 1860
Affiliation: Christian nondenominational
Freshman admissions: more selective; 2013-2014: 1,941 applied, 1,364 accepted. Either SAT or ACT required. ACT 25/75 percentile: 27-32. High school rank: 58% in top tenth, 82% in top quarter, 97% in top half
Early decision deadline: N/A, notification date: N/A
Early action deadline: 11/1, notification date: 12/31
Application deadline (fall): 1/10
Undergraduate student body: 2,378 full time, 66 part time; 49% male, 51% female; 0% American Indian, 8% Asian, 2% black, 5% Hispanic, 5% multiracial, 0% Pacific Islander, 78% white, 2% international; 26% from in state; 90% live on campus; N/A of students in fraternities, N/A in sororities
Most popular majors: 8% Business, Management, Marketing, and Related Support Services, 8% English Language and Literature/Letters, 14% Social Sciences, 8% Theology and Religious Vocations, 8% Visual and Performing Arts
Expenses: 2014-2015: $31,900; room/board: $8,820
Financial aid: (630) 752-5021; 52% of undergrads determined to have financial need; average aid package $23,691

Anderson University

Anderson IN
(765) 641-4080
U.S. News ranking: Reg. U. (Mid. W), No. 41
Website: www.anderson.edu
Admissions email: info@anderson.edu
Private; founded 1917
Affiliation: Church of God
Freshman admissions: selective; 2013-2014: 2,734 applied, 1,516 accepted. Either SAT or ACT required. SAT 25/75 percentile: 940-1140. High school rank: 20% in top tenth, 52% in top quarter, 82% in top half
Early decision deadline: N/A, notification date: N/A
Early action deadline: N/A, notification date: N/A
Application deadline (fall): rolling
Undergraduate student body: 1,737 full time, 279 part time; 40% male, 60% female; 0% American Indian, 1% Asian, 6% black, 3% Hispanic, 0% multiracial, 0% Pacific Islander, 81% white, 3% international; 74% from in state; 64% live on campus; N/A of students in fraternities, N/A in sororities
Most popular majors: 24% Business, Management, Marketing, and Related Support Services, 15% Education, 10% Health Professions and Related Programs, 6% Psychology, 10% Visual and Performing Arts
Expenses: 2014-2015: $26,850; room/board: $9,250
Financial aid: (765) 641-4180; 84% of undergrads determined to have financial need; average aid package $21,552

Ball State University

Muncie IN
(765) 285-8300
U.S. News ranking: Nat. U., No. 173
Website: www.bsu.edu
Admissions email: askus@bsu.edu
Public; founded 1918
Freshman admissions: selective; 2013-2014: 17,118 applied, 10,367 accepted. Neither SAT nor ACT required. SAT 25/75 percentile: 980-1170. High school rank: 19% in top tenth, 52% in top quarter, 90% in top half
Early decision deadline: N/A, notification date: N/A
Early action deadline: N/A, notification date: N/A
Application deadline (fall): 8/15
Undergraduate student body: 15,128 full time, 1,172 part time; 42% male, 58% female; 0% American Indian, 1% Asian, 7% black, 3% Hispanic, 2% multiracial, 0% Pacific Islander, 82% white, 3% international; 88% from in state; 41% live on campus; 10% of students in fraternities, 13% in sororities
Most popular majors: 13% Business, Management, Marketing, and Related Support Services, 13% Communication, Journalism, and Related Programs, 13% Education, 10% Health Professions and Related Programs, 7% Liberal Arts and Sciences, General Studies and Humanities
Expenses: 2014-2015: $9,344 in state, $24,610 out of state; room/board: $9,246

Financial aid: (765) 285-5600; 67% of undergrads determined to have financial need; average aid package $11,277

Bethel College

Mishawaka IN
(800) 422-4101
U.S. News ranking: Reg. Coll. (Mid. W), No. 19
Website: www.bethelcollege.edu
Admissions email: admissions@bethelcollege.edu
Private; founded 1947
Affiliation: Missionary Church
Freshman admissions: selective; 2013-2014: 1,241 applied, 889 accepted. Either SAT or ACT required. SAT 25/75 percentile: 900-1130. High school rank: 24% in top tenth, 51% in top quarter, 87% in top half
Early decision deadline: N/A, notification date: N/A
Early action deadline: N/A, notification date: N/A
Application deadline (fall): rolling
Undergraduate student body: 1,304 full time, 351 part time; 34% male, 66% female; 0% American Indian, 0% Asian, 12% black, 5% Hispanic, 2% multiracial, 0% Pacific Islander, 77% white, 2% international; 74% from in state; 47% live on campus; 0% of students in fraternities, 0% in sororities
Most popular majors: 31% Business, Management, Marketing, and Related Support Services, 11% Education, 11% Health Professions and Related Programs, 6% Public Administration and Social Service Professions, 7% Theology and Religious Vocations
Expenses: 2014-2015: $25,830; room/board: $7,780
Financial aid: (574) 257-3316; 86% of undergrads determined to have financial need; average aid package $17,321

Butler University

Indianapolis IN
(888) 940-8100
U.S. News ranking: Reg. U. (Mid. W), No. 2
Website: www.butler.edu
Admissions email: admission@butler.edu
Private; founded 1855
Freshman admissions: more selective; 2013-2014: 9,357 applied, 6,185 accepted. Either SAT or ACT required. ACT 25/75 percentile: 25-30. High school rank: 49% in top tenth, 81% in top quarter, 97% in top half
Early decision deadline: N/A, notification date: N/A
Early action deadline: 11/1, notification date: 12/15
Application deadline (fall): 2/1
Undergraduate student body: 4,049 full time, 77 part time; 39% male, 61% female; 0% American Indian, 3% Asian, 3% black, 3% Hispanic, 1% multiracial, 0% Pacific Islander, 83% white, 2% international; 48% from in state; 67% live on campus; 29% of students in fraternities, 33% in sororities
Most popular majors: 21% Business, Management, Marketing, and Related Support Services, 9% Communication, Journalism, and Related Programs, 14% Education, 8%

Social Sciences, 12% Visual and Performing Arts
Expenses: 2014-2015: $35,652; room/board: $11,920
Financial aid: (317) 940-8200; 66% of undergrads determined to have financial need; average aid package $22,443

Calumet College of St. Joseph

Whiting IN
(219) 473-4295
U.S. News ranking: Reg. U. (Mid. W), second tier
Website: www.ccsj.edu
Admissions email: admissions@ccsj.edu
Private; founded 1951
Affiliation: Roman Catholic
Freshman admissions: least selective; 2013-2014: 545 applied, 218 accepted. Neither SAT nor ACT required. SAT 25/75 percentile: 780-940. High school rank: 5% in top tenth, 14% in top quarter, 44% in top half
Early decision deadline: N/A, notification date: N/A
Early action deadline: N/A, notification date: N/A
Application deadline (fall): rolling
Undergraduate student body: 580 full time, 408 part time; 56% male, 44% female; 1% American Indian, 0% Asian, 27% black, 31% Hispanic, 1% multiracial, 0% Pacific Islander, 40% white, 0% international; 57% from in state; 0% live on campus; N/A of students in fraternities, N/A in sororities
Most popular majors: 6% Business Administration and Management, General, 12% Business Administration, Management and Operations, Other, 55% Criminal Justice/Safety Studies, 5% Elementary Education and Teaching, 3% Psychology, General
Expenses: 2014-2015: $16,440; room/board: N/A
Financial aid: (219) 473-4213; 83% of undergrads determined to have financial need; average aid package $12,356

DePauw University

Greencastle IN
(765) 658-4006
U.S. News ranking: Nat. Lib. Arts, No. 51
Website: www.depauw.edu
Admissions email: admission@depauw.edu
Private; founded 1837
Affiliation: United Methodist
Freshman admissions: more selective; 2013-2014: 5,086 applied, 3,113 accepted. Either SAT or ACT required. ACT 25/75 percentile: 25-29. High school rank: 49% in top tenth, 78% in top quarter, 100% in top half
Early decision deadline: 11/1, notification date: 1/1
Early action deadline: 12/1, notification date: 1/31
Application deadline (fall): 2/1
Undergraduate student body: 2,280 full time, 24 part time; 45% male, 55% female; 0% American Indian, 3% Asian, 6% black, 3% Hispanic, 6% multiracial, 0% Pacific Islander, 68% white, 10% international; 40% from in state; 96% live on campus; 78% of students in fraternities, 64% in sororities

Most popular majors: 13% Biological and Biomedical Sciences, 10% Communication, Journalism, and Related Programs, 10% English Language and Literature/Letters, 7% Foreign Languages, Literatures, and Linguistics, 23% Social Sciences
Expenses: 2014-2015: $42,746; room/board: $11,200
Financial aid: (765) 658-4030; 53% of undergrads determined to have financial need; average aid package $34,151

Earlham College

Richmond IN
(765) 983-1600
U.S. News ranking: Nat. Lib. Arts, No. 73
Website: www.earlham.edu/admissions
Admissions email: admission@earlham.edu
Private; founded 1847
Affiliation: Quaker
Freshman admissions: more selective; 2013-2014: 1,890 applied, 1,204 accepted. Neither SAT nor ACT required. SAT 25/75 percentile: 1150-1340. High school rank: 29% in top tenth, 60% in top quarter, 92% in top half
Early decision deadline: 11/1, notification date: 12/1
Early action deadline: 12/1, notification date: 2/1
Application deadline (fall): 2/15
Undergraduate student body: 1,031 full time, 33 part time; 45% male, 55% female; 1% American Indian, 4% Asian, 14% black, 6% Hispanic, 0% multiracial, 0% Pacific Islander, 54% white, 18% international; 33% from in state; 96% live on campus; 0% of students in fraternities, 0% in sororities
Most popular majors: 16% Biology, General, 9% Fine and Studio Arts, 15% Multi-/Interdisciplinary Studies, Other, 9% Psychology, General, 11% Sociology
Expenses: 2014-2015: $42,870; room/board: $8,600
Financial aid: (765) 983-1217; 66% of undergrads determined to have financial need; average aid package $37,334

Franklin College[1]

Franklin IN
(317) 738-8062
U.S. News ranking: Reg. Coll. (Mid. W), No. 6
Website: www.franklincollege.edu
Admissions email: admissions@franklincollege.edu
Private; founded 1834
Affiliation: American Baptist
Application deadline (fall): rolling
Undergraduate student body: N/A full time, N/A part time
Expenses: 2013-2014: $27,695; room/board: $8,190
Financial aid: (317) 738-8075

Goshen College

Goshen IN
(574) 535-7535
U.S. News ranking: Nat. Lib. Arts, No. 129
Website: www.goshen.edu
Admissions email: admissions@goshen.edu
Private; founded 1894
Affiliation: Mennonite Church USA

Freshman admissions: selective; 2013-2014: 770 applied, 424 accepted. Either SAT or ACT required. SAT 25/75 percentile: 950-1250. High school rank: 25% in top tenth, 33% in top quarter, 89% in top half
Early decision deadline: N/A, notification date: N/A
Early action deadline: N/A, notification date: N/A
Application deadline (fall): 8/1
Undergraduate student body: 745 full time, 83 part time; 43% male, 57% female; 0% American Indian, 1% Asian, 4% black, 12% Hispanic, 3% multiracial, 0% Pacific Islander, 72% white, 8% international; 50% from in state; 66% live on campus; N/A of students in fraternities, N/A in sororities
Most popular majors: 10% Biological and Biomedical Sciences, 15% Business, Management, Marketing, and Related Support Services, 7% Education, 19% Health Professions and Related Programs, 10% Visual and Performing Arts
Expenses: 2014-2015: $29,700; room/board: $9,700
Financial aid: (574) 535-7583; 74% of undergrads determined to have financial need; average aid package $23,539

Grace College and Seminary

Winona Lake IN
(574) 372-5100
U.S. News ranking: Reg. Coll. (Mid. W), No. 46
Website: www.grace.edu
Admissions email: enroll@grace.edu
Private; founded 1948
Affiliation: Fellowship of Grace Brethren Churches
Freshman admissions: selective; 2013-2014: 3,572 applied, 2,789 accepted. Either SAT or ACT required. SAT 25/75 percentile: 910-1150. High school rank: 21% in top tenth, 47% in top quarter, 79% in top half
Early decision deadline: N/A, notification date: N/A
Early action deadline: 12/1, notification date: 12/20
Application deadline (fall): 3/1
Undergraduate student body: 1,275 full time, 340 part time; 41% male, 59% female; 0% American Indian, 1% Asian, 4% black, 3% Hispanic, 3% multiracial, 0% Pacific Islander, 82% white, 0% international; 62% from in state; 70% live on campus; 0% of students in fraternities, 0% in sororities
Most popular majors: 19% Business Administration, Management and Operations, Other, 7% Counseling Psychology, 13% Elementary Education and Teaching, 5% Graphic Design, 5% Psychology, General
Expenses: 2014-2015: $24,670; room/board: $7,930
Financial aid: (574) 372-5100; 52% of undergrads determined to have financial need; average aid package $15,916

Hanover College

Hanover IN
(812) 866-7021
U.S. News ranking: Nat. Lib. Arts, No. 113
Website: www.hanover.edu
Admissions email: admission@hanover.edu
Private; founded 1827
Affiliation: Presbyterian
Freshman admissions: selective; 2013-2014: 3,174 applied, 2,118 accepted. Either SAT or ACT required. SAT 25/75 percentile: 1000-1200. High school rank: 32% in top tenth, 66% in top quarter, 95% in top half
Early decision deadline: N/A, notification date: N/A
Early action deadline: 12/1, notification date: 12/20
Application deadline (fall): 3/1
Undergraduate student body: 1,158 full time, 5 part time; 43% male, 57% female; 0% American Indian, 1% Asian, 4% black, 2% Hispanic, 2% multiracial, 0% Pacific Islander, 82% white, 5% international; 69% from in state; 95% live on campus; 44% of students in fraternities, 29% in sororities
Most popular majors: 8% Biology/Biological Sciences, General, 7% Economics, General, 9% Elementary Education and Teaching, 8% Kinesiology and Exercise Science, 10% Psychology, General
Expenses: 2014-2015: $33,023; room/board: $10,050
Financial aid: (800) 213-2178; 77% of undergrads determined to have financial need; average aid package $26,398

Holy Cross College[1]

Notre Dame IN
(574) 239-8400
U.S. News ranking: Nat. Lib. Arts, second tier
Website: www.hcc-nd.edu/home
Admissions email: admissions@hcc-nd.edu
Private; founded 1966
Affiliation: Roman Catholic
Application deadline (fall): rolling
Undergraduate student body: N/A full time, N/A part time
Expenses: 2014-2015: $27,150; room/board: $9,500
Financial aid: (574) 239-8408

Huntington University

Huntington IN
(800) 642-6493
U.S. News ranking: Reg. Coll. (Mid. W), No. 14
Website: www.huntington.edu
Admissions email: admissions@huntington.edu
Private; founded 1897
Affiliation: United Brethren in Christ
Freshman admissions: selective; 2013-2014: 780 applied, 759 accepted. Either SAT or ACT required. SAT 25/75 percentile: 880-1130. High school rank: 26% in top tenth, 53% in top quarter, 80% in top half
Early decision deadline: N/A, notification date: N/A
Early action deadline: N/A, notification date: N/A
Application deadline (fall): 8/1

Undergraduate student body: 961 full time, 92 part time; 43% male, 57% female; 0% American Indian, 0% Asian, 2% black, 3% Hispanic, 1% multiracial, 0% Pacific Islander, 88% white, 4% international; 65% from in state; 76% live on campus; 0% of students in fraternities, 0% in sororities
Most popular majors: 19% Business, Management, Marketing, and Related Support Services, 15% Education, 9% Health Professions and Related Programs, 13% Theology and Religious Vocations, 9% Visual and Performing Arts
Expenses: 2014-2015: $24,771; room/board: $8,306
Financial aid: (260) 359-4015; 81% of undergrads determined to have financial need; average aid package $18,334

Indiana Institute of Technology

Fort Wayne IN
(800) 937-2448
U.S. News ranking: Business, unranked
Website: www.indianatech.edu
Admissions email: admissions@indianatech.edu
Private; founded 1930
Freshman admissions: selective; 2013-2014: 2,324 applied, 1,679 accepted. Either SAT or ACT required. ACT 25/75 percentile: 17-23. High school rank: 8% in top tenth, 28% in top quarter, 59% in top half
Early decision deadline: N/A, notification date: N/A
Early action deadline: N/A, notification date: N/A
Application deadline (fall): rolling
Undergraduate student body: 3,710 full time, 2,007 part time; 38% male, 62% female; 0% American Indian, 0% Asian, 39% black, 4% Hispanic, 2% multiracial, 0% Pacific Islander, 48% white, 1% international; 83% from in state; N/A live on campus; 2% of students in fraternities, 1% in sororities
Most popular majors: 9% Accounting, 41% Business Administration and Management, General, 11% Business/Commerce, General, 4% General Studies, 10% Organizational Leadership
Expenses: 2014-2015: $24,860; room/board: $11,150
Financial aid: (260) 422-5561; 91% of undergrads determined to have financial need; average aid package $15,351

Indiana State University

Terre Haute IN
(812) 237-2121
U.S. News ranking: Nat. U., second tier
Website: web.indstate.edu/
Admissions email: admissions@indstate.edu
Public; founded 1865
Freshman admissions: less selective; 2013-2014: 11,016 applied, 9,150 accepted. Either SAT or ACT required. SAT 25/75 percentile: 800-1020. High school rank: 8% in top tenth, 28% in top quarter, 67% in top half

Early decision deadline: N/A, notification date: N/A
Early action deadline: N/A, notification date: N/A
Application deadline (fall): 8/15
Undergraduate student body: 9,131 full time, 1,137 part time; 46% male, 54% female; 0% American Indian, 1% Asian, 18% black, 3% Hispanic, 3% multiracial, 0% Pacific Islander, 67% white, 6% international; 84% from in state; 40% live on campus; 2% of students in fraternities, 2% in sororities
Most popular majors: 17% Business, Management, Marketing, and Related Support Services, 9% Education, 6% Engineering Technologies and Engineering-Related Fields, 18% Health Professions and Related Programs, 12% Social Sciences
Expenses: 2014-2015: $8,416 in state, $18,346 out of state; room/board: $9,182
Financial aid: (812) 237-2215; 74% of undergrads determined to have financial need; average aid package $10,252

Indiana University–Bloomington

Bloomington IN
(812) 855-0661
U.S. News ranking: Nat. U., No. 76
Website: www.iub.edu
Admissions email: iuadmit@indiana.edu
Public; founded 1820
Freshman admissions: more selective; 2013-2014: 37,826 applied, 27,300 accepted. Either SAT or ACT required. SAT 25/75 percentile: 1060-1290. High school rank: 35% in top tenth, 70% in top quarter, 95% in top half
Early decision deadline: N/A, notification date: N/A
Early action deadline: N/A, notification date: N/A
Application deadline (fall): rolling
Undergraduate student body: 31,050 full time, 5,812 part time; 49% male, 51% female; 0% American Indian, 4% Asian, 4% black, 4% Hispanic, 3% multiracial, 0% Pacific Islander, 73% white, 11% international; 71% from in state; 28% live on campus; 21% of students in fraternities, 23% in sororities
Most popular majors: 5% Biological and Biomedical Sciences, 18% Business, Management, Marketing, and Related Support Services, 6% Parks, Recreation, Leisure, and Fitness Studies, 5% Psychology, 7% Public Administration and Social Service Professions
Expenses: 2014-2015: $10,388 in state, $33,241 out of state; room/board: $9,493
Financial aid: (812) 855-0321; 44% of undergrads determined to have financial need; average aid package $11,991

Indiana University East

Richmond IN
(765) 973-8208
U.S. News ranking: Reg. Coll. (Mid. W), second tier
Website: www.iue.edu
Admissions email: eaadmit@indiana.edu

Public; founded 1971
Freshman admissions: less selective; 2013-2014: 1,219 applied, 656 accepted. Either SAT or ACT required. SAT 25/75 percentile: 820-1030. High school rank: 8% in top tenth, 29% in top quarter, 68% in top half
Early decision deadline: N/A, notification date: N/A
Early action deadline: N/A, notification date: N/A
Application deadline (fall): rolling
Undergraduate student body: 1,948 full time, 2,378 part time; 35% male, 65% female; 0% American Indian, 1% Asian, 4% black, 2% Hispanic, 2% multiracial, 0% Pacific Islander, 89% white, 0% international; 78% from in state; 0% live on campus; N/A of students in fraternities, N/A in sororities
Most popular majors: 29% Business, Management, Marketing, and Related Support Services, 9% Education, 18% Health Professions and Related Programs, 13% Liberal Arts and Sciences, General Studies and Humanities, 6% Public Administration and Social Service Professions
Expenses: 2014-2015: $6,787 in state, $18,081 out of state; room/board: $8
Financial aid: (765) 973-8206; 83% of undergrads determined to have financial need; average aid package $8,814

Indiana University–Kokomo

Kokomo IN
(765) 455-9217
U.S. News ranking: Reg. Coll. (Mid. W), second tier
Website: www.iuk.edu
Admissions email: iuadmiss@iuk.edu
Public; founded 1945
Freshman admissions: less selective; 2013-2014: 1,066 applied, 784 accepted. Either SAT or ACT required. SAT 25/75 percentile: 850-1040. High school rank: 9% in top tenth, 29% in top quarter, 68% in top half
Early decision deadline: N/A, notification date: N/A
Early action deadline: N/A, notification date: N/A
Application deadline (fall): 8/6
Undergraduate student body: 2,012 full time, 1,969 part time; 36% male, 64% female; 0% American Indian, 1% Asian, 4% black, 4% Hispanic, 3% multiracial, 0% Pacific Islander, 84% white, 0% international; 99% from in state; 0% live on campus; 0% of students in fraternities, 0% in sororities
Most popular majors: 10% Business, Management, Marketing, and Related Support Services, 9% Education, 33% Health Professions and Related Programs, 13% Liberal Arts and Sciences, General Studies and Humanities, 6% Psychology
Expenses: 2014-2015: $6,811 in state, $18,081 out of state; room/board: N/A
Financial aid: (765) 455-9216; 75% of undergrads determined to have financial need; average aid package $8,303

Indiana University Northwest

Gary IN
(219) 980-6991
U.S. News ranking: Reg. U. (Mid. W), second tier
Website: www.iun.edu
Admissions email: admit@iun.edu
Public; founded 1948
Freshman admissions: less selective; 2013-2014: 1,773 applied, 1,352 accepted. Either SAT or ACT required. SAT 25/75 percentile: 780-1020. High school rank: 10% in top tenth, 32% in top quarter, 62% in top half
Early decision deadline: N/A, notification date: N/A
Early action deadline: N/A, notification date: N/A
Application deadline (fall): rolling
Undergraduate student body: 3,221 full time, 2,683 part time; 34% male, 66% female; 0% American Indian, 2% Asian, 20% black, 17% Hispanic, 2% multiracial, 0% Pacific Islander, 56% white, 0% international; 98% from in state; 0% live on campus; 0% of students in fraternities, 0% in sororities
Most popular majors: 12% Business, Management, Marketing, and Related Support Services, 14% Health Professions and Related Programs, 10% Homeland Security, Law Enforcement, Firefighting and Related Protective Services, 14% Liberal Arts and Sciences, General Studies and Humanities, 11% Psychology
Expenses: 2014-2015: $6,854 in state, $18,081 out of state; room/board: N/A
Financial aid: (877) 280-4593; 73% of undergrads determined to have financial need; average aid package $8,206

Indiana University–Purdue University–Fort Wayne

Fort Wayne IN
(260) 481-6812
U.S. News ranking: Reg. U. (Mid. W), second tier
Website: www.ipfw.edu
Admissions email: ask@ipfw.edu
Public; founded 1964
Freshman admissions: selective; 2013-2014: 3,702 applied, 3,076 accepted. Either SAT or ACT required. SAT 25/75 percentile: 890-1090. High school rank: 13% in top tenth, 38% in top quarter, 77% in top half
Early decision deadline: N/A, notification date: N/A
Early action deadline: N/A, notification date: N/A
Application deadline (fall): 8/1
Undergraduate student body: 7,418 full time, 5,510 part time; 45% male, 55% female; 0% American Indian, 2% Asian, 5% black, 5% Hispanic, 3% multiracial, 0% Pacific Islander, 82% white, 2% international; 97% from in state; 7% live on campus; 1% of students in fraternities, 0% in sororities
Most popular majors: 18% Business Administration and Management, General, 11% Education, General, 14% General Studies, 11% Health Services/Allied Health/Health Sciences, General, 7% Visual and Performing Arts, General

---

Expenses: 2014-2015: $8,040 in state, $19,183 out of state; room/board: $9,242
Financial aid: (260) 481-6820; 78% of undergrads determined to have financial need; average aid package $9,274

Indiana University–Purdue University–Indianapolis

Indianapolis IN
(317) 274-4591
U.S. News ranking: Nat. U., No. 194
Website: www.iupui.edu
Admissions email: apply@iupui.edu
Public; founded 1969
Freshman admissions: selective; 2013-2014: 12,230 applied, 8,510 accepted. Either SAT or ACT required. SAT 25/75 percentile: 890-1120. High school rank: 15% in top tenth, 45% in top quarter, 86% in top half
Early decision deadline: N/A, notification date: N/A
Early action deadline: N/A, notification date: N/A
Application deadline (fall): 5/1
Undergraduate student body: 16,760 full time, 5,649 part time; 43% male, 57% female; 0% American Indian, 4% Asian, 10% black, 5% Hispanic, 3% multiracial, 0% Pacific Islander, 72% white, 3% international; 98% from in state; 10% live on campus; 3% of students in fraternities, 4% in sororities
Most popular majors: 13% Business, Management, Marketing, and Related Support Services, 5% Education, 11% Health Professions and Related Programs, 12% Liberal Arts and Sciences, General Studies and Humanities, 5% Psychology
Expenses: 2014-2015: $8,909 in state, $30,089 out of state; room/board: $7,981
Financial aid: (317) 274-4162; 71% of undergrads determined to have financial need; average aid package $9,848

Indiana University–South Bend

South Bend IN
(574) 520-4839
U.S. News ranking: Reg. U. (Mid. W), second tier
Website: www.iusb.edu
Admissions email: admissions@iusb.edu
Public; founded 1922
Freshman admissions: less selective; 2013-2014: 2,456 applied, 1,720 accepted. Either SAT or ACT required. SAT 25/75 percentile: 860-1060. High school rank: 9% in top tenth, 29% in top quarter, 65% in top half
Early decision deadline: N/A, notification date: N/A
Early action deadline: N/A, notification date: N/A
Application deadline (fall): rolling
Undergraduate student body: 3,984 full time, 3,528 part time; 39% male, 61% female; 0% American Indian, 1% Asian, 7% black, 7% Hispanic, 3% multiracial, 0% Pacific Islander, 77% white, 2% international; 97% from in state; 6% live on campus; N/A of students in fraternities, N/A in sororities

---

Most popular majors: 18% Business, Management, Marketing, and Related Support Services, 7% Education, 11% Health Professions and Related Programs, 15% Liberal Arts and Sciences, General Studies and Humanities, 5% Psychology
Expenses: 2014-2015: $6,905 in state, $18,081 out of state; room/board: N/A
Financial aid: (574) 237-4357; 78% of undergrads determined to have financial need; average aid package $8,655

Indiana University Southeast

New Albany IN
(812) 941-2212
U.S. News ranking: Reg. U. (Mid. W), second tier
Website: www.ius.edu
Admissions email: admissions@ius.edu
Public; founded 1941
Freshman admissions: less selective; 2013-2014: 2,097 applied, 1,666 accepted. Either SAT or ACT required. SAT 25/75 percentile: 850-1050. High school rank: 10% in top tenth, 34% in top quarter, 71% in top half
Early decision deadline: N/A, notification date: N/A
Early action deadline: N/A, notification date: N/A
Application deadline (fall): rolling
Undergraduate student body: 3,665 full time, 2,483 part time; 42% male, 58% female; 0% American Indian, 1% Asian, 6% black, 3% Hispanic, 2% multiracial, 0% Pacific Islander, 86% white, 0% international; 70% from in state; 6% live on campus; N/A of students in fraternities, N/A in sororities
Most popular majors: 18% Business, Management, Marketing, and Related Support Services, 10% Education, 10% Health Professions and Related Programs, 16% Liberal Arts and Sciences, General Studies and Humanities, 7% Psychology
Expenses: 2014-2015: $6,827 in state, $18,081 out of state; room/board: N/A
Financial aid: (812) 941-2246; 69% of undergrads determined to have financial need; average aid package $7,669

Indiana Wesleyan University

Marion IN
(866) 468-6498
U.S. News ranking: Reg. U. (Mid. W), No. 26
Website: www.indwes.edu
Admissions email: admissions@indwes.edu
Private; founded 1920
Affiliation: Wesleyan Church
Freshman admissions: selective; 2013-2014: 2,606 applied, 2,521 accepted. Either SAT or ACT required. ACT 25/75 percentile: 21-27. High school rank: 28% in top tenth, 57% in top quarter, 85% in top half
Early decision deadline: N/A, notification date: N/A
Early action deadline: N/A, notification date: N/A
Application deadline (fall): rolling

Undergraduate student body: 2,761 full time, 172 part time; 35% male, 65% female; 0% American Indian, 1% Asian, 2% black, 3% Hispanic, 2% multiracial, 0% Pacific Islander, 90% white, 0% international; 55% from in state; 80% live on campus; 0% of students in fraternities, 0% in sororities
Most popular majors: 3% Business Administration and Management, General, 8% Elementary Education and Teaching, 5% Psychology, General, 19% Registered Nursing/Registered Nurse, 3% Social Work
Expenses: 2014-2015: $24,102; room/board: $7,712
Financial aid: (765) 677-2116; 79% of undergrads determined to have financial need; average aid package $21,892

Manchester University

North Manchester IN
(800) 852-3648
U.S. News ranking: Reg. Coll. (Mid. W), No. 27
Website: www.manchester.edu
Admissions email: admitinfo@manchester.edu
Private; founded 1889
Affiliation: Church of the Brethren
Freshman admissions: selective; 2013-2014: 2,195 applied, 1,562 accepted. Either SAT or ACT required. SAT 25/75 percentile: 890-1130. High school rank: 20% in top tenth, 48% in top quarter, 83% in top half
Early decision deadline: N/A, notification date: N/A
Early action deadline: N/A, notification date: N/A
Application deadline (fall): rolling
Undergraduate student body: 1,177 full time, 22 part time; 47% male, 53% female; 0% American Indian, 1% Asian, 4% black, 5% Hispanic, 3% multiracial, 0% Pacific Islander, 84% white, 2% international; 89% from in state; 72% live on campus; N/A of students in fraternities, N/A in sororities
Most popular majors: 21% Business, Management, Marketing, and Related Support Services, 16% Education, 11% Health Professions and Related Programs, 10% Parks, Recreation, Leisure, and Fitness Studies, 7% Psychology
Expenses: 2014-2015: $29,040; room/board: $9,300
Financial aid: (260) 982-5066; 87% of undergrads determined to have financial need; average aid package $25,180

Marian University

Indianapolis IN
(317) 955-6300
U.S. News ranking: Reg. Coll. (Mid. W), No. 25
Website: www.marian.edu
Admissions email: admissions@marian.edu
Private; founded 1851
Affiliation: Roman Catholic
Freshman admissions: selective; 2013-2014: 2,064 applied, 1,196 accepted. Either SAT or ACT required. ACT 25/75 percentile: 19-25. High school rank: 11% in top tenth, 43% in top quarter, 82% in top half

Early decision deadline: N/A, notification date: N/A
Early action deadline: N/A, notification date: N/A
Application deadline (fall): 8/1
Undergraduate student body: 1,679 full time, 525 part time; 36% male, 64% female; 0% American Indian, 1% Asian, 14% black, 4% Hispanic, 2% multiracial, 0% Pacific Islander, 75% white, 0% international; 91% from in state; 34% live on campus; 0% of students in fraternities, 0% in sororities
Most popular majors: 3% Accounting, 10% Business Administration and Management, General, 3% Kinesiology and Exercise Science, 8% Marketing/Marketing Management, General, 38% Registered Nursing/Registered Nurse
Expenses: 2014-2015: $29,400; room/board: $9,140
Financial aid: (317) 955-6040; 85% of undergrads determined to have financial need; average aid package $22,292

Martin University[1]

Indianapolis IN
(317) 543-3243
U.S. News ranking: Nat. Lib. Arts, unranked
Website: www.martin.edu
Admissions email: bshaheed@martin.edu
Private
Application deadline (fall): N/A
Undergraduate student body: N/A full time, N/A part time
Expenses: 2013-2014: $11,960; room/board: N/A
Financial aid: (317) 543-3258

Oakland City University

Oakland City IN
(800) 737-5125
U.S. News ranking: Reg. U. (Mid. W), No. 105
Website: www.oak.edu
Admissions email: admission@oak.edu
Private; founded 1885
Affiliation: General Association of General Baptist
Freshman admissions: less selective; 2013-2014: 652 applied, 475 accepted. Neither SAT nor ACT required. SAT 25/75 percentile: 870-1070. High school rank: N/A
Early decision deadline: N/A, notification date: N/A
Early action deadline: N/A, notification date: N/A
Application deadline (fall): 9/8
Undergraduate student body: 461 full time, 1,850 part time; 39% male, 61% female; 0% American Indian, 1% Asian, 6% black, 2% Hispanic, 1% multiracial, 0% Pacific Islander, 77% white, 6% international; 85% from in state; 50% live on campus; N/A of students in fraternities, N/A in sororities
Most popular majors: 8% Biological and Biomedical Sciences, 35% Business, Management, Marketing, and Related Support Services, 29% Education, 7% Homeland Security, Law Enforcement, Firefighting and Related Protective Services, 5% Psychology

Expenses: 2013-2014: $19,200; room/board: $8,300
Financial aid: (812) 749-1224

Purdue University–Calumet

Hammond IN
(219) 989-2213
U.S. News ranking: Reg. U. (Mid. W), second tier
Website: www.purduecal.edu/
Admissions email: adms@purduecal.edu
Public; founded 1946
Freshman admissions: selective; 2013-2014: 1,945 applied, 1,470 accepted. Either SAT or ACT required. SAT 25/75 percentile: 870-1080. High school rank: 12% in top tenth, 36% in top quarter, 71% in top half
Early decision deadline: N/A, notification date: N/A
Early action deadline: N/A, notification date: N/A
Application deadline (fall): 8/1
Undergraduate student body: 4,836 full time, 3,554 part time; 43% male, 57% female; 0% American Indian, 2% Asian, 14% black, 17% Hispanic, 2% multiracial, 0% Pacific Islander, 57% white, 6% international; 78% from in state; 6% live on campus; 1% of students in fraternities, 1% in sororities
Most popular majors: 20% Business, Management, Marketing, and Related Support Services, 6% Communication, Journalism, and Related Programs, 5% Engineering, 6% Engineering Technologies and Engineering-Related Fields, 33% Health Professions and Related Programs
Expenses: 2014-2015: $7,241 in state, $16,356 out of state; room/board: $8,075
Financial aid: (219) 989-2301; 64% of undergrads determined to have financial need; average aid package $4,522

Purdue University–North Central

Westville IN
(219) 785-5505
U.S. News ranking: Reg. Coll. (Mid. W), second tier
Website: www.pnc.edu/admissions
Admissions email: admissions@pnc.edu
Public; founded 1946
Freshman admissions: less selective; 2013-2014: 1,567 applied, 1,143 accepted. Neither SAT nor ACT required. SAT 25/75 percentile: 860-1050. High school rank: 7% in top tenth, 25% in top quarter, 63% in top half
Early decision deadline: N/A, notification date: N/A
Early action deadline: N/A, notification date: N/A
Application deadline (fall): rolling
Undergraduate student body: 2,732 full time, 3,322 part time; 40% male, 60% female; 1% American Indian, 1% Asian, 5% black, 8% Hispanic, 2% multiracial, 0% Pacific Islander, 82% white, 1% international; 98% from in state; N/A live on campus; N/A of students in fraternities, N/A in sororities
Most popular majors: Information not available
Expenses: 2014-2015: $7,329 in state, $17,445 out of state; room/board: N/A

Financial aid: (219) 785-5653; 74% of undergrads determined to have financial need; average aid package $7,608

Purdue University–West Lafayette

West Lafayette IN
(765) 494-1776
U.S. News ranking: Nat. U., No. 62
Website: www.purdue.edu
Admissions email: admissions@purdue.edu
Public; founded 1869
Freshman admissions: more selective; 2013-2014: 30,955 applied, 18,684 accepted. Either SAT or ACT required. SAT 25/75 percentile: 1080-1320. High school rank: 47% in top tenth, 80% in top quarter, 98% in top half
Early decision deadline: N/A, notification date: N/A
Early action deadline: 11/1, notification date: 12/13
Application deadline (fall): rolling
Undergraduate student body: 28,142 full time, 1,298 part time; 57% male, 43% female; 0% American Indian, 5% Asian, 3% black, 4% Hispanic, 2% multiracial, 0% Pacific Islander, 67% white, 17% international; 68% from in state; 36% live on campus; 10% of students in fraternities, 8% in sororities
Most popular majors: 8% Agriculture, Agriculture Operations, and Related Sciences, 17% Business, Management, Marketing, and Related Support Services, 6% Education, 20% Engineering, 15% Liberal Arts and Sciences, General Studies and Humanities
Expenses: 2014-2015: $10,002 in state, $28,804 out of state; room/board: $10,030
Financial aid: (765) 494-5090; 46% of undergrads determined to have financial need; average aid package $13,081

Rose-Hulman Institute of Technology

Terre Haute IN
(812) 877-8213
U.S. News ranking: Engineering, unranked
Website: www.rose-hulman.edu
Admissions email: admissions@rose-hulman.edu
Private; founded 1874
Freshman admissions: more selective; 2013-2014: 5,046 applied, 2,837 accepted. Either SAT or ACT required. ACT 25/75 percentile: 27-32. High school rank: 66% in top tenth, 92% in top quarter, 100% in top half
Early decision deadline: N/A, notification date: N/A
Early action deadline: 11/1, notification date: 12/15
Application deadline (fall): 3/1
Undergraduate student body: 2,186 full time, 19 part time; 78% male, 22% female; 0% American Indian, 4% Asian, 2% black, 3% Hispanic, 3% multiracial, 0% Pacific Islander, 78% white, 9% international; 37% from in state; 60% live on campus; 36% of students in fraternities, 33% in sororities

Most popular majors: 10% Bioengineering and Biomedical Engineering, 11% Chemical Engineering, 9% Civil Engineering, General, 13% Electrical and Electronics Engineering, 28% Mechanical Engineering
Expenses: 2014-2015: $41,283; room/board: $12,057
Financial aid: (812) 877-8259; 65% of undergrads determined to have financial need; average aid package $28,577

St. Joseph's College

Rensselaer IN
(219) 866-6170
U.S. News ranking: Reg. Coll. (Mid. W), No. 28
Website: www.saintjoe.edu
Admissions email: admissions@saintjoe.edu
Private; founded 1889
Affiliation: Roman Catholic
Freshman admissions: selective; 2013-2014: 1,639 applied, 1,052 accepted. Either SAT or ACT required. SAT 25/75 percentile: 890-1080. High school rank: 12% in top tenth, 35% in top quarter, 73% in top half
Early decision deadline: N/A, notification date: N/A
Early action deadline: N/A, notification date: N/A
Application deadline (fall): rolling
Undergraduate student body: 1,036 full time, 112 part time; 41% male, 59% female; 1% American Indian, 0% Asian, 9% black, 5% Hispanic, 2% multiracial, 0% Pacific Islander, 80% white, 1% international; 77% from in state; 61% live on campus; N/A of students in fraternities, N/A in sororities
Most popular majors: 12% Biology/Biological Sciences, General, 15% Business/Commerce, General, 5% Criminal Justice/Safety Studies, 6% Elementary Education and Teaching, 35% Registered Nursing/Registered Nurse
Expenses: 2014-2015: $27,890; room/board: $8,610
Financial aid: (219) 866-6163; 85% of undergrads determined to have financial need; average aid package $27,592

St. Mary-of-the-Woods College

St. Mary-of-the-Woods IN
(800) 926-7692
U.S. News ranking: Reg. Coll. (Mid. W), No. 16
Website: www.smwc.edu
Admissions email: smwcadms@smwc.edu
Private; founded 1840
Affiliation: Roman Catholic
Freshman admissions: less selective; 2013-2014: 325 applied, 317 accepted. Either SAT or ACT required. SAT 25/75 percentile: 780-1020. High school rank: 14% in top tenth, 41% in top quarter, 70% in top half
Early decision deadline: N/A, notification date: N/A
Early action deadline: N/A, notification date: N/A
Application deadline (fall): rolling
Undergraduate student body: 384 full time, 265 part time; 3% male, 97% female; 1% American Indian, 0% Asian, 4% black, 1% Hispanic, 0% multiracial, 0% Pacific Islander, 85% white,

0% international; N/A from in state; 60% live on campus; 0% of students in fraternities, 0% in sororities
Most popular majors: 4% Accounting, 10% Business Administration and Management, General, 29% Education, 5% Human Resources Management and Services, 11% Psychology
Expenses: 2014-2015: $28,226; room/board: $10,250
Financial aid: (812) 535-5109; 90% of undergrads determined to have financial need; average aid package $17,832

St. Mary's College
Notre Dame IN
(574) 284-4587
U.S. News ranking: Nat. Lib. Arts, No. 96
Website: www.saintmarys.edu
Admissions email: admission@saintmarys.edu
Private; founded 1844
Affiliation: Roman Catholic
Freshman admissions: selective; 2013-2014: 1,529 applied, 1,310 accepted. Either SAT or ACT required. ACT 25/75 percentile: 23-28. High school rank: 27% in top tenth, 57% in top quarter, 90% in top half
Early decision deadline: 11/15, notification date: 12/15
Early action deadline: N/A, notification date: N/A
Application deadline (fall): rolling
Undergraduate student body: 1,469 full time, 10 part time; 0% male, 100% female; 0% American Indian, 1% Asian, 1% black, 12% Hispanic, 3% multiracial, 0% Pacific Islander, 77% white, 2% international; 25% from in state; 91% live on campus; 0% of students in fraternities, 0% in sororities
Most popular majors: 9% Biology/Biological Sciences, General, 11% Elementary Education and Teaching, 8% Psychology, General, 14% Registered Nursing/Registered Nurse, 8% Speech Communication and Rhetoric
Expenses: 2014-2015: $35,970; room/board: $10,930
Financial aid: (574) 284-4557; 56% of undergrads determined to have financial need; average aid package $29,077

Taylor University
Upland IN
(765) 998-5134
U.S. News ranking: Reg. Coll. (Mid. W), No. 1
Website: www.taylor.edu
Admissions email: admissions_u@taylor.edu
Private; founded 1846
Affiliation: Christian interdenominational
Freshman admissions: more selective; 2013-2014: 1,637 applied, 1,434 accepted. Either SAT or ACT required. ACT 25/75 percentile: 24-31. High school rank: 37% in top tenth, 67% in top quarter, 89% in top half
Early decision deadline: N/A, notification date: N/A
Early action deadline: N/A, notification date: N/A
Application deadline (fall): rolling
Undergraduate student body: 1,852 full time, 294 part time; 45% male, 55% female; 0% American Indian, 3% Asian, 2% black, 3% Hispanic, 1% multiracial,

0% Pacific Islander, 87% white, 4% international; 36% from in state; 87% live on campus; 0% of students in fraternities, 0% in sororities
Most popular majors: 14% Business, Management, Marketing, and Related Support Services, 7% Communication, Journalism, and Related Programs, 18% Education, 7% Psychology, 10% Visual and Performing Arts
Expenses: 2014-2015: $29,538; room/board: $8,283
Financial aid: (765) 998-5358; 61% of undergrads determined to have financial need; average aid package $19,190

Trine University
Angola IN
(260) 665-4100
U.S. News ranking: Reg. Coll. (Mid. W), No. 32
Website: www.trine.edu
Admissions email: admit@trine.edu
Private; founded 1884
Freshman admissions: selective; 2013-2014: 2,711 applied, 2,036 accepted. Either SAT or ACT required. SAT 25/75 percentile: 980-1190. High school rank: 25% in top tenth, 57% in top quarter, 87% in top half
Early decision deadline: N/A, notification date: N/A
Early action deadline: N/A, notification date: N/A
Application deadline (fall): 8/1
Undergraduate student body: 1,430 full time, 445 part time; 65% male, 35% female; 0% American Indian, 0% Asian, 2% black, 3% Hispanic, 2% multiracial, 0% Pacific Islander, 84% white, 4% international; 61% from in state; 69% live on campus; 26% of students in fraternities, 19% in sororities
Most popular majors: 19% Business/Commerce, General, 8% Criminal Justice/Law Enforcement Administration, 9% Education, General, 33% Engineering, General, 7% Psychology, General
Expenses: 2014-2015: $29,600; room/board: $9,800
Financial aid: (260) 665-4175; 84% of undergrads determined to have financial need; average aid package $24,095

University of Evansville
Evansville IN
(812) 488-2468
U.S. News ranking: Reg. U. (Mid. W), No. 9
Website: www.evansville.edu
Admissions email: admission@evansville.edu
Private; founded 1854
Affiliation: Methodist
Freshman admissions: more selective; 2013-2014: 2,935 applied, 2,468 accepted. Either SAT or ACT required. ACT 25/75 percentile: 23-29. High school rank: 33% in top tenth, 66% in top quarter, 91% in top half
Early decision deadline: N/A, notification date: N/A
Early action deadline: 12/1, notification date: 12/15
Application deadline (fall): rolling
Undergraduate student body: 2,290 full time, 187 part time; 42% male, 58% female; 0% American Indian, 1% Asian, 3% black, 3% Hispanic, 2% multiracial, 0%

Pacific Islander, 78% white, 9% international; 55% from in state; 65% live on campus; 30% of students in fraternities, 28% in sororities
Most popular majors: 12% Business, Management, Marketing, and Related Support Services, 9% Engineering, 10% Health Professions and Related Programs, 9% Parks, Recreation, Leisure, and Fitness Studies, 12% Visual and Performing Arts
Expenses: 2014-2015: $31,776; room/board: $10,880
Financial aid: (812) 488-2364; 69% of undergrads determined to have financial need; average aid package $25,721

University of Indianapolis
Indianapolis IN
(317) 788-3216
U.S. News ranking: Reg. U. (Mid. W), No. 26
Website: www.uindy.edu
Admissions email: admissions@uindy.edu
Private; founded 1902
Affiliation: United Methodist
Freshman admissions: selective; 2013-2014: 5,530 applied, 4,504 accepted. Either SAT or ACT required. SAT 25/75 percentile: 910-1120. High school rank: 23% in top tenth, 56% in top quarter, 88% in top half
Early decision deadline: N/A, notification date: N/A
Early action deadline: N/A, notification date: N/A
Application deadline (fall): 8/20
Undergraduate student body: 3,169 full time, 993 part time; 33% male, 67% female; 0% American Indian, 1% Asian, 11% black, 3% Hispanic, 2% multiracial, 0% Pacific Islander, 69% white, 8% international; 93% from in state; 35% live on campus; 0% of students in fraternities, 0% in sororities
Most popular majors: 13% Business Administration and Management, General, 6% Kinesiology and Exercise Science, 7% Liberal Arts and Sciences/Liberal Studies, 10% Psychology, General, 15% Registered Nursing/Registered Nurse
Expenses: 2014-2015: $25,414; room/board: $9,550
Financial aid: (317) 788-3217; 74% of undergrads determined to have financial need; average aid package $17,356

University of Notre Dame
Notre Dame IN
(574) 631-7505
U.S. News ranking: Nat. U., No. 16
Website: www.nd.edu
Admissions email: admissions@nd.edu
Private; founded 1842
Affiliation: Roman Catholic
Freshman admissions: most selective; 2013-2014: 17,647 applied, 3,936 accepted. Either SAT or ACT required. ACT 25/75 percentile: 32-34. High school rank: 90% in top tenth, 98% in top quarter, 100% in top half
Early decision deadline: N/A, notification date: N/A
Early action deadline: 11/1, notification date: 12/21

Application deadline (fall): 1/1
Undergraduate student body: 8,459 full time, 18 part time; 53% male, 47% female; 0% American Indian, 6% Asian, 4% black, 10% Hispanic, 4% multiracial, 0% Pacific Islander, 71% white, 4% international; 8% from in state; 80% live on campus; N/A of students in fraternities, N/A in sororities
Most popular majors: 8% Accounting, 5% Economics, General, 11% Finance, General, 7% Political Science and Government, General, 7% Psychology, General
Expenses: 2014-2015: $46,237; room/board: $13,224
Financial aid: (574) 631-6436; 49% of undergrads determined to have financial need; average aid package $40,352

University of Southern Indiana
Evansville IN
(812) 464-1765
U.S. News ranking: Reg. U. (Mid. W), second tier
Website: www.usi.edu
Admissions email: enroll@usi.edu
Public; founded 1965
Freshman admissions: selective; 2013-2014: 6,204 applied, 4,302 accepted. Either SAT or ACT required. SAT 25/75 percentile: 890-1110. High school rank: 13% in top tenth, 36% in top quarter, 73% in top half
Early decision deadline: N/A, notification date: N/A
Early action deadline: N/A, notification date: N/A
Undergraduate student body: 7,375 full time, 1,538 part time; 41% male, 59% female; 0% American Indian, 1% Asian, 4% black, 1% Hispanic, 2% multiracial, 0% Pacific Islander, 86% white, 3% international; 89% from in state; 27% live on campus; 7% of students in fraternities, 8% in sororities
Most popular majors: 15% Business, Management, Marketing, and Related Support Services, 6% Communication, Journalism, and Related Programs, 12% Education, 26% Health Professions and Related Programs, 5% Social Sciences
Expenses: 2014-2015: $6,977 in state, $16,317 out of state; room/board: $7,680
Financial aid: (812) 464-1767; 66% of undergrads determined to have financial need; average aid package $8,892

University of St. Francis
Fort Wayne IN
(260) 399-8000
U.S. News ranking: Reg. U. (Mid. W), No. 69
Website: www.sf.edu
Admissions email: admis@sf.edu
Private; founded 1890
Affiliation: Roman Catholic
Freshman admissions: less selective; 2013-2014: 1,057 applied, 1,023 accepted. Either SAT or ACT required. SAT 25/75 percentile: 890-1060. High school rank: 11% in top tenth, 38% in top quarter, 80% in top half
Early decision deadline: N/A, notification date: N/A

Early action deadline: N/A, notification date: N/A
Application deadline (fall): rolling
Undergraduate student body: 1,616 full time, 364 part time; 29% male, 71% female; 1% American Indian, 1% Asian, 6% black, 6% Hispanic, 2% multiracial, 0% Pacific Islander, 82% white, 0% international; 90% from in state; 19% live on campus; 0% of students in fraternities, 0% in sororities
Most popular majors: 8% Biological and Biomedical Sciences, 10% Business, Management, Marketing, and Related Support Services, 9% Education, 36% Health Professions and Related Programs, 10% Visual and Performing Arts
Expenses: 2014-2015: $25,930; room/board: $8,640
Financial aid: (260) 434-3283; 87% of undergrads determined to have financial need; average aid package $17,054

Valparaiso University
Valparaiso IN
(888) 468-2576
U.S. News ranking: Reg. U. (Mid. W), No. 5
Website: www.valpo.edu
Admissions email: undergrad.admission@valpo.edu
Private; founded 1859
Affiliation: Lutheran
Freshman admissions: more selective; 2013-2014: 6,124 applied, 4,880 accepted. Either SAT or ACT required. ACT 25/75 percentile: 23-29. High school rank: 36% in top tenth, 68% in top quarter, 93% in top half
Early decision deadline: N/A, notification date: N/A
Early action deadline: N/A, notification date: N/A
Application deadline (fall): rolling
Undergraduate student body: 3,136 full time, 115 part time; 48% male, 52% female; 0% American Indian, 2% Asian, 5% black, 7% Hispanic, 2% multiracial, 0% Pacific Islander, 75% white, 8% international; 40% from in state; 68% live on campus; 21% of students in fraternities, 19% in sororities
Most popular majors: 5% Biology/Biological Sciences, General, 4% Civil Engineering, General, 5% English Language and Literature, General, 4% Marketing/Marketing Management, General, 19% Registered Nursing/Registered Nurse
Expenses: 2014-2015: $34,760; room/board: $10,180
Financial aid: (219) 464-5015; 72% of undergrads determined to have financial need; average aid package $26,875

Vincennes University
Vincennes IN
(800) 742-9198
U.S. News ranking: Reg. Coll. (Mid. W), unranked
Website: www.vinu.edu
Admissions email: N/A
Public
Freshman admissions: N/A; 2013-2014: N/A applied, N/A accepted. Neither SAT nor ACT required. ACT 25/75 percentile: N/A. High school rank: N/A
Early decision deadline: N/A, notification date: N/A

Early action deadline: N/A, notification date: N/A
Application deadline (fall): rolling
Undergraduate student body: 6,049 full time, 12,334 part time; 56% male, 44% female; 0% American Indian, 1% Asian, 12% black, 3% Hispanic, 2% multiracial, 0% Pacific Islander, 70% white, 0% international; 83% from in state; N/A live on campus; N/A of students in fraternities, N/A in sororities
Most popular majors: Information not available
Expenses: 2014-2015: $5,174 in state, $12,234 out of state; room/board: $8,732
Financial aid: (812) 888-4361

Wabash College

Crawfordsville IN
(800) 345-5385
U.S. News ranking: Nat. Lib. Arts, No. 61
Website: www.wabash.edu
Admissions email: admissions@wabash.edu
Private; founded 1832
Freshman admissions: more selective; 2013-2014: 1,129 applied, 786 accepted. Either SAT or ACT required. SAT 25/75 percentile: 1028-1250. High school rank: 33% in top tenth, 72% in top quarter, 93% in top half
Early decision deadline: 11/15, notification date: 11/30
Early action deadline: 12/1, notification date: 12/19
Application deadline (fall): rolling
Undergraduate student body: 902 full time, 0 part time; 100% male, 0% female; 0% American Indian, 1% Asian, 6% black, 6% Hispanic, 3% multiracial, 0% Pacific Islander, 76% white, 7% international; 75% from in state; 89% live on campus; 60% of students in fraternities, N/A in sororities
Most popular majors: 11% Economics, General, 12% English Language and Literature, General, 12% History, General, 9% Mathematics, General, 9% Political Science and Government, General
Expenses: 2014-2015: $37,750; room/board: $9,130
Financial aid: (765) 361-6370; 80% of undergrads determined to have financial need; average aid package $34,725

IOWA

AIB College of Business

Des Moines IA
(515) 246-5358
U.S. News ranking: Business, unranked
Website: www.aib.edu
Admissions email: admissions@aib.edu
Private; founded 1921
Freshman admissions: less selective; 2013-2014: 424 applied, 292 accepted. Neither SAT nor ACT required. ACT 25/75 percentile: 17-23. High school rank: 10% in top tenth, 25% in top quarter, 50% in top half
Early decision deadline: N/A, notification date: N/A
Early action deadline: N/A, notification date: N/A

Application deadline (fall): rolling
Undergraduate student body: 732 full time, 287 part time; 44% male, 56% female; 1% American Indian, 2% Asian, 5% black, 6% Hispanic, 2% multiracial, 0% Pacific Islander, 63% white, 3% international; 86% from in state; 44% live on campus; 0% of students in fraternities, 0% in sororities
Most popular majors: 24% Accounting, 48% Business Administration and Management, General, 3% Sport and Fitness Administration/Management
Expenses: 2014-2015: $15,600; room/board: N/A
Financial aid: N/A; 78% of undergrads determined to have financial need; average aid package $13,329

Ashford University[1]

Clinton IA
(563) 242-4153
U.S. News ranking: Reg. U. (Mid. W), unranked
Website: www.ashford.edu
Admissions email: admissions@ashford.edu
For-profit
Application deadline (fall): N/A
Undergraduate student body: N/A full time, N/A part time
Expenses: 2013-2014: $10,312; room/board: $6,000
Financial aid: (563) 242-4023

Briar Cliff University

Sioux City IA
(712) 279-5200
U.S. News ranking: Reg. Coll. (Mid. W), No. 38
Website: www.briarcliff.edu
Admissions email: admissions@briarcliff.edu
Private; founded 1930
Affiliation: Roman Catholic
Freshman admissions: selective; 2013-2014: 1,728 applied, 931 accepted. Either SAT or ACT required. ACT 25/75 percentile: 19-25. High school rank: 9% in top tenth, 32% in top quarter, 70% in top half
Early decision deadline: N/A, notification date: N/A
Early action deadline: N/A, notification date: N/A
Application deadline (fall): rolling
Undergraduate student body: 848 full time, 194 part time; 43% male, 57% female; 1% American Indian, 2% Asian, 7% black, 9% Hispanic, 2% multiracial, 0% Pacific Islander, 76% white, 4% international; 55% from in state; 46% live on campus; N/A of students in fraternities, N/A in sororities
Most popular majors: 6% Biological and Biomedical Sciences, 22% Business, Management, Marketing, and Related Support Services, 12% Education, 23% Health Professions and Related Programs, 8% Visual and Performing Arts
Expenses: 2014-2015: $27,102; room/board: $7,888
Financial aid: (712) 279-5239; 93% of undergrads determined to have financial need; average aid package $21,148

Buena Vista University

Storm Lake IA
(800) 383-9600
U.S. News ranking: Reg. Coll. (Mid. W), No. 11
Website: www.bvu.edu
Admissions email: admissions@bvu.edu
Private; founded 1891
Affiliation: Presbyterian
Freshman admissions: selective; 2013-2014: 1,409 applied, 980 accepted. Either SAT or ACT required. ACT 25/75 percentile: 20-25. High school rank: 14% in top tenth, 42% in top quarter, 74% in top half
Early decision deadline: N/A, notification date: N/A
Early action deadline: N/A, notification date: N/A
Application deadline (fall): rolling
Undergraduate student body: 899 full time, 21 part time; 49% male, 51% female; 0% American Indian, 2% Asian, 3% black, 8% Hispanic, 2% multiracial, 0% Pacific Islander, 77% white, 4% international; 80% from in state; 87% live on campus; 0% of students in fraternities, 0% in sororities
Most popular majors: 14% Biological and Biomedical Sciences, 17% Business, Management, Marketing, and Related Support Services, 9% Education, 6% Homeland Security, Law Enforcement, Firefighting and Related Protective Services, 7% Parks, Recreation, Leisure, and Fitness Studies
Expenses: 2014-2015: $30,406; room/board: $8,782
Financial aid: (712) 749-2164; 85% of undergrads determined to have financial need; average aid package $32,113

Central College

Pella IA
(641) 628-5286
U.S. News ranking: Nat. Lib. Arts, No. 139
Website: www.central.edu
Admissions email: admission@central.edu
Private; founded 1853
Affiliation: Reformed Church in America
Freshman admissions: selective; 2013-2014: 2,842 applied, 1,870 accepted. Either SAT or ACT required. ACT 25/75 percentile: 21-26. High school rank: 21% in top tenth, 53% in top quarter, 85% in top half
Early decision deadline: N/A, notification date: N/A
Early action deadline: N/A, notification date: N/A
Application deadline (fall): 8/15
Undergraduate student body: 1,340 full time, 46 part time; 47% male, 53% female; 0% American Indian, 1% Asian, 2% black, 3% Hispanic, 1% multiracial, 0% Pacific Islander, 90% white, 0% international; 81% from in state; 94% live on campus; 4% of students in fraternities, 3% in sororities
Most popular majors: 13% Business, Management, Marketing, and Related Support Services, 9% Education, 9% Foreign Languages, Literatures, and Linguistics, 11% Parks,

Recreation, Leisure, and Fitness Studies, 11% Social Sciences
Expenses: 2014-2015: $32,124; room/board: $9,980
Financial aid: (641) 628-5187; 80% of undergrads determined to have financial need; average aid package $24,341

Clarke University

Dubuque IA
(563) 588-6316
U.S. News ranking: Reg. Coll. (Mid. W), No. 17
Website: www.clarke.edu
Admissions email: admissions@clarke.edu
Private; founded 1843
Affiliation: Roman Catholic
Freshman admissions: selective; 2013-2014: 1,250 applied, 969 accepted. Either SAT or ACT required. ACT 25/75 percentile: 20-25. High school rank: 18% in top tenth, 46% in top quarter, 83% in top half
Early decision deadline: N/A, notification date: N/A
Early action deadline: N/A, notification date: N/A
Application deadline (fall): rolling
Undergraduate student body: 877 full time, 134 part time; 34% male, 66% female; 1% American Indian, 1% Asian, 3% black, 3% Hispanic, 0% multiracial, 0% Pacific Islander, 88% white, 1% international; 59% from in state; 56% live on campus; 0% of students in fraternities, 0% in sororities
Most popular majors: 15% Business Administration and Management, General, 10% Education, General, 9% Psychology, General, 29% Registered Nursing/Registered Nurse
Expenses: 2014-2015: $28,900; room/board: $8,700
Financial aid: (563) 588-6327; 87% of undergrads determined to have financial need; average aid package $22,591

Coe College

Cedar Rapids IA
(319) 399-8500
U.S. News ranking: Nat. Lib. Arts, No. 120
Website: www.coe.edu
Admissions email: admission@coe.edu
Private; founded 1851
Affiliation: Presbyterian
Freshman admissions: more selective; 2013-2014: 2,972 applied, 1,834 accepted. Either SAT or ACT required. ACT 25/75 percentile: 23-28. High school rank: 31% in top tenth, 61% in top quarter, 91% in top half
Early decision deadline: N/A, notification date: N/A
Early action deadline: 12/10, notification date: 1/20
Application deadline (fall): 3/1
Undergraduate student body: 1,351 full time, 69 part time; 46% male, 54% female; 0% American Indian, 2% Asian, 4% black, 5% Hispanic, 3% multiracial, 0% Pacific Islander, 79% white, 2% international; 51% from in state; 86% live on campus; 12% of students in fraternities, 13% in sororities

Most popular majors: 22% Business, Management, Marketing, and Related Support Services, 8% Communication, Journalism, and Related Programs, 9% Health Professions and Related Programs, 12% Psychology, 7% Social Sciences
Expenses: 2014-2015: $37,230; room/board: $8,230
Financial aid: (319) 399-8540; 82% of undergrads determined to have financial need; average aid package $28,412

Cornell College

Mount Vernon IA
(800) 747-1112
U.S. News ranking: Nat. Lib. Arts, No. 105
Website: www.cornellcollege.edu
Admissions email: admissions@cornellcollege.edu
Private; founded 1853
Affiliation: United Methodist
Freshman admissions: more selective; 2013-2014: 2,498 applied, 1,471 accepted. Either SAT or ACT required. ACT 25/75 percentile: 23-29. High school rank: 39% in top tenth, 69% in top quarter, 90% in top half
Early decision deadline: 11/1, notification date: 12/15
Early action deadline: 12/1, notification date: 2/1
Application deadline (fall): 2/1
Undergraduate student body: 1,117 full time, 8 part time; 45% male, 55% female; 1% American Indian, 3% Asian, 5% black, 13% Hispanic, 3% multiracial, 0% Pacific Islander, 65% white, 6% international; 18% from in state; 92% live on campus; 16% of students in fraternities, 22% in sororities
Most popular majors: 12% Biological and Biomedical Sciences, 8% English Language and Literature/Letters, 13% Psychology, 8% Social Sciences, 9% Visual and Performing Arts
Expenses: 2014-2015: $37,500; room/board: $8,500
Financial aid: (319) 895-4216; 77% of undergrads determined to have financial need; average aid package $28,332

Dordt College

Sioux Center IA
(800) 343-6738
U.S. News ranking: Reg. Coll. (Mid. W), No. 5
Website: www.dordt.edu
Admissions email: admissions@dordt.edu
Private; founded 1955
Affiliation: Christian Reformed
Freshman admissions: selective; 2013-2014: 1,344 applied, 1,016 accepted. Either SAT or ACT required. ACT 25/75 percentile: 21-28. High school rank: 21% in top tenth, 44% in top quarter, 73% in top half
Early decision deadline: N/A, notification date: N/A
Early action deadline: N/A, notification date: N/A
Application deadline (fall): 8/1
Undergraduate student body: 1,345 full time, 31 part time; 54% male, 46% female; 0% American Indian, 1% Asian, 1% black, 1% Hispanic, 3% multiracial, 0% Pacific Islander, 85% white, 8% international; 46% from in

state; 89% live on campus; 0% of students in fraternities, 0% in sororities
Most popular majors: 8% Agricultural Business and Management, General, 8% Business/Commerce, General, 22% Elementary Education and Teaching, 8% Health and Wellness, General, 7% Parks, Recreation and Leisure Studies
Expenses: 2014-2015: $27,460; room/board: $8,000
Financial aid: (712) 722-6087; 71% of undergrads determined to have financial need; average aid package $21,345

Drake University
Des Moines IA
(800) 443-7253
U.S. News ranking: Reg. U. (Mid. W), No. 3
Website: www.drake.edu
Admissions email: admission@ drake.edu
Private; founded 1881
Freshman admissions: more selective; 2013-2014: 5,930 applied, 3,911 accepted. Either SAT or ACT required. ACT 25/75 percentile: 25-30. High school rank: 44% in top tenth, 73% in top quarter, 95% in top half
Early decision deadline: N/A, notification date: N/A
Early action deadline: N/A, notification date: N/A
Application deadline (fall): rolling
Undergraduate student body: 3,185 full time, 198 part time; 44% male, 56% female; 0% American Indian, 4% Asian, 3% black, 3% Hispanic, 1% multiracial, 0% Pacific Islander, 79% white, 7% international; 35% from in state; 75% live on campus; 34% of students in fraternities, 28% in sororities
Most popular majors: 36% Business, Management, Marketing, and Related Support Services, 12% Communication, Journalism, and Related Programs, 7% Social Sciences, 7% Visual and Performing Arts
Expenses: 2014-2015: $32,246; room/board: $9,270
Financial aid: (515) 271-2905; 60% of undergrads determined to have financial need; average aid package $23,125

Graceland University
Lamoni IA
(866) 472-2352
U.S. News ranking: Reg. U. (Mid. W), No. 103
Website: www.graceland.edu
Admissions email: admissions@ graceland.edu
Private; founded 1895
Affiliation: Community of Christ
Freshman admissions: selective; 2013-2014: 1,981 applied, 994 accepted. Either SAT or ACT required. ACT 25/75 percentile: 18-24. High school rank: 12% in top tenth, 34% in top quarter, 62% in top half
Early decision deadline: N/A, notification date: N/A
Early action deadline: N/A, notification date: N/A
Application deadline (fall): rolling
Undergraduate student body: 1,293 full time, 266 part time; 43% male, 57% female; 1% American Indian, 1% Asian, 9% black,

7% Hispanic, 4% multiracial, 1% Pacific Islander, 64% white, 7% international; 25% from in state; 68% live on campus; 0% of students in fraternities, 0% in sororities
Most popular majors: 4% Biological and Biomedical Sciences, 11% Business, Management, Marketing, and Related Support Services, 29% Education, 30% Health Professions and Related Programs, 4% Parks, Recreation, Leisure, and Fitness Studies
Expenses: 2014-2015: $24,920; room/board: $8,060
Financial aid: (641) 784-5136; 76% of undergrads determined to have financial need; average aid package $20,935

Grand View University[1]
Des Moines IA
(515) 263-2810
U.S. News ranking: Reg. Coll. (Mid. W), No. 54
Website: www.grandview.edu/
Admissions email: admissions@ grandview.edu
Private; founded 1896
Affiliation: Evangelical Lutheran Church in America
Application deadline (fall): 8/15
Undergraduate student body: N/A full time, N/A part time
Expenses: 2014-2015: $23,516; room/board: $7,554
Financial aid: (515) 263-2820; 82% of undergrads determined to have financial need; average aid package $15,640

Grinnell College
Grinnell IA
(800) 247-0113
U.S. News ranking: Nat. Lib. Arts, No. 19
Website: www.grinnell.edu
Admissions email: askgrin@ grinnell.edu
Private; founded 1846
Freshman admissions: most selective; 2013-2014: 3,979 applied, 1,395 accepted. Either SAT or ACT required. ACT 25/75 percentile: 28-32. High school rank: 63% in top tenth, 88% in top quarter, 98% in top half
Early decision deadline: 11/15, notification date: 12/15
Early action deadline: N/A, notification date: N/A
Application deadline (fall): 1/15
Undergraduate student body: 1,664 full time, 57 part time; 46% male, 54% female; 0% American Indian, 8% Asian, 6% black, 8% Hispanic, 4% multiracial, 0% Pacific Islander, 58% white, 13% international; 12% from in state; 88% live on campus; 0% of students in fraternities, 0% in sororities
Most popular majors: 13% Biology/Biological Sciences, General, 10% Foreign Languages and Literatures, General, 8% History, General, 26% Social Sciences, General, 7% Visual and Performing Arts, General
Expenses: 2014-2015: $45,620; room/board: $10,997
Financial aid: (641) 269-3250; 72% of undergrads determined to have financial need; average aid package $41,315

Iowa State University
Ames IA
(800) 262-3810
U.S. News ranking: Nat. U., No. 106
Website: www.iastate.edu
Admissions email: admissions@ iastate.edu
Public; founded 1858
Freshman admissions: more selective; 2013-2014: 17,525 applied, 14,975 accepted. Either SAT or ACT required. ACT 25/75 percentile: 22-28. High school rank: 25% in top tenth, 56% in top quarter, 89% in top half
Early decision deadline: N/A, notification date: N/A
Early action deadline: N/A, notification date: N/A
Application deadline (fall): 7/1
Undergraduate student body: 26,171 full time, 1,488 part time; 57% male, 43% female; 0% American Indian, 3% Asian, 3% black, 4% Hispanic, 2% multiracial, 0% Pacific Islander, 77% white, 7% international; 71% from in state; 34% live on campus; 11% of students in fraternities, 16% in sororities
Most popular majors: 10% Agriculture, Agriculture Operations, and Related Sciences, 6% Biological and Biomedical Sciences, 18% Business, Management, Marketing, and Related Support Services, 19% Engineering, 6% Visual and Performing Arts
Expenses: 2014-2015: $7,731 in state, $20,617 out of state; room/board: $7,830
Financial aid: (515) 294-2223; 55% of undergrads determined to have financial need; average aid package $11,841

Iowa Wesleyan College[1]
Mount Pleasant IA
(319) 385-6231
U.S. News ranking: Reg. Coll. (Mid. W), second tier
Website: www.iwc.edu
Admissions email: admit@iwc.edu
Private
Application deadline (fall): N/A
Undergraduate student body: N/A full time, N/A part time
Expenses: 2013-2014: $25,550; room/board: $8,800
Financial aid: (319) 385-6242

Kaplan University[1]
Davenport IA
(800) 987-7734
U.S. News ranking: Reg. U. (Mid. W), unranked
Website: www.kaplan.edu
Admissions email: N/A
For-profit
Application deadline (fall): N/A
Undergraduate student body: N/A full time, N/A part time
Expenses: N/A
Financial aid: (866) 428-2008

Loras College
Dubuque IA
(800) 245-6727
U.S. News ranking: Reg. Coll. (Mid. W), No. 11
Website: www.loras.edu
Admissions email: admissions@ loras.edu
Private; founded 1839
Affiliation: Roman Catholic

Freshman admissions: selective; 2013-2014: 1,873 applied, 1,293 accepted. Either SAT or ACT required. ACT 25/75 percentile: 21-26. High school rank: 16% in top tenth, 39% in top quarter, 76% in top half
Early decision deadline: N/A, notification date: N/A
Early action deadline: N/A, notification date: N/A
Application deadline (fall): rolling
Undergraduate student body: 1,484 full time, 70 part time; 52% male, 48% female; 0% American Indian, 1% Asian, 2% black, 6% Hispanic, 2% multiracial, 0% Pacific Islander, 83% white, 2% international; 37% from in state; 65% live on campus; 4% of students in fraternities, 4% in sororities
Most popular majors: 8% Biological and Biomedical Sciences, 16% Business, Management, Marketing, and Related Support Services, 7% Communication, Journalism, and Related Programs, 18% Education, 9% English Language and Literature/Letters
Expenses: 2014-2015: $29,729; room/board: $8,353
Financial aid: (563) 588-7136; 73% of undergrads determined to have financial need; average aid package $23,000

Luther College
Decorah IA
(563) 387-1287
U.S. News ranking: Nat. Lib. Arts, No. 89
Website: www.luther.edu
Admissions email: admissions@ luther.edu
Private; founded 1861
Affiliation: Lutheran
Freshman admissions: more selective; 2013-2014: 3,490 applied, 2,517 accepted. Either SAT or ACT required. ACT 25/75 percentile: 23-29. High school rank: 32% in top tenth, 56% in top quarter, 87% in top half
Early decision deadline: N/A, notification date: N/A
Early action deadline: N/A, notification date: N/A
Application deadline (fall): rolling
Undergraduate student body: 2,413 full time, 53 part time; 43% male, 57% female; 0% American Indian, 2% Asian, 2% black, 3% Hispanic, 2% multiracial, 0% Pacific Islander, 86% white, 6% international; 32% from in state; 84% live on campus; 1% of students in fraternities, 2% in sororities
Most popular majors: 13% Biology/Biological Sciences, General, 8% Business Administration and Management, General, 5% Mathematics, General, 11% Music, General, 7% Psychology, General
Expenses: 2014-2015: $38,370; room/board: $7,350
Financial aid: (563) 387-1018; 71% of undergrads determined to have financial need; average aid package $28,581

Maharishi University of Management[1]
Fairfield IA
(641) 472-1110
U.S. News ranking: Reg. U. (Mid. W), unranked
Website: www.mum.edu
Admissions email: admissions@ mum.edu
Private
Application deadline (fall): N/A
Undergraduate student body: N/A full time, N/A part time
Expenses: 2013-2014: $26,430; room/board: $7,400
Financial aid: (641) 472-1156

Morningside College
Sioux City IA
(712) 274-5111
U.S. News ranking: Reg. Coll. (Mid. W), No. 23
Website: www.morningside.edu
Admissions email: mscadm@ morningside.edu
Private; founded 1894
Affiliation: United Methodist
Freshman admissions: selective; 2013-2014: 3,721 applied, 1,986 accepted. Either SAT or ACT required. ACT 25/75 percentile: 20-25. High school rank: 19% in top tenth, 46% in top quarter, 78% in top half
Early decision deadline: N/A, notification date: N/A
Early action deadline: N/A, notification date: N/A
Application deadline (fall): rolling
Undergraduate student body: 1,263 full time, 42 part time; 47% male, 53% female; 0% American Indian, 1% Asian, 1% black, 5% Hispanic, 2% multiracial, 0% Pacific Islander, 84% white, 2% international; 64% from in state; 63% live on campus; 5% of students in fraternities, 3% in sororities
Most popular majors: 13% Biology/Biological Sciences, General, 22% Business, Management, Marketing, and Related Support Services, 19% Elementary Education and Teaching, 7% Psychology, General, 9% Registered Nursing/Registered Nurse
Expenses: 2014-2015: $27,180; room/board: $8,250
Financial aid: (712) 274-5159; 87% of undergrads determined to have financial need; average aid package $25,931

Mount Mercy University
Cedar Rapids IA
(319) 368-6460
U.S. News ranking: Reg. Coll. (Mid. W), No. 21
Website: www.mtmercy.edu
Admissions email: admission@ mtmercy.edu
Private; founded 1928
Affiliation: Roman Catholic
Freshman admissions: selective; 2013-2014: 542 applied, 371 accepted. Either SAT or ACT required. ACT 25/75 percentile: 20-24. High school rank: 12% in top tenth, 41% in top quarter, 76% in top half
Early decision deadline: N/A, notification date: N/A
Early action deadline: N/A, notification date: N/A
Application deadline (fall): rolling

Undergraduate student body: 882 full time, 594 part time; 31% male, 69% female; 0% American Indian, 2% Asian, 4% black, 2% Hispanic, 1% multiracial, 0% Pacific Islander, 83% white, 3% international; 95% from in state; 37% live on campus; N/A of students in fraternities, N/A in sororities
Most popular majors: 7% Accounting, 9% Business/Commerce, General, 1% Criminal Justice/Law Enforcement Administration, 5% Elementary Education and Teaching, 22% Registered Nursing/Registered Nurse
Expenses: 2014-2015: $27,010; room/board: $8,310
Financial aid: (319) 368-6467; 77% of undergrads determined to have financial need; average aid package $18,114

Northwestern College

Orange City IA
(712) 707-7130
U.S. News ranking: Reg. Coll. (Mid. W), No. 6
Website: www.nwciowa.edu
Admissions email: admissions@nwciowa.edu
Private; founded 1882
Affiliation: Reformed Church in America
Freshman admissions: selective; 2013-2014: 1,221 applied, 929 accepted. Either SAT or ACT required. ACT 25/75 percentile: 22-27. High school rank: 19% in top tenth, 49% in top quarter, 81% in top half
Early decision deadline: N/A, notification date: N/A
Early action deadline: N/A, notification date: N/A
Application deadline (fall): rolling
Undergraduate student body: 1,133 full time, 100 part time; 43% male, 57% female; 0% American Indian, 1% Asian, 2% black, 6% Hispanic, 2% multiracial, 0% Pacific Islander, 85% white, 3% international; 52% from in state; 87% live on campus; 0% of students in fraternities, 0% in sororities
Most popular majors: 8% Biology/Biological Sciences, General, 17% Business Administration and Management, General, 17% Elementary Education and Teaching, 6% Psychology, General, 8% Registered Nursing/Registered Nurse
Expenses: 2014-2015: $27,930; room/board: $8,410
Financial aid: (712) 707-7131; 80% of undergrads determined to have financial need; average aid package $22,344

Simpson College

Indianola IA
(515) 961-1624
U.S. News ranking: Nat. Lib. Arts, No. 139
Website: www.simpson.edu
Admissions email: admiss@simpson.edu
Private; founded 1860
Affiliation: United Methodist
Freshman admissions: more selective; 2013-2014: 1,302 applied, 1,146 accepted. Either SAT or ACT required. ACT 25/75 percentile: 21-27. High school rank: 29% in top tenth, 58% in top quarter, 88% in top half

Early decision deadline: N/A, notification date: N/A
Early action deadline: N/A, notification date: N/A
Application deadline (fall): rolling
Undergraduate student body: 1,486 full time, 26 part time; 44% male, 56% female; 1% American Indian, 1% Asian, 2% black, 2% Hispanic, 2% multiracial, 0% Pacific Islander, 87% white, 1% international; 86% from in state; 86% live on campus; 23% of students in fraternities, 22% in sororities
Most popular majors: 7% Accounting, 5% Biology/Biological Sciences, General, 13% Business/Commerce, General, 7% Elementary Education and Teaching, 5% Mathematics, General
Expenses: 2014-2015: $32,550; room/board: $7,963
Financial aid: (515) 961-1630; 83% of undergrads determined to have financial need; average aid package $28,770

St. Ambrose University

Davenport IA
(563) 333-6300
U.S. News ranking: Reg. U. (Mid. W), No. 34
Website: www.sau.edu
Admissions email: admit@sau.edu
Private; founded 1882
Affiliation: Roman Catholic
Freshman admissions: selective; 2013-2014: 3,948 applied, 2,803 accepted. Either SAT or ACT required. ACT 25/75 percentile: 20-25. High school rank: 15% in top tenth, 36% in top quarter, 67% in top half
Early decision deadline: N/A, notification date: N/A
Early action deadline: N/A, notification date: N/A
Application deadline (fall): rolling
Undergraduate student body: 2,440 full time, 303 part time; 41% male, 59% female; 0% American Indian, 1% Asian, 4% black, 6% Hispanic, 2% multiracial, 0% Pacific Islander, 82% white, 2% international; 44% from in state; 62% live on campus; 0% of students in fraternities, 0% in sororities
Most popular majors: 21% Business, Management, Marketing, and Related Support Services, 13% Education, 11% Health Professions and Related Programs, 13% Parks, Recreation, Leisure, and Fitness Studies, 11% Psychology
Expenses: 2014-2015: $27,540; room/board: $9,280
Financial aid: (563) 333-6314; 77% of undergrads determined to have financial need; average aid package $18,817

University of Dubuque

Dubuque IA
(800) 722-5583
U.S. News ranking: Reg. U. (Mid. W), second tier
Website: www.dbq.edu
Admissions email: admssns@univ.dbq.edu
Private; founded 1852
Affiliation: Presbyterian

Freshman admissions: less selective; 2013-2014: 1,457 applied, 1,128 accepted. Either SAT or ACT required. ACT 25/75 percentile: 17-22. High school rank: N/A
Early decision deadline: N/A, notification date: N/A*
Early action deadline: N/A, notification date: N/A
Application deadline (fall): rolling
Undergraduate student body: 1,545 full time, 150 part time; 57% male, 43% female; 1% American Indian, 1% Asian, 10% black, 6% Hispanic, 2% multiracial, 0% Pacific Islander, 70% white, 1% international
Most popular majors: Information not available
Expenses: 2013-2014: $25,520; room/board: $8,160
Financial aid: (563) 589-3396

University of Iowa

Iowa City IA
(319) 335-3847
U.S. News ranking: Nat. U., No. 71
Website: www.uiowa.edu
Admissions email: admissions@uiowa.edu
Public; founded 1847
Freshman admissions: more selective; 2013-2014: 21,644 applied, 17,363 accepted. Either SAT or ACT required. ACT 25/75 percentile: 23-28. High school rank: 24% in top tenth, 57% in top quarter, 90% in top half
Early decision deadline: N/A, notification date: N/A
Early action deadline: N/A, notification date: N/A
Application deadline (fall): 4/1
Undergraduate student body: 19,522 full time, 2,452 part time; 48% male, 52% female; 0% American Indian, 3% Asian, 3% black, 6% Hispanic, 2% multiracial, 0% Pacific Islander, 72% white, 10% international; 66% from in state; 25% live on campus; 12% of students in fraternities, 17% in sororities
Most popular majors: 19% Business, Management, Marketing, and Related Support Services, 8% Communication, Journalism, and Related Programs, 8% Parks, Recreation, Leisure, and Fitness Studies, 9% Social Sciences, 7% Visual and Performing Arts
Expenses: 2014-2015: $8,079 in state, $27,409 out of state; room/board: $9,614
Financial aid: (319) 335-1450; 48% of undergrads determined to have financial need; average aid package $11,805

University of Northern Iowa

Cedar Falls IA
(800) 772-2037
U.S. News ranking: Reg. U. (Mid. W), No. 18
Website: www.uni.edu/
Admissions email: admissions@uni.edu
Public; founded 1876
Freshman admissions: selective; 2013-2014: 4,081 applied, 3,403 accepted. Either SAT or ACT required. ACT 25/75 percentile: 20-24. High school rank: 17% in top tenth, 45% in top quarter, 81% in top half

Early decision deadline: N/A, notification date: N/A
Early action deadline: N/A, notification date: N/A
Application deadline (fall): 8/15
Undergraduate student body: 9,330 full time, 1,050 part time; 43% male, 57% female; 0% American Indian, 1% Asian, 3% black, 3% Hispanic, 2% multiracial, 0% Pacific Islander, 87% white, 3% international; 94% from in state; 66% live on campus; N/A of students in fraternities, N/A in sororities
Most popular majors: 20% Business, Management, Marketing, and Related Support Services, 6% Communication, Journalism, and Related Programs, 17% Education, 7% Parks, Recreation, Leisure, and Fitness Studies, 7% Social Sciences
Expenses: 2014-2015: $7,749 in state, $17,647 out of state; room/board: $8,046
Financial aid: (319) 273-2700; 64% of undergrads determined to have financial need; average aid package $7,642

Upper Iowa University

Fayette IA
(563) 425-5281
U.S. News ranking: Reg. U. (Mid. W), No. 109
Website: www.uiu.edu
Admissions email: admission@uiu.edu
Private; founded 1857
Freshman admissions: selective; 2013-2014: 1,229 applied, 715 accepted. SAT required. ACT 25/75 percentile: 19-25. High school rank: 11% in top tenth, 32% in top quarter, 59% in top half
Early decision deadline: N/A, notification date: N/A
Early action deadline: N/A, notification date: N/A
Application deadline (fall): rolling
Undergraduate student body: 2,997 full time, 1,635 part time; 40% male, 60% female; 0% American Indian, 1% Asian, 19% black, 4% Hispanic, 1% multiracial, 0% Pacific Islander, 66% white, 3% international; 40% from in state; 5% live on campus; 10% of students in fraternities, 12% in sororities
Most popular majors: 43% Business, Management, Marketing, and Related Support Services, 7% Health Professions and Related Programs, 11% Psychology, 20% Public Administration and Social Service Professions, 15% Social Sciences
Expenses: 2014-2015: $26,834; room/board: $7,824
Financial aid: (563) 425-5274; 88% of undergrads determined to have financial need; average aid package $7,201

Waldorf College[1]

Forest City IA
(641) 585-8112
U.S. News ranking: Reg. Coll. (Mid. W), second tier
Website: www.waldorf.edu
Admissions email: admissions@waldorf.edu
For-profit
Application deadline (fall): N/A

Undergraduate student body: N/A full time, N/A part time
Expenses: 2013-2014: $20,316; room/board: $6,856
Financial aid: (641) 585-8120

Wartburg College

Waverly IA
(319) 352-8264
U.S. News ranking: Nat. Lib. Arts, No. 159
Website: www.wartburg.edu
Admissions email: admissions@wartburg.edu
Private; founded 1852
Affiliation: Lutheran
Freshman admissions: selective; 2013-2014: 2,268 applied, 1,761 accepted. Either SAT or ACT required. ACT 25/75 percentile: 21-26. High school rank: 26% in top tenth, 55% in top quarter, 79% in top half
Early decision deadline: N/A, notification date: N/A
Early action deadline: 12/1, notification date: N/A
Application deadline (fall): rolling
Undergraduate student body: 1,643 full time, 71 part time; 47% male, 53% female; 0% American Indian, 1% Asian, 6% black, 2% Hispanic, 2% multiracial, 0% Pacific Islander, 78% white, 10% international; 74% from in state; 81% live on campus; 0% of students in fraternities, 0% in sororities
Most popular majors: 15% Biology/Biological Sciences, General, 20% Business/Commerce, General, 15% Elementary Education and Teaching, 7% Speech Communication and Rhetoric, 8% Visual and Performing Arts, General
Expenses: 2014-2015: $36,120; room/board: $8,920
Financial aid: (319) 352-8262; 75% of undergrads determined to have financial need; average aid package $25,732

William Penn University[1]

Oskaloosa IA
(641) 673-1012
U.S. News ranking: Reg. Coll. (Mid. W), second tier
Website: www.wmpenn.edu
Admissions email: admissions@wmpenn.edu
Private
Application deadline (fall): N/A
Undergraduate student body: N/A full time, N/A part time
Expenses: 2013-2014: $23,210; room/board: $5,472
Financial aid: (641) 673-1040

KANSAS

Baker University

Baldwin City KS
(800) 873-4282
U.S. News ranking: Reg. U. (Mid. W), No. 44
Website: www.bakeru.edu
Admissions email: admission@bakeru.edu
Private; founded 1858
Affiliation: United Methodist
Freshman admissions: selective; 2013-2014: 949 applied, 832 accepted. Either SAT or ACT required. ACT 25/75 percentile: 21-26. High school rank: 15%

in top tenth, 42% in top quarter, 77% in top half
Early decision deadline: N/A, notification date: N/A
Early action deadline: N/A, notification date: N/A
Application deadline (fall): rolling
Undergraduate student body: 800 full time, 142 part time; 49% male, 51% female; 3% American Indian, 1% Asian, 10% black, 5% Hispanic, 1% multiracial, 1% Pacific Islander, 74% white, 0% international; 70% from in state; 76% live on campus; 27% of students in fraternities, 42% in sororities
Most popular majors: 20% Business, Management, Marketing, and Related Support Services, 7% Communication, Journalism, and Related Programs, 15% Education, 13% Parks, Recreation, Leisure, and Fitness Studies, 8% Social Sciences
Expenses: 2014-2015: $26,290; room/board: $8,040
Financial aid: (785) 594-4595; 82% of undergrads determined to have financial need; average aid package $20,157

Benedictine College
Atchison KS
(800) 467-5340
U.S. News ranking: Reg. Coll. (Mid. W), No. 20
Website: www.benedictine.edu
Admissions email: bcadmiss@ benedictine.edu
Private; founded 1859
Affiliation: Roman Catholic
Freshman admissions: selective; 2013-2014: 2,195 applied, 2,130 accepted. Either SAT or ACT required. ACT 25/75 percentile: 22-28. High school rank: 25% in top tenth, 46% in top quarter, 74% in top half
Early decision deadline: N/A, notification date: N/A
Early action deadline: N/A, notification date: N/A
Application deadline (fall): rolling
Undergraduate student body: 1,750 full time, 363 part time; 48% male, 52% female; 0% American Indian, 1% Asian, 3% black, 6% Hispanic, 3% multiracial, 0% Pacific Islander, 80% white, 3% international; 27% from in state; 85% live on campus; 0% of students in fraternities, 0% in sororities
Most popular majors: 14% Business, Management, Marketing, and Related Support Services, 6% Communication, Journalism, and Related Programs, 20% Education, 10% Social Sciences, 9% Theology and Religious Vocations
Expenses: 2014-2015: $25,100; room/board: $8,750
Financial aid: (913) 360-7484; 72% of undergrads determined to have financial need; average aid package $18,934

Bethany College
Lindsborg KS
(800) 826-2281
U.S. News ranking: Reg. Coll. (Mid. W), No. 68
Website: www.bethanylb.edu
Admissions email: admissions@ bethanylb.edu
Private
Affiliation: Evangelical Lutheran Chuch in America (ELCA)

Freshman admissions: selective; 2013-2014: 1,139 applied, 670 accepted. Either SAT or ACT required. ACT 25/75 percentile: 18-23. High school rank: 8% in top tenth, 20% in top quarter, 63% in top half
Early decision deadline: N/A, notification date: N/A
Early action deadline: N/A, notification date: N/A
Application deadline (fall): rolling
Undergraduate student body: 603 full time, 62 part time; 60% male, 40% female; 1% American Indian, 1% Asian, 12% black, 12% Hispanic, 4% multiracial, 1% Pacific Islander, 69% white, 0% international; 55% from in state; 67% live on campus; 6% of students in fraternities, 16% in sororities
Most popular majors: 14% Biology/ Biological Sciences, General, 11% Criminology, 10% Elementary Education and Teaching, 8% Sport and Fitness Administration/ Management
Expenses: 2014-2015: $24,390; room/board: $7,610
Financial aid: (785) 227-3311; 83% of undergrads determined to have financial need; average aid package $24,733

Bethel College
North Newton KS
(800) 522-1887
U.S. News ranking: Reg. Coll. (Mid. W), No. 25
Website: www.bethelks.edu
Admissions email: admissions@ bethelks.edu
Private; founded 1887
Affiliation: Mennonite Church USA
Freshman admissions: selective; 2013-2014: 854 applied, 550 accepted. Either SAT or ACT required. ACT 25/75 percentile: 19-26. High school rank: 17% in top tenth, 21% in top quarter, 70% in top half
Early decision deadline: N/A, notification date: N/A
Early action deadline: N/A, notification date: N/A
Application deadline (fall): rolling
Undergraduate student body: 464 full time, 18 part time; 49% male, 51% female; 1% American Indian, 1% Asian, 13% black, 10% Hispanic, 3% multiracial, 0% Pacific Islander, 71% white, 2% international; 66% from in state; 73% live on campus; 0% of students in fraternities, 0% in sororities
Most popular majors: 6% Biological and Biomedical Sciences, 11% Business, Management, Marketing, and Related Support Services, 7% Education, 22% Health Professions and Related Programs, 12% Public Administration and Social Service Professions
Expenses: 2014-2015: $24,200; room/board: $8,240
Financial aid: (316) 284-5232; 85% of undergrads determined to have financial need; average aid package $24,337

Central Christian College[1]
McPherson KS
(800) 835-0078
U.S. News ranking: Reg. Coll. (Mid. W), second tier
Website: www.centralchristian.edu/
Admissions email: rick.wyatt@ centralchristian.edu
Private
Application deadline (fall): N/A
Undergraduate student body: N/A full time, N/A part time
Expenses: 2013-2014: $14,800; room/board: $6,500
Financial aid: (620) 241-0723

Donnelly College[1]
Kansas City KS
(913) 621-8700
U.S. News ranking: Reg. Coll. (Mid. W), unranked
Website: donnelly.edu
Admissions email: N/A
Private
Application deadline (fall): N/A
Undergraduate student body: N/A full time, N/A part time
Expenses: 2013-2014: $6,579; room/board: $6,224
Financial aid: (913) 621-8700

Emporia State University
Emporia KS
(620) 341-5465
U.S. News ranking: Reg. U. (Mid. W), No. 103
Website: www.emporia.edu
Admissions email: go2esu@ emporia.edu
Public; founded 1863
Freshman admissions: selective; 2013-2014: 2,452 applied, 1,488 accepted. Either SAT or ACT required. ACT 25/75 percentile: 19-25. High school rank: 14% in top tenth, 36% in top quarter, 72% in top half
Early decision deadline: N/A, notification date: N/A
Early action deadline: N/A, notification date: N/A
Application deadline (fall): rolling
Undergraduate student body: 3,445 full time, 428 part time; 40% male, 60% female; 0% American Indian, 1% Asian, 6% black, 7% Hispanic, 5% multiracial, 0% Pacific Islander, 72% white, 8% international; 92% from in state; 26% live on campus; 16% of students in fraternities, 12% in sororities
Most popular majors: 15% Business, Management, Marketing, and Related Support Services, 22% Education, 10% Health Professions and Related Programs, 10% Social Sciences, 6% Visual and Performing Arts
Expenses: 2014-2015: $5,746 in state, $17,896 out of state; room/ board: $7,582
Financial aid: (620) 341-5457; 66% of undergrads determined to have financial need; average aid package $8,590

Fort Hays State University
Hays KS
(800) 628-3478
U.S. News ranking: Reg. U. (Mid. W), second tier
Website: www.fhsu.edu
Admissions email: tigers@fhsu.edu

Public; founded 1902
Freshman admissions: less selective; 2013-2014: 2,511 applied, 2,239 accepted. Either SAT or ACT required. SAT 25/75 percentile: 740-1230. High school rank: 10% in top tenth, 31% in top quarter, 61% in top half
Early decision deadline: N/A, notification date: N/A
Early action deadline: N/A, notification date: N/A
Application deadline (fall): rolling
Undergraduate student body: 5,449 full time, 5,984 part time; 41% male, 59% female; 0% American Indian, 1% Asian, 4% black, 5% Hispanic, 2% multiracial, 0% Pacific Islander, 55% white, 31% international
Most popular majors: Information not available
Expenses: 2013-2014: $5,054 in state, $12,003 out of state; room/ board: $7,130
Financial aid: (785) 628-4408; 73% of undergrads determined to have financial need; average aid package $6,966

Friends University[1]
Wichita KS
(316) 295-5100
U.S. News ranking: Reg. U. (Mid. W), second tier
Website: www.friends.edu
Admissions email: learn@friends.edu
Private
Application deadline (fall): N/A
Undergraduate student body: N/A full time, N/A part time
Expenses: 2013-2014: $23,430; room/board: $6,800
Financial aid: (316) 295-5200

Kansas State University
Manhattan KS
(785) 532-6250
U.S. News ranking: Nat. U., No. 142
Website: www.k-state.edu
Admissions email: k-state@k-state.edu
Public; founded 1863
Freshman admissions: selective; 2013-2014: 9,839 applied, 9,437 accepted. Neither SAT nor ACT required. ACT 25/75 percentile: 21-27. High school rank: 22% in top tenth, 48% in top quarter, 77% in top half
Early decision deadline: N/A, notification date: N/A
Early action deadline: N/A, notification date: N/A
Application deadline (fall): rolling
Undergraduate student body: 18,110 full time, 2,059 part time; 52% male, 48% female; 0% American Indian, 1% Asian, 4% black, 6% Hispanic, 3% multiracial, 0% Pacific Islander, 78% white, 6% international; 84% from in state; 25% live on campus; 14% of students in fraternities, 20% in sororities
Most popular majors: 12% Agriculture, Agriculture Operations, and Related Sciences, 17% Business, Management, Marketing, and Related Support Services, 9% Education, 10% Engineering, 10% Social Sciences
Expenses: 2014-2015: $9,034 in state, $22,624 out of state; room/ board: $8,060

Financial aid: (785) 532-6420; 53% of undergrads determined to have financial need; average aid package $10,873

Kansas Wesleyan University
Salina KS
(785) 827-5541
U.S. News ranking: Reg. Coll. (Mid. W), No. 54
Website: www.kwu.edu
Admissions email: admissions@ kwu.edu
Private; founded 1886
Affiliation: United Methodist
Freshman admissions: selective; 2013-2014: 689 applied, 370 accepted. Either SAT or ACT required. ACT 25/75 percentile: 20-24. High school rank: 11% in top tenth, 43% in top quarter, 81% in top half
Early decision deadline: N/A, notification date: N/A
Early action deadline: N/A, notification date: N/A
Application deadline (fall): rolling
Undergraduate student body: 624 full time, 60 part time; 46% male, 54% female; 1% American Indian, 1% Asian, 8% black, 13% Hispanic, 2% multiracial, 0% Pacific Islander, 72% white, 4% international; 59% from in state; 60% live on campus; 0% of students in fraternities, 0% in sororities
Most popular majors: 9% Business Administration and Management, General, 8% Criminal Justice/ Law Enforcement Administration, 8% Elementary Education and Teaching, 20% Registered Nursing/Registered Nurse, 7% Secondary Education and Teaching
Expenses: 2014-2015: $25,200; room/board: $8,000
Financial aid: (785) 827-5541; 82% of undergrads determined to have financial need; average aid package $18,643

McPherson College
McPherson KS
(800) 365-7402
U.S. News ranking: Reg. Coll. (Mid. W), No. 52
Website: www.mcpherson.edu
Admissions email: admissions@ mcpherson.edu
Private; founded 1887
Freshman admissions: selective; 2013-2014: 887 applied, 556 accepted. Either SAT or ACT required. ACT 25/75 percentile: 19-24. High school rank: N/A
Early decision deadline: N/A, notification date: N/A
Early action deadline: N/A, notification date: N/A
Application deadline (fall): 8/1
Undergraduate student body: 602 full time, 35 part time; 59% male, 41% female; 0% American Indian, 1% Asian, 14% black, 9% Hispanic, 4% multiracial, 0% Pacific Islander, 70% white, 2% international; 48% from in state; 73% live on campus; 0% of students in fraternities, 0% in sororities
Most popular majors: 30% Business, Management, Marketing, and Related Support Services, 6% Education, 23% Engineering Technologies and Engineering-Related Fields, 12% Visual and Performing Arts

Expenses: 2014-2015: $24,035; room/board: $8,411
Financial aid: (620) 241-0731; 86% of undergrads determined to have financial need; average aid package $25,781

MidAmerica Nazarene University[1]

Olathe KS
(913) 971-3380
U.S. News ranking: Reg. U. (Mid. W), second tier
Website: www.mnu.edu
Admissions email: admissions@mnu.edu
Private
Application deadline (fall): N/A
Undergraduate student body: N/A full time, N/A part time
Expenses: 2013-2014: $22,290; room/board: $7,250
Financial aid: (913) 791-3298

Newman University

Wichita KS
(877) 639-6268
U.S. News ranking: Reg. U. (Mid. W), second tier
Website: www.newmanu.edu
Admissions email: admissions@newmanu.edu
Private; founded 1933
Affiliation: Roman Catholic
Freshman admissions: more selective; 2013-2014: 2,378 applied, 1,050 accepted. Neither SAT nor ACT required. ACT 25/75 percentile: 20-27. High school rank: 19% in top tenth, 51% in top quarter, 77% in top half
Early decision deadline: N/A, notification date: N/A
Early action deadline: N/A, notification date: N/A
Application deadline (fall): rolling
Undergraduate student body: 1,121 full time, 1,674 part time; 38% male, 62% female; 1% American Indian, 5% Asian, 6% black, 13% Hispanic, 3% multiracial, 0% Pacific Islander, 66% white, 6% international; 86% from in state; 25% live on campus; 0% of students in fraternities, 0% in sororities
Most popular majors: 12% Biology/Biological Sciences, General, 11% Business Administration and Management, General, 17% Elementary Education and Teaching, 7% Multi/Interdisciplinary Studies, 23% Registered Nursing/Registered Nurse
Expenses: 2014-2015: $24,800; room/board: $7,060
Financial aid: (316) 942-4291; 76% of undergrads determined to have financial need; average aid package $17,256

Ottawa University

Ottawa KS
(785) 242-5200
U.S. News ranking: Reg. Coll. (Mid. W), No. 59
Website: www.ottawa.edu
Admissions email: admiss@ottawa.edu
Private; founded 1865
Affiliation: American Baptist
Freshman admissions: selective; 2013-2014: 263 applied, 260 accepted. Either SAT or ACT required. ACT 25/75 percentile: 19-25. High school rank: 17% in top tenth, 38% in top quarter, 72% in top half

Early decision deadline: N/A, notification date: N/A
Early action deadline: N/A, notification date: N/A
Application deadline (fall): rolling
Undergraduate student body: 515 full time, 24 part time; 56% male, 44% female; 5% American Indian, 1% Asian, 12% black, 7% Hispanic, 0% multiracial, 0% Pacific Islander, 63% white, 1% international; 60% from in state; 72% live on campus; 0% of students in fraternities, 0% in sororities
Most popular majors: 10% Biology/Biological Sciences, General, 15% Business Administration and Management, General, 8% Elementary Education and Teaching, 7% Human Services, General, 15% Kinesiology and Exercise Science
Expenses: 2014-2015: $25,154; room/board: $8,432
Financial aid: (785) 242-5200; 86% of undergrads determined to have financial need; average aid package $12,326

Pittsburg State University

Pittsburg KS
(800) 854-7488
U.S. News ranking: Reg. U. (Mid. W), No. 84
Website: www.pittstate.edu
Admissions email: psuadmit@pittstate.edu
Public; founded 1903
Freshman admissions: selective; 2013-2014: 3,073 applied, 2,427 accepted. Either SAT or ACT required. ACT 25/75 percentile: 19-24. High school rank: 20% in top tenth, 38% in top quarter, 70% in top half
Early decision deadline: N/A, notification date: N/A
Early action deadline: N/A, notification date: N/A
Application deadline (fall): rolling
Undergraduate student body: 5,625 full time, 611 part time; 52% male, 48% female; 2% American Indian, 1% Asian, 4% black, 5% Hispanic, 4% multiracial, 0% Pacific Islander, 81% white, 3% international; N/A from in state; 19% live on campus; N/A of students in fraternities, N/A in sororities
Most popular majors: 5% Biology/Biological Sciences, General, 5% Business/Commerce, General, 7% Multicultural Education, 5% Psychology, General, 8% Registered Nursing/Registered Nurse
Expenses: 2014-2015: $6,230 in state, $16,336 out of state; room/board: $6,936
Financial aid: (620) 235-4240; average aid package $6,481

Southwestern College

Winfield KS
(620) 229-6236
U.S. News ranking: Reg. U. (Mid. W), No. 84
Website: www.sckans.edu
Admissions email: scadmit@sckans.edu
Private; founded 1885
Affiliation: United Methodist
Freshman admissions: selective; 2013-2014: 436 applied, 391 accepted. Either SAT or ACT required. ACT 25/75 percentile: 20-25. High school rank: 22%

in top tenth, 49% in top quarter, 77% in top half
Early decision deadline: N/A, notification date: N/A
Early action deadline: N/A, notification date: N/A
Application deadline (fall): 8/25
Undergraduate student body: 553 full time, 805 part time; 57% male, 43% female; 2% American Indian, 1% Asian, 10% black, 8% Hispanic, 4% multiracial, 0% Pacific Islander, 61% white, 3% international; 59% from in state; 72% live on campus; N/A of students in fraternities, N/A in sororities
Most popular majors: 11% Biological and Biomedical Sciences, 26% Business, Management, Marketing, and Related Support Services, 12% Education, 10% Parks, Recreation, Leisure, and Fitness Studies, 10% Psychology
Expenses: 2014-2015: $24,835; room/board: $6,846
Financial aid: (620) 229-6215; 80% of undergrads determined to have financial need; average aid package $19,966

Sterling College

Sterling KS
(800) 346-1017
U.S. News ranking: Reg. Coll. (Mid. W), No. 67
Website: www.sterling.edu
Admissions email: admissions@sterling.edu
Private; founded 1887
Freshman admissions: selective; 2013-2014: 883 applied, 389 accepted. Either SAT or ACT required. ACT 25/75 percentile: 19-25. High school rank: 12% in top tenth, 29% in top quarter, 63% in top half
Early decision deadline: N/A, notification date: N/A
Early action deadline: N/A, notification date: N/A
Application deadline (fall): rolling
Undergraduate student body: 595 full time, 95 part time; 54% male, 46% female; 1% American Indian, 0% Asian, 9% black, 10% Hispanic, 0% multiracial, 1% Pacific Islander, 70% white, 0% international; 52% from in state; 77% live on campus; N/A of students in fraternities, N/A in sororities
Most popular majors: 19% Business, Management, Marketing, and Related Support Services, 23% Education, 15% Parks, Recreation, Leisure, and Fitness Studies, 8% Philosophy and Religious Studies, 6% Visual and Performing Arts
Expenses: 2014-2015: $22,100; room/board: $6,911
Financial aid: (620) 278-4207; 86% of undergrads determined to have financial need; average aid package $21,695

Tabor College

Hillsboro KS
(620) 947-3121
U.S. News ranking: Reg. Coll. (Mid. W), No. 49
Website: www.tabor.edu
Admissions email: admissions@tabor.edu
Private; founded 1908
Affiliation: Mennonite Brethren
Freshman admissions: selective; 2013-2014: 517 applied, 380 accepted. Either SAT or ACT

required. ACT 25/75 percentile: 19-25. High school rank: 14% in top tenth, 20% in top quarter, 69% in top half
Early decision deadline: N/A, notification date: N/A
Early action deadline: N/A, notification date: N/A
Application deadline (fall): rolling
Undergraduate student body: 565 full time, 160 part time; 52% male, 48% female; 1% American Indian, 1% Asian, 7% black, 10% Hispanic, 3% multiracial, 0% Pacific Islander, 60% white, 3% international; 49% from in state; 89% live on campus; 0% of students in fraternities, 0% in sororities
Most popular majors: 12% Business Administration and Management, General, 7% Elementary Education and Teaching, 12% Health and Physical Education/Fitness, General, 9% Psychology, General, 20% Registered Nursing, Nursing Administration, Nursing Research and Clinical Nursing, Other
Expenses: 2014-2015: $23,900; room/board: $8,620
Financial aid: (620) 947-3121; 82% of undergrads determined to have financial need; average aid package $20,544

University of Kansas

Lawrence KS
(785) 864-3911
U.S. News ranking: Nat. U., No. 106
Website: www.ku.edu/
Admissions email: adm@ku.edu
Public; founded 1866
Freshman admissions: more selective; 2013-2014: 13,256 applied, 11,715 accepted. Either SAT or ACT required. ACT 25/75 percentile: 22-28. High school rank: 26% in top tenth, 59% in top quarter, 90% in top half
Early decision deadline: N/A, notification date: N/A
Early action deadline: N/A, notification date: N/A
Application deadline (fall): rolling
Undergraduate student body: 17,193 full time, 2,024 part time; 50% male, 50% female; 1% American Indian, 4% Asian, 4% black, 6% Hispanic, 4% multiracial, 0% Pacific Islander, 75% white, 5% international; 77% from in state; 25% live on campus; 16% of students in fraternities, 21% in sororities
Most popular majors: 13% Business, Management, Marketing, and Related Support Services, 9% Communication, Journalism, and Related Programs, 7% Engineering, 16% Health Professions and Related Programs, 7% Social Sciences
Expenses: 2014-2015: $10,448 in state, $25,731 out of state; room/board: $7,896
Financial aid: (785) 864-4700; 49% of undergrads determined to have financial need; average aid package $8,799

University of St. Mary

Leavenworth KS
(913) 758-6118
U.S. News ranking: Reg. U. (Mid. W), second tier
Website: www.stmary.edu
Admissions email: admiss@stmary.edu
Private; founded 1923
Affiliation: Roman Catholic
Freshman admissions: less selective; 2013-2014: 767 applied, 361 accepted. Either SAT or ACT required. ACT 25/75 percentile: 19-24. High school rank: 2% in top tenth, 3% in top quarter, 32% in top half
Early decision deadline: N/A, notification date: N/A
Early action deadline: N/A, notification date: N/A
Application deadline (fall): rolling
Undergraduate student body: 566 full time, 324 part time; 35% male, 65% female; 0% American Indian, 1% Asian, 11% black, 6% Hispanic, 2% multiracial, 1% Pacific Islander, 53% white, 1% international; 58% from in state; 30% live on campus; N/A of students in fraternities, N/A in sororities
Most popular majors: 7% Business Administration and Management, General, 5% Elementary Education and Teaching, 9% Psychology, General, 45% Registered Nursing/Registered Nurse, 10% Sport and Fitness Administration/Management
Expenses: 2013-2014: $23,170; room/board: $7,386
Financial aid: (800) 752-7043

Washburn University

Topeka KS
(785) 670-1030
U.S. News ranking: Reg. U. (Mid. W), No. 91
Website: www.washburn.edu
Admissions email: admissions@washburn.edu
Public; founded 1865
Freshman admissions: selective; 2013-2014: 2,079 applied, 2,041 accepted. ACT required. ACT 25/75 percentile: 19-25. High school rank: 13% in top tenth, 38% in top quarter, 69% in top half
Early decision deadline: N/A, notification date: N/A
Early action deadline: N/A, notification date: N/A
Application deadline (fall): 8/1
Undergraduate student body: 4,072 full time, 2,107 part time; 41% male, 59% female; N/A American Indian, N/A Asian, N/A black, N/A Hispanic, N/A multiracial, N/A Pacific Islander, N/A white, N/A international; 91% from in state; 15% live on campus; 7% of students in fraternities, 7% in sororities
Most popular majors: 14% Business, Management, Marketing, and Related Support Services, 6% Communication, Journalism, and Related Programs, 8% Education, 30% Health Professions and Related Programs, 7% Homeland Security, Law Enforcement, Firefighting and Related Protective Services
Expenses: 2014-2015: $6,038 in state, $13,526 out of state; room/board: $6,541

Financial aid: (785) 670-1151; 64% of undergrads determined to have financial need; average aid package $9,341

Wichita State University
Wichita KS
(316) 978-3085
U.S. News ranking: Nat. U., second tier
Website: www.wichita.edu
Admissions email: admissions@wichita.edu
Public; founded 1895
Freshman admissions: selective; 2013-2014: 3,492 applied, 3,344 accepted. Neither SAT nor ACT required. ACT 25/75 percentile: 21-26. High school rank: 23% in top tenth, 50% in top quarter, 79% in top half
Early decision deadline: N/A, notification date: N/A
Early action deadline: N/A, notification date: N/A
Application deadline (fall): rolling
Undergraduate student body: 8,807 full time, 2,980 part time; 48% male, 52% female; 1% American Indian, 7% Asian, 6% black, 9% Hispanic, 2% multiracial, 0% Pacific Islander, 65% white, 6% international; 95% from in state; 7% live on campus; 4% of students in fraternities, 4% in sororities
Most popular majors: 19% Business, Management, Marketing, and Related Support Services, 9% Education, 10% Engineering, 17% Health Professions and Related Programs, 6% Homeland Security, Law Enforcement, Firefighting and Related Protective Services
Expenses: 2014-2015: $7,267 in state, $16,697 out of state; room/board: $8,373
Financial aid: (316) 978-3430

KENTUCKY

Alice Lloyd College
Pippa Passes KY
(888) 280-4252
U.S. News ranking: Reg. Coll. (S), No. 29
Website: www.alc.edu
Admissions email: admissions@alc.edu
Private; founded 1923
Freshman admissions: selective; 2013-2014: 3,807 applied, 359 accepted. Either SAT or ACT required. ACT 25/75 percentile: 18-23. High school rank: 18% in top tenth, 51% in top quarter, 90% in top half
Early decision deadline: N/A, notification date: N/A
Early action deadline: N/A, notification date: N/A
Application deadline (fall): 7/1
Undergraduate student body: 606 full time, 25 part time; 46% male, 54% female; 0% American Indian, 0% Asian, 1% black, 1% Hispanic, 0% multiracial, 0% Pacific Islander, 96% white, 0% international; 78% from in state; 85% live on campus; N/A of students in fraternities, N/A in sororities
Most popular majors: 33% Biological and Biomedical Sciences, 12% Business, Management, Marketing, and Related Support Services, 21%

Education, 8% History, 13% Social Sciences
Expenses: 2014-2015: $10,980; room/board: $5,660
Financial aid: (606) 368-6059; 91% of undergrads determined to have financial need; average aid package $12,581

Asbury University
Wilmore KY
(800) 888-1818
U.S. News ranking: Reg. Coll. (S), No. 1
Website: www.asbury.edu
Admissions email: admissions@asbury.edu
Private; founded 1890
Affiliation: non-denominational
Freshman admissions: more selective; 2013-2014: 1,211 applied, 796 accepted. Either SAT or ACT required. ACT 25/75 percentile: 21-27. High school rank: 27% in top tenth, 54% in top quarter, 85% in top half
Early decision deadline: N/A, notification date: N/A
Early action deadline: N/A, notification date: N/A
Application deadline (fall): rolling
Undergraduate student body: 1,326 full time, 206 part time; 40% male, 60% female; 0% American Indian, 1% Asian, 3% black, 2% Hispanic, 5% multiracial, 0% Pacific Islander, 84% white, 2% international; 50% from in state; 86% live on campus; 0% of students in fraternities, 0% in sororities
Most popular majors: 5% Business Administration and Management, General, 5% Communication, General, 9% Elementary Education and Teaching, 19% Radio, Television, and Digital Communication, Other, 4% Social Work
Expenses: 2013-2014: $26,076; room/board: $5,962
Financial aid: (800) 888-1818

Bellarmine University
Louisville KY
(502) 272-8131
U.S. News ranking: Reg. U. (S), No. 13
Website: www.bellarmine.edu
Admissions email: admissions@bellarmine.edu
Private; founded 1950
Affiliation: Roman Catholic
Freshman admissions: selective; 2013-2014: 4,160 applied, 3,943 accepted. Either SAT or ACT required. ACT 25/75 percentile: 22-27. High school rank: 25% in top tenth, 54% in top quarter, 82% in top half
Early decision deadline: N/A, notification date: N/A
Early action deadline: 11/1, notification date: 11/15
Application deadline (fall): 8/15
Undergraduate student body: 2,378 full time, 215 part time; 36% male, 64% female; 0% American Indian, 2% Asian, 4% black, 3% Hispanic, 2% multiracial, 0% Pacific Islander, 84% white, 1% international; 68% from in state; 43% live on campus; 1% of students in fraternities, 1% in sororities
Most popular majors: 6% Biological and Biomedical Sciences, 14% Business, Management, Marketing, and Related Support

Services, 6% Education, 31% Health Professions and Related Programs, 8% Psychology
Expenses: 2014-2015: $36,290; room/board: $10,700
Financial aid: (502) 452-8124; 77% of undergrads determined to have financial need; average aid package $27,406

Berea College
Berea KY
(859) 985-3500
U.S. News ranking: Nat. Lib. Arts, No. 69
Website: www.berea.edu
Admissions email: admissions@berea.edu
Private; founded 1855
Freshman admissions: more selective; 2013-2014: 1,620 applied, 551 accepted. Either SAT or ACT required. ACT 25/75 percentile: 22-26. High school rank: 25% in top tenth, 73% in top quarter, 95% in top half
Early decision deadline: N/A, notification date: N/A
Early action deadline: N/A, notification date: N/A
Application deadline (fall): 4/30
Undergraduate student body: 1,587 full time, 36 part time; 43% male, 57% female; 0% American Indian, 2% Asian, 15% black, 4% Hispanic, 5% multiracial, 0% Pacific Islander, 64% white, 8% international; 46% from in state; 81% live on campus; N/A of students in fraternities, N/A in sororities
Most popular majors: 8% Education, 8% English Language and Literature/Letters, 7% Family and Consumer Sciences/Human Sciences, 7% Social Sciences, 9% Visual and Performing Arts
Expenses: 2014-2015: $870; room/board: $6,322
Financial aid: (859) 985-3310; 100% of undergrads determined to have financial need; average aid package $29,179

Brescia University
Owensboro KY
(270) 686-4241
U.S. News ranking: Reg. Coll. (S), No. 43
Website: www.brescia.edu
Admissions email: admissions@brescia.edu
Private; founded 1950
Affiliation: Roman Catholic
Freshman admissions: selective; 2013-2014: 3,582 applied, 1,612 accepted. Either SAT or ACT required. ACT 25/75 percentile: 19-24. High school rank: N/A
Early decision deadline: N/A, notification date: N/A
Early action deadline: N/A, notification date: N/A
Application deadline (fall): rolling
Undergraduate student body: 688 full time, 240 part time; 28% male, 72% female; 1% American Indian, 1% Asian, 13% black, 7% Hispanic, 0% multiracial, 0% Pacific Islander, 67% white, 1% international
Most popular majors: Information not available
Expenses: 2014-2015: $19,990; room/board: $9,500
Financial aid: (270) 686-4253

Campbellsville University
Campbellsville KY
(270) 789-5220
U.S. News ranking: Reg. U. (S), No. 81
Website: www.campbellsville.edu
Admissions email: admissions@campbellsville.edu
Private; founded 1906
Affiliation: Baptist
Freshman admissions: selective; 2013-2014: 2,649 applied, 1,813 accepted. Either SAT or ACT required. ACT 25/75 percentile: 18-24. High school rank: N/A
Early decision deadline: N/A, notification date: N/A
Early action deadline: N/A, notification date: N/A
Application deadline (fall): 8/1
Undergraduate student body: 1,996 full time, 1,105 part time; 41% male, 59% female; 0% American Indian, 0% Asian, 13% black, 2% Hispanic, 2% multiracial, 0% Pacific Islander, 74% white, 8% international; 84% from in state; 52% live on campus; N/A of students in fraternities, N/A in sororities
Most popular majors: 18% Business, Management, Marketing, and Related Support Services, 20% Education, 8% Homeland Security, Law Enforcement, Firefighting and Related Protective Services, 10% Public Administration and Social Service Professions, 9% Theology and Religious Vocations
Expenses: 2014-2015: $22,842; room/board: $7,550
Financial aid: (270) 789-5013; 89% of undergrads determined to have financial need; average aid package $18,489

Centre College
Danville KY
(859) 238-5350
U.S. News ranking: Nat. Lib. Arts, No. 45
Website: www.centre.edu
Admissions email: admission@centre.edu
Private; founded 1819
Affiliation: Presbyterian Church (USA)
Freshman admissions: more selective; 2013-2014: 2,533 applied, 1,737 accepted. Either SAT or ACT required. ACT 25/75 percentile: 26-31. High school rank: 52% in top tenth, 81% in top quarter, 96% in top half
Early decision deadline: 12/1, notification date: 12/31
Early action deadline: 12/1, notification date: 1/15
Application deadline (fall): 1/15
Undergraduate student body: 1,378 full time, 3 part time; 49% male, 51% female; 0% American Indian, 2% Asian, 5% black, 2% Hispanic, 3% multiracial, 0% Pacific Islander, 83% white, 4% international; 54% from in state; 98% live on campus; 53% of students in fraternities, 53% in sororities
Most popular majors: 10% Biology/Biological Sciences, General, 14% Economics, Other, 13% History, General, 7% International/Global Studies, 7% Mathematics, General
Expenses: 2014-2015: $37,100; room/board: $9,520

Financial aid: (859) 238-5365; 59% of undergrads determined to have financial need; average aid package $27,581

Eastern Kentucky University
Richmond KY
(800) 465-9191
U.S. News ranking: Reg. U. (S), No. 62
Website: www.eku.edu
Admissions email: admissions@eku.edu
Public; founded 1906
Freshman admissions: selective; 2013-2014: 9,000 applied, 6,642 accepted. Either SAT or ACT required. ACT 25/75 percentile: 19-25. High school rank: N/A
Early decision deadline: N/A, notification date: N/A
Early action deadline: N/A, notification date: N/A
Application deadline (fall): 8/1
Undergraduate student body: 10,969 full time, 2,922 part time; 44% male, 56% female; 0% American Indian, 1% Asian, 5% black, 2% Hispanic, 2% multiracial, 0% Pacific Islander, 85% white, 0% international; 87% from in state; 30% live on campus; N/A of students in fraternities, N/A in sororities
Most popular majors: 9% Criminal Justice/Law Enforcement Administration, 4% Elementary Education and Teaching, 10% General Studies, 5% Psychology, General, 7% Registered Nursing/Registered Nurse
Expenses: 2014-2015: $7,920 in state, $17,448 out of state; room/board: $7,720
Financial aid: (859) 622-2361; 71% of undergrads determined to have financial need; average aid package $10,170

Georgetown College
Georgetown KY
(502) 863-8009
U.S. News ranking: Nat. Lib. Arts, No. 155
Website: www.georgetowncollege.edu/admission/
Admissions email: admissions@georgetowncollege.edu
Private; founded 1787
Affiliation: Baptist
Freshman admissions: selective; 2013-2014: 1,448 applied, 1,242 accepted. Either SAT or ACT required. ACT 25/75 percentile: 20-25. High school rank: 20% in top tenth, 48% in top quarter, 83% in top half
Early decision deadline: 10/15, notification date: N/A
Early action deadline: 11/1, notification date: N/A
Application deadline (fall): 8/1
Undergraduate student body: 1,000 full time, 43 part time; 46% male, 54% female; 0% American Indian, 1% Asian, 10% black, 3% Hispanic, 2% multiracial, 0% Pacific Islander, 76% white, 2% international; 77% from in state; 91% live on campus; 27% of students in fraternities, 35% in sororities
Most popular majors: 10% Biological and Biomedical Sciences, 12% Business, Management, Marketing, and Related Support Services, 9% Parks, Recreation, Leisure, and

Fitness Studies, 13% Psychology, 11% Social Sciences
Expenses: 2014-2015: $32,960; room/board: $8,480
Financial aid: (502) 863-8027; 83% of undergrads determined to have financial need; average aid package $32,160

Kentucky Christian University

Grayson KY
(800) 522-3181
U.S. News ranking: Reg. Coll. (S), No. 56
Website: www.kcu.edu
Admissions email: knights@kcu.edu
Private; founded 1919
Affiliation: Christian Church/Church of Christ
Freshman admissions: selective; 2013-2014: 590 applied, 303 accepted. Either SAT or ACT required. ACT 25/75 percentile: 18-23. High school rank: 10% in top tenth, 32% in top quarter, 64% in top half
Early decision deadline: N/A, notification date: N/A
Early action deadline: N/A, notification date: N/A
Application deadline (fall): 8/1
Undergraduate student body: 494 full time, 57 part time; 54% male, 46% female; 0% American Indian, 0% Asian, 12% black, 1% Hispanic, 1% multiracial, 0% Pacific Islander, 70% white, 1% international; 48% from in state; 81% live on campus; 0% of students in fraternities, 0% in sororities
Most popular majors: 8% Business Administration and Management, General, 8% Elementary Education and Teaching, 18% Multi-/Interdisciplinary Studies, Other, 12% Registered Nursing/Registered Nurse, 8% Social Work
Expenses: 2014-2015: $16,860; room/board: $7,200
Financial aid: (606) 474-3226; 93% of undergrads determined to have financial need; average aid package $15,487

Kentucky State University

Frankfort KY
(800) 325-1716
U.S. News ranking: Nat. Lib. Arts, second tier
Website: www.kysu.edu
Admissions email: admissions@kysu.edu
Public; founded 1886
Freshman admissions: less selective; 2013-2014: 6,399 applied, 2,414 accepted. Either SAT or ACT required. ACT 25/75 percentile: 16-20. High school rank: N/A
Early decision deadline: N/A, notification date: N/A
Early action deadline: N/A, notification date: N/A
Application deadline (fall): rolling
Undergraduate student body: 1,813 full time, 557 part time; 41% male, 59% female; 0% American Indian, 1% Asian, 62% black, 1% Hispanic, 2% multiracial, 0% Pacific Islander, 20% white, 0% international; 58% from in state; 34% live on campus; 5% of students in fraternities, 4% in sororities

Most popular majors: 9% Biology/Biological Sciences, General, 9% Business/Commerce, General, 12% Liberal Arts and Sciences/Liberal Studies, 8% Psychology, General, 16% Registered Nursing/Registered Nurse
Expenses: 2014-2015: $7,404 in state, $17,214 out of state; room/board: $6,690
Financial aid: (502) 597-5960; 85% of undergrads determined to have financial need; average aid package $11,284

Kentucky Wesleyan College

Owensboro KY
(800) 999-0592
U.S. News ranking: Reg. Coll. (S), No. 31
Website: www.kwc.edu/page.php?page=354
Admissions email: rsmith@kwc.edu
Private; founded 1858
Affiliation: United Methodist
Freshman admissions: selective; 2013-2014: 1,006 applied, 675 accepted. Either SAT or ACT required. ACT 25/75 percentile: 19-25. High school rank: 13% in top tenth, 39% in top quarter, 69% in top half
Early decision deadline: N/A, notification date: N/A
Early action deadline: N/A, notification date: N/A
Application deadline (fall): rolling
Undergraduate student body: 621 full time, 36 part time; 52% male, 48% female; 0% American Indian, 0% Asian, 13% black, 2% Hispanic, 0% multiracial, 0% Pacific Islander, 73% white, 2% international; 71% from in state; 50% live on campus; 16% of students in fraternities, 23% in sororities
Most popular majors: 11% Biological and Biomedical Sciences, 12% Business, Management, Marketing, and Related Support Services, 11% Education, 11% Homeland Security, Law Enforcement, Firefighting and Related Protective Services, 11% Visual and Performing Arts
Expenses: 2014-2015: $22,030; room/board: $7,800
Financial aid: (270) 926-3111; 87% of undergrads determined to have financial need; average aid package $17,166

Lindsey Wilson College

Columbia KY
(270) 384-8100
U.S. News ranking: Reg. U. (S), second tier
Website: www.lindsey.edu
Admissions email: admissions@lindsey.edu
Private; founded 1903
Affiliation: United Methodist
Freshman admissions: selective; 2013-2014: 2,711 applied, 1,939 accepted. Neither SAT nor ACT required. ACT 25/75 percentile: 19-24. High school rank: 13% in top tenth, 33% in top quarter, 70% in top half
Early decision deadline: N/A, notification date: N/A
Early action deadline: N/A, notification date: N/A
Application deadline (fall): rolling

Undergraduate student body: 2,101 full time, 99 part time; 41% male, 59% female; 0% American Indian, 1% Asian, 9% black, 1% Hispanic, 2% multiracial, 0% Pacific Islander, 71% white, 0% international; 81% from in state; 52% live on campus; 0% of students in fraternities, 0% in sororities
Most popular majors: 2% Biology/Biological Sciences, General, 7% Business Administration and Management, General, 8% Criminal Justice/Safety Studies, 52% Human Services, General, 4% Registered Nursing/Registered Nurse
Expenses: 2014-2015: $22,550; room/board: $8,670
Financial aid: (270) 384-8022; 94% of undergrads determined to have financial need; average aid package $15,688

Mid-Continent University[1]

Mayfield KY
(270) 247-8475
U.S. News ranking: Reg. Coll. (S), second tier
Website: www.midcontinent.edu
Admissions email: advantage@midcontinent.edu
Private; founded 1949
Affiliation: Southern Baptist Convention
Application deadline (fall): rolling
Undergraduate student body: N/A full time, N/A part time
Expenses: 2013-2014: $13,350; room/board: $6,900
Financial aid: (270) 247-8521

Midway College[1]

Midway KY
(800) 755-0031
U.S. News ranking: Reg. Coll. (S), No. 61
Website: www.midway.edu
Admissions email: admissions@midway.edu
Private
Application deadline (fall): N/A
Undergraduate student body: N/A full time, N/A part time
Expenses: 2013-2014: $22,150; room/board: $8,000
Financial aid: (859) 846-5745

Morehead State University

Morehead KY
(606) 783-2000
U.S. News ranking: Reg. U. (S), No. 53
Website: www.moreheadstate.edu
Admissions email: admissions@moreheadstate.edu
Public; founded 1922
Freshman admissions: selective; 2013-2014: 5,241 applied, 4,364 accepted. Either SAT or ACT required. ACT 25/75 percentile: 19-25. High school rank: 19% in top tenth, 46% in top quarter, 78% in top half
Early decision deadline: N/A, notification date: N/A
Early action deadline: N/A, notification date: N/A
Application deadline (fall): rolling
Undergraduate student body: 6,209 full time, 3,867 part time; 39% male, 61% female; 0% American Indian, 0% Asian, 4% black, 1% Hispanic, 1% multiracial,

0% Pacific Islander, 91% white, 1% international; 87% from in state; 39% live on campus; 10% of students in fraternities, 9% in sororities
Most popular majors: 5% Agriculture, Agriculture Operations, and Related Sciences, 6% Elementary Education and Teaching, 13% General Studies, 5% Registered Nursing/Registered Nurse, 8% Social Work
Expenses: 2014-2015: $7,866 in state, $19,666 out of state; room/board: $7,888
Financial aid: (606) 783-2011; 78% of undergrads determined to have financial need; average aid package $10,749

Murray State University

Murray KY
(270) 809-3741
U.S. News ranking: Reg. U. (S), No. 26
Website: www.murraystate.edu
Admissions email: admissions@murraystate.edu
Public; founded 1922
Freshman admissions: selective; 2013-2014: 4,956 applied, 4,068 accepted. Either SAT or ACT required. ACT 25/75 percentile: 20-26. High school rank: 19% in top tenth, 43% in top quarter, 73% in top half
Early decision deadline: N/A, notification date: N/A
Early action deadline: N/A, notification date: N/A
Application deadline (fall): 8/15
Undergraduate student body: 7,153 full time, 2,019 part time; 42% male, 58% female; 0% American Indian, 1% Asian, 7% black, 2% Hispanic, 2% multiracial, 0% Pacific Islander, 83% white, 4% international; 69% from in state; 33% live on campus; 14% of students in fraternities, 15% in sororities
Most popular majors: 11% Business, Management, Marketing, and Related Support Services, 13% Education, 7% Engineering Technologies and Engineering-Related Fields, 15% Health Professions and Related Programs, 10% Liberal Arts and Sciences, General Studies and Humanities
Expenses: 2014-2015: $7,392 in state, $10,073 out of state; room/board: $7,912
Financial aid: (270) 809-2546; 63% of undergrads determined to have financial need; average aid package $10,679

Northern Kentucky University

Highland Heights KY
(800) 637-9948
U.S. News ranking: Reg. U. (S), No. 70
Website: www.nku.edu
Admissions email: admitnku@nku.edu
Public; founded 1968
Freshman admissions: selective; 2013-2014: 8,724 applied, 5,105 accepted. Either SAT or ACT required. ACT 25/75 percentile: 20-25. High school rank: 11% in top tenth, 32% in top quarter, 64% in top half
Early decision deadline: N/A, notification date: N/A

Early action deadline: N/A, notification date: N/A
Undergraduate student body: 9,736 full time, 3,058 part time; 45% male, 55% female; 0% American Indian, 1% Asian, 7% black, 2% Hispanic, 2% multiracial, 0% Pacific Islander, 82% white, 4% international; 66% from in state; 14% live on campus; 4% of students in fraternities, 4% in sororities
Most popular majors: 12% Health Services/Allied Health/Health Sciences, General
Expenses: 2014-2015: $8,856 in state, $17,328 out of state; room/board: $8,610
Financial aid: (859) 572-5143; 65% of undergrads determined to have financial need; average aid package $10,384

Spalding University[1]

Louisville KY
(502) 585-7111
U.S. News ranking: Nat. U., No. 181
Website: www.spalding.edu
Admissions email: admissions@spalding.edu
Private; founded 1814
Affiliation: Roman Catholic
Application deadline (fall): rolling
Undergraduate student body: N/A full time, N/A part time
Expenses: 2013-2014: $22,425; room/board: $10,400
Financial aid: (502) 585-9911

St. Catharine College[1]

St. Catharine KY
(800) 599-2000
U.S. News ranking: Reg. Coll. (S), unranked
Website: www.sccky.edu
Admissions email: admissions@sccky.edu
Private
Application deadline (fall): N/A
Undergraduate student body: N/A full time, N/A part time
Expenses: 2013-2014: $18,026; room/board: $9,031
Financial aid: (859) 336-5082

Sullivan University[1]

Louisville KY
(502) 456-6504
U.S. News ranking: Reg. U. (S), unranked
Website: www.sullivan.edu
Admissions email: admissions@sullivan.edu
Private
Application deadline (fall): N/A
Undergraduate student body: N/A full time, N/A part time
Expenses: 2013-2014: $17,970; room/board: $9,120
Financial aid: (800) 844-1354

Thomas More College

Crestview Hills KY
(800) 825-4557
U.S. News ranking: Reg. U. (S), No. 49
Website: www.thomasmore.edu
Admissions email: admissions@thomasmore.edu
Private; founded 1921
Affiliation: Roman Catholic
Freshman admissions: selective; 2013-2014: 1,053 applied, 924 accepted. Either SAT or ACT required. ACT 25/75 percentile:

20-25. High school rank: 11% in top tenth, 27% in top quarter, 64% in top half
Early decision deadline: N/A, notification date: N/A
Early action deadline: N/A, notification date: N/A
Application deadline (fall): 8/1
Undergraduate student body: 1,140 full time, 362 part time; 48% male, 52% female; 0% American Indian, 1% Asian, 7% black, 2% Hispanic, 2% multiracial, 0% Pacific Islander, 75% white, 1% international; 47% from in state; 30% live on campus; 2% of students in fraternities, 2% in sororities
Most popular majors: 7% Biological and Biomedical Sciences, 44% Business, Management, Marketing, and Related Support Services, 8% Education, 11% Health Professions and Related Programs, 5% Liberal Arts and Sciences, General Studies and Humanities
Expenses: 2014-2015: $28,618; room/board: $7,770
Financial aid: (859) 344-3319; 58% of undergrads determined to have financial need; average aid package $21,066

Transylvania University
Lexington KY
(859) 233-8242
U.S. News ranking: Nat. Lib. Arts, No. 81
Website: www.transy.edu
Admissions email: admissions@transy.edu
Private; founded 1780
Affiliation: Christian Church (Disciples of Christ)
Freshman admissions: more selective; 2013-2014: 1,539 applied, 1,275 accepted. Either SAT or ACT required. ACT 25/75 percentile: 24-30. High school rank: 39% in top tenth, 75% in top quarter, 95% in top half.
Early decision deadline: N/A, notification date: N/A
Early action deadline: 12/1, notification date: 1/15
Application deadline (fall): 2/1
Undergraduate student body: 1,066 full time, 15 part time; 43% male, 57% female; 0% American Indian, 2% Asian, 3% black, 3% Hispanic, 3% multiracial, 0% Pacific Islander, 83% white, 2% international; 77% from in state; 75% live on campus; 44% of students in fraternities, 60% in sororities
Most popular majors: 13% Biology/Biological Sciences, General, 17% Business/Commerce, General, 8% English Language and Literature, General, 8% Psychology, General, 15% Social Sciences, General
Expenses: 2014-2015: $33,360; room/board: $9,300
Financial aid: (859) 233-8239; 68% of undergrads determined to have financial need; average aid package $26,801

Union College
Barbourville KY
(800) 489-8646
U.S. News ranking: Reg. U. (S), No. 81
Website: www.unionky.edu
Admissions email: enroll@unionky.edu
Private; founded 1879

Affiliation: United Methodist
Freshman admissions: selective; 2013-2014: 1,390 applied, 1,038 accepted. Either SAT or ACT required. ACT 25/75 percentile: 19-24. High school rank: N/A
Early decision deadline: N/A, notification date: N/A
Early action deadline: N/A, notification date: N/A
Application deadline (fall): rolling
Undergraduate student body: 729 full time, 89 part time; 51% male, 49% female; 0% American Indian, 0% Asian, 10% black, 2% Hispanic, 2% multiracial, 0% Pacific Islander, 79% white, 6% international; 76% from in state; 48% live on campus; 0% of students in fraternities, 0% in sororities
Most popular majors: 9% Athletic Training/Trainer, 8% Business Administration and Management, General, 8% Criminal Justice/Law Enforcement Administration, 10% Psychology, General
Expenses: 2014-2015: $22,980; room/board: $6,975
Financial aid: (606) 546-1229; 87% of undergrads determined to have financial need; average aid package $20,468

University of Kentucky
Lexington KY
(859) 257-2000
U.S. News ranking: Nat. U., No. 129
Website: www.uky.edu
Admissions email: admissions@uky.edu
Public; founded 1865
Freshman admissions: more selective; 2013-2014: 19,810 applied, 13,592 accepted. Either SAT or ACT required. ACT 25/75 percentile: 22-28. High school rank: 31% in top tenth, 58% in top quarter, 85% in top half
Early decision deadline: N/A, notification date: N/A
Early action deadline: N/A, notification date: N/A
Application deadline (fall): rolling
Undergraduate student body: 19,884 full time, 1,557 part time; 49% male, 51% female; 0% American Indian, 2% Asian, 8% black, 3% Hispanic, 3% multiracial, 0% Pacific Islander, 78% white, 3% international; 68% from in state; 15% live on campus; 18% of students in fraternities, 28% in sororities
Most popular majors: 4% Accounting, 5% Biology/Biological Sciences, General, 4% Finance, General, 5% Psychology, General, 4% Registered Nursing/Registered Nurse
Expenses: 2014-2015: $10,616 in state, $22,888 out of state; room/board: $10,506
Financial aid: (859) 257-3172; 52% of undergrads determined to have financial need; average aid package $10,872

University of Louisville
Louisville KY
(502) 852-6531
U.S. News ranking: Nat. U., No. 161
Website: www.louisville.edu
Admissions email: admitme@louisville.edu

Public; founded 1798
Freshman admissions: selective; 2013-2014: 9,142 applied, 6,496 accepted. Either SAT or ACT required. ACT 25/75 percentile: 22-28. High school rank: 20% in top tenth, 33% in top quarter, 61% in top half
Early decision deadline: N/A, notification date: N/A
Early action deadline: N/A, notification date: N/A
Application deadline (fall): 8/25
Undergraduate student body: 12,426 full time, 3,531 part time; 49% male, 51% female; 0% American Indian, 3% Asian, 11% black, 4% Hispanic, 4% multiracial, 0% Pacific Islander, 77% white, 1% international; 85% from in state; 27% live on campus; 18% of students in fraternities, 13% in sororities
Most popular majors: 15% Business, Management, Marketing, and Related Support Services, 10% Engineering, 8% Health Professions and Related Programs, 9% Parks, Recreation, Leisure, and Fitness Studies, 8% Social Sciences
Expenses: 2014-2015: $10,432 in state, $24,320 out of state; room/board: $7,710
Financial aid: (502) 852-5511; 63% of undergrads determined to have financial need; average aid package $10,965

University of Pikeville
Pikeville KY
(606) 218-5251
U.S. News ranking: Nat. Lib. Arts, second tier
Website: www.pc.edu/
Admissions email: wewantyou@pc.edu
Private; founded 1889
Affiliation: Presbyterian Church (USA)
Freshman admissions: selective; 2013-2014: 1,804 applied, 1,804 accepted. Either SAT or ACT required. ACT 25/75 percentile: 17-22. High school rank: 15% in top tenth, 36% in top quarter, 65% in top half
Early decision deadline: N/A, notification date: N/A
Early action deadline: N/A, notification date: N/A
Application deadline (fall): 8/16
Undergraduate student body: 1,282 full time, 455 part time; 47% male, 53% female; 0% American Indian, 0% Asian, 13% black, 1% Hispanic, 0% multiracial, 0% Pacific Islander, 82% white, 3% international; 81% from in state; 59% live on campus; N/A of students in fraternities, N/A in sororities
Most popular majors: 10% Biological and Biomedical Sciences, 23% Business, Management, Marketing, and Related Support Services, 12% Homeland Security, Law Enforcement, Firefighting and Related Protective Services, 10% Psychology, 12% Social Sciences
Expenses: 2014-2015: $18,290; room/board: $7,210
Financial aid: (606) 218-5253; 98% of undergrads determined to have financial need; average aid package $18,056

University of the Cumberlands
Williamsburg KY
(800) 343-1609
U.S. News ranking: Reg. U. (S), No. 92
Website: www.ucumberlands.edu
Admissions email: admiss@ucumberlands.edu
Private; founded 1888
Affiliation: Baptist
Freshman admissions: selective; 2013-2014: 2,529 applied, 1,803 accepted. Either SAT or ACT required. ACT 25/75 percentile: 19-25. High school rank: 15% in top tenth, 38% in top quarter, 71% in top half
Early decision deadline: N/A, notification date: N/A
Early action deadline: N/A, notification date: N/A
Application deadline (fall): 8/15
Undergraduate student body: 1,514 full time, 582 part time; 50% male, 50% female; 0% American Indian, 0% Asian, 8% black, 2% Hispanic, 1% multiracial, 0% Pacific Islander, 80% white, 6% international; 69% from in state; 75% live on campus; 0% of students in fraternities, 0% in sororities
Most popular majors: 12% Biological and Biomedical Sciences, 16% Business, Management, Marketing, and Related Support Services, 13% Education, 8% Health Professions and Related Programs, 8% Public Administration and Social Service Professions
Expenses: 2013-2014: $20,000; room/board: $7,500
Financial aid: (800) 532-0828

Western Kentucky University
Bowling Green KY
(270) 745-2551
U.S. News ranking: Reg. U. (S), No. 31
Website: www.wku.edu
Admissions email: admission@wku.edu
Public; founded 1906
Freshman admissions: selective; 2013-2014: 8,114 applied, 7,491 accepted. Either SAT or ACT required. ACT 25/75 percentile: 19-25. High school rank: 25% in top tenth, 50% in top quarter, 76% in top half
Early decision deadline: N/A, notification date: N/A
Early action deadline: N/A, notification date: N/A
Application deadline (fall): 8/1
Undergraduate student body: 13,382 full time, 4,127 part time; 43% male, 57% female; 0% American Indian, 1% Asian, 11% black, 2% Hispanic, 2% multiracial, 0% Pacific Islander, 77% white, 5% international; 83% from in state; 29% live on campus; 12% of students in fraternities, 13% in sororities
Most popular majors: 14% Business, Management, Marketing, and Related Support Services, 12% Education, 9% Health Professions and Related Programs, 9% Liberal Arts and Sciences, General Studies and Humanities, 9% Social Sciences
Expenses: 2014-2015: $9,140 in state, $23,352 out of state; room/board: N/A

Financial aid: (270) 745-2755; 65% of undergrads determined to have financial need; average aid package $13,809

Centenary College of Louisiana
Shreveport LA
(800) 234-4448
U.S. News ranking: Nat. Lib. Arts, No. 148
Website: www.centenary.edu
Admissions email: admissions@centenary.edu
Private; founded 1825
Affiliation: Methodist
Freshman admissions: more selective; 2013-2014: 670 applied, 442 accepted. Either SAT or ACT required. ACT 25/75 percentile: 22-28. High school rank: 25% in top tenth, 58% in top quarter, 86% in top half
Early decision deadline: N/A, notification date: N/A
Early action deadline: 12/15, notification date: N/A
Application deadline (fall): 8/1
Undergraduate student body: 571 full time, 15 part time; 44% male, 56% female; 1% American Indian, 3% Asian, 15% black, 5% Hispanic, 3% multiracial, 0% Pacific Islander, 69% white, 4% international; 64% from in state; 60% live on campus; 27% of students in fraternities, 38% in sororities
Most popular majors: 10% Accounting, 29% Biology/Biological Sciences, General, 17% Communication and Media Studies, 14% Music Performance, General, 24% Psychology, General
Expenses: 2014-2015: $32,000; room/board: $10,230
Financial aid: (318) 869-5137; 75% of undergrads determined to have financial need; average aid package $24,661

Dillard University
New Orleans LA
(800) 216-6637
U.S. News ranking: Nat. Lib. Arts, second tier
Website: www.dillard.edu
Admissions email: admissions@dillard.edu
Private; founded 1869
Affiliation: United Methodist
Freshman admissions: selective; 2013-2014: 4,726 applied, 1,675 accepted. Either SAT or ACT required. ACT 25/75 percentile: 17-20. High school rank: 14% in top tenth, 31% in top quarter, 62% in top half
Early decision deadline: N/A, notification date: N/A
Early action deadline: N/A, notification date: N/A
Application deadline (fall): 8/1
Undergraduate student body: 1,127 full time, 56 part time; 29% male, 71% female; 0% American Indian, 0% Asian, 90% black, 1% Hispanic, 1% multiracial, 0% Pacific Islander, 0% white, 5% international; 65% from in state; 41% live on campus; 5% of students in fraternities, 5% in sororities

Most popular majors: 9% Biology/Biological Sciences, General, 10% Mass Communication/Media Studies, 10% Public Health, General, 10% Registered Nursing/Registered Nurse, 9% Sociology
Expenses: 2013-2014: $16,191; room/board: $8,878
Financial aid: (504) 816-4677

Grambling State University

Grambling LA
(318) 274-6183
U.S. News ranking: Reg. U. (S), second tier
Website: www.gram.edu/
Admissions email: admissions@gram.edu
Public
Freshman admissions: less selective; 2013-2014: 4,248 applied, 1,888 accepted. Either SAT or ACT required. ACT 25/75 percentile: 16-20. High school rank: 8% in top tenth, 22% in top quarter, 52% in top half
Early decision deadline: N/A, notification date: N/A
Early action deadline: N/A, notification date: N/A
Application deadline (fall): 8/15
Undergraduate student body: 3,860 full time, 295 part time; 40% male, 60% female; 0% American Indian, 0% Asian, 90% black, 1% Hispanic, 1% multiracial, 0% Pacific Islander, 1% white, 6% international; 65% from in state; N/A live on campus; N/A of students in fraternities, N/A in sororities
Most popular majors: 7% Biology/Biological Sciences, General, 8% Business Administration and Management, General, 21% Criminal Justice/Safety Studies, 7% Mass Communication/Media Studies, 11% Registered Nursing/Registered Nurse
Expenses: 2014-2015: $6,545 in state, $15,744 out of state; room/board: $8,412
Financial aid: (318) 274-6056; 91% of undergrads determined to have financial need; average aid package $3,522

Louisiana College[1]

Pineville LA
(318) 487-7259
U.S. News ranking: Reg. Coll. (S), No. 74
Website: www.lacollege.edu
Admissions email: admissions@lacollege.edu
Private
Application deadline (fall): N/A
Undergraduate student body: N/A full time, N/A part time
Expenses: 2013-2014: $14,520; room/board: $5,720
Financial aid: (318) 487-7386

Louisiana State University–Alexandria

Alexandria LA
(318) 473-6417
U.S. News ranking: Nat. Lib. Arts, second tier
Website: www.lsua.edu
Admissions email: admissions@lsua.edu
Public; founded 1960
Freshman admissions: selective; 2013-2014: 1,080 applied, 656 accepted. ACT required. ACT 25/75 percentile: 18-22.

High school rank: 13% in top tenth, 39% in top quarter, 69% in top half
Early decision deadline: N/A, notification date: N/A
Early action deadline: N/A, notification date: N/A
Application deadline (fall): 8/1
Undergraduate student body: 1,257 full time, 954 part time; 30% male, 70% female; 1% American Indian, 1% Asian, 15% black, 4% Hispanic, 2% multiracial, 0% Pacific Islander, 75% white, 0% international; 97% from in state; 11% live on campus; 0% of students in fraternities, 0% in sororities
Most popular majors: 20% Business Administration and Management, General, 11% Criminal Justice/Safety Studies, 9% Elementary Education and Teaching, 20% General Studies, 14% Psychology, General
Expenses: 2014-2015: $5,315 in state, $12,173 out of state; room/board: $7,650
Financial aid: (318) 473-6423; 64% of undergrads determined to have financial need; average aid package $6,647

Louisiana State University–Baton Rouge

Baton Rouge LA
(225) 578-1175
U.S. News ranking: Nat. U., No. 129
Website: www.lsu.edu
Admissions email: admissions@lsu.edu
Public; founded 1860
Freshman admissions: more selective; 2013-2014: 16,005 applied, 12,002 accepted. Either SAT or ACT required. ACT 25/75 percentile: 23-28. High school rank: 25% in top tenth, 53% in top quarter, 82% in top half
Early decision deadline: N/A, notification date: N/A
Early action deadline: N/A, notification date: N/A
Application deadline (fall): 4/15
Undergraduate student body: 22,811 full time, 2,112 part time; 48% male, 52% female; 0% American Indian, 3% Asian, 11% black, 5% Hispanic, 2% multiracial, 0% Pacific Islander, 76% white, 2% international; 81% from in state; 25% live on campus; 17% of students in fraternities, 26% in sororities
Most popular majors: 8% Biological and Biomedical Sciences, 18% Business, Management, Marketing, and Related Support Services, 8% Communication, Journalism, and Related Programs, 10% Education, 11% Engineering
Expenses: 2014-2015: $8,750 in state, $26,467 out of state; room/board: $10,804
Financial aid: (225) 578-3103; 43% of undergrads determined to have financial need; average aid package $14,693

Louisiana State University–Shreveport

Shreveport LA
(318) 797-5061
U.S. News ranking: Reg. U. (S), second tier
Website: www.lsus.edu
Admissions email: admissions@pilot.lsus.edu
Public; founded 1967
Freshman admissions: selective; 2013-2014: 695 applied, 621 accepted. Either SAT or ACT required. ACT 25/75 percentile: 20-24. High school rank: N/A
Early decision deadline: N/A, notification date: N/A
Early action deadline: N/A, notification date: N/A
Application deadline (fall): rolling
Undergraduate student body: 2,097 full time, 1,577 part time; 41% male, 59% female; 1% American Indian, 2% Asian, 22% black, 4% Hispanic, 3% multiracial, 0% Pacific Islander, 61% white, 2% international
Most popular majors: 11% Biological and Biomedical Sciences, 23% Business, Management, Marketing, and Related Support Services, 9% Education, 14% Liberal Arts and Sciences, General Studies and Humanities, 11% Psychology
Expenses: 2013-2014: $5,606 in state, $5,606 out of state; room/board: N/A
Financial aid: (318) 797-5363

Louisiana Tech University

Ruston LA
(318) 257-3036
U.S. News ranking: Nat. U., No. 201
Website: www.latech.edu
Admissions email: bulldog@latech.edu
Public; founded 1894
Freshman admissions: more selective; 2013-2014: 5,080 applied, 3,424 accepted. Either SAT or ACT required. ACT 25/75 percentile: 21-26. High school rank: 24% in top tenth, 51% in top quarter, 80% in top half
Early decision deadline: N/A, notification date: N/A
Early action deadline: N/A, notification date: N/A
Application deadline (fall): 7/31
Undergraduate student body: 6,585 full time, 2,660 part time; 53% male, 47% female; 0% American Indian, 1% Asian, 15% black, 1% Hispanic, 1% multiracial, 0% Pacific Islander, 68% white, 4% international; 90% from in state; 5% live on campus; N/A of students in fraternities, N/A in sororities
Most popular majors: 6% Biological and Biomedical Sciences, 16% Business, Management, Marketing, and Related Support Services, 6% Education, 16% Engineering, 5% Social Sciences
Expenses: 2014-2015: $8,052 in state, $22,635 out of state; room/board: $6,495
Financial aid: (318) 257-2643; 53% of undergrads determined to have financial need; average aid package $9,932

Loyola University New Orleans

New Orleans LA
(800) 456-9652
U.S. News ranking: Reg. U. (S), No. 11
Website: www.loyno.edu
Admissions email: admit@loyno.edu
Private; founded 1912
Affiliation: Roman Catholic (Jesuit)
Freshman admissions: selective; 2013-2014: 4,827 applied, 4,203 accepted. Either SAT or ACT required. ACT 25/75 percentile: 22-28. High school rank: 15% in top tenth, 43% in top quarter, 76% in top half
Early decision deadline: N/A, notification date: N/A
Early action deadline: N/A, notification date: N/A
Application deadline (fall): rolling
Undergraduate student body: 2,741 full time, 205 part time; 41% male, 59% female; 1% American Indian, 4% Asian, 16% black, 16% Hispanic, 4% multiracial, 0% Pacific Islander, 51% white, 3% international; 46% from in state; 43% live on campus; 3% of students in fraternities, 7% in sororities
Most popular majors: 8% English Language and Literature, General, 7% Marketing/Marketing Management, General, 6% Music Management, 9% Psychology, General, 9% Speech Communication and Rhetoric
Expenses: 2014-2015: $36,610; room/board: $12,660
Financial aid: (504) 865-3231; 69% of undergrads determined to have financial need; average aid package $27,599

McNeese State University

Lake Charles LA
(337) 475-5356
U.S. News ranking: Reg. U. (S), No. 87
Website: www.mcneese.edu
Admissions email: admissions@mcneese.edu
Public; founded 1939
Freshman admissions: selective; 2013-2014: 3,638 applied, 2,165 accepted. Either SAT or ACT required. ACT 25/75 percentile: 20-24. High school rank: 18% in top tenth, 41% in top quarter, 72% in top half
Early decision deadline: N/A, notification date: N/A
Early action deadline: N/A, notification date: N/A
Application deadline (fall): 8/19
Undergraduate student body: 5,959 full time, 1,542 part time; 38% male, 62% female; 1% American Indian, 1% Asian, 19% black, 2% Hispanic, 2% multiracial, 0% Pacific Islander, 71% white, 4% international; 93% from in state; N/A live on campus; 6% of students in fraternities, 6% in sororities
Most popular majors: 6% Business Administration and Management, General, 5% Criminal Justice/Safety Studies, 6% Engineering, General, 15% General Studies, 16% Registered Nursing/Registered Nurse

Expenses: 2013-2014: $5,701 in state, $16,603 out of state; room/board: $7,230
Financial aid: (337) 475-5065

Nicholls State University

Thibodaux LA
(985) 448-4507
U.S. News ranking: Reg. U. (S), No. 87
Website: www.nicholls.edu
Admissions email: nicholls@nicholls.edu
Public; founded 1948
Freshman admissions: selective; 2013-2014: 2,404 applied, 2,090 accepted. Either SAT or ACT required. ACT 25/75 percentile: 20-24. High school rank: 16% in top tenth, 40% in top quarter, 73% in top half
Early decision deadline: N/A, notification date: N/A
Early action deadline: N/A, notification date: N/A
Application deadline (fall): rolling
Undergraduate student body: 4,729 full time, 1,163 part time; 38% male, 62% female; 2% American Indian, 1% Asian, 20% black, 3% Hispanic, 3% multiracial, 0% Pacific Islander, 68% white, 2% international; 95% from in state; 25% live on campus; 11% of students in fraternities, 11% in sororities
Most popular majors: 22% Business, Management, Marketing, and Related Support Services, 11% Education, 19% Health Professions and Related Programs, 14% Liberal Arts and Sciences, General Studies and Humanities, 5% Personal and Culinary Services
Expenses: 2014-2015: $7,234 in state, $17,481 out of state; room/board: $8,673
Financial aid: (985) 448-4048; 64% of undergrads determined to have financial need; average aid package $8,075

Northwestern State University of Louisiana

Natchitoches LA
(800) 426-3754
U.S. News ranking: Reg. U. (S), No. 87
Website: www.nsula.edu
Admissions email: admissions@nsula.edu
Public; founded 1884
Freshman admissions: selective; 2013-2014: 4,088 applied, 2,366 accepted. Either SAT or ACT required. ACT 25/75 percentile: 19-24. High school rank: 19% in top tenth, 44% in top quarter, 75% in top half
Early decision deadline: N/A, notification date: N/A
Early action deadline: N/A, notification date: N/A
Application deadline (fall): 7/6
Undergraduate student body: 5,013 full time, 2,823 part time; 32% male, 68% female; 1% American Indian, 1% Asian, 29% black, 5% Hispanic, 3% multiracial, 0% Pacific Islander, 56% white, 1% international; 89% from in state; 19% live on campus; N/A of students in fraternities, N/A in sororities

Most popular majors: 12% Business, Management, Marketing, and Related Support Services, 6% Education, 26% Health Professions and Related Programs, 13% Liberal Arts and Sciences, General Studies and Humanities, 8% Psychology
Expenses: 2014-2015: $6,807 in state, $17,595 out of state; room/board: $6,846
Financial aid: (318) 357-5961; 72% of undergrads determined to have financial need; average aid package $10,556

Our Lady of Holy Cross College[1]
New Orleans LA
(504) 398-2175
U.S. News ranking: Reg. U. (S), second tier
Website: www.olhcc.edu
Admissions email: admissions@olhcc.edu
Private
Application deadline (fall): N/A
Undergraduate student body: N/A full time, N/A part time
Expenses: 2014-2015: $12,620; room/board: N/A
Financial aid: (504) 398-2165; 91% of undergrads determined to have financial need; average aid package $7,396

Southeastern Louisiana University
Hammond LA
(985) 549-5637
U.S. News ranking: Reg. U. (S), second tier
Website: www.selu.edu
Admissions email: admissions@selu.edu
Public; founded 1925
Freshman admissions: selective; 2013-2014: 3,818 applied, 3,405 accepted. Either SAT or ACT required. ACT 25/75 percentile: 20-24. High school rank: 11% in top tenth, 30% in top quarter, 63% in top half
Early decision deadline: N/A, notification date: N/A
Early action deadline: N/A, notification date: N/A
Application deadline (fall): 8/1
Undergraduate student body: 9,999 full time, 3,745 part time; 40% male, 60% female; 0% American Indian, 1% Asian, 16% black, 6% Hispanic, 4% multiracial, 0% Pacific Islander, 69% white, 2% international; 96% from in state; 19% live on campus; 6% of students in fraternities, 6% in sororities
Most popular majors: 23% Business, Management, Marketing, and Related Support Services, 15% Education, 12% Health Professions and Related Programs, 13% Liberal Arts and Sciences, General Studies and Humanities, 5% Psychology
Expenses: 2013-2014: $5,715 in state, $17,734 out of state; room/board: $6,714
Financial aid: (985) 549-2244

Southern University and A&M College
Baton Rouge LA
(225) 771-2430
U.S. News ranking: Reg. U. (S), second tier
Website: www.subr.edu/
Admissions email: admit@subr.edu
Public; founded 1880
Freshman admissions: less selective; 2013-2014: N/A applied, N/A accepted. Either SAT or ACT required. ACT 25/75 percentile: 17-20. High school rank: 9% in top tenth, 23% in top quarter, 49% in top half
Early decision deadline: N/A, notification date: N/A
Early action deadline: N/A, notification date: N/A
Application deadline (fall): 7/1
Undergraduate student body: 4,631 full time, 967 part time; 37% male, 63% female; 0% American Indian, 0% Asian, 94% black, 1% Hispanic, 1% multiracial, 0% Pacific Islander, 3% white, 0% international
Most popular majors: Information not available
Expenses: 2013-2014: $6,630 in state, $8,274 out of state; room/board: $8,003
Financial aid: (225) 771-2790

Southern University–New Orleans[1]
New Orleans LA
(504) 286-5314
U.S. News ranking: Reg. U. (S), second tier
Website: www.suno.edu
Admissions email: N/A
Public
Application deadline (fall): N/A
Undergraduate student body: N/A full time, N/A part time
Expenses: 2013-2014: $4,911 in state, $4,911 out of state; room/board: $7,080
Financial aid: (504) 286-5263

Tulane University
New Orleans LA
(504) 865-5731
U.S. News ranking: Nat. U., No. 54
Website: www.tulane.edu
Admissions email: undergrad.admission@tulane.edu
Private; founded 1834
Freshman admissions: more selective; 2013-2014: 30,122 applied, 7,961 accepted. Either SAT or ACT required. ACT 25/75 percentile: 29-32. High school rank: 58% in top tenth, 83% in top quarter, 95% in top half
Early decision deadline: N/A, notification date: N/A
Early action deadline: 11/15, notification date: 12/15
Application deadline (fall): 1/15
Undergraduate student body: 6,487 full time, 1,865 part time; 42% male, 58% female; 0% American Indian, 4% Asian, 9% black, 6% Hispanic, 3% multiracial, 0% Pacific Islander, 71% white, 3% international; 27% from in state; 43% live on campus; 26% of students in fraternities, 43% in sororities
Most popular majors: 10% Biological and Biomedical Sciences, 22% Business, Management, Marketing, and Related Support Services, 5%

Health Professions and Related Programs, 6% Psychology, 18% Social Sciences
Expenses: 2014-2015: $48,305; room/board: $13,102
Financial aid: (504) 865-5723; 38% of undergrads determined to have financial need; average aid package $44,160

University of Louisiana–Lafayette
Lafayette LA
(337) 482-6553
U.S. News ranking: Nat. U., second tier
Website: www.louisiana.edu
Admissions email: enroll@louisiana.edu
Public; founded 1898
Freshman admissions: selective; 2013-2014: 8,506 applied, 5,044 accepted. Either SAT or ACT required. ACT 25/75 percentile: 21-25. High school rank: 17% in top tenth, 43% in top quarter, 75% in top half
Early decision deadline: N/A, notification date: N/A
Early action deadline: N/A, notification date: N/A
Application deadline (fall): rolling
Undergraduate student body: 12,295 full time, 2,758 part time; 45% male, 55% female; 0% American Indian, 2% Asian, 21% black, 3% Hispanic, 2% multiracial, 0% Pacific Islander, 68% white, 2% international; 94% from in state; 18% live on campus; 9% of students in fraternities, 10% in sororities
Most popular majors: 20% Business, Management, Marketing, and Related Support Services, 13% Education, 7% Engineering, 9% Health Professions and Related Programs, 14% Liberal Arts and Sciences, General Studies and Humanities
Expenses: 2014-2015: $6,948 in state, $19,348 out of state; room/board: $8,566
Financial aid: (337) 482-6506; 57% of undergrads determined to have financial need; average aid package $8,339

University of Louisiana–Monroe
Monroe LA
(318) 342-5430
U.S. News ranking: Reg. U. (S), No. 81
Website: www.ulm.edu
Admissions email: admissions@ulm.edu
Public; founded 1931
Freshman admissions: selective; 2013-2014: 3,454 applied, 2,668 accepted. Either SAT or ACT required. ACT 25/75 percentile: 20-25. High school rank: 25% in top tenth, 50% in top quarter, 80% in top half
Early decision deadline: N/A, notification date: N/A
Early action deadline: N/A, notification date: N/A
Application deadline (fall): rolling
Undergraduate student body: 4,894 full time, 2,382 part time; 37% male, 63% female; 0% American Indian, 2% Asian, 28% black, 2% Hispanic, 2% multiracial, 0% Pacific Islander, 62% white, 2% international; 92% from in state; N/A live on campus; 6% of students in fraternities, N/A in sororities

Most popular majors: 6% Business Administration and Management, General, 6% Elementary Education and Teaching, 15% General Studies, 6% Psychology, General, 7% Registered Nursing/Registered Nurse
Expenses: 2014-2015: $6,963 in state, $19,121 out of state; room/board: $6,830
Financial aid: (318) 342-5320

University of New Orleans
New Orleans LA
(504) 280-6595
U.S. News ranking: Nat. U., second tier
Website: www.uno.edu
Admissions email: unopec@uno.edu
Public; founded 1956
Freshman admissions: selective; 2013-2014: 3,197 applied, 1,610 accepted. Either SAT or ACT required. ACT 25/75 percentile: 21-25. High school rank: 16% in top tenth, 41% in top quarter, 66% in top half
Early decision deadline: N/A, notification date: N/A
Early action deadline: N/A, notification date: N/A
Application deadline (fall): 7/25
Undergraduate student body: 5,376 full time, 1,768 part time; 50% male, 50% female; 0% American Indian, 8% Asian, 15% black, 10% Hispanic, 3% multiracial, 0% Pacific Islander, 56% white, 3% international; 95% from in state; 10% live on campus; 2% of students in fraternities, 2% in sororities
Most popular majors: 8% Biological and Biomedical Sciences, 34% Business, Management, Marketing, and Related Support Services, 11% Engineering, 10% Multi/Interdisciplinary Studies, 11% Visual and Performing Arts
Expenses: 2014-2015: $7,482 in state, $21,092 out of state; room/board: $9,274
Financial aid: (504) 280-6603; 76% of undergrads determined to have financial need; average aid package $8,762

Xavier University of Louisiana
New Orleans LA
(504) 520-7388
U.S. News ranking: Nat. Lib. Arts, No. 178
Website: www.xula.edu
Admissions email: apply@xula.edu
Private; founded 1915
Affiliation: Roman Catholic
Freshman admissions: more selective; 2013-2014: 4,703 applied, 2,560 accepted. Either SAT or ACT required. ACT 25/75 percentile: 20-26. High school rank: 28% in top tenth, 56% in top quarter, 81% in top half
Early decision deadline: N/A, notification date: N/A
Early action deadline: 1/15, notification date: 2/15
Application deadline (fall): 7/1
Undergraduate student body: 2,380 full time, 124 part time; 28% male, 72% female; 0% American Indian, 10% Asian, 77% black, 2% Hispanic, 3% multiracial, 0% Pacific Islander, 4% white,

2% international; 50% from in state; 47% live on campus; 1% of students in fraternities, 3% in sororities
Most popular majors: 23% Biological and Biomedical Sciences, 11% Business, Management, Marketing, and Related Support Services, 20% Physical Sciences, 17% Psychology, 8% Social Sciences
Expenses: 2014-2015: $21,552; room/board: $8,500
Financial aid: (504) 520-7517; 84% of undergrads determined to have financial need; average aid package $20,877

MAINE

Bates College
Lewiston ME
(855) 228-3755
U.S. News ranking: Nat. Lib. Arts, No. 19
Website: www.bates.edu
Admissions email: admission@bates.edu
Private; founded 1855
Freshman admissions: more selective; 2013-2014: 5,243 applied, 1,267 accepted. Neither SAT nor ACT required. SAT 25/75 percentile: 1260-1430. High school rank: 56% in top tenth, 87% in top quarter, 98% in top half
Early decision deadline: 11/15, notification date: 12/20
Early action deadline: N/A, notification date: N/A
Application deadline (fall): 1/1
Undergraduate student body: 1,791 full time, 0 part time; 50% male, 50% female; 0% American Indian, 5% Asian, 5% black, 6% Hispanic, 4% multiracial, 0% Pacific Islander, 72% white, 6% international; 10% from in state; 93% live on campus; 0% of students in fraternities, 0% in sororities
Most popular majors: 14% Biological and Biomedical Sciences, 9% English Language and Literature/Letters, 8% History, 11% Psychology, 21% Social Sciences
Expenses: 2014-2015 tuition/fees/room/board: $60,720
Financial aid: (207) 786-6096; 48% of undergrads determined to have financial need; average aid package $40,233

Bowdoin College
Brunswick ME
(207) 725-3100
U.S. News ranking: Nat. Lib. Arts, No. 5
Website: www.bowdoin.edu
Admissions email: admissions@bowdoin.edu
Private; founded 1794
Freshman admissions: most selective; 2013-2014: 7,052 applied, 1,054 accepted. Neither SAT nor ACT required. SAT 25/75 percentile: 1360-1510. High school rank: 83% in top tenth, 94% in top quarter, 100% in top half
Early decision deadline: 11/15, notification date: 12/15
Early action deadline: N/A, notification date: N/A
Application deadline (fall): 1/1

Undergraduate student body: 1,791 full time, 4 part time; 50% male, 50% female; 0% American Indian, 7% Asian, 5% black, 12% Hispanic, 6% multiracial, 0% Pacific Islander, 64% white, 5% international; 11% from in state; 92% live on campus; N/A of students in fraternities, N/A in sororities
Most popular majors: 17% Economics, General, 8% Environmental Studies, 8% History, General, 9% Mathematics, General, 18% Political Science and Government, General
Expenses: 2014-2015: $46,808; room/board: $12,760
Financial aid: (207) 725-3273; 45% of undergrads determined to have financial need; average aid package $41,712

Colby College

Waterville ME
(800) 723-3032
U.S. News ranking: Nat. Lib. Arts, No. 15
Website: www.colby.edu
Admissions email: admissions@colby.edu
Private; founded 1813
Freshman admissions: most selective; 2013-2014: 5,407 applied, 1,408 accepted. Neither SAT nor ACT required. SAT 25/75 percentile: 1260-1430. High school rank: 64% in top tenth, 93% in top quarter, 99% in top half
Early decision deadline: 11/15, notification date: 12/15
Early action deadline: N/A, notification date: N/A
Application deadline (fall): 1/1
Undergraduate student body: 1,820 full time, 0 part time; 48% male, 52% female; 0% American Indian, 5% Asian, 3% black, 6% Hispanic, 5% multiracial, 0% Pacific Islander, 60% white, 9% international; 13% from in state; 95% live on campus; 0% of students in fraternities, 0% in sororities
Most popular majors: 9% Biological and Biomedical Sciences, 7% English Language and Literature/Letters, 13% Multi/Interdisciplinary Studies, 6% Psychology, 22% Social Sciences
Expenses: 2014-2015: $47,350; room/board: $12,150
Financial aid: (800) 723-3032; 45% of undergrads determined to have financial need; average aid package $40,489

College of the Atlantic

Bar Harbor ME
(800) 528-0025
U.S. News ranking: Nat. Lib. Arts, No. 99
Website: www.coa.edu/
Admissions email: inquiry@coa.edu
Private; founded 1969
Freshman admissions: more selective; 2013-2014: 455 applied, 333 accepted. Neither SAT nor ACT required. SAT 25/75 percentile: 1110-1330. High school rank: 10% in top tenth, 69% in top quarter, 95% in top half
Early decision deadline: 12/1, notification date: 12/15

Early action deadline: N/A, notification date: N/A
Application deadline (fall): 2/15
Undergraduate student body: 344 full time, 18 part time; 33% male, 67% female; 1% American Indian, 2% Asian, 1% black, 5% Hispanic, 3% multiracial, 0% Pacific Islander, 70% white, 16% international; 17% from in state; 42% live on campus; 0% of students in fraternities, 0% in sororities
Most popular majors: Information not available
Expenses: 2014-2015: $40,491; room/board: $9,300
Financial aid: (800) 528-0025; 89% of undergrads determined to have financial need; average aid package $35,649

Husson University

Bangor ME
(207) 941-7100
U.S. News ranking: Reg. U. (N), second tier
Website: www.husson.edu
Admissions email: admit@husson.edu
Private; founded 1898
Freshman admissions: selective; 2013-2014: 1,581 applied, 1,263 accepted. Either SAT or ACT required. SAT 25/75 percentile: 850-1080. High school rank: 18% in top tenth, 59% in top quarter, 84% in top half
Early decision deadline: N/A, notification date: N/A
Early action deadline: N/A, notification date: N/A
Application deadline (fall): 8/15
Undergraduate student body: 1,869 full time, 484 part time; 41% male, 59% female; 1% American Indian, 1% Asian, 4% black, 1% Hispanic, 1% multiracial, 0% Pacific Islander, 88% white, 3% international; 84% from in state; 34% live on campus; 3% of students in fraternities, 6% in sororities
Most popular majors: 34% Business, Management, Marketing, and Related Support Services, 5% Computer and Information Sciences and Support Services, 25% Health Professions and Related Programs, 16% Homeland Security, Law Enforcement, Firefighting and Related Protective Services, 10% Psychology
Expenses: 2014-2015: $15,590; room/board: $8,579
Financial aid: (207) 941-7156; 96% of undergrads determined to have financial need; average aid package $10,388

Maine College of Art

Portland ME
(800) 699-1509
U.S. News ranking: Arts, unranked
Website: www.meca.edu
Admissions email: admissions@meca.edu
Private; founded 1882
Freshman admissions: N/A; 2013-2014: 527 applied, 357 accepted. Neither SAT nor ACT required. SAT 25/75 percentile: N/A. High school rank: N/A
Early decision deadline: N/A, notification date: N/A
Early action deadline: 12/1, notification date: 12/24
Application deadline (fall): rolling

Undergraduate student body: 361 full time, 17 part time; 29% male, 71% female; 1% American Indian, 2% Asian, 2% black, 5% Hispanic, 4% multiracial, 0% Pacific Islander, 81% white, 1% international; 30% from in state; 18% live on campus; 0% of students in fraternities, 0% in sororities
Most popular majors: 12% Ceramic Arts and Ceramics, 13% Illustration, 17% Painting, 12% Printmaking, 13% Sculpture
Expenses: 2014-2015: $31,620; room/board: $10,660
Financial aid: (207) 775-3052; 84% of undergrads determined to have financial need

Maine Maritime Academy

Castine ME
(207) 326-2206
U.S. News ranking: Reg. Coll. (N), No. 8
Website: www.mainemaritime.edu
Admissions email: admissions@mma.edu
Public; founded 1941
Freshman admissions: selective; 2013-2014: 791 applied, 514 accepted. Either SAT or ACT required. SAT 25/75 percentile: 920-1130. High school rank: 8% in top tenth, 32% in top quarter, 76% in top half
Early decision deadline: N/A, notification date: N/A
Early action deadline: 12/31, notification date: 2/15
Application deadline (fall): 3/31
Undergraduate student body: 979 full time, 15 part time; 87% male, 13% female; 0% American Indian, 1% Asian, 1% black, 0% Hispanic, 0% multiracial, 0% Pacific Islander, 96% white, 0% international; 71% from in state; 68% live on campus; 0% of students in fraternities, 0% in sororities
Most popular majors: 6% Biological and Biomedical Sciences, Other, 28% Engineering Technologies and Engineering-Related Fields, Other, 12% International Business/Trade/Commerce, 25% Marine Science/Merchant Marine Officer, 29% Naval Architecture and Marine Engineering
Expenses: 2014-2015: $17,120 in state, $24,040 out of state; room/board: $9,830
Financial aid: (207) 326-2339; 85% of undergrads determined to have financial need; average aid package $9,368

St. Joseph's College[1]

Standish ME
(207) 893-7746
U.S. News ranking: Reg. U. (N), second tier
Website: www.sjcme.edu
Admissions email: admission@sjcme.edu
Private
Application deadline (fall): N/A
Undergraduate student body: N/A full time, N/A part time
Expenses: 2013-2014: $29,900; room/board: $11,900
Financial aid: (800) 752-1266

Thomas College

Waterville ME
(800) 339-7001
U.S. News ranking: Reg. Coll. (N), No. 44
Website: www.thomas.edu
Admissions email: admiss@thomas.edu
Private; founded 1894
Freshman admissions: less selective; 2013-2014: 1,129 applied, 829 accepted. Either SAT or ACT required. SAT 25/75 percentile: 790-1010. High school rank: 21% in top tenth, 34% in top quarter, 64% in top half
Early decision deadline: N/A, notification date: N/A
Early action deadline: N/A, notification date: N/A
Application deadline (fall): rolling
Undergraduate student body: 780 full time, 559 part time; 48% male, 52% female; 1% American Indian, 0% Asian, 3% black, 3% Hispanic, 9% multiracial, 0% Pacific Islander, 75% white, 3% international; 78% from in state; 65% live on campus; 2% of students in fraternities, 0% in sororities
Most popular majors: 9% Accounting, 14% Business Administration and Management, General, 16% Criminal Justice/Safety Studies, 10% Elementary Education and Teaching, 10% Psychology, General
Expenses: 2014-2015: $23,460; room/board: $10,100
Financial aid: (207) 859-1112; 87% of undergrads determined to have financial need; average aid package $19,704

Unity College

Unity ME
(207) 948-3131
U.S. News ranking: Reg. Coll. (N), No. 31
Website: www.unity.edu
Admissions email: admissions@unity.edu
Private
Freshman admissions: less selective; 2013-2014: 519 applied, 461 accepted. Neither SAT nor ACT required. SAT 25/75 percentile: 910-1110. High school rank: 6% in top tenth, 29% in top quarter, 73% in top half
Early decision deadline: N/A, notification date: N/A
Early action deadline: 12/15, notification date: 12/31
Application deadline (fall): 6/15
Undergraduate student body: 548 full time, 6 part time; 49% male, 51% female; 1% American Indian, 1% Asian, 1% black, 3% Hispanic, 3% multiracial, 0% Pacific Islander, 91% white, 0% international; 23% from in state; 71% live on campus; N/A of students in fraternities, N/A in sororities
Most popular majors: 9% Agroecology and Sustainable Agriculture, 58% Natural Resources Law Enforcement and Protective Services, 4% Outdoor Education, 27% Wildlife Biology
Expenses: 2014-2015: $25,320; room/board: $9,330
Financial aid: (207) 948-3131; 87% of undergrads determined to have financial need; average aid package $18,932

Thomas College

University of Maine

Orono ME
(877) 486-2364
U.S. News ranking: Nat. U., No. 173
Website: www.umaine.edu
Admissions email: um-admit@maine.edu
Public; founded 1865
Freshman admissions: selective; 2013-2014: 9,336 applied, 7,789 accepted. Either SAT or ACT required. SAT 25/75 percentile: 950-1190. High school rank: 19% in top tenth, 46% in top quarter, 78% in top half
Early decision deadline: N/A, notification date: N/A
Early action deadline: 12/15, notification date: 1/31
Application deadline (fall): rolling
Undergraduate student body: 7,922 full time, 1,260 part time; 52% male, 48% female; 1% American Indian, 1% Asian, 2% black, 2% Hispanic, 3% multiracial, 0% Pacific Islander, 81% white, 3% international; 80% from in state; 40% live on campus; N/A of students in fraternities, N/A in sororities
Most popular majors: 10% Business, Management, Marketing, and Related Support Services, 12% Education, 12% Engineering, 7% Health Professions and Related Programs, 7% Psychology
Expenses: 2014-2015: $10,604 in state, $28,484 out of state; room/board: $9,296
Financial aid: (207) 581-1324; 71% of undergrads determined to have financial need; average aid package $15,176

University of Maine–Augusta

Augusta ME
(207) 621-3465
U.S. News ranking: Reg. Coll. (N), second tier
Website: www.uma.edu
Admissions email: umaadm@maine.edu
Public; founded 1965
Freshman admissions: least selective; 2013-2014: 828 applied, 790 accepted. Neither SAT nor ACT required. SAT 25/75 percentile: 760-1010. High school rank: 2% in top tenth, 9% in top quarter, 34% in top half
Early decision deadline: N/A, notification date: N/A
Early action deadline: N/A, notification date: N/A
Application deadline (fall): 8/15
Undergraduate student body: 1,726 full time, 3,044 part time; 29% male, 71% female; 2% American Indian, 0% Asian, 1% black, 1% Hispanic, 2% multiracial, 0% Pacific Islander, 86% white, 0% international; 97% from in state; 0% live on campus; 0% of students in fraternities, 0% in sororities
Most popular majors: 17% Business, Management, Marketing, and Related Support Services, 31% Health Professions and Related Programs, 5% Homeland Security, Law Enforcement, Firefighting and Related Protective Services, 26% Liberal Arts and Sciences, General Studies and Humanities, 8% Library Science

Expenses: 2014-2015: $7,500 in state, $16,740 out of state; room/board: N/A
Financial aid: (207) 621-3163; 87% of undergrads determined to have financial need; average aid package $8,873

University of Maine–Farmington

Farmington ME
(207) 778-7050
U.S. News ranking: Reg. Coll. (N), No. 18
Website: www.farmington.edu
Admissions email: umfadmit@maine.edu
Public; founded 1864
Freshman admissions: selective; 2013-2014: 1,638 applied, 1,371 accepted. Neither SAT nor ACT required. SAT 25/75 percentile: 880-1150. High school rank: 14% in top tenth, 43% in top quarter, 79% in top half
Early decision deadline: N/A, notification date: N/A
Early action deadline: 11/15, notification date: 12/15
Application deadline (fall): rolling
Undergraduate student body: 1,783 full time, 118 part time; 34% male, 66% female; 1% American Indian, 1% Asian, 1% black, 2% Hispanic, 3% multiracial, 0% Pacific Islander, 84% white, 0% international; 85% from in state; 48% live on campus; N/A of students in fraternities, N/A in sororities
Most popular majors: 39% Education, 9% English Language and Literature/Letters, 13% Health Professions and Related Programs, 9% Psychology, 5% Social Sciences
Expenses: 2014-2015: $9,217 in state, $18,305 out of state; room/board: $8,970
Financial aid: (207) 778-7100; 81% of undergrads determined to have financial need; average aid package $13,342

University of Maine–Fort Kent

Fort Kent ME
(207) 834-7600
U.S. News ranking: Reg. Coll. (N), No. 37
Website: www.umfk.maine.edu
Admissions email: umfkadm@maine.edu
Public; founded 1878
Freshman admissions: less selective; 2013-2014: 464 applied, 292 accepted. Neither SAT nor ACT required. SAT 25/75 percentile: 818-1000. High school rank: 0% in top tenth, 10% in top quarter, 34% in top half
Early decision deadline: N/A, notification date: N/A
Early action deadline: N/A, notification date: N/A
Application deadline (fall): rolling
Undergraduate student body: 594 full time, 615 part time; 29% male, 71% female; 1% American Indian, 0% Asian, 2% black, 1% Hispanic, 2% multiracial, 0% Pacific Islander, 78% white, 11% international; 93% from in state; 24% live on campus; 1% of students in fraternities, 2% in sororities

Most popular majors: 14% Business, Management, Marketing, and Related Support Services, 19% Education, 49% Health Professions and Related Programs, 4% Public Administration and Social Service Professions, 7% Social Sciences
Expenses: 2014-2015: $7,575 in state, $10,875 out of state; room/board: $7,400
Financial aid: (888) 879-8635; 77% of undergrads determined to have financial need; average aid package $11,454

University of Maine–Machias

Machias ME
(888) 468-6866
U.S. News ranking: Nat. Lib. Arts, second tier
Website: www.umm.maine.edu
Admissions email: ummadmissions@maine.edu
Public; founded 1909
Freshman admissions: less selective; 2013-2014: 452 applied, 386 accepted. Either SAT or ACT required. SAT 25/75 percentile: 820-1050. High school rank: N/A
Early decision deadline: N/A, notification date: N/A
Early action deadline: 12/15, notification date: N/A
Application deadline (fall): 8/15
Undergraduate student body: 439 full time, 453 part time; 30% male, 70% female; 2% American Indian, 0% Asian, 4% black, 4% Hispanic, 3% multiracial, 0% Pacific Islander, 81% white, 1% international; 79% from in state; 37% live on campus; 11% of students in fraternities, 8% in sororities
Most popular majors: 20% Biology/Biological Sciences, General, 15% Community Psychology, 7% Entrepreneurial and Small Business Operations, 9% General Studies, 14% Parks, Recreation and Leisure Studies
Expenses: 2013-2014: $7,490 in state, $19,370 out of state; room/board: $8,178
Financial aid: (207) 255-1203

University of Maine–Presque Isle

Presque Isle ME
(207) 768-9532
U.S. News ranking: Reg. Coll. (N), No. 46
Website: www.umpi.edu
Admissions email: admissions@umpi.edu
Public; founded 1903
Freshman admissions: less selective; 2013-2014: 530 applied, 413 accepted. Neither SAT nor ACT required. ACT 25/75 percentile: N/A. High school rank: 13% in top tenth, 25% in top quarter, 49% in top half
Early decision deadline: N/A, notification date: N/A
Early action deadline: N/A, notification date: N/A
Application deadline (fall): rolling
Undergraduate student body: 718 full time, 545 part time; 37% male, 63% female; 3% American Indian, 0% Asian, 1% black, 1% Hispanic, 2% multiracial, 0% Pacific Islander, 79% white, 8% international; 98% from in

state; 28% live on campus; N/A of students in fraternities, N/A in sororities
Most popular majors: 14% Business, Management, Marketing, and Related Support Services, 16% Education, 17% Liberal Arts and Sciences, General Studies and Humanities, 8% Psychology, 5% Public Administration and Social Service Professions
Expenses: 2014-2015: $7,436 in state, $10,736 out of state; room/board: $7,656
Financial aid: (207) 768-9511; 78% of undergrads determined to have financial need; average aid package $11,581

University of New England

Biddeford ME
(207) 283-0171
U.S. News ranking: Reg. U. (N), No. 79
Website: www.une.edu
Admissions email: admissions@une.edu
Private; founded 1831
Freshman admissions: selective; 2013-2014: 4,231 applied, 3,632 accepted. Either SAT or ACT required. SAT 25/75 percentile: 950-1150. High school rank: N/A
Early decision deadline: N/A, notification date: N/A
Early action deadline: 12/1, notification date: 12/31
Application deadline (fall): 2/15
Undergraduate student body: 2,156 full time, 497 part time; 29% male, 71% female; 1% American Indian, 2% Asian, 1% black, 0% Hispanic, 1% multiracial, 0% Pacific Islander, 70% white, 1% international; 34% from in state; 65% live on campus; 0% of students in fraternities, 0% in sororities
Most popular majors: 30% Biological and Biomedical Sciences, 5% Business, Management, Marketing, and Related Support Services, 32% Health Professions and Related Programs, 13% Parks, Recreation, Leisure, and Fitness Studies, 5% Psychology
Expenses: 2014-2015: $34,080; room/board: $13,390
Financial aid: (207) 602-2342

University of Southern Maine

Gorham ME
(207) 780-5670
U.S. News ranking: Reg. U. (N), second tier
Website: www.usm.maine.edu
Admissions email: usmadm@usm.maine.edu
Public; founded 1878
Freshman admissions: less selective; 2013-2014: 3,993 applied, 3,284 accepted. Either SAT or ACT required. SAT 25/75 percentile: 870-1100. High school rank: 12% in top tenth, 34% in top quarter, 74% in top half
Early decision deadline: N/A, notification date: N/A
Early action deadline: N/A, notification date: N/A
Application deadline (fall): rolling
Undergraduate student body: 4,281 full time, 2,817 part time; 43% male, 57% female; 1% American Indian, 2% Asian, 3% black,

2% Hispanic, 2% multiracial, 0% Pacific Islander, 81% white, 1% international; 90% from in state; 18% live on campus; N/A of students in fraternities, N/A in sororities
Most popular majors: 17% Business, Management, Marketing, and Related Support Services, 18% Health Professions and Related Programs, 5% Psychology, 15% Social Sciences, 5% Visual and Performing Arts
Expenses: 2013-2014: $8,920 in state, $21,280 out of state; room/board: $9,820
Financial aid: (207) 780-5250; 76% of undergrads determined to have financial need; average aid package $13,008

Bowie State University

Bowie MD
(301) 860-3415
U.S. News ranking: Nat. U., second tier
Website: www.bowiestate.edu
Admissions email: ugradadmissions@bowiestate.edu
Public; founded 1865
Freshman admissions: less selective; 2013-2014: 3,986 applied, 2,063 accepted. Either SAT or ACT required. SAT 25/75 percentile: 810-960. High school rank: N/A
Early decision deadline: N/A, notification date: N/A
Early action deadline: N/A, notification date: N/A
Application deadline (fall): rolling
Undergraduate student body: 3,521 full time, 837 part time; 38% male, 62% female; 0% American Indian, 1% Asian, 83% black, 3% Hispanic, 3% multiracial, 0% Pacific Islander, 2% white, 1% international; 91% from in state; 45% live on campus; 20% of students in fraternities, 15% in sororities
Most popular majors: Information not available
Expenses: 2013-2014: $6,971 in state, $17,538 out of state; room/board: $9,336
Financial aid: (301) 860-3540

Capitol College[1]

Laurel MD
(800) 950-1992
U.S. News ranking: Engineering, unranked
Website: www.capitol-college.edu
Admissions email: admissions@capitol-college.edu
Private
Application deadline (fall): N/A
Undergraduate student body: N/A full time, N/A part time
Expenses: 2013-2014: $22,176; room/board: $5,364
Financial aid: (301) 369-2800

Coppin State University[1]

Baltimore MD
(410) 951-3600
U.S. News ranking: Reg. U. (N), second tier
Website: www.coppin.edu
Admissions email: admissions@coppin.edu
Public
Application deadline (fall): N/A

Undergraduate student body: N/A full time, N/A part time
Expenses: 2013-2014: $5,076 in state, $10,010 out of state; room/board: $8,654
Financial aid: (410) 951-3636

Frostburg State University

Frostburg MD
(301) 687-4201
U.S. News ranking: Reg. U. (N), No. 125
Website: www.frostburg.edu
Admissions email: fsuadmissions@frostburg.edu
Public; founded 1898
Freshman admissions: less selective; 2013-2014: 3,872 applied, 2,302 accepted. Either SAT or ACT required. SAT 25/75 percentile: 860-1070. High school rank: 10% in top tenth, 27% in top quarter, 61% in top half
Early decision deadline: 12/15, notification date: N/A
Early action deadline: N/A, notification date: N/A
Application deadline (fall): rolling
Undergraduate student body: 4,189 full time, 515 part time; 51% male, 49% female; 0% American Indian, 1% Asian, 28% black, 5% Hispanic, 4% multiracial, 0% Pacific Islander, 61% white, 1% international; 93% from in state; 32% live on campus; 10% of students in fraternities, 10% in sororities
Most popular majors: 11% Business Administration and Management, General, 5% Criminal Justice/Safety Studies, 5% Early Childhood Education and Teaching, 7% Psychology, General, 5% Registered Nursing/Registered Nurse
Expenses: 2014-2015: $7,982 in state, $19,274 out of state; room/board: $9,800
Financial aid: (301) 687-4301; 64% of undergrads determined to have financial need; average aid package $9,365

Goucher College

Baltimore MD
(410) 337-6100
U.S. News ranking: Nat. Lib. Arts, No. 105
Website: www.goucher.edu
Admissions email: admissions@goucher.edu
Private; founded 1885
Freshman admissions: more selective; 2013-2014: 3,466 applied, 2,505 accepted. Neither SAT nor ACT required. SAT 25/75 percentile: 1010-1280. High school rank: 31% in top tenth, 58% in top quarter, 88% in top half
Early decision deadline: 11/15, notification date: 12/15
Early action deadline: 12/1, notification date: 2/1
Application deadline (fall): rolling
Undergraduate student body: 1,424 full time, 25 part time; 34% male, 66% female; 0% American Indian, 3% Asian, 9% black, 7% Hispanic, 4% multiracial, 0% Pacific Islander, 68% white, 2% international; 26% from in state; 84% live on campus; 0% of students in fraternities, 0% in sororities

Most popular majors: 10% Communication, Journalism, and Related Programs, 7% Foreign Languages, Literatures, and Linguistics, 15% Psychology, 13% Social Sciences, 13% Visual and Performing Arts
Expenses: 2014-2015: $40,558; room/board: $11,482
Financial aid: (410) 337-6141; 64% of undergrads determined to have financial need; average aid package $29,199

Hood College
Frederick MD
(800) 922-1599
U.S. News ranking: Reg. U. (N), No. 31
Website: www.hood.edu
Admissions email: admission@hood.edu
Private; founded 1893
Affiliation: United Church of Christ
Freshman admissions: selective; 2013-2014: 1,686 applied, 1,366 accepted. Neither SAT nor ACT required. SAT 25/75 percentile: 910-1160. High school rank: 12% in top tenth, 45% in top quarter, 77% in top half
Early decision deadline: N/A, notification date: N/A
Early action deadline: N/A, notification date: N/A
Application deadline (fall): rolling
Undergraduate student body: 1,265 full time, 122 part time; 34% male, 66% female; 0% American Indian, 3% Asian, 12% black, 8% Hispanic, 5% multiracial, 0% Pacific Islander, 66% white, 2% international; 76% from in state; 56% live on campus; 0% of students in fraternities, 0% in sororities
Most popular majors: 10% Biological and Biomedical Sciences, 10% Business, Management, Marketing, and Related Support Services, 14% Education, 13% Psychology, 7% Social Sciences
Expenses: 2014-2015: $34,120; room/board: $11,610
Financial aid: (301) 696-3411; 85% of undergrads determined to have financial need; average aid package $26,534

Johns Hopkins University
Baltimore MD
(410) 516-8171
U.S. News ranking: Nat. U., No. 12
Website: www.jhu.edu
Admissions email: gotojhu@jhu.edu
Private; founded 1876
Freshman admissions: most selective; 2013-2014: 20,614 applied, 3,519 accepted. Either SAT or ACT required. SAT 25/75 percentile: 1340-1520. High school rank: 84% in top tenth, 98% in top quarter, 99% in top half
Early decision deadline: 11/1, notification date: 12/15
Early action deadline: N/A, notification date: N/A
Application deadline (fall): 1/1
Undergraduate student body: 6,012 full time, 239 part time; 48% male, 52% female; 0% American Indian, 18% Asian, 5% black, 10% Hispanic, 4% multiracial, 0% Pacific Islander, 49% white,

10% international; 13% from in state; 55% live on campus; 27% of students in fraternities, 32% in sororities
Most popular majors: 9% Bioengineering and Biomedical Engineering, 7% Cell/Cellular and Molecular Biology, 9% International Relations and Affairs, 8% Neuroscience, 8% Public Health, General
Expenses: 2014-2015: $47,060; room/board: $14,246
Financial aid: (410) 516-8028; 46% of undergrads determined to have financial need; average aid package $37,345

Loyola University Maryland
Baltimore MD
(410) 617-5012
U.S. News ranking: Reg. U. (N), No. 3
Website: www.loyola.edu
Admissions email: admissions@loyola.edu
Private; founded 1852
Affiliation: Roman Catholic
Freshman admissions: more selective; 2013-2014: 13,604 applied, 7,891 accepted. Neither SAT nor ACT required. SAT 25/75 percentile: 1100-1268. High school rank: 28% in top tenth, 67% in top quarter, 91% in top half
Early decision deadline: N/A, notification date: N/A
Early action deadline: 11/1, notification date: 1/15
Application deadline (fall): 1/15
Undergraduate student body: 3,951 full time, 53 part time; 41% male, 59% female; 0% American Indian, 3% Asian, 5% black, 9% Hispanic, 2% multiracial, 0% Pacific Islander, 79% white, 0% international; 17% from in state; 81% live on campus; 0% of students in fraternities, 0% in sororities
Most popular majors: 30% Business/Commerce, General, 7% Psychology, General, 10% Social Sciences, General, 13% Speech Communication and Rhetoric, 7% Speech-Language Pathology/Pathologist
Expenses: 2014-2015: $44,255; room/board: $12,790
Financial aid: (410) 617-2576; 56% of undergrads determined to have financial need; average aid package $27,655

Maryland Institute College of Art
Baltimore MD
(410) 225-2222
U.S. News ranking: Arts, unranked
Website: www.mica.edu
Admissions email: admissions@mica.edu
Private; founded 1826
Freshman admissions: N/A; 2013-2014: 2,914 applied, 1,691 accepted. Either SAT or ACT required. SAT 25/75 percentile: N/A. High school rank: N/A
Early decision deadline: 11/15, notification date: 12/13
Early action deadline: N/A, notification date: N/A
Application deadline (fall): 2/1
Undergraduate student body: 1,759 full time, 19 part time; 29% male, 71% female; 0% American Indian, 12% Asian, 5% black, 4% Hispanic, 8% multiracial,

0% Pacific Islander, 55% white, 8% international; N/A from in state; 88% live on campus; N/A of students in fraternities, N/A in sororities
Most popular majors: Information not available
Expenses: 2014-2015: $42,390; room/board: $11,710
Financial aid: (410) 225-2285

McDaniel College
Westminster MD
(800) 638-5005
U.S. News ranking: Nat. Lib. Arts, No. 129
Website: www.mcdaniel.edu
Admissions email: admissions@mcdaniel.edu
Private; founded 1867
Freshman admissions: selective; 2013-2014: 2,942 applied, 2,232 accepted. Either SAT or ACT required. SAT 25/75 percentile: 1000-1210. High school rank: 26% in top tenth, 52% in top quarter, 87% in top half
Early decision deadline: N/A, notification date: N/A
Early action deadline: 12/1, notification date: 12/21
Application deadline (fall): 6/1
Undergraduate student body: 1,658 full time, 34 part time; 47% male, 53% female; 1% American Indian, 4% Asian, 13% black, 6% Hispanic, 0% multiracial, 0% Pacific Islander, 74% white, 1% international; 64% from in state; 83% live on campus; 17% of students in fraternities, 18% in sororities
Most popular majors: 7% English Language and Literature/Letters, 10% Parks, Recreation, Leisure, and Fitness Studies, 9% Psychology, 16% Social Sciences, 7% Visual and Performing Arts
Expenses: 2014-2015: $38,350; room/board: $9,100
Financial aid: (410) 857-2233; 74% of undergrads determined to have financial need; average aid package $31,352

Morgan State University
Baltimore MD
(800) 332-6674
U.S. News ranking: Nat. U., second tier
Website: www.morgan.edu
Admissions email: admissions@morgan.edu
Public; founded 1867
Freshman admissions: less selective; 2013-2014: 4,925 applied, 2,764 accepted. Neither SAT nor ACT required. SAT 25/75 percentile: 820-980. High school rank: 3% in top tenth, 9% in top quarter, 38% in top half
Early decision deadline: N/A, notification date: N/A
Early action deadline: 11/15, notification date: 2/15
Application deadline (fall): rolling
Undergraduate student body: 5,504 full time, 748 part time; 45% male, 55% female; 0% American Indian, 1% Asian, 85% black, 3% Hispanic, 3% multiracial, 0% Pacific Islander, 2% white, 4% international; 80% from in state; 32% live on campus; N/A of students in fraternities, N/A in sororities

Most popular majors: 20% Business, Management, Marketing, and Related Support Services, 9% Communication, Journalism, and Related Programs, 10% Engineering, 13% Health Professions and Related Programs, 9% Public Administration and Social Service Professions
Expenses: 2014-2015: $7,378 in state, $16,862 out of state; room/board: $9,492
Financial aid: (443) 885-3170; 82% of undergrads determined to have financial need; average aid package $21,438

Mount St. Mary's University
Emmitsburg MD
(800) 448-4347
U.S. News ranking: Reg. U. (N), No. 19
Website: www.msmary.edu
Admissions email: admissions@msmary.edu
Private; founded 1808
Affiliation: Roman Catholic
Freshman admissions: selective; 2013-2014: 4,942 applied, 3,332 accepted. Either SAT or ACT required. SAT 25/75 percentile: 990-1180. High school rank: 15% in top tenth, 35% in top quarter, 68% in top half
Early decision deadline: N/A, notification date: N/A
Early action deadline: 12/1, notification date: 12/25
Application deadline (fall): 3/1
Undergraduate student body: 1,650 full time, 91 part time; 45% male, 55% female; 0% American Indian, 2% Asian, 10% black, 9% Hispanic, 3% multiracial, 0% Pacific Islander, 73% white, 1% international; 51% from in state; 82% live on campus; 0% of students in fraternities, 0% in sororities
Most popular majors: 7% Accounting, 9% Biology/Biological Sciences, General, 20% Business/Commerce, General, 10% Criminology, 8% Elementary Education and Teaching
Expenses: 2014-2015: $36,021; room/board: $11,975
Financial aid: (301) 447-5207; 70% of undergrads determined to have financial need; average aid package $23,441

National Labor College[1]
Silver Spring MD
(301) 431-6400
U.S. News ranking: Business, unranked
Website: www.nlc.edu/
Admissions email: N/A
Private
Application deadline (fall): N/A
Undergraduate student body: N/A full time, N/A part time
Expenses: 2013-2014: $9,528; room/board: N/A
Financial aid: (301) 628-5592

Notre Dame of Maryland University
Baltimore MD
(410) 532-5330
U.S. News ranking: Reg. U. (N), No. 50
Website: www.ndm.edu
Admissions email: admiss@ndm.edu

Private; founded 1873
Affiliation: Roman Catholic
Freshman admissions: selective; 2013-2014: 838 applied, 416 accepted. Either SAT or ACT required. SAT 25/75 percentile: 930-1150. High school rank: 33% in top tenth, 61% in top quarter, 88% in top half
Early decision deadline: N/A, notification date: N/A
Early action deadline: 12/1, notification date: 12/15
Application deadline (fall): rolling
Undergraduate student body: 525 full time, 709 part time; 5% male, 95% female; 1% American Indian, 5% Asian, 28% black, 5% Hispanic, 0% multiracial, 0% Pacific Islander, 57% white, 1% international; N/A from in state; 47% live on campus; N/A of students in fraternities, N/A in sororities
Most popular majors: 4% Biology, General, 9% Business/Commerce, General, 13% Education, General, 11% Liberal Arts and Sciences, General Studies and Humanities, 47% Registered Nursing, Nursing Administration, Nursing Research and Clinical Nursing, Other
Expenses: 2014-2015: $33,010; room/board: $10,716
Financial aid: (410) 532-5369; 84% of undergrads determined to have financial need; average aid package $23,572

Salisbury University
Salisbury MD
(410) 543-6161
U.S. News ranking: Reg. U. (N), No. 65
Website: www.salisbury.edu/
Admissions email: admissions@salisbury.edu
Public; founded 1925
Freshman admissions: selective; 2013-2014: 8,905 applied, 4,895 accepted. Neither SAT nor ACT required. SAT 25/75 percentile: 1080-1230. High school rank: 23% in top tenth, 59% in top quarter, 93% in top half
Early decision deadline: 11/15, notification date: 12/15
Early action deadline: 12/1, notification date: 1/15
Application deadline (fall): 1/15
Undergraduate student body: 7,405 full time, 599 part time; 43% male, 57% female; 0% American Indian, 2% Asian, 11% black, 4% Hispanic, 4% multiracial, 0% Pacific Islander, 74% white, 1% international; 86% from in state; 28% live on campus; 6% of students in fraternities, 4% in sororities
Most popular majors: 13% Business Administration and Management, General, 12% Elementary Education and Teaching, 9% Psychology, General, 8% Registered Nursing/Registered Nurse, 10% Speech Communication and Rhetoric
Expenses: 2014-2015: $8,560 in state, $16,906 out of state; room/board: $10,620
Financial aid: (410) 543-6165; 52% of undergrads determined to have financial need; average aid package $7,537

Sojourner-Douglass College[1]

Baltimore MD
(800) 732-2630
U.S. News ranking: Reg. Coll. (N), unranked
Website: www.sdc.edu/
Admissions email: N/A
Private
Application deadline (fall): N/A
Undergraduate student body: N/A full time, N/A part time
Expenses: 2013-2014: $9,830; room/board: N/A
Financial aid: (410) 276-0306

Stevenson University

Stevenson MD
(410) 486-7001
U.S. News ranking: Reg. U. (N), No. 98
Website: www.stevenson.edu/
Admissions email: admissions@stevenson.edu
Private; founded 1947
Freshman admissions: less selective; 2013-2014: 5,318 applied, 3,169 accepted. Either SAT or ACT required. SAT 25/75 percentile: 890-1100. High school rank: 11% in top tenth, 31% in top quarter, 58% in top half
Early decision deadline: N/A, notification date: N/A
Early action deadline: N/A, notification date: N/A
Application deadline (fall): rolling
Undergraduate student body: 3,300 full time, 547 part time; 35% male, 65% female; 0% American Indian, 3% Asian, 29% black, 4% Hispanic, 2% multiracial, 0% Pacific Islander, 57% white, 0% international; 79% from in state; 48% live on campus; 0% of students in fraternities, 2% in sororities
Most popular majors: 19% Business, Management, Marketing, and Related Support Services, 6% Computer and Information Sciences and Support Services, 7% Education, 28% Health Professions and Related Programs, 6% Visual and Performing Arts
Expenses: 2014-2015: $28,980; room/board: $12,490
Financial aid: (443) 334-2559; 76% of undergrads determined to have financial need; average aid package $18,305

St. John's College

Annapolis MD
(410) 626-2522
U.S. News ranking: Nat. Lib. Arts, No. 56
Website: sjc.edu
Admissions email: annapolis.admissions@sjc.edu
Private; founded 1696
Freshman admissions: selective; 2013-2014: 318 applied, 277 accepted. Neither SAT nor ACT required. SAT 25/75 percentile: 1140-1410. High school rank: 19% in top tenth, 37% in top quarter, 77% in top half
Early decision deadline: N/A, notification date: N/A
Early action deadline: 1/15, notification date: 2/15
Application deadline (fall): rolling
Undergraduate student body: 440 full time, 3 part time; 55% male, 45% female; 0% American Indian, 2% Asian, 2% black, 6% Hispanic, 3% multiracial, 0% Pacific Islander, 70% white,

11% international; 25% from in state; 75% live on campus; 0% of students in fraternities, 0% in sororities
Most popular majors: 100% Liberal Arts and Sciences, General Studies and Humanities
Expenses: 2014-2015: $47,826; room/board: $11,270
Financial aid: (410) 626-2502; 71% of undergrads determined to have financial need; average aid package $35,091

St. Mary's College of Maryland

St. Mary's City MD
(800) 492-7181
U.S. News ranking: Nat. Lib. Arts, No. 89
Website: www.smcm.edu
Admissions email: admissions@smcm.edu
Public; founded 1840
Freshman admissions: selective; 2013-2014: 2,321 applied, 1,704 accepted. Either SAT or ACT required. SAT 25/75 percentile: 1070-1310. High school rank: 28% in top tenth, 64% in top quarter, 87% in top half
Early decision deadline: 11/1, notification date: 12/15
Early action deadline: N/A, notification date: N/A
Application deadline (fall): 1/1
Undergraduate student body: 1,762 full time, 57 part time; 41% male, 59% female; 0% American Indian, 3% Asian, 8% black, 6% Hispanic, 4% multiracial, 0% Pacific Islander, 75% white, 1% international; 90% from in state; 87% live on campus; 0% of students in fraternities, 0% in sororities
Most popular majors: 9% Biology/Biological Sciences, General, 8% Economics, General, 10% English Language and Literature, General, 8% Political Science and Government, General, 14% Psychology, General
Expenses: 2014-2015: $14,874 in state, $28,674 out of state; room/board: $11,930
Financial aid: (240) 895-3000; 47% of undergrads determined to have financial need; average aid package $14,332

Towson University

Towson MD
(410) 704-2113
U.S. News ranking: Reg. U. (N), No. 60
Website: www.towson.edu
Admissions email: admissions@towson.edu
Public; founded 1866
Freshman admissions: selective; 2013-2014: 17,750 applied, 10,710 accepted. Either SAT or ACT required. SAT 25/75 percentile: 990-1170. High school rank: 18% in top tenth, 49% in top quarter, 87% in top half
Early decision deadline: N/A, notification date: N/A
Early action deadline: N/A, notification date: N/A
Application deadline (fall): 2/15
Undergraduate student body: 16,588 full time, 2,191 part time; 40% male, 60% female; 0% American Indian, 5% Asian, 15% black, 5% Hispanic, 3% multiracial, 0% Pacific Islander,

65% white, 2% international; 85% from in state; 25% live on campus; 9% of students in fraternities, 7% in sororities
Most popular majors: 14% Business, Management, Marketing, and Related Support Services, 12% Education, 11% Health Professions and Related Programs, 8% Psychology, 12% Social Sciences
Expenses: 2013-2014: $8,342 in state, $20,020 out of state; room/board: $10,662
Financial aid: (410) 704-4236

United States Naval Academy

Annapolis MD
(410) 293-4361
U.S. News ranking: Nat. Lib. Arts, No. 13
Website: www.usna.edu
Admissions email: webmail@usna.edu
Public; founded 1845
Freshman admissions: more selective; 2013-2014: 19,146 applied, 1,408 accepted. Either SAT or ACT required. SAT 25/75 percentile: 1180-1380. High school rank: 54% in top tenth, 81% in top quarter, 96% in top half
Early decision deadline: N/A, notification date: N/A
Early action deadline: N/A, notification date: N/A
Application deadline (fall): 1/31
Undergraduate student body: 4,526 full time, 0 part time; 78% male, 22% female; 0% American Indian, 6% Asian, 7% black, 11% Hispanic, 7% multiracial, 1% Pacific Islander, 65% white, 1% international; 7% from in state; 100% live on campus; 0% of students in fraternities, 0% in sororities
Most popular majors: 9% Economics, General, 9% History, General, 8% Oceanography, Chemical and Physical, 13% Political Science and Government, General, 9% Systems Engineering
Expenses: N/A
Financial aid: N/A

University of Baltimore[1]

Baltimore MD
(410) 837-4777
U.S. News ranking: Reg. U. (N), No. 115
Website: www.ubalt.edu
Admissions email: admissions@ubalt.edu
Public; founded 1925
Application deadline (fall): rolling
Undergraduate student body: N/A full time, N/A part time
Expenses: 2013-2014: $7,838 in state, $16,288 out of state; room/board: N/A
Financial aid: (410) 837-4763

University of Maryland– Baltimore County

Baltimore MD
(410) 455-2291
U.S. News ranking: Nat. U., No. 149
Website: www.umbc.edu
Admissions email: admissions@umbc.edu
Public; founded 1963

Freshman admissions: more selective; 2013-2014: 9,755 applied, 6,160 accepted. SAT required. SAT 25/75 percentile: 1110-1310. High school rank: 25% in top tenth, 57% in top quarter, 86% in top half
Early decision deadline: N/A, notification date: N/A
Early action deadline: 11/1, notification date: 12/15
Application deadline (fall): 2/1
Undergraduate student body: 9,508 full time, 1,628 part time; 55% male, 45% female; 0% American Indian, 20% Asian, 16% black, 6% Hispanic, 4% multiracial, 0% Pacific Islander, 45% white, 4% international; 94% from in state; 34% live on campus; 4% of students in fraternities, 4% in sororities
Most popular majors: 14% Biological and Biomedical Sciences, 14% Computer and Information Sciences and Support Services, 13% Psychology, 16% Social Sciences, 8% Visual and Performing Arts
Expenses: 2013-2014: $10,068 in state, $21,642 out of state; room/board: $10,716
Financial aid: (410) 455-2387

University of Maryland– College Park

College Park MD
(301) 314-8385
U.S. News ranking: Nat. U., No. 62
Website: www.maryland.edu
Admissions email: um-admit@umd.edu
Public; founded 1856
Freshman admissions: more selective; 2013-2014: 26,205 applied, 12,293 accepted. Either SAT or ACT required. SAT 25/75 percentile: 1200-1420. High school rank: 71% in top tenth, 88% in top quarter, 98% in top half
Early decision deadline: N/A, notification date: N/A
Early action deadline: 11/1, notification date: 1/31
Application deadline (fall): 1/20
Undergraduate student body: 24,522 full time, 2,136 part time; 53% male, 47% female; 0% American Indian, 16% Asian, 12% black, 9% Hispanic, 4% multiracial, 0% Pacific Islander, 54% white, 3% international; 78% from in state; 44% live on campus; 12% of students in fraternities, 17% in sororities
Most popular majors: 8% Biology/Biological Sciences, General, 5% Criminology, 5% Economics, General, 4% Political Science and Government, General, 5% Psychology, General
Expenses: 2014-2015: $9,427 in state, $29,720 out of state; room/board: $10,633
Financial aid: (301) 314-9000; 43% of undergrads determined to have financial need; average aid package $13,271

University of Maryland– Eastern Shore

Princess Anne MD
(410) 651-6410
U.S. News ranking: Reg. U. (N), second tier
Website: www.umes.edu
Admissions email: umesadmissions@umes.edu
Public; founded 1886
Freshman admissions: less selective; 2013-2014: 4,073 applied, 2,241 accepted. Either SAT or ACT required. SAT 25/75 percentile: 790-960. High school rank: N/A
Early decision deadline: N/A, notification date: N/A
Early action deadline: N/A, notification date: N/A
Application deadline (fall): 6/30
Undergraduate student body: 3,171 full time, 360 part time; 45% male, 55% female; 0% American Indian, 1% Asian, 74% black, 2% Hispanic, 8% multiracial, 0% Pacific Islander, 11% white, 3% international; 81% from in state; 60% live on campus; N/A of students in fraternities, N/A in sororities
Most popular majors: 7% Biology/Biological Sciences, General, 15% Criminal Justice/Police Science, 8% Family and Consumer Sciences/Human Sciences, General, 7% Hotel/Motel Administration/Management, 8% Sociology
Expenses: 2014-2015: $7,287 in state, $16,311 out of state; room/board: $8,906
Financial aid: (410) 651-6172; 82% of undergrads determined to have financial need; average aid package $10,080

University of Maryland– University College

Adelphi MD
(800) 888-8682
U.S. News ranking: Reg. U. (N), unranked
Website: www.umuc.edu/
Admissions email: enroll@umuc.edu
Public; founded 1947
Freshman admissions: N/A; 2013-2014: 2,251 applied, 2,251 accepted. Neither SAT nor ACT required. ACT 25/75 percentile: N/A. High school rank: N/A
Early decision deadline: N/A, notification date: N/A
Early action deadline: N/A, notification date: N/A
Application deadline (fall): rolling
Undergraduate student body: 5,917 full time, 20,823 part time; 51% male, 49% female; 0% American Indian, 4% Asian, 29% black, 9% Hispanic, 3% multiracial, 1% Pacific Islander, 42% white, 1% international; 57% from in state; N/A live on campus; N/A of students in fraternities, N/A in sororities
Most popular majors: 41% Business, Management, Marketing, and Related Support Services, 23% Computer and Information Sciences and Support Services, 8% Homeland Security, Law Enforcement, Firefighting and Related Protective Services, 8% Psychology

Expenses: 2013-2014: $6,552 in state, $12,336 out of state; room/board: N/A
Financial aid: (301) 985-7510; 63% of undergrads determined to have financial need; average aid package $7,607

Washington Adventist University

Takoma Park MD
(301) 891-4080
U.S. News ranking: Reg. Coll. (N), No. 46
Website: www.wau.edu
Admissions email: enroll@wau.edu
Private; founded 1904
Affiliation: Seventh-day Adventist
Freshman admissions: least selective; 2013-2014: 1,116 applied, 596 accepted. Either SAT or ACT required. SAT 25/75 percentile: 720-960. High school rank: N/A
Early decision deadline: N/A, notification date: N/A
Early action deadline: N/A, notification date: N/A
Application deadline (fall): 8/1
Undergraduate student body: 806 full time, 205 part time; 35% male, 65% female; 1% American Indian, 7% Asian, 59% black, 11% Hispanic, 1% multiracial, 0% Pacific Islander, 9% white, 2% international; 60% from in state; N/A live on campus; N/A of students in fraternities, N/A in sororities
Most popular majors: 9% Business, Management, Marketing, and Related Support Services, 57% Health Professions and Related Programs, 9% Liberal Arts and Sciences, General Studies and Humanities, 8% Psychology, 4% Theology and Religious Vocations
Expenses: 2014-2015: $21,395; room/board: $8,300
Financial aid: (301) 891-4005; 95% of undergrads determined to have financial need; average aid package $11,026

Washington College

Chestertown MD
(410) 778-7700
U.S. News ranking: Nat. Lib. Arts, No. 105
Website: www.washcoll.edu
Admissions email: adm.off@washcoll.edu
Private; founded 1782
Freshman admissions: more selective; 2013-2014: 4,647 applied, 3,088 accepted. Neither SAT nor ACT required. SAT 25/75 percentile: 1050-1280. High school rank: 33% in top tenth, 62% in top quarter, 88% in top half
Early decision deadline: 11/1, notification date: 12/1
Early action deadline: 12/1, notification date: 12/20
Application deadline (fall): 2/15
Undergraduate student body: 1,440 full time, 43 part time; 42% male, 58% female; 0% American Indian, 2% Asian, 4% black, 4% Hispanic, 2% multiracial, 0% Pacific Islander, 79% white, 5% international; 52% from in state; 85% live on campus; 8% of students in fraternities, 11% in sororities
Most popular majors: 9% Biological and Biomedical Sciences, 14% Business, Management, Marketing, and Related Support Services, 7% English Language and Literature/Letters, 10% Psychology, 25% Social Sciences
Expenses: 2014-2015: $42,592; room/board: $10,010
Financial aid: (410) 778-7214; 60% of undergrads determined to have financial need; average aid package $31,604

MASSACHUSETTS

American International College

Springfield MA
(413) 205-3201
U.S. News ranking: Reg. U. (N), second tier
Website: www.aic.edu
Admissions email: inquiry@aic.edu
Private; founded 1885
Freshman admissions: least selective; 2013-2014: 1,928 applied, 1,306 accepted. Either SAT or ACT required. SAT 25/75 percentile: 836-869. High school rank: N/A
Early decision deadline: N/A, notification date: N/A
Early action deadline: N/A, notification date: N/A
Application deadline (fall): rolling
Undergraduate student body: 1,397 full time, 116 part time; 42% male, 58% female; 0% American Indian, 2% Asian, 25% black, 7% Hispanic, 4% multiracial, 1% Pacific Islander, 44% white, 1% international; 63% from in state; 48% live on campus; 2% of students in fraternities, 2% in sororities
Most popular majors: 18% Business, Management, Marketing, and Related Support Services, 30% Health Professions and Related Programs, 12% Homeland Security, Law Enforcement, Firefighting and Related Protective Services, 9% Liberal Arts and Sciences, General Studies and Humanities, 9% Psychology
Expenses: 2014-2015: $30,941; room/board: $12,514
Financial aid: (413) 205-3259; 95% of undergrads determined to have financial need; average aid package $23,969

Amherst College

Amherst MA
(413) 542-2328
U.S. News ranking: Nat. Lib. Arts, No. 2
Website: www.amherst.edu
Admissions email: admission@amherst.edu
Private; founded 1821
Freshman admissions: most selective; 2013-2014: 7,927 applied, 1,132 accepted. Either SAT or ACT required. SAT 25/75 percentile: 1350-1530. High school rank: 86% in top tenth, 98% in top quarter, 100% in top half
Early decision deadline: 11/15, notification date: 12/15
Early action deadline: N/A, notification date: N/A
Application deadline (fall): 1/1
Undergraduate student body: 1,785 full time, N/A part time; 50% male, 50% female; 0% American Indian, 13% Asian, 12% black, 13% Hispanic, 6% multiracial, 0% Pacific Islander, 42% white, 10% international; 12% from in state; 98% live on campus; 0% of students in fraternities, 0% in sororities
Most popular majors: 15% Economics, General, 9% English Language and Literature, General, 11% History, General, 10% Political Science and Government, General, 8% Psychology, General
Expenses: 2014-2015: $48,526; room/board: $12,680
Financial aid: (413) 542-2296; 56% of undergrads determined to have financial need; average aid package $46,809

Anna Maria College

Paxton MA
(508) 849-3360
U.S. News ranking: Reg. U. (N), second tier
Website: www.annamaria.edu
Admissions email: admissions@annamaria.edu
Private; founded 1946
Affiliation: Roman Catholic
Freshman admissions: least selective; 2013-2014: 2,071 applied, 1,607 accepted. Neither SAT nor ACT required. SAT 25/75 percentile: 765-975. High school rank: N/A
Early decision deadline: N/A, notification date: N/A
Early action deadline: N/A, notification date: N/A
Application deadline (fall): rolling
Undergraduate student body: 845 full time, 298 part time; 43% male, 57% female; 0% American Indian, 1% Asian, 8% black, 7% Hispanic, 2% multiracial, 0% Pacific Islander, 72% white, 0% international
Most popular majors: Information not available
Expenses: 2014-2015: $34,330; room/board: $12,730
Financial aid: (508) 849-3366; 72% of undergrads determined to have financial need; average aid package $23,637

Assumption College

Worcester MA
(866) 477-7776
U.S. News ranking: Reg. U. (N), No. 31
Website: www.assumption.edu
Admissions email: admiss@assumption.edu
Private; founded 1904
Affiliation: Roman Catholic
Freshman admissions: selective; 2013-2014: 4,659 applied, 3,458 accepted. Neither SAT nor ACT required. SAT 25/75 percentile: 1020-1215. High school rank: 10% in top tenth, 40% in top quarter, 79% in top half
Early decision deadline: N/A, notification date: N/A
Early action deadline: 11/1, notification date: 12/15
Application deadline (fall): 2/15
Undergraduate student body: 2,003 full time, 12 part time; 40% male, 60% female; 0% American Indian, 2% Asian, 4% black, 7% Hispanic, 2% multiracial, 0% Pacific Islander, 74% white, 1% international; 64% from in state; 87% live on campus; N/A of students in fraternities, N/A in sororities
Most popular majors: 25% Business, Management, Marketing, and Related Support Services, 11% English Language and Literature/Letters, 9% Health Professions and Related Programs, 10% Psychology, 12% Social Sciences
Expenses: 2014-2015: $36,160; room/board: $10,962
Financial aid: (508) 767-7158; 78% of undergrads determined to have financial need; average aid package $25,672

Babson College

Babson Park MA
(781) 239-5522
U.S. News ranking: Business, unranked
Website: www.babson.edu
Admissions email: ugradadmission@babson.edu
Private; founded 1919
Freshman admissions: more selective; 2013-2014: 6,086 applied, 1,717 accepted. Either SAT or ACT required. SAT 25/75 percentile: 1160-1350. High school rank: N/A
Early decision deadline: 11/1, notification date: 12/15
Early action deadline: 11/1, notification date: 1/1
Application deadline (fall): 1/1
Undergraduate student body: 2,106 full time, N/A part time; 55% male, 45% female; 0% American Indian, 12% Asian, 4% black, 10% Hispanic, 2% multiracial, 0% Pacific Islander, 39% white, 26% international; 30% from in state; 81% live on campus; 15% of students in fraternities, 25% in sororities
Most popular majors: Information not available
Expenses: 2014-2015: $45,120; room/board: $14,494
Financial aid: (781) 239-4219; 43% of undergrads determined to have financial need; average aid package $37,060

Bard College at Simon's Rock

Great Barrington MA
(800) 234-7186
U.S. News ranking: Reg. Coll. (N), No. 12
Website: www.simons-rock.edu
Admissions email: admit@simons-rock.edu
Private; founded 1966
Freshman admissions: more selective; 2013-2014: 218 applied, 201 accepted. Neither SAT nor ACT required. SAT 25/75 percentile: 1290-1460. High school rank: 46% in top tenth, 67% in top quarter, 89% in top half
Early decision deadline: N/A, notification date: N/A
Early action deadline: N/A, notification date: N/A
Application deadline (fall): 5/1
Undergraduate student body: 341 full time, 9 part time; 42% male, 58% female; 0% American Indian, 6% Asian, 7% black, 2% Hispanic, 9% multiracial, 0% Pacific Islander, 57% white, 10% international; N/A from in state; 90% live on campus; N/A of students in fraternities, N/A in sororities
Most popular majors: 6% Engineering, 10% English Language and Literature/Letters, 16% Multi/Interdisciplinary Studies, 11% Social Sciences, 18% Visual and Performing Arts
Expenses: 2014-2015: $48,551; room/board: $13,198
Financial aid: (413) 528-7297; 81% of undergrads determined to have financial need; average aid package $38,911

Bay Path University

Longmeadow MA
(413) 565-1331
U.S. News ranking: Nat. Lib. Arts, second tier
Website: www.baypath.edu
Admissions email: admiss@baypath.edu
Private; founded 1897
Freshman admissions: selective; 2013-2014: 908 applied, 523 accepted. Neither SAT nor ACT required. SAT 25/75 percentile: 840-1090. High school rank: 14% in top tenth, 49% in top quarter, 84% in top half
Early decision deadline: N/A, notification date: N/A
Early action deadline: 12/15, notification date: 1/2
Application deadline (fall): rolling
Undergraduate student body: 1,179 full time, 279 part time; 0% male, 100% female; 0% American Indian, 1% Asian, 12% black, 15% Hispanic, 2% multiracial, 0% Pacific Islander, 59% white, 0% international; 58% from in state; 53% live on campus; 0% of students in fraternities, 0% in sororities
Most popular majors: 26% Business, Management, Marketing, and Related Support Services, 9% Homeland Security, Law Enforcement, Firefighting and Related Protective Services, 8% Legal Professions and Studies, 25% Liberal Arts and Sciences, General Studies and Humanities, 17% Psychology
Expenses: 2014-2015: $30,859; room/board: $12,240
Financial aid: (413) 565-1261; 97% of undergrads determined to have financial need; average aid package $24,093

Bay State College

Boston MA
(617) 217-9000
U.S. News ranking: Reg. Coll. (N), second tier
Website: www.baystate.edu
Admissions email: N/A
For-profit
Freshman admissions: least selective; 2013-2014: 1,669 applied, 985 accepted. Neither SAT nor ACT required. ACT 25/75 percentile: N/A. High school rank: N/A
Early decision deadline: N/A, notification date: N/A
Early action deadline: N/A, notification date: N/A
Application deadline (fall): rolling
Undergraduate student body: 769 full time, 427 part time; 28% male, 72% female; 0% American Indian, 5% Asian, 23% black, 18% Hispanic, 8% multiracial, 0% Pacific Islander, 41% white, 2% international
Most popular majors: 18% Arts, Entertainment,and Media Management, General, 33% Business Administration and

Management, General, 15%
Criminal Justice/Law Enforcement
Administration, 14% Fashion
Merchandising, 13% Licensed
Practical/Vocational Nurse Training
Expenses: 2014-2015: $25,280;
room/board: $11,800
Financial aid: (617) 217-9186

Becker College
Worcester MA
(877) 523-2537
U.S. News ranking: Reg. Coll. (N),
second tier
Website: www.beckercollege.edu
Admissions email: admissions@
beckercollege.edu
Private; founded 1784
Freshman admissions: selective;
2013-2014: 3,936 applied,
2,462 accepted. Either SAT
or ACT required. SAT 25/75
percentile: 890-1120. High
school rank: 7% in top tenth, 26%
in top quarter, 57% in top half
Early decision deadline: N/A,
notification date: N/A
Early action deadline: 11/15,
notification date: 12/15
Application deadline (fall): rolling
Undergraduate student body: 1,449
full time, 453 part time; 43%
male, 57% female; 0% American
Indian, 1% Asian, 8% black,
10% Hispanic, 3% multiracial,
0% Pacific Islander, 67% white,
1% international; 67% from in
state; 41% live on campus; 0%
of students in fraternities, 0% in
sororities
Most popular majors: 27%
Business, Management,
Marketing, and Related Support
Services, 12% Communications
Technologies/Technicians and
Support Services, 9% Health
Professions and Related Programs,
11% Parks, Recreation, Leisure,
and Fitness Studies, 17%
Psychology
Expenses: 2013-2014: $31,500;
room/board: $11,500
Financial aid: (508) 791-9241

Benjamin Franklin Institute of Technology[1]
Boston MA
(617) 423-4630
U.S. News ranking: Engineering,
unranked
Website: www.bfit.edu
Admissions email:
admissions@bfit.edu
Private
Application deadline (fall): N/A
Undergraduate student body: N/A
full time, N/A part time
Expenses: 2013-2014: $16,950;
room/board: $16,900
Financial aid: (617) 423-4630

Bentley University
Waltham MA
(781) 891-2244
U.S. News ranking: Reg. U. (N),
No. 6
Website: www.bentley.edu
Admissions email: ugadmission@
bentley.edu
Private; founded 1917
Freshman admissions: more
selective; 2013-2014: 7,493
applied, 3,281 accepted. Either
SAT or ACT required. SAT 25/75
percentile: 1140-1310. High
school rank: 41% in top tenth,
75% in top quarter, 98% in
top half

Early decision deadline: 11/15,
notification date: 12/28
Early action deadline: 11/15,
notification date: 2/7
Application deadline (fall): 1/7
Undergraduate student body: 4,142
full time, 105 part time; 60%
male, 40% female; 0% American
Indian, 8% Asian, 3% black, 7%
Hispanic, 2% multiracial, 0%
Pacific Islander, 61% white, 15%
international; 47% from in state;
78% live on campus; 11% of
students in fraternities, 11% in
sororities
Most popular majors: 14%
Accounting, 14% Accounting
and Finance, 13% Business,
Management, Marketing, and
Related Support Services, Other,
14% Finance, General, 15%
Marketing/Marketing Management,
General
Expenses: 2014-2015: $42,511;
room/board: $13,949
Financial aid: (781) 891-3441;
45% of undergrads determined to
have financial need; average aid
package $33,956

Berklee College of Music
Boston MA
(800) 237-5533
U.S. News ranking: Arts, unranked
Website: www.berklee.edu
Admissions email: admissions@
berklee.edu
Private; founded 1945
Freshman admissions: N/A; 2013-
2014: 6,412 applied, 2,319
accepted. Neither SAT nor ACT
required. SAT 25/75 percentile:
N/A. High school rank: N/A
Early decision deadline: N/A,
notification date: N/A
Early action deadline: 11/1,
notification date: 1/31
Application deadline (fall): 1/15
Undergraduate student body: 3,950
full time, 452 part time; 69%
male, 31% female; 5% American
Indian, 0% Asian, 0% black,
9% Hispanic, 4% multiracial,
39% Pacific Islander, 3% white,
31% international; 16% from in
state; 17% live on campus; 0%
of students in fraternities, 0% in
sororities
Most popular majors: 12% Music
Management, 16% Music
Performance, General, 21% Music
Theory and Composition, 20%
Music, General, 14% Recording
Arts Technology/Technician
Expenses: 2014-2015: $38,910;
room/board: $17,372
Financial aid: (617) 747-2274

Boston Architectural College
Boston MA
(617) 585-0123
U.S. News ranking: Arts, unranked
Website: www.the-bac.edu
Admissions email: admissions@
the-bac.edu
Private; founded 1889
Freshman admissions: N/A; 2013-
2014: 24 applied, 24 accepted.
Neither SAT nor ACT required.
SAT 25/75 percentile: N/A. High
school rank: N/A
Early decision deadline: N/A,
notification date: N/A
Early action deadline: N/A,
notification date: N/A
Application deadline (fall): rolling

Undergraduate student body: 396
full time, 11 part time; 70%
male, 30% female; 1% American
Indian, 9% Asian, 6% black, 16%
Hispanic, 2% multiracial, 0%
Pacific Islander, 59% white, 1%
international
Most popular majors: Information
not available
Expenses: 2014-2015: $19,706;
room/board: N/A
Financial aid: (617) 585-0125;
96% of undergrads determined to
have financial need; average aid
package $9,907

Boston College
Chestnut Hill MA
(617) 552-3100
U.S. News ranking: Nat. U.,
No. 31
Website: www.bc.edu
Admissions email: N/A
Private; founded 1863
Affiliation: Roman Catholic (Jesuit)
Freshman admissions: most
selective; 2013-2014: 24,538
applied, 7,905 accepted. Either
SAT or ACT required. SAT 25/75
percentile: 1270-1450. High
school rank: 81% in top tenth,
97% in top quarter, 99% in
top half
Early decision deadline: N/A,
notification date: N/A
Early action deadline: 11/1,
notification date: 12/25
Application deadline (fall): 1/1
Undergraduate student body: 9,049
full time, N/A part time; 46%
male, 54% female; 0% American
Indian, 10% Asian, 4% black,
11% Hispanic, 3% multiracial,
0% Pacific Islander, 60% white,
5% international; 26% from in
state; 85% live on campus; 0%
of students in fraternities, 0% in
sororities
Most popular majors: 8% Biology/
Biological Sciences, General,
9% Economics, General,
10% Finance, General, 7%
Psychology, General, 8% Speech
Communication and Rhetoric
Expenses: 2014-2015: $47,436;
room/board: $13,186
Financial aid: (617) 552-3320;
43% of undergrads determined to
have financial need; average aid
package $36,779

Boston Conservatory[1]
Boston MA
(617) 912-9153
U.S. News ranking: Arts, unranked
Website:
www.bostonconservatory.edu
Admissions email: admissions@
bostonconservatory.edu
Private
Application deadline (fall): N/A
Undergraduate student body: N/A
full time, N/A part time
Expenses: 2013-2014: $40,900;
room/board: $17,195
Financial aid: (617) 912-9147

Boston University
Boston MA
(617) 353-2300
U.S. News ranking: Nat. U.,
No. 42
Website: www.bu.edu
Admissions email:
admissions@bu.edu
Private; founded 1839
Freshman admissions: more
selective; 2013-2014: 52,705
applied, 19,420 accepted. Either

SAT or ACT required. SAT 25/75
percentile: 1190-1390. High
school rank: 58% in top tenth,
89% in top quarter, 99% in
top half
Early decision deadline: 11/1,
notification date: 12/15
Early action deadline: N/A,
notification date: N/A
Application deadline (fall): 1/1
Undergraduate student body:
16,593 full time, 1,572 part
time; 40% male, 60% female;
0% American Indian, 13% Asian,
3% black, 9% Hispanic, 4%
multiracial, 0% Pacific Islander,
47% white, 16% international;
26% from in state; 75% live
on campus; 7% of students in
fraternities, 11% in sororities
Most popular majors: 8% Biological
and Biomedical Sciences,
18% Business, Management,
Marketing, and Related Support
Services, 15% Communication,
Journalism, and Related Programs,
9% Health Professions and
Related Programs, 16% Social
Sciences
Expenses: 2014-2015: $46,664;
room/board: $14,030
Financial aid: (617) 353-2965;
40% of undergrads determined to
have financial need; average aid
package $35,633

Brandeis University
Waltham MA
(781) 736-3500
U.S. News ranking: Nat. U.,
No. 35
Website: www.brandeis.edu
Admissions email: admissions@
brandeis.edu
Private; founded 1948
Freshman admissions: more
selective; 2013-2014: 9,496
applied, 3,517 accepted. Either
SAT or ACT required. SAT 25/75
percentile: 1230-1470. High
school rank: 65% in top tenth,
89% in top quarter, 99% in
top half
Early decision deadline: 11/1,
notification date: 12/15
Early action deadline: N/A,
notification date: N/A
Application deadline (fall): 1/1
Undergraduate student body: 3,599
full time, 15 part time; 43%
male, 57% female; 0% American
Indian, 12% Asian, 5% black,
7% Hispanic, 3% multiracial,
0% Pacific Islander, 50% white,
15% international; 27% from in
state; 79% live on campus; 0%
of students in fraternities, 0% in
sororities
Most popular majors: 10% Biology/
Biological Sciences, General,
7% Business Administration,
Management and Operations,
Other, 9% Economics, General,
6% Health Policy Analysis, 9%
Psychology, General
Expenses: 2014-2015: $47,833;
room/board: $13,192
Financial aid: (781) 736-3700;
53% of undergrads determined to
have financial need; average aid
package $37,333

Bridgewater State University
Bridgewater MA
(508) 531-1237
U.S. News ranking: Reg. U. (N),
second tier
Website:
www.bridgew.edu/admissions

Admissions email: admission@
bridgew.edu
Public; founded 1840
Freshman admissions: less
selective; 2013-2014: 5,918
applied, 4,651 accepted. Either
SAT or ACT required. SAT 25/75
percentile: 890-1090. High
school rank: N/A
Early decision deadline: N/A,
notification date: N/A
Early action deadline: 11/15,
notification date: 12/15
Application deadline (fall): rolling
Undergraduate student body: 8,034
full time, 1,581 part time; 42%
male, 58% female; 0% American
Indian, 2% Asian, 8% black,
5% Hispanic, 3% multiracial,
0% Pacific Islander, 81% white,
0% international; 96% from in
state; 39% live on campus; 5%
of students in fraternities, 5% in
sororities
Most popular majors: 16%
Business, Management,
Marketing, and Related Support
Services, 9% Communication,
Journalism, and Related Programs,
16% Education, 11% Homeland
Security, Law Enforcement,
Firefighting and Related Protective
Services, 12% Psychology
Expenses: 2013-2014: $8,228 in
state, $14,368 out of state; room/
board: $11,100
Financial aid: (508) 531-1341

Cambridge College[1]
Cambridge MA
(800) 877-4723
U.S. News ranking: Reg. U. (N),
unranked
Website:
www.cambridgecollege.edu
Admissions email: N/A
Private; founded 1971
Application deadline (fall): rolling
Undergraduate student body: N/A
full time, N/A part time
Expenses: 2014-2015: $13,392;
room/board: N/A
Financial aid: (800) 877-4723;
average aid package $8,418

Clark University
Worcester MA
(508) 793-7431
U.S. News ranking: Nat. U.,
No. 76
Website: www.clarku.edu
Admissions email: admissions@
clarku.edu
Private; founded 1887
Freshman admissions: more
selective; 2013-2014: 5,551
applied, 3,416 accepted. Neither
SAT nor ACT required. SAT
25/75 percentile: 1110-1320.
High school rank: 38% in top
tenth, 73% in top quarter, 98%
in top half
Early decision deadline: N/A,
notification date: N/A
Early action deadline: 11/15,
notification date: 12/23
Application deadline (fall): 1/15
Undergraduate student body: 2,270
full time, 110 part time; 42%
male, 58% female; 0% American
Indian, 6% Asian, 4% black,
6% Hispanic, 2% multiracial,
0% Pacific Islander, 62% white,
12% international; 39% from in
state; 71% live on campus; 0%
of students in fraternities, 0% in
sororities
Most popular majors: 6% Biology,
General, 5% Economics, 6%
International Relations and
National Security Studies, 9%

Political Science and Government, 17% Psychology
Expenses: 2014-2015: $40,730; room/board: $7,800
Financial aid: (508) 793-7478; 62% of undergrads determined to have financial need; average aid package $33,320

College of Our Lady of the Elms

Chicopee MA
(800) 255-3567
U.S. News ranking: Reg. Coll. (N), No. 24
Website: www.elms.edu
Admissions email: admissions@elms.edu
Private
Affiliation: Roman Catholic, founded by Sisters of Saint Joseph of Springfield
Freshman admissions: less selective; 2013-2014: 993 applied, 744 accepted. Either SAT or ACT required. SAT 25/75 percentile: 820-1040. High school rank: N/A
Early decision deadline: N/A, notification date: N/A
Early action deadline: N/A, notification date: N/A
Application deadline (fall): rolling
Undergraduate student body: 1,006 full time, 341 part time; 24% male, 76% female; 1% American Indian, 3% Asian, 8% black, 11% Hispanic, 0% multiracial, 0% Pacific Islander, 56% white, 1% international; 82% from in state; 28% live on campus; 0% of students in fraternities, 0% in sororities
Most popular majors: 5% Biological and Biomedical Sciences, 16% Business, Management, Marketing, and Related Support Services, 41% Health Professions and Related Programs, 6% Psychology, 11% Public Administration and Social Service Professions
Expenses: 2014-2015: $31,188; room/board: $11,312
Financial aid: (413) 594-2761; 74% of undergrads determined to have financial need; average aid package $18,695

College of the Holy Cross

Worcester MA
(508) 793-2443
U.S. News ranking: Nat. Lib. Arts, No. 34
Website: www.holycross.edu
Admissions email: admissions@holycross.edu
Private; founded 1843
Affiliation: Roman Catholic (Jesuit)
Freshman admissions: more selective; 2013-2014: 7,115 applied, 2,346 accepted. Neither SAT nor ACT required. SAT 25/75 percentile: 1220-1390. High school rank: 57% in top tenth, 90% in top quarter, 100% in top half
Early decision deadline: 12/15, notification date: 1/15
Early action deadline: N/A, notification date: N/A
Application deadline (fall): 1/15
Undergraduate student body: 2,877 full time, 35 part time; 50% male, 50% female; 0% American Indian, 5% Asian, 4% black, 11% Hispanic, 3% multiracial,

0% Pacific Islander, 68% white, 1% international; 37% from in state; 92% live on campus; 0% of students in fraternities, 0% in sororities
Most popular majors: 9% English Language and Literature/Letters, 7% Foreign Languages, Literatures, and Linguistics, 8% History, 16% Psychology, 31% Social Sciences
Expenses: 2014-2015: $45,692; room/board: $12,350
Financial aid: (508) 793-2266; 58% of undergrads determined to have financial need; average aid package $31,877

Curry College

Milton MA
(800) 669-0686
U.S. News ranking: Reg. U. (N), second tier
Website: www.curry.edu
Admissions email: curryadm@curry.edu
Private; founded 1879
Freshman admissions: less selective; 2013-2014: 5,192 applied, 4,537 accepted. Neither SAT nor ACT required. SAT 25/75 percentile: 840-1030. High school rank: 5% in top tenth, 20% in top quarter, 58% in top half
Early decision deadline: N/A, notification date: N/A
Early action deadline: 12/1, notification date: 12/15
Application deadline (fall): rolling
Undergraduate student body: 2,068 full time, 781 part time; 37% male, 63% female; 0% American Indian, 2% Asian, 9% black, 5% Hispanic, 2% multiracial, 0% Pacific Islander, 67% white, 1% international; 78% from in state; 51% live on campus; 0% of students in fraternities, 0% in sororities
Most popular majors: 12% Business, Management, Marketing, and Related Support Services, 10% Communication, Journalism, and Related Programs, 44% Health Professions and Related Programs; 12% Homeland Security, Law Enforcement, Firefighting and Related Protective Services, 8% Psychology
Expenses: 2014-2015: $35,415; room/board: $13,510
Financial aid: (617) 333-2146; 75% of undergrads determined to have financial need; average aid package $21,860

Dean College

Franklin MA
(508) 541-1508
U.S. News ranking: Reg. Coll. (N), No. 26
Website: www.dean.edu
Admissions email: admission@dean.edu
Private; founded 1865
Freshman admissions: least selective; 2013-2014: 2,594 applied, 1,773 accepted. Either SAT or ACT required. SAT 25/75 percentile: 750-950. High school rank: 4% in top tenth, 11% in top quarter, 22% in top half
Early decision deadline: N/A, notification date: N/A
Early action deadline: 12/1, notification date: 1/15
Application deadline (fall): rolling
Undergraduate student body: 1,076 full time, 224 part time; 53% male, 47% female; 0% American

Indian, 1% Asian, 16% black, 6% Hispanic, 3% multiracial, 0% Pacific Islander, 46% white, 12% international; N/A from in state; 89% live on campus; N/A of students in fraternities, N/A in sororities
Most popular majors: Information not available
Expenses: 2014-2015: $34,390; room/board: $14,760
Financial aid: (508) 541-1519; 74% of undergrads determined to have financial need; average aid package $23,345

Eastern Nazarene College

Quincy MA
(617) 745-3711
U.S. News ranking: Nat. Lib. Arts, second tier
Website: www.enc.edu
Admissions email: info@enc.edu
Private; founded 1918
Affiliation: Nazarene
Freshman admissions: less selective; 2013-2014: 1,070 applied, 549 accepted. Either SAT or ACT required. SAT 25/75 percentile: 820-1090. High school rank: 9% in top tenth, 25% in top quarter, 59% in top half
Early decision deadline: N/A, notification date: N/A
Early action deadline: N/A, notification date: N/A
Application deadline (fall): rolling
Undergraduate student body: 1,302 full time, 19 part time; 27% male, 73% female; 0% American Indian, 2% Asian, 21% black, 11% Hispanic, 3% multiracial, 0% Pacific Islander, 58% white, 2% international; 52% from in state; 72% live on campus; 0% of students in fraternities, 0% in sororities
Most popular majors: 5% Biological and Biomedical Sciences, 28% Business, Management, Marketing, and Related Support Services, 30% Education, 11% Psychology
Expenses: 2013-2014: $27,922; room/board: $8,700
Financial aid: (617) 745-3869

Emerson College

Boston MA
(617) 824-8600
U.S. News ranking: Reg. U. (N), No. 14
Website: www.emerson.edu
Admissions email: admission@emerson.edu
Private; founded 1880
Freshman admissions: more selective; 2013-2014: 8,198 applied, 3,933 accepted. Either SAT or ACT required. SAT 25/75 percentile: 1140-1320. High school rank: 29% in top tenth, 68% in top quarter, 95% in top half
Early decision deadline: N/A, notification date: N/A
Early action deadline: 11/1, notification date: 12/15
Application deadline (fall): 1/15
Undergraduate student body: 3,668 full time, 63 part time; 38% male, 62% female; 0% American Indian, 4% Asian, 3% black, 10% Hispanic, 5% multiracial, 0% Pacific Islander, 65% white, 5% international; 24% from in state; 58% live on campus; 3% of students in fraternities, 4% in sororities

Most popular majors: 6% Broadcast Journalism, 14% Cinematography and Film/Video Production, 16% Creative Writing, 14% Marketing/Marketing Management, General, 7% Radio and Television
Expenses: 2014-2015: $37,350; room/board: $15,096
Financial aid: (617) 824-8655; 55% of undergrads determined to have financial need; average aid package $21,243

Emmanuel College

Boston MA
(617) 735-9715
U.S. News ranking: Reg. U. (N), No. 60
Website: www.emmanuel.edu
Admissions email: enroll@emmanuel.edu
Private; founded 1919
Affiliation: Roman Catholic
Freshman admissions: selective; 2013-2014: 6,623 applied, 4,006 accepted. Neither SAT nor ACT required. SAT 25/75 percentile: 1000-1180. High school rank: 17% in top tenth, 54% in top quarter, 85% in top half
Early decision deadline: N/A, notification date: N/A
Early action deadline: 11/1, notification date: 12/15
Application deadline (fall): 2/15
Undergraduate student body: 1,857 full time, 319 part time; 27% male, 73% female; 0% American Indian, 3% Asian, 5% black, 6% Hispanic, 2% multiracial, 0% Pacific Islander, 70% white, 1% international; 58% from in state; 72% live on campus; N/A of students in fraternities, N/A in sororities
Most popular majors: 10% Biological and Biomedical Sciences, 21% Business, Management, Marketing, and Related Support Services, 10% Communication, Journalism, and Related Programs, 7% English Language and Literature/Letters, 9% Psychology
Expenses: 2014-2015: $35,532; room/board: $13,580
Financial aid: (617) 735-9938; 79% of undergrads determined to have financial need; average aid package $27,623

Endicott College

Beverly MA
(978) 921-1000
U.S. News ranking: Reg. U. (N), No. 74
Website: www.endicott.edu
Admissions email: admission@endicott.edu
Private; founded 1939
Freshman admissions: selective; 2013-2014: 3,732 applied, 2,682 accepted. Either SAT or ACT required. SAT 25/75 percentile: 980-1160. High school rank: 15% in top tenth, 39% in top quarter, 81% in top half
Early decision deadline: N/A, notification date: N/A
Early action deadline: N/A, notification date: N/A
Application deadline (fall): 2/15
Undergraduate student body: 2,531 full time, 321 part time; 41% male, 59% female; 0% American Indian, 1% Asian, 3% black, 4% Hispanic, 2% multiracial, 0% Pacific Islander, 82% white,

2% international; 48% from in state; 82% live on campus; N/A of students in fraternities, N/A in sororities
Most popular majors: 26% Business, Management, Marketing, and Related Support Services, 9% Education, 10% Parks, Recreation, Leisure, and Fitness Studies, 10% Psychology, 10% Visual and Performing Arts
Expenses: 2014-2015: $29,494; room/board: $13,734
Financial aid: (978) 232-2070; 67% of undergrads determined to have financial need; average aid package $20,065

Fisher College

Boston MA
(617) 236-8818
U.S. News ranking: Reg. Coll. (N), second tier
Website: www.fisher.edu
Admissions email: admissions@fisher.edu
Private; founded 1903
Freshman admissions: least selective; 2013-2014: 2,281 applied, 1,492 accepted. Neither SAT nor ACT required. SAT 25/75 percentile: 730-920. High school rank: N/A
Early decision deadline: N/A, notification date: N/A
Early action deadline: N/A, notification date: N/A
Application deadline (fall): rolling
Undergraduate student body: 1,229 full time, 701 part time; 26% male, 74% female; 0% American Indian, 1% Asian, 10% black, 8% Hispanic, 1% multiracial, 0% Pacific Islander, 32% white, 6% international; 83% from in state; 16% live on campus; N/A of students in fraternities, N/A in sororities
Most popular majors: 41% Business Administration and Management, General, 9% Early Childhood Education and Teaching, 21% Health/Health Care Administration/Management, 14% Liberal Arts and Sciences/Liberal Studies, 5% Public Administration and Social Service Professions, Other
Expenses: 2014-2015: $28,260; room/board: $14,714
Financial aid: (617) 236-8821; 66% of undergrads determined to have financial need

Fitchburg State University

Fitchburg MA
(978) 665-3144
U.S. News ranking: Reg. U. (N), second tier
Website: www.fitchburgstate.edu
Admissions email: admissions@fitchburgstate.edu
Public; founded 1894
Freshman admissions: less selective; 2013-2014: 3,818 applied, 2,834 accepted. Either SAT or ACT required. SAT 25/75 percentile: 900-1090. High school rank: N/A
Early decision deadline: N/A, notification date: N/A
Early action deadline: N/A, notification date: N/A
Application deadline (fall): rolling
Undergraduate student body: 3,438 full time, 801 part time; 45% male, 55% female; 0% American Indian, 2% Asian, 6% black, 9% Hispanic, 2% multiracial,

0% Pacific Islander, 77% white, 0% international; 92% from in state; 41% live on campus; 1% of students in fraternities, 3% in sororities
Most popular majors: 14% Business, Management, Marketing, and Related Support Services, 9% Education, 8% Health Professions and Related Programs, 10% Multi/Interdisciplinary Studies, 15% Visual and Performing Arts
Expenses: 2014-2015: $9,260 in state, $15,340 out of state; room/board: $8,912
Financial aid: (978) 665-3156; 67% of undergrads determined to have financial need; average aid package $9,970

Framingham State University

Framingham MA
(508) 626-4500
U.S. News ranking: Reg. U. (N), second tier
Website: www.framingham.edu
Admissions email: admissions@framingham.edu
Public; founded 1839
Freshman admissions: selective; 2013-2014: 5,400 applied, 3,020 accepted. Either SAT or ACT required. SAT 25/75 percentile: 930-1100. High school rank: 8% in top tenth, 28% in top quarter, 71% in top half
Early decision deadline: N/A, notification date: N/A
Early action deadline: 11/15, notification date: 12/15
Application deadline (fall): rolling
Undergraduate student body: 3,884 full time, 700 part time; 36% male, 64% female; 0% American Indian, 2% Asian, 7% black, 9% Hispanic, 3% multiracial, 0% Pacific Islander, 76% white, 0% international; 96% from in state; 52% live on campus; 0% of students in fraternities, 0% in sororities
Most popular majors: 15% Business, Management, Marketing, and Related Support Services, 8% Communications Technologies/Technicians and Support Services, 14% Family and Consumer Sciences/Human Sciences, 10% Psychology, 14% Social Sciences
Expenses: 2013-2014: $8,080 in state, $14,160 out of state; room/board: $10,074
Financial aid: (508) 626-4534

Franklin W. Olin College of Engineering

Needham MA
(781) 292-2222
U.S. News ranking: Engineering, unranked
Website: www.olin.edu/
Admissions email: info@olin.edu
Private; founded 1997
Freshman admissions: most selective; 2013-2014: 782 applied, 131 accepted. Either SAT or ACT required. SAT 25/75 percentile: 1428-1550. High school rank: N/A
Early decision deadline: N/A, notification date: N/A
Early action deadline: N/A, notification date: N/A
Application deadline (fall): 1/1

Undergraduate student body: 355 full time, 0 part time; 50% male, 50% female; 0% American Indian, 17% Asian, 1% black, 4% Hispanic, 6% multiracial, 0% Pacific Islander, 53% white, 7% international; 15% from in state; 100% live on campus; 0% of students in fraternities, 0% in sororities
Most popular majors: 20% Electrical and Electronics Engineering, 36% Engineering, General, 20% Mechanical Engineering
Expenses: 2014-2015: $44,025; room/board: $15,200
Financial aid: N/A; 52% of undergrads determined to have financial need; average aid package $37,674

Gordon College

Wenham MA
(866) 464-6736
U.S. News ranking: Nat. Lib. Arts, No. 139
Website: www.gordon.edu
Admissions email: admissions@gordon.edu
Private; founded 1889
Affiliation: multi-denominational
Freshman admissions: selective; 2013-2014: 3,843 applied, 1,657 accepted. Either SAT or ACT required. SAT 25/75 percentile: 1015-1292. High school rank: 34% in top tenth, 55% in top quarter, 85% in top half
Early decision deadline: 11/1, notification date: 12/1
Early action deadline: 11/15, notification date: 12/1
Application deadline (fall): 8/15
Undergraduate student body: 1,669 full time, 38 part time; 38% male, 62% female; 0% American Indian, 3% Asian, 3% black, 7% Hispanic, 3% multiracial, 0% Pacific Islander, 78% white, 5% international; 35% from in state; 89% live on campus; 0% of students in fraternities, 0% in sororities
Most popular majors: 8% Biology/Biological Sciences, General, 6% Business Administration and Management, General, 7% English Language and Literature, General, 10% Psychology, General, 8% Speech Communication and Rhetoric
Expenses: 2014-2015: $34,390; room/board: $9,930
Financial aid: (978) 867-4246; 72% of undergrads determined to have financial need; average aid package $20,999

Hampshire College

Amherst MA
(413) 559-5471
U.S. News ranking: Nat. Lib. Arts, unranked
Website: www.hampshire.edu
Admissions email: admissions@hampshire.edu
Private; founded 1965
Freshman admissions: N/A; 2013-2014: 2,827 applied, 1,990 accepted. Neither SAT nor ACT required. ACT 25/75 percentile: N/A. High school rank: N/A
Early decision deadline: 11/15, notification date: 12/15
Early action deadline: 12/1, notification date: 2/15
Application deadline (fall): 1/15

Undergraduate student body: 1,492 full time, N/A part time; 43% male, 57% female; 0% American Indian, 2% Asian, 2% black, 9% Hispanic, 5% multiracial, 0% Pacific Islander, 67% white, 6% international
Most popular majors: Information not available
Expenses: 2013-2014: $46,625; room/board: $12,030
Financial aid: (413) 559-5484

Harvard University

Cambridge MA
(617) 495-1551
U.S. News ranking: Nat. U., No. 2
Website: www.college.harvard.edu
Admissions email: college@fas.harvard.edu
Private; founded 1636
Freshman admissions: most selective; 2013-2014: 35,023 applied, 2,047 accepted. Either SAT or ACT required. SAT 25/75 percentile: 1410-1600. High school rank: 95% in top tenth, 99% in top quarter, 100% in top half
Early decision deadline: N/A, notification date: N/A
Early action deadline: 11/1, notification date: 12/16
Application deadline (fall): 1/1
Undergraduate student body: 6,710 full time, 12 part time; 52% male, 48% female; 0% American Indian, 19% Asian, 7% black, 9% Hispanic, 6% multiracial, 0% Pacific Islander, 45% white, 11% international; 16% from in state; 99% live on campus; N/A of students in fraternities, N/A in sororities
Most popular majors: 15% Biology/Biological Sciences, General, 9% History, General, 7% Mathematics, General, 6% Psychology, General, 33% Social Sciences, General
Expenses: 2014-2015: $43,938; room/board: $14,669
Financial aid: (617) 495-1581; 58% of undergrads determined to have financial need; average aid package $47,759

Lasell College

Newton MA
(617) 243-2225
U.S. News ranking: Reg. Coll. (N), No. 27
Website: www.lasell.edu?ctschool=lasell&cttype=referral&ctsource=usnmain
Admissions email: info@lasell.edu
Private; founded 1851
Freshman admissions: less selective; 2013-2014: 3,584 applied, 2,729 accepted. Either SAT or ACT required. SAT 25/75 percentile: 880-1070. High school rank: N/A
Early decision deadline: N/A, notification date: N/A
Early action deadline: 11/15, notification date: 12/15
Application deadline (fall): rolling
Undergraduate student body: 1,649 full time, 38 part time; 36% male, 64% female; 0% American Indian, 2% Asian, 7% black, 9% Hispanic, 3% multiracial, 0% Pacific Islander, 71% white, 3% international; 56% from in state; 77% live on campus; 0% of students in fraternities, 0% in sororities

---

Most popular majors: 11% Communication and Media Studies, 14% Fashion Merchandising, 8% Fashion/Apparel Design, 6% Psychology, General, 7% Sport and Fitness Administration/Management
Expenses: 2014-2015: $31,000; room/board: $12,750
Financial aid: (617) 243-2227; 81% of undergrads determined to have financial need; average aid package $25,070

Lesley University

Cambridge MA
(617) 349-8800
U.S. News ranking: Reg. U. (N), No. 111
Website: www.lesley.edu
Admissions email: lcadmissions@lesley.edu
Private; founded 1909
Freshman admissions: selective; 2013-2014: N/A applied, N/A accepted. Either SAT or ACT required. SAT 25/75 percentile: 970-1180. High school rank: N/A
Early decision deadline: N/A, notification date: N/A
Early action deadline: 12/1, notification date: 12/31
Application deadline (fall): rolling
Undergraduate student body: N/A full time, N/A part time; N/A male, N/A female; N/A American Indian, N/A Asian, N/A black, N/A Hispanic, N/A multiracial, N/A Pacific Islander, N/A white, N/A international
Most popular majors: 8% Business, Management, Marketing, and Related Support Services, 14% Education, 10% English Language and Literature/Letters, 23% Psychology, 24% Visual and Performing Arts
Expenses: 2014-2015: $24,560; room/board: $15,000
Financial aid: (617) 349-8581; 71% of undergrads determined to have financial need; average aid package $20,133

Massachusetts College of Art and Design

Boston MA
(617) 879-7222
U.S. News ranking: Arts, unranked
Website: www.massart.edu
Admissions email: admissions@massart.edu
Public; founded 1873
Freshman admissions: N/A; 2013-2014: 1,403 applied, 980 accepted. Either SAT or ACT required. SAT 25/75 percentile: N/A. High school rank: N/A
Early decision deadline: N/A, notification date: N/A
Early action deadline: 12/1, notification date: 1/5
Application deadline (fall): 2/1
Undergraduate student body: 1,677 full time, 443 part time; 30% male, 70% female; 0% American Indian, 6% Asian, 3% black, 7% Hispanic, 2% multiracial, 0% Pacific Islander, 69% white, 2% international; 69% from in state; 38% live on campus; N/A of students in fraternities, N/A in sororities
Most popular majors: Information not available
Expenses: 2014-2015: $11,225 in state, $29,925 out of state; room/board: $13,000

Financial aid: (617) 879-7850; 62% of undergrads determined to have financial need; average aid package $10,452

Massachusetts College of Liberal Arts

North Adams MA
(413) 662-5410
U.S. News ranking: Nat. Lib. Arts, No. 165
Website: www.mcla.edu
Admissions email: admissions@mcla.edu
Public; founded 1894
Freshman admissions: selective; 2013-2014: 1,786 applied, 1,200 accepted. Either SAT or ACT required. SAT 25/75 percentile: 910-1150. High school rank: 25% in top tenth, 58% in top quarter, 83% in top half
Early decision deadline: N/A, notification date: N/A
Early action deadline: 12/1, notification date: 12/15
Application deadline (fall): rolling
Undergraduate student body: 1,353 full time, 185 part time; 40% male, 60% female; 0% American Indian, 1% Asian, 10% black, 7% Hispanic, 2% multiracial, 0% Pacific Islander, 76% white, 0% international; 76% from in state; 67% live on campus; N/A of students in fraternities, N/A in sororities
Most popular majors: 18% Business, Management, Marketing, and Related Support Services, 14% English Language and Literature/Letters, 10% Multi/Interdisciplinary Studies, 9% Psychology, 16% Social Sciences
Expenses: 2014-2015: $8,975 in state, $17,920 out of state; room/board: $9,638
Financial aid: (413) 662-5219; 76% of undergrads determined to have financial need; average aid package $14,468

Massachusetts Institute of Technology

Cambridge MA
(617) 253-3400
U.S. News ranking: Nat. U., No. 7
Website: web.mit.edu/
Admissions email: admissions@mit.edu
Private; founded 1861
Freshman admissions: most selective; 2013-2014: 18,989 applied, 1,548 accepted. Either SAT or ACT required. SAT 25/75 percentile: 1430-1570. High school rank: 99% in top tenth, 100% in top quarter, 100% in top half
Early decision deadline: N/A, notification date: N/A
Early action deadline: 11/1, notification date: 12/20
Application deadline (fall): 1/1
Undergraduate student body: 4,499 full time, 29 part time; 55% male, 45% female; 0% American Indian, 24% Asian, 5% black, 16% Hispanic, 5% multiracial, 0% Pacific Islander, 37% white, 10% international; 9% from in state; 88% live on campus; 49% of students in fraternities, 32% in sororities

---

Most popular majors: 9% Biological and Biomedical Sciences, 18% Computer Science, 44% Engineering, 6% Mathematics, General, 10% Physical Sciences
Expenses: 2014-2015: $45,016; room/board: $13,224
Financial aid: (617) 253-4971; 58% of undergrads determined to have financial need; average aid package $41,325

Massachusetts Maritime Academy
Buzzards Bay MA
(800) 544-3411
U.S. News ranking: Reg. Coll. (N), No. 7
Website: www.maritime.edu
Admissions email: admissions@maritime.edu
Public; founded 1891
Freshman admissions: selective; 2013-2014: 957 applied, 561 accepted. Either SAT or ACT required. SAT 25/75 percentile: 980-1170. High school rank: N/A
Early decision deadline: N/A, notification date: N/A
Early action deadline: 11/1, notification date: 12/15
Application deadline (fall): rolling
Undergraduate student body: 1,333 full time, 43 part time; 88% male, 12% female; 2% American Indian, 3% Asian, 2% black, 1% Hispanic, 0% multiracial, 0% Pacific Islander, 90% white, 1% international; 75% from in state; 95% live on campus; 0% of students in fraternities, 0% in sororities
Most popular majors: 10% Environmental Science, 11% Homeland Security, Law Enforcement, Firefighting and Related Protective Services, Other, 16% Marine Science/Merchant Marine Officer, 46% Naval Architecture and Marine Engineering
Expenses: 2014-2015: $7,203 in state, $22,109 out of state; room/board: $11,120
Financial aid: (508) 830-5087; 56% of undergrads determined to have financial need; average aid package $13,343

Merrimack College
North Andover MA
(978) 837-5100
U.S. News ranking: Reg. Coll. (N), No. 9
Website: www.merrimack.edu
Admissions email: Admission@Merrimack.edu
Private; founded 1947
Affiliation: Roman Catholic
Freshman admissions: selective; 2013-2014: 6,314 applied, 4,963 accepted. Neither SAT nor ACT required. SAT 25/75 percentile: 920-1130. High school rank: 11% in top tenth, 34% in top quarter, 69% in top half
Early decision deadline: 11/15, notification date: 12/1
Early action deadline: 11/15, notification date: 12/1
Application deadline (fall): 2/15
Undergraduate student body: 2,604 full time, 148 part time; 51% male, 49% female; 0% American Indian, 2% Asian, 3% black, 6% Hispanic, 1% multiracial, 0% Pacific Islander, 67% white, 6% international; 73% from in

state; 72% live on campus; 1% of students in fraternities, 4% in sororities
Most popular majors: 32% Business, Management, Marketing, and Related Support Services, 6% Communication, Journalism, and Related Programs, 9% Health Professions and Related Programs, 6% Homeland Security, Law Enforcement, Firefighting and Related Protective Services, 8% Social Sciences
Expenses: 2014-2015: $36,215; room/board: $13,255
Financial aid: (978) 837-5196; 71% of undergrads determined to have financial need; average aid package $21,798

Montserrat College of Art[1]
Beverly MA
(978) 921-4242
U.S. News ranking: Arts, unranked
Website: www.montserrat.edu
Admissions email: admissions@montserrat.edu
Private
Application deadline (fall): N/A
Undergraduate student body: N/A full time, N/A part time
Expenses: 2013-2014: $27,770; room/board: N/A
Financial aid: (978) 921-4242

Mount Holyoke College
South Hadley MA
(413) 538-2023
U.S. News ranking: Nat. Lib. Arts, No. 41
Website: www.mtholyoke.edu
Admissions email: admission@mtholyoke.edu
Private; founded 1837
Freshman admissions: more selective; 2013-2014: 3,732 applied, 1,747 accepted. Neither SAT nor ACT required. SAT 25/75 percentile: 1220-1430. High school rank: 57% in top tenth, 84% in top quarter, 97% in top half
Early decision deadline: 11/15, notification date: 1/1
Early action deadline: N/A, notification date: N/A
Application deadline (fall): 1/15
Undergraduate student body: 2,151 full time, 32 part time; 0% male, 100% female; 0% American Indian, 9% Asian, 6% black, 8% Hispanic, 3% multiracial, 0% Pacific Islander, 47% white, 25% international; 23% from in state; 95% live on campus; 0% of students in fraternities, 0% in sororities
Most popular majors: 9% Biology/Biological Sciences, General, 7% Economics, General, 10% English Language and Literature, General, 7% International Relations and Affairs, 10% Psychology, General
Expenses: 2014-2015: $42,656; room/board: $12,490
Financial aid: (413) 538-2291; 68% of undergrads determined to have financial need; average aid package $35,454

Mount Ida College
Newton MA
(617) 928-4535
U.S. News ranking: Reg. Coll. (N), No. 40
Website: www.mountida.edu

Admissions email: admissions@mountida.edu
Private; founded 1899
Freshman admissions: least selective; 2013-2014: 1,770 applied, 1,201 accepted. Either SAT or ACT required. SAT 25/75 percentile: 790-980. High school rank: N/A
Early decision deadline: N/A, notification date: N/A
Early action deadline: N/A, notification date: N/A
Application deadline (fall): rolling
Undergraduate student body: 1,167 full time, 101 part time; 34% male, 66% female; 0% American Indian, 2% Asian, 12% black, 11% Hispanic, 3% multiracial, 0% Pacific Islander, 59% white, 5% international; 37% from in state; 60% live on campus; 0% of students in fraternities, 0% in sororities
Most popular majors: 12% Business Administration and Management, General, 12% Dental Hygiene/Hygienist, 7% Fashion Merchandising, 7% Funeral Service and Mortuary Science, General, 18% Veterinary/Animal Health Technology/Technician and Veterinary Assistant
Expenses: 2014-2015: $30,447; room/board: $12,500
Financial aid: (617) 928-4785; 82% of undergrads determined to have financial need; average aid package $19,475

National Graduate School of Quality Management[1]
Falmouth MA
(800) 838-2580
U.S. News ranking: Business, unranked
Website: www.ngs.edu
Admissions email: N/A
Private
Application deadline (fall): N/A
Undergraduate student body: N/A full time, N/A part time
Expenses: N/A
Financial aid: (800) 838-2580

Newbury College[1]
Brookline MA
(617) 730-7007
U.S. News ranking: Reg. Coll. (N), unranked
Website: www.newbury.edu/
Admissions email: info@newbury.edu
Private
Application deadline (fall): N/A
Undergraduate student body: N/A full time, N/A part time
Expenses: 2014-2015: $29,930; room/board: $13,340
Financial aid: (617) 730-7100; 91% of undergrads determined to have financial need; average aid package $12,503

New England Conservatory of Music
Boston MA
(617) 585-1101
U.S. News ranking: Arts, unranked
Website: www.newenglandconservatory.edu
Admissions email: admission@newenglandconservatory.edu
Private; founded 1867

Freshman admissions: N/A; 2013-2014: 1,253 applied, 348 accepted. Neither SAT nor ACT required. SAT 25/75 percentile: N/A. High school rank: N/A
Early decision deadline: N/A, notification date: N/A
Early action deadline: N/A, notification date: N/A
Application deadline (fall): 12/1
Undergraduate student body: 396 full time, 35 part time; 59% male, 41% female; 0% American Indian, 12% Asian, 5% black, 2% Hispanic, 4% multiracial, 0% Pacific Islander, 45% white, 29% international
Most popular majors: Information not available
Expenses: 2014-2015: $41,405; room/board: $12,850
Financial aid: (617) 585-1110; 48% of undergrads determined to have financial need; average aid package $23,718

New England Institute of Art[1]
Brookline MA
(800) 903-4425
U.S. News ranking: Arts, unranked
Website: www.artinstitutes.edu/boston/
Admissions email: N/A
For-profit
Application deadline (fall): N/A
Undergraduate student body: N/A full time, N/A part time
Expenses: 2013-2014: $18,760; room/board: $15,252
Financial aid: N/A

Nichols College
Dudley MA
(800) 470-3379
U.S. News ranking: Reg. Coll. (N), No. 40
Website: www.nichols.edu/
Admissions email: admissions@nichols.edu
Private; founded 1815
Freshman admissions: less selective; 2013-2014: 2,344 applied, 1,919 accepted. Neither SAT nor ACT required. SAT 25/75 percentile: 840-1030. High school rank: 9% in top tenth, 16% in top quarter, 48% in top half
Early decision deadline: N/A, notification date: N/A
Early action deadline: 12/1, notification date: N/A
Application deadline (fall): rolling
Undergraduate student body: 1,100 full time, 181 part time; 59% male, 41% female; 0% American Indian, 1% Asian, 6% black, 7% Hispanic, 3% multiracial, 0% Pacific Islander, 82% white, 1% international; 62% from in state; 80% live on campus; 0% of students in fraternities, 0% in sororities
Most popular majors: 12% Accounting, 8% Business Administration and Management, General, 33% Business/Commerce, General, 8% Criminal Justice/Law Enforcement Administration, 12% Sport and Fitness Administration/Management
Expenses: 2014-2015: $32,370; room/board: $12,235
Financial aid: (508) 213-2278; 86% of undergrads determined to have financial need; average aid package $25,024

Northeastern University
Boston MA
(617) 373-2200
U.S. News ranking: Nat. U., No. 42
Website: www.northeastern.edu/
Admissions email: admissions@neu.edu
Private; founded 1898
Freshman admissions: most selective; 2013-2014: 47,364 applied, 15,301 accepted. Either SAT or ACT required. SAT 25/75 percentile: 1300-1480. High school rank: 64% in top tenth, 91% in top quarter, 98% in top half
Early decision deadline: 11/1, notification date: 12/15
Early action deadline: 11/1, notification date: 12/31
Application deadline (fall): 1/1
Undergraduate student body: 13,204 full time, N/A part time; 49% male, 51% female; 0% American Indian, 10% Asian, 3% black, 7% Hispanic, 4% multiracial, 0% Pacific Islander, 50% white, 18% international; 33% from in state; N/A live on campus; 8% of students in fraternities, 12% in sororities
Most popular majors: 21% Business, Management, Marketing, and Related Support Services, 8% Communication, Journalism, and Related Programs, 12% Engineering, 13% Health Professions and Related Programs, 11% Social Sciences
Expenses: 2014-2015: $43,440; room/board: $14,570
Financial aid: (617) 373-3190; 39% of undergrads determined to have financial need; average aid package $24,099

Pine Manor College
Chestnut Hill MA
(617) 731-7104
U.S. News ranking: Nat. Lib. Arts, second tier
Website: www.pmc.edu
Admissions email: admission@pmc.edu
Private; founded 1911
Freshman admissions: least selective; 2013-2014: 535 applied, 343 accepted. Either SAT or ACT required. SAT 25/75 percentile: 660-860. High school rank: N/A
Early decision deadline: N/A, notification date: N/A
Early action deadline: N/A, notification date: N/A
Application deadline (fall): rolling
Undergraduate student body: 305 full time, 8 part time; 15% male, 85% female; 0% American Indian, 5% Asian, 20% black, 15% Hispanic, 12% multiracial, 0% Pacific Islander, 8% white, 29% international
Most popular majors: 22% Biology/Biological Sciences, General, 6% Communication and Media Studies, 17% Management Science, 20% Psychology, General, 18% Social Sciences, General
Expenses: 2014-2015: $26,180; room/board: $12,820
Financial aid: (617) 731-7129; 64% of undergrads determined to have financial need; average aid package $24,014

Salem State University
Salem MA
(978) 542-6200
U.S. News ranking: Reg. U. (N), second tier
Website: www.salemstate.edu
Admissions email: admissions@salemstate.edu
Public; founded 1854
Freshman admissions: less selective; 2013-2014: 5,216 applied, 3,739 accepted. Either SAT or ACT required. SAT 25/75 percentile: 890-1080. High school rank: N/A
Early decision deadline: N/A, notification date: N/A
Early action deadline: 11/15, notification date: 12/1
Application deadline (fall): rolling
Undergraduate student body: 5,834 full time, 1,830 part time; 39% male, 61% female; 0% American Indian, 3% Asian, 8% black, 11% Hispanic, 2% multiracial, 0% Pacific Islander, 70% white, 3% international; 97% from in state; 28% live on campus; N/A of students in fraternities, N/A in sororities
Most popular majors: 22% Business, Management, Marketing, and Related Support Services, 9% Education, 13% Health Professions and Related Programs, 9% Homeland Security, Law Enforcement, Firefighting and Related Protective Services, 8% Psychology
Expenses: 2013-2014: $8,130 in state, $14,270 out of state; room/board: $11,304
Financial aid: (978) 542-6139

Simmons College
Boston MA
(800) 345-8468
U.S. News ranking: Reg. U. (N), No. 16
Website: www.simmons.edu
Admissions email: ugadm@simmons.edu
Private; founded 1899
Freshman admissions: selective; 2013-2014: 4,239 applied, 2,076 accepted. Either SAT or ACT required. SAT 25/75 percentile: 1040-1250. High school rank: 26% in top tenth, 61% in top quarter, 90% in top half
Early decision deadline: N/A, notification date: N/A
Early action deadline: 11/1, notification date: 12/15
Application deadline (fall): 2/1
Undergraduate student body: 1,577 full time, 155 part time; 0% male, 100% female; 0% American Indian, 9% Asian, 6% black, 6% Hispanic, 3% multiracial, 0% Pacific Islander, 68% white, 3% international; 63% from in state; 58% live on campus; N/A of students in fraternities, 0% in sororities
Most popular majors: 9% Business, Management, Marketing, and Related Support Services, 8% Communication, Journalism, and Related Programs, 37% Health Services/Allied Health/Health Sciences, General, 9% Psychology, 9% Social Sciences, General
Expenses: 2014-2015: $36,230; room/board: $13,736

Smith College
Northampton MA
(413) 585-2500
U.S. News ranking: Nat. Lib. Arts, No. 19
Website: www.smith.edu
Admissions email: admission@smith.edu
Private; founded 1871
Freshman admissions: more selective; 2013-2014: 4,403 applied, 1,897 accepted. Neither SAT nor ACT required. SAT 25/75 percentile: 1220-1450. High school rank: 62% in top tenth, 89% in top quarter, 99% in top half
Early decision deadline: 11/15, notification date: 12/15
Early action deadline: N/A, notification date: N/A
Application deadline (fall): 1/15
Undergraduate student body: 2,585 full time, 21 part time; 0% male, 100% female; 0% American Indian, 13% Asian, 5% black, 10% Hispanic, 5% multiracial, 0% Pacific Islander, 46% white, 13% international; 23% from in state; 95% live on campus; 0% of students in fraternities, 0% in sororities
Most popular majors: 9% Area, Ethnic, Cultural, Gender, and Group Studies, 10% Foreign Languages, Literatures, and Linguistics, 10% Psychology, 23% Social Sciences, 10% Visual and Performing Arts
Expenses: 2014-2015: $44,724; room/board: $14,950
Financial aid: (413) 585-2530; 63% of undergrads determined to have financial need; average aid package $39,958

Springfield College
Springfield MA
(413) 748-3136
U.S. News ranking: Reg. U. (N), No. 31
Website: www.springfieldcollege.edu
Admissions email: admissions@springfiledcollege.edu
Private; founded 1885
Freshman admissions: selective; 2013-2014: 2,231 applied, 1,560 accepted. Either SAT or ACT required. SAT 25/75 percentile: 920-1130. High school rank: 13% in top tenth, 35% in top quarter, 69% in top half
Early decision deadline: 12/1, notification date: 2/1
Early action deadline: N/A, notification date: N/A
Application deadline (fall): 4/1
Undergraduate student body: 2,142 full time, 62 part time; 52% male, 48% female; 1% American Indian, 1% Asian, 5% black, 5% Hispanic, 1% multiracial, 0% Pacific Islander, 82% white, 1% international; 40% from in state; 85% live on campus; N/A of students in fraternities, N/A in sororities
Most popular majors: 6% Business, Management, Marketing, and Related Support Services, 9% Education, 33% Health Professions and Related Programs, 6% Homeland Security, Law

Enforcement, Firefighting and Related Protective Services, 23% Parks, Recreation, Leisure, and Fitness Studies
Expenses: 2014-2015: $33,455; room/board: $11,210
Financial aid: (413) 748-3108; 83% of undergrads determined to have financial need; average aid package $23,220

Stonehill College
Easton MA
(508) 565-1373
U.S. News ranking: Nat. Lib. Arts, No. 105
Website: www.stonehill.edu
Admissions email: admission@stonehill.edu
Private; founded 1948
Affiliation: Roman Catholic
Freshman admissions: more selective; 2013-2014: 6,547 applied, 4,643 accepted. Neither SAT nor ACT required. SAT 25/75 percentile: 1030-1230. High school rank: 31% in top tenth, 69% in top quarter, 95% in top half
Early decision deadline: 12/1, notification date: 12/31
Early action deadline: 11/1, notification date: 12/31
Application deadline (fall): 1/15
Undergraduate student body: 2,458 full time, 23 part time; 38% male, 62% female; 0% American Indian, 2% Asian, 3% black, 4% Hispanic, 2% multiracial, 0% Pacific Islander, 85% white, 1% international; 55% from in state; 90% live on campus; N/A of students in fraternities, N/A in sororities
Most popular majors: 10% Biological and Biomedical Sciences, 19% Business, Management, Marketing, and Related Support Services, 7% Communication, Journalism, and Related Programs, 11% Psychology, 19% Social Sciences
Expenses: 2014-2015: $37,426; room/board: $14,290
Financial aid: (508) 565-1088; 59% of undergrads determined to have financial need; average aid package $27,915

Suffolk University
Boston MA
(617) 573-8460
U.S. News ranking: Reg. U. (N), No. 60
Website: www.suffolk.edu
Admissions email: admission@suffolk.edu
Private; founded 1906
Freshman admissions: selective; 2013-2014: 9,275 applied, 7,652 accepted. Either SAT or ACT required. SAT 25/75 percentile: 890-1130. High school rank: 13% in top tenth, 42% in top quarter, 79% in top half
Early decision deadline: N/A, notification date: N/A
Early action deadline: 11/15, notification date: 11/20
Application deadline (fall): 2/15
Undergraduate student body: 5,356 full time, 423 part time; 45% male, 55% female; 0% American Indian, 7% Asian, 5% black, 11% Hispanic, 1% multiracial, 0% Pacific Islander, 41% white, 19% international; 69% from in state; 21% live on campus; N/A of students in fraternities, N/A in sororities

Most popular majors: 39% Business, Management, Marketing, and Related Support Services, 16% Communication, Journalism, and Related Programs, 6% Psychology, 15% Social Sciences, 6% Visual and Performing Arts
Expenses: 2014-2015: $32,660; room/board: $14,638
Financial aid: (617) 573-8470; 64% of undergrads determined to have financial need; average aid package $23,254

Tufts University
Medford MA
(617) 627-3170
U.S. News ranking: Nat. U., No. 27
Website: www.tufts.edu
Admissions email: admissions.inquiry@ase.tufts.edu
Private; founded 1852
Freshman admissions: most selective; 2013-2014: 18,406 applied, 3,469 accepted. Either SAT or ACT required. SAT 25/75 percentile: 1370-1520. High school rank: 91% in top tenth, 99% in top quarter, 100% in top half
Early decision deadline: 11/1, notification date: 12/15
Early action deadline: N/A, notification date: N/A
Application deadline (fall): 1/1
Undergraduate student body: 5,138 full time, 42 part time; 49% male, 51% female; 0% American Indian, 11% Asian, 4% black, 6% Hispanic, 4% multiracial, 0% Pacific Islander, 56% white, 8% international; 23% from in state; 63% live on campus; 14% of students in fraternities, 19% in sororities
Most popular majors: 7% Art/Art Studies, General, 6% Biology/Biological Sciences, General, 9% Economics, General, 6% English Language and Literature, General, 15% International Relations and Affairs
Expenses: 2014-2015: $48,643; room/board: $12,634
Financial aid: (617) 627-2000; 39% of undergrads determined to have financial need; average aid package $38,008

University of Massachusetts–Amherst
Amherst MA
(413) 545-0222
U.S. News ranking: Nat. U., No. 76
Website: www.umass.edu
Admissions email: mail@admissions.umass.edu
Public; founded 1863
Freshman admissions: more selective; 2013-2014: 35,868 applied, 22,556 accepted. Either SAT or ACT required. SAT 25/75 percentile: 1110-1310. High school rank: 28% in top tenth, 69% in top quarter, 97% in top half
Early decision deadline: N/A, notification date: N/A
Early action deadline: 11/1, notification date: 12/31
Application deadline (fall): 1/15
Undergraduate student body: 20,505 full time, 1,629 part time; 51% male, 49% female; 0% American Indian, 8% Asian, 4% black, 5% Hispanic, 2%

multiracial, 0% Pacific Islander, 67% white, 2% international; 78% from in state; 64% live on campus; 7% of students in fraternities, 6% in sororities
Most popular majors: 4% Accounting, 4% Biology/Biological Sciences, General, 3% Political Science and Government, General, 8% Psychology, General, 5% Speech Communication and Rhetoric
Expenses: 2014-2015: $13,258 in state, $28,813 out of state; room/board: $11,457
Financial aid: (413) 545-0801; 60% of undergrads determined to have financial need; average aid package $15,543

University of Massachusetts–Boston
Boston MA
(617) 287-6000
U.S. News ranking: Nat. U., second tier
Website: www.umb.edu
Admissions email: enrollment.info@umb.edu
Public; founded 1964
Freshman admissions: selective; 2013-2014: 8,170 applied, 5,709 accepted. SAT required. SAT 25/75 percentile: 950-1160. High school rank: N/A
Early decision deadline: N/A, notification date: N/A
Early action deadline: N/A, notification date: N/A
Application deadline (fall): rolling
Undergraduate student body: 8,759 full time, 3,607 part time; 44% male, 56% female; 0% American Indian, 12% Asian, 16% black, 12% Hispanic, 2% multiracial, 0% Pacific Islander, 42% white, 10% international; 95% from in state; N/A live on campus; N/A of students in fraternities, N/A in sororities
Most popular majors: 7% Biological and Biomedical Sciences, 20% Business, Management, Marketing, and Related Support Services, 18% Health Professions and Related Programs, 12% Psychology, 12% Social Sciences
Expenses: 2014-2015: $13,680 in state, $22,218 out of state; room/board: N/A
Financial aid: (617) 287-6300; 68% of undergrads determined to have financial need; average aid package $15,265

University of Massachusetts–Dartmouth
North Dartmouth MA
(508) 999-8605
U.S. News ranking: Reg. U. (N), No. 87
Website: www.umassd.edu
Admissions email: admissions@umassd.edu
Public; founded 1895
Freshman admissions: selective; 2013-2014: 8,119 applied, 6,094 accepted. Either SAT or ACT required. SAT 25/75 percentile: 980-1180. High school rank: 21% in top tenth, 46% in top quarter, 80% in top half
Early decision deadline: N/A, notification date: N/A
Early action deadline: 11/15, notification date: 12/15
Application deadline (fall): rolling

Undergraduate student body: 6,373 full time, 1,064 part time; 52% male, 48% female; 0% American Indian, 3% Asian, 12% black, 7% Hispanic, 4% multiracial, 0% Pacific Islander, 69% white, 1% international; 95% from in state; 56% live on campus; 1% of students in fraternities, 1% in sororities
Most popular majors: 30% Business, Management, Marketing, and Related Support Services, 10% Engineering, 14% Health Professions and Related Programs, 10% Social Sciences, 8% Visual and Performing Arts
Expenses: 2014-2015: $11,681 in state, $18,363 out of state; room/board: $11,069
Financial aid: (508) 999-8632; 72% of undergrads determined to have financial need; average aid package $16,048

University of Massachusetts–Lowell

Lowell MA
(978) 934-3931
U.S. News ranking: Nat. U., No. 156
Website: www.uml.edu
Admissions email: admissions@uml.edu
Public; founded 1894
Freshman admissions: selective; 2013-2014: 9,110 applied, 5,824 accepted. Either SAT or ACT required. SAT 25/75 percentile: 1030-1230. High school rank: 22% in top tenth, 51% in top quarter, 85% in top half
Early decision deadline: N/A, notification date: N/A
Early action deadline: 11/15, notification date: 12/20
Application deadline (fall): 2/15
Undergraduate student body: 9,034 full time, 3,700 part time; 61% male, 39% female; 0% American Indian, 9% Asian, 6% black, 9% Hispanic, 2% multiracial, 0% Pacific Islander, 66% white, 2% international; 91% from in state; 36% live on campus; N/A of students in fraternities, N/A in sororities
Most popular majors: 17% Business, Management, Marketing, and Related Support Services, 10% Computer and Information Sciences and Support Services, 14% Engineering, 11% Health Professions and Related Programs, 12% Homeland Security, Law Enforcement, Firefighting and Related Protective Services
Expenses: 2014-2015: $12,447 in state, $19,560 out of state; room/board: $11,278
Financial aid: (978) 934-4226; 63% of undergrads determined to have financial need; average aid package $14,730

Wellesley College

Wellesley MA
(781) 283-2270
U.S. News ranking: Nat. Lib. Arts, No. 4
Website: www.wellesley.edu
Admissions email: admission@wellesley.edu
Private; founded 1870

Freshman admissions: most selective; 2013-2014: 4,765 applied, 1,387 accepted. Either SAT or ACT required. SAT 25/75 percentile: 1310-1510. High school rank: 83% in top tenth, 99% in top quarter, 100% in top half
Early decision deadline: 11/1, notification date: 12/15
Early action deadline: N/A, notification date: N/A
Application deadline (fall): 1/15
Undergraduate student body: 2,344 full time, 130 part time; 2% male, 98% female; 0% American Indian, 23% Asian, 6% black, 10% Hispanic, 6% multiracial, 0% Pacific Islander, 43% white, 11% international; 15% from in state; 97% live on campus; N/A of students in fraternities, N/A in sororities
Most popular majors: 6% Biology/Biological Sciences, General, 18% Economics, General, 8% English Language and Literature, General, 6% Political Science and Government, General, 10% Psychology, General
Expenses: 2014-2015: $45,078; room/board: $13,960
Financial aid: (781) 283-2360; 61% of undergrads determined to have financial need; average aid package $41,847

Wentworth Institute of Technology

Boston MA
(617) 989-4000
U.S. News ranking: Reg. Coll. (N), No. 12
Website: www.wit.edu
Admissions email: admissions@wit.edu
Private; founded 1904
Freshman admissions: selective; 2013-2014: 6,124 applied, 3,519 accepted. Either SAT or ACT required. SAT 25/75 percentile: 1010-1210. High school rank: 12% in top tenth, 40% in top quarter, 76% in top half
Early decision deadline: N/A, notification date: N/A
Early action deadline: N/A, notification date: N/A
Application deadline (fall): rolling
Undergraduate student body: 3,634 full time, 358 part time; 82% male, 18% female; 0% American Indian, 6% Asian, 5% black, 4% Hispanic, 3% multiracial, 0% Pacific Islander, 60% white, 6% international; 63% from in state; 50% live on campus; 0% of students in fraternities, 0% in sororities
Most popular majors: 22% Architecture, 27% Business, Management, Marketing, and Related Support Services, 9% Computer and Information Sciences and Support Services, 9% Construction Trades, 32% Engineering Technologies and Engineering-Related Fields
Expenses: 2014-2015: $29,320; room/board: $12,840
Financial aid: (617) 989-4020; 73% of undergrads determined to have financial need; average aid package $20,610

Western New England University

Springfield MA
(413) 782-1321
U.S. News ranking: Reg. U. (N), No. 65
Website: www.wne.edu
Admissions email: ugradmis@wne.edu
Private; founded 1919
Freshman admissions: selective; 2013-2014: 5,988 applied, 4,881 accepted. Either SAT or ACT required. SAT 25/75 percentile: 960-1180. High school rank: 17% in top tenth, 44% in top quarter, 74% in top half
Early decision deadline: N/A, notification date: N/A
Early action deadline: N/A, notification date: N/A
Application deadline (fall): rolling
Undergraduate student body: 2,498 full time, 169 part time; 60% male, 40% female; 0% American Indian, 3% Asian, 5% black, 8% Hispanic, 2% multiracial, 0% Pacific Islander, 77% white, 2% international; 47% from in state; 65% live on campus; 0% of students in fraternities, 0% in sororities
Most popular majors: 31% Business, Management, Marketing, and Related Support Services, 15% Engineering, 8% Homeland Security, Law Enforcement, Firefighting and Related Protective Services, 8% Psychology, General, 7% Sport and Fitness Administration/Management
Expenses: 2014-2015: $33,466; room/board: $12,688
Financial aid: (413) 796-2080; 79% of undergrads determined to have financial need; average aid package $23,023

Westfield State University

Westfield MA
(413) 572-5218
U.S. News ranking: Reg. U. (N), No. 115
Website: www.westfield.ma.edu
Admissions email: admissions@westfield.ma.edu
Public; founded 1838
Freshman admissions: less selective; 2013-2014: 5,145 applied, 3,853 accepted. Either SAT or ACT required. SAT 25/75 percentile: 910-1090. High school rank: 9% in top tenth, 22% in top quarter, 62% in top half
Early decision deadline: N/A, notification date: N/A
Early action deadline: N/A, notification date: N/A
Application deadline (fall): 3/1
Undergraduate student body: 4,999 full time, 692 part time; 48% male, 52% female; 0% American Indian, 1% Asian, 4% black, 7% Hispanic, 4% multiracial, 0% Pacific Islander, 80% white, 0% international; 92% from in state; 55% live on campus; 0% of students in fraternities, 0% in sororities
Most popular majors: 12% Business, Management, Marketing, and Related Support Services, 11% Education, 15% Homeland Security, Law Enforcement, Firefighting and Related Protective Services, 15%

Liberal Arts and Sciences, General Studies and Humanities, 7% Psychology
Expenses: 2013-2014: $8,697 in state, $14,777 out of state; room/board: $9,795
Financial aid: (413) 572-5218

Wheaton College

Norton MA
(508) 286-8251
U.S. News ranking: Nat. Lib. Arts, No. 69
Website: www.wheatoncollege.edu
Admissions email: admission@wheatoncollege.edu
Private; founded 1834
Freshman admissions: more selective; 2013-2014: 3,433 applied, 2,537 accepted. Neither SAT nor ACT required. SAT 25/75 percentile: 1110-1340. High school rank: 37% in top tenth, 70% in top quarter, 93% in top half
Early decision deadline: 11/15, notification date: 12/15
Early action deadline: 11/15, notification date: 1/15
Application deadline (fall): 1/15
Undergraduate student body: 1,647 full time, 9 part time; 35% male, 65% female; 0% American Indian, 4% Asian, 5% black, 7% Hispanic, 3% multiracial, 0% Pacific Islander, 69% white, 9% international; 40% from in state; 97% live on campus; 0% of students in fraternities, 0% in sororities
Most popular majors: 6% Biology/Biological Sciences, General, 8% Economics, General, 8% English Language and Literature, General, 6% Neuroscience, 14% Psychology, General
Expenses: 2014-2015: $46,423; room/board: $11,840
Financial aid: (508) 286-8232; 69% of undergrads determined to have financial need; average aid package $35,559

Wheelock College

Boston MA
(617) 879-2206
U.S. News ranking: Reg. U. (N), No. 79
Website: www.wheelock.edu
Admissions email: undergrad@wheelock.edu
Private; founded 1888
Freshman admissions: selective; 2013-2014: 1,570 applied, 1,149 accepted. Either SAT or ACT required. SAT 25/75 percentile: 890-1090. High school rank: 12% in top tenth, 38% in top quarter, 64% in top half
Early decision deadline: N/A, notification date: N/A
Early action deadline: 12/1, notification date: 12/20
Application deadline (fall): 5/1
Undergraduate student body: 809 full time, 71 part time; 12% male, 88% female; 0% American Indian, 3% Asian, 11% black, 12% Hispanic, 3% multiracial, 0% Pacific Islander, 58% white, 2% international; 66% from in state; 63% live on campus; 0% of students in fraternities, 0% in sororities
Most popular majors: 38% Education, 21% Family and Consumer Sciences/Human Sciences, 4% Liberal Arts and Sciences, General Studies and

Humanities, 7% Psychology, 19% Public Administration and Social Service Professions
Expenses: 2014-2015: $32,830; room/board: $13,600
Financial aid: (617) 879-2206; 83% of undergrads determined to have financial need; average aid package $21,783

Williams College

Williamstown MA
(413) 597-2211
U.S. News ranking: Nat. Lib. Arts, No. 1
Website: www.williams.edu
Admissions email: admission@williams.edu
Private; founded 1793
Freshman admissions: most selective; 2013-2014: 6,853 applied, 1,200 accepted. Either SAT or ACT required. SAT 25/75 percentile: 1330-1540. High school rank: 88% in top tenth, 98% in top quarter, 100% in top half
Early decision deadline: 11/10, notification date: 12/15
Early action deadline: N/A, notification date: N/A
Application deadline (fall): 1/1
Undergraduate student body: 2,045 full time, 32 part time; 49% male, 51% female; 0% American Indian, 11% Asian, 8% black, 12% Hispanic, 6% multiracial, 0% Pacific Islander, 56% white, 7% international; 13% from in state; 93% live on campus; N/A of students in fraternities, N/A in sororities
Most popular majors: 12% Economics, General, 13% English Language and Literature, General, 13% History, General, 13% Mathematics, General, 12% Political Science and Government, General
Expenses: 2014-2015: $48,310; room/board: $12,760
Financial aid: (413) 597-4181; 52% of undergrads determined to have financial need; average aid package $44,933

Worcester Polytechnic Institute

Worcester MA
(508) 831-5286
U.S. News ranking: Nat. U., No. 68
Website: admissions.wpi.edu
Admissions email: admissions@wpi.edu
Private; founded 1865
Freshman admissions: more selective; 2013-2014: 8,578 applied, 4,425 accepted. Neither SAT nor ACT required. SAT 25/75 percentile: 1220-1410. High school rank: 64% in top tenth, 91% in top quarter, 99% in top half
Early decision deadline: N/A, notification date: N/A
Early action deadline: 1/1, notification date: 2/10
Application deadline (fall): 2/1
Undergraduate student body: 3,959 full time, 175 part time; 67% male, 33% female; 0% American Indian, 5% Asian, 3% black, 7% Hispanic, 3% multiracial, 0% Pacific Islander, 65% white, 13% international; 45% from in state; 49% live on campus; 29% of students in fraternities, 41% in sororities

Most popular majors: 10% Bioengineering and Biomedical Engineering, 8% Chemical Engineering, 7% Civil Engineering, General, 9% Electrical and Electronics Engineering, 20% Mechanical Engineering
Expenses: 2013-2014: $42,778; room/board: $13,082
Financial aid: (508) 831-5469

Worcester State University

Worcester MA
(508) 929-8040
U.S. News ranking: Reg. U. (N), No. 125
Website: www.worcester.edu
Admissions email: admissions@worcester.edu
Public; founded 1874
Freshman admissions: selective; 2013-2014: 4,149 applied, 2,515 accepted. Either SAT or ACT required. SAT 25/75 percentile: 920-1110. High school rank: N/A
Early decision deadline: N/A, notification date: N/A
Early action deadline: N/A, notification date: N/A
Application deadline (fall): 5/1
Undergraduate student body: 4,115 full time, 1,441 part time; 40% male, 60% female; 1% American Indian, 4% Asian, 6% black, 8% Hispanic, 2% multiracial, 0% Pacific Islander, 74% white, 1% international; 97% from in state; 22% live on campus; 0% of students in fraternities, 0% in sororities
Most popular majors: 8% Biological and Biomedical Sciences, 17% Business, Management, Marketing, and Related Support Services, 19% Health Professions and Related Programs, 9% Homeland Security, Law Enforcement, Firefighting and Related Protective Services, 12% Psychology
Expenses: 2014-2015: $8,557 in state, $14,637 out of state; room/board: $11,255
Financial aid: (508) 929-8056; 60% of undergrads determined to have financial need; average aid package $11,078

MICHIGAN

Adrian College

Adrian MI
(800) 877-2246
U.S. News ranking: Reg. Coll. (Mid. W), No. 22
Website: www.adrian.edu
Admissions email: admissions@adrian.edu
Private; founded 1859
Affiliation: The United Methodist Church
Freshman admissions: selective; 2013-2014: 4,675 applied, 2,631 accepted. Either SAT or ACT required. ACT 25/75 percentile: 19-24. High school rank: N/A
Early decision deadline: N/A, notification date: N/A
Early action deadline: N/A, notification date: N/A
Application deadline (fall): rolling
Undergraduate student body: 1,582 full time, 67 part time; 51% male, 49% female; 0% American Indian, 0% Asian, 9% black, 2%

Hispanic, 4% multiracial, 0% Pacific Islander, 80% white, 0% international; 79% from in state; 88% live on campus; 18% of students in fraternities, 19% in sororities
Most popular majors: 11% Biological and Biomedical Sciences, 25% Business, Management, Marketing, and Related Support Services, 7% Education, 6% Homeland Security, Law Enforcement, Firefighting and Related Protective Services, 10% Parks, Recreation, Leisure, and Fitness Studies
Expenses: 2014-2015: $32,660; room/board: $9,740
Financial aid: (517) 264-3107; 87% of undergrads determined to have financial need; average aid package $25,978

Albion College

Albion MI
(800) 858-6770
U.S. News ranking: Nat. Lib. Arts, No. 99
Website: albion.edu/
Admissions email: admission@albion.edu
Private; founded 1835
Affiliation: United Methodist
Freshman admissions: more selective; 2013-2014: 4,430 applied, 2,498 accepted. Either SAT or ACT required. ACT 25/75 percentile: 22-28. High school rank: 21% in top tenth, 52% in top quarter, 84% in top half
Early decision deadline: N/A, notification date: N/A
Early action deadline: 12/1, notification date: 1/15
Application deadline (fall): rolling
Undergraduate student body: 1,272 full time, 35 part time; 51% male, 49% female; 0% American Indian, 2% Asian, 3% black, 3% Hispanic, 3% multiracial, 0% Pacific Islander, 82% white, 3% international; 91% from in state; 89% live on campus; 53% of students in fraternities, 42% in sororities
Most popular majors: 11% Biology/Biological Sciences, General, 11% Economics, General, 5% History, General, 5% Kinesiology and Exercise Science, 15% Psychology, General
Expenses: 2014-2015: $37,300; room/board: $10,550
Financial aid: (517) 629-0440; 71% of undergrads determined to have financial need; average aid package $27,997

Alma College

Alma MI
(800) 321-2562
U.S. News ranking: Nat. Lib. Arts, No. 139
Website: www.alma.edu
Admissions email: admissions@alma.edu
Private; founded 1886
Affiliation: Presbyterian
Freshman admissions: selective; 2013-2014: 2,554 applied, 1,772 accepted. Either SAT or ACT required. ACT 25/75 percentile: 22-27. High school rank: 27% in top tenth, 53% in top quarter, 84% in top half
Early decision deadline: N/A, notification date: N/A
Early action deadline: N/A, notification date: N/A

Application deadline (fall): rolling
Undergraduate student body: 1,378 full time, 41 part time; 45% male, 55% female; 1% American Indian, 2% Asian, 2% black, 3% Hispanic, 2% multiracial, 0% Pacific Islander, 86% white, 0% international; 92% from in state; 90% live on campus; 24% of students in fraternities, 30% in sororities
Most popular majors: 9% Biology, General, 19% Business Administration, Management and Operations, 13% Health and Physical Education/Fitness, 8% Psychology, General, 11% Teacher Education and Professional Development, Specific Levels and Methods
Expenses: 2014-2015: $34,220; room/board: $9,490
Financial aid: (989) 463-7347; 82% of undergrads determined to have financial need; average aid package $24,779

Andrews University

Berrien Springs MI
(800) 253-2874
U.S. News ranking: Nat. U., No. 168
Website: www.andrews.edu
Admissions email: enroll@andrews.edu
Private; founded 1874
Affiliation: Seventh-day Adventist
Freshman admissions: more selective; 2013-2014: 2,480 applied, 957 accepted. Either SAT or ACT required. ACT 25/75 percentile: 20-27. High school rank: 22% in top tenth, 46% in top quarter, 74% in top half
Early decision deadline: N/A, notification date: N/A
Early action deadline: N/A, notification date: N/A
Application deadline (fall): rolling
Undergraduate student body: 1,618 full time, 287 part time; 44% male, 56% female; 0% American Indian, 13% Asian, 22% black, 14% Hispanic, 3% multiracial, 0% Pacific Islander, 29% white, 18% international; 35% from in state; 62% live on campus; 0% of students in fraternities, 0% in sororities
Most popular majors: 7% Business, Management, Marketing, and Related Support Services, 8% Communication, Journalism, and Related Programs, 9% Education, 7% Health Professions and Related Programs, 13% Visual and Performing Arts
Expenses: 2014-2015: $26,262; room/board: $8,302
Financial aid: (269) 471-3334; 65% of undergrads determined to have financial need; average aid package $27,093

Aquinas College

Grand Rapids MI
(616) 732-4460
U.S. News ranking: Reg. U. (Mid. W), No. 44
Website: www.aquinas.edu
Admissions email: admissions@aquinas.edu
Private; founded 1886
Affiliation: Roman Catholic
Freshman admissions: selective; 2013-2014: 2,602 applied, 1,847 accepted. Either SAT or ACT required. ACT 25/75 percentile: 21-26. High school

rank: 19% in top tenth, 45% in top quarter, 77% in top half
Early decision deadline: N/A, notification date: N/A
Early action deadline: N/A, notification date: N/A
Application deadline (fall): rolling
Undergraduate student body: 1,634 full time, 211 part time; 38% male, 62% female; 0% American Indian, 1% Asian, 3% black, 5% Hispanic, 2% multiracial, 0% Pacific Islander, 85% white, 1% international; 94% from in state; 47% live on campus; N/A of students in fraternities, N/A in sororities
Most popular majors: 16% Business, Management, Marketing, and Related Support Services, 8% Education, 7% Psychology, 8% Social Sciences, 7% Visual and Performing Arts
Expenses: 2014-2015: $27,726; room/board: $8,350
Financial aid: (616) 632-2893; 85% of undergrads determined to have financial need; average aid package $20,130

Baker College of Flint[1]

Flint MI
(810) 766-4000
U.S. News ranking: Reg. Coll. (Mid. W), unranked
Website: www.baker.edu
Admissions email: troy.crowe@baker.edu
Private
Application deadline (fall): N/A
Undergraduate student body: N/A full time, N/A part time
Expenses: 2013-2014: $8,100; room/board: $5,400
Financial aid: (810) 766-4202

Calvin College

Grand Rapids MI
(616) 526-6106
U.S. News ranking: Nat. Lib. Arts, No. 116
Website: www.calvin.edu
Admissions email: admissions@calvin.edu
Private; founded 1876
Affiliation: Christian Reformed
Freshman admissions: more selective; 2013-2014: 4,001 applied, 2,792 accepted. Neither SAT nor ACT required. ACT 25/75 percentile: 23-29. High school rank: 30% in top tenth, 55% in top quarter, 82% in top half
Early decision deadline: N/A, notification date: N/A
Early action deadline: N/A, notification date: N/A
Application deadline (fall): 8/15
Undergraduate student body: 3,814 full time, 145 part time; 45% male, 55% female; 0% American Indian, 4% Asian, 3% black, 3% Hispanic, 3% multiracial, 0% Pacific Islander, 75% white, 10% international; 56% from in state; 61% live on campus; 0% of students in fraternities, 0% in sororities
Most popular majors: 5% Biology/Biological Sciences, General, 10% Business/Commerce, General, 8% Engineering, General, 8% Psychology, General, 8% Registered Nursing/Registered Nurse
Expenses: 2014-2015: $29,635; room/board: $9,485

Financial aid: (616) 526-6137; 63% of undergrads determined to have financial need; average aid package $20,765

Central Michigan University

Mount Pleasant MI
(989) 774-3076
U.S. News ranking: Nat. U., No. 194
Website: www.cmich.edu
Admissions email: cmuadmit@cmich.edu
Public; founded 1892
Freshman admissions: selective; 2013-2014: 19,253 applied, 12,142 accepted. Either SAT or ACT required. ACT 25/75 percentile: 20-24. High school rank: 15% in top tenth, 38% in top quarter, 73% in top half
Early decision deadline: N/A, notification date: N/A
Early action deadline: N/A, notification date: N/A
Application deadline (fall): 7/1
Undergraduate student body: 17,880 full time, 2,654 part time; 44% male, 56% female; 1% American Indian, 1% Asian, 7% black, 3% Hispanic, 2% multiracial, 0% Pacific Islander, 80% white, 1% international; 96% from in state; 30% live on campus; 5% of students in fraternities, 7% in sororities
Most popular majors: 24% Business, Management, Marketing, and Related Support Services, 7% Communication, Journalism, and Related Programs, 12% Education, 9% Parks, Recreation, Leisure, and Fitness Studies, 7% Psychology
Expenses: 2014-2015: $11,550 in state, $23,670 out of state; room/board: $8,780
Financial aid: (989) 774-3674; 65% of undergrads determined to have financial need; average aid package $12,569

Cleary University[1]

Ann Arbor MI
(734) 332-4477
U.S. News ranking: Business, unranked
Website: www.cleary.edu
Admissions email: admissions@cleary.edu
Private
Application deadline (fall): N/A
Undergraduate student body: N/A full time, N/A part time
Expenses: 2013-2014: $13,860; room/board: N/A
Financial aid: (800) 686-1883

College for Creative Studies

Detroit MI
(313) 664-7425
U.S. News ranking: Arts, unranked
Website: www.collegeforcreativestudies.edu
Admissions email: admissions@collegeforcreativestudies.edu
Private; founded 1906
Freshman admissions: N/A; 2013-2014: 1,284 applied, 624 accepted. Either SAT or ACT required. SAT 25/75 percentile: N/A. High school rank: N/A
Early decision deadline: N/A, notification date: N/A
Early action deadline: 12/1, notification date: N/A

Application deadline (fall): rolling
Undergraduate student body: 1,082 full time, 281 part time; 51% male, 49% female; 0% American Indian, 5% Asian, 8% black, 4% Hispanic, 3% multiracial, 0% Pacific Islander, 60% white, 6% international; 91% from in state; 32% live on campus; N/A of students in fraternities, N/A in sororities
Most popular majors: 100% Visual and Performing Arts
Expenses: 2014-2015: $37,092; room/board: $8,250
Financial aid: (313) 664-7495

Cornerstone University

Grand Rapids MI
(616) 222-1426
U.S. News ranking: Reg. U. (Mid. W), second tier
Website: www.cornerstone.edu
Admissions email: admissions@cornerstone.edu
Private; founded 1941
Affiliation: Evangelical
Freshman admissions: selective; 2013-2014: 2,349 applied, 1,599 accepted. Either SAT or ACT required. ACT 25/75 percentile: 21-26. High school rank: 18% in top tenth, 49% in top quarter, 79% in top half
Early decision deadline: N/A, notification date: N/A
Early action deadline: N/A, notification date: N/A
Application deadline (fall): 8/15
Undergraduate student body: 1,610 full time, 590 part time; 41% male, 59% female; 1% American Indian, 1% Asian, 11% black, 4% Hispanic, 1% multiracial, 0% Pacific Islander, 81% white, 2% international; 79% from in state; 55% live on campus; N/A of students in fraternities, N/A in sororities
Most popular majors: Information not available
Expenses: 2014-2015: $25,682; room/board: $8,226
Financial aid: (616) 222-1424; 83% of undergrads determined to have financial need; average aid package $19,455

Davenport University

Grand Rapids MI
(866) 925-3884
U.S. News ranking: Reg. U. (Mid. W), second tier
Website: www.davenport.edu
Admissions email: Davenport.Admissions@davenport.edu
Private; founded 1866
Freshman admissions: less selective; 2013-2014: 1,385 applied, 1,270 accepted. Neither SAT nor ACT required. ACT 25/75 percentile: N/A. High school rank: N/A
Early decision deadline: N/A, notification date: N/A
Early action deadline: N/A, notification date: N/A
Application deadline (fall): rolling
Undergraduate student body: 2,580 full time, 4,776 part time; 38% male, 62% female; 0% American Indian, 2% Asian, 5% black, 0% Hispanic, 2% multiracial, 0% Pacific Islander, 70% white, 3% international; N/A from in state; 5% live on campus; N/A of students in fraternities, N/A in sororities

Most popular majors: Information not available
Expenses: 2014-2015: $14,066; room/board: $8,434
Financial aid: (616) 451-3511

Eastern Michigan University

Ypsilanti MI
(734) 487-3060
U.S. News ranking: Reg. U. (Mid. W), No. 77
Website: www.emich.edu/
Admissions email: undergraduate.admissions@emich.edu
Public; founded 1849
Freshman admissions: selective; 2013-2014: 12,936 applied, 7,901 accepted. Either SAT or ACT required. ACT 25/75 percentile: 19-25. High school rank: 14% in top tenth, 40% in top quarter, 76% in top half
Early decision deadline: N/A, notification date: N/A
Early action deadline: N/A, notification date: N/A
Application deadline (fall): rolling
Undergraduate student body: 13,498 full time, 5,586 part time; 42% male, 58% female; 0% American Indian, 2% Asian, 21% black, 4% Hispanic, 3% multiracial, 0% Pacific Islander, 65% white, 2% international; 91% from in state; 23% live on campus; 4% of students in fraternities, 4% in sororities
Most popular majors: 20% Business, Management, Marketing, and Related Support Services, 14% Education, 12% Health Professions and Related Programs, 8% Social Sciences, 6% Visual and Performing Arts
Expenses: 2014-2015: $9,604 in state, $25,614 out of state; room/board: $8,940
Financial aid: (734) 487-0455; 70% of undergrads determined to have financial need; average aid package $9,187

Ferris State University

Big Rapids MI
(231) 591-2100
U.S. News ranking: Reg. U. (Mid. W), No. 54
Website: www.ferris.edu
Admissions email: admissions@ferris.edu
Public; founded 1884
Freshman admissions: selective; 2013-2014: 10,708 applied, 8,128 accepted. Either SAT or ACT required. ACT 25/75 percentile: 19-24. High school rank: N/A
Early decision deadline: N/A, notification date: N/A
Early action deadline: N/A, notification date: N/A
Application deadline (fall): 8/1
Undergraduate student body: 9,255 full time, 4,214 part time; 48% male, 52% female; 1% American Indian, 1% Asian, 7% black, 3% Hispanic, 3% multiracial, 0% Pacific Islander, 79% white, 2% international; 95% from in state; 28% live on campus; 4% of students in fraternities, 2% in sororities
Most popular majors: 5% Business, Management, Marketing, and Related Support Services, 4% Education, 9% Homeland Security, Law Enforcement, Firefighting and Related Protective Services, 6% Pharmacy, 7%

Registered Nursing/Registered Nurse
Expenses: 2014-2015: $10,677 in state, $16,467 out of state; room/board: $9,208
Financial aid: (231) 591-2110; 74% of undergrads determined to have financial need; average aid package $10,755

Finlandia University[1]

Hancock MI
(906) 487-7274
U.S. News ranking: Reg. Coll. (Mid. W), second tier
Website: www.finlandia.edu
Admissions email: N/A
Private
Application deadline (fall): N/A
Undergraduate student body: N/A full time, N/A part time
Expenses: 2013-2014: $20,480; room/board: $7,210
Financial aid: (906) 487-7240

Grace Bible College[1]

Grand Rapids MI
(616) 538-2330
U.S. News ranking: Reg. Coll. (Mid. W), second tier
Website: www.gbcol.edu
Admissions email: enrollment@gbcol.edu
Private
Application deadline (fall): N/A
Undergraduate student body: N/A full time, N/A part time
Expenses: 2013-2014: $12,235; room/board: $7,150
Financial aid: (800) 968-1887

Grand Valley State University

Allendale MI
(800) 748-0246
U.S. News ranking: Reg. U. (Mid. W), No. 26
Website: www.gvsu.edu
Admissions email: admissions@gvsu.edu
Public; founded 1960
Freshman admissions: selective; 2013-2014: 18,120 applied, 14,967 accepted. Either SAT or ACT required. ACT 25/75 percentile: 21-26. High school rank: 18% in top tenth, 50% in top quarter, 86% in top half
Early decision deadline: N/A, notification date: N/A
Early action deadline: N/A, notification date: N/A
Application deadline (fall): 5/1
Undergraduate student body: 18,686 full time, 2,549 part time; 42% male, 58% female; 0% American Indian, 2% Asian, 5% black, 4% Hispanic, 3% multiracial, 0% Pacific Islander, 84% white, 1% international; 95% from in state; 28% live on campus; N/A of students in fraternities, N/A in sororities
Most popular majors: 7% Biological and Biomedical Sciences, 19% Business, Management, Marketing, and Related Support Services, 11% Health Professions and Related Programs, 6% Psychology, 9% Social Sciences
Expenses: 2014-2015: $10,752 in state, $15,408 out of state; room/board: $8,200
Financial aid: (616) 331-3234; 65% of undergrads determined to have financial need; average aid package $9,280

Hillsdale College

Hillsdale MI
(517) 607-2327
U.S. News ranking: Nat. Lib. Arts, No. 69
Website: www.hillsdale.edu
Admissions email: admissions@hillsdale.edu
Private; founded 1844
Freshman admissions: more selective; 2013-2014: 1,902 applied, 942 accepted. Either SAT or ACT required. ACT 25/75 percentile: 27-31. High school rank: 56% in top tenth, 85% in top quarter, 99% in top half
Early decision deadline: 11/15, notification date: 12/1
Early action deadline: 12/15, notification date: 2/15
Application deadline (fall): 2/15
Undergraduate student body: 1,462 full time, 24 part time; 47% male, 53% female; N/A American Indian, N/A Asian, N/A black, N/A Hispanic, N/A multiracial, N/A Pacific Islander, N/A white, N/A international; 37% from in state; 80% live on campus; 33% of students in fraternities, 44% in sororities
Most popular majors: 10% Biological and Biomedical Sciences, 13% Business, Management, Marketing, and Related Support Services, 14% English Language and Literature/Letters, 10% History, 16% Social Sciences
Expenses: 2014-2015: $23,616; room/board: $9,250
Financial aid: (517) 607-2350; 43% of undergrads determined to have financial need; average aid package $18,298

Hope College

Holland MI
(616) 395-7850
U.S. News ranking: Nat. Lib. Arts, No. 99
Website: www.hope.edu
Admissions email: admissions@hope.edu
Private; founded 1866
Affiliation: Reformed Church in America
Freshman admissions: more selective; 2013-2014: 4,158 applied, 2,931 accepted. Either SAT or ACT required. ACT 25/75 percentile: 24-29. High school rank: 34% in top tenth, 64% in top quarter, 92% in top half
Early decision deadline: N/A, notification date: N/A
Early action deadline: N/A, notification date: N/A
Application deadline (fall): rolling
Undergraduate student body: 3,235 full time, 153 part time; 40% male, 60% female; 0% American Indian, 2% Asian, 2% black, 7% Hispanic, 2% multiracial, 0% Pacific Islander, 85% white, 2% international; 69% from in state; 81% live on campus; 12% of students in fraternities, 14% in sororities
Most popular majors: 6% Biology/Biological Sciences, General, 9% Business Administration and Management, General, 7% Chemistry, General, 7% Kinesiology and Exercise Science, 12% Psychology, General
Expenses: 2014-2015: $29,560; room/board: $9,090

Financial aid: (616) 395-7765; 60% of undergrads determined to have financial need; average aid package $23,019

Kalamazoo College

Kalamazoo MI
(800) 253-3602
U.S. News ranking: Nat. Lib. Arts, No. 64
Website: www.kzoo.edu
Admissions email: admission@kzoo.edu
Private; founded 1833
Freshman admissions: more selective; 2013-2014: 2,528 applied, 1,691 accepted. Either SAT or ACT required. ACT 25/75 percentile: 25-30. High school rank: 38% in top tenth, 80% in top quarter, 98% in top half
Early decision deadline: 11/15, notification date: 12/1
Early action deadline: 11/15, notification date: 12/20
Application deadline (fall): 2/15
Undergraduate student body: 1,446 full time, 12 part time; 44% male, 56% female; 0% American Indian, 6% Asian, 4% black, 8% Hispanic, 4% multiracial, 0% Pacific Islander, 63% white, 7% international; 70% from in state; 61% live on campus; 0% of students in fraternities, 0% in sororities
Most popular majors: 12% Biological and Biomedical Sciences, 10% English Language and Literature/Letters, 12% Physical Sciences, 10% Psychology, 17% Social Sciences
Expenses: 2014-2015: $41,061; room/board: $8,679
Financial aid: (269) 337-7192; 67% of undergrads determined to have financial need; average aid package $33,209

Kettering University

Flint MI
(800) 955-4464
U.S. News ranking: Reg. U. (Mid. W), No. 20
Website: www.kettering.edu
Admissions email: admissions@kettering.edu
Private; founded 1919
Freshman admissions: more selective; 2013-2014: 2,056 applied, 1,336 accepted. Either SAT or ACT required. ACT 25/75 percentile: 25-30. High school rank: 28% in top tenth, 66% in top quarter, 96% in top half
Early decision deadline: N/A, notification date: N/A
Early action deadline: N/A, notification date: N/A
Application deadline (fall): rolling
Undergraduate student body: 1,590 full time, 94 part time; 82% male, 18% female; 0% American Indian, 3% Asian, 3% black, 3% Hispanic, 3% multiracial, 0% Pacific Islander, 78% white, 4% international; 72% from in state; 30% live on campus; 36% of students in fraternities, 31% in sororities
Most popular majors: 2% Biological and Biomedical Sciences, 2% Business, Management, Marketing, and Related Support Services, 4% Computer and Information Sciences and Support Services, 91% Engineering, 1% Mathematics and Statistics

Expenses: 2013-2014: $35,600; room/board: $6,980
Financial aid: (810) 762-7859

Kuyper College[1]
Grand Rapids MI
(800) 511-3749
U.S. News ranking: Reg. Coll. (Mid. W), No. 64
Website: www.kuyper.edu
Admissions email: admissions@kuyper.edu
Private
Application deadline (fall): N/A
Undergraduate student body: N/A full time, N/A part time
Expenses: 2013-2014: $18,454; room/board: $7,050
Financial aid: (616) 222-3000

Lake Superior State University
Sault Ste. Marie MI
(906) 635-2231
U.S. News ranking: Reg. Coll. (Mid. W), No. 69
Website: www.lssu.edu
Admissions email: admissions@lssu.edu
Public; founded 1946
Freshman admissions: selective; 2013-2014: 1,465 applied, 1,319 accepted. Either SAT or ACT required. ACT 25/75 percentile: 20-25. High school rank: 14% in top tenth, 40% in top quarter, 76% in top half
Early decision deadline: N/A, notification date: N/A
Early action deadline: N/A, notification date: N/A
Undergraduate student body: 1,967 full time, 462 part time; 50% male, 50% female; 8% American Indian, 1% Asian, 1% black, 2% Hispanic, 0% multiracial, 0% Pacific Islander, 79% white, 7% international
Most popular majors: 6% Biological and Biomedical Sciences, 14% Business, Management, Marketing, and Related Support Services, 9% Education, 12% Health Professions and Related Programs, 24% Homeland Security, Law Enforcement, Firefighting and Related Protective Services
Expenses: 2013-2014: $9,960 in state, $15,000 out of state; room/board: $8,728
Financial aid: (906) 635-2678; 69% of undergrads determined to have financial need; average aid package $9,515

Lawrence Technological University
Southfield MI
(248) 204-3160
U.S. News ranking: Reg. U. (Mid. W), No. 54
Website: www.ltu.edu
Admissions email: admissions@ltu.edu
Private; founded 1932
Freshman admissions: more selective; 2013-2014: 2,076 applied, 1,196 accepted. ACT 25/75 percentile: 22-29. High school rank: 25% in top tenth, 52% in top quarter, 80% in top half
Early decision deadline: N/A, notification date: N/A

Early action deadline: N/A, notification date: N/A
Application deadline (fall): rolling
Undergraduate student body: 1,536 full time, 1,497 part time; 76% male, 24% female; 1% American Indian, 6% Asian, 8% black, 3% Hispanic, 0% multiracial, 0% Pacific Islander, 68% white, 8% international; 97% from in state; 20% live on campus; 6% of students in fraternities, 6% in sororities
Most popular majors: 34% Architecture, 5% Business Administration and Management, General, 9% Computer Science, 8% Engineering Technology, General, 30% Engineering, General
Expenses: 2014-2015: $30,200; room/board: $8,986
Financial aid: (248) 204-2280; 61% of undergrads determined to have financial need; average aid package $22,880

Madonna University
Livonia MI
(734) 432-5339
U.S. News ranking: Reg. U. (Mid. W), No. 84
Website: www.madonna.edu
Admissions email: admissions@madonna.edu
Private; founded 1947
Affiliation: Roman Catholic
Freshman admissions: selective; 2013-2014: 1,071 applied, 665 accepted. Either SAT or ACT required. ACT 25/75 percentile: 19-25. High school rank: 15% in top tenth, 40% in top quarter, 76% in top half
Early decision deadline: N/A, notification date: N/A
Early action deadline: N/A, notification date: N/A
Application deadline (fall): rolling
Undergraduate student body: 1,678 full time, 1,674 part time; 33% male, 67% female; 0% American Indian, 1% Asian, 13% black, 2% Hispanic, 2% multiracial, 0% Pacific Islander, 62% white, 17% international; 99% from in state; 8% live on campus; 0% of students in fraternities, 0% in sororities
Most popular majors: 4% Biological and Biomedical Sciences, 15% Business, Management, Marketing, and Related Support Services, 5% Family and Consumer Sciences/Human Sciences, 23% Health Professions and Related Programs, 20% Homeland Security, Law Enforcement, Firefighting and Related Protective Services
Expenses: 2014-2015: $17,390; room/board: $8,610
Financial aid: (734) 432-5662; 73% of undergrads determined to have financial need; average aid package $10,252

Marygrove College
Detroit MI
(313) 927-1240
U.S. News ranking: Reg. U. (Mid. W), second tier
Website: www.marygrove.edu
Admissions email: info@marygrove.edu
Private
Affiliation: Roman Catholic

Freshman admissions: least selective; 2013-2014: 916 applied, 859 accepted. Neither SAT nor ACT required. ACT 25/75 percentile: 14-18. High school rank: N/A
Early decision deadline: N/A, notification date: N/A
Early action deadline: N/A, notification date: N/A
Application deadline (fall): rolling
Undergraduate student body: 801 full time, 240 part time; 25% male, 75% female; 0% American Indian, 0% Asian, 73% black, 3% Hispanic, 3% multiracial, 0% Pacific Islander, 14% white, 1% international
Most popular majors: 10% Business, Management, Marketing, and Related Support Services, 11% Health Professions and Related Programs, 34% Public Administration and Social Service Professions, 8% Social Sciences, 6% Visual and Performing Arts
Expenses: 2013-2014: $19,850; room/board: $7,600
Financial aid: (313) 927-1692

Michigan State University
East Lansing MI
(517) 355-8332
U.S. News ranking: Nat. U., No. 85
Website: www.msu.edu/
Admissions email: admis@msu.edu
Public; founded 1855
Freshman admissions: more selective; 2013-2014: 31,479 applied, 21,610 accepted. Either SAT or ACT required. ACT 25/75 percentile: 23-28. High school rank: 28% in top tenth, 66% in top quarter, 94% in top half
Early decision deadline: N/A, notification date: N/A
Early action deadline: N/A, notification date: N/A
Application deadline (fall): rolling
Undergraduate student body: 34,840 full time, 3,148 part time; 50% male, 50% female; 0% American Indian, 4% Asian, 7% black, 4% Hispanic, 2% multiracial, 0% Pacific Islander, 70% white, 12% international; 90% from in state; 40% live on campus; 8% of students in fraternities, 7% in sororities
Most popular majors: 11% Biological and Biomedical Sciences, 17% Business, Management, Marketing, and Related Support Services, 11% Communication, Journalism, and Related Programs, 6% Engineering, 10% Social Sciences
Expenses: 2014-2015: $13,200 in state, $34,980 out of state; room/board: $9,154
Financial aid: (517) 353-5940; 49% of undergrads determined to have financial need; average aid package $12,041

Michigan Technological University
Houghton MI
(906) 487-2335
U.S. News ranking: Nat. U., No. 116
Website: www.mtu.edu
Admissions email: mtu4u@mtu.edu
Public; founded 1885

Freshman admissions: more selective; 2013-2014: 4,905 applied, 3,815 accepted. Either SAT or ACT required. ACT 25/75 percentile: 24-29. High school rank: 30% in top tenth, 65% in top quarter, 91% in top half
Early decision deadline: N/A, notification date: N/A
Early action deadline: N/A, notification date: N/A
Application deadline (fall): rolling
Undergraduate student body: 5,198 full time, 423 part time; 75% male, 25% female; 1% American Indian, 1% Asian, 1% black, 2% Hispanic, 2% multiracial, 0% Pacific Islander, 84% white, 6% international; 76% from in state; 48% live on campus; 6% of students in fraternities, 3% in sororities
Most popular majors: 5% Biological and Biomedical Sciences, 10% Business, Management, Marketing, and Related Support Services, 6% Computer and Information Sciences and Support Services, 57% Engineering, 3% Natural Resources and Conservation
Expenses: 2014-2015: $14,040 in state, $29,520 out of state; room/board: $9,516
Financial aid: (906) 487-2622; 65% of undergrads determined to have financial need; average aid package $13,659

Northern Michigan University[1]
Marquette MI
(906) 227-2650
U.S. News ranking: Reg. U. (Mid. W), No. 91
Website: www.nmu.edu
Admissions email: admiss@nmu.edu
Public; founded 1899
Application deadline (fall): rolling
Undergraduate student body: N/A full time, N/A part time
Expenses: 2014-2015: $9,220 in state, $14,400 out of state; room/board: $8,950
Financial aid: (906) 227-2327; 70% of undergrads determined to have financial need; average aid package $9,298

Northwood University
Midland MI
(989) 837-4273
U.S. News ranking: Business, unranked
Website: www.northwood.edu
Admissions email: miadmit@northwood.edu
Private; founded 1959
Freshman admissions: selective; 2013-2014: 1,447 applied, 946 accepted. Either SAT or ACT required. ACT 25/75 percentile: 20-24. High school rank: 11% in top tenth, 31% in top quarter, 75% in top half
Early decision deadline: N/A, notification date: N/A
Early action deadline: N/A, notification date: N/A
Application deadline (fall): rolling
Undergraduate student body: 1,406 full time, 62 part time; 62% male, 38% female; 0% American Indian, 0% Asian, 7% black, 1% Hispanic, 1% multiracial, 1% Pacific Islander, 78% white, 5% international; 85% from in state;

43% live on campus; 13% of students in fraternities, 13% in sororities
Most popular majors: 16% Accounting, 20% Business Administration and Management, General, 8% International Business/Trade/Commerce, 15% Marketing/Marketing Management, General, 10% Sport and Fitness Administration/Management
Expenses: 2014-2015: $23,132; room/board: $9,310
Financial aid: (989) 837-4230; 66% of undergrads determined to have financial need; average aid package $19,950

Oakland University
Rochester MI
(248) 370-3360
U.S. News ranking: Nat. U., second tier
Website: www.oakland.edu
Admissions email: visit@oakland.edu
Public; founded 1957
Freshman admissions: selective; 2013-2014: 12,019 applied, 7,933 accepted. Either SAT or ACT required. ACT 25/75 percentile: 20-26. High school rank: 17% in top tenth, 44% in top quarter, 80% in top half
Early decision deadline: N/A, notification date: N/A
Early action deadline: N/A, notification date: N/A
Application deadline (fall): 8/1
Undergraduate student body: 12,252 full time, 4,342 part time; 41% male, 59% female; 0% American Indian, 4% Asian, 8% black, 3% Hispanic, 2% multiracial, 0% Pacific Islander, 77% white, 1% international; 99% from in state; 14% live on campus; 2% of students in fraternities, 3% in sororities
Most popular majors: 16% Business, Management, Marketing, and Related Support Services, 8% Communication, Journalism, and Related Programs, 7% Education, 25% Health Professions and Related Programs, 7% Psychology
Expenses: 2014-2015: $11,460 in state, $24,735 out of state; room/board: $8,894
Financial aid: (248) 370-2550; 65% of undergrads determined to have financial need; average aid package $12,636

Olivet College
Olivet MI
(269) 749-7635
U.S. News ranking: Reg. Coll. (Mid. W), No. 47
Website: www.olivetcollege.edu
Admissions email: admissions@olivetcollege.edu
Private; founded 1844
Affiliation: United Church of Christ
Freshman admissions: selective; 2013-2014: 1,995 applied, 1,027 accepted. Either SAT or ACT required. ACT 25/75 percentile: 17-22. High school rank: N/A
Early decision deadline: N/A, notification date: N/A
Early action deadline: N/A, notification date: N/A
Application deadline (fall): rolling
Undergraduate student body: 982 full time, 137 part time; 57% male, 43% female; 1% American Indian, 0% Asian, 10% black,

6% Hispanic, 2% multiracial, 0% Pacific Islander, 80% white, 0% international
Most popular majors: 12% Biology/Biological Sciences, General, 15% Criminal Justice/Safety Studies, 11% Insurance, 7% Psychology, General, 8% Sport and Fitness Administration/Management
Expenses: 2014-2015: $23,802; room/board: $7,900
Financial aid: (269) 749-7102; 92% of undergrads determined to have financial need; average aid package $17,931

Robert B. Miller College[1]

Battle Creek MI
(269) 660-8021
U.S. News ranking: Reg. Coll. (Mid. W), unranked
Website: www.millercollege.edu
Admissions email: N/A
Private
Application deadline (fall): N/A
Undergraduate student body: N/A full time, N/A part time
Expenses: N/A
Financial aid: (269) 660-8021

Rochester College

Rochester Hills MI
(248) 218-2031
U.S. News ranking: Reg. Coll. (Mid. W), No. 61
Website: www.rc.edu
Admissions email: admissions@rc.edu
Private; founded 1959
Affiliation: Church of Christ
Freshman admissions: less selective; 2013-2014: 1,171 applied, 769 accepted. Neither SAT nor ACT required. ACT 25/75 percentile: 18-24. High school rank: N/A
Early decision deadline: N/A, notification date: N/A
Early action deadline: N/A, notification date: N/A
Application deadline (fall): rolling
Undergraduate student body: 712 full time, 405 part time; 40% male, 60% female; 0% American Indian, 2% Asian, 16% black, 2% Hispanic, 2% multiracial, 0% Pacific Islander, 52% white, 3% international; 97% from in state; 22% live on campus; N/A of students in fraternities, N/A in sororities
Most popular majors: 35% Business, Management, Marketing, and Related Support Services, 12% Communication, Journalism, and Related Programs, 14% Education, 6% Multi/Interdisciplinary Studies, 21% Psychology
Expenses: 2014-2015: $21,350; room/board: $6,554
Financial aid: (248) 218-2028

Saginaw Valley State University

University Center MI
(989) 964-4200
U.S. News ranking: Reg. U. (Mid. W), second tier
Website: www.svsu.edu
Admissions email: admissions@svsu.edu
Public; founded 1963

Freshman admissions: selective; 2013-2014: 6,010 applied, 4,733 accepted. ACT required. ACT 25/75 percentile: 19-24. High school rank: 18% in top tenth, 39% in top quarter, 72% in top half
Early decision deadline: N/A, notification date: N/A
Early action deadline: N/A, notification date: N/A
Application deadline (fall): rolling
Undergraduate student body: 7,594 full time, 1,381 part time; 43% male, 57% female; 0% American Indian, 1% Asian, 11% black, 3% Hispanic, 1% multiracial, 0% Pacific Islander, 73% white, 4% international; 99% from in state; 31% live on campus; 3% of students in fraternities, 3% in sororities
Most popular majors: 7% Criminal Justice/Safety Studies, 7% Education, 10% Health Professions and Related Programs, 5% Health/Medical Preparatory Programs, Other, 7% Social Work
Expenses: 2014-2015: $8,691 in state, $20,409 out of state; room/board: N/A
Financial aid: (989) 964-4103; 71% of undergrads determined to have financial need

Siena Heights University

Adrian MI
(517) 264-7180
U.S. News ranking: Reg. U. (Mid. W), second tier
Website: www.sienaheights.edu
Admissions email: admissions@sienaheights.edu
Private; founded 1919
Affiliation: Roman Catholic
Freshman admissions: selective; 2013-2014: 1,422 applied, 962 accepted. Either SAT or ACT required. ACT 25/75 percentile: 19-23. High school rank: 8% in top tenth, 33% in top quarter, 68% in top half
Early decision deadline: N/A, notification date: N/A
Early action deadline: N/A, notification date: N/A
Application deadline (fall): 8/1
Undergraduate student body: 1,237 full time, 1,187 part time; 43% male, 57% female; 1% American Indian, 1% Asian, 13% black, 5% Hispanic, 2% multiracial, 0% Pacific Islander, 76% white, 0% international; 88% from in state; 19% live on campus; 2% of students in fraternities, 2% in sororities
Most popular majors: 22% Business, Management, Marketing, and Related Support Services, 24% Health Professions and Related Programs, 11% Homeland Security, Law Enforcement, Firefighting and Related Protective Services, 6% Liberal Arts and Sciences, General Studies and Humanities, 7% Public Administration and Social Service Professions
Expenses: 2014-2015: $22,740; room/board: $9,300
Financial aid: (517) 264-7130; 80% of undergrads determined to have financial need; average aid package $2,194

Spring Arbor University

Spring Arbor MI
(800) 968-0011
U.S. News ranking: Reg. U. (Mid. W), No. 49
Website: www.arbor.edu/
Admissions email: admissions@arbor.edu
Private; founded 1873
Affiliation: Free Methodist
Freshman admissions: selective; 2013-2014: 2,698 applied, 1,755 accepted. Either SAT or ACT required. ACT 25/75 percentile: 20-26. High school rank: 22% in top tenth, 48% in top quarter, 77% in top half
Early decision deadline: N/A, notification date: N/A
Early action deadline: N/A, notification date: N/A
Application deadline (fall): 8/1
Undergraduate student body: 2,005 full time, 962 part time; 31% male, 69% female; 1% American Indian, 1% Asian, 12% black, 3% Hispanic, 2% multiracial, 0% Pacific Islander, 73% white, 1% international; 88% from in state; 72% live on campus; 0% of students in fraternities, 0% in sororities
Most popular majors: 10% Business Administration and Management, General, 9% Christian Studies, 10% Psychology, General, 10% Social Work, 19% Teacher Education and Professional Development, Specific Subject Areas
Expenses: 2014-2015: $24,350; room/board: $8,460
Financial aid: (517) 750-6463; 87% of undergrads determined to have financial need; average aid package $21,465

University of Detroit Mercy

Detroit MI
(313) 993-1245
U.S. News ranking: Reg. U. (Mid. W), No. 41
Website: www.udmercy.edu
Admissions email: admissions@udmercy.edu
Private; founded 1877
Affiliation: Roman Catholic (Jesuit/Sisters of Mercy)
Freshman admissions: selective; 2013-2014: 3,959 applied, 2,450 accepted. Either SAT or ACT required. ACT 25/75 percentile: 21-26. High school rank: 26% in top tenth, 55% in top quarter, 90% in top half
Early decision deadline: N/A, notification date: N/A
Early action deadline: 11/1, notification date: 12/15
Application deadline (fall): 3/1
Undergraduate student body: 2,196 full time, 687 part time; 35% male, 65% female; 0% American Indian, 3% Asian, 10% black, 3% Hispanic, 3% multiracial, 0% Pacific Islander, 54% white, 6% international
Most popular majors: Information not available
Expenses: 2014-2015: $37,320; room/board: $8,528
Financial aid: (313) 993-3350; 72% of undergrads determined to have financial need; average aid package $28,137

University of Michigan–Ann Arbor

Ann Arbor MI
(734) 764-7433
U.S. News ranking: Nat. U., No. 29
Website: www.umich.edu
Admissions email: N/A
Public; founded 1817
Freshman admissions: more selective; 2013-2014: 46,813 applied, 15,570 accepted. Either SAT or ACT required. ACT 25/75 percentile: 28-32. High school rank: N/A
Early decision deadline: N/A, notification date: N/A
Early action deadline: 11/1, notification date: 12/24
Application deadline (fall): 2/1
Undergraduate student body: 27,316 full time, 967 part time; 51% male, 49% female; 0% American Indian, 12% Asian, 4% black, 4% Hispanic, 3% multiracial, 0% Pacific Islander, 63% white, 7% international; 66% from in state; 33% live on campus; 17% of students in fraternities, 22% in sororities
Most popular majors: 6% Business Administration and Management, General, 7% Economics, General, 4% English Language and Literature, General, 8% Experimental Psychology, 6% Political Science and Government, General
Expenses: 2014-2015: $13,977 in state, $41,811 out of state; room/board: $9,996
Financial aid: (734) 763-4119; 39% of undergrads determined to have financial need; average aid package $20,188

University of Michigan–Dearborn

Dearborn MI
(313) 593-5100
U.S. News ranking: Reg. U. (Mid. W), No. 35
Website: www.umd.umich.edu
Admissions email: admissions@umd.umich.edu
Public; founded 1959
Freshman admissions: more selective; 2013-2014: 4,908 applied, 3,084 accepted. Either SAT or ACT required. ACT 25/75 percentile: 22-27. High school rank: 24% in top tenth, 57% in top quarter, 92% in top half
Early decision deadline: N/A, notification date: N/A
Early action deadline: N/A, notification date: N/A
Application deadline (fall): rolling
Undergraduate student body: 4,814 full time, 2,330 part time; 50% male, 50% female; 0% American Indian, 6% Asian, 11% black, 5% Hispanic, 3% multiracial, 0% Pacific Islander, 70% white, 1% international; 95% from in state; 0% live on campus; N/A of students in fraternities, N/A in sororities
Most popular majors: 8% Biological and Biomedical Sciences, 18% Business, Management, Marketing, and Related Support Services, 10% Engineering, 10% Psychology, 9% Social Sciences
Expenses: 2014-2015: $11,188 in state, $23,386 out of state; room/board: N/A
Financial aid: (313) 593-5300; 67% of undergrads determined to have financial need; average aid package $11,298

University of Michigan–Flint

Flint MI
(810) 762-3300
U.S. News ranking: Reg. U. (Mid. W), No. 99
Website: www.umflint.edu
Admissions email: admissions@umflint.edu
Public; founded 1956
Freshman admissions: selective; 2013-2014: 3,003 applied, 2,345 accepted. Either SAT or ACT required. ACT 25/75 percentile: 18-24. High school rank: 15% in top tenth, 42% in top quarter, 76% in top half
Early decision deadline: N/A, notification date: N/A
Early action deadline: N/A, notification date: N/A
Application deadline (fall): 8/20
Undergraduate student body: 4,490 full time, 2,653 part time; 40% male, 60% female; 1% American Indian, 2% Asian, 12% black, 4% Hispanic, 3% multiracial, 0% Pacific Islander, 68% white, 6% international; 98% from in state; 4% live on campus; 5% of students in fraternities, 4% in sororities
Most popular majors: 7% Biological and Biomedical Sciences, 16% Business, Management, Marketing, and Related Support Services, 8% Education, 30% Health Professions and Related Programs, 6% Public Administration and Social Service Professions
Expenses: 2014-2015: $10,138 in state, $19,360 out of state; room/board: $7,911
Financial aid: (810) 762-3444

Walsh College of Accountancy and Business Administration[1]

Troy MI
(248) 823-1610
U.S. News ranking: Business, unranked
Website: www.walshcollege.edu
Admissions email: admissions@walshcollege.edu
Private
Application deadline (fall): N/A
Undergraduate student body: N/A full time, N/A part time
Expenses: N/A
Financial aid: (248) 823-1665

Wayne State University

Detroit MI
(313) 577-3577
U.S. News ranking: Nat. U., second tier
Website: www.wayne.edu/
Admissions email: admissions@wayne.edu
Public; founded 1868
Freshman admissions: selective; 2013-2014: 11,524 applied, 8,786 accepted. Either SAT or ACT required. ACT 25/75 percentile: 19-26. High school rank: 23% in top tenth, 46% in top quarter, 77% in top half
Early decision deadline: N/A, notification date: N/A
Early action deadline: N/A, notification date: N/A
Application deadline (fall): rolling

Undergraduate student body: 12,221 full time, 6,381 part time; 44% male, 56% female; 0% American Indian, 8% Asian, 21% black, 4% Hispanic, 3% multiracial, 0% Pacific Islander, 53% white, 2% international; 99% from in state; 10% live on campus; N/A of students in fraternities, N/A in sororities
Most popular majors: 6% Biology/Biological Sciences, General, 4% Criminal Justice/Safety Studies, 4% Organizational Behavior Studies, 12% Psychology, General, 4% Social Work
Expenses: 2014-2015: $12,350 in state, $26,592 out of state; room/board: $9,713
Financial aid: (313) 577-3378; 76% of undergrads determined to have financial need; average aid package $10,248

Western Michigan University
Kalamazoo MI
(269) 387-2000
U.S. News ranking: Nat. U., No. 173
Website: www.wmich.edu
Admissions email: ask-wmu@wmich.edu
Public; founded 1903
Freshman admissions: selective; 2013-2014: 14,621 applied, 12,113 accepted. Either SAT or ACT required. ACT 25/75 percentile: 19-25. High school rank: 12% in top tenth, 35% in top quarter, 70% in top half
Early decision deadline: N/A, notification date: N/A
Early action deadline: N/A, notification date: N/A
Application deadline (fall): rolling
Undergraduate student body: 15,879 full time, 3,319 part time; 50% male, 50% female; 0% American Indian, 1% Asian, 11% black, 5% Hispanic, 3% multiracial, 0% Pacific Islander, 75% white, 3% international; 93% from in state; 28% live on campus; 5% of students in fraternities, 6% in sororities
Most popular majors: 20% Business, Management, Marketing, and Related Support Services, 6% Communication, Journalism, and Related Programs, 10% Education, 9% Health Professions and Related Programs, 8% Multi/Interdisciplinary Studies
Expenses: 2014-2015: $10,685 in state, $24,917 out of state; room/board: $8,943
Financial aid: (269) 387-6000; 61% of undergrads determined to have financial need; average aid package $14,400

MINNESOTA

Augsburg College
Minneapolis MN
(612) 330-1001
U.S. News ranking: Reg. U. (Mid. W), No. 23
Website: www.augsburg.edu
Admissions email: admissions@augsburg.edu
Private; founded 1869
Affiliation: Lutheran
Freshman admissions: selective; 2013-2014: 2,334 applied, 1,718 accepted. Either SAT or ACT required. ACT 25/75

percentile: 20-24. High school rank: 14% in top tenth, 43% in top quarter, 74% in top half
Early decision deadline: N/A, notification date: N/A
Early action deadline: N/A, notification date: N/A
Application deadline (fall): 8/15
Undergraduate student body: 2,038 full time, 678 part time; 45% male, 55% female; 1% American Indian, 8% Asian, 10% black, 6% Hispanic, 4% multiracial, 0% Pacific Islander, 58% white, 2% international
Most popular majors: 38% Business, Management, Marketing, and Related Support Services, 9% Communication, Journalism, and Related Programs, 15% Education, 8% Visual and Performing Arts
Expenses: 2013-2014: $33,209; room/board: $8,556
Financial aid: (612) 330-1046

Bemidji State University
Bemidji MN
(218) 755-2040
U.S. News ranking: Reg. U. (Mid. W), No. 99
Website: www.bemidjistate.edu
Admissions email: admissions@bemidjistate.edu
Public; founded 1919
Freshman admissions: selective; 2013-2014: 3,606 applied, 2,408 accepted. Either SAT or ACT required. ACT 25/75 percentile: 19-23. High school rank: 7% in top tenth, 23% in top quarter, 57% in top half
Early decision deadline: N/A, notification date: N/A
Early action deadline: N/A, notification date: N/A
Application deadline (fall): rolling
Undergraduate student body: 3,516 full time, 1,213 part time; 44% male, 56% female; 3% American Indian, 1% Asian, 2% black, 2% Hispanic, 3% multiracial, 0% Pacific Islander, 86% white, 2% international; 89% from in state; 28% live on campus; N/A of students in fraternities, N/A in sororities
Most popular majors: 6% Biological and Biomedical Sciences, 20% Business, Management, Marketing, and Related Support Services, 15% Education, 13% Health Professions and Related Programs, 7% Homeland Security, Law Enforcement, Firefighting and Related Protective Services
Expenses: 2014-2015: $8,134 in state, $8,134 out of state; room/board: $7,470
Financial aid: (218) 755-4143; 66% of undergrads determined to have financial need; average aid package $9,060

Bethany Lutheran College
Mankato MN
(507) 344-7331
U.S. News ranking: Nat. Lib. Arts, second tier
Website: www.blc.edu
Admissions email: admiss@blc.edu
Private; founded 1927
Affiliation: Evangelical Lutheran Synod
Freshman admissions: selective; 2013-2014: 531 applied, 396 accepted. Either SAT or ACT required. ACT 25/75 percentile:

20-26. High school rank: 14% in top tenth, 32% in top quarter, 67% in top half
Early decision deadline: N/A, notification date: N/A
Early action deadline: N/A, notification date: N/A
Application deadline (fall): 7/1
Undergraduate student body: 552 full time, 27 part time; 49% male, 51% female; 1% American Indian, 1% Asian, 1% black, 1% Hispanic, 3% multiracial, 0% Pacific Islander, 88% white, 1% international; 75% from in state; 60% live on campus; 0% of students in fraternities, 0% in sororities
Most popular majors: 11% Biology/Biological Sciences, General, 19% Business Administration and Management, General, 13% Communication, General, 10% Psychology, General, 12% Visual and Performing Arts
Expenses: 2014-2015: $24,450; room/board: $7,710
Financial aid: (507) 344-7307; 88% of undergrads determined to have financial need; average aid package $19,087

Bethel University
St. Paul MN
(800) 255-8706
U.S. News ranking: Reg. U. (Mid. W), No. 20
Website: www.bethel.edu
Admissions email: BUadmissions-cas@bethel.edu
Private; founded 1871
Affiliation: Converge Worldwide (former Baptist General Conference)
Freshman admissions: more selective; 2013-2014: 2,118 applied, 2,009 accepted. Either SAT or ACT required. ACT 25/75 percentile: 22-28. High school rank: 29% in top tenth, 60% in top quarter, 86% in top half
Early decision deadline: N/A, notification date: N/A
Early action deadline: N/A, notification date: N/A
Application deadline (fall): rolling
Undergraduate student body: 2,617 full time, 663 part time; 37% male, 63% female; 0% American Indian, 3% Asian, 6% black, 2% Hispanic, 2% multiracial, 0% Pacific Islander, 84% white, 0% international; 77% from in state; 69% live on campus; 0% of students in fraternities, 0% in sororities
Most popular majors: 7% Biological and Biomedical Sciences, 15% Business, Management, Marketing, and Related Support Services, 8% Communication, Journalism, and Related Programs, 13% Education, 15% Health Professions and Related Programs
Expenses: 2014-2015: $32,990; room/board: $9,440
Financial aid: (800) 255-8706; 73% of undergrads determined to have financial need; average aid package $23,686

Capella University[1]
Minneapolis MN
(888) 227-3552
U.S. News ranking: Nat. U., unranked
Website: www.capella.edu
Admissions email: admissionsoffice@capella.edu
For-profit

Application deadline (fall): N/A
Undergraduate student body: N/A full time, N/A part time
Expenses: 2013-2014: $12,348; room/board: N/A
Financial aid: (612) 977-5233

Carleton College
Northfield MN
(507) 222-4190
U.S. News ranking: Nat. Lib. Arts, No. 8
Website: www.carleton.edu
Admissions email: admissions@carleton.edu
Private; founded 1866
Freshman admissions: most selective; 2013-2014: 7,045 applied, 1,476 accepted. Either SAT or ACT required. SAT 25/75 percentile: 1340-1520. High school rank: 79% in top tenth, 96% in top quarter, 100% in top half
Early decision deadline: 11/15, notification date: 12/15
Early action deadline: N/A, notification date: N/A
Application deadline (fall): 1/15
Undergraduate student body: 2,025 full time, 20 part time; 47% male, 53% female; 0% American Indian, 9% Asian, 4% black, 6% Hispanic, 4% multiracial, 0% Pacific Islander, 66% white, 9% international; 21% from in state; 96% live on campus; 0% of students in fraternities, 0% in sororities
Most popular majors: 11% Biological and Biomedical Sciences, 7% Mathematics and Statistics, 12% Physical Sciences, 20% Social Sciences, 12% Visual and Performing Arts
Expenses: 2014-2015: $47,736; room/board: $12,366
Financial aid: (507) 646-4138; 55% of undergrads determined to have financial need; average aid package $37,888

College of St. Benedict
St. Joseph MN
(320) 363-5055
U.S. News ranking: Nat. Lib. Arts, No. 89
Website: www.csbsju.edu
Admissions email: admissions@csbsju.edu
Private; founded 1913
Affiliation: Roman Catholic (Benedictine)
Freshman admissions: more selective; 2013-2014: 2,077 applied, 1,569 accepted. Either SAT or ACT required. ACT 25/75 percentile: 23-28. High school rank: 33% in top tenth, 70% in top quarter, 94% in top half
Early decision deadline: N/A, notification date: N/A
Early action deadline: 11/15, notification date: 12/15
Application deadline (fall): 1/15
Undergraduate student body: 2,015 full time, 36 part time; 0% male, 100% female; 0% American Indian, 6% Asian, 2% black, 5% Hispanic, 1% multiracial, 0% Pacific Islander, 80% white, 6% international; 83% from in state; 88% live on campus; 0% of students in fraternities, 0% in sororities
Most popular majors: 11% Biology/Biological Sciences, General, 7% Nutrition Sciences, 10% Psychology, General, 10%

Registered Nursing/Registered Nurse, 9% Rhetoric and Composition
Expenses: 2014-2015: $39,402; room/board: $9,957
Financial aid: (320) 363-5388; 71% of undergrads determined to have financial need; average aid package $30,121

College of St. Scholastica
Duluth MN
(218) 723-6046
U.S. News ranking: Reg. U. (Mid. W), No. 23
Website: www.css.edu
Admissions email: admissions@css.edu
Private; founded 1912
Affiliation: Roman Catholic
Freshman admissions: selective; 2013-2014: 1,809 applied, 1,315 accepted. Either SAT or ACT required. ACT 25/75 percentile: 21-26. High school rank: 20% in top tenth, 55% in top quarter, 85% in top half
Early decision deadline: N/A, notification date: N/A
Early action deadline: N/A, notification date: N/A
Application deadline (fall): rolling
Undergraduate student body: 2,423 full time, 513 part time; 31% male, 69% female; 2% American Indian, 2% Asian, 3% black, 2% Hispanic, 2% multiracial, 0% Pacific Islander, 80% white, 4% international; 85% from in state; 36% live on campus; 0% of students in fraternities, 0% in sororities
Most popular majors: 13% Biological and Biomedical Sciences, 19% Business, Management, Marketing, and Related Support Services, 39% Health Professions and Related Programs, 7% Psychology, 6% Public Administration and Social Service Professions
Expenses: 2014-2015: $32,842; room/board: $8,598
Financial aid: (218) 723-6047; 80% of undergrads determined to have financial need; average aid package $20,760

Concordia College–Moorhead
Moorhead MN
(800) 699-9897
U.S. News ranking: Nat. Lib. Arts, No. 129
Website: www.concordiacollege.edu
Admissions email: admissions@cord.edu
Private; founded 1891
Affiliation: Evangelical Lutheran Church in America
Freshman admissions: more selective; 2013-2014: 2,493 applied, 1,944 accepted. Either SAT or ACT required. ACT 25/75 percentile: 22-28. High school rank: 30% in top tenth, 62% in top quarter, 90% in top half
Early decision deadline: N/A, notification date: N/A
Early action deadline: N/A, notification date: N/A
Application deadline (fall): rolling
Undergraduate student body: 2,488 full time, 43 part time; 38% male, 62% female; 1% American Indian, 2% Asian, 2% black, 2% Hispanic, 1% multiracial, 0% Pacific Islander, 84% white,

3% international; 70% from in state; 64% live on campus; 0% of students in fraternities, 0% in sororities
Most popular majors: 9% Biology, General, 10% Business Administration, Management and Operations, 13% Education, General, 7% Linguistic, Comparative, and Related Language Studies and Services, 8% Visual and Performing Arts, General
Expenses: 2014-2015: $34,114; room/board: $7,370
Financial aid: (218) 299-3010; 73% of undergrads determined to have financial need; average aid package $27,251

Concordia University–St. Paul
St. Paul MN
(651) 641-8230
U.S. News ranking: Reg. U. (Mid. W), No. 106
Website: www.csp.edu
Admissions email: admissions@csp.edu
Private; founded 1893
Affiliation: Lutheran Church-Missouri Synod
Freshman admissions: selective; 2013-2014: 1,349 applied, 720 accepted. ACT required. ACT 25/75 percentile: 18-24. High school rank: 7% in top tenth, 22% in top quarter, 58% in top half
Early decision deadline: N/A, notification date: N/A
Early action deadline: N/A, notification date: N/A
Application deadline (fall): rolling
Undergraduate student body: 1,217 full time, 954 part time; 42% male, 58% female; 0% American Indian, 7% Asian, 13% black, 4% Hispanic, 4% multiracial, 0% Pacific Islander, 64% white, 3% international; 79% from in state; 23% live on campus; 0% of students in fraternities, 0% in sororities
Most popular majors: 39% Business, Management, Marketing, and Related Support Services, 8% Education, 10% Family and Consumer Sciences/Human Sciences, 7% Homeland Security, Law Enforcement, Firefighting and Related Protective Services, 9% Parks, Recreation, Leisure, and Fitness Studies
Expenses: 2014-2015: $20,250; room/board: $8,000
Financial aid: (651) 603-6300; 80% of undergrads determined to have financial need; average aid package $14,086

Crown College[1]
St. Bonifacius MN
(952) 446-4142
U.S. News ranking: Reg. Coll. (Mid. W), No. 54
Website: www.crown.edu
Admissions email: admissions@crown.edu
Private; founded 1916
Affiliation: Christian and Missionary Alliance
Application deadline (fall): 8/20
Undergraduate student body: N/A full time, N/A part time
Expenses: 2013-2014: $22,430; room/board: $7,480
Financial aid: (952) 446-4177

Dunwoody College of Technology
Minneapolis MN
(800) 292-4625
U.S. News ranking: Reg. Coll. (Mid. W), No. 64
Website: www.dunwoody.edu
Admissions email: admissions@dunwoody.edu
Private; founded 1914
Freshman admissions: less selective; 2013-2014: 739 applied, 563 accepted. Neither SAT nor ACT required. ACT 25/75 percentile: N/A. High school rank: 1% in top tenth, 1% in top quarter, 21% in top half
Early decision deadline: N/A, notification date: N/A
Early action deadline: N/A, notification date: N/A
Application deadline (fall): rolling
Undergraduate student body: 855 full time, 216 part time; 88% male, 12% female; 1% American Indian, 5% Asian, 5% black, 2% Hispanic, 4% multiracial, 0% Pacific Islander, 73% white, 0% international
Most popular majors: 55% Business Administration and Management, General, 19% Industrial Technology/Technician, 26% Interior Design
Expenses: 2014-2015: $19,454; room/board: N/A
Financial aid: N/A; 90% of undergrads determined to have financial need; average aid package $7,851

Gustavus Adolphus College
St. Peter MN
(507) 933-7676
U.S. News ranking: Nat. Lib. Arts, No. 64
Website: www.gac.edu
Admissions email: admission@gac.edu
Private; founded 1862
Affiliation: Lutheran–ELCA
Freshman admissions: more selective; 2013-2014: 4,804 applied, 3,037 accepted. Neither SAT nor ACT required. ACT 25/75 percentile: 24-30. High school rank: 33% in top tenth, 67% in top quarter, 95% in top half
Early decision deadline: N/A, notification date: N/A
Early action deadline: 11/1, notification date: 11/20
Application deadline (fall): rolling
Undergraduate student body: 2,423 full time, 32 part time; 46% male, 54% female; 0% American Indian, 4% Asian, 2% black, 3% Hispanic, 3% multiracial, 0% Pacific Islander, 84% white, 3% international; 81% from in state; 85% live on campus; 17% of students in fraternities, 19% in sororities
Most popular majors: 15% Biology/Biological Sciences, General, 11% Business/Commerce, General, 6% Education, General, 10% Psychology, General, 6% Speech Communication and Rhetoric
Expenses: 2014-2015: $40,020; room/board: $9,250
Financial aid: (507) 933-7527; 72% of undergrads determined to have financial need; average aid package $30,614

Hamline University
St. Paul MN
(651) 523-2207
U.S. News ranking: Reg. U. (Mid. W), No. 12
Website: www.hamline.edu
Admissions email: admission@hamline.edu
Private; founded 1854
Affiliation: United Methodist
Freshman admissions: selective; 2013-2014: 3,427 applied, 2,247 accepted. Either SAT or ACT required. ACT 25/75 percentile: 21-27. High school rank: 19% in top tenth, 47% in top quarter, 84% in top half
Early decision deadline: 11/1, notification date: 11/20
Early action deadline: 12/1, notification date: 12/20
Application deadline (fall): rolling
Undergraduate student body: 2,101 full time, 110 part time; 41% male, 59% female; 0% American Indian, 6% Asian, 6% black, 6% Hispanic, 5% multiracial, 0% Pacific Islander, 72% white, 2% international; 80% from in state; 40% live on campus; 5% of students in fraternities, 5% in sororities
Most popular majors: 16% Business, Management, Marketing, and Related Support Services, 7% English Language and Literature/Letters, 7% Legal Professions and Studies, 12% Psychology, 17% Social Sciences
Expenses: 2014-2015: $36,260; room/board: $9,392
Financial aid: (651) 523-3000; 85% of undergrads determined to have financial need; average aid package $27,515

Macalester College
St. Paul MN
(651) 696-6357
U.S. News ranking: Nat. Lib. Arts, No. 24
Website: www.macalester.edu
Admissions email: admissions@macalester.edu
Private; founded 1874
Freshman admissions: most selective; 2013-2014: 6,680 applied, 2,283 accepted. Either SAT or ACT required. SAT 25/75 percentile: 1240-1460. High school rank: 64% in top tenth, 90% in top quarter, 99% in top half
Early decision deadline: 11/15, notification date: 12/15
Early action deadline: N/A, notification date: N/A
Application deadline (fall): 1/15
Undergraduate student body: 2,011 full time, 28 part time; 39% male, 61% female; 0% American Indian, 7% Asian, 3% black, 6% Hispanic, 5% multiracial, 0% Pacific Islander, 67% white, 12% international; 18% from in state; 64% live on campus; 0% of students in fraternities, 0% in sororities
Most popular majors: 9% Biological and Biomedical Sciences, 7% English Language and Literature/Letters, 9% Foreign Languages, Literatures, and Linguistics, 9% Multi/Interdisciplinary Studies, 26% Social Sciences
Expenses: 2014-2015: $47,195; room/board: $10,496
Financial aid: (651) 696-6214; 69% of undergrads determined to have financial need; average aid package $39,234

Martin Luther College[1]
New Ulm MN
(877) 652-1995
U.S. News ranking: Reg. Coll. (Mid. W), No. 40
Website: www.mlc-wels.edu
Admissions email: N/A
Private
Application deadline (fall): N/A
Undergraduate student body: N/A full time, N/A part time
Expenses: 2013-2014: $12,300; room/board: $4,860
Financial aid: (507) 354-8221

Metropolitan State University[1]
St. Paul MN
(651) 772-7600
U.S. News ranking: Reg. U. (Mid. W), second tier
Website: www.metrostate.edu
Admissions email: admissions@metrostate.edu
Public
Application deadline (fall): N/A
Undergraduate student body: N/A full time, N/A part time
Expenses: 2013-2014: $6,642 in state, $13,227 out of state; room/board: N/A
Financial aid: (651) 772-7670

Minneapolis College of Art and Design
Minneapolis MN
(612) 874-3760
U.S. News ranking: Arts, unranked
Website: www.mcad.edu
Admissions email: admissions@mcad.edu
Private; founded 1886
Freshman admissions: N/A; 2013-2014: N/A applied, N/A accepted. Either SAT or ACT required. SAT 25/75 percentile: N/A. High school rank: N/A
Early decision deadline: N/A, notification date: N/A
Early action deadline: 12/1, notification date: 12/15
Application deadline (fall): 5/1
Undergraduate student body: 665 full time, 23 part time; 36% male, 64% female; N/A American Indian, N/A Asian, N/A black, N/A Hispanic, N/A multiracial, N/A Pacific Islander, N/A white, N/A international; 90% from in state; 25% live on campus; 0% of students in fraternities, 0% in sororities
Most popular majors: Information not available
Expenses: 2014-2015: $34,146; room/board: N/A
Financial aid: (612) 874-3782; 80% of undergrads determined to have financial need; average aid package $21,791

Minnesota State University–Mankato
Mankato MN
(507) 389-1822
U.S. News ranking: Reg. U. (Mid. W), No. 69
Website: www.mnsu.edu
Admissions email: admissions@mnsu.edu
Public; founded 1867
Freshman admissions: selective; 2013-2014: 9,938 applied, 6,514 accepted. ACT required. ACT 25/75 percentile: 20-24. High school rank: 6% in top tenth, 23% in top quarter, 64% in top half

Early decision deadline: N/A, notification date: N/A
Early action deadline: N/A, notification date: N/A
Application deadline (fall): rolling
Undergraduate student body: 11,419 full time, 2,048 part time; 48% male, 52% female; 0% American Indian, 3% Asian, 5% black, 3% Hispanic, 2% multiracial, 0% Pacific Islander, 79% white, 5% international; 88% from in state; 20% live on campus; N/A of students in fraternities, N/A in sororities
Most popular majors: 21% Business, Management, Marketing, and Related Support Services, 9% Education, 12% Health Professions and Related Programs, 6% Homeland Security, Law Enforcement, Firefighting and Related Protective Services, 7% Social Sciences
Expenses: 2013-2014: $7,531 in state, $15,010 out of state; room/board: $7,368
Financial aid: (507) 389-1866

Minnesota State University–Moorhead
Moorhead MN
(800) 593-7246
U.S. News ranking: Reg. U. (Mid. W), No. 106
Website: www.mnstate.edu
Admissions email: admissions@mnstate.edu
Public; founded 1887
Freshman admissions: selective; 2013-2014: 3,562 applied, 3,174 accepted. Either SAT or ACT required. ACT 25/75 percentile: 20-25. High school rank: 9% in top tenth, 30% in top quarter, 64% in top half
Early decision deadline: N/A, notification date: N/A
Early action deadline: N/A, notification date: N/A
Application deadline (fall): 8/1
Undergraduate student body: 5,107 full time, 1,051 part time; 40% male, 60% female; 1% American Indian, 1% Asian, 3% black, 1% Hispanic, 3% multiracial, 0% Pacific Islander, 78% white, 7% international; 65% from in state; 25% live on campus; N/A of students in fraternities, N/A in sororities
Most popular majors: 10% Art/Art Studies, General, 15% Business Administration and Management, General, 15% Elementary Education and Teaching, 7% Mass Communication/Media Studies, 11% Registered Nursing/Registered Nurse
Expenses: 2014-2015: $7,838 in state, $14,736 out of state; room/board: $7,398
Financial aid: (218) 477-2251; 62% of undergrads determined to have financial need

North Central University
Minneapolis MN
(800) 289-6222
U.S. News ranking: Reg. Coll. (Mid. W), No. 66
Website: www.northcentral.edu
Admissions email: admissions@northcentral.edu
Private; founded 1930
Affiliation: Assemblies of God
Freshman admissions: selective; 2013-2014: 601 applied, 476 accepted. Either SAT or ACT

required. ACT 25/75 percentile: 19-26. High school rank: 15% in top tenth, 40% in top quarter, 67% in top half
Early decision deadline: N/A, notification date: N/A
Early action deadline: N/A, notification date: N/A
Application deadline (fall): 6/1
Undergraduate student body: 1,086 full time, 211 part time; 46% male, 54% female; 0% American Indian, 1% Asian, 3% black, 5% Hispanic, 3% multiracial, 0% Pacific Islander, 70% white, 1% international
Most popular majors: 7% Business Administration and Management, General, 7% Elementary Education and Teaching, 7% Intercultural/Multicultural and Diversity Studies, 11% Pastoral Studies/Counseling, 9% Youth Ministry
Expenses: 2014-2015: $20,776; room/board: $6,360
Financial aid: (612) 343-4485; 83% of undergrads determined to have financial need; average aid package $14,026

Southwest Minnesota State University

Marshall MN
(507) 537-6286
U.S. News ranking: Reg. U. (Mid. W), second tier
Website: www.smsu.edu
Admissions email: N/A
Public; founded 1963
Freshman admissions: selective; 2013-2014: 2,076 applied, 1,359 accepted. ACT required. ACT 25/75 percentile: 19-24. High school rank: 8% in top tenth, 27% in top quarter, 60% in top half
Early decision deadline: N/A, notification date: N/A
Early action deadline: N/A, notification date: N/A
Application deadline (fall): 9/1
Undergraduate student body: 2,108 full time, 4,118 part time; 41% male, 59% female; 1% American Indian, 3% Asian, 5% black, 2% Hispanic, 0% multiracial, 0% Pacific Islander, 85% white, 3% international
Most popular majors: 22% Business Administration and Management, General, 6% Early Childhood Education and Teaching, 6% Elementary Education and Teaching, 5% Finance, General, 5% Psychology, General
Expenses: 2013-2014: $8,280 in state, $8,280 out of state; room/board: $7,146
Financial aid: (507) 537-6281

St. Catherine University

St. Paul MN
(800) 945-4599
U.S. News ranking: Reg. U. (Mid. W), No. 13
Website: www.stkate.edu
Admissions email: admissions@stkate.edu
Private; founded 1905
Affiliation: Roman Catholic
Freshman admissions: more selective; 2013-2014: 2,685 applied, 1,571 accepted. Either SAT or ACT required. ACT 25/75 percentile: 22-26. High school rank: 23% in top tenth, 52% in top quarter, 87% in top half

Early decision deadline: N/A, notification date: N/A
Early action deadline: N/A, notification date: N/A
Application deadline (fall): rolling
Undergraduate student body: 2,188 full time, 1,371 part time; 3% male, 97% female; 1% American Indian, 11% Asian, 10% black, 5% Hispanic, 2% multiracial, 0% Pacific Islander, 66% white, 1% international; 89% from in state; 44% live on campus; N/A of students in fraternities, N/A in sororities
Most popular majors: 5% Business Administration and Management, General, 6% Psychology, General, 6% Public Health Education and Promotion, 23% Registered Nursing/Registered Nurse, 7% Social Work
Expenses: 2014-2015: $34,280; room/board: $8,894
Financial aid: (651) 690-6540; 88% of undergrads determined to have financial need; average aid package $30,944

St. Cloud State University

St. Cloud MN
(320) 308-2244
U.S. News ranking: Reg. U. (Mid. W), No. 99
Website: www.stcloudstate.edu
Admissions email: scsu4u@stcloudstate.edu
Public; founded 1869
Freshman admissions: selective; 2013-2014: 5,965 applied, 4,905 accepted. Either SAT or ACT required. ACT 25/75 percentile: 18-24: High school rank: 7% in top tenth, 24% in top quarter, 58% in top half
Early decision deadline: N/A, notification date: N/A
Early action deadline: N/A, notification date: N/A
Application deadline (fall): 8/1
Undergraduate student body: 9,860 full time, 4,781 part time; 48% male, 52% female; 0% American Indian, 4% Asian, 6% black, 3% Hispanic, 3% multiracial, 0% Pacific Islander, 77% white, 5% international
Most popular majors: Information not available
Expenses: 2013-2014: $7,514 in state, $15,156 out of state; room/board: $7,236
Financial aid: (320) 308-2047

St. John's University

Collegeville MN
(320) 363-5055
U.S. News ranking: Nat. Lib. Arts, No. 73
Website: www.csbsju.edu
Admissions email: admissions@csbsju.edu
Private; founded 1857
Affiliation: Roman Catholic (Benedictine)
Freshman admissions: more selective; 2013-2014: 1,747 applied, 1,313 accepted. Either SAT or ACT required. ACT 25/75 percentile: 22% in top tenth, 52% in top quarter, 83% in top half
Early decision deadline: N/A, notification date: N/A
Early action deadline: 11/15, notification date: 12/15
Application deadline (fall): 1/15

Undergraduate student body: 1,850 full time, 21 part time; 100% male, 0% female; 1% American Indian, 3% Asian, 3% black, 4% Hispanic, 1% multiracial, 0% Pacific Islander, 83% white, 5% international; 82% from in state; 85% live on campus; 0% of students in fraternities, 0% in sororities
Most popular majors: 9% Accounting, 6% Biology/Biological Sciences, General, 18% Business Administration and Management, General, 5% Political Science and Government, General, 6% Psychology, General
Expenses: 2014-2015: $38,704; room/board: $9,280
Financial aid: (320) 363-3664; 66% of undergrads determined to have financial need; average aid package $28,897

St. Mary's University of Minnesota

Winona MN
(507) 457-1700
U.S. News ranking: Nat. U., No. 181
Website: www.smumn.edu
Admissions email: admissions@smumn.edu
Private; founded 1912
Affiliation: Roman Catholic
Freshman admissions: selective; 2013-2014: 1,551 applied, 1,161 accepted. Either SAT or ACT required. ACT 25/75 percentile: 20-26. High school rank: 18% in top tenth, 35% in top quarter, 73% in top half
Early decision deadline: N/A, notification date: N/A
Early action deadline: N/A, notification date: N/A
Application deadline (fall): 5/1
Undergraduate student body: 1,307 full time, 625 part time; 45% male, 55% female; 1% American Indian, 2% Asian, 5% black, 5% Hispanic, 0% multiracial, 0% Pacific Islander, 53% white, 2% international; 60% from in state; 88% live on campus; 4% of students in fraternities, 3% in sororities
Most popular majors: 8% Accounting, 17% Business/Commerce, General, 6% Criminal Justice/Police Science, 5% Human Services, General, 8% Marketing/Marketing Management, General
Expenses: 2014-2015: $30,315; room/board: $7,965
Financial aid: (507) 457-1438; 77% of undergrads determined to have financial need; average aid package $22,086

St. Olaf College

Northfield MN
(507) 786-3025
U.S. News ranking: Nat. Lib. Arts, No. 54
Website: wp.stolaf.edu/
Admissions email: admissions@stolaf.edu
Private; founded 1874
Affiliation: Lutheran
Freshman admissions: more selective; 2013-2014: 4,011 applied, 2,372 accepted. Either SAT or ACT required. ACT 25/75 percentile: 26-31. High school rank: 54% in top tenth, 76% in top quarter, 98% in top half
Early decision deadline: 11/15, notification date: 12/17

Early action deadline: N/A, notification date: N/A
Application deadline (fall): 1/15
Undergraduate student body: 3,081 full time, 44 part time; 44% male, 56% female; 0% American Indian, 5% Asian, 1% black, 4% Hispanic, 4% multiracial, 0% Pacific Islander, 78% white, 6% international; 50% from in state; 92% live on campus; 0% of students in fraternities, 0% in sororities
Most popular majors: 12% Biological and Biomedical Sciences, 9% Physical Sciences, 8% Psychology, 16% Social Sciences, 11% Visual and Performing Arts
Expenses: 2014-2015: $41,700; room/board: $9,500
Financial aid: (507) 646-3019; 65% of undergrads determined to have financial need; average aid package $33,317

University of Minnesota–Crookston

Crookston MN
(800) 232-6466
U.S. News ranking: Reg. Coll. (Mid. W), No. 40
Website: www.crk.umn.edu
Admissions email: UMCinfo@umn.edu
Public; founded 1966
Freshman admissions: selective; 2013-2014: 762 applied, 527 accepted. Either SAT or ACT required. ACT 25/75 percentile: 19-24. High school rank: 10% in top tenth, 28% in top quarter, 63% in top half
Early decision deadline: N/A, notification date: N/A
Early action deadline: N/A, notification date: N/A
Application deadline (fall): rolling
Undergraduate student body: 1,305 full time, 1,534 part time; 47% male, 53% female; 1% American Indian, 2% Asian, 6% black, 2% Hispanic, 2% multiracial, 0% Pacific Islander, 78% white, 6% international; 72% from in state; 45% live on campus; 1% of students in fraternities, 0% in sororities
Most popular majors: 20% Agriculture, Agriculture Operations, and Related Sciences, 31% Business, Management, Marketing, and Related Support Services, 5% Health Professions and Related Programs, 8% Multi/Interdisciplinary Studies, 16% Natural Resources and Conservation
Expenses: 2014-2015: $11,468 in state, $11,468 out of state; room/board: $7,350
Financial aid: (218) 281-8576; 69% of undergrads determined to have financial need; average aid package $11,543

University of Minnesota–Duluth

Duluth MN
(218) 726-7171
U.S. News ranking: Reg. U. (Mid. W), No. 36
Website: www.d.umn.edu
Admissions email: umdadmis@d.umn.edu
Public; founded 1947
Freshman admissions: selective; 2013-2014: 7,074 applied, 5,533 accepted. Either SAT or ACT required. ACT 25/75

percentile: 22-26. High school rank: 16% in top tenth, 44% in top quarter, 84% in top half
Early decision deadline: N/A, notification date: N/A
Early action deadline: N/A, notification date: N/A
Application deadline (fall): 8/1
Undergraduate student body: 8,989 full time, 1,090 part time; 53% male, 47% female; 0% American Indian, 3% Asian, 2% black, 2% Hispanic, 2% multiracial, 0% Pacific Islander, 88% white, 2% international; 90% from in state; 31% live on campus; N/A of students in fraternities, N/A in sororities
Most popular majors: 11% Biological and Biomedical Sciences, 20% Business, Management, Marketing, and Related Support Services, 8% Education, 10% Engineering, 10% Social Sciences
Expenses: 2014-2015: $12,802 in state, $16,467 out of state; room/board: $7,004
Financial aid: (218) 726-8000; 60% of undergrads determined to have financial need; average aid package $10,879

University of Minnesota–Morris

Morris MN
(888) 866-3382
U.S. News ranking: Nat. Lib. Arts, No. 139
Website: www.morris.umn.edu
Admissions email: admissions@morris.umn.edu
Public; founded 1959
Freshman admissions: selective; 2013-2014: 2,649 applied, 1,527 accepted. Either SAT or ACT required. ACT 25/75 percentile: 23-28. High school rank: 31% in top tenth, 59% in top quarter, 92% in top half
Early decision deadline: N/A, notification date: N/A
Early action deadline: N/A, notification date: N/A
Application deadline (fall): 3/15
Undergraduate student body: 1,815 full time, 131 part time; 45% male, 55% female; 6% American Indian, 3% Asian, 2% black, 3% Hispanic, 11% multiracial, 0% Pacific Islander, 66% white, 9% international; 88% from in state; 51% live on campus; N/A of students in fraternities, N/A in sororities
Most popular majors: 10% Biological and Biomedical Sciences, 8% Business, Management, Marketing, and Related Support Services, 6% English Language and Literature/Letters, 5% History, 10% Psychology
Expenses: 2013-2014: $12,584 in state, $12,584 out of state; room/board: $7,482
Financial aid: (320) 589-6035

University of Minnesota– Twin Cities

Minneapolis MN
(800) 752-1000
U.S. News ranking: Nat. U., No. 71
Website: www.umn.edu
Admissions email: N/A
Public; founded 1851

Freshman admissions: more selective; 2013-2014: 43,048 applied, 19,121 accepted. Either SAT or ACT required. ACT 25/75 percentile: 26-30. High school rank: 45% in top tenth, 82% in top quarter, 100% in top half Early decision deadline: N/A, notification date: N/A
Early action deadline: N/A, notification date: N/A
Application deadline (fall): rolling Undergraduate student body: 28,940 full time, 5,509 part time; 49% male, 51% female; 0% American Indian, 9% Asian, 4% black, 3% Hispanic, 3% multiracial, 0% Pacific Islander, 71% white, 9% international; 74% from in state; 23% live on campus; N/A of students in fraternities, N/A in sororities
Most popular majors: 8% Biological and Biomedical Sciences, 9% Business, Management, Marketing, and Related Support Services, 11% Engineering, 8% Psychology, 12% Social Sciences
Expenses: 2014-2015: $13,626 in state, $20,876 out of state; room/board: $8,920
Financial aid: (612) 624-1111; 51% of undergrads determined to have financial need; average aid package $13,244

University of Northwestern– St. Paul

St. Paul MN
(800) 827-6827
U.S. News ranking: Reg. Coll. (Mid. W), No. 10
Website: www.unwsp.edu
Admissions email: admissions@ unwsp.edu
Private; founded 1902
Affiliation: Christian nondenominational
Freshman admissions: more selective; 2013-2014: N/A applied, N/A accepted. Either SAT or ACT required. ACT 25/75 percentile: 22-27. High school rank: 28% in top tenth, 50% in top quarter, 83% in top half Early decision deadline: N/A, notification date: N/A
Early action deadline: N/A, notification date: N/A
Application deadline (fall): 8/1 Undergraduate student body: 1,685 full time, 52 part time; 40% male, 60% female; N/A American Indian, N/A Asian, N/A black, N/A Hispanic, N/A multiracial, N/A Pacific Islander, N/A white, N/A international
Most popular majors: Information not available
Expenses: 2014-2015: $28,676; room/board: N/A
Financial aid: (651) 631-5212

University of St. Thomas

St. Paul MN
(651) 962-6150
U.S. News ranking: Nat. U., No. 113
Website: www.stthomas.edu
Admissions email: admissions@ stthomas.edu
Private; founded 1885
Affiliation: Roman Catholic
Freshman admissions: selective; 2013-2014: 5,540 applied, 4,774 accepted. Either SAT or ACT required. ACT 25/75

percentile: 23-28. High school rank: 22% in top tenth, 50% in top quarter, 86% in top half Early decision deadline: N/A, notification date: N/A
Early action deadline: N/A, notification date: N/A
Application deadline (fall): rolling Undergraduate student body: 6,094 full time, 256 part time; 53% male, 47% female; 0% American Indian, 4% Asian, 3% black, 4% Hispanic, 3% multiracial, 0% Pacific Islander, 82% white, 3% international; 80% from in state; 39% live on campus; 0% of students in fraternities, 0% in sororities
Most popular majors: 7% Biological and Biomedical Sciences, 38% Business, Management, Marketing, and Related Support Services, 6% Communication, Journalism, and Related Programs, 8% Philosophy and Religious Studies, 9% Social Sciences
Expenses: 2014-2015: $34,442; room/board: $9,166
Financial aid: (651) 962-6550; 58% of undergrads determined to have financial need; average aid package $23,731

Walden University

Minneapolis MN
(866) 492-5336
U.S. News ranking: Nat. U., unranked
Website: www.waldenu.edu/
Admissions email: N/A
For-profit; founded 1970
Freshman admissions: N/A; 2013-2014: 687 applied, 673 accepted. Neither SAT nor ACT required. ACT 25/75 percentile: N/A. High school rank: N/A
Early decision deadline: N/A, notification date: N/A
Early action deadline: N/A, notification date: N/A
Application deadline (fall): rolling Undergraduate student body: 815 full time, 7,390 part time; 23% male, 77% female; 0% American Indian, 2% Asian, 35% black, 6% Hispanic, 2% multiracial, 0% Pacific Islander, 42% white, 1% international; 2% from in state; N/A live on campus; N/A of students in fraternities, N/A in sororities
Most popular majors: 19% Business Administration and Management, General, 5% Criminal Justice/Law Enforcement Administration, 6% Human Development and Family Studies, General, 17% Psychology, General, 32% Registered Nursing/ Registered Nurse
Expenses: 2014-2015: $14,300; room/board: N/A
Financial aid: N/A; 77% of undergrads determined to have financial need; average aid package $13,677

Winona State University

Winona MN
(507) 457-5100
U.S. News ranking: Reg. U. (Mid. W), No. 61
Website: www.winona.edu
Admissions email: admissions@ winona.edu
Public; founded 1858

Freshman admissions: selective; 2013-2014: 7,212 applied, 4,381 accepted. Either SAT or ACT required. ACT 25/75 percentile: 21-25. High school rank: 8% in top tenth, 31% jn top quarter, 72% in top half
Early decision deadline: N/A, notification date: N/A
Early action deadline: N/A, notification date: N/A
Application deadline (fall): rolling Undergraduate student body: 7,351 full time, 903 part time; 39% male, 61% female; 0% American Indian, 2% Asian, 2% black, 3% Hispanic, 2% multiracial, 0% Pacific Islander, 88% white, 2% international; 69% from in state; 29% live on campus; N/A of students in fraternities, N/A in sororities
Most popular majors: 17% Business, Management, Marketing, and Related Support Services, 6% Communication, Journalism, and Related Programs, 16% Education, 16% Health Professions and Related Programs, 8% Parks, Recreation, Leisure, and Fitness Studies
Expenses: 2014-2015: $8,750 in state, $14,250 out of state; room/board: $7,890
Financial aid: (507) 457-5090; 61% of undergrads determined to have financial need; average aid package $7,374

MISSISSIPPI

Alcorn State University

Alcorn State MS
(601) 877-6147
U.S. News ranking: Reg. U. (S), No. 73
Website: www.alcorn.edu
Admissions email: ebarnes@alcorn.edu
Public; founded 1871
Freshman admissions: less selective; 2013-2014: 2,265 applied, 1,878 accepted. Either SAT or ACT required. ACT 25/75 percentile: 16-19. High school rank: N/A in top tenth, N/A in top quarter, 68% in top half
Early decision deadline: N/A, notification date: N/A
Early action deadline: N/A, notification date: N/A
Application deadline (fall): rolling Undergraduate student body: 2,732 full time, 425 part time; 35% male, 65% female; 0% American Indian, 0% Asian, 93% black, 1% Hispanic, 1% multiracial, 0% Pacific Islander, 3% white, 1% international; 87% from in state; 50% live on campus; N/A of students in fraternities, N/A in sororities
Most popular majors: 11% Biological and Biomedical Sciences, 15% Health Professions and Related Programs, 12% Liberal Arts and Sciences, General Studies and Humanities, 8% Military Technologies and Applied Sciences, 6% Social Sciences
Expenses: 2013-2014: $6,096 in state, $15,096 out of state; room/board: $8,430
Financial aid: (601) 877-6190

Belhaven University

Jackson MS
(601) 968-5940
U.S. News ranking: Reg. U. (S), No. 65
Website: www.belhaven.edu
Admissions email: admission@ belhaven.edu
Private; founded 1883
Affiliation: Presbyterian
Freshman admissions: selective; 2013-2014: 1,980 applied, 1,104 accepted. Either SAT or ACT required. ACT 25/75 percentile: 19-25. High school rank: 8% in top tenth, 26% in top quarter, 56% in top half
Early decision deadline: N/A, notification date: N/A
Early action deadline: N/A, notification date: N/A
Application deadline (fall): rolling Undergraduate student body: 1,188 full time, 830 part time; 39% male, 61% female; 1% American Indian, 2% Asian, 40% black, 5% Hispanic, 2% multiracial, 0% Pacific Islander, 42% white, 0% international; 33% from in state; 45% live on campus; 0% of students in fraternities, 0% in sororities
Most popular majors: 41% Business, Management, Marketing, and Related Support Services, 8% Health Professions and Related Programs, 7% Parks, Recreation, Leisure, and Fitness Studies, 11% Social Sciences, 13% Visual and Performing Arts
Expenses: 2014-2015: $20,780; room/board: $7,700
Financial aid: (601) 968-5934; 75% of undergrads determined to have financial need; average aid package $15,058

Blue Mountain College

Blue Mountain MS
(662) 685-4161
U.S. News ranking: Reg. Coll. (S), No. 23
Website: www.bmc.edu
Admissions email: admissions@ bmc.edu
Private; founded 1873
Affiliation: Southern Baptist Convention
Freshman admissions: selective; 2013-2014: 315 applied, 162 accepted. Either SAT or ACT required. ACT 25/75 percentile: 18-23. High school rank: 14% in top tenth, 38% in top quarter, 68% in top half
Early decision deadline: N/A, notification date: N/A
Early action deadline: N/A, notification date: N/A
Application deadline (fall): rolling Undergraduate student body: 453 full time, 67 part time; 42% male, 58% female; 0% American Indian, 1% Asian, 10% black, 2% Hispanic, 0% multiracial, 0% Pacific Islander, 86% white, 2% international; 81% from in state; 56% live on campus; 0% of students in fraternities, 0% in sororities
Most popular majors: 17% Bible/ Biblical Studies, 6% Biology/ Biological Sciences, General, 7% Business Administration and Management, General, 48% Education, General, 8% Psychology, General

Expenses: 2014-2015: $10,534; room/board: $4,800
Financial aid: (662) 685-4771; 84% of undergrads determined to have financial need; average aid package $9,738

Delta State University

Cleveland MS
(662) 846-4018
U.S. News ranking: Reg. U. (S), No. 92
Website: www.deltastate.edu
Admissions email: admissions@ deltastate.edu
Public; founded 1924
Freshman admissions: selective; 2013-2014: 472 applied, 422 accepted. ACT required. ACT 25/75 percentile: 18-22. High school rank: 17% in top tenth, 40% in top quarter, 77% in top half
Early decision deadline: N/A, notification date: N/A
Early action deadline: N/A, notification date: N/A
Application deadline (fall): 8/1 Undergraduate student body: 2,166 full time, 472 part time; 40% male, 60% female; 0% American Indian, 1% Asian, 35% black, 1% Hispanic, 1% multiracial, 0% Pacific Islander, 59% white, 3% international; 88% from in state; 36% live on campus; N/A of students in fraternities, N/A in sororities
Most popular majors: 8% Biology/ Biological Sciences, General, 13% Elementary Education and Teaching, 6% Physical Education Teaching and Coaching, 8% Registered Nursing/Registered Nurse, 10% Social Work
Expenses: 2014-2015: $6,187 in state, $6,187 out of state; room/ board: $7,045
Financial aid: (662) 846-4670; 67% of undergrads determined to have financial need; average aid package $8,914

Jackson State University[1]

Jackson MS
(601) 979-2100
U.S. News ranking: Nat. U., second tier
Website: www.jsums.edu
Admissions email: admappl@ jsums.edu
Public
Application deadline (fall): N/A
Undergraduate student body: N/A full time, N/A part time
Expenses: 2013-2014: $6,348 in state, $15,552 out of state; room/ board: $7,192
Financial aid: (601) 979-2227

Millsaps College

Jackson MS
(601) 974-1050
U.S. News ranking: Nat. Lib. Arts, No. 89
Website: www.millsaps.edu
Admissions email: admissions@ millsaps.edu
Private; founded 1890
Affiliation: United Methodist
Freshman admissions: more selective; 2013-2014: 1,901 applied, 902 accepted. Either SAT or ACT required. ACT 25/75 percentile: 23-28. High school rank: 31% in top tenth, 59% in top quarter, 85% in top half

Early decision deadline: N/A, notification date: N/A
Early action deadline: 11/15, notification date: 1/15
Application deadline (fall): 2/1
Undergraduate student body: 730 full time, 14 part time; 52% male, 48% female; 1% American Indian, 5% Asian, 10% black, 3% Hispanic, 0% multiracial, 0% Pacific Islander, 76% white, 3% international; 42% from in state; 88% live on campus; 60% of students in fraternities, 64% in sororities
Most popular majors: 20% Biological and Biomedical Sciences, 24% Business, Management, Marketing, and Related Support Services, 8% Psychology, 10% Social Sciences, 7% Visual and Performing Arts
Expenses: 2014-2015: $33,982; room/board: $11,878
Financial aid: (601) 974-1220; 58% of undergrads determined to have financial need; average aid package $27,915

Mississippi College

Clinton MS
(601) 925-3800
U.S. News ranking: Reg. U. (S), No. 29
Website: www.mc.edu
Admissions email: enrollment-services@mc.edu
Private; founded 1826
Affiliation: Mississippi Baptist Convention
Freshman admissions: selective; 2013-2014: 1,936 applied, 1,303 accepted. Either SAT or ACT required. ACT 25/75 percentile: 21-27. High school rank: 24% in top tenth, 42% in top quarter, 57% in top half
Early decision deadline: N/A, notification date: N/A
Early action deadline: N/A, notification date: N/A
Application deadline (fall): rolling
Undergraduate student body: 2,589 full time, 316 part time; 41% male, 59% female; 1% American Indian, 2% Asian, 22% black, 2% Hispanic, 1% multiracial, 0% Pacific Islander, 68% white, 3% international; 74% from in state; 59% live on campus; 7% of students in fraternities, 18% in sororities
Most popular majors: 7% Accounting, 7% Biomedical Sciences, General, 8% Business Administration and Management, General, 9% Kinesiology and Exercise Science, 10% Registered Nursing/Registered Nurse
Expenses: 2014-2015: $15,458; room/board: $8,408
Financial aid: (601) 925-3319; 55% of undergrads determined to have financial need; average aid package $13,596

Mississippi State University

Mississippi State MS
(662) 325-2224
U.S. News ranking: Nat. U., No. 156
Website: www.msstate.edu
Admissions email: admit@admissions.msstate.edu
Public; founded 1878

Freshman admissions: more selective; 2013-2014: 11,117 applied, 7,938 accepted. Either SAT or ACT required. ACT 25/75 percentile: 20-28. High school rank: 28% in top tenth, 53% in top quarter, 83% in top half
Early decision deadline: N/A, notification date: N/A
Early action deadline: N/A, notification date: N/A
Application deadline (fall): rolling
Undergraduate student body: 15,048 full time, 1,351 part time; 52% male, 48% female; 1% American Indian, 1% Asian, 21% black, 2% Hispanic, 1% multiracial, 0% Pacific Islander, 72% white, 1% international; 76% from in state; 28% live on campus; 15% of students in fraternities, 24% in sororities
Most popular majors: 5% Biological and Biomedical Sciences, 18% Business, Management, Marketing, and Related Support Services, 19% Education, 11% Engineering, 5% Psychology
Expenses: 2013-2014: $6,772 in state, $16,960 out of state; room/board: $8,647
Financial aid: (662) 325-2450; 62% of undergrads determined to have financial need; average aid package $12,990

Mississippi University for Women

Columbus MS
(662) 329-7106
U.S. News ranking: Reg. U. (S), No. 47
Website: www.muw.edu
Admissions email: admissions@muw.edu
Public; founded 1884
Freshman admissions: selective; 2013-2014: 1,274 applied, 554 accepted. Either SAT or ACT required. ACT 25/75 percentile: 18-24. High school rank: 26% in top tenth, 59% in top quarter, 87% in top half
Early decision deadline: N/A, notification date: N/A
Early action deadline: N/A, notification date: N/A
Application deadline (fall): rolling
Undergraduate student body: 1,945 full time, 484 part time; 18% male, 82% female; 0% American Indian, 1% Asian, 39% black, 1% Hispanic, 1% multiracial, 0% Pacific Islander, 56% white, 2% international; 91% from in state; 22% live on campus; 8% of students in fraternities, 12% in sororities
Most popular majors: 6% Business Administration and Management, General, 6% Elementary Education and Teaching, 7% Liberal Arts and Sciences/Liberal Studies, 48% Registered Nursing/Registered Nurse, 4% Speech-Language Pathology/Pathologist
Expenses: 2014-2015: $5,640 in state, $15,360 out of state; room/board: $6,183
Financial aid: (662) 329-7114; 76% of undergrads determined to have financial need; average aid package $8,948

Mississippi Valley State University[1]

Itta Bena MS
(662) 254-3344
U.S. News ranking: Reg. U. (S), second tier
Website: www.mvsu.edu
Admissions email: admsn@mvsu.edu
Public
Application deadline (fall): N/A
Undergraduate student body: N/A full time, N/A part time
Expenses: 2013-2014: $5,916 in state, $5,916 out of state; room/board: $6,836
Financial aid: (662) 254-3335

Rust College

Holly Springs MS
(662) 252-8000
U.S. News ranking: Nat. Lib. Arts, second tier
Website: www.rustcollege.edu
Admissions email: admissions@rustcollege.edu
Private; founded 1866
Affiliation: United Methodist
Freshman admissions: less selective; 2013-2014: 3,152 applied, 437 accepted. ACT required. ACT 25/75 percentile: 13-14. High school rank: N/A
Early decision deadline: N/A, notification date: N/A
Early action deadline: N/A, notification date: N/A
Application deadline (fall): rolling
Undergraduate student body: 854 full time, 68 part time; 39% male, 61% female; 0% American Indian, 0% Asian, 95% black, 0% Hispanic, 0% multiracial, 0% Pacific Islander, 0% white, 3% international; 49% from in state; 93% live on campus; 15% of students in fraternities, 15% in sororities
Most popular majors: 34% Biology/Biological Sciences, General, 12% Broadcast Journalism, 9% Computer Science, 8% Education, General, 14% Social Sciences, General
Expenses: 2014-2015: $9,286; room/board: $4,000
Financial aid: (662) 252-8000; 93% of undergrads determined to have financial need; average aid package $11,915

Tougaloo College

Tougaloo MS
(601) 977-7765
U.S. News ranking: Nat. Lib. Arts, second tier
Website: www.tougaloo.edu
Admissions email: information@mail.tougaloo.edu
Private; founded 1869
Affiliation: United Church Disciples of Christ
Freshman admissions: less selective; 2013-2014: 3,018 applied, 1,028 accepted. Either SAT or ACT required. ACT 25/75 percentile: 15-21. High school rank: 19% in top tenth, 25% in top quarter, 82% in top half
Early decision deadline: N/A, notification date: N/A
Early action deadline: 11/1, notification date: 12/1
Application deadline (fall): 7/1
Undergraduate student body: 848 full time, 30 part time; 35% male, 65% female; 0% American Indian, 0% Asian, 98% black, 0% Hispanic, 0% multiracial,

0% Pacific Islander, 1% white, 1% international; 84% from in state; 65% live on campus; 6% of students in fraternities, 8% in sororities
Most popular majors: 9% Biology/Biological Sciences, General, 7% Chemistry, General, 8% Economics, General, 8% Psychology, General, 27% Sociology
Expenses: 2014-2015: $10,210; room/board: $6,330
Financial aid: (601) 977-7769; 96% of undergrads determined to have financial need; average aid package $13,500

University of Mississippi

University MS
(662) 915-7226
U.S. News ranking: Nat. U., No. 149
Website: www.olemiss.edu
Admissions email: admissions@olemiss.edu
Public; founded 1844
Freshman admissions: more selective; 2013-2014: 14,258 applied, 8,464 accepted. Neither SAT nor ACT required. ACT 25/75 percentile: 21-27. High school rank: 24% in top tenth, 48% in top quarter, 77% in top half
Early decision deadline: N/A, notification date: N/A
Early action deadline: N/A, notification date: N/A
Application deadline (fall): 7/20
Undergraduate student body: 15,628 full time, 1,049 part time; 45% male, 55% female; 0% American Indian, 2% Asian, 16% black, 3% Hispanic, 2% multiracial, 0% Pacific Islander, 77% white, 1% international; 63% from in state; 32% live on campus; 29% of students in fraternities, 36% in sororities
Most popular majors: 5% Accounting, 5% Business/Managerial Economics, 8% Elementary Education and Teaching, 6% Marketing/Marketing Management, General, 5% Psychology, General
Expenses: 2014-2015: $7,096 in state, $19,144 out of state; room/board: $9,908
Financial aid: (662) 915-7175; 54% of undergrads determined to have financial need; average aid package $7,890

University of Southern Mississippi

Hattiesburg MS
(601) 266-5000
U.S. News ranking: Nat. U., second tier
Website: www.usm.edu/admissions
Admissions email: admissions@usm.edu
Public; founded 1910
Freshman admissions: selective; 2013-2014: 6,120 applied, 4,058 accepted. Either SAT or ACT required. ACT 25/75 percentile: 19-25. High school rank: 6% in top tenth, 35% in top quarter, 71% in top half
Early decision deadline: N/A, notification date: N/A
Early action deadline: N/A, notification date: N/A
Application deadline (fall): rolling

0% Pacific Islander, 1% white, 1% international; 84% from in state; 65% live on campus; 6% of students in fraternities, 8% in sororities

Undergraduate student body: 10,841 full time, 1,634 part time; 36% male, 64% female; 0% American Indian, 1% Asian, 32% black, 3% Hispanic, 2% multiracial, 0% Pacific Islander, 61% white, 1% international; 85% from in state; 27% live on campus; 15% of students in fraternities, 17% in sororities
Most popular majors: 4% Business Administration and Management, General, 8% Elementary Education and Teaching, 5% Multi-/Interdisciplinary Studies, Other, 6% Psychology, General, 8% Registered Nursing/Registered Nurse
Expenses: 2013-2014: $6,744 in state, $15,024 out of state; room/board: $7,206
Financial aid: (601) 266-4774

William Carey University

Hattiesburg MS
(601) 318-6103
U.S. News ranking: Reg. U. (S), No. 37
Website: www.wmcarey.edu
Admissions email: admissions@wmcarey.edu
Private; founded 1892
Affiliation: Baptist
Freshman admissions: more selective; 2013-2014: 712 applied, 357 accepted. Either SAT or ACT required. ACT 25/75 percentile: 21-28. High school rank: 39% in top tenth, 59% in top quarter, 81% in top half
Early decision deadline: N/A, notification date: N/A
Early action deadline: N/A, notification date: N/A
Application deadline (fall): rolling
Undergraduate student body: 1,886 full time, 371 part time; 36% male, 64% female; 1% American Indian, 1% Asian, 30% black, 2% Hispanic, 0% multiracial, 0% Pacific Islander, 61% white, 4% international; 89% from in state; 31% live on campus; 0% of students in fraternities, 2% in sororities
Most popular majors: 4% Biology/Biological Sciences, General, 11% Business Administration and Management, General, 18% Elementary Education and Teaching, 19% Psychology, General, 23% Registered Nursing/Registered Nurse
Expenses: 2014-2015: $11,400; room/board: $4,140
Financial aid: (601) 318-6153; 91% of undergrads determined to have financial need; average aid package $16,000

MISSOURI

Avila University[1]

Kansas City MO
(816) 501-2400
U.S. News ranking: Reg. U. (Mid. W), second tier
Website: www.Avila.edu
Admissions email: admissions@mail.avila.edu
Private
Application deadline (fall): N/A
Undergraduate student body: N/A full time, N/A part time
Expenses: 2013-2014: $24,950; room/board: $6,908
Financial aid: (816) 501-3600

Central Methodist University

Fayette MO
(660) 248-6251
U.S. News ranking: Reg. Coll. (Mid. W), No. 40
Website: www.centralmethodist.edu
Admissions email: admissions@centralmethodist.edu
Private; founded 1854
Affiliation: United Methodist
Freshman admissions: selective; 2013-2014: 1,285 applied, 836 accepted. Either SAT or ACT required. ACT 25/75 percentile: 19-24. High school rank: 18% in top tenth, 43% in top quarter, 79% in top half
Early decision deadline: N/A, notification date: N/A
Early action deadline: N/A, notification date: N/A
Application deadline (fall): rolling
Undergraduate student body: 1,024 full time, 83 part time; 49% male, 51% female; 3% American Indian, 0% Asian, 0% black, 1% Hispanic, 0% multiracial, 63% Pacific Islander, 1% white, 0% international; 88% from in state; 61% live on campus; 17% of students in fraternities, 14% in sororities
Most popular majors: 10% Biological and Biomedical Sciences, 16% Business, Management, Marketing, and Related Support Services, 24% Education, 16% Health Professions and Related Programs, 8% Multi/Interdisciplinary Studies
Expenses: 2014-2015: $21,830; room/board: $7,130
Financial aid: (660) 248-6244; 81% of undergrads determined to have financial need; average aid package $19,231

College of the Ozarks

Point Lookout MO
(800) 222-0525
U.S. News ranking: Reg. Coll. (Mid. W), No. 4
Website: www.cofo.edu
Admissions email: admiss4@cofo.edu
Private; founded 1906
Affiliation: Evangelical Christian Interdenominational
Freshman admissions: selective; 2013-2014: 3,050 applied, 371 accepted. Either SAT or ACT required. ACT 25/75 percentile: 20-25. High school rank: 19% in top tenth, 50% in top quarter, 94% in top half
Early decision deadline: N/A, notification date: N/A
Early action deadline: N/A, notification date: N/A
Application deadline (fall): rolling
Undergraduate student body: 1,498 full time, 33 part time; 47% male, 53% female; 1% American Indian, 1% Asian; 1% black, 2% Hispanic, 2% multiracial, 0% Pacific Islander, 92% white, 2% international; 84% from in state; 81% live on campus; 0% of students in fraternities, 0% in sororities
Most popular majors: 10% Agriculture, Agriculture Operations, and Related Sciences, 12% Business, Management, Marketing, and Related Support Services, 17% Education,

General, 9% Homeland Security, Law Enforcement, Firefighting and Related Protective Services, 9% Speech Communication and Rhetoric
Expenses: 2014-2015: $18,530; room/board: $6,200
Financial aid: (417) 334-6411; 94% of undergrads determined to have financial need; average aid package $17,434

Columbia College

Columbia MO
(573) 875-7352
U.S. News ranking: Reg. U. (Mid. W), unranked
Website: www.ccis.edu
Admissions email: admissions@ccis.edu
Private; founded 1851
Affiliation: Christian Church (Disciples of Christ)
Freshman admissions: N/A; 2013-2014: N/A applied, N/A accepted. Neither SAT nor ACT required. ACT 25/75 percentile: N/A. High school rank: N/A
Early decision deadline: N/A, notification date: N/A
Early action deadline: N/A, notification date: N/A
Application deadline (fall): rolling
Undergraduate student body: N/A full time, N/A part time; N/A male, N/A female; N/A American Indian, N/A Asian, N/A black, N/A Hispanic, N/A multiracial, N/A Pacific Islander, N/A white, N/A international
Most popular majors: Information not available
Expenses: 2013-2014: $19,386; room/board: N/A
Financial aid: (573) 875-7390

Culver-Stockton College

Canton MO
(800) 537-1883
U.S. News ranking: Reg. Coll. (Mid. W), No. 34
Website: www.culver.edu
Admissions email: admissions@culver.edu
Private; founded 1853
Affiliation: Christian Church (Disciples of Christ)
Freshman admissions: selective; 2013-2014: 2,040 applied, 1,209 accepted. Either SAT or ACT required. ACT 25/75 percentile: 18-23. High school rank: 11% in top tenth, 25% in top quarter, 59% in top half
Early decision deadline: N/A, notification date: N/A
Early action deadline: N/A, notification date: N/A
Application deadline (fall): rolling
Undergraduate student body: 772 full time, 58 part time; 50% male, 50% female; 0% American Indian, 0% Asian, 12% black, 4% Hispanic, 2% multiracial, 1% Pacific Islander, 79% white, 2% international; 65% from in state; 74% live on campus; 36% of students in fraternities, 39% in sororities
Most popular majors: 12% Business Administration and Management, General, 6% Criminal Justice/Law Enforcement Administration, 9% Psychology, General, 8% Registered Nursing/Registered Nurse, 10% Sport and Fitness Administration/Management

Expenses: 2014-2015: $24,050; room/board: $7,780
Financial aid: (573) 288-6307; 90% of undergrads determined to have financial need; average aid package $20,649

Drury University

Springfield MO
(417) 873-7205
U.S. News ranking: Reg. U. (Mid. W), No. 8
Website: www.drury.edu
Admissions email: druryad@drury.edu
Private; founded 1873
Affiliation: Christian Church (Disciples of Christ)
Freshman admissions: more selective; 2013-2014: 1,244 applied, 909 accepted. Either SAT or ACT required. ACT 25/75 percentile: 22-28. High school rank: 30% in top tenth, 59% in top quarter, 87% in top half
Early decision deadline: N/A, notification date: N/A
Early action deadline: N/A, notification date: N/A
Application deadline (fall): rolling
Undergraduate student body: 1,549 full time, 26 part time; 47% male, 53% female; 1% American Indian, 2% Asian, 3% black, 3% Hispanic, 1% multiracial, 0% Pacific Islander, 81% white, 10% international; 85% from in state; 52% live on campus; 25% of students in fraternities, 26% in sororities
Most popular majors: 11% Biological and Biomedical Sciences, 12% Business, Management, Marketing, and Related Support Services, 11% Education, 14% Psychology, 9% Social Sciences
Expenses: 2014-2015: $23,885; room/board: $7,394
Financial aid: (417) 873-7312; 70% of undergrads determined to have financial need; average aid package $17,945

Evangel University

Springfield MO
(800) 382-6435
U.S. News ranking: Reg. Coll. (Mid. W), No. 49
Website: www.evangel.edu
Admissions email: admissions@evangel.edu
Private; founded 1955
Affiliation: Assemblies of God
Freshman admissions: selective; 2013-2014: N/A applied, N/A accepted. Either SAT or ACT required. ACT 25/75 percentile: 19-26. High school rank: N/A
Early decision deadline: N/A, notification date: N/A
Early action deadline: N/A, notification date: N/A
Application deadline (fall): rolling
Undergraduate student body: 1,887 full time, 190 part time; 44% male, 56% female; 1% American Indian, 2% Asian, 5% black, 6% Hispanic, 3% multiracial, 0% Pacific Islander, 70% white, 1% international; 55% from in state; 68% live on campus; N/A of students in fraternities, N/A in sororities
Most popular majors: Information not available
Expenses: 2014-2015: $20,676; room/board: $7,200

Financial aid: (417) 865-2815; 96% of undergrads determined to have financial need; average aid package $14,653

Fontbonne University

St. Louis MO
(314) 889-1400
U.S. News ranking: Reg. U. (Mid. W), No. 109
Website: www.fontbonne.edu
Admissions email: admissions@fontbonne.edu
Private; founded 1923
Affiliation: Roman Catholic
Freshman admissions: selective; 2013-2014: 676 applied, 441 accepted. Either SAT or ACT required. ACT 25/75 percentile: 21-25. High school rank: N/A
Early decision deadline: N/A, notification date: N/A
Early action deadline: N/A, notification date: N/A
Application deadline (fall): rolling
Undergraduate student body: 956 full time, 372 part time; 33% male, 67% female; 0% American Indian, 1% Asian, 17% black, 2% Hispanic, 1% multiracial, 0% Pacific Islander, 68% white, 9% international; 87% from in state; 19% live on campus; N/A of students in fraternities, N/A in sororities
Most popular majors: 16% Business Administration and Management, General, 4% Dietetics/Dietitian, 5% Psychology, General, 7% Special Education and Teaching, General, 6% Speech-Language Pathology/Pathologist
Expenses: 2013-2014: $22,684; room/board: $8,400
Financial aid: (314) 889-1414

Hannibal-LaGrange University

Hannibal MO
(800) 454-1119
U.S. News ranking: Reg. Coll. (Mid. W), second tier
Website: www.hlg.edu
Admissions email: admissions@hlg.edu
Private; founded 1858
Affiliation: Southern Baptist Convention
Freshman admissions: selective; 2013-2014: 703 applied, 480 accepted. Either SAT or ACT required. ACT 25/75 percentile: 19-25. High school rank: N/A
Early decision deadline: N/A, notification date: N/A
Early action deadline: N/A, notification date: N/A
Application deadline (fall): 8/27
Undergraduate student body: 850 full time, 349 part time; 42% male, 58% female; 1% American Indian, 1% Asian, 4% black, 4% Hispanic, 2% multiracial, 1% Pacific Islander, 79% white, 9% international; 77% from in state; 43% live on campus; N/A of students in fraternities, N/A in sororities
Most popular majors: 8% Business Administration and Management, General, 11% Criminal Justice/Safety Studies, 15% Elementary Education and Teaching, 12% Organizational Leadership, 11% Registered Nursing/Registered Nurse
Expenses: 2013-2014: $18,770; room/board: $6,840
Financial aid: (573) 221-3675

Harris-Stowe State University[1]

St. Louis MO
(314) 340-3300
U.S. News ranking: Reg. Coll. (Mid. W), unranked
Website: www.hssu.edu
Admissions email: admissions@hssu.edu
Public
Application deadline (fall): N/A
Undergraduate student body: N/A full time, N/A part time
Expenses: 2013-2014: $5,220 in state, $9,853 out of state; room/board: $8,900
Financial aid: (314) 340-3500

Kansas City Art Institute

Kansas City MO
(800) 522-5224
U.S. News ranking: Arts, unranked
Website: www.kcai.edu
Admissions email: admiss@kcai.edu
Private; founded 1885
Freshman admissions: N/A; 2013-2014: 577 applied, 397 accepted. Either SAT or ACT required. SAT 25/75 percentile: N/A. High school rank: 13% in top tenth, 36% in top quarter, 66% in top half
Early decision deadline: N/A, notification date: N/A
Early action deadline: N/A, notification date: N/A
Application deadline (fall): rolling
Undergraduate student body: 735 full time, 4 part time; 37% male, 63% female; 0% American Indian, 2% Asian, 5% black, 7% Hispanic, 7% multiracial, 0% Pacific Islander, 63% white, 0% international; 40% from in state; 11% live on campus; 0% of students in fraternities, 0% in sororities
Most popular majors: 14% Animation, Interactive Technology, Video Graphics and Special Effects, 11% Graphic Design, 14% Illustration, 16% Painting, 11% Sculpture
Expenses: 2013-2014: $33,712; room/board: $9,650
Financial aid: (816) 802-3448

Lincoln University[1]

Jefferson City MO
(573) 681-5599
U.S. News ranking: Reg. U. (Mid. W), unranked
Website: www.lincolnu.edu
Admissions email: enroll@lincolnu.edu
Public
Application deadline (fall): N/A
Undergraduate student body: N/A full time, N/A part time
Expenses: 2013-2014: $6,838 in state, $13,228 out of state; room/board: $5,531
Financial aid: (573) 681-6156

Lindenwood University

St. Charles MO
(636) 949-4949
U.S. News ranking: Reg. U. (Mid. W), No. 95
Website: www.lindenwood.edu
Admissions email: admissions@lindenwood.edu
Private; founded 1827
Affiliation: Presbyterian

Freshman admissions: selective; 2013-2014: 3,379 applied, 2,240 accepted. Either SAT or ACT required. ACT 25/75 percentile: 20-25. High school rank: 12% in top tenth, 33% in top quarter, 69% in top half **Early decision deadline:** N/A, notification date: N/A **Early action deadline:** N/A, notification date: N/A **Application deadline (fall):** rolling **Undergraduate student body:** 7,502 full time, 951 part time; 46% male, 54% female; 0% American Indian, 1% Asian, 14% black, 4% Hispanic, 3% multiracial, 0% Pacific Islander, 59% white, 11% international; 69% from in state; 51% live on campus; 2% of students in fraternities, 3% in sororities **Most popular majors:** 23% Business/Commerce, General, 10% Criminology, 5% Elementary Education and Teaching, 4% Human Resources Management/ Personnel Administration, General, 4% Mass Communication/Media Studies **Expenses:** 2014-2015: $15,580; room/board: $7,880 **Financial aid:** (636) 949-4923; 59% of undergrads determined to have financial need; average aid package $9,739

Maryville University of St. Louis

St Louis MO
(800) 627-9855
U.S. News ranking: Nat. U., No. 156
Website: www.maryville.edu
Admissions email: admissions@ maryville.edu
Private; founded 1872
Freshman admissions: more selective; 2013-2014: 1,595 applied, 1,214 accepted. Either SAT or ACT required. ACT 25/75 percentile: 23-27. High school rank: 27% in top tenth, 61% in top quarter, 91% in top half **Early decision deadline:** N/A, notification date: N/A **Early action deadline:** N/A, notification date: N/A **Application deadline (fall):** 8/15 **Undergraduate student body:** 1,786 full time, 1,043 part time; 29% male, 71% female; 0% American Indian, 2% Asian, 8% black, 2% Hispanic, 2% multiracial, 0% Pacific Islander, 76% white, 3% international; 80% from in state; 24% live on campus; 0% of students in fraternities, 0% in sororities **Most popular majors:** 6% Accounting, 8% Business/ Commerce, General, 6% Health Professions and Related Clinical Sciences, Other, 5% Psychology, General, 31% Registered Nursing/ Registered Nurse **Expenses:** 2014-2015: $25,884; room/board: $10,284 **Financial aid:** (314) 529-9360; 71% of undergrads determined to have financial need; average aid package $22,335

Missouri Baptist University[1]

St. Louis MO
(314) 434-2290
U.S. News ranking: Reg. U. (Mid. W), second tier
Website: www.mobap.edu
Admissions email: admissions@ mobap.edu
Private; founded 1964
Affiliation: Baptist
Application deadline (fall): rolling **Undergraduate student body:** N/A full time, N/A part time
Expenses: 2013-2014: $21,670; room/board: $8,640
Financial aid: (314) 392-2366

Missouri Southern State University

Joplin MO
(417) 781-6778
U.S. News ranking: Reg. Coll. (Mid. W), second tier
Website: www.mssu.edu
Admissions email: admissions@ mssu.edu
Public; founded 1937
Freshman admissions: less selective; 2013-2014: 1,726 applied, 1,679 accepted. Either SAT or ACT required. ACT 25/75 percentile: 18-24. High school rank: 12% in top tenth, 33% in top quarter, 67% in top half **Early decision deadline:** N/A, notification date: N/A **Early action deadline:** N/A, notification date: N/A **Application deadline (fall):** rolling **Undergraduate student body:** 4,125 full time, 1,462 part time; 42% male, 58% female; 3% American Indian, 2% Asian, 5% black, 4% Hispanic, 1% multiracial, 0% Pacific Islander, 80% white, 2% international; 85% from in state; 8% live on campus; N/A of students in fraternities, N/A in sororities **Most popular majors:** 13% Business, Management, Marketing, and Related Support Services, 29% Education, 14% Health Professions and Related Programs, 16% Homeland Security, Law Enforcement, Firefighting and Related Protective Services, 7% Liberal Arts and Sciences, General Studies and Humanities **Expenses:** 2014-2015: $5,416 in state, $10,450 out of state; room/ board: $6,299 **Financial aid:** (417) 625-9325; 80% of undergrads determined to have financial need; average aid package $7,486

Missouri State University

Springfield MO
(800) 492-7900
U.S. News ranking: Reg. U. (Mid. W), No. 67
Website: www.missouristate.edu
Admissions email: info@missouristate.edu
Public; founded 1906
Freshman admissions: selective; 2013-2014: 7,464 applied, 6,368 accepted. Either SAT or ACT required. ACT 25/75 percentile: 21-26. High school rank: 24% in top tenth, 53% in top quarter, 84% in top half **Early decision deadline:** N/A, notification date: N/A

Early action deadline: N/A, notification date: N/A **Application deadline (fall):** 7/20 **Undergraduate student body:** 13,805 full time, 4,222 part time; 43% male, 57% female; 1% American Indian, 1% Asian, 4% black, 3% Hispanic, 3% multiracial, 0% Pacific Islander, 82% white, 4% international; 92% from in state; 24% live on campus; 21% of students in fraternities, 19% in sororities **Most popular majors:** 29% Business, Management, Marketing, and Related Support Services, 15% Education, 6% Health Professions and Related Programs, 6% Psychology, 9% Social Sciences **Expenses:** 2014-2015: $7,008 in state, $13,668 out of state; room/ board: $7,678 **Financial aid:** (417) 836-5262; 63% of undergrads determined to have financial need; average aid package $11,129

Missouri University of Science & Technology

Rolla MO
(573) 341-4165
U.S. News ranking: Nat. U., No. 138
Website: www.mst.edu
Admissions email: admissions@mst.edu
Public; founded 1870
Freshman admissions: more selective; 2013-2014: 3,297 applied, 2,709 accepted. Either SAT or ACT required. ACT 25/75 percentile: 25-31. High school rank: 41% in top tenth, 71% in top quarter, 93% in top half **Early decision deadline:** N/A, notification date: N/A **Early action deadline:** N/A, notification date: N/A **Application deadline (fall):** 7/1 **Undergraduate student body:** 5,472 full time, 674 part time; 77% male, 23% female; 0% American Indian, 2% Asian, 4% black, 2% Hispanic, 2% multiracial, 0% Pacific Islander, 79% white, 6% international; 84% from in state; 43% live on campus; 21% of students in fraternities, 19% in sororities **Most popular majors:** 4% Biological and Biomedical Sciences, 8% Computer and Information Sciences and Support Services, 70% Engineering, 4% Physical Sciences, 4% Psychology **Expenses:** 2014-2015: $9,537 in state, $25,404 out of state; room/ board: $9,540 **Financial aid:** (573) 341-4282; 61% of undergrads determined to have financial need; average aid package $10,052

Missouri Valley College[1]

Marshall MO
(660) 831-4114
U.S. News ranking: Reg. Coll. (Mid. W), second tier
Website: www.moval.edu
Admissions email: admissions@ moval.edu
Private
Application deadline (fall): N/A **Undergraduate student body:** N/A full time, N/A part time

Expenses: 2013-2014: $18,300; room/board: $7,700
Financial aid: (660) 831-4171

Missouri Western State University

St. Joseph MO
(816) 271-4266
U.S. News ranking: Reg. Coll. (Mid. W), second tier
Website: www.missouriwestern.edu
Admissions email: admission@ missouriwestern.edu
Public; founded 1969
Freshman admissions: less selective; 2013-2014: 3,376 applied, 3,376 accepted. Neither SAT nor ACT required. ACT 25/75 percentile: 17-23. High school rank: 10% in top tenth, 28% in top quarter, 61% in top half **Early decision deadline:** N/A, notification date: N/A **Early action deadline:** N/A, notification date: N/A **Application deadline (fall):** rolling **Undergraduate student body:** 3,945 full time, 1,671 part time; 43% male, 57% female; 1% American Indian, 1% Asian, 11% black, 1% Hispanic, 3% multiracial, 0% Pacific Islander, 79% white, 1% international; 91% from in state; 24% live on campus; N/A of students in fraternities, N/A in sororities **Most popular majors:** 6% Business Administration and Management, General, 7% Criminal Justice/ Safety Studies, 6% Elementary Education and Teaching, 6% Health and Physical Education/ Fitness, General, 13% Registered Nursing/Registered Nurse **Expenses:** 2014-2015: $6,497 in state, $12,489 out of state; room/ board: $7,128 **Financial aid:** (816) 271-4361; 74% of undergrads determined to have financial need; average aid package $8,007

Northwest Missouri State University

Maryville MO
(800) 633-1175
U.S. News ranking: Reg. U. (Mid. W), No. 80
Website: www.nwmissouri.edu
Admissions email: admissions@ nwmissouri.edu
Public; founded 1905
Freshman admissions: selective; 2013-2014: 5,619 applied, 4,111 accepted. Either SAT or ACT required. ACT 25/75 percentile: 20-25. High school rank: 14% in top tenth, 40% in top quarter, 77% in top half **Early decision deadline:** N/A, notification date: N/A **Early action deadline:** N/A, notification date: N/A **Application deadline (fall):** rolling **Undergraduate student body:** 4,988 full time, 554 part time; 45% male, 55% female; 0% American Indian, 1% Asian, 6% black, 3% Hispanic, 3% multiracial, 0% Pacific Islander, 83% white, 2% international; 73% from in state; 39% live on campus; 21% of students in fraternities, 20% in sororities **Most popular majors:** 6% Agriculture, Agriculture Operations, and Related Sciences, 27% Business, Management, Marketing, and Related Support

Services, 21% Education, 9% Parks, Recreation, Leisure, and Fitness Studies, 8% Psychology **Expenses:** 2014-2015: $8,156 in state, $14,407 out of state; room/ board: $8,709 **Financial aid:** (660) 562-1363; 69% of undergrads determined to have financial need; average aid package $8,841

Park University[1]

Parkville MO
(800) 745-7275
U.S. News ranking: Reg. U. (Mid. W), second tier
Website: www.park.edu
Admissions email: admissions@ mail.park.edu
Private; founded 1875
Application deadline (fall): 8/1 **Undergraduate student body:** N/A full time, N/A part time
Expenses: 2013-2014: $10,600; room/board: $7,152
Financial aid: (816) 584-6190

Ranken Technical College[1]

Saint Louis MO
(866) 472-6536
U.S. News ranking: Reg. Coll. (Mid. W), unranked
Website: www.ranken.edu
Admissions email: N/A
Private
Application deadline (fall): N/A **Undergraduate student body:** N/A full time, N/A part time
Expenses: 2013-2014: $14,457; room/board: $5,200
Financial aid: (314) 286-4862

Rockhurst University

Kansas City MO
(816) 501-4100
U.S. News ranking: Reg. U. (Mid. W), No. 14
Website: www.rockhurst.edu
Admissions email: admissions@ rockhurst.edu
Private; founded 1910
Affiliation: Roman Catholic (Jesuit)
Freshman admissions: more selective; 2013-2014: 2,576 applied, 1,943 accepted. Either SAT or ACT required. ACT 25/75 percentile: 23-28. High school rank: 30% in top tenth, 53% in top quarter, 87% in top half **Early decision deadline:** N/A, notification date: N/A **Early action deadline:** N/A, notification date: N/A **Application deadline (fall):** rolling **Undergraduate student body:** 1,546 full time, 695 part time; 40% male, 60% female; 1% American Indian, 3% Asian, 5% black, 5% Hispanic, 1% multiracial, 0% Pacific Islander, 78% white, 1% international; 57% from in state; 54% live on campus; 26% of students in fraternities, 34% in sororities **Most popular majors:** 8% Biological and Biomedical Sciences, 16% Business, Management, Marketing, and Related Support Services, 24% Health Professions and Related Programs, 11% Psychology, 9% Social Sciences **Expenses:** 2014-2015: $32,865; room/board: $8,680 **Financial aid:** (816) 501-4100; 59% of undergrads determined to have financial need; average aid package $30,086

Southeast Missouri State University

Cape Girardeau MO
(573) 651-2590
U.S. News ranking: Reg. U. (Mid. W), No. 95
Website: www.semo.edu
Admissions email: admissions@semo.edu
Public; founded 1873
Freshman admissions: selective; 2013-2014: 4,388 applied, 3,840 accepted. Either SAT or ACT required. ACT 25/75 percentile: 20-25. High school rank: 17% in top tenth, 43% in top quarter, 73% in top half
Early decision deadline: N/A, notification date: N/A
Early action deadline: N/A, notification date: N/A
Application deadline (fall): 7/1
Undergraduate student body: 8,094 full time, 2,661 part time; 43% male, 57% female; 1% American Indian, 1% Asian, 10% black, 2% Hispanic, 0% multiracial, 0% Pacific Islander, 79% white, 6% international; 85% from in state; 26% live on campus; 14% of students in fraternities, 11% in sororities
Most popular majors: 8% Communication and Media Studies, 9% Liberal Arts and Sciences, General Studies and Humanities, 7% Registered Nursing, Nursing Administration, Nursing Research and Clinical Nursing, 7% Teacher Education and Professional Development, Specific Levels and Methods, 7% Teacher Education and Professional Development, Specific Subject Areas
Expenses: 2014-2015: $6,938 in state, $12,270 out of state; room/board: N/A
Financial aid: (573) 651-2253; 62% of undergrads determined to have financial need; average aid package $8,419

Southwest Baptist University[1]

Bolivar MO
(800) 526-5859
U.S. News ranking: Reg. U. (Mid. W), second tier
Website: www.sbuniv.edu
Admissions email: dcrowder@sbuniv.edu
Private
Application deadline (fall): N/A
Undergraduate student body: N/A full time, N/A part time
Expenses: 2013-2014: $20,040; room/board: $6,800
Financial aid: (417) 328-1822

Stephens College

Columbia MO
(800) 876-7207
U.S. News ranking: Reg. Coll. (Mid. W), No. 23
Website: www.stephens.edu
Admissions email: apply@stephens.edu
Private; founded 1833
Freshman admissions: selective; 2013-2014: 783 applied, 529 accepted. Either SAT or ACT required. ACT 25/75 percentile: 19-26. High school rank: 17% in top tenth, 39% in top quarter, 73% in top half
Early decision deadline: 11/15, notification date: 12/1

Early action deadline: 1/1, notification date: 1/15
Application deadline (fall): rolling
Undergraduate student body: 521 full time, 129 part time; 2% male, 98% female; 0% American Indian, 2% Asian, 18% black, 2% Hispanic, 6% multiracial, 0% Pacific Islander, 70% white, 0% international; 55% from in state; 71% live on campus; N/A of students in fraternities, N/A in sororities
Most popular majors: 25% Business/Commerce, General, 33% Drama and Dramatics/Theatre Arts, General, 6% Education, General, 13% Health Information/Medical Records Administration/Administrator, 5% Liberal Arts and Sciences/Liberal Studies
Expenses: 2014-2015: $28,510; room/board: $9,533
Financial aid: (573) 876-7106; 84% of undergrads determined to have financial need; average aid package $25,673

St. Louis University

St. Louis MO
(314) 977-2500
U.S. News ranking: Nat. U., No. 99
Website: www.slu.edu
Admissions email: admission@slu.edu
Private; founded 1818
Affiliation: Roman Catholic
Freshman admissions: more selective; 2013-2014: 13,091 applied, 8,327 accepted. Either SAT or ACT required. ACT 25/75 percentile: 25-30. High school rank: 41% in top tenth, 74% in top quarter, 91% in top half
Early decision deadline: N/A, notification date: N/A
Early action deadline: N/A, notification date: N/A
Application deadline (fall): 8/20
Undergraduate student body: 7,795 full time, 892 part time; 41% male, 59% female; 0% American Indian, 8% Asian, 7% black, 4% Hispanic, 5% multiracial, 0% Pacific Islander, 65% white, 7% international; 39% from in state; 50% live on campus; 12% of students in fraternities, 16% in sororities
Most popular majors: 5% Accounting, 6% Biology/Biological Sciences, General, 5% Kinesiology and Exercise Science, 5% Psychology, General, 12% Registered Nursing/Registered Nurse
Expenses: 2014-2015: $37,966; room/board: $10,380
Financial aid: (314) 977-2350; 58% of undergrads determined to have financial need; average aid package $24,852

Truman State University

Kirksville MO
(660) 785-4114
U.S. News ranking: Reg. U. (Mid. W), No. 9
Website: www.truman.edu
Admissions email: admissions@truman.edu
Public; founded 1867
Freshman admissions: more selective; 2013-2014: 4,462 applied, 3,221 accepted. Either SAT or ACT required. ACT 25/75

percentile: 25-30. High school rank: 47% in top tenth, 80% in top quarter, 98% in top half
Early decision deadline: N/A, notification date: N/A
Early action deadline: N/A, notification date: N/A
Application deadline (fall): rolling
Undergraduate student body: 5,375 full time, 523 part time; 40% male, 60% female; 0% American Indian, 2% Asian, 3% black, 3% Hispanic, 2% multiracial, 0% Pacific Islander, 82% white, 6% international; 83% from in state; 42% live on campus; 21% of students in fraternities, 18% in sororities
Most popular majors: 8% Biology/Biological Sciences, General, 17% Business Administration and Management, General, 9% English Language and Literature, General, 14% Health and Physical Education/Fitness, General, 7% Psychology, General
Expenses: 2014-2015: $7,374 in state, $13,438 out of state; room/board: $8,167
Financial aid: (660) 785-4130; 53% of undergrads determined to have financial need; average aid package $11,389

University of Central Missouri

Warrensburg MO
(660) 543-4290
U.S. News ranking: Reg. U. (Mid. W), No. 84
Website: www.ucmo.edu
Admissions email: admit@ucmo.edu
Public
Freshman admissions: selective; 2013-2014: 4,611 applied, 3,727 accepted. Either SAT or ACT required. ACT 25/75 percentile: 19-24. High school rank: 10% in top tenth, 32% in top quarter, 67% in top half
Early decision deadline: N/A, notification date: N/A
Early action deadline: N/A, notification date: N/A
Application deadline (fall): 8/19
Undergraduate student body: 8,290 full time, 1,684 part time; 46% male, 54% female; 0% American Indian, 1% Asian, 8% black, 3% Hispanic, 2% multiracial, 0% Pacific Islander, 67% white, 2% international; 92% from in state; N/A live on campus; N/A of students in fraternities, N/A in sororities
Most popular majors: 15% Business, Management, Marketing, and Related Support Services, 17% Education, 7% Engineering Technologies and Engineering-Related Fields, 11% Health Professions and Related Programs, 9% Homeland Security, Law Enforcement, Firefighting and Related Protective Services
Expenses: 2014-2015: $7,265 in state, $13,659 out of state; room/board: $7,734
Financial aid: (660) 543-4040; 63% of undergrads determined to have financial need; average aid package $8,758

University of Missouri

Columbia MO
(573) 882-7786
U.S. News ranking: Nat. U., No. 99
Website: www.missouri.edu
Admissions email: mu4u@missouri.edu
Public; founded 1839
Freshman admissions: more selective; 2013-2014: 20,956 applied, 16,473 accepted. Either SAT or ACT required. ACT 25/75 percentile: 23-28. High school rank: 27% in top tenth, 58% in top quarter, 88% in top half
Early decision deadline: N/A, notification date: N/A
Early action deadline: N/A, notification date: N/A
Application deadline (fall): rolling
Undergraduate student body: 25,258 full time, 1,707 part time; 48% male, 52% female; 0% American Indian, 2% Asian, 8% black, 3% Hispanic, 3% multiracial, 0% Pacific Islander, 80% white, 3% international; 77% from in state; 25% live on campus; 24% of students in fraternities, 31% in sororities
Most popular majors: 16% Business, Management, Marketing, and Related Support Services, 12% Communication, Journalism, and Related Programs, 7% Engineering, 11% Health Professions and Related Programs, 6% Social Sciences
Expenses: 2014-2015: $9,433 in state, $24,460 out of state; room/board: $9,386
Financial aid: (573) 882-7506; 49% of undergrads determined to have financial need; average aid package $14,050

University of Missouri–Kansas City

Kansas City MO
(816) 235-1111
U.S. News ranking: Nat. U., No. 189
Website: www.umkc.edu
Admissions email: admit@umkc.edu
Public; founded 1929
Freshman admissions: more selective; 2013-2014: 4,471 applied, 2,919 accepted. Either SAT or ACT required. ACT 25/75 percentile: 21-27. High school rank: 26% in top tenth, 55% in top quarter, 81% in top half
Early decision deadline: N/A, notification date: N/A
Early action deadline: N/A, notification date: N/A
Application deadline (fall): rolling
Undergraduate student body: 6,813 full time, 3,434 part time; 42% male, 58% female; 0% American Indian, 6% Asian, 16% black, 7% Hispanic, 3% multiracial, 0% Pacific Islander, 58% white, 4% international; 77% from in state; 8% live on campus; 4% of students in fraternities, 6% in sororities
Most popular majors: 13% Business, Management, Marketing, and Related Support Services, 14% Health Professions and Related Programs, 11% Liberal Arts and Sciences, General Studies and Humanities, 8% Physical Sciences, 7% Psychology

Expenses: 2014-2015: $9,582 in state, $22,641 out of state; room/board: $9,815
Financial aid: (816) 235-1154; 70% of undergrads determined to have financial need; average aid package $9,869

University of Missouri–St. Louis

St. Louis MO
(314) 516-5451
U.S. News ranking: Nat. U., second tier
Website: www.umsl.edu
Admissions email: admissions@umsl.edu
Public; founded 1963
Freshman admissions: more selective; 2013-2014: 1,753 applied, 1,300 accepted. Either SAT or ACT required. ACT 25/75 percentile: 21-26. High school rank: 30% in top tenth, 63% in top quarter, 87% in top half
Early decision deadline: N/A, notification date: N/A
Early action deadline: N/A, notification date: N/A
Application deadline (fall): 8/25
Undergraduate student body: 6,035 full time, 7,539 part time; 42% male, 58% female; 0% American Indian, 4% Asian, 19% black, 2% Hispanic, 2% multiracial, 0% Pacific Islander, 62% white, 3% international; 89% from in state; 9% live on campus; 1% of students in fraternities, 1% in sororities
Most popular majors: 22% Business, Management, Marketing, and Related Support Services, 12% Education, 11% Health Professions and Related Programs, 7% Psychology, 12% Social Sciences
Expenses: 2014-2015: $9,474 in state, $24,795 out of state; room/board: $8,960
Financial aid: (314) 516-5526; 71% of undergrads determined to have financial need; average aid package $12,241

Washington University in St. Louis

St. Louis MO
(800) 638-0700
U.S. News ranking: Nat. U., No. 14
Website: www.wustl.edu
Admissions email: admissions@wustl.edu
Private; founded 1853
Freshman admissions: most selective; 2013-2014: 30,117 applied, 4,684 accepted. Either SAT or ACT required. ACT 25/75 percentile: 32-34. High school rank: 95% in top tenth, 99% in top quarter, 100% in top half
Early decision deadline: 11/15, notification date: 12/15
Early action deadline: N/A, notification date: N/A
Application deadline (fall): 1/15
Undergraduate student body: 6,587 full time, 749 part time; 49% male, 51% female; 0% American Indian, 17% Asian, 6% black, 6% Hispanic, 4% multiracial, 0% Pacific Islander, 55% white, 8% international; 7% from in state; 78% live on campus; 25% of students in fraternities, 25% in sororities

Most popular majors: 10% Biological and Biomedical Sciences, 9% Business, Management, Marketing, and Related Support Services, 16% Engineering, 14% Pre-Medicine/ Pre-Medical Studies, 17% Social Sciences
Expenses: 2014-2015: $46,467; room/board: $14,377
Financial aid: (888) 547-6670; 40% of undergrads determined to have financial need; average aid package $36,101

Webster University
St. Louis MO
(314) 968-6991
U.S. News ranking: Reg. U. (Mid. W), No. 26
Website: www.webster.edu
Admissions email: admit@webster.edu
Private; founded 1915
Freshman admissions: selective; 2013-2014: 1,769 applied, 1,014 accepted. Either SAT or ACT required. ACT 25/75 percentile: 20-27. High school rank: 17% in top tenth, 42% in top quarter, 73% in top half
Early decision deadline: N/A, notification date: N/A
Early action deadline: N/A, notification date: N/A
Application deadline (fall): 8/1
Undergraduate student body: 2,458 full time, 504 part time; 46% male, 54% female; 0% American Indian, 3% Asian, 11% black, 4% Hispanic, 2% multiracial, 0% Pacific Islander, 70% white, 2% international; 77% from in state; 25% live on campus; N/A of students in fraternities, 3% in sororities
Most popular majors: 6% Art/Art Studies, General, 18% Business Administration and Management, General, 5% Computer Science, 6% Education, General, 5% Psychology, General
Expenses: 2014-2015: $24,500; room/board: $10,600
Financial aid: (314) 968-6992; 74% of undergrads determined to have financial need; average aid package $16,809

Westminster College
Fulton MO
(800) 475-3361
U.S. News ranking: Nat. Lib. Arts, No. 159
Website: www.westminster-mo.edu
Admissions email: admissions@ westminster-mo.edu
Private; founded 1851
Affiliation: Presbyterian
Freshman admissions: more selective; 2013-2014: 1,308 applied, 902 accepted. Either SAT or ACT required. ACT 25/75 percentile: 21-27. High school rank: 28% in top tenth, 50% in top quarter, 77% in top half
Early decision deadline: N/A, notification date: N/A
Early action deadline: N/A, notification date: N/A
Application deadline (fall): rolling
Undergraduate student body: 1,036 full time, 8 part time; 56% male, 44% female; 2% American Indian, 1% Asian, 6% black, 4% Hispanic, 1% multiracial, 0% Pacific Islander, 66% white, 17% international; 79% from in state; 85% live on campus; 46% of students in fraternities, 33% in sororities

William Jewell College
Liberty MO
(888) 253-9355
U.S. News ranking: Nat. Lib. Arts, No. 155
Website: www.jewell.edu
Admissions email: admission@ william.jewell.edu
Private; founded 1849
Freshman admissions: more selective; 2013-2014: 1,433 applied, 828 accepted. Neither SAT nor ACT required. ACT 25/75 percentile: 22-28. High school rank: 23% in top tenth, 58% in top quarter, 90% in top half
Early decision deadline: N/A, notification date: N/A
Early action deadline: N/A, notification date: N/A
Application deadline (fall): 8/15
Undergraduate student body: 1,011 full time, 32 part time; 43% male, 57% female; 1% American Indian, 5% Asian, 6% black, 4% Hispanic, 5% multiracial, 0% Pacific Islander, 77% white, 3% international; 62% from in state; 83% live on campus; 31% of students in fraternities, 31% in sororities
Most popular majors: 16% Business, Management, Marketing, and Related Support Services, 6% Education, 26% Health Professions and Related Programs, 10% Psychology, 7% Social Sciences
Expenses: 2014-2015: $31,620; room/board: $8,410
Financial aid: (888) 253-9355; 74% of undergrads determined to have financial need; average aid package $26,119

William Woods University
Fulton MO
(573) 592-4221
U.S. News ranking: Reg. U. (Mid. W), No. 95
Website: www.williamwoods.edu
Admissions email: admissions@ williamwoods.edu
Private; founded 1870
Affiliation: Disciples of Christ
Freshman admissions: selective; 2013-2014: 819 applied, 639 accepted. Either SAT or ACT required. ACT 25/75 percentile: 19-25. High school rank: 12% in top tenth, 37% in top quarter, 70% in top half
Early decision deadline: N/A, notification date: N/A
Early action deadline: N/A, notification date: N/A
Application deadline (fall): rolling
Undergraduate student body: 843 full time, 159 part time; 27% male, 73% female; 0% American Indian, 0% Asian, 4% black, 1% Hispanic, 2% multiracial, 1% Pacific Islander, 85% white,

0% international; 64% from in state; 65% live on campus; 25% of students in fraternities, 41% in sororities
Most popular majors: 5% Biology/ Biological Sciences, General, 17% Business Administration and Management, General, 6% Elementary Education and Teaching, 5% Legal Professions and Studies, Other, 3% Physical Education Teaching and Coaching
Expenses: 2014-2015: $21,260; room/board: $8,680
Financial aid: (573) 592-4232; 59% of undergrads determined to have financial need; average aid package $16,691

MONTANA

Carroll College
Helena MT
(406) 447-4384
U.S. News ranking: Reg. Coll. (W), No. 1
Website: www.carroll.edu
Admissions email: admission@carroll.edu
Private; founded 1909
Affiliation: Roman Catholic
Freshman admissions: more selective; 2013-2014: 3,279 applied, 1,740 accepted. Either SAT or ACT required. ACT 25/75 percentile: 22-27. High school rank: 25% in top tenth, 61% in top quarter, 90% in top half
Early decision deadline: N/A, notification date: N/A
Early action deadline: 12/1, notification date: 1/1
Application deadline (fall): 5/1
Undergraduate student body: 1,349 full time, 82 part time; 42% male, 58% female; 1% American Indian, 1% Asian, 1% black, 4% Hispanic, 1% multiracial, 0% Pacific Islander, 81% white, 1% international; 46% from in state; 57% live on campus; N/A of students in fraternities, N/A in sororities
Most popular majors: 11% Biological and Biomedical Sciences, 11% Business, Management, Marketing, and Related Support Services, 10% Education, 26% Health Professions and Related Programs, 8% Social Sciences
Expenses: 2014-2015: $29,280; room/board: $8,950
Financial aid: (406) 447-5423; 64% of undergrads determined to have financial need; average aid package $20,251

Montana State University
Bozeman MT
(406) 994-2452
U.S. News ranking: Nat. U., second tier
Website: www.montana.edu
Admissions email: admissions@ montana.edu
Public; founded 1893
Freshman admissions: selective; 2013-2014: 12,578 applied, 10,630 accepted. Either SAT or ACT required. ACT 25/75 percentile: 21-27. High school rank: 19% in top tenth, 44% in top quarter, 72% in top half
Early decision deadline: N/A, notification date: N/A
Early action deadline: N/A, notification date: N/A

Application deadline (fall): rolling
Undergraduate student body: 11,012 full time, 2,252 part time; 55% male, 45% female; 1% American Indian, 0% Asian, 1% black, 3% Hispanic, 3% multiracial, 87% Pacific Islander, 1% white, 3% international; 61% from in state; 25% live on campus; 2% of students in fraternities, 2% in sororities
Most popular majors: 11% Business, Management, Marketing, and Related Support Services, 11% Engineering, 9% Family and Consumer Sciences/ Human Sciences, 9% Health Professions and Related Programs, 8% Visual and Performing Arts
Expenses: 2014-2015: $6,894 in state, $21,296 out of state; room/ board: $8,380
Financial aid: (406) 994-2845; 56% of undergrads determined to have financial need; average aid package $11,983

Montana State University–Billings
Billings MT
(406) 657-2158
U.S. News ranking: Reg. U. (W), second tier
Website: www.msubillings.edu
Admissions email: admissions@ msubillings.edu
Public; founded 1927
Freshman admissions: selective; 2013-2014: 1,407 applied, 1,397 accepted. Either SAT or ACT required. ACT 25/75 percentile: 18-23. High school rank: 8% in top tenth, 31% in top quarter, 62% in top half
Early decision deadline: N/A, notification date: N/A
Early action deadline: N/A, notification date: N/A
Application deadline (fall): 7/1
Undergraduate student body: 3,164 full time, 1,301 part time; 39% male, 61% female; 5% American Indian, 1% Asian, 1% black, 5% Hispanic, 3% multiracial, 0% Pacific Islander, 83% white, 3% international; 91% from in state; 18% live on campus; 0% of students in fraternities, 0% in sororities
Most popular majors: 24% Business/Commerce, General, 23% Elementary Education and Teaching, 11% Liberal Arts and Sciences/Liberal Studies, 6% Mass Communication/Media Studies, 6% Psychology, General
Expenses: 2014-2015: $5,780 in state, $17,342 out of state; room/ board: $6,980
Financial aid: (406) 657-2188; 64% of undergrads determined to have financial need; average aid package $10,148

Montana State University–Northern[1]
Havre MT
(406) 265-3704
U.S. News ranking: Reg. Coll. (W), unranked
Website: www.msun.edu
Admissions email: admissions@msun.edu
Public
Application deadline (fall): N/A
Undergraduate student body: N/A full time, N/A part time

Expenses: 2013-2014: $5,480 in state, $17,312 out of state; room/ board: $7,500
Financial aid: (406) 265-3787

Montana Tech of the University of Montana
Butte MT
(406) 496-4256
U.S. News ranking: Reg. Coll. (W), unranked
Website: www.mtech.edu
Admissions email: enrollment@ mtech.edu
Public; founded 1893
Freshman admissions: N/A; 2013-2014: 877 applied, 773 accepted. Either SAT or ACT required. ACT 25/75 percentile: 22-26. High school rank: 26% in top tenth, 57% in top quarter, 86% in top half
Early decision deadline: N/A, notification date: N/A
Early action deadline: N/A, notification date: N/A
Application deadline (fall): rolling
Undergraduate student body: 2,190 full time, 567 part time; 60% male, 40% female; 2% American Indian, 1% Asian, 1% black, 2% Hispanic, 0% multiracial, 0% Pacific Islander, 83% white, 7% international; 87% from in state; 11% live on campus; 0% of students in fraternities, 0% in sororities
Most popular majors: 15% Business/Commerce, General, 5% Computer Systems Networking and Telecommunications, 17% Engineering, General, 5% Occupational Health and Industrial Hygiene, 21% Petroleum Engineering
Expenses: 2014-2015: $6,752 in state, $20,068 out of state; room/ board: $8,238
Financial aid: (406) 496-4212; 62% of undergrads determined to have financial need; average aid package $10,848

Rocky Mountain College
Billings MT
(406) 657-1026
U.S. News ranking: Reg. Coll. (W), No. 13
Website: www.rocky.edu
Admissions email: admissions@ rocky.edu
Private; founded 1878
Affiliation: United Church of Christ, Methodist, and Presbyterian
Freshman admissions: selective; 2013-2014: 1,396 applied, 933 accepted. Either SAT or ACT required. ACT 25/75 percentile: 19-25. High school rank: 15% in top tenth, 35% in top quarter, 70% in top half
Early decision deadline: N/A, notification date: N/A
Early action deadline: 2/15, notification date: 2/15
Application deadline (fall): rolling
Undergraduate student body: 947 full time, 41 part time; 52% male, 48% female; 2% American Indian, 1% Asian, 2% black, 4% Hispanic, 3% multiracial, 1% Pacific Islander, 80% white, 4% international; 54% from in state; 49% live on campus; 0% of students in fraternities, 0% in sororities

Most popular majors: Information not available
Expenses: 2014-2015: $24,530; room/board: $7,712
Financial aid: (406) 657-1031; 77% of undergrads determined to have financial need; average aid package $19,265

University of Great Falls

Great Falls MT
(406) 791-5200
U.S. News ranking: Reg. Coll. (W), No. 22
Website: www.ugf.edu
Admissions email: enroll@ugf.edu
Private; founded 1932
Affiliation: Roman Catholic
Freshman admissions: less selective; 2013-2014: N/A applied, N/A accepted. Either SAT or ACT required. SAT 25/75 percentile: 840-1090. High school rank: N/A
Early decision deadline: N/A, notification date: N/A
Early action deadline: N/A, notification date: N/A
Application deadline (fall): 9/1
Undergraduate student body: 665 full time, 381 part time; 32% male, 68% female; 3% American Indian, 2% Asian, 2% black, 5% Hispanic, 2% multiracial, 1% Pacific Islander, 79% white, 0% international; 52% from in state; 37% live on campus; N/A of students in fraternities, N/A in sororities
Most popular majors: 9% Biological and Biomedical Sciences, 12% Education, 29% Health Professions and Related Programs, 10% Homeland Security, Law Enforcement, Firefighting and Related Protective Services, 10% Psychology
Expenses: 2014-2015: $20,960; room/board: $6,800
Financial aid: (406) 791-5235; 80% of undergrads determined to have financial need; average aid package $16,916

University of Montana

Missoula MT
(800) 462-8636
U.S. News ranking: Nat. U., No. 194
Website: www.umt.edu
Admissions email: admiss@umontana.edu
Public; founded 1893
Freshman admissions: selective; 2013-2014: 4,064 applied, 3,889 accepted. Either SAT or ACT required. ACT 25/75 percentile: 21-26. High school rank: 18% in top tenth, 40% in top quarter, 70% in top half
Early decision deadline: N/A, notification date: N/A
Early action deadline: N/A, notification date: N/A
Application deadline (fall): rolling
Undergraduate student body: 8,182 full time, 1,605 part time; 47% male, 53% female; 3% American Indian, 1% Asian, 1% black, 4% Hispanic, 4% multiracial, 0% Pacific Islander, 81% white, 2% international; 81% from in state; 28% live on campus; 6% of students in fraternities, 6% in sororities

Most popular majors: 6% Biological and Biomedical Sciences, 19% Business, Management, Marketing, and Related Support Services, 10% Natural Resources and Conservation, 7% Psychology, 13% Social Sciences
Expenses: 2014-2015: $6,330 in state, $23,146 out of state; room/board: $8,006
Financial aid: (406) 243-5373; 62% of undergrads determined to have financial need; average aid package $7,780

University of Montana–Western

Dillon MT
(877) 683-7331
U.S. News ranking: Reg. Coll. (W), unranked
Website: www.umwestern.edu
Admissions email: admissions@umwestern.edu
Public; founded 1893
Freshman admissions: N/A; 2013-2014: 553 applied, 414 accepted. Either SAT or ACT required. ACT 25/75 percentile: 17-22. High school rank: 5% in top tenth, 18% in top quarter, 48% in top half
Early decision deadline: N/A, notification date: N/A
Early action deadline: N/A, notification date: N/A
Application deadline (fall): rolling
Undergraduate student body: 1,206 full time, 305 part time; 42% male, 58% female; 2% American Indian, 1% Asian, 1% black, 2% Hispanic, 2% multiracial, 1% Pacific Islander, 86% white, 0% international; 77% from in state; 24% live on campus; N/A of students in fraternities, N/A in sororities
Most popular majors: 16% Business/Commerce, General, 4% Early Childhood Education and Teaching, 15% Elementary Education and Teaching, 6% Secondary Education and Teaching, 10% Teacher Education, Multiple Levels
Expenses: 2014-2015: $5,370 in state, $15,212 out of state; room/board: $6,536
Financial aid: (406) 683-7511; 65% of undergrads determined to have financial need; average aid package $3,327

NEBRASKA

Bellevue University[1]

Bellevue NE
(800) 756-7920
U.S. News ranking: Reg. U. (Mid. W), unranked
Website: www.bellevue.edu
Admissions email: info@bellevue.edu
Private
Application deadline (fall): N/A
Undergraduate student body: N/A full time, N/A part time
Expenses: 2014-2015: $7,950; room/board: N/A
Financial aid: (402) 293-3763; 100% of undergrads determined to have financial need; average aid package $2,658

Chadron State College[1]

Chadron NE
(308) 432-6263
U.S. News ranking: Reg. Coll. (Mid. W), unranked
Website: www.csc.edu
Admissions email: inquire@csc.edu
Public
Application deadline (fall): N/A
Undergraduate student body: N/A full time, N/A part time
Expenses: 2013-2014: $5,600 in state, $5,630 out of state; room/board: $5,760
Financial aid: (308) 432-6230

College of St. Mary

Omaha NE
(402) 399-2407
U.S. News ranking: Reg. U. (Mid. W), No. 69
Website: www.csm.edu
Admissions email: enroll@csm.edu
Private; founded 1923
Affiliation: Catholic
Freshman admissions: selective; 2013-2014: 347 applied, 189 accepted. Either SAT or ACT required. ACT 25/75 percentile: 20-26. High school rank: 28% in top tenth, 51% in top quarter, 87% in top half
Early decision deadline: N/A, notification date: N/A
Early action deadline: N/A, notification date: N/A
Application deadline (fall): rolling
Undergraduate student body: 639 full time, 96 part time; 1% male, 99% female; 0% American Indian, 1% Asian, 6% black, 11% Hispanic, 2% multiracial, 0% Pacific Islander, 78% white, 1% international; 80% from in state; 32% live on campus; 0% of students in fraternities, 0% in sororities
Most popular majors: 6% Biological and Biomedical Sciences, 15% Business, Management, Marketing, and Related Support Services, 6% Education, 58% Health Professions and Related Programs, 4% Psychology
Expenses: 2014-2015: $27,984; room/board: $7,200
Financial aid: (402) 399-2362; 92% of undergrads determined to have financial need; average aid package $18,759

Concordia University

Seward NE
(800) 535-5494
U.S. News ranking: Reg. U. (Mid. W), No. 44
Website: www.cune.edu
Admissions email: admiss@cune.edu
Private; founded 1894
Affiliation: Lutheran Church-Missouri Synod
Freshman admissions: selective; 2013-2014: 1,299 applied, 929 accepted. Either SAT or ACT required. ACT 25/75 percentile: 21-27. High school rank: 18% in top tenth, 43% in top quarter, 78% in top half
Early decision deadline: N/A, notification date: N/A
Early action deadline: N/A, notification date: N/A
Application deadline (fall): 8/1
Undergraduate student body: 1,134 full time, 374 part time; 49% male, 51% female; 0% American

Indian, 1% Asian, 4% black, 4% Hispanic, 1% multiracial, 0% Pacific Islander, 82% white, 1% international; 47% from in state; 70% live on campus; N/A of students in fraternities, N/A in sororities
Most popular majors: 8% Biological and Biomedical Sciences, 37% Education, 8% Parks, Recreation, Leisure, and Fitness Studies, 12% Theology and Religious Vocations, 7% Visual and Performing Arts
Expenses: 2014-2015: $25,950; room/board: $7,080
Financial aid: (402) 643-7270; 77% of undergrads determined to have financial need; average aid package $19,350

Creighton University

Omaha NE
(800) 282-5835
U.S. News ranking: Reg. U. (Mid. W), No. 1
Website: www.creighton.edu
Admissions email: admissions@creighton.edu
Private; founded 1878
Affiliation: Roman Catholic (Jesuit)
Freshman admissions: more selective; 2013-2014: 5,336 applied, 4,090 accepted. Either SAT or ACT required. ACT 25/75 percentile: 24-30. High school rank: 40% in top tenth, 68% in top quarter, 93% in top half
Early decision deadline: N/A, notification date: N/A
Early action deadline: N/A, notification date: N/A
Application deadline (fall): 2/15
Undergraduate student body: 3,815 full time, 261 part time; 41% male, 59% female; 0% American Indian, 9% Asian, 2% black, 7% Hispanic, 4% multiracial, 0% Pacific Islander, 74% white, 2% international; 30% from in state; 62% live on campus; 30% of students in fraternities, 30% in sororities
Most popular majors: 9% Biological and Biomedical Sciences, 15% Business, Management, Marketing, and Related Support Services, 28% Health Professions and Related Clinical Sciences, Other, 8% Psychology, 7% Social Sciences
Expenses: 2014-2015: $35,360; room/board: $9,996
Financial aid: (402) 280-2731; 57% of undergrads determined to have financial need; average aid package $27,558

Doane College

Crete NE
(402) 826-8222
U.S. News ranking: Nat. Lib. Arts, No. 164
Website: www.doane.edu
Admissions email: admissions@doane.edu
Private; founded 1872
Freshman admissions: selective; 2013-2014: 1,822 applied, 1,307 accepted. ACT required. ACT 25/75 percentile: 21-26. High school rank: 20% in top tenth, 46% in top quarter, 81% in top half
Early decision deadline: N/A, notification date: N/A
Early action deadline: N/A, notification date: N/A
Application deadline (fall): rolling

Undergraduate student body: 1,106 full time, 7 part time; 50% male, 50% female; 0% American Indian, 2% Asian, 4% black, 6% Hispanic, 2% multiracial, 0% Pacific Islander, 84% white, 1% international; 83% from in state; 75% live on campus; 18% of students in fraternities, 23% in sororities
Most popular majors: 16% Biological and Biomedical Sciences, 13% Business, Management, Marketing, and Related Support Services, 24% Education, 9% Psychology, 14% Visual and Performing Arts
Expenses: 2014-2015: $27,200; room/board: $7,880
Financial aid: (402) 826-8260; 77% of undergrads determined to have financial need; average aid package $19,454

Grace University[1]

Omaha NE
(402) 449-2831
U.S. News ranking: Reg. Coll. (Mid. W), second tier
Website: www.graceuniversity.edu
Admissions email: admissions@graceuniversity.edu
Private
Application deadline (fall): N/A
Undergraduate student body: N/A full time, N/A part time
Expenses: 2013-2014: $18,256; room/board: $6,552
Financial aid: (402) 449-2810

Hastings College

Hastings NE
(800) 532-7642
U.S. News ranking: Reg. Coll. (Mid. W), No. 18
Website: www.hastings.edu
Admissions email: hcadmissions@hastings.edu
Private; founded 1882
Affiliation: Presbyterian Church (USA)
Freshman admissions: selective; 2013-2014: 1,529 applied, 1,126 accepted. Either SAT or ACT required. ACT 25/75 percentile: 21-26. High school rank: 16% in top tenth, 40% in top quarter, 65% in top half
Early decision deadline: N/A, notification date: N/A
Early action deadline: N/A, notification date: N/A
Application deadline (fall): rolling
Undergraduate student body: 1,060 full time, 58 part time; 51% male, 49% female; 1% American Indian, 2% Asian, 3% black, 5% Hispanic, 2% multiracial, 1% Pacific Islander, 85% white, 1% international; 68% from in state; 70% live on campus; 27% of students in fraternities, 27% in sororities
Most popular majors: 8% Biological and Biomedical Sciences, 20% Business, Management, Marketing, and Related Support Services, 18% Education, 8% Social Sciences, 8% Visual and Performing Arts
Expenses: 2014-2015: $26,280; room/board: $7,500
Financial aid: (402) 461-7391; 77% of undergrads determined to have financial need; average aid package $19,961

Midland University[1]
Fremont NE
(402) 941-6501
U.S. News ranking: Reg. Coll.
(Mid. W), No. 69
Website: www.midlandu.edu/
Admissions email: admissions@
midlandu.edu
Private; founded 1883
Affiliation: Lutheran
Application deadline (fall): rolling
Undergraduate student body: N/A
full time, N/A part time
Expenses: 2013-2014: $27,146;
room/board: $6,850
Financial aid: (402) 941-6520

Nebraska Wesleyan University
Lincoln NE
(402) 465-2218
U.S. News ranking: Nat. Lib. Arts,
No. 148
Website: www.nebrwesleyan.edu/
undergraduate-admissions
Admissions email: admissions@
nebrwesleyan.edu
Private; founded 1887
Affiliation: United Methodist
Freshman admissions: selective;
2013-2014: 2,315 applied,
1,780 accepted. Either SAT
or ACT required. ACT 25/75
percentile: 22-26. High school
rank: 23% in top tenth, 50% in
top quarter, 82% in top half
Early decision deadline: N/A,
notification date: N/A
Early action deadline: N/A,
notification date: N/A
Application deadline (fall): 8/15
Undergraduate student body: 1,606
full time, 321 part time; 38%
male, 62% female; 0% American
Indian, 2% Asian, 3% black, 4%
Hispanic, 2% multiracial, 0%
Pacific Islander, 82% white, 1%
international
Most popular majors: 9% Biological
and Biomedical Sciences,
13% Business, Management,
Marketing, and Related Support
Services, 11% Education, 12%
Health Professions and Related
Programs, 8% Parks, Recreation,
Leisure, and Fitness Studies
Expenses: 2014-2015: $28,500;
room/board: $7,950
Financial aid: (402) 465-2212;
72% of undergrads determined to
have financial need; average aid
package $17,642

Peru State College[1]
Peru NE
(402) 872-2221
U.S. News ranking: Reg. U.
(Mid. W), unranked
Website: www.peru.edu
Admissions email:
admissions@peru.edu
Public
Application deadline (fall): N/A
Undergraduate student body: N/A
full time, N/A part time
Expenses: 2013-2014: $6,188 in
state, $6,188 out of state; room/
board: $6,656
Financial aid: (402) 872-2228

Union College
Lincoln NE
(800) 228-4600
U.S. News ranking: Reg. Coll.
(Mid. W), No. 49
Website: www.ucollege.edu
Admissions email:
ucenroll@ucollege.edu

Private; founded 1891
Affiliation: Seventh-day Adventist
Freshman admissions: selective;
2013-2014: 1,415 applied, 742
accepted. Either SAT or ACT
required. ACT 25/75 percentile:
19-26. High school rank: 11%
in top tenth, 28% in top quarter,
56% in top half
Early decision deadline: N/A,
notification date: N/A
Early action deadline: N/A,
notification date: N/A
Application deadline (fall): rolling
Undergraduate student body: 713
full time, 108 part time; 43%
male, 57% female; 1% American
Indian, 3% Asian, 6% black,
15% Hispanic, 4% multiracial,
1% Pacific Islander, 60% white,
9% international; 29% from in
state; 70% live on campus; 0%
of students in fraternities, 0% in
sororities
Most popular majors: 6% Bible/
Biblical Studies, 13% Business
Administration and Management,
General, 14% Education, General,
7% Psychology, General, 36%
Registered Nursing/Registered
Nurse
Expenses: 2014-2015: $21,080;
room/board: $6,520
Financial aid: (402) 486-2505;
70% of undergrads determined to
have financial need; average aid
package $15,641

University of Nebraska–Kearney
Kearney NE
(308) 865-8526
U.S. News ranking: Reg. U.
(Mid. W), No. 54
Website: www.unk.edu
Admissions email:
admissionsug@unk.edu
Public; founded 1903
Freshman admissions: selective;
2013-2014: 2,589 applied,
2,197 accepted. Either SAT
or ACT required. ACT 25/75
percentile: 20-25. High school
rank: 18% in top tenth, 41% in
top quarter, 76% in top half
Early decision deadline: N/A,
notification date: N/A
Early action deadline: N/A,
notification date: N/A
Application deadline (fall): 9/1
Undergraduate student body: 4,777
full time, 725 part time; 43%
male, 57% female; 0% American
Indian, 1% Asian, 2% black, 9%
Hispanic, 1% multiracial, 0%
Pacific Islander, 80% white, 6%
international; 91% from in state;
36% live on campus; 12% of
students in fraternities, 13% in
sororities
Most popular majors: 12%
Business Administration and
Management, General, 13%
Elementary Education and
Teaching, 8% Operations
Management and Supervision,
6% Parks, Recreation and Leisure
Studies, 5% Physical Education
Teaching and Coaching
Expenses: 2014-2015: $6,584 in
state, $12,742 out of state; room/
board: $8,880
Financial aid: (308) 865-8520;
61% of undergrads determined to
have financial need; average aid
package $9,525

University of Nebraska–Lincoln
Lincoln NE
(800) 742-8800
U.S. News ranking: Nat. U.,
No. 99
Website: www.unl.edu
Admissions email:
Admissions@unl.edu
Public; founded 1869
Freshman admissions: more
selective; 2013-2014: 10,929
applied, 6,999 accepted. Either
SAT or ACT required. ACT 25/75
percentile: 22-28. High school
rank: 26% in top tenth, 52% in
top quarter, 83% in top half
Early decision deadline: N/A,
notification date: N/A
Early action deadline: N/A,
notification date: N/A
Application deadline (fall): 5/1
Undergraduate student body:
18,102 full time, 1,274 part
time; 54% male, 46% female;
0% American Indian, 2% Asian,
2% black, 5% Hispanic, 2%
multiracial, 0% Pacific Islander,
80% white, 6% international;
81% from in state; 39% live
on campus; 18% of students in
fraternities, 22% in sororities
Most popular majors: 8%
Agriculture, Agriculture
Operations, and Related Sciences,
22% Business, Management,
Marketing, and Related Support
Services, 8% Education, 10%
Engineering, 9% Family and
Consumer Sciences/Human
Sciences
Expenses: 2013-2014: $8,060 in
state, $21,388 out of state; room/
board: $9,532
Financial aid: (402) 472-2030

University of Nebraska–Omaha
Omaha NE
(402) 554-2393
U.S. News ranking: Nat. U.,
second tier
Website: www.unomaha.edu
Admissions email: unoadm@
unomaha.edu
Public; founded 1908
Freshman admissions: selective;
2013-2014: 4,955 applied,
3,507 accepted. Either SAT
or ACT required. ACT 25/75
percentile: 20-26. High school
rank: 15% in top tenth, 40% in
top quarter, 75% in top half
Early decision deadline: N/A,
notification date: N/A
Early action deadline: N/A,
notification date: N/A
Application deadline (fall): 8/1
Undergraduate student body: 9,511
full time, 2,824 part time; 48%
male, 52% female; 0% American
Indian, 3% Asian, 6% black,
9% Hispanic, 3% multiracial,
0% Pacific Islander, 72% white,
3% international; 93% from in
state; 14% live on campus; 3%
of students in fraternities, 4% in
sororities
Most popular majors: 5%
Accounting, 9% Business
Administration and Management,
General, 9% Criminal Justice/
Safety Studies, 8% Elementary
Education and Teaching, 6%
Secondary Education and
Teaching
Expenses: 2014-2015: $6,750 in
state, $18,070 out of state; room/
board: $8,408

Financial aid: (402) 554-2327;
59% of undergrads determined to
have financial need; average aid
package $9,038

Wayne State College
Wayne NE
(800) 228-9972
U.S. News ranking: Reg. U.
(Mid. W), No. 84
Website: www.wsc.edu
Admissions email:
admit1@wsc.edu
Public; founded 1909
Freshman admissions: selective;
2013-2014: 2,070 applied,
2,070 accepted. Neither SAT
nor ACT required. ACT 25/75
percentile: 19-24. High school
rank: 10% in top tenth, 29% in
top quarter, 59% in top half
Early decision deadline: N/A,
notification date: N/A
Early action deadline: N/A,
notification date: N/A
Application deadline (fall): rolling
Undergraduate student body: 2,735
full time, 256 part time; 43%
male, 57% female; 1% American
Indian, 0% Asian, 3% black,
7% Hispanic, 2% multiracial,
0% Pacific Islander, 80% white,
1% international; 87% from in
state; 46% live on campus; N/A
of students in fraternities, N/A in
sororities
Most popular majors: 15%
Business, Management,
Marketing, and Related Support
Services, 28% Education,
8% Homeland Security, Law
Enforcement, Firefighting and
Related Protective Services, 5%
Parks, Recreation, Leisure, and
Fitness Studies, 9% Psychology
Expenses: 2014-2015: $5,604 in
state, $9,804 out of state; room/
board: $6,420
Financial aid: (402) 375-7230;
68% of undergrads determined to
have financial need; average aid
package $8,584

York College
York NE
(800) 950-9675
U.S. News ranking: Reg. Coll.
(Mid. W), second tier
Website: www.york.edu
Admissions email: enroll@york.edu
Private; founded 1890
Affiliation: Church of Christ
Freshman admissions: selective;
2013-2014: 546 applied, 267
accepted. Either SAT or ACT
required. ACT 25/75 percentile:
17-22. High school rank: 5% in
top tenth, 24% in top quarter,
60% in top half
Early decision deadline: N/A,
notification date: N/A
Early action deadline: N/A,
notification date: N/A
Application deadline (fall): 8/31
Undergraduate student body: 442
full time, 17 part time; 54%
male, 46% female; 2% American
Indian, 1% Asian, 14% black,
7% Hispanic, 0% multiracial,
0% Pacific Islander, 72% white,
1% international; 35% from in
state; 90% live on campus; N/A
of students in fraternities, N/A in
sororities
Most popular majors: 5% Biological
and Biomedical Sciences,
24% Business, Management,
Marketing, and Related Support
Services, 28% Education,
12% Liberal Arts and Sciences,

General Studies and Humanities,
12% Psychology
Expenses: 2014-2015: $16,080;
room/board: $6,100
Financial aid: (402) 363-5624;
89% of undergrads determined to
have financial need; average aid
package $13,720

NEVADA

College of Southern Nevada
Las Vegas NV
(702) 651-5610
U.S. News ranking: Reg. Coll. (W),
unranked
Website: www.csn.edu
Admissions email: N/A
Public; founded 1971
Freshman admissions: N/A; 2013-
2014: N/A applied, N/A accepted.
Neither SAT nor ACT required.
ACT 25/75 percentile: N/A. High
school rank: N/A
Early decision deadline: N/A,
notification date: N/A
Early action deadline: N/A,
notification date: N/A
Application deadline (fall): rolling
Undergraduate student body: 8,903
full time, 25,274 part time; 45%
male, 55% female; 1% American
Indian, 10% Asian, 11% black,
26% Hispanic, 4% multiracial,
2% Pacific Islander, 38% white,
1% international; 8% from in
state; 0% live on campus; 0%
of students in fraternities, 0% in
sororities
Most popular majors: 13%
Business Administration and
Management, General, 5%
Criminal Justice/Safety Studies,
15% Liberal Arts and Sciences/
Liberal Studies, 8% Registered
Nursing/Registered Nurse, 8%
Science Technologies/Technicians,
Other
Expenses: 2013-2014: $2,700 in
state, $9,345 out of state; room/
board: N/A
Financial aid: (702) 651-5660

Great Basin College[1]
Elko NV
(775) 753-2102
U.S. News ranking: Reg. Coll. (W),
unranked
Website: www.gbcnv.edu
Admissions email: N/A
Public
Application deadline (fall): N/A
Undergraduate student body: N/A
full time, N/A part time
Expenses: 2013-2014: $2,700 in
state, $9,345 out of state; room/
board: $6,800
Financial aid: (775) 753-2399

Nevada State College[1]
Henderson NV
(702) 992-2130
U.S. News ranking: Reg. Coll. (W),
second tier
Website: nsc.nevada.edu
Admissions email: N/A
Public
Application deadline (fall): N/A
Undergraduate student body: N/A
full time, N/A part time
Expenses: 2013-2014: $4,482 in
state, $14,758 out of state; room/
board: N/A
Financial aid: (702) 992-2150

Sierra Nevada College

Incline Village NV
(866) 412-4636
U.S. News ranking: Reg. U. (W),
second tier
Website: www.sierranevada.edu
Admissions email: admissions@
sierranevada.edu
Private; founded 1969
Freshman admissions: less
selective; 2013-2014: 604
applied, 524 accepted. Either
SAT or ACT required. SAT 25/75
percentile: 870-1070. High
school rank: 0% in top tenth, 20%
in top quarter, 50% in top half
Early decision deadline: N/A,
notification date: N/A
Early action deadline: 11/30,
notification date: 11/30
Application deadline (fall): 8/28
Undergraduate student body: 494
full time, 53 part time; 57%
male, 43% female; 3% American
Indian, 1% Asian, 1% black,
1% Hispanic, 0% multiracial,
1% Pacific Islander, 72% white,
7% international; 16% from in
state; 52% live on campus; 0%
of students in fraternities, 0% in
sororities
Most popular majors: 41%
Business, Management,
Marketing, and Related
Support Services, 13% Multi/
Interdisciplinary Studies,
6% Physical Sciences, 14%
Psychology, 14% Visual and
Performing Arts
Expenses: 2014-2015: $29,149;
room/board: $12,066
Financial aid: (775) 831-1314;
66% of undergrads determined to
have financial need; average aid
package $21,452

University of Nevada–Las Vegas

Las Vegas NV
(702) 774-8658
U.S. News ranking: Nat. U.,
second tier
Website: www.unlv.edu
Admissions email: undergraduate.
recruitment@unlv.edu
Public; founded 1957
Freshman admissions: selective;
2013-2014: 7,343 applied,
6,250 accepted. Either SAT
or ACT required. SAT 25/75
percentile: 890-1110. High school
rank: 21% in top tenth, 48% in
top quarter, 80% in top half
Early decision deadline: N/A,
notification date: N/A
Early action deadline: N/A,
notification date: N/A
Application deadline (fall): 7/1
Undergraduate student body:
16,523 full time, 6,576 part
time; 44% male, 56% female;
0% American Indian, 16% Asian,
8% black, 23% Hispanic, 8%
multiracial, 2% Pacific Islander,
38% white, 4% international;
86% from in state; 5% live
on campus; 5% of students in
fraternities, 3% in sororities
Most popular majors: 35%
Business, Management,
Marketing, and Related Support
Services, 6% Education, 7%
Psychology, 6% Social Sciences,
5% Visual and Performing Arts
Expenses: 2014-2015: $6,690 in
state, $20,600 out of state; room/
board: $10,524

Financial aid: (702) 895-3424;
64% of undergrads determined to
have financial need; average aid
package $9,204

University of Nevada–Reno

Reno NV
(775) 784-4700
U.S. News ranking: Nat. U.,
No. 194
Website: www.unr.edu
Admissions email:
asknevada@unr.edu
Public; founded 1864
Freshman admissions: selective;
2013-2014: 7,974 applied,
6,720 accepted. Either SAT
or ACT required. SAT 25/75
percentile: 960-1190. High school
rank: 23% in top tenth, 55% in
top quarter, 87% in top half
Early decision deadline: N/A,
notification date: N/A
Early action deadline: N/A,
notification date: N/A
Application deadline (fall): 5/31
Undergraduate student body:
12,934 full time, 2,760 part
time; 47% male, 53% female;
1% American Indian, 7% Asian,
4% black, 16% Hispanic, 6%
multiracial, 1% Pacific Islander,
65% white, 1% international;
76% from in state; 17% live
on campus; 9% of students in
fraternities, 8% in sororities
Most popular majors: 8% Biological
and Biomedical Sciences,
15% Business, Management,
Marketing, and Related Support
Services, 9% Engineering, 11%
Health Professions and Related
Programs, 12% Social Sciences
Expenses: 2014-2015: $6,415 in
state, $20,325 out of state; room/
board: $9,769
Financial aid: (775) 784-4666;
53% of undergrads determined to
have financial need; average aid
package $9,560

Western Nevada College[1]

Carson City NV
(775) 445-3000
U.S. News ranking: Reg. Coll. (W),
unranked
Website: www.wnc.edu
Admissions email: N/A
Public; founded 1971
Application deadline (fall): rolling
Undergraduate student body: N/A
full time, N/A part time
Expenses: 2013-2014: $2,700 in
state, $9,345 out of state; room/
board: N/A
Financial aid: (775) 445-3264

NEW HAMPSHIRE

Colby-Sawyer College[1]

New London NH
(800) 272-1015
U.S. News ranking: Reg. Coll. (N),
unranked
Website: www.colby-sawyer.edu
Admissions email:
admissions@colby-sawyer.edu
Private
Application deadline (fall): N/A
Undergraduate student body: N/A
full time, N/A part time
Expenses: 2013-2014: $37,300;
room/board: $12,500
Financial aid: (603) 526-3717

Daniel Webster College[1]

Nashua NH
(800) 325-6876
U.S. News ranking: Reg. Coll. (N),
second tier
Website: www.dwc.edu
Admissions email:
admissions@dwc.edu
Private; founded 1965
Application deadline (fall): rolling
Undergraduate student body: N/A
full time, N/A part time
Expenses: 2013-2014: $15,630;
room/board: $10,650
Financial aid: (603) 577-6590

Dartmouth College

Hanover NH
(603) 646-2875
U.S. News ranking: Nat. U.,
No. 11
Website: www.dartmouth.edu
Admissions email: admissions.
office@dartmouth.edu
Private; founded 1769
Freshman admissions: most
selective; 2013-2014: 22,428
applied, 2,337 accepted. Either
SAT or ACT required. SAT 25/75
percentile: 1360-1560. High
school rank: 90% in top tenth,
98% in top quarter, 100% in
top half
Early decision deadline: 11/1,
notification date: 12/15
Early action deadline: N/A,
notification date: N/A
Application deadline (fall): 1/1
Undergraduate student body: 4,200
full time, 76 part time; 51%
male, 49% female; 2% American
Indian, 14% Asian, 7% black,
8% Hispanic, 5% multiracial, 0%
Pacific Islander, 47% white, 8%
international; 3% from in state;
88% live on campus; 47% of
students in fraternities, 46% in
sororities
Most popular majors: 17%
Economics, General, 7%
Engineering, General, 8% History,
General, 10% Political Science
and Government, General, 6%
Psychology, General
Expenses: 2014-2015: $48,108;
room/board: $13,839
Financial aid: (603) 646-2451;
51% of undergrads determined to
have financial need; average aid
package $44,011

Franklin Pierce University

Rindge NH
(800) 437-0048
U.S. News ranking: Reg. U. (N),
second tier
Website: www.franklinpierce.edu/
Admissions email: admissions@
franklinpierce.edu
Private; founded 1962
Freshman admissions: less
selective; 2013-2014: 4,656
applied, 4,315 accepted. Either
SAT or ACT required. SAT 25/75
percentile: 860-1060. High
school rank: 9% in top tenth, 20%
in top quarter, 56% in top half
Early decision deadline: N/A,
notification date: N/A
Early action deadline: N/A,
notification date: N/A
Application deadline (fall): rolling
Undergraduate student body: 1,307
full time, 380 part time; 41%
male, 59% female; 0% American
Indian, 1% Asian, 3% black,

5% Hispanic, 2% multiracial,
0% Pacific Islander, 74% white,
1% international; 22% from in
state; 85% live on campus; 0%
of students in fraternities, 0% in
sororities
Most popular majors: 8% Biological
and Biomedical Sciences,
19% Business, Management,
Marketing, and Related Support
Services, 7% Education, 15%
Health Professions and Related
Programs, 6% Visual and
Performing Arts
Expenses: 2014-2015: $31,782;
room/board: $12,060
Financial aid: (603) 899-4186;
83% of undergrads determined to
have financial need; average aid
package $23,887

Granite State College

Concord NH
(603) 513-1391
U.S. News ranking: Nat. Lib. Arts,
unranked
Website: www.granite.edu
Admissions email: gsc.admissions@
granite.edu
Public; founded 1972
Freshman admissions: N/A;
2013-2014: 267 applied, 267
accepted. Neither SAT nor ACT
required. ACT 25/75 percentile:
N/A. High school rank: N/A
Early decision deadline: N/A,
notification date: N/A
Early action deadline: N/A,
notification date: N/A
Application deadline (fall): rolling
Undergraduate student body: 918
full time, 805 part time; 30%
male, 70% female; 1% American
Indian, 1% Asian, 1% black,
2% Hispanic, 2% multiracial,
0% Pacific Islander, 82% white,
0% international; 88% from in
state; 0% live on campus; 0%
of students in fraternities, 0% in
sororities
Most popular majors: 26%
Business Administration and
Management, General, 8%
Criminal Justice/Safety Studies,
10% Education, 15% Liberal Arts
and Sciences/Liberal Studies,
30% Multi-/Interdisciplinary
Studies, Other
Expenses: 2014-2015: $8,775 in
state, $9,675 out of state; room/
board: N/A
Financial aid: (603) 228-3000;
84% of undergrads determined to
have financial need

Keene State College

Keene NH
(603) 358-2276
U.S. News ranking: Reg. U. (N),
No. 74
Website: www.keene.edu
Admissions email: admissions@
keene.edu
Public; founded 1909
Freshman admissions: less
selective; 2013-2014: 6,144
applied, 5,026 accepted. Either
SAT or ACT required. SAT 25/75
percentile: 860-1080. High
school rank: 4% in top tenth, 19%
in top quarter, 56% in top half
Early decision deadline: N/A,
notification date: N/A
Early action deadline: N/A,
notification date: N/A
Application deadline (fall): 4/1
Undergraduate student body: 4,541
full time, 263 part time; 43%
male, 57% female; 0% American

Indian, 1% Asian, 1% black,
3% Hispanic, 2% multiracial,
0% Pacific Islander, 82% white,
0% international; 49% from in
state; 55% live on campus; 8%
of students in fraternities, 5% in
sororities
Most popular majors: 9%
Communication, Journalism,
and Related Programs, 17%
Education, 9% Psychology, 12%
Social Sciences, 9% Visual and
Performing Arts
Expenses: 2014-2015: $12,864
in state, $20,784 out of state;
room/board: $9,368
Financial aid: (603) 358-2280;
67% of undergrads determined to
have financial need; average aid
package $10,551

Mount Washington College[1]

Manchester NH
(888) 971-2190
U.S. News ranking: Reg. Coll. (N),
unranked
Website:
www.mountwashington.edu
Admissions email: N/A
For-profit
Application deadline (fall): N/A
Undergraduate student body: N/A
full time, N/A part time
Expenses: 2013-2014: $8,016;
room/board: N/A
Financial aid: N/A

New England College

Henniker NH
(800) 521-7642
U.S. News ranking: Reg. U. (N),
second tier
Website: www.nec.edu
Admissions email:
admission@nec.edu
Private; founded 1946
Freshman admissions: least
selective; 2013-2014: 5,843
applied, 5,251 accepted. Neither
SAT nor ACT required. SAT 25/75
percentile: 810-1020. High
school rank: 2% in top tenth, 12%
in top quarter, 36% in top half
Early decision deadline: N/A,
notification date: N/A
Early action deadline: N/A,
notification date: N/A
Application deadline (fall): rolling
Undergraduate student body: 1,548
full time, 59 part time; 44%
male, 56% female; 1% American
Indian, 1% Asian, 19% black,
3% Hispanic, 1% multiracial,
0% Pacific Islander, 59% white,
4% international; 25% from in
state; 44% live on campus; 4%
of students in fraternities, 10%
in sororities
Most popular majors: 15%
Business, Management,
Marketing, and Related Support
Services, 14% Education, 8%
Health Professions and Related
Programs, 8% Homeland Security,
Law Enforcement, Firefighting and
Related Protective Services, 8%
Social Sciences
Expenses: 2014-2015: $34,250;
room/board: $13,126
Financial aid: (603) 428-2414;
77% of undergrads determined to
have financial need; average aid
package $24,794

Plymouth State University

Plymouth NH
(603) 535-2237
U.S. News ranking: Reg. U. (N), No. 103
Website: www.plymouth.edu
Admissions email: plymouthadmit@plymouth.edu
Public; founded 1871
Freshman admissions: less selective; 2013-2014: 5,084 applied, 3,967 accepted. Either SAT or ACT required. SAT 25/75 percentile: 860-1070. High school rank: 4% in top tenth, 20% in top quarter, 52% in top half
Early decision deadline: N/A, notification date: N/A
Early action deadline: N/A, notification date: N/A
Application deadline (fall): 4/1
Undergraduate student body: 3,795 full time, 270 part time; 52% male, 48% female; 0% American Indian, 2% Asian, 2% black, 3% Hispanic, 1% multiracial, 0% Pacific Islander, 79% white, 1% international; 59% from in state; 52% live on campus; 0% of students in fraternities, 4% in sororities
Most popular majors: 22% Business, Management, Marketing, and Related Support Services, 14% Education, 8% Homeland Security, Law Enforcement, Firefighting and Related Protective Services, 8% Parks, Recreation, Leisure, and Fitness Studies, 7% Visual and Performing Arts
Expenses: 2014-2015: $12,677 in state, $20,587 out of state; room/board: $10,728
Financial aid: (603) 535-2338; 65% of undergrads determined to have financial need; average aid package $9,345

Rivier University

Nashua NH
(603) 888-1311
U.S. News ranking: Reg. U. (N), second tier
Website: rivier.edu
Admissions email: admissions@rivier.edu
Private
Freshman admissions: less selective; 2013-2014: N/A applied, N/A accepted. Neither SAT nor ACT required. SAT 25/75 percentile: 860-1020. High school rank: N/A
Early decision deadline: N/A, notification date: N/A
Early action deadline: N/A, notification date: N/A
Application deadline (fall): rolling
Undergraduate student body: 891 full time, 700 part time; 18% male, 82% female; 0% American Indian, 2% Asian, 3% black, 5% Hispanic, 1% multiracial, 0% Pacific Islander, 77% white, 0% international; 60% from in state; N/A live on campus; N/A of students in fraternities, N/A in sororities
Most popular majors: 8% Business Administration and Management, General, 7% Elementary Education and Teaching, 8% Human Development and Family Studies, General, 8% Psychology, General, 45% Registered Nursing/Registered Nurse

Expenses: 2013-2014: $28,055; room/board: $10,570
Financial aid: (603) 897-8533

Southern New Hampshire University

Manchester NH
(603) 645-9611
U.S. News ranking: Reg. U. (N), unranked
Website: www.snhu.edu
Admissions email: admission@snhu.edu
Private; founded 1932
Freshman admissions: N/A; 2013-2014: 4,393 applied, 3,414 accepted. Neither SAT nor ACT required. SAT 25/75 percentile: 890-1100. High school rank: 7% in top tenth, 19% in top quarter, 61% in top half
Early decision deadline: N/A, notification date: N/A
Early action deadline: 11/15, notification date: 12/15
Application deadline (fall): rolling
Undergraduate student body: 9,283 full time, 8,820 part time; 40% male, 60% female; 0% American Indian, 1% Asian, 5% black, 2% Hispanic, 0% multiracial, 0% Pacific Islander, 29% white, 2% international; 44% from in state; 68% live on campus; 4% of students in fraternities, 5% in sororities
Most popular majors: 6% Accounting, 37% Business Administration and Management, General, 5% Computer and Information Sciences, General, 5% Hospitality Administration/Management, General, 8% Psychology, General
Expenses: 2014-2015: $29,924; room/board: $11,442
Financial aid: (603) 645-9645; 76% of undergrads determined to have financial need; average aid package $21,914

St. Anselm College

Manchester NH
(603) 641-7500
U.S. News ranking: Nat. Lib. Arts, No. 120
Website: www.anselm.edu
Admissions email: admission@anselm.edu
Private; founded 1889
Affiliation: Roman Catholic (Benedictine)
Freshman admissions: selective; 2013-2014: 3,829 applied, 2,820 accepted. Neither SAT nor ACT required. SAT 25/75 percentile: 1060-1230. High school rank: 22% in top tenth, 58% in top quarter, 90% in top half
Early decision deadline: N/A, notification date: N/A
Early action deadline: 11/15, notification date: 1/15
Application deadline (fall): 2/1
Undergraduate student body: 1,878 full time, 45 part time; 41% male, 59% female; 0% American Indian, 1% Asian, 2% black, 3% Hispanic, 2% multiracial, 0% Pacific Islander, 79% white, 1% international; 24% from in state; 89% live on campus; 0% of students in fraternities, 0% in sororities
Most popular majors: 11% Business/Commerce, General, 12% Criminology, 6% History,

General, 8% Psychology, General, 18% Registered Nursing/Registered Nurse
Expenses: 2014-2015: $36,336; room/board: $13,040
Financial aid: (603) 641-7110; 74% of undergrads determined to have financial need; average aid package $26,660

Thomas More College of Liberal Arts

Merrimack NH
(800) 880-8308
U.S. News ranking: Nat. Lib. Arts, unranked
Website: www.thomasmorecollege.edu
Admissions email: admissions@thomasmorecollege.edu
Private
Affiliation: Roman Catholic
Freshman admissions: N/A; 2013-2014: N/A applied, N/A accepted. Neither SAT nor ACT required. ACT 25/75 percentile: N/A. High school rank: N/A
Early decision deadline: N/A, notification date: N/A
Early action deadline: N/A, notification date: N/A
Application deadline (fall): rolling
Undergraduate student body: 80 full time, 0 part time; 50% male, 50% female; 0% American Indian, 5% Asian, 0% black, 3% Hispanic, 0% multiracial, 0% Pacific Islander, 85% white, 3% international; 11% from in state; 93% live on campus; 0% of students in fraternities, 0% in sororities
Most popular majors: Information not available
Expenses: 2014-2015: $20,400; room/board: $9,400
Financial aid: (800) 880-8308; 79% of undergrads determined to have financial need; average aid package $20,109

University of New Hampshire

Durham NH
(603) 862-1360
U.S. News ranking: Nat. U., No. 99
Website: www.unh.edu
Admissions email: admissions@unh.edu
Public; founded 1866
Freshman admissions: selective; 2013-2014: 17,938 applied, 13,963 accepted. Either SAT or ACT required. SAT 25/75 percentile: 1000-1210. High school rank: 20% in top tenth, 50% in top quarter, 88% in top half
Early decision deadline: N/A, notification date: N/A
Early action deadline: 11/15, notification date: 1/15
Application deadline (fall): 2/1
Undergraduate student body: 12,060 full time, 471 part time; 46% male, 54% female; 0% American Indian, 2% Asian, 1% black, 3% Hispanic, 2% multiracial, 0% Pacific Islander, 80% white, 1% international; 54% from in state; 58% live on campus; 10% of students in fraternities, 11% in sororities
Most popular majors: 16% Business Administration and Management, General, 4% Mechanical Engineering,

3% Political Science and Government, General, 9% Psychology, General, 5% Speech Communication and Rhetoric
Expenses: 2014-2015: $16,552 in state, $29,532 out of state; room/board: $10,360
Financial aid: (603) 862-3600; 68% of undergrads determined to have financial need; average aid package $21,879

NEW JERSEY

Berkeley College

Woodland Park NJ
(800) 446-5400
U.S. News ranking: Business, unranked
Website: www.berkeleycollege.edu
Admissions email: admissions@berkeleycollege.edu
For-profit; founded 1931
Freshman admissions: less selective; 2013-2014: 2,097 applied, 1,986 accepted. Neither SAT nor ACT required. ACT 25/75 percentile: N/A. High school rank: N/A
Early decision deadline: N/A, notification date: N/A
Early action deadline: N/A, notification date: N/A
Application deadline (fall): rolling
Undergraduate student body: 2,954 full time, 717 part time; 29% male, 71% female; 0% American Indian, 3% Asian, 23% black, 38% Hispanic, 0% multiracial, 0% Pacific Islander, 20% white, 1% international
Most popular majors: 10% Accounting, 32% Business Administration and Management, General, 23% Criminal Justice/Law Enforcement Administration, 11% Fashion Merchandising, 8% Health/Health Care Administration/Management
Expenses: 2014-2015: $23,700; room/board: N/A
Financial aid: (973) 278-5400

Bloomfield College

Bloomfield NJ
(800) 848-4555
U.S. News ranking: Nat. Lib. Arts, second tier
Website: www.bloomfield.edu
Admissions email: admission@bloomfield.edu
Private; founded 1868
Affiliation: Presbyterian
Freshman admissions: less selective; 2013-2014: 2,987 applied, 1,758 accepted. Either SAT or ACT required. SAT 25/75 percentile: 770-930. High school rank: 6% in top tenth, 24% in top quarter, 55% in top half
Early decision deadline: N/A, notification date: N/A
Early action deadline: 12/1, notification date: 12/23
Application deadline (fall): 8/1
Undergraduate student body: 1,765 full time, 204 part time; 35% male, 65% female; 0% American Indian, 4% Asian, 50% black, 22% Hispanic, 1% multiracial, 0% Pacific Islander, 13% white, 3% international; 94% from in state; 26% live on campus; 4% of students in fraternities, 2% in sororities
Most popular majors: 13% Business, Management, Marketing, and Related Support Services, 12% Health Professions and Related Programs,

14% Psychology, 19% Social Sciences, 20% Visual and Performing Arts
Expenses: 2014-2015: $26,750; room/board: $11,100
Financial aid: (973) 748-9000; 94% of undergrads determined to have financial need; average aid package $24,037

Caldwell University

Caldwell NJ
(973) 618-3500
U.S. News ranking: Reg. U. (N), No. 115
Website: www.caldwell.edu
Admissions email: admissions@caldwell.edu
Private; founded 1939
Affiliation: Roman Catholic
Freshman admissions: less selective; 2013-2014: 2,881 applied, 1,902 accepted. Either SAT or ACT required. SAT 25/75 percentile: 830-1070. High school rank: 10% in top tenth, 25% in top quarter, 62% in top half
Early decision deadline: N/A, notification date: N/A
Early action deadline: 12/1, notification date: 1/1
Application deadline (fall): rolling
Undergraduate student body: 1,302 full time, 274 part time; 31% male, 69% female; 0% American Indian, 4% Asian, 15% black, 16% Hispanic, 1% multiracial, 0% Pacific Islander, 45% white, 4% international; 92% from in state; 32% live on campus; N/A of students in fraternities, N/A in sororities
Most popular majors: 16% Business Administration and Management, General, 11% Education, General, 12% English Language and Literature, General, 8% Health Professions and Related Programs, 14% Psychology, General
Expenses: 2014-2015: $30,050; room/board: $11,700
Financial aid: (973) 618-3221; 81% of undergrads determined to have financial need; average aid package $13,193

Centenary College

Hackettstown NJ
(800) 236-8679
U.S. News ranking: Reg. U. (N), second tier
Website: www.centenarycollege.edu
Admissions email: admissions@centenarycollege.edu
Private; founded 1867
Affiliation: United Methodist
Freshman admissions: less selective; 2013-2014: 1,038 applied, 944 accepted. Either SAT or ACT required. SAT 25/75 percentile: 820-1090. High school rank: 10% in top tenth, 28% in top quarter, 58% in top half
Early decision deadline: N/A, notification date: N/A
Early action deadline: N/A, notification date: N/A
Application deadline (fall): 8/15
Undergraduate student body: 1,610 full time, 98 part time; 40% male, 60% female; 1% American Indian, 1% Asian, 10% black, 9% Hispanic, 1% multiracial, 0% Pacific Islander, 60% white, 5% international; 80% from in state; 61% live on campus; 0% of students in fraternities, 1% in sororities

Most popular majors: Information not available
Expenses: 2014-2015: $30,942; room/board: $10,420
Financial aid: (908) 852-1400; 79% of undergrads determined to have financial need; average aid package $25,324

College of New Jersey

Ewing NJ
(609) 771-2131
U.S. News ranking: Reg. U. (N), No. 3
Website: www.tcnj.edu
Admissions email: admiss@tcnj.edu
Public; founded 1855
Freshman admissions: more selective; 2013-2014: 11,145 applied, 4,805 accepted. Either SAT or ACT required. SAT 25/75 percentile: 1130-1340. High school rank: 84% in top tenth, 89% in top quarter, 99% in top half
Early decision deadline: 11/15, notification date: 12/15
Early action deadline: N/A, notification date: N/A
Application deadline (fall): 1/15
Undergraduate student body: 6,455 full time, 198 part time; 43% male, 57% female; 0% American Indian, 9% Asian, 5% black, 11% Hispanic, 1% multiracial, 0% Pacific Islander, 66% white, 0% international; 94% from in state; 55% live on campus; 9% of students in fraternities, 11% in sororities
Most popular majors: 7% Biology/Biological Sciences, General, 18% Business Administration and Management, General, 23% Elementary Education and Teaching, 7% Engineering, General, 7% Psychology, General
Expenses: 2014-2015: $15,024 in state, $25,637 out of state; room/board: $11,677
Financial aid: (609) 771-2211; 52% of undergrads determined to have financial need; average aid package $11,078

College of St. Elizabeth

Morristown NJ
(973) 290-4700
U.S. News ranking: Reg. U. (N), No. 87
Website: www.cse.edu
Admissions email: apply@cse.edu
Private; founded 1899
Affiliation: Catholic
Freshman admissions: least selective; 2013-2014: 2,496 applied, 1,207 accepted. Either SAT or ACT required. SAT 25/75 percentile: 748-960. High school rank: 1% in top tenth, 10% in top quarter, 49% in top half
Early decision deadline: N/A, notification date: N/A
Early action deadline: N/A, notification date: N/A
Application deadline (fall): rolling
Undergraduate student body: 554 full time, 433 part time; 8% male, 92% female; 0% American Indian, 3% Asian, 26% black, 15% Hispanic, 1% multiracial, 0% Pacific Islander, 39% white, 4% international; 94% from in state; 33% live on campus; 0% of students in fraternities, 0% in sororities

Most popular majors: 6% Business Administration and Management, General, 7% Dietetics/Dietitian, 12% Multi-/Interdisciplinary Studies, Other, 12% Psychology, General, 38% Registered Nursing/Registered Nurse
Expenses: 2014-2015: $31,095; room/board: $12,744
Financial aid: (973) 290-4445; 89% of undergrads determined to have financial need; average aid package $26,055

Drew University

Madison NJ
(973) 408-3739
U.S. News ranking: Nat. Lib. Arts, No. 99
Website: www.drew.edu
Admissions email: cadm@drew.edu
Private; founded 1867
Affiliation: Methodist
Freshman admissions: selective; 2013-2014: 3,430 applied, 2,656 accepted. Either SAT or ACT required. SAT 25/75 percentile: 990-1220. High school rank: 31% in top tenth, 62% in top quarter, 89% in top half
Early decision deadline: 12/1, notification date: 12/16
Early action deadline: N/A, notification date: N/A
Application deadline (fall): 2/15
Undergraduate student body: 1,434 full time, 59 part time; 38% male, 62% female; 0% American Indian, 5% Asian, 11% black, 14% Hispanic, 3% multiracial, 0% Pacific Islander, 56% white, 3% international; 69% from in state; 77% live on campus; 0% of students in fraternities, 0% in sororities
Most popular majors: 6% Drama and Dramatics/Theatre Arts, General, 7% Economics, General, 8% English Language and Literature, General, 7% Political Science and Government, General, 10% Psychology, General
Expenses: 2014-2015: $45,214; room/board: $12,302
Financial aid: (973) 408-3112; 72% of undergrads determined to have financial need; average aid package $35,618

Fairleigh Dickinson University

Teaneck NJ
(800) 338-8803
U.S. News ranking: Reg. U. (N), No. 79
Website: www.fdu.edu
Admissions email: admissions@fdu.edu
Private; founded 1942
Freshman admissions: selective; 2013-2014: 12,561 applied, 6,616 accepted. Either SAT or ACT required. SAT 25/75 percentile: 900-1100. High school rank: 17% in top tenth, 43% in top quarter, 76% in top half
Early decision deadline: N/A, notification date: N/A
Early action deadline: N/A, notification date: N/A
Application deadline (fall): rolling
Undergraduate student body: 4,843 full time, 3,539 part time; 42% male, 58% female; 0% American Indian, 4% Asian, 13% black, 27% Hispanic, 1% multiracial, 0% Pacific Islander, 39% white, 5% international; 89% from in

state; 34% live on campus; N/A of students in fraternities, N/A in sororities
Most popular majors: Information not available
Expenses: 2013-2014: $34,882; room/board: $13,068
Financial aid: (201) 692-2823

Felician College

Lodi NJ
(201) 559-6131
U.S. News ranking: Reg. U. (N), second tier
Website: www.felician.edu
Admissions email: admissions@felician.edu
Private; founded 1942
Affiliation: Roman Catholic
Freshman admissions: least selective; 2013-2014: 1,567 applied, 1,382 accepted. Either SAT or ACT required. SAT 25/75 percentile: 780-980. High school rank: 2% in top tenth, 24% in top quarter, 57% in top half
Early decision deadline: N/A, notification date: N/A
Early action deadline: N/A, notification date: N/A
Application deadline (fall): rolling
Undergraduate student body: 1,340 full time, 281 part time; 28% male, 72% female; 1% American Indian, 8% Asian, 20% black, 24% Hispanic, 1% multiracial, 1% Pacific Islander, 38% white, 2% international; 92% from in state; N/A live on campus; N/A of students in fraternities, N/A in sororities
Most popular majors: 18% Business, Management, Marketing, and Related Support Services, 6% Education, 39% Health Professions and Related Programs, 9% Homeland Security, Law Enforcement, Firefighting and Related Protective Services, 8% Multi/Interdisciplinary Studies
Expenses: 2014-2015: $30,615; room/board: $11,650
Financial aid: (201) 559-6010; 87% of undergrads determined to have financial need; average aid package $25,793

Georgian Court University

Lakewood NJ
(800) 458-8422
U.S. News ranking: Reg. U. (N), No. 125
Website: www.georgian.edu
Admissions email: admissions@georgian.edu
Private; founded 1908
Affiliation: Roman Catholic
Freshman admissions: less selective; 2013-2014: 1,276 applied, 994 accepted. Either SAT or ACT required. SAT 25/75 percentile: 790-1010. High school rank: 6% in top tenth, 30% in top quarter, 65% in top half
Early decision deadline: N/A, notification date: N/A
Early action deadline: N/A, notification date: N/A
Application deadline (fall): rolling
Undergraduate student body: 1,261 full time, 306 part time; 19% male, 81% female; 0% American Indian, 2% Asian, 15% black, 12% Hispanic, 2% multiracial, 0% Pacific Islander, 53% white, 1% international; 94% from in state; 28% live on campus; N/A of students in fraternities, N/A in sororities

Most popular majors: 6% Business, Management, Marketing, and Related Support Services, 17% Education, 12% English Language and Literature/Letters, 8% Health Professions and Related Programs, 24% Psychology
Expenses: 2014-2015: $30,998; room/board: $10,596
Financial aid: (732) 364-2200; 83% of undergrads determined to have financial need; average aid package $25,096

Kean University

Union NJ
(908) 737-7100
U.S. News ranking: Reg. U. (N), second tier
Website: www.kean.edu
Admissions email: admitme@kean.edu
Public; founded 1855
Freshman admissions: less selective; 2013-2014: 4,952 applied, 3,980 accepted. Either SAT or ACT required. SAT 25/75 percentile: 810-1000. High school rank: 8% in top tenth, 26% in top quarter, 63% in top half
Early decision deadline: N/A, notification date: N/A
Early action deadline: N/A, notification date: N/A
Application deadline (fall): 5/31
Undergraduate student body: 9,251 full time, 2,827 part time; 40% male, 60% female; 0% American Indian, 6% Asian, 19% black, 24% Hispanic, 2% multiracial, 0% Pacific Islander, 39% white, 1% international; 98% from in state; 14% live on campus; N/A of students in fraternities, N/A in sororities
Most popular majors: 6% Accounting, 5% Biology/Biological Sciences, General, 8% Business Administration and Management, General, 6% Criminal Justice/Law Enforcement Administration, 14% Psychology, General
Expenses: 2013-2014: $10,918 in state, $17,141 out of state; room/board: $10,064
Financial aid: (908) 737-3190; 70% of undergrads determined to have financial need; average aid package $9,917

Monmouth University

West Long Branch NJ
(800) 543-9671
U.S. News ranking: Reg. U. (N), No. 37
Website: www.monmouth.edu
Admissions email: admission@monmouth.edu
Private; founded 1933
Freshman admissions: selective; 2013-2014: 5,537 applied, 4,314 accepted. Either SAT or ACT required. SAT 25/75 percentile: 970-1150. High school rank: 19% in top tenth, 49% in top quarter, 82% in top half
Early decision deadline: N/A, notification date: N/A
Early action deadline: 12/1, notification date: 1/15
Application deadline (fall): 3/1
Undergraduate student body: 4,304 full time, 303 part time; 41% male, 59% female; 0% American Indian, 3% Asian, 5% black, 9% Hispanic, 2% multiracial, 0% Pacific Islander, 77% white, 1% international; 88% from in state; 15% live on campus; 13% of students in fraternities, 15% in sororities

Most popular majors: 24% Business, Management, Marketing, and Related Support Services, 12% Communication, Journalism, and Related Programs, 13% Education, 8% Health Professions and Related Programs, 8% Psychology
Expenses: 2014-2015: $32,310; room/board: $11,798
Financial aid: (732) 571-3463; 70% of undergrads determined to have financial need; average aid package $21,048

Montclair State University

Montclair NJ
(973) 655-4444
U.S. News ranking: Reg. U. (N), No. 50
Website: www.montclair.edu
Admissions email: undergraduate.admissions@montclair.edu
Public; founded 1908
Freshman admissions: selective; 2013-2014: 13,012 applied, 8,500 accepted. SAT required. SAT 25/75 percentile: 880-1060. High school rank: 11% in top tenth, 35% in top quarter, 79% in top half
Early decision deadline: N/A, notification date: N/A
Early action deadline: N/A, notification date: N/A
Application deadline (fall): 3/1
Undergraduate student body: 13,356 full time, 2,075 part time; 39% male, 61% female; 0% American Indian, 5% Asian, 9% black, 23% Hispanic, 3% multiracial, 0% Pacific Islander, 47% white, 2% international; 3% from in state; 32% live on campus; N/A of students in fraternities, N/A in sororities
Most popular majors: 14% Business Administration and Management, General, 6% English Language and Literature, General, 8% Family and Consumer Sciences/Human Sciences, General, 5% Multi-/Interdisciplinary Studies, Other, 9% Psychology, General
Expenses: 2014-2015: $11,616 in state, $21,153 out of state; room/board: $14,140
Financial aid: (973) 655-4461; 71% of undergrads determined to have financial need; average aid package $15,857

New Jersey City University

Jersey City NJ
(888) 441-6528
U.S. News ranking: Reg. U. (N), second tier
Website: www.njcu.edu/
Admissions email: admissions@njcu.edu
Public; founded 1927
Freshman admissions: less selective; 2013-2014: 4,183 applied, 1,727 accepted. Either SAT or ACT required. SAT 25/75 percentile: 820-1012. High school rank: 17% in top tenth, 37% in top quarter, 74% in top half
Early decision deadline: N/A, notification date: N/A
Early action deadline: N/A, notification date: N/A
Undergraduate student body: 4,777 full time, 1,661 part time; 40% male, 60% female; 0% American Indian, 9% Asian, 21% black, 34% Hispanic, 1% multiracial,

0% Pacific Islander, 25% white, 1% international; 99% from in state; 4% live on campus; 0% of students in fraternities, 0% in sororities
Most popular majors: 8% Accounting, 10% Business Administration and Management, General, 8% Corrections and Criminal Justice, Other, 11% Psychology, General, 12% Registered Nursing, Nursing Administration, Nursing Research and Clinical Nursing, Other
Expenses: 2014-2015: $10,852 in state, $19,424 out of state; room/board: $10,604
Financial aid: (201) 200-3173; 87% of undergrads determined to have financial need; average aid package $16,087

New Jersey Institute of Technology

Newark NJ
(973) 596-3300
U.S. News ranking: Nat. U., No. 149
Website: www.njit.edu
Admissions email: admissions@njit.edu
Public; founded 1881
Freshman admissions: more selective; 2013-2014: 4,344 applied, 2,844 accepted. Either SAT or ACT required. SAT 25/75 percentile: 1030-1250. High school rank: 27% in top tenth, 54% in top quarter, 85% in top half
Early decision deadline: N/A, notification date: N/A
Early action deadline: N/A, notification date: N/A
Application deadline (fall): 3/1
Undergraduate student body: 5,709 full time, 1,577 part time; 76% male, 24% female; 0% American Indian, 20% Asian, 9% black, 20% Hispanic, 2% multiracial, 0% Pacific Islander, 33% white, 5% international; 95% from in state; 23% live on campus; 5% of students in fraternities, 3% in sororities
Most popular majors: 11% Architecture and Related Services, 9% Business, Management, Marketing, and Related Support Services, 15% Computer and Information Sciences and Support Services, 36% Engineering, 14% Engineering Technologies and Engineering-Related Fields
Expenses: 2014-2015: $15,602 in state, $28,274 out of state; room/board: $12,500
Financial aid: (973) 596-3479; 72% of undergrads determined to have financial need; average aid package $14,123

Princeton University

Princeton NJ
(609) 258-3060
U.S. News ranking: Nat. U., No. 1
Website: www.princeton.edu
Admissions email: uaoffice@princeton.edu
Private; founded 1746
Freshman admissions: most selective; 2013-2014: 26,498 applied, 1,963 accepted. Either SAT or ACT required. SAT 25/75 percentile: 1410-1600. High school rank: 95% in top tenth, 98% in top quarter, 100% in top half

Early decision deadline: N/A, notification date: N/A
Early action deadline: 11/1, notification date: 12/15
Application deadline (fall): 1/1
Undergraduate student body: 5,244 full time, 79 part time; 51% male, 49% female; 0% American Indian, 20% Asian, 8% black, 8% Hispanic, 4% multiracial, 0% Pacific Islander, 47% white, 11% international; 18% from in state; 97% live on campus; 0% of students in fraternities, 0% in sororities
Most popular majors: 11% Economics, General, 6% Molecular Biology, 8% Political Science and Government, General, 6% Psychology, General, 6% Public Policy Analysis, General
Expenses: 2014-2015: $41,820; room/board: $13,620
Financial aid: (609) 258-3330; 59% of undergrads determined to have financial need; average aid package $40,732

Ramapo College of New Jersey

Mahwah NJ
(201) 684-7300
U.S. News ranking: Reg. U. (N), No. 28
Website: www.ramapo.edu
Admissions email: admissions@ramapo.edu
Public; founded 1969
Freshman admissions: selective; 2013-2014: 6,297 applied, 3,480 accepted. Either SAT or ACT required. SAT 25/75 percentile: 990-1200. High school rank: 22% in top tenth, 52% in top quarter, 85% in top half
Early decision deadline: N/A, notification date: N/A
Early action deadline: 11/15, notification date: 12/15
Application deadline (fall): 3/1
Undergraduate student body: 4,992 full time, 622 part time; 44% male, 56% female; 0% American Indian, 6% Asian, 5% black, 14% Hispanic, 1% multiracial, 0% Pacific Islander, 66% white, 1% international; 95% from in state; 50% live on campus; 7% of students in fraternities, 11% in sororities
Most popular majors: 6% Accounting, 15% Business Administration and Management, General, 8% Nursing Science, 15% Psychology, General, 11% Speech Communication and Rhetoric
Expenses: 2014-2015: $13,388 in state, $22,038 out of state; room/board: $11,550
Financial aid: (201) 684-7549; 61% of undergrads determined to have financial need; average aid package $11,083

Richard Stockton College of New Jersey

Galloway NJ
(609) 652-4261
U.S. News ranking: Reg. U. (N), No. 41
Website: www.stockton.edu
Admissions email: admissions@stockton.edu
Public; founded 1969
Freshman admissions: selective; 2013-2014: 6,126 applied,

3,805 accepted. Either SAT or ACT required. SAT 25/75 percentile: 980-1170. High school rank: 23% in top tenth, 60% in top quarter, 95% in top half
Early decision deadline: N/A, notification date: N/A
Early action deadline: N/A, notification date: N/A
Application deadline (fall): 5/1
Undergraduate student body: 6,953 full time, 586 part time; 40% male, 60% female; 0% American Indian, 5% Asian, 6% black, 10% Hispanic, 3% multiracial, 0% Pacific Islander, 74% white, 0% international; 99% from in state; 36% live on campus; N/A of students in fraternities, N/A in sororities
Most popular majors: 8% Biology/Biological Sciences, General, 15% Business Administration and Management, General, 9% Criminology, 13% Psychology, General, 6% Teacher Education, Multiple Levels
Expenses: 2014-2015: $12,568 in state, $19,089 out of state; room/board: $11,164
Financial aid: (609) 652-4201; 74% of undergrads determined to have financial need; average aid package $16,417

Rider University

Lawrenceville NJ
(609) 896-5042
U.S. News ranking: Reg. U. (N), No. 23
Website: www.rider.edu
Admissions email: admissions@rider.edu
Private; founded 1865
Freshman admissions: selective; 2013-2014: 8,076 applied, 5,604 accepted. Either SAT or ACT required. SAT 25/75 percentile: 930-1150. High school rank: 14% in top tenth, 38% in top quarter, 68% in top half
Early decision deadline: N/A, notification date: N/A
Early action deadline: 11/15, notification date: 12/15
Application deadline (fall): rolling
Undergraduate student body: 3,792 full time, 627 part time; 41% male, 59% female; 0% American Indian, 4% Asian, 10% black, 10% Hispanic, 2% multiracial, 0% Pacific Islander, 66% white, 3% international; 78% from in state; 57% live on campus; 5% of students in fraternities, 9% in sororities
Most popular majors: 10% Accounting, 7% Business Administration and Management, General, 8% Elementary Education and Teaching, 9% Psychology, General, 6% Rhetoric and Composition
Expenses: 2014-2015: $36,830; room/board: $13,330
Financial aid: (609) 896-5360; 71% of undergrads determined to have financial need; average aid package $23,474

Rowan University

Glassboro NJ
(856) 256-4200
U.S. News ranking: Reg. U. (N), No. 19
Website: www.rowan.edu
Admissions email: admissions@rowan.edu
Public; founded 1923

Freshman admissions: selective; 2013-2014: 9,082 applied, 5,464 accepted. Either SAT or ACT required. SAT 25/75 percentile: 1000-1230. High school rank: 36% in top tenth, 63% in top quarter, 88% in top half
Early decision deadline: N/A, notification date: N/A
Early action deadline: N/A, notification date: N/A
Application deadline (fall): 5/1
Undergraduate student body: 9,348 full time, 1,603 part time; 51% male, 49% female; 0% American Indian, 6% Asian, 8% black, 9% Hispanic, 3% multiracial, 0% Pacific Islander, 70% white, 1% international; 94% from in state; 33% live on campus; 8% of students in fraternities, 7% in sororities
Most popular majors: 14% Business, Management, Marketing, and Related Support Services, 8% Communication, Journalism, and Related Programs, 20% Education, 5% Homeland Security, Law Enforcement, Firefighting and Related Protective Services, 9% Psychology
Expenses: 2014-2015: $12,616 in state, $20,570 out of state; room/board: $14,022
Financial aid: (856) 256-4250; 66% of undergrads determined to have financial need; average aid package $9,627

Rutgers, The State University of New Jersey–Camden

Camden NJ
(856) 225-6104
U.S. News ranking: Reg. U. (N), No. 28
Website: www.rutgers.edu/
Admissions email: camden@ugadm.rutgers.edu
Public; founded 1927
Freshman admissions: selective; 2013-2014: 7,437 applied, 4,357 accepted. Either SAT or ACT required. SAT 25/75 percentile: 930-1140. High school rank: 17% in top tenth, 43% in top quarter, 80% in top half
Early decision deadline: N/A, notification date: N/A
Early action deadline: N/A, notification date: N/A
Application deadline (fall): rolling
Undergraduate student body: 3,939 full time, 903 part time; 45% male, 55% female; 0% American Indian, 9% Asian, 17% black, 11% Hispanic, 3% multiracial, 0% Pacific Islander, 56% white, 1% international; 98% from in state; 9% live on campus; N/A of students in fraternities, N/A in sororities
Most popular majors: 8% Biology/Biological Sciences, General, 13% Business Administration and Management, General, 8% Criminal Justice/Safety Studies, 12% Psychology, General, 10% Registered Nursing/Registered Nurse
Expenses: 2014-2015: $13,683 in state, $27,978 out of state; room/board: $11,438
Financial aid: (856) 225-6039; 78% of undergrads determined to have financial need; average aid package $12,097

Rutgers, The State University of New Jersey–Newark

Newark NJ
(973) 353-5205
U.S. News ranking: Nat. U., No. 126
Website: rutgers-newark.rutgers.edu
Admissions email: admissions@ugadm.rutgers.edu
Public; founded 1908
Freshman admissions: selective; 2013-2014: 13,282 applied, 7,173 accepted. Either SAT or ACT required. SAT 25/75 percentile: 960-1158. High school rank: 22% in top tenth, 52% in top quarter, 88% in top half
Early decision deadline: N/A, notification date: N/A
Early action deadline: N/A, notification date: N/A
Application deadline (fall): rolling
Undergraduate student body: 5,827 full time, 1,390 part time; 50% male, 50% female; 0% American Indian, 22% Asian, 19% black, 24% Hispanic, 3% multiracial, 0% Pacific Islander, 26% white, 3% international; 98% from in state; 9% live on campus; N/A of students in fraternities, N/A in sororities
Most popular majors: 13% Criminal Justice/Safety Studies, 9% Finance, General, 9% Psychology, General, 9% Registered Nursing/Registered Nurse, 15% Regular/General High School/Secondary Diploma Program
Expenses: 2014-2015: $13,297 in state, $28,075 out of state; room/board: $12,509
Financial aid: (973) 353-5151; 77% of undergrads determined to have financial need; average aid package $13,074

Rutgers, The State University of New Jersey–New Brunswick

Piscataway NJ
(732) 932-4636
U.S. News ranking: Nat. U., No. 70
Website: www.rutgers.edu
Admissions email: admissions@ugadm.rutgers.edu
Public; founded 1766
Freshman admissions: more selective; 2013-2014: 30,631 applied, 18,230 accepted. Either SAT or ACT required. SAT 25/75 percentile: 1090-1330. High school rank: 38% in top tenth, 74% in top quarter, 96% in top half
Early decision deadline: N/A, notification date: N/A
Early action deadline: N/A, notification date: N/A
Application deadline (fall): rolling
Undergraduate student body: 31,759 full time, 2,141 part time; 50% male, 50% female; 0% American Indian, 26% Asian, 8% black, 12% Hispanic, 3% multiracial, 0% Pacific Islander, 45% white, 4% international; 94% from in state; 48% live on campus; N/A of students in fraternities, N/A in sororities
Most popular majors: 5% Biology/Biological Sciences, General, 5% Economics, General, 4% Political Science and Government,

General, 9% Psychology, General, 7% Speech Communication and Rhetoric
Expenses: 2014-2015: $13,813 in state, $28,591 out of state; room/board: $11,749
Financial aid: (732) 932-7057; 56% of undergrads determined to have financial need; average aid package $13,041

Seton Hall University

South Orange NJ
(973) 761-9332
U.S. News ranking: Nat. U., No. 126
Website: www.shu.edu
Admissions email: thehall@shu.edu
Private; founded 1856
Affiliation: Roman Catholic
Freshman admissions: selective; 2013-2014: 10,730 applied, 8,498 accepted. Either SAT or ACT required. SAT 25/75 percentile: 1020-1220. High school rank: 35% in top tenth, 62% in top quarter, 88% in top half
Early decision deadline: N/A, notification date: N/A
Early action deadline: 11/15, notification date: 12/30
Application deadline (fall): rolling
Undergraduate student body: 5,380 full time, 459 part time; 41% male, 59% female; 0% American Indian, 8% Asian, 13% black, 17% Hispanic, 2% multiracial, 0% Pacific Islander, 50% white, 3% international; 77% from in state; 39% live on campus; 9% of students in fraternities, 11% in sororities
Most popular majors: 6% Biology/Biological Sciences, General, 5% Finance, General, 5% Humanities/Humanistic Studies, 6% International Relations and Affairs, 22% Registered Nursing/Registered Nurse
Expenses: 2014-2015: $36,926; room/board: $13,742
Financial aid: (973) 761-9350

Stevens Institute of Technology

Hoboken NJ
(201) 216-5194
U.S. News ranking: Nat. U., No. 76
Website: www.stevens.edu
Admissions email: admissions@stevens.edu
Private; founded 1870
Freshman admissions: more selective; 2013-2014: 4,977 applied, 1,899 accepted. Either SAT or ACT required. SAT 25/75 percentile: 1210-1390. High school rank: 68% in top tenth, 89% in top quarter, 98% in top half
Early decision deadline: 11/15, notification date: 12/15
Early action deadline: N/A, notification date: N/A
Application deadline (fall): 2/1
Undergraduate student body: 2,661 full time, 30 part time; 72% male, 28% female; 0% American Indian, 10% Asian, 2% black, 9% Hispanic, 0% multiracial, 0% Pacific Islander, 61% white, 4% international; 66% from in state; 73% live on campus; 25% of students in fraternities, 25% in sororities

Most popular majors: Information not available
Expenses: 2013-2014: $44,490; room/board: $14,214
Financial aid: (201) 216-5555

St. Peter's University

Jersey City NJ
(201) 761-7100
U.S. News ranking: Reg. U. (N), No. 98
Website: www.spc.edu
Admissions email: admissions@spc.edu
Private; founded 1872
Affiliation: Roman Catholic (Jesuit)
Freshman admissions: less selective; 2013-2014: 6,145 applied, 3,323 accepted. Either SAT or ACT required. SAT 25/75 percentile: 830-1000. High school rank: 15% in top tenth, 38% in top quarter, 70% in top half
Early decision deadline: N/A, notification date: N/A
Early action deadline: N/A, notification date: N/A
Application deadline (fall): rolling
Undergraduate student body: 2,068 full time, 416 part time; 39% male, 61% female; 1% American Indian, 9% Asian, 28% black, 28% Hispanic, 2% multiracial, 0% Pacific Islander, 24% white, 2% international; 87% from in state; 36% live on campus; N/A of students in fraternities, N/A in sororities
Most popular majors: 11% Biological and Biomedical Sciences, 33% Business, Management, Marketing, and Related Support Services, 8% Health Professions and Related Programs, 7% Homeland Security, Law Enforcement, Firefighting and Related Protective Services, 6% Liberal Arts and Sciences, General Studies and Humanities
Expenses: 2014-2015: $33,232; room/board: $13,996
Financial aid: (201) 915-4929; 89% of undergrads determined to have financial need; average aid package $27,280

Thomas Edison State College[1]

Trenton NJ
(888) 442-8372
U.S. News ranking: Reg. U. (N), unranked
Website: www.tesc.edu
Admissions email: admissions@tesc.edu
Public; founded 1972
Application deadline (fall): rolling
Undergraduate student body: N/A full time, N/A part time
Expenses: 2013-2014: $5,821 in state, $8,516 out of state; room/board: N/A
Financial aid: (609) 633-9658

William Paterson University of New Jersey

Wayne NJ
(973) 720-2125
U.S. News ranking: Reg. U. (N), No. 103
Website: www.wpunj.edu/
Admissions email: admissions@wpunj.edu
Public; founded 1855
Freshman admissions: selective; 2013-2014: 8,935 applied, 6,086 accepted. Either SAT

or ACT required. SAT 25/75 percentile: 920-1100. High school rank: N/A
Early decision deadline: N/A, notification date: N/A
Early action deadline: 12/1, notification date: 1/15
Application deadline (fall): 6/1
Undergraduate student body: 8,271 full time, 1,756 part time; 45% male, 55% female; 0% American Indian, 7% Asian, 14% black, 25% Hispanic, 2% multiracial, 0% Pacific Islander, 47% white, 1% international; 98% from in state; 22% live on campus; 1% of students in fraternities, 1% in sororities
Most popular majors: 19% Business, Management, Marketing, and Related Support Services, 10% Communication, Journalism, and Related Programs, 12% Education, 9% Psychology, 12% Social Sciences
Expenses: 2013-2014: $11,918 in state, $19,458 out of state; room/board: $10,600
Financial aid: (973) 720-2202; 73% of undergrads determined to have financial need; average aid package $9,749

NEW MEXICO

Eastern New Mexico University[1]

Portales NM
(505) 562-2178
U.S. News ranking: Reg. U. (W), second tier
Website: www.enmu.edu
Admissions email: admissions.office@enmu.edu
Public
Application deadline (fall): N/A
Undergraduate student body: N/A full time, N/A part time
Expenses: 2013-2014: $4,558 in state, $10,069 out of state; room/board: $6,266
Financial aid: (800) 367-3668

New Mexico Highlands University

Las Vegas NM
(505) 454-3439
U.S. News ranking: Reg. U. (W), unranked
Website: www.nmhu.edu
Admissions email: admissions@nmhu.edu
Public; founded 1893
Freshman admissions: N/A; 2013-2014: 1,575 applied, 1,575 accepted. Neither SAT nor ACT required. ACT 25/75 percentile: 16-20. High school rank: 5% in top tenth, 16% in top quarter, 47% in top half
Early decision deadline: N/A, notification date: N/A
Early action deadline: N/A, notification date: N/A
Application deadline (fall): rolling
Undergraduate student body: 1,646 full time, 750 part time; 40% male, 60% female; 16% American Indian, 1% Asian, 13% black, 11% Hispanic, 4% multiracial, 1% Pacific Islander, 39% white, 13% international
Most popular majors: Information not available
Expenses: 2013-2014: $4,000 in state, $6,383 out of state; room/board: $5,720

Financial aid: (505) 454-3430; 75% of undergrads determined to have financial need; average aid package $1,816

New Mexico Institute of Mining and Technology

Socorro NM
(505) 835-5424
U.S. News ranking: Reg. U. (W), No. 23
Website: www.nmt.edu
Admissions email: admission@admin.nmt.edu
Public; founded 1889
Freshman admissions: more selective; 2013-2014: 1,088 applied, 350 accepted. Either SAT or ACT required. ACT 25/75 percentile: 23-29. High school rank: 40% in top tenth, 67% in top quarter, 87% in top half
Early decision deadline: N/A, notification date: N/A
Early action deadline: N/A, notification date: N/A
Application deadline (fall): 8/1
Undergraduate student body: 1,418 full time, 186 part time; 70% male, 30% female; 4% American Indian, 3% Asian, 2% black, 25% Hispanic, 4% multiracial, 0% Pacific Islander, 59% white, 3% international
Most popular majors: 10% Biology/Biological Sciences, General, 8% Chemical Engineering, 8% Computer and Information Sciences, General, 26% Mechanical Engineering, 7% Petroleum Engineering
Expenses: 2014-2015: $6,256 in state, $18,184 out of state; room/board: $6,740
Financial aid: (505) 835-5333; 53% of undergrads determined to have financial need; average aid package $11,806

New Mexico State University

Las Cruces NM
(505) 646-3121
U.S. News ranking: Nat. U., second tier
Website: www.nmsu.edu
Admissions email: admissions@nmsu.edu
Public; founded 1888
Freshman admissions: selective; 2013-2014: 5,285 applied, 4,505 accepted. Either SAT or ACT required. ACT 25/75 percentile: 18-24. High school rank: 21% in top tenth, 47% in top quarter, 80% in top half
Early decision deadline: N/A, notification date: N/A
Early action deadline: N/A, notification date: N/A
Application deadline (fall): rolling
Undergraduate student body: 11,297 full time, 2,285 part time; 47% male, 53% female; 2% American Indian, 1% Asian, 3% black, 52% Hispanic, 1% multiracial, 0% Pacific Islander, 32% white, 4% international; 75% from in state; 18% live on campus; 2% of students in fraternities, 3% in sororities
Most popular majors: 3% Biology/Biological Sciences, General, 6% Criminal Justice/Safety Studies, 3% Education, General, 4% General Studies, 3% Psychology, General

Expenses: 2014-2015: $6,573 in state, $20,658 out of state; room/board: $7,530
Financial aid: (505) 646-4105; 65% of undergrads determined to have financial need; average aid package $8,800

Northern New Mexico College[1]

Espanola NM
(505) 747-2111
U.S. News ranking: Reg. Coll. (W), unranked
Website: nnmc.edu
Admissions email: N/A
Public
Application deadline (fall): N/A
Undergraduate student body: N/A full time, N/A part time
Expenses: 2013-2014: $4,060 in state, $11,523 out of state; room/board: $7,180
Financial aid: (505) 747-2128

Santa Fe University of Art and Design

Santa Fe NM
(505) 473-6937
U.S. News ranking: Arts, unranked
Website: www.santafeuniversity.edu
Admissions email: admissions@santafeuniversity.edu
For-profit; founded 1859
Freshman admissions: N/A; 2013-2014: 397 applied, 396 accepted. Neither SAT nor ACT required. SAT 25/75 percentile: N/A. High school rank: N/A
Early decision deadline: N/A, notification date: N/A
Early action deadline: N/A, notification date: N/A
Application deadline (fall): rolling
Undergraduate student body: 819 full time, 7 part time; 47% male, 53% female; 3% American Indian, 1% Asian, 7% black, 25% Hispanic, 5% multiracial, 1% Pacific Islander, 48% white, 5% international; 25% from in state; 70% live on campus; N/A of students in fraternities, N/A in sororities
Most popular majors: 29% Cinematography and Film/Video Production, 18% Drama and Dramatics/Theatre Arts, General, 11% Fine/Studio Arts, General, 14% Graphic Design, 11% Music, General
Expenses: 2014-2015: $30,136; room/board: $9,379
Financial aid: (505) 473-6454; 80% of undergrads determined to have financial need; average aid package $22,334

St. John's College

Santa Fe NM
(505) 984-6060
U.S. News ranking: Nat. Lib. Arts, No. 89
Website: www.sjc.edu/admissions-and-aid
Admissions email: santafe.admissions@sjc.edu
Private; founded 1964
Freshman admissions: more selective; 2013-2014: 181 applied, 169 accepted. Neither SAT nor ACT required. SAT 25/75 percentile: 1160-1450.

High school rank: 25% in top tenth, 39% in top quarter, 71% in top half
Early decision deadline: N/A, notification date: N/A
Early action deadline: 1/15, notification date: 2/15
Application deadline (fall): rolling
Undergraduate student body: 339 full time, 5 part time; 54% male, 46% female; 1% American Indian, 3% Asian, 1% black, 11% Hispanic, 7% multiracial, 0% Pacific Islander, 59% white, 15% international; 8% from in state; 84% live on campus; 0% of students in fraternities, 0% in sororities
Most popular majors: 100% Liberal Arts and Sciences/Liberal Studies
Expenses: 2014-2015: $47,626; room/board: $10,582
Financial aid: (505) 984-6073; 80% of undergrads determined to have financial need; average aid package $36,918

University of New Mexico
Albuquerque NM
(505) 277-8900
U.S. News ranking: Nat. U., No. 189
Website: www.unm.edu
Admissions email: apply@unm.edu
Public; founded 1889
Freshman admissions: selective; 2013-2014: 11,995 applied, 6,799 accepted. Either SAT or ACT required. ACT 25/75 percentile: 19-25. High school rank: N/A
Early decision deadline: N/A, notification date: N/A
Early action deadline: N/A, notification date: N/A
Application deadline (fall): rolling
Undergraduate student body: 17,187 full time, 3,951 part time; 44% male, 56% female; 6% American Indian, 3% Asian, 3% black, 44% Hispanic, 3% multiracial, 0% Pacific Islander, 38% white, 1% international; 90% from in state; 13% live on campus; 5% of students in fraternities, 6% in sororities
Most popular majors: 8% Biological and Biomedical Sciences, 14% Business, Management, Marketing, and Related Support Services, 12% Education, 10% Psychology, 8% Social Sciences
Expenses: 2013-2014: $6,846 in state, $20,688 out of state; room/board: $8,454
Financial aid: (505) 277-3012

University of the Southwest[1]
Hobbs NM
(575) 392-6563
U.S. News ranking: Reg. Coll. (W), unranked
Website: www.usw.edu
Admissions email: admissions@usw.edu
Private; founded 1962
Application deadline (fall): rolling
Undergraduate student body: N/A full time, N/A part time
Expenses: 2013-2014: $14,280; room/board: $6,960
Financial aid: (505) 392-6561

Western New Mexico University[1]
Silver City NM
(505) 538-6127
U.S. News ranking: Reg. U. (W), unranked
Website: www.wnmu.edu
Admissions email: admissions@wnmu.edu
Public; founded 1893
Application deadline (fall): 8/1
Undergraduate student body: N/A full time, N/A part time
Expenses: 2013-2014: $4,723 in state, $12,763 out of state; room/board: $10,156
Financial aid: (575) 538-6173

NEW YORK

Adelphi University
Garden City NY
(800) 233-5744
U.S. News ranking: Nat. U., No. 149
Website: www.adelphi.edu
Admissions email: admissions@adelphi.edu
Private; founded 1896
Freshman admissions: selective; 2013-2014: 8,654 applied, 5,897 accepted. Neither SAT nor ACT required. SAT 25/75 percentile: 1020-1220. High school rank: 26% in top tenth, 64% in top quarter, 92% in top half
Early decision deadline: N/A, notification date: N/A
Early action deadline: 12/1, notification date: 12/31
Application deadline (fall): rolling
Undergraduate student body: 4,531 full time, 509 part time; 31% male, 69% female; 0% American Indian, 8% Asian, 11% black, 13% Hispanic, 2% multiracial, 0% Pacific Islander, 53% white, 4% international; 92% from in state; 23% live on campus; 11% of students in fraternities, 9% in sororities
Most popular majors: 27% Health Services/Allied Health/Health Sciences, General
Expenses: 2014-2015: $32,340; room/board: $13,620
Financial aid: (516) 877-3365; 72% of undergrads determined to have financial need; average aid package $20,000

Alfred University
Alfred NY
(800) 541-9229
U.S. News ranking: Reg. U. (N), No. 38
Website: www.alfred.edu
Admissions email: admissions@alfred.edu
Private; founded 1836
Freshman admissions: selective; 2013-2014: 3,417 applied, 2,385 accepted. Either SAT or ACT required. SAT 25/75 percentile: 1000-1200. High school rank: 16% in top tenth, 43% in top quarter, 84% in top half
Early decision deadline: 12/1, notification date: 12/15
Early action deadline: N/A, notification date: N/A
Application deadline (fall): rolling
Undergraduate student body: 1,909 full time, 51 part time; 49% male, 51% female; 0% American Indian, 2% Asian, 8% black,

7% Hispanic, 3% multiracial, 0% Pacific Islander, 67% white, 3% international; 76% from in state; 75% live on campus; 0% of students in fraternities, 0% in sororities
Most popular majors: 8% Biological and Biomedical Sciences, 8% Business, Management, Marketing, and Related Support Services, 17% Engineering, 8% Psychology, 31% Visual and Performing Arts
Expenses: 2014-2015: $29,610; room/board: $11,790
Financial aid: (607) 871-2159; 87% of undergrads determined to have financial need; average aid package $28,178

Bard College
Annandale on Hudson NY
(845) 758-7472
U.S. News ranking: Nat. Lib. Arts, No. 45
Website: www.bard.edu
Admissions email: admission@bard.edu
Private; founded 1860
Freshman admissions: more selective; 2013-2014: 5,466 applied, 2,056 accepted. Neither SAT nor ACT required. SAT 25/75 percentile: 1170-1380. High school rank: 58% in top tenth, 92% in top quarter, 99% in top half
Early decision deadline: N/A, notification date: N/A
Early action deadline: 11/1, notification date: 1/1
Application deadline (fall): 1/1
Undergraduate student body: 1,925 full time, 97 part time; 44% male, 56% female; 1% American Indian, 4% Asian, 6% black, 2% Hispanic, 0% multiracial, 0% Pacific Islander, 62% white, 11% international; 35% from in state; 73% live on campus; 0% of students in fraternities, 0% in sororities
Most popular majors: 7% Biological and Biomedical Sciences, 13% English Language and Literature/Letters, 7% Foreign Languages, Literatures, and Linguistics, 15% Social Sciences, 31% Visual and Performing Arts
Expenses: 2014-2015: $48,240; room/board: $13,772
Financial aid: (845) 758-7525; 68% of undergrads determined to have financial need; average aid package $40,706

Barnard College
New York NY
(212) 854-2014
U.S. News ranking: Nat. Lib. Arts, No. 32
Website: www.barnard.edu
Admissions email: admissions@barnard.edu
Private; founded 1889
Freshman admissions: most selective; 2013-2014: 5,606 applied, 1,151 accepted. Either SAT or ACT required. SAT 25/75 percentile: 1240-1440. High school rank: 77% in top tenth, 97% in top quarter, 100% in top half
Early decision deadline: 11/1, notification date: 12/15
Early action deadline: N/A, notification date: N/A
Application deadline (fall): 1/1

Undergraduate student body: 2,463 full time, 26 part time; 0% male, 100% female; 0% American Indian, 15% Asian, 5% black, 11% Hispanic, 5% multiracial, 0% Pacific Islander, 57% white, 7% international; 31% from in state; 91% live on campus; N/A of students in fraternities, 19% in sororities
Most popular majors: 9% Biological and Biomedical Sciences, 12% English Language and Literature/Letters, 14% Psychology, 27% Social Sciences, 11% Visual and Performing Arts
Expenses: 2014-2015: $46,040; room/board: $14,660
Financial aid: (212) 854-2154; 40% of undergrads determined to have financial need; average aid package $42,579

Berkeley College
New York NY
(212) 986-4343
U.S. News ranking: Business, unranked
Website: www.berkeleycollege.edu
Admissions email: admissions@berkeleycollege.edu
For-profit; founded 1931
Freshman admissions: least selective; 2013-2014: 2,158 applied, 2,033 accepted. Neither SAT nor ACT required. ACT 25/75 percentile: N/A. High school rank: N/A
Early decision deadline: N/A, notification date: N/A
Early action deadline: N/A, notification date: N/A
Application deadline (fall): rolling
Undergraduate student body: 4,058 full time, 698 part time; 35% male, 65% female; 0% American Indian, 3% Asian, 28% black, 22% Hispanic, 0% multiracial, 0% Pacific Islander, 9% white, 17% international
Most popular majors: 12% Accounting, 13% Criminal Justice/Law Enforcement Administration, 19% Fashion Merchandising, 12% International Business/Trade/Commerce, 18% Management Information Systems, General
Expenses: 2014-2015: $23,700; room/board: $12,600
Financial aid: (212) 986-4343

Binghamton University–SUNY
Binghamton NY
(607) 777-2171
U.S. News ranking: Nat. U., No. 88
Website: www.binghamton.edu
Admissions email: admit@binghamton.edu
Public; founded 1946
Freshman admissions: more selective; 2013-2014: 29,067 applied, 12,134 accepted. Either SAT or ACT required. SAT 25/75 percentile: 1203-1385. High school rank: 52% in top tenth, 84% in top quarter, 96% in top half
Early decision deadline: N/A, notification date: N/A
Early action deadline: 11/15, notification date: 1/15
Application deadline (fall): rolling
Undergraduate student body: 12,559 full time, 438 part time; 53% male, 47% female; 0% American Indian, 14% Asian, 5% black, 10% Hispanic, 2% multiracial, 0% Pacific Islander,

54% white, 11% international; 89% from in state; 59% live on campus; 10% of students in fraternities, 10% in sororities
Most popular majors: 9% Biology/Biological Sciences, General, 12% Business Administration and Management, General, 10% Engineering, General, 8% English Language and Literature, General, 10% Psychology, General
Expenses: 2014-2015: $8,619 in state, $20,259 out of state; room/board: $13,028
Financial aid: (607) 777-2428; 49% of undergrads determined to have financial need; average aid package $11,897

Boricua College[1]
New York NY
(212) 694-1000
U.S. News ranking: Reg. Coll. (N), unranked
Website: www.boricuacollege.edu/
Admissions email: acruz@boricuacollege.edu
Private; founded 1973
Application deadline (fall): rolling
Undergraduate student body: N/A full time, N/A part time
Expenses: 2013-2014: $11,025; room/board: N/A
Financial aid: (212) 694-1000

Briarcliffe College[1]
Bethpage NY
(888) 348-4999
U.S. News ranking: Reg. Coll. (N), unranked
Website: www.briarcliffe.edu
Admissions email: N/A
For-profit
Application deadline (fall): N/A
Undergraduate student body: N/A full time, N/A part time
Expenses: 2013-2014: $16,665; room/board: N/A
Financial aid: N/A

Canisius College
Buffalo NY
(800) 843-1517
U.S. News ranking: Reg. U. (N), No. 27
Website: www.canisius.edu
Admissions email: admissions@canisius.edu
Private; founded 1870
Affiliation: Roman Catholic
Freshman admissions: selective; 2013-2014: 4,322 applied, 3,134 accepted. Either SAT or ACT required. SAT 25/75 percentile: 980-1200. High school rank: 22% in top tenth, 53% in top quarter, 87% in top half
Early decision deadline: N/A, notification date: N/A
Early action deadline: N/A, notification date: N/A
Undergraduate student body: 2,825 full time, 259 part time; 50% male, 50% female; 0% American Indian, 2% Asian, 7% black, 3% Hispanic, 2% multiracial, 0% Pacific Islander, 75% white, 4% international; 91% from in state; 48% live on campus; 1% of students in fraternities, 1% in sororities
Most popular majors: 12% Biological and Biomedical Sciences, 27% Business, Management, Marketing, and Related Support Services, 14% Education, 10% Psychology, 10% Social Sciences

Expenses: 2014-2015: $34,000; room/board: $12,516
Financial aid: (716) 888-2300; 78% of undergrads determined to have financial need; average aid package $28,042

Cazenovia College

Cazenovia NY
(800) 654-3210
U.S. News ranking: Reg. Coll. (N), No. 24
Website: www.cazenovia.edu
Admissions email: admission@cazenovia.edu
Private; founded 1824
Freshman admissions: selective; 2013-2014: 2,440 applied, 1,902 accepted. Neither SAT nor ACT required. SAT 25/75 percentile: 860-1070. High school rank: 14% in top tenth, 40% in top quarter, 78% in top half
Early decision deadline: N/A, notification date: N/A
Early action deadline: N/A, notification date: N/A
Application deadline (fall): rolling
Undergraduate student body: 937 full time, 140 part time; 28% male, 72% female; 1% American Indian, 1% Asian, 8% black, 7% Hispanic, 5% multiracial, 0% Pacific Islander, 75% white, 0% international; 88% from in state; 92% live on campus; N/A of students in fraternities, N/A in sororities
Most popular majors: 28% Business, Management, Marketing, and Related Support Services, 13% Public Administration and Social Service Professions, 27% Visual and Performing Arts
Expenses: 2014-2015: $30,560; room/board: $12,344
Financial aid: (315) 655-7887; 91% of undergrads determined to have financial need; average aid package $27,200

Clarkson University

Potsdam NY
(800) 527-6577
U.S. News ranking: Nat. U., No. 121
Website: www.clarkson.edu
Admissions email: admission@clarkson.edu
Private; founded 1896
Freshman admissions: more selective; 2013-2014: 6,747 applied, 4,320 accepted. Either SAT or ACT required. SAT 25/75 percentile: 1090-1290. High school rank: 40% in top tenth, 76% in top quarter, 96% in top half
Early decision deadline: 12/1, notification date: 1/1
Early action deadline: N/A, notification date: N/A
Application deadline (fall): 1/15
Undergraduate student body: 3,084 full time, 26 part time; 72% male, 28% female; 0% American Indian, 4% Asian, 2% black, 4% Hispanic, 2% multiracial, 0% Pacific Islander, 83% white, 3% international; 74% from in state; 83% live on campus; 12% of students in fraternities, 15% in sororities
Most popular majors: 7% Biology/Biological Sciences, General, 27% Business Administration and Management, General, 50% Engineering, General, 4% Psychology, General

---

Expenses: 2014-2015: $42,530; room/board: $13,720
Financial aid: (315) 268-6479; 85% of undergrads determined to have financial need; average aid package $38,840

Colgate University

Hamilton NY
(315) 228-7401
U.S. News ranking: Nat. Lib. Arts, No. 22
Website: www.colgate.edu
Admissions email: admission@mail.colgate.edu
Private; founded 1819
Freshman admissions: most selective; 2013-2014: 8,375 applied, 2,238 accepted. Either SAT or ACT required. SAT 25/75 percentile: 1270-1450. High school rank: 76% in top tenth, 93% in top quarter, 99% in top half
Early decision deadline: 11/15, notification date: 12/15
Early action deadline: N/A, notification date: N/A
Application deadline (fall): 1/15
Undergraduate student body: 2,871 full time, 19 part time; 45% male, 55% female; 0% American Indian, 3% Asian, 4% black, 8% Hispanic, 4% multiracial, 0% Pacific Islander, 68% white, 8% international; 27% from in state; 84% live on campus; 27% of students in fraternities, 36% in sororities
Most popular majors: 11% Economics, General, 10% English Language and Literature, General, 9% History, General, 6% International Relations and Affairs, 9% Political Science and Government, General
Expenses: 2014-2015: $48,175; room/board: $11,970
Financial aid: (315) 228-7431; 36% of undergrads determined to have financial need; average aid package $43,436

College at Brockport—SUNY

Brockport NY
(585) 395-2751
U.S. News ranking: Reg. U. (N), No. 60
Website: www.brockport.edu
Admissions email: admit@brockport.edu
Public; founded 1835
Freshman admissions: selective; 2013-2014: 8,831 applied, 4,245 accepted. Either SAT or ACT required. SAT 25/75 percentile: 960-1150. High school rank: 12% in top tenth, 39% in top quarter, 83% in top half
Early decision deadline: N/A, notification date: N/A
Early action deadline: N/A, notification date: N/A
Application deadline (fall): rolling
Undergraduate student body: 6,411 full time, 679 part time; 45% male, 55% female; 0% American Indian, 1% Asian, 8% black, 5% Hispanic, 2% multiracial, 0% Pacific Islander, 74% white, 1% international; 99% from in state; 37% live on campus; 2% of students in fraternities, 2% in sororities
Most popular majors: 16% Business, Management, Marketing, and Related Support Services, 16% Health Professions and Related Programs, 8%

Homeland Security, Law Enforcement, Firefighting and Related Protective Services, 7% Parks, Recreation, Leisure, and Fitness Studies, 8% Psychology
Expenses: 2014-2015: $7,562 in state, $17,212 out of state; room/board: $11,440
Financial aid: (585) 395-2501; 73% of undergrads determined to have financial need; average aid package $10,050

College of Mount St. Vincent

Riverdale NY
(718) 405-3267
U.S. News ranking: Reg. U. (N), No. 120
Website: www.mountsaintvincent.edu
Admissions email: admissions.office@mountsaintvincent.edu
Private; founded 1847
Affiliation: Roman Catholic
Freshman admissions: less selective; 2013-2014: 2,416 applied, 2,202 accepted. Either SAT or ACT required. SAT 25/75 percentile: 810-990. High school rank: 8% in top tenth, 26% in top quarter, 58% in top half
Early decision deadline: N/A, notification date: N/A
Early action deadline: 11/1, notification date: 12/1
Application deadline (fall): rolling
Undergraduate student body: 1,489 full time, 160 part time; 28% male, 72% female; 0% American Indian, 10% Asian, 17% black, 34% Hispanic, 6% multiracial, 0% Pacific Islander, 27% white, 1% international; 88% from in state; 48% live on campus; 0% of students in fraternities, 0% in sororities
Most popular majors: 8% Business/Commerce, General, 10% Liberal Arts and Sciences/Liberal Studies, 15% Psychology, General, 34% Registered Nursing/Registered Nurse, 9% Speech Communication and Rhetoric
Expenses: 2013-2014: $30,290; room/board: $12,060
Financial aid: (718) 405-3290

College of New Rochelle[1]

New Rochelle NY
(800) 933-5923
U.S. News ranking: Reg. U. (N), second tier
Website: www.cnr.edu
Admissions email: admission@cnr.edu
Private; founded 1904
Application deadline (fall): 8/31
Undergraduate student body: N/A full time, N/A part time
Expenses: 2013-2014: $31,260; room/board: $11,690
Financial aid: (914) 654-5224

College of St. Rose

Albany NY
(518) 454-5150
U.S. News ranking: Reg. U. (N), No. 41
Website: www.strose.edu
Admissions email: admit@strose.edu
Private; founded 1920
Freshman admissions: selective; 2013-2014: 4,651 applied, 3,605 accepted. Neither SAT

---

nor ACT required. SAT 25/75 percentile: 940-1150. High school rank: 11% in top tenth, 44% in top quarter, 75% in top half
Early decision deadline: N/A, notification date: N/A
Early action deadline: 12/1, notification date: 12/15
Application deadline (fall): 5/1
Undergraduate student body: 2,664 full time, 227 part time; 34% male, 66% female; 1% American Indian, 2% Asian, 7% black, 6% Hispanic, 5% multiracial, 0% Pacific Islander, 73% white, 1% international; 89% from in state; 45% live on campus; 0% of students in fraternities, 0% in sororities
Most popular majors: 13% Business, Management, Marketing, and Related Support Services, 7% Communication, Journalism, and Related Programs, 38% Education, 6% Psychology, 9% Visual and Performing Arts
Expenses: 2014-2015: $29,016; room/board: $11,532
Financial aid: (518) 458-5424; 84% of undergrads determined to have financial need; average aid package $17,366

Columbia University

New York NY
(212) 854-2522
U.S. News ranking: Nat. U., No. 4
Website: www.columbia.edu
Admissions email: ugrad-ask@columbia.edu
Private; founded 1754
Freshman admissions: most selective; 2013-2014: 33,531 applied, 2,311 accepted. Either SAT or ACT required. SAT 25/75 percentile: 1400-1570. High school rank: 93% in top tenth, 98% in top quarter, 100% in top half
Early decision deadline: 11/1, notification date: 12/15
Early action deadline: N/A, notification date: N/A
Application deadline (fall): 1/1
Undergraduate student body: 6,084 full time, N/A part time; 52% male, 48% female; 2% American Indian, 22% Asian, 11% black, 13% Hispanic, 0% multiracial, 0% Pacific Islander, 36% white, 13% international; 23% from in state; 94% live on campus; 19% of students in fraternities, 9% in sororities
Most popular majors: 10% Biological and Biomedical Sciences, 21% Engineering, 5% English Language and Literature/Letters, 22% Social Sciences, 5% Visual and Performing Arts
Expenses: 2013-2014: $49,138; room/board: $11,978
Financial aid: (212) 854-3711; 50% of undergrads determined to have financial need; average aid package $43,766

Concordia College[1]

Bronxville NY
(800) 937-2655
U.S. News ranking: Reg. Coll. (N), No. 31
Website: www.concordia-ny.edu
Admissions email: admission@concordia-ny.edu
Private; founded 1881
Affiliation: Lutheran
Application deadline (fall): rolling

Undergraduate student body: 814 full time, 73 part time
Expenses: 2014-2015: $28,770; room/board: $10,265
Financial aid: (914) 337-9300

Cooper Union

New York NY
(212) 353-4120
U.S. News ranking: Reg. Coll. (N), No. 2
Website: www.cooper.edu
Admissions email: admissions@cooper.edu
Private; founded 1859
Freshman admissions: most selective; 2013-2014: 3,193 applied, 247 accepted. Either SAT or ACT required. SAT 25/75 percentile: 1220-1490. High school rank: 92% in top tenth, 95% in top quarter, 96% in top half
Early decision deadline: 12/1, notification date: 12/22
Early action deadline: N/A, notification date: N/A
Application deadline (fall): 1/1
Undergraduate student body: 863 full time, 5 part time; 64% male, 36% female; 1% American Indian, 20% Asian, 6% black, 10% Hispanic, 4% multiracial, 0% Pacific Islander, 40% white, 2% international; 55% from in state; 20% live on campus; 10% of students in fraternities, N/A in sororities
Most popular majors: 15% Architecture and Related Services, 55% Engineering, 30% Visual and Performing Arts
Expenses: 2014-2015: $41,400; room/board: $11,220
Financial aid: (212) 353-4113; 28% of undergrads determined to have financial need; average aid package $39,600

Cornell University

Ithaca NY
(607) 255-5241
U.S. News ranking: Nat. U., No. 15
Website: www.cornell.edu
Admissions email: admissions@cornell.edu
Private; founded 1865
Freshman admissions: most selective; 2013-2014: 39,999 applied, 6,222 accepted. Either SAT or ACT required. SAT 25/75 percentile: 1320-1520. High school rank: 87% in top tenth, 98% in top quarter, 99% in top half
Early decision deadline: 11/1, notification date: 12/15
Early action deadline: N/A, notification date: N/A
Application deadline (fall): 1/2
Undergraduate student body: 14,393 full time, N/A part time; 49% male, 51% female; 0% American Indian, 16% Asian, 6% black, 11% Hispanic, 4% multiracial, 0% Pacific Islander, 43% white, 9% international; 36% from in state; 55% live on campus; 27% of students in fraternities, 25% in sororities
Most popular majors: 12% Agriculture, Agriculture Operations, and Related Sciences, 13% Biological and Biomedical Sciences, 14% Business, Management, Marketing, and Related Support Services, 17% Engineering, 10% Social Sciences

Expenses: 2014-2015: $47,286; room/board: $13,678
Financial aid: (607) 255-5145; 50% of undergrads determined to have financial need; average aid package $42,258

CUNY–Baruch College

New York NY
(646) 312-1400
U.S. News ranking: Reg. U. (N), No. 25
Website: www.baruch.cuny.edu
Admissions email: admissions@baruch.cuny.edu
Public; founded 1919
Freshman admissions: more selective; 2013-2014: 19,423 applied, 5,153 accepted. Either SAT or ACT required. SAT 25/75 percentile: 1130-1330. High school rank: 41% in top tenth, 70% in top quarter, 89% in top half
Early decision deadline: 12/13, notification date: 1/7
Early action deadline: N/A, notification date: N/A
Application deadline (fall): 2/1
Undergraduate student body: 10,396 full time, 3,686 part time; 52% male, 48% female; 0% American Indian, 35% Asian, 10% black, 13% Hispanic, 1% multiracial, 0% Pacific Islander, 29% white, 12% international; 97% from in state; 2% live on campus; 1% of students in fraternities, 1% in sororities
Most popular majors: 20% Accounting, 8% Business/ Corporate Communications, 23% Finance, General, 5% Psychology, General, 10% Sales, Distribution, and Marketing Operations, General
Expenses: 2014-2015: $6,555 in state, $16,575 out of state; room/ board: $12,400
Financial aid: (646) 312-1360; 66% of undergrads determined to have financial need; average aid package $5,265

CUNY–Brooklyn College

Brooklyn NY
(718) 951-5001
U.S. News ranking: Reg. U. (N), No. 70
Website: www.brooklyn.cuny.edu
Admissions email: adminqry@ brooklyn.cuny.edu
Public; founded 1930
Freshman admissions: selective; 2013-2014: 20,145 applied, 6,768 accepted. Either SAT or ACT required. SAT 25/75 percentile: 980-1170. High school rank: 18% in top tenth, 50% in top quarter, 77% in top half
Early decision deadline: N/A, notification date: N/A
Early action deadline: N/A, notification date: N/A
Undergraduate student body: 9,543 full time, 4,053 part time; 41% male, 59% female; 0% American Indian, 17% Asian, 22% black, 18% Hispanic, 1% multiracial, 0% Pacific Islander, 38% white, 3% international; 98% from in state; 0% live on campus; 3% of students in fraternities, 3% in sororities
Most popular majors: 10% Accounting, 21% Business Administration and Management, General, 5% Early Childhood Education and Teaching,

4% Elementary Education and Teaching, 13% Psychology, General
Expenses: 2014-2015: $6,535 in state, $13,345 out of state; room/ board: N/A
Financial aid: (718) 951-5045; 87% of undergrads determined to have financial need; average aid package $7,500

CUNY–City College

New York NY
(212) 650-6977
U.S. News ranking: Reg. U. (N), No. 65
Website: www.ccny.cuny.edu
Admissions email: admissions@ ccny.cuny.edu
Public; founded 1847
Freshman admissions: selective; 2013-2014: 26,628 applied, 9,031 accepted. SAT required. SAT 25/75 percentile: 970-1090. High school rank: 29% in top tenth, 44% in top quarter, 85% in top half
Early decision deadline: N/A, notification date: N/A
Early action deadline: N/A, notification date: N/A
Application deadline (fall): 1/15
Undergraduate student body: 9,274 full time, 3,355 part time; 48% male, 52% female; 0% American Indian, 25% Asian, 19% black, 30% Hispanic, 0% multiracial, 0% Pacific Islander, 19% white, 8% international; 99% from in state; N/A live on campus; N/A of students in fraternities, N/A in sororities
Most popular majors: 13% Engineering, 7% English Language and Literature/Letters, 14% Psychology, 11% Social Sciences, 10% Visual and Performing Arts
Expenses: 2014-2015: $6,440 in state, $15,710 out of state; room/ board: N/A
Financial aid: (212) 650-5819; 91% of undergrads determined to have financial need; average aid package $8,874

CUNY–College of Staten Island

Staten Island NY
(718) 982-2010
U.S. News ranking: Reg. U. (N), No. 115
Website: www.csi.cuny.edu
Admissions email: admissions@csi.cuny.edu
Public; founded 1976
Freshman admissions: less selective; 2013-2014: 12,123 applied, 12,123 accepted. Either SAT or ACT required. SAT 25/75 percentile: 920-1100. High school rank: N/A
Early decision deadline: N/A, notification date: N/A
Early action deadline: N/A, notification date: N/A
Application deadline (fall): rolling
Undergraduate student body: 9,784 full time, 3,681 part time; 45% male, 55% female; 0% American Indian, 10% Asian, 10% black, 18% Hispanic, 1% multiracial, 0% Pacific Islander, 39% white, 3% international; 99% from in state; 3% live on campus; 0% of students in fraternities, 0% in sororities
Most popular majors: 21% Business, Management, Marketing, and Related Support Services, 6% English Language

and Literature/Letters, 6% Health Professions and Related Programs, 13% Psychology, 18% Social Sciences
Expenses: 2014-2015: $6,509 in state, $16,529 out of state; room/ board: $13,864
Financial aid: (718) 982-2030; 68% of undergrads determined to have financial need; average aid package $8,200

CUNY–Hunter College

New York NY
(212) 772-4490
U.S. News ranking: Reg. U. (N), No. 50
Website: www.hunter.cuny.edu
Admissions email: admissions@ hunter.cuny.edu
Public; founded 1870
Freshman admissions: more selective; 2013-2014: 32,868 applied, 10,193 accepted. Either SAT or ACT required. SAT 25/75 percentile: 1070-1270. High school rank: 22% in top tenth, 56% in top quarter, 86% in top half
Early decision deadline: N/A, notification date: N/A
Early action deadline: N/A, notification date: N/A
Application deadline (fall): 3/15
Undergraduate student body: 11,747 full time, 4,942 part time; 35% male, 65% female; 0% American Indian, 26% Asian, 11% black, 19% Hispanic, 0% multiracial, 0% Pacific Islander, 37% white, 7% international
Most popular majors: 13% English Language and Literature/ Letters, 9% Health Professions and Related Programs, 22% Psychology, 18% Social Sciences, 9% Visual and Performing Arts
Expenses: 2014-2015: $6,129 in state, $15,699 out of state; room/ board: $10,386
Financial aid: (212) 772-4820; 83% of undergrads determined to have financial need; average aid package $7,641

CUNY–John Jay College of Criminal Justice

New York NY
(212) 237-8866
U.S. News ranking: Reg. U. (N), No. 122
Website: www.jjay.cuny.edu/
Admissions email: admissions@ jjay.cuny.edu
Public; founded 1965
Freshman admissions: less selective; 2013-2014: 14,297 applied, 7,515 accepted. Either SAT or ACT required. SAT 25/75 percentile: 840-1030. High school rank: N/A
Early decision deadline: N/A, notification date: N/A
Early action deadline: N/A, notification date: N/A
Application deadline (fall): 5/31
Undergraduate student body: 10,374 full time, 2,843 part time; 44% male, 56% female; 0% American Indian, 12% Asian, 21% black, 40% Hispanic, 0% multiracial, 0% Pacific Islander, 25% white, 3% international; 96% from in state; 0% live on campus; 0% of students in fraternities, 0% in sororities

Most popular majors: 55% Criminal Justice/Law Enforcement Administration, 3% English Language and Literature, General, 17% Forensic Psychology, 4% Legal Studies, General, 16% Social Sciences, Other
Expenses: 2014-2015: $6,359 in state, $16,379 out of state; room/ board: N/A
Financial aid: (212) 237-8151; 75% of undergrads determined to have financial need; average aid package $9,445

CUNY–Lehman College

Bronx NY
(718) 960-8131
U.S. News ranking: Reg. U. (N), No. 125
Website: www.lehman.cuny.edu
Admissions email: undergraduate. admissions@lehman.cuny.edu
Public; founded 1968
Freshman admissions: selective; 2013-2014: 15,717 applied, 3,996 accepted. Either SAT or ACT required. SAT 25/75 percentile: 890-1050. High school rank: N/A
Early decision deadline: N/A, notification date: N/A
Early action deadline: N/A, notification date: N/A
Application deadline (fall): 10/1
Undergraduate student body: 5,643 full time, 4,243 part time; 32% male, 68% female; 0% American Indian, 6% Asian, 31% black, 50% Hispanic, 0% multiracial, 0% Pacific Islander, 9% white, 4% international; 100% from in state; 0% live on campus; 0% of students in fraternities, 0% in sororities
Most popular majors: Information not available
Expenses: 2014-2015: $6,230 in state, $13,040 out of state; room/ board: N/A
Financial aid: (718) 960-8545; 80% of undergrads determined to have financial need

CUNY– Medgar Evers College

Brooklyn NY
(718) 270-6024
U.S. News ranking: Reg. Coll. (N), second tier
Website: www.mec.cuny.edu
Admissions email: enroll@mec.cuny.edu
Public; founded 1969
Freshman admissions: least selective; 2013-2014: 7,586 applied, 7,586 accepted. Neither SAT nor ACT required. SAT 25/75 percentile: 690-860. High school rank: N/A
Early decision deadline: N/A, notification date: N/A
Early action deadline: N/A, notification date: N/A
Application deadline (fall): rolling
Undergraduate student body: 4,275 full time, 2,216 part time; 26% male, 74% female; 1% American Indian, 2% Asian, 72% black, 10% Hispanic, 0% multiracial, 0% Pacific Islander, 1% white, 1% international
Most popular majors: 12% Biology/ Biological Sciences, General, 39% Business/Commerce, General, 8% Health Professions and Related Programs, 11% Psychology,

General, 9% Public Administration and Social Service Professions
Expenses: 2013-2014: $6,032 in state, $12,542 out of state; room/ board: N/A
Financial aid: (718) 270-6038

CUNY–New York City College of Technology

Brooklyn NY
(718) 260-5500
U.S. News ranking: Reg. Coll. (N), second tier
Website: www.citytech.cuny.edu
Admissions email: admissions@ citytech.cuny.edu
Public; founded 1946
Freshman admissions: least selective; 2013-2014: 17,465 applied, 12,326 accepted. Neither SAT nor ACT required. ACT 25/75 percentile: N/A. High school rank: N/A
Early decision deadline: N/A, notification date: N/A
Early action deadline: N/A, notification date: N/A
Application deadline (fall): 2/1
Undergraduate student body: 10,318 full time, 6,542 part time; 56% male, 44% female; 0% American Indian, 18% Asian, 32% black, 31% Hispanic, 1% multiracial, 0% Pacific Islander, 13% white, 5% international
Most popular majors: 8% Architectural Technology/ Technician, 16% Hospitality Administration/Management, General, 16% Information Science/Studies, 10% Public Administration and Social Service Professions, 11% Registered Nursing/Registered Nurse
Expenses: 2013-2014: $6,069 in state, $15,639 out of state; room/ board: N/A
Financial aid: (718) 260-5700

CUNY–Queens College

Flushing NY
(718) 997-5600
U.S. News ranking: Reg. U. (N), No. 31
Website: www.qc.edu/
Admissions email: applyto@uapc.cuny.edu
Public; founded 1937
Freshman admissions: more selective; 2013-2014: 24,323 applied, 8,929 accepted. Either SAT or ACT required. SAT 25/75 percentile: 1030-1220. High school rank: 35% in top tenth, 65% in top quarter, 99% in top half
Early decision deadline: N/A, notification date: N/A
Early action deadline: N/A, notification date: N/A
Application deadline (fall): 2/1
Undergraduate student body: 10,769 full time, 4,582 part time; 44% male, 56% female; 0% American Indian, 26% Asian, 8% black, 19% Hispanic, 0% multiracial, 0% Pacific Islander, 42% white, 5% international; 99% from in state; 3% live on campus; 1% of students in fraternities, 1% in sororities
Most popular majors: Information not available
Expenses: 2014-2015: $6,207 in state, $15,777 out of state; room/ board: $13,554

Financial aid: (718) 997-5101; 75% of undergrads determined to have financial need; average aid package $6,450

CUNY–York College

Jamaica NY
(718) 262-2165
U.S. News ranking: Reg. Coll. (N), second tier
Website: www.york.cuny.edu
Admissions email: admissions@york.cuny.edu
Public; founded 1966
Freshman admissions: least selective; 2013-2014: 14,674 applied, 9,477 accepted. SAT required. Average composite SAT score: 871. High school rank: N/A
Early decision deadline: N/A, notification date: N/A
Early action deadline: N/A, notification date: N/A
Application deadline (fall): 6/1
Undergraduate student body: 5,152 full time, 3,107 part time; 35% male, 65% female; 1% American Indian, 23% Asian, 44% black, 20% Hispanic, 0% multiracial, 0% Pacific Islander, 8% white, 4% international
Most popular majors: 7% Accounting, 11% Business Administration and Management, General, 6% Health Teacher Education, 20% Psychology, General, 8% Social Work
Expenses: 2014-2015: $6,396 in state, $16,416 out of state; room/board: N/A
Financial aid: (718) 262-2230; 63% of undergrads determined to have financial need; average aid package $6,930

Daemen College

Amherst NY
(800) 462-7652
U.S. News ranking: Reg. U. (N), second tier
Website: www.daemen.edu
Admissions email: admissions@daemen.edu
Private; founded 1947
Freshman admissions: selective; 2013-2014: 3,061 applied, 1,489 accepted. Neither SAT nor ACT required. SAT 25/75 percentile: 920-1140. High school rank: 15% in top tenth, 51% in top quarter, 85% in top half
Early decision deadline: N/A, notification date: N/A
Early action deadline: N/A, notification date: N/A
Application deadline (fall): rolling
Undergraduate student body: 1,720 full time, 436 part time; 27% male, 73% female; 0% American Indian, 2% Asian, 11% black, 5% Hispanic, 1% multiracial, 0% Pacific Islander, 75% white, 1% international; 95% from in state; 37% live on campus; 4% of students in fraternities, 4% in sororities
Most popular majors: 6% Business Administration and Management, General, 5% Elementary Education and Teaching, 16% Natural Sciences, 8% Physician Assistant, 31% Registered Nursing/Registered Nurse
Expenses: 2014-2015: $24,990; room/board: $11,800
Financial aid: (716) 839-8254; 77% of undergrads determined to have financial need; average aid package $18,236

Dominican College

Orangeburg NY
(845) 359-3533
U.S. News ranking: Reg. U. (N), second tier
Website: www.dc.edu
Admissions email: admissions@dc.edu
Private; founded 1952
Freshman admissions: less selective; 2013-2014: 1,594 applied, 1,146 accepted. Either SAT or ACT required. SAT 25/75 percentile: 810-1000. High school rank: N/A
Early decision deadline: N/A, notification date: N/A
Early action deadline: N/A, notification date: N/A
Application deadline (fall): rolling
Undergraduate student body: 1,280 full time, 247 part time; 34% male, 66% female; 0% American Indian, 6% Asian, 13% black, 27% Hispanic, 0% multiracial, 0% Pacific Islander, 25% white, 0% international; 74% from in state; 46% live on campus; N/A of students in fraternities, N/A in sororities
Most popular majors: 14% Business, Management, Marketing, and Related Support Services, 8% Education, 29% Health Professions and Related Programs, 5% Homeland Security, Law Enforcement, Firefighting and Related Protective Services, 26% Social Sciences
Expenses: 2014-2015: $25,702; room/board: $11,880
Financial aid: (845) 359-7800; 91% of undergrads determined to have financial need; average aid package $16,841

Dowling College

Oakdale Long Island NY
(631) 244-3030
U.S. News ranking: Reg. U. (N), second tier
Website: www.dowling.edu
Admissions email: admissions@dowling.edu
Private; founded 1955
Freshman admissions: less selective; 2013-2014: 1,897 applied, 1,402 accepted. Neither SAT nor ACT required. ACT 25/75 percentile: N/A. High school rank: N/A
Early decision deadline: N/A, notification date: N/A
Early action deadline: 12/31, notification date: 1/31
Application deadline (fall): rolling
Undergraduate student body: 1,439 full time, 859 part time; 44% male, 56% female; 0% American Indian, 1% Asian, 9% black, 7% Hispanic, 0% multiracial, 0% Pacific Islander, 45% white, 4% international; 89% from in state; 15% live on campus; N/A of students in fraternities, N/A in sororities
Most popular majors: 29% Business Administration and Management, General, 9% Finance, General, 6% Hospital and Health Care Facilities Administration/Management, 6% Special Education and Teaching, General, 8% Special Education and Teaching, General
Expenses: 2014-2015: $29,100; room/board: $10,770
Financial aid: (631) 244-3303; 73% of undergrads determined to have financial need; average aid package $19,348

D'Youville College

Buffalo NY
(716) 829-7600
U.S. News ranking: Reg. U. (N), second tier
Website: www.dyc.edu
Admissions email: admissions@dyc.edu
Private; founded 1908
Freshman admissions: selective; 2013-2014: 1,168 applied, 925 accepted. Either SAT or ACT required. SAT 25/75 percentile: 950-1140. High school rank: 27% in top tenth, 47% in top quarter, 84% in top half
Early decision deadline: N/A, notification date: N/A
Early action deadline: N/A, notification date: N/A
Application deadline (fall): rolling
Undergraduate student body: 1,614 full time, 409 part time; 27% male, 73% female; 1% American Indian, 3% Asian, 9% black, 5% Hispanic, 2% multiracial, 0% Pacific Islander, 72% white, 7% international; 96% from in state; 15% live on campus; 0% of students in fraternities, 0% in sororities
Most popular majors: 8% Biological and Biomedical Sciences, 14% Business, Management, Marketing, and Related Support Services, 65% Health Professions and Related Programs, 7% Multi/Interdisciplinary Studies, 3% Psychology
Expenses: 2014-2015: $23,462; room/board: $10,800
Financial aid: (716) 829-7500; 84% of undergrads determined to have financial need; average aid package $17,087

Elmira College

Elmira NY
(800) 935-6472
U.S. News ranking: Reg. Coll. (N), No. 9
Website: www.elmira.edu
Admissions email: admissions@elmira.edu
Private; founded 1855
Freshman admissions: selective; 2013-2014: 2,302 applied, 1,836 accepted. Either SAT or ACT required. SAT 25/75 percentile: 940-1160. High school rank: 28% in top tenth, 58% in top quarter, 84% in top half
Early decision deadline: 11/15, notification date: 12/15
Early action deadline: N/A, notification date: N/A
Application deadline (fall): rolling
Undergraduate student body: 1,188 full time, 220 part time; 28% male, 72% female; 1% American Indian, 1% Asian, 3% black, 3% Hispanic, 2% multiracial, 0% Pacific Islander, 70% white, 3% international
Most popular majors: 17% Business Administration and Management, General, 19% Education, 9% Psychology, General, 13% Registered Nursing/Registered Nurse, 9% Social Sciences
Expenses: 2014-2015: $38,150; room/board: $11,800
Financial aid: (607) 735-1728; 84% of undergrads determined to have financial need; average aid package $29,925

Excelsior College[1]

Albany NY
(518) 464-8500
U.S. News ranking: Reg. U. (N), unranked
Website: www.excelsior.edu
Admissions email: admissions@excelsior.edu
Private; founded 1971
Application deadline (fall): rolling
Undergraduate student body: N/A full time, N/A part time
Expenses: N/A
Financial aid: (518) 464-8500

Farmingdale State College–SUNY

Farmingdale NY
(631) 420-2200
U.S. News ranking: Reg. Coll. (N), No. 28
Website: www.farmingdale.edu
Admissions email: admissions@farmingdale.edu
Public; founded 1912
Freshman admissions: selective; 2013-2014: 5,282 applied, 2,677 accepted. Either SAT or ACT required. SAT 25/75 percentile: 950-1110. High school rank: 17% in top tenth, 36% in top quarter, 69% in top half
Early decision deadline: N/A, notification date: N/A
Early action deadline: N/A, notification date: N/A
Application deadline (fall): rolling
Undergraduate student body: 6,074 full time, 2,088 part time; 58% male, 42% female; 0% American Indian, 7% Asian, 11% black, 15% Hispanic, 2% multiracial, 0% Pacific Islander, 61% white, 3% international; 99% from in state; 8% live on campus; 2% of students in fraternities, 2% in sororities
Most popular majors: 37% Business, Management, Marketing, and Related Support Services, 7% Computer and Information Sciences and Support Services, 13% Engineering Technologies and Engineering-Related Fields, 7% Health Professions and Related Programs, 8% Multi/Interdisciplinary Studies
Expenses: 2014-2015: $7,483 in state, $17,133 out of state; room/board: $12,190
Financial aid: (631) 420-2328; 55% of undergrads determined to have financial need; average aid package $9,242

Fashion Institute of Technology

New York NY
(212) 217-3760
U.S. News ranking: Reg. U. (N), unranked
Website: www.fitnyc.edu
Admissions email: fitinfo@fitsuny.edu
Public; founded 1944
Freshman admissions: N/A; 2013-2014: 4,567 applied, 2,044 accepted. Neither SAT nor ACT required. ACT 25/75 percentile: N/A. High school rank: N/A
Early decision deadline: N/A, notification date: N/A
Early action deadline: N/A, notification date: N/A
Application deadline (fall): 1/1
Undergraduate student body: 7,257 full time, 2,309 part time; 15% male, 85% female; 0% American Indian, 9% Asian, 9% black,

17% Hispanic, 3% multiracial, 0% Pacific Islander, 47% white, 14% international; 59% from in state; 22% live on campus; N/A of students in fraternities, N/A in sororities
Most popular majors: 37% Business, Management, Marketing, and Related Support Services, 16% Communication, Journalism, and Related Programs, 1% Communications Technologies/Technicians and Support Services, 5% Family and Consumer Sciences/Human Sciences, 41% Visual and Performing Arts
Expenses: 2013-2014: $5,105 in state, $13,955 out of state; room/board: N/A
Financial aid: (212) 217-7439; 52% of undergrads determined to have financial need; average aid package $11,605

Five Towns College

Dix Hills NY
(631) 424-7000
U.S. News ranking: Reg. Coll. (N), second tier
Website: www.ftc.edu
Admissions email: admissions@ftc.edu
For-profit; founded 1972
Freshman admissions: less selective; 2013-2014: 452 applied, 249 accepted. Either SAT or ACT required. SAT 25/75 percentile: 770-1000. High school rank: 11% in top tenth, 36% in top quarter, 47% in top half
Early decision deadline: 10/15, notification date: 11/1
Early action deadline: N/A, notification date: N/A
Application deadline (fall): rolling
Undergraduate student body: 695 full time, 57 part time; 70% male, 30% female; 0% American Indian, 3% Asian, 21% black, 13% Hispanic, 6% multiracial, 0% Pacific Islander, 51% white, 0% international; 92% from in state; 26% live on campus; N/A of students in fraternities, N/A in sororities
Most popular majors: 58% Business, Management, Marketing, and Related Support Services, 11% Education, 31% Visual and Performing Arts
Expenses: 2014-2015: $21,300; room/board: $13,270
Financial aid: (631) 424-7000; 81% of undergrads determined to have financial need; average aid package $13,922

Fordham University

New York NY
(800) 367-3426
U.S. News ranking: Nat. U., No. 58
Website: www.fordham.edu
Admissions email: enroll@fordham.edu
Private; founded 1841
Affiliation: Roman Catholic
Freshman admissions: more selective; 2013-2014: 36,189 applied, 17,055 accepted. Either SAT or ACT required. SAT 25/75 percentile: 1160-1350. High school rank: 47% in top tenth, 82% in top quarter, 97% in top half
Early decision deadline: N/A, notification date: N/A
Early action deadline: 11/1, notification date: 12/25

Application deadline (fall): 1/15
Undergraduate student body: 7,694
full time, 651 part time; 46%
male, 54% female; 0% American
Indian, 9% Asian, 4% black,
14% Hispanic, 3% multiracial,
0% Pacific Islander, 61% white,
6% international; 51% from in
state; 57% live on campus; 0%
of students in fraternities, 0% in
sororities
Most popular majors: 14%
Business Administration and
Management, General, 6%
Economics, General, 7% Finance,
General, 7% Psychology, General,
13% Speech Communication and
Rhetoric
Expenses: 2013-2014: $43,577;
room/board: $15,835
Financial aid: (718) 817-3800

Hamilton College

Clinton NY
(800) 843-2655
U.S. News ranking: Nat. Lib. Arts,
No. 15
Website: www.hamilton.edu
Admissions email: admission@
hamilton.edu
Private; founded 1812
Freshman admissions: most
selective; 2013-2014: 5,017
applied, 1,364 accepted. Either
SAT or ACT required. SAT 25/75
percentile: 1300-1470. High
school rank: 72% in top tenth,
97% in top quarter, 99% in
top half
Early decision deadline: 11/15,
notification date: 12/15
Early action deadline: N/A,
notification date: N/A
Application deadline (fall): 1/1
Undergraduate student body: 1,905
full time, 21 part time; 49%
male, 51% female; 0% American
Indian, 7% Asian, 4% black, 8%
Hispanic, 3% multiracial, 0%
Pacific Islander, 62% white, 5%
international; 31% from in state;
97% live on campus; 27% of
students in fraternities, 20% in
sororities
Most popular majors: 13%
Economics, General, 6% History,
General, 10% Mathematics,
General, 8% Political Science
and Government, General, 7%
Psychology, General
Expenses: 2014-2015: $47,820;
room/board: $12,150
Financial aid: (315) 859-4434;
47% of undergrads determined to
have financial need; average aid
package $40,858

Hartwick College

Oneonta NY
(607) 431-4150
U.S. News ranking: Nat. Lib. Arts,
No. 165
Website: www.hartwick.edu
Admissions email: admissions@
hartwick.edu
Private; founded 1797
Freshman admissions: selective;
2013-2014: 5,392 applied,
4,542 accepted. Neither SAT
nor ACT required. SAT 25/75
percentile: 1010-1230. High
school rank: 20% in top tenth,
47% in top quarter, 86% in
top half
Early decision deadline: 11/15,
notification date: 11/25
Early action deadline: N/A,
notification date: N/A
Application deadline (fall): rolling

Undergraduate student body: 1,576
full time, 39 part time; 41%
male, 59% female; 1% American
Indian, 2% Asian, 6% black,
6% Hispanic, 0% multiracial,
0% Pacific Islander, 69% white,
3% international; 74% from in
state; 77% live on campus; 3%
of students in fraternities, 5% in
sororities
Most popular majors: 11% Biology/
Biological Sciences, General,
17% Business Administration
and Management, General,
10% Psychology, General, 12%
Registered Nursing, Nursing
Administration, Nursing Research
and Clinical Nursing, 12%
Sociology
Expenses: 2014-2015: $40,070;
room/board: $10,800
Financial aid: (607) 431-4130;
82% of undergrads determined to
have financial need; average aid
package $30,926

Hilbert College[1]

Hamburg NY
(716) 649-7900
U.S. News ranking: Reg. Coll. (N),
unranked
Website: www.hilbert.edu/
Admissions email:
admissions@hilbert.edu
Private
Application deadline (fall): N/A
Undergraduate student body: N/A
full time, N/A part time
Expenses: 2013-2014: $19,940;
room/board: $8,650
Financial aid: (716) 649-7900

Hobart and William Smith Colleges

Geneva NY
(315) 781-3622
U.S. News ranking: Nat. Lib. Arts,
No. 61
Website: www.hws.edu
Admissions email:
admissions@hws.edu
Private; founded 1822
Freshman admissions: more
selective; 2013-2014: 4,380
applied, 2,190 accepted. Neither
SAT nor ACT required. SAT
25/75 percentile: 1120-1290.
High school rank: 36% in top
tenth, 63% in top quarter, 87%
in top half
Early decision deadline: 11/15,
notification date: 12/15
Early action deadline: N/A,
notification date: N/A
Application deadline (fall): 2/1
Undergraduate student body: 2,324
full time, 44 part time; 46%
male, 54% female; 1% American
Indian, 2% Asian, 4% black,
4% Hispanic, 0% multiracial,
0% Pacific Islander, 69% white,
5% international; 43% from in
state; 90% live on campus; 18%
of students in fraternities, 0% in
sororities
Most popular majors: 8%
Architecture and Related
Services, Other, 7% Biology/
Biological Sciences, General, 8%
Economics, General, 7% Mass
Communication/Media Studies,
7% Psychology, General
Expenses: 2014-2015: $47,908;
room/board: $12,126
Financial aid: (315) 781-3315;
67% of undergrads determined to
have financial need; average aid
package $32,064

Hofstra University

Hempstead NY
(516) 463-6700
U.S. News ranking: Nat. U.,
No. 135
Website: www.hofstra.edu
Admissions email: admission@
hofstra,edu
Private; founded 1935
Freshman admissions: selective;
2013-2014: 27,700 applied,
16,354 accepted. Neither SAT
nor ACT required. SAT 25/75
percentile: 1050-1230. High
school rank: 24% in top tenth,
56% in top quarter, 88% in
top half
Early decision deadline: N/A,
notification date: N/A
Early action deadline: 11/15,
notification date: 12/15
Application deadline (fall): rolling
Undergraduate student body: 6,378
full time, 448 part time; 47%
male, 53% female; 0% American
Indian, 8% Asian, 9% black,
13% Hispanic, 3% multiracial,
1% Pacific Islander, 59% white,
3% international; 65% from in
state; 47% live on campus; 6%
of students in fraternities, 8% in
sororities
Most popular majors: 6%
Accounting, 4% Business
Administration and Management,
General, 6% English Language
and Literature, General, 6%
Marketing/Marketing Management,
General, 8% Psychology, General
Expenses: 2014-2015: $38,900;
room/board: $12,910
Financial aid: (516) 463-6680;
68% of undergrads determined to
have financial need; average aid
package $25,000

Houghton College

Houghton NY
(800) 777-2556
U.S. News ranking: Nat. Lib. Arts,
No. 139
Website: www.houghton.edu
Admissions email: admission@
houghton.edu
Private; founded 1883
Affiliation: The Wesleyan Church
Freshman admissions: selective;
2013-2014: 807 applied, 735
accepted. Either SAT or ACT
required. SAT 25/75 percentile:
980-1235. High school rank:
35% in top tenth, 61% in top
quarter, 88% in top half
Early decision deadline: N/A,
notification date: N/A
Early action deadline: N/A,
notification date: N/A
Application deadline (fall): rolling
Undergraduate student body: 1,023
full time, 58 part time; 36%
male, 64% female; 0% American
Indian, 1% Asian, 3% black,
2% Hispanic, 3% multiracial,
0% Pacific Islander, 85% white,
6% international; 62% from in
state; 87% live on campus; N/A
of students in fraternities, N/A in
sororities
Most popular majors: 11%
Biological and Biomedical
Sciences, 21% Business,
Management, Marketing, and
Related Support Services, 7%
Communication, Journalism,
and Related Programs, 13%
Education, 8% Visual and
Performing Arts
Expenses: 2014-2015: $28,556;
room/board: $8,252

Financial aid: (585) 567-9328;
82% of undergrads determined to
have financial need; average aid
package $18,935

Iona College

New Rochelle NY
(914) 633-2502
U.S. News ranking: Reg. U. (N),
No. 74
Website: www.iona.edu/info
Admissions email:
admissions@iona.edu
Private; founded 1940
Affiliation: Roman Catholic
Freshman admissions: less
selective; 2013-2014: 5,911
applied, 5,445 accepted. Either
SAT or ACT required. SAT 25/75
percentile: 900-1110. High school
rank: 10% in top tenth, 31% in
top quarter, 66% in top half
Early decision deadline: N/A,
notification date: N/A
Early action deadline: 12/1,
notification date: 12/21
Application deadline (fall): 2/15
Undergraduate student body: 3,110
full time, 429 part time; 46%
male, 54% female; 0% American
Indian, 2% Asian, 8% black,
19% Hispanic, 2% multiracial,
0% Pacific Islander, 59% white,
2% international; 76% from in
state; 43% live on campus; 8%
of students in fraternities, 4% in
sororities
Most popular majors: 37%
Business, Management,
Marketing, and Related Support
Services, 15% Communication,
Journalism, and Related Programs,
8% Education, 7% Health
Professions and Related Programs,
11% Psychology
Expenses: 2014-2015: $34,030;
room/board: $13,570
Financial aid: (914) 633-2497;
81% of undergrads determined to
have financial need; average aid
package $21,368

Ithaca College

Ithaca NY
(800) 429-4274
U.S. News ranking: Reg. U. (N),
No. 9
Website: www.ithaca.edu
Admissions email:
admission@ithaca.edu
Private; founded 1892
Freshman admissions: more
selective; 2013-2014: 15,658
applied, 10,429 accepted. Neither
SAT nor ACT required. SAT
25/75 percentile: 1080-1270.
High school rank: 27% in top
tenth, 63% in top quarter, 91%
in top half
Early decision deadline: 11/1,
notification date: 12/15
Early action deadline: 12/1,
notification date: 2/1
Application deadline (fall): 2/1
Undergraduate student body: 6,131
full time, 103 part time; 44%
male, 56% female; 0% American
Indian, 3% Asian, 5% black,
7% Hispanic, 3% multiracial,
0% Pacific Islander, 69% white,
2% international; 45% from in
state; 73% live on campus; 1%
of students in fraternities, 1% in
sororities
Most popular majors: 11%
Business, Management,
Marketing, and Related Support
Services, 21% Communication,
Journalism, and Related Programs,

13% Health Professions and
Related Programs, 6% Social
Sciences, 18% Visual and
Performing Arts
Expenses: 2014-2015: $39,532;
room/board: $14,332
Financial aid: (607) 274-3131;
68% of undergrads determined to
have financial need; average aid
package $32,139

Juilliard School[1]

New York NY
(212) 799-5000
U.S. News ranking: Arts, unranked
Website: www.juilliard.edu
Admissions email: admissions@
juilliard.edu
Private; founded 1905
Application deadline (fall): 12/1
Undergraduate student body: N/A
full time, N/A part time
Expenses: 2013-2014: $36,920;
room/board: $13,810
Financial aid: (212) 799-5000

Keuka College

Keuka Park NY
(315) 279-5254
U.S. News ranking: Reg. U. (N),
No. 125
Website: www.keuka.edu
Admissions email: admissions@
mail.keuka.edu
Private; founded 1890
Affiliation: American Baptist
Freshman admissions: less
selective; 2013-2014: 1,375
applied, 1,207 accepted. Either
SAT or ACT required. SAT 25/75
percentile: 860-1050. High
school rank: 7% in top tenth, 27%
in top quarter, 75% in top half
Early decision deadline: N/A,
notification date: N/A
Early action deadline: N/A,
notification date: N/A
Application deadline (fall): rolling
Undergraduate student body: 1,514
full time, 315 part time; 23%
male, 77% female; 1% American
Indian, 1% Asian, 8% black,
4% Hispanic, 1% multiracial,
0% Pacific Islander, 79% white,
0% international; 94% from in
state; 80% live on campus; N/A
of students in fraternities, N/A in
sororities
Most popular majors: 29%
Business, Management,
Marketing, and Related Support
Services, 16% Education, 22%
Health Professions and Related
Programs, 14% Homeland
Security, Law Enforcement,
Firefighting and Related
Protective Services, 9% Public
Administration and Social Service
Professions
Expenses: 2014-2015: $28,010;
room/board: $10,800
Financial aid: (315) 279-5232;
88% of undergrads determined to
have financial need; average aid
package $18,079

The King's College

New York NY
(212) 659-3610
U.S. News ranking: Nat. Lib. Arts,
second tier
Website: www.tkc.edu/
Admissions email:
admissions@tkc.edu
Private; founded 1938
Affiliation: Christian
nondenominational

Freshman admissions: selective; 2013-2014: 3,033 applied, 2,158 accepted. Either SAT or ACT required. SAT 25/75 percentile: 1050-1230. High school rank: 15% in top tenth, 48% in top quarter, 98% in top half
Early decision deadline: N/A, notification date: N/A
Early action deadline: 11/15, notification date: 12/15
Application deadline (fall): rolling
Undergraduate student body: 493 full time, 23 part time; 40% male, 60% female; 0% American Indian, 3% Asian, 3% black, 8% Hispanic, 5% multiracial, 0% Pacific Islander, 78% white, 4% international; 7% from in state; 76% live on campus; 0% of students in fraternities, 0% in sororities
Most popular majors: 17% Business Administration and Management, General, 83% Humanities/Humanistic Studies
Expenses: 2014-2015: $32,300; room/board: $12,400
Financial aid: (212) 659-7200; 74% of undergrads determined to have financial need; average aid package $24,910

Le Moyne College
Syracuse NY
(315) 445-4300
U.S. News ranking: Reg. U. (N), No. 19
Website: www.lemoyne.edu
Admissions email: admission@lemoyne.edu
Private; founded 1946
Affiliation: Roman Catholic (Jesuit)
Freshman admissions: selective; 2013-2014: 5,924 applied, 3,667 accepted. Either SAT or ACT required. SAT 25/75 percentile: 980-1170. High school rank: 21% in top tenth, 51% in top quarter, 88% in top half
Early decision deadline: N/A, notification date: N/A
Early action deadline: 11/15, notification date: 12/15
Application deadline (fall): rolling
Undergraduate student body: 2,401 full time, 384 part time; 41% male, 59% female; 1% American Indian, 3% Asian, 6% black, 6% Hispanic, 2% multiracial, 0% Pacific Islander, 78% white, 1% international; 94% from in state; 60% live on campus; 0% of students in fraternities, 0% in sororities
Most popular majors: 6% Accounting, 12% Biology/Biological Sciences, General, 7% Business Administration, Management and Operations, Other, 6% Marketing/Marketing Management, General, 21% Psychology, General
Expenses: 2014-2015: $31,340; room/board: $12,130
Financial aid: (315) 445-4400; 83% of undergrads determined to have financial need; average aid package $23,164

LIM College[1]
New York NY
(800) 677-1323
U.S. News ranking: Business, unranked
Website: www.limcollege.edu/html/home.htm
Admissions email: admissions@limcollege.edu
For-profit; founded 1939

Application deadline (fall): rolling
Undergraduate student body: N/A full time, N/A part time
Expenses: 2014-2015: $24,225; room/board: $19,850
Financial aid: (800) 677-1323; 69% of undergrads determined to have financial need; average aid package $9,527

LIU Post
Brookville NY
(516) 299-2900
U.S. News ranking: Reg. U. (N), second tier
Website: www.liu.edu
Admissions email: post-enroll@liu.edu
Private; founded 1954
Freshman admissions: less selective; 2013-2014: 6,006 applied, 4,844 accepted. Either SAT or ACT required. SAT 25/75 percentile: 880-1060. High school rank: N/A
Early decision deadline: N/A, notification date: N/A
Early action deadline: N/A, notification date: N/A
Application deadline (fall): rolling
Undergraduate student body: 3,661 full time, 4,322 part time; 42% male, 58% female; 0% American Indian, 4% Asian, 10% black, 13% Hispanic, 1% multiracial, 0% Pacific Islander, 48% white, 11% international; 93% from in state; 32% live on campus; N/A of students in fraternities, N/A in sororities
Most popular majors: 5% Audiology/Audiologist and Speech-Language Pathology/Pathologist, 14% Business Administration and Management, General, 10% Criminal Justice/Law Enforcement Administration, 6% Elementary Education and Teaching, 7% Psychology, General
Expenses: 2014-2015: $34,852; room/board: $12,808
Financial aid: (516) 299-2338; 72% of undergrads determined to have financial need; average aid package $18,445

Manhattan College
Riverdale NY
(718) 862-7200
U.S. News ranking: Reg. U. (N), No. 18
Website: www.manhattan.edu
Admissions email: admit@manhattan.edu
Private; founded 1853
Affiliation: Roman Catholic
Freshman admissions: selective; 2013-2014: 7,268 applied, 4,809 accepted. SAT required. SAT 25/75 percentile: 970-1190. High school rank: 24% in top tenth, 52% in top quarter, 81% in top half
Early decision deadline: 11/15, notification date: 12/15
Early action deadline: N/A, notification date: N/A
Application deadline (fall): rolling
Undergraduate student body: 3,195 full time, 208 part time; 56% male, 44% female; 0% American Indian, 4% Asian, 4% black, 18% Hispanic, 2% multiracial, 0% Pacific Islander, 60% white, 2% international; 72% from in state; 62% live on campus; 2% of students in fraternities, 5% in sororities

Most popular majors: 18% Business, Management, Marketing, and Related Support Services, 7% Communication, Journalism, and Related Programs, 13% Education, 26% Engineering, 9% Multi/Interdisciplinary Studies
Expenses: 2013-2014: $35,725; room/board: $13,080
Financial aid: (718) 862-7100

Manhattan School of Music[1]
New York NY
(212) 749-2802
U.S. News ranking: Arts, unranked
Website: www.msmnyc.edu
Admissions email: admission@msmnyc.edu
Private
Application deadline (fall): N/A
Undergraduate student body: N/A full time, N/A part time
Expenses: 2013-2014: $36,500; room/board: $13,750
Financial aid: (212) 749-2802

Manhattanville College
Purchase NY
(914) 323-5464
U.S. News ranking: Reg. U. (N), No. 83
Website: www.mville.edu
Admissions email: admissions@mville.edu
Private; founded 1841
Freshman admissions: selective; 2013-2014: 3,930 applied, 3,016 accepted. Neither SAT nor ACT required. SAT 25/75 percentile: 970-1180. High school rank: N/A
Early decision deadline: 12/15, notification date: 12/31
Early action deadline: N/A, notification date: N/A
Application deadline (fall): rolling
Undergraduate student body: 1,611 full time, 108 part time; 36% male, 64% female; 0% American Indian, 1% Asian, 7% black, 12% Hispanic, 1% multiracial, 0% Pacific Islander, 23% white, 10% international; 62% from in state; 66% live on campus; N/A of students in fraternities, N/A in sororities
Most popular majors: 20% Business Administration and Management, General, 10% Finance, General, 8% Psychology, General, 8% Sociology, 9% Speech Communication and Rhetoric
Expenses: 2014-2015: $36,220; room/board: $14,520
Financial aid: (914) 323-5357; 79% of undergrads determined to have financial need; average aid package $34,835

Marist College
Poughkeepsie NY
(845) 575-3226
U.S. News ranking: Reg. U. (N), No. 11
Website: www.marist.edu
Admissions email: admissions@marist.edu
Private; founded 1929
Freshman admissions: more selective; 2013-2014: 10,351 applied, 3,876 accepted. Neither SAT nor ACT required. SAT 25/75 percentile: 1090-1260. High

school rank: 32% in top tenth, 64% in top quarter, 92% in top half
Early decision deadline: 11/1, notification date: 12/15
Early action deadline: 11/15, notification date: 1/30
Application deadline (fall): 2/1
Undergraduate student body: 4,924 full time, 642 part time; 41% male, 59% female; 0% American Indian, 3% Asian, 4% black, 9% Hispanic, 2% multiracial, 0% Pacific Islander, 73% white, 2% international; 56% from in state; 73% live on campus; 3% of students in fraternities, 3% in sororities
Most popular majors: 23% Business, Management, Marketing, and Related Support Services, 18% Communication, Journalism, and Related Programs, 5% Education, 16% Psychology, 10% Visual and Performing Arts
Expenses: 2014-2015: $32,500; room/board: $14,325
Financial aid: (845) 575-3230; 59% of undergrads determined to have financial need; average aid package $18,315

Marymount Manhattan College
New York NY
(212) 517-0430
U.S. News ranking: Nat. Lib. Arts, second tier
Website: www.mmm.edu
Admissions email: admissions@mmm.edu
Private; founded 1936
Freshman admissions: selective; 2013-2014: 4,145 applied, 3,096 accepted. Either SAT or ACT required. SAT 25/75 percentile: 930-1153. High school rank: N/A
Early decision deadline: N/A, notification date: N/A
Early action deadline: N/A, notification date: N/A
Application deadline (fall): rolling
Undergraduate student body: 1,593 full time, 240 part time; 23% male, 77% female; 1% American Indian, 4% Asian, 11% black, 16% Hispanic, 1% multiracial, 0% Pacific Islander, 58% white, 5% international; 41% from in state; 40% live on campus; N/A of students in fraternities, N/A in sororities
Most popular majors: 7% Business, Management, Marketing, and Related Support Services, 21% Communication, Journalism, and Related Programs, 6% English Language and Literature/Letters, 9% Psychology, 40% Visual and Performing Arts
Expenses: 2014-2015: $27,636; room/board: $15,000
Financial aid: (212) 517-0480; 68% of undergrads determined to have financial need; average aid package $14,102

Medaille College
Buffalo NY
(716) 880-2200
U.S. News ranking: Reg. U. (N), second tier
Website: www.medaille.edu
Admissions email: admissionsug@medaille.edu
Private; founded 1937

Freshman admissions: less selective; 2013-2014: 1,505 applied, 817 accepted. Either SAT or ACT required. SAT 25/75 percentile: 760-970. High school rank: N/A
Early decision deadline: N/A, notification date: N/A
Early action deadline: N/A, notification date: N/A
Application deadline (fall): rolling
Undergraduate student body: 1,586 full time, 142 part time; 33% male, 67% female; 1% American Indian, 1% Asian, 21% black, 5% Hispanic, 0% multiracial, 1% Pacific Islander, 65% white, 2% international; 94% from in state; N/A live on campus; 0% of students in fraternities, 0% in sororities
Most popular majors: 31% Business Administration and Management, General, 9% Criminal Justice/Police Science, 12% Elementary Education and Teaching, 10% Psychology, General, 10% Veterinary/Animal Health Technology/Technician and Veterinary Assistant
Expenses: 2014-2015: $25,002; room/board: $11,866
Financial aid: (716) 880-2256; 95% of undergrads determined to have financial need; average aid package $11,000

Mercy College
Dobbs Ferry NY
(877) 637-2946
U.S. News ranking: Reg. U. (N), unranked
Website: www.mercy.edu
Admissions email: admissions@mercy.edu
Private; founded 1950
Freshman admissions: N/A; 2013-2014: 6,394 applied, 4,013 accepted. Neither SAT nor ACT required. ACT 25/75 percentile: N/A. High school rank: N/A
Early decision deadline: N/A, notification date: N/A
Early action deadline: N/A, notification date: N/A
Application deadline (fall): rolling
Undergraduate student body: 5,547 full time, 2,607 part time; 31% male, 69% female; 0% American Indian, 3% Asian, 27% black, 35% Hispanic, 2% multiracial, 0% Pacific Islander, 27% white, 0% international; 93% from in state; 7% live on campus; N/A of students in fraternities, N/A in sororities
Most popular majors: 14% Business, Management, Marketing, and Related Support Services, 22% Health Professions and Related Programs, 6% Homeland Security, Law Enforcement, Firefighting and Related Protective Services, 10% Psychology, 31% Social Sciences
Expenses: 2014-2015: $17,766; room/board: $12,790
Financial aid: (914) 378-3421; 87% of undergrads determined to have financial need; average aid package $13,414

Metropolitan College of New York

New York NY
(800) 338-4465
U.S. News ranking: Reg. U. (N), unranked
Website: www.metropolitan.edu/
Admissions email: N/A
Private
Freshman admissions: N/A; 2013-2014: 639 applied, 334 accepted. Neither SAT nor ACT required. ACT 25/75 percentile: N/A. High school rank: N/A
Early decision deadline: N/A, notification date: N/A
Early action deadline: N/A, notification date: N/A
Application deadline (fall): rolling
Undergraduate student body: 851 full time, 60 part time; 29% male, 71% female; 1% American Indian, 2% Asian, 59% black, 20% Hispanic, 2% multiracial, 1% Pacific Islander, 5% white, 3% international; 97% from in state; 0% live on campus; 0% of students in fraternities, 0% in sororities
Most popular majors: 29% Business/Commerce, General, 53% Community Organization and Advocacy, 7% Health Information/Medical Records Administration/Administrator, 11% Urban Studies/Affairs
Expenses: 2013-2014: $17,530; room/board: N/A
Financial aid: (212) 343-1234; 93% of undergrads determined to have financial need; average aid package $15,731

Molloy College

Rockville Centre NY
(888) 466-5569
U.S. News ranking: Reg. U. (N), No. 41
Website: www.molloy.edu
Admissions email: admissions@molloy.edu
Private; founded 1955
Affiliation: Roman Catholic
Freshman admissions: selective; 2013-2014: 3,242 applied, 2,356 accepted. Either SAT or ACT required. SAT 25/75 percentile: 970-1140. High school rank: 38% in top tenth, 56% in top quarter, 92% in top half
Early decision deadline: N/A, notification date: N/A
Early action deadline: 12/1, notification date: 12/15
Application deadline (fall): rolling
Undergraduate student body: 2,693 full time, 682 part time; 26% male, 74% female; 0% American Indian, 7% Asian, 13% black, 14% Hispanic, 1% multiracial, 1% Pacific Islander, 62% white, 0% international; 99% from in state; 5% live on campus; N/A of students in fraternities, N/A in sororities
Most popular majors: 9% Business, Management, Marketing, and Related Support Services, 14% Education, 48% Health Professions and Related Programs, 5% Homeland Security, Law Enforcement, Firefighting and Related Protective Services, 5% Public Administration and Social Service Professions
Expenses: 2014-2015: $26,850; room/board: $13,590

Financial aid: (516) 256-2217; 84% of undergrads determined to have financial need; average aid package $14,394

Monroe College

Bronx NY
(800) 556-6676
U.S. News ranking: Reg. U. (N), second tier
Website: www.monroecollege.edu
Admissions email: N/A
For-profit; founded 1933
Freshman admissions: less selective; 2013-2014: 4,419 applied, 1,946 accepted. Neither SAT nor ACT required. ACT 25/75 percentile: N/A. High school rank: N/A
Early decision deadline: N/A, notification date: N/A
Early action deadline: N/A, notification date: N/A
Application deadline (fall): rolling
Undergraduate student body: 4,895 full time, 1,899 part time; 36% male, 64% female; 0% American Indian, 2% Asian, 45% black, 41% Hispanic, 0% multiracial, 0% Pacific Islander, 2% white, 7% international; 88% from in state; 13% live on campus; 0% of students in fraternities, 0% in sororities
Most popular majors: 14% Accounting, 20% Business Administration and Management, General, 26% Criminal Justice/Law Enforcement Administration, 12% Health Services Administration, 11% Hospitality Administration/Management, General
Expenses: 2014-2015: $13,740; room/board: $9,200
Financial aid: N/A; 90% of undergrads determined to have financial need; average aid package $14,103

Morrisville State College

Morrisville NY
(315) 684-6046
U.S. News ranking: Reg. Coll. (N), No. 43
Website: www.morrisville.edu
Admissions email: admissions@morrisville.edu
Public; founded 1908
Freshman admissions: less selective; 2013-2014: 4,049 applied, 2,388 accepted. Neither SAT nor ACT required. SAT 25/75 percentile: 840-1030. High school rank: 5% in top tenth, 16% in top quarter, 65% in top half
Early decision deadline: N/A, notification date: N/A
Early action deadline: N/A, notification date: N/A
Application deadline (fall): rolling
Undergraduate student body: 2,668 full time, 360 part time; 52% male, 48% female; 1% American Indian, 1% Asian, 18% black, 7% Hispanic, 2% multiracial, 0% Pacific Islander, 68% white, 1% international; 96% from in state; 55% live on campus; 0% of students in fraternities, 0% in sororities
Most popular majors: 25% Agriculture, Agriculture Operations, and Related Sciences, 33% Business, Management, Marketing, and Related Support Services, 12% Computer and

Information Sciences and Support Services, 13% Homeland Security, Law Enforcement, Firefighting and Related Protective Services, 6% Mechanic and Repair Technologies/Technicians
Expenses: 2014-2015: $6,670 in state, $12,140 out of state; room/board: $13,370
Financial aid: (315) 684-6289; 87% of undergrads determined to have financial need; average aid package $9,627

Mount St. Mary College

Newburgh NY
(845) 569-3488
U.S. News ranking: Reg. U. (N), No. 109
Website: www.msmc.edu
Admissions email: admissions@msmc.edu
Private; founded 1959
Affiliation: Roman Catholic
Freshman admissions: selective; 2013-2014: 3,551 applied, 3,054 accepted. Either SAT or ACT required. SAT 25/75 percentile: 910-1093. High school rank: 10% in top tenth, 38% in top quarter, 71% in top half
Early decision deadline: N/A, notification date: N/A
Early action deadline: N/A, notification date: N/A
Application deadline (fall): 8/15
Undergraduate student body: 1,742 full time, 461 part time; 30% male, 70% female; 1% American Indian, 2% Asian, 7% black, 12% Hispanic, 1% multiracial, 0% Pacific Islander, 64% white, 0% international; 89% from in state; 46% live on campus; N/A of students in fraternities, N/A in sororities
Most popular majors: 18% Business, Management, Marketing, and Related Support Services, 8% English Language and Literature/Letters, 19% Health Professions and Related Programs, 11% History, 11% Psychology
Expenses: 2014-2015: $27,312; room/board: $13,556
Financial aid: (845) 569-3298; 81% of undergrads determined to have financial need; average aid package $17,409

Nazareth College

Rochester NY
(585) 389-2860
U.S. News ranking: Reg. U. (N), No. 31
Website: www.naz.edu
Admissions email: admissions@naz.edu
Private; founded 1924
Freshman admissions: selective; 2013-2014: 3,838 applied, 2,624 accepted. Neither SAT nor ACT required. SAT 25/75 percentile: 1020-1180. High school rank: 30% in top tenth, 65% in top quarter, 91% in top half
Early decision deadline: 11/1, notification date: 12/1
Early action deadline: 12/1, notification date: 1/15
Application deadline (fall): 2/1
Undergraduate student body: 1,901 full time, 133 part time; 27% male, 73% female; 1% American Indian, 2% Asian, 5% black,

5% Hispanic, 1% multiracial, 0% Pacific Islander, 73% white, 2% international; 93% from in state; 53% live on campus; N/A of students in fraternities, N/A in sororities
Most popular majors: 10% Business, Management, Marketing, and Related Support Services, 17% Education, 17% Health Professions and Related Programs, 10% Psychology, 8% Visual and Performing Arts
Expenses: 2014-2015: $30,572; room/board: $12,570
Financial aid: (585) 389-2310; 81% of undergrads determined to have financial need; average aid package $24,450

New School

New York NY
(800) 292-3040
U.S. News ranking: Nat. U., No. 135
Website: www.newschool.edu
Admissions email: admission@newschool.edu
Private; founded 1919
Freshman admissions: selective; 2013-2014: 4,976 applied, 3,314 accepted. Neither SAT nor ACT required. SAT 25/75 percentile: 990-1240. High school rank: 15% in top tenth, 42% in top quarter, 74% in top half
Early decision deadline: 11/1, notification date: 12/30
Early action deadline: N/A, notification date: N/A
Undergraduate student body: 5,971 full time, 903 part time; 28% male, 72% female; 0% American Indian, 1% Asian, 5% black, 10% Hispanic, 4% multiracial, 0% Pacific Islander, 36% white, 31% international; 30% from in state; 23% live on campus; N/A of students in fraternities, N/A in sororities
Most popular majors: 5% English Language and Literature/Letters, 12% Liberal Arts and Sciences, General Studies and Humanities, 2% Psychology, 7% Social Sciences, 68% Visual and Performing Arts
Expenses: 2014-2015: $41,836; room/board: $18,190
Financial aid: (212) 229-8930; 51% of undergrads determined to have financial need; average aid package $21,350

New York Institute of Technology

Old Westbury NY
(516) 686-7520
U.S. News ranking: Reg. U. (N), No. 50
Website: www.nyit.edu
Admissions email: admissions@nyit.edu
Private; founded 1955
Freshman admissions: selective; 2013-2014: 5,619 applied, 4,181 accepted. Either SAT or ACT required. SAT 25/75 percentile: 1020-1220. High school rank: 22% in top tenth, 52% in top quarter, 88% in top half
Early decision deadline: N/A, notification date: N/A
Early action deadline: 12/1, notification date: 12/31
Application deadline (fall): rolling

Undergraduate student body: 3,704 full time, 752 part time; 63% male, 37% female; 0% American Indian, 13% Asian, 8% black, 13% Hispanic, 1% multiracial, 0% Pacific Islander, 19% white, 12% international; 91% from in state; 12% live on campus; 3% of students in fraternities, 2% in sororities
Most popular majors: 18% Architecture and Related Services, 11% Biological and Biomedical Sciences, 16% Business, Management, Marketing, and Related Support Services, 10% Communication, Journalism, and Related Programs, 12% Engineering
Expenses: 2014-2015: $32,180; room/board: $12,830
Financial aid: (516) 686-7680; 75% of undergrads determined to have financial need; average aid package $18,348

New York University

New York NY
(212) 998-4500
U.S. News ranking: Nat. U., No. 32
Website: www.nyu.edu
Admissions email: admissions@nyu.edu
Private; founded 1831
Freshman admissions: more selective; 2013-2014: 45,779 applied, 14,829 accepted. Either SAT or ACT required. SAT 25/75 percentile: 1260-1460. High school rank: 63% in top tenth, 96% in top quarter, 99% in top half
Early decision deadline: 11/1, notification date: 12/15
Early action deadline: N/A, notification date: N/A
Application deadline (fall): 1/1
Undergraduate student body: 21,365 full time, 1,250 part time; 40% male, 60% female; 0% American Indian, 18% Asian, 5% black, 11% Hispanic, 3% multiracial, 0% Pacific Islander, 38% white, 14% international; 34% from in state; 47% live on campus; 5% of students in fraternities, 7% in sororities
Most popular majors: 13% Business, Management, Marketing, and Related Support Services, 9% Health Professions and Related Programs, 10% Liberal Arts and Sciences, General Studies and Humanities, 16% Social Sciences, 21% Visual and Performing Arts
Expenses: 2014-2015: $46,170; room/board: $16,782
Financial aid: (212) 998-4444; 52% of undergrads determined to have financial need; average aid package $27,544

Niagara University

Niagara University NY
(716) 286-8700
U.S. News ranking: Reg. U. (N), No. 50
Website: www.niagara.edu
Admissions email: admissions@niagara.edu
Private; founded 1856
Affiliation: Roman Catholic (Vincentian)
Freshman admissions: selective; 2013-2014: 3,716 applied, 2,465 accepted. Either SAT or ACT required. SAT 25/75

percentile: 930-1120. High school rank: 15% in top tenth, 41% in top quarter, 77% in top half **Early decision deadline:** N/A, notification date: N/A **Early action deadline:** N/A, notification date: N/A **Application deadline (fall):** rolling **Undergraduate student body:** 2,865 full time, 362 part time; 40% male, 60% female; 1% American Indian, 1% Asian, 5% black, 4% Hispanic, 1% multiracial, 0% Pacific Islander, 68% white, 14% international; 91% from in state; 43% live on campus; 1% of students in fraternities, 2% in sororities **Most popular majors:** 5% Biological and Biomedical Sciences, 32% Business, Management, Marketing, and Related Support Services, 15% Education, 10% Homeland Security, Law Enforcement, Firefighting and Related Protective Services, 5% Parks, Recreation, Leisure, and Fitness Studies **Expenses:** 2014-2015: $29,060; room/board: $11,950 **Financial aid:** (716) 286-8686; 76% of undergrads determined to have financial need; average aid package $23,087

Nyack College[1]

Nyack NY
(800) 336-9225
U.S. News ranking: Reg. U. (N), second tier
Website: www.nyack.edu
Admissions email: admissions@nyack.edu
Private
Application deadline (fall): N/A
Undergraduate student body: N/A full time, N/A part time
Expenses: 2013-2014: $23,250; room/board: $8,650
Financial aid: (845) 358-1710

Pace University

New York NY
(212) 346-1323
U.S. News ranking: Nat. U., No. 173
Website: www.pace.edu
Admissions email: infoctr@pace.edu
Private; founded 1906
Freshman admissions: selective; 2013-2014: 14,590 applied, 11,853 accepted. Either SAT or ACT required. SAT 25/75 percentile: 940-1150. High school rank: 13% in top tenth, 40% in top quarter, 76% in top half
Early decision deadline: N/A, notification date: N/A
Early action deadline: 12/1, notification date: 1/1
Application deadline (fall): 2/15
Undergraduate student body: 7,116 full time, 1,173 part time; 41% male, 59% female; 0% American Indian, 9% Asian, 11% black, 16% Hispanic, 4% multiracial, 0% Pacific Islander, 48% white, 6% international; 55% from in state; 40% live on campus; 11% of students in fraternities, 7% in sororities
Most popular majors: 36% Business, Management, Marketing, and Related Support Services, 13% Communication, Journalism, and Related Programs, 6% Health Professions and Related Programs, 8% Psychology, 6% Visual and Performing Arts

Expenses: 2014-2015: $39,747; room/board: $13,620 **Financial aid:** (212) 346-1300; 75% of undergrads determined to have financial need; average aid package $28,893

Paul Smith's College[1]

Paul Smiths NY
(800) 421-2605
U.S. News ranking: Reg. Coll. (N), No. 40
Website: www.paulsmiths.edu
Admissions email: admiss@paulsmiths.edu
Private
Application deadline (fall): N/A
Undergraduate student body: N/A full time, N/A part time
Expenses: 2013-2014: $25,454; room/board: $10,696
Financial aid: (518) 327-6220

Plaza College[1]

Jackson Heights NY
(718) 779-1430
U.S. News ranking: Reg. Coll. (N), unranked
Website: www.plazacollege.edu
Admissions email: N/A
For-profit
Application deadline (fall): rolling
Undergraduate student body: N/A full time, N/A part time
Expenses: 2013-2014: $11,350; room/board: N/A
Financial aid: (718) 779-1430

Pratt Institute

Brooklyn NY
(718) 636-3514
U.S. News ranking: Reg. U. (N), No. 19
Website: www.pratt.edu
Admissions email: admissions@pratt.edu
Private; founded 1887
Freshman admissions: selective; 2013-2014: 4,446 applied, 2,977 accepted. Either SAT or ACT required. SAT 25/75 percentile: 1070-1300. High school rank: N/A
Early decision deadline: N/A, notification date: N/A
Early action deadline: 11/1, notification date: 12/22
Application deadline (fall): 1/5
Undergraduate student body: 3,041 full time, 108 part time; 34% male, 66% female; 0% American Indian, 15% Asian, 5% black, 10% Hispanic, 0% multiracial, 0% Pacific Islander, 40% white, 28% international; 31% from in state; 53% live on campus; 6% of students in fraternities, 3% in sororities
Most popular majors: 17% Architecture, 11% Design and Visual Communications, General, 12% Graphic Design, 9% Industrial and Product Design, 8% Interior Design
Expenses: 2014-2015: $44,804; room/board: $11,152
Financial aid: (718) 636-3599; 54% of undergrads determined to have financial need; average aid package $23,204

Purchase College–SUNY

Purchase NY
(914) 251-6300
U.S. News ranking: Nat. Lib. Arts, No. 171
Website: www.purchase.edu
Admissions email: admissions@purchase.edu
Public; founded 1967
Freshman admissions: selective; 2013-2014: 8,405 applied, 2,790 accepted. Either SAT or ACT required. SAT 25/75 percentile: 980-1180. High school rank: 13% in top tenth, 36% in top quarter, 73% in top half
Early decision deadline: N/A, notification date: N/A
Early action deadline: 11/15, notification date: 12/15
Application deadline (fall): 7/15
Undergraduate student body: 3,860 full time, 405 part time; 44% male, 56% female; 0% American Indian, 3% Asian, 8% black, 18% Hispanic, 8% multiracial, 0% Pacific Islander, 54% white, 3% international; 85% from in state; 66% live on campus; N/A of students in fraternities, N/A in sororities
Most popular majors: 7% Communication, Journalism, and Related Programs, 20% Liberal Arts and Sciences, General Studies and Humanities, 6% Psychology, 10% Social Sciences, 40% Visual and Performing Arts
Expenses: 2014-2015: $7,873 in state, $17,523 out of state; room/board: $11,806
Financial aid: (914) 251-6350; 62% of undergrads determined to have financial need; average aid package $10,456

Rensselaer Polytechnic Institute

Troy NY
(518) 276-6216
U.S. News ranking: Nat. U., No. 42
Website: www.rpi.edu
Admissions email: admissions@rpi.edu
Private; founded 1824
Freshman admissions: most selective; 2013-2014: 16,150 applied, 6,654 accepted. Either SAT or ACT required. SAT 25/75 percentile: 1290-1488. High school rank: 72% in top tenth, 95% in top quarter, 98% in top half
Early decision deadline: 11/1, notification date: 12/14
Early action deadline: N/A, notification date: N/A
Application deadline (fall): 1/15
Undergraduate student body: 5,423 full time, 29 part time; 70% male, 30% female; 0% American Indian, 10% Asian, 2% black, 7% Hispanic, 6% multiracial, 0% Pacific Islander, 65% white, 7% international; 34% from in state; 57% live on campus; 30% of students in fraternities, 16% in sororities
Most popular majors: 6% Biological and Biomedical Sciences, 6% Business, Management, Marketing, and Related Support Services, 9% Computer and Information Sciences and Support Services, 54% Engineering, 6% Physical Sciences
Expenses: 2014-2015: $47,908; room/board: $13,620

Financial aid: (518) 276-6813; 65% of undergrads determined to have financial need; average aid package $32,603

Roberts Wesleyan College

Rochester NY
(585) 594-6400
U.S. News ranking: Reg. U. (N), No. 87
Website: www.roberts.edu
Admissions email: admissions@roberts.edu
Private; founded 1866
Affiliation: Free Methodist
Freshman admissions: selective; 2013-2014: 814 applied, 591 accepted. Either SAT or ACT required. SAT 25/75 percentile: 920-1170. High school rank: 21% in top tenth, 52% in top quarter, 87% in top half
Early decision deadline: N/A, notification date: N/A
Early action deadline: N/A, notification date: N/A
Application deadline (fall): 8/15
Undergraduate student body: 1,325 full time, 90 part time; 35% male, 65% female; 0% American Indian, 1% Asian, 13% black, 6% Hispanic, 3% multiracial, 0% Pacific Islander, 74% white, 3% international; 92% from in state; 58% live on campus; 0% of students in fraternities, 0% in sororities
Most popular majors: 22% Business, Management, Marketing, and Related Support Services, 18% Education, 27% Health Professions and Related Programs, 4% Liberal Arts and Sciences, General Studies and Humanities, 6% Psychology
Expenses: 2013-2014: $27,364; room/board: $9,630
Financial aid: (585) 594-6150

Rochester Institute of Technology

Rochester NY
(585) 475-6631
U.S. News ranking: Reg. U. (N), No. 8
Website: www.rit.edu
Admissions email: admissions@rit.edu
Private; founded 1829
Freshman admissions: more selective; 2013-2014: 16,354 applied, 9,839 accepted. Either SAT or ACT required. SAT 25/75 percentile: 1110-1320. High school rank: 31% in top tenth, 64% in top quarter, 94% in top half
Early decision deadline: 12/1, notification date: 1/15
Early action deadline: N/A, notification date: N/A
Application deadline (fall): rolling
Undergraduate student body: 12,106 full time, 1,774 part time; 68% male, 32% female; 0% American Indian, 6% Asian, 5% black, 6% Hispanic, 2% multiracial, 0% Pacific Islander, 63% white, 5% international; N/A from in state; 55% live on campus; N/A of students in fraternities, N/A in sororities
Most popular majors: 10% Business, Management, Marketing, and Related Support Services, 16% Computer and

Information Sciences and Support Services, 16% Engineering, 12% Engineering Technologies and Engineering-Related Fields, 13% Visual and Performing Arts
Expenses: 2014-2015: $35,768; room/board: $11,568
Financial aid: (585) 475-2186; 76% of undergrads determined to have financial need; average aid package $23,800

The Sage Colleges

Troy NY
(888) 837-9724
U.S. News ranking: Reg. U. (N), No. 87
Website: www.sage.edu
Admissions email: tscadm@sage.edu
Private; founded 1916
Freshman admissions: selective; 2013-2014: 2,237 applied, 1,267 accepted. Neither SAT nor ACT required. SAT 25/75 percentile: 840-1090. High school rank: 14% in top tenth, 43% in top quarter, 83% in top half
Early decision deadline: N/A, notification date: N/A
Early action deadline: N/A, notification date: N/A
Application deadline (fall): rolling
Undergraduate student body: 1,446 full time, 253 part time; 21% male, 79% female; 0% American Indian, 3% Asian, 13% black, 9% Hispanic, 3% multiracial, 0% Pacific Islander, 61% white, 0% international; 94% from in state; 53% live on campus; 0% of students in fraternities, N/A in sororities
Most popular majors: 9% Biological and Biomedical Sciences, 14% Business, Management, Marketing, and Related Support Services, 9% Education, 8% Health Professions and Related Programs, 25% Visual and Performing Arts
Expenses: 2014-2015: $28,200; room/board: $11,830
Financial aid: (518) 244-2215; 93% of undergrads determined to have financial need

Sarah Lawrence College

Bronxville NY
(914) 395-2510
U.S. News ranking: Nat. Lib. Arts, No. 59
Website: www.slc.edu
Admissions email: slcadmit@sarahlawrence.edu
Private; founded 1926
Freshman admissions: more selective; 2013-2014: 2,236 applied, 1,723 accepted. Neither SAT nor ACT required. SAT 25/75 percentile: 1150-1350. High school rank: 35% in top tenth, 66% in top quarter, 96% in top half
Early decision deadline: 11/1, notification date: 12/15
Early action deadline: N/A, notification date: N/A
Application deadline (fall): 1/15
Undergraduate student body: 1,441 full time, 30 part time; 28% male, 72% female; 0% American Indian, 4% Asian, 4% black, 10% Hispanic, 5% multiracial, 0% Pacific Islander, 58% white, 11% international; 21% from in state; 82% live on campus; 0% of students in fraternities, 0% in sororities

Most popular majors: 100% Liberal Arts and Sciences/Liberal Studies
Expenses: 2014-2015: $50,780; room/board: $14,212
Financial aid: (914) 395-2570; 68% of undergrads determined to have financial need; average aid package $34,855

School of Visual Arts

New York NY
(212) 592-2100
U.S. News ranking: Arts, unranked
Website: www.schoolofvisualarts.edu/
Admissions email: admissions@sva.edu
For-profit; founded 1947
Freshman admissions: N/A; 2013-2014: 3,280 applied, 2,485 accepted. Either SAT or ACT required. SAT 25/75 percentile: N/A. High school rank: N/A
Early decision deadline: N/A, notification date: N/A
Early action deadline: 12/1, notification date: N/A
Application deadline (fall): rolling
Undergraduate student body: 3,349 full time, 287 part time; 39% male, 61% female; 1% American Indian, 14% Asian, 6% black, 8% Hispanic, 0% multiracial, 1% Pacific Islander, 41% white, 28% international
Most popular majors: Information not available
Expenses: 2014-2015: $33,560; room/board: $17,000
Financial aid: (212) 592-2030; 50% of undergrads determined to have financial need; average aid package $15,761

Siena College

Loudonville NY
(888) 287-4362
U.S. News ranking: Nat. Lib. Arts, No. 113
Website: www.siena.edu
Admissions email: admissions@siena.edu
Private; founded 1937
Affiliation: Roman Catholic
Freshman admissions: selective; 2013-2014: 9,438 applied, 5,428 accepted. Either SAT or ACT required. SAT 25/75 percentile: 1000-1200. High school rank: 24% in top tenth, 58% in top quarter, 90% in top half
Early decision deadline: 12/1, notification date: 12/15
Early action deadline: 12/1, notification date: 1/1
Application deadline (fall): 2/15
Undergraduate student body: 3,009 full time, 152 part time; 47% male, 53% female; 0% American Indian, 4% Asian, 4% black, 7% Hispanic, 2% multiracial, 0% Pacific Islander, 81% white, 2% international; 81% from in state; 78% live on campus; N/A of students in fraternities, N/A in sororities
Most popular majors: 14% Accounting, 11% Biology, General, 8% Finance, General, 10% Marketing/Marketing Management, General, 10% Psychology, General
Expenses: 2014-2015: $32,293; room/board: $13,060
Financial aid: (518) 783-2427; 77% of undergrads determined to have financial need; average aid package $24,441

Skidmore College

Saratoga Springs NY
(518) 580-5570
U.S. News ranking: Nat. Lib. Arts, No. 37
Website: www.skidmore.edu
Admissions email: admissions@skidmore.edu
Private; founded 1903
Freshman admissions: more selective; 2013-2014: 8,285 applied, 2,904 accepted. Either SAT or ACT required. SAT 25/75 percentile: 1130-1350. High school rank: 45% in top tenth, 81% in top quarter, 97% in top half
Early decision deadline: 11/15, notification date: 12/15
Early action deadline: N/A, notification date: N/A
Application deadline (fall): 1/15
Undergraduate student body: 2,647 full time, 37 part time; 39% male, 61% female; 0% American Indian, 6% Asian, 4% black, 9% Hispanic, 4% multiracial, 0% Pacific Islander, 63% white, 7% international; 33% from in state; 87% live on campus; 0% of students in fraternities, 0% in sororities
Most popular majors: 12% Business, Management, Marketing, and Related Support Services, 11% English Language and Literature/Letters, 9% Psychology, 17% Social Sciences, 15% Visual and Performing Arts
Expenses: 2014-2015: $47,314; room/board: $12,628
Financial aid: (518) 580-5750; 43% of undergrads determined to have financial need; average aid package $41,000

St. Bonaventure University

St. Bonaventure NY
(800) 462-5050
U.S. News ranking: Reg. U. (N), No. 24
Website: www.sbu.edu
Admissions email: admissions@sbu.edu
Private; founded 1858
Affiliation: Roman Catholic
Freshman admissions: selective; 2013-2014: 2,754 applied, 2,203 accepted. Either SAT or ACT required. SAT 25/75 percentile: 930-1180. High school rank: 18% in top tenth, 45% in top quarter, 77% in top half
Early decision deadline: N/A, notification date: N/A
Early action deadline: N/A, notification date: N/A
Application deadline (fall): 7/1
Undergraduate student body: 1,780 full time, 46 part time; 49% male, 51% female; 0% American Indian, 4% Asian, 5% black, 7% Hispanic, 1% multiracial, 0% Pacific Islander, 68% white, 2% international; 77% from in state; 75% live on campus; 0% of students in fraternities, 0% in sororities
Most popular majors: 20% Journalism, 27% Marketing/Marketing Management, General, 7% Psychology, General, 15% Special Education and Teaching, General, 6% Sports Studies
Expenses: 2014-2015: $30,475; room/board: $10,727
Financial aid: (716) 375-2528; 76% of undergrads determined to have financial need; average aid package $22,796

St. Francis College

Brooklyn Heights NY
(718) 489-5200
U.S. News ranking: Reg. Coll. (N), No. 20
Website: www.sfc.edu
Admissions email: admissions@stfranciscollege.edu
Private; founded 1884
Freshman admissions: less selective; 2013-2014: 2,815 applied, 1,811 accepted. Either SAT or ACT required. SAT 25/75 percentile: 850-1030. High school rank: N/A
Early decision deadline: N/A, notification date: N/A
Early action deadline: N/A, notification date: N/A
Application deadline (fall): rolling
Undergraduate student body: 2,456 full time, 308 part time; 44% male, 56% female; 0% American Indian, 3% Asian, 20% black, 22% Hispanic, 2% multiracial, 1% Pacific Islander, 37% white, 5% international; 90% from in state; 4% live on campus; 0% of students in fraternities, N/A in sororities
Most popular majors: 10% Accounting and Related Services, 10% Business Administration, Management and Operations, 14% Communication and Media Studies, 9% Health Professions and Related Clinical Sciences, Other, 9% Liberal Arts and Sciences, General Studies and Humanities
Expenses: 2014-2015: $22,300; room/board: $14,250
Financial aid: (718) 489-5255; 67% of undergrads determined to have financial need; average aid package $14,300

St. John Fisher College

Rochester NY
(585) 385-8064
U.S. News ranking: Nat. U., No. 142
Website: www.sjfc.edu
Admissions email: admissions@sjfc.edu
Private; founded 1948
Affiliation: Roman Catholic
Freshman admissions: selective; 2013-2014: 4,016 applied, 2,521 accepted. Either SAT or ACT required. SAT 25/75 percentile: 990-1170. High school rank: 26% in top tenth, 60% in top quarter, 90% in top half
Early decision deadline: 12/1, notification date: 1/15
Early action deadline: N/A, notification date: N/A
Application deadline (fall): rolling
Undergraduate student body: 2,738 full time, 221 part time; 40% male, 60% female; 0% American Indian, 3% Asian, 4% black, 4% Hispanic, 1% multiracial, 0% Pacific Islander, 84% white, 0% international; 97% from in state; 46% live on campus; 0% of students in fraternities, 0% in sororities
Most popular majors: 23% Business, Management, Marketing, and Related Support Services, 20% Education, 18% Health Professions and Related Programs, 6% Psychology, 8% Social Sciences
Expenses: 2014-2015: $29,550; room/board: $11,158

Financial aid: (585) 385-8042; 83% of undergrads determined to have financial need; average aid package $20,162

St. John's University

Queens NY
(718) 990-2000
U.S. News ranking: Nat. U., No. 145
Website: www.stjohns.edu/
Admissions email: admhelp@stjohns.edu
Private; founded 1870
Affiliation: Roman Catholic
Freshman admissions: selective; 2013-2014: 51,207 applied, 26,932 accepted. Either SAT or ACT required. SAT 25/75 percentile: 990-1210. High school rank: 17% in top tenth, 42% in top quarter, 73% in top half
Early decision deadline: N/A, notification date: N/A
Early action deadline: N/A, notification date: N/A
Application deadline (fall): rolling
Undergraduate student body: 10,908 full time, 4,865 part time; 45% male, 55% female; 0% American Indian, 19% Asian, 19% black, 16% Hispanic, 4% multiracial, 0% Pacific Islander, 34% white, 5% international; 70% from in state; 31% live on campus; 9% of students in fraternities, 8% in sororities
Most popular majors: 7% Biological and Biomedical Sciences, 22% Business, Management, Marketing, and Related Support Services, 11% Communication, Journalism, and Related Programs, 9% Health Professions and Related Programs, 8% Psychology
Expenses: 2014-2015: $38,680; room/board: $16,390
Financial aid: (718) 990-2000; 81% of undergrads determined to have financial need; average aid package $23,166

St. Joseph's College New York

Brooklyn NY
(718) 940-5800
U.S. News ranking: Reg. U. (N), No. 70
Website: www.sjcny.edu
Admissions email: longislandas@sjcny.edu
Private; founded 1916
Freshman admissions: selective; 2013-2014: 3,148 applied, 2,373 accepted. Either SAT or ACT required. SAT 25/75 percentile: 950-1150. High school rank: N/A
Early decision deadline: N/A, notification date: N/A
Early action deadline: N/A, notification date: N/A
Application deadline (fall): 8/15
Undergraduate student body: 3,591 full time, 938 part time; 31% male, 69% female; 1% American Indian, 3% Asian, 10% black, 12% Hispanic, 1% multiracial, 0% Pacific Islander, 59% white, 5% international; 99% from in state; 1% live on campus; 1% of students in fraternities, 4% in sororities
Most popular majors: 5% Accounting, 9% Business Administration and Management, General, 7% Psychology, General, 7% Rhetoric and Composition, 25% Special Education and Teaching, General

Expenses: 2014-2015: $22,835; room/board: N/A
Financial aid: (718) 636-6808; 77% of undergrads determined to have financial need; average aid package $11,353

St. Lawrence University

Canton NY
(315) 229-5261
U.S. News ranking: Nat. Lib. Arts, No. 56
Website: www.stlawu.edu
Admissions email: admissions@stlawu.edu
Private; founded 1856
Freshman admissions: more selective; 2013-2014: 4,424 applied, 2,054 accepted. Neither SAT nor ACT required. SAT 25/75 percentile: 1120-1310. High school rank: 34% in top tenth, 71% in top quarter, 95% in top half
Early decision deadline: 11/1, notification date: N/A
Early action deadline: N/A, notification date: N/A
Application deadline (fall): 2/1
Undergraduate student body: 2,397 full time, 17 part time; 45% male, 55% female; 0% American Indian, 2% Asian, 3% black, 4% Hispanic, 2% multiracial, 0% Pacific Islander, 80% white, 8% international; 43% from in state; 98% live on campus; 8% of students in fraternities, 18% in sororities
Most popular majors: 13% Biological and Biomedical Sciences, 6% Communication, Journalism, and Related Programs, 11% Psychology, 31% Social Sciences, 6% Visual and Performing Arts
Expenses: 2014-2015: $47,696; room/board: $12,286
Financial aid: (315) 229-5265; 60% of undergrads determined to have financial need; average aid package $41,005

Stony Brook University–SUNY

Stony Brook NY
(631) 632-6868
U.S. News ranking: Nat. U., No. 88
Website: www.stonybrook.edu
Admissions email: enroll@stonybrook.edu
Public; founded 1957
Freshman admissions: more selective; 2013-2014: 30,300 applied, 11,963 accepted. Either SAT or ACT required. SAT 25/75 percentile: 1150-1350. High school rank: 47% in top tenth, 78% in top quarter, 96% in top half
Early decision deadline: N/A, notification date: N/A
Early action deadline: N/A, notification date: N/A
Application deadline (fall): rolling
Undergraduate student body: 14,892 full time, 1,100 part time; 54% male, 46% female; 0% American Indian, 24% Asian, 6% black, 10% Hispanic, 2% multiracial, 0% Pacific Islander, 38% white, 10% international; 91% from in state; 60% live on campus; 4% of students in fraternities, 3% in sororities

Most popular majors: 4% Applied Mathematics, General, 10% Biology/Biological Sciences, General, 9% Business Administration and Management, General, 10% Health Professions and Related Clinical Sciences, Other, 12% Psychology, General
Expenses: 2014-2015: $8,430 in state, $21,850 out of state; room/board: $11,538
Financial aid: (631) 632-6840; 59% of undergrads determined to have financial need; average aid package $13,093

St. Thomas Aquinas College

Sparkill NY
(845) 398-4100
U.S. News ranking: Reg. U. (N), No. 125
Website: www.stac.edu
Admissions email: admissions@stac.edu
Private; founded 1952
Freshman admissions: less selective; 2013-2014: 1,841 applied, 1,514 accepted. Either SAT or ACT required. SAT 25/75 percentile: 830-1050. High school rank: 11% in top tenth, 30% in top quarter, 60% in top half
Early decision deadline: 12/15, notification date: 3/1
Early action deadline: N/A, notification date: N/A
Application deadline (fall): rolling
Undergraduate student body: 1,259 full time, 542 part time; 47% male, 53% female; 0% American Indian, 3% Asian, 8% black, 19% Hispanic, 2% multiracial, 0% Pacific Islander, 56% white, 2% international
Most popular majors: 10% Business Administration and Management, General, 12% Criminal Justice/Law Enforcement Administration, 9% Education/Teaching of Individuals in Early Childhood Special Education Programs, 11% Psychology, General, 10% Sociology
Expenses: 2014-2015: $27,630; room/board: $11,680
Financial aid: (845) 398-4097; 76% of undergrads determined to have financial need; average aid package $20,600

SUNY Buffalo State

Buffalo NY
(716) 878-4017
U.S. News ranking: Reg. U. (N), No. 106
Website: www.buffalostate.edu
Admissions email: admissions@buffalostate.edu
Public; founded 1871
Freshman admissions: less selective; 2013-2014: 11,251 applied, 5,463 accepted. SAT or ACT required. SAT 25/75 percentile: 890-1060. High school rank: 3% in top tenth, 32% in top quarter, 74% in top half
Early decision deadline: 11/15, notification date: 12/15
Early action deadline: N/A, notification date: N/A
Undergraduate student body: 8,293 full time, 1,062 part time; 43% male, 57% female; 0% American Indian, 2% Asian, 21% black, 9% Hispanic, 3% multiracial, 0% Pacific Islander, 63% white,

1% international; 99% from in state; 26% live on campus; 1% of students in fraternities, 1% in sororities
Most popular majors: 13% Business, Management, Marketing, and Related Support Services, 7% Communication, Journalism, and Related Programs, 21% Education, 8% Homeland Security, Law Enforcement, Firefighting and Related Protective Services, 8% Social Sciences
Expenses: 2014-2015: $7,347 in state, $16,997 out of state; room/board: $11,964
Financial aid: (716) 878-4901; 87% of undergrads determined to have financial need; average aid package $9,232

SUNY College–Cortland

Cortland NY
(607) 753-4711
U.S. News ranking: Reg. U. (N), No. 70
Website: www.cortland.edu/admissions
Admissions email: admissions@cortland.edu
Public; founded 1868
Freshman admissions: selective; 2013-2014: 11,518 applied, 5,394 accepted. Neither SAT nor ACT required. SAT 25/75 percentile: 980-1130. High school rank: N/A
Early decision deadline: N/A, notification date: N/A
Early action deadline: 11/15, notification date: 1/1
Application deadline (fall): rolling
Undergraduate student body: 6,281 full time, 119 part time; 44% male, 56% female; 0% American Indian, 1% Asian, 4% black, 10% Hispanic, 2% multiracial, 0% Pacific Islander, 71% white, 1% international; 97% from in state; 53% live on campus; N/A of students in fraternities, N/A in sororities
Most popular majors: 6% Communication, Journalism, and Related Programs, 36% Education, 8% Health Professions and Related Programs, 15% Parks, Recreation, Leisure, and Fitness Studies, 9% Social Sciences
Expenses: 2014-2015: $7,327 in state, $16,777 out of state; room/board: $11,790
Financial aid: (607) 753-4717

SUNY College of Agriculture and Technology–Cobleskill

Cobleskill NY
(518) 255-5525
U.S. News ranking: Reg. Coll. (N), No. 28
Website: www.cobleskill.edu
Admissions email: admissionsoffice@cobleskill.edu
Public; founded 1911
Freshman admissions: less selective; 2013-2014: 2,765 applied, 2,021 accepted. Neither SAT nor ACT required. SAT 25/75 percentile: 760-1000. High school rank: 6% in top tenth, 22% in top quarter, 56% in top half
Early decision deadline: N/A, notification date: N/A

Early action deadline: N/A, notification date: N/A
Application deadline (fall): rolling
Undergraduate student body: 2,321 full time, 149 part time; 48% male, 52% female; 0% American Indian, 1% Asian, 12% black, 7% Hispanic, 0% multiracial, 0% Pacific Islander, 74% white, 1% international; 90% from in state; 57% live on campus; 0% of students in fraternities, 0% in sororities
Most popular majors: 43% Agriculture, Agriculture Operations, and Related Sciences, 15% Business, Management, Marketing, and Related Support Services, 5% Communication, Journalism, and Related Programs, 6% Computer and Information Sciences and Support Services, 13% Natural Resources and Conservation
Expenses: 2014-2015: $7,609 in state, $17,259 out of state; room/board: $12,140
Financial aid: (518) 255-5623; 76% of undergrads determined to have financial need; average aid package $7,894

SUNY College of Environmental Science and Forestry

Syracuse NY
(315) 470-6600
U.S. News ranking: Nat. U., No. 76
Website: www.esf.edu
Admissions email: esfinfo@esf.edu
Public; founded 1911
Freshman admissions: more selective; 2013-2014: 1,538 applied, 777 accepted. Either SAT or ACT required. SAT 25/75 percentile: 1080-1260. High school rank: 27% in top tenth, 66% in top quarter, 95% in top half
Early decision deadline: 12/1, notification date: 1/15
Early action deadline: N/A, notification date: N/A
Application deadline (fall): rolling
Undergraduate student body: 1,640 full time, 158 part time; 57% male, 43% female; 0% American Indian, 3% Asian, 1% black, 3% Hispanic, 3% multiracial, 0% Pacific Islander, 87% white, 2% international; 81% from in state; 35% live on campus; 5% of students in fraternities, 5% in sororities
Most popular majors: 19% Engineering, General, 37% Environmental Biology, 22% Environmental Science, 9% Landscape Architecture, 11% Natural Resources Management and Policy
Expenses: 2014-2015: $7,303 in state, $16,953 out of state; room/board: $14,610
Financial aid: (315) 470-6706; 67% of undergrads determined to have financial need; average aid package $14,000

SUNY College of Technology–Alfred

Alfred NY
(800) 425-3733
U.S. News ranking: Reg. Coll. (N), No. 22
Website: www.alfredstate.edu/alfred/Default.asp
Admissions email: admissions@alfredstate.edu
Public; founded 1908
Freshman admissions: least selective; 2013-2014: 5,761 applied, 3,165 accepted. Neither SAT nor ACT required. SAT 25/75 percentile: 840-1070. High school rank: N/A
Early decision deadline: N/A, notification date: N/A
Early action deadline: N/A, notification date: N/A
Application deadline (fall): rolling
Undergraduate student body: 3,216 full time, 333 part time; 60% male, 40% female; 0% American Indian, 2% Asian, 9% black, 6% Hispanic, 2% multiracial, 0% Pacific Islander, 77% white, 0% international; 94% from in state; 68% live on campus; 3% of students in fraternities, 3% in sororities
Most popular majors: Information not available
Expenses: 2014-2015: $7,646 in state, $17,296 out of state; room/board: $11,944
Financial aid: (607) 587-4251; 82% of undergrads determined to have financial need; average aid package $10,914

SUNY College of Technology–Canton

Canton NY
(800) 388-7123
U.S. News ranking: Reg. Coll. (N), second tier
Website: www.canton.edu/
Admissions email: admissions@canton.edu
Public; founded 1906
Freshman admissions: less selective; 2013-2014: 3,438 applied, 2,698 accepted. Neither SAT nor ACT required. SAT 25/75 percentile: 820-1020. High school rank: 4% in top tenth, 15% in top quarter, 50% in top half
Early decision deadline: N/A, notification date: N/A
Early action deadline: N/A, notification date: N/A
Application deadline (fall): 7/1
Undergraduate student body: 2,938 full time, 612 part time; 45% male, 55% female; 1% American Indian, 1% Asian, 14% black, 8% Hispanic, 1% multiracial, 0% Pacific Islander, 68% white, 2% international; 97% from in state; 36% live on campus; N/A of students in fraternities, N/A in sororities
Most popular majors: 23% Business, Management, Marketing, and Related Support Services, Other, 25% Criminal Justice/Law Enforcement Administration, 7% Engineering Technologies and Engineering-Related Fields, Other, 17% Health/Health Care Administration/Management, 8% Legal Assistant/Paralegal
Expenses: 2013-2014: $7,129 in state, $16,969 out of state; room/board: $10,540
Financial aid: (315) 386-7616

SUNY College of Technology–Delhi

Delhi NY
(607) 746-4550
U.S. News ranking: Reg. Coll. (N), No. 33
Website: www.delhi.edu/
Admissions email: enroll@delhi.edu
Public; founded 1913
Freshman admissions: less selective; 2013-2014: 4,846 applied, 2,843 accepted. Neither SAT nor ACT required. SAT 25/75 percentile: 808-983. High school rank: 3% in top tenth, 14% in top quarter, 42% in top half
Early decision deadline: N/A, notification date: N/A
Early action deadline: N/A, notification date: N/A
Application deadline (fall): rolling
Undergraduate student body: 2,627 full time, 799 part time; 46% male, 54% female; 1% American Indian, 2% Asian, 16% black, 12% Hispanic, 0% multiracial, 0% Pacific Islander, 64% white, 1% international; 97% from in state; 60% live on campus; N/A of students in fraternities, N/A in sororities
Most popular majors: 6% Architectural and Building Sciences/Technology, 15% Business Administration and Management, General, 15% Business, Management, Marketing, and Related Support Services, Other, 28% Hospitality Administration/Management, General, 26% Registered Nursing/Registered Nurse
Expenses: 2014-2015: $7,740 in state, $17,390 out of state; room/board: $10,970
Financial aid: (607) 746-4570; 96% of undergrads determined to have financial need

SUNY College–Old Westbury

Old Westbury NY
(516) 876-3073
U.S. News ranking: Nat. Lib. Arts, second tier
Website: www.oldwestbury.edu
Admissions email: enroll@oldwestbury.edu
Public; founded 1965
Freshman admissions: selective; 2013-2014: 3,341 applied, 1,939 accepted. Either SAT or ACT required. SAT 25/75 percentile: 920-1080. High school rank: N/A
Early decision deadline: N/A, notification date: N/A
Early action deadline: N/A, notification date: N/A
Application deadline (fall): rolling
Undergraduate student body: 3,556 full time, 602 part time; 42% male, 58% female; 0% American Indian, 9% Asian, 31% black, 21% Hispanic, 3% multiracial, 0% Pacific Islander, 32% white, 0% international; 98% from in state; 21% live on campus; 2% of students in fraternities, 2% in sororities
Most popular majors: 12% Accounting, 7% Criminology, 16% Psychology, General, 8% Social Sciences, Other, 9% Speech Communication and Rhetoric
Expenses: 2014-2015: $8,436 in state, $18,086 out of state; room/board: $10,390

Financial aid: (516) 876-3222; 81% of undergrads determined to have financial need; average aid package $9,420

SUNY College–Oneonta

Oneonta NY
(607) 436-2524
U.S. News ranking: Reg. U. (N), No. 41
Website: www.oneonta.edu
Admissions email: admissions@oneonta.edu
Public; founded 1889
Freshman admissions: selective; 2013-2014: 12,360 applied, 5,319 accepted. Either SAT or ACT required. SAT 25/75 percentile: 1020-1180. High school rank: 21% in top tenth, 58% in top quarter, 92% in top half
Early decision deadline: N/A, notification date: N/A
Early action deadline: 11/15, notification date: 12/1
Application deadline (fall): rolling
Undergraduate student body: 5,688 full time, 132 part time; 40% male, 60% female; 0% American Indian, 2% Asian, 3% black, 9% Hispanic, 0% multiracial, 0% Pacific Islander, 82% white, 1% international; 99% from in state; 50% live on campus; 1% of students in fraternities, 1% in sororities
Most popular majors: 7% Business, Management, Marketing, and Related Support Services, 18% Education, 16% Family and Consumer Sciences/Human Sciences, 9% Psychology, 11% Visual and Performing Arts
Expenses: 2014-2015: $7,220 in state, $16,670 out of state; room/board: $11,100
Financial aid: (607) 436-2532; 59% of undergrads determined to have financial need; average aid package $9,155

SUNY College–Potsdam

Potsdam NY
(315) 267-2180
U.S. News ranking: Reg. U. (N), No. 87
Website: www.potsdam.edu
Admissions email: admissions@potsdam.edu
Public; founded 1816
Freshman admissions: selective; 2013-2014: 4,764 applied, 3,257 accepted. Neither SAT nor ACT required. SAT 25/75 percentile: 930-1170. High school rank: 10% in top tenth, 23% in top quarter, 61% in top half
Early decision deadline: N/A, notification date: N/A
Early action deadline: N/A, notification date: N/A
Application deadline (fall): rolling
Undergraduate student body: 3,596 full time, 111 part time; 43% male, 57% female; 1% American Indian, 1% Asian, 7% black, 8% Hispanic, 3% multiracial, 0% Pacific Islander, 72% white, 1% international; 97% from in state; 61% live on campus; 1% of students in fraternities, 2% in sororities
Most popular majors: 23% Education, 9% English Language and Literature/Letters, 8% Psychology, 9% Social Sciences, 14% Visual and Performing Arts

Expenses: 2014-2015: $7,553 in state, $17,203 out of state; room/board: $11,370
Financial aid: (315) 267-2162; 72% of undergrads determined to have financial need; average aid package $13,626

SUNY Empire State College

Saratoga Springs NY
(518) 587-2100
U.S. News ranking: Reg. U. (N), unranked
Website: www.esc.edu
Admissions email: admissions@esc.edu
Public; founded 1971
Freshman admissions: N/A; 2013-2014: 1,342 applied, 1,100 accepted. Neither SAT nor ACT required. ACT 25/75 percentile: N/A. High school rank: N/A
Early decision deadline: N/A, notification date: N/A
Early action deadline: N/A, notification date: N/A
Application deadline (fall): rolling
Undergraduate student body: 4,231 full time, 6,620 part time; 38% male, 62% female; 1% American Indian, 2% Asian, 17% black, 9% Hispanic, 2% multiracial, 0% Pacific Islander, 66% white, 1% international; 93% from in state; 0% live on campus; 0% of students in fraternities, 0% in sororities
Most popular majors: 38% Business, Management, Marketing, and Related Support Services, 7% English Language and Literature/Letters, 8% Psychology, 25% Public Administration and Social Service Professions
Expenses: 2013-2014: $6,315 in state, $15,765 out of state; room/board: N/A
Financial aid: (518) 587-2100

SUNY–Fredonia

Fredonia NY
(800) 252-1212
U.S. News ranking: Reg. U. (N), No. 41
Website: www.fredonia.edu
Admissions email: admissions.office@fredonia.edu
Public; founded 1826
Freshman admissions: selective; 2013-2014: 6,040 applied, 3,156 accepted. Either SAT or ACT required. SAT 25/75 percentile: 950-1140. High school rank: 12% in top tenth, 39% in top quarter, 81% in top half
Early decision deadline: 11/1, notification date: 12/1
Early action deadline: N/A, notification date: N/A
Application deadline (fall): rolling
Undergraduate student body: 4,958 full time, 145 part time; 45% male, 55% female; 0% American Indian, 1% Asian, 4% black, 5% Hispanic, 2% multiracial, 0% Pacific Islander, 81% white, 3% international; 98% from in state; 44% live on campus; 1% of students in fraternities, 1% in sororities
Most popular majors: 11% Business Administration and Management, General, 5% Education/Teaching of Individuals with Multiple Disabilities, 5% Elementary Education and

Teaching, 5% Music Teacher Education, 5% Psychology, General
Expenses: 2014-2015: $7,700 in state, $16,850 out of state; room/board: $11,900
Financial aid: (716) 673-3253; 69% of undergrads determined to have financial need; average aid package $10,068

SUNY–Geneseo

Geneseo NY
(585) 245-5571
U.S. News ranking: Reg. U. (N), No. 14
Website: www.geneseo.edu
Admissions email: admissions@geneseo.edu
Public; founded 1871
Freshman admissions: more selective; 2013-2014: 9,069 applied, 4,786 accepted. Either SAT or ACT required. SAT 25/75 percentile: 1178-1360. High school rank: 48% in top tenth, 84% in top quarter, 99% in top half
Early decision deadline: 11/15, notification date: 12/15
Early action deadline: N/A, notification date: N/A
Application deadline (fall): 1/1
Undergraduate student body: 5,386 full time, 118 part time; 42% male, 58% female; 0% American Indian, 7% Asian, 3% black, 6% Hispanic, 2% multiracial, 0% Pacific Islander, 75% white, 2% international; 98% from in state; 55% live on campus; 15% of students in fraternities, 24% in sororities
Most popular majors: 12% Biological and Biomedical Sciences, 11% Business, Management, Marketing, and Related Support Services, 20% Education, 11% Psychology, 15% Social Sciences
Expenses: 2014-2015: $7,774 in state, $17,424 out of state; room/board: $11,518
Financial aid: (585) 245-5731; 48% of undergrads determined to have financial need; average aid package $10,658

SUNY Institute of Technology–Utica/Rome

Utica NY
(315) 792-7500
U.S. News ranking: Reg. U. (N), No. 106
Website: www.sunyit.edu
Admissions email: admissions@sunyit.edu
Public; founded 1966
Freshman admissions: selective; 2013-2014: 1,952 applied, 930 accepted. Either SAT or ACT required. SAT 25/75 percentile: 1010-1160. High school rank: 13% in top tenth, 45% in top quarter, 87% in top half
Early decision deadline: N/A, notification date: N/A
Early action deadline: 11/15, notification date: 12/15
Application deadline (fall): 8/1
Undergraduate student body: 1,424 full time, 383 part time; 59% male, 41% female; 0% American Indian, 3% Asian, 8% black, 5% Hispanic, 0% multiracial, 0% Pacific Islander, 82% white, 1% international; 99% from in

state; 34% live on campus; N/A of students in fraternities, N/A in sororities
Most popular majors: 18% Business Administration and Management, General, 7% Health Information/Medical Records Administration/Administrator, 8% Mechanical Engineering/Mechanical Technology/Technician, 9% Psychology, General, 10% Registered Nursing/Registered Nurse
Expenses: 2014-2015: $7,530 in state, $17,155 out of state; room/board: $12,250
Financial aid: (315) 792-7210; 65% of undergrads determined to have financial need; average aid package $8,816

SUNY Maritime College

Throggs Neck NY
(718) 409-7221
U.S. News ranking: Reg. Coll. (N), No. 20
Website: www.sunymaritime.edu
Admissions email: admissions@sunymaritime.edu
Public; founded 1874
Freshman admissions: selective; 2013-2014: 1,279 applied, 818 accepted. Either SAT or ACT required. SAT 25/75 percentile: 930-1170. High school rank: 7% in top tenth, 30% in top quarter, 73% in top half
Early decision deadline: 11/1, notification date: 12/20
Early action deadline: N/A, notification date: N/A
Application deadline (fall): 1/31
Undergraduate student body: 1,518 full time, 83 part time; 89% male, 11% female; 0% American Indian, 4% Asian, 4% black, 9% Hispanic, 0% multiracial, 0% Pacific Islander, 72% white, 3% international; 76% from in state; 84% live on campus; 0% of students in fraternities, 0% in sororities
Most popular majors: 20% Business, Management, Marketing, and Related Support Services, Other, 34% Hospitality Administration/Management, 7% Industrial Engineering, 9% Mechanical Engineering, 20% Naval Architecture and Marine Engineering
Expenses: 2014-2015: $7,446 in state, $17,096 out of state; room/board: $11,040
Financial aid: (718) 409-7254; 36% of undergrads determined to have financial need

SUNY–New Paltz

New Paltz NY
(845) 257-3200
U.S. News ranking: Reg. U. (N), No. 25
Website: www.newpaltz.edu
Admissions email: admissions@newpaltz.edu
Public; founded 1828
Freshman admissions: more selective; 2013-2014: 13,541 applied, 5,899 accepted. Either SAT or ACT required. SAT 25/75 percentile: 1030-1220. High school rank: 38% in top tenth, 70% in top quarter, 92% in top half
Early decision deadline: N/A, notification date: N/A

Early action deadline: 11/15, notification date: 12/15
Application deadline (fall): 4/1
Undergraduate student body: 6,060 full time, 510 part time; 37% male, 63% female; 0% American Indian, 5% Asian, 5% black, 14% Hispanic, 2% multiracial, 0% Pacific Islander, 66% white, 2% international; 97% from in state; 43% live on campus; 4% of students in fraternities, 4% in sororities
Most popular majors: 12% Business, Management, Marketing, and Related Support Services, 10% Communication, Journalism, and Related Programs, 17% Education, 12% Social Sciences, 12% Visual and Performing Arts
Expenses: 2014-2015: $7,408 in state, $17,058 out of state; room/board: $10,895
Financial aid: (845) 257-3250; 56% of undergrads determined to have financial need; average aid package $9,904

SUNY–Oswego

Oswego NY
(315) 312-2250
U.S. News ranking: Reg. U. (N), No. 56
Website: www.oswego.edu
Admissions email: admiss@oswego.edu
Public; founded 1861
Freshman admissions: selective; 2013-2014: 10,351 applied, 5,034 accepted. Either SAT or ACT required. SAT 25/75 percentile: 1040-1180. High school rank: 15% in top tenth, 55% in top quarter, 87% in top half
Early decision deadline: 11/30, notification date: 12/15
Early action deadline: N/A, notification date: N/A
Application deadline (fall): rolling
Undergraduate student body: 6,954 full time, 374 part time; 48% male, 52% female; 0% American Indian, 2% Asian, 6% black, 9% Hispanic, 2% multiracial, 0% Pacific Islander, 79% white, 2% international; 98% from in state; 58% live on campus; 7% of students in fraternities, 6% in sororities
Most popular majors: 22% Business, Management, Marketing, and Related Support Services, 11% Communication, Journalism, and Related Programs, 19% Education, 10% Psychology, 8% Visual and Performing Arts
Expenses: 2014-2015: $7,501 in state, $17,151 out of state; room/board: $12,690
Financial aid: (315) 312-2248; 66% of undergrads determined to have financial need; average aid package $9,973

SUNY–Plattsburgh

Plattsburgh NY
(888) 673-0012
U.S. News ranking: Reg. U. (N), No. 74
Website: www.plattsburgh.edu
Admissions email: admissions@plattsburgh.edu
Public; founded 1889
Freshman admissions: selective; 2013-2014: 8,193 applied, 3,739 accepted. Either SAT or ACT required. SAT 25/75 percentile: 930-1120. High

school rank: 12% in top tenth, 45% in top quarter, 85% in top half
Early decision deadline: N/A, notification date: N/A
Early action deadline: N/A, notification date: N/A
Application deadline (fall): rolling
Undergraduate student body: 5,186 full time, 453 part time; 44% male, 56% female; 0% American Indian, 2% Asian, 6% black, 8% Hispanic, 2% multiracial, 0% Pacific Islander, 71% white, 6% international; 96% from in state; 44% live on campus; 6% of students in fraternities, 5% in sororities
Most popular majors: 22% Business, Management, Marketing, and Related Support Services, 10% Communication, Journalism, and Related Programs, 10% Education, 9% Homeland Security, Law Enforcement, Firefighting and Related Protective Services, 7% Psychology
Expenses: 2014-2015: $7,497 in state, $17,147 out of state; room/board: $10,972
Financial aid: (518) 564-4061; 65% of undergrads determined to have financial need; average aid package $12,391

Syracuse University

Syracuse NY
(315) 443-3611
U.S. News ranking: Nat. U., No. 58
Website: syr.edu
Admissions email: orange@syr.edu
Private; founded 1870
Freshman admissions: more selective; 2013-2014: 28,269 applied, 13,990 accepted. Either SAT or ACT required. SAT 25/75 percentile: 1040-1270. High school rank: 39% in top tenth, 71% in top quarter, 94% in top half
Early decision deadline: 11/15, notification date: 1/1
Early action deadline: N/A, notification date: N/A
Application deadline (fall): 1/1
Undergraduate student body: 14,422 full time, 675 part time; 45% male, 55% female; 1% American Indian, 8% Asian, 9% black, 11% Hispanic, 3% multiracial, 0% Pacific Islander, 56% white, 9% international; 44% from in state; 75% live on campus; 22% of students in fraternities, 27% in sororities
Most popular majors: 16% Business, Management, Marketing, and Related Support Services, 13% Communication, Journalism, and Related Programs, 8% Engineering, 12% Social Sciences, 11% Visual and Performing Arts
Expenses: 2014-2015: $41,886; room/board: $14,460
Financial aid: (315) 443-1513; 58% of undergrads determined to have financial need; average aid package $32,540

Touro College

New York NY
(212) 436-0400
U.S. News ranking: Reg. U. (N), second tier
Website: www.touro.edu/
Admissions email: lasadmit@touro.edu
Private; founded 1971

Freshman admissions: selective; 2013-2014: 1,220 applied, 793 accepted. Neither SAT nor ACT required. SAT 25/75 percentile: 1040-1260. High school rank: N/A
Early decision deadline: N/A, notification date: N/A
Early action deadline: N/A, notification date: N/A
Application deadline (fall): rolling
Undergraduate student body: 5,118 full time, 1,687 part time; 31% male, 69% female; 0% American Indian, 3% Asian, 14% black, 9% Hispanic, 0% multiracial, 0% Pacific Islander, 64% white, 3% international
Most popular majors: 13% Accounting, 12% Biology/Biological Sciences, General, 6% Business Administration and Management, General, 33% Psychology, General, 5% Speech Communication and Rhetoric
Expenses: 2014-2015: $15,600; room/board: $12,359
Financial aid: (718) 252-7800; 75% of undergrads determined to have financial need; average aid package $8,612

Union College

Schenectady NY
(888) 843-6688
U.S. News ranking: Nat. Lib. Arts, No. 41
Website: www.union.edu
Admissions email: admissions@union.edu
Private; founded 1795
Freshman admissions: more selective; 2013-2014: 5,725 applied, 2,134 accepted. Neither SAT nor ACT required. SAT 25/75 percentile: 1220-1400. High school rank: 64% in top tenth, 84% in top quarter, 97% in top half
Early decision deadline: 11/15, notification date: 12/15
Early action deadline: N/A, notification date: N/A
Application deadline (fall): 1/15
Undergraduate student body: 2,225 full time, 21 part time; 54% male, 46% female; 0% American Indian, 6% Asian, 4% black, 7% Hispanic, 2% multiracial, 0% Pacific Islander, 75% white, 6% international; 38% from in state; 86% live on campus; 39% of students in fraternities, 39% in sororities
Most popular majors: 7% Biology/Biological Sciences, General, 11% Economics, General, 6% History, General, 6% Mechanical Engineering, 13% Psychology, General
Expenses: 2014-2015: $48,384; room/board: $11,856
Financial aid: (518) 388-6123; 47% of undergrads determined to have financial need; average aid package $36,845

United States Merchant Marine Academy

Kings Point NY
(516) 773-5391
U.S. News ranking: Reg. Coll. (N), No. 3
Website: www.usmma.edu
Admissions email: admissions@usmma.edu
Public; founded 1943

Freshman admissions: more selective; 2013-2014: 2,252 applied, 409 accepted. Either SAT or ACT required. SAT 25/75 percentile: 1183-1351. High school rank: 33% in top tenth, 57% in top quarter, 92% in top half
Early decision deadline: N/A, notification date: N/A
Early action deadline: N/A, notification date: N/A
Application deadline (fall): 3/1
Undergraduate student body: 958 full time, 0 part time; 85% male, 15% female; 1% American Indian, 6% Asian, 3% black, 9% Hispanic, 0% multiracial, 0% Pacific Islander, 79% white, 1% international; N/A from in state; 100% live on campus; N/A of students in fraternities, N/A in sororities
Most popular majors: 22% Logistics, Materials, and Supply Chain Management, 15% Marine Science/Merchant Marine Officer, 22% Marine Transportation, Other, 18% Naval Architecture and Marine Engineering, 23% Naval Architecture and Marine Engineering
Expenses: 2014-2015: $1,032 in state, $1,032 out of state; room/board: $0
Financial aid: (516) 773-5295; 100% of undergrads determined to have financial need; average aid package $4,082

United States Military Academy

West Point NY
(845) 938-4041
U.S. News ranking: Nat. Lib. Arts, No. 24
Website: www.usma.edu
Admissions email: admissions@usma.edu
Public; founded 1802
Freshman admissions: more selective; 2013-2014: 15,408 applied, 1,380 accepted. Either SAT or ACT required. SAT 25/75 percentile: 1180-1385. High school rank: 46% in top tenth, 74% in top quarter, 94% in top half
Early decision deadline: N/A, notification date: N/A
Early action deadline: N/A, notification date: N/A
Application deadline (fall): 2/28
Undergraduate student body: 4,591 full time, 0 part time; 83% male, 17% female; 1% American Indian, 6% Asian, 8% black, 10% Hispanic, 4% multiracial, 1% Pacific Islander, 69% white, 1% international; 7% from in state; 100% live on campus; 0% of students in fraternities, 0% in sororities
Most popular majors: 7% Business, Management, Marketing, and Related Support Services, 23% Engineering, 5% Engineering Technologies and Engineering-Related Fields, 8% Foreign Languages, Literatures, and Linguistics, 19% Social Sciences
Expenses: N/A
Financial aid: (845) 938-4262; 0% of undergrads determined to have financial need; average aid package $0

University at Albany–SUNY

Albany NY
(518) 442-5435
U.S. News ranking: Nat. U., No. 126
Website: www.albany.edu
Admissions email: ugadmissions@albany.edu
Public; founded 1844
Freshman admissions: selective; 2013-2014: 21,591 applied, 12,028 accepted. Either SAT or ACT required. SAT 25/75 percentile: 1010-1180. High school rank: 19% in top tenth, 53% in top quarter, 88% in top half
Early decision deadline: N/A, notification date: N/A
Early action deadline: 11/15, notification date: 1/15
Application deadline (fall): 3/1
Undergraduate student body: 12,055 full time, 767 part time; 52% male, 48% female; 0% American Indian, 8% Asian, 14% black, 13% Hispanic, 3% multiracial, 0% Pacific Islander, 53% white, 5% international; 94% from in state; 59% live on campus; 1% of students in fraternities, 2% in sororities
Most popular majors: 10% Biological and Biomedical Sciences, 10% Business, Management, Marketing, and Related Support Services, 13% English Language and Literature/Letters, 11% Psychology, 27% Social Sciences
Expenses: 2014-2015: $8,527 in state, $20,167 out of state; room/board: $11,986
Financial aid: (518) 442-5757; 64% of undergrads determined to have financial need; average aid package $10,279

University at Buffalo–SUNY

Buffalo NY
(716) 645-6900
U.S. News ranking: Nat. U., No. 103
Website: www.buffalo.edu
Admissions email: ub-admissions@buffalo.edu
Public; founded 1846
Freshman admissions: more selective; 2013-2014: 23,207 applied, 13,134 accepted. Either SAT or ACT required. SAT 25/75 percentile: 1050-1260. High school rank: 28% in top tenth, 63% in top quarter, 93% in top half
Early decision deadline: 11/1, notification date: 12/15
Early action deadline: N/A, notification date: N/A
Application deadline (fall): rolling
Undergraduate student body: 18,091 full time, 1,740 part time; 54% male, 46% female; 0% American Indian, 13% Asian, 7% black, 7% Hispanic, 2% multiracial, 0% Pacific Islander, 50% white, 16% international; 96% from in state; 35% live on campus; 2% of students in fraternities, 2% in sororities
Most popular majors: 9% Biological and Biomedical Sciences, 17% Business, Management, Marketing, and Related Support Services, 13% Engineering, 12% Psychology, 15% Social Sciences

Expenses: 2014-2015: $8,426 in state, $20,366 out of state; room/board: $12,200
Financial aid: (866) 838-7257; 68% of undergrads determined to have financial need; average aid package $9,395

University of Rochester

Rochester NY
(585) 275-3221
U.S. News ranking: Nat. U., No. 33
Website: www.rochester.edu
Admissions email: admit@admissions.rochester.edu
Private; founded 1850
Freshman admissions: most selective; 2013-2014: 17,244 applied, 6,153 accepted. Neither SAT nor ACT required. SAT 25/75 percentile: 1250-1450. High school rank: 75% in top tenth, 97% in top quarter, 100% in top half
Early decision deadline: 11/1, notification date: 12/15
Early action deadline: N/A, notification date: N/A
Application deadline (fall): 1/1
Undergraduate student body: 5,837 full time, 340 part time; 48% male, 52% female; 0% American Indian, 11% Asian, 5% black, 6% Hispanic, 3% multiracial, 0% Pacific Islander, 52% white, 16% international; 42% from in state; 93% live on campus; 20% of students in fraternities, 23% in sororities
Most popular majors: 13% Biological and Biomedical Sciences, 11% Engineering, 10% Health Professions and Related Programs, 13% Psychology, 20% Social Sciences
Expenses: 2014-2015: $46,960; room/board: $13,708
Financial aid: (585) 275-3226; 52% of undergrads determined to have financial need; average aid package $38,021

Utica College

Utica NY
(315) 792-3006
U.S. News ranking: Reg. U. (N), No. 120
Website: www.utica.edu
Admissions email: admiss@utica.edu
Private; founded 1946
Freshman admissions: less selective; 2013-2014: 3,689 applied, 3,151 accepted. Neither SAT nor ACT required. SAT 25/75 percentile: 830-1050. High school rank: 11% in top tenth, 28% in top quarter, 60% in top half
Early decision deadline: N/A, notification date: N/A
Early action deadline: N/A, notification date: N/A
Application deadline (fall): rolling
Undergraduate student body: 2,230 full time, 651 part time; 39% male, 61% female; 1% American Indian, 3% Asian, 10% black, 8% Hispanic, 2% multiracial, 0% Pacific Islander, 70% white, 2% international; 85% from in state; 44% live on campus; 2% of students in fraternities, 2% in sororities
Most popular majors: 4% Biological and Biomedical Sciences, 9% Business, Management, Marketing, and Related Support Services, 36% Health Professions

and Related Programs, 21% Homeland Security, Law Enforcement, Firefighting and Related Protective Services, 7% Psychology
Expenses: 2014-2015: $33,736; room/board: $11,934
Financial aid: (315) 792-3179; 91% of undergrads determined to have financial need; average aid package $25,160

Vassar College

Poughkeepsie NY
(845) 437-7300
U.S. News ranking: Nat. Lib. Arts, No. 11
Website: www.vassar.edu
Admissions email: admission@vassar.edu
Private; founded 1861
Freshman admissions: most selective; 2013-2014: 7,597 applied, 1,832 accepted. Either SAT or ACT required. SAT 25/75 percentile: 1310-1480. High school rank: 66% in top tenth, 93% in top quarter, 99% in top half
Early decision deadline: 11/15, notification date: 12/15
Early action deadline: N/A, notification date: N/A
Application deadline (fall): 1/1
Undergraduate student body: 2,437 full time, 40 part time; 44% male, 56% female; 0% American Indian, 10% Asian, 6% black, 11% Hispanic, 6% multiracial, 0% Pacific Islander, 61% white, 6% international; 27% from in state; 95% live on campus; 0% of students in fraternities, 0% in sororities
Most popular majors: 13% Biological and Biomedical Sciences, 6% English Language and Literature/Letters, 9% Psychology, 28% Social Sciences, 13% Visual and Performing Arts
Expenses: 2014-2015: $49,570; room/board: $11,570
Financial aid: (845) 437-5320; 58% of undergrads determined to have financial need; average aid package $46,214

Vaughn College of Aeronautics and Technology

Flushing NY
(718) 429-6600
U.S. News ranking: Reg. Coll. (N), No. 22
Website: www.vaughn.edu
Admissions email: admitme@vaughn.edu
Private; founded 1932
Freshman admissions: less selective; 2013-2014: 837 applied, 645 accepted. SAT required. SAT 25/75 percentile: 885-1093. High school rank: N/A
Early decision deadline: N/A, notification date: N/A
Early action deadline: N/A, notification date: N/A
Application deadline (fall): rolling
Undergraduate student body: 1,308 full time, 417 part time; 88% male, 12% female; 1% American Indian, 10% Asian, 20% black, 35% Hispanic, 6% multiracial, 3% Pacific Islander, 17% white, 2% international; 86% from in state; 10% live on campus; 0% of students in fraternities, 0% in sororities

Most popular majors: 70% Aviation/Airway Management and Operations, 1% Business Administration and Management, General, 13% Electrical and Electronic Engineering Technologies/Technicians, Other, 1% Mechanical Engineering, 12% Mechanical Engineering/Mechanical Technology/Technician
Expenses: 2014-2015: $21,740; room/board: $12,355
Financial aid: (718) 429-6600; 70% of undergrads determined to have financial need; average aid package $22,266

Wagner College

Staten Island NY
(718) 390-3411
U.S. News ranking: Reg. U. (N), No. 28
Website: www.wagner.edu
Admissions email: adm@wagner.edu
Private; founded 1883
Freshman admissions: selective; 2013-2014: 2,942 applied, 2,056 accepted. Neither SAT nor ACT required. SAT 25/75 percentile: 1050-1270. High school rank: 15% in top tenth, 73% in top quarter, 92% in top half
Early decision deadline: 12/1, notification date: 1/2
Early action deadline: N/A, notification date: N/A
Application deadline (fall): 2/15
Undergraduate student body: 1,761 full time, 77 part time; 35% male, 65% female; 0% American Indian, 3% Asian, 6% black, 9% Hispanic, 2% multiracial, 0% Pacific Islander, 66% white, 3% international; 52% from in state; 69% live on campus; 9% of students in fraternities, 15% in sororities
Most popular majors: 16% Business, Management, Marketing, and Related Support Services, 25% Health Professions and Related Programs, 7% Psychology, 7% Social Sciences, 21% Visual and Performing Arts
Expenses: 2014-2015: $40,750; room/board: $12,450
Financial aid: (718) 390-3183; 65% of undergrads determined to have financial need; average aid package $25,502

Webb Institute

Glen Cove NY
(516) 671-8355
U.S. News ranking: Engineering, unranked
Website: www.webb.edu
Admissions email: admissions@webb.edu
Private; founded 1889
Freshman admissions: most selective; 2013-2014: 105 applied, 31 accepted. SAT required. SAT 25/75 percentile: 1360-1510. High school rank: 83% in top tenth, 83% in top quarter, 100% in top half
Early decision deadline: 10/15, notification date: 12/15
Early action deadline: N/A, notification date: N/A
Application deadline (fall): 2/15
Undergraduate student body: 82 full time, N/A part time; 79% male, 21% female; 0% American Indian, 9% Asian, 0% black, 0% Hispanic, 6% multiracial,

0% Pacific Islander, 85% white, 0% international; 27% from in state; 100% live on campus; 0% of students in fraternities, 0% in sororities
Most popular majors: 100% Naval Architecture and Marine Engineering
Expenses: 2014-2015: $44,000; room/board: $14,050
Financial aid: (516) 671-2213; 21% of undergrads determined to have financial need; average aid package $49,015

Wells College

Aurora NY
(800) 952-9355
U.S. News ranking: Nat. Lib. Arts, No. 148
Website: www.wells.edu
Admissions email: admissions@wells.edu
Private
Freshman admissions: selective; 2013-2014: 2,214 applied, 1,321 accepted. Neither SAT nor ACT required. SAT 25/75 percentile: 930-1070. High school rank: 32% in top tenth, 64% in top quarter, 86% in top half
Early decision deadline: N/A, notification date: N/A
Early action deadline: N/A, notification date: N/A
Application deadline (fall): N/A
Undergraduate student body: 524 full time, 10 part time; 34% male, 66% female; 1% American Indian, 2% Asian, 11% black, 8% Hispanic, 3% multiracial, 0% Pacific Islander, 63% white, 4% international
Most popular majors: Information not available
Expenses: 2014-2015: $36,700; room/board: $12,700
Financial aid: (315) 364-3289; 92% of undergrads determined to have financial need; average aid package $31,346

Yeshiva University

New York NY
(212) 960-5277
U.S. News ranking: Nat. U., No. 48
Website: www.yu.edu
Admissions email: yuadmit@ymail.yu.edu
Private; founded 1886
Freshman admissions: more selective; 2013-2014: 1,580 applied, 1,299 accepted. Either SAT or ACT required. SAT 25/75 percentile: 1100-1370. High school rank: 45% in top tenth, 75% in top quarter, 97% in top half
Early decision deadline: 11/1, notification date: 12/15
Early action deadline: N/A, notification date: N/A
Application deadline (fall): 2/1
Undergraduate student body: 2,832 full time, 53 part time; 53% male, 47% female; 0% American Indian, 0% Asian, 0% black, 0% Hispanic, 0% multiracial, 0% Pacific Islander, 92% white, 6% international; 35% from in state; 69% live on campus; 0% of students in fraternities, 0% in sororities
Most popular majors: 10% Accounting, 18% Biology/Biological Sciences, General, 12% Business Administration and Management, General, 15% Psychology, General, 10% Social Sciences, General

Expenses: 2014-2015: $38,730; room/board: $11,250
Financial aid: (212) 960-5399; 58% of undergrads determined to have financial need; average aid package $31,293

NORTH CAROLINA

Appalachian State University

Boone NC
(828) 262-2120
U.S. News ranking: Reg. U. (S), No. 9
Website: www.appstate.edu
Admissions email: admissions@appstate.edu
Public; founded 1899
Freshman admissions: selective; 2013-2014: 13,673 applied, 8,992 accepted. Either SAT or ACT required. SAT 25/75 percentile: 1050-1220. High school rank: 21% in top tenth, 58% in top quarter, 92% in top half
Early decision deadline: N/A, notification date: N/A
Early action deadline: N/A, notification date: N/A
Application deadline (fall): 3/15
Undergraduate student body: 15,115 full time, 910 part time; 47% male, 53% female; 0% American Indian, 1% Asian, 3% black, 4% Hispanic, 2% multiracial, 0% Pacific Islander, 86% white, 1% international; 92% from in state; 36% live on campus; 9% of students in fraternities, 13% in sororities
Most popular majors: 20% Business, Management, Marketing, and Related Support Services, 7% Communication, Journalism, and Related Programs, 14% Education, 8% Psychology, 7% Social Sciences
Expenses: 2014-2015: $6,553 in state, $19,720 out of state; room/board: $7,675
Financial aid: (828) 262-2190; 51% of undergrads determined to have financial need; average aid package $10,581

Barton College

Wilson NC
(800) 345-4973
U.S. News ranking: Reg. Coll. (S), No. 25
Website: www.barton.edu
Admissions email: enroll@barton.edu
Private; founded 1902
Affiliation: Christian Church (Disciples of Christ)
Freshman admissions: selective; 2013-2014: 2,933 applied, 1,225 accepted. Either SAT or ACT required. SAT 25/75 percentile: 840-1020. High school rank: 13% in top tenth, 38% in top quarter, 72% in top half
Early decision deadline: N/A, notification date: N/A
Early action deadline: N/A, notification date: N/A
Application deadline (fall): rolling
Undergraduate student body: 900 full time, 157 part time; 31% male, 69% female; 0% American Indian, 1% Asian, 25% black, 4% Hispanic, 3% multiracial, 0% Pacific Islander, 59% white, 3% international; 87% from in state; 38% live on campus; 19% of students in fraternities, 13% in sororities

Most popular majors: 14% Business Administration and Management, General, 6% Elementary Education and Teaching, 6% Liberal Arts and Sciences/Liberal Studies, 8% Registered Nursing/Registered Nurse, 20% Social Work
Expenses: 2014-2015: $26,664; room/board: $8,906
Financial aid: (252) 399-6323; 90% of undergrads determined to have financial need; average aid package $18,922

Belmont Abbey College

Belmont NC
(704) 461-6665
U.S. News ranking: Reg. Coll. (S), No. 37
Website: www.belmontabbeycollege.edu
Admissions email: admissions@bac.edu
Private; founded 1876
Affiliation: Roman Catholic
Freshman admissions: less selective; 2013-2014: 1,976 applied, 1,336 accepted. Neither SAT nor ACT required. SAT 25/75 percentile: 868-1070. High school rank: 8% in top tenth, 26% in top quarter, 60% in top half
Early decision deadline: N/A, notification date: N/A
Early action deadline: N/A, notification date: N/A
Application deadline (fall): 8/1
Undergraduate student body: 1,549 full time, 98 part time; 42% male, 58% female; 0% American Indian, 1% Asian, 27% black, 2% Hispanic, 0% multiracial, 0% Pacific Islander, 37% white, 2% international; 72% from in state; 42% live on campus; 2% of students in fraternities, 3% in sororities
Most popular majors: 10% Accounting, 23% Business Administration and Management, General, 11% Education, General, 9% Elementary Education and Teaching, 8% Liberal Arts and Sciences/Liberal Studies
Expenses: 2014-2015: $18,500; room/board: $10,094
Financial aid: (704) 825-6718; 78% of undergrads determined to have financial need; average aid package $11,718

Bennett College[1]

Greensboro NC
(336) 370-8624
U.S. News ranking: Nat. Lib. Arts, second tier
Website: www.bennett.edu
Admissions email: admiss@bennett.edu
Private; founded 1873
Affiliation: United Methodist
Application deadline (fall): rolling
Undergraduate student body: N/A full time, N/A part time
Expenses: 2013-2014: $17,130; room/board: $7,576
Financial aid: (336) 517-2205

Brevard College

Brevard NC
(828) 884-8300
U.S. News ranking: Nat. Lib. Arts, second tier
Website: www.brevard.edu
Admissions email: admissions@brevard.edu
Private; founded 1853

Affiliation: Methodist
Freshman admissions: less selective; 2013-2014: 2,299 applied, 1,032 accepted. Either SAT or ACT required. SAT 25/75 percentile: 850-1050. High school rank: 5% in top tenth, 24% in top quarter, 57% in top half
Early decision deadline: N/A, notification date: N/A
Early action deadline: N/A, notification date: N/A
Application deadline (fall): rolling
Undergraduate student body: 690 full time, 11 part time; 62% male, 38% female; 1% American Indian, 1% Asian, 10% black, 0% Hispanic, 2% multiracial, 0% Pacific Islander, 75% white, 6% international; 54% from in state; 76% live on campus; 0% of students in fraternities, 0% in sororities
Most popular majors: 15% Business/Commerce, General, 10% Homeland Security, Law Enforcement, Firefighting and Related Protective Services, 21% Parks, Recreation and Leisure Studies, 8% Psychology, General, 14% Visual and Performing Arts
Expenses: 2014-2015: $26,170; room/board: $9,100
Financial aid: (828) 884-8287; 78% of undergrads determined to have financial need; average aid package $10,572

Campbell University
Buies Creek NC
(910) 893-1320
U.S. News ranking: Reg. U. (S), No. 31
Website: www.campbell.edu
Admissions email: adm@ mailcenter.campbell.edu
Private; founded 1887
Affiliation: Baptist
Freshman admissions: selective; 2013-2014: 11,716 applied, 8,180 accepted. Either SAT or ACT required. SAT 25/75 percentile: 820-1290. High school rank: 26% in top tenth, 54% in top quarter, 88% in top half
Early decision deadline: N/A, notification date: N/A
Early action deadline: N/A, notification date: N/A
Application deadline (fall): rolling
Undergraduate student body: 3,537 full time, 928 part time; 50% male, 50% female; 1% American Indian, 2% Asian, 17% black, 6% Hispanic, 2% multiracial, 0% Pacific Islander, 55% white, 2% international; 14% from in state; 34% live on campus; 7% of students in fraternities, 6% in sororities
Most popular majors: 5% Accounting, 12% Business Administration and Management, General, 7% Psychology, General, 10% Science Technologies/ Technicians, Other, 7% Social Sciences, General
Expenses: 2014-2015: $27,530; room/board: $9,860
Financial aid: (910) 893-1310; 78% of undergrads determined to have financial need; average aid package $20,052

Catawba College
Salisbury NC
(800) 228-2922
U.S. News ranking: Reg. Coll. (S), No. 16
Website: www.catawba.edu
Admissions email: admission@ catawba.edu
Private; founded 1851
Affiliation: United Church of Christ
Freshman admissions: selective; 2013-2014: 3,226 applied, 1,309 accepted. Neither SAT nor ACT required. SAT 25/75 percentile: 850-1090. High school rank: 11% in top tenth, 22% in top quarter, 61% in top half
Early decision deadline: N/A, notification date: N/A
Early action deadline: N/A, notification date: N/A
Application deadline (fall): rolling
Undergraduate student body: 1,210 full time, 88 part time; 48% male, 52% female; 1% American Indian, 1% Asian, 21% black, 3% Hispanic, 1% multiracial, 0% Pacific Islander, 70% white, 3% international; 81% from in state; 53% live on campus; 0% of students in fraternities, 0% in sororities
Most popular majors: 29% Business, Management, Marketing, and Related Support Services, 23% Education, 10% Parks, Recreation, Leisure, and Fitness Studies, 6% Social Sciences, 10% Visual and Performing Arts
Expenses: 2014-2015: $27,360; room/board: $9,880
Financial aid: (704) 637-4416; 85% of undergrads determined to have financial need; average aid package $21,343

Chowan University
Murfreesboro NC
(252) 398-1236
U.S. News ranking: Reg. Coll. (S), second tier
Website: www.chowan.edu
Admissions email: admission@ chowan.edu
Private; founded 1848
Affiliation: Baptist
Freshman admissions: least selective; 2013-2014: 3,708 applied, 2,282 accepted. Either SAT or ACT required. SAT 25/75 percentile: 700-870. High school rank: 2% in top tenth, 11% in top quarter, 39% in top half
Early decision deadline: N/A, notification date: N/A
Early action deadline: N/A, notification date: N/A
Application deadline (fall): rolling
Undergraduate student body: 1,285 full time, 76 part time; 47% male, 53% female; 1% American Indian, 0% Asian, 70% black, 3% Hispanic, 4% multiracial, 0% Pacific Islander, 21% white, 1% international; 51% from in state; 81% live on campus; 11% of students in fraternities, 12% in sororities
Most popular majors: 18% Business Administration and Management, General, 12% Criminal Justice/Safety Studies, 9% Elementary Education and Teaching, 11% Health and Physical Education/Fitness, General, 11% Psychology, General
Expenses: 2014-2015: $23,050; room/board: $8,380

Financial aid: (252) 398-1229; 86% of undergrads determined to have financial need; average aid package $21,880

Davidson College
Davidson NC
(800) 768-0380
U.S. News ranking: Nat. Lib. Arts, No. 11
Website: www.davidson.edu
Admissions email: admission@ davidson.edu
Private; founded 1837
Affiliation: Presbyterian Church (USA)
Freshman admissions: more selective; 2013-2014: 4,745 applied, 1,215 accepted. Either SAT or ACT required. SAT 25/75 percentile: 1230-1440. High school rank: 81% in top tenth, 97% in top quarter, 100% in top half
Early decision deadline: 11/15, notification date: 12/15
Early action deadline: N/A, notification date: N/A
Application deadline (fall): 1/2
Undergraduate student body: 1,788 full time, 0 part time; 50% male, 50% female; 1% American Indian, 5% Asian, 7% black, 6% Hispanic, 4% multiracial, 0% Pacific Islander, 69% white, 5% international; 23% from in state; 92% live on campus; 34% of students in fraternities, 1% in sororities
Most popular majors: 10% Biology/ Biological Sciences, General, 11% Economics, General, 10% English Language and Literature, General, 13% Political Science and Government, General, 8% Psychology, General
Expenses: 2014-2015: $45,377; room/board: $12,769
Financial aid: (704) 894-2232; 46% of undergrads determined to have financial need; average aid package $35,646

Duke University
Durham NC
(919) 684-3214
U.S. News ranking: Nat. U., No. 8
Website: www.duke.edu/
Admissions email: N/A
Private; founded 1838
Affiliation: Methodist
Freshman admissions: most selective; 2013-2014: 30,546 applied, 3,801 accepted. Either SAT or ACT required. SAT 25/75 percentile: 1360-1550. High school rank: 90% in top tenth, 98% in top quarter, 100% in top half
Early decision deadline: 11/1, notification date: 12/15
Early action deadline: N/A, notification date: N/A
Application deadline (fall): 1/2
Undergraduate student body: 6,629 full time, 17 part time; 50% male, 50% female; 1% American Indian, 21% Asian, 10% black, 6% Hispanic, 2% multiracial, 0% Pacific Islander, 49% white, 9% international; 12% from in state; 82% live on campus; 29% of students in fraternities, 42% in sororities
Most popular majors: Information not available
Expenses: 2014-2015: $47,488; room/board: $12,576

Financial aid: (919) 684-6225; 45% of undergrads determined to have financial need; average aid package $43,338

East Carolina University
Greenville NC
(252) 328-6640
U.S. News ranking: Nat. U., second tier
Website: www.ecu.edu
Admissions email: admis@ecu.edu
Public; founded 1907
Freshman admissions: selective; 2013-2014: 15,320 applied, 11,238 accepted. Either SAT or ACT required. SAT 25/75 percentile: 960-1170. High school rank: 15% in top tenth, 43% in top quarter, 81% in top half
Early decision deadline: N/A, notification date: N/A
Early action deadline: N/A, notification date: N/A
Application deadline (fall): 3/15
Undergraduate student body: 18,610 full time, 2,898 part time; 40% male, 60% female; 1% American Indian, 3% Asian, 16% black, 5% Hispanic, 3% multiracial, 0% Pacific Islander, 71% white, 0% international; 88% from in state; 28% live on campus; 10% of students in fraternities, 11% in sororities
Most popular majors: 16% Business, Management, Marketing, and Related Support Services, 6% Communication, Journalism, and Related Programs, 13% Education, 7% Engineering Technologies and Engineering-Related Fields, 16% Health Professions and Related Programs
Expenses: 2014-2015: $6,143 in state, $21,340 out of state; room/ board: $8,833
Financial aid: (252) 328-6610; 62% of undergrads determined to have financial need; average aid package $10,534

Elizabeth City State University
Elizabeth City NC
(252) 335-3305
U.S. News ranking: Reg. Coll. (S), No. 29
Website: www.ecsu.edu
Admissions email: admissions@ mail.ecsu.edu
Public; founded 1891
Freshman admissions: least selective; 2013-2014: 3,040 applied, 1,575 accepted. Either SAT or ACT required. SAT 25/75 percentile: 780-945. High school rank: 2% in top tenth, 5% in top quarter, 33% in top half
Early decision deadline: N/A, notification date: N/A
Early action deadline: N/A, notification date: N/A
Application deadline (fall): 6/30
Undergraduate student body: 2,146 full time, 190 part time; 41% male, 59% female; 1% American Indian, 0% Asian, 75% black, 1% Hispanic, 1% multiracial, 0% Pacific Islander, 14% white, 0% international; 89% from in state; 46% live on campus; N/A of students in fraternities, N/A in sororities
Most popular majors: 18% Business, Management, Marketing, and Related Support Services, 19% Education,

7% English Language and Literature/Letters, 12% Homeland Security, Law Enforcement, Firefighting and Related Protective Services, 24% Transportation and Materials Moving
Expenses: 2014-2015: $4,497 in state, $16,172 out of state; room/ board: $7,213
Financial aid: (252) 335-3282; 84% of undergrads determined to have financial need

Elon University
Elon NC
(800) 334-8448
U.S. News ranking: Reg. U. (S), No. 1
Website: www.elon.edu
Admissions email: admissions@ elon.edu
Private; founded 1889
Freshman admissions: more selective; 2013-2014: 9,949 applied, 5,370 accepted. Either SAT or ACT required. SAT 25/75 percentile: 1120-1320. High school rank: 26% in top tenth, 63% in top quarter, 92% in top half
Early decision deadline: 11/1, notification date: 12/1
Early action deadline: 11/10, notification date: 12/20
Application deadline (fall): 1/10
Undergraduate student body: 5,464 full time, 135 part time; 41% male, 59% female; 0% American Indian, 2% Asian, 6% black, 5% Hispanic, 2% multiracial, 0% Pacific Islander, 82% white, 2% international; 22% from in state; 62% live on campus; 23% of students in fraternities, 38% in sororities
Most popular majors: 21% Business/Commerce, General, 19% Communication and Media Studies, 4% International Relations and Affairs, 4% Political Science and Government, General, 7% Psychology, General
Expenses: 2014-2015: $31,247; room/board: $10,667
Financial aid: (336) 278-7640; 35% of undergrads determined to have financial need; average aid package $16,804

Fayetteville State University
Fayetteville NC
(910) 672-1371
U.S. News ranking: Reg. U. (S), second tier
Website: www.uncfsu.edu
Admissions email: admissions@ uncfsu.edu
Public; founded 1867
Freshman admissions: least selective; 2013-2014: 4,106 applied, 2,496 accepted. Either SAT or ACT required. SAT 25/75 percentile: 770-910. High school rank: 4% in top tenth, 17% in top quarter, 52% in top half
Early decision deadline: N/A, notification date: N/A
Early action deadline: N/A, notification date: N/A
Application deadline (fall): 6/30
Undergraduate student body: 3,971 full time, 1,439 part time; 31% male, 69% female; 2% American Indian, 1% Asian, 67% black, 6% Hispanic, 0% multiracial, 0% Pacific Islander, 17% white, 1% international; N/A from in

state; N/A live on campus; 1% of students in fraternities, 1% in sororities
Most popular majors: 13% Business Administration and Management, General, 15% Criminal Justice/Safety Studies, 11% Psychology, General, 7% Registered Nursing/Registered Nurse, 7% Sociology
Expenses: 2014-2015: $5,035 in state, $16,643 out of state; room/board: $6,445
Financial aid: (910) 672-1325; 89% of undergrads determined to have financial need; average aid package $10,559

Gardner-Webb University
Boiling Springs NC
(800) 253-6472
U.S. News ranking: Reg. U. (S), No. 34
Website: www.gardner-webb.edu
Admissions email: admissions@gardner-webb.edu
Private; founded 1905
Affiliation: Baptist
Freshman admissions: selective; 2013-2014: 5,484 applied, 2,642 accepted. Either SAT or ACT required. SAT 25/75 percentile: 900-1120. High school rank: 23% in top tenth, 55% in top quarter, 82% in top half
Early decision deadline: N/A, notification date: N/A
Early action deadline: N/A, notification date: N/A
Application deadline (fall): rolling
Undergraduate student body: 2,088 full time, 471 part time; 35% male, 65% female; 1% American Indian, 1% Asian, 16% black, 2% Hispanic, 0% multiracial, 0% Pacific Islander, 68% white, 2% international; 78% from in state; 48% live on campus; 0% of students in fraternities, 0% in sororities
Most popular majors: 23% Business, Management, Marketing, and Related Support Services, 6% Education, 15% Health Professions and Related Programs, 6% Homeland Security, Law Enforcement, Firefighting and Related Protective Services, 24% Psychology
Expenses: 2014-2015: $27,080; room/board: $8,850
Financial aid: (704) 406-4243; 82% of undergrads determined to have financial need; average aid package $20,596

Greensboro College[1]
Greensboro NC
(336) 272-7102
U.S. News ranking: Reg. Coll. (S), second tier
Website: www.gborocollege.edu
Admissions email: admissions@gborocollege.edu
Private
Application deadline (fall): N/A
Undergraduate student body: N/A full time, N/A part time
Expenses: 2013-2014: $26,306; room/board: $10,420
Financial aid: (336) 272-7102

Guilford College
Greensboro NC
(800) 992-7759
U.S. News ranking: Nat. Lib. Arts, No. 172
Website: www.guilford.edu
Admissions email: admission@guilford.edu
Private; founded 1837
Affiliation: Quaker
Freshman admissions: selective; 2013-2014: 3,030 applied, 2,066 accepted. Neither SAT nor ACT required. SAT 25/75 percentile: 970-1220. High school rank: 11% in top tenth, 33% in top quarter, 69% in top half
Early decision deadline: N/A, notification date: N/A
Early action deadline: 11/15, notification date: 2/15
Application deadline (fall): 8/10
Undergraduate student body: 1,928 full time, 374 part time; 44% male, 56% female; 0% American Indian, 2% Asian, 25% black, 6% Hispanic, 3% multiracial, 0% Pacific Islander, 62% white, 1% international; 55% from in state; 77% live on campus; 0% of students in fraternities, 0% in sororities
Most popular majors: 6% Biological and Biomedical Sciences, 17% Business, Management, Marketing, and Related Support Services, 10% Homeland Security, Law Enforcement, Firefighting and Related Protective Services, 12% Psychology, 9% Social Sciences
Expenses: 2014-2015: $33,430; room/board: $9,370
Financial aid: (336) 316-2165; 92% of undergrads determined to have financial need; average aid package $20,980

High Point University
High Point NC
(800) 345-6993
U.S. News ranking: Reg. Coll. (S), No. 1
Website: www.highpoint.edu
Admissions email: admiss@highpoint.edu
Private; founded 1924
Affiliation: United Methodist
Freshman admissions: selective; 2013-2014: 6,598 applied, 5,569 accepted. Either SAT or ACT required. SAT 25/75 percentile: 980-1170. High school rank: 22% in top tenth, 51% in top quarter, 80% in top half
Early decision deadline: 11/1, notification date: 11/26
Early action deadline: 11/8, notification date: 12/17
Application deadline (fall): 7/1
Undergraduate student body: 3,962 full time, 37 part time; 41% male, 59% female; 1% American Indian, 1% Asian, 6% black, 3% Hispanic, 1% multiracial, 0% Pacific Islander, 84% white, 1% international; 21% from in state; 93% live on campus; 17% of students in fraternities, 47% in sororities
Most popular majors: 30% Business/Commerce, General, 14% Communication, General, 9% Elementary Education and Teaching, 8% Organizational Behavior Studies, 5% Psychology, General
Expenses: 2014-2015: $31,480; room/board: $11,480

Financial aid: (336) 841-9128; 48% of undergrads determined to have financial need; average aid package $14,065

Johnson C. Smith University
Charlotte NC
(704) 378-1010
U.S. News ranking: Nat. Lib. Arts, second tier
Website: www.jcsu.edu
Admissions email: admissions@jcsu.edu
Private; founded 1867
Freshman admissions: less selective; 2013-2014: 4,777 applied, 1,751 accepted. Either SAT or ACT required. SAT 25/75 percentile: 733-920. High school rank: 8% in top tenth, 25% in top quarter, 55% in top half
Early decision deadline: N/A, notification date: N/A
Early action deadline: N/A, notification date: N/A
Application deadline (fall): rolling
Undergraduate student body: 1,324 full time, 63 part time; 41% male, 59% female; 0% American Indian, 0% Asian, 73% black, 6% Hispanic, 2% multiracial, 0% Pacific Islander, 1% white, 4% international; 56% from in state; 61% live on campus; 1% of students in fraternities, 2% in sororities
Most popular majors: 7% Biology/Biological Sciences, General, 22% Business Administration and Management, General, 8% Computer and Information Sciences, General, 9% Criminology, 12% Mass Communication/Media Studies
Expenses: 2014-2015: $18,336; room/board: $7,100
Financial aid: (704) 378-1035; 85% of undergrads determined to have financial need; average aid package $15,003

Lees-McRae College
Banner Elk NC
(828) 898-8723
U.S. News ranking: Reg. Coll. (S), No. 54
Website: www.lmc.edu
Admissions email: admissions@lmc.edu
Private; founded 1900
Affiliation: Presbyterian Church (U.S.A.)
Freshman admissions: less selective; 2013-2014: 1,751 applied, 1,164 accepted. Neither SAT nor ACT required. SAT 25/75 percentile: 840-1060. High school rank: 8% in top tenth, 29% in top quarter, 58% in top half
Early decision deadline: N/A, notification date: N/A
Early action deadline: N/A, notification date: N/A
Application deadline (fall): rolling
Undergraduate student body: 883 full time, 7 part time; 40% male, 60% female; 0% American Indian, 0% Asian, 5% black, 1% Hispanic, 0% multiracial, 0% Pacific Islander, 39% white, 2% international; 71% from in state; 64% live on campus; N/A of students in fraternities, N/A in sororities
Most popular majors: 7% Biological and Biomedical Sciences, 9% Business, Management, Marketing, and Related Support

Services, 19% Education, 25% Health Professions and Related Programs, 19% Social Sciences
Expenses: 2014-2015: $24,150; room/board: $9,810
Financial aid: (828) 898-8793; 80% of undergrads determined to have financial need; average aid package $23,324

Lenoir-Rhyne University
Hickory NC
(828) 328-7300
U.S. News ranking: Reg. Coll. (S), No. 20
Website: www.lr.edu
Admissions email: admission@lr.edu
Private; founded 1891
Affiliation: Evangelical Lutheran Church in America
Freshman admissions: selective; 2013-2014: 4,762 applied, 3,241 accepted. Either SAT or ACT required. SAT 25/75 percentile: 880-1080. High school rank: 15% in top tenth, 44% in top quarter, 82% in top half
Early decision deadline: N/A, notification date: N/A
Early action deadline: 8/15, notification date: N/A
Application deadline (fall): rolling
Undergraduate student body: 1,306 full time, 185 part time; 42% male, 58% female; 1% American Indian, 2% Asian, 15% black, 5% Hispanic, 2% multiracial, 0% Pacific Islander, 68% white, 1% international; 79% from in state; 44% live on campus; 0% of students in fraternities, 3% in sororities
Most popular majors: 16% Business, Management, Marketing, and Related Support Services, 13% Education, 15% Health Professions and Related Programs, 19% Parks, Recreation, Leisure, and Fitness Studies, 9% Psychology
Expenses: 2014-2015: $30,922; room/board: $10,740
Financial aid: (828) 328-7304; 89% of undergrads determined to have financial need; average aid package $24,753

Livingstone College
Salisbury NC
(704) 216-6001
U.S. News ranking: Reg. Coll. (S), second tier
Website: www.livingstone.edu/
Admissions email: admissions@livingstone.edu
Private; founded 1879
Affiliation: African Methodist Episcopal Zion
Freshman admissions: least selective; 2013-2014: 3,110 applied, 2,250 accepted. Either SAT or ACT required. ACT 25/75 percentile: 11-16. High school rank: 2% in top tenth, 6% in top quarter, 25% in top half
Early decision deadline: N/A, notification date: N/A
Early action deadline: N/A, notification date: N/A
Application deadline (fall): rolling
Undergraduate student body: 1,164 full time, 11 part time; 56% male, 44% female; 1% American Indian, 0% Asian, 91% black, 1% Hispanic, 0% multiracial, 0% Pacific Islander, 0% white,

0% international; 65% from in state; 80% live on campus; 30% of students in fraternities, 37% in sororities
Most popular majors: 8% Biology/Biological Sciences, General, 18% Business Administration and Management, General, 15% Criminal Justice/Safety Studies, 11% Psychology, General, 6% Social Work
Expenses: 2014-2015: $16,825; room/board: $6,596
Financial aid: (704) 216-6069; 98% of undergrads determined to have financial need; average aid package $13,835

Mars Hill University
Mars Hill NC
(866) 642-4968
U.S. News ranking: Reg. Coll. (S), No. 37
Website: www.mhc.edu
Admissions email: admissions@mhc.edu
Private; founded 1856
Freshman admissions: less selective; 2013-2014: 2,899 applied, 1,869 accepted. Either SAT or ACT required. SAT 25/75 percentile: 830-1040. High school rank: 8% in top tenth, 26% in top quarter, 59% in top half
Early decision deadline: N/A, notification date: N/A
Early action deadline: N/A, notification date: N/A
Application deadline (fall): rolling
Undergraduate student body: 1,319 full time, 107 part time; 50% male, 50% female; 3% American Indian, 1% Asian, 19% black, 3% Hispanic, 0% multiracial, 0% Pacific Islander, 70% white, 0% international; 75% from in state; 69% live on campus; N/A of students in fraternities, 10% in sororities
Most popular majors: 7% Biology/Biological Sciences, General, 21% Business Administration and Management, General, 21% Elementary Education and Teaching, 12% Social Work, 7% Sociology
Expenses: 2013-2014: $25,636; room/board: $8,548
Financial aid: (828) 689-1103

Meredith College
Raleigh NC
(919) 760-8581
U.S. News ranking: Reg. Coll. (S), No. 6
Website: www.meredith.edu
Admissions email: admissions@meredith.edu
Private; founded 1891
Freshman admissions: selective; 2013-2014: 1,762 applied, 1,098 accepted. Neither SAT nor ACT required. SAT 25/75 percentile: 930-1140. High school rank: 23% in top tenth, 52% in top quarter, 84% in top half
Early decision deadline: 10/30, notification date: 11/15
Early action deadline: N/A, notification date: N/A
Application deadline (fall): rolling
Undergraduate student body: 1,490 full time, 81 part time; 0% male, 100% female; 1% American Indian, 3% Asian, 11% black, 3% Hispanic, 3% multiracial, 0% Pacific Islander, 72% white, 4% international; 91% from in state; 59% live on campus; N/A of students in fraternities, N/A in sororities

Most popular majors: 10% Biology/Biological Sciences, General, 8% Business/Commerce, General, 7% Child Development, 5% Interior Design, 10% Psychology, General
Expenses: 2014-2015: $32,140; room/board: $9,516
Financial aid: (919) 760-8565; 76% of undergrads determined to have financial need; average aid package $22,795

Methodist University[1]
Fayetteville NC
(910) 630-7027
U.S. News ranking: Reg. Coll. (S), No. 62
Website: www.methodist.edu
Admissions email: admissions@methodist.edu
Private
Application deadline (fall): N/A
Undergraduate student body: N/A full time, N/A part time
Expenses: 2013-2014: $27,830; room/board: $10,340
Financial aid: (910) 630-7193

Mid-Atlantic Christian University
Elizabeth City NC
(866) 996-6228
U.S. News ranking: Reg. Coll. (S), unranked
Website: www.macuniversity.edu
Admissions email: admissions@macuniversity.edu
Private
Freshman admissions: N/A; 2013-2014: N/A applied, 74 accepted. Either SAT or ACT required. SAT 25/75 percentile: 778-943. High school rank: 13% in top tenth, 28% in top quarter, 55% in top half
Early decision deadline: N/A, notification date: N/A
Early action deadline: N/A, notification date: N/A
Application deadline (fall): rolling
Undergraduate student body: 129 full time, 32 part time; 47% male, 53% female; 1% American Indian, 1% Asian, 25% black, 4% Hispanic, 0% multiracial, 0% Pacific Islander, 70% white, 0% international; 68% from in state; 62% live on campus; N/A of students in fraternities, N/A in sororities
Most popular majors: 12% Education, 10% Family and Consumer Sciences/Human Sciences, 14% Psychology, 62% Theology and Religious Vocations
Expenses: 2014-2015: $13,105; room/board: $8,100
Financial aid: N/A

Montreat College[1]
Montreat NC
(800) 622-6968
U.S. News ranking: Reg. U. (S), second tier
Website: www.montreat.edu
Admissions email: admissions@montreat.edu
Private
Application deadline (fall): N/A
Undergraduate student body: N/A full time, N/A part time
Expenses: 2013-2014: $23,420; room/board: $7,778
Financial aid: (800) 545-4656

North Carolina A&T State University
Greensboro NC
(336) 334-7946
U.S. News ranking: Nat. U., second tier
Website: www.ncat.edu
Admissions email: uadmit@ncat.edu
Public; founded 1891
Freshman admissions: less selective; 2013-2014: 6,461 applied, 3,651 accepted. Either SAT or ACT required. SAT 25/75 percentile: 830-990. High school rank: 10% in top tenth, 31% in top quarter, 73% in top half
Early decision deadline: N/A, notification date: N/A
Early action deadline: N/A, notification date: N/A
Application deadline (fall): rolling
Undergraduate student body: 8,102 full time, 770 part time; 46% male, 54% female; 0% American Indian, 1% Asian, 87% black, 2% Hispanic, 2% multiracial, 0% Pacific Islander, 4% white, 2% international; 82% from in state; 44% live on campus; 1% of students in fraternities, 1% in sororities
Most popular majors: 10% Business, Management, Marketing, and Related Support Services, 8% Communication, Journalism, and Related Programs, 14% Engineering, 8% Liberal Arts and Sciences, General Studies and Humanities, 10% Psychology
Expenses: 2013-2014: $5,422 in state, $16,503 out of state; room/board: $7,643
Financial aid: (336) 334-7973

North Carolina Central University
Durham NC
(919) 530-6298
U.S. News ranking: Reg. U. (S), No. 65
Website: www.nccu.edu
Admissions email: admissions@nccu.edu
Public; founded 1910
Freshman admissions: less selective; 2013-2014: 7,989 applied, 3,098 accepted. Either SAT or ACT required. SAT 25/75 percentile: 800-950. High school rank: 6% in top tenth, 22% in top quarter, 63% in top half
Early decision deadline: N/A, notification date: N/A
Early action deadline: N/A, notification date: N/A
Application deadline (fall): rolling
Undergraduate student body: 5,297 full time, 923 part time; 33% male, 67% female; 0% American Indian, 1% Asian, 83% black, 3% Hispanic, 3% multiracial, 0% Pacific Islander, 5% white, 1% international; 90% from in state; 43% live on campus; N/A of students in fraternities, N/A in sororities
Most popular majors: 11% Business Administration and Management, General, 11% Criminal Justice/Safety Studies, 11% Family and Consumer Sciences/Human Sciences, General, 6% Psychology, General, 8% Registered Nursing/Registered Nurse
Expenses: 2014-2015: $5,525 in state, $16,940 out of state; room/board: $8,165
Financial aid: (919) 530-6180

North Carolina State University–Raleigh
Raleigh NC
(919) 515-2434
U.S. News ranking: Nat. U., No. 95
Website: www.ncsu.edu
Admissions email: undergrad_admissions@ncsu.edu
Public; founded 1887
Freshman admissions: more selective; 2013-2014: 21,610 applied, 10,128 accepted. Either SAT or ACT required. SAT 25/75 percentile: 1150-1320. High school rank: 50% in top tenth, 80% in top quarter, 99% in top half
Early decision deadline: N/A, notification date: N/A
Early action deadline: 11/1, notification date: 1/30
Application deadline (fall): 1/15
Undergraduate student body: 21,469 full time, 3,067 part time; 56% male, 44% female; 0% American Indian, 5% Asian, 7% black, 4% Hispanic, 3% multiracial, 0% Pacific Islander, 75% white, 3% international; 90% from in state; 27% live on campus; 1% of students in fraternities, 15% in sororities
Most popular majors: 7% Agriculture, Agriculture Operations, and Related Sciences, 11% Biological and Biomedical Sciences, 13% Business, Management, Marketing, and Related Support Services, 23% Engineering, 6% Social Sciences
Expenses: 2014-2015: $8,296 in state, $23,551 out of state; room/board: $10,030
Financial aid: (919) 515-2421; 50% of undergrads determined to have financial need; average aid package $12,567

North Carolina Wesleyan College
Rocky Mount NC
(800) 488-6292
U.S. News ranking: Reg. Coll. (S), No. 71
Website: www.ncwc.edu
Admissions email: adm@ncwc.edu
Private; founded 1956
Affiliation: Methodist
Freshman admissions: less selective; 2013-2014: 1,790 applied, 834 accepted. Neither SAT nor ACT required. SAT 25/75 percentile: 760-970. High school rank: 5% in top tenth, 14% in top quarter, 45% in top half
Early decision deadline: N/A, notification date: N/A
Early action deadline: N/A, notification date: N/A
Application deadline (fall): rolling
Undergraduate student body: 1,231 full time, 371 part time; 41% male, 59% female; 1% American Indian, 0% Asian, 49% black, 2% Hispanic, 1% multiracial, 0% Pacific Islander, 30% white, 3% international; 87% from in state; 29% live on campus; N/A of students in fraternities, N/A in sororities
Most popular majors: 10% Accounting, 33% Business Administration and Management, General, 6% Computer and Information Sciences, General, 19% Criminal Justice/Law Enforcement Administration, 17% Psychology, General

Expenses: 2013-2014: $26,981; room/board: $8,679
Financial aid: (252) 985-5200

Pfeiffer University
Misenheimer NC
(800) 338-2060
U.S. News ranking: Reg. U. (S), No. 62
Website: www.pfeiffer.edu
Admissions email: admissions@pfeiffer.edu
Private; founded 1885
Affiliation: Methodist
Freshman admissions: less selective; 2013-2014: 1,711 applied, 1,682 accepted. Either SAT or ACT required. SAT 25/75 percentile: 870-1080. High school rank: 11% in top tenth, 35% in top quarter, 70% in top half
Early decision deadline: N/A, notification date: N/A
Early action deadline: N/A, notification date: N/A
Application deadline (fall): rolling
Undergraduate student body: 856 full time, 95 part time; 40% male, 60% female; 1% American Indian, 1% Asian, 16% black, 4% Hispanic, 2% multiracial, 0% Pacific Islander, 49% white, 5% international; 67% from in state; 65% live on campus; 0% of students in fraternities, 0% in sororities
Most popular majors: 20% Business Administration and Management, General, 12% Criminal Justice/Safety Studies, 11% Elementary Education and Teaching, 5% Psychology, General, 6% Registered Nursing/Registered Nurse
Expenses: 2014-2015: $25,590; room/board: $10,215
Financial aid: (800) 338-2060; 81% of undergrads determined to have financial need; average aid package $24,169

Queens University of Charlotte
Charlotte NC
(800) 849-0202
U.S. News ranking: Reg. U. (S), No. 18
Website: www.queens.edu
Admissions email: admissions@queens.edu
Private; founded 1857
Affiliation: Presbyterian
Freshman admissions: selective; 2013-2014: 1,949 applied, 1,498 accepted. Either SAT or ACT required. SAT 25/75 percentile: 940-1140. High school rank: 18% in top tenth, 42% in top quarter, 78% in top half
Early decision deadline: N/A, notification date: N/A
Early action deadline: 11/1, notification date: 12/1
Application deadline (fall): 8/1
Undergraduate student body: 1,410 full time, 324 part time; 28% male, 72% female; 1% American Indian, 3% Asian, 18% black, 5% Hispanic, 1% multiracial, 0% Pacific Islander, 56% white, 6% international; 61% from in state; 71% live on campus; 13% of students in fraternities, 21% in sororities
Most popular majors: 12% Business, Management, Marketing, and Related Support Services, 11% Communication, Journalism, and Related Programs,

30% Health Professions and Related Programs, 8% Psychology, 6% Social Sciences
Expenses: 2014-2015: $30,850; room/board: $10,630
Financial aid: (704) 337-2225; 67% of undergrads determined to have financial need; average aid package $20,035

Salem College
Winston-Salem NC
(336) 721-2621
U.S. News ranking: Nat. Lib. Arts, No. 148
Website: www.salem.edu
Admissions email: admissions@salem.edu
Private; founded 1772
Affiliation: Moravian Church in America
Freshman admissions: more selective; 2013-2014: 855 applied, 498 accepted. Either SAT or ACT required. SAT 25/75 percentile: 1000-1200. High school rank: 39% in top tenth, 75% in top quarter, 96% in top half
Early decision deadline: N/A, notification date: N/A
Early action deadline: N/A, notification date: N/A
Application deadline (fall): rolling
Undergraduate student body: 827 full time, 152 part time; 5% male, 95% female; 0% American Indian, 3% Asian, 23% black, 7% Hispanic, 3% multiracial, 0% Pacific Islander, 55% white, 1% international; 79% from in state; 52% live on campus; 0% of students in fraternities, 0% in sororities
Most popular majors: 14% Business Administration and Management, General, 6% Communication, General, 16% Education, General, 8% Psychology, General, 9% Sociology
Expenses: 2014-2015: $25,356; room/board: $11,764
Financial aid: (336) 721-2808

Shaw University[1]
Raleigh NC
(800) 214-6683
U.S. News ranking: Reg. Coll. (S), second tier
Website: www.shawu.edu
Admissions email: admission@shawu.edu
Private; founded 1865
Affiliation: Baptist
Application deadline (fall): 7/30
Undergraduate student body: N/A full time, N/A part time
Expenses: 2013-2014: $16,480; room/board: $8,158
Financial aid: (919) 546-8240

St. Augustine's University
Raleigh NC
(919) 516-4012
U.S. News ranking: Reg. Coll. (S), second tier
Website: www.st-aug.edu
Admissions email: admissions@st-aug.edu
Private; founded 1867
Affiliation: Episcopal
Freshman admissions: least selective; 2013-2014: 2,560 applied, 1,725 accepted. Either SAT or ACT required. SAT 25/75 percentile: 665-858. High school rank: N/A

More at usnews.com/college

Early decision deadline: N/A, notification date: N/A
Early action deadline: N/A, notification date: N/A
Application deadline (fall): rolling
Undergraduate student body: 1,265 full time, 34 part time; 50% male, 50% female; 0% American Indian, 0% Asian, 96% black, 0% Hispanic, 0% multiracial, 0% Pacific Islander, 1% white, 2% international; 57% from in state; 75% live on campus; N/A of students in fraternities, N/A in sororities
Most popular majors: 24% Business, Management, Marketing, and Related Support Services, 9% Health Professions and Related Programs, 9% Homeland Security, Law Enforcement, Firefighting and Related Protective Services, 13% Parks, Recreation, Leisure, and Fitness Studies, 11% Social Sciences
Expenses: 2014-2015: $17,890; room/board: $7,692
Financial aid: (919) 516-4131; 100% of undergrads determined to have financial need; average aid package $8,306

University of Mount Olive

Mount Olive NC
(919) 658-2502
U.S. News ranking: Reg. Coll. (S), No. 56
Website: www.umo.edu/
Admissions email: admissions@umo.edu
Private; founded 1951
Affiliation: Original Free Will Baptist
Freshman admissions: less selective; 2013-2014: 1,798 applied, 859 accepted. Neither SAT nor ACT required. SAT 25/75 percentile: 833-1060. High school rank: N/A
Early decision deadline: N/A, notification date: N/A
Early action deadline: N/A, notification date: N/A
Application deadline (fall): rolling
Undergraduate student body: 1,386 full time, 2,028 part time; 33% male, 67% female; 2% American Indian, 1% Asian, 34% black, 4% Hispanic, 0% multiracial, 0% Pacific Islander, 47% white, 3% international
Most popular majors: 28% Business Administration and Management, General, 15% Early Childhood Education and Teaching, 20% Health/Health Care Administration/Management
Expenses: 2013-2014: $17,300; room/board: $7,000
Financial aid: (919) 658-2502

University of North Carolina– Asheville

Asheville NC
(828) 251-6481
U.S. News ranking: Nat. Lib. Arts, No. 159
Website: www.unca.edu
Admissions email: admissions@unca.edu
Public; founded 1927
Freshman admissions: selective; 2013-2014: 3,173 applied, 2,181 accepted. Either SAT or ACT required. SAT 25/75

percentile: 1100-1290. High school rank: 22% in top tenth, 54% in top quarter, 90% in top half
Early decision deadline: N/A, notification date: N/A
Early action deadline: N/A, notification date: N/A
Application deadline (fall): 2/15
Undergraduate student body: 3,129 full time, 607 part time; 43% male, 57% female; 0% American Indian, 1% Asian, 3% black, 4% Hispanic, 3% multiracial, 0% Pacific Islander, 83% white, 0% international; 88% from in state; 40% live on campus; 3% of students in fraternities, 3% in sororities
Most popular majors: 6% Art/Art Studies, General, 7% English Language and Literature, General, 6% Environmental Studies, 7% Liberal Arts and Sciences/Liberal Studies, 12% Psychology, General
Expenses: 2014-2015: $6,392 in state, $21,263 out of state; room/board: $8,332
Financial aid: (828) 251-6535; 59% of undergrads determined to have financial need; average aid package $11,789

University of North Carolina– Chapel Hill

Chapel Hill NC
(919) 966-3621
U.S. News ranking: Nat. U., No. 30
Website: www.unc.edu
Admissions email: unchelp@admissions.unc.edu
Public; founded 1789
Freshman admissions: most selective; 2013-2014: 30,835 applied, 8,243 accepted. Either SAT or ACT required. SAT 25/75 percentile: 1200-1410. High school rank: 78% in top tenth, 96% in top quarter, 99% in top half
Early decision deadline: N/A, notification date: N/A
Early action deadline: 10/15, notification date: 1/31
Application deadline (fall): 1/10
Undergraduate student body: 17,570 full time, 800 part time; 42% male, 58% female; 0% American Indian, 9% Asian, 8% black, 7% Hispanic, 4% multiracial, 0% Pacific Islander, 66% white, 2% international; 82% from in state; 53% live on campus; 17% of students in fraternities, 18% in sororities
Most popular majors: 8% Biology, General, 6% Business Administration, Management and Operations, 10% Communication and Media Studies, 6% Economics, 9% Psychology, General
Expenses: 2014-2015: $8,374 in state, $33,624 out of state; room/board: $10,592
Financial aid: (919) 962-8396; 44% of undergrads determined to have financial need; average aid package $16,798

University of North Carolina– Charlotte

Charlotte NC
(704) 687-5507
U.S. News ranking: Nat. U., No. 201
Website: www.uncc.edu/
Admissions email: admissions@uncc.edu
Public; founded 1946
Freshman admissions: selective; 2013-2014: 14,300 applied, 8,967 accepted. Either SAT or ACT required. SAT 25/75 percentile: 1000-1170. High school rank: 19% in top tenth, 55% in top quarter, 89% in top half
Early decision deadline: N/A, notification date: N/A
Early action deadline: N/A, notification date: N/A
Application deadline (fall): 7/1
Undergraduate student body: 18,309 full time, 3,194 part time; 52% male, 48% female; 0% American Indian, 5% Asian, 17% black, 7% Hispanic, 3% multiracial, 0% Pacific Islander, 61% white, 2% international; 93% from in state; 24% live on campus; 3% of students in fraternities, 4% in sororities
Most popular majors: 19% Business, Management, Marketing, and Related Support Services, 7% Engineering, 7% Homeland Security, Law Enforcement, Firefighting and Related Protective Services, 7% Psychology, 9% Social Sciences
Expenses: 2014-2015: $6,179 in state, $18,708 out of state; room/board: $11,646
Financial aid: (704) 687-2461; 66% of undergrads determined to have financial need; average aid package $9,524

University of North Carolina– Greensboro

Greensboro NC
(336) 334-5243
U.S. News ranking: Nat. U., No. 181
Website: www.uncg.edu/
Admissions email: admissions@uncg.edu
Public; founded 1891
Freshman admissions: selective; 2013-2014: 10,154 applied, 5,909 accepted. Either SAT or ACT required. SAT 25/75 percentile: 950-1120. High school rank: 22% in top tenth, 48% in top quarter, 84% in top half
Early decision deadline: N/A, notification date: N/A
Early action deadline: N/A, notification date: N/A
Application deadline (fall): 3/1
Undergraduate student body: 12,354 full time, 1,994 part time; 35% male, 65% female; 0% American Indian, 4% Asian, 25% black, 6% Hispanic, 4% multiracial, 0% Pacific Islander, 58% white, 2% international; 94% from in state; 32% live on campus; 4% of students in fraternities, 4% in sororities
Most popular majors: 17% Business, Management, Marketing, and Related Support Services, 11% Education, 13%

Health Professions and Related Programs, 8% Social Sciences, 8% Visual and Performing Arts
Expenses: 2014-2015: $6,442 in state, $21,304 out of state; room/board: $7,688
Financial aid: (336) 334-5702; 80% of undergrads determined to have financial need; average aid package $10,090

University of North Carolina– Pembroke

Pembroke NC
(910) 521-6262
U.S. News ranking: Reg. U. (S), No. 87
Website: www.uncp.edu
Admissions email: admissions@uncp.edu
Public; founded 1887
Freshman admissions: less selective; 2013-2014: 3,678 applied, 2,600 accepted. Either SAT or ACT required. SAT 25/75 percentile: 840-1010. High school rank: 11% in top tenth, 35% in top quarter, 72% in top half
Early decision deadline: N/A, notification date: N/A
Early action deadline: N/A, notification date: N/A
Application deadline (fall): 7/31
Undergraduate student body: 4,230 full time, 1,199 part time; 38% male, 62% female; 16% American Indian, 2% Asian, 35% black, 5% Hispanic, 2% multiracial, 0% Pacific Islander, 38% white, 1% international; 96% from in state; 37% live on campus; 7% of students in fraternities, 9% in sororities
Most popular majors: 13% Business Administration and Management, General, 10% Criminal Justice/Safety Studies, 14% Education, General, 10% Health and Physical Education/Fitness, General, 11% Sociology
Expenses: 2014-2015: $5,287 in state, $15,238 out of state; room/board: $8,101
Financial aid: (910) 521-6255; 81% of undergrads determined to have financial need; average aid package $9,522

University of North Carolina School of the Arts

Winston-Salem NC
(336) 770-3291
U.S. News ranking: Arts, unranked
Website: www.uncsa.edu
Admissions email: admissions@uncsa.edu
Public; founded 1963
Freshman admissions: N/A; 2013-2014: 803 applied, 359 accepted. Either SAT or ACT required. SAT 25/75 percentile: N/A. High school rank: 14% in top tenth, 45% in top quarter, 80% in top half
Early decision deadline: N/A, notification date: N/A
Early action deadline: N/A, notification date: N/A
Undergraduate student body: 781 full time, 16 part time; 55% male, 45% female; 1% American Indian, 1% Asian, 7% black, 9% Hispanic, 4% multiracial, 0% Pacific Islander, 74% white, 1% international; 49% from in

state; 64% live on campus; N/A of students in fraternities, N/A in sororities
Most popular majors: 35% Cinematography and Film/Video Production, 7% Dance, General, 17% Drama and Dramatics/Theatre Arts, General, 16% Music Performance, General, 25% Technical Theatre/Theatre Design and Technology
Expenses: 2014-2015: $8,378 in state, $23,862 out of state; room/board: $8,570
Financial aid: (336) 770-3297; 62% of undergrads determined to have financial need; average aid package $13,246

University of North Carolina– Wilmington

Wilmington NC
(910) 962-3243
U.S. News ranking: Reg. U. (S), No. 16
Website: www.uncw.edu
Admissions email: admissions@uncw.edu
Public; founded 1947
Freshman admissions: more selective; 2013-2014: 10,838 applied, 6,160 accepted. Either SAT or ACT required. SAT 25/75 percentile: 1110-1270. High school rank: 27% in top tenth, 64% in top quarter, 96% in top half
Early decision deadline: N/A, notification date: N/A
Early action deadline: 11/1, notification date: 1/20
Application deadline (fall): 2/1
Undergraduate student body: 11,408 full time, 1,020 part time; 40% male, 60% female; 0% American Indian, 2% Asian, 5% black, 6% Hispanic, 3% multiracial, 0% Pacific Islander, 80% white, 1% international; 86% from in state; 33% live on campus; 50% of students in fraternities, 8% in sororities
Most popular majors: 20% Business, Management, Marketing, and Related Support Services, 10% Education, 8% Health Professions and Related Programs, 9% Psychology, 9% Social Sciences
Expenses: 2014-2015: $6,392 in state, $20,517 out of state; room/board: $9,124
Financial aid: (910) 962-3177; 54% of undergrads determined to have financial need; average aid package $10,402

Wake Forest University

Winston-Salem NC
(336) 758-5201
U.S. News ranking: Nat. U., No. 27
Website: www.wfu.edu
Admissions email: admissions@wfu.edu
Private; founded 1834
Freshman admissions: most selective; 2013-2014: 11,121 applied, 3,915 accepted. Neither SAT nor ACT required. SAT 25/75 percentile: 1230-1420. High school rank: 76% in top tenth, 93% in top quarter, 99% in top half
Early decision deadline: 1/1, notification date: N/A

Early action deadline: N/A, notification date: N/A
Application deadline (fall): 1/1
Undergraduate student body: 4,756 full time, 67 part time; 48% male, 52% female; 0% American Indian, 5% Asian, 7% black, 6% Hispanic, 3% multiracial, 0% Pacific Islander, 76% white, 4% international; 23% from in state; 74% live on campus; 39% of students in fraternities, 58% in sororities
Most popular majors: 18% Business, Management, Marketing, and Related Support Services, 9% Communication, Journalism, and Related Programs, 7% Parks, Recreation, Leisure, and Fitness Studies, 8% Psychology, 20% Social Sciences
Expenses: 2014-2015: $46,200; room/board: $12,638
Financial aid: (336) 758-5154; 40% of undergrads determined to have financial need; average aid package $37,377

Warren Wilson College

Asheville NC
(800) 934-3536
U.S. News ranking: Nat. Lib. Arts, No. 165
Website: www.warren-wilson.edu
Admissions email: admit@warren-wilson.edu
Private; founded 1894
Freshman admissions: selective; 2013-2014: 1,214 applied, 845 accepted. Either SAT or ACT required. SAT 25/75 percentile: 1010-1250. High school rank: 22% in top tenth, 50% in top quarter, 81% in top half
Early decision deadline: 11/15, notification date: 12/1
Early action deadline: 11/1, notification date: 12/1
Application deadline (fall): 2/1
Undergraduate student body: 824 full time, 6 part time; 39% male, 61% female; 1% American Indian, 1% Asian, 4% black, 5% Hispanic, 2% multiracial, 0% Pacific Islander, 85% white, 2% international; 23% from in state; 90% live on campus; 0% of students in fraternities, 0% in sororities
Most popular majors: 7% Creative Writing, 24% Environmental Studies, 9% International/Global Studies, 9% Social Sciences, Other, 8% Visual and Performing Arts, General
Expenses: 2014-2015: $30,852; room/board: $9,280
Financial aid: (828) 771-2082; 69% of undergrads determined to have financial need; average aid package $25,309

Western Carolina University

Cullowhee NC
(828) 227-7317
U.S. News ranking: Reg. U. (S), No. 37
Website: www.wcu.edu
Admissions email: admiss@email.wcu.edu
Public; founded 1889
Freshman admissions: selective; 2013-2014: 15,142 applied, 5,878 accepted. Either SAT or ACT required. SAT 25/75 percentile: 940-1120. High school rank: 11% in top tenth, 38% in top quarter, 79% in top half

Early decision deadline: N/A, notification date: N/A
Early action deadline: 11/15, notification date: 12/15
Application deadline (fall): 3/1
Undergraduate student body: 7,081 full time, 1,367 part time; 45% male, 55% female; 1% American Indian, 1% Asian, 6% black, 4% Hispanic, 3% multiracial, 0% Pacific Islander, 81% white, 2% international; 91% from in state; 48% live on campus; 9% of students in fraternities, 7% in sororities
Most popular majors: 12% Business, Management, Marketing, and Related Support Services, 17% Education, 15% Health Professions and Related Programs, 8% Homeland Security, Law Enforcement, Firefighting and Related Protective Services, 6% Visual and Performing Arts
Expenses: 2014-2015: $6,531 in state, $16,924 out of state; room/board: $8,016
Financial aid: (828) 227-7290; 68% of undergrads determined to have financial need; average aid package $9,291

William Peace University[1]

Raleigh NC
(919) 508-2214
U.S. News ranking: Nat. Lib. Arts, second tier
Website: www.peace.edu
Admissions email: admissions@peace.edu
Private; founded 1857
Affiliation: Presbyterian Church (USA)
Application deadline (fall): rolling
Undergraduate student body: N/A full time, N/A part time
Expenses: 2013-2014: $23,900; room/board: $9,000
Financial aid: (919) 508-2249

Wingate University

Wingate NC
(800) 755-5550
U.S. News ranking: Reg. U. (S), No. 43
Website: www.wingate.edu/admissions
Admissions email: admit@wingate.edu
Private; founded 1896
Freshman admissions: selective; 2013-2014: 5,323 applied, 4,221 accepted. Either SAT or ACT required. SAT 25/75 percentile: 910-1120. High school rank: 18% in top tenth, 50% in top quarter, 85% in top half
Early decision deadline: N/A, notification date: N/A
Early action deadline: N/A, notification date: N/A
Application deadline (fall): rolling
Undergraduate student body: 1,953 full time, 56 part time; 41% male, 59% female; 1% American Indian, 2% Asian, 15% black, 2% Hispanic, 4% multiracial, 0% Pacific Islander, 64% white, 4% international; 83% from in state; 80% live on campus; 4% of students in fraternities, 10% in sororities
Most popular majors: 14% Biological and Biomedical Sciences, 20% Business, Management, Marketing, and Related Support Services,

10% Communication, Journalism, and Related Programs, 9% Education, 10% Parks, Recreation, Leisure, and Fitness Studies
Expenses: 2014-2015: $26,300; room/board: $10,400
Financial aid: (704) 233-8209; 86% of undergrads determined to have financial need; average aid package $23,080

Winston-Salem State University[1]

Winston-Salem NC
(336) 750-2070
U.S. News ranking: Reg. U. (S), No. 60
Website: www.wssu.edu
Admissions email: admissions@wssu.edu
Public; founded 1892
Application deadline (fall): 3/15
Undergraduate student body: N/A full time, N/A part time
Expenses: 2013-2014: $5,468 in state, $14,281 out of state; room/board: $7,968
Financial aid: (336) 750-3280

NORTH DAKOTA

Bismarck State College

Bismarck ND
(701) 224-2459
U.S. News ranking: Reg. Coll. (Mid. W), No. 69
Website: www.bismarckstate.edu
Admissions email: admissions@bismarckstate.edu
Public; founded 1959
Freshman admissions: less selective; 2013-2014: 1,141 applied, 1,141 accepted. Neither SAT nor ACT required. ACT 25/75 percentile: 17-23. High school rank: N/A
Early decision deadline: N/A, notification date: N/A
Early action deadline: N/A, notification date: N/A
Application deadline (fall): rolling
Undergraduate student body: 2,365 full time, 1,697 part time; 56% male, 44% female; N/A American Indian, N/A Asian, N/A black, N/A Hispanic, N/A multiracial, N/A Pacific Islander, N/A white, N/A international; 75% from in state; 9% live on campus; 0% of students in fraternities, 0% in sororities
Most popular majors: 100% Business, Management, Marketing, and Related Support Services
Expenses: 2014-2015: $4,222 in state, $10,084 out of state; room/board: $6,801
Financial aid: (701) 224-5494

Dickinson State University

Dickinson ND
(701) 483-2175
U.S. News ranking: Reg. Coll. (Mid. W), No. 62
Website: www.dickinsonstate.com
Admissions email: dsu.hawks@dsu.nodak.edu
Public
Freshman admissions: selective; 2013-2014: 421 applied, 206 accepted. Either SAT or ACT required. ACT 25/75 percentile: 18-23. High school rank: N/A

Early decision deadline: N/A, notification date: N/A
Early action deadline: 4/15, notification date: N/A
Application deadline (fall): 8/1
Undergraduate student body: 1,018 full time, 431 part time; 39% male, 61% female; 1% American Indian, 1% Asian, 4% black, 5% Hispanic, 2% multiracial, 0% Pacific Islander, 76% white, 7% international; N/A from in state; 19% live on campus; N/A of students in fraternities, N/A in sororities
Most popular majors: 38% Business, Management, Marketing, and Related Support Services, 18% Education, 9% Multi/Interdisciplinary Studies, 4% Parks, Recreation, Leisure, and Fitness Studies, 4% Psychology
Expenses: 2013-2014: $5,848 in state, $8,200 out of state; room/board: $5,582
Financial aid: (701) 483-2371

Mayville State University

Mayville ND
(701) 788-4667
U.S. News ranking: Reg. Coll. (Mid. W), second tier
Website: www.mayvillestate.edu
Admissions email: masuadmissions@mayvillestate.edu
Public; founded 1889
Freshman admissions: selective; 2013-2014: 317 applied, 163 accepted. Either SAT or ACT required. ACT 25/75 percentile: 17-21. High school rank: N/A in top tenth, 34% in top quarter, 67% in top half
Early decision deadline: N/A, notification date: N/A
Early action deadline: N/A, notification date: N/A
Application deadline (fall): rolling
Undergraduate student body: 587 full time, 449 part time; 44% male, 56% female; 2% American Indian, 0% Asian, 7% black, 5% Hispanic, 2% multiracial, 0% Pacific Islander, 79% white, 3% international; 60% from in state; 41% live on campus; 0% of students in fraternities, 0% in sororities
Most popular majors: 22% Business Administration and Management, General, 9% Child Care and Support Services Management, 20% Elementary Education and Teaching, 7% General Studies, 9% Health and Physical Education/Fitness, General
Expenses: 2014-2015: $6,489 in state, $8,894 out of state; room/board: $5,430
Financial aid: (701) 788-4767; 63% of undergrads determined to have financial need; average aid package $12,504

Minot State University

Minot ND
(701) 858-3350
U.S. News ranking: Reg. U. (Mid. W), No. 106
Website: www.minotstateu.edu
Admissions email: askmsu@minotstateu.edu
Public; founded 1913
Freshman admissions: selective; 2013-2014: 959 applied, 543 accepted. Either SAT or ACT

required. ACT 25/75 percentile: 19-24. High school rank: 11% in top tenth, 22% in top quarter, 67% in top half
Early decision deadline: N/A, notification date: N/A
Early action deadline: N/A, notification date: N/A
Application deadline (fall): rolling
Undergraduate student body: 2,151 full time, 1,103 part time; 39% male, 61% female; 2% American Indian, 1% Asian, 4% black, 4% Hispanic, 3% multiracial, 0% Pacific Islander, 71% white, 12% international; 82% from in state; 21% live on campus; N/A of students in fraternities, N/A in sororities
Most popular majors: 34% Business Administration and Management, General, 6% Criminal Justice/Safety Studies, 18% Elementary Education and Teaching, 16% Registered Nursing/Registered Nurse, 5% Social Work
Expenses: 2014-2015: $6,224 in state, $6,224 out of state; room/board: $5,620
Financial aid: (701) 858-3375

North Dakota State University

Fargo ND
(701) 231-8643
U.S. News ranking: Nat. U., No. 181
Website: www.ndsu.edu
Admissions email: NDSU.Admission@ndsu.edu
Public; founded 1890
Freshman admissions: selective; 2013-2014: 5,812 applied, 4,888 accepted. Either SAT or ACT required. ACT 25/75 percentile: 21-26. High school rank: 16% in top tenth, 40% in top quarter, 75% in top half
Early decision deadline: N/A, notification date: N/A
Early action deadline: N/A, notification date: N/A
Application deadline (fall): 8/1
Undergraduate student body: 10,707 full time, 1,241 part time; 56% male, 44% female; 1% American Indian, 1% Asian, 2% black, 1% Hispanic, 2% multiracial, 0% Pacific Islander, 88% white, 4% international; 44% from in state; 34% live on campus; N/A of students in fraternities, N/A in sororities
Most popular majors: 7% Agriculture, Agriculture Operations, and Related Sciences, 7% Biological and Biomedical Sciences, 17% Business, Management, Marketing, and Related Support Services, 14% Engineering, 11% Health Professions and Related Programs
Expenses: 2013-2014: $7,660 in state, $18,242 out of state; room/board: $7,300
Financial aid: (800) 726-3188

University of Jamestown

Jamestown ND
(701) 252-3467
U.S. News ranking: Reg. Coll. (Mid. W), No. 37
Website: www.jc.edu
Admissions email: admissions@jc.edu
Private; founded 1884
Affiliation: Presbyterian

Freshman admissions: selective; 2013-2014: 1,088 applied, 619 accepted. Either SAT or ACT required. ACT 25/75 percentile: 21-24. High school rank: 12% in top tenth, 36% in top quarter, 69% in top half
Early decision deadline: N/A, notification date: N/A
Early action deadline: N/A, notification date: N/A
Application deadline (fall): rolling
Undergraduate student body: 882 full time, 73 part time; 47% male, 53% female; 1% American Indian, 2% Asian, 3% black, 5% Hispanic, 0% multiracial, 0% Pacific Islander, 84% white, 5% international; 45% from in state; 69% live on campus; N/A of students in fraternities, N/A in sororities
Most popular majors: 7% Biology/Biological Sciences, General, 18% Business Administration and Management, General, 8% Criminal Justice/Police Science, 10% Elementary Education and Teaching, 21% Registered Nursing, Nursing Administration, Nursing Research and Clinical Nursing
Expenses: 2014-2015: $19,170; room/board: $6,780
Financial aid: (701) 252-3467; 67% of undergrads determined to have financial need; average aid package $13,741

University of Mary[1]
Bismarck ND
(701) 355-8030
U.S. News ranking: Reg. U. (Mid. W), second tier
Website: www.umary.edu
Admissions email: marauder@umary.edu
Private
Application deadline (fall): N/A
Undergraduate student body: N/A full time, N/A part time
Expenses: 2013-2014: $14,730; room/board: $5,505
Financial aid: (701) 355-8079

University of North Dakota
Grand Forks ND
(800) 225-5863
U.S. News ranking: Nat. U., No. 168
Website: und.edu
Admissions email: admissions@und.edu
Public; founded 1883
Freshman admissions: selective; 2013-2014: 4,734 applied, 3,362 accepted. Either SAT or ACT required. ACT 25/75 percentile: 21-26. High school rank: 15% in top tenth, 39% in top quarter, 71% in top half
Early decision deadline: N/A, notification date: N/A
Early action deadline: N/A, notification date: N/A
Application deadline (fall): rolling
Undergraduate student body: 9,385 full time, 2,339 part time; 57% male, 43% female; 2% American Indian, 2% Asian, 2% black, 3% Hispanic, 3% multiracial, 0% Pacific Islander, 81% white, 0% international; 41% from in state; 27% live on campus; 9% of students in fraternities, 11% in sororities

Most popular majors: 4% Airline/Commercial/Professional Pilot and Flight Crew, 5% Biology/Biological Sciences, General, 4% Elementary Education and Teaching, 6% Psychology, General, 8% Registered Nursing/Registered Nurse
Expenses: 2013-2014: $7,508 in state, $17,794 out of state; room/board: $6,400
Financial aid: (701) 777-3121

Valley City State University
Valley City ND
(701) 845-7101
U.S. News ranking: Reg. Coll. (Mid. W), No. 44
Website: www.vcsu.edu
Admissions email: enrollment.services@vcsu.edu
Public; founded 1890
Freshman admissions: selective; 2013-2014: 345 applied, 286 accepted. Either SAT or ACT required. ACT 25/75 percentile: 18-23. High school rank: 6% in top tenth, 21% in top quarter, 61% in top half
Early decision deadline: N/A, notification date: N/A
Early action deadline: N/A, notification date: N/A
Application deadline (fall): rolling
Undergraduate student body: 759 full time, 452 part time; 44% male, 56% female; 1% American Indian, 1% Asian, 4% black, 5% Hispanic, 2% multiracial, 0% Pacific Islander, 81% white, 5% international; 64% from in state; 23% live on campus; 1% of students in fraternities, 1% in sororities
Most popular majors: 13% Business Administration and Management, General, 4% Computer and Information Sciences, General, 56% Elementary Education and Teaching, 4% Physical Education Teaching and Coaching, 5% Wildlife, Fish and Wildlands Science and Management
Expenses: 2014-2015: $6,704 in state, $15,099 out of state; room/board: $5,938
Financial aid: (701) 845-7412; 63% of undergrads determined to have financial need; average aid package $8,621

OHIO

Antioch University[1]
Yellow Springs OH
(937) 769-1818
U.S. News ranking: Reg. U. (Mid. W), unranked
Website: midwest.antioch.edu
Admissions email: N/A
Private
Application deadline (fall): N/A
Undergraduate student body: N/A full time, N/A part time
Expenses: N/A
Financial aid: N/A

Art Academy of Cincinnati[1]
Cincinnati OH
(513) 562-8740
U.S. News ranking: Arts, unranked
Website: www.artacademy.edu
Admissions email: admissions@artacademy.edu
Private

Application deadline (fall): N/A
Undergraduate student body: N/A full time, N/A part time
Expenses: 2013-2014: $24,330; room/board: $8,700
Financial aid: (513) 562-8751

Ashland University
Ashland OH
(419) 289-5052
U.S. News ranking: Nat. U., second tier
Website: www.ashland.edu/admissions
Admissions email: enrollme@ashland.edu
Private; founded 1878
Affiliation: Brethren Church
Freshman admissions: selective; 2013-2014: 2,943 applied, 2,130 accepted. Either SAT or ACT required. ACT 25/75 percentile: 20-25. High school rank: 19% in top tenth, 49% in top quarter, 83% in top half
Early decision deadline: N/A, notification date: N/A
Early action deadline: N/A, notification date: N/A
Application deadline (fall): rolling
Undergraduate student body: 2,389 full time, 809 part time; 49% male, 51% female; 1% American Indian, 0% Asian, 13% black, 2% Hispanic, 1% multiracial, 0% Pacific Islander, 79% white, 3% international; 85% from in state; 64% live on campus; 13% of students in fraternities, 21% in sororities
Most popular majors: 9% Early Childhood Education and Teaching, 4% Education/Teaching of Individuals with Multiple Disabilities, 4% Exercise Physiology, 6% Junior High/Intermediate/Middle School Education and Teaching, 12% Nursing Practice
Expenses: 2014-2015: $19,852; room/board: $9,502
Financial aid: (419) 289-5002; 82% of undergrads determined to have financial need; average aid package $25,115

Baldwin Wallace University
Berea OH
(440) 826-2222
U.S. News ranking: Reg. U. (Mid. W), No. 14
Website: www.bw.edu
Admissions email: admission@bw.edu
Private; founded 1845
Affiliation: United Methodist
Freshman admissions: selective; 2013-2014: 4,220 applied, 2,699 accepted. Neither SAT nor ACT required. ACT 25/75 percentile: 21-27. High school rank: 19% in top tenth, 50% in top quarter, 80% in top half
Early decision deadline: N/A, notification date: N/A
Early action deadline: N/A, notification date: N/A
Application deadline (fall): rolling
Undergraduate student body: 3,003 full time, 422 part time; 45% male, 55% female; 0% American Indian, 1% Asian, 9% black, 5% Hispanic, 4% multiracial, 0% Pacific Islander, 80% white, 1% international; 83% from in state; 61% live on campus; 12% of students in fraternities, 19% in sororities

Most popular majors: 10% Biological and Biomedical Sciences, 27% Business, Management, Marketing, and Related Support Services, 7% Communication, Journalism, and Related Programs, 8% Education, 9% Visual and Performing Arts
Expenses: 2014-2015: $28,814; room/board: $8,048
Financial aid: (440) 826-2108; 78% of undergrads determined to have financial need; average aid package $23,639

Bluffton University
Bluffton OH
(800) 488-3257
U.S. News ranking: Reg. Coll. (Mid. W), No. 28
Website: www.bluffton.edu
Admissions email: admissions@bluffton.edu
Private; founded 1899
Affiliation: Mennonite Church USA
Freshman admissions: selective; 2013-2014: 1,784 applied, 947 accepted. Either SAT or ACT required. ACT 25/75 percentile: 19-25. High school rank: 12% in top tenth, 36% in top quarter, 62% in top half
Early decision deadline: N/A, notification date: N/A
Early action deadline: N/A, notification date: N/A
Application deadline (fall): 8/15
Undergraduate student body: 838 full time, 215 part time; 50% male, 50% female; 0% American Indian, 0% Asian, 7% black, 4% Hispanic, 1% multiracial, 0% Pacific Islander, 84% white, 1% international; 86% from in state; 90% live on campus; 0% of students in fraternities, 0% in sororities
Most popular majors: 11% Business Administration and Management, General, 8% Elementary Education and Teaching, 23% Organizational Behavior Studies, 12% Social Work, 7% Sport and Fitness Administration/Management
Expenses: 2014-2015: $29,316; room/board: $9,632
Financial aid: (419) 358-3266; 82% of undergrads determined to have financial need; average aid package $25,740

Bowling Green State University
Bowling Green OH
(419) 372-2478
U.S. News ranking: Nat. U., No. 173
Website: www.bgsu.edu
Admissions email: choosebgsu@bgsu.edu
Public; founded 1910
Freshman admissions: selective; 2013-2014: 15,689 applied, 11,370 accepted. Either SAT or ACT required. ACT 25/75 percentile: 20-25. High school rank: 12% in top tenth, 34% in top quarter, 70% in top half
Early decision deadline: N/A, notification date: N/A
Early action deadline: N/A, notification date: N/A
Application deadline (fall): 7/15
Undergraduate student body: 13,387 full time, 1,090 part time; 44% male, 56% female; 0% American Indian, 1% Asian,

10% black, 4% Hispanic, 2% multiracial, 0% Pacific Islander, 78% white, 2% international; 88% from in state; 44% live on campus; 8% of students in fraternities, 12% in sororities
Most popular majors: 4% Education, Other, 5% Kindergarten/Preschool Education and Teaching, 5% Liberal Arts and Sciences/Liberal Studies, 3% Sport and Fitness Administration/Management, 4% Teacher Education, Multiple Levels
Expenses: 2014-2015: $10,726 in state, $18,034 out of state; room/board: $8,244
Financial aid: (419) 372-2651; 67% of undergrads determined to have financial need; average aid package $13,852

Capital University
Columbus OH
(866) 544-6175
U.S. News ranking: Reg. U. (Mid. W), No. 36
Website: www.capital.edu
Admissions email: admission@capital.edu
Private; founded 1830
Affiliation: Lutheran
Freshman admissions: selective; 2013-2014: 3,640 applied, 2,767 accepted. Either SAT or ACT required. ACT 25/75 percentile: 21-27. High school rank: 16% in top tenth, 45% in top quarter, 78% in top half
Early decision deadline: N/A, notification date: N/A
Early action deadline: N/A, notification date: N/A
Application deadline (fall): rolling
Undergraduate student body: 2,481 full time, 307 part time; 42% male, 58% female; 0% American Indian, 1% Asian, 9% black, 3% Hispanic, 4% multiracial, 0% Pacific Islander, 80% white, 1% international; 91% from in state; 57% live on campus; 3% of students in fraternities, 3% in sororities
Most popular majors: 13% Business, Management, Marketing, and Related Support Services, 14% Education, 17% Health Professions and Related Programs, 7% Social Sciences, 11% Visual and Performing Arts
Expenses: 2014-2015: $31,990; room/board: $9,060
Financial aid: (614) 236-6511; 82% of undergrads determined to have financial need; average aid package $25,447

Case Western Reserve University
Cleveland OH
(216) 368-4450
U.S. News ranking: Nat. U., No. 38
Website: www.case.edu
Admissions email: admission@case.edu
Private; founded 1826
Freshman admissions: most selective; 2013-2014: 18,418 applied, 7,713 accepted. Either SAT or ACT required. SAT 25/75 percentile: 1270-1480. High school rank: 67% in top tenth, 92% in top quarter, 99% in top half
Early decision deadline: 11/1, notification date: 12/15

Early action deadline: 11/1, notification date: 12/15
Application deadline (fall): 1/15
Undergraduate student body: 4,528 full time, 133 part time; 55% male, 45% female; 0% American Indian, 19% Asian, 5% black, 5% Hispanic, 4% multiracial, 0% Pacific Islander, 54% white, 8% international; 36% from in state; 89% live on campus; 40% of students in fraternities, 37% in sororities
Most popular majors: 10% Bioengineering and Biomedical Engineering, 9% Biology/Biological Sciences, General, 7% Mechanical Engineering, 9% Psychology, General, 7% Registered Nursing/Registered Nurse
Expenses: 2014-2015: $43,158; room/board: $13,376
Financial aid: (216) 368-3866; 62% of undergrads determined to have financial need; average aid package $34,243

Cedarville University

Cedarville OH
(800) 233-2784
U.S. News ranking: Reg. Coll. (Mid. W), No. 6
Website: www.cedarville.edu
Admissions email: admissions@cedarville.edu
Private; founded 1887
Affiliation: Baptist
Freshman admissions: more selective; 2013-2014: 3,267 applied, 2,418 accepted. Either SAT or ACT required. ACT 25/75 percentile: 24-29. High school rank: 31% in top tenth, 61% in top quarter, 89% in top half
Early decision deadline: N/A, notification date: N/A
Early action deadline: N/A, notification date: N/A
Application deadline (fall): 8/14
Undergraduate student body: 3,044 full time, 194 part time; 47% male, 53% female; 0% American Indian, 2% Asian, 2% black, 2% Hispanic, 2% multiracial, 0% Pacific Islander, 88% white, 1% international; 38% from in state; 82% live on campus; 0% of students in fraternities, 0% in sororities
Most popular majors: 12% Business, Management, Marketing, and Related Support Services, 10% Education, 9% Engineering, 11% Health Professions and Related Programs, 9% Theology and Religious Vocations
Expenses: 2014-2015: $26,400; room/board: $6,460
Financial aid: (937) 766-7866; 68% of undergrads determined to have financial need; average aid package $16,554

Central State University

Wilberforce OH
(937) 376-6348
U.S. News ranking: Reg. Coll. (Mid. W), second tier
Website: www.centralstate.edu
Admissions email: admissions@centralstate.edu
Public; founded 1887
Freshman admissions: less selective; 2013-2014: 7,142 applied, 2,377 accepted. Either SAT or ACT required. ACT 25/75

percentile: 15-19. High school rank: 5% in top tenth, 18% in top quarter, 49% in top half
Early decision deadline: N/A, notification date: N/A
Early action deadline: N/A, notification date: N/A
Application deadline (fall): rolling
Undergraduate student body: 1,840 full time, 196 part time; 47% male, 53% female; 0% American Indian, 0% Asian, 95% black, 1% Hispanic, 1% multiracial, 0% Pacific Islander, 2% white, 0% international; 63% from in state; 56% live on campus; 1% of students in fraternities, 1% in sororities
Most popular majors: 30% Business, Management, Marketing, and Related Support Services, 8% Communication, Journalism, and Related Programs, 17% Education, 7% Homeland Security, Law Enforcement, Firefighting and Related Protective Services, 6% Psychology
Expenses: 2014-2015: $7,916 in state, $14,056 out of state; room/board: $9,318
Financial aid: (937) 376-6579; 98% of undergrads determined to have financial need; average aid package $7,159

Cleveland Institute of Art

Cleveland OH
(216) 421-7418
U.S. News ranking: Arts, unranked
Website: www.cia.edu
Admissions email: admissions@cia.edu
Private; founded 1882
Freshman admissions: N/A; 2013-2014: 633 applied, 432 accepted. Either SAT or ACT required. SAT 25/75 percentile: N/A. High school rank: 14% in top tenth, 37% in top quarter, 65% in top half
Early decision deadline: N/A, notification date: N/A
Early action deadline: 12/1, notification date: 12/15
Application deadline (fall): rolling
Undergraduate student body: 558 full time, 10 part time; 42% male, 58% female; 0% American Indian, 3% Asian, 10% black, 5% Hispanic, 2% multiracial, 0% Pacific Islander, 75% white, 5% international; 72% from in state; 25% live on campus; 0% of students in fraternities, 1% in sororities
Most popular majors: 17% Illustration, 20% Industrial and Product Design, 6% Interior Design, 8% Medical Illustration/Medical Illustrator, 8% Painting
Expenses: 2014-2015: $37,565; room/board: $11,120
Financial aid: (216) 421-7425; 83% of undergrads determined to have financial need; average aid package $26,213

Cleveland Institute of Music

Cleveland OH
(216) 795-3107
U.S. News ranking: Arts, unranked
Website: www.cim.edu/
Admissions email: admission@cim.edu
Private; founded 1920
Freshman admissions: N/A; 2013-2014: 358 applied, 196 accepted. Neither SAT nor ACT

required. SAT 25/75 percentile: N/A. High school rank: N/A
Early decision deadline: N/A, notification date: N/A
Early action deadline: N/A, notification date: N/A
Application deadline (fall): 12/1
Undergraduate student body: 236 full time, 1 part time; 50% male, 50% female; 0% American Indian, 3% Asian, 1% black, 2% Hispanic, 0% multiracial, 0% Pacific Islander, 19% white, 18% international; N/A from in state; 41% live on campus; 0% of students in fraternities, 0% in sororities
Most popular majors: Information not available
Expenses: 2013-2014: $44,039; room/board: $12,844
Financial aid: (216) 791-5000

Cleveland State University

Cleveland OH
(216) 687-2100
U.S. News ranking: Nat. U., second tier
Website: www.csuohio.edu
Admissions email: admissions@csuohio.edu
Public; founded 1964
Freshman admissions: selective; 2013-2014: 6,768 applied, 4,255 accepted. Either SAT or ACT required. ACT 25/75 percentile: 19-25. High school rank: 14% in top tenth, 39% in top quarter, 71% in top half
Early decision deadline: N/A, notification date: N/A
Early action deadline: 5/1, notification date: N/A
Application deadline (fall): 8/16
Undergraduate student body: 9,027 full time, 3,349 part time; 46% male, 54% female; 0% American Indian, 2% Asian, 19% black, 5% Hispanic, 3% multiracial, 0% Pacific Islander, 63% white, 5% international; 92% from in state; 9% live on campus; 1% of students in fraternities, 1% in sororities
Most popular majors: 19% Business, Management, Marketing, and Related Support Services, 6% Education, 15% Health Professions and Related Programs, 10% Psychology, 11% Social Sciences
Expenses: 2014-2015: $9,473 in state, $12,653 out of state; room/board: $12,100
Financial aid: (216) 687-2054; 79% of undergrads determined to have financial need; average aid package $8,707

College of Wooster

Wooster OH
(800) 877-9905
U.S. News ranking: Nat. Lib. Arts, No. 69
Website: www.wooster.edu/
Admissions email: admissions@wooster.edu
Private; founded 1866
Freshman admissions: more selective; 2013-2014: 5,583 applied, 3,145 accepted. Either SAT or ACT required. ACT 25/75 percentile: 25-30. High school rank: 40% in top tenth, 73% in top quarter, 92% in top half
Early decision deadline: 11/1, notification date: 11/15
Early action deadline: 11/15, notification date: 12/31

Application deadline (fall): 2/15
Undergraduate student body: 2,077 full time, 39 part time; 44% male, 56% female; 1% American Indian, 3% Asian, 8% black, 4% Hispanic, 0% multiracial, 0% Pacific Islander, 72% white, 7% international; 39% from in state; 99% live on campus; 15% of students in fraternities, 21% in sororities
Most popular majors: 6% Biological and Biomedical Sciences, 9% English Language and Literature/Letters, 8% History, 8% Psychology, 15% Social Sciences
Expenses: 2014-2015: $43,350; room/board: $10,250
Financial aid: (330) 263-2317; 58% of undergrads determined to have financial need; average aid package $37,614

Columbus College of Art and Design

Columbus OH
(614) 222-3261
U.S. News ranking: Arts, unranked
Website: www.ccad.edu
Admissions email: admissions@ccad.edu
Private; founded 1879
Freshman admissions: N/A; 2013-2014: 666 applied, 582 accepted. Either SAT or ACT required. SAT 25/75 percentile: N/A. High school rank: 6% in top tenth, 18% in top quarter, 59% in top half
Early decision deadline: N/A, notification date: N/A
Early action deadline: 12/1, notification date: 12/20
Application deadline (fall): 8/22
Undergraduate student body: 1,212 full time, 121 part time; 38% male, 62% female; 0% American Indian, 3% Asian, 8% black, 5% Hispanic, 4% multiracial, 0% Pacific Islander, 68% white, 8% international; N/A from in state; 65% live on campus; N/A of students in fraternities, N/A in sororities
Most popular majors: Information not available
Expenses: 2014-2015: $31,322; room/board: $7,740
Financial aid: (614) 222-3295; 81% of undergrads determined to have financial need; average aid package $20,042

Defiance College

Defiance OH
(800) 520-4632
U.S. News ranking: Reg. Coll. (Mid. W), No. 40
Website: www.defiance.edu
Admissions email: admissions@defiance.edu
Private; founded 1850
Affiliation: United Church of Christ
Freshman admissions: selective; 2013-2014: 1,704 applied, 1,220 accepted. Either SAT or ACT required. ACT 25/75 percentile: 18-23. High school rank: 7% in top tenth, 25% in top quarter, 56% in top half
Early decision deadline: N/A, notification date: N/A
Early action deadline: N/A, notification date: N/A
Application deadline (fall): rolling
Undergraduate student body: 732 full time, 160 part time; 52% male, 48% female; 2% American Indian, 1% Asian, 11% black, 6% Hispanic, 0% multiracial,

0% Pacific Islander, 76% white, 1% international; 73% from in state; 50% live on campus; 6% of students in fraternities, 6% in sororities
Most popular majors: 23% Business Administration and Management, General, 11% Criminal Justice/Police Science, 15% Education, General, 8% Health Professions and Related Programs, 13% Sport and Fitness Administration/Management
Expenses: 2014-2015: $29,916; room/board: $9,522
Financial aid: (419) 783-2376; 90% of undergrads determined to have financial need; average aid package $23,246

Denison University

Granville OH
(740) 587-6276
U.S. News ranking: Nat. Lib. Arts, No. 51
Website: www.denison.edu
Admissions email: admissions@denison.edu
Private; founded 1831
Freshman admissions: more selective; 2013-2014: 4,770 applied, 2,193 accepted. Neither SAT nor ACT required. ACT 25/75 percentile: 27-31. High school rank: 45% in top tenth, 88% in top quarter, 100% in top half
Early decision deadline: 11/15, notification date: N/A
Early action deadline: N/A, notification date: N/A
Application deadline (fall): 1/15
Undergraduate student body: 2,253 full time, 21 part time; 42% male, 58% female; 0% American Indian, 3% Asian, 7% black, 9% Hispanic, 4% multiracial, 0% Pacific Islander, 69% white, 7% international; 28% from in state; 99% live on campus; 34% of students in fraternities, 45% in sororities
Most popular majors: 11% Biological and Biomedical Sciences, 9% Communication, Journalism, and Related Programs, 5% History, 23% Social Sciences, 8% Visual and Performing Arts
Expenses: 2014-2015: $45,670; room/board: $11,180
Financial aid: (740) 587-6279; 51% of undergrads determined to have financial need; average aid package $38,369

Franciscan University of Steubenville

Steubenville OH
(740) 283-6226
U.S. News ranking: Reg. U. (Mid. W), No. 30
Website: www.franciscan.edu
Admissions email: admissions@franciscan.edu
Private; founded 1946
Affiliation: Roman Catholic
Freshman admissions: more selective; 2013-2014: 1,889 applied, 1,437 accepted. Either SAT or ACT required. ACT 25/75 percentile: 23-28. High school rank: 31% in top tenth, 52% in top quarter, 83% in top half
Early decision deadline: N/A, notification date: N/A
Early action deadline: N/A, notification date: N/A
Application deadline (fall): rolling
Undergraduate student body: 1,989 full time, 123 part time; 38% male, 62% female; 0% American

Indian, 2% Asian, 0% black, 10% Hispanic, 2% multiracial, 0% Pacific Islander, 81% white, 1% international; 21% from in state; 79% live on campus; 0% of students in fraternities, 0% in sororities
Most popular majors: 10% Business Administration and Management, General, 10% Elementary Education and Teaching, 7% Philosophy, 7% Religious Education, 29% Theology/Theological Studies
Expenses: 2014-2015: $23,930; room/board: $8,000
Financial aid: (740) 283-6226; 66% of undergrads determined to have financial need; average aid package $13,503

Franklin University[1]

Columbus OH
(614) 341-6256
U.S. News ranking: Business, unranked
Website: www.franklin.edu
Admissions email: info@franklin.edu
Private; founded 1902
Application deadline (fall): rolling
Undergraduate student body: N/A full time, N/A part time
Expenses: 2013-2014: $10,681; room/board: N/A
Financial aid: (614) 797-4700

Heidelberg University

Tiffin OH
(419) 448-2330
U.S. News ranking: Reg. U. (Mid. W), No. 49
Website: www.heidelberg.edu
Admissions email: adminfo@heidelberg.edu
Private; founded 1850
Affiliation: United Church of Christ
Freshman admissions: selective; 2013-2014: 1,797 applied, 1,328 accepted. Either SAT or ACT required. ACT 25/75 percentile: 19-25. High school rank: N/A
Early decision deadline: N/A, notification date: N/A
Early action deadline: N/A, notification date: N/A
Application deadline (fall): rolling
Undergraduate student body: 1,065 full time, 51 part time; 50% male, 50% female; 1% American Indian, 1% Asian, 7% black, 2% Hispanic, 3% multiracial, 0% Pacific Islander, 75% white, 0% international; 86% from in state; 77% live on campus; 12% of students in fraternities, 22% in sororities
Most popular majors: 16% Business, Management, Marketing, and Related Support Services, 17% Education, 10% Parks, Recreation, Leisure, and Fitness Studies, 7% Psychology, 6% Social Sciences
Expenses: 2014-2015: $27,480; room/board: $9,226
Financial aid: (419) 448-2293; 90% of undergrads determined to have financial need; average aid package $21,855

Hiram College

Hiram OH
(800) 362-5280
U.S. News ranking: Nat. Lib. Arts, No. 148
Website: www.hiram.edu
Admissions email: admission@hiram.edu
Private; founded 1850
Freshman admissions: selective; 2013-2014: 2,530 applied, 1,449 accepted. Either SAT or ACT required. ACT 25/75 percentile: 19-25. High school rank: 12% in top tenth, 37% in top quarter, 67% in top half
Early decision deadline: N/A, notification date: N/A
Early action deadline: N/A, notification date: N/A
Application deadline (fall): rolling
Undergraduate student body: 1,117 full time, 166 part time; 45% male, 55% female; 0% American Indian, 1% Asian, 14% black, 4% Hispanic, 2% multiracial, 0% Pacific Islander, 71% white, 4% international; 82% from in state; 80% live on campus; N/A of students in fraternities, N/A in sororities
Most popular majors: 14% Biological and Biomedical Sciences, 29% Business, Management, Marketing, and Related Support Services, 5% Education, 5% Health Professions and Related Programs, 13% Social Sciences
Expenses: 2014-2015: $30,290; room/board: $10,010
Financial aid: (330) 569-5107; 86% of undergrads determined to have financial need; average aid package $25,110

John Carroll University

University Heights OH
(216) 397-4294
U.S. News ranking: Reg. U. (Mid. W), No. 7
Website: www.jcu.edu
Admissions email: admission@jcu.edu
Private; founded 1886
Affiliation: Roman Catholic (Jesuit)
Freshman admissions: selective; 2013-2014: 3,721 applied, 3,101 accepted. Either SAT or ACT required. ACT 25/75 percentile: 22-27. High school rank: 22% in top tenth, 51% in top quarter, 82% in top half
Early decision deadline: N/A, notification date: N/A
Early action deadline: N/A, notification date: N/A
Application deadline (fall): 2/1
Undergraduate student body: 2,962 full time, 90 part time; 52% male, 48% female; 0% American Indian, 2% Asian, 4% black, 4% Hispanic, 2% multiracial, 0% Pacific Islander, 83% white, 1% international; 70% from in state; 54% live on campus; 6% of students in fraternities, 11% in sororities
Most popular majors: 9% Biological and Biomedical Sciences, 30% Business, Management, Marketing, and Related Support Services, 9% Communication, Journalism, and Related Programs, 9% Education, 10% Social Sciences
Expenses: 2014-2015: $35,800; room/board: $10,500

Financial aid: (216) 397-4248; 74% of undergrads determined to have financial need; average aid package $27,861

Kent State University

Kent OH
(330) 672-2444
U.S. News ranking: Nat. U., No. 194
Website: www.kent.edu
Admissions email: kentadm@kent.edu
Public; founded 1910
Freshman admissions: selective; 2013-2014: 16,083 applied, 13,368 accepted. Either SAT or ACT required. ACT 25/75 percentile: 20-25. High school rank: 14% in top tenth, 40% in top quarter, 77% in top half
Early decision deadline: N/A, notification date: N/A
Early action deadline: N/A, notification date: N/A
Application deadline (fall): 8/1
Undergraduate student body: 19,865 full time, 3,103 part time; 41% male, 59% female; 0% American Indian, 1% Asian, 9% black, 3% Hispanic, 3% multiracial, 0% Pacific Islander, 76% white, 6% international; 88% from in state; 28% live on campus; N/A of students in fraternities, N/A in sororities
Most popular majors: 19% Business, Management, Marketing, and Related Support Services, 8% Communication, Journalism, and Related Programs, 9% Education, 18% Health Professions and Related Programs, 6% Visual and Performing Arts
Expenses: 2014-2015: $10,012 in state, $17,972 out of state; room/board: $9,768
Financial aid: (330) 672-2972; 67% of undergrads determined to have financial need; average aid package $9,749

Kenyon College

Gambier OH
(740) 427-5776
U.S. News ranking: Nat. Lib. Arts, No. 30
Website: www.kenyon.edu
Admissions email: admissions@kenyon.edu
Private; founded 1824
Freshman admissions: more selective; 2013-2014: 4,051 applied, 1,555 accepted. Either SAT or ACT required. SAT 25/75 percentile: 1230-1410. High school rank: 65% in top tenth, 88% in top quarter, 98% in top half
Early decision deadline: 11/15, notification date: 12/15
Early action deadline: N/A, notification date: N/A
Application deadline (fall): 1/15
Undergraduate student body: 1,695 full time, 10 part time; 46% male, 54% female; 1% American Indian, 6% Asian, 3% black, 5% Hispanic, 2% multiracial, 0% Pacific Islander, 76% white, 4% international; 14% from in state; 99% live on campus; 10% of students in fraternities, 10% in sororities

Most popular majors: 8% Economics, General, 18% English Language and Literature, General, 7% History, General, 9% Political Science and Government, General, 9% Psychology, General
Expenses: 2014-2015: $47,330; room/board: $11,560
Financial aid: (740) 427-5430; 39% of undergrads determined to have financial need; average aid package $38,495

Lake Erie College

Painesville OH
(800) 916-0904
U.S. News ranking: Reg. U. (Mid. W), second tier
Website: www.lec.edu
Admissions email: admissions@lec.edu
Private; founded 1856
Freshman admissions: selective; 2013-2014: 1,160 applied, 645 accepted. Either SAT or ACT required. ACT 25/75 percentile: 19-23. High school rank: 6% in top tenth, 28% in top quarter, 63% in top half
Early decision deadline: N/A, notification date: N/A
Early action deadline: N/A, notification date: N/A
Application deadline (fall): 8/1
Undergraduate student body: 852 full time, 72 part time; 51% male, 49% female; 0% American Indian, 0% Asian, 11% black, 2% Hispanic, 3% multiracial, 0% Pacific Islander, 78% white, 4% international; 73% from in state; 62% live on campus; N/A of students in fraternities, N/A in sororities
Most popular majors: 8% Biology/Biological Sciences, General, 38% Business Administration and Management, General, 6% Equestrian/Equine Studies, 6% Psychology, General, 9% Sport and Fitness Administration/Management
Expenses: 2014-2015: $28,355; room/board: $8,912
Financial aid: (440) 375-7100; 80% of undergrads determined to have financial need; average aid package $21,312

Lourdes University

Sylvania OH
(419) 885-5291
U.S. News ranking: Reg. U. (Mid. W), unranked
Website: www.lourdes.edu
Admissions email: admissionslcadmits@lourdes.edu
Private; founded 1958
Affiliation: Roman Catholic
Freshman admissions: N/A; 2013-2014: 1,307 applied, 906 accepted. Neither SAT nor ACT required. ACT 25/75 percentile: N/A. High school rank: 9% in top tenth, 24% in top quarter, 59% in top half
Early decision deadline: N/A, notification date: N/A
Early action deadline: N/A, notification date: N/A
Application deadline (fall): rolling
Undergraduate student body: 1,137 full time, 669 part time; 30% male, 70% female; 0% American Indian, 1% Asian, 11% black, 13% Hispanic, 3% multiracial, 0% Pacific Islander, 69% white, 0% international; 84% from in state; 16% live on campus; 0% of students in fraternities, 0% in sororities

Most popular majors: 4% Business Administration, Management and Operations, 4% Criminal Justice and Corrections, 14% Multi/Interdisciplinary Studies, Other, 36% Registered Nursing, Nursing Administration, Nursing Research and Clinical Nursing, 5% Social Work
Expenses: 2013-2014: $17,656; room/board: $8,400
Financial aid: (419) 824-3732

Malone University

Canton OH
(330) 471-8145
U.S. News ranking: Reg. U. (Mid. W), No. 54
Website: www.malone.edu
Admissions email: admissions@malone.edu
Private; founded 1892
Affiliation: Evangelical Friends
Freshman admissions: selective; 2013-2014: 1,333 applied, 957 accepted. Either SAT or ACT required. ACT 25/75 percentile: 19-26. High school rank: 19% in top tenth, 42% in top quarter, 76% in top half
Early decision deadline: N/A, notification date: N/A
Early action deadline: N/A, notification date: N/A
Application deadline (fall): rolling
Undergraduate student body: 1,453 full time, 203 part time; 43% male, 57% female; 0% American Indian, 1% Asian, 8% black, 3% Hispanic, 2% multiracial, 0% Pacific Islander, 85% white, 2% international; 86% from in state; 55% live on campus; 0% of students in fraternities, 0% in sororities
Most popular majors: 7% Business Administration and Management, General, 16% Business Administration, Management and Operations, Other, 4% Education/Teaching of Individuals with Specific Learning Disabilities, 4% Kinesiology and Exercise Science, 15% Registered Nursing/Registered Nurse
Expenses: 2014-2015: $26,416; room/board: $8,948
Financial aid: (330) 471-8159; 83% of undergrads determined to have financial need; average aid package $20,320

Marietta College

Marietta OH
(800) 331-7896
U.S. News ranking: Reg. Coll. (Mid. W), No. 6
Website: www.marietta.edu
Admissions email: admit@marietta.edu
Private; founded 1797
Freshman admissions: selective; 2013-2014: 4,053 applied, 2,579 accepted. Either SAT or ACT required. ACT 25/75 percentile: 21-27. High school rank: 32% in top tenth, 59% in top quarter, 85% in top half
Early decision deadline: N/A, notification date: N/A
Early action deadline: N/A, notification date: N/A
Application deadline (fall): 4/15
Undergraduate student body: 1,352 full time, 64 part time; 58% male, 42% female; 0% American Indian, 1% Asian, 6% black, 3% Hispanic, 2% multiracial, 0% Pacific Islander, 71% white,

12% international; 53% from in state; 77% live on campus; 13% of students in fraternities, 30% in sororities
Most popular majors: Information not available
Expenses: 2014-2015: $33,490; room/board: $10,395
Financial aid: (740) 376-4712; 68% of undergrads determined to have financial need; average aid package $24,569

Miami University–Oxford
Oxford OH
(513) 529-2531
U.S. News ranking: Nat. U., No. 76
Website: www.MiamiOH.edu
Admissions email: admission@MiamiOH.edu
Public; founded 1809
Freshman admissions: more selective; 2013-2014: 22,520 applied, 15,034 accepted. Either SAT or ACT required. ACT 25/75 percentile: 25-30. High school rank: 39% in top tenth, 71% in top quarter, 95% in top half
Early decision deadline: 11/15, notification date: 12/15
Early action deadline: 12/1, notification date: 2/1
Application deadline (fall): 2/1
Undergraduate student body: 15,001 full time, 461 part time; 48% male, 52% female; 0% American Indian, 2% Asian, 4% black, 3% Hispanic, 3% multiracial, 0% Pacific Islander, 81% white, 6% international; 68% from in state; 47% live on campus; 23% of students in fraternities, 28% in sororities
Most popular majors: 6% Biological and Biomedical Sciences, 24% Business, Management, Marketing, and Related Support Services, 11% Education, 6% Parks, Recreation, Leisure, and Fitness Studies, 9% Social Sciences
Expenses: 2014-2015: $14,287 in state, $30,394 out of state; room/board: $11,109
Financial aid: (513) 529-8734; 40% of undergrads determined to have financial need; average aid package $11,902

Mount St. Joseph University
Cincinnati OH
(513) 244-4531
U.S. News ranking: Reg. U. (Mid. W), No. 61
Website: www.msj.edu
Admissions email: admission@mail.msj.edu
Private; founded 1920
Affiliation: Catholic
Freshman admissions: selective; 2013-2014: 1,180 applied, 1,036 accepted. Either SAT or ACT required. ACT 25/75 percentile: 19-24. High school rank: 7% in top tenth, 29% in top quarter, 58% in top half
Early decision deadline: N/A, notification date: N/A
Early action deadline: N/A, notification date: N/A
Application deadline (fall): 8/1
Undergraduate student body: 1,223 full time, 572 part time; 37% male, 63% female; 0% American Indian, 0% Asian, 10% black, 2% Hispanic, 2% multiracial, 0% Pacific Islander, 82% white,

0% international; 84% from in state; 23% live on campus; N/A of students in fraternities, N/A in sororities
Most popular majors: 5% Biology, General, 10% Business Administration and Management, General, 10% General Studies, 8% Graphic Design, 36% Registered Nursing/Registered Nurse
Expenses: 2014-2015: $26,850; room/board: $8,710
Financial aid: (513) 244-4418; 81% of undergrads determined to have financial need; average aid package $18,794

Mount Vernon Nazarene University
Mount Vernon OH
(866) 462-6868
U.S. News ranking: Reg. U. (Mid. W), No. 67
Website: www.gotomvnu.com
Admissions email: admissions@mvnu.edu
Private; founded 1968
Affiliation: Nazarene
Freshman admissions: selective; 2013-2014: 1,275 applied, 811 accepted. Either SAT or ACT required. ACT 25/75 percentile: 20-26. High school rank: 23% in top tenth, 49% in top quarter, 78% in top half
Early decision deadline: N/A, notification date: N/A
Early action deadline: N/A, notification date: N/A
Application deadline (fall): 7/15
Undergraduate student body: 1,450 full time, 379 part time; 36% male, 64% female; 0% American Indian, 0% Asian, 5% black, 2% Hispanic, 2% multiracial, 0% Pacific Islander, 83% white, 0% international; 92% from in state; 54% live on campus; 0% of students in fraternities, 0% in sororities
Most popular majors: 35% Business, Management, Marketing, and Related Support Services, 13% Education, 7% Health Professions and Related Programs, 12% Public Administration and Social Service Professions
Expenses: 2013-2014: $23,690; room/board: $6,980
Financial aid: (740) 392-6868

Muskingum University
New Concord OH
(740) 826-8137
U.S. News ranking: Reg. U. (Mid. W), No. 61
Website: www.muskingum.edu
Admissions email: adminfo@muskingum.edu
Private; founded 1837
Affiliation: Presbyterian Church (USA)
Freshman admissions: selective; 2013-2014: 2,001 applied, 1,520 accepted. Either SAT or ACT required. ACT 25/75 percentile: 18-24. High school rank: 28% in top tenth, 43% in top quarter, 70% in top half
Early decision deadline: N/A, notification date: N/A
Early action deadline: N/A, notification date: N/A
Application deadline (fall): 8/1
Undergraduate student body: 1,438 full time, 290 part time; 45% male, 55% female; 0% American Indian, 0% Asian, 6% black,

2% Hispanic, 3% multiracial, 0% Pacific Islander, 82% white, 4% international; 92% from in state; 71% live on campus; 25% of students in fraternities, 34% in sororities
Most popular majors: 18% Business, Management, Marketing, and Related Support Services, 8% Communication, Journalism, and Related Programs, 17% Education, 10% Health Professions and Related Programs, 10% Psychology
Expenses: 2014-2015: $24,826; room/board: $9,760
Financial aid: (740) 826-8139; 84% of undergrads determined to have financial need; average aid package $20,803

Notre Dame College of Ohio[1]
Cleveland OH
(216) 373-5355
U.S. News ranking: Reg. Coll. (Mid. W), No. 59
Website: www.notredamecollege.edu
Admissions email: admission@ndc.edu
Private; founded 1922
Affiliation: Roman Catholic
Application deadline (fall): rolling
Undergraduate student body: N/A full time, N/A part time
Expenses: 2013-2014: $26,344; room/board: $8,598
Financial aid: (216) 373-5263

Oberlin College
Oberlin OH
(440) 775-8411
U.S. News ranking: Nat. Lib. Arts, No. 23
Website: www.oberlin.edu
Admissions email: college.admissions@oberlin.edu
Private; founded 1833
Freshman admissions: more selective; 2013-2014: 7,438 applied, 2,262 accepted. Either SAT or ACT required. SAT 25/75 percentile: 1270-1455. High school rank: 62% in top tenth, 87% in top quarter, 99% in top half
Early decision deadline: 11/15, notification date: 12/10
Early action deadline: N/A, notification date: N/A
Application deadline (fall): 1/15
Undergraduate student body: 2,861 full time, 33 part time; 46% male, 54% female; 0% American Indian, 4% Asian, 5% black, 7% Hispanic, 5% multiracial, 0% Pacific Islander, 70% white, 7% international; 8% from in state; 90% live on campus; 0% of students in fraternities, 0% in sororities
Most popular majors: 9% Biology, General, 8% English Language and Literature, General, 15% Music Performance, General, 9% Political Science and Government, 6% Psychology, General
Expenses: 2014-2015: $48,682; room/board: $13,106
Financial aid: (440) 775-8142; 49% of undergrads determined to have financial need; average aid package $37,656

Ohio Christian University[1]
Circleville OH
(877) 762-8669
U.S. News ranking: Reg. Coll. (Mid. W), second tier
Website: www.ohiochristian.edu/
Admissions email: enroll@ohiochristian.edu
Private
Application deadline (fall): N/A
Undergraduate student body: N/A full time, N/A part time
Expenses: 2013-2014: $17,720; room/board: $6,998
Financial aid: (740) 477-7758

Ohio Dominican University
Columbus OH
(614) 251-4500
U.S. News ranking: Reg. U. (Mid. W), No. 84
Website: www.ohiodominican.edu
Admissions email: admissions@ohiodominican.edu
Private; founded 1911
Affiliation: Roman Catholic
Freshman admissions: selective; 2013-2014: 2,652 applied, 1,310 accepted. Either SAT or ACT required. ACT 25/75 percentile: 20-24. High school rank: 22% in top tenth, 46% in top quarter, 80% in top half
Early decision deadline: N/A, notification date: N/A
Early action deadline: N/A, notification date: N/A
Application deadline (fall): rolling
Undergraduate student body: 1,391 full time, 614 part time; 42% male, 58% female; 0% American Indian, 1% Asian, 26% black, 3% Hispanic, 4% multiracial, 0% Pacific Islander, 63% white, 1% international
Most popular majors: 5% Accounting, 5% Biology/Biological Sciences, General, 36% Business Administration and Management, General, 9% Elementary Education and Teaching, 5% Sport and Fitness Administration/Management
Expenses: 2013-2014: $28,932; room/board: $9,978
Financial aid: (614) 251-4778

Ohio Northern University
Ada OH
(888) 408-4668
U.S. News ranking: Reg. Coll. (Mid. W), No. 2
Website: www.onu.edu
Admissions email: admissions-ug@onu.edu
Private; founded 1871
Affiliation: Methodist
Freshman admissions: more selective; 2013-2014: 3,325 applied, 2,256 accepted. Either SAT or ACT required. ACT 25/75 percentile: 23-29. High school rank: 38% in top tenth, 69% in top quarter, 90% in top half
Early decision deadline: N/A, notification date: N/A
Early action deadline: N/A, notification date: N/A
Application deadline (fall): 8/15
Undergraduate student body: 2,194 full time, 508 part time; 52% male, 48% female; 0% American Indian, 1% Asian, 4% black, 2% Hispanic, 3% multiracial, 0% Pacific Islander, 85% white, 4% international; 86% from in state;

78% live on campus; 21% of students in fraternities, 21% in sororities
Most popular majors: 19% Business, Management, Marketing, and Related Support Services, 5% Communication, Journalism, and Related Programs, 9% Education, 15% Engineering, 10% Health Professions and Related Programs
Expenses: 2014-2015: $28,050; room/board: $10,910
Financial aid: (419) 772-2272

Ohio State University–Columbus
Columbus OH
(614) 292-3980
U.S. News ranking: Nat. U., No. 54
Website: www.osu.edu
Admissions email: askabuckeye@osu.edu
Public; founded 1870
Freshman admissions: more selective; 2013-2014: 31,359 applied, 17,413 accepted. Either SAT or ACT required. ACT 25/75 percentile: 27-31. High school rank: 58% in top tenth, 92% in top quarter, 99% in top half
Early decision deadline: N/A, notification date: N/A
Early action deadline: 11/1, notification date: 12/15
Application deadline (fall): 2/1
Undergraduate student body: 40,020 full time, 4,181 part time; 53% male, 47% female; 0% American Indian, 5% Asian, 6% black, 3% Hispanic, 3% multiracial, 0% Pacific Islander, 72% white, 7% international; 86% from in state; 26% live on campus; 6% of students in fraternities, 6% in sororities
Most popular majors: 3% Biology/Biological Sciences, General, 4% Finance, General, 3% Marketing/Marketing Management, General, 6% Psychology, General, 4% Speech Communication and Rhetoric
Expenses: 2014-2015: $10,037 in state, $26,537 out of state; room/board: $9,850
Financial aid: (614) 292-0300; 52% of undergrads determined to have financial need; average aid package $12,183

Ohio University
Athens OH
(740) 593-4100
U.S. News ranking: Nat. U., No. 129
Website: www.ohio.edu
Admissions email: admissions@ohio.edu
Public; founded 1804
Freshman admissions: selective; 2013-2014: 20,765 applied, 15,149 accepted. Either SAT or ACT required. ACT 25/75 percentile: 22-26. High school rank: 17% in top tenth, 42% in top quarter, 82% in top half
Early decision deadline: N/A, notification date: N/A
Early action deadline: N/A, notification date: N/A
Undergraduate student body: 16,756 full time, 6,748 part time; 40% male, 60% female; 0% American Indian, 1% Asian, 5% black, 2% Hispanic, 3% multiracial, 0% Pacific Islander, 83% white, 4% international; 86% from in state; 44% live

on campus; 8% of students in fraternities, 8% in sororities
Most popular majors: 4% Liberal Arts and Sciences, General Studies and Humanities, Other, 4% Psychology, General, 30% Registered Nursing/Registered Nurse, 4% Secondary Education and Teaching, 5% Speech Communication and Rhetoric
Expenses: 2014-2015: $10,536 in state, $19,500 out of state; room/board: $11,532
Financial aid: (740) 593-4141; 60% of undergrads determined to have financial need; average aid package $8,800

Ohio Wesleyan University

Delaware OH
(740) 368-3020
U.S. News ranking: Nat. Lib. Arts, No. 99
Website: web.owu.edu
Admissions email: owuadmit@owu.edu
Private; founded 1842
Affiliation: Methodist
Freshman admissions: more selective; 2013-2014: 4,029 applied, 3,035 accepted. Neither SAT nor ACT required. ACT 25/75 percentile: 22-27. High school rank: 32% in top tenth, 55% in top quarter, 82% in top half
Early decision deadline: 11/15, notification date: 11/30
Early action deadline: 1/15, notification date: N/A
Application deadline (fall): rolling
Undergraduate student body: 1,809 full time, 21 part time; 46% male, 54% female; 0% American Indian, 3% Asian, 6% black, 5% Hispanic, 4% multiracial, 0% Pacific Islander, 72% white, 7% international; N/A from in state; 33% live on campus; 44% of students in fraternities, 44% in sororities
Most popular majors: 15% Biological and Biomedical Sciences, 8% Business, Management, Marketing, and Related Support Services, 8% Psychology, 16% Social Sciences, 7% Visual and Performing Arts
Expenses: 2014-2015: $41,920; room/board: $11,210
Financial aid: (740) 368-3050; 65% of undergrads determined to have financial need; average aid package $32,026

Otterbein University

Westerville OH
(614) 823-1500
U.S. News ranking: Reg. U. (Mid. W), No. 20
Website: www.otterbein.edu
Admissions email: UOtterB@Otterbein.edu
Private; founded 1847
Affiliation: United Methodist
Freshman admissions: selective; 2013-2014: 3,175 applied, 2,341 accepted. Either SAT or ACT required. ACT 25/75 percentile: 22-27. High school rank: 23% in top tenth, 54% in top quarter, 86% in top half
Early decision deadline: N/A, notification date: N/A
Early action deadline: N/A, notification date: N/A
Application deadline (fall): rolling

Undergraduate student body: 2,206 full time, 273 part time; 38% male, 62% female; 0% American Indian, 1% Asian, 7% black, 2% Hispanic, 3% multiracial, 0% Pacific Islander, 79% white, 3% international; 89% from in state; 65% live on campus; 27% of students in fraternities, 18% in sororities
Most popular majors: 11% Business Administration, Management and Operations, 7% Communication and Media Studies, 10% Health Services/Allied Health/Health Sciences, General, 11% Registered Nursing, Nursing Administration, Nursing Research and Clinical Nursing, 7% Teacher Education and Professional Development, Specific Levels and Methods
Expenses: 2014-2015: $31,624; room/board: $9,460
Financial aid: (614) 823-1502; 76% of undergrads determined to have financial need; average aid package $21,407

Shawnee State University

Portsmouth OH
(800) 959-2778
U.S. News ranking: Nat. Lib. Arts, second tier
Website: www.shawnee.edu
Admissions email: To_SSU@shawnee.edu
Public; founded 1986
Freshman admissions: selective; 2013-2014: 4,426 applied, 3,688 accepted. Neither SAT nor ACT required. ACT 25/75 percentile: 17-23. High school rank: 12% in top tenth, 43% in top quarter, 64% in top half
Early decision deadline: N/A, notification date: N/A
Early action deadline: N/A, notification date: N/A
Application deadline (fall): rolling
Undergraduate student body: 3,635 full time, 620 part time; 42% male, 58% female; 1% American Indian, 0% Asian, 6% black, 1% Hispanic, 1% multiracial, 0% Pacific Islander, 86% white, 1% international; 90% from in state; 22% live on campus; 1% of students in fraternities, 1% in sororities
Most popular majors: 6% Business Administration and Management, General, 6% General Studies, 5% Nursing Administration, 8% Psychology, General, 7% Sociology
Expenses: 2014-2015: $7,364 in state, $12,617 out of state; room/board: $9,552
Financial aid: (740) 351-4243

Tiffin University

Tiffin OH
(419) 448-3423
U.S. News ranking: Reg. U. (Mid. W), second tier
Website: www.tiffin.edu
Admissions email: admiss@tiffin.edu
Private; founded 1888
Freshman admissions: selective; 2013-2014: 3,998 applied, 2,377 accepted. Neither SAT nor ACT required. ACT 25/75 percentile: 18-23. High school rank: N/A
Early decision deadline: N/A, notification date: N/A
Early action deadline: N/A, notification date: N/A

Application deadline (fall): rolling
Undergraduate student body: 2,145 full time, 1,619 part time; 41% male, 59% female; 0% American Indian, 0% Asian, 17% black, 2% Hispanic, 3% multiracial, 0% Pacific Islander, 33% white, 3% international; 66% from in state; 25% live on campus; 1% of students in fraternities, 1% in sororities
Most popular majors: Information not available
Expenses: 2014-2015: $21,510; room/board: $9,870
Financial aid: (419) 448-3357; 89% of undergrads determined to have financial need; average aid package $15,597

Union Institute and University[1]

Cincinnati OH
(513) 487-1239
U.S. News ranking: Nat. U., unranked
Website: www.myunion.edu
Admissions email: admissions@myunion.edu
Private
Application deadline (fall): N/A
Undergraduate student body: N/A full time, N/A part time
Expenses: 2013-2014: $11,904; room/board: N/A
Financial aid: (513) 487-1127

University of Akron

Akron OH
(330) 972-7077
U.S. News ranking: Nat. U., second tier
Website: www.uakron.edu
Admissions email: admissions@uakron.edu
Public; founded 1870
Freshman admissions: selective; 2013-2014: 10,575 applied, 10,204 accepted. Either SAT or ACT required. ACT 25/75 percentile: 18-25. High school rank: 13% in top tenth, 33% in top quarter, 62% in top half
Early decision deadline: N/A, notification date: N/A
Early action deadline: 11/1, notification date: 12/15
Application deadline (fall): 7/1
Undergraduate student body: 15,869 full time, 4,604 part time; 52% male, 48% female; 0% American Indian, 2% Asian, 14% black, 2% Hispanic, 3% multiracial, 0% Pacific Islander, 74% white, 1% international; 97% from in state; 14% live on campus; 4% of students in fraternities, 4% in sororities
Most popular majors: 18% Business, Management, Marketing, and Related Support Services, 8% Communication, Journalism, and Related Programs, 11% Education, 9% Engineering, 15% Health Professions and Related Programs
Expenses: 2014-2015: $10,320 in state, $18,851 out of state; room/board: $11,332
Financial aid: (330) 972-7032; 78% of undergrads determined to have financial need; average aid package $7,051

University of Cincinnati

Cincinnati OH
(513) 556-1100
U.S. News ranking: Nat. U., No. 129
Website: www.uc.edu
Admissions email: admissions@uc.edu
Public; founded 1819
Freshman admissions: more selective; 2013-2014: 16,069 applied, 11,680 accepted. Either SAT or ACT required. ACT 25/75 percentile: 22-28. High school rank: 22% in top tenth, 50% in top quarter, 81% in top half
Early decision deadline: N/A, notification date: N/A
Early action deadline: N/A, notification date: N/A
Application deadline (fall): 2/1
Undergraduate student body: 18,857 full time, 3,374 part time; 49% male, 51% female; 0% American Indian, 3% Asian, 8% black, 3% Hispanic, 2% multiracial, 0% Pacific Islander, 76% white, 4% international; 89% from in state; 21% live on campus; 10% of students in fraternities, 11% in sororities
Most popular majors: 8% Biological and Biomedical Sciences, 51% Business, Management, Marketing, and Related Support Services, 4% Computer and Information Sciences and Support Services, 4% Foreign Languages, Literatures, and Linguistics, 14% Social Sciences
Expenses: 2014-2015: $11,000 in state, $26,334 out of state; room/board: $10,496
Financial aid: (513) 556-6982; 59% of undergrads determined to have financial need; average aid package $8,330

University of Cincinnati–UC Blue Ash College[1]

Cincinnati OH
(513) 745-5700
U.S. News ranking: Reg. Coll. (Mid. W), unranked
Website: www.rwc.uc.edu/
Admissions email: N/A
Public
Application deadline (fall): N/A
Undergraduate student body: N/A full time, N/A part time
Expenses: 2013-2014: $5,890 in state, $14,516 out of state; room/board: N/A
Financial aid: (513) 745-5700

University of Dayton

Dayton OH
(937) 229-4411
U.S. News ranking: Nat. U., No. 103
Website: www.udayton.edu
Admissions email: admission@udayton.edu
Private; founded 1850
Affiliation: Roman Catholic (Marianist)
Freshman admissions: more selective; 2013-2014: 16,279 applied, 8,507 accepted. Either SAT or ACT required. ACT 25/75 percentile: 24-29. High school rank: 24% in top tenth, 54% in top quarter, 87% in top half
Early decision deadline: N/A, notification date: N/A

Early action deadline: 12/15, notification date: 2/1
Application deadline (fall): 3/1
Undergraduate student body: 7,454 full time, 521 part time; 52% male, 48% female; 0% American Indian, 1% Asian, 3% black, 3% Hispanic, 1% multiracial, 0% Pacific Islander, 82% white, 9% international; 55% from in state; 72% live on campus; 17% of students in fraternities, 23% in sororities
Most popular majors: 29% Business, Management, Marketing, and Related Support Services, 7% Communication, Journalism, and Related Programs, 9% Education, 13% Engineering, 6% Psychology
Expenses: 2014-2015: $37,230; room/board: $11,840
Financial aid: (937) 229-4311; 53% of undergrads determined to have financial need; average aid package $22,338

University of Findlay

Findlay OH
(800) 548-0932
U.S. News ranking: Reg. U. (Mid. W), No. 49
Website: www.findlay.edu
Admissions email: admissions@findlay.edu
Private; founded 1882
Affiliation: Churches of God General Conference
Freshman admissions: selective; 2013-2014: 2,951 applied, 1,940 accepted. Either SAT or ACT required. ACT 25/75 percentile: 20-25. High school rank: 42% in top tenth, 44% in top quarter, 89% in top half
Early decision deadline: N/A, notification date: N/A
Early action deadline: N/A, notification date: N/A
Application deadline (fall): rolling
Undergraduate student body: 2,490 full time, 1,382 part time; 38% male, 62% female; 0% American Indian, 1% Asian, 4% black, 2% Hispanic, 2% multiracial, 0% Pacific Islander, 82% white, 8% international; 82% from in state; 45% live on campus; 2% of students in fraternities, 2% in sororities
Most popular majors: 14% Agriculture, Agriculture Operations, and Related Sciences, 6% Biological and Biomedical Sciences, 16% Business, Management, Marketing, and Related Support Services, 12% Education, 21% Health Professions and Related Programs
Expenses: 2014-2015: $30,640; room/board: $9,350
Financial aid: (419) 434-4792; 80% of undergrads determined to have financial need; average aid package $18,435

University of Mount Union

Alliance OH
(330) 823-2590
U.S. News ranking: Reg. Coll. (Mid. W), No. 11
Website: www.mountunion.edu/
Admissions email: admission@mountunion.edu
Private; founded 1846
Affiliation: United Methodist
Freshman admissions: selective; 2013-2014: 2,660 applied, 1,894 accepted. Either SAT

or ACT required. ACT 25/75 percentile: 20-25. High school rank: 10% in top tenth, 34% in top quarter, 66% in top half
Early decision deadline: N/A, notification date: N/A
Early action deadline: N/A, notification date: N/A
Application deadline (fall): rolling
Undergraduate student body: 2,056 full time, 40 part time; 50% male, 50% female; 0% American Indian, 0% Asian, 6% black, 2% Hispanic, 4% multiracial, 0% Pacific Islander, 81% white, 3% international; 82% from in state; 76% live on campus; 14% of students in fraternities, 32% in sororities
Most popular majors: 10% Biological and Biomedical Sciences, 14% Business, Management, Marketing, and Related Support Services, 20% Education, 13% Parks, Recreation, Leisure, and Fitness Studies, 6% Psychology
Expenses: 2014-2015: $27,990; room/board: $9,200
Financial aid: (877) 543-9185; 86% of undergrads determined to have financial need; average aid package $21,406

University of Northwestern Ohio[1]
Lima OH
(419) 998-3120
U.S. News ranking: Reg. Coll. (Mid. W), unranked
Website: www.unoh.edu/
Admissions email: info@unoh.edu
Private
Application deadline (fall): N/A
Undergraduate student body: N/A full time, N/A part time
Expenses: 2013-2014: $9,565; room/board: $6,750
Financial aid: (419) 998-3140

University of Rio Grande
Rio Grande OH
(740) 245-7208
U.S. News ranking: Reg. U. (Mid. W), unranked
Website: www.rio.edu
Admissions email: admissions@rio.edu
Private; founded 1876
Freshman admissions: N/A; 2013-2014: 1,709 applied, 1,277 accepted. Neither SAT nor ACT required. ACT 25/75 percentile: N/A. High school rank: 9% in top tenth, 28% in top quarter, 58% in top half
Early decision deadline: N/A, notification date: N/A
Early action deadline: N/A, notification date: N/A
Application deadline (fall): rolling
Undergraduate student body: 1,800 full time, 405 part time; 38% male, 62% female; 0% American Indian, 0% Asian, 5% black, 1% Hispanic, 0% multiracial, 0% Pacific Islander, 83% white, 0% international; 95% from in state; 17% live on campus; 2% of students in fraternities, 1% in sororities
Most popular majors: 6% Biology/Biological Sciences, General, 14% Business Administration and Management, General, 5% Elementary Education and Teaching, 12% Registered Nursing, Nursing Administration, Nursing Research and Clinical

Nursing, Other, 8% Sport and Fitness Administration/Management
Expenses: 2014-2015: $21,930; room/board: $9,450
Financial aid: (740) 245-7218; 93% of undergrads determined to have financial need; average aid package $6,686

University of Toledo
Toledo OH
(419) 530-8888
U.S. News ranking: Nat. U., second tier
Website: www.utoledo.edu
Admissions email: enroll@utnet.utoledo.edu
Public; founded 1872
Freshman admissions: selective; 2013-2014: 11,066 applied, 10,040 accepted. Either SAT or ACT required. ACT 25/75 percentile: 19-25. High school rank: 17% in top tenth, 40% in top quarter, 70% in top half
Early decision deadline: N/A, notification date: N/A
Early action deadline: N/A, notification date: N/A
Application deadline (fall): rolling
Undergraduate student body: 13,069 full time, 3,123 part time; 51% male, 49% female; 0% American Indian, 2% Asian, 14% black, 4% Hispanic, 3% multiracial, 0% Pacific Islander, 69% white, 4% international; 84% from in state; 19% live on campus; 7% of students in fraternities, 7% in sororities
Most popular majors: 18% Business, Management, Marketing, and Related Support Services, 9% Education, 11% Engineering, 19% Health Professions and Related Programs
Expenses: 2014-2015: $9,280 in state, $19,158 out of state; room/board: $10,094
Financial aid: (419) 530-8700; 69% of undergrads determined to have financial need; average aid package $10,665

Urbana University[1]
Urbana OH
(937) 484-1356
U.S. News ranking: Reg. Coll. (Mid. W), unranked
Website: www.urbana.edu
Admissions email: admiss@urbana.edu
Private
Application deadline (fall): N/A
Undergraduate student body: N/A full time, N/A part time
Expenses: 2013-2014: $21,566; room/board: $8,120
Financial aid: (937) 484-1355

Ursuline College
Pepper Pike OH
(440) 449-4203
U.S. News ranking: Reg. U. (Mid. W), No. 54
Website: www.ursuline.edu
Admissions email: admission@ursuline.edu
Private; founded 1871
Affiliation: Roman Catholic
Freshman admissions: selective; 2013-2014: 441 applied, 255 accepted. Either SAT or ACT required. ACT 25/75 percentile: 19-24. High school rank: 12% in top tenth, 38% in top quarter, 80% in top half

Early decision deadline: N/A, notification date: N/A
Early action deadline: N/A, notification date: N/A
Application deadline (fall): 2/1
Undergraduate student body: 547 full time, 258 part time; 8% male, 92% female; 0% American Indian, 1% Asian, 28% black, 2% Hispanic, 3% multiracial, 0% Pacific Islander, 62% white, 1% international; 94% from in state; 23% live on campus; 0% of students in fraternities, 0% in sororities
Most popular majors: 12% Business, Management, Marketing, and Related Support Services, 58% Health Professions and Related Programs, 4% Legal Professions and Studies, 8% Psychology, 3% Public Administration and Social Service Professions
Expenses: 2014-2015: $27,690; room/board: $9,212
Financial aid: (440) 646-8309; 90% of undergrads determined to have financial need; average aid package $17,815

Walsh University
North Canton OH
(800) 362-9846
U.S. News ranking: Reg. U. (Mid. W), No. 65
Website: www.walsh.edu
Admissions email: admissions@walsh.edu
Private; founded 1958
Affiliation: Roman Catholic
Freshman admissions: selective; 2013-2014: 1,640 applied, 1,265 accepted. Either SAT or ACT required. ACT 25/75 percentile: 20-25. High school rank: 15% in top tenth, 46% in top quarter, 79% in top half
Early decision deadline: N/A, notification date: N/A
Early action deadline: N/A, notification date: N/A
Application deadline (fall): 8/15
Undergraduate student body: 1,916 full time, 469 part time; 39% male, 61% female; 0% American Indian, 0% Asian, 5% black, 2% Hispanic, 2% multiracial, 0% Pacific Islander, 78% white, 3% international; 96% from in state; 48% live on campus; 0% of students in fraternities, 0% in sororities
Most popular majors: 10% Biological and Biomedical Sciences, 32% Business, Management, Marketing, and Related Support Services, 15% Education, 20% Health Professions and Related Programs, 6% Social Sciences
Expenses: 2014-2015: $26,670; room/board: $9,580
Financial aid: (330) 490-7150; 93% of undergrads determined to have financial need; average aid package $21,862

Wilberforce University[1]
Wilberforce OH
(800) 367-8568
U.S. News ranking: Reg. Coll. (Mid. W), second tier
Website: www.wilberforce.edu
Admissions email: admissions@wilberforce.edu
Private
Application deadline (fall): N/A

Undergraduate student body: N/A full time, N/A part time
Expenses: 2013-2014: $15,140; room/board: $6,100
Financial aid: (800) 367-8565

Wilmington College
Wilmington OH
(937) 382-6661
U.S. News ranking: Reg. Coll. (Mid. W), No. 58
Website: www2.wilmington.edu
Admissions email: admission@wilmington.edu
Private; founded 1870
Affiliation: Religious Society of Friends
Freshman admissions: less selective; 2013-2014: N/A applied, N/A accepted. Neither SAT nor ACT required. ACT 25/75 percentile: N/A. High school rank: N/A
Early decision deadline: N/A, notification date: N/A
Early action deadline: N/A, notification date: N/A
Undergraduate student body: 1,030 full time, 133 part time; 47% male, 53% female; 1% American Indian, 0% Asian, 8% black, 1% Hispanic, 3% multiracial, 0% Pacific Islander, 75% white, 1% international
Most popular majors: Information not available
Expenses: 2013-2014: $28,190; room/board: $9,392
Financial aid: (937) 382-6661

Wittenberg University
Springfield OH
(937) 327-6314
U.S. News ranking: Nat. Lib. Arts, No. 139
Website: www5.wittenberg.edu
Admissions email: admission@wittenberg.edu
Private; founded 1845
Affiliation: Lutheran
Freshman admissions: selective; 2013-2014: 5,160 applied, 4,612 accepted. Neither SAT nor ACT required. ACT 25/75 percentile: 23-28. High school rank: 22% in top tenth, 49% in top quarter, 81% in top half
Early decision deadline: 11/15, notification date: 12/15
Early action deadline: 12/1, notification date: 1/1
Application deadline (fall): rolling
Undergraduate student body: 1,853 full time, 106 part time; 43% male, 57% female; 0% American Indian, 1% Asian, 7% black, 3% Hispanic, 4% multiracial, 0% Pacific Islander, 81% white, 2% international; 71% from in state; 84% live on campus; 25% of students in fraternities, 35% in sororities
Most popular majors: 16% Biological and Biomedical Sciences, 8% Communication, Journalism, and Related Programs, 7% Education, 7% Psychology, 16% Social Sciences
Expenses: 2014-2015: $38,030; room/board: $9,932
Financial aid: (937) 327-7321; 78% of undergrads determined to have financial need; average aid package $31,471

Wright State University
Dayton OH
(937) 775-5700
U.S. News ranking: Nat. U., second tier
Website: www.wright.edu
Admissions email: admissions@wright.edu
Public; founded 1964
Freshman admissions: selective; 2013-2014: 5,049 applied, 4,863 accepted. Either SAT or ACT required. ACT 25/75 percentile: 19-25. High school rank: 15% in top tenth, 36% in top quarter, 65% in top half
Early decision deadline: N/A, notification date: N/A
Early action deadline: N/A, notification date: N/A
Application deadline (fall): rolling
Undergraduate student body: 9,987 full time, 2,809 part time; 49% male, 51% female; 0% American Indian, 2% Asian, 12% black, 3% Hispanic, 4% multiracial, 0% Pacific Islander, 73% white, 5% international; 97% from in state; 14% live on campus; 2% of students in fraternities, 5% in sororities
Most popular majors: 5% Biology/Biological Sciences, General, 15% Business Administration and Management, General, 4% Mechanical Engineering, 8% Psychology, General, 11% Registered Nursing/Registered Nurse
Expenses: 2014-2015: $8,730 in state, $16,910 out of state; room/board: $9,108
Financial aid: (937) 873-5721; 67% of undergrads determined to have financial need; average aid package $10,250

Xavier University
Cincinnati OH
(877) 982-3648
U.S. News ranking: Reg. U. (Mid. W), No. 5
Website: www.xavier.edu
Admissions email: xuadmit@xavier.edu
Private; founded 1831
Affiliation: Roman Catholic (Jesuit)
Freshman admissions: more selective; 2013-2014: 10,907 applied, 7,632 accepted. Either SAT or ACT required. ACT 25/75 percentile: 23-27. High school rank: 22% in top tenth, 54% in top quarter, 85% in top half
Early decision deadline: N/A, notification date: N/A
Early action deadline: N/A, notification date: N/A
Application deadline (fall): rolling
Undergraduate student body: 4,150 full time, 502 part time; 46% male, 54% female; 0% American Indian, 2% Asian, 10% black, 4% Hispanic, 3% multiracial, 0% Pacific Islander, 73% white, 2% international; 53% from in state; 51% live on campus; N/A of students in fraternities, N/A in sororities
Most popular majors: 30% Business, Management, Marketing, and Related Support Services, 8% Health Professions and Related Programs, 13% Liberal Arts and Sciences, General Studies and Humanities, 6% Psychology, 7% Social Sciences
Expenses: 2013-2014: $33,000; room/board: $10,520
Financial aid: (513) 745-3142

Youngstown State University

Youngstown OH
(877) 468-6978
U.S. News ranking: Reg. U. (Mid. W), second tier
Website: www.ysu.edu
Admissions email: enroll@ysu.edu
Public; founded 1908
Freshman admissions: selective; 2013-2014: 4,343 applied, 3,756 accepted. Either SAT or ACT required. ACT 25/75 percentile: 17-23. High school rank: 11% in top tenth, 17% in top quarter, 57% in top half
Early decision deadline: N/A, notification date: N/A
Early action deadline: N/A, notification date: N/A
Application deadline (fall): 8/1
Undergraduate student body: 9,473 full time, 2,699 part time; 47% male, 53% female; 0% American Indian, 1% Asian, 14% black, 3% Hispanic, 2% multiracial, 0% Pacific Islander, 75% white, 1% international; 89% from in state; 10% live on campus; 1% of students in fraternities, 1% in sororities
Most popular majors: 5% Accounting, 5% Biology/Biological Sciences, General, 7% Criminal Justice/Safety Studies, 5% General Studies, 4% Social Work
Expenses: 2014-2015: $8,317 in state, $14,317 out of state; room/board: $8,645
Financial aid: (330) 941-3399; 76% of undergrads determined to have financial need; average aid package $8,669

OKLAHOMA

Bacone College[1]

Muskogee OK
(888) 682-5514
U.S. News ranking: Reg. Coll. (W), second tier
Website: www.bacone.edu/
Admissions email: admissions@bacone.edu
Private
Application deadline (fall): N/A
Undergraduate student body: N/A full time, N/A part time
Expenses: 2013-2014: $14,050; room/board: $9,560
Financial aid: (888) 682-5514

Cameron University

Lawton OK
(580) 581-2289
U.S. News ranking: Reg. U. (W), second tier
Website: www.cameron.edu
Admissions email: admissions@cameron.edu
Public; founded 1908
Freshman admissions: less selective; 2013-2014: 1,356 applied, 1,353 accepted. Neither SAT nor ACT required. ACT 25/75 percentile: 16-21. High school rank: 4% in top tenth, 15% in top quarter, 44% in top half
Early decision deadline: N/A, notification date: N/A
Early action deadline: N/A, notification date: N/A
Application deadline (fall): rolling
Undergraduate student body: 3,590 full time, 1,768 part time; 39% male, 61% female; 6% American Indian, 2% Asian, 17% black, 12% Hispanic, 8% multiracial, 1% Pacific Islander, 48% white,

4% international; 85% from in state; 8% live on campus; 2% of students in fraternities, 1% in sororities
Most popular majors: 13% Business Administration and Management, General, 13% Corrections and Criminal Justice, Other, 6% Elementary Education and Teaching, 12% General Studies, 7% Psychology, General
Expenses: 2014-2015: $5,340 in state, $13,380 out of state; room/board $4,664
Financial aid: (580) 581-2293; 67% of undergrads determined to have financial need; average aid package $9,080

East Central University[1]

Ada OK
(580) 559-5239
U.S. News ranking: Reg. U. (W), second tier
Website: www.ecok.edu
Admissions email: parmstro@ecok.edu
Public
Application deadline (fall): N/A
Undergraduate student body: N/A full time, N/A part time
Expenses: 2013-2014: $5,241 in state, $12,643 out of state; room/board: $4,982
Financial aid: (580) 559-5242

Langston University

Langston OK
(405) 466-3231
U.S. News ranking: Reg. U. (W), unranked
Website: www.lunet.edu
Admissions email: admission@speedy.lunet.edu
Public
Freshman admissions: N/A; 2013-2014: 6,965 applied, 3,520 accepted. Neither SAT nor ACT required. ACT 25/75 percentile: N/A. High school rank: N/A
Early decision deadline: N/A, notification date: N/A
Early action deadline: N/A, notification date: N/A
Application deadline (fall): rolling
Undergraduate student body: 1,841 full time, 234 part time; 40% male, 60% female; 2% American Indian, 1% Asian, 85% black, 1% Hispanic, 0% multiracial, 0% Pacific Islander, 10% white, 1% international
Most popular majors: 18% Business, Management, Marketing, and Related Support Services, 20% Health Professions and Related Programs, 5% Homeland Security, Law Enforcement, Firefighting and Related Protective Services, 8% Liberal Arts and Sciences, General Studies and Humanities, 11% Psychology
Expenses: 2014-2015: $6,298 in state, $13,285 out of state; room/board: $7,026
Financial aid: (405) 466-3282; 89% of undergrads determined to have financial need; average aid package $9,840

Mid-America Christian University[1]

Oklahoma City OK
(888) 436-3035
U.S. News ranking: Reg. Coll. (W), unranked
Website: www.macu.edu
Admissions email: info@macu.edu
Private
Application deadline (fall): N/A
Undergraduate student body: N/A full time, N/A part time
Expenses: 2013-2014: $15,688; room/board: $6,430
Financial aid: (405) 691-3800

Northeastern State University

Tahlequah OK
(918) 444-2200
U.S. News ranking: Reg. U. (W), No. 84
Website: www.nsuok.edu
Admissions email: nsuinfo@nsuok.edu
Public; founded 1846
Freshman admissions: selective; 2013-2014: 1,889 applied, 1,386 accepted. ACT required. ACT 25/75 percentile: 18-23. High school rank: 18% in top tenth, 43% in top quarter, 78% in top half
Early decision deadline: N/A, notification date: N/A
Early action deadline: N/A, notification date: N/A
Application deadline (fall): rolling
Undergraduate student body: 5,307 full time, 2,124 part time; 40% male, 60% female; 23% American Indian, 2% Asian, 5% black, 4% Hispanic, 11% multiracial, 0% Pacific Islander, 52% white, 1% international; 94% from in state; 19% live on campus; 2% of students in fraternities, 17% in sororities
Most popular majors: 6% Biology/Biological Sciences, General, 8% Criminal Justice/Law Enforcement Administration, 7% Elementary Education and Teaching, 6% General Studies, 9% Psychology, General
Expenses: 2014-2015: $4,994 in state, $12,012 out of state; room/board: $6,670
Financial aid: (918) 456-5511; 69% of undergrads determined to have financial need; average aid package $11,880

Northwestern Oklahoma State University

Alva OK
(580) 327-8545
U.S. News ranking: Reg. U. (W), second tier
Website: www.nwosu.edu
Admissions email: recruit@nwosu.edu
Public; founded 1897
Freshman admissions: selective; 2013-2014: 1,010 applied, 663 accepted. Either SAT or ACT required. ACT 25/75 percentile: 18-22. High school rank: 12% in top tenth, 28% in top quarter, 64% in top half
Early decision deadline: N/A, notification date: N/A
Early action deadline: N/A, notification date: N/A
Application deadline (fall): rolling

percentile: 22-28. High school rank: 30% in top tenth, 58% in top quarter, 81% in top half
Early decision deadline: N/A, notification date: N/A
Early action deadline: N/A, notification date: N/A
Application deadline (fall): rolling
Undergraduate student body: 1,725 full time, 424 part time; 44% male, 56% female; 7% American Indian, 1% Asian, 7% black, 6% Hispanic, 1% multiracial, 0% Pacific Islander, 67% white, 4% international; 78% from in state; 48% live on campus; N/A of students in fraternities, N/A in sororities
Most popular majors: 10% Business Administration and Management, General, 7% Early Childhood Education and Teaching, 12% Parks, Recreation, Leisure, and Fitness Studies, Other, 9% Psychology, General, 9% Registered Nursing/Registered Nurse
Expenses: 2013-2014: $5,054 in state, $10,987 out of state; room/board: $3,900
Financial aid: (580) 327-8542

Oklahoma Baptist University

Shawnee OK
(405) 585-5000
U.S. News ranking: Reg. Coll. (W), No. 4
Website: www.okbu.edu
Admissions email: admissions@okbu.edu
Private; founded 1910
Affiliation: Southern Baptist Convention
Freshman admissions: more selective; 2013-2014: 6,560 applied, 3,704 accepted. Either SAT or ACT required. ACT 25/75 percentile: 21-27. High school rank: 27% in top tenth, 58% in top quarter, 87% in top half
Early decision deadline: N/A, notification date: N/A
Early action deadline: N/A, notification date: N/A
Application deadline (fall): 8/1
Undergraduate student body: 1,868 full time, 151 part time; 41% male, 59% female; 5% American Indian, 1% Asian, 5% black, 5% Hispanic, 7% multiracial, 0% Pacific Islander, 69% white, 4% international; 64% from in state; 63% live on campus; 2% of students in fraternities, 11% in sororities
Most popular majors: 8% Business, Management, Marketing, and Related Support Services, 7% Communication, Journalism, and Related Programs, 18% Education, 19% Health Professions and Related Programs, 6% Philosophy and Religious Studies
Expenses: 2014-2015: $22,800; room/board: $6,520
Financial aid: (405) 878-2016; 74% of undergrads determined to have financial need; average aid package $19,312

Oklahoma Christian University

Oklahoma City OK
(405) 425-5050
U.S. News ranking: Reg. U. (W), No. 40
Website: www.oc.edu/
Admissions email: info@oc.edu
Private; founded 1950
Affiliation: Church of Christ
Freshman admissions: more selective; 2013-2014: 1,984 applied, 1,254 accepted. Either SAT or ACT required. ACT 25/75

rank: 30% in top tenth, 58% in top quarter, 81% in top half
Early decision deadline: N/A, notification date: N/A
Early action deadline: N/A, notification date: N/A
Application deadline (fall): rolling
Undergraduate student body: 1,907 full time, 59 part time; 51% male, 49% female; 2% American Indian, 1% Asian, 6% black, 5% Hispanic, 6% multiracial, 0% Pacific Islander, 70% white, 11% international; 41% from in state; 82% live on campus; 0% of students in fraternities, 0% in sororities
Most popular majors: 7% Biological and Biomedical Sciences, 16% Business, Management, Marketing, and Related Support Services, 9% Communication, Journalism, and Related Programs, 7% Education, 11% Engineering
Expenses: 2014-2015: $19,120; room/board: $6,670
Financial aid: (405) 425-5190; 63% of undergrads determined to have financial need; average aid package $21,444

Oklahoma City University

Oklahoma City OK
(405) 208-5050
U.S. News ranking: Reg. U. (W), No. 25
Website: www.okcu.edu
Admissions email: uadmissions@okcu.edu
Private; founded 1904
Affiliation: United Methodist
Freshman admissions: more selective; 2013-2014: 1,432 applied, 1,008 accepted. Either SAT or ACT required. ACT 25/75 percentile: 23-29. High school rank: 35% in top tenth, 61% in top quarter, 91% in top half
Early decision deadline: N/A, notification date: N/A
Early action deadline: N/A, notification date: N/A
Application deadline (fall): rolling
Undergraduate student body: 1,646 full time, 175 part time; 39% male, 61% female; 3% American Indian, 2% Asian, 6% black, 8% Hispanic, 7% multiracial, 0% Pacific Islander, 59% white, 15% international; 53% from in state; 51% live on campus; 29% of students in fraternities, 18% in sororities
Most popular majors: 4% Biological and Biomedical Sciences, 14% Business, Management, Marketing, and Related Support Services, 14% Health Professions and Related Programs, 15% Liberal Arts and Sciences, General Studies and Humanities, 32% Visual and Performing Arts
Expenses: 2014-2015: $30,726; room/board: $9,534
Financial aid: (405) 208-5211; 60% of undergrads determined to have financial need; average aid package $19,715

Oklahoma Panhandle State University[1]

Goodwell OK
(800) 664-6778
U.S. News ranking: Reg. Coll. (W), second tier
Website: www.opsu.edu
Admissions email: opsu@opsu.edu
Public; founded 1909

Application deadline (fall): rolling
Undergraduate student body: N/A
full time, N/A part time
Expenses: 2014-2015: $6,777 in
state, $8,293 out of state; room/
board: $4,200
Financial aid: (580) 349-1580;
93% of undergrads determined to
have financial need; average aid
package $8,549

Oklahoma State University

Stillwater OK
(405) 744-5358
U.S. News ranking: Nat. U.,
No. 145
Website: osu.okstate.edu
Admissions email: admissions@
okstate.edu
Public; founded 1890
Freshman admissions: more
selective; 2013-2014: 11,064
applied, 8,411 accepted. Either
SAT or ACT required. ACT 25/75
percentile: 22-28. High school
rank: 28% in top tenth, 56% in
top quarter, 87% in top half
Early decision deadline: N/A,
notification date: N/A
Early action deadline: N/A,
notification date: N/A
Application deadline (fall): rolling
Undergraduate student body:
17,746 full time, 2,747 part
time; 51% male, 49% female;
6% American Indian, 2% Asian,
5% black, 5% Hispanic, 7%
multiracial, 0% Pacific Islander,
72% white, 3% international;
74% from in state; 45% live
on campus; 18% of students in
fraternities, 25% in sororities
Most popular majors: 9%
Agriculture, Agriculture
Operations, and Related Sciences,
24% Business, Management,
Marketing, and Related Support
Services, 8% Education, 9%
Engineering, 8% Family and
Consumer Sciences/Human
Sciences
Expenses: 2014-2015: $7,442 in
state, $20,027 out of state; room/
board: $7,390
Financial aid: (405) 744-6604;
52% of undergrads determined to
have financial need; average aid
package $12,835

Oklahoma State University Institute of Technology– Okmulgee

Okmulgee OK
(918) 293-4680
U.S. News ranking: Reg. Coll. (W),
No. 24
Website: www.osuit.edu/
admissions
Admissions email: osuit.
admissions@okstate.edu
Public; founded 1946
Freshman admissions: less
selective; 2013-2014: 2,026
applied, 1,090 accepted. Either
SAT or ACT required. ACT 25/75
percentile: 16-21. High school
rank: 5% in top tenth, 18% in top
quarter, 47% in top half
Early decision deadline: N/A,
notification date: N/A
Early action deadline: N/A,
notification date: N/A
Application deadline (fall): rolling
Undergraduate student body: 2,207
full time, 1,411 part time; 65%
male, 35% female; 20% American
Indian, 1% Asian, 6% black,

5% Hispanic, 7% multiracial,
0% Pacific Islander, 56% white,
1% international; 88% from in
state; 29% live on campus; 0%
of students in fraternities, 0% in
sororities
Most popular majors: 10%
Civil Engineering Technology/
Technician, 59% Computer and
Information Systems Security/
Information Assurance, 31%
Instrumentation Technology/
Technician
Expenses: 2013-2014: $5,118 in
state, $16,329 out of state; room/
board: $3,137
Financial aid: (800) 722-4471;
71% of undergrads determined to
have financial need; average aid
package $7,500

Oklahoma State University– Oklahoma City

Oklahoma City OK
(405) 945-3224
U.S. News ranking: Reg. Coll. (W),
unranked
Website: www.osuokc.edu/
Admissions email: admissions@
osuokc.edu
Public; founded 1961
Freshman admissions: N/A; 2013-
2014: 2,555 applied, 2,555
accepted. Neither SAT nor ACT
required. ACT 25/75 percentile:
N/A. High school rank: N/A
Early decision deadline: N/A,
notification date: N/A
Early action deadline: N/A,
notification date: N/A
Application deadline (fall): rolling
Undergraduate student body: 2,251
full time, 4,745 part time; 40%
male, 60% female; 4% American
Indian, 3% Asian, 16% black,
8% Hispanic, 7% multiracial, 0%
Pacific Islander, 59% white, 0%
international
Most popular majors: Information
not available
Expenses: 2013-2014: $3,323 in
state, $9,026 out of state; room/
board: $5,534
Financial aid: (405) 945-3319

Oklahoma Wesleyan University

Bartlesville OK
(866) 222-8226
U.S. News ranking: Reg. Coll. (W),
No. 6
Website: www.okwu.edu
Admissions email:
admissions@okwu.edu
Private; founded 1972
Affiliation: The Wesleyan Church
Freshman admissions: selective;
2013-2014: 2,293 applied, 549
accepted. Either SAT or ACT
required. ACT 25/75 percentile:
18-24. High school rank: N/A
Early decision deadline: N/A,
notification date: N/A
Early action deadline: N/A,
notification date: N/A
Application deadline (fall): rolling
Undergraduate student body: 571
full time, 643 part time; 39%
male, 61% female; 7% American
Indian, 0% Asian, 7% black,
7% Hispanic, 4% multiracial,
0% Pacific Islander, 68% white,
5% international; 56% from in
state; 62% live on campus; 0%
of students in fraternities, 0% in
sororities

Most popular majors: 14%
Business Administration and
Management, General, 5% Human
Resources Management/Personnel
Administration, General, 29%
Nursing Science, 5% Pastoral
Counseling and Specialized
Ministries, Other
Expenses: 2014-2015: $23,180;
room/board: $7,488
Financial aid: (918) 335-6282;
78% of undergrads determined to
have financial need; average aid
package $12,566

Oral Roberts University

Tulsa OK
(800) 678-8876
U.S. News ranking: Reg. U. (W),
No. 46
Website: www.oru.edu
Admissions email:
admissions@oru.edu
Private; founded 1963
Affiliation: Christian
interdenominational
Freshman admissions: selective;
2013-2014: 1,417 applied, 617
accepted. Either SAT or ACT
required. ACT 25/75 percentile:
20-25. High school rank: N/A
Early decision deadline: N/A,
notification date: N/A
Early action deadline: N/A,
notification date: N/A
Application deadline (fall): rolling
Undergraduate student body: 2,517
full time, 367 part time; 44%
male, 56% female; 3% American
Indian, 2% Asian, 15% black,
8% Hispanic, 4% multiracial,
0% Pacific Islander, 52% white,
6% international; 42% from in
state; 63% live on campus; 0%
of students in fraternities, 0% in
sororities
Most popular majors: 23%
Business, Management,
Marketing, and Related Support
Services, 10% Communication,
Journalism, and Related Programs,
9% Health Professions and
Related Programs, 12% Theology
and Religious Vocations, 8%
Visual and Performing Arts
Expenses: 2014-2015: $23,410;
room/board: $10,768
Financial aid: (918) 495-7088;
71% of undergrads determined to
have financial need; average aid
package $22,081

Rogers State University

Claremore OK
(918) 343-7545
U.S. News ranking: Reg. Coll. (W),
second tier
Website: www.rsu.edu/
Admissions email: info@rsu.edu
Public; founded 1909
Freshman admissions: less
selective; 2013-2014: 1,864
applied, 1,015 accepted. Either
SAT or ACT required. ACT 25/75
percentile: 17-23. High school
rank: 9% in top tenth, 20% in top
quarter, 42% in top half
Early decision deadline: N/A,
notification date: N/A
Early action deadline: N/A,
notification date: N/A
Application deadline (fall): rolling
Undergraduate student body: 2,576
full time, 1,713 part time; 37%
male, 63% female; 3% American
Indian, 0% Asian, 14% black,
4% Hispanic, 16% multiracial,
61% Pacific Islander, 2% white,

1% international; 96% from in
state; 10% live on campus; N/A
of students in fraternities, N/A in
sororities
Most popular majors: 11%
Biological and Biomedical
Sciences, 32% Business,
Management, Marketing, and
Related Support Services,
8% Health Professions and
Related Programs, 8% Multi/
Interdisciplinary Studies, 9%
Social Sciences
Expenses: 2013-2014: $5,144 in
state, $11,864 out of state; room/
board: $8,430
Financial aid: (918) 343-7553;
71% of undergrads determined to
have financial need; average aid
package $9,008

Southeastern Oklahoma State University

Durant OK
(580) 745-2060
U.S. News ranking: Reg. U. (W),
second tier
Website: www.se.edu
Admissions email:
admissions@se.edu
Public; founded 1909
Freshman admissions: selective;
2013-2014: 1,001 applied, 800
accepted. Either SAT or ACT
required. ACT 25/75 percentile:
18-22. High school rank: 17%
in top tenth, 38% in top quarter,
74% in top half
Early decision deadline: N/A,
notification date: N/A
Early action deadline: N/A,
notification date: N/A
Application deadline (fall): rolling
Undergraduate student body: 2,650
full time, 790 part time; 46%
male, 54% female; 31% American
Indian, 1% Asian, 7% black,
4% Hispanic, 0% multiracial,
0% Pacific Islander, 55% white,
3% international; 75% from in
state; 16% live on campus; N/A
of students in fraternities, N/A in
sororities
Most popular majors: 13%
Business, Management,
Marketing, and Related Support
Services, 13% Education, 14%
Engineering Technologies and
Engineering-Related Fields, 13%
Liberal Arts and Sciences, General
Studies and Humanities, 7%
Psychology
Expenses: 2013-2014: $5,315 in
state, $13,440 out of state; room/
board: $2,470
Financial aid: (580) 745-2186;
85% of undergrads determined to
have financial need; average aid
package $10,109

Southern Nazarene University

Bethany OK
(405) 491-6324
U.S. News ranking: Reg. U. (W),
No. 84
Website: www.snu.edu
Admissions email:
admissions@snu.edu
Private; founded 1899
Affiliation: Nazarene
Freshman admissions: selective;
2013-2014: N/A applied, N/A
accepted. Either SAT or ACT
required. ACT 25/75 percentile:
19-24. High school rank: 26%
in top tenth, 49% in top quarter,
78% in top half

Early decision deadline: N/A,
notification date: N/A
Early action deadline: N/A,
notification date: N/A
Application deadline (fall): 8/6
Undergraduate student body: 1,549
full time, 111 part time; 48%
male, 52% female; 5% American
Indian, 3% Asian, 14% black,
6% Hispanic, 0% multiracial,
1% Pacific Islander, 68% white,
2% international; 60% from in
state; 63% live on campus; N/A
of students in fraternities, N/A in
sororities
Most popular majors: 15%
Business Administration and
Management, General, 9% Health/
Health Care Administration/
Management, 10% Human
Development and Family Studies,
General, 6% Marriage and
Family Therapy/Counseling, 27%
Organizational Behavior Studies
Expenses: 2014-2015: $22,680;
room/board: $7,970
Financial aid: (405) 491-6310

Southwestern Christian University[1]

Bethany OK
(405) 789-7661
U.S. News ranking: Reg. Coll. (W),
No. 23
Website: www.swcu.edu/
Admissions email: admissions@
swcu.edu
Private; founded 1946
Affiliation: Pentecostal
Application deadline (fall): rolling
Undergraduate student body: N/A
full time, N/A part time
Expenses: 2013-2014: $14,220;
room/board: $6,100
Financial aid: N/A

Southwestern Oklahoma State University

Weatherford OK
(580) 774-3782
U.S. News ranking: Reg. U. (W),
second tier
Website: www.swosu.edu
Admissions email: admissions@
swosu.edu
Public; founded 1901
Freshman admissions: selective;
2013-2014: 2,536 applied,
2,289 accepted. Either SAT
or ACT required. ACT 25/75
percentile: 18-24. High school
rank: 22% in top tenth, 43% in
top quarter, 76% in top half
Early decision deadline: N/A,
notification date: N/A
Early action deadline: N/A,
notification date: N/A
Application deadline (fall): rolling
Undergraduate student body: 3,368
full time, 794 part time; 42%
male, 58% female; 4% American
Indian, 2% Asian, 5% black,
8% Hispanic, 7% multiracial,
0% Pacific Islander, 70% white,
3% international; 89% from in
state; 32% live on campus; 3%
of students in fraternities, 5% in
sororities
Most popular majors: 18%
Business, Management,
Marketing, and Related Support
Services, 15% Education, 3%
Engineering Technologies and
Engineering-Related Fields, 26%
Health Professions and Related
Programs, 10% Parks, Recreation,
Leisure, and Fitness Studies

Expenses: 2013-2014: $5,460 in state, $11,820 out of state; room/board: $4,920
Financial aid: (580) 774-3786; 63% of undergrads determined to have financial need; average aid package $5,380

St. Gregory's University

Shawnee OK
(405) 878-5444
U.S. News ranking: Reg. Coll. (W), No. 25
Website: www.stgregorys.edu
Admissions email: admissions@stgregorys.edu
Private
Affiliation: Roman Catholic–Benedictine
Freshman admissions: less selective; 2013-2014: 455 applied, 259 accepted. Neither SAT nor ACT required. ACT 25/75 percentile: N/A. High school rank: N/A
Early decision deadline: N/A, notification date: N/A
Early action deadline: N/A, notification date: N/A
Application deadline (fall): N/A
Undergraduate student body: 578 full time, 55 part time; 43% male, 57% female; 8% American Indian, 1% Asian, 8% black, 12% Hispanic, 8% multiracial, 0% Pacific Islander, 46% white, 4% international
Most popular majors: Information not available
Expenses: 2013-2014: $20,765; room/board: $7,206
Financial aid: (405) 878-5412

University of Central Oklahoma

Edmond OK
(405) 974-2338
U.S. News ranking: Reg. U. (W), No. 75
Website: www.uco.edu
Admissions email: 4ucoinfo@uco.edu
Public; founded 1890
Freshman admissions: selective; 2013-2014: 4,629 applied, 3,684 accepted. Either SAT or ACT required. ACT 25/75 percentile: 20-24. High school rank: 16% in top tenth, 37% in top quarter, 73% in top half
Early decision deadline: N/A, notification date: N/A
Early action deadline: N/A, notification date: N/A
Application deadline (fall): rolling
Undergraduate student body: 10,981 full time, 4,386 part time; 43% male, 57% female; 4% American Indian, 3% Asian, 9% black, 7% Hispanic, 7% multiracial, 0% Pacific Islander, 60% white, 7% international; 91% from in state; 9% live on campus; 6% of students in fraternities, 6% in sororities
Most popular majors: 4% Accounting, 8% Business Administration and Management, General, 12% General Studies, 4% Psychology, General, 5% Registered Nursing/Registered Nurse
Expenses: 2014-2015: $5,437 in state, $13,552 out of state; room/board: $6,940
Financial aid: (405) 974-3334; 60% of undergrads determined to have financial need; average aid package $9,073

University of Oklahoma

Norman OK
(405) 325-2252
U.S. News ranking: Nat. U., No. 106
Website: www.ou.edu
Admissions email: admrec@ou.edu
Public; founded 1890
Freshman admissions: more selective; 2013-2014: 10,991 applied, 8,841 accepted. Either SAT or ACT required. ACT 25/75 percentile: 23-29. High school rank: 33% in top tenth, 64% in top quarter, 92% in top half
Early decision deadline: N/A, notification date: N/A
Early action deadline: N/A, notification date: N/A
Application deadline (fall): 4/1
Undergraduate student body: 18,324 full time, 3,494 part time; 49% male, 51% female; 4% American Indian, 6% Asian, 5% black, 9% Hispanic, 7% multiracial, 0% Pacific Islander, 63% white, 4% international; 70% from in state; 31% live on campus; 23% of students in fraternities, 28% in sororities
Most popular majors: 3% Business, Management, Marketing, and Related Support Services, 2% Communication, Journalism, and Related Programs, 7% Health Professions and Related Programs, 11% Multi/Interdisciplinary Studies, 3% Psychology
Expenses: 2014-2015: $7,695 in state, $20,469 out of state; room/board: $9,126
Financial aid: (405) 325-4521; 50% of undergrads determined to have financial need; average aid package $12,520

University of Science and Arts of Oklahoma

Chickasha OK
(405) 574-1357
U.S. News ranking: Nat. Lib. Arts, second tier
Website: www.usao.edu
Admissions email: usao-admissions@usao.edu
Public; founded 1908
Freshman admissions: selective; 2013-2014: 594 applied, 371 accepted. Either SAT or ACT required. ACT 25/75 percentile: 19-24. High school rank: 29% in top tenth, 62% in top quarter, 87% in top half
Early decision deadline: N/A, notification date: N/A
Early action deadline: N/A, notification date: N/A
Application deadline (fall): 8/30
Undergraduate student body: 806 full time, 111 part time; 36% male, 64% female; 13% American Indian, 1% Asian, 4% black, 6% Hispanic, 0% multiracial, 0% Pacific Islander, 69% white, 6% international; 90% from in state; 44% live on campus; 3% of students in fraternities, 6% in sororities
Most popular majors: 18% Business Administration and Management, General, 20% Education, 9% Psychology, General, 14% Visual and Performing Arts
Expenses: 2014-2015: $6,270 in state, $15,210 out of state; room/board: $5,470

Financial aid: (405) 574-1240; 65% of undergrads determined to have financial need; average aid package $9,473

University of Tulsa

Tulsa OK
(918) 631-2307
U.S. News ranking: Nat. U., No. 88
Website: www.utulsa.edu
Admissions email: admission@utulsa.edu
Private; founded 1894
Affiliation: Presbyterian
Freshman admissions: most selective; 2013-2014: 7,304 applied, 2,965 accepted. Either SAT or ACT required. ACT 25/75 percentile: 25-32. High school rank: 74% in top tenth, 90% in top quarter, 97% in top half
Early decision deadline: N/A, notification date: N/A
Early action deadline: 11/1, notification date: 11/25
Application deadline (fall): rolling
Undergraduate student body: 3,293 full time, 135 part time; 58% male, 42% female; 4% American Indian, 3% Asian, 5% black, 4% Hispanic, 2% multiracial, 0% Pacific Islander, 55% white, 26% international; 58% from in state; 74% live on campus; 21% of students in fraternities, 23% in sororities
Most popular majors: 19% Business, Management, Marketing, and Related Support Services, 21% Engineering, 7% Health Professions and Related Programs, 6% Social Sciences, 5% Visual and Performing Arts
Expenses: 2014-2015: $34,704; room/board: $10,426
Financial aid: (918) 631-2526; 38% of undergrads determined to have financial need; average aid package $24,867

OREGON

Art Institute of Portland[1]

Portland OR
(888) 228-6528
U.S. News ranking: Arts, unranked
Website: www.artinstitutes.edu/portland/
Admissions email: N/A
For-profit
Application deadline (fall): N/A
Undergraduate student body: N/A full time, N/A part time
Expenses: 2013-2014: $17,416; room/board: $9,522
Financial aid: N/A

Concordia University[1]

Portland OR
(503) 280-8501
U.S. News ranking: Reg. U. (W), No. 80
Website: www.cu-portland.edu
Admissions email: admissions@cu-portland.edu
Private; founded 1905
Affiliation: Lutheran
Application deadline (fall): 7/1
Undergraduate student body: N/A full time, N/A part time
Expenses: 2013-2014: $27,492; room/board: $8,030
Financial aid: (503) 280-8514

Corban University

Salem OR
(800) 845-3005
U.S. News ranking: Reg. Coll. (W), No. 7
Website: www.corban.edu
Admissions email: admissions@corban.edu
Private; founded 1935
Affiliation: Baptist
Freshman admissions: selective; 2013-2014: 2,711 applied, 934 accepted. Either SAT or ACT required. SAT 25/75 percentile: 950-1180. High school rank: 33% in top tenth, 63% in top quarter, 89% in top half
Early decision deadline: N/A, notification date: N/A
Early action deadline: N/A, notification date: N/A
Application deadline (fall): 8/1
Undergraduate student body: 797 full time, 88 part time; 40% male, 60% female; 1% American Indian, 2% Asian, 1% black, 4% Hispanic, 2% multiracial, 1% Pacific Islander, 83% white, 1% international; 53% from in state; 62% live on campus; N/A of students in fraternities, N/A in sororities
Most popular majors: 14% Business, Management, Marketing, and Related Support Services, 16% Education, 7% English Language and Literature/Letters, 33% Psychology, 9% Theology and Religious Vocations
Expenses: 2014-2015: $28,640; room/board: $8,892
Financial aid: (503) 375-7006; 83% of undergrads determined to have financial need; average aid package $19,380

Eastern Oregon University[1]

La Grande OR
(541) 962-3393
U.S. News ranking: Reg. U. (W), second tier
Website: www.eou.edu
Admissions email: admissions@eou.edu
Public; founded 1929
Application deadline (fall): 9/1
Undergraduate student body: N/A full time, N/A part time
Expenses: 2013-2014: $7,530 in state, $16,755 out of state; room/board: $9,183
Financial aid: (541) 962-3551

George Fox University

Newberg OR
(800) 765-4369
U.S. News ranking: Reg. U. (W), No. 30
Website: www.georgefox.edu
Admissions email: admissions@georgefox.edu
Private; founded 1891
Affiliation: Evangelical Friends
Freshman admissions: selective; 2013-2014: 2,431 applied, 1,830 accepted. Either SAT or ACT required. SAT 25/75 percentile: 940-1200. High school rank: 27% in top tenth, 57% in top quarter, 85% in top half
Early decision deadline: N/A, notification date: N/A
Early action deadline: 11/15, notification date: 12/15
Application deadline (fall): rolling
Undergraduate student body: 2,108 full time, 275 part time; 43% male, 57% female; 0% American Indian, 4% Asian, 2% black,

7% Hispanic, 5% multiracial, 0% Pacific Islander, 70% white, 6% international; 65% from in state; 56% live on campus; N/A of students in fraternities, N/A in sororities
Most popular majors: 25% Business, Management, Marketing, and Related Support Services, 7% Education, 7% Health Professions and Related Programs, 12% Multi/Interdisciplinary Studies, 7% Visual and Performing Arts
Expenses: 2014-2015: $31,866; room/board: $9,864
Financial aid: (503) 554-2290; 76% of undergrads determined to have financial need; average aid package $27,155

Lewis & Clark College

Portland OR
(800) 444-4111
U.S. News ranking: Nat. Lib. Arts, No. 77
Website: www.lclark.edu
Admissions email: admissions@lclark.edu
Private; founded 1867
Freshman admissions: more selective; 2013-2014: 6,456 applied, 4,059 accepted. Neither SAT nor ACT required. SAT 25/75 percentile: 1180-1370. High school rank: 39% in top tenth, 76% in top quarter, 96% in top half
Early decision deadline: 11/1, notification date: 12/1
Early action deadline: 11/1, notification date: 12/31
Application deadline (fall): 3/1
Undergraduate student body: 2,086 full time, 40 part time; 41% male, 59% female; 1% American Indian, 6% Asian, 2% black, 8% Hispanic, 1% multiracial, 0% Pacific Islander, 64% white, 6% international; 18% from in state; 65% live on campus; 0% of students in fraternities, 0% in sororities
Most popular majors: 11% Biological and Biomedical Sciences, 8% English Language and Literature/Letters, 14% Psychology, 24% Social Sciences, 12% Visual and Performing Arts
Expenses: 2014-2015: $43,382; room/board: $11,000
Financial aid: (503) 768-7090; 66% of undergrads determined to have financial need; average aid package $32,902

Linfield College

McMinnville OR
(800) 640-2287
U.S. News ranking: Nat. Lib. Arts, No. 124
Website: www.linfield.edu
Admissions email: admission@linfield.edu
Private; founded 1858
Affiliation: American Baptist
Freshman admissions: selective; 2013-2014: 2,139 applied, 1,972 accepted. Either SAT or ACT required. SAT 25/75 percentile: 980-1200. High school rank: 34% in top tenth, 72% in top quarter, 94% in top half
Early decision deadline: N/A, notification date: N/A
Early action deadline: 11/15, notification date: 1/15
Application deadline (fall): rolling

Undergraduate student body: 1,630 full time, 41 part time; 40% male, 60% female; 1% American Indian, 6% Asian, 2% black, 9% Hispanic, 10% multiracial, 1% Pacific Islander, 64% white, 4% international; 48% from in state; 74% live on campus; 22% of students in fraternities, 25% in sororities
Most popular majors: 21% Business, Management, Marketing, and Related Support Services, 7% Communication, Journalism, and Related Programs, 12% Education, 8% Parks, Recreation, Leisure, and Fitness Studies, 10% Social Sciences
Expenses: 2014-2015: $37,346; room/board: $10,330
Financial aid: (503) 883-2225; 74% of undergrads determined to have financial need; average aid package $28,439

Marylhurst University[1]

Marylhurst OR
(503) 699-6268
U.S. News ranking: Reg. U. (W), unranked
Website: www.marylhurst.edu
Admissions email: admissions@marylhurst.edu
Private
Application deadline (fall): N/A
Undergraduate student body: N/A full time, N/A part time
Expenses: 2013-2014: $19,665; room/board: N/A
Financial aid: (503) 699-6253

Northwest Christian University

Eugene OR
(541) 684-7201
U.S. News ranking: Reg. Coll. (W), No. 20
Website: www.nwcu.edu
Admissions email: admissions@nwcu.edu
Private; founded 1895
Affiliation: Christian Church (Disciples of Christ)
Freshman admissions: less selective; 2013-2014: 318 applied, 224 accepted. Either SAT or ACT required. SAT 25/75 percentile: 885-1065. High school rank: N/A
Early decision deadline: N/A, notification date: N/A
Early action deadline: N/A, notification date: N/A
Application deadline (fall): rolling
Undergraduate student body: 382 full time, 102 part time; 36% male, 64% female; 2% American Indian, 3% Asian, 2% black, 8% Hispanic, 3% multiracial, 0% Pacific Islander, 81% white, 0% international; 79% from in state; 28% live on campus; 0% of students in fraternities, 0% in sororities
Most popular majors: 7% Biological and Biomedical Sciences, 33% Business, Management, Marketing, and Related Support Services, 17% Education, 9% Multi/Interdisciplinary Studies, 14% Psychology
Expenses: 2014-2015: $26,180; room/board: $8,200
Financial aid: (541) 684-7203; 91% of undergrads determined to have financial need; average aid package $19,400

Oregon College of Art and Craft

Portland OR
(800) 390-0632
U.S. News ranking: Arts, unranked
Website: www.ocac.edu/
Admissions email: admissions@ocac.edu
Private; founded 1907
Freshman admissions: N/A; 2013-2014: 37 applied, 36 accepted. Neither SAT nor ACT required. SAT 25/75 percentile: N/A. High school rank: 29% in top tenth, 57% in top quarter, 71% in top half
Early decision deadline: N/A, notification date: N/A
Early action deadline: N/A, notification date: N/A
Application deadline (fall): rolling
Undergraduate student body: 117 full time, 22 part time; 19% male, 81% female; 1% American Indian, 2% Asian, 1% black, 11% Hispanic, 9% multiracial, 2% Pacific Islander, 63% white, 0% international; 40% from in state; 13% live on campus; 0% of students in fraternities, 0% in sororities
Most popular majors: 100% Crafts/Craft Design, Folk Art and Artisanry
Expenses: 2013-2014: $27,145; room/board: $7,800
Financial aid: N/A

Oregon Institute of Technology

Klamath Falls OR
(541) 885-1155
U.S. News ranking: Reg. Coll. (W), No. 8
Website: www.oit.edu
Admissions email: oit@oit.edu
Public; founded 1947
Freshman admissions: selective; 2013-2014: 2,778 applied, 1,982 accepted. Either SAT or ACT required. SAT 25/75 percentile: 880-1140. High school rank: 25% in top tenth, 59% in top quarter, 88% in top half
Early decision deadline: N/A, notification date: N/A
Early action deadline: N/A, notification date: N/A
Application deadline (fall): 9/8
Undergraduate student body: 2,321 full time, 2,052 part time; 52% male, 48% female; 1% American Indian, 4% Asian, 1% black, 6% Hispanic, 4% multiracial, 0% Pacific Islander, 76% white, 3% international; 76% from in state; 16% live on campus; 0% of students in fraternities, N/A in sororities
Most popular majors: 6% Business, Management, Marketing, and Related Support Services, 5% Computer and Information Sciences and Support Services, 16% Engineering, 15% Engineering Technologies and Engineering-Related Fields, 36% Health Professions and Related Programs
Expenses: 2014-2015: $8,445 in state, $23,670 out of state; room/board: $9,032
Financial aid: (541) 885-1280; 73% of undergrads determined to have financial need; average aid package $8,059

Oregon State University

Corvallis OR
(541) 737-4411
U.S. News ranking: Nat. U., No. 138
Website: oregonstate.edu
Admissions email: osuadmit@oregonstate.edu
Public; founded 1868
Freshman admissions: selective; 2013-2014: 14,239 applied, 11,303 accepted. Either SAT or ACT required. SAT 25/75 percentile: 970-1220. High school rank: 25% in top tenth, 53% in top quarter, 88% in top half
Early decision deadline: N/A, notification date: N/A
Early action deadline: 11/1, notification date: 12/20
Application deadline (fall): 9/1
Undergraduate student body: 18,486 full time, 4,675 part time; 54% male, 46% female; 1% American Indian, 7% Asian, 1% black, 7% Hispanic, 6% multiracial, 0% Pacific Islander, 69% white, 6% international; 75% from in state; 13% live on campus; 13% of students in fraternities, 18% in sororities
Most popular majors: 7% Agriculture, Agriculture Operations, and Related Sciences, 13% Business, Management, Marketing, and Related Support Services, 14% Engineering, 11% Family and Consumer Sciences/Human Sciences, 7% Natural Resources and Conservation
Expenses: 2014-2015: $8,276 in state, $23,540 out of state; room/board: N/A
Financial aid: (541) 737-2241; 59% of undergrads determined to have financial need; average aid package $12,973

Pacific Northwest College of Art[1]

Portland OR
(800) 818-7622
U.S. News ranking: Arts, unranked
Website: www.pnca.edu
Admissions email: admissions@pnca.edu
Private
Application deadline (fall): N/A
Undergraduate student body: N/A full time, N/A part time
Expenses: 2013-2014: $32,417; room/board: $12,814
Financial aid: (503) 821-8976

Pacific University

Forest Grove OR
(800) 677-6712
U.S. News ranking: Reg. U. (W), No. 25
Website: www.pacificu.edu
Admissions email: admissions@pacificu.edu
Private; founded 1849
Freshman admissions: selective; 2013-2014: 2,658 applied, 2,291 accepted. Either SAT or ACT required. SAT 25/75 percentile: 990-1210. High school rank: N/A
Early decision deadline: N/A, notification date: N/A
Early action deadline: N/A, notification date: N/A
Application deadline (fall): 8/15

Undergraduate student body: 1,729 full time, 56 part time; 42% male, 58% female; 1% American Indian, 13% Asian, 1% black, 10% Hispanic, 12% multiracial, 2% Pacific Islander, 53% white, 2% international; 32% from in state; 58% live on campus; 6% of students in fraternities, 9% in sororities
Most popular majors: 10% Biological and Biomedical Sciences, 9% Education, 9% Health Professions and Related Programs, 13% Parks, Recreation, Leisure, and Fitness Studies, 9% Social Sciences
Expenses: 2014-2015: $38,510; room/board: $11,116
Financial aid: (503) 352-2222; 83% of undergrads determined to have financial need; average aid package $29,308

Portland State University[1]

Portland OR
(503) 725-3511
U.S. News ranking: Nat. U., second tier
Website: www.pdx.edu
Admissions email: admissions@pdx.edu
Public; founded 1946
Application deadline (fall): rolling
Undergraduate student body: N/A full time, N/A part time
Expenses: 2013-2014: $7,878 in state, $23,088 out of state; room/board: $10,050
Financial aid: (503) 725-3461

Reed College[1]

Portland OR
(503) 777-7511
U.S. News ranking: Nat. Lib. Arts, No. 77
Website: www.reed.edu/
Admissions email: admission@reed.edu
Private
Application deadline (fall): N/A
Undergraduate student body: N/A full time, N/A part time
Expenses: 2013-2014: $46,010; room/board: $11,770
Financial aid: (503) 777-7223

Southern Oregon University

Ashland OR
(541) 552-6411
U.S. News ranking: Reg. U. (W), No. 79
Website: www.sou.edu
Admissions email: admissions@sou.edu
Public; founded 1926
Freshman admissions: less selective; 2013-2014: 1,985 applied, 1,837 accepted. Either SAT or ACT required. SAT 25/75 percentile: 890-1120. High school rank: N/A
Early decision deadline: N/A, notification date: N/A
Early action deadline: N/A, notification date: N/A
Application deadline (fall): rolling
Undergraduate student body: 3,667 full time, 1,635 part time; 43% male, 57% female; 1% American Indian, 1% Asian, 2% black, 8% Hispanic, 5% multiracial, 0% Pacific Islander, 53% white,

2% international; 69% from in state; 22% live on campus; N/A of students in fraternities, N/A in sororities
Most popular majors: 15% Business, Management, Marketing, and Related Support Services, 7% Homeland Security, Law Enforcement, Firefighting and Related Protective Services, 12% Psychology, 9% Social Sciences, 11% Visual and Performing Arts
Expenses: 2013-2014: $7,863 in state, $20,238 out of state; room/board: $11,340
Financial aid: (541) 552-6754

University of Oregon

Eugene OR
(800) 232-3825
U.S. News ranking: Nat. U., No. 106
Website: www.uoregon.edu
Admissions email: uoadmit@uoregon.edu
Public; founded 1876
Freshman admissions: selective; 2013-2014: 21,938 applied, 16,206 accepted. Either SAT or ACT required. SAT 25/75 percentile: 990-1240. High school rank: 25% in top tenth, 64% in top quarter, 94% in top half
Early decision deadline: N/A, notification date: N/A
Early action deadline: 11/1, notification date: 12/15
Application deadline (fall): 1/15
Undergraduate student body: 18,892 full time, 1,905 part time; 48% male, 52% female; 1% American Indian, 5% Asian, 2% black, 8% Hispanic, 6% multiracial, 0% Pacific Islander, 64% white, 12% international; 64% from in state; 20% live on campus; 13% of students in fraternities, 17% in sororities
Most popular majors: 10% Business/Commerce, General, 5% Economics, General, 5% Physiology, General, 9% Psychology, General, 6% Sociology
Expenses: 2014-2015: $9,918 in state, $30,888 out of state; room/board: $11,442
Financial aid: (541) 346-3221; 46% of undergrads determined to have financial need; average aid package $10,172

University of Portland

Portland OR
(888) 627-5601
U.S. News ranking: Reg. U. (W), No. 8
Website: www.up.edu
Admissions email: admission@up.edu
Private; founded 1901
Affiliation: Roman Catholic
Freshman admissions: more selective; 2013-2014: 9,523 applied, 6,361 accepted. Either SAT or ACT required. SAT 25/75 percentile: 1090-1300. High school rank: 37% in top tenth, 70% in top quarter, 94% in top half
Early decision deadline: N/A, notification date: N/A
Early action deadline: N/A, notification date: N/A
Application deadline (fall): 2/1
Undergraduate student body: 3,410 full time, 84 part time; 42% male, 58% female; 0% American Indian, 10% Asian, 1% black, 10% Hispanic, 8% multiracial,

1% Pacific Islander, 64% white, 3% international; 34% from in state; 54% live on campus; 0% of students in fraternities, 0% in sororities
Most popular majors: 11% Biological and Biomedical Sciences, 13% Business, Management, Marketing, and Related Support Services, 12% Engineering, 20% Health Professions and Related Programs, 8% Social Sciences
Expenses: 2014-2015: $38,520; room/board: $13,158
Financial aid: (503) 943-7311; 65% of undergrads determined to have financial need; average aid package $27,750

Warner Pacific College
Portland OR
(503) 517-1020
U.S. News ranking: Reg. Coll. (W), No. 8
Website: www.warnerpacific.edu
Admissions email: admissions@warnerpacific.edu
Private; founded 1937
Affiliation: Church of God
Freshman admissions: less selective; 2013-2014: 948 applied, 500 accepted. Either SAT or ACT required. SAT 25/75 percentile: 830-1100. High school rank: 8% in top tenth, 25% in top quarter, 77% in top half
Early decision deadline: N/A, notification date: N/A
Early action deadline: N/A, notification date: N/A
Application deadline (fall): rolling
Undergraduate student body: 469 full time, 34 part time; 44% male, 56% female; 0% American Indian, 4% Asian, 8% black, 11% Hispanic, 8% multiracial, 2% Pacific Islander, 61% white, 0% international; 65% from in state; 43% live on campus; N/A of students in fraternities, N/A in sororities
Most popular majors: 8% Biological and Biomedical Sciences, 16% Business, Management, Marketing, and Related Support Services, 14% Education, 15% Family and Consumer Sciences/Human Sciences, 12% Theology and Religious Vocations
Expenses: 2014-2015: $20,300; room/board: $8,230
Financial aid: (503) 517-1017; 85% of undergrads determined to have financial need; average aid package $16,136

Western Oregon University
Monmouth OR
(503) 838-8211
U.S. News ranking: Reg. U. (W), No. 84
Website: www.wou.edu
Admissions email: wolfgram@wou.edu
Public; founded 1856
Freshman admissions: less selective; 2013-2014: 2,789 applied, 2,533 accepted. Either SAT or ACT required. SAT 25/75 percentile: 840-1070. High school rank: 14% in top tenth, 32% in top quarter, 65% in top half
Early decision deadline: N/A, notification date: N/A
Early action deadline: N/A, notification date: N/A

Application deadline (fall): rolling
Undergraduate student body: 4,454 full time, 812 part time; 42% male, 58% female; 2% American Indian, 3% Asian, 4% black, 9% Hispanic, 1% multiracial, 3% Pacific Islander, 69% white, 6% international
Most popular majors: 13% Business/Commerce, General, 8% Criminal Justice/Law Enforcement Administration, 21% Education, General, 4% Health and Wellness, General, 7% Psychology, General
Expenses: 2014-2015: $9,105 in state, $22,200 out of state; room/board: $9,579
Financial aid: (503) 838-8475; 72% of undergrads determined to have financial need; average aid package $9,263

Willamette University
Salem OR
(877) 542-2787
U.S. News ranking: Nat. Lib. Arts, No. 64
Website: www.willamette.edu
Admissions email: LIBARTS@willamette.edu
Private; founded 1842
Freshman admissions: more selective; 2013-2014: 8,109 applied, 4,690 accepted. Either SAT or ACT required. SAT 25/75 percentile: 1080-1310. High school rank: 41% in top tenth, 75% in top quarter, 94% in top half
Early decision deadline: N/A, notification date: N/A
Early action deadline: 12/1, notification date: 1/15
Application deadline (fall): 2/1
Undergraduate student body: 2,019 full time, 209 part time; 44% male, 56% female; 2% American Indian, 7% Asian, 2% black, 10% Hispanic, 9% multiracial, 1% Pacific Islander, 63% white, 1% international; 28% from in state; 66% live on campus; 23% of students in fraternities, 28% in sororities
Most popular majors: 9% Biological and Biomedical Sciences, 7% Foreign Languages, Literatures, and Linguistics, 11% Physical Sciences, 18% Social Sciences, 17% Visual and Performing Arts
Expenses: 2014-2015: $44,076; room/board: $10,820
Financial aid: (503) 370-6273; 65% of undergrads determined to have financial need; average aid package $33,652

PENNSYLVANIA

Albright College
Reading PA
(800) 252-1856
U.S. News ranking: Nat. Lib. Arts, No. 177
Website: www.albright.edu
Admissions email: admission@alb.edu
Private; founded 1856
Affiliation: United Methodist
Freshman admissions: selective; 2013-2014: 6,060 applied, 3,776 accepted. Neither SAT nor ACT required. SAT 25/75 percentile: 930-1130. High school rank: 20% in top tenth, 49% in top quarter, 77% in top half
Early decision deadline: N/A, notification date: N/A

Early action deadline: N/A, notification date: N/A
Application deadline (fall): rolling
Undergraduate student body: 2,315 full time, 34 part time; 42% male, 58% female; 1% American Indian, 3% Asian, 18% black, 9% Hispanic, 2% multiracial, 0% Pacific Islander, 62% white, 4% international; 63% from in state; 69% live on campus; 14% of students in fraternities, 19% in sororities
Most popular majors: 28% Business, Management, Marketing, and Related Support Services, 5% Education, 16% Psychology, 14% Social Sciences, 12% Visual and Performing Arts
Expenses: 2014-2015: $38,220; room/board: $10,400
Financial aid: (610) 921-7515; 94% of undergrads determined to have financial need; average aid package $30,789

Allegheny College
Meadville PA
(800) 521-5293
U.S. News ranking: Nat. Lib. Arts, No. 81
Website: www.allegheny.edu
Admissions email: admissions@allegheny.edu
Private; founded 1815
Affiliation: United Methodist
Freshman admissions: more selective; 2013-2014: 4,512 applied, 2,927 accepted. Either SAT or ACT required. SAT 25/75 percentile: 1070-1290. High school rank: 41% in top tenth, 70% in top quarter, 95% in top half
Early decision deadline: 11/15, notification date: 12/15
Early action deadline: N/A, notification date: N/A
Application deadline (fall): 2/15
Undergraduate student body: 2,125 full time, 36 part time; 46% male, 54% female; 0% American Indian, 3% Asian, 4% black, 6% Hispanic, 4% multiracial, 0% Pacific Islander, 80% white, 2% international; 54% from in state; 90% live on campus; 31% of students in fraternities, 33% in sororities
Most popular majors: 11% Biology/Biological Sciences, General, 11% Economics, General, 8% English Language and Literature, General, 6% Neuroscience, 14% Psychology, General
Expenses: 2014-2015: $40,660; room/board: $10,320
Financial aid: (800) 835-7780; 72% of undergrads determined to have financial need; average aid package $32,250

Alvernia University
Reading PA
(610) 796-8220
U.S. News ranking: Reg. U. (N), No. 111
Website: www.alvernia.edu
Admissions email: admissions@alvernia.edu
Private; founded 1958
Affiliation: Roman Catholic
Freshman admissions: less selective; 2013-2014: 1,792 applied, 1,391 accepted. Either SAT or ACT required. SAT 25/75 percentile: 890-1070. High school rank: 8% in top tenth, 33% in top quarter, 67% in top half

Early decision deadline: N/A, notification date: N/A
Early action deadline: N/A, notification date: N/A
Application deadline (fall): rolling
Undergraduate student body: 1,719 full time, 652 part time; 28% male, 72% female; 0% American Indian, 1% Asian, 14% black, 7% Hispanic, 2% multiracial, 0% Pacific Islander, 70% white, 0% international; 75% from in state; 57% live on campus; 0% of students in fraternities, 0% in sororities
Most popular majors: 21% Business, Management, Marketing, and Related Support Services, 5% Education, 41% Health Professions and Related Programs, 11% Homeland Security, Law Enforcement, Firefighting and Related Protective Services, 5% Psychology
Expenses: 2014-2015: $30,080; room/board: $10,450
Financial aid: (610) 796-8356; 86% of undergrads determined to have financial need; average aid package $18,210

Arcadia University
Glenside PA
(215) 572-2910
U.S. News ranking: Reg. U. (N), No. 41
Website: www.arcadia.edu
Admissions email: admiss@arcadia.edu
Private; founded 1853
Freshman admissions: selective; 2013-2014: 9,608 applied, 5,735 accepted. Either SAT or ACT required. SAT 25/75 percentile: 1000-1178. High school rank: 28% in top tenth, 62% in top quarter, 90% in top half
Early decision deadline: N/A, notification date: N/A
Early action deadline: N/A, notification date: N/A
Application deadline (fall): rolling
Undergraduate student body: 2,260 full time, 193 part time; 32% male, 68% female; 0% American Indian, 5% Asian, 8% black, 6% Hispanic, 4% multiracial, 0% Pacific Islander, 73% white, 2% international; 61% from in state; 58% live on campus; 0% of students in fraternities, 0% in sororities
Most popular majors: 15% Biology/Biological Sciences, General, 5% History, General, 7% International Business/Trade/Commerce, 5% International/Global Studies, 14% Psychology, General
Expenses: 2014-2015: $38,160; room/board: $12,740
Financial aid: (215) 572-2980; 82% of undergrads determined to have financial need; average aid package $28,613

Art Institute of Pittsburgh[1]
Pittsburgh PA
(800) 275-2470
U.S. News ranking: Arts, unranked
Website: www.artinstitutes.edu/pittsburgh/Admissions
Admissions email: aip@aii.edu
For-profit
Application deadline (fall): N/A
Undergraduate student body: N/A full time, N/A part time

Expenses: 2013-2014: $17,632; room/board: $9,450
Financial aid: N/A

Bloomsburg University of Pennsylvania
Bloomsburg PA
(570) 389-4316
U.S. News ranking: Reg. U. (N), No. 98
Website: www.bloomu.edu
Admissions email: buadmiss@bloomu.edu
Public; founded 1839
Freshman admissions: less selective; 2013-2014: 9,248 applied, 8,190 accepted. Either SAT or ACT required. SAT 25/75 percentile: 890-1070. High school rank: 7% in top tenth, 26% in top quarter, 66% in top half
Early decision deadline: N/A, notification date: N/A
Early action deadline: N/A, notification date: 5/1
Application deadline (fall): rolling
Undergraduate student body: 8,813 full time, 603 part time; 44% male, 56% female; 0% American Indian, 1% Asian, 8% black, 5% Hispanic, 2% multiracial, 0% Pacific Islander, 81% white, 1% international; 89% from in state; 43% live on campus; 6% of students in fraternities, 6% in sororities
Most popular majors: 16% Business Administration, Management and Operations, 5% Criminal Justice and Corrections, 5% Psychology, General, 7% Public Relations, Advertising, and Applied Communication, 7% Teacher Education and Professional Development, Specific Levels and Methods
Expenses: 2014-2015: $8,914 in state, $19,144 out of state; room/board: $8,168
Financial aid: (570) 389-4297; 64% of undergrads determined to have financial need; average aid package $8,740

Bryn Athyn College of the New Church
Bryn Athyn PA
(267) 502-6000
U.S. News ranking: Nat. Lib. Arts, second tier
Website: www.brynathyn.edu
Admissions email: admissions@brynathyn.edu
Private; founded 1877
Affiliation: General Church of the New Jerusalem
Freshman admissions: selective; 2013-2014: 396 applied, 207 accepted. Either SAT or ACT required. SAT 25/75 percentile: 920-1130. High school rank: N/A
Early decision deadline: N/A, notification date: N/A
Early action deadline: N/A, notification date: N/A
Application deadline (fall): rolling
Undergraduate student body: 259 full time, 9 part time; 48% male, 52% female; 0% American Indian, 3% Asian, 14% black, 6% Hispanic, 0% multiracial, 1% Pacific Islander, 68% white, 8% international
Most popular majors: Information not available

Expenses: 2014-2015: $18,610; room/board: $10,773
Financial aid: (267) 502-2630; 76% of undergrads determined to have financial need; average aid package $17,450

Bryn Mawr College
Bryn Mawr PA
(610) 526-5152
U.S. News ranking: Nat. Lib. Arts, No. 27
Website: www.brynmawr.edu
Admissions email: admissions@brynmawr.edu
Private; founded 1885
Freshman admissions: more selective; 2013-2014: 2,708 applied, 1,081 accepted. Either SAT or ACT required. SAT 25/75 percentile: 1210-1470. High school rank: 65% in top tenth, 93% in top quarter, 99% in top half
Early decision deadline: 11/15, notification date: 12/15
Early action deadline: N/A, notification date: N/A
Application deadline (fall): 1/15
Undergraduate student body: 1,315 full time, 13 part time; 0% male, 100% female; 0% American Indian, 11% Asian, 5% black, 10% Hispanic, 4% multiracial, 0% Pacific Islander, 37% white, 23% international; 19% from in state; 93% live on campus; N/A of students in fraternities, N/A in sororities
Most popular majors: 6% Biology/Biological Sciences, General, 10% English Language and Literature, General, 11% Mathematics, General, 7% Political Science and Government, General, 8% Psychology, General
Expenses: 2014-2015: $45,540; room/board: $14,350
Financial aid: (610) 526-5245; 54% of undergrads determined to have financial need; average aid package $41,195

Bucknell University
Lewisburg PA
(570) 577-3000
U.S. News ranking: Nat. Lib. Arts, No. 32
Website: www.bucknell.edu
Admissions email: admissions@bucknell.edu
Private; founded 1846
Freshman admissions: more selective; 2013-2014: 7,947 applied, 2,345 accepted. Either SAT or ACT required. SAT 25/75 percentile: 1200-1400. High school rank: 62% in top tenth, 87% in top quarter, 98% in top half
Early decision deadline: 11/15, notification date: 12/20
Early action deadline: N/A, notification date: N/A
Application deadline (fall): 1/15
Undergraduate student body: 3,504 full time, 28 part time; 48% male, 52% female; 0% American Indian, 4% Asian, 3% black, 5% Hispanic, 3% multiracial, 0% Pacific Islander, 79% white, 5% international; 24% from in state; 86% live on campus; 44% of students in fraternities, 41% in sororities
Most popular majors: 5% Biology/Biological Sciences, General, 9% Business Administration and Management, General,

9% Economics, General, 7% Political Science and Government, General, 8% Psychology, General
Expenses: 2014-2015: $48,498; room/board: $11,642
Financial aid: (570) 577-1331; 45% of undergrads determined to have financial need; average aid package $29,000

Cabrini College
Radnor PA
(610) 902-8552
U.S. News ranking: Reg. U. (N), No. 133
Website: www.cabrini.edu
Admissions email: admit@cabrini.edu
Private; founded 1957
Affiliation: Roman Catholic
Freshman admissions: least selective; 2013-2014: 2,127 applied, 1,580 accepted. Either SAT or ACT required. SAT 25/75 percentile: 780-1000. High school rank: 4% in top tenth, 21% in top quarter, 51% in top half
Early decision deadline: N/A, notification date: N/A
Early action deadline: N/A, notification date: N/A
Application deadline (fall): rolling
Undergraduate student body: 1,228 full time, 109 part time; 36% male, 64% female; 0% American Indian, 1% Asian, 13% black, 5% Hispanic, 3% multiracial, 0% Pacific Islander, 72% white, 0% international; 65% from in state; 58% live on campus; 0% of students in fraternities, 0% in sororities
Most popular majors: 24% Business, Management, Marketing, and Related Support Services, Other, 15% Education, General, 12% Psychology, General, 9% Social Sciences, General, 8% Speech Communication and Rhetoric
Expenses: 2014-2015: $29,842; room/board: $12,026
Financial aid: (610) 902-8420; 79% of undergrads determined to have financial need; average aid package $16,794

Cairn University
Langhorne PA
(215) 702-4235
U.S. News ranking: Reg. U. (N), No. 111
Website: cairn.edu/
Admissions email: admissions@cairn.edu
Private; founded 1913
Affiliation: Evangelical
Freshman admissions: selective; 2013-2014: 376 applied, 256 accepted. Either SAT or ACT required. SAT 25/75 percentile: 900-1170. High school rank: 26% in top tenth, 49% in top quarter, 71% in top half
Early decision deadline: N/A, notification date: N/A
Early action deadline: N/A, notification date: N/A
Application deadline (fall): rolling
Undergraduate student body: 781 full time, 65 part time; 46% male, 54% female; 1% American Indian, 3% Asian, 14% black, 5% Hispanic, 2% multiracial, 0% Pacific Islander, 73% white, 1% international; 57% from in state; 56% live on campus; 0% of students in fraternities, 0% in sororities

Most popular majors: 6% Business, Management, Marketing, and Related Support Services, 13% Education, 69% Philosophy and Religious Studies, 9% Public Administration and Social Service Professions, 3% Visual and Performing Arts
Expenses: 2014-2015: $23,110; room/board: $9,085
Financial aid: (215) 702-4246; 81% of undergrads determined to have financial need; average aid package $18,284

California University of Pennsylvania
California PA
(724) 938-4404
U.S. News ranking: Reg. U. (N), second tier
Website: www.calu.edu/
Admissions email: inquiry@calu.edu
Public
Freshman admissions: less selective; 2013-2014: 3,125 applied, 2,814 accepted. SAT required. SAT 25/75 percentile: 850-1040. High school rank: 6% in top tenth, 25% in top quarter, 61% in top half
Early decision deadline: N/A, notification date: N/A
Early action deadline: N/A, notification date: N/A
Application deadline (fall): 8/22
Undergraduate student body: 5,649 full time, 801 part time; 48% male, 52% female; 0% American Indian, 1% Asian, 10% black, 3% Hispanic, 3% multiracial, 0% Pacific Islander, 77% white, 1% international; 90% from in state; 27% live on campus; 6% of students in fraternities, 5% in sororities
Most popular majors: 13% Business, Management, Marketing, and Related Support Services, 12% Education, 9% Health Professions and Related Programs, 8% Homeland Security, Law Enforcement, Firefighting and Related Protective Services, 12% Parks, Recreation, Leisure, and Fitness Studies
Expenses: 2014-2015: $9,556 in state, $12,966 out of state; room/board: $10,086
Financial aid: (724) 938-4415; 76% of undergrads determined to have financial need; average aid package $9,476

Carlow University[1]
Pittsburgh PA
(412) 578-6059
U.S. News ranking: Reg. U. (N), second tier
Website: www.carlow.edu
Admissions email: admissions@carlow.edu
Private
Application deadline (fall): N/A
Undergraduate student body: N/A full time, N/A part time
Expenses: 2013-2014: $25,416; room/board: $10,014
Financial aid: (412) 578-6058

Carnegie Mellon University
Pittsburgh PA
(412) 268-2082
U.S. News ranking: Nat. U., No. 25
Website: www.cmu.edu
Admissions email: undergraduate-admissions@andrew.cmu.edu
Private; founded 1900
Freshman admissions: most selective; 2013-2014: 18,884 applied, 4,813 accepted. Either SAT or ACT required. SAT 25/75 percentile: 1340-1530. High school rank: 80% in top tenth, 96% in top quarter, 99% in top half
Early decision deadline: 11/1, notification date: 12/15
Early action deadline: N/A, notification date: N/A
Application deadline (fall): 1/1
Undergraduate student body: 6,104 full time, 202 part time; 57% male, 43% female; 0% American Indian, 23% Asian, 5% black, 7% Hispanic, 4% multiracial, 0% Pacific Islander, 36% white, 19% international; 18% from in state; 36% live on campus; 15% of students in fraternities, 16% in sororities
Most popular majors: 5% Chemical Engineering, 11% Computer Science, 9% Electrical and Electronics Engineering, 7% Mechanical Engineering, 4% Systems Science and Theory
Expenses: 2014-2015: $48,786; room/board: $12,090
Financial aid: (412) 268-8186; 50% of undergrads determined to have financial need; average aid package $33,041

Cedar Crest College
Allentown PA
(800) 360-1222
U.S. News ranking: Reg. Coll. (N), No. 16
Website: www.cedarcrest.edu
Admissions email: cccadmis@cedarcrest.edu
Private; founded 1867
Freshman admissions: less selective; 2013-2014: 1,063 applied, 625 accepted. Either SAT or ACT required. SAT 25/75 percentile: 840-1050. High school rank: 10% in top tenth, 43% in top quarter, 81% in top half
Early decision deadline: N/A, notification date: N/A
Early action deadline: N/A, notification date: N/A
Application deadline (fall): rolling
Undergraduate student body: 640 full time, 646 part time; 7% male, 93% female; 0% American Indian, 3% Asian, 9% black, 13% Hispanic, 1% multiracial, 0% Pacific Islander, 70% white, 1% international; 87% from in state; 22% live on campus; 0% of students in fraternities, 0% in sororities
Most popular majors: 6% Business, Management, Marketing, and Related Support Services, 35% Health Professions and Related Programs, 15% Psychology, 6% Public Administration and Social Service Professions, 5% Visual and Performing Arts
Expenses: 2014-2015: $34,304; room/board: $10,409

Financial aid: (610) 740-3785; 93% of undergrads determined to have financial need; average aid package $24,855

Central Penn College[1]
Summerdale PA
(800) 759-2727
U.S. News ranking: Reg. Coll. (N), unranked
Website: www.centralpenn.edu
Admissions email: admissions@centralpenn.edu
For-profit
Application deadline (fall): N/A
Undergraduate student body: N/A full time, N/A part time
Expenses: 2013-2014: $16,167; room/board: $6,480
Financial aid: (800) 759-2727

Chatham University
Pittsburgh PA
(800) 837-1290
U.S. News ranking: Reg. U. (N), No. 56
Website: www.chatham.edu
Admissions email: admissions@chatham.edu
Private; founded 1869
Freshman admissions: selective; 2013-2014: 594 applied, 361 accepted. Neither SAT nor ACT required. SAT 25/75 percentile: 950-1190. High school rank: 42% in top tenth, 65% in top quarter, 94% in top half
Early decision deadline: N/A, notification date: N/A
Early action deadline: N/A, notification date: N/A
Application deadline (fall): 8/1
Undergraduate student body: 611 full time, 366 part time; 9% male, 91% female; 0% American Indian, 2% Asian, 12% black, 2% Hispanic, 3% multiracial, 0% Pacific Islander, 68% white, 9% international; 83% from in state; 46% live on campus; N/A of students in fraternities, N/A in sororities
Most popular majors: 11% Biological and Biomedical Sciences, 13% Business, Management, Marketing, and Related Support Services, 20% Health Professions and Related Programs, 12% Psychology, 8% Visual and Performing Arts
Expenses: 2014-2015: $33,429; room/board: $10,410
Financial aid: (412) 365-1777; 65% of undergrads determined to have financial need; average aid package $27,154

Chestnut Hill College
Philadelphia PA
(215) 248-7001
U.S. News ranking: Reg. U. (N), second tier
Website: www.chc.edu
Admissions email: chcapply@chc.edu
Private; founded 1924
Affiliation: Roman Catholic
Freshman admissions: less selective; 2013-2014: 1,855 applied, 1,064 accepted. Either SAT or ACT required. SAT 25/75 percentile: 850-1060. High school rank: 10% in top tenth, 29% in top quarter, 65% in top half
Early decision deadline: N/A, notification date: N/A
Early action deadline: N/A, notification date: N/A

Application deadline (fall): rolling
Undergraduate student body: 1,161 full time, 346 part time; 32% male, 68% female; 0% American Indian, 2% Asian, 35% black, 7% Hispanic, 3% multiracial, 0% Pacific Islander, 41% white, 1% international; 77% from in state; 38% live on campus; 0% of students in fraternities, 0% in sororities
Most popular majors: 14% Business, Management, Marketing, and Related Support Services, 32% Education, 10% Homeland Security, Law Enforcement, Firefighting and Related Protective Services, 7% Psychology, 17% Public Administration and Social Service Professions
Expenses: 2014-2015: $32,510; room/board: $10,000
Financial aid: (215) 248-7182; 62% of undergrads determined to have financial need; average aid package $19,039

Cheyney University of Pennsylvania

Cheyney PA
(610) 399-2275
U.S. News ranking: Reg. U. (N), second tier
Website: www.cheyney.edu
Admissions email: abrown@cheyney.edu
Public; founded 1837
Freshman admissions: least selective; 2013-2014: 1,451 applied, 1,273 accepted. Either SAT or ACT required. SAT 25/75 percentile: 670-850. High school rank: 2% in top tenth, 9% in top quarter, 40% in top half
Early decision deadline: N/A, notification date: N/A
Early action deadline: N/A, notification date: N/A
Application deadline (fall): rolling
Undergraduate student body: 1,114 full time, 65 part time; 48% male, 52% female; 0% American Indian, 0% Asian, 88% black, 5% Hispanic, 3% multiracial, 0% Pacific Islander, 1% white, 0% international; 78% from in state; 73% live on campus; N/A of students in fraternities, N/A in sororities
Most popular majors: 25% Business, Management, Marketing, and Related Support Services, 9% Education, 7% Parks, Recreation, Leisure, and Fitness Studies, 11% Psychology, 23% Social Sciences
Expenses: 2014-2015: $8,842 in state, $13,148 out of state; room/board: $11,270
Financial aid: (610) 399-2302; 98% of undergrads determined to have financial need; average aid package $11,339

Clarion University of Pennsylvania

Clarion PA
(814) 393-2306
U.S. News ranking: Reg. U. (N), second tier
Website: www.clarion.edu
Admissions email: admissions@clarion.edu
Public; founded 1867
Freshman admissions: less selective; 2013-2014: 2,071 applied, 1,936 accepted. Either SAT or ACT required. SAT 25/75 percentile: 840-1030. High

school rank: 2% in top tenth, 9% in top quarter, 39% in top half
Early decision deadline: N/A, notification date: N/A
Early action deadline: N/A, notification date: N/A
Application deadline (fall): 8/1
Undergraduate student body: 4,373 full time, 826 part time; 37% male, 63% female; 0% American Indian, 0% Asian, 7% black, 1% Hispanic, 2% multiracial, 0% Pacific Islander, 88% white, 1% international; 90% from in state; 35% live on campus; 1% of students in fraternities, 1% in sororities
Most popular majors: 13% Business, Management, Marketing, and Related Support Services, 9% Communication, Journalism, and Related Programs, 14% Education, 16% Health Professions and Related Programs, 12% Liberal Arts and Sciences, General Studies and Humanities
Expenses: 2014-2015: $9,788 in state, $13,198 out of state; room/board: $8,285
Financial aid: (814) 393-2315; 81% of undergrads determined to have financial need; average aid package $8,130

Curtis Institute of Music

Philadelphia PA
(215) 717-3117
U.S. News ranking: Arts, unranked
Website: www.curtis.edu
Admissions email: admissions@curtis.edu
Private; founded 1924
Freshman admissions: N/A; 2013-2014: 289 applied, 14 accepted. SAT required. SAT 25/75 percentile: N/A. High school rank: N/A
Early decision deadline: N/A, notification date: N/A
Early action deadline: N/A, notification date: N/A
Application deadline (fall): 12/12
Undergraduate student body: 122 full time, N/A part time; 53% male, 47% female; 0% American Indian, 20% Asian, 2% black, 2% Hispanic, 0% multiracial, 0% Pacific Islander, 39% white, 37% international
Most popular majors: Information not available
Expenses: 2014-2015: $2,475; room/board: $14,363
Financial aid: (215) 717-3165; 50% of undergrads determined to have financial need; average aid package $16,455

Delaware Valley College

Doylestown PA
(215) 489-2211
U.S. News ranking: Reg. Coll. (N), No. 19
Website: www.delval.edu
Admissions email: admitme@delval.edu
Private; founded 1896
Freshman admissions: selective; 2013-2014: 1,895 applied, 1,295 accepted. Either SAT or ACT required. SAT 25/75 percentile: 880-1123. High school rank: 16% in top tenth, 41% in top quarter, 74% in top half
Early decision deadline: N/A, notification date: N/A

Early action deadline: N/A, notification date: N/A
Application deadline (fall): rolling
Undergraduate student body: 1,608 full time, 199 part time; 37% male, 63% female; 1% American Indian, 1% Asian, 6% black, 6% Hispanic, 1% multiracial, 0% Pacific Islander, 81% white, 0% international; 62% from in state; 53% live on campus; 1% of students in fraternities, 1% in sororities
Most popular majors: 39% Agriculture, Agriculture Operations, and Related Sciences, 15% Biological and Biomedical Sciences, 16% Business, Management, Marketing, and Related Support Services, 4% Homeland Security, Law Enforcement, Firefighting and Related Protective Services, 14% Natural Resources and Conservation
Expenses: 2014-2015: $33,826; room/board: $12,076
Financial aid: (215) 489-2272; 79% of undergrads determined to have financial need; average aid package $22,385

DeSales University

Center Valley PA
(610) 282-4443
U.S. News ranking: Reg. U. (N), No. 70
Website: www.desales.edu
Admissions email: admiss@desales.edu
Private; founded 1964
Affiliation: Roman Catholic
Freshman admissions: selective; 2013-2014: 2,624 applied, 1,989 accepted. Either SAT or ACT required. SAT 25/75 percentile: 930-1190. High school rank: 23% in top tenth, 47% in top quarter, 80% in top half
Early decision deadline: N/A, notification date: N/A
Early action deadline: N/A, notification date: N/A
Application deadline (fall): 8/1
Undergraduate student body: 1,836 full time, 646 part time; 38% male, 62% female; 1% American Indian, 2% Asian, 5% black, 9% Hispanic, 0% multiracial, 0% Pacific Islander, 76% white, 0% international; 69% from in state; 64% live on campus; 0% of students in fraternities, 0% in sororities
Most popular majors: 20% Business, Management, Marketing, and Related Support Services, 23% Health Professions and Related Programs, 6% Parks, Recreation, Leisure, and Fitness Studies, 8% Psychology, 11% Visual and Performing Arts
Expenses: 2014-2015: $32,350; room/board: $11,620
Financial aid: (610) 282-1100; 80% of undergrads determined to have financial need; average aid package $22,148

Dickinson College

Carlisle PA
(800) 644-1773
U.S. News ranking: Nat. Lib. Arts, No. 37
Website: www.dickinson.edu
Admissions email: admissions@dickinson.edu
Private; founded 1783
Freshman admissions: more selective; 2013-2014: 5,817 applied, 2,589 accepted. Neither

SAT nor ACT required. SAT 25/75 percentile: 1190-1365. High school rank: 46% in top tenth, 78% in top quarter, 93% in top half
Early decision deadline: 11/15, notification date: 12/15
Early action deadline: 12/1, notification date: 2/1
Application deadline (fall): 2/1
Undergraduate student body: 2,356 full time, 40 part time; 44% male, 56% female; 0% American Indian, 2% Asian, 4% black, 6% Hispanic, 3% multiracial, 0% Pacific Islander, 76% white, 7% international; 23% from in state; 95% live on campus; 12% of students in fraternities, 20% in sororities
Most popular majors: 7% Biology/Biological Sciences, General, 6% Economics, General, 8% International Business/Trade/Commerce, 6% Political Science and Government, General, 6% Psychology, General
Expenses: 2014-2015: $47,692; room/board: $11,972
Financial aid: (717) 245-1308; 53% of undergrads determined to have financial need; average aid package $36,427

Drexel University

Philadelphia PA
(800) 237-3935
U.S. News ranking: Nat. U., No. 95
Website: www.drexel.edu
Admissions email: enroll@drexel.edu
Private; founded 1891
Freshman admissions: more selective; 2013-2014: 43,945 applied, 35,815 accepted. Either SAT or ACT required. SAT 25/75 percentile: 1070-1310. High school rank: 33% in top tenth, 61% in top quarter, 86% in top half
Early decision deadline: N/A, notification date: N/A
Early action deadline: 11/1, notification date: 12/15
Application deadline (fall): 1/15
Undergraduate student body: 11,480 full time, 2,628 part time; 52% male, 48% female; 0% American Indian, 12% Asian, 7% black, 6% Hispanic, 3% multiracial, 1% Pacific Islander, 56% white, 14% international; 47% from in state; 26% live on campus; 9% of students in fraternities, 8% in sororities
Most popular majors: 20% Business, Management, Marketing, and Related Support Services, 6% Computer and Information Sciences and Support Services, 19% Engineering, 23% Health Professions and Related Programs, 9% Visual and Performing Arts
Expenses: 2014-2015: $47,051; room/board: $14,367
Financial aid: (215) 895-2537

Duquesne University

Pittsburgh PA
(412) 396-6222
U.S. News ranking: Nat. U., No. 116
Website: www.duq.edu
Admissions email: admissions@duq.edu
Private; founded 1878
Affiliation: Roman Catholic

Freshman admissions: selective; 2013-2014: 6,793 applied, 5,033 accepted. Neither SAT nor ACT required. SAT 25/75 percentile: 1050-1220. High school rank: 27% in top tenth, 60% in top quarter, 89% in top half
Early decision deadline: 11/1, notification date: 11/15
Early action deadline: 12/1, notification date: 1/15
Application deadline (fall): 7/1
Undergraduate student body: 5,740 full time, 230 part time; 41% male, 59% female; 0% American Indian, 2% Asian, 4% black, 3% Hispanic, 2% multiracial, 0% Pacific Islander, 84% white, 4% international; 75% from in state; 61% live on campus; 17% of students in fraternities, 21% in sororities
Most popular majors: 6% Biological and Biomedical Sciences, 25% Business, Management, Marketing, and Related Support Services, 8% Communication, Journalism, and Related Programs, 8% Education, 23% Health Professions and Related Programs
Expenses: 2014-2015: $32,636; room/board: $11,084
Financial aid: (412) 396-6607; 71% of undergrads determined to have financial need; average aid package $25,135

Eastern University

St. Davids PA
(610) 341-5967
U.S. News ranking: Reg. U. (N), No. 98
Website: www.eastern.edu
Admissions email: ugadm@eastern.edu
Private; founded 1952
Affiliation: American Baptist
Freshman admissions: selective; 2013-2014: 1,485 applied, 1,111 accepted. Either SAT or ACT required. SAT 25/75 percentile: 920-1160. High school rank: 19% in top tenth, 51% in top quarter, 81% in top half
Early decision deadline: N/A, notification date: N/A
Early action deadline: N/A, notification date: N/A
Application deadline (fall): rolling
Undergraduate student body: 2,076 full time, 465 part time; 30% male, 70% female; 1% American Indian, 2% Asian, 21% black, 15% Hispanic, 0% multiracial, 0% Pacific Islander, 54% white, 2% international; 55% from in state; 73% live on campus; N/A of students in fraternities, N/A in sororities
Most popular majors: 14% Business Administration and Management, General, 17% Early Childhood Education and Teaching, 11% Nursing Practice, 5% Organizational Leadership, 5% Registered Nursing/Registered Nurse
Expenses: 2014-2015: $29,600; room/board: $9,940
Financial aid: (610) 341-5842; 90% of undergrads determined to have financial need; average aid package $18,115

East Stroudsburg University of Pennsylvania

East Stroudsburg PA
(570) 422-3542
U.S. News ranking: Reg. U. (N), No. 133
Website: www.esu.edu
Admissions email: undergrads@po-box.esu.edu
Public; founded 1893
Freshman admissions: least selective; 2013-2014: 5,642 applied, 4,409 accepted. Either SAT or ACT required. SAT 25/75 percentile: 880-1010. High school rank: 2% in top tenth, 10% in top quarter, 39% in top half
Early decision deadline: N/A, notification date: N/A
Early action deadline: N/A, notification date: N/A
Application deadline (fall): 4/1
Undergraduate student body: 5,495 full time, 691 part time; 45% male, 55% female; 0% American Indian, 1% Asian, 9% black, 10% Hispanic, 2% multiracial, 0% Pacific Islander, 63% white, 1% international; 77% from in state; 36% live on campus; N/A of students in fraternities, N/A in sororities
Most popular majors: 13% Business, Management, Marketing, and Related Support Services, 23% Education, 10% Health Professions and Related Programs, 9% Parks, Recreation, Leisure, and Fitness Studies, 11% Social Sciences
Expenses: 2014-2015: $9,376 in state, $19,606 out of state; room/board: $7,980
Financial aid: (570) 422-2800; 53% of undergrads determined to have financial need; average aid package $7,330

Edinboro University of Pennsylvania

Edinboro PA
(888) 846-2676
U.S. News ranking: Reg. U. (N), No. 135
Website: www.edinboro.edu
Admissions email: eup_admissions@edinboro.edu
Public; founded 1857
Freshman admissions: less selective; 2013-2014: 3,187 applied, 2,784 accepted. Either SAT or ACT required. SAT 25/75 percentile: 820-1040. High school rank: 6% in top tenth, 24% in top quarter, 54% in top half
Early decision deadline: N/A, notification date: N/A
Early action deadline: N/A, notification date: N/A
Application deadline (fall): rolling
Undergraduate student body: 5,320 full time, 544 part time; 42% male, 58% female; 0% American Indian, 1% Asian, 7% black, 1% Hispanic, 4% multiracial, 0% Pacific Islander, 84% white, 2% international; 88% from in state; 37% live on campus; 0% of students in fraternities, 1% in sororities
Most popular majors: 9% Business, Management, Marketing, and Related Support Services, 11% Education, 11% Health Professions and Related Programs, 8% Social Sciences, 15% Visual and Performing Arts

Expenses: 2014-2015: $9,222 in state, $12,632 out of state; room/board: $8,612
Financial aid: (814) 732-5555; 64% of undergrads determined to have financial need; average aid package $8,425

Elizabethtown College

Elizabethtown PA
(717) 361-1400
U.S. News ranking: Reg. Coll. (N), No. 4
Website: www.etown.edu
Admissions email: admissions@etown.edu
Private; founded 1899
Freshman admissions: selective; 2013-2014: 3,815 applied, 2,654 accepted. Either SAT or ACT required. SAT 25/75 percentile: 1000-1230. High school rank: 34% in top tenth, 65% in top quarter, 88% in top half
Early decision deadline: N/A, notification date: N/A
Early action deadline: N/A, notification date: N/A
Application deadline (fall): rolling
Undergraduate student body: 1,808 full time, 36 part time; 36% male, 64% female; 0% American Indian, 2% Asian, 2% black, 3% Hispanic, 1% multiracial, 0% Pacific Islander, 88% white, 3% international; 66% from in state; 88% live on campus; 0% of students in fraternities, 0% in sororities
Most popular majors: 10% Biological and Biomedical Sciences, 15% Business, Management, Marketing, and Related Support Services, 10% Education, 11% Health Professions and Related Programs, 10% Social Sciences
Expenses: 2014-2015: $39,920; room/board: $9,820
Financial aid: (717) 361-1404; 78% of undergrads determined to have financial need; average aid package $26,636

Franklin and Marshall College

Lancaster PA
(717) 291-3953
U.S. News ranking: Nat. Lib. Arts, No. 37
Website: www.fandm.edu
Admissions email: admission@fandm.edu
Private; founded 1787
Freshman admissions: more selective; 2013-2014: 5,347 applied, 1,936 accepted. Neither SAT nor ACT required. SAT 25/75 percentile: 1220-1410. High school rank: 56% in top tenth, 86% in top quarter, 100% in top half
Early decision deadline: 11/15, notification date: 12/15
Early action deadline: N/A, notification date: N/A
Application deadline (fall): 1/15
Undergraduate student body: 2,258 full time, 39 part time; 48% male, 52% female; 0% American Indian, 4% Asian, 5% black, 7% Hispanic, 2% multiracial, 0% Pacific Islander, 63% white, 13% international; 29% from in state; 97% live on campus; 28% of students in fraternities, 36% in

Most popular majors: 6% Biology/Biological Sciences, General, 12% Business/Commerce, General, 5% Economics, General, 11% Political Science and Government, General, 6% Psychology, General
Expenses: 2014-2015: $48,514; room/board: $12,285
Financial aid: (717) 291-3991; 49% of undergrads determined to have financial need; average aid package $40,929

Gannon University

Erie PA
(814) 871-7240
U.S. News ranking: Reg. U. (N), No. 60
Website: www.gannon.edu
Admissions email: admissions@gannon.edu
Private; founded 1925
Affiliation: Roman Catholic
Freshman admissions: selective; 2013-2014: 3,983 applied, 3,203 accepted. Either SAT or ACT required. SAT 25/75 percentile: 930-1150. High school rank: 27% in top tenth, 54% in top quarter, 82% in top half
Early decision deadline: N/A, notification date: N/A
Early action deadline: N/A, notification date: N/A
Application deadline (fall): rolling
Undergraduate student body: 2,556 full time, 555 part time; 43% male, 57% female; 0% American Indian, 2% Asian, 5% black, 3% Hispanic, 1% multiracial, 0% Pacific Islander, 81% white, 7% international; 75% from in state; 42% live on campus; 14% of students in fraternities, 18% in sororities
Most popular majors: 10% Biological and Biomedical Sciences, 11% Business, Management, Marketing, and Related Support Services, 31% Health Professions and Related Programs, 7% Homeland Security, Law Enforcement, Firefighting and Related Protective Services, 8% Parks, Recreation, Leisure, and Fitness Studies
Expenses: 2014-2015: $28,368; room/board: $11,240
Financial aid: (814) 871-7337; 80% of undergrads determined to have financial need; average aid package $23,171

Geneva College

Beaver Falls PA
(724) 847-6500
U.S. News ranking: Reg. Coll. (N), No. 14
Website: www.geneva.edu
Admissions email: admissions@geneva.edu
Private; founded 1848
Affiliation: Reformed Presbyterian of N.A.
Freshman admissions: selective; 2013-2014: 1,652 applied, 1,136 accepted. Either SAT or ACT required. SAT 25/75 percentile: 950-1190. High school rank: 22% in top tenth, 45% in top quarter, 78% in top half
Early decision deadline: N/A, notification date: N/A
Early action deadline: N/A, notification date: N/A
Application deadline (fall): rolling
Undergraduate student body: 1,475 full time, 66 part time; 48% male,

52% female; 0% American Indian, 1% Asian, 6% black, 1% Hispanic, 2% multiracial, 0% Pacific Islander, 89% white, 1% international; 71% from in state; 70% live on campus; 0% of students in fraternities, 0% in sororities
Most popular majors: 17% Business, Management, Marketing, and Related Support Services, 11% Education, 14% Engineering, 6% Psychology, 6% Public Administration and Social Service Professions
Expenses: 2014-2015: $25,220; room/board: $9,460
Financial aid: (724) 847-6530; 82% of undergrads determined to have financial need; average aid package $19,770

Gettysburg College

Gettysburg PA
(800) 431-0803
U.S. News ranking: Nat. Lib. Arts, No. 50
Website: www.gettysburg.edu
Admissions email: admiss@gettysburg.edu
Private; founded 1832
Affiliation: Lutheran
Freshman admissions: more selective; 2013-2014: 5,453 applied, 2,270 accepted. Neither SAT nor ACT required. SAT 25/75 percentile: 1200-1370. High school rank: 69% in top tenth, 89% in top quarter, 99% in top half
Early decision deadline: 11/15, notification date: 12/15
Early action deadline: N/A, notification date: N/A
Application deadline (fall): 2/1
Undergraduate student body: 2,515 full time, 18 part time; 48% male, 52% female; 0% American Indian, 1% Asian, 3% black, 4% Hispanic, 3% multiracial, 0% Pacific Islander, 82% white, 2% international; N/A from in state; 93% live on campus; 41% of students in fraternities, 33% in sororities
Most popular majors: 11% Biology/Biological Sciences, General, 10% Business/Commerce, General, 8% English Language and Literature, General, 8% History, General, 23% Social Sciences, General
Expenses: 2014-2015: $47,480; room/board: $11,340
Financial aid: (717) 337-6611; 61% of undergrads determined to have financial need; average aid package $33,652

Gratz College[1]

Melrose Park PA
(215) 635-7300
U.S. News ranking: Reg. U. (N), unranked
Website: www.gratzcollege.edu
Admissions email: admissions@gratz.edu
Private
Affiliation: Jewish
Application deadline (fall): N/A
Undergraduate student body: N/A full time, N/A part time
Expenses: N/A
Financial aid: (215) 635-7300

Grove City College

Grove City PA
(724) 458-2100
U.S. News ranking: Nat. Lib. Arts, No. 139
Website: www.gcc.edu
Admissions email: admissions@gcc.edu
Private; founded 1876
Affiliation: Presbyterian
Freshman admissions: more selective; 2013-2014: 1,530 applied, 1,233 accepted. Either SAT or ACT required. SAT 25/75 percentile: 1079-1334. High school rank: 41% in top tenth, 65% in top quarter, 90% in top half
Early decision deadline: 11/15, notification date: 12/15
Early action deadline: N/A, notification date: N/A
Application deadline (fall): 2/1
Undergraduate student body: 2,438 full time, 53 part time; 49% male, 51% female; 0% American Indian, 2% Asian, 1% black, 1% Hispanic, 2% multiracial, 0% Pacific Islander, 93% white, 1% international; 48% from in state; 94% live on campus; 16% of students in fraternities, 18% in sororities
Most popular majors: 6% Biology/Biological Sciences, General, 8% English Language and Literature, General, 6% History, General, 7% Mechanical Engineering, 6% Speech Communication and Rhetoric
Expenses: 2014-2015: $15,550; room/board: $8,472
Financial aid: (724) 458-3300; 41% of undergrads determined to have financial need; average aid package $6,541

Gwynedd Mercy University

Gwynedd Valley PA
(215) 681-5510
U.S. News ranking: Reg. U. (N), No. 109
Website: www.gmercyu.edu/
Admissions email: admissions@gmercyu.edu
Private; founded 1948
Affiliation: Roman Catholic
Freshman admissions: less selective; 2013-2014: 1,232 applied, 812 accepted. Either SAT or ACT required. SAT 25/75 percentile: 850-1050. High school rank: 7% in top tenth, 21% in top quarter, 52% in top half
Early decision deadline: N/A, notification date: N/A
Early action deadline: N/A, notification date: N/A
Application deadline (fall): 8/20
Undergraduate student body: 1,851 full time, 211 part time; 25% male, 75% female; 0% American Indian, 5% Asian, 25% black, 4% Hispanic, 0% multiracial, 0% Pacific Islander, 61% white, 0% international; 90% from in state; 22% live on campus; N/A of students in fraternities, N/A in sororities
Most popular majors: 30% Business, Management, Marketing, and Related Support Services, 9% Education, 42% Health Professions and Related Programs, 5% Homeland Security, Law Enforcement, Firefighting and Related Protective Services, 5% Psychology

Expenses: 2014-2015: $30,460; room/board: $11,040
Financial aid: (215) 641-5570; 74% of undergrads determined to have financial need; average aid package $20,075

Harrisburg University of Science and Technology

Harrisburg PA
(717) 901-5150
U.S. News ranking: Nat. Lib. Arts, second tier
Website: www.harrisburgu.edu
Admissions email: admissions@harrisburgu.edu
Private; founded 2001
Freshman admissions: less selective; 2013-2014: N/A applied, N/A accepted. Neither SAT nor ACT required. SAT 25/75 percentile: 830-1050. High school rank: N/A
Early decision deadline: N/A, notification date: N/A
Early action deadline: N/A, notification date: N/A
Application deadline (fall): rolling
Undergraduate student body: 263 full time, 17 part time; 51% male, 49% female; 0% American Indian, 6% Asian, 33% black, 4% Hispanic, 6% multiracial, 0% Pacific Islander, 47% white, 0% international; 79% from in state; 33% live on campus; 0% of students in fraternities, 0% in sororities
Most popular majors: 21% Biotechnology, 27% Computer and Information Sciences, General, 3% Geological and Earth Sciences/Geosciences, Other, 48% Natural Sciences
Expenses: 2014-2015: $23,900; room/board: $9,700
Financial aid: N/A; 97% of undergrads determined to have financial need; average aid package $3,418

Haverford College

Haverford PA
(610) 896-1350
U.S. News ranking: Nat. Lib. Arts, No. 8
Website: www.haverford.edu
Admissions email: admission@haverford.edu
Private; founded 1833
Freshman admissions: most selective; 2013-2014: 3,585 applied, 842 accepted. Either SAT or ACT required. SAT 25/75 percentile: 1310-1490. High school rank: 95% in top tenth, 98% in top quarter, 100% in top half
Early decision deadline: 11/15, notification date: 12/15
Early action deadline: N/A, notification date: N/A
Application deadline (fall): 1/15
Undergraduate student body: 1,187 full time, 0 part time; 48% male, 52% female; 0% American Indian, 7% Asian, 6% black, 9% Hispanic, 7% multiracial, 0% Pacific Islander, 65% white, 6% international; 13% from in state; 98% live on campus; 0% of students in fraternities, 0% in sororities
Most popular majors: 13% Biology/Biological Sciences, General, 9% Economics, General, 10% English Language and Literature,

General, 9% Political Science and Government, General, 12% Psychology, General
Expenses: 2014-2015: $47,214; room/board: $14,350
Financial aid: (610) 896-1350; 51% of undergrads determined to have financial need; average aid package $41,254

Holy Family University

Philadelphia PA
(215) 637-3050
U.S. News ranking: Reg. U. (N), No. 125
Website: www.holyfamily.edu
Admissions email: admissions@holyfamily.edu
Private; founded 1954
Affiliation: Roman Catholic
Freshman admissions: less selective; 2013-2014: 1,287 applied, 999 accepted. Either SAT or ACT required. SAT 25/75 percentile: 850-1020. High school rank: 11% in top tenth, 35% in top quarter, 70% in top half
Early decision deadline: N/A, notification date: N/A
Early action deadline: N/A, notification date: N/A
Application deadline (fall): rolling
Undergraduate student body: 1,499 full time, 683 part time; 26% male, 74% female; 0% American Indian, 4% Asian, 7% black, 6% Hispanic, 0% multiracial, 0% Pacific Islander, 56% white, 0% international; 84% from in state; 11% live on campus; 0% of students in fraternities, 0% in sororities
Most popular majors: 16% Business, Management, Marketing, and Related Support Services, 23% Education, 27% Health Professions and Related Programs, 6% Homeland Security, Law Enforcement, Firefighting and Related Protective Services, 13% Psychology
Expenses: 2014-2015: $28,456; room/board: $13,576
Financial aid: (215) 637-5538; 86% of undergrads determined to have financial need; average aid package $19,506

Immaculata University

Immaculata PA
(877) 428-6329
U.S. News ranking: Nat. U., No. 181
Website: www.immaculata.edu
Admissions email: admiss@immaculata.edu
Private; founded 1920
Affiliation: Roman Catholic
Freshman admissions: less selective; 2013-2014: 1,770 applied, 1,449 accepted. Either SAT or ACT required. SAT 25/75 percentile: 830-1060. High school rank: N/A
Early decision deadline: N/A, notification date: N/A
Early action deadline: N/A, notification date: N/A
Application deadline (fall): rolling
Undergraduate student body: 1,184 full time, 1,376 part time; 24% male, 76% female; 0% American Indian, 3% Asian, 17% black, 5% Hispanic, 2% multiracial, 0% Pacific Islander, 72% white, 1% international; 76% from in state; 22% live on campus; 3% of students in fraternities, 4% in sororities

Most popular majors: 18% Business, Management, Marketing, and Related Support Services, 5% Education, 57% Health Professions and Related Programs, 3% Parks, Recreation, Leisure, and Fitness Studies, 6% Psychology
Expenses: 2013-2014: $30,740; room/board: $12,260
Financial aid: (610) 647-4400

Indiana University of Pennsylvania

Indiana PA
(800) 442-6830
U.S. News ranking: Nat. U., second tier
Website: www.iup.edu
Admissions email: admissions-inquiry@iup.edu
Public; founded 1875
Freshman admissions: less selective; 2013-2014: 9,367 applied, 8,476 accepted. Either SAT or ACT required. SAT 25/75 percentile: 880-1070. High school rank: 8% in top tenth, 23% in top quarter, 58% in top half
Early decision deadline: N/A, notification date: N/A
Early action deadline: N/A, notification date: N/A
Application deadline (fall): rolling
Undergraduate student body: 11,748 full time, 723 part time; 45% male, 55% female; 0% American Indian, 1% Asian, 11% black, 3% Hispanic, 3% multiracial, 0% Pacific Islander, 79% white, 2% international; 93% from in state; 32% live on campus; 7% of students in fraternities, 6% in sororities
Most popular majors: 23% Business, Management, Marketing, and Related Support Services, 7% Communication, Journalism, and Related Programs, 9% Health Professions and Related Programs, 16% Social Sciences, 7% Visual and Performing Arts
Expenses: 2014-2015: $9,470 in state, $19,700 out of state; room/board: $11,346
Financial aid: (724) 357-2218; 73% of undergrads determined to have financial need; average aid package $8,726

Juniata College

Huntingdon PA
(877) 586-4282
U.S. News ranking: Nat. Lib. Arts, No. 105
Website: www.juniata.edu
Admissions email: admissions@juniata.edu
Private; founded 1876
Freshman admissions: selective; 2013-2014: 2,227 applied, 1,650 accepted. Neither SAT nor ACT required. SAT 25/75 percentile: 1040-1260. High school rank: 34% in top tenth, 73% in top quarter, 98% in top half
Early decision deadline: 11/15, notification date: 12/23
Early action deadline: N/A, notification date: N/A
Application deadline (fall): 3/15
Undergraduate student body: 1,555 full time, 70 part time; 45% male, 55% female; 0% American Indian, 3% Asian, 3% black, 4% Hispanic, 2% multiracial,

0% Pacific Islander, 74% white, 8% international; 64% from in state; 79% live on campus; 0% of students in fraternities, 0% in sororities
Most popular majors: 15% Biological and Biomedical Sciences, 12% Business, Management, Marketing, and Related Support Services, 8% Natural Resources and Conservation, 8% Physical Sciences, 10% Psychology
Expenses: 2014-2015: $38,630; room/board: $10,710
Financial aid: (814) 641-3142; 70% of undergrads determined to have financial need; average aid package $29,631

Keystone College

La Plume PA
(570) 945-8000
U.S. News ranking: Reg. Coll. (N), No. 38
Website: www.keystone.edu
Admissions email: admissions@keystone.edu
Private; founded 1868
Freshman admissions: less selective; 2013-2014: 1,120 applied, 807 accepted. Either SAT or ACT required. SAT 25/75 percentile: 800-1000. High school rank: N/A
Early decision deadline: N/A, notification date: N/A
Early action deadline: N/A, notification date: N/A
Application deadline (fall): 6/1
Undergraduate student body: 1,304 full time, 270 part time; 41% male, 59% female; 0% American Indian, 1% Asian, 5% black, 3% Hispanic, 1% multiracial, 0% Pacific Islander, 75% white, 1% international; 86% from in state; 30% live on campus; 0% of students in fraternities, 0% in sororities
Most popular majors: 25% Business, Management, Marketing, and Related Support Services, 15% Education, 12% Homeland Security, Law Enforcement, Firefighting and Related Protective Services, 12% Parks, Recreation, Leisure, and Fitness Studies, 8% Visual and Performing Arts
Expenses: 2013-2014: $21,200; room/board: $9,800
Financial aid: (877) 426-5534

King's College

Wilkes-Barre PA
(888) 546-4772
U.S. News ranking: Reg. U. (N), No. 41
Website: www.kings.edu
Admissions email: admissions@kings.edu
Private; founded 1946
Affiliation: Catholic
Freshman admissions: selective; 2013-2014: 2,780 applied, 1,988 accepted. Neither SAT nor ACT required. SAT 25/75 percentile: 940-1150. High school rank: 14% in top tenth, 38% in top quarter, 74% in top half
Early decision deadline: N/A, notification date: N/A
Early action deadline: N/A, notification date: N/A
Application deadline (fall): rolling
Undergraduate student body: 1,925 full time, 219 part time; 51% male, 49% female;

0% American Indian, 2% Asian, 3% black, 7% Hispanic, 2% multiracial, 0% Pacific Islander, 80% white, 0% international; 28% from in state; 50% live on campus; 0% of students in fraternities, 0% in sororities
Most popular majors: 10% Accounting, 9% Business Administration and Management, General, 9% Criminal Justice/Safety Studies, 9% Elementary Education and Teaching, 9% Psychology, General
Expenses: 2014-2015: $31,816; room/board: $11,658
Financial aid: (570) 208-5868; 84% of undergrads determined to have financial need; average aid package $20,673

Kutztown University of Pennsylvania

Kutztown PA
(610) 683-4060
U.S. News ranking: Reg. U. (N), No. 125
Website: www.kutztown.edu
Admissions email: admissions@kutztown.edu
Public; founded 1866
Freshman admissions: less selective; 2013-2014: 8,533 applied, 6,406 accepted. Either SAT or ACT required. SAT 25/75 percentile: 870-1050. High school rank: 5% in top tenth, 20% in top quarter, 54% in top half
Early decision deadline: N/A, notification date: N/A
Early action deadline: N/A, notification date: N/A
Application deadline (fall): rolling
Undergraduate student body: 8,279 full time, 536 part time; 43% male, 57% female; 0% American Indian, 1% Asian, 7% black, 6% Hispanic, 2% multiracial, 0% Pacific Islander, 81% white, 1% international; 89% from in state; 44% live on campus; 6% of students in fraternities, 7% in sororities
Most popular majors: 19% Business Administration and Management, General, 6% Criminal Justice/Safety Studies, 6% English Language and Literature, General, 4% Parks, Recreation and Leisure Studies, 8% Psychology, General
Expenses: 2014-2015: $8,833 in state, $19,063 out of state; room/board: $8,430
Financial aid: (610) 683-4077; 71% of undergrads determined to have financial need; average aid package $7,840

Lafayette College

Easton PA
(610) 330-5100
U.S. News ranking: Nat. Lib. Arts, No. 35
Website: www.lafayette.edu
Admissions email: admissions@lafayette.edu
Private; founded 1826
Freshman admissions: more selective; 2013-2014: 6,766 applied, 2,310 accepted. Either SAT or ACT required. SAT 25/75 percentile: 1180-1370. High school rank: 62% in top tenth, 89% in top quarter, 97% in top half
Early decision deadline: 11/15, notification date: 12/15

Early action deadline: N/A, notification date: N/A
Application deadline (fall): 1/15
Undergraduate student body: 2,435 full time, 51 part time; 53% male, 47% female; 0% American Indian, 3% Asian, 5% black, 6% Hispanic, 2% multiracial, 0% Pacific Islander, 68% white, 6% international; 21% from in state; 92% live on campus; 18% of students in fraternities, 38% in sororities
Most popular majors: 6% Engineering, 7% English Language and Literature/Letters, 7% Psychology, 12% Social Sciences, 8% Social Sciences
Expenses: 2014-2015: $45,635; room/board: $13,520
Financial aid: (610) 330-5055; 40% of undergrads determined to have financial need; average aid package $39,420

La Roche College

Pittsburgh PA
(800) 838-4572
U.S. News ranking: Reg. Coll. (N), No. 33
Website: www.laroche.edu
Admissions email: admissions@laroche.edu
Private; founded 1963
Affiliation: Roman Catholic
Freshman admissions: less selective; 2013-2014: 1,488 applied, 828 accepted. Either SAT or ACT required. SAT 25/75 percentile: 800-1040. High school rank: 9% in top tenth, 26% in top quarter, 61% in top half
Early decision deadline: N/A, notification date: N/A
Early action deadline: N/A, notification date: N/A
Application deadline (fall): rolling
Undergraduate student body: 1,130 full time, 233 part time; 43% male, 57% female; 0% American Indian, 1% Asian, 7% black, 1% Hispanic, 1% multiracial, 0% Pacific Islander, 65% white, 13% international; 95% from in state; 42% live on campus; 0% of students in fraternities, 0% in sororities
Most popular majors: 8% Accounting, 7% Criminal Justice/Safety Studies, 6% Elementary Education and Teaching, 11% Medical Radiologic Technology/Science - Radiation Therapist, 9% Psychology, General
Expenses: 2014-2015: $25,500; room/board: $10,324
Financial aid: (412) 536-1120; 73% of undergrads determined to have financial need; average aid package $25,820

La Salle University

Philadelphia PA
(215) 951-1500
U.S. News ranking: Reg. U. (N), No. 31
Website: www.lasalle.edu
Admissions email: admiss@lasalle.edu
Private; founded 1863
Affiliation: Roman Catholic
Freshman admissions: selective; 2013-2014: 5,547 applied, 4,449 accepted. Either SAT or ACT required. SAT 25/75 percentile: 880-1100. High school rank: 15% in top tenth, 38% in top quarter, 73% in top half
Early decision deadline: N/A, notification date: N/A
Early action deadline: 11/15, notification date: 12/15
Application deadline (fall): rolling
Undergraduate student body: 3,542 full time, 867 part time; 35% male, 65% female; 0% American Indian, 5% Asian, 19% black, 10% Hispanic, 5% multiracial, 0% Pacific Islander, 55% white, 2% international; 62% from in state; 55% live on campus; 6% of students in fraternities, 13% in sororities
Most popular majors: 6% Accounting, 7% Marketing, 25% Nursing Science, 6% Psychology, General, 8% Speech Communication and Rhetoric
Expenses: 2014-2015: $39,800; room/board: $13,580
Financial aid: (215) 951-1070; 81% of undergrads determined to have financial need; average aid package $28,610

Lebanon Valley College

Annville PA
(717) 867-6181
U.S. News ranking: Reg. Coll. (N), No. 6
Website: www.lvc.edu
Admissions email: admission@lvc.edu
Private; founded 1866
Affiliation: Methodist
Freshman admissions: selective; 2013-2014: 3,793 applied, 2,536 accepted. Neither SAT nor ACT required. SAT 25/75 percentile: 1000-1220. High school rank: 37% in top tenth, 74% in top quarter, 92% in top half
Early decision deadline: N/A, notification date: N/A
Early action deadline: N/A, notification date: N/A
Application deadline (fall): rolling
Undergraduate student body: 1,648 full time, 118 part time; 47% male, 53% female; 0% American Indian, 2% Asian, 2% black, 5% Hispanic, 2% multiracial, 0% Pacific Islander, 85% white, 0% international; 80% from in state; 76% live on campus; 7% of students in fraternities, 10% in sororities
Most popular majors: 18% Business, Management, Marketing, and Related Support Services, 13% Education, 12% Health Professions and Related Programs, 9% Social Sciences, 9% Visual and Performing Arts
Expenses: 2014-2015: $37,470; room/board: $10,100
Financial aid: (717) 867-6126; 84% of undergrads determined to have financial need; average aid package $25,885

Lehigh University

Bethlehem PA
(610) 758-3100
U.S. News ranking: Nat. U., No. 40
Website: www.lehigh.edu
Admissions email: admissions@lehigh.edu
Private; founded 1865
Freshman admissions: more selective; 2013-2014: 12,589 applied, 3,882 accepted. Either SAT or ACT required. SAT 25/75 percentile: 1220-1410. High school rank: 60% in top tenth, 88% in top quarter, 98% in top half
Early decision deadline: 11/15, notification date: 12/15
Early action deadline: N/A, notification date: N/A
Application deadline (fall): 1/1
Undergraduate student body: 4,862 full time, 69 part time; 56% male, 44% female; 0% American Indian, 7% Asian, 3% black, 8% Hispanic, 3% multiracial, 0% Pacific Islander, 69% white, 7% international; 26% from in state; 68% live on campus; 40% of students in fraternities, 43% in sororities
Most popular majors: 6% Accounting, 4% Civil Engineering, General, 12% Finance, General, 5% Marketing/Marketing Management, General, 10% Mechanical Engineering
Expenses: 2014-2015: $44,890; room/board: $11,880
Financial aid: (610) 758-3181; 42% of undergrads determined to have financial need; average aid package $37,984

Lincoln University

Lincoln University PA
(800) 790-0191
U.S. News ranking: Reg. U. (N), second tier
Website: www.lincoln.edu
Admissions email: admiss@lu.lincoln.edu
Public; founded 1854
Freshman admissions: less selective; 2013-2014: 3,240 applied, 1,987 accepted. Either SAT or ACT required. SAT 25/75 percentile: 770-960. High school rank: 10% in top tenth, 28% in top quarter, 58% in top half
Early decision deadline: N/A, notification date: N/A
Early action deadline: N/A, notification date: N/A
Application deadline (fall): rolling
Undergraduate student body: 1,488 full time, 136 part time; 41% male, 59% female; 0% American Indian, 0% Asian, 84% black, 2% Hispanic, 1% multiracial, 0% Pacific Islander, 0% white, 3% international; 42% from in state; 98% live on campus; 5% of students in fraternities, 5% in sororities
Most popular majors: 9% Broadcast Journalism, 9% Business Administration and Management, General, 12% Criminal Justice/Safety Studies, 12% Human Services, General, 9% Sociology
Expenses: 2014-2015: $7,160 in state, $11,836 out of state; room/board: $8,686
Financial aid: (800) 561-2606; 97% of undergrads determined to have financial need; average aid package $12,004

Lock Haven University of Pennsylvania

Lock Haven PA
(570) 893-2027
U.S. News ranking: Reg. U. (N), second tier
Website: www.lhup.edu
Admissions email: admissions@lhup.edu
Public; founded 1870
Freshman admissions: less selective; 2013-2014: 3,849 applied, 3,311 accepted. Either SAT or ACT required. SAT 25/75 percentile: 840-1050. High school rank: 9% in top tenth, 30% in top quarter, 64% in top half
Early decision deadline: N/A, notification date: N/A
Early action deadline: N/A, notification date: N/A
Application deadline (fall): rolling
Undergraduate student body: 4,519 full time, 336 part time; 43% male, 57% female; 0% American Indian, 1% Asian, 8% black, 2% Hispanic, 1% multiracial, 0% Pacific Islander, 87% white, 0% international; 94% from in state; 40% live on campus; 3% of students in fraternities, 4% in sororities
Most popular majors: 7% Business Administration and Management, General, 10% Criminal Justice/Law Enforcement Administration, 9% Health Services/Allied Health/Health Sciences, General, 6% Health and Physical Education/Fitness, Other, 8% Sport and Fitness Administration/Management
Expenses: 2014-2015: $9,276 in state, $17,506 out of state; room/board: $8,752
Financial aid: (570) 893-2344; 58% of undergrads determined to have financial need; average aid package $8,361

Lycoming College

Williamsport PA
(800) 345-3920
U.S. News ranking: Nat. Lib. Arts, No. 159
Website: www.lycoming.edu
Admissions email: admissions@lycoming.edu
Private; founded 1812
Affiliation: Methodist
Freshman admissions: selective; 2013-2014: 1,737 applied, 1,244 accepted. Neither SAT nor ACT required. SAT 25/75 percentile: 930-1150. High school rank: 19% in top tenth, 43% in top quarter, 75% in top half
Early decision deadline: N/A, notification date: N/A
Early action deadline: N/A, notification date: N/A
Application deadline (fall): 3/1
Undergraduate student body: 1,290 full time, 17 part time; 44% male, 56% female; 0% American Indian, 1% Asian, 5% black, 3% Hispanic, 2% multiracial, 0% Pacific Islander, 77% white, 4% international; 66% from in state; 87% live on campus; 16% of students in fraternities, 21% in sororities
Most popular majors: 11% Biological and Biomedical Sciences, 25% Business, Management, Marketing, and Related Support Services, 14% Psychology, 16% Social Sciences, 6% Visual and Performing Arts
Expenses: 2014-2015: $34,706; room/board: $10,376
Financial aid: (570) 321-4040; 84% of undergrads determined to have financial need; average aid package $27,877

Mansfield University of Pennsylvania

Mansfield PA
(800) 577-6826
U.S. News ranking: Reg. U. (N), No. 135
Website: www.mansfield.edu
Admissions email: admissns@mansfield.edu
Public; founded 1857
Freshman admissions: less selective; 2013-2014: 2,023 applied, 1,867 accepted. Either SAT or ACT required. SAT 25/75 percentile: 850-1070. High school rank: 8% in top tenth, 29% in top quarter, 63% in top half
Early decision deadline: N/A, notification date: N/A
Early action deadline: N/A, notification date: N/A
Application deadline (fall): rolling
Undergraduate student body: 2,453 full time, 264 part time; 41% male, 59% female; 0% American Indian, 1% Asian, 9% black, 3% Hispanic, 2% multiracial, 0% Pacific Islander, 81% white, 1% international; 80% from in state; 51% live on campus; 7% of students in fraternities, 6% in sororities
Most popular majors: 13% Health Professions and Related Programs, 11% Homeland Security, Law Enforcement, Firefighting and Related Protective Services, 9% Psychology, 9% Social Sciences, 12% Visual and Performing Arts
Expenses: 2014-2015: $9,526 in state, $19,756 out of state; room/board: $10,582
Financial aid: (570) 662-4878; 86% of undergrads determined to have financial need; average aid package $9,945

Marywood University

Scranton PA
(570) 348-6234
U.S. News ranking: Reg. U. (N), No. 38
Website: www.marywood.edu
Admissions email: YourFuture@marywood.edu
Private; founded 1915
Affiliation: Roman Catholic
Freshman admissions: selective; 2013-2014: 2,059 applied, 1,443 accepted. Either SAT or ACT required. SAT 25/75 percentile: 950-1150. High school rank: 20% in top tenth, 47% in top quarter, 84% in top half
Early decision deadline: N/A, notification date: N/A
Early action deadline: N/A, notification date: N/A
Application deadline (fall): rolling
Undergraduate student body: 1,961 full time, 187 part time; 33% male, 67% female; 0% American Indian, 2% Asian, 2% black, 5% Hispanic, 1% multiracial, 0% Pacific Islander, 81% white, 1% international; 70% from in state; 46% live on campus; 0% of students in fraternities, 4% in sororities
Most popular majors: 17% Education, 23% Health Professions and Related Programs, 12% High School/Secondary Diplomas and Certificates, 7% Psychology, 14% Visual and Performing Arts
Expenses: 2014-2015: $31,695; room/board: $13,900
Financial aid: (570) 348-6225; 84% of undergrads determined to have financial need; average aid package $23,894

More at usnews.com/college

Mercyhurst University

Erie PA
(814) 824-2202
U.S. News ranking: Reg. U. (N),
No. 56
Website: www.mercyhurst.edu
Admissions email: ccoons@
mercyhurst.edu
Private; founded 1926
Affiliation: Roman Catholic
Freshman admissions: selective;
2013-2014: 2,938 applied,
2,214 accepted. Either SAT
or ACT required. SAT 25/75
percentile: 940-1160. High school
rank: 21% in top tenth, 29% in
top quarter, 87% in top half
Early decision deadline: N/A,
notification date: N/A
Early action deadline: N/A,
notification date: N/A
Application deadline (fall): rolling
Undergraduate student body: 2,552
full time, 128 part time; 44%
male, 56% female; 0% American
Indian, 1% Asian, 4% black,
2% Hispanic, 0% multiracial,
0% Pacific Islander, 77% white,
8% international; 52% from in
state; 68% live on campus; 0%
of students in fraternities, 0% in
sororities
Most popular majors: 21%
Business, Management,
Marketing, and Related Support
Services, 9% Health Professions
and Related Programs, 8%
Homeland Security, Law
Enforcement, Firefighting and
Related Protective Services, 14%
Multi/Interdisciplinary Studies, 8%
Visual and Performing Arts
Expenses: 2014-2015: $31,485;
room/board: $10,800
Financial aid: (814) 824-2288;
75% of undergrads determined to
have financial need; average aid
package $17,705

Messiah College

Mechanicsburg PA
(717) 691-6000
U.S. News ranking: Reg. Coll. (N),
No. 5
Website: www.messiah.edu
Admissions email:
admiss@messiah.edu
Private; founded 1909
Affiliation: Christian
interdenominational
Freshman admissions: more
selective; 2013-2014: 2,836
applied, 1,869 accepted. Either
SAT or ACT required. SAT 25/75
percentile: 1030-1260. High
school rank: 36% in top tenth,
68% in top quarter, 92% in
top half
Early decision deadline: N/A,
notification date: N/A
Early action deadline: N/A,
notification date: N/A
Application deadline (fall): rolling
Undergraduate student body: 2,701
full time, 71 part time; 39%
male, 61% female; 0% American
Indian, 2% Asian, 2% black,
3% Hispanic, 3% multiracial,
0% Pacific Islander, 86% white,
2% international; 59% from in
state; 87% live on campus; 0%
of students in fraternities, 0% in
sororities
Most popular majors:
5% Business Administration
and Management, General,
4% Elementary Education and
Teaching, 8% Engineering,

General, 6% Psychology, General,
5% Registered Nursing/Registered
Nurse
Expenses: 2014-2015: $31,340;
room/board: $9,350
Financial aid: (717) 691-6007;
73% of undergrads determined to
have financial need; average aid
package $21,592

Millersville University of Pennsylvania

Millersville PA
(717) 872-3371
U.S. News ranking: Reg. U. (N),
No. 87
Website: www.millersville.edu
Admissions email: Admissions@
millersville.edu
Public; founded 1855
Freshman admissions: selective;
2013-2014: 6,034 applied,
3,920 accepted. Either SAT
or ACT required. SAT 25/75
percentile: 920-1110. High school
rank: 12% in top tenth, 34% in
top quarter, 71% in top half
Early decision deadline: N/A,
notification date: N/A
Early action deadline: N/A,
notification date: N/A
Application deadline (fall): rolling
Undergraduate student body: 6,584
full time, 804 part time; 45%
male, 55% female; 0% American
Indian, 2% Asian, 9% black,
7% Hispanic, 2% multiracial,
0% Pacific Islander, 78% white,
1% international; 95% from in
state; 33% live on campus; 3%
of students in fraternities, 4% in
sororities
Most popular majors: 10%
Biological and Biomedical
Sciences, 12% Business,
Management, Marketing, and
Related Support Services, 6%
Communication, Journalism, and
Related Programs, 7% Psychology,
5% Public Administration and
Social Service Professions
Expenses: 2014-2015: $10,268
in state, $23,648 out of state;
room/board: $11,380
Financial aid: (717) 872-3026;
68% of undergrads determined to
have financial need; average aid
package $8,491

Misericordia University

Dallas PA
(570) 674-6264
U.S. News ranking: Reg. U. (N),
No. 41
Website: www.misericordia.edu/
Admissions email: admiss@
misericordia.edu
Private; founded 1924
Affiliation: Roman Catholic
Freshman admissions: selective;
2013-2014: 2,125 applied,
1,379 accepted. Either SAT
or ACT required. SAT 25/75
percentile: 970-1140. High school
rank: 24% in top tenth, 56% in
top quarter, 86% in top half
Early decision deadline: N/A,
notification date: N/A
Early action deadline: N/A,
notification date: N/A
Application deadline (fall): rolling
Undergraduate student body: 1,790
full time, 627 part time; 32%
male, 68% female; 0% American
Indian, 1% Asian, 1% black,
3% Hispanic, 1% multiracial,
0% Pacific Islander, 94% white,

0% international; 77% from in
state; 45% live on campus; 0%
of students in fraternities, 0% in
sororities
Most popular majors: 12%
Business Administration and
Management, General, 8%
General Studies, 10% Health
Services/Allied Health/Health
Sciences, General, 10%
Psychology, General, 12%
Registered Nursing/Registered
Nurse
Expenses: 2014-2015: $29,010;
room/board: $12,050
Financial aid: (570) 674-6280;
82% of undergrads determined to
have financial need; average aid
package $19,729

Moore College of Art & Design

Philadelphia PA
(215) 965-4015
U.S. News ranking: Arts, unranked
Website: www.moore.edu
Admissions email:
admiss@moore.edu
Private
Freshman admissions: N/A;
2013-2014: 672 applied, 377
accepted. Neither SAT nor ACT
required. SAT 25/75 percentile:
N/A. High school rank: N/A
Early decision deadline: N/A,
notification date: N/A
Early action deadline: N/A,
notification date: N/A
Application deadline (fall): 8/1
Undergraduate student body: 411
full time, 26 part time; 0% male,
100% female; 0% American
Indian, 3% Asian, 14% black,
6% Hispanic, 5% multiracial,
0% Pacific Islander, 66% white,
3% international; 60% from in
state; N/A live on campus; N/A
of students in fraternities, N/A in
sororities
Most popular majors: 21% Fashion/
Apparel Design, 20% Fine/Studio
Arts, General, 13% Graphic
Design, 25% Illustration, 7%
Interior Design
Expenses: 2013-2014: $34,048;
room/board: $12,790
Financial aid: (215) 965-4042

Moravian College

Bethlehem PA
(610) 861-1320
U.S. News ranking: Nat. Lib. Arts,
No. 133
Website: www.moravian.edu
Admissions email: admissions@
moravian.edu
Private; founded 1742
Affiliation: Moravian Church
in America
Freshman admissions: selective;
2013-2014: 1,636 applied,
1,308 accepted. Neither SAT
nor ACT required. SAT 25/75
percentile: 940-1170. High school
rank: 19% in top tenth, 48% in
top quarter, 83% in top half
Early decision deadline: N/A,
notification date: N/A
Early action deadline: N/A,
notification date: N/A
Application deadline (fall): 3/1
Undergraduate student body: 1,425
full time, 160 part time; 41%
male, 59% female; 0% American
Indian, 2% Asian, 4% black,
5% Hispanic, 0% multiracial,
0% Pacific Islander, 79% white,
0% international; 68% from in

state; 75% live on campus; 15%
of students in fraternities, 25%
in sororities
Most popular majors: 18%
Business, Management,
Marketing, and Related Support
Services, 13% Health Professions
and Related Programs, 8%
Psychology, 11% Social Sciences,
9% Visual and Performing Arts
Expenses: 2014-2015: $36,800;
room/board: $11,082
Financial aid: (610) 861-1330;
86% of undergrads determined to
have financial need; average aid
package $27,055

Mount Aloysius College

Cresson PA
(814) 886-6383
U.S. News ranking: Reg. Coll. (N),
No. 38
Website: www.mtaloy.edu
Admissions email: admissions@
mtaloy.edu
Private; founded 1853
Affiliation: Roman Catholic (Sisters
of Mercy)
Freshman admissions: least
selective; 2013-2014: 1,563
applied, 1,114 accepted. Either
SAT or ACT required. SAT 25/75
percentile: 830-1030. High
school rank: N/A
Early decision deadline: N/A,
notification date: N/A
Early action deadline: N/A,
notification date: N/A
Application deadline (fall): rolling
Undergraduate student body: 1,248
full time, 533 part time; 28%
male, 72% female; 0% American
Indian, 0% Asian, 2% black,
1% Hispanic, 0% multiracial,
0% Pacific Islander, 79% white,
1% international; 96% from in
state; 31% live on campus; N/A
of students in fraternities, N/A in
sororities
Most popular majors: 12%
Biological and Biomedical
Sciences, 18% Business,
Management, Marketing, and
Related Support Services, 7%
Computer and Information
Sciences and Support Services,
30% Health Professions and
Related Programs, 11% Liberal
Arts and Sciences, General
Studies and Humanities
Expenses: 2014-2015: $20,790;
room/board: $9,186
Financial aid: (814) 886-6357;
96% of undergrads determined to
have financial need; average aid
package $15,830

Muhlenberg College

Allentown PA
(484) 664-3200
U.S. News ranking: Nat. Lib. Arts,
No. 64
Website: www.muhlenberg.edu
Admissions email: admissions@
muhlenberg.edu
Private; founded 1848
Affiliation: Lutheran
Freshman admissions: more
selective; 2013-2014: 5,152
applied, 2,378 accepted. Neither
SAT nor ACT required. SAT
25/75 percentile: 1140-1340.
High school rank: 45% in top
tenth, 73% in top quarter, 92%
in top half
Early decision deadline: 2/15,
notification date: 12/1

Early action deadline: N/A,
notification date: N/A
Application deadline (fall): 2/15
Undergraduate student body: 2,323
full time, 125 part time; 41%
male, 59% female; 0% American
Indian, 3% Asian, 3% black, 5%
Hispanic, 2% multiracial, 0%
Pacific Islander, 77% white, 1%
international; 22% from in state;
92% live on campus; 18% of
students in fraternities, 24% in
sororities
Most popular majors: 12%
Business Administration and
Management, General, 8% Drama
and Dramatics/Theatre Arts,
General, 5% English Language
and Literature, General, 13%
Psychology, General, 8% Speech
Communication and Rhetoric
Expenses: 2014-2015: $44,145;
room/board: $10,335
Financial aid: (484) 664-3174;
51% of undergrads determined to
have financial need; average aid
package $27,092

Neumann University

Aston PA
(610) 558-5616
U.S. News ranking: Reg. U. (N),
second tier
Website: www.neumann.edu
Admissions email: neumann@
neumann.edu
Private; founded 1965
Affiliation: Roman Catholic
Freshman admissions: least
selective; 2013-2014: 2,637
applied, 2,479 accepted. Either
SAT or ACT required. SAT 25/75
percentile: 770-950. High school
rank: N/A
Early decision deadline: N/A,
notification date: N/A
Early action deadline: N/A,
notification date: N/A
Application deadline (fall): rolling
Undergraduate student body: 2,080
full time, 493 part time; 36%
male, 64% female; 1% American
Indian, 0% Asian, 18% black,
3% Hispanic, 2% multiracial,
0% Pacific Islander, 52% white,
2% international; 66% from in
state; 35% live on campus; N/A
of students in fraternities, N/A in
sororities
Most popular majors: 8% Business
Administration and Management,
General, 12% Elementary
Education and Teaching, 18%
Liberal Arts and Sciences/
Liberal Studies, 10% Psychology,
General, 16% Registered Nursing,
Nursing Administration, Nursing
Research and Clinical Nursing,
Other
Expenses: 2013-2014: $24,948;
room/board: $11,512
Financial aid: (610) 558-5521

Peirce College

Philadelphia PA
(888) 467-3472
U.S. News ranking: Reg. Coll. (N),
unranked
Website: www.peirce.edu
Admissions email: info@peirce.edu
Private; founded 1865
Freshman admissions: N/A; 2013-
2014: N/A applied, N/A accepted.
Neither SAT nor ACT required.
ACT 25/75 percentile: N/A. High
school rank: N/A
Early decision deadline: N/A,
notification date: N/A
Early action deadline: N/A,
notification date: N/A

Application deadline (fall): rolling
Undergraduate student body: 358 full time, 1,401 part time; 28% male, 72% female; 0% American Indian, 2% Asian, 68% black, 7% Hispanic, 1% multiracial, 0% Pacific Islander, 21% white, 0% international; 91% from in state; N/A live on campus; N/A of students in fraternities, N/A in sororities
Most popular majors: 63% Business, Management, Marketing, and Related Support Services, 18% Computer and Information Sciences and Support Services, 19% Legal Professions and Studies
Expenses: 2013-2014: $17,040; room/board: N/A
Financial aid: (215) 670-9370

Pennsylvania College of Art and Design[1]

Lancaster PA
(717) 396-7833
U.S. News ranking: Arts, unranked
Website: www.pcad.edu
Admissions email: N/A
Private
Application deadline (fall): N/A
Undergraduate student body: N/A full time, N/A part time
Expenses: 2013-2014: $20,680; room/board: N/A
Financial aid: (800) 689-0379

Pennsylvania College of Technology

Williamsport PA
(570) 327-4761
U.S. News ranking: Reg. Coll. (N), No. 28
Website: www.pct.edu
Admissions email: admissions@pct.edu
Public; founded 1941
Freshman admissions: least selective; 2013-2014: 3,763 applied, 3,386 accepted. Neither SAT nor ACT required. ACT 25/75 percentile: N/A. High school rank: N/A in top tenth, N/A in top quarter, 26% in top half
Early decision deadline: N/A, notification date: N/A
Early action deadline: N/A, notification date: N/A
Application deadline (fall): 7/1
Undergraduate student body: 4,774 full time, 904 part time; 63% male, 37% female; 0% American Indian, 1% Asian, 4% black, 3% Hispanic, 2% multiracial, 0% Pacific Islander, 85% white, 1% international; 87% from in state; 30% live on campus; 1% of students in fraternities, 0% in sororities
Most popular majors:
5% Adult Health Nurse/Nursing, 8% Business Administration, Management and Operations, Other, 4% Computer Systems Networking and Telecommunications, 5% Industrial Production Technologies/Technicians, Other, 6% Physician Assistant
Expenses: 2014-2015: $15,270 in state, $21,660 out of state; room/board: $10,024
Financial aid: (570) 327-4766; 87% of undergrads determined to have financial need

Pennsylvania State University–University Park

University Park PA
(814) 865-5471
U.S. News ranking: Nat. U., No. 48
Website: www.psu.edu
Admissions email: admissions@psu.edu
Public; founded 1855
Freshman admissions: more selective; 2013-2014: 42,570 applied, 23,603 accepted. Either SAT or ACT required. SAT 25/75 percentile: 1070-1280. High school rank: 36% in top tenth, 78% in top quarter, 98% in top half
Early decision deadline: N/A, notification date: N/A
Early action deadline: N/A, notification date: N/A
Application deadline (fall): rolling
Undergraduate student body: 38,826 full time, 1,259 part time; 54% male, 46% female; 0% American Indian, 5% Asian, 4% black, 5% Hispanic, 2% multiracial, 0% Pacific Islander, 72% white, 9% international; 69% from in state; 37% live on campus; 19% of students in fraternities, 16% in sororities
Most popular majors: 6% Biological and Biomedical Sciences, 15% Business, Management, Marketing, and Related Support Services, 9% Communication, Journalism, and Related Programs, 15% Engineering, 8% Social Sciences
Expenses: 2014-2015: $17,502 in state, $30,452 out of state; room/board: $10,520
Financial aid: (814) 865-6301; 50% of undergrads determined to have financial need; average aid package $11,035

Philadelphia University

Philadelphia PA
(215) 951-2800
U.S. News ranking: Reg. U. (N), No. 79
Website: www.philau.edu
Admissions email: admissions@philau.edu
Private; founded 1884
Freshman admissions: selective; 2013-2014: 4,701 applied, 2,982 accepted. Either SAT or ACT required. SAT 25/75 percentile: 960-1160. High school rank: 17% in top tenth, 45% in top quarter, 79% in top half
Early decision deadline: N/A, notification date: N/A
Early action deadline: N/A, notification date: N/A
Application deadline (fall): rolling
Undergraduate student body: 2,531 full time, 280 part time; 35% male, 65% female; 0% American Indian, 4% Asian, 13% black, 7% Hispanic, 2% multiracial, 0% Pacific Islander, 60% white, 3% international; 56% from in state; 50% live on campus; 1% of students in fraternities, 1% in sororities
Most popular majors: 18% Architecture and Related Services, 33% Business, Management, Marketing, and Related Support Services, 12% Health Professions and Related Programs, 6% Psychology, 22% Visual and Performing Arts

Expenses: 2014-2015: $35,080; room/board: $11,610
Financial aid: (215) 951-2940; 79% of undergrads determined to have financial need; average aid package $24,123

Point Park University

Pittsburgh PA
(800) 321-0129
U.S. News ranking: Reg. U. (N), No. 122
Website: www.pointpark.edu
Admissions email: enroll@pointpark.edu
Private; founded 1960
Freshman admissions: selective; 2013-2014: 3,237 applied, 2,393 accepted. Either SAT or ACT required. SAT 25/75 percentile: 870-1100. High school rank: 11% in top tenth, 31% in top quarter, 66% in top half
Early decision deadline: N/A, notification date: N/A
Early action deadline: N/A, notification date: N/A
Application deadline (fall): rolling
Undergraduate student body: 2,551 full time, 675 part time; 43% male, 57% female; 0% American Indian, 1% Asian, 16% black, 3% Hispanic, 4% multiracial, 0% Pacific Islander, 72% white, 3% international; 79% from in state; 29% live on campus; 0% of students in fraternities, 0% in sororities
Most popular majors: 9% Business Administration and Management, General, 8% Business, Management, Marketing, and Related Support Services, Other, 8% Criminal Justice/Safety Studies, 8% Dance, General, 10% Drama and Dramatics/Theatre Arts, General
Expenses: 2014-2015: $27,190; room/board: $10,320
Financial aid: (412) 392-3930; 91% of undergrads determined to have financial need; average aid package $19,935

Robert Morris University

Moon Township PA
(412) 397-5200
U.S. News ranking: Reg. U. (N), No. 96
Website: www.rmu.edu
Admissions email: admissions@rmu.edu
Private; founded 1921
Freshman admissions: selective; 2013-2014: 5,689 applied, 4,570 accepted. Either SAT or ACT required. SAT 25/75 percentile: 940-1140. High school rank: 14% in top tenth, 42% in top quarter, 77% in top half
Early decision deadline: N/A, notification date: N/A
Early action deadline: N/A, notification date: N/A
Application deadline (fall): rolling
Undergraduate student body: 3,935 full time, 561 part time; 54% male, 46% female; 0% American Indian, 1% Asian, 7% black, 2% Hispanic, 2% multiracial, 0% Pacific Islander, 77% white, 8% international; 88% from in state; 44% live on campus; 10% of students in fraternities, 11% in sororities

Most popular majors: 11% Accounting, 11% Business Administration and Management, General, 7% Elementary Education and Teaching, 9% Registered Nursing/Registered Nurse, 8% Speech Communication and Rhetoric
Expenses: 2014-2015: $26,054; room/board: $11,810
Financial aid: (412) 262-8545; 76% of undergrads determined to have financial need; average aid package $18,933

Rosemont College

Rosemont PA
(800) 331-0708
U.S. News ranking: Reg. U. (N), No. 96
Website: www.rosemont.edu
Admissions email: admissions@rosemont.edu
Private; founded 1921
Affiliation: Roman Catholic
Freshman admissions: selective; 2013-2014: 1,014 applied, 592 accepted. Either SAT or ACT required. SAT 25/75 percentile: 800-1040. High school rank: 27% in top tenth, 49% in top quarter, 76% in top half
Early decision deadline: N/A, notification date: N/A
Early action deadline: N/A, notification date: N/A
Application deadline (fall): rolling
Undergraduate student body: 415 full time, 116 part time; 34% male, 66% female; 0% American Indian, 5% Asian, 36% black, 8% Hispanic, 2% multiracial, 0% Pacific Islander, 37% white, 2% international; 73% from in state; 72% live on campus; 0% of students in fraternities, 0% in sororities
Most popular majors: 25% Biology/Biological Sciences, General, 24% Business/Commerce, General, 12% Education, General, 6% Psychology, General, 10% Speech Communication and Rhetoric
Expenses: 2014-2015: $31,550; room/board: $12,880
Financial aid: (610) 527-0200; 90% of undergrads determined to have financial need; average aid package $29,879

Seton Hill University

Greensburg PA
(724) 838-4255
U.S. News ranking: Reg. Coll. (N), No. 11
Website: www.setonhill.edu
Admissions email: admit@setonhill.edu
Private; founded 1883
Affiliation: Roman Catholic
Freshman admissions: selective; 2013-2014: 2,414 applied, 1,574 accepted. Neither SAT nor ACT required. SAT 25/75 percentile: 900-1150. High school rank: 20% in top tenth, 47% in top quarter, 77% in top half
Early decision deadline: N/A, notification date: N/A
Early action deadline: N/A, notification date: N/A
Application deadline (fall): 8/15
Undergraduate student body: 1,472 full time, 177 part time; 36% male, 64% female; 0% American Indian, 0% Asian, 9% black, 3% Hispanic, 3% multiracial, 0% Pacific Islander, 82% white,

3% international; 77% from in state; 43% live on campus; 0% of students in fraternities, 0% in sororities
Most popular majors: 7% Biological and Biomedical Sciences, 31% Business, Management, Marketing, and Related Support Services, 7% Psychology, 6% Public Administration and Social Service Professions, 8% Visual and Performing Arts
Expenses: 2014-2015: $31,280; room/board: $10,476
Financial aid: (724) 838-4293; 87% of undergrads determined to have financial need; average aid package $24,161

Shippensburg University of Pennsylvania

Shippensburg PA
(717) 477-1231
U.S. News ranking: Reg. U. (N), No. 87
Website: www.ship.edu
Admissions email: admiss@ship.edu
Public; founded 1871
Freshman admissions: less selective; 2013-2014: 5,950 applied, 4,962 accepted. Either SAT or ACT required. SAT 25/75 percentile: 890-1080. High school rank: 7% in top tenth, 26% in top quarter, 58% in top half
Early decision deadline: N/A, notification date: N/A
Early action deadline: N/A, notification date: N/A
Application deadline (fall): rolling
Undergraduate student body: 6,219 full time, 331 part time; 50% male, 50% female; 0% American Indian, 1% Asian, 9% black, 4% Hispanic, 3% multiracial, 0% Pacific Islander, 80% white, 1% international; 93% from in state; 36% live on campus; 6% of students in fraternities, 7% in sororities
Most popular majors: 6% Business Administration and Management, General, 9% Criminal Justice/Safety Studies, 6% Journalism, 6% Marketing/Marketing Management, General, 10% Psychology, General
Expenses: 2014-2015: $9,774 in state, $18,520 out of state; room/board: $11,160
Financial aid: (717) 477-1131; 69% of undergrads determined to have financial need; average aid package $8,479

Slippery Rock University of Pennsylvania

Slippery Rock PA
(800) 929-4778
U.S. News ranking: Reg. U. (N), No. 83
Website: www.sru.edu
Admissions email: asktherock@sru.edu
Public; founded 1889
Freshman admissions: selective; 2013-2014: 5,475 applied, 3,667 accepted. Either SAT or ACT required. SAT 25/75 percentile: 910-1090. High school rank: 12% in top tenth, 36% in top quarter, 77% in top half
Early decision deadline: N/A, notification date: N/A

More at usnews.com/college

Early action deadline: N/A, notification date: N/A
Application deadline (fall): rolling
Undergraduate student body: 7,057 full time, 538 part time; 44% male, 56% female; 0% American Indian, 1% Asian, 5% black, 2% Hispanic, 2% multiracial, 0% Pacific Islander, 86% white, 1% international; 89% from in state; 36% live on campus; 6% of students in fraternities, 7% in sororities
Most popular majors: 12% Business, Management, Marketing, and Related Support Services, 15% Education, 19% Health Professions and Related Programs, 10% Parks, Recreation, Leisure, and Fitness Studies, 7% Social Sciences
Expenses: 2014-2015: $9,309 in state, $12,719 out of state; room/board: $9,794
Financial aid: (724) 738-2044; 70% of undergrads determined to have financial need; average aid package $8,915

St. Francis University
Loretto PA
(814) 472-3100
U.S. News ranking: Reg. U. (N), No. 56
Website: www.francis.edu/undergraduate_admissions
Admissions email: admissions@francis.edu
Private; founded 1847
Affiliation: Roman Catholic
Freshman admissions: selective; 2013-2014: 1,679 applied, 1,277 accepted. Either SAT or ACT required. SAT 25/75 percentile: 930-1160. High school rank: 20% in top tenth, 42% in top quarter, 60% in top half
Early decision deadline: N/A, notification date: N/A
Early action deadline: N/A, notification date: N/A
Application deadline (fall): 7/30
Undergraduate student body: 1,547 full time, 148 part time; 38% male, 62% female; 0% American Indian, 1% Asian, 6% black, 2% Hispanic, 1% multiracial, 0% Pacific Islander, 80% white, 4% international; 78% from in state; 88% live on campus; 23% of students in fraternities, 24% in sororities
Most popular majors: 23% Business Administration and Management, General, 34% Health Professions and Related Programs
Expenses: 2014-2015: $31,078; room/board: $10,760
Financial aid: (814) 472-3010; 80% of undergrads determined to have financial need; average aid package $19,008

St. Joseph's University
Philadelphia PA
(610) 660-1300
U.S. News ranking: Reg. U. (N), No. 11
Website: www.sju.edu
Admissions email: admit@sju.edu
Private; founded 1851
Affiliation: Roman Catholic (Jesuit)
Freshman admissions: selective; 2013-2014: 7,831 applied, 6,165 accepted. Neither SAT nor ACT required. SAT 25/75 percentile: 1020-1200. High school rank: 22% in top tenth, 52% in top quarter, 87% in top half

Early decision deadline: N/A, notification date: N/A
Early action deadline: 11/15, notification date: 12/25
Application deadline (fall): 2/1
Undergraduate student body: 4,489 full time, 885 part time; 46% male, 54% female; 0% American Indian, 2% Asian, 7% black, 5% Hispanic, 2% multiracial, 0% Pacific Islander, 80% white, 2% international; 46% from in state; 60% live on campus; 6% of students in fraternities, 15% in sororities
Most popular majors: 6% Accounting, 9% Finance, General, 12% Marketing/Marketing Management, General, 6% Special Education and Teaching, Other, 9% Special Products Marketing Operations
Expenses: 2014-2015: $40,580; room/board: $14,513
Financial aid: (610) 660-1556; 58% of undergrads determined to have financial need; average aid package $24,321

St. Vincent College
Latrobe PA
(800) 782-5549
U.S. News ranking: Nat. Lib. Arts, No. 148
Website: www.stvincent.edu
Admissions email: admission@stvincent.edu
Private; founded 1846
Affiliation: Roman Catholic
Freshman admissions: selective; 2013-2014: 2,035 applied, 1,399 accepted. Either SAT or ACT required. SAT 25/75 percentile: 910-1150. High school rank: 20% in top tenth, 53% in top quarter, 83% in top half
Early decision deadline: N/A, notification date: N/A
Early action deadline: N/A, notification date: N/A
Application deadline (fall): 4/1
Undergraduate student body: 1,532 full time, 64 part time; 52% male, 48% female; 0% American Indian, 2% Asian, 5% black, 4% Hispanic, 1% multiracial, 0% Pacific Islander, 85% white, 1% international; 82% from in state; 72% live on campus; 0% of students in fraternities, 0% in sororities
Most popular majors: 10% Biological and Biomedical Sciences, 26% Business, Management, Marketing, and Related Support Services, 5% Communication, Journalism, and Related Programs, 5% English Language and Literature/Letters, 8% Psychology
Expenses: 2014-2015: $31,370; room/board: $9,862
Financial aid: (724) 537-4540; 83% of undergrads determined to have financial need; average aid package $27,374

Susquehanna University
Selinsgrove PA
(800) 326-9672
U.S. News ranking: Nat. Lib. Arts, No. 116
Website: www.susqu.edu
Admissions email: suadmiss@susqu.edu
Private; founded 1858
Affiliation: Lutheran

Freshman admissions: selective; 2013-2014: 3,217 applied, 2,327 accepted. Neither SAT nor ACT required. SAT 25/75 percentile: 1020-1230. High school rank: 26% in top tenth, 52% in top quarter, 80% in top half
Early decision deadline: 11/1, notification date: 11/15
Early action deadline: 11/1, notification date: 11/15
Application deadline (fall): 2/1
Undergraduate student body: 2,126 full time, 53 part time; 44% male, 56% female; 0% American Indian, 1% Asian, 5% black, 5% Hispanic, 2% multiracial, 0% Pacific Islander, 84% white, 1% international; 49% from in state; 86% live on campus; 17% of students in fraternities, 16% in sororities
Most popular majors: 6% Biology/Biological Sciences, General, 21% Business/Commerce, General, 17% Communication, General, 8% Creative Writing, 9% Psychology, General
Expenses: 2014-2015: $40,350; room/board: $10,800
Financial aid: (570) 372-4450; 73% of undergrads determined to have financial need; average aid package $29,510

Swarthmore College
Swarthmore PA
(610) 328-8300
U.S. News ranking: Nat. Lib. Arts, No. 3
Website: www.swarthmore.edu
Admissions email: admissions@swarthmore.edu
Private; founded 1864
Freshman admissions: most selective; 2013-2014: 6,615 applied, 947 accepted. Either SAT or ACT required. SAT 25/75 percentile: 1350-1530. High school rank: 89% in top tenth, 99% in top quarter, 100% in top half
Early decision deadline: 11/15, notification date: 12/15
Early action deadline: N/A, notification date: N/A
Application deadline (fall): 1/1
Undergraduate student body: 1,526 full time, 8 part time; 49% male, 51% female; 0% American Indian, 15% Asian, 6% black, 14% Hispanic, 8% multiracial, 0% Pacific Islander, 43% white, 9% international; 13% from in state; 94% live on campus; 13% of students in fraternities, 6% in sororities
Most popular majors: 11% Biological and Biomedical Sciences, 7% Foreign Languages, Literatures, and Linguistics, 7% Psychology, 24% Social Sciences, 9% Visual and Performing Arts
Expenses: 2014-2015: $46,060; room/board: $13,550
Financial aid: (610) 328-8358; 50% of undergrads determined to have financial need; average aid package $40,340

Temple University
Philadelphia PA
(215) 204-7200
U.S. News ranking: Nat. U., No. 121
Website: www.temple.edu
Admissions email: tuadm@temple.edu
Public; founded 1888

Freshman admissions: selective; 2013-2014: 18,813 applied, 12,016 accepted. Neither SAT nor ACT required. SAT 25/75 percentile: 1010-1230. High school rank: 20% in top tenth, 52% in top quarter, 88% in top half
Early decision deadline: N/A, notification date: N/A
Early action deadline: N/A, notification date: N/A
Application deadline (fall): 3/1
Undergraduate student body: 24,743 full time, 3,325 part time; 49% male, 51% female; 0% American Indian, 10% Asian, 14% black, 5% Hispanic, 2% multiracial, 0% Pacific Islander, 60% white, 3% international; 79% from in state; 18% live on campus; 4% of students in fraternities, 4% in sororities
Most popular majors: 20% Business, Management, Marketing, and Related Support Services, 11% Communication, Journalism, and Related Programs, 6% Health Professions and Related Programs, 7% Psychology, 11% Visual and Performing Arts
Expenses: 2014-2015: $14,770 in state, $25,450 out of state; room/board: $11,860
Financial aid: (215) 204-8760; 71% of undergrads determined to have financial need; average aid package $15,918

Thiel College
Greenville PA
(800) 248-4435
U.S. News ranking: Reg. Coll. (N), No. 33
Website: www.thiel.edu
Admissions email: admission@thiel.edu
Private; founded 1866
Affiliation: Lutheran
Freshman admissions: less selective; 2013-2014: 2,519 applied, 1,650 accepted. Either SAT or ACT required. SAT 25/75 percentile: 870-1060. High school rank: 12% in top tenth, 34% in top quarter, 69% in top half
Early decision deadline: N/A, notification date: N/A
Early action deadline: N/A, notification date: N/A
Application deadline (fall): rolling
Undergraduate student body: 1,061 full time, 39 part time; 50% male, 50% female; 0% American Indian, 1% Asian, 8% black, 2% Hispanic, 2% multiracial, 0% Pacific Islander, 76% white, 0% international; N/A from in state; 90% live on campus; 22% of students in fraternities, 27% in sororities
Most popular majors: 14% Biological and Biomedical Sciences, 20% Business, Management, Marketing, and Related Support Services, 12% Education, 19% Homeland Security, Law Enforcement, Firefighting and Related Protective Services, 14% Psychology
Expenses: 2014-2015: $27,828; room/board: $10,900
Financial aid: (724) 589-2178; 88% of undergrads determined to have financial need; average aid package $22,273

University of Pennsylvania
Philadelphia PA
(215) 898-7507
U.S. News ranking: Nat. U., No. 8
Website: www.upenn.edu
Admissions email: info@admissions.ugao.upenn.edu
Private; founded 1740
Freshman admissions: most selective; 2013-2014: 31,282 applied, 3,830 accepted. Either SAT or ACT required. SAT 25/75 percentile: 1360-1540. High school rank: 94% in top tenth, 99% in top quarter, 100% in top half
Early decision deadline: 11/1, notification date: 12/15
Early action deadline: N/A, notification date: N/A
Application deadline (fall): 1/1
Undergraduate student body: 9,407 full time, 305 part time; 50% male, 50% female; 0% American Indian, 19% Asian, 7% black, 10% Hispanic, 4% multiracial, 0% Pacific Islander, 45% white, 11% international; 18% from in state; 54% live on campus; 31% of students in fraternities, 28% in sororities
Most popular majors: 9% Biological and Biomedical Sciences, 22% Business, Management, Marketing, and Related Support Services, 10% Engineering, 5% History, 16% Social Sciences
Expenses: 2014-2015: $47,668; room/board: $13,464
Financial aid: (215) 898-1988; 47% of undergrads determined to have financial need; average aid package $41,961

University of Pittsburgh
Pittsburgh PA
(412) 624-7488
U.S. News ranking: Nat. U., No. 62
Website: www.oafa.pitt.edu/
Admissions email: oafa@pitt.edu
Public; founded 1787
Freshman admissions: more selective; 2013-2014: 27,634 applied, 15,047 accepted. Either SAT or ACT required. SAT 25/75 percentile: 1180-1360. High school rank: 53% in top tenth, 86% in top quarter, 99% in top half
Early decision deadline: N/A, notification date: N/A
Early action deadline: N/A, notification date: N/A
Application deadline (fall): rolling
Undergraduate student body: 17,483 full time, 1,132 part time; 50% male, 50% female; 0% American Indian, 8% Asian, 5% black, 3% Hispanic, 3% multiracial, 0% Pacific Islander, 77% white, 3% international; 74% from in state; 44% live on campus; 10% of students in fraternities, 9% in sororities
Most popular majors: 15% Business, Management, Marketing, and Related Support Services, 9% Engineering, 9% English Language and Literature/Letters, 12% Health Professions and Related Programs, 13% Social Sciences
Expenses: 2014-2015: $16,872 in state, $27,268 out of state; room/board: N/A

Financial aid: (412) 624-7488; 56% of undergrads determined to have financial need; average aid package $12,404

University of Scranton

Scranton PA
(570) 941-7540
U.S. News ranking: Reg. U. (N), No. 7
Website: www.scranton.edu
Admissions email: admissions@scranton.edu
Private; founded 1888
Affiliation: Roman Catholic (Jesuit)
Freshman admissions: selective; 2013-2014: 9,087 applied, 6,824 accepted. Either SAT or ACT required. SAT 25/75 percentile: 1030-1210. High school rank: 25% in top tenth, 59% in top quarter, 85% in top half
Early decision deadline: N/A, notification date: N/A
Early action deadline: 11/15, notification date: 12/15
Application deadline (fall): 3/1
Undergraduate student body: 3,756 full time, 186 part time; 45% male, 55% female; 0% American Indian, 3% Asian, 2% black, 7% Hispanic, 2% multiracial, 0% Pacific Islander, 81% white, 0% international; 41% from in state; 63% live on campus; N/A of students in fraternities, N/A in sororities
Most popular majors: 6% Accounting, 8% Biology/Biological Sciences, General, 6% Kinesiology and Exercise Science, 5% Psychology, General, 8% Registered Nursing/Registered Nurse
Expenses: 2014-2015: $39,906; room/board: $13,566
Financial aid: (570) 941-7700; 74% of undergrads determined to have financial need; average aid package $24,193

University of the Arts

Philadelphia PA
(215) 717-6049
U.S. News ranking: Arts, unranked
Website: www.uarts.edu
Admissions email: admissions@uarts.edu
Private; founded 1876
Freshman admissions: N/A; 2013-2014: 1,479 applied, 1,115 accepted. Either SAT or ACT required. SAT 25/75 percentile: N/A. High school rank: N/A
Early decision deadline: N/A, notification date: N/A
Early action deadline: N/A, notification date: N/A
Application deadline (fall): rolling
Undergraduate student body: 1,860 full time, 30 part time; 42% male, 58% female; 0% American Indian, 3% Asian, 13% black, 9% Hispanic, 4% multiracial, 1% Pacific Islander, 62% white, 5% international; 38% from in state; 33% live on campus; 0% of students in fraternities, 0% in sororities
Most popular majors: 15% Dance, General, 9% Graphic Design, 11% Illustration, 6% Music Performance, General, 8% Photography
Expenses: 2014-2015: $38,410; room/board: $14,004
Financial aid: (215) 717-6170

Ursinus College

Collegeville PA
(610) 409-3200
U.S. News ranking: Nat. Lib. Arts, unranked
Website: www.ursinus.edu
Admissions email: Admissions@Ursinus.edu
Private; founded 1869
Freshman admissions: N/A; 2013-2014: 3,947 applied, 2,618 accepted. Neither SAT nor ACT required. SAT 25/75 percentile: 1060-1280. High school rank: 33% in top tenth, 67% in top quarter, 92% in top half
Early decision deadline: 1/15, notification date: 2/1
Early action deadline: 12/1, notification date: 1/15
Application deadline (fall): rolling
Undergraduate student body: 1,582 full time, 14 part time; 49% male, 51% female; 0% American Indian, 5% Asian, 6% black, 5% Hispanic, 3% multiracial, 0% Pacific Islander, 77% white, 1% international; 50% from in state; 95% live on campus; 10% of students in fraternities, 15% in sororities
Most popular majors: 24% Biological and Biomedical Sciences, 7% English Language and Literature/Letters, 7% Parks, Recreation, Leisure, and Fitness Studies, 11% Psychology, 19% Social Sciences
Expenses: 2014-2015: $46,075; room/board: $11,500
Financial aid: (610) 409-3600; 74% of undergrads determined to have financial need; average aid package $33,601

Valley Forge Christian College[1]

Phoenixville PA
(800) 432-8322
U.S. News ranking: Reg. Coll. (N), No. 44
Website: www.vfcc.edu
Admissions email: admissions@vfcc.edu
Private
Application deadline (fall): N/A
Undergraduate student body: N/A full time, N/A part time
Expenses: 2013-2014: $19,394; room/board: $7,794
Financial aid: (610) 917-1498

Villanova University

Villanova PA
(610) 519-4000
U.S. News ranking: Reg. U. (N), No. 1
Website: www.villanova.edu
Admissions email: gotovu@villanova.edu
Private; founded 1842
Affiliation: Roman Catholic
Freshman admissions: more selective; 2013-2014: 14,966 applied, 7,319 accepted. Either SAT or ACT required. SAT 25/75 percentile: 1210-1400. High school rank: 60% in top tenth, 88% in top quarter, 99% in top half
Early decision deadline: N/A, notification date: N/A
Early action deadline: 11/1, notification date: 12/20
Application deadline (fall): 1/15
Undergraduate student body: 6,547 full time, 495 part time; 48% male, 52% female; 0% American Indian, 7% Asian, 4% black, 7% Hispanic, 2% multiracial,

0% Pacific Islander, 76% white, 2% international; 21% from in state; 2% live on campus; 18% of students in fraternities, 37% in sororities
Most popular majors: 29% Business, Management, Marketing, and Related Support Services, 8% Communication, Journalism, and Related Programs, 11% Engineering, 11% Health Professions and Related Programs, 10% Social Sciences
Expenses: 2014-2015: $45,966; room/board: $12,252
Financial aid: (610) 519-4010; 48% of undergrads determined to have financial need; average aid package $32,184

Washington and Jefferson College

Washington PA
(724) 223-6025
U.S. News ranking: Nat. Lib. Arts, No. 96
Website: www.washjeff.edu
Admissions email: admission@washjeff.edu
Private; founded 1781
Freshman admissions: more selective; 2013-2014: 7,176 applied, 2,851 accepted. Neither SAT nor ACT required. SAT 25/75 percentile: 1050-1230. High school rank: 37% in top tenth, 70% in top quarter, 94% in top half
Early decision deadline: 12/1, notification date: 12/15
Early action deadline: 1/15, notification date: 2/15
Application deadline (fall): 3/1
Undergraduate student body: 1,318 full time, 10 part time; 49% male, 51% female; 0% American Indian, 3% Asian, 3% black, 3% Hispanic, 3% multiracial, 0% Pacific Islander, 84% white, 1% international; 73% from in state; 94% live on campus; 43% of students in fraternities, 46% in sororities
Most popular majors: 8% Accounting, 11% Business/Commerce, General, 6% Economics, General, 7% History, General, 17% Psychology, General
Expenses: 2014-2015: $41,282; room/board: $10,884
Financial aid: (724) 223-6019; 78% of undergrads determined to have financial need; average aid package $29,320

Waynesburg University

Waynesburg PA
(800) 225-7393
U.S. News ranking: Reg. U. (N), No. 106
Website: www.waynesburg.edu/
Admissions email: admissions@waynesburg.edu
Private; founded 1849
Affiliation: Presbyterian
Freshman admissions: selective; 2013-2014: 1,681 applied, 1,396 accepted. SAT required. SAT 25/75 percentile: 890-1110. High school rank: 18% in top tenth, 47% in top quarter, 85% in top half
Early decision deadline: N/A, notification date: N/A
Early action deadline: N/A, notification date: N/A
Application deadline (fall): rolling

Undergraduate student body: 1,481 full time, 117 part time; 39% male, 61% female; 0% American Indian, 1% Asian, 3% black, 1% Hispanic, 1% multiracial, 0% Pacific Islander, 88% white, 0% international; 80% from in state; 67% live on campus; N/A of students in fraternities, N/A in sororities
Most popular majors: 7% Biology/Biological Sciences, General, 11% Business/Commerce, General, 7% Elementary Education and Teaching, 33% Registered Nursing/Registered Nurse, 7% Speech Communication and Rhetoric
Expenses: 2014-2015: $21,290; room/board: $8,860
Financial aid: (724) 852-3208; 67% of undergrads determined to have financial need; average aid package $15,426

West Chester University of Pennsylvania

West Chester PA
(610) 436-3414
U.S. News ranking: Reg. U. (N), No. 65
Website: www.wcupa.edu/
Admissions email: ugadmiss@wcupa.edu
Public; founded 1871
Freshman admissions: selective; 2013-2014: 13,438 applied, 6,922 accepted. Either SAT or ACT required. SAT 25/75 percentile: 1020-1190. High school rank: 14% in top tenth, 45% in top quarter, 85% in top half
Early decision deadline: N/A, notification date: N/A
Early action deadline: N/A, notification date: N/A
Application deadline (fall): rolling
Undergraduate student body: 12,484 full time, 1,227 part time; 40% male, 60% female; 0% American Indian, 2% Asian, 9% black, 5% Hispanic, 2% multiracial, 0% Pacific Islander, 81% white, 0% international; 87% from in state; 36% live on campus; 10% of students in fraternities, 13% in sororities
Most popular majors: 16% Business, Management, Marketing, and Related Support Services, 10% Education, 9% English Language and Literature/Letters, 15% Health Professions and Related Programs, 9% Liberal Arts and Sciences, General Studies and Humanities
Expenses: 2014-2015: $9,144 in state, $19,374 out of state; room/board: $8,042
Financial aid: (610) 436-2627; 61% of undergrads determined to have financial need; average aid package $7,619

Westminster College

New Wilmington PA
(800) 942-8033
U.S. News ranking: Nat. Lib. Arts, No. 116
Website: www.westminster.edu
Admissions email: admis@westminster.edu
Private; founded 1852
Affiliation: Presbyterian Church (USA)
Freshman admissions: selective; 2013-2014: 3,378 applied, 2,478 accepted. Either SAT

or ACT required. SAT 25/75 percentile: 920-1150. High school rank: 17% in top tenth, 50% in top quarter, 85% in top half
Early decision deadline: N/A, notification date: N/A
Early action deadline: 11/15, notification date: 12/1
Application deadline (fall): 1/5
Undergraduate student body: 1,254 full time, 52 part time; 41% male, 59% female; 0% American Indian, 0% Asian, 1% black, 1% Hispanic, 2% multiracial, 0% Pacific Islander, 83% white, 0% international; 78% from in state; 73% live on campus; 31% of students in fraternities, 42% in sororities
Most popular majors: 12% Biological and Biomedical Sciences, 19% Business, Management, Marketing, and Related Support Services, 9% Communication, Journalism, and Related Programs, 17% Education, 11% Social Sciences
Expenses: 2014-2015: $33,410; room/board: $10,160
Financial aid: (724) 946-7102; 81% of undergrads determined to have financial need; average aid package $25,879

Widener University

Chester PA
(610) 499-4126
U.S. News ranking: Nat. U., No. 189
Website: www.widener.edu
Admissions email: admissions.office@widener.edu
Private; founded 1821
Freshman admissions: selective; 2013-2014: 5,461 applied, 3,673 accepted. Either SAT or ACT required. SAT 25/75 percentile: 920-1130. High school rank: 15% in top tenth, 38% in top quarter, 71% in top half
Early decision deadline: N/A, notification date: N/A
Early action deadline: N/A, notification date: N/A
Application deadline (fall): rolling
Undergraduate student body: 2,903 full time, 631 part time; 44% male, 56% female; 0% American Indian, 3% Asian, 15% black, 5% Hispanic, 3% multiracial, 0% Pacific Islander, 70% white, 3% international; 59% from in state; 48% live on campus; 10% of students in fraternities, 9% in sororities
Most popular majors: 24% Business, Management, Marketing, and Related Support Services, 12% Engineering, 20% Health Professions and Related Programs, 10% Psychology, 5% Social Sciences
Expenses: 2014-2015: $39,830; room/board: $12,588
Financial aid: (610) 499-4174; 80% of undergrads determined to have financial need; average aid package $27,822

Wilkes University

Wilkes-Barre PA
(570) 408-4400
U.S. News ranking: Reg. U. (N), No. 83
Website: www.wilkes.edu
Admissions email: admissions@wilkes.edu
Private; founded 1933
Freshman admissions: selective; 2013-2014: 3,120 applied, 2,500 accepted. Either SAT

or ACT required. SAT 25/75 percentile: 930-1150. High school rank: 21% in top tenth, 53% in top quarter, 80% in top half
Early decision deadline: N/A, notification date: N/A
Early action deadline: N/A, notification date: N/A
Application deadline (fall): rolling
Undergraduate student body: 2,181 full time, 207 part time; 53% male, 47% female; 0% American Indian, 3% Asian, 3% black, 5% Hispanic, 3% multiracial, 0% Pacific Islander, 77% white, 7% international; 83% from in state; 44% live on campus; 0% of students in fraternities, 0% in sororities
Most popular majors: 15% Business, Management, Marketing, and Related Support Services, 7% Communication, Journalism, and Related Programs, 10% Engineering, 15% Health Professions and Related Programs, 6% Psychology
Expenses: 2014-2015: $31,262; room/board: $12,808
Financial aid: (570) 408-4346; 81% of undergrads determined to have financial need; average aid package $22,941

Wilson College

Chambersburg PA
(800) 421-8402
U.S. News ranking: Reg. Coll. (N), No. 17
Website: www.wilson.edu
Admissions email: admissions@wilson.edu
Private; founded 1869
Affiliation: Presbyterian Church (USA)
Freshman admissions: selective; 2013-2014: 450 applied, 237 accepted. Neither SAT nor ACT required. SAT 25/75 percentile: 860-1120. High school rank: 19% in top tenth, 53% in top quarter, 77% in top half
Early decision deadline: N/A, notification date: N/A
Early action deadline: N/A, notification date: N/A
Application deadline (fall): rolling
Undergraduate student body: 330 full time, 241 part time; 12% male, 88% female; 0% American Indian, 0% Asian, 3% black, 3% Hispanic, 2% multiracial, 0% Pacific Islander, 68% white, 5% international; 77% from in state; 51% live on campus; 0% of students in fraternities, 0% in sororities
Most popular majors: 9% Biology/ Biological Sciences, General, 8% Business Administration and Management, General, 12% Elementary Education and Teaching, 8% Equestrian/Equine Studies, 30% Veterinary/Animal Health Technology/Technician and Veterinary Assistant
Expenses: 2014-2015: $24,381; room/board: $10,700
Financial aid: (717) 262-2016; 94% of undergrads determined to have financial need; average aid package $23,486

York College of Pennsylvania

York PA
(717) 849-1600
U.S. News ranking: Reg. U. (N), No. 87
Website: www.ycp.edu
Admissions email: admissions@ycp.edu
Private; founded 1787
Freshman admissions: selective; 2013-2014: 9,934 applied, 7,302 accepted. Either SAT or ACT required. SAT 25/75 percentile: 950-1138. High school rank: 12% in top tenth, 40% in top quarter, 77% in top half
Early decision deadline: N/A, notification date: N/A
Early action deadline: N/A, notification date: N/A
Application deadline (fall): rolling
Undergraduate student body: 4,453 full time, 555 part time; 45% male, 55% female; 0% American Indian, 1% Asian, 5% black, 5% Hispanic, 3% multiracial, 0% Pacific Islander, 83% white, 0% international; 58% from in state; 52% live on campus; 11% of students in fraternities, 14% in sororities
Most popular majors: 18% Business, Management, Marketing, and Related Support Services, 13% Education, 14% Health Professions and Related Programs, 9% Homeland Security, Law Enforcement, Firefighting and Related Protective Services, 10% Parks, Recreation, Leisure, and Fitness Studies
Expenses: 2014-2015: $17,630; room/board: $9,870
Financial aid: (717) 849-1682; 69% of undergrads determined to have financial need; average aid package $13,115

RHODE ISLAND

Brown University

Providence RI
(401) 863-2378
U.S. News ranking: Nat. U., No. 16
Website: www.brown.edu
Admissions email: admission@brown.edu
Private; founded 1764
Freshman admissions: most selective; 2013-2014: 28,919 applied, 2,654 accepted. Either SAT or ACT required. SAT 25/75 percentile: 1330-1540. High school rank: 94% in top tenth, 98% in top quarter, 100% in top half
Early decision deadline: 11/1, notification date: 12/15
Early action deadline: N/A, notification date: N/A
Application deadline (fall): 1/1
Undergraduate student body: 6,168 full time, 287 part time; 48% male, 52% female; 0% American Indian, 12% Asian, 6% black, 11% Hispanic, 5% multiracial, 0% Pacific Islander, 43% white, 12% international; 5% from in state; 78% live on campus; 18% of students in fraternities, 8% in sororities
Most popular majors: 10% Biology/ Biological Sciences, General, 11% Economics, General, 4% Engineering, General, 4% International Relations and Affairs, 4% Political Science and Government, General

Expenses: 2014-2015: $47,434; room/board: $11,994
Financial aid: (401) 863-2721; 46% of undergrads determined to have financial need; average aid package $41,577

Bryant University

Smithfield RI
(800) 622-7001
U.S. News ranking: Reg. U. (N), No. 11
Website: www.bryant.edu
Admissions email: admission@bryant.edu
Private; founded 1863
Freshman admissions: selective; 2013-2014: 6,013 applied, 4,603 accepted. Neither SAT nor ACT required. SAT 25/75 percentile: 1050-1220. High school rank: 18% in top tenth, 50% in top quarter, 88% in top half
Early decision deadline: 11/15, notification date: 12/16
Early action deadline: 12/2, notification date: 1/15
Application deadline (fall): 2/3
Undergraduate student body: 3,200 full time, 87 part time; 58% male, 42% female; 0% American Indian, 4% Asian, 4% black, 6% Hispanic, 0% multiracial, 0% Pacific Islander, 83% white, 7% international; 13% from in state; 81% live on campus; 6% of students in fraternities, 8% in sororities
Most popular majors: 79% Business, Management, Marketing, and Related Support Services, 5% Communication, Journalism, and Related Programs, 3% Computer and Information Sciences and Support Services, 5% Mathematics and Statistics, 3% Social Sciences
Expenses: 2014-2015: $38,574; room/board: $13,827
Financial aid: (401) 232-6020; 66% of undergrads determined to have financial need; average aid package $23,104

Johnson & Wales University

Providence RI
(800) 342-5598
U.S. News ranking: Reg. U. (N), No. 65
Website: www.jwu.edu
Admissions email: admissions.pvd@jwu.edu
Private; founded 1914
Freshman admissions: less selective; 2013-2014: 12,364 applied, 9,399 accepted. Neither SAT nor ACT required. ACT 25/75 percentile: N/A. High school rank: N/A
Early decision deadline: N/A, notification date: N/A
Early action deadline: N/A, notification date: N/A
Application deadline (fall): rolling
Undergraduate student body: 8,754 full time, 647 part time; 42% male, 58% female; 0% American Indian, 1% Asian, 9% black, 10% Hispanic, 4% multiracial, 0% Pacific Islander, 55% white, 8% international; 18% from in state; 40% live on campus; N/A of students in fraternities, N/A in sororities
Most popular majors: 9% Business Administration and Management, General, 6% Culinary Arts/ Chef Training, 21% Foodservice

Systems Administration/ Management, 9% Hotel/Motel Administration/Management, 11% Parks, Recreation and Leisure Facilities Management, General
Expenses: 2014-2015: $28,539; room/board: $11,604
Financial aid: (401) 598-1468; 72% of undergrads determined to have financial need; average aid package $18,932

New England Institute of Technology

East Greenwich RI
(401) 467-7744
U.S. News ranking: Reg. Coll. (N), unranked
Website: www.neit.edu/
Admissions email: neit@neit.edu
Private; founded 1940
Freshman admissions: N/A; 2013-2014: N/A applied, N/A accepted. Neither SAT nor ACT required. ACT 25/75 percentile: N/A. High school rank: N/A
Early decision deadline: N/A, notification date: N/A
Early action deadline: N/A, notification date: N/A
Application deadline (fall): rolling
Undergraduate student body: 2,396 full time, 464 part time; 69% male, 31% female; 1% American Indian, 2% Asian, 5% black, 9% Hispanic, 1% multiracial, 0% Pacific Islander, 68% white, 4% international
Most popular majors: Information not available
Expenses: 2014-2015: $22,230; room/board: N/A
Financial aid: (800) 736-7744

Providence College

Providence RI
(401) 865-2535
U.S. News ranking: Reg. U. (N), No. 2
Website: www.providence.edu
Admissions email: pcadmiss@providence.edu
Private; founded 1917
Affiliation: Roman Catholic
Freshman admissions: more selective; 2013-2014: 9,660 applied, 5,776 accepted. Neither SAT nor ACT required. SAT 25/75 percentile: 1050-1260. High school rank: 37% in top tenth, 67% in top quarter, 92% in top half
Early decision deadline: 12/1, notification date: 1/1
Early action deadline: 11/1, notification date: 1/1
Application deadline (fall): 1/15
Undergraduate student body: 3,902 full time, 337 part time; 43% male, 57% female; 0% American Indian, 1% Asian, 4% black, 7% Hispanic, 2% multiracial, 0% Pacific Islander, 77% white, 2% international; 10% from in state; 77% live on campus; 0% of students in fraternities, 0% in sororities
Most popular majors: 8% Biological and Biomedical Sciences, 33% Business, Management, Marketing, and Related Support Services, 9% Education, 6% History, 11% Social Sciences
Expenses: 2014-2015: $43,245; room/board: $12,750
Financial aid: (401) 865-2286; 56% of undergrads determined to have financial need; average aid package $28,068

Rhode Island College

Providence RI
(800) 669-5760
U.S. News ranking: Reg. U. (N), No. 122
Website: www.ric.edu
Admissions email: admissions@ric.edu
Public; founded 1854
Freshman admissions: less selective; 2013-2014: 4,690 applied, 3,363 accepted. Either SAT or ACT required. SAT 25/75 percentile: 820-1030. High school rank: 12% in top tenth, 40% in top quarter, 79% in top half
Early decision deadline: N/A, notification date: N/A
Early action deadline: N/A, notification date: N/A
Application deadline (fall): 3/15
Undergraduate student body: 5,600 full time, 1,905 part time; 33% male, 67% female; 0% American Indian, 2% Asian, 7% black, 12% Hispanic, 2% multiracial, 0% Pacific Islander, 64% white, 0% international; 85% from in state; 16% live on campus; N/A of students in fraternities, N/A in sororities
Most popular majors: 14% Business, Management, Marketing, and Related Support Services, 15% Education, 15% Health Professions and Related Programs, 13% Psychology, 8% Visual and Performing Arts
Expenses: 2014-2015: $7,602 in state, $18,300 out of state; room/board: $10,094
Financial aid: (401) 456-8033; 69% of undergrads determined to have financial need; average aid package $9,019

Rhode Island School of Design

Providence RI
(401) 454-6300
U.S. News ranking: Arts, unranked
Website: www.risd.edu
Admissions email: admissions@risd.edu
Private; founded 1877
Freshman admissions: N/A; 2013-2014: 3,215 applied, 878 accepted. Either SAT or ACT required. SAT 25/75 percentile: N/A. High school rank: N/A
Early decision deadline: 11/1, notification date: 12/1
Early action deadline: N/A, notification date: N/A
Application deadline (fall): 2/1
Undergraduate student body: 2,005 full time, 0 part time; 34% male, 66% female; 0% American Indian, 16% Asian, 2% black, 8% Hispanic, 3% multiracial, 0% Pacific Islander, 33% white, 24% international; 1% from in state; 70% live on campus; N/A of students in fraternities, N/A in sororities
Most popular majors: 14% Architecture, 9% Film/Cinema/ Video Studies, 11% Graphic Design, 18% Illustration, 17% Industrial and Product Design
Expenses: 2014-2015: $44,594; room/board: $12,640
Financial aid: (401) 454-6636; 41% of undergrads determined to have financial need; average aid package $28,500

Roger Williams University

Bristol RI
(401) 254-3500
U.S. News ranking: Reg. U. (N), No. 41
Website: www.rwu.edu
Admissions email: admit@rwu.edu
Private; founded 1956
Freshman admissions: selective; 2013-2014: 9,021 applied, 7,305 accepted. Neither SAT nor ACT required. SAT 25/75 percentile: 1020-1200. High school rank: 14% in top tenth, 37% in top quarter, 75% in top half
Early decision deadline: N/A, notification date: N/A
Early action deadline: 11/1, notification date: 12/15
Application deadline (fall): 2/1
Undergraduate student body: 3,875 full time, 536 part time; 50% male, 50% female; 0% American Indian, 1% Asian, 2% black, 5% Hispanic, 2% multiracial, 0% Pacific Islander, 75% white, 5% international; 17% from in state; 63% live on campus; 0% of students in fraternities, 0% in sororities
Most popular majors: 10% Architecture and Related Services, 24% Business, Management, Marketing, and Related Support Services, 8% Communication, Journalism, and Related Programs, 9% Homeland Security, Law Enforcement, Firefighting and Related Protective Services, 7% Psychology
Expenses: 2014-2015: $31,750; room/board: $14,546
Financial aid: (401) 254-3100; 61% of undergrads determined to have financial need; average aid package $20,050

Salve Regina University

Newport RI
(888) 467-2583
U.S. News ranking: Reg. U. (N), No. 50
Website: www.salve.edu
Admissions email: sruadmis@salve.edu
Private; founded 1934
Affiliation: Roman Catholic
Freshman admissions: selective; 2013-2014: 5,070 applied, 3,400 accepted. Neither SAT nor ACT required. SAT 25/75 percentile: 1020-1190. High school rank: 16% in top tenth, 45% in top quarter, 83% in top half
Early decision deadline: N/A, notification date: N/A
Early action deadline: 11/1, notification date: 12/25
Application deadline (fall): rolling
Undergraduate student body: 1,873 full time, 153 part time; 30% male, 70% female; 0% American Indian, 1% Asian, 2% black, 6% Hispanic, 2% multiracial, 0% Pacific Islander, 76% white, 1% international; 20% from in state; 58% live on campus; 0% of students in fraternities, 0% in sororities
Most popular majors: 13% Criminal Justice/Law Enforcement Administration, 7% Marketing/Marketing Management, General, 7% Psychology, General, 14% Registered Nursing/Registered Nurse, 8% Special Education and Teaching, General

Expenses: 2014-2015: $35,690; room/board: $12,860
Financial aid: (401) 341-2901; 78% of undergrads determined to have financial need; average aid package $23,401

University of Rhode Island

Kingston RI
(401) 874-7100
U.S. News ranking: Nat. U., No. 161
Website: www.uri.edu
Admissions email: admission@uri.edu
Public; founded 1892
Freshman admissions: selective; 2013-2014: 20,907 applied, 15,844 accepted. Either SAT or ACT required. SAT 25/75 percentile: 1000-1210. High school rank: 19% in top tenth, 47% in top quarter, 83% in top half
Early decision deadline: N/A, notification date: N/A
Early action deadline: 12/1, notification date: 1/31
Application deadline (fall): 2/1
Undergraduate student body: 11,829 full time, 1,525 part time; 46% male, 54% female; 0% American Indian, 3% Asian, 5% black, 9% Hispanic, 2% multiracial, 0% Pacific Islander, 69% white, 1% international; 59% from in state; 44% live on campus; 15% of students in fraternities, 15% in sororities
Most popular majors: 5% Human Development and Family Studies, General, 6% Kinesiology and Exercise Science, 6% Psychology, General, 6% Registered Nursing/Registered Nurse, 8% Speech Communication and Rhetoric
Expenses: 2014-2015: $12,506 in state, $28,072 out of state; room/board: $11,496
Financial aid: (401) 874-9500; 84% of undergrads determined to have financial need; average aid package $15,482

SOUTH CAROLINA

Allen University

Columbia SC
(803) 376-5735
U.S. News ranking: Nat. Lib. Arts, second tier
Website: www.allenuniversity.edu
Admissions email: admissions@allenuniversity.edu
Private; founded 1870
Affiliation: African Methodist Episcopal
Freshman admissions: less selective; 2013-2014: 2,659 applied, 1,333 accepted. Neither SAT nor ACT required. Average composite ACT score: 16. High school rank: N/A
Early decision deadline: N/A, notification date: N/A
Early action deadline: N/A, notification date: N/A
Application deadline (fall): rolling
Undergraduate student body: 635 full time, 16 part time; 38% male, 62% female; 0% American Indian, 0% Asian, 100% black, 0% Hispanic, 0% multiracial, 0% Pacific Islander, 0% white, 0% international; 98% from in state; 82% live on campus; 1% of students in fraternities, 10% in sororities

Most popular majors: 15% Biology/Biological Sciences, General, 21% Business Administration and Management, General, 12% English Language and Literature, General, 8% Mathematics, General, 29% Social Sciences, General
Expenses: 2014-2015: $12,970; room/board: $6,560
Financial aid: (803) 376-5736; 97% of undergrads determined to have financial need; average aid package $12,418

Anderson University

Anderson SC
(864) 231-5607
U.S. News ranking: Reg. Coll. (S), No. 21
Website: www.andersonuniversity.edu
Admissions email: admission@andersonuniversity.edu
Private; founded 1911
Affiliation: South Carolina Baptist Convention
Freshman admissions: selective; 2013-2014: 2,190 applied, 1,424 accepted. Either SAT or ACT required. SAT 25/75 percentile: 960-1180. High school rank: 39% in top tenth, 64% in top quarter, 89% in top half
Early decision deadline: N/A, notification date: N/A
Early action deadline: N/A, notification date: N/A
Application deadline (fall): rolling
Undergraduate student body: 2,131 full time, 522 part time; 33% male, 67% female; 1% American Indian, 1% Asian, 10% black, 3% Hispanic, 0% multiracial, 1% Pacific Islander, 81% white, 1% international; 82% from in state; 47% live on campus; N/A of students in fraternities, N/A in sororities
Most popular majors: 26% Business, Management, Marketing, and Related Support Services, 23% Education, 5% Multi/Interdisciplinary Studies, 6% Parks, Recreation, Leisure, and Fitness Studies, 15% Visual and Performing Arts
Expenses: 2014-2015: $23,750; room/board: $8,690
Financial aid: (864) 231-2070; 84% of undergrads determined to have financial need; average aid package $17,688

Benedict College[1]

Columbia SC
(803) 253-5143
U.S. News ranking: Reg. Coll. (S), unranked
Website: www.benedict.edu
Admissions email: admissions@benedict.edu
Private
Application deadline (fall): N/A
Undergraduate student body: N/A full time, N/A part time
Expenses: 2013-2014: $18,254; room/board: $8,104
Financial aid: (803) 253-5105

Charleston Southern University

Charleston SC
(843) 863-7050
U.S. News ranking: Reg. U. (S), second tier
Website: www.csuniv.edu
Admissions email: enroll@csuniv.edu
Private; founded 1964
Affiliation: Baptist
Freshman admissions: less selective; 2013-2014: 3,640 applied, 2,507 accepted. Either SAT or ACT required. SAT 25/75 percentile: 870-1080. High school rank: N/A
Early decision deadline: N/A, notification date: N/A
Early action deadline: N/A, notification date: N/A
Application deadline (fall): rolling
Undergraduate student body: 2,601 full time, 311 part time; 36% male, 64% female; 1% American Indian, 1% Asian, 30% black, 3% Hispanic, 2% multiracial, 0% Pacific Islander, 59% white, 1% international
Most popular majors: Information not available
Expenses: 2014-2015: $22,840; room/board: $9,000
Financial aid: (843) 863-7050

The Citadel

Charleston SC
(843) 953-5230
U.S. News ranking: Reg. U. (S), No. 4
Website: www.citadel.edu/root/
Admissions email: admissions@citadel.edu
Public; founded 1842
Freshman admissions: selective; 2013-2014: 2,768 applied, 2,116 accepted. Either SAT or ACT required. SAT 25/75 percentile: 970-1190. High school rank: 12% in top tenth, 34% in top quarter, 71% in top half
Early decision deadline: N/A, notification date: N/A
Early action deadline: N/A, notification date: N/A
Application deadline (fall): rolling
Undergraduate student body: 2,517 full time, 218 part time; 91% male, 9% female; 1% American Indian, 3% Asian, 8% black, 6% Hispanic, 2% multiracial, 0% Pacific Islander, 78% white, 1% international; 58% from in state; 100% live on campus; 0% of students in fraternities, 0% in sororities
Most popular majors: 25% Business Administration and Management, General, 17% Civil Engineering, General, 14% Criminal Justice/Law Enforcement Administration, 11% Political Science and Government, General, 9% Secondary Education and Teaching
Expenses: 2014-2015: $12,568 in state, $32,176 out of state; room/board: $6,381
Financial aid: (843) 953-5187; 57% of undergrads determined to have financial need; average aid package $13,923

Claflin University

Orangeburg SC
(803) 535-5340
U.S. News ranking: Nat. Lib. Arts, second tier
Website: www.claflin.edu
Admissions email: mike.zeigler@claflin.edu
Private; founded 1869
Affiliation: United Methodist
Freshman admissions: less selective; 2013-2014: 4,073 applied, 2,469 accepted. Either SAT or ACT required. SAT 25/75 percentile: 710-960. High school rank: 13% in top tenth, 35% in top quarter, 68% in top half
Early decision deadline: N/A, notification date: N/A
Early action deadline: N/A, notification date: N/A
Application deadline (fall): rolling
Undergraduate student body: 1,767 full time, 67 part time; 37% male, 63% female; 1% American Indian, 0% Asian, 92% black, 2% Hispanic, 0% multiracial, 0% Pacific Islander, 2% white, 3% international; 81% from in state; 70% live on campus; 3% of students in fraternities, 6% in sororities
Most popular majors: 13% Biotechnology, 34% Business, Management, Marketing, and Related Support Services, Other, 12% Criminal Justice/Law Enforcement Administration, 7% Mass Communication/Media Studies, 14% Sociology
Expenses: 2014-2015: $15,210; room/board: $10,540
Financial aid: (803) 535-5334; 96% of undergrads determined to have financial need; average aid package $14,045

Clemson University

Clemson SC
(864) 656-2287
U.S. News ranking: Nat. U., No. 62
Website: www.clemson.edu
Admissions email: cuadmissions@clemson.edu
Public; founded 1889
Freshman admissions: more selective; 2013-2014: 18,604 applied, 10,645 accepted. Either SAT or ACT required. SAT 25/75 percentile: 1150-1340. High school rank: 56% in top tenth, 86% in top quarter, 98% in top half
Early decision deadline: N/A, notification date: N/A
Early action deadline: N/A, notification date: N/A
Application deadline (fall): 5/1
Undergraduate student body: 16,050 full time, 881 part time; 54% male, 46% female; 0% American Indian, 2% Asian, 6% black, 3% Hispanic, 1% multiracial, 0% Pacific Islander, 85% white, 1% international; 65% from in state; 41% live on campus; 22% of students in fraternities, 48% in sororities
Most popular majors: 9% Biological and Biomedical Sciences, 19% Business, Management, Marketing, and Related Support Services, 17% Engineering, 7% Health Professions and Related Programs, 7% Social Sciences
Expenses: 2013-2014: $13,382 in state, $30,816 out of state; room/board: $8,142
Financial aid: (864) 656-2280

More at usnews.com/college

Coastal Carolina University

Conway SC
(843) 349-2170
U.S. News ranking: Reg. U. (S), No. 57
Website: www.coastal.edu
Admissions email: admissions@coastal.edu
Public; founded 1954
Freshman admissions: selective; 2013-2014: 14,050 applied, 9,014 accepted. Either SAT or ACT required. SAT 25/75 percentile: 910-1090. High school rank: 10% in top tenth, 33% in top quarter, 70% in top half
Early decision deadline: N/A, notification date: N/A
Early action deadline: N/A, notification date: N/A
Application deadline (fall): 8/1
Undergraduate student body: 8,032 full time, 835 part time; 46% male, 54% female; 0% American Indian, 1% Asian, 21% black, 4% Hispanic, 4% multiracial, 0% Pacific Islander, 69% white, 1% international; 53% from in state; 39% live on campus; 3% of students in fraternities, 6% in sororities
Most popular majors: 10% Business Administration and Management, General, 6% Marine Biology and Biological Oceanography, 6% Marketing/Marketing Management, General, 7% Speech Communication and Rhetoric, 6% Sport and Fitness Administration/Management
Expenses: 2014-2015: $10,140 in state, $23,480 out of state; room/board: $8,440
Financial aid: (843) 349-2313; 72% of undergrads determined to have financial need; average aid package $9,829

Coker College

Hartsville SC
(843) 383-8050
U.S. News ranking: Reg. Coll. (S), No. 16
Website: www.coker.edu
Admissions email: admissions@coker.edu
Private; founded 1908
Freshman admissions: less selective; 2013-2014: 1,273 applied, 678 accepted. Either SAT or ACT required. SAT 25/75 percentile: 870-1050. High school rank: 7% in top tenth, 21% in top quarter, 66% in top half
Early decision deadline: N/A, notification date: N/A
Early action deadline: N/A, notification date: N/A
Application deadline (fall): 8/1
Undergraduate student body: 1,007 full time, 137 part time; 37% male, 63% female; 0% American Indian, 0% Asian, 36% black, 3% Hispanic, 2% multiracial, 0% Pacific Islander, 51% white, 2% international; 80% from in state; 49% live on campus; 0% of students in fraternities, 0% in sororities
Most popular majors: 19% Business Administration and Management, General, 13% Elementary Education and Teaching, 8% Psychology, General, 8% Social Work, 14% Sociology
Expenses: 2014-2015: $25,536; room/board: $7,830

Financial aid: (843) 383-8055; 88% of undergrads determined to have financial need; average aid package $18,385

College of Charleston

Charleston SC
(843) 953-5670
U.S. News ranking: Reg. U. (S), No. 13
Website: www.cofc.edu
Admissions email: admissions@cofc.edu
Public; founded 1770
Freshman admissions: selective; 2013-2014: 11,532 applied, 8,330 accepted. Either SAT or ACT required. SAT 25/75 percentile: 1070-1250. High school rank: 26% in top tenth, 60% in top quarter, 92% in top half
Early decision deadline: N/A, notification date: N/A
Early action deadline: 11/1, notification date: N/A
Application deadline (fall): 4/1
Undergraduate student body: 9,708 full time, 780 part time; 38% male, 62% female; 0% American Indian, 2% Asian, 6% black, 4% Hispanic, 3% multiracial, 0% Pacific Islander, 82% white, 1% international; 63% from in state; 29% live on campus; 17% of students in fraternities, 23% in sororities
Most popular majors: 10% Biology/Biological Sciences, General, 21% Business/Commerce, General, 11% Social Sciences, General, 10% Speech Communication and Rhetoric, 10% Visual and Performing Arts, General
Expenses: 2014-2015: $11,018 in state, $28,008 out of state; room/board: $11,127
Financial aid: (843) 953-5540; 49% of undergrads determined to have financial need; average aid package $12,946

Columbia College

Columbia SC
(800) 277-1301
U.S. News ranking: Reg. U. (S), No. 37
Website: www.columbiasc.edu
Admissions email: admissions@columbiasc.edu
Private; founded 1854
Affiliation: United Methodist
Freshman admissions: selective; 2013-2014: 446 applied, 287 accepted. Either SAT or ACT required. SAT 25/75 percentile: 920-1130. High school rank: 22% in top tenth, 63% in top quarter, 90% in top half
Early decision deadline: N/A, notification date: N/A
Early action deadline: N/A, notification date: N/A
Application deadline (fall): rolling
Undergraduate student body: 722 full time, 290 part time; 5% male, 95% female; 2% American Indian, 1% Asian, 38% black, 3% Hispanic, 0% multiracial, 0% Pacific Islander, 52% white, 0% international; 92% from in state; 42% live on campus; 0% of students in fraternities, 0% in sororities
Most popular majors: 6% Business Administration and Management, General, 12% Human Development, Family Studies, and Related Services, Other, 13% Psychology, General, 7% Speech Communication and Rhetoric,

---

7% Speech-Language Pathology/Pathologist
Expenses: 2014-2015: $27,350; room/board: $7,200
Financial aid: (803) 786-3612; 91% of undergrads determined to have financial need; average aid package $20,665

Columbia International University

Columbia SC
(800) 777-2227
U.S. News ranking: Reg. U. (S), No. 37
Website: www.ciu.edu
Admissions email: N/A
Private; founded 1923
Affiliation: Evangelical multi-denominational
Freshman admissions: selective; 2013-2014: 302 applied, 189 accepted. Either SAT or ACT required. SAT 25/75 percentile: 940-1200. High school rank: 15% in top tenth, 37% in top quarter, 73% in top half
Early decision deadline: N/A, notification date: N/A
Early action deadline: N/A, notification date: N/A
Undergraduate student body: 511 full time, 74 part time; 54% male, 46% female; 0% American Indian, 2% Asian, 11% black, 4% Hispanic, 1% multiracial, 0% Pacific Islander, 77% white, 3% international; 58% from in state; 71% live on campus; 0% of students in fraternities, 0% in sororities
Most popular majors: 17% General Studies, 16% Humanities/Humanistic Studies, 10% Intercultural/Multicultural and Diversity Studies, 7% Mass Communication/Media Studies, 14% Psychology, General
Expenses: 2014-2015: $19,480; room/board: $7,310
Financial aid: (803) 754-4100; 81% of undergrads determined to have financial need; average aid package $15,728

Converse College

Spartanburg SC
(864) 596-9040
U.S. News ranking: Reg. U. (S), No. 23
Website: www.converse.edu
Admissions email: info@converse.edu
Private; founded 1889
Freshman admissions: selective; 2013-2014: 1,504 applied, 784 accepted. Either SAT or ACT required. SAT 25/75 percentile: 960-1160. High school rank: 18% in top tenth, 43% in top quarter, 80% in top half
Early decision deadline: N/A, notification date: N/A
Early action deadline: N/A, notification date: N/A
Application deadline (fall): 8/1
Undergraduate student body: 665 full time, 83 part time; 0% male, 100% female; 0% American Indian, 1% Asian, 7% black, 4% Hispanic, 3% multiracial, 0% Pacific Islander, 55% white, 1% international
Most popular majors: 9% Business, Management, Marketing, and Related Support Services, 24% Education, 10% English Language

---

and Literature/Letters, 15% Psychology, 16% Visual and Performing Arts
Expenses: 2014-2015: $16,500; room/board: $9,500
Financial aid: (864) 596-9019; 90% of undergrads determined to have financial need; average aid package $23,249

Erskine College

Due West SC
(864) 379-8838
U.S. News ranking: Nat. Lib. Arts, No. 178
Website: www.erskine.edu
Admissions email: admissions@erskine.edu
Private
Affiliation: Associate Reformed Presbyterian
Freshman admissions: selective; 2013-2014: 750 applied, 523 accepted. Either SAT or ACT required. SAT 25/75 percentile: 910-1110. High school rank: N/A
Early decision deadline: N/A, notification date: N/A
Early action deadline: N/A, notification date: N/A
Application deadline (fall): rolling
Undergraduate student body: 565 full time, 40 part time; 52% male, 48% female; 0% American Indian, 1% Asian, 10% black, 4% Hispanic, 0% multiracial, 0% Pacific Islander, 67% white, 0% international
Most popular majors: 20% Biological and Biomedical Sciences, 12% Business, Management, Marketing, and Related Support Services, 11% English Language and Literature/Letters, 7% Parks, Recreation, Leisure, and Fitness Studies, 8% Physical Sciences
Expenses: 2014-2015: $31,280; room/board: $10,105
Financial aid: (864) 379-8832; 100% of undergrads determined to have financial need; average aid package $22,000

Francis Marion University

Florence SC
(843) 661-1231
U.S. News ranking: Reg. U. (S), No. 76
Website: www.fmarion.edu
Admissions email: admission@fmarion.edu
Public; founded 1970
Freshman admissions: selective; 2013-2014: 3,951 applied, 2,239 accepted. Either SAT or ACT required. SAT 25/75 percentile: 830-1060. High school rank: 15% in top tenth, 42% in top quarter, 81% in top half
Early decision deadline: N/A, notification date: N/A
Early action deadline: N/A, notification date: N/A
Application deadline (fall): 8/15
Undergraduate student body: 3,316 full time, 398 part time; 31% male, 69% female; 0% American Indian, 1% Asian, 50% black, 1% Hispanic, 0% multiracial, 0% Pacific Islander, 45% white, 1% international; 97% from in state; 39% live on campus; 1% of students in fraternities, 1% in sororities
Most popular majors: 15% Biological and Biomedical Sciences, 17% Business, Management, Marketing, and

---

Related Support Services, 16% Health Professions and Related Programs, 8% Psychology, 11% Social Sciences
Expenses: 2014-2015: $9,738 in state, $19,004 out of state; room/board: $7,256
Financial aid: (843) 661-1190; 80% of undergrads determined to have financial need; average aid package $7,224

Furman University

Greenville SC
(864) 294-2034
U.S. News ranking: Nat. Lib. Arts, No. 51
Website: www.furman.edu/
Admissions email: admissions@furman.edu
Private; founded 1826
Freshman admissions: more selective; 2013-2014: 5,935 applied, 3,802 accepted. Neither SAT nor ACT required. SAT 25/75 percentile: 1130-1340. High school rank: 48% in top tenth, 76% in top quarter, 93% in top half
Early decision deadline: 11/1, notification date: 11/30
Early action deadline: 11/15, notification date: 2/1
Application deadline (fall): 1/15
Undergraduate student body: 2,675 full time, 123 part time; 42% male, 58% female; 0% American Indian, 2% Asian, 5% black, 3% Hispanic, 2% multiracial, 0% Pacific Islander, 80% white, 4% international; 28% from in state; 96% live on campus; 31% of students in fraternities, 54% in sororities
Most popular majors: 6% Biology, General, 11% Business Administration, Management and Operations, 7% Health Professions and Related Clinical Sciences, Other, 6% History, 10% Political Science and Government
Expenses: 2014-2015: $44,668; room/board: $11,204
Financial aid: (864) 294-2204; 44% of undergrads determined to have financial need; average aid package $28,539

Lander University[1]

Greenwood SC
(864) 388-8307
U.S. News ranking: Reg. Coll. (S), No. 64
Website: www.lander.edu
Admissions email: admissions@lander.edu
Public
Application deadline (fall): N/A
Undergraduate student body: N/A full time, N/A part time
Expenses: 2013-2014: $10,100 in state, $19,136 out of state; room/board: $7,500
Financial aid: (864) 388-8340

Limestone College

Gaffney SC
(864) 488-4554
U.S. News ranking: Reg. Coll. (S), No. 64
Website: www.limestone.edu
Admissions email: admiss@limestone.edu
Private; founded 1845
Affiliation: Christian nondenominational
Freshman admissions: less selective; 2013-2014: 2,318 applied, 1,244 accepted. Either

SAT or ACT required. SAT 25/75 percentile: 930-1090. High school rank: 3% in top tenth, 19% in top quarter, 51% in top half **Early decision deadline:** N/A, notification date: N/A **Early action deadline:** N/A, notification date: N/A **Application deadline (fall):** 8/22 **Undergraduate student body:** 1,041 full time, 18 part time; 62% male, 38% female; 0% American Indian, 0% Asian, 29% black, 4% Hispanic, 2% multiracial, 0% Pacific Islander, 54% white, 9% international; 58% from in state; 58% live on campus; 3% of students in fraternities, 0% in sororities **Most popular majors:** 28% Business, Management, Marketing, and Related Support Services, 14% Education, 6% Homeland Security, Law Enforcement, Firefighting and Related Protective Services, 8% Liberal Arts and Sciences, General Studies and Humanities, 12% Parks, Recreation, Leisure, and Fitness Studies **Expenses:** 2014-2015: $23,000; room/board: $7,800 **Financial aid:** (864) 488-8231; 85% of undergrads determined to have financial need; average aid package $17,351

Morris College[1]

Sumter SC
(803) 934-3225
U.S. News ranking: Reg. Coll. (S), unranked
Website: www.morris.edu
Admissions email:
dcalhoun@morris.edu
Private
Application deadline (fall): N/A
Undergraduate student body: N/A full time, N/A part time
Expenses: 2013-2014: $11,087; room/board: $4,919
Financial aid: (803) 934-3238

Newberry College

Newberry SC
(800) 845-4955
U.S. News ranking: Reg. Coll. (S), No. 33
Website: www.newberry.edu/
Admissions email:
admissions@newberry.edu
Private; founded 1856
Affiliation: Evangelical Lutheran Church of America
Freshman admissions: less selective; 2013-2014: 887 applied, 524 accepted. Either SAT or ACT required. SAT 25/75 percentile: 830-1060. High school rank: 8% in top tenth, 16% in top quarter, 54% in top half **Early decision deadline:** N/A, notification date: N/A **Early action deadline:** N/A, notification date: N/A **Application deadline (fall):** rolling **Undergraduate student body:** 1,007 full time, 32 part time; 54% male, 46% female; 1% American Indian, 1% Asian, 26% black, 4% Hispanic, 2% multiracial, 0% Pacific Islander, 61% white, 3% international; 79% from in state; 72% live on campus; 13% of students in fraternities, 25% in sororities **Most popular majors:** 9% Biology/ Biological Sciences, General, 18% Business Administration and Management, General,

18% Education, General, 11% Parks, Recreation and Leisure Studies, 9% Registered Nursing/ Registered Nurse **Expenses:** 2014-2015: $24,300; room/board: $9,300 **Financial aid:** (803) 321-5120; 87% of undergrads determined to have financial need; average aid package $20,448

North Greenville University

Tigerville SC
(864) 977-7001
U.S. News ranking: Reg. Coll. (S), No. 25
Website: www.ngu.edu
Admissions email:
admissions@ngu.edu
Private; founded 1892
Affiliation: Southern Baptist Convention
Freshman admissions: selective; 2013-2014: 1,782 applied, 1,032 accepted. Either SAT or ACT required. SAT 25/75 percentile: 920-1340. High school rank: 19% in top tenth, 39% in top quarter, 80% in top half **Early decision deadline:** N/A, notification date: N/A **Early action deadline:** N/A, notification date: N/A **Application deadline (fall):** rolling **Undergraduate student body:** 1,994 full time, 269 part time; 50% male, 50% female; 0% American Indian, 0% Asian, 6% black, 2% Hispanic, 2% multiracial, 0% Pacific Islander, 85% white, 0% international; 78% from in state; 66% live on campus; 0% of students in fraternities, 0% in sororities **Most popular majors:** 19% Business, Management, Marketing, and Related Support Services, 10% Communication, Journalism, and Related Programs, 17% Education, 13% Liberal Arts and Sciences, General Studies and Humanities, 14% Theology and Religious Vocations **Expenses:** 2014-2015: $15,510; room/board: $9,180 **Financial aid:** (864) 977-7058; 59% of undergrads determined to have financial need; average aid package $13,615

Presbyterian College

Clinton SC
(864) 833-8230
U.S. News ranking: Nat. Lib. Arts, No. 124
Website: www.presby.edu
Admissions email:
admissions@presby.edu
Private; founded 1880
Affiliation: Presbyterian Church (USA)
Freshman admissions: selective; 2013-2014: 1,650 applied, 1,089 accepted. Neither SAT nor ACT required. SAT 25/75 percentile: 1000-1210. High school rank: 35% in top tenth, 61% in top quarter, 92% in top half **Early decision deadline:** 11/1, notification date: 12/1 **Early action deadline:** 11/15, notification date: 12/15 **Application deadline (fall):** 6/30 **Undergraduate student body:** 1,087 full time, 36 part time; 45% male, 55% female; 0% American

Indian, 1% Asian, 11% black, 1% Hispanic, 1% multiracial, 0% Pacific Islander, 82% white, 2% international; 65% from in state; 99% live on campus; 38% of students in fraternities, 47% in sororities **Most popular majors:** 14% Biological and Biomedical Sciences, 18% Business, Management, Marketing, and Related Support Services, 11% English Language and Literature/ Letters, 10% History, 11% Psychology **Expenses:** 2013-2014: $33,650; room/board: $9,028 **Financial aid:** (864) 833-8289

South Carolina State University

Orangeburg SC
(803) 536-7185
U.S. News ranking: Nat. U., second tier
Website: www.scsu.edu
Admissions email:
admissions@scsu.edu
Public; founded 1896
Freshman admissions: least selective; 2013-2014: 1,999 applied, 1,838 accepted. Either SAT or ACT required. SAT 25/75 percentile: 720-870. High school rank: 2% in top tenth, 30% in top quarter, 43% in top half **Early decision deadline:** N/A, notification date: N/A **Early action deadline:** N/A, notification date: N/A **Application deadline (fall):** 5/31 **Undergraduate student body:** 2,714 full time, 223 part time; 48% male, 52% female; 0% American Indian, 1% Asian, 95% black, 1% Hispanic, 0% multiracial, 0% Pacific Islander, 3% white, 0% international; 79% from in state; 58% live on campus; N/A of students in fraternities, N/A in sororities **Most popular majors:** 8% Biology/ Biological Sciences, General, 6% Business Administration and Management, General, 8% Criminal Justice/Law Enforcement Administration, 10% Family and Consumer Sciences/Human Sciences, General, 8% Registered Nursing/Registered Nurse **Expenses:** 2013-2014: $9,776 in state, $18,910 out of state; room/ board: $9,286 **Financial aid:** (803) 536-7067

Southern Wesleyan University[1]

Central SC
(864) 644-5550
U.S. News ranking: Reg. U. (S), second tier
Website: www.swu.edu
Admissions email:
admissions@swu.edu
Private
Application deadline (fall): N/A
Undergraduate student body: N/A full time, N/A part time
Expenses: 2013-2014: $22,200; room/board: $8,360
Financial aid: (864) 644-5500

University of South Carolina

Columbia SC
(803) 777-7700
U.S. News ranking: Nat. U., No. 113
Website: www.sc.edu
Admissions email:
admissions-ugrad@sc.edu
Public; founded 1801
Freshman admissions: more selective; 2013-2014: 23,035 applied, 14,844 accepted. Either SAT or ACT required. SAT 25/75 percentile: 1110-1300. High school rank: 30% in top tenth, 66% in top quarter, 94% in top half **Early decision deadline:** N/A, notification date: N/A **Early action deadline:** 10/15, notification date: 12/20 **Application deadline (fall):** 12/1 **Undergraduate student body:** 22,533 full time, 1,647 part time; 46% male, 54% female; 0% American Indian, 2% Asian, 10% black, 4% Hispanic, 3% multiracial, 0% Pacific Islander, 77% white, 1% international; 69% from in state; 30% live on campus; 13% of students in fraternities, 28% in sororities **Most popular majors:** 5% Biology, General, 6% Business Administration, Management and Operations, 4% Physiology, Pathology and Related Sciences, 5% Registered Nursing, Nursing Administration, Nursing Research and Clinical Nursing, 6% Research and Experimental Psychology **Expenses:** 2014-2015: $11,158 in state, $29,440 out of state; room/board: $9,248 **Financial aid:** (803) 777-8134; 52% of undergrads determined to have financial need; average aid package $13,332

University of South Carolina–Aiken

Aiken SC
(803) 641-3366
U.S. News ranking: Reg. Coll. (S), No. 18
Website: web.usca.edu/
Admissions email: admit@sc.edu
Public; founded 1961
Freshman admissions: selective; 2013-2014: 1,839 applied, 1,294 accepted. Either SAT or ACT required. SAT 25/75 percentile: 860-1070. High school rank: 11% in top tenth, 36% in top quarter, 74% in top half **Early decision deadline:** N/A, notification date: N/A **Early action deadline:** N/A, notification date: N/A **Application deadline (fall):** 8/1 **Undergraduate student body:** 2,406 full time, 769 part time; 37% male, 63% female; 0% American Indian, 1% Asian, 27% black, 4% Hispanic, 3% multiracial, 0% Pacific Islander, 60% white, 2% international; 89% from in state; 27% live on campus; 6% of students in fraternities, 11% in sororities **Most popular majors:** 9% Biological and Biomedical Sciences, 24% Business, Management, Marketing, and Related Support Services, 12% Education, 16% Health Professions and Related Programs, 8% Social Sciences

Expenses: 2014-2015: $9,602 in state, $18,926 out of state; room/board: $7,110 **Financial aid:** (803) 641-3476; 71% of undergrads determined to have financial need; average aid package $10,094

University of South Carolina– Beaufort

Bluffton SC
(843) 208-8000
U.S. News ranking: Reg. Coll. (S), No. 59
Website: www.uscb.edu
Admissions email:
admissions@uscb.edu
Public; founded 1959
Freshman admissions: less selective; 2013-2014: 1,666 applied, 1,135 accepted. Either SAT or ACT required. SAT 25/75 percentile: 830-1010. High school rank: 5% in top tenth, 24% in top quarter, 57% in top half **Early decision deadline:** N/A, notification date: N/A **Early action deadline:** N/A, notification date: N/A **Application deadline (fall):** rolling **Undergraduate student body:** 1,376 full time, 348 part time; 39% male, 61% female; 0% American Indian, 1% Asian, 19% black, 5% Hispanic, 3% multiracial, 0% Pacific Islander, 62% white, 1% international; 84% from in state; 32% live on campus; 0% of students in fraternities, 0% in sororities **Most popular majors:** 23% Business Administration and Management, General, 15% Hospitality Administration/ Management, General, 9% Psychology, General, 12% Registered Nursing/Registered Nurse, 8% Social Sciences, General **Expenses:** 2014-2015: $9,092 in state, $19,478 out of state; room/board: $8,186 **Financial aid:** (843) 521-3104

University of South Carolina– Upstate

Spartanburg SC
(864) 503-5246
U.S. News ranking: Reg. Coll. (S), No. 32
Website: www.uscupstate.edu/
Admissions email: admissions@uscupstate.edu
Public; founded 1967
Freshman admissions: less selective; 2013-2014: 2,971 applied, 1,690 accepted. Either SAT or ACT required. SAT 25/75 percentile: 870-1038. High school rank: 14% in top tenth, 40% in top quarter, 77% in top half **Early decision deadline:** N/A, notification date: N/A **Early action deadline:** N/A, notification date: N/A **Application deadline (fall):** rolling **Undergraduate student body:** 4,189 full time, 1,035 part time; 35% male, 65% female; 0% American Indian, 2% Asian, 29% black, 4% Hispanic, 3% multiracial, 0% Pacific Islander, 57% white, 2% international; 96% from in state; 19% live on campus; 6% of students in fraternities, 2% in sororities

Most popular majors: 14% Business Administration and Management, General, 16% Education, General, 7% Multi-/Interdisciplinary Studies, General, 8% Psychology, General, 27% Registered Nursing/Registered Nurse
Expenses: 2014-2015: $10,518 in state, $20,868 out of state; room/board: $7,682
Financial aid: (864) 503-5340; 78% of undergrads determined to have financial need; average aid package $9,484

Voorhees College[1]
Denmark SC
(803) 780-1030
U.S. News ranking: Reg. Coll. (S), second tier
Website: www.voorhees.edu
Admissions email: admissions@voorhees.edu
Private
Application deadline (fall): N/A
Undergraduate student body: N/A full time, N/A part time
Expenses: 2013-2014: $10,780; room/board: $7,346
Financial aid: (803) 780-1150

Winthrop University
Rock Hill SC
(803) 323-2191
U.S. News ranking: Reg. U. (S), No. 25
Website: www.winthrop.edu
Admissions email: admissions@winthrop.edu
Public; founded 1886
Freshman admissions: selective; 2013-2014: 4,285 applied, 3,096 accepted. Either SAT or ACT required. SAT 25/75 percentile: 920-1140. High school rank: 22% in top tenth, 51% in top quarter, 84% in top half
Early decision deadline: N/A, notification date: N/A
Early action deadline: N/A, notification date: N/A
Application deadline (fall): rolling
Undergraduate student body: 4,432 full time, 616 part time; 33% male, 67% female; 0% American Indian, 1% Asian, 31% black, 3% Hispanic, 2% multiracial, 0% Pacific Islander, 58% white, 3% international; 92% from in state; 47% live on campus; N/A of students in fraternities, N/A in sororities
Most popular majors: 28% Business, Management, Marketing, and Related Support Services, 15% Education, 7% Psychology, 7% Social Sciences, 11% Visual and Performing Arts
Expenses: 2014-2015: $13,812 in state, $26,738 out of state; room/board: $8,182
Financial aid: (803) 323-2189; 74% of undergrads determined to have financial need; average aid package $11,837

Wofford College
Spartanburg SC
(864) 597-4130
U.S. News ranking: Nat. Lib. Arts, No. 77
Website: www.wofford.edu
Admissions email: admissions@wofford.edu
Private; founded 1854
Affiliation: United Methodist

Freshman admissions: more selective; 2013-2014: 2,718 applied, 1,870 accepted. Either SAT or ACT required. SAT 25/75 percentile: 1080-1260. High school rank: 42% in top tenth, 77% in top quarter, 96% in top half
Early decision deadline: 11/1, notification date: 12/1
Early action deadline: 11/15, notification date: 2/1
Application deadline (fall): 2/1
Undergraduate student body: 1,549 full time, 35 part time; 52% male, 48% female; 0% American Indian, 3% Asian, 8% black, 3% Hispanic, 3% multiracial, 0% Pacific Islander, 81% white, 2% international; 56% from in state; 93% live on campus; 43% of students in fraternities, 55% in sororities
Most popular majors: 7% Accounting, 20% Biology/Biological Sciences, General, 9% Business/Managerial Economics, 11% Finance, General, 7% Spanish Language and Literature
Expenses: 2014-2015: $37,120; room/board: $10,730
Financial aid: (864) 597-4160; 59% of undergrads determined to have financial need; average aid package $28,377

SOUTH DAKOTA

Augustana College
Sioux Falls SD
(605) 274-5516
U.S. News ranking: Reg. Coll. (Mid. W), No. 3
Website: www.augie.edu
Admissions email: admission@augie.edu
Private; founded 1860
Affiliation: ELCA Lutheran
Freshman admissions: more selective; 2013-2014: 1,147 applied, 781 accepted. Either SAT or ACT required. ACT 25/75 percentile: 23-28. High school rank: 30% in top tenth, 63% in top quarter, 93% in top half
Early decision deadline: N/A, notification date: N/A
Early action deadline: N/A, notification date: N/A
Application deadline (fall): rolling
Undergraduate student body: 1,585 full time, 112 part time; 41% male, 59% female; 0% American Indian, 1% Asian, 2% black, 1% Hispanic, 2% multiracial, 0% Pacific Islander, 88% white, 6% international
Most popular majors: 13% Biological and Biomedical Sciences, 16% Business, Management, Marketing, and Related Support Services, 11% Education, General, 18% Health Professions and Related Programs, 7% Social Sciences
Expenses: 2014-2015: $29,214; room/board: $7,170
Financial aid: (605) 274-5216; 62% of undergrads determined to have financial need; average aid package $23,156

Black Hills State University[1]
Spearfish SD
(800) 255-2478
U.S. News ranking: Reg. U. (Mid. W), second tier
Website: www.bhsu.edu
Admissions email: admissions@bhsu.edu
Public
Application deadline (fall): N/A
Undergraduate student body: N/A full time, N/A part time
Expenses: 2013-2014: $7,617 in state, $9,617 out of state; room/board: $5,945
Financial aid: (605) 642-6145

Dakota State University
Madison SD
(888) 378-9988
U.S. News ranking: Reg. U. (Mid. W), No. 80
Website: www.dsu.edu
Admissions email: admissions@dsu.edu
Public; founded 1881
Freshman admissions: selective; 2013-2014: 781 applied, 648 accepted. Either SAT or ACT required. ACT 25/75 percentile: 19-24. High school rank: 6% in top tenth, 23% in top quarter, 56% in top half
Early decision deadline: N/A, notification date: N/A
Early action deadline: N/A, notification date: N/A
Application deadline (fall): rolling
Undergraduate student body: 1,190 full time, 1,686 part time; 52% male, 48% female; 1% American Indian, 1% Asian, 3% black, 3% Hispanic, 3% multiracial, 0% Pacific Islander, 86% white, 1% international; 73% from in state; 33% live on campus; 0% of students in fraternities, 0% in sororities
Most popular majors: 24% Business, Management, Marketing, and Related Support Services, 34% Computer and Information Sciences and Support Services, 18% Education, 5% Health Professions and Related Programs, 7% Parks, Recreation, Leisure, and Fitness Studies
Expenses: 2014-2015: $8,286 in state, $10,286 out of state; room/board: $5,941
Financial aid: (605) 256-5152; 69% of undergrads determined to have financial need; average aid package $7,997

Dakota Wesleyan University
Mitchell SD
(800) 333-8506
U.S. News ranking: Reg. Coll. (Mid. W), No. 54
Website: www.dwu.edu
Admissions email: admissions@dwu.edu
Private; founded 1885
Affiliation: United Methodist
Freshman admissions: selective; 2013-2014: N/A applied, N/A accepted. Either SAT or ACT required. ACT 25/75 percentile: 19-27. High school rank: 9% in top tenth, 26% in top quarter, 61% in top half
Early decision deadline: N/A, notification date: N/A

Early action deadline: N/A, notification date: N/A
Application deadline (fall): rolling
Undergraduate student body: 699 full time, 111 part time; 45% male, 55% female; 1% American Indian, 0% Asian, 2% black, 4% Hispanic, 2% multiracial, 0% Pacific Islander, 89% white, 1% international; N/A from in state; 45% live on campus; N/A of students in fraternities, N/A in sororities
Most popular majors: 10% Biology/Biological Sciences, General, 20% Business Administration and Management, General, 13% Education, General, 10% Registered Nursing/Registered Nurse, 10% Sport and Fitness Administration/Management
Expenses: 2014-2015: $23,650; room/board: $6,900
Financial aid: (605) 995-2656; 83% of undergrads determined to have financial need; average aid package $19,100

Mount Marty College
Yankton SD
(800) 658-4552
U.S. News ranking: Reg. Coll. (Mid. W), No. 45
Website: www.mtmc.edu
Admissions email: mmcadmit@mtmc.edu
Private; founded 1936
Affiliation: Roman Catholic
Freshman admissions: selective; 2013-2014: 402 applied, 291 accepted. Either SAT or ACT required. ACT 25/75 percentile: 19-24. High school rank: 19% in top tenth, 44% in top quarter, 74% in top half
Early decision deadline: N/A, notification date: N/A
Early action deadline: N/A, notification date: N/A
Application deadline (fall): 8/30
Undergraduate student body: 522 full time, 546 part time; 38% male, 62% female; 4% American Indian, 1% Asian, 4% black, 8% Hispanic, 0% multiracial, 1% Pacific Islander, 80% white, 0% international; 65% from in state; 66% live on campus; 0% of students in fraternities, 0% in sororities
Most popular majors: 18% Business Administration and Management, General, 8% Criminal Justice/Safety Studies, 22% Education, General, 22% Registered Nursing/Registered Nurse
Expenses: 2014-2015: $22,892; room/board: $6,978
Financial aid: (605) 668-1589; 78% of undergrads determined to have financial need; average aid package $23,247

National American University[1]
Rapid City SD
(855) 448-2318
U.S. News ranking: Reg. U. (Mid. W), unranked
Website: www.national.edu/rc
Admissions email: N/A
For-profit
Application deadline (fall): N/A
Undergraduate student body: N/A full time, N/A part time
Expenses: N/A
Financial aid: (605) 394-4880

Northern State University
Aberdeen SD
(800) 678-5330
U.S. News ranking: Reg. Coll. (Mid. W), No. 47
Website: www.northern.edu
Admissions email: admissions@northern.edu
Public; founded 1901
Freshman admissions: selective; 2013-2014: 1,157 applied, 1,080 accepted. Either SAT or ACT required. ACT 25/75 percentile: 19-25. High school rank: 7% in top tenth, 26% in top quarter, 63% in top half
Early decision deadline: N/A, notification date: N/A
Early action deadline: N/A, notification date: N/A
Application deadline (fall): rolling
Undergraduate student body: 1,534 full time, 1,295 part time; 42% male, 58% female; 2% American Indian, 1% Asian, 2% black, 3% Hispanic, 2% multiracial, 0% Pacific Islander, 86% white, 4% international; 79% from in state; 41% live on campus; N/A of students in fraternities, N/A in sororities
Most popular majors: 7% Biological and Biomedical Sciences, 27% Business, Management, Marketing, and Related Support Services, 22% Education, 8% Parks, Recreation, Leisure, and Fitness Studies, 11% Social Sciences
Expenses: 2014-2015: $7,563 in state, $9,563 out of state; room/board: $6,941
Financial aid: (605) 626-2640; 66% of undergrads determined to have financial need; average aid package $10,097

Presentation College[1]
Aberdeen SD
(800) 437-6060
U.S. News ranking: Reg. Coll. (Mid. W), second tier
Website: www.presentation.edu/
Admissions email: N/A
Private
Application deadline (fall): N/A
Undergraduate student body: N/A full time, N/A part time
Expenses: 2013-2014: $17,014; room/board: $7,000
Financial aid: (800) 437-6060

South Dakota School of Mines and Technology
Rapid City SD
(605) 394-2414
U.S. News ranking: Engineering, unranked
Website: www.sdsmt.edu
Admissions email: admissions@sdsmt.edu
Public; founded 1885
Freshman admissions: selective; 2013-2014: 1,350 applied, 1,155 accepted. Either SAT or ACT required. ACT 25/75 percentile: 24-28. High school rank: 17% in top tenth, 38% in top quarter, 62% in top half
Early decision deadline: N/A, notification date: N/A
Early action deadline: N/A, notification date: N/A
Application deadline (fall): rolling

Undergraduate student body: 1,950 full time, 379 part time; 77% male, 23% female; 1% American Indian, 1% Asian, 2% black, 3% Hispanic, 4% multiracial, 1% Pacific Islander, 85% white, 2% international; 54% from in state; 38% live on campus; 2% of students in fraternities, 5% in sororities
Most popular majors: 13% Chemical Engineering, 15% Civil Engineering, General, 12% Electrical and Electronics Engineering, 10% Industrial Engineering, 19% Mechanical Engineering
Expenses: 2014-2015: $10,040 in state, $12,870 out of state; room/board: $6,370
Financial aid: (605) 394-2274; 55% of undergrads determined to have financial need; average aid package $13,717

South Dakota State University

Brookings SD
(605) 688-4121
U.S. News ranking: Nat. U., No. 181
Website: www.sdstate.edu
Admissions email: SDSU_Admissions@sdstate.edu
Public; founded 1881
Freshman admissions: selective; 2013-2014: 4,851 applied, 4,458 accepted. Either SAT or ACT required. ACT 25/75 percentile: 20-25. High school rank: 13% in top tenth, 35% in top quarter, 69% in top half
Early decision deadline: N/A, notification date: N/A
Early action deadline: N/A, notification date: N/A
Application deadline (fall): rolling
Undergraduate student body: 8,646 full time, 2,352 part time; 48% male, 52% female; 1% American Indian, 1% Asian, 2% black, 2% Hispanic, 2% multiracial, 0% Pacific Islander, 90% white, 2% international; 63% from in state; 42% live on campus; N/A of students in fraternities, N/A in sororities
Most popular majors: Information not available
Expenses: 2014-2015: $7,713 in state, $9,795 out of state; room/board: $7,311
Financial aid: (605) 688-4695

University of Sioux Falls

Sioux Falls SD
(605) 331-6600
U.S. News ranking: Reg. Coll. (Mid. W), No. 38
Website: www.usiouxfalls.edu
Admissions email: admissions@usiouxfalls.edu
Private; founded 1883
Affiliation: American Baptist
Freshman admissions: selective; 2013-2014: 1,385 applied, 1,343 accepted. Either SAT or ACT required. ACT 25/75 percentile: 20-26. High school rank: 14% in top tenth, 46% in top quarter, 76% in top half
Early decision deadline: N/A, notification date: N/A
Early action deadline: N/A, notification date: N/A
Application deadline (fall): rolling

Undergraduate student body: 929 full time, 171 part time; 41% male, 59% female; 0% American Indian, 0% Asian, 4% black, 3% Hispanic, 3% multiracial, 0% Pacific Islander, 88% white, 1% international; 50% from in state; 56% live on campus; 0% of students in fraternities, 0% in sororities
Most popular majors: 19% Business Administration and Management, General, 6% Criminal Justice/Safety Studies, 12% Elementary Education and Teaching, 9% Kinesiology and Exercise Science, 21% Registered Nursing/Registered Nurse
Expenses: 2014-2015: $25,480; room/board: $6,700
Financial aid: (605) 331-6623; 77% of undergrads determined to have financial need; average aid package $19,348

University of South Dakota

Vermillion SD
(605) 677-5434
U.S. News ranking: Nat. U., No. 168
Website: www.usd.edu
Admissions email: admiss@usd.edu
Public; founded 1862
Freshman admissions: selective; 2013-2014: 3,606 applied, 3,169 accepted. Either SAT or ACT required. ACT 25/75 percentile: 21-26. High school rank: 15% in top tenth, 38% in top quarter, 73% in top half
Early decision deadline: N/A, notification date: N/A
Early action deadline: N/A, notification date: N/A
Application deadline (fall): rolling
Undergraduate student body: 4,732 full time, 2,901 part time; 37% male, 63% female; 2% American Indian, 1% Asian, 2% black, 3% Hispanic, 3% multiracial, 0% Pacific Islander, 87% white, 1% international; 67% from in state; 32% live on campus; 18% of students in fraternities, 11% in sororities
Most popular majors: 15% Business, Management, Marketing, and Related Support Services, 11% Education, 21% Health Professions and Related Programs, 9% Psychology, 7% Social Sciences
Expenses: 2014-2015: $8,022 in state, $10,104 out of state; room/board: $7,454
Financial aid: (605) 677-5446; 67% of undergrads determined to have financial need; average aid package $6,439

TENNESSEE

Aquinas College

Nashville TN
(800) 649-9956
U.S. News ranking: Reg. Coll. (S), No. 14
Website: www.aquinascollege.edu
Admissions email: admissions@aquinascollege.edu
Private; founded 1961
Affiliation: Roman Catholic
Freshman admissions: selective; 2013-2014: 119 applied, 62 accepted. Either SAT or ACT required. ACT 25/75 percentile: 23-27. High school rank: 21% in top tenth, 43% in top quarter, 86% in top half

Early decision deadline: N/A, notification date: N/A
Early action deadline: N/A, notification date: N/A
Application deadline (fall): rolling
Undergraduate student body: 187 full time, 321 part time; 18% male, 82% female; 0% American Indian, 4% Asian, 8% black, 4% Hispanic, 2% multiracial, 1% Pacific Islander, 73% white, 3% international; 84% from in state; 8% live on campus; 0% of students in fraternities, 0% in sororities
Most popular majors: 33% Business Administration and Management, General, 12% Elementary Education and Teaching, 39% Registered Nursing/Registered Nurse
Expenses: 2014-2015: $20,550; room/board: $4,350
Financial aid: (615) 297-7545

Austin Peay State University

Clarksville TN
(931) 221-7661
U.S. News ranking: Reg. U. (S), No. 62
Website: www.apsu.edu
Admissions email: admissions@apsu.edu
Public; founded 1927
Freshman admissions: selective; 2013-2014: 3,551 applied, 3,054 accepted. Neither SAT nor ACT required. ACT 25/75 percentile: 19-24. High school rank: 14% in top tenth, 37% in top quarter, 72% in top half
Early decision deadline: N/A, notification date: N/A
Early action deadline: N/A, notification date: N/A
Application deadline (fall): 8/5
Undergraduate student body: 6,866 full time, 2,684 part time; 40% male, 60% female; 0% American Indian, 1% Asian, 19% black, 6% Hispanic, 5% multiracial, 0% Pacific Islander, 66% white, 0% international; 89% from in state; 15% live on campus; 12% of students in fraternities, 11% in sororities
Most popular majors: 16% Business, Management, Marketing, and Related Support Services, 6% Communication, Journalism, and Related Programs, 8% Education, 10% Health Professions and Related Programs, 7% Homeland Security, Law Enforcement, Firefighting and Related Protective Services
Expenses: 2014-2015: $7,462 in state, $23,860 out of state; room/board: $8,106
Financial aid: (931) 221-7907; 81% of undergrads determined to have financial need; average aid package $9,812

Belmont University

Nashville TN
(615) 460-6785
U.S. News ranking: Reg. U. (S), No. 5
Website: www.belmont.edu
Admissions email: buadmission@mail.belmont.edu
Private; founded 1890
Affiliation: Nondenominational Christian
Freshman admissions: more selective; 2013-2014: 5,111 applied, 4,082 accepted. Either SAT or ACT required. ACT 25/75

percentile: 24-29. High school rank: 31% in top tenth, 61% in top quarter, 91% in top half
Early decision deadline: N/A, notification date: N/A
Early action deadline: N/A, notification date: N/A
Application deadline (fall): 8/1
Undergraduate student body: 5,117 full time, 389 part time; 40% male, 60% female; 0% American Indian, 2% Asian, 4% black, 4% Hispanic, 3% multiracial, 0% Pacific Islander, 82% white, 1% international; 35% from in state; 50% live on campus; N/A of students in fraternities, N/A in sororities
Most popular majors: 18% Business, Management, Marketing, and Related Support Services, 5% Communication, Journalism, and Related Programs, 5% Communications Technologies/Technicians and Support Services, 11% Health Professions and Related Programs, 28% Visual and Performing Arts
Expenses: 2014-2015: $28,660; room/board: $10,530
Financial aid: (615) 460-6403; 54% of undergrads determined to have financial need; average aid package $13,958

Bethel University

McKenzie TN
(731) 352-4030
U.S. News ranking: Reg. U. (S), second tier
Website: www.bethel-college.edu
Admissions email: admissions@bethel-college.edu
Private
Affiliation: Cumberland Presbyterian Church
Freshman admissions: less selective; 2013-2014: 1,573 applied, 969 accepted. Neither SAT nor ACT required. ACT 25/75 percentile: 17-23. High school rank: N/A
Early decision deadline: N/A, notification date: N/A
Early action deadline: N/A, notification date: N/A
Application deadline (fall): rolling
Undergraduate student body: 3,606 full time, 633 part time; 44% male, 56% female; 0% American Indian, 0% Asian, 40% black, 1% Hispanic, 1% multiracial, 0% Pacific Islander, 55% white, 2% international; 86% from in state; 16% live on campus; N/A of students in fraternities, N/A in sororities
Most popular majors: 2% Biological and Biomedical Sciences, 54% Business, Management, Marketing, and Related Support Services, 4% Education, 3% Liberal Arts and Sciences, General Studies and Humanities, 2% Parks, Recreation, Leisure, and Fitness Studies
Expenses: 2013-2014: $15,714; room/board: $8,782
Financial aid: (731) 352-4233

Bryan College

Dayton TN
(800) 277-9522
U.S. News ranking: Reg. Coll. (S), No. 22
Website: www.bryan.edu
Admissions email: admissions@bryan.edu
Private; founded 1930

Affiliation: Christian nondenominational
Freshman admissions: more selective; 2013-2014: 1,151 applied, 433 accepted. Either SAT or ACT required. ACT 25/75 percentile: 20-25. High school rank: N/A
Early decision deadline: N/A, notification date: N/A
Early action deadline: N/A, notification date: N/A
Application deadline (fall): rolling
Undergraduate student body: 1,129 full time, 444 part time; 44% male, 56% female; 0% American Indian, 0% Asian, 6% black, 2% Hispanic, 2% multiracial, 0% Pacific Islander, 86% white, 2% international
Most popular majors: 60% Business, Management, Marketing, and Related Support Services, 4% Communication, Journalism, and Related Programs, 5% Education, 4% Psychology, 4% Visual and Performing Arts
Expenses: 2014-2015: $22,200; room/board: $6,550
Financial aid: (423) 775-7339; 81% of undergrads determined to have financial need; average aid package $22,005

Carson-Newman University

Jefferson City TN
(800) 678-9061
U.S. News ranking: Reg. Coll. (S), No. 15
Website: www.cn.edu
Admissions email: admitme@cn.edu
Private; founded 1851
Affiliation: Baptist
Freshman admissions: selective; 2013-2014: 3,916 applied, 2,607 accepted. Either SAT or ACT required. ACT 25/75 percentile: 20-26. High school rank: N/A
Early decision deadline: N/A, notification date: N/A
Early action deadline: N/A, notification date: N/A
Application deadline (fall): 8/8
Undergraduate student body: 1,658 full time, 55 part time; 45% male, 55% female; 0% American Indian, 1% Asian, 9% black, 1% Hispanic, 2% multiracial, 0% Pacific Islander, 82% white, 4% international; 81% from in state; 60% live on campus; N/A of students in fraternities, N/A in sororities
Most popular majors: Information not available
Expenses: 2014-2015: $24,440; room/board: $7,060
Financial aid: (865) 471-3247; 81% of undergrads determined to have financial need; average aid package $21,286

Christian Brothers University

Memphis TN
(901) 321-3205
U.S. News ranking: Reg. U. (S), No. 26
Website: www.cbu.edu
Admissions email: admissions@cbu.edu
Private; founded 1871
Affiliation: Roman Catholic
Freshman admissions: more selective; 2013-2014: 1,817 applied, 921 accepted. Either SAT or ACT required. ACT 25/75

percentile: 21-27. High school rank: 28% in top tenth, 60% in top quarter, 93% in top half
Early decision deadline: N/A, notification date: N/A
Early action deadline: N/A, notification date: N/A
Application deadline (fall): rolling
Undergraduate student body: 1,023 full time, 148 part time; 46% male, 54% female; 0% American Indian, 7% Asian, 32% black, 6% Hispanic, 3% multiracial, 0% Pacific Islander, 46% white, 3% international; 82% from in state; 45% live on campus; N/A of students in fraternities, N/A in sororities
Most popular majors: 10% Biological and Biomedical Sciences, 26% Business, Management, Marketing, and Related Support Services, 14% Engineering, 8% Health Professions and Related Programs, 16% Psychology
Expenses: 2014-2015: $29,190; room/board: $6,680
Financial aid: (901) 321-3305; 84% of undergrads determined to have financial need; average aid package $22,040

Cumberland University
Lebanon TN
(615) 444-2562
U.S. News ranking: Reg. U. (S), second tier
Website: www.cumberland.edu
Admissions email: admissions@cumberland.edu
Private; founded 1842
Freshman admissions: selective; 2013-2014: 795 applied, 376 accepted. ACT required. ACT 25/75 percentile: 19-23. High school rank: 9% in top tenth, 29% in top quarter, 66% in top half
Early decision deadline: N/A, notification date: N/A
Early action deadline: N/A, notification date: N/A
Application deadline (fall): rolling
Undergraduate student body: 1,056 full time, 213 part time; 46% male, 54% female; 0% American Indian, 1% Asian, 12% black, 3% Hispanic, 0% multiracial, 0% Pacific Islander, 67% white, 4% international
Most popular majors: 4% Accounting, 7% Business/Commerce, General, 4% Physical Education Teaching and Coaching, 53% Registered Nursing/Registered Nurse
Expenses: 2014-2015: $20,200; room/board: $8,000
Financial aid: (615) 444-2562; 86% of undergrads determined to have financial need; average aid package $16,665

East Tennessee State University[1]
Johnson City TN
(423) 439-4213
U.S. News ranking: Nat. U., second tier
Website: www.etsu.edu
Admissions email: go2etsu@etsu.edu
Public; founded 1911
Application deadline (fall): rolling
Undergraduate student body: N/A full time, N/A part time
Expenses: 2014-2015: $7,985 in state, $17,917 out of state; room/board: $7,822

Financial aid: (423) 439-4300; 82% of undergrads determined to have financial need; average aid package $9,043

Fisk University
Nashville TN
(888) 702-0022
U.S. News ranking: Nat. Lib. Arts, No. 165
Website: www.fisk.edu
Admissions email: admissions@fisk.edu
Private
Freshman admissions: selective; 2013-2014: 1,269 applied, 269 accepted. Either SAT or ACT required. ACT 25/75 percentile: 17-23. High school rank: N/A
Early decision deadline: N/A, notification date: N/A
Early action deadline: N/A, notification date: N/A
Application deadline (fall): 5/1
Undergraduate student body: 585 full time, 22 part time; 34% male, 66% female; 0% American Indian, 1% Asian, 87% black, 1% Hispanic, 1% multiracial, 0% Pacific Islander, 1% white, 0% international
Most popular majors: 12% Biology/Biological Sciences, General, 10% Business/Commerce, General, 12% English Language and Literature, General, 2% History, General, 18% Psychology, General
Expenses: 2014-2015: $20,858; room/board: $10,160
Financial aid: (615) 329-8585

Freed-Hardeman University
Henderson TN
(800) 630-3480
U.S. News ranking: Reg. U. (S), No. 43
Website: www.fhu.edu
Admissions email: admissions@fhu.edu
Private; founded 1869
Affiliation: Church of Christ
Freshman admissions: selective; 2013-2014: 1,042 applied, 959 accepted. Either SAT or ACT required. ACT 25/75 percentile: 21-27. High school rank: 28% in top tenth, 55% in top quarter, 80% in top half
Early decision deadline: N/A, notification date: N/A
Early action deadline: N/A, notification date: N/A
Application deadline (fall): rolling
Undergraduate student body: 1,262 full time, 123 part time; 42% male, 58% female; 0% American Indian, 0% Asian, 6% black, 1% Hispanic, 2% multiracial, 0% Pacific Islander, 88% white, 2% international; 61% from in state; 81% live on campus; N/A of students in fraternities, N/A in sororities
Most popular majors: 8% Biological and Biomedical Sciences, 9% Business, Management, Marketing, and Related Support Services, 13% Education, 11% Multi/Interdisciplinary Studies, 13% Theology and Religious Vocations
Expenses: 2014-2015: $20,468; room/board: $7,464
Financial aid: (731) 989-6662; 82% of undergrads determined to have financial need; average aid package $16,915

King University
Bristol TN
(423) 652-4861
U.S. News ranking: Reg. U. (S), No. 85
Website: www.king.edu
Admissions email: admissions@king.edu
Private; founded 1867
Affiliation: Presbyterian
Freshman admissions: selective; 2013-2014: 933 applied, 595 accepted. Either SAT or ACT required. ACT 25/75 percentile: 20-25. High school rank: 16% in top tenth, 40% in top quarter, 74% in top half
Early decision deadline: N/A, notification date: N/A
Early action deadline: N/A, notification date: N/A
Application deadline (fall): rolling
Undergraduate student body: 2,043 full time, 153 part time; 34% male, 66% female; 0% American Indian, 1% Asian, 6% black, 2% Hispanic, 1% multiracial, 0% Pacific Islander, 81% white, 3% international; 65% from in state; 42% live on campus; 0% of students in fraternities, 0% in sororities
Most popular majors: 35% Business Administration and Management, General, 2% Elementary Education and Teaching, 5% Information Technology, 3% Psychology, General, 42% Registered Nursing/Registered Nurse
Expenses: 2014-2015: $25,708; room/board: $8,180
Financial aid: (423) 652-4725; 88% of undergrads determined to have financial need; average aid package $15,001

Lane College[1]
Jackson TN
(731) 426-7533
U.S. News ranking: Nat. Lib. Arts, second tier
Website: www.lanecollege.edu
Admissions email: admissions@lanecollege.edu
Private; founded 1882
Affiliation: Christian Methodist Episcopal
Application deadline (fall): 8/1
Undergraduate student body: N/A full time, N/A part time
Expenses: 2013-2014: $9,180; room/board: $6,520
Financial aid: (731) 426-7535

Lee University
Cleveland TN
(423) 614-8500
U.S. News ranking: Reg. U. (S), No. 57
Website: www.leeuniversity.edu
Admissions email: admissions@leeuniversity.edu
Private; founded 1918
Affiliation: Pentecostal
Freshman admissions: selective; 2013-2014: 1,689 applied, 1,548 accepted. Either SAT or ACT required. ACT 25/75 percentile: 21-27. High school rank: 25% in top tenth, 49% in top quarter, 74% in top half
Early decision deadline: N/A, notification date: N/A
Early action deadline: N/A, notification date: N/A
Application deadline (fall): rolling

Undergraduate student body: 3,830 full time, 720 part time; 43% male, 57% female; 0% American Indian, 1% Asian, 6% black, 4% Hispanic, 1% multiracial, 0% Pacific Islander, 78% white, 5% international; 43% from in state; 47% live on campus; 9% of students in fraternities, 8% in sororities
Most popular majors: 8% Business, Management, Marketing, and Related Support Services, 24% Education, 10% Health Professions and Related Programs, 12% Psychology, 17% Theology and Religious Vocations
Expenses: 2014-2015: $14,280; room/board: $6,865
Financial aid: (423) 614-8300; 72% of undergrads determined to have financial need; average aid package $10,481

LeMoyne-Owen College
Memphis TN
(901) 435-1500
U.S. News ranking: Reg. Coll. (S), second tier
Website: www.loc.edu/
Admissions email: admission@loc.edu
Private; founded 1862
Affiliation: United Church of Christ
Freshman admissions: less selective; 2013-2014: 1,247 applied, 342 accepted. Either SAT or ACT required. ACT 25/75 percentile: N/A. High school rank: N/A
Early decision deadline: N/A, notification date: N/A
Early action deadline: N/A, notification date: N/A
Application deadline (fall): 7/1
Undergraduate student body: 879 full time, 144 part time; 36% male, 64% female; 0% American Indian, 0% Asian, 99% black, 0% Hispanic, 0% multiracial, 0% Pacific Islander, 0% white, 1% international; 88% from in state; 10% live on campus; 5% of students in fraternities, 5% in sororities
Most popular majors: Information not available
Expenses: 2014-2015: $5,450; room/board: $5,910
Financial aid: (901) 942-7313; 97% of undergrads determined to have financial need; average aid package $9,981

Lincoln Memorial University
Harrogate TN
(423) 869-6280
U.S. News ranking: Reg. U. (S), No. 53
Website: www.lmunet.edu
Admissions email: admissions@lmunet.edu
Private; founded 1897
Freshman admissions: selective; 2013-2014: 975 applied, 682 accepted. Either SAT or ACT required. ACT 25/75 percentile: 19-27. High school rank: N/A
Early decision deadline: N/A, notification date: N/A
Early action deadline: N/A, notification date: N/A
Application deadline (fall): rolling
Undergraduate student body: 1,185 full time, 528 part time; 29% male, 71% female; 0% American

Indian, 1% Asian, 4% black, 2% Hispanic, 1% multiracial, 0% Pacific Islander, 84% white, 2% international; 74% from in state; 37% live on campus; 3% of students in fraternities, 4% in sororities
Most popular majors: Information not available
Expenses: 2014-2015: $19,970; room/board: $9,700
Financial aid: (423) 869-6336; 86% of undergrads determined to have financial need; average aid package $17,135

Lipscomb University
Nashville TN
(615) 966-1776
U.S. News ranking: Reg. U. (S), No. 18
Website: www.lipscomb.edu
Admissions email: admissions@lipscomb.edu
Private; founded 1891
Affiliation: Church of Christ
Freshman admissions: more selective; 2013-2014: 3,467 applied, 1,827 accepted. Either SAT or ACT required. ACT 25/75 percentile: 22-28. High school rank: 31% in top tenth, 55% in top quarter, 85% in top half
Early decision deadline: N/A, notification date: N/A
Early action deadline: N/A, notification date: N/A
Application deadline (fall): rolling
Undergraduate student body: 2,590 full time, 300 part time; 40% male, 60% female; 0% American Indian, 3% Asian, 8% black, 5% Hispanic, 2% multiracial, 0% Pacific Islander, 77% white, 2% international; 67% from in state; 52% live on campus; 16% of students in fraternities, 17% in sororities
Most popular majors: 12% Biological and Biomedical Sciences, 22% Business, Management, Marketing, and Related Support Services, 12% Education, 9% Health Professions and Related Programs, 7% Psychology
Expenses: 2014-2015: $27,390; room/board: $10,350
Financial aid: (615) 269-1791; 66% of undergrads determined to have financial need; average aid package $21,711

Martin Methodist College[1]
Pulaski TN
(931) 363-9804
U.S. News ranking: Reg. Coll. (S), unranked
Website: www.martinmethodist.edu
Admissions email: admit@martinmethodist.edu
Private
Application deadline (fall): N/A
Undergraduate student body: N/A full time, N/A part time
Expenses: 2014-2015: $23,100; room/board: $8,400
Financial aid: (931) 363-9821; 83% of undergrads determined to have financial need; average aid package $10,700

Maryville College
Maryville TN
(865) 981-8092
U.S. News ranking: Nat. Lib. Arts, second tier
Website: www.maryvillecollege.edu
Admissions email: admissions@maryvillecollege.edu
Private; founded 1819
Affiliation: Presbyterian
Freshman admissions: selective; 2013-2014: 2,196 applied, 1,594 accepted. Either SAT or ACT required. ACT 25/75 percentile: 21-26. High school rank: 14% in top tenth, 42% in top quarter, 79% in top half
Early decision deadline: N/A, notification date: N/A
Early action deadline: N/A, notification date: N/A
Application deadline (fall): 5/1
Undergraduate student body: 1,132 full time, 36 part time; 44% male, 56% female; 1% American Indian, 1% Asian, 7% black, 3% Hispanic, 2% multiracial, 0% Pacific Islander, 82% white, 4% international; 75% from in state; 70% live on campus; 0% of students in fraternities, 0% in sororities
Most popular majors: 10% Biological and Biomedical Sciences, 17% Business, Management, Marketing, and Related Support Services, 11% Education, 12% Psychology, 9% Visual and Performing Arts
Expenses: 2014-2015: $31,754; room/board: $10,088
Financial aid: (865) 981-8100; 85% of undergrads determined to have financial need; average aid package $30,274

Memphis College of Art[1]
Memphis TN
(800) 727-1088
U.S. News ranking: Arts, unranked
Website: www.mca.edu
Admissions email: info@mca.edu
Private
Application deadline (fall): N/A
Undergraduate student body: N/A full time, N/A part time
Expenses: 2014-2015: $28,870; room/board: $8,600
Financial aid: (901) 272-5136; 88% of undergrads determined to have financial need; average aid package $21,314

Middle Tennessee State University
Murfreesboro TN
(615) 898-2111
U.S. News ranking: Nat. U., second tier
Website: www.mtsu.edu
Admissions email: admissions@mtsu.edu
Public; founded 1911
Freshman admissions: selective; 2013-2014: 9,845 applied, 6,888 accepted. Either SAT or ACT required. ACT 25/75 percentile: 19-24. High school rank: 16% in top tenth, 43% in top quarter, 77% in top half
Early decision deadline: N/A, notification date: N/A
Early action deadline: N/A, notification date: N/A
Application deadline (fall): rolling

Undergraduate student body: 17,381 full time, 3,781 part time; 47% male, 53% female; 0% American Indian, 3% Asian, 21% black, 4% Hispanic, 3% multiracial, 0% Pacific Islander, 67% white, 1% international; 96% from in state; 19% live on campus; 5% of students in fraternities, 8% in sororities
Most popular majors: 13% Business, Management, Marketing, and Related Support Services, 7% Communication, Journalism, and Related Programs, 8% Education, 10% Liberal Arts and Sciences, General Studies and Humanities, 10% Visual and Performing Arts
Expenses: 2014-2015: $7,370 in state, $24,434 out of state; room/board: $8,302
Financial aid: (615) 898-2830; 78% of undergrads determined to have financial need; average aid package $8,850

Milligan College
Milligan College TN
(423) 461-8730
U.S. News ranking: Reg. Coll. (S), No. 9
Website: www.milligan.edu
Admissions email: admissions@milligan.edu
Private; founded 1866
Affiliation: Christian Churches/Churches of Christ
Freshman admissions: more selective; 2013-2014: 612 applied, 418 accepted. Either SAT or ACT required. ACT 25/75 percentile: 22-26. High school rank: N/A
Early decision deadline: N/A, notification date: N/A
Early action deadline: N/A, notification date: N/A
Application deadline (fall): 8/1
Undergraduate student body: 884 full time, 89 part time; 38% male, 62% female; 1% American Indian, 1% Asian, 5% black, 4% Hispanic, 2% multiracial, 0% Pacific Islander, 84% white, 3% international
Most popular majors: Information not available
Expenses: 2014-2015: $28,730; room/board: $6,250
Financial aid: (423) 461-8949; 83% of undergrads determined to have financial need; average aid package $21,085

Rhodes College
Memphis TN
(800) 844-5969
U.S. News ranking: Nat. Lib. Arts, No. 54
Website: www.rhodes.edu
Admissions email: adminfo@rhodes.edu
Private; founded 1848
Affiliation: Presbyterian (USA)
Freshman admissions: more selective; 2013-2014: 3,555 applied, 2,049 accepted. Either SAT or ACT required. ACT 25/75 percentile: 27-31. High school rank: 50% in top tenth, 82% in top quarter, 95% in top half
Early decision deadline: 11/1, notification date: 12/1
Early action deadline: 11/15, notification date: 1/15
Application deadline (fall): 1/15

Undergraduate student body: 2,014 full time, 13 part time; 42% male, 58% female; 0% American Indian, 6% Asian, 6% black, 3% Hispanic, 3% multiracial, 0% Pacific Islander, 76% white, 2% international; 27% from in state; 69% live on campus; 39% of students in fraternities, 60% in sororities
Most popular majors: 17% Biological and Biomedical Sciences, 15% Business, Management, Marketing, and Related Support Services, 11% English Language and Literature/Letters, 7% Physical Sciences, 22% Social Sciences
Expenses: 2014-2015: $41,572; room/board: $10,328
Financial aid: (901) 843-3810; 52% of undergrads determined to have financial need; average aid package $31,684

Sewanee–University of the South
Sewanee TN
(800) 522-2234
U.S. News ranking: Nat. Lib. Arts, No. 45
Website: www.sewanee.edu
Admissions email: admiss@sewanee.edu
Private; founded 1857
Affiliation: Episcopal
Freshman admissions: more selective; 2013-2014: 3,285 applied, 1,980 accepted. Neither SAT nor ACT required. ACT 25/75 percentile: 26-30. High school rank: 42% in top tenth, 72% in top quarter, 96% in top half
Early decision deadline: 11/15, notification date: 12/15
Early action deadline: 12/1, notification date: 1/25
Application deadline (fall): 2/1
Undergraduate student body: 1,602 full time, 18 part time; 49% male, 51% female; 0% American Indian, 2% Asian, 5% black, 4% Hispanic, 4% multiracial, 0% Pacific Islander, 83% white, 3% international; 24% from in state; 96% live on campus; 67% of students in fraternities, 72% in sororities
Most popular majors: 12% Biological and Biomedical Sciences, 13% English Language and Literature/Letters, 9% History, 10% Multi/Interdisciplinary Studies, 17% Social Sciences
Expenses: 2014-2015: $37,100; room/board: $10,600
Financial aid: (931) 598-1312; 58% of undergrads determined to have financial need; average aid package $26,381

South College[1]
Knoxville TN
(865) 251-1800
U.S. News ranking: Reg. Coll. (S), unranked
Website: www.southcollegetn.edu/
Admissions email: N/A
For-profit
Application deadline (fall): N/A
Undergraduate student body: N/A full time, N/A part time
Expenses: 2013-2014: $18,875; room/board: N/A
Financial aid: (865) 251-1800

Southern Adventist University[1]
Collegedale TN
(423) 236-2844
U.S. News ranking: Reg. Coll. (S), No. 34
Website: www.southern.edu
Admissions email: admissions@southern.edu
Private; founded 1892
Affiliation: Seventh-day Adventist
Application deadline (fall): rolling
Undergraduate student body: N/A full time, N/A part time
Expenses: 2014-2015: $20,240; room/board: $5,850
Financial aid: (423) 236-2835

Tennessee State University
Nashville TN
(615) 963-5101
U.S. News ranking: Nat. U., second tier
Website: www.tnstate.edu
Admissions email: jcade@tnstate.edu
Public; founded 1912
Freshman admissions: less selective; 2013-2014: 6,286 applied, 3,328 accepted. Either SAT or ACT required. ACT 25/75 percentile: 16-20. High school rank: N/A
Early decision deadline: N/A, notification date: N/A
Early action deadline: N/A, notification date: N/A
Application deadline (fall): 7/1
Undergraduate student body: 5,356 full time, 1,393 part time; 39% male, 61% female; 0% American Indian, 1% Asian, 77% black, 1% Hispanic, 0% multiracial, 0% Pacific Islander, 15% white, 5% international; 77% from in state; N/A live on campus; N/A of students in fraternities, N/A in sororities
Most popular majors: Information not available
Expenses: 2014-2015: $6,776 in state, $20,132 out of state; room/board: $7,126
Financial aid: (615) 963-5701; 90% of undergrads determined to have financial need; average aid package $10,159

Tennessee Technological University
Cookeville TN
(800) 255-8881
U.S. News ranking: Reg. U. (S), No. 34
Website: www.tntech.edu
Admissions email: admissions@tntech.edu
Public; founded 1915
Freshman admissions: selective; 2013-2014: 4,973 applied, 4,633 accepted. Either SAT or ACT required. ACT 25/75 percentile: 20-26. High school rank: 25% in top tenth, 55% in top quarter, 83% in top half
Early decision deadline: N/A, notification date: N/A
Early action deadline: N/A, notification date: N/A
Application deadline (fall): rolling
Undergraduate student body: 9,140 full time, 943 part time; 56% male, 44% female; 0% American

Indian, 1% Asian, 4% black, 2% Hispanic, 2% multiracial, 0% Pacific Islander, 82% white, 7% international; 98% from in state; 53% live on campus; 9% of students in fraternities, 11% in sororities
Most popular majors: 5% Accounting, 7% Liberal Arts and Sciences/Liberal Studies, 5% Mechanical Engineering, 5% Registered Nursing/Registered Nurse, 16% Teacher Education, Multiple Levels
Expenses: 2014-2015: $7,950 in state, $23,450 out of state; room/board: $8,700
Financial aid: (931) 372-3073; 68% of undergrads determined to have financial need; average aid package $11,110

Tennessee Wesleyan College
Athens TN
(423) 746-5286
U.S. News ranking: Reg. Coll. (S), No. 41
Website: www.twcnet.edu
Admissions email: admissions@twcnet.edu
Private; founded 1857
Affiliation: United Methodist
Freshman admissions: selective; 2013-2014: 790 applied, 564 accepted. Either SAT or ACT required. ACT 25/75 percentile: 19-24. High school rank: 20% in top tenth, 20% in top quarter, 80% in top half
Early decision deadline: N/A, notification date: N/A
Early action deadline: N/A, notification date: N/A
Application deadline (fall): 8/31
Undergraduate student body: 988 full time, 77 part time; 38% male, 62% female; 0% American Indian, 1% Asian, 8% black, 2% Hispanic, 2% multiracial, 0% Pacific Islander, 83% white, 1% international; 90% from in state; 32% live on campus; 4% of students in fraternities, 8% in sororities
Most popular majors: 28% Business, Management, Marketing, and Related Support Services, 13% Education, 23% Health Professions and Related Programs, 7% Multi/Interdisciplinary Studies, 8% Parks, Recreation, Leisure, and Fitness Studies
Expenses: 2014-2015: $22,300; room/board: $7,100
Financial aid: (423) 746-5209; 83% of undergrads determined to have financial need; average aid package $15,994

Trevecca Nazarene University
Nashville TN
(615) 248-1320
U.S. News ranking: Nat. U., second tier
Website: www.trevecca.edu
Admissions email: admissions_und@trevecca.edu
Private; founded 1901
Affiliation: Nazarene
Freshman admissions: selective; 2013-2014: 903 applied, 618 accepted. Either SAT or ACT required. ACT 25/75 percentile: 21-26. High school rank: N/A
Early decision deadline: N/A, notification date: N/A

Early action deadline: N/A, notification date: N/A
Application deadline (fall): 8/1
Undergraduate student body: 1,016 full time, 476 part time; 45% male, 55% female; 1% American Indian, 1% Asian, 8% black, 3% Hispanic, 2% multiracial, 0% Pacific Islander, 71% white, 1% international; 63% from in state; 50% live on campus; 0% of students in fraternities, 0% in sororities
Most popular majors: 46% Business, Management, Marketing, and Related Support Services, 8% Computer and Information Sciences and Support Services, 10% Education, 6% Health Professions and Related Programs, 6% Theology and Religious Vocations
Expenses: 2014-2015: $23,126; room/board: $8,060
Financial aid: (615) 248-1242

Tusculum College[1]

Greeneville TN
(800) 729-0256
U.S. News ranking: Reg. U. (S), second tier
Website: www.tusculum.edu
Admissions email: admissions@tusculum.edu
Private
Application deadline (fall): N/A
Undergraduate student body: N/A full time, N/A part time
Expenses: 2013-2014: $22,250; room/board: $8,500
Financial aid: (423) 636-7377

Union University

Jackson TN
(800) 338-6466
U.S. News ranking: Reg. U. (S), No. 12
Website: www.uu.edu
Admissions email: info@uu.edu
Private; founded 1823
Affiliation: Southern Baptist
Freshman admissions: more selective; 2013-2014: 1,930 applied, 1,432 accepted. Either SAT or ACT required. ACT 25/75 percentile: 22-29. High school rank: 33% in top tenth, 62% in top quarter, 85% in top half
Early decision deadline: N/A, notification date: N/A
Early action deadline: N/A, notification date: N/A
Application deadline (fall): 8/15
Undergraduate student body: 2,172 full time, 657 part time; 39% male, 61% female; 0% American Indian, 1% Asian, 14% black, 2% Hispanic, 2% multiracial, 0% Pacific Islander, 77% white, 2% international; 69% from in state; 65% live on campus; 27% of students in fraternities, 23% in sororities
Most popular majors: Information not available
Expenses: 2014-2015: $28,190; room/board: $8,430
Financial aid: (731) 661-5015; 76% of undergrads determined to have financial need; average aid package $18,303

University of Memphis

Memphis TN
(901) 678-2111
U.S. News ranking: Nat. U., second tier
Website: www.memphis.edu
Admissions email: recruitment@memphis.edu
Public; founded 1912
Freshman admissions: selective; 2013-2014: 6,107 applied, 4,470 accepted. Either SAT or ACT required. ACT 25/75 percentile: 20-26. High school rank: 16% in top tenth, 43% in top quarter, 75% in top half
Early decision deadline: N/A, notification date: N/A
Early action deadline: N/A, notification date: N/A
Application deadline (fall): 7/1
Undergraduate student body: 12,317 full time, 4,904 part time; 40% male, 60% female; 0% American Indian, 3% Asian, 38% black, 3% Hispanic, 3% multiracial, 0% Pacific Islander, 51% white, 1% international; 97% from in state; 13% live on campus; 3% of students in fraternities, 8% in sororities
Most popular majors: 18% Business, Management, Marketing, and Related Support Services, 9% Education, 9% Health Professions and Related Programs, 6% Liberal Arts and Sciences, General Studies and Humanities, 10% Multi/Interdisciplinary Studies
Expenses: 2014-2015: $8,619 in state, $13,275 out of state; room/board: $8,976
Financial aid: (901) 678-4825; 78% of undergrads determined to have financial need; average aid package $9,087

University of Tennessee

Knoxville TN
(865) 974-2184
U.S. News ranking: Nat. U., No. 106
Website: admissions.utk.edu/undergraduate
Admissions email: admissions@utk.edu
Public; founded 1794
Freshman admissions: more selective; 2013-2014: 14,396 applied, 10,435 accepted. Either SAT or ACT required. ACT 25/75 percentile: 24-29. High school rank: 52% in top tenth, 91% in top quarter, 100% in top half
Early decision deadline: N/A, notification date: N/A
Early action deadline: N/A, notification date: N/A
Application deadline (fall): 12/1
Undergraduate student body: 19,799 full time, 1,383 part time; 51% male, 49% female; 0% American Indian, 3% Asian, 7% black, 3% Hispanic, 3% multiracial, 0% Pacific Islander, 81% white, 2% international; 91% from in state; 37% live on campus; 14% of students in fraternities, 21% in sororities
Most popular majors: 20% Business, Management, Marketing, and Related Support Services, 8% Communication, Journalism, and Related Programs, 9% Engineering, 10% Psychology, 10% Social Sciences

Expenses: 2014-2015: $11,246 in state, $29,696 out of state; room/board: $10,296
Financial aid: (865) 974-3131; 61% of undergrads determined to have financial need; average aid package $12,126

University of Tennessee–Chattanooga

Chattanooga TN
(423) 425-4662
U.S. News ranking: Reg. U. (S), No. 57
Website: www.utc.edu
Admissions email: utcmocs@utc.edu
Public; founded 1886
Freshman admissions: selective; 2013-2014: 7,628 applied, 5,917 accepted. Either SAT or ACT required. ACT 25/75 percentile: 21-25. High school rank: N/A in top tenth, 45% in top quarter, 86% in top half
Early decision deadline: N/A, notification date: N/A
Early action deadline: N/A, notification date: N/A
Application deadline (fall): 5/1
Undergraduate student body: 9,066 full time, 1,231 part time; 45% male, 55% female; 0% American Indian, 2% Asian, 11% black, 3% Hispanic, 8% multiracial, 0% Pacific Islander, 74% white, 1% international; 94% from in state; 31% live on campus; 9% of students in fraternities, 13% in sororities
Most popular majors: 22% Business Administration and Management, General, 11% Education, General, 6% Engineering, General, 7% Kinesiology and Exercise Science, 8% Psychology, General
Expenses: 2014-2015: $8,138 in state, $24,256 out of state; room/board: $8,110
Financial aid: (423) 425-4677; 62% of undergrads determined to have financial need; average aid package $9,571

University of Tennessee–Martin

Martin TN
(800) 829-8861
U.S. News ranking: Reg. U. (S), No. 53
Website: www.utm.edu
Admissions email: admitme@utm.edu
Public; founded 1900
Freshman admissions: selective; 2013-2014: 3,640 applied, 2,791 accepted. Either SAT or ACT required. ACT 25/75 percentile: 20-25. High school rank: 27% in top tenth, 59% in top quarter, 87% in top half
Early decision deadline: N/A, notification date: N/A
Early action deadline: N/A, notification date: N/A
Application deadline (fall): 8/1
Undergraduate student body: 5,927 full time, 1,098 part time; 42% male, 58% female; 0% American Indian, 0% Asian, 17% black, 2% Hispanic, 2% multiracial, 0% Pacific Islander, 76% white, 3% international; 96% from in state; 30% live on campus; 8% of students in fraternities, 10% in sororities

Most popular majors: 7% Agriculture, Agriculture Operations, and Related Sciences, 18% Marketing/Marketing Management, General, 13% Multi/Interdisciplinary Studies, Other, 9% Parks, Recreation, Leisure, and Fitness Studies, 12% Teacher Education and Professional Development, Specific Levels and Methods
Expenses: 2014-2015: $7,880 in state, $22,660 out of state; room/board: $7,141
Financial aid: (731) 587-7040; 77% of undergrads determined to have financial need; average aid package $13,357

Vanderbilt University

Nashville TN
(800) 288-0432
U.S. News ranking: Nat. U., No. 16
Website: www.vanderbilt.edu
Admissions email: admissions@vanderbilt.edu
Private; founded 1873
Freshman admissions: most selective; 2013-2014: 31,099 applied, 3,963 accepted. Either SAT or ACT required. ACT 25/75 percentile: 32-34. High school rank: 88% in top tenth, 95% in top quarter, 98% in top half
Early decision deadline: 11/1, notification date: 12/15
Early action deadline: N/A, notification date: N/A
Application deadline (fall): 1/1
Undergraduate student body: 6,764 full time, 71 part time; 50% male, 50% female; 0% American Indian, 8% Asian, 8% black, 8% Hispanic, 5% multiracial, 0% Pacific Islander, 61% white, 6% international; 12% from in state; 86% live on campus; 30% of students in fraternities, 55% in sororities
Most popular majors: 11% Economics, General, 5% Mathematics, General, 9% Multi-/Interdisciplinary Studies, Other, 5% Political Science and Government, General, 9% Social Sciences, General
Expenses: 2014-2015: $43,838; room/board: $14,382
Financial aid: (615) 322-3591; 49% of undergrads determined to have financial need; average aid package $44,720

Victory University[1]

Memphis TN
(901) 320-9797
U.S. News ranking: Reg. Coll. (S), second tier
Website: www.victory.edu
Admissions email: admissions@victory.edu
For-profit
Application deadline (fall): N/A
Undergraduate student body: N/A full time, N/A part time
Expenses: 2013-2014: $9,760; room/board: $10,116
Financial aid: (901) 320-9787

Watkins College of Art, Design & Film[1]

Nashville TN
(615) 383-4848
U.S. News ranking: Arts, unranked
Website: www.watkins.edu
Admissions email: admission@watkins.edu
Private
Application deadline (fall): N/A
Undergraduate student body: N/A full time, N/A part time
Expenses: 2013-2014: $19,710; room/board: $9,390
Financial aid: (615) 383-4848

Welch College

Nashville TN
(888) 979-3524
U.S. News ranking: Reg. Coll. (S), No. 52
Website: www.welch.edu
Admissions email: Recruit@welch.edu
Private; founded 1942
Affiliation: Free Will Baptist
Freshman admissions: selective; 2013-2014: 167 applied, 87 accepted. Either SAT or ACT required. ACT 25/75 percentile: 18-25. High school rank: 22% in top tenth, 42% in top quarter, 60% in top half
Early decision deadline: N/A, notification date: N/A
Early action deadline: N/A, notification date: N/A
Application deadline (fall): rolling
Undergraduate student body: 234 full time, 104 part time; 51% male, 49% female; 0% American Indian, 1% Asian, 10% black, 2% Hispanic, 1% multiracial, 0% Pacific Islander, 85% white, 1% international; 46% from in state; 68% live on campus; 84% of students in fraternities, 96% in sororities
Most popular majors: 8% Biological and Biomedical Sciences, 8% Business, Management, Marketing, and Related Support Services, 30% Education, 8% Psychology, 32% Theology and Religious Vocations
Expenses: 2014-2015: $16,891; room/board: $6,842
Financial aid: (615) 844-5250; 89% of undergrads determined to have financial need; average aid package $12,160

TEXAS

Abilene Christian University

Abilene TX
(800) 460-6228
U.S. News ranking: Reg. U. (W), No. 17
Website: www.acu.edu
Admissions email: info@admissions.acu.edu
Private; founded 1906
Affiliation: Church of Christ
Freshman admissions: more selective; 2013-2014: 10,188 applied, 4,986 accepted. Either SAT or ACT required. ACT 25/75 percentile: 21-27. High school rank: 25% in top tenth, 57% in top quarter, 87% in top half
Early decision deadline: N/A, notification date: N/A
Early action deadline: 11/1, notification date: 12/1

Application deadline (fall): 2/15
Undergraduate student body: 3,510 full time, 217 part time; 43% male, 57% female; 0% American Indian, 1% Asian, 8% black, 12% Hispanic, 4% multiracial, 0% Pacific Islander, 71% white, 4% international; 84% from in state; 48% live on campus; 24% of students in fraternities, 24% in sororities
Most popular majors: 7% Accounting, 7% Business Administration and Management, General, 4% Elementary Education and Teaching, 7% Human Development and Family Studies, General, 5% Psychology, General
Expenses: 2014-2015: $29,450; room/board: $9,000
Financial aid: (325) 674-2643; 68% of undergrads determined to have financial need; average aid package $20,300

Amberton University[1]
Garland TX
(972) 279-6511
U.S. News ranking: Reg. U. (W), unranked
Website: www.amberton.edu
Admissions email: advisor@amberton.edu
Private
Application deadline (fall): N/A
Undergraduate student body: N/A full time, N/A part time
Expenses: N/A
Financial aid: (972) 279-6511

Angelo State University
San Angelo TX
(325) 942-2041
U.S. News ranking: Reg. U. (W), second tier
Website: www.angelo.edu
Admissions email: admissions@angelo.edu
Public; founded 1928
Freshman admissions: selective; 2013-2014: 2,599 applied, 2,092 accepted. Either SAT or ACT required. ACT 25/75 percentile: 18-23. High school rank: 11% in top tenth, 35% in top quarter, 73% in top half
Early decision deadline: N/A, notification date: N/A
Early action deadline: N/A, notification date: N/A
Undergraduate student body: 4,726 full time, 820 part time; 46% male, 54% female; 0% American Indian, 1% Asian, 8% black, 30% Hispanic, 2% multiracial, 0% Pacific Islander, 55% white, 3% international; 97% from in state; 20% live on campus; 5% of students in fraternities, 3% in sororities
Most popular majors: 6% Agriculture, Agriculture Operations, and Related Sciences, 13% Business, Management, Marketing, and Related Support Services, 14% Health Professions and Related Programs, 14% Multi/Interdisciplinary Studies, 7% Psychology
Expenses: 2014-2015: $7,642 in state, $18,502 out of state; room/board; $7,484
Financial aid: (325) 942-2246; 69% of undergrads determined to have financial need; average aid package $10,579

Art Institute of Houston[1]
Houston TX
(800) 275-4244
U.S. News ranking: Arts, unranked
Website: www.artinstitute.edu/houston/
Admissions email: N/A
For-profit
Application deadline (fall): N/A
Undergraduate student body: N/A full time, N/A part time
Expenses: 2013-2014: $17,668; room/board: $11,367
Financial aid: (713) 353-4311

Austin College
Sherman TX
(800) 442-5363
U.S. News ranking: Nat. Lib. Arts, No. 89
Website: www.austincollege.edu
Admissions email: admission@austincollege.edu
Private; founded 1849
Affiliation: Presbyterian
Freshman admissions: more selective; 2013-2014: 3,138 applied, 1,839 accepted. Either SAT or ACT required. SAT 25/75 percentile: 1100-1330. High school rank: 35% in top tenth, 74% in top quarter, 95% in top half
Early decision deadline: N/A, notification date: N/A
Early action deadline: 1/15, notification date: 3/1
Application deadline (fall): 5/1
Undergraduate student body: 1,204 full time, 4 part time; 49% male, 51% female; 1% American Indian, 15% Asian, 6% black, 16% Hispanic, 1% multiracial, 0% Pacific Islander, 58% white, 3% international; 91% from in state; 81% live on campus; 20% of students in fraternities, 16% in sororities
Most popular majors: 7% Biological and Biomedical Sciences, 11% Business, Management, Marketing, and Related Support Services, 7% Foreign Languages, Literatures, and Linguistics, 16% Psychology, 18% Social Sciences
Expenses: 2014-2015: $34,840; room/board: $11,503
Financial aid: (903) 813-2900; 67% of undergrads determined to have financial need; average aid package $28,827

Baylor University
Waco TX
(800) 229-5678
U.S. News ranking: Nat. U., No. 71
Website: www.baylor.edu
Admissions email: Admissions@Baylor.edu
Private; founded 1845
Affiliation: Baptist
Freshman admissions: more selective; 2013-2014: 29,249 applied, 16,809 accepted. Either SAT or ACT required. ACT 25/75 percentile: 24-29. High school rank: 42% in top tenth, 75% in top quarter, 97% in top half
Early decision deadline: N/A, notification date: N/A
Early action deadline: 11/1, notification date: 1/15
Application deadline (fall): 2/1
Undergraduate student body: 13,059 full time, 233 part time; 42% male, 58% female;

0% American Indian, 6% Asian, 7% black, 14% Hispanic, 5% multiracial, 0% Pacific Islander, 64% white, 3% international; 76% from in state; 40% live on campus; 14% of students in fraternities, 22% in sororities
Most popular majors: 4% Accounting, 9% Biology/Biological Sciences, General, 4% Finance, General, 6% Psychology, General, 6% Registered Nursing/Registered Nurse
Expenses: 2014-2015: $38,290; room/board: $11,309
Financial aid: (254) 710-2611; 58% of undergrads determined to have financial need; average aid package $24,975

Brazosport College[1]
Lake Jackson TX
(979) 230-3020
U.S. News ranking: Reg. Coll. (W), unranked
Website: www.brazosport.edu
Admissions email: N/A
Public
Application deadline (fall): N/A
Undergraduate student body: N/A full time, N/A part time
Expenses: 2013-2014: $3,315 in state, $4,725 out of state; room/board: N/A
Financial aid: (979) 230-0337

College of Saints John Fisher & Thomas More[1]
Fort Worth TX
(817) 923-8459
U.S. News ranking: Nat. Lib. Arts, second tier
Website: fishermore.edu/
Admissions email: more-Info@cstm.edu
Private
Application deadline (fall): N/A
Undergraduate student body: N/A full time, N/A part time
Expenses: N/A
Financial aid: (325) 673-1934

Concordia University Texas[1]
Austin TX
(800) 865-4282
U.S. News ranking: Reg. U. (W), second tier
Website: www.concordia.edu
Admissions email: admissions@concordia.edu
Private; founded 1926
Affiliation: Lutheran Church-Missouri Synod
Application deadline (fall): 8/1
Undergraduate student body: N/A full time, N/A part time
Expenses: 2014-2015: $26,960; room/board: $8,980
Financial aid: (512) 486-1283; 76% of undergrads determined to have financial need; average aid package $18,951

Dallas Baptist University
Dallas TX
(214) 333-5360
U.S. News ranking: Reg. U. (W), No. 35
Website: www.dbu.edu
Admissions email: admiss@dbu.edu
Private; founded 1898
Affiliation: Baptist

Freshman admissions: selective; 2013-2014: 2,631 applied, 1,113 accepted. Either SAT or ACT required. ACT 25/75 percentile: 18-27. High school rank: 20% in top tenth, 46% in top quarter, 77% in top half
Early decision deadline: N/A, notification date: N/A
Early action deadline: N/A, notification date: N/A
Application deadline (fall): rolling
Undergraduate student body: 2,463 full time, 972 part time; 42% male, 58% female; 1% American Indian, 2% Asian, 16% black, 12% Hispanic, 0% multiracial, 0% Pacific Islander, 62% white, 6% international; 90% from in state; 54% live on campus; 7% of students in fraternities, 10% in sororities
Most popular majors: 15% Business Administration and Management, General, 15% Multi-/Interdisciplinary Studies, Other, 9% Psychology, General, 9% Religious Education, 7% Speech Communication and Rhetoric
Expenses: 2014-2015: $23,650; room/board: $6,930
Financial aid: (214) 333-5460; 64% of undergrads determined to have financial need; average aid package $15,400

East Texas Baptist University
Marshall TX
(800) 804-3828
U.S. News ranking: Reg. Coll. (W), No. 13
Website: www.etbu.edu
Admissions email: admissions@etbu.edu
Private; founded 1912
Affiliation: Baptist
Freshman admissions: selective; 2013-2014: 709 applied, 522 accepted. Either SAT or ACT required. ACT 25/75 percentile: 18-22. High school rank: 16% in top tenth, 40% in top quarter, 75% in top half
Early decision deadline: N/A, notification date: N/A
Early action deadline: N/A, notification date: N/A
Application deadline (fall): 8/21
Undergraduate student body: 1,066 full time, 130 part time; 47% male, 53% female; 1% American Indian, 0% Asian, 18% black, 10% Hispanic, 3% multiracial, 0% Pacific Islander, 66% white, 1% international; 93% from in state; 85% live on campus; 2% of students in fraternities, 1% in sororities
Most popular majors: 15% Business, Management, Marketing, and Related Support Services, 19% Education, 11% Health Professions and Related Programs, 14% Multi/Interdisciplinary Studies, 8% Psychology
Expenses: 2014-2015: $23,280; room/board: $8,297
Financial aid: (903) 923-2137; 86% of undergrads determined to have financial need; average aid package $17,276

Hardin-Simmons University
Abilene TX
(325) 670-1206
U.S. News ranking: Reg. U. (W), No. 35
Website: www.hsutx.edu/
Admissions email: enroll@hsutx.edu
Private; founded 1891
Affiliation: Baptist
Freshman admissions: selective; 2013-2014: 2,091 applied, 786 accepted. Either SAT or ACT required. ACT 25/75 percentile: 20-25. High school rank: 19% in top tenth, 56% in top quarter, 83% in top half
Early decision deadline: N/A, notification date: N/A
Early action deadline: N/A, notification date: N/A
Application deadline (fall): rolling
Undergraduate student body: 1,561 full time, 229 part time; 48% male, 52% female; 0% American Indian, 2% Asian, 6% black, 15% Hispanic, 2% multiracial, 0% Pacific Islander, 71% white, 2% international; 96% from in state; 45% live on campus; 3% of students in fraternities, 5% in sororities
Most popular majors: 9% Biological and Biomedical Sciences, 12% Business, Management, Marketing, and Related Support Services, 13% Education, 12% Health Professions and Related Programs, 14% Parks, Recreation, Leisure, and Fitness Studies
Expenses: 2014-2015: $22,350; room/board: $6,962
Financial aid: (325) 670-5891; 72% of undergrads determined to have financial need; average aid package $20,386

Houston Baptist University
Houston TX
(281) 649-3211
U.S. News ranking: Reg. U. (W), No. 68
Website: www.hbu.edu
Admissions email: admissions@hbu.edu
Private; founded 1960
Affiliation: Baptist
Freshman admissions: selective; 2013-2014: 11,892 applied, 4,310 accepted. Either SAT or ACT required. SAT 25/75 percentile: 960-1170. High school rank: 21% in top tenth, 53% in top quarter, 80% in top half
Early decision deadline: N/A, notification date: N/A
Early action deadline: N/A, notification date: N/A
Application deadline (fall): rolling
Undergraduate student body: 2,005 full time, 166 part time; 37% male, 63% female; 0% American Indian, 13% Asian, 19% black, 26% Hispanic, 7% multiracial, 0% Pacific Islander, 28% white, 4% international; 96% from in state; 33% live on campus; 10% of students in fraternities, 11% in sororities
Most popular majors: 16% Biology/Biological Sciences, General, 17% Business/Commerce, General, 8% Education, General, 8% Psychology, General, 14% Registered Nursing/Registered Nurse
Expenses: 2014-2015: $28,750; room/board: $6,740

Financial aid: (281) 649-3389; 76% of undergrads determined to have financial need; average aid package $24,867

Howard Payne University

Brownwood TX
(325) 649-8020
U.S. News ranking: Reg. Coll. (W), No. 15
Website: www.hputx.edu
Admissions email: enroll@hputx.edu
Private; founded 1889
Affiliation: Baptist
Freshman admissions: less selective; 2013-2014: 1,572 applied, 844 accepted. Either SAT or ACT required. SAT 25/75 percentile: 860-1050. High school rank: 5% in top tenth, 24% in top quarter, 61% in top half
Early decision deadline: N/A, notification date: N/A
Early action deadline: N/A, notification date: N/A
Application deadline (fall): rolling
Undergraduate student body: 983 full time, 117 part time; 53% male, 47% female; 0% American Indian, 0% Asian, 9% black, 20% Hispanic, 3% multiracial, 0% Pacific Islander, 65% white, 0% international; 98% from in state; 59% live on campus; 7% of students in fraternities, 10% in sororities
Most popular majors: 14% Business, Management, Marketing, and Related Support Services, 11% Education, 10% Parks, Recreation, Leisure, and Fitness Studies, 9% Social Sciences, 11% Theology and Religious Vocations
Expenses: 2014-2015: $24,600; room/board: $7,154
Financial aid: (325) 649-8014; 85% of undergrads determined to have financial need; average aid package $17,043

Huston-Tillotson University[1]

Austin TX
(512) 505-3029
U.S. News ranking: Nat. Lib. Arts, second tier
Website: htu.edu/
Admissions email: admission@htu.edu
Private
Application deadline (fall): N/A
Undergraduate student body: N/A full time, N/A part time
Expenses: 2013-2014: $13,494; room/board: $7,242
Financial aid: (512) 505-3031

Jarvis Christian College

Hawkins TX
(903) 730-4890
U.S. News ranking: Reg. Coll. (W), second tier
Website: www.jarvis.edu
Admissions email: Recruitment@jarvis.edu
Private; founded 1912
Affiliation: Christian Church (Disciples of Christ)
Freshman admissions: least selective; 2013-2014: 453 applied, 453 accepted. Either SAT or ACT required. ACT 25/75

percentile: 13-18. High school rank: 1% in top tenth, 8% in top quarter, 26% in top half
Early decision deadline: N/A, notification date: N/A
Early action deadline: N/A, notification date: N/A
Application deadline (fall): 8/1
Undergraduate student body: 569 full time, 40 part time; 54% male, 46% female; 0% American Indian, 0% Asian, 88% black, 7% Hispanic, 0% multiracial, 0% Pacific Islander, 4% white, 0% international; 84% from in state; 77% live on campus; 12% of students in fraternities, 2% in sororities
Most popular majors: 14% Biological and Biomedical Sciences, 14% Business, Management, Marketing, and Related Support Services, 21% Education, 33% Homeland Security, Law Enforcement, Firefighting and Related Protective Services, 7% Public Administration and Social Service Professions
Expenses: 2014-2015: $11,369; room/board: $8,183
Financial aid: (903) 769-5740; 96% of undergrads determined to have financial need; average aid package $17,996

Lamar University

Beaumont TX
(409) 880-8888
U.S. News ranking: Nat. U., second tier
Website: www.lamar.edu
Admissions email: admissions@lamar.edu
Public; founded 1923
Freshman admissions: selective; 2013-2014: 4,720 applied, 3,616 accepted. Either SAT or ACT required. SAT 25/75 percentile: 870-1080. High school rank: 15% in top tenth, 37% in top quarter, 70% in top half
Early decision deadline: N/A, notification date: N/A
Early action deadline: N/A, notification date: N/A
Application deadline (fall): 8/1
Undergraduate student body: 6,604 full time, 2,778 part time; 42% male, 58% female; 0% American Indian, 4% Asian, 30% black, 11% Hispanic, 2% multiracial, 0% Pacific Islander, 49% white, 2% international; 95% from in state; 21% live on campus; 4% of students in fraternities, 2% in sororities
Most popular majors: 14% Business, Management, Marketing, and Related Support Services, 7% Engineering, 8% General Studies, 11% Health Professions and Related Programs, 19% Multi-/Interdisciplinary Studies, Other
Expenses: 2014-2015: $9,361 in state, $19,681 out of state; room/board: $8,052
Financial aid: (409) 880-8450; 66% of undergrads determined to have financial need; average aid package $6,782

LeTourneau University

Longview TX
(903) 233-4300
U.S. News ranking: Reg. U. (W), No. 27
Website: www.letu.edu
Admissions email: admissions@letu.edu
Private; founded 1946
Affiliation: Christian interdenominational
Freshman admissions: more selective; 2013-2014: 1,831 applied, 758 accepted. Neither SAT nor ACT required. SAT 25/75 percentile: 1030-1300. High school rank: 47% in top tenth, 67% in top quarter, 89% in top half
Early decision deadline: N/A, notification date: N/A
Early action deadline: N/A, notification date: N/A
Application deadline (fall): rolling
Undergraduate student body: 1,332 full time, 973 part time; 53% male, 47% female; 0% American Indian, 1% Asian, 9% black, 9% Hispanic, 3% multiracial, 0% Pacific Islander, 64% white, 4% international; 54% from in state; 74% live on campus; N/A of students in fraternities, N/A in sororities
Most popular majors: 37% Business, Management, Marketing, and Related Support Services, 17% Education, 11% Engineering, 7% Engineering Technologies and Engineering-Related Fields, 7% Psychology
Expenses: 2014-2015: $26,910; room/board: $9,300
Financial aid: (903) 233-3430; 73% of undergrads determined to have financial need; average aid package $21,666

Lubbock Christian University

Lubbock TX
(806) 720-7151
U.S. News ranking: Reg. U. (W), No. 84
Website: www.lcu.edu
Admissions email: admissions@lcu.edu
Private; founded 1957
Affiliation: Churches of Christ
Freshman admissions: selective; 2013-2014: 783 applied, 743 accepted. Either SAT or ACT required. ACT 25/75 percentile: 19-24. High school rank: 17% in top tenth, 39% in top quarter, 77% in top half
Early decision deadline: N/A, notification date: N/A
Early action deadline: N/A, notification date: N/A
Application deadline (fall): 6/1
Undergraduate student body: 1,258 full time, 273 part time; 39% male, 61% female; 1% American Indian, 0% Asian, 6% black, 21% Hispanic, 0% multiracial, 0% Pacific Islander, 70% white, 2% international; 91% from in state; 33% live on campus; 19% of students in fraternities, 17% in sororities
Most popular majors: 18% Business, Management, Marketing, and Related Support Services, 17% Education, 25% Health Professions and Related Programs, 5% Parks, Recreation, Leisure, and Fitness Studies, 5% Public Administration and Social Service Professions

Expenses: 2014-2015: $19,400; room/board: $5,860
Financial aid: (800) 933-7601; 74% of undergrads determined to have financial need; average aid package $14,728

McMurry University

Abilene TX
(325) 793-4700
U.S. News ranking: Reg. Coll. (W), No. 18
Website: www.mcm.edu
Admissions email: admissions@mcm.edu
Private; founded 1923
Affiliation: Methodist
Freshman admissions: selective; 2013-2014: 1,396 applied, 827 accepted. Either SAT or ACT required. SAT 25/75 percentile: 860-1090. High school rank: 16% in top tenth, 37% in top quarter, 72% in top half
Early decision deadline: N/A, notification date: N/A
Early action deadline: N/A, notification date: N/A
Application deadline (fall): 8/15
Undergraduate student body: 1,032 full time, 180 part time; 51% male, 49% female; 1% American Indian, 1% Asian, 16% black, 21% Hispanic, 2% multiracial, 0% Pacific Islander, 58% white, 1% international; 94% from in state; 45% live on campus; 16% of students in fraternities, 19% in sororities
Most popular majors: 18% Business, Management, Marketing, and Related Support Services, 20% Education, 9% Psychology, 9% Social Sciences, 7% Visual and Performing Arts
Expenses: 2014-2015: $24,844; room/board: $7,988
Financial aid: (325) 793-4709; 85% of undergrads determined to have financial need; average aid package $20,125

Midland College[1]

Midland TX
(432) 685-5502
U.S. News ranking: Reg. Coll. (W), unranked
Website: www.midland.edu/
Admissions email: pebensberger@midland.edu
Public
Application deadline (fall): N/A
Undergraduate student body: N/A full time, N/A part time
Expenses: 2013-2014: $4,007 in state, $5,177 out of state; room/board: $4,821
Financial aid: (432) 685-4757

Midwestern State University

Wichita Falls TX
(800) 842-1922
U.S. News ranking: Reg. U. (W), second tier
Website: www.mwsu.edu
Admissions email: admissions@mwsu.edu
Public; founded 1922
Freshman admissions: less selective; 2013-2014: 3,023 applied, 2,170 accepted. Either SAT or ACT required. SAT 25/75 percentile: 900-1090. High school rank: 12% in top tenth, 36% in top quarter, 73% in top half
Early decision deadline: N/A, notification date: N/A

Early action deadline: 8/7, notification date: N/A
Application deadline (fall): 8/7
Undergraduate student body: 3,861 full time, 1,332 part time; 42% male, 58% female; 1% American Indian, 3% Asian, 15% black, 15% Hispanic, 2% multiracial, 0% Pacific Islander, 58% white, 5% international; 92% from in state; 26% live on campus; 7% of students in fraternities, 8% in sororities
Most popular majors: 5% Accounting, 5% Business Administration and Management, General, 13% Multi-/Interdisciplinary Studies, Other, 11% Radiologic Technology/Science - Radiographer, 15% Registered Nursing/Registered Nurse
Expenses: 2014-2015: $7,753 in state, $9,703 out of state; room/board: $6,810
Financial aid: (940) 397-4214; 61% of undergrads determined to have financial need; average aid package $9,475

Our Lady of the Lake University

San Antonio TX
(800) 436-6558
U.S. News ranking: Nat. U., second tier
Website: www.ollusa.edu
Admissions email: admission@lake.ollusa.edu
Private; founded 1895
Affiliation: Roman Catholic
Freshman admissions: less selective; 2013-2014: 7,262 applied, 1,649 accepted. Either SAT or ACT required. SAT 25/75 percentile: 870-960. High school rank: 12% in top tenth, 33% in top quarter, 68% in top half
Early decision deadline: N/A, notification date: N/A
Early action deadline: N/A, notification date: N/A
Application deadline (fall): rolling
Undergraduate student body: 1,312 full time, 243 part time; 28% male, 72% female; 1% American Indian, 1% Asian, 8% black, 73% Hispanic, 0% multiracial, 0% Pacific Islander, 12% white, 1% international; 86% from in state; 38% live on campus; 2% of students in fraternities, 4% in sororities
Most popular majors: 5% Business Administration, Management and Operations, 8% Communication Sciences and Disorders, General, 4% Criminal Justice/Law Enforcement Administration, 6% Psychology, General, 9% Social Work
Expenses: 2014-2015: $24,596; room/board: $7,436
Financial aid: (210) 434-6711; 89% of undergrads determined to have financial need; average aid package $19,833

Prairie View A&M University

Prairie View TX
(877) PVA-MU30
U.S. News ranking: Reg. U. (W), second tier
Website: www.pvamu.edu
Admissions email: admission@pvamu.edu
Public; founded 1876

Freshman admissions: less selective; 2013-2014: 4,548 applied, 3,871 accepted. Either SAT or ACT required. SAT 25/75 percentile: 750-940. High school rank: 5% in top tenth, 14% in top quarter, 52% in top half
Early decision deadline: N/A, notification date: N/A
Early action deadline: N/A, notification date: N/A
Application deadline (fall): 6/1
Undergraduate student body: 6,234 full time, 497 part time; 42% male, 58% female; 0% American Indian, 2% Asian, 86% black, 6% Hispanic, 1% multiracial, 0% Pacific Islander, 3% white, 1% international; 92% from in state; 25% live on campus; 1% of students in fraternities, 2% in sororities
Most popular majors: 10% Business, Management, Marketing, and Related Support Services, 12% Engineering, 24% Health Professions and Related Programs, 8% Legal Professions and Studies, 8% Psychology
Expenses: 2014-2015: $8,098 in state, $18,718 out of state; room/board: $7,467
Financial aid: (936) 857-2424; 72% of undergrads determined to have financial need; average aid package $14,265

Rice University
Houston TX
(713) 348-7423
U.S. News ranking: Nat. U., No. 19
Website: www.rice.edu
Admissions email: admission@rice.edu
Private; founded 1912
Freshman admissions: most selective; 2013-2014: 15,415 applied, 2,581 accepted. Either SAT or ACT required. SAT 25/75 percentile: 1370-1550. High school rank: 87% in top tenth, 97% in top quarter, 100% in top half
Early decision deadline: 11/1, notification date: 12/15
Early action deadline: N/A, notification date: N/A
Application deadline (fall): 1/1
Undergraduate student body: 3,904 full time, 61 part time; 51% male, 49% female; 0% American Indian, 21% Asian, 6% black, 15% Hispanic, 5% multiracial, 0% Pacific Islander, 39% white, 11% international; 51% from in state; 71% live on campus; 0% of students in fraternities, 0% in sororities
Most popular majors: 7% Biochemistry, 6% Chemical Engineering, 5% Economics, General, 5% Electrical and Electronics Engineering, 6% Psychology, General
Expenses: 2014-2015: $40,566; room/board: $13,400
Financial aid: (713) 348-4958; 41% of undergrads determined to have financial need; average aid package $36,556

Sam Houston State University
Huntsville TX
(936) 294-1828
U.S. News ranking: Nat. U., second tier
Website: www.shsu.edu
Admissions email: admissions@shsu.edu
Public; founded 1879
Freshman admissions: less selective; 2013-2014: 8,291 applied, 6,126 accepted. Either SAT or ACT required. SAT 25/75 percentile: 880-1090. High school rank: 14% in top tenth, 38% in top quarter, 87% in top half
Early decision deadline: N/A, notification date: N/A
Early action deadline: N/A, notification date: N/A
Application deadline (fall): 8/1
Undergraduate student body: 13,359 full time, 2,896 part time; 41% male, 59% female; 0% American Indian, 1% Asian, 18% black, 19% Hispanic, 2% multiracial, 0% Pacific Islander, 56% white, 1% international; 99% from in state; 21% live on campus; 2% of students in fraternities, 3% in sororities
Most popular majors: 6% Agriculture, Agriculture Operations, and Related Sciences, 21% Business, Management, Marketing, and Related Support Services, 18% Homeland Security, Law Enforcement, Firefighting and Related Protective Services, 12% Multi/Interdisciplinary Studies, 6% Parks, Recreation, Leisure, and Fitness Studies
Expenses: 2014-2015: $8,932 in state, $19,792 out of state; room/board: $8,324
Financial aid: (936) 294-1774; 64% of undergrads determined to have financial need; average aid package $10,279

Schreiner University[1]
Kerrville TX
(800) 343-4919
U.S. News ranking: Reg. Coll. (W), unranked
Website: www.schreiner.edu
Admissions email: admissions@schreiner.edu
Private; founded 1923
Affiliation: Presbyterian
Application deadline (fall): 8/1
Undergraduate student body: N/A full time, N/A part time
Expenses: 2013-2014: $22,484; room/board: $10,250
Financial aid: (830) 792-7217

Southern Methodist University
Dallas TX
(800) 323-0672
U.S. News ranking: Nat. U., No. 58
Website: www.smu.edu
Admissions email: ugadmission@smu.edu
Private; founded 1911
Affiliation: United Methodist
Freshman admissions: more selective; 2013-2014: 12,080 applied, 6,125 accepted. Either SAT or ACT required. ACT 25/75 percentile: 27-31. High school rank: 48% in top tenth, 80% in top quarter, 95% in top half
Early decision deadline: 11/1, notification date: 12/31

Early action deadline: 11/1, notification date: 12/31
Application deadline (fall): 1/15
Undergraduate student body: 6,119 full time, 238 part time; 49% male, 51% female; 0% American Indian, 7% Asian, 5% black, 12% Hispanic, 3% multiracial, 0% Pacific Islander, 66% white, 7% international; 50% from in state; 38% live on campus; 32% of students in fraternities, 48% in sororities
Most popular majors: 21% Business, Management, Marketing, and Related Support Services, 9% Communication, Journalism, and Related Programs, 8% Engineering, 7% Psychology, 16% Social Sciences
Expenses: 2014-2015: $45,940; room/board: $14,645
Financial aid: (214) 768-3016; 40% of undergrads determined to have financial need; average aid package $35,977

South Texas College[1]
McAllen TX
(956) 872-8323
U.S. News ranking: Reg. Coll. (W), unranked
Website: www.southtexascollege.edu/
Admissions email: N/A
Public
Application deadline (fall): N/A
Undergraduate student body: N/A full time, N/A part time
Expenses: 2013-2014: $3,530 in state, $7,260 out of state; room/board: N/A
Financial aid: (956) 872-8375

Southwestern Adventist University
Keene TX
(817) 645-3921
U.S. News ranking: Reg. Coll. (W), unranked
Website: www.swau.edu
Admissions email: admissions@swau.edu
Private; founded 1893
Affiliation: Seventh-day Adventist
Freshman admissions: N/A; 2013-2014: 746 applied, 235 accepted. SAT required. SAT 25/75 percentile: 830-1060. High school rank: 14% in top tenth, 26% in top quarter, 65% in top half
Early decision deadline: N/A, notification date: N/A
Early action deadline: N/A, notification date: N/A
Application deadline (fall): rolling
Undergraduate student body: 640 full time, 150 part time; 42% male, 58% female; 0% American Indian, 4% Asian, 12% black, 41% Hispanic, 4% multiracial, 1% Pacific Islander, 24% white, 14% international; 73% from in state; 30% live on campus; 0% of students in fraternities, 0% in sororities
Most popular majors: Information not available
Expenses: 2014-2015: $19,460; room/board: $7,400
Financial aid: (817) 645-3921

Southwestern Assemblies of God University
Waxahachie TX
(888) 937-7248
U.S. News ranking: Reg. U. (W), second tier
Website: www.sagu.edu/
Admissions email: admissions@sagu.edu
Private; founded 1927
Affiliation: Assemblies of God
Freshman admissions: selective; 2013-2014: 1,837 applied, 550 accepted. Either SAT or ACT required. ACT 25/75 percentile: 19-24. High school rank: N/A
Early decision deadline: N/A, notification date: N/A
Early action deadline: N/A, notification date: N/A
Application deadline (fall): rolling
Undergraduate student body: 1,434 full time, 266 part time; 48% male, 52% female; 2% American Indian, 1% Asian, 10% black, 20% Hispanic, 1% multiracial, 1% Pacific Islander, 64% white, 0% international; 63% from in state; N/A live on campus; N/A of students in fraternities, N/A in sororities
Most popular majors: 29% Bible/ Biblical Studies, 6% Elementary Education and Teaching, 6% General Studies, 2% Psychology, General, 13% Religious Education
Expenses: 2014-2015: $18,580; room/board: $6,340
Financial aid: N/A; 86% of undergrads determined to have financial need; average aid package $7,487

Southwestern Christian College[1]
Terrell TX
(972) 524-3341
U.S. News ranking: Reg. Coll. (W), unranked
Website: www.swcc.edu
Admissions email: N/A
Private
Application deadline (fall): N/A
Undergraduate student body: N/A full time, N/A part time
Expenses: 2013-2014: $7,620; room/board: $5,155
Financial aid: (972) 524-3341

Southwestern University
Georgetown TX
(800) 252-3166
U.S. News ranking: Nat. Lib. Arts, No. 87
Website: www.southwestern.edu
Admissions email: admission@southwestern.edu
Private; founded 1840
Affiliation: United Methodist
Freshman admissions: more selective; 2013-2014: 3,546 applied, 1,850 accepted. Either SAT or ACT required. SAT 25/75 percentile: 1055-1280. High school rank: 37% in top tenth, 72% in top quarter, 95% in top half
Early decision deadline: N/A, notification date: N/A
Early action deadline: 11/15, notification date: 2/15
Application deadline (fall): rolling
Undergraduate student body: 1,519 full time, 16 part time; 43% male, 57% female; 1% American

Indian, 4% Asian, 5% black, 19% Hispanic, 2% multiracial, 0% Pacific Islander, 67% white, 1% international; 90% from in state; 77% live on campus; 37% of students in fraternities, 29% in sororities
Most popular majors: 13% Biological and Biomedical Sciences, 11% Business, Management, Marketing, and Related Support Services, 9% Psychology, 19% Social Sciences, 10% Visual and Performing Arts
Expenses: 2014-2015: $36,120; room/board: $11,760
Financial aid: (512) 863-1259; 65% of undergrads determined to have financial need; average aid package $30,966

St. Edward's University
Austin TX
(512) 448-8500
U.S. News ranking: Reg. U. (W), No. 13
Website: www.stedwards.edu
Admissions email: seu.admit@stedwards.edu
Private; founded 1885
Affiliation: Roman Catholic
Freshman admissions: selective; 2013-2014: 3,694 applied, 2,901 accepted. Either SAT or ACT required. SAT 25/75 percentile: 1020-1220. High school rank: 20% in top tenth, 54% in top quarter, 83% in top half
Early decision deadline: N/A, notification date: N/A
Early action deadline: N/A, notification date: N/A
Application deadline (fall): 5/1
Undergraduate student body: 3,442 full time, 647 part time; 39% male, 61% female; 0% American Indian, 3% Asian, 4% black, 37% Hispanic, 3% multiracial, 0% Pacific Islander, 43% white, 8% international; 88% from in state; 39% live on campus; N/A of students in fraternities, N/A in sororities
Most popular majors: 4% Biology/ Biological Sciences, General, 8% Business Administration and Management, General, 8% Communication and Media Studies, Other, 11% Psychology, General, 4% Teacher Education and Professional Development, Specific Subject Areas, Other
Expenses: 2014-2015: $36,550; room/board: $11,234
Financial aid: (512) 448-8520; 66% of undergrads determined to have financial need; average aid package $26,026

Stephen F. Austin State University
Nacogdoches TX
(936) 468-2504
U.S. News ranking: Reg. U. (W), No. 84
Website: www.sfasu.edu
Admissions email: admissions@sfasu.edu
Public; founded 1923
Freshman admissions: selective; 2013-2014: 11,383 applied, 6,474 accepted. Either SAT or ACT required. SAT 25/75 percentile: 890-1090. High school rank: 13% in top tenth, 41% in top quarter, 77% in top half

Early decision deadline: N/A, notification date: N/A
Early action deadline: N/A, notification date: N/A
Application deadline (fall): rolling
Undergraduate student body: 9,333 full time, 1,673 part time; 37% male, 63% female; 1% American Indian, 1% Asian, 22% black, 14% Hispanic, 2% multiracial, 0% Pacific Islander, 57% white, 1% international; 98% from in state; 45% live on campus; 14% of students in fraternities, 9% in sororities
Most popular majors: 4% Business Administration and Management, General, 4% Human Development and Family Studies, General, 8% Kinesiology and Exercise Science, 15% Multi-/Interdisciplinary Studies, Other, 7% Registered Nursing/Registered Nurse
Expenses: 2014-2015: $8,892 in state, $19,752 out of state; room/board: $8,868
Financial aid: (936) 468-2403

St. Mary's University of San Antonio
San Antonio TX
(210) 436-3126
U.S. News ranking: Reg. U. (W), No. 21
Website: www.stmarytx.edu
Admissions email: uadm@stmarytx.edu
Private; founded 1852
Affiliation: Roman Catholic
Freshman admissions: selective; 2013-2014: 5,147 applied, 2,997 accepted. Either SAT or ACT required. SAT 25/75 percentile: 950-1150. High school rank: 28% in top tenth, 57% in top quarter, 83% in top half
Early decision deadline: N/A, notification date: N/A
Early action deadline: N/A, notification date: N/A
Application deadline (fall): rolling
Undergraduate student body: 2,284 full time, 109 part time; 44% male, 56% female; 0% American Indian, 3% Asian, 4% black, 73% Hispanic, 0% multiracial, 0% Pacific Islander, 14% white, 3% international; 93% from in state; 58% live on campus; 1% of students in fraternities, 3% in sororities
Most popular majors: 11% Biological and Biomedical Sciences, 23% Business, Management, Marketing, and Related Support Services, 7% Homeland Security, Law Enforcement, Firefighting and Related Protective Services, 7% Psychology, 18% Social Sciences
Expenses: 2013-2014: $25,126; room/board: $8,666
Financial aid: (210) 436-3141

Sul Ross State University
Alpine TX
(432) 837-8050
U.S. News ranking: Reg. U. (W), second tier
Website: www.sulross.edu
Admissions email: admissions@sulross.edu
Public; founded 1917
Freshman admissions: least selective; 2013-2014: N/A applied, N/A accepted. Either SAT or ACT required. ACT 25/75 percentile: 14-19. High school

rank: 3% in top tenth, 16% in top quarter, 49% in top half
Early decision deadline: N/A, notification date: N/A
Early action deadline: N/A, notification date: N/A
Application deadline (fall): rolling
Undergraduate student body: 1,213 full time, 790 part time; 44% male, 56% female; 0% American Indian, 1% Asian, 11% black, 48% Hispanic, 0% multiracial, 0% Pacific Islander, 37% white, 1% international
Most popular majors: Information not available
Expenses: 2013-2014: $4,764 in state, $12,276 out of state; room/board: $6,810
Financial aid: (432) 837-8059

Tarleton State University
Stephenville TX
(800) 687-8236
U.S. News ranking: Reg. U. (W), second tier
Website: www.tarleton.edu
Admissions email: uadm@tarleton.edu
Public; founded 1899
Freshman admissions: less selective; 2013-2014: 5,013 applied, 3,844 accepted. Either SAT or ACT required. SAT 25/75 percentile: 870-1060. High school rank: 8% in top tenth, 24% in top quarter, 68% in top half
Early decision deadline: N/A, notification date: N/A
Early action deadline: 3/1, notification date: N/A
Application deadline (fall): 7/21
Undergraduate student body: 7,413 full time, 2,172 part time; 40% male, 60% female; 1% American Indian, 1% Asian, 7% black, 15% Hispanic, 2% multiracial, 0% Pacific Islander, 73% white, 1% international; 98% from in state; 33% live on campus; N/A of students in fraternities, N/A in sororities
Most popular majors: 11% Agriculture, Agriculture Operations, and Related Sciences, 17% Business, Management, Marketing, and Related Support Services, 16% Multi-/Interdisciplinary Studies, 8% Parks, Recreation, Leisure, and Fitness Studies, 6% Psychology
Expenses: 2014-2015: $7,237 in state, $18,097 out of state; room/board: $7,556
Financial aid: (254) 968-9070; 67% of undergrads determined to have financial need; average aid package $9,517

Texas A&M International University
Laredo TX
(956) 326-2200
U.S. News ranking: Reg. U. (W), No. 63
Website: www.tamiu.edu
Admissions email: enroll@tamiu.edu
Public; founded 1970
Freshman admissions: selective; 2013-2014: 4,917 applied, 2,404 accepted. Either SAT or ACT required. SAT 25/75 percentile: 800-1010. High school rank: 20% in top tenth, 53% in top quarter, 86% in top half

Early decision deadline: N/A, notification date: N/A
Early action deadline: N/A, notification date: N/A
Application deadline (fall): 7/1
Undergraduate student body: 4,022 full time, 2,563 part time; 42% male, 58% female; 0% American Indian, 1% Asian, 1% black, 92% Hispanic, 0% multiracial, 0% Pacific Islander, 2% white, 2% international; 99% from in state; 9% live on campus; 1% of students in fraternities, 1% in sororities
Most popular majors: 21% Business, Management, Marketing, and Related Support Services, 19% Health Professions and Related Programs, 14% Homeland Security, Law Enforcement, Firefighting and Related Protective Services, 8% Multi/Interdisciplinary Studies, 9% Psychology
Expenses: 2014-2015: $9,180 in state, $18,054 out of state; room/board: $8,028
Financial aid: (956) 326-2225; 88% of undergrads determined to have financial need; average aid package $9,480

Texas A&M University–College Station
College Station TX
(979) 845-3741
U.S. News ranking: Nat. U., No. 68
Website: www.tamu.edu
Admissions email: admissions@tamu.edu
Public; founded 1876
Freshman admissions: more selective; 2013-2014: 31,388 applied, 21,725 accepted. Either SAT or ACT required. SAT 25/75 percentile: 1070-1290. High school rank: 53% in top tenth, 78% in top quarter, 98% in top half
Early decision deadline: N/A, notification date: N/A
Early action deadline: N/A, notification date: N/A
Application deadline (fall): 12/1
Undergraduate student body: 39,856 full time, 4,459 part time; 52% male, 48% female; 0% American Indian, 5% Asian, 3% black, 20% Hispanic, 2% multiracial, 0% Pacific Islander, 68% white, 1% international; 96% from in state; 25% live on campus; 6% of students in fraternities, 11% in sororities
Most popular majors: 11% Agriculture, Agriculture Operations, and Related Sciences, 8% Biological and Biomedical Sciences, 17% Business, Management, Marketing, and Related Support Services, 14% Engineering, 9% Multi/Interdisciplinary Studies
Expenses: 2014-2015: $9,180 in state, $26,356 out of state; room/board: $9,522
Financial aid: (979) 845-3236; 42% of undergrads determined to have financial need; average aid package $14,855

Texas A&M University–Commerce
Commerce TX
(903) 886-5000
U.S. News ranking: Nat. U., second tier
Website: www.tamuc.edu/
Admissions email: Admissions@tamuc.edu
Public; founded 1889
Freshman admissions: selective; 2013-2014: 4,236 applied, 2,888 accepted. Either SAT or ACT required. SAT 25/75 percentile: 880-1090. High school rank: 16% in top tenth, 40% in top quarter, 72% in top half
Early decision deadline: N/A, notification date: N/A
Early action deadline: N/A, notification date: N/A
Application deadline (fall): 8/15
Undergraduate student body: 5,086 full time, 1,804 part time; 41% male, 59% female; 1% American Indian, 2% Asian, 20% black, 14% Hispanic, 3% multiracial, 0% Pacific Islander, 55% white, 4% international; 98% from in state; 28% live on campus; 9% of students in fraternities, 7% in sororities
Most popular majors: 15% Business, Management, Marketing, and Related Support Services, 5% Liberal Arts and Sciences, General Studies and Humanities, 38% Multi/Interdisciplinary Studies, 5% Parks, Recreation, Leisure, and Fitness Studies, 6% Psychology
Expenses: 2014-2015: $7,096 in state, $17,956 out of state; room/board: N/A
Financial aid: (903) 886-5096; 74% of undergrads determined to have financial need; average aid package $9,884

Texas A&M University–Corpus Christi
Corpus Christi TX
(361) 825-2624
U.S. News ranking: Nat. U., second tier
Website: www.tamucc.edu
Admissions email: admiss@tamucc.edu
Public; founded 1947
Freshman admissions: less selective; 2013-2014: 7,217 applied, 6,281 accepted. Either SAT or ACT required. SAT 25/75 percentile: 870-1060. High school rank: 10% in top tenth, 34% in top quarter, 72% in top half
Early decision deadline: N/A, notification date: N/A
Early action deadline: N/A, notification date: N/A
Application deadline (fall): 7/1
Undergraduate student body: 7,237 full time, 1,915 part time; 42% male, 58% female; 0% American Indian, 2% Asian, 5% black, 46% Hispanic, 2% multiracial, 0% Pacific Islander, 40% white, 3% international; 97% from in state; 17% live on campus; 5% of students in fraternities, 5% in sororities
Most popular majors: 10% Biological and Biomedical Sciences, 18% Business, Management, Marketing, and Related Support Services,

15% Health Professions and Related Programs, 14% Multi/Interdisciplinary Studies, 7% Psychology
Expenses: 2013-2014: $7,778 in state, $18,398 out of state; room/board: $9,965
Financial aid: (361) 825-2338; 62% of undergrads determined to have financial need; average aid package $8,898

Texas A&M University–Kingsville
Kingsville TX
(361) 593-2315
U.S. News ranking: Nat. U., second tier
Website: www.tamuk.edu
Admissions email: admissions@tamuk.edu
Public; founded 1925
Freshman admissions: less selective; 2013-2014: 6,499 applied, 5,720 accepted. Either SAT or ACT required. ACT 25/75 percentile: 16-21. High school rank: 9% in top tenth, 35% in top quarter, 76% in top half
Early decision deadline: N/A, notification date: N/A
Early action deadline: N/A, notification date: N/A
Application deadline (fall): rolling
Undergraduate student body: 4,935 full time, 1,186 part time; 51% male, 49% female; 0% American Indian, 1% Asian, 7% black, 68% Hispanic, 1% multiracial, 0% Pacific Islander, 20% white, 2% international; 99% from in state; 33% live on campus; 5% of students in fraternities, 5% in sororities
Most popular majors: 15% Communication Sciences and Disorders, General, 5% Criminology, 5% Kinesiology and Exercise Science, 10% Multi-/Interdisciplinary Studies, General, 5% Psychology, General
Expenses: 2014-2015: $7,434 in state, $18,294 out of state; room/board: $8,131
Financial aid: (361) 593-2173; 80% of undergrads determined to have financial need; average aid package $11,872

Texas A&M University–Texarkana
Texarkana TX
(903) 223-3069
U.S. News ranking: Reg. U. (W), second tier
Website: www.tamut.edu
Admissions email: admissions@tamut.edu
Public; founded 1971
Freshman admissions: selective; 2013-2014: 730 applied, 262 accepted. Either SAT or ACT required. ACT 25/75 percentile: 19-24. High school rank: 16% in top tenth, 39% in top quarter, 72% in top half
Early decision deadline: N/A, notification date: N/A
Early action deadline: N/A, notification date: N/A
Application deadline (fall): rolling
Undergraduate student body: 924 full time, 477 part time; 36% male, 64% female; N/A American Indian, N/A Asian, N/A black, N/A Hispanic, N/A multiracial, N/A Pacific Islander, N/A white, N/A international

Most popular majors: Information not available
Expenses: 2013-2014: $5,578 in state, $14,002 out of state; room/board: $8,800
Financial aid: (903) 223-3060

Texas Christian University
Fort Worth TX
(817) 257-7490
U.S. News ranking: Nat. U., No. 76
Website: www.tcu.edu
Admissions email: frogmail@tcu.edu
Private; founded 1873
Affiliation: Christian Church (Disciples of Christ)
Freshman admissions: more selective; 2013-2014: 18,551 applied, 8,791 accepted. Either SAT or ACT required. ACT 25/75 percentile: 25-29. High school rank: 42% in top tenth, 75% in top quarter, 96% in top half
Early decision deadline: 11/1, notification date: 1/1
Early action deadline: 11/1, notification date: 1/1
Application deadline (fall): 2/15
Undergraduate student body: 8,326 full time, 314 part time; 40% male, 60% female; 1% American Indian, 2% Asian, 5% black, 11% Hispanic, 1% multiracial, 0% Pacific Islander, 74% white, 5% international; 61% from in state; 48% live on campus; 42% of students in fraternities, 53% in sororities
Most popular majors: 24% Business, Management, Marketing, and Related Support Services, 16% Communication, Journalism, and Related Programs, 6% Education, 13% Health Professions and Related Programs, 8% Social Sciences
Expenses: 2014-2015: $38,600; room/board: $11,380
Financial aid: (817) 257-7858; 41% of undergrads determined to have financial need; average aid package $22,885

Texas College[1]
Tyler TX
(903) 593-8311
U.S. News ranking: Reg. Coll. (W), unranked
Website: www.texascollege.edu
Admissions email: cmarshall-biggins@texascollege.edu
Private
Application deadline (fall): N/A
Undergraduate student body: N/A full time, N/A part time
Expenses: 2013-2014: $10,008; room/board: $7,200
Financial aid: (903) 593-8311

Texas Lutheran University
Seguin TX
(800) 771-8521
U.S. News ranking: Reg. Coll. (W), No. 2
Website: www.tlu.edu
Admissions email: admissions@tlu.edu
Private; founded 1891
Affiliation: Evangelical Lutheran Church in America

Freshman admissions: selective; 2013-2014: 1,734 applied, 882 accepted. Either SAT or ACT required. SAT 25/75 percentile: 930-1140. High school rank: 20% in top tenth, 53% in top quarter, 87% in top half
Early decision deadline: N/A, notification date: N/A
Early action deadline: N/A, notification date: N/A
Application deadline (fall): rolling
Undergraduate student body: 1,258 full time, 71 part time; 48% male, 52% female; 0% American Indian, 1% Asian, 8% black, 31% Hispanic, 0% multiracial, 0% Pacific Islander, 56% white, 0% international; 97% from in state; 56% live on campus; 3% of students in fraternities, 7% in sororities
Most popular majors: 10% Biological and Biomedical Sciences, 21% Business, Management, Marketing, and Related Support Services, 11% Education, 17% Parks, Recreation, Leisure, and Fitness Studies, 7% Psychology
Expenses: 2014-2015: $26,800; room/board: $9,240
Financial aid: (830) 372-8075; 82% of undergrads determined to have financial need; average aid package $22,076

Texas Southern University
Houston TX
(713) 313-7071
U.S. News ranking: Nat. U., second tier
Website: www.tsu.edu
Admissions email: admissions@tsu.edu
Public; founded 1947
Freshman admissions: least selective; 2013-2014: 9,746 applied, 4,389 accepted. Either SAT or ACT required. SAT 25/75 percentile: 750-920. High school rank: 5% in top tenth, 20% in top quarter, 62% in top half
Early decision deadline: 12/1, notification date: N/A
Early action deadline: N/A, notification date: N/A
Application deadline (fall): 8/1
Undergraduate student body: 5,321 full time, 967 part time; 41% male, 59% female; 0% American Indian, 3% Asian, 84% black, 6% Hispanic, 0% multiracial, 0% Pacific Islander, 2% white, 5% international; 90% from in state; 24% live on campus; 2% of students in fraternities, 3% in sororities
Most popular majors: 5% Accounting, 8% Biology/Biological Sciences, General, 9% Business Administration and Management, General, 6% Criminal Justice/Law Enforcement Administration, 11% General Studies
Expenses: 2013-2014: $7,946 in state, $18,566 out of state; room/board: $15,170
Financial aid: (713) 313-7071; 90% of undergrads determined to have financial need; average aid package $7,816

Texas State University
San Marcos TX
(512) 245-2364
U.S. News ranking: Reg. U. (W), No. 50
Website: www.txstate.edu
Admissions email: admissions@txstate.edu
Public; founded 1899
Freshman admissions: selective; 2013-2014: 18,937 applied, 13,976 accepted. Either SAT or ACT required. SAT 25/75 percentile: 940-1130. High school rank: 14% in top tenth, 49% in top quarter, 93% in top half
Early decision deadline: N/A, notification date: N/A
Early action deadline: N/A, notification date: N/A
Application deadline (fall): 5/1
Undergraduate student body: 25,683 full time, 5,322 part time; 44% male, 56% female; 0% American Indian, 2% Asian, 7% black, 31% Hispanic, 3% multiracial, 0% Pacific Islander, 54% white, 0% international; 98% from in state; 19% live on campus; 5% of students in fraternities, 5% in sororities
Most popular majors: 6% Business Administration and Management, General, 4% Marketing/Marketing Management, General, 10% Multi-/Interdisciplinary Studies, Other, 6% Parks, Recreation and Leisure Facilities Management, General, 6% Psychology, General
Expenses: 2014-2015: $9,516 in state, $20,376 out of state; room/board: $7,612
Financial aid: (512) 245-2315; 59% of undergrads determined to have financial need; average aid package $10,055

Texas Tech University
Lubbock TX
(806) 742-1480
U.S. News ranking: Nat. U., No. 156
Website: www.ttu.edu
Admissions email: admissions@ttu.edu
Public; founded 1923
Freshman admissions: selective; 2013-2014: 19,170 applied, 12,709 accepted. Either SAT or ACT required. SAT 25/75 percentile: 1010-1210. High school rank: 22% in top tenth, 55% in top quarter, 86% in top half
Early decision deadline: N/A, notification date: N/A
Early action deadline: N/A, notification date: N/A
Application deadline (fall): 8/1
Undergraduate student body: 24,338 full time, 2,706 part time; 56% male, 44% female; 0% American Indian, 3% Asian, 6% black, 21% Hispanic, 3% multiracial, 0% Pacific Islander, 63% white, 4% international; 94% from in state; 26% live on campus; 3% of students in fraternities, 6% in sororities
Most popular majors: 21% Business, Management, Marketing, and Related Support Services, 11% Engineering, 8% Family and Consumer Sciences/Human Sciences, 10% Multi/Interdisciplinary Studies, 6% Social Sciences
Expenses: 2014-2015: $9,308 in state, $20,168 out of state; room/board: $8,405

Financial aid: (806) 742-3681; 50% of undergrads determined to have financial need; average aid package $9,469

Texas Wesleyan University
Fort Worth TX
(817) 531-4422
U.S. News ranking: Reg. U. (W), No. 49
Website: www.txwes.edu
Admissions email: admission@txwes.edu
Private; founded 1890
Affiliation: Methodist
Freshman admissions: selective; 2013-2014: 3,336 applied, 1,538 accepted. Either SAT or ACT required. SAT 25/75 percentile: 940-1090. High school rank: 12% in top tenth, 30% in top quarter, 71% in top half
Early decision deadline: N/A, notification date: N/A
Early action deadline: N/A, notification date: N/A
Application deadline (fall): rolling
Undergraduate student body: 1,429 full time, 512 part time; 49% male, 51% female; 1% American Indian, 2% Asian, 15% black, 20% Hispanic, 3% multiracial, 0% Pacific Islander, 33% white, 22% international; 95% from in state; 38% live on campus; 3% of students in fraternities, 3% in sororities
Most popular majors: 18% Business, Management, Marketing, and Related Support Services, 13% Education, 9% Homeland Security, Law Enforcement, Firefighting and Related Protective Services, 14% Multi/Interdisciplinary Studies, 8% Psychology
Expenses: 2014-2015: $23,144; room/board: $8,238
Financial aid: (817) 531-4420; 70% of undergrads determined to have financial need; average aid package $17,154

Texas Woman's University
Denton TX
(940) 898-3188
U.S. News ranking: Nat. U., second tier
Website: www.twu.edu
Admissions email: admissions@twu.edu
Public; founded 1901
Freshman admissions: selective; 2013-2014: 4,431 applied, 3,812 accepted. Neither SAT nor ACT required. SAT 25/75 percentile: 840-1070. High school rank: 16% in top tenth, 48% in top quarter, 82% in top half
Early decision deadline: N/A, notification date: N/A
Early action deadline: N/A, notification date: N/A
Application deadline (fall): 7/15
Undergraduate student body: 6,722 full time, 2,793 part time; 11% male, 89% female; 1% American Indian, 8% Asian, 21% black, 25% Hispanic, 3% multiracial, 0% Pacific Islander, 41% white, 1% international; 100% from in state; 21% live on campus; 1% of students in fraternities, 3% in sororities
Most popular majors: 7% Business, Management, Marketing, and Related Support Services, 6% Family and Consumer Sciences/

Human Sciences, 28% Health Professions and Related Programs, 13% Liberal Arts and Sciences, General Studies and Humanities, 14% Multi/Interdisciplinary Studies
Expenses: 2014-2015: $7,560 in state, $18,420 out of state; room/board: $7,191
Financial aid: (940) 898-3050; 72% of undergrads determined to have financial need; average aid package $8,111

Trinity University
San Antonio TX
(800) 874-6489
U.S. News ranking: Reg. U. (W), No. 1
Website: www.trinity.edu
Admissions email: admissions@trinity.edu
Private; founded 1869
Affiliation: Presbyterian
Freshman admissions: more selective; 2013-2014: 4,505 applied, 2,880 accepted. Either SAT or ACT required. SAT 25/75 percentile: 1150-1370. High school rank: 45% in top tenth, 73% in top quarter, 93% in top half
Early decision deadline: 11/1, notification date: 12/15
Early action deadline: 1/1, notification date: 2/15
Application deadline (fall): 2/1
Undergraduate student body: 2,186 full time, 51 part time; 47% male, 53% female; 0% American Indian, 7% Asian, 4% black, 17% Hispanic, 4% multiracial, 0% Pacific Islander, 58% white, 7% international; 72% from in state; 74% live on campus; 16% of students in fraternities, 18% in sororities
Most popular majors: 10% Biological and Biomedical Sciences, 20% Business, Management, Marketing, and Related Support Services, 6% Communication, Journalism, and Related Programs, 9% Foreign Languages, Literatures, and Linguistics, 19% Social Sciences
Expenses: 2014-2015: $36,214; room/board: $11,936
Financial aid: (210) 999-8315; 48% of undergrads determined to have financial need; average aid package $31,800

University of Dallas
Irving TX
(800) 628-6999
U.S. News ranking: Reg. U. (W), No. 13
Website: www.udallas.edu
Admissions email: ugadmis@udallas.edu
Private; founded 1956
Affiliation: Roman Catholic
Freshman admissions: more selective; 2013-2014: 1,224 applied, 1,103 accepted. Either SAT or ACT required. SAT 25/75 percentile: 1090-1330. High school rank: 54% in top tenth, 68% in top quarter, 88% in top half
Early decision deadline: N/A, notification date: N/A
Early action deadline: 11/1, notification date: 12/1
Application deadline (fall): 7/1
Undergraduate student body: 1,365 full time, 15 part time; 46% male, 54% female; 0% American

Indian, 4% Asian, 1% black, 19% Hispanic, 3% multiracial, 0% Pacific Islander, 67% white, 3% international; 46% from in state; 63% live on campus; N/A of students in fraternities, N/A in sororities
Most popular majors: 12% Biology/Biological Sciences, General, 13% English Language and Literature, General, 9% History, General, 15% Social Sciences, General, 11% Theology/Theological Studies
Expenses: 2014-2015: $34,430; room/board: $11,070
Financial aid: (972) 721-5266; 64% of undergrads determined to have financial need; average aid package $28,291

University of Houston

Houston TX
(713) 743-1010
U.S. News ranking: Nat. U., No. 189
Website: www.uh.edu
Admissions email: admissions@uh.edu
Public; founded 1927
Freshman admissions: more selective; 2013-2014: 17,407 applied, 10,167 accepted. Either SAT or ACT required. SAT 25/75 percentile: 1030-1250. High school rank: 34% in top tenth, 69% in top quarter, 92% in top half
Early decision deadline: N/A, notification date: N/A
Early action deadline: N/A, notification date: N/A
Application deadline (fall): 4/1
Undergraduate student body: 22,829 full time, 8,758 part time; 50% male, 50% female; 0% American Indian, 21% Asian, 12% black, 30% Hispanic, 3% multiracial, 0% Pacific Islander, 28% white, 5% international; 98% from in state; 18% live on campus; 4% of students in fraternities, 3% in sororities
Most popular majors: 6% Biological and Biomedical Sciences, 29% Business, Management, Marketing, and Related Support Services, 6% Communication, Journalism, and Related Programs, 8% Psychology, 7% Social Sciences
Expenses: 2014-2015: $10,518 in state, $24,378 out of state; room/board: $9,278
Financial aid: (713) 743-1010; 64% of undergrads determined to have financial need; average aid package $12,977

University of Houston–Clear Lake

Houston TX
(281) 283-2500
U.S. News ranking: Reg. U. (W), second tier
Website: www.uhcl.edu
Admissions email: admissions@uhcl.edu
Public; founded 1974
Freshman admissions: less selective; 2013-2014: N/A applied, N/A accepted. Either SAT or ACT required. ACT 25/75 percentile: N/A. High school rank: N/A
Early decision deadline: N/A, notification date: N/A
Early action deadline: N/A, notification date: N/A
Application deadline (fall): 6/1

Undergraduate student body: 2,084 full time, 2,533 part time; 32% male, 68% female; 0% American Indian, 6% Asian, 8% black, 34% Hispanic, 2% multiracial, 0% Pacific Islander, 46% white, 2% international; N/A from in state; 2% live on campus; N/A of students in fraternities, N/A in sororities
Most popular majors: 25% Business, Management, Marketing, and Related Support Services, 26% Multi/Interdisciplinary Studies, 5% Parks, Recreation, Leisure, and Fitness Studies, 8% Psychology, 6% Social Sciences
Expenses: 2014-2015: $7,131 in state, $20,091 out of state; room/board: $9,682
Financial aid: (281) 283-2480; 68% of undergrads determined to have financial need; average aid package $8,936

University of Houston–Downtown

Houston TX
(713) 221-8522
U.S. News ranking: Reg. Coll. (W), unranked
Website: www.uhd.edu
Admissions email: uhdadmit@uhd.edu
Public; founded 1974
Freshman admissions: N/A; 2013-2014: 3,096 applied, 2,944 accepted. Either SAT or ACT required. SAT 25/75 percentile: 800-990. High school rank: 8% in top tenth, 29% in top quarter, 67% in top half
Early decision deadline: N/A, notification date: N/A
Early action deadline: N/A, notification date: N/A
Application deadline (fall): 7/1
Undergraduate student body: 6,896 full time, 6,590 part time; 40% male, 60% female; 0% American Indian, 9% Asian, 25% black, 39% Hispanic, 1% multiracial, 0% Pacific Islander, 18% white, 5% international; 99% from in state; 0% live on campus; 0% of students in fraternities, 0% in sororities
Most popular majors: 36% Business, Management, Marketing, and Related Support Services, 10% Homeland Security, Law Enforcement, Firefighting and Related Protective Services, 26% Multi/Interdisciplinary Studies, 8% Psychology, 4% Social Sciences
Expenses: 2014-2015: $6,614 in state, $17,474 out of state; room/board: N/A
Financial aid: (713) 221-8041; 74% of undergrads determined to have financial need; average aid package $8,573

University of Houston–Victoria

Victoria TX
(877) 970-4848
U.S. News ranking: Reg. U. (W), second tier
Website: www.uhv.edu/
Admissions email: N/A
Public
Freshman admissions: less selective; 2013-2014: 2,873 applied, 1,491 accepted. Neither SAT nor ACT required. SAT 25/75 percentile: 810-1005. High school rank: 7% in top tenth, 23% in top quarter, 68% in top half

Early decision deadline: N/A, notification date: N/A
Early action deadline: N/A, notification date: N/A
Application deadline (fall): 8/15
Undergraduate student body: 1,466 full time, 1,423 part time; 34% male, 66% female; 0% American Indian, 7% Asian, 17% black, 31% Hispanic, 2% multiracial, 0% Pacific Islander, 40% white, 1% international; 100% from in state; N/A live on campus; N/A of students in fraternities, N/A in sororities
Most popular majors: 5% Biological and Biomedical Sciences, 31% Business, Management, Marketing, and Related Support Services, 15% Health Professions and Related Programs, 25% Multi/Interdisciplinary Studies, 10% Psychology
Expenses: 2013-2014: $6,248 in state, $16,868 out of state; room/board: $7,216
Financial aid: (877) 970-4848

University of Mary Hardin-Baylor

Belton TX
(254) 295-4520
U.S. News ranking: Reg. U. (W), No. 43
Website: www.umhb.edu
Admissions email: admission@umhb.edu
Private; founded 1845
Affiliation: Baptist
Freshman admissions: selective; 2013-2014: 5,540 applied, 4,691 accepted. Either SAT or ACT required. SAT 25/75 percentile: 940-1140. High school rank: 22% in top tenth, 51% in top quarter, 82% in top half
Early decision deadline: N/A, notification date: N/A
Early action deadline: N/A, notification date: N/A
Application deadline (fall): rolling
Undergraduate student body: 2,793 full time, 270 part time; 38% male, 62% female; 1% American Indian, 1% Asian, 14% black, 17% Hispanic, 2% multiracial, 0% Pacific Islander, 60% white, 2% international; 98% from in state; 50% live on campus; N/A of students in fraternities, N/A in sororities
Most popular majors: 9% Business, Management, Marketing, and Related Support Services, 16% Education, 29% Health Professions and Related Programs, 6% Liberal Arts and Sciences, General Studies and Humanities, 8% Psychology
Expenses: 2014-2015: $25,750; room/board: $7,020
Financial aid: (254) 295-4517; 86% of undergrads determined to have financial need; average aid package $15,789

University of North Texas

Denton TX
(940) 565-2681
U.S. News ranking: Nat. U., second tier
Website: www.unt.edu
Admissions email: undergrad@unt.edu
Public; founded 1890
Freshman admissions: selective; 2013-2014: 16,326 applied,

10,037 accepted. Either SAT or ACT required. SAT 25/75 percentile: 1000-1210. High school rank: 20% in top tenth, 52% in top quarter, 90% in top half
Early decision deadline: N/A, notification date: N/A
Early action deadline: N/A, notification date: N/A
Application deadline (fall): 8/1
Undergraduate student body: 23,669 full time, 5,812 part time; 48% male, 52% female; 1% American Indian, 6% Asian, 13% black, 20% Hispanic, 3% multiracial, 0% Pacific Islander, 53% white, 3% international; 96% from in state; 19% live on campus; 2% of students in fraternities, 2% in sororities
Most popular majors: 19% Business, Management, Marketing, and Related Support Services, 15% Multi/Interdisciplinary Studies, 6% Psychology, 9% Social Sciences, 8% Visual and Performing Arts
Expenses: 2014-2015: $9,706 in state, $20,566 out of state; room/board: $7,760
Financial aid: (940) 565-2302; 62% of undergrads determined to have financial need; average aid package $10,767

University of St. Thomas

Houston TX
(713) 525-3500
U.S. News ranking: Reg. U. (W), No. 27
Website: www.stthom.edu
Admissions email: admissions@stthom.edu
Private; founded 1947
Affiliation: Roman Catholic
Freshman admissions: selective; 2013-2014: 780 applied, 602 accepted. Either SAT or ACT required. SAT 25/75 percentile: 1000-1210. High school rank: 22% in top tenth, 54% in top quarter, 84% in top half
Early decision deadline: N/A, notification date: N/A
Early action deadline: 12/1, notification date: 12/15
Application deadline (fall): 8/1
Undergraduate student body: 1,269 full time, 341 part time; 37% male, 63% female; 0% American Indian, 12% Asian, 6% black, 38% Hispanic, 2% multiracial, 0% Pacific Islander, 31% white, 9% international; 96% from in state; 18% live on campus; N/A of students in fraternities, N/A in sororities
Most popular majors: 10% Biological and Biomedical Sciences, 23% Business, Management, Marketing, and Related Support Services, 10% Liberal Arts and Sciences, General Studies and Humanities, 10% Psychology, 10% Social Sciences
Expenses: 2014-2015: $29,440; room/board: $8,250
Financial aid: (713) 525-2170; 61% of undergrads determined to have financial need; average aid package $19,320

University of Texas–Arlington

Arlington TX
(817) 272-6287
U.S. News ranking: Nat. U., second tier
Website: www.uta.edu
Admissions email: admissions@uta.edu
Public; founded 1895
Freshman admissions: selective; 2013-2014: 10,679 applied, 6,405 accepted. Either SAT or ACT required. SAT 25/75 percentile: 960-1200. High school rank: 28% in top tenth, 75% in top quarter, 98% in top half
Early decision deadline: N/A, notification date: N/A
Early action deadline: N/A, notification date: N/A
Application deadline (fall): rolling
Undergraduate student body: 15,938 full time, 9,752 part time; 44% male, 56% female; 0% American Indian, 12% Asian, 15% black, 26% Hispanic, 3% multiracial, 0% Pacific Islander, 40% white, 4% international; 97% from in state; 11% live on campus; 5% of students in fraternities, 3% in sororities
Most popular majors: 6% Biological and Biomedical Sciences, 13% Business, Management, Marketing, and Related Support Services, 6% Engineering, 33% Health Professions and Related Programs, 6% Multi/Interdisciplinary Studies
Expenses: 2014-2015: $8,878 in state, $20,274 out of state; room/board: $8,156
Financial aid: (817) 272-3568; 68% of undergrads determined to have financial need; average aid package $12,738

University of Texas–Austin

Austin TX
(512) 475-7440
U.S. News ranking: Nat. U., No. 53
Website: www.utexas.edu
Admissions email: N/A
Public; founded 1883
Freshman admissions: more selective; 2013-2014: 38,161 applied, 15,335 accepted. Either SAT or ACT required. SAT 25/75 percentile: 1140-1380. High school rank: 75% in top tenth, 91% in top quarter, 98% in top half
Early decision deadline: N/A, notification date: N/A
Early action deadline: N/A, notification date: N/A
Application deadline (fall): 12/1
Undergraduate student body: 36,899 full time, 3,080 part time; 48% male, 52% female; 0% American Indian, 18% Asian, 4% black, 22% Hispanic, 3% multiracial, 0% Pacific Islander, 48% white, 5% international; 95% from in state; 18% live on campus; 15% of students in fraternities, 17% in sororities
Most popular majors: 9% Biological and Biomedical Sciences, 12% Business, Management, Marketing, and Related Support Services, 12% Communication, Journalism, and Related Programs, 12% Engineering, 12% Social Sciences

Expenses: 2014-2015: $9,798 in state, $34,722 out of state; room/board: $11,456
Financial aid: (512) 475-6203; 45% of undergrads determined to have financial need; average aid package $12,427

University of Texas–Brownsville

Brownsville TX
(956) 882-8295
U.S. News ranking: Reg. U. (W), second tier
Website: www.utb.edu
Admissions email: admissions@utb.edu
Public; founded 1926
Freshman admissions: less selective; 2013-2014: 2,843 applied, 2,479 accepted. Either SAT or ACT required. SAT 25/75 percentile: 810-1000. High school rank: 17% in top tenth, 43% in top quarter, 75% in top half
Early decision deadline: N/A, notification date: N/A
Early action deadline: N/A, notification date: N/A
Application deadline (fall): 8/1
Undergraduate student body: 4,553 full time, 2,994 part time; 43% male, 57% female; 0% American Indian, 1% Asian, 1% black, 89% Hispanic, 0% multiracial, 0% Pacific Islander, 4% white, 5% international
Most popular majors: 8% Biology, General, 13% Business Administration, Management and Operations, 10% Health and Physical Education/Fitness, 20% Multi/Interdisciplinary Studies, Other, 9% Psychology, General
Expenses: 2013-2014: $5,372 in state, $14,834 out of state; room/board: $3,360
Financial aid: (956) 882-8277

University of Texas–Dallas

Richardson TX
(972) 883-2270
U.S. News ranking: Nat. U., No. 145
Website: www.utdallas.edu
Admissions email: interest@utdallas.edu
Public; founded 1969
Freshman admissions: more selective; 2013-2014: 8,750 applied, 5,125 accepted. Either SAT or ACT required. SAT 25/75 percentile: 1150-1370. High school rank: 38% in top tenth, 71% in top quarter, 91% in top half
Early decision deadline: N/A, notification date: N/A
Early action deadline: N/A, notification date: N/A
Application deadline (fall): 7/1
Undergraduate student body: 10,635 full time, 2,414 part time; 57% male, 43% female; 0% American Indian, 27% Asian, 6% black, 17% Hispanic, 4% multiracial, 0% Pacific Islander, 40% white, 4% international; 97% from in state; 26% live on campus; 3% of students in fraternities, 2% in sororities
Most popular majors: 14% Biological and Biomedical Sciences, 32% Business, Management, Marketing, and Related Support Services, 9% Engineering, 9% Psychology, 7% Social Sciences

Expenses: 2013-2014: $11,806 in state, $30,378 out of state; room/board: $9,240
Financial aid: (972) 883-2941; 55% of undergrads determined to have financial need; average aid package $12,421

University of Texas–El Paso

El Paso TX
(915) 747-5890
U.S. News ranking: Nat. U., second tier
Website: www.utep.edu
Admissions email: futureminer@utep.edu
Public; founded 1914
Freshman admissions: selective; 2013-2014: N/A applied, N/A accepted. Neither SAT nor ACT required. ACT 25/75 percentile: 17-22. High school rank: N/A
Early decision deadline: N/A, notification date: N/A
Early action deadline: N/A, notification date: N/A
Application deadline (fall): rolling
Undergraduate student body: N/A full time, N/A part time; N/A male, N/A female; N/A American Indian, N/A Asian, N/A black, N/A Hispanic, N/A multiracial, N/A Pacific Islander, N/A white, N/A international
Most popular majors: Information not available
Expenses: 2014-2015: $7,018 in state, $17,639 out of state; room/board: $9,300
Financial aid: (915) 747-5204; 79% of undergrads determined to have financial need; average aid package $11,702

University of Texas of the Permian Basin

Odessa TX
(432) 552-2605
U.S. News ranking: Reg. U. (W), second tier
Website: www.utpb.edu
Admissions email: admissions@utpb.edu
Public; founded 1969
Freshman admissions: selective; 2013-2014: 973 applied, 799 accepted. Either SAT or ACT required. SAT 25/75 percentile: 910-1122. High school rank: 26% in top tenth, 60% in top quarter, 94% in top half
Early decision deadline: N/A, notification date: N/A
Early action deadline: N/A, notification date: N/A
Application deadline (fall): rolling
Undergraduate student body: 1,924 full time, 2,322 part time; 41% male, 59% female; 1% American Indian, 2% Asian, 6% black, 46% Hispanic, 1% multiracial, 0% Pacific Islander, 42% white, 1% international; 98% from in state; 14% live on campus; 0% of students in fraternities, 0% in sororities
Most popular majors: 7% Biological and Biomedical Sciences, 25% Business, Management, Marketing, and Related Support Services, 8% Multi/Interdisciplinary Studies, 7% Parks, Recreation, Leisure, and Fitness Studies, 7% Psychology
Expenses: 2013-2014: $6,776 in state, $17,308 out of state; room/board: $7,978
Financial aid: (432) 552-2620

University of Texas–Pan American

Edinburg TX
(956) 665-2999
U.S. News ranking: Reg. U. (W), second tier
Website: www.utpa.edu
Admissions email: admissions@utpa.edu
Public; founded 1927
Freshman admissions: selective; 2013-2014: 9,832 applied, 6,825 accepted. Either SAT or ACT required. ACT 25/75 percentile: 18-22. High school rank: 22% in top tenth, 53% in top quarter, 83% in top half
Early decision deadline: N/A, notification date: N/A
Early action deadline: N/A, notification date: N/A
Application deadline (fall): 8/11
Undergraduate student body: 13,215 full time, 4,387 part time; 45% male, 55% female; 0% American Indian, 1% Asian, 1% black, 90% Hispanic, 0% multiracial, 0% Pacific Islander, 3% white, 2% international; 99% from in state; 5% live on campus; 99% of students in fraternities, 100% in sororities
Most popular majors: 8% Biological and Biomedical Sciences, 13% Business, Management, Marketing, and Related Support Services, 16% Health Professions and Related Programs, 8% Homeland Security, Law Enforcement, Firefighting and Related Protective Services, 9% Multi/Interdisciplinary Studies
Expenses: 2014-2015: $6,134 in state, $17,132 out of state; room/board: N/A
Financial aid: (956) 381-2501

University of Texas–San Antonio

San Antonio TX
(210) 458-4599
U.S. News ranking: Nat. U., second tier
Website: www.utsa.edu
Admissions email: prospects@utsa.edu
Public; founded 1969
Freshman admissions: selective; 2013-2014: 13,988 applied, 8,671 accepted. Either SAT or ACT required. SAT 25/75 percentile: 950-1180. High school rank: 19% in top tenth, 73% in top quarter, 96% in top half
Early decision deadline: N/A, notification date: N/A
Early action deadline: N/A, notification date: N/A
Application deadline (fall): 6/1
Undergraduate student body: 20,033 full time, 4,309 part time; 53% male, 47% female; 0% American Indian, 5% Asian, 9% black, 49% Hispanic, 3% multiracial, 0% Pacific Islander, 28% white, 5% international; 98% from in state; 5% live on campus; 3% of students in fraternities, 3% in sororities
Most popular majors: 7% Biological and Biomedical Sciences, 24% Business, Management, Marketing, and Related Support Services, 6% Engineering, 9% Multi/Interdisciplinary Studies, 7% Psychology
Expenses: 2014-2015: $8,737 in state, $20,050 out of state; room/board: $7,624

Financial aid: (210) 458-8000; 65% of undergrads determined to have financial need; average aid package $9,193

University of Texas–Tyler

Tyler TX
(903) 566-7202
U.S. News ranking: Reg. U. (W), No. 68
Website: www.uttyler.edu
Admissions email: admrequest@uttyler.edu
Public; founded 1971
Freshman admissions: selective; 2013-2014: 2,104 applied, 1,726 accepted. Either SAT or ACT required. SAT 25/75 percentile: 960-1158. High school rank: 13% in top tenth, 44% in top quarter, 68% in top half
Early decision deadline: N/A, notification date: N/A
Early action deadline: N/A, notification date: N/A
Application deadline (fall): 8/20
Undergraduate student body: 4,090 full time, 1,501 part time; 43% male, 57% female; 0% American Indian, 3% Asian, 9% black, 14% Hispanic, 8% multiracial, 0% Pacific Islander, 63% white, 1% international; 98% from in state; 14% live on campus; 3% of students in fraternities, 2% in sororities
Most popular majors: 18% Business, Management, Marketing, and Related Support Services, 27% Health Professions and Related Programs, 11% Multi/Interdisciplinary Studies, 7% Parks, Recreation, Leisure, and Fitness Studies
Expenses: 2013-2014: $7,222 in state, $17,842 out of state; room/board: $8,979
Financial aid: (903) 566-7180

University of the Incarnate Word

San Antonio TX
(210) 829-6005
U.S. News ranking: Reg. U. (W), No. 63
Website: www.uiw.edu
Admissions email: admis@uiwtx.edu
Private; founded 1881
Affiliation: Roman Catholic
Freshman admissions: selective; 2013-2014: 4,062 applied, 3,781 accepted. Either SAT or ACT required. SAT 25/75 percentile: 870-1060. High school rank: 18% in top tenth, 43% in top quarter, 71% in top half
Early decision deadline: N/A, notification date: N/A
Early action deadline: N/A, notification date: N/A
Application deadline (fall): rolling
Undergraduate student body: 4,201 full time, 2,290 part time; 39% male, 61% female; 0% American Indian, 2% Asian, 7% black, 61% Hispanic, 1% multiracial, 0% Pacific Islander, 20% white, 3% international; 94% from in state; 12% live on campus; 1% of students in fraternities, 1% in sororities
Most popular majors: 8% Biology, General, 37% Business Administration, Management and Operations, 8% Design and Applied Arts, 9% Registered

Nursing, Nursing Administration, Nursing Research and Clinical Nursing, 8% Teacher Education and Professional Development, Specific Levels and Methods
Expenses: 2014-2015: $26,490; room/board: $10,826
Financial aid: (210) 829-6008; 79% of undergrads determined to have financial need; average aid package $18,126

Wayland Baptist University

Plainview TX
(806) 291-3500
U.S. News ranking: Reg. U. (W), second tier
Website: www.wbu.edu
Admissions email: admityou@wbu.edu
Private; founded 1908
Affiliation: Southern Baptist Convention
Freshman admissions: less selective; 2013-2014: 581 applied, 573 accepted. Either SAT or ACT required. ACT 25/75 percentile: 17-23. High school rank: 11% in top tenth, 28% in top quarter, 65% in top half
Early decision deadline: N/A, notification date: N/A
Early action deadline: N/A, notification date: N/A
Application deadline (fall): rolling
Undergraduate student body: 1,143 full time, 3,372 part time; 50% male, 50% female; 1% American Indian, 2% Asian, 17% black, 27% Hispanic, 4% multiracial, 1% Pacific Islander, 43% white, 1% international; 68% from in state; 17% live on campus; 1% of students in fraternities, 1% in sororities
Most popular majors: 36% Business Administration and Management, General, 7% Criminal Justice/Law Enforcement Administration, 6% Human Services, General, 31% Liberal Arts and Sciences, General Studies and Humanities, Other, 6% Registered Nursing/Registered Nurse
Expenses: 2014-2015: $15,930; room/board: $5,852
Financial aid: (806) 291-3520; 61% of undergrads determined to have financial need; average aid package $10,545

West Texas A&M University

Canyon TX
(806) 651-2020
U.S. News ranking: Reg. U. (W), No. 80
Website: www.wtamu.edu
Admissions email: admissions@mail.wtamu.edu
Public; founded 1910
Freshman admissions: selective; 2013-2014: 4,632 applied, 3,429 accepted. Either SAT or ACT required. ACT 25/75 percentile: 19-24. High school rank: 15% in top tenth, 42% in top quarter, 77% in top half
Early decision deadline: N/A, notification date: N/A
Early action deadline: N/A, notification date: N/A
Application deadline (fall): rolling
Undergraduate student body: 5,523 full time, 1,385 part time; 45% male, 55% female; 1% American

Indian, 1% Asian, 5% black, 23% Hispanic, 2% multiracial, 0% Pacific Islander, 64% white, 2% international; 90% from in state; 28% live on campus; 6% of students in fraternities, 7% in sororities
Most popular majors: 9% Agriculture, Agriculture Operations, and Related Sciences, 15% Business, Management, Marketing, and Related Support Services, 10% Health Professions and Related Programs, 12% Liberal Arts and Sciences, General Studies and Humanities, 15% Multi/Interdisciplinary Studies
Expenses: 2014-2015: $7,361 in state, $8,312 out of state; room/board: $7,196
Financial aid: (806) 651-2055; 62% of undergrads determined to have financial need; average aid package $9,843

Wiley College
Marshall TX
(800) 658-6889
U.S. News ranking: Reg. Coll. (W), second tier
Website: www.wileyc.edu
Admissions email: admissions@wileyc.edu
Private; founded 1873
Affiliation: United Methodist
Freshman admissions: least selective; 2013-2014: 1,544 applied, 1,458 accepted. Neither SAT nor ACT required. ACT 25/75 percentile: 14-18. High school rank: 1% in top tenth, 8% in top quarter, 39% in top half
Early decision deadline: N/A, notification date: N/A
Early action deadline: N/A, notification date: N/A
Application deadline (fall): rolling
Undergraduate student body: 1,324 full time, 64 part time; 44% male, 56% female; 0% American Indian, 0% Asian, 85% black, 7% Hispanic, 0% multiracial, 0% Pacific Islander, 2% white, 5% international; 57% from in state; 67% live on campus; 3% of students in fraternities, 6% in sororities
Most popular majors: 7% Business Administration and Management, General, 8% Criminal Justice/Law Enforcement Administration, 12% Criminal Justice/Police Science, 6% Early Childhood Education and Teaching, 15% Non-Profit/Public/Organizational Management
Expenses: 2014-2015: $11,482; room/board: $6,846
Financial aid: (903) 927-3210; 95% of undergrads determined to have financial need; average aid package $8,596

UTAH

Brigham Young University–Provo
Provo UT
(801) 422-2507
U.S. News ranking: Nat. U., No. 62
Website: www.byu.edu
Admissions email: admissions@byu.edu
Private; founded 1875
Affiliation: Church of Jesus Christ of Latter-day Saints
Freshman admissions: more selective; 2013-2014: 11,603 applied, 5,645 accepted. Either SAT or ACT required. ACT 25/75

percentile: 26-31. High school rank: 54% in top tenth, 85% in top quarter, 97% in top half
Early decision deadline: N/A, notification date: N/A
Early action deadline: N/A, notification date: N/A
Application deadline (fall): 2/1
Undergraduate student body: 25,084 full time, 2,681 part time; 54% male, 46% female; 0% American Indian, 2% Asian, 0% black, 5% Hispanic, 3% multiracial, 1% Pacific Islander, 84% white, 3% international; 34% from in state; 19% live on campus; N/A of students in fraternities, N/A in sororities
Most popular majors: 11% Biological and Biomedical Sciences, 12% Business, Management, Marketing, and Related Support Services, 10% Education, 8% Health Professions and Related Programs, 8% Social Sciences
Expenses: 2014-2015: $5,000; room/board: $7,964
Financial aid: (801) 422-4104; 49% of undergrads determined to have financial need; average aid package $7,082

Dixie State College of Utah
Saint George UT
(435) 652-7702
U.S. News ranking: Reg. Coll. (W), unranked
Website: www.dixie.edu
Admissions email: admissions@dixie.edu
Public; founded 1911
Freshman admissions: N/A; 2013-2014: 3,321 applied, 3,321 accepted. Neither SAT nor ACT required. ACT 25/75 percentile: 17-23. High school rank: 9% in top tenth, 28% in top quarter, 57% in top half
Early decision deadline: N/A, notification date: N/A
Early action deadline: N/A, notification date: N/A
Application deadline (fall): 8/15
Undergraduate student body: 5,165 full time, 3,185 part time; 47% male, 53% female; 1% American Indian, 1% Asian, 2% black, 8% Hispanic, 2% multiracial, 2% Pacific Islander, 80% white, 2% international; 84% from in state; N/A live on campus; N/A of students in fraternities, N/A in sororities
Most popular majors: Information not available
Expenses: 2014-2015: $4,456 in state, $12,792 out of state; room/board: $5,048
Financial aid: (435) 652-7575; 73% of undergrads determined to have financial need; average aid package $7,501

Southern Utah University
Cedar City UT
(435) 586-7740
U.S. News ranking: Reg. U. (W), No. 58
Website: www.suu.edu
Admissions email: admissionsinfo@suu.edu
Public; founded 1897
Freshman admissions: selective; 2013-2014: 8,318 applied, 4,749 accepted. Either SAT or ACT required. ACT 25/75 percentile: 20-26. High school

rank: 18% in top tenth, 42% in top quarter, 75% in top half
Early decision deadline: N/A, notification date: N/A
Early action deadline: N/A, notification date: N/A
Application deadline (fall): 5/1
Undergraduate student body: 5,254 full time, 1,763 part time; 45% male, 55% female; 2% American Indian, 1% Asian, 1% black, 4% Hispanic, 1% multiracial, 1% Pacific Islander, 81% white, 5% international; 82% from in state; 10% live on campus; N/A of students in fraternities, N/A in sororities
Most popular majors: 8% Biological and Biomedical Sciences, 11% Business, Management, Marketing, and Related Support Services, 6% Communication, Journalism, and Related Programs, 23% Education, 7% Psychology
Expenses: 2014-2015: $6,138 in state, $18,596 out of state; room/board: $6,890
Financial aid: (435) 586-7735; 65% of undergrads determined to have financial need; average aid package $8,927

University of Utah
Salt Lake City UT
(801) 581-8761
U.S. News ranking: Nat. U., No. 129
Website: www.utah.edu
Admissions email: admissions@utah.edu
Public; founded 1850
Freshman admissions: selective; 2013-2014: 11,354 applied, 9,281 accepted. Either SAT or ACT required. ACT 25/75 percentile: 21-27. High school rank: 21% in top tenth, 48% in top quarter, 83% in top half
Early decision deadline: N/A, notification date: N/A
Early action deadline: N/A, notification date: N/A
Application deadline (fall): 4/1
Undergraduate student body: 17,319 full time, 7,173 part time; 55% male, 45% female; 1% American Indian, 5% Asian, 1% black, 9% Hispanic, 3% multiracial, 1% Pacific Islander, 72% white, 7% international; 81% from in state; 13% live on campus; 2% of students in fraternities, 3% in sororities
Most popular majors: 4% Economics, General, 4% Human Development and Family Studies, General, 5% Kinesiology and Exercise Science, 6% Mass Communication/Media Studies, 6% Psychology, General
Expenses: 2014-2015: $7,935 in state, $25,267 out of state; room/board: $8,528
Financial aid: (801) 581-8788; 46% of undergrads determined to have financial need; average aid package $16,604

Utah State University
Logan UT
(435) 797-1079
U.S. News ranking: Nat. U., No. 194
Website: www.usu.edu
Admissions email: admit@usu.edu
Public; founded 1888
Freshman admissions: selective; 2013-2014: 10,935 applied, 10,768 accepted. Either SAT or ACT required. ACT 25/75

percentile: 20-26. High school rank: 19% in top tenth, 44% in top quarter, 74% in top half
Early decision deadline: N/A, notification date: N/A
Early action deadline: N/A, notification date: N/A
Application deadline (fall): rolling
Undergraduate student body: 15,260 full time, 9,125 part time; 46% male, 54% female; 2% American Indian, 1% Asian, 1% black, 5% Hispanic, 2% multiracial, 0% Pacific Islander, 80% white, 2% international; 76% from in state; N/A live on campus; 2% of students in fraternities, 2% in sororities
Most popular majors: 11% Communication Sciences and Disorders, General, 7% Economics, General, 4% Elementary Education and Teaching, 5% Multi-/Interdisciplinary Studies, Other, 4% Physical Education Teaching and Coaching
Expenses: 2014-2015: $6,384 in state, $18,491 out of state; room/board: $2,840
Financial aid: (435) 797-0173; 57% of undergrads determined to have financial need; average aid package $8,800

Utah Valley University
Orem UT
(801) 863-8466
U.S. News ranking: Reg. Coll. (W), unranked
Website: www.uvu.edu/
Admissions email: InstantInfo@uvu.edu
Public; founded 1941
Freshman admissions: N/A; 2013-2014: 6,934 applied, 6,934 accepted. Either SAT or ACT required. ACT 25/75 percentile: 18-24. High school rank: 5% in top tenth, 14% in top quarter, 44% in top half
Early decision deadline: N/A, notification date: N/A
Early action deadline: N/A, notification date: N/A
Application deadline (fall): 8/1
Undergraduate student body: 15,751 full time, 14,619 part time; 56% male, 44% female; 1% American Indian, 1% Asian, 1% black, 10% Hispanic, 2% multiracial, 1% Pacific Islander, 81% white, 2% international; 90% from in state; 0% live on campus; N/A of students in fraternities, N/A in sororities
Most popular majors: 3% Accounting, 5% Airline/Commercial/Professional Pilot and Flight Crew, 6% Business Administration and Management, General, 4% Elementary Education and Teaching, 7% Psychology, General
Expenses: 2014-2015: $5,270 in state, $14,802 out of state; room/board: N/A
Financial aid: (801) 863-8442; 68% of undergrads determined to have financial need; average aid package $5,081

Weber State University
Ogden UT
(801) 626-6744
U.S. News ranking: Reg. U. (W), No. 68
Website: weber.edu
Admissions email: admissions@weber.edu
Public; founded 1889
Freshman admissions: selective; 2013-2014: 5,296 applied, 5,296 accepted. Neither SAT nor ACT required. ACT 25/75 percentile: 18-24. High school rank: N/A
Early decision deadline: N/A, notification date: N/A
Early action deadline: N/A, notification date: N/A
Application deadline (fall): 8/21
Undergraduate student body: 10,879 full time, 13,619 part time; 47% male, 53% female; 1% American Indian, 2% Asian, 2% black, 9% Hispanic, 2% multiracial, 0% Pacific Islander, 71% white, 2% international; 91% from in state; 4% live on campus; 1% of students in fraternities, 1% in sororities
Most popular majors: 2% Accounting, 2% Computer Science, 2% Medical Radiologic Technology/Science - Radiation Therapist, 8% Registered Nursing/Registered Nurse, 3% Selling Skills and Sales Operations
Expenses: 2014-2015: $5,126 in state, $13,780 out of state; room/board: $8,000
Financial aid: (801) 626-7569; 61% of undergrads determined to have financial need; average aid package $1,952

Western Governors University
Salt Lake City UT
(866) 225-5948
U.S. News ranking: Reg. U. (W), unranked
Website: www.wgu.edu/
Admissions email: info@wgu.edu
Private; founded 1996
Freshman admissions: N/A; 2013-2014: N/A applied, N/A accepted. Neither SAT nor ACT required. ACT 25/75 percentile: N/A. High school rank: N/A
Early decision deadline: N/A, notification date: N/A
Early action deadline: N/A, notification date: N/A
Application deadline (fall): rolling
Undergraduate student body: 35,493 full time, 0 part time; 41% male, 59% female; 1% American Indian, 3% Asian, 9% black, 7% Hispanic, 3% multiracial, 0% Pacific Islander, 73% white, 0% international
Most popular majors: 15% Business Administration and Management, General, 7% Education, General, 6% Nursing Administration, 23% Registered Nursing/Registered Nurse, 5% Special Education and Teaching, General
Expenses: 2014-2015: $6,070; room/board: N/A
Financial aid: (801) 327-8104; 62% of undergrads determined to have financial need; average aid package $5,846

Westminster College

Salt Lake City UT
(801) 832-2200
U.S. News ranking: Reg. U. (W),
No. 20
Website:
www.westminstercollege.edu
Admissions email: admission@
westminstercollege.edu
Private; founded 1875
Freshman admissions: more
selective; 2013-2014: 2,461
applied, 1,850 accepted. Either
SAT or ACT required. ACT 25/75
percentile: 22-28. High school
rank: 23% in top tenth, 55% in
top quarter, 88% in top half
Early decision deadline: N/A,
notification date: N/A
Early action deadline: N/A,
notification date: N/A
Application deadline (fall): 8/15
Undergraduate student body: 2,140
full time, 155 part time; 44%
male, 56% female; 1% American
Indian, 2% Asian, 1% black,
10% Hispanic, 2% multiracial,
0% Pacific Islander, 69% white,
5% international; 60% from in
state; 27% live on campus; 0%
of students in fraternities, 0% in
sororities
Most popular majors: 26%
Business, Management,
Marketing, and Related Support
Services, 19% Health Professions
and Related Programs, 5% Natural
Resources and Conservation, 9%
Psychology, 8% Social Sciences
Expenses: 2014-2015: $30,364;
room/board: $8,456
Financial aid: (801) 832-2500;
59% of undergrads determined to
have financial need; average aid
package $22,755

VERMONT

Bennington College

Bennington VT
(800) 833-6845
U.S. News ranking: Nat. Lib. Arts,
No. 89
Website: www.bennington.edu
Admissions email: admissions@
bennington.edu
Private; founded 1925
Freshman admissions: more
selective; 2013-2014: 1,130
applied, 733 accepted. Neither
SAT nor ACT required. SAT
25/75 percentile: 1180-1380.
High school rank: 44% in top
tenth, 75% in top quarter, 97%
in top half
Early decision deadline: 11/15,
notification date: 12/20
Early action deadline: 12/1,
notification date: 2/1
Application deadline (fall): 1/3
Undergraduate student body: 609
full time, 10 part time; 35%
male, 65% female; 0% American
Indian, 3% Asian, 2% black,
5% Hispanic, 4% multiracial,
0% Pacific Islander, 76% white,
8% international; 4% from in
state; 99% live on campus; 0%
of students in fraternities, 0% in
sororities
Most popular majors: 11%
English Language and Literature/
Letters, 5% Foreign Languages,
Literatures, and Linguistics, 5%
Physical Sciences, 9% Social
Sciences, 44% Visual and
Performing Arts
Expenses: 2014-2015: $46,658;
room/board: $13,652

Financial aid: (802) 440-4325;
63% of undergrads determined to
have financial need; average aid
package $37,681

Burlington College

Burlington VT
(802) 862-9616
U.S. News ranking: Nat. Lib. Arts,
second tier
Website: www.burlington.edu
Admissions email: admissions@
burlington.edu
Private; founded 1972
Freshman admissions: less
selective; 2013-2014: 255
applied, 211 accepted. Neither
SAT nor ACT required. SAT 25/75
percentile: 820-1130. High
school rank: 5% in top tenth, 13%
in top quarter, 45% in top half
Early decision deadline: N/A,
notification date: N/A
Early action deadline: N/A,
notification date: N/A
Application deadline (fall): rolling
Undergraduate student body: 160
full time, 56 part time; 51%
male, 49% female; 1% American
Indian, 1% Asian, 2% black, 7%
Hispanic, 1% multiracial, 0%
Pacific Islander, 35% white, 1%
international
Most popular majors: Information
not available
Expenses: 2014-2015: $23,546;
room/board: $8,600
Financial aid: (802) 862-9616;
79% of undergrads determined to
have financial need; average aid
package $14,385

Castleton State College

Castleton VT
(800) 639-8521
U.S. News ranking: Nat. Lib. Arts,
second tier
Website: www.castleton.edu
Admissions email:
info@castleton.edu
Public; founded 1787
Freshman admissions: less
selective; 2013-2014: 2,600
applied, 2,051 accepted. Either
SAT or ACT required. SAT 25/75
percentile: 850-1060. High
school rank: 8% in top tenth, 25%
in top quarter, 56% in top half
Early decision deadline: N/A,
notification date: N/A
Early action deadline: N/A,
notification date: N/A
Application deadline (fall): rolling
Undergraduate student body: 1,916
full time, 153 part time; 48%
male, 52% female; 1% American
Indian, 1% Asian, 1% black, 2%
Hispanic, 1% multiracial, 0%
Pacific Islander, 85% white, 1%
international; N/A from in state;
53% live on campus; 0% of
students in fraternities, 11% in
sororities
Most popular majors: Information
not available
Expenses: 2013-2014: $10,286
in state, $24,014 out of state;
room/board: $9,138
Financial aid: (802) 468-1292

Champlain College

Burlington VT
(800) 570-5858
U.S. News ranking: Reg. Coll. (N),
No. 14
Website: www.champlain.edu
Admissions email: admission@
champlain.edu

Private; founded 1878
Freshman admissions: selective;
2013-2014: 5,047 applied,
3,573 accepted. Either SAT
or ACT required. SAT 25/75
percentile: 990-1240. High school
rank: 15% in top tenth, 39% in
top quarter, 68% in top half
Early decision deadline: 11/15,
notification date: 12/15
Early action deadline: N/A,
notification date: N/A
Application deadline (fall): 1/31
Undergraduate student body: 2,332
full time, 566 part time; 60%
male, 40% female; 0% American
Indian, 1% Asian, 3% black,
4% Hispanic, 2% multiracial,
0% Pacific Islander, 71% white,
1% international; 24% from in
state; 46% live on campus; N/A
of students in fraternities, N/A in
sororities
Most popular majors: 7%
Accounting, 13% Business
Administration and Management,
General, 7% Computer Graphics,
7% Computer and Information
Sciences and Support Services,
Other, 8% Graphic Design
Expenses: 2014-2015: $32,900;
room/board: $13,750
Financial aid: (800) 570-5858;
68% of undergrads determined to
have financial need; average aid
package $19,612

College of St. Joseph

Rutland VT
(802) 773-5286
U.S. News ranking: Reg. U. (N),
second tier
Website: www.csj.edu
Admissions email:
admissions@csj.edu
Private; founded 1956
Affiliation: Roman Catholic
Freshman admissions: least
selective; 2013-2014: 179
applied, 130 accepted. Either
SAT or ACT required. SAT 25/75
percentile: 705-985. High school
rank: N/A
Early decision deadline: N/A,
notification date: N/A
Early action deadline: N/A,
notification date: N/A
Application deadline (fall): rolling
Undergraduate student body: 120
full time, 56 part time; 48%
male, 52% female; 0% American
Indian, 1% Asian, 23% black,
1% Hispanic, 0% multiracial,
1% Pacific Islander, 74% white,
0% international; 69% from in
state; 49% live on campus; 0%
of students in fraternities, 0% in
sororities
Most popular majors: 11%
Behavioral Sciences, 13% Human
Services, General, 11% Liberal
Arts and Sciences/Liberal Studies,
16% Organizational Leadership,
11% Psychology, General
Expenses: 2014-2015: $21,200;
room/board: $9,400
Financial aid: (802) 773-5900;
95% of undergrads determined to
have financial need; average aid
package $25,177

Goddard College

Plainfield VT
(800) 906-8312
U.S. News ranking: Reg. U. (N),
unranked
Website: www.goddard.edu
Admissions email:
admissions@goddard.edu
Private; founded 1863

Freshman admissions: N/A; 2013-
2014: 5 applied, 4 accepted.
Neither SAT nor ACT required.
ACT 25/75 percentile: N/A. High
school rank: N/A
Early decision deadline: N/A,
notification date: N/A
Early action deadline: N/A,
notification date: N/A
Application deadline (fall): rolling
Undergraduate student body:
209 full time, 0 part time; 35%
male, 65% female; 0% American
Indian, 1% Asian, 2% black, 6%
Hispanic, 4% multiracial, 0%
Pacific Islander, 73% white, 0%
international
Most popular majors: Information
not available
Expenses: 2014-2015: $14,930;
room/board: $1,488
Financial aid: (800) 468-4888;
46% of undergrads determined to
have financial need; average aid
package $7,964

Green Mountain College

Poultney VT
(802) 287-8208
U.S. News ranking: Nat. Lib. Arts,
second tier
Website: www.greenmtn.edu
Admissions email:
admiss@greenmtn.edu
Private; founded 1834
Affiliation: United Methodist
Freshman admissions: selective;
2013-2014: 773 applied, 584
accepted. Neither SAT nor ACT
required. SAT 25/75 percentile:
920-1200. High school rank: N/A
Early decision deadline: N/A,
notification date: N/A
Early action deadline: 11/1,
notification date: 12/14
Application deadline (fall): rolling
Undergraduate student body: 568
full time, 23 part time; 45%
male, 55% female; 1% American
Indian, 2% Asian, 6% black,
2% Hispanic, 2% multiracial,
0% Pacific Islander, 63% white,
4% international; 13% from in
state; 84% live on campus; N/A
of students in fraternities, N/A in
sororities
Most popular majors: Information
not available
Expenses: 2013-2014: $32,436;
room/board: $11,266
Financial aid: (802) 287-8210

Johnson State College

Johnson VT
(800) 635-2356
U.S. News ranking: Reg. U. (N),
second tier
Website: www.jsc.edu
Admissions email:
JSCAdmissions@jsc.edu
Public
Freshman admissions: less
selective; 2013-2014: N/A
applied, N/A accepted. Neither
SAT nor ACT required. ACT 25/75
percentile: N/A. High school
rank: N/A
Early decision deadline: N/A,
notification date: N/A
Early action deadline: N/A,
notification date: N/A
Application deadline (fall): N/A
Undergraduate student body: 1,004
full time, 531 part time; 35%
male, 65% female; N/A American
Indian, N/A Asian, N/A black, N/A
Hispanic, N/A multiracial, N/A
Pacific Islander, N/A white, N/A
international

Most popular majors: Information
not available
Expenses: 2013-2014: $10,286
in state, $21,950 out of state;
room/board: $9,138
Financial aid: (802) 635-1380

Lyndon State College[1]

Lyndonville VT
(802) 626-6413
U.S. News ranking: Reg. Coll. (N),
second tier
Website: www.lyndonstate.edu
Admissions email: admissions@
lyndonstate.edu
Public
Application deadline (fall): N/A
Undergraduate student body: N/A
full time, N/A part time
Expenses: 2013-2014: $10,286
in state, $20,942 out of state;
room/board: $9,138
Financial aid: (802) 626-6218

Marlboro College[1]

Marlboro VT
(800) 343-0049
U.S. News ranking: Nat. Lib. Arts,
unranked
Website: www.marlboro.edu
Admissions email:
admissions@marlboro.edu
Private
Application deadline (fall): N/A
Undergraduate student body: N/A
full time, N/A part time
Expenses: 2013-2014: $38,110;
room/board: $10,280
Financial aid: (802) 258-9237

Middlebury College

Middlebury VT
(802) 443-3000
U.S. News ranking: Nat. Lib. Arts,
No. 7
Website: www.middlebury.edu
Admissions email: admissions@
middlebury.edu
Private; founded 1800
Freshman admissions: most
selective; 2013-2014: 9,109
applied, 1,595 accepted. Either
SAT or ACT required. SAT 25/75
percentile: 1280-1490. High
school rank: 74% in top tenth,
93% in top quarter, 99% in
top half
Early decision deadline: 11/1,
notification date: 12/15
Early action deadline: N/A,
notification date: N/A
Application deadline (fall): 1/1
Undergraduate student body: 2,477
full time, 18 part time; 49%
male, 51% female; 0% American
Indian, 6% Asian, 3% black,
7% Hispanic, 4% multiracial,
0% Pacific Islander, 66% white,
10% international; 6% from in
state; 95% live on campus; 0%
of students in fraternities, 0% in
sororities
Most popular majors: 13%
Economics, General, 6% English
Language and Literature/Letters,
Other, 7% Environmental
Studies, 7% Political Science
and Government, General, 6%
Psychology, General
Expenses: 2014-2015: $46,044;
room/board: $13,116
Financial aid: (802) 443-5158;
40% of undergrads determined to
have financial need; average aid
package $40,419

Norwich University
Northfield VT
(800) 468-6679
U.S. News ranking: Reg. U. (N),
No. 74
Website: www.norwich.edu
Admissions email:
nuadm@norwich.edu
Private; founded 1819
Freshman admissions: selective;
2013-2014: 3,081 applied,
1,956 accepted. Either SAT
or ACT required. SAT 25/75
percentile: 950-1160. High school
rank: 11% in top tenth, 33% in
top quarter, 70% in top half
Early decision deadline: N/A,
notification date: N/A
Early action deadline: N/A,
notification date: N/A
Application deadline (fall): rolling
Undergraduate student body: 2,186
full time, 70 part time; 74%
male, 26% female; 1% American
Indian, 2% Asian, 2% black,
3% Hispanic, 2% multiracial,
0% Pacific Islander, 56% white,
1% international; 12% from in
state; 93% live on campus; 0%
of students in fraternities, 0% in
sororities
Most popular majors: 7%
Architecture, 6% Business
Administration and Management,
General, 22% Criminal Justice/
Law Enforcement Administration,
7% Mechanical Engineering, 7%
Registered Nursing/Registered
Nurse
Expenses: 2014-2015: $34,704;
room/board: $11,984
Financial aid: (802) 485-2015;
79% of undergrads determined to
have financial need; average aid
package $27,656

Southern Vermont College
Bennington VT
(802) 447-6304
U.S. News ranking: Reg. Coll. (N),
second tier
Website: www.svc.edu
Admissions email: admis@svc.edu
Private
Freshman admissions: least
selective; 2013-2014: N/A
applied, N/A accepted. Neither
SAT nor ACT required. ACT 25/75
percentile: N/A. High school
rank: N/A
Early decision deadline: N/A,
notification date: N/A
Early action deadline: N/A,
notification date: N/A
Application deadline (fall): N/A
Undergraduate student body: 453
full time, 27 part time; 38%
male, 62% female; 0% American
Indian, 1% Asian, 9% black, 9%
Hispanic, 1% multiracial, 0%
Pacific Islander, 63% white, 1%
international
Most popular majors: Information
not available
Expenses: 2014-2015: $22,370;
room/board: $10,500
Financial aid: (877) 563-6076

Sterling College[1]
Craftsbury Common VT
(802) 586-7711
U.S. News ranking: Nat. Lib. Arts,
unranked
Website: www.sterlingcollege.edu
Admissions email: admissions@
sterlingcollege.edu
Private; founded 1958
Application deadline (fall): rolling

Undergraduate student body: N/A
full time, N/A part time
Expenses: 2013-2014: $29,894;
room/board: $8,498
Financial aid: (802) 586-7711

St. Michael's College
Colchester VT
(800) 762-8000
U.S. News ranking: Nat. Lib. Arts,
No. 99
Website: www.smcvt.edu
Admissions email:
admission@smcvt.edu
Private; founded 1904
Affiliation: Roman Catholic
Freshman admissions: selective;
2013-2014: 4,431 applied,
3,328 accepted. Neither SAT
nor ACT required. SAT 25/75
percentile: 1060-1290. High
school rank: 26% in top tenth,
54% in top quarter, 81% in
top half
Early decision deadline: N/A,
notification date: N/A
Early action deadline: 11/1,
notification date: 1/1
Application deadline (fall): 2/1
Undergraduate student body: 1,959
full time, 39 part time; 45%
male, 55% female; 0% American
Indian, 2% Asian, 2% black,
4% Hispanic, 2% multiracial,
0% Pacific Islander, 86% white,
3% international; 20% from in
state; 96% live on campus; 0%
of students in fraternities, 0% in
sororities
Most popular majors: 11%
Biological and Biomedical
Sciences, 18% Business,
Management, Marketing, and
Related Support Services, 8%
English Language and Literature/
Letters, 10% Psychology, 13%
Social Sciences
Expenses: 2014-2015: $39,375;
room/board: $10,600
Financial aid: (802) 654-3243;
69% of undergrads determined to
have financial need; average aid
package $26,858

University of Vermont
Burlington VT
(802) 656-3370
U.S. News ranking: Nat. U.,
No. 85
Website: www.uvm.edu
Admissions email:
admissions@uvm.edu
Public; founded 1791
Freshman admissions: more
selective; 2013-2014: 22,381
applied, 17,357 accepted. Either
SAT or ACT required. SAT 25/75
percentile: 1080-1290. High
school rank: 33% in top tenth,
68% in top quarter, 96% in
top half
Early decision deadline: N/A,
notification date: N/A
Early action deadline: 11/1,
notification date: 12/15
Application deadline (fall): 1/15
Undergraduate student body: 9,764
full time, 1,148 part time; 44%
male, 56% female; 0% American
Indian, 2% Asian, 1% black,
4% Hispanic, 3% multiracial,
0% Pacific Islander, 83% white,
2% international; 34% from in
state; 50% live on campus; 6%
of students in fraternities, 6% in
sororities
Most popular majors: 8% Business
Administration and Management,
General, 5% English Language

---

and Literature, General,
5% Environmental Studies,
5% Political Science and
Government, General,
6% Psychology, General
Expenses: 2014-2015: $16,226
in state, $37,874 out of state;
room/board: $10,780
Financial aid: (802) 656-5700;
58% of undergrads determined to
have financial need; average aid
package $21,989

Vermont Technical College
Randolph Center VT
(802) 728-1244
U.S. News ranking: Reg. Coll. (N),
No. 36
Website: www.vtc.edu
Admissions email:
admissions@vtc.edu
Public; founded 1866
Freshman admissions: less
selective; 2013-2014: 841
applied, 560 accepted. Neither
SAT nor ACT required. SAT 25/75
percentile: 810-1040. High
school rank: 7% in top tenth, 27%
in top quarter, 58% in top half
Early decision deadline: N/A,
notification date: N/A
Early action deadline: N/A,
notification date: N/A
Application deadline (fall): rolling
Undergraduate student body: 1,042
full time, 503 part time; 58%
male, 42% female; 1% American
Indian, 1% Asian, 1% black,
1% Hispanic, 0% multiracial,
0% Pacific Islander, 88% white,
4% international; 86% from in
state; N/A live on campus; N/A
of students in fraternities, N/A in
sororities
Most popular majors: Information
not available
Expenses: 2014-2015: $13,200
in state, $24,048 out of state;
room/board: $9,414
Financial aid: (800) 965-8790;
77% of undergrads determined to
have financial need; average aid
package $11,282

Averett University
Danville VA
(800) 283-7388
U.S. News ranking: Reg. Coll. (S),
No. 25
Website: www.averett.edu
Admissions email:
admit@averett.edu
Private; founded 1859
Affiliation: Baptist General
Association of Virginia
Freshman admissions: less
selective; 2013-2014: 1,697
applied, 1,491 accepted. Either
SAT or ACT required. SAT 25/75
percentile: 840-1030. High school
rank: 11% in top tenth, 30% in
top quarter, 60% in top half
Early decision deadline: N/A,
notification date: N/A
Early action deadline: N/A,
notification date: N/A
Application deadline (fall): rolling
Undergraduate student body: 858
full time, 28 part time; 50%
male, 50% female; 1% American
Indian, 1% Asian, 23% black,
3% Hispanic, 0% multiracial,
0% Pacific Islander, 63% white,
9% international; 70% from in
state; 57% live on campus; 0%
of students in fraternities, 1% in
sororities

Most popular majors: 12%
Criminal Justice/Law Enforcement
Administration, 28% Education,
General, 13% Health Services/
Allied Health/Health Sciences,
General, 5% Liberal Arts and
Sciences/Liberal Studies, 17%
Marketing/Marketing Management,
General
Expenses: 2014-2015: $29,150;
room/board: $8,600
Financial aid: (434) 791-5646;
85% of undergrads determined to
have financial need; average aid
package $22,442

Bluefield College
Bluefield VA
(276) 326-4231
U.S. News ranking: Reg. Coll. (S),
No. 54
Website: www.bluefield.edu
Admissions email: admissions@
bluefield.edu
Private; founded 1922
Affiliation: Baptist
Freshman admissions: less
selective; 2013-2014: 1,044
applied, 598 accepted. Either
SAT or ACT required. SAT 25/75
percentile: 800-1010. High
school rank: 8% in top tenth, 27%
in top quarter, 64% in top half
Early decision deadline: N/A,
notification date: N/A
Early action deadline: N/A,
notification date: N/A
Application deadline (fall): rolling
Undergraduate student body: 723
full time, 114 part time; 45%
male, 55% female; 0% American
Indian, 0% Asian, 23% black,
3% Hispanic, 3% multiracial,
0% Pacific Islander, 67% white,
2% international; 24% from in
state; 66% live on campus; 11%
of students in fraternities, 41%
in sororities
Most popular majors: 28%
Business Administration and
Management, General, 19%
Criminal Justice/Safety Studies,
8% Human Services, General,
10% Kinesiology and Exercise
Science, 8% Psychology, Other
Expenses: 2014-2015: $22,840;
room/board: $8,456
Financial aid: (276) 326-4215;
87% of undergrads determined to
have financial need; average aid
package $14,942

Bridgewater College
Bridgewater VA
(800) 759-8328
U.S. News ranking: Nat. Lib. Arts,
No. 178
Website: www.bridgewater.edu
Admissions email: admissions@
bridgewater.edu
Private; founded 1880
Affiliation: Church of the Brethren
Freshman admissions: selective;
2013-2014: 5,401 applied,
2,967 accepted. Either SAT
or ACT required. SAT 25/75
percentile: 930-1130. High school
rank: 20% in top tenth, 45% in
top quarter, 82% in top half
Early decision deadline: N/A,
notification date: N/A
Early action deadline: N/A,
notification date: N/A
Application deadline (fall): 5/1
Undergraduate student body:
1,840 full time, 8 part time; 45%
male, 55% female; 0% American
Indian, 1% Asian, 9% black,
3% Hispanic, 4% multiracial,

0% Pacific Islander, 79% white,
1% international; 78% from in
state; 83% live on campus; 0%
of students in fraternities, 0% in
sororities
Most popular majors: 11% Biology/
Biological Sciences, General,
11% Business Administration and
Management, General, 5% Family
and Consumer Sciences/Human
Sciences, General, 10% Health
and Physical Education/Fitness,
General, 6% Liberal Arts and
Sciences/Liberal Studies
Expenses: 2014-2015: $30,380;
room/board: $11,070
Financial aid: (540) 828-5376;
82% of undergrads determined to
have financial need; average aid
package $25,654

Christopher Newport University
Newport News VA
(757) 594-7015
U.S. News ranking: Reg. U. (S),
No. 17
Website: www.cnu.edu
Admissions email: admit@cnu.edu
Public; founded 1960
Freshman admissions: selective;
2013-2014: 7,016 applied,
4,141 accepted. Neither SAT
nor ACT required. SAT 25/75
percentile: 1070-1250. High
school rank: 20% in top tenth,
53% in top quarter, 91% in
top half
Early decision deadline: 11/15,
notification date: 12/15
Early action deadline: 12/1,
notification date: 1/15
Application deadline (fall): 2/1
Undergraduate student body: 4,962
full time, 132 part time; 43%
male, 57% female; 0% American
Indian, 2% Asian, 8% black,
5% Hispanic, 5% multiracial,
0% Pacific Islander, 75% white,
0% international; 93% from in
state; 73% live on campus; 3%
of students in fraternities, 0% in
sororities
Most popular majors: 12% Biology/
Biological Sciences, General,
12% Business Administration
and Management, General,
9% History, General, 14%
Psychology, General, 10% Speech
Communication and Rhetoric
Expenses: 2014-2015: $11,646
in state, $21,578 out of state;
room/board: $10,314
Financial aid: (757) 594-7170;
46% of undergrads determined to
have financial need; average aid
package $8,359

College of William and Mary
Williamsburg VA
(757) 221-4223
U.S. News ranking: Nat. U.,
No. 33
Website: www.wm.edu
Admissions email:
admission@wm.edu
Public; founded 1693
Freshman admissions: most
selective; 2013-2014: 14,046
applied, 4,665 accepted. Either
SAT or ACT required. SAT 25/75
percentile: 1270-1460. High
school rank: 80% in top tenth,
97% in top quarter, 99% in
top half
Early decision deadline: 11/1,
notification date: 12/1

Early action deadline: N/A,
notification date: N/A
Application deadline (fall): 1/1
Undergraduate student body: 6,195
full time, 76 part time; 45%
male, 55% female; 0% American
Indian, 7% Asian, 7% black, 9%
Hispanic, 5% multiracial, 0%
Pacific Islander, 60% white, 4%
international; 69% from in state;
73% live on campus; 25% of
students in fraternities, 30% in
sororities
Most popular majors: 9% Biological
and Biomedical Sciences,
12% Business, Management,
Marketing, and Related Support
Services, 7% English Language
and Literature/Letters, 8%
Psychology, 23% Social Sciences
Expenses: 2014-2015: $17,656
in state, $39,360 out of state;
room/board: $10,344
Financial aid: (757) 221-2420;
34% of undergrads determined to
have financial need; average aid
package $18,125

Eastern Mennonite University

Harrisonburg VA
(800) 368-2665
U.S. News ranking: Nat. Lib. Arts,
No. 172
Website: www.emu.edu
Admissions email:
admiss@emu.edu
Private; founded 1917
Affiliation: Mennonite Church USA
Freshman admissions: selective;
2013-2014: 1,073 applied, 698
accepted. Either SAT or ACT
required. SAT 25/75 percentile:
863-1128. High school rank:
16% in top tenth, 36% in top
quarter, 75% in top half
Early decision deadline: N/A,
notification date: N/A
Early action deadline: N/A,
notification date: N/A
Application deadline (fall): rolling
Undergraduate student body: 1,122
full time, 62 part time; 35%
male, 65% female; 0% American
Indian, 2% Asian, 6% black,
7% Hispanic, 2% multiracial,
0% Pacific Islander, 77% white,
3% international; 57% from in
state; 58% live on campus; N/A
of students in fraternities, N/A in
sororities
Most popular majors: 8% Biological
and Biomedical Sciences,
7% Business, Management,
Marketing, and Related Support
Services, 18% Health Professions
and Related Programs, 17%
Liberal Arts and Sciences, General
Studies and Humanities, 9%
Psychology
Expenses: 2013-2014: $29,350;
room/board: $9,500
Financial aid: (540) 432-4139

ECPI University[1]

Virginia Beach VA
(866) 499-0336
U.S. News ranking: Reg. Coll. (S),
unranked
Website: www.ecpi.edu/
Admissions email:
ssaunders@ecpi.edu
For-profit
Application deadline (fall): N/A
Undergraduate student body: N/A
full time, N/A part time
Expenses: 2013-2014: $14,245;
room/board: N/A
Financial aid: N/A

Emory and Henry College

Emory VA
(800) 848-5493
U.S. News ranking: Nat. Lib. Arts,
No. 172
Website: www.ehc.edu
Admissions email:
ehadmiss@ehc.edu
Private; founded 1836
Affiliation: United Methodist
Freshman admissions: selective;
2013-2014: 1,663 applied,
1,093 accepted. Either SAT
or ACT required. SAT 25/75
percentile: 880-1120. High
school rank: N/A
Early decision deadline: 11/15,
notification date: 12/15
Early action deadline: N/A,
notification date: N/A
Application deadline (fall): rolling
Undergraduate student body: 889
full time, 47 part time; 52%
male, 48% female; 1% American
Indian, 0% Asian, 9% black,
2% Hispanic, 2% multiracial,
0% Pacific Islander, 81% white,
1% international; 64% from in
state; 79% live on campus; N/A
of students in fraternities, N/A in
sororities
Most popular majors: 8% Biology/
Biological Sciences, General,
6% Environmental Science, 6%
History Teacher Education, 5%
Psychology, General, 7% Sociology
Expenses: 2014-2015: $30,226;
room/board: $10,258
Financial aid: (276) 944-6229;
83% of undergrads determined to
have financial need; average aid
package $26,671

Ferrum College

Ferrum VA
(800) 868-9797
U.S. News ranking: Reg. Coll. (S),
No. 47
Website: www.ferrum.edu
Admissions email:
admissions@ferrum.edu
Private; founded 1913
Affiliation: United Methodist
Freshman admissions: least
selective; 2013-2014: 3,273
applied, 2,426 accepted. Either
SAT or ACT required. SAT 25/75
percentile: 780-990. High school
rank: 2% in top tenth, 15% in top
quarter, 48% in top half
Early decision deadline: N/A,
notification date: N/A
Early action deadline: N/A,
notification date: N/A
Application deadline (fall): rolling
Undergraduate student body: 1,492
full time, 20 part time; 57%
male, 43% female; 0% American
Indian, 0% Asian, 32% black,
5% Hispanic, 5% multiracial,
0% Pacific Islander, 52% white,
1% international; 82% from in
state; 91% live on campus; 12%
of students in fraternities, 17%
in sororities
Most popular majors: 11%
Business, Management,
Marketing, and Related Support
Services, 8% Education, 11%
Health Professions and Related
Programs, 7% Homeland Security,
Law Enforcement, Firefighting and
Related Protective Services, 10%
Liberal Arts and Sciences, General
Studies and Humanities
Expenses: 2014-2015: $29,795;
room/board: $9,970
Financial aid: (540) 365-4282

George Mason University

Fairfax VA
(703) 993-2400
U.S. News ranking: Nat. U.,
No. 138
Website: www.gmu.edu
Admissions email:
admissions@gmu.edu
Public; founded 1972
Freshman admissions: selective;
2013-2014: 20,805 applied,
12,905 accepted. Neither SAT
nor ACT required. SAT 25/75
percentile: 1050-1250. High
school rank: 20% in top tenth,
56% in top quarter, 94% in
top half
Early decision deadline: N/A,
notification date: N/A
Early action deadline: 11/1,
notification date: 12/15
Application deadline (fall): 1/15
Undergraduate student body:
17,261 full time, 4,729 part
time; 48% male, 52% female;
0% American Indian, 17% Asian,
10% black, 12% Hispanic, 5%
multiracial, 0% Pacific Islander,
46% white, 4% international;
89% from in state; 27% live
on campus; 7% of students in
fraternities, 9% in sororities
Most popular majors: 6%
Accounting, 5% Biology/
Biological Sciences, General,
6% Information Technology, 8%
Psychology, General, 6% Speech
Communication and Rhetoric
Expenses: 2014-2015: $10,382
in state, $29,960 out of state;
room/board: $10,100
Financial aid: (703) 993-2353;
53% of undergrads determined to
have financial need; average aid
package $11,731

Hampden-Sydney College

Hampden-Sydney VA
(800) 755-0733
U.S. News ranking: Nat. Lib. Arts,
No. 105
Website: www.hsc.edu
Admissions email: hsapp@hsc.edu
Private; founded 1775
Affiliation: Presbyterian
Freshman admissions: selective;
2013-2014: 2,623 applied,
1,439 accepted. Either SAT
or ACT required. SAT 25/75
percentile: 1005-1215. High
school rank: 13% in top tenth,
28% in top quarter, 85% in
top half
Early decision deadline: 11/15,
notification date: 12/15
Early action deadline: 1/15,
notification date: 2/15
Application deadline (fall): 3/1
Undergraduate student body: 1,070
full time, N/A part time; 100%
male, 0% female; 1% American
Indian, 2% Asian, 8% black,
2% Hispanic, 5% multiracial,
0% Pacific Islander, 81% white,
0% international; 71% from in
state; 95% live on campus; 34%
of students in fraternities, 0% in
sororities
Most popular majors: 8% American
Government and Politics (United
States), 12% Business/Managerial
Economics, 13% Economics,
General, 19% History, General,
10% Psychology, Other
Expenses: 2014-2015: $39,272;
room/board: $12,312

Financial aid: (434) 223-6119;
64% of undergrads determined to
have financial need; average aid
package $29,135

Hampton University

Hampton VA
(757) 727-5328
U.S. News ranking: Reg. U. (S),
No. 18
Website: www.hamptonu.edu
Admissions email: admissions@
hamptonu.edu
Private; founded 1868
Freshman admissions: selective;
2013-2014: 15,337 applied,
5,529 accepted. Neither SAT
nor ACT required. SAT 25/75
percentile: 920-1090. High school
rank: 20% in top tenth, 45% in
top quarter, 89% in top half
Early decision deadline: N/A,
notification date: N/A
Early action deadline: 11/1,
notification date: 12/31
Application deadline (fall): 3/1
Undergraduate student body: 3,464
full time, 278 part time; 36%
male, 64% female; 0% American
Indian, 1% Asian, 94% black,
1% Hispanic, 0% multiracial,
0% Pacific Islander, 3% white,
1% international; 21% from in
state; 56% live on campus; 5%
of students in fraternities, 4% in
sororities
Most popular majors: 7% Biology/
Biological Sciences, General,
6% Business Administration
and Management, General,
5% Journalism, Other, 17%
Psychology, General, 13%
Registered Nursing/Registered
Nurse
Expenses: 2014-2015: $22,010;
room/board: $9,692
Financial aid: (800) 624-3341;
59% of undergrads determined to
have financial need; average aid
package $5,632

Hollins University

Roanoke VA
(800) 456-9595
U.S. News ranking: Nat. Lib. Arts,
No. 112
Website: www.hollins.edu
Admissions email:
huadm@hollins.edu
Private; founded 1842
Freshman admissions: selective;
2013-2014: 824 applied, 571
accepted. Either SAT or ACT
required. SAT 25/75 percentile:
970-1220. High school rank:
24% in top tenth, 54% in top
quarter, 83% in top half
Early decision deadline: 11/1,
notification date: 11/15
Early action deadline: 12/1,
notification date: 12/15
Application deadline (fall): rolling
Undergraduate student body:
559 full time, 21 part time; 1%
male, 99% female; 0% American
Indian, 3% Asian, 10% black,
6% Hispanic, 3% multiracial,
0% Pacific Islander, 72% white,
5% international; 55% from in
state; 79% live on campus; N/A
of students in fraternities, N/A in
sororities
Most popular majors: 7% Biological
and Biomedical Sciences, 21%
English Language and Literature/
Letters, 6% Psychology, 17%
Social Sciences, 21% Visual and
Performing Arts
Expenses: 2014-2015: $34,295;
room/board: $11,940

Financial aid: (540) 362-6332;
77% of undergrads determined to
have financial need; average aid
package $30,402

James Madison University

Harrisonburg VA
(540) 568-5681
U.S. News ranking: Reg. U. (S),
No. 6
Website: www.jmu.edu
Admissions email:
admissions@jmu.edu
Public; founded 1908
Freshman admissions: selective;
2013-2014: 23,400 applied,
14,168 accepted. Either SAT
or ACT required. SAT 25/75
percentile: 1050-1240. High
school rank: 27% in top tenth,
45% in top quarter, 99% in
top half
Early decision deadline: N/A,
notification date: N/A
Early action deadline: 11/1,
notification date: 1/15
Application deadline (fall): 1/15
Undergraduate student body:
17,526 full time, 905 part time;
41% male, 59% female; 0%
American Indian, 4% Asian,
4% black, 5% Hispanic, 3%
multiracial, 0% Pacific Islander,
79% white, 2% international;
71% from in state; 33% live
on campus; 10% of students in
fraternities, 12% in sororities
Most popular majors: 9%
Communication, Journalism, and
Related Programs, 7% Liberal Arts
and Sciences, General Studies
and Humanities, 6% Parks,
Recreation, Leisure, and Fitness
Studies, 6% Psychology, 8%
Social Sciences
Expenses: 2014-2015: $9,662 in
state, $24,522 out of state; room/
board: $8,828
Financial aid: (540) 568-7820;
42% of undergrads determined to
have financial need; average aid
package $9,509

Liberty University

Lynchburg VA
(800) 543-5317
U.S. News ranking: Reg. U. (S),
No. 80
Website: www.liberty.edu
Admissions email: admissions@
liberty.edu
Private; founded 1971
Affiliation: Southern Baptist
Freshman admissions: selective;
2013-2014: 27,458 applied,
5,821 accepted. Either SAT
or ACT required. SAT 25/75
percentile: 900-1150. High school
rank: 16% in top tenth, 38% in
top quarter, 70% in top half
Early decision deadline: N/A,
notification date: N/A
Early action deadline: N/A,
notification date: N/A
Application deadline (fall): rolling
Undergraduate student body:
25,911 full time, 21,549 part
time; 41% male, 59% female;
1% American Indian, 1% Asian,
15% black, 2% Hispanic, 2%
multiracial, 0% Pacific Islander,
49% white, 3% international;
42% from in state; 60% live
on campus; N/A of students in
fraternities, N/A in sororities
Most popular majors: Information
not available

More at usnews.com/college

Expenses: 2014-2015: $21,706; room/board: $8,200
Financial aid: (434) 582-2270; 81% of undergrads determined to have financial need; average aid package $8,498

Longwood University
Farmville VA
(434) 395-2060
U.S. News ranking: Reg. U. (S), No. 30
Website: www.whylongwood.com
Admissions email: admissions@longwood.edu
Public; founded 1839
Freshman admissions: selective; 2013-2014: 4,055 applied, 3,299 accepted. Either SAT or ACT required. SAT 25/75 percentile: 920-1090. High school rank: 10% in top tenth, 33% in top quarter, 73% in top half
Early decision deadline: N/A, notification date: N/A
Early action deadline: 12/1, notification date: 1/15
Application deadline (fall): rolling
Undergraduate student body: 4,123 full time, 374 part time; 34% male, 66% female; 0% American Indian, 1% Asian, 8% black, 5% Hispanic, 4% multiracial, 0% Pacific Islander, 78% white, 1% international; 97% from in state; 71% live on campus; 22% of students in fraternities, 22% in sororities
Most popular majors: 7% Biology/Biological Sciences, General, 12% Business Administration and Management, General, 19% Liberal Arts and Sciences/Liberal Studies, 7% Social Sciences, General, 7% Visual and Performing Arts, General
Expenses: 2014-2015: $11,580 in state, $25,350 out of state; room/board: $9,948
Financial aid: (434) 395-2077; 54% of undergrads determined to have financial need; average aid package $13,155

Lynchburg College
Lynchburg VA
(434) 544-8300
U.S. News ranking: Reg. U. (S), No. 33
Website: www.lynchburg.edu
Admissions email: admissions@lynchburg.edu
Private; founded 1903
Affiliation: Christian Church (Disciples of Christ)
Freshman admissions: selective; 2013-2014: 5,695 applied, 3,627 accepted. Either SAT or ACT required. SAT 25/75 percentile: 890-1110. High school rank: N/A
Early decision deadline: 11/15, notification date: 12/15
Early action deadline: N/A, notification date: N/A
Application deadline (fall): rolling
Undergraduate student body: 2,089 full time, 89 part time; 40% male, 60% female; 0% American Indian, 1% Asian, 11% black, 4% Hispanic, 3% multiracial, 0% Pacific Islander, 77% white, 1% international; 68% from in state; 73% live on campus; 11% of students in fraternities, 14% in sororities
Most popular majors: 10% Biological and Biomedical Sciences, 10% Business, Management, Marketing, and Related Support Services,

---

9% Education, 14% Health Professions and Related Programs, 15% Social Sciences
Expenses: 2014-2015: $34,545; room/board: $9,330
Financial aid: (434) 544-8228; 76% of undergrads determined to have financial need; average aid package $24,284

Mary Baldwin College
Staunton VA
(800) 468-2262
U.S. News ranking: Reg. U. (S), No. 49
Website: www.mbc.edu
Admissions email: admit@mbc.edu
Private; founded 1842
Affiliation: Presbyterian
Freshman admissions: less selective; 2013-2014: 2,952 applied, 2,731 accepted. Either SAT or ACT required. SAT 25/75 percentile: 830-1060. High school rank: 16% in top tenth, 46% in top quarter, 80% in top half
Early decision deadline: 11/15, notification date: 12/1
Early action deadline: N/A, notification date: N/A
Application deadline (fall): rolling
Undergraduate student body: 1,033 full time, 404 part time; 6% male, 94% female; 1% American Indian, 4% Asian; 26% black, 7% Hispanic, 3% multiracial, 0% Pacific Islander, 55% white, 0% international; 61% from in state; 52% live on campus; 0% of students in fraternities, 0% in sororities
Most popular majors: 9% Area, Ethnic, Cultural, Gender, and Group Studies, 8% Business, Management, Marketing, and Related Support Services, 10% History, 16% Psychology, 17% Social Sciences
Expenses: 2014-2015: $29,595; room/board: $8,650
Financial aid: (540) 887-7022; 82% of undergrads determined to have financial need; average aid package $21,761

Marymount University
Arlington VA
(703) 284-1500
U.S. News ranking: Reg. U. (S), No. 37
Website: www.marymount.edu
Admissions email: admissions@marymount.edu
Private; founded 1950
Affiliation: Roman Catholic
Freshman admissions: selective; 2013-2014: 2,082 applied, 1,718 accepted. Either SAT or ACT required. SAT 25/75 percentile: 930-1130. High school rank: 22% in top tenth, 44% in top quarter, 78% in top half
Early decision deadline: N/A, notification date: N/A
Early action deadline: N/A, notification date: N/A
Application deadline (fall): rolling
Undergraduate student body: 2,141 full time, 255 part time; 32% male, 68% female; 0% American Indian, 9% Asian, 15% black, 15% Hispanic, 3% multiracial, 1% Pacific Islander, 43% white, 9% international; 63% from in state; 36% live on campus; 0% of students in fraternities, 0% in sororities
Most popular majors: 17% Business Administration and Management, General, 5% Fashion Merchandising,

---

5% Interior Design, 6% Public Health Education and Promotion, 30% Registered Nursing/Registered Nurse
Expenses: 2014-2015: $27,470; room/board: $12,010
Financial aid: (703) 284-1530; 66% of undergrads determined to have financial need; average aid package $17,589

Norfolk State University
Norfolk VA
(757) 823-8396
U.S. News ranking: Reg. U. (S), second tier
Website: www.nsu.edu
Admissions email: admissions@nsu.edu
Public
Freshman admissions: less selective; 2013-2014: 3,373 applied, 2,192 accepted. Either SAT or ACT required. SAT 25/75 percentile: 770-948. High school rank: N/A
Early decision deadline: N/A, notification date: N/A
Early action deadline: N/A, notification date: N/A
Undergraduate student body: 4,976 full time, 1,045 part time; 36% male, 64% female; 0% American Indian, 0% Asian, 84% black, 3% Hispanic, 3% multiracial, 0% Pacific Islander, 5% white, 0% international; 85% from in state; 37% live on campus; N/A of students in fraternities, N/A in sororities
Most popular majors: 15% Business, Management, Marketing, and Related Support Services, 10% Health Professions and Related Programs, 10% Multi/Interdisciplinary Studies, 10% Psychology, 10% Social Sciences
Expenses: 2014-2015: $8,850 in state, $21,540 out of state; room/board: $8,624
Financial aid: (757) 823-8381

Old Dominion University
Norfolk VA
(757) 683-3685
U.S. News ranking: Nat. U., second tier
Website: www.odu.edu
Admissions email: admissions@odu.edu
Public; founded 1930
Freshman admissions: selective; 2013-2014: 10,202 applied, 7,834 accepted. Either SAT or ACT required. SAT 25/75 percentile: 930-1130. High school rank: 10% in top tenth, 33% in top quarter, 75% in top half
Early decision deadline: N/A, notification date: N/A
Early action deadline: 12/1, notification date: 1/15
Application deadline (fall): rolling
Undergraduate student body: 15,102 full time, 4,717 part time; 46% male, 54% female; 0% American Indian, 4% Asian, 26% black, 7% Hispanic, 6% multiracial, 0% Pacific Islander, 52% white, 1% international; 93% from in state; 24% live on campus; 6% of students in fraternities, 5% in sororities
Most popular majors: 16% Business, Management, Marketing, and Related Support Services, 8% English Language

---

and Literature/Letters, 14% Health Professions and Related Programs, 7% Multi/Interdisciplinary Studies, 14% Social Sciences
Expenses: 2014-2015: $9,280 in state, $25,030 out of state; room/board: $10,396
Financial aid: (757) 683-3683; 63% of undergrads determined to have financial need; average aid package $9,677

Radford University
Radford VA
(540) 831-5371
U.S. News ranking: Reg. U. (S), No. 34
Website: www.radford.edu
Admissions email: admissions@radford.edu
Public; founded 1910
Freshman admissions: less selective; 2013-2014: 7,774 applied, 6,088 accepted. Either SAT or ACT required. SAT 25/75 percentile: 900-1080. High school rank: 6% in top tenth, 22% in top quarter, 61% in top half
Early decision deadline: N/A, notification date: N/A
Early action deadline: 12/1, notification date: 1/15
Application deadline (fall): 2/1
Undergraduate student body: 8,545 full time, 368 part time; 44% male, 56% female; 0% American Indian, 1% Asian, 10% black, 5% Hispanic, 4% multiracial, 0% Pacific Islander, 78% white, 1% international; 95% from in state; 36% live on campus; 9% of students in fraternities, 12% in sororities
Most popular majors: 7% Criminal Justice/Safety Studies, 10% Multi-/Interdisciplinary Studies, Other, 7% Physical Education Teaching and Coaching, 7% Psychology, General, 6% Registered Nursing/Registered Nurse
Expenses: 2014-2015: $9,360 in state, $21,600 out of state; room/board: $8,406
Financial aid: (540) 831-5408; 56% of undergrads determined to have financial need; average aid package $9,316

Randolph College
Lynchburg VA
(800) 745-7692
U.S. News ranking: Nat. Lib. Arts, No. 133
Website: www.randolphcollege.edu/
Admissions email: admissions@randolphcollege.edu
Private; founded 1891
Affiliation: United Methodist
Freshman admissions: selective; 2013-2014: 1,056 applied, 881 accepted. Either SAT or ACT required. SAT 25/75 percentile: 970-1200. High school rank: 17% in top tenth, 54% in top quarter, 91% in top half
Early decision deadline: N/A, notification date: N/A
Early action deadline: 12/1, notification date: 1/1
Application deadline (fall): 2/1
Undergraduate student body: 649 full time, 16 part time; 36% male, 64% female; 1% American Indian, 2% Asian, 9% black, 6% Hispanic, 3% multiracial, 0% Pacific Islander, 69% white, 11% international; 55% from in

---

state; 86% live on campus; 0% of students in fraternities, 0% in sororities
Most popular majors: 9% Biological and Biomedical Sciences, 9% Education, 10% History, 11% Psychology, 16% Social Sciences
Expenses: 2014-2015: $34,107; room/board: $11,650
Financial aid: (434) 947-8128; 67% of undergrads determined to have financial need; average aid package $26,014

Randolph-Macon College
Ashland VA
(800) 888-1762
U.S. News ranking: Nat. Lib. Arts, No. 124
Website: www.rmc.edu
Admissions email: admissions@rmc.edu
Private; founded 1830
Affiliation: United Methodist
Freshman admissions: selective; 2013-2014: 2,997 applied, 1,909 accepted. Either SAT or ACT required. SAT 25/75 percentile: 970-1180. High school rank: 14% in top tenth, 48% in top quarter, 83% in top half
Early decision deadline: N/A, notification date: N/A
Early action deadline: 11/15, notification date: 1/1
Application deadline (fall): 3/1
Undergraduate student body: 1,295 full time, 20 part time; 47% male, 53% female; 0% American Indian, 2% Asian, 10% black, 4% Hispanic, 3% multiracial, 0% Pacific Islander, 76% white, 3% international; 75% from in state; 78% live on campus; 26% of students in fraternities, 27% in sororities
Most popular majors: 11% Biology/Biological Sciences, General, 9% Business/Managerial Economics, 9% Communication, General, 10% Political Science and Government, General, 9% Psychology, General
Expenses: 2014-2015: $36,340; room/board: $10,750
Financial aid: (804) 752-7259; 75% of undergrads determined to have financial need; average aid package $25,779

Regent University
Virginia Beach VA
(888) 718-1222
U.S. News ranking: Nat. U., second tier
Website: www.regent.edu
Admissions email: admissions@regent.edu
Private; founded 1977
Affiliation: non-denominational
Freshman admissions: selective; 2013-2014: 1,243 applied, 1,062 accepted. Either SAT or ACT required. SAT 25/75 percentile: 940-1170. High school rank: 14% in top tenth, 30% in top quarter, 85% in top half
Early decision deadline: N/A, notification date: N/A
Early action deadline: N/A, notification date: N/A
Application deadline (fall): 7/28
Undergraduate student body: 1,537 full time, 924 part time; 39% male, 61% female; 1% American Indian, 2% Asian, 20% black, 5% Hispanic, 0% multiracial, 0% Pacific Islander, 57% white, 1% international; 48% from in

state; 23% live on campus; N/A of students in fraternities, N/A in sororities
Most popular majors: 22% Business Administration and Management, General, 17% Divinity/Ministry, 8% English Language and Literature, General, 19% Psychology, General, 20% Speech Communication and Rhetoric
Expenses: 2014-2015: $16,638; room/board: $8,250
Financial aid: (757) 226-4125; 77% of undergrads determined to have financial need; average aid package $11,621

Roanoke College

Salem VA
(540) 375-2270
U.S. News ranking: Nat. Lib. Arts, No. 133
Website: www.roanoke.edu
Admissions email: admissions@roanoke.edu
Private; founded 1842
Affiliation: Lutheran
Freshman admissions: selective; 2013-2014: 4,167 applied, 3,034 accepted. Either SAT or ACT required. SAT 25/75 percentile: 980-1190. High school rank: 18% in top tenth, 42% in top quarter, 76% in top half
Early decision deadline: 11/1, notification date: 12/1
Early action deadline: N/A, notification date: N/A
Application deadline (fall): 3/15
Undergraduate student body: 1,964 full time, 65 part time; 41% male, 59% female; 0% American Indian, 1% Asian, 5% black, 3% Hispanic, 4% multiracial, 0% Pacific Islander, 85% white, 1% international; 53% from in state; 78% live on campus; 26% of students in fraternities, 22% in sororities
Most popular majors: 7% Biology/Biological Sciences, General, 18% Business Administration and Management, General, 6% English Language and Literature, General, 9% History, General, 13% Psychology, General
Expenses: 2014-2015: $37,802; room/board: $11,924
Financial aid: (540) 375-2235; 74% of undergrads determined to have financial need; average aid package $27,864

Shenandoah University

Winchester VA
(540) 665-4581
U.S. News ranking: Reg. U. (S), No. 47
Website: www.su.edu
Admissions email: admit@su.edu
Private; founded 1875
Affiliation: United Methodist
Freshman admissions: less selective; 2013-2014: 1,632 applied, 1,377 accepted. Either SAT or ACT required. SAT 25/75 percentile: 850-1090. High school rank: 13% in top tenth, 36% in top quarter, 74% in top half
Early decision deadline: N/A, notification date: N/A
Early action deadline: N/A, notification date: N/A
Application deadline (fall): rolling
Undergraduate student body: 1,791 full time, 359 part time; 39% male, 61% female; 2% American Indian, 4% Asian, 14% black,

4% Hispanic, 0% multiracial, 0% Pacific Islander, 66% white, 5% international; 62% from in state; 47% live on campus; N/A of students in fraternities, N/A in sororities
Most popular majors: 12% Business Administration and Management, General, 17% Musical Theatre, 12% Physical Education Teaching and Coaching, 6% Psychology, General, 31% Registered Nursing/Registered Nurse
Expenses: 2014-2015: $30,188; room/board: $9,728
Financial aid: (540) 665-4538; 75% of undergrads determined to have financial need; average aid package $28,336

Sweet Briar College

Sweet Briar VA
(800) 381-6142
U.S. News ranking: Nat. Lib. Arts, No. 116
Website: www.sbc.edu
Admissions email: admissions@sbc.edu
Private; founded 1901
Freshman admissions: selective; 2013-2014: 905 applied, 763 accepted. Either SAT or ACT required. SAT 25/75 percentile: 938-1210. High school rank: 30% in top tenth, 58% in top quarter, 82% in top half
Early decision deadline: N/A, notification date: N/A
Early action deadline: N/A, notification date: N/A
Application deadline (fall): 2/1
Undergraduate student body: 680 full time, 23 part time; 2% male, 98% female; 1% American Indian, 3% Asian, 10% black, 7% Hispanic, 2% multiracial, 0% Pacific Islander, 74% white, 2% international; 47% from in state; 96% live on campus; 0% of students in fraternities, 0% in sororities
Most popular majors: 8% Biological and Biomedical Sciences, 22% Business, Management, Marketing, and Related Support Services, 9% Psychology, 11% Social Sciences, 14% Visual and Performing Arts
Expenses: 2014-2015: $34,935; room/board: $12,160
Financial aid: (434) 381-6156; 78% of undergrads determined to have financial need; average aid package $27,921

University of Mary Washington

Fredericksburg VA
(540) 654-2000
U.S. News ranking: Reg. U. (S), No. 13
Website: www.umw.edu
Admissions email: admit@umw.edu
Public; founded 1908
Freshman admissions: selective; 2013-2014: 4,501 applied, 3,637 accepted. Either SAT or ACT required. SAT 25/75 percentile: 1010-1210. High school rank: 16% in top tenth, 50% in top quarter, 86% in top half
Early decision deadline: N/A, notification date: N/A
Early action deadline: 11/15, notification date: 1/31
Application deadline (fall): 2/1

Undergraduate student body: 3,843 full time, 540 part time; 36% male, 64% female; 0% American Indian, 4% Asian, 6% black, 7% Hispanic, 4% multiracial, 0% Pacific Islander, 66% white, 1% international; 89% from in state; 61% live on campus; 0% of students in fraternities, 0% in sororities
Most popular majors: 15% Business, Management, Marketing, and Related Support Services, 9% English Language and Literature/Letters, 9% Multi/Interdisciplinary Studies, 12% Psychology, 16% Social Sciences
Expenses: 2014-2015: $10,252 in state, $23,538 out of state; room/board: $9,430
Financial aid: (540) 654-2468; 41% of undergrads determined to have financial need; average aid package $8,055

University of Richmond

Univ. of Richmond VA
(804) 289-8640
U.S. News ranking: Nat. Lib. Arts, No. 30
Website: www.richmond.edu
Admissions email: admissions@richmond.edu
Private; founded 1830
Freshman admissions: more selective; 2013-2014: 9,825 applied, 3,061 accepted. Either SAT or ACT required. SAT 25/75 percentile: 1210-1410. High school rank: 64% in top tenth, 93% in top quarter, 99% in top half
Early decision deadline: 11/15, notification date: 12/15
Early action deadline: N/A, notification date: N/A
Application deadline (fall): 1/15
Undergraduate student body: 2,942 full time, 41 part time; 48% male, 52% female; 0% American Indian, 6% Asian, 6% black, 7% Hispanic, 4% multiracial, 0% Pacific Islander, 58% white, 9% international; 20% from in state; 87% live on campus; 13% of students in fraternities, 22% in sororities
Most popular majors: 9% Biological and Biomedical Sciences, 39% Business, Management, Marketing, and Related Support Services, 6% Multi/Interdisciplinary Studies, 6% Psychology, 16% Social Sciences
Expenses: 2014-2015: $46,680; room/board: $10,790
Financial aid: (804) 289-8438; 40% of undergrads determined to have financial need; average aid package $42,003

University of Virginia

Charlottesville VA
(434) 982-3200
U.S. News ranking: Nat. U., No. 23
Website: www.virginia.edu
Admissions email: undergradadmission@virginia.edu
Public; founded 1819
Freshman admissions: most selective; 2013-2014: 29,021 applied, 8,728 accepted. Either SAT or ACT required. SAT 25/75 percentile: 1250-1460. High school rank: 92% in top tenth, 98% in top quarter, 99% in top half
Early decision deadline: N/A, notification date: N/A

Early decision deadline: N/A, notification date: N/A
Early action deadline: 11/1, notification date: 1/31
Application deadline (fall): 1/1
Undergraduate student body: 15,090 full time, 997 part time; 44% male, 56% female; 0% American Indian, 12% Asian, 6% black, 6% Hispanic, 4% multiracial, 0% Pacific Islander, 61% white, 6% international
Most popular majors: 8% Biology/Biological Sciences, General, 9% Business/Commerce, General, 8% Economics, General, 9% International Relations and Affairs, 8% Psychology, General
Expenses: 2014-2015: $12,998 in state, $42,184 out of state; room/board: $10,052
Financial aid: (434) 982-6000; 34% of undergrads determined to have financial need; average aid package $23,789

University of Virginia–Wise

Wise VA
(888) 282-9324
U.S. News ranking: Nat. Lib. Arts, second tier
Website: www.uvawise.edu
Admissions email: admissions@uvawise.edu
Public; founded 1954
Freshman admissions: less selective; 2013-2014: 970 applied, 727 accepted. Either SAT or ACT required. SAT 25/75 percentile: 860-1050. High school rank: 15% in top tenth, 40% in top quarter, 76% in top half
Early decision deadline: N/A, notification date: N/A
Early action deadline: 12/1, notification date: 12/15
Application deadline (fall): 8/15
Undergraduate student body: 1,471 full time, 820 part time; 42% male, 58% female; 0% American Indian, 1% Asian, 10% black, 2% Hispanic, 0% multiracial, 0% Pacific Islander, 80% white, 0% international; 97% from in state; 37% live on campus; 1% of students in fraternities, 2% in sororities
Most popular majors: Information not available
Expenses: 2014-2015: $8,868 in state, $23,870 out of state; room/board: $10,340
Financial aid: (276) 328-0103; 72% of undergrads determined to have financial need; average aid package $11,156

Virginia Commonwealth University

Richmond VA
(800) 841-3638
U.S. News ranking: Nat. U., No. 156
Website: www.vcu.edu
Admissions email: ugrad@vcu.edu
Public; founded 1838
Freshman admissions: selective; 2013-2014: 15,399 applied, 9,860 accepted. Either SAT or ACT required. SAT 25/75 percentile: 1000-1210. High school rank: 20% in top tenth, 50% in top quarter, 85% in top half
Early decision deadline: N/A, notification date: N/A

Early action deadline: N/A, notification date: N/A
Application deadline (fall): 1/15
Undergraduate student body: 19,989 full time, 3,668 part time; 43% male, 57% female; 0% American Indian, 12% Asian, 18% black, 8% Hispanic, 5% multiracial, 0% Pacific Islander, 51% white, 3% international; 92% from in state; 25% live on campus; 8% of students in fraternities, 6% in sororities
Most popular majors: 13% Business, Management, Marketing, and Related Support Services, 7% Health Professions and Related Programs, 7% Homeland Security, Law Enforcement, Firefighting and Related Protective Services, 10% Psychology, 12% Visual and Performing Arts
Expenses: 2014-2015: $12,398 in state, $29,847 out of state; room/board: $10,742
Financial aid: (804) 828-6669; 57% of undergrads determined to have financial need; average aid package $10,502

Virginia Intermont College[1]

Bristol VA
(276) 466-7867
U.S. News ranking: Nat. Lib. Arts, second tier
Website: www.vic.edu
Admissions email: viadmit@vic.edu
Private; founded 1884
Affiliation: Virginia Baptist
Application deadline (fall): rolling
Undergraduate student body: N/A full time, N/A part time
Expenses: 2013-2014: $24,642; room/board: $7,769
Financial aid: (276) 466-7873

Virginia Military Institute

Lexington VA
(800) 767-4207
U.S. News ranking: Nat. Lib. Arts, No. 64
Website: www.vmi.edu
Admissions email: admissions@vmi.edu
Public; founded 1839
Freshman admissions: selective; 2013-2014: 1,864 applied, 890 accepted. Either SAT or ACT required. SAT 25/75 percentile: 1050-1250. High school rank: 16% in top tenth, 48% in top quarter, 87% in top half
Early decision deadline: 11/15, notification date: 12/15
Early action deadline: N/A, notification date: N/A
Application deadline (fall): 2/1
Undergraduate student body: 1,675 full time, N/A part time; 89% male, 11% female; 0% American Indian, 4% Asian, 4% black, 4% Hispanic, 2% multiracial, 1% Pacific Islander, 83% white, 1% international; 59% from in state; 100% live on campus; N/A of students in fraternities, N/A in sororities
Most popular majors: 11% Civil Engineering, General, 15% Economics, General, 13% History, General, 18% International Relations and Affairs, 8% Psychology, General
Expenses: 2014-2015: $15,518 in state, $37,574 out of state; room/board: $8,372

Financial aid: (540) 464-7208; 54% of undergrads determined to have financial need; average aid package $21,056

Virginia State University

Petersburg VA
(804) 524-5902
U.S. News ranking: Reg. U. (S), No. 92
Website: www.vsu.edu
Admissions email: admiss@vsu.edu
Public
Freshman admissions: least selective; 2013-2014: 9,107 applied, 4,922 accepted. Either SAT or ACT required. SAT 25/75 percentile: 730-910. High school rank: 5% in top tenth, 17% in top quarter, 55% in top half
Early decision deadline: N/A, notification date: N/A
Early action deadline: N/A, notification date: N/A
Application deadline (fall): 5/1
Undergraduate student body: 4,817 full time, 256 part time; 40% male, 60% female; 0% American Indian, 0% Asian, 86% black, 2% Hispanic, 0% multiracial, 0% Pacific Islander, 2% white, 0% international
Most popular majors: 6% Business Administration and Management, General, 11% Criminal Justice/ Safety Studies, 8% Mass Communication/Media Studies, 11% Physical Education Teaching and Coaching, 9% Psychology, General
Expenses: 2014-2015: $8,002 in state, $17,258 out of state; room/ board: $10,128
Financial aid: (804) 524-5992; 90% of undergrads determined to have financial need; average aid package $12,401

Virginia Tech

Blacksburg VA
(540) 231-6267
U.S. News ranking: Nat. U., No. 71
Website: www.vt.edu
Admissions email: vtadmiss@vt.edu
Public; founded 1872
Freshman admissions: more selective; 2013-2014: 19,112 applied, 13,432 accepted. Either SAT or ACT required. SAT 25/75 percentile: 1120-1320. High school rank: 41% in top tenth, 83% in top quarter, 98% in top half
Early decision deadline: 11/1, notification date: 12/15
Early action deadline: N/A, notification date: N/A
Application deadline (fall): 1/15
Undergraduate student body: 23,512 full time, 522 part time; 59% male, 41% female; 0% American Indian, 8% Asian, 3% black, 5% Hispanic, 4% multiracial, 0% Pacific Islander, 72% white, 4% international; N/A from in state; 37% live on campus; 3% of students in fraternities, 1% in sororities
Most popular majors: 9% Biological and Biomedical Sciences, 18% Business, Management, Marketing, and Related Support Services, 21% Engineering, 9% Family and Consumer Sciences/ Human Sciences, 8% Social Sciences

Expenses: 2014-2015: $12,017 in state, $27,444 out of state; room/board: $8,270
Financial aid: (540) 231-5179; 45% of undergrads determined to have financial need; average aid package $16,280

Virginia Union University

Richmond VA
(804) 257-5600
U.S. News ranking: Reg. Coll. (S), No. 68
Website: www.vuu.edu/
Admissions email: admissions@vuu.edu
Private; founded 1865
Affiliation: Baptist
Freshman admissions: least selective; 2013-2014: 2,670 applied, 2,217 accepted. Either SAT or ACT required. SAT 25/75 percentile: 670-840. High school rank: 6% in top tenth, 18% in top quarter, 45% in top half
Early decision deadline: N/A, notification date: N/A
Early action deadline: N/A, notification date: N/A
Application deadline (fall): 6/30
Undergraduate student body: 1,329 full time, 30 part time; 45% male, 55% female; 0% American Indian, 0% Asian, 95% black, 1% Hispanic, 1% multiracial, 0% Pacific Islander, 1% white, 1% international; 53% from in state; 54% live on campus; N/A of students in fraternities, N/A in sororities
Most popular majors: 7% Biological and Biomedical Sciences, 24% Business, Management, Marketing, and Related Support Services, 9% Computer and Information Sciences and Support Services, 11% Psychology, 33% Social Sciences
Expenses: 2014-2015: $14,930; room/board: $8,074
Financial aid: (804) 257-5882; 95% of undergrads determined to have financial need; average aid package $12,592

Virginia Wesleyan College

Norfolk VA
(800) 737-8684
U.S. News ranking: Nat. Lib. Arts, second tier
Website: www.vwc.edu
Admissions email: admissions@vwc.edu
Private; founded 1961
Affiliation: United Methodist
Freshman admissions: less selective; 2013-2014: 3,727 applied, 3,463 accepted. Neither SAT nor ACT required. SAT 25/75 percentile: 907-1142. High school rank: 14% in top tenth, 36% in top quarter, 61% in top half
Early decision deadline: N/A, notification date: N/A
Early action deadline: N/A, notification date: N/A
Application deadline (fall): rolling
Undergraduate student body: 1,348 full time, 111 part time; 39% male, 61% female; 1% American Indian, 1% Asian, 23% black, 6% Hispanic, 7% multiracial, 0% Pacific Islander, 58% white, 1% international; 76% from in state; 60% live on campus; N/A of students in fraternities, N/A in sororities

Most popular majors: 6% Biology/ Biological Sciences, General, 21% Business Administration and Management, General, 9% Criminal Justice/Safety Studies, 7% Psychology, General, 6% Social Sciences, General
Expenses: 2014-2015: $33,286; room/board: $8,594
Financial aid: (757) 455-3345; 80% of undergrads determined to have financial need; average aid package $19,980

Washington and Lee University

Lexington VA
(540) 463-8710
U.S. News ranking: Nat. Lib. Arts, No. 14
Website: www.wlu.edu
Admissions email: admissions@wlu.edu
Private; founded 1749
Freshman admissions: most selective; 2013-2014: 6,222 applied, 1,147 accepted. Either SAT or ACT required. ACT 25/75 percentile: 30-33. High school rank: 80% in top tenth, 98% in top quarter, 100% in top half
Early decision deadline: 11/1, notification date: 12/21
Early action deadline: N/A, notification date: N/A
Application deadline (fall): 1/1
Undergraduate student body: 1,851 full time, 4 part time; 50% male, 50% female; 0% American Indian, 4% Asian, 2% black, 3% Hispanic, 2% multiracial, 0% Pacific Islander, 83% white, 3% international; 14% from in state; 56% live on campus; 82% of students in fraternities, 82% in sororities
Most popular majors: 5% Accounting and Business/ Management, 5% Biology/ Biological Sciences, General, 14% Business Administration and Management, General, 8% Economics, General, 6% English Language and Literature, General
Expenses: 2014-2015: $45,617; room/board: $10,645
Financial aid: (540) 458-8717; 42% of undergrads determined to have financial need; average aid package $45,619

WASHINGTON

Art Institute of Seattle[1]

Seattle WA
(800) 275-2471
U.S. News ranking: Arts, unranked
Website: www.ais.edu
Admissions email: N/A
For-profit
Application deadline (fall): N/A
Undergraduate student body: N/A full time, N/A part time
Expenses: 2013-2014: $17,560; room/board: $12,132
Financial aid: N/A

Bellevue College[1]

Bellevue WA
(425) 564-1000
U.S. News ranking: Reg. Coll. (W), unranked
Website: bellevuecollege.edu
Admissions email: N/A
Public
Application deadline (fall): N/A

Undergraduate student body: N/A full time, N/A part time
Expenses: 2013-2014: $3,754 in state, $8,944 out of state; room/board: N/A
Financial aid: (425) 564-2227

Central Washington University

Ellensburg WA
(866) 298-4968
U.S. News ranking: Reg. U. (W), No. 51
Website: www.cwu.edu
Admissions email: cwuadmis@cwu.edu
Public; founded 1891
Freshman admissions: less selective; 2013-2014: 4,507 applied, 3,703 accepted. Either SAT or ACT required. SAT 25/75 percentile: 880-1100. High school rank: N/A
Early decision deadline: N/A, notification date: N/A
Early action deadline: N/A, notification date: N/A
Application deadline (fall): rolling
Undergraduate student body: 8,996 full time, 1,427 part time; 50% male, 50% female; 1% American Indian, 3% Asian, 3% black, 12% Hispanic, 5% multiracial, 0% Pacific Islander, 64% white, 4% international; 95% from in state; 23% live on campus; 0% of students in fraternities, 0% in sororities
Most popular majors: 19% Business, Management, Marketing, and Related Support Services, 15% Education, 8% Homeland Security, Law Enforcement, Firefighting and Related Protective Services, 5% Psychology, 14% Social Sciences
Expenses: 2014-2015: $8,976 in state, $20,522 out of state; room/board: $9,795
Financial aid: (509) 963-1611; 66% of undergrads determined to have financial need; average aid package $11,191

City University of Seattle

Seattle WA
(206) 239-4500
U.S. News ranking: Reg. U. (W), unranked
Website: www.cityu.edu
Admissions email: info@cityu.edu
Private; founded 1973
Freshman admissions: N/A; 2013-2014: 364 applied, 364 accepted. Neither SAT nor ACT required. ACT 25/75 percentile: N/A. High school rank: N/A
Early decision deadline: N/A, notification date: N/A
Early action deadline: N/A, notification date: N/A
Application deadline (fall): rolling
Undergraduate student body: 638 full time, 634 part time; 47% male, 53% female; 1% American Indian, 3% Asian, 4% black, 7% Hispanic, 0% multiracial, 1% Pacific Islander, 40% white, 18% international
Most popular majors: 8% Accounting, 6% Applied Psychology, 55% Business Administration and Management, General, 5% Computer and Information Sciences, General, 19% Education, General
Expenses: 2013-2014: $14,880; room/board: N/A
Financial aid: (800) 426-5596

Cornish College of the Arts

Seattle WA
(800) 726-ARTS
U.S. News ranking: Arts, unranked
Website: www.cornish.edu
Admissions email: admission@cornish.edu
Private; founded 1914
Freshman admissions: N/A; 2013-2014: 1,186 applied, 691 accepted. Neither SAT nor ACT required. SAT 25/75 percentile: N/A. High school rank: N/A
Early decision deadline: N/A, notification date: N/A
Early action deadline: N/A, notification date: N/A
Application deadline (fall): 8/15
Undergraduate student body: 746 full time, 29 part time; 35% male, 65% female; 1% American Indian, 6% Asian, 4% black, 9% Hispanic, 8% multiracial, 0% Pacific Islander, 63% white, 3% international; 54% from in state; 12% live on campus; N/A of students in fraternities, N/A in sororities
Most popular majors: 12% Dance, General, 23% Design and Visual Communications, General, 23% Drama and Dramatics/ Theatre Arts, General, 19% Fine/ Studio Arts, General, 16% Music Performance, General
Expenses: 2014-2015: $35,800; room/board: $9,600
Financial aid: (206) 726-5014; 81% of undergrads determined to have financial need; average aid package $18,090

Eastern Washington University

Cheney WA
(509) 359-2397
U.S. News ranking: Reg. U. (W), No. 66
Website: www.ewu.edu
Admissions email: admissions@ewu.edu
Public; founded 1882
Freshman admissions: less selective; 2013-2014: 5,108 applied, 3,993 accepted. Either SAT or ACT required. SAT 25/75 percentile: 870-1090. High school rank: N/A
Early decision deadline: N/A, notification date: N/A
Early action deadline: N/A, notification date: N/A
Application deadline (fall): 5/15
Undergraduate student body: 9,715 full time, 1,963 part time; 46% male, 54% female; 1% American Indian, 3% Asian, 4% black, 12% Hispanic, 4% multiracial, 0% Pacific Islander, 66% white, 3% international; 95% from in state; 16% live on campus; 5% of students in fraternities, 5% in sororities
Most popular majors: 18% Business, Management, Marketing, and Related Support Services, 8% Education, 10% Health Professions and Related Programs, 9% Psychology, 9% Social Sciences
Expenses: 2014-2015: $7,982 in state, $21,113 out of state; room/board: $9,628
Financial aid: (509) 359-2314; 68% of undergrads determined to have financial need; average aid package $13,826

Evergreen State College

Olympia WA
(360) 867-6170
U.S. News ranking: Reg. U. (W), No. 31
Website: www.evergreen.edu
Admissions email: admissions@evergreen.edu
Public; founded 1967
Freshman admissions: selective; 2013-2014: 1,583 applied, 1,537 accepted. Either SAT or ACT required. SAT 25/75 percentile: 950-1210. High school rank: 10% in top tenth, 23% in top quarter, 54% in top half
Early decision deadline: N/A, notification date: N/A
Early action deadline: N/A, notification date: N/A
Application deadline (fall): rolling
Undergraduate student body: 3,766 full time, 321 part time; 47% male, 53% female; 2% American Indian, 2% Asian, 5% black, 7% Hispanic, 7% multiracial, 0% Pacific Islander, 66% white, 0% international; 76% from in state; 20% live on campus; N/A of students in fraternities, N/A in sororities
Most popular majors: 13% Environmental Studies, 19% Humanities/Humanistic Studies, 12% Liberal Arts and Sciences/Liberal Studies, 15% Natural Sciences, 21% Social Sciences, Other
Expenses: 2014-2015: $8,682 in state, $21,735 out of state; room/board: $9,492
Financial aid: (360) 867-6205; 69% of undergrads determined to have financial need; average aid package $9,236

Gonzaga University

Spokane WA
(800) 322-2584
U.S. News ranking: Reg. U. (W), No. 3
Website: www.gonzaga.edu
Admissions email: mcculloh@gu.gonzaga.edu
Private; founded 1887
Affiliation: Roman Catholic
Freshman admissions: more selective; 2013-2014: 7,031 applied, 4,790 accepted. Either SAT or ACT required. SAT 25/75 percentile: 1100-1290. High school rank: 39% in top tenth, 68% in top quarter, 95% in top half
Early decision deadline: N/A, notification date: N/A
Early action deadline: 11/15, notification date: 1/15
Application deadline (fall): 2/1
Undergraduate student body: 4,826 full time, 70 part time; 46% male, 54% female; 1% American Indian, 4% Asian, 1% black, 9% Hispanic, 6% multiracial, 0% Pacific Islander, 74% white, 3% international; 49% from in state; 60% live on campus; 0% of students in fraternities, 0% in sororities
Most popular majors: 8% Biological and Biomedical Sciences, 24% Business, Management, Marketing, and Related Support Services, 9% Engineering, 8% Psychology, 13% Social Sciences
Expenses: 2014-2015: $36,535; room/board: $9,906

Financial aid: (509) 323-4049; 58% of undergrads determined to have financial need; average aid package $25,512

Heritage University[1]

Toppenish WA
(509) 865-8508
U.S. News ranking: Reg. U. (W), unranked
Website: www.heritage.edu
Admissions email: admissions@heritage.edu
Private
Application deadline (fall): N/A
Undergraduate student body: N/A full time, N/A part time
Expenses: 2013-2014: $17,744; room/board: N/A
Financial aid: (509) 865-8502

Northwest University

Kirkland WA
(425) 889-5231
U.S. News ranking: Reg. Coll. (W), No. 16
Website: www.northwestu.edu
Admissions email: admissions@northwestu.edu
Private; founded 1934
Affiliation: Assembly of God
Freshman admissions: less selective; 2013-2014: 419 applied, 362 accepted. Either SAT or ACT required. SAT 25/75 percentile: 950-1170. High school rank: N/A
Early decision deadline: N/A, notification date: N/A
Early action deadline: 11/15, notification date: 12/15
Application deadline (fall): rolling
Undergraduate student body: 1,221 full time, 217 part time; 41% male, 59% female; 1% American Indian, 5% Asian, 3% black, 8% Hispanic, 2% multiracial, 1% Pacific Islander, 74% white, 2% international
Most popular majors: 10% Business Administration, Management and Operations, Other, 6% Organizational Communication, General, 12% Psychology, General, 13% Registered Nursing/Registered Nurse, 12% Theological and Ministerial Studies, Other
Expenses: 2014-2015: $26,968; room/board: $7,620
Financial aid: (425) 889-5336; 84% of undergrads determined to have financial need; average aid package $19,633

Olympic College[1]

Bremerton WA
(360) 792-6050
U.S. News ranking: Reg. Coll. (W), unranked
Website: www.olympic.edu
Admissions email: N/A
Public
Application deadline (fall): N/A
Undergraduate student body: N/A full time, N/A part time
Expenses: 2013-2014: $3,726 in state, $4,197 out of state; room/board: $9,492
Financial aid: (800) 259-6718

Pacific Lutheran University

Tacoma WA
(800) 274-6758
U.S. News ranking: Reg. U. (W), No. 17
Website: www.plu.edu
Admissions email: admission@plu.edu
Private; founded 1890
Affiliation: Lutheran
Freshman admissions: selective; 2013-2014: 3,443 applied, 2,643 accepted. Either SAT or ACT required. SAT 25/75 percentile: 980-1220. High school rank: 35% in top tenth, 70% in top quarter, 92% in top half
Early decision deadline: N/A, notification date: N/A
Early action deadline: N/A, notification date: N/A
Application deadline (fall): rolling
Undergraduate student body: 3,010 full time, 132 part time; 38% male, 62% female; 1% American Indian, 6% Asian, 3% black, 7% Hispanic, 7% multiracial, 1% Pacific Islander, 71% white, 4% international; 79% from in state; 43% live on campus; N/A of students in fraternities, N/A in sororities
Most popular majors: 9% Biological and Biomedical Sciences, 11% Business, Management, Marketing, and Related Support Services, 10% Health Professions and Related Programs, 7% Psychology, 13% Social Sciences
Expenses: 2014-2015: $36,530; room/board: $10,230
Financial aid: (253) 535-7134; 76% of undergrads determined to have financial need; average aid package $32,765

Peninsula College[1]

Port Angeles WA
(360) 417-6340
U.S. News ranking: Reg. Coll. (W), unranked
Website: www.pencol.edu
Admissions email: N/A
Public
Application deadline (fall): N/A
Undergraduate student body: N/A full time, N/A part time
Expenses: 2013-2014: $4,246 in state, $4,687 out of state; room/board: N/A
Financial aid: (360) 417-6390

Seattle Pacific University

Seattle WA
(800) 366-3344
U.S. News ranking: Reg. U. (W), No. 19
Website: www.spu.edu
Admissions email: admissions@spu.edu
Private; founded 1891
Affiliation: Free Methodist
Freshman admissions: selective; 2013-2014: 4,477 applied, 3,724 accepted. Either SAT or ACT required. SAT 25/75 percentile: 1030-1250. High school rank: 28% in top tenth, 57% in top quarter, 87% in top half
Early decision deadline: N/A, notification date: N/A
Early action deadline: 11/15, notification date: 1/5
Application deadline (fall): 2/1

Undergraduate student body: 3,230 full time, 136 part time; 34% male, 66% female; 0% American Indian, 11% Asian, 4% black, 8% Hispanic, 8% multiracial, 0% Pacific Islander, 66% white, 2% international; 63% from in state; 51% live on campus; N/A of students in fraternities, N/A in sororities
Most popular majors: Information not available
Expenses: 2014-2015: $35,472; room/board: $10,086
Financial aid: (206) 281-2061; 74% of undergrads determined to have financial need; average aid package $29,857

Seattle University

Seattle WA
(206) 296-2000
U.S. News ranking: Reg. U. (W), No. 5
Website: www.seattleu.edu
Admissions email: admissions@seattleu.edu
Private; founded 1891
Affiliation: Roman Catholic (Jesuit)
Freshman admissions: more selective; 2013-2014: 7,159 applied, 5,243 accepted. Either SAT or ACT required. SAT 25/75 percentile: 1050-1260. High school rank: 23% in top tenth, 62% in top quarter, 90% in top half
Early decision deadline: N/A, notification date: N/A
Early action deadline: 11/15, notification date: 12/23
Application deadline (fall): rolling
Undergraduate student body: 4,429 full time, 237 part time; 42% male, 58% female; 1% American Indian, 16% Asian, 3% black, 8% Hispanic, 7% multiracial, 1% Pacific Islander, 47% white, 12% international; 45% from in state; 45% live on campus; 0% of students in fraternities, 0% in sororities
Most popular majors: 26% Business, Management, Marketing, and Related Support Services, 6% Engineering, 14% Health Professions and Related Programs, 5% Liberal Arts and Sciences, General Studies and Humanities, 5% Social Sciences
Expenses: 2014-2015: $38,205; room/board: $10,830
Financial aid: (206) 296-2000; 61% of undergrads determined to have financial need; average aid package $29,704

South Seattle Community College[1]

Seattle WA
(206) 764-5300
U.S. News ranking: Reg. Coll. (W), unranked
Website: southseattle.edu
Admissions email: N/A
Public
Application deadline (fall): N/A
Undergraduate student body: N/A full time, N/A part time
Expenses: 2013-2014: $3,824 in state, $9,014 out of state; room/board: N/A
Financial aid: (206) 934-5317

St. Martin's University

Lacey WA
(800) 368-8803
U.S. News ranking: Reg. U. (W), No. 46
Website: www.stmartin.edu
Admissions email: admissions@stmartin.edu
Private; founded 1895
Affiliation: Roman Catholic (Benedictine)
Freshman admissions: selective; 2013-2014: 651 applied, 572 accepted. Either SAT or ACT required. SAT 25/75 percentile: 950-1190. High school rank: 24% in top tenth, 52% in top quarter, 85% in top half
Early decision deadline: N/A, notification date: N/A
Early action deadline: N/A, notification date: N/A
Application deadline (fall): rolling
Undergraduate student body: 1,110 full time, 302 part time; 50% male, 50% female; 1% American Indian, 6% Asian, 6% black, 12% Hispanic, 8% multiracial, 2% Pacific Islander, 54% white, 5% international; 70% from in state; 33% live on campus; 0% of students in fraternities, 0% in sororities
Most popular majors: 26% Biological and Biomedical Sciences, 26% Business, Management, Marketing, and Related Support Services, 9% Education, 10% Engineering, 17% Psychology
Expenses: 2014-2015: $31,688; room/board: $9,990
Financial aid: (360) 438-4397; 89% of undergrads determined to have financial need; average aid package $21,463

Trinity Lutheran College[1]

Everett WA
(425) 249-4741
U.S. News ranking: Reg. Coll. (W), unranked
Website: www.tlc.edu/
Admissions email: admissions@tlc.edu
Private
Application deadline (fall): N/A
Undergraduate student body: N/A full time, N/A part time
Expenses: 2013-2014: $27,042; room/board: $8,200
Financial aid: (425) 249-4777

University of Puget Sound

Tacoma WA
(253) 879-3211
U.S. News ranking: Nat. Lib. Arts, No. 81
Website: www.pugetsound.edu
Admissions email: admission@pugetsound.edu
Private; founded 1888
Freshman admissions: selective; 2013-2014: 4,588 applied, 3,910 accepted. Either SAT or ACT required. SAT 25/75 percentile: 1120-1330. High school rank: 26% in top tenth, 51% in top quarter, 89% in top half
Early decision deadline: 11/15, notification date: 12/15
Early action deadline: N/A, notification date: N/A
Application deadline (fall): 1/15

More at usnews.com/college

Undergraduate student body: 2,520 full time, 21 part time; 43% male, 57% female; 0% American Indian, 7% Asian, 1% black, 7% Hispanic, 9% multiracial, 0% Pacific Islander, 75% white, 0% international; 24% from in state; 64% live on campus; 24% of students in fraternities, 29% in sororities
Most popular majors: 12% Biological and Biomedical Sciences, 12% Business, Management, Marketing, and Related Support Services, 11% Psychology, 18% Social Sciences, 8% Visual and Performing Arts
Expenses: 2014-2015: $43,428; room/board: $11,180
Financial aid: (800) 396-7192; 59% of undergrads determined to have financial need; average aid package $29,075

University of Washington

Seattle WA
(206) 543-9686
U.S. News ranking: Nat. U., No. 48
Website: www.washington.edu
Admissions email: askuwadm@u. washington.edu
Public; founded 1861
Freshman admissions: more selective; 2013-2014: 30,226 applied, 16,679 accepted. Either SAT or ACT required. SAT 25/75 percentile: 1100-1360. High school rank: 92% in top tenth, 98% in top quarter, 100% in top half
Early decision deadline: N/A, notification date: N/A
Early action deadline: N/A, notification date: N/A
Application deadline (fall): 12/1
Undergraduate student body: 27,048 full time, 2,706 part time; 48% male, 52% female; 1% American Indian, 24% Asian, 3% black, 6% Hispanic, 4% multiracial, 1% Pacific Islander, 49% white, 11% international; 85% from in state; 24% live on campus; 15% of students in fraternities, 13% in sororities
Most popular majors: 12% Biological and Biomedical Sciences, 10% Business, Management, Marketing, and Related Support Services, 8% Engineering, 18% Social Sciences, 8% Visual and Performing Arts
Expenses: 2014-2015: $12,394 in state, $33,513 out of state; room/board: $10,833
Financial aid: (206) 543-6101; 47% of undergrads determined to have financial need; average aid package $18,600

Walla Walla University

College Place WA
(509) 527-2327
U.S. News ranking: Reg. U. (W), No. 58
Website: www.wallawalla.edu
Admissions email: info@wallawalla.edu
Private; founded 1892
Affiliation: Seventh-day Adventist
Freshman admissions: less selective; 2013-2014: 1,102 applied, 1,034 accepted. Neither SAT nor ACT required. SAT 25/75 percentile: 930-1190. High school rank: N/A

percentile: 990-1220. High school rank: 21% in top tenth, 50% in top quarter, 84% in top half
Early decision deadline: N/A, notification date: N/A
Early action deadline: N/A, notification date: N/A
Application deadline (fall): 1/31
Undergraduate student body: 12,942 full time, 1,084 part time; 45% male, 55% female; 0% American Indian, 6% Asian, 2% black, 7% Hispanic, 8% multiracial, 0% Pacific Islander, 75% white, 1% international; 91% from in state; 29% live on campus; N/A of students in fraternities, N/A in sororities
Most popular majors: Information not available
Expenses: 2014-2015: $8,964 in state, $20,406 out of state; room/board: $10,042
Financial aid: (360) 650-3470; 50% of undergrads determined to have financial need; average aid package $14,893

Washington State University

Pullman WA
(888) 468-6978
U.S. News ranking: Nat. U., No. 138
Website: www.wsu.edu
Admissions email: admissions@wsu.edu
Public; founded 1890
Freshman admissions: selective; 2013-2014: 14,887 applied, 12,219 accepted. Either SAT or ACT required. SAT 25/75 percentile: 910-1150. High school rank: 30% in top tenth, 52% in top quarter, 83% in top half
Early decision deadline: N/A, notification date: N/A
Early action deadline: N/A, notification date: N/A
Application deadline (fall): rolling
Undergraduate student body: 20,312 full time, 2,758 part time; 49% male, 51% female; 1% American Indian, 5% Asian, 3% black, 11% Hispanic, 7% multiracial, 0% Pacific Islander, 66% white, 4% international; 92% from in state; 26% live on campus; 17% of students in fraternities, 17% in sororities
Most popular majors: 17% Business, Management, Marketing, and Related Support Services, 7% Communication, Journalism, and Related Programs, 9% Engineering, 8% Health Professions and Related Programs, 15% Social Sciences
Expenses: 2014-2015: $12,428 in state, $25,510 out of state; room/board: $11,276
Financial aid: (509) 335-9711; 68% of undergrads determined to have financial need; average aid package $12,537

Western Washington University

Bellingham WA
(360) 650-3440
U.S. News ranking: Reg. U. (W), No. 21
Website: www.wwu.edu
Admissions email: admit@cc.wwu.edu
Public; founded 1893
Freshman admissions: selective; 2013-2014: 9,508 applied, 7,958 accepted. Either SAT or ACT required. SAT 25/75

Whitman College

Walla Walla WA
(509) 527-5176
U.S. News ranking: Nat. Lib. Arts, No. 37
Website: www.whitman.edu
Admissions email: admission@whitman.edu
Private; founded 1883
Freshman admissions: more selective; 2013-2014: 2,586 applied, 1,473 accepted. Either SAT or ACT required. SAT 25/75 percentile: 1220-1422. High school rank: 61% in top tenth, 84% in top quarter, 97% in top half
Early decision deadline: 11/15, notification date: 12/21
Early action deadline: N/A, notification date: N/A
Application deadline (fall): 1/15
Undergraduate student body: 1,505 full time, 36 part time; 43% male, 57% female; 1% American Indian, 6% Asian, 1% black, 8% Hispanic, 4% multiracial, 0% Pacific Islander, 72% white, 3% international; 36% from in state; 67% live on campus; 46% of students in fraternities, 40% in sororities
Most popular majors: 6% Biochemistry and Molecular Biology, 11% Biology/Biological Sciences, General, 6% Economics, General, 7% English Language and Literature, General, 8% Psychology, General
Expenses: 2014-2015: $44,800; room/board: $11,228
Financial aid: (509) 527-5178; 46% of undergrads determined to have financial need; average aid package $33,555

Whitworth University

Spokane WA
(800) 533-4668
U.S. News ranking: Reg. U. (W), No. 9
Website: www.whitworth.edu
Admissions email: admissions@whitworth.edu
Private; founded 1890
Affiliation: Presbyterian Church
Freshman admissions: selective; 2013-2014: 3,357 applied, 2,610 accepted. Neither SAT nor ACT required. SAT 25/75 percentile: 1090-1290. High school rank: N/A

Early decision deadline: N/A, notification date: N/A
Early action deadline: 11/30, notification date: 12/20
Application deadline (fall): 3/1
Undergraduate student body: 2,316 full time, 42 part time; 40% male, 60% female; 1% American Indian, 3% Asian, 1% black, 8% Hispanic, 5% multiracial, 0% Pacific Islander, 79% white, 2% international; 65% from in state; 60% live on campus; N/A of students in fraternities, N/A in sororities
Most popular majors: 14% Business, Management, Marketing, and Related Support Services, 7% Communication, Journalism, and Related Programs, 7% Multi/Interdisciplinary Studies, 10% Social Sciences, 8% Visual and Performing Arts
Expenses: 2014-2015: $37,456; room/board: $10,278
Financial aid: (800) 533-4668; 70% of undergrads determined to have financial need; average aid package $29,205

WEST VIRGINIA

Alderson Broaddus University

Philippi WV
(800) 263-1549
U.S. News ranking: Reg. Coll. (S), No. 37
Website: www.ab.edu
Admissions email: admissions@ab.edu
Private; founded 1871
Affiliation: American Baptist
Freshman admissions: selective; 2013-2014: 4,892 applied, 2,114 accepted. Either SAT or ACT required. ACT 25/75 percentile: 19-24. High school rank: 11% in top tenth, 36% in top quarter, 67% in top half
Early decision deadline: N/A, notification date: N/A
Early action deadline: N/A, notification date: N/A
Application deadline (fall): 8/25
Undergraduate student body: 995 full time, 57 part time; 52% male, 48% female; 1% American Indian, 1% Asian, 16% black, 4% Hispanic, 1% multiracial, 0% Pacific Islander, 74% white, 3% international; 44% from in state; 81% live on campus; 4% of students in fraternities, 5% in sororities
Most popular majors: 6% Athletic Training/Trainer, 17% Biology/Biological Sciences, General, 5% Elementary Education and Teaching, 5% Music Teacher Education, 15% Registered Nursing/Registered Nurse
Expenses: 2014-2015: $22,740; room/board: $7,236
Financial aid: (304) 457-6354; 87% of undergrads determined to have financial need; average aid package $18,600

American Public University System

Charles Town WV
(877) 777-9081
U.S. News ranking: Reg. U. (S), unranked
Website: www.apus.edu
Admissions email: N/A
For-profit; founded 1991

Freshman admissions: N/A; 2013-2014: N/A applied, N/A accepted. Neither SAT nor ACT required. ACT 25/75 percentile: N/A. High school rank: N/A
Early decision deadline: N/A, notification date: N/A
Early action deadline: N/A, notification date: N/A
Application deadline (fall): rolling
Undergraduate student body: 3,275 full time, 40,689 part time; 60% male, 40% female; 1% American Indian, 2% Asian, 24% black, 10% Hispanic, 3% multiracial, 1% Pacific Islander, 54% white, 1% international
Most popular majors: 13% Business Administration and Management, General, 7% Criminal Justice/Safety Studies, 10% General Studies, 6% Homeland Security, 14% International/Global Studies
Expenses: 2014-2015: $8,000; room/board: N/A
Financial aid: (877) 372-3535

Bethany College

Bethany WV
(304) 829-7611
U.S. News ranking: Nat. Lib. Arts, second tier
Website: www.bethanywv.edu
Admissions email: admission@bethanywv.edu
Private; founded 1840
Affiliation: Christian Church (Disciples of Christ)
Freshman admissions: less selective; 2013-2014: 1,736 applied, 859 accepted. Either SAT or ACT required. SAT 25/75 percentile: 770-1040. High school rank: 12% in top tenth, 30% in top quarter, 47% in top half
Early decision deadline: N/A, notification date: N/A
Early action deadline: N/A, notification date: N/A
Application deadline (fall): rolling
Undergraduate student body: 690 full time, 4 part time; 56% male, 44% female; 0% American Indian, 0% Asian, 20% black, 3% Hispanic, 2% multiracial, 0% Pacific Islander, 58% white, 1% international; 20% from in state; 99% live on campus; 29% of students in fraternities, 29% in sororities
Most popular majors: 7% Biology/Biological Sciences, General, 8% Elementary Education and Teaching, 13% Physical Education Teaching and Coaching, 21% Psychology, General, 14% Speech Communication and Rhetoric
Expenses: 2014-2015: $25,736; room/board: $9,746
Financial aid: (304) 829-7141; 88% of undergrads determined to have financial need; average aid package $24,972

Bluefield State College

Bluefield WV
(304) 327-4065
U.S. News ranking: Reg. Coll. (S), second tier
Website: www.bluefieldstate.edu
Admissions email: bscadmit@bluefieldstate.edu
Public; founded 1895
Freshman admissions: less selective; 2013-2014: 1,059 applied, 435 accepted. Either SAT or ACT required. ACT 25/75

percentile: 16-21. High school rank: N/A
Early decision deadline: N/A, notification date: N/A
Early action deadline: N/A, notification date: N/A
Application deadline (fall): rolling
Undergraduate student body: 1,440 full time, 307 part time; 38% male, 62% female; 0% American Indian, 0% Asian, 10% black, 1% Hispanic, 1% multiracial, 0% Pacific Islander, 85% white, 3% international; 98% from in state; 0% live on campus; 4% of students in fraternities, 4% in sororities
Most popular majors: 15% Business, Management, Marketing, and Related Support Services, 12% Education, 19% Engineering Technologies and Engineering-Related Fields, 8% Health Professions and Related Programs, 27% Liberal Arts and Sciences, General Studies and Humanities
Expenses: 2014-2015: $5,832 in state, $11,064 out of state; room/board: N/A
Financial aid: (304) 327-4020; 81% of undergrads determined to have financial need; average aid package $3,582

Concord University

Athens WV
(304) 384-5249
U.S. News ranking: Reg. Coll. (S), No. 50
Website: www.concord.edu
Admissions email: admissions@concord.edu
Public; founded 1872
Freshman admissions: selective; 2013-2014: 2,778 applied, 1,251 accepted. Either SAT or ACT required. ACT 25/75 percentile: 18-24. High school rank: 19% in top tenth, 44% in top quarter, 75% in top half
Early decision deadline: N/A, notification date: N/A
Early action deadline: N/A, notification date: N/A
Application deadline (fall): rolling
Undergraduate student body: 2,275 full time, 245 part time; 43% male, 57% female; 0% American Indian, 1% Asian, 6% black, 1% Hispanic, 0% multiracial, 0% Pacific Islander, 87% white, 4% international; 85% from in state; 36% live on campus; N/A of students in fraternities, N/A in sororities
Most popular majors: 6% Biological and Biomedical Sciences, 17% Business, Management, Marketing, and Related Support Services, 21% Education, 22% Liberal Arts and Sciences, General Studies and Humanities, 6% Social Sciences
Expenses: 2014-2015: $6,422 in state, $14,118 out of state; room/board: $7,818
Financial aid: (304) 384-6069; 76% of undergrads determined to have financial need; average aid package $8,632

Davis and Elkins College[1]

Elkins WV
(304) 637-1230
U.S. News ranking: Reg. Coll. (S), No. 50
Website: www.davisandelkins.edu
Admissions email: admiss@davisandelkins.edu
Private
Application deadline (fall): N/A
Undergraduate student body: N/A full time, N/A part time
Expenses: 2013-2014: $24,992; room/board: $8,750
Financial aid: (304) 637-1373

Fairmont State University

Fairmont WV
(304) 367-4892
U.S. News ranking: Reg. U. (S), second tier
Website: www.fairmontstate.edu
Admissions email: admit@fairmontstate.edu
Public; founded 1865
Freshman admissions: selective; 2013-2014: 2,799 applied, 1,861 accepted. Either SAT or ACT required. ACT 25/75 percentile: 18-23. High school rank: 13% in top tenth, 39% in top quarter, 74% in top half
Early decision deadline: N/A, notification date: N/A
Early action deadline: N/A, notification date: N/A
Application deadline (fall): rolling
Undergraduate student body: 3,435 full time, 523 part time; 45% male, 55% female; 0% American Indian, 0% Asian, 5% black, 2% Hispanic, 2% multiracial, 0% Pacific Islander, 86% white, 2% international; 92% from in state; 21% live on campus; 1% of students in fraternities, 2% in sororities
Most popular majors: 15% Business Administration and Management, General, 11% Criminal Justice/Safety Studies, 11% Education, General, 10% General Studies, 7% Psychology, General
Expenses: 2014-2015: $5,824 in state, $12,288 out of state; room/board: $7,686
Financial aid: (304) 367-4213; 76% of undergrads determined to have financial need; average aid package $8,360

Glenville State College

Glenville WV
(304) 462-4128
U.S. News ranking: Reg. Coll. (S), No. 71
Website: www.glenville.edu
Admissions email: admissions@glenville.edu
Public; founded 1872
Freshman admissions: less selective; 2013-2014: 1,198 applied, 802 accepted. Either SAT or ACT required. ACT 25/75 percentile: 16-21. High school rank: 8% in top tenth, 20% in top quarter, 40% in top half
Early decision deadline: N/A, notification date: N/A
Early action deadline: N/A, notification date: N/A
Application deadline (fall): rolling

Undergraduate student body: 1,114 full time, 736 part time; 57% male, 43% female; 0% American Indian, 0% Asian, 17% black, 1% Hispanic, 1% multiracial, 0% Pacific Islander, 78% white, 0% international; 86% from in state; 29% live on campus; 2% of students in fraternities, 4% in sororities
Most popular majors: Information not available
Expenses: 2014-2015: $6,696 in state, $15,120 out of state; room/board: $9,492
Financial aid: (304) 462-4103; 81% of undergrads determined to have financial need; average aid package $12,805

Marshall University

Huntington WV
(800) 642-3499
U.S. News ranking: Reg. U. (S), No. 46
Website: www.marshall.edu
Admissions email: admissions@marshall.edu
Public; founded 1837
Freshman admissions: selective; 2013-2014: 2,866 applied, 2,255 accepted. Either SAT or ACT required. ACT 25/75 percentile: 20-24. High school rank: N/A
Early decision deadline: N/A, notification date: N/A
Early action deadline: N/A, notification date: N/A
Application deadline (fall): rolling
Undergraduate student body: 8,268 full time, 1,488 part time; 44% male, 56% female; 0% American Indian, 1% Asian, 6% black, 2% Hispanic, 2% multiracial, 0% Pacific Islander, 86% white, 1% international; 77% from in state; N/A live on campus; N/A of students in fraternities, N/A in sororities
Most popular majors: 5% Biological and Biomedical Sciences, 17% Business, Management, Marketing, and Related Support Services, 14% Education, 11% Health Professions and Related Programs, 16% Liberal Arts and Sciences, General Studies and Humanities
Expenses: 2014-2015: $6,526 in state, $15,026 out of state; room/board: $8,722
Financial aid: (304) 696-3162; 71% of undergrads determined to have financial need; average aid package $9,956

Ohio Valley University

Vienna WV
(877) 446-8668
U.S. News ranking: Reg. Coll. (S), No. 56
Website: www.ovu.edu
Admissions email: admissions@ovu.edu
Private; founded 1958
Affiliation: Church of Christ
Freshman admissions: selective; 2013-2014: 846 applied, 321 accepted. Either SAT or ACT required. ACT 25/75 percentile: 19-23. High school rank: 10% in top tenth, 29% in top quarter, 59% in top half
Early decision deadline: N/A, notification date: N/A
Early action deadline: N/A, notification date: N/A
Application deadline (fall): 8/15

Undergraduate student body: 371 full time, 47 part time; 54% male, 46% female; 0% American Indian, 1% Asian, 7% black, 3% Hispanic, 2% multiracial, 0% Pacific Islander, 72% white, 8% international; 34% from in state; 53% live on campus; 66% of students in fraternities, 66% in sororities
Most popular majors: 25% Business, Management, Marketing, and Related Support Services, 20% Education, 8% Liberal Arts and Sciences, General Studies and Humanities, 13% Psychology, 10% Theology and Religious Vocations
Expenses: 2014-2015: $19,260; room/board: $7,010
Financial aid: (304) 865-6075; 76% of undergrads determined to have financial need; average aid package $14,612

Salem International University[1]

Salem WV
(888) 235-5024
U.S. News ranking: Reg. U. (S), unranked
Website: www.salemu.edu
Admissions email: admissions@salemu.edu
For-profit
Application deadline (fall): N/A
Undergraduate student body: N/A full time, N/A part time
Expenses: 2013-2014: $17,700; room/board: $7,000
Financial aid: (304) 782-5303

Shepherd University

Shepherdstown WV
(304) 876-5212
U.S. News ranking: Reg. U. (S), second tier
Website: www.shepherd.edu
Admissions email: admissions@shepherd.edu
Public; founded 1871
Freshman admissions: less selective; 2013-2014: 1,746 applied, 1,647 accepted. SAT or ACT required. SAT 25/75 percentile: 900-1080. High school rank: N/A
Early decision deadline: N/A, notification date: N/A
Early action deadline: 11/15, notification date: 12/1
Application deadline (fall): rolling
Undergraduate student body: 3,289 full time, 701 part time; 43% male, 57% female; 0% American Indian, 2% Asian, 8% black, 3% Hispanic, 0% multiracial, 0% Pacific Islander, 83% white, 0% international; 63% from in state; 33% live on campus; 3% of students in fraternities, 4% in sororities
Most popular majors: 12% Business, Management, Marketing, and Related Support Services, 12% Education, 9% Health Professions and Related Programs, 17% Liberal Arts and Sciences, General Studies and Humanities, 8% Social Sciences
Expenses: 2014-2015: $6,570 in state, $16,628 out of state; room/board: $9,308
Financial aid: (304) 876-5470; 64% of undergrads determined to have financial need; average aid package $11,094

University of Charleston

Charleston WV
(800) 995-4682
U.S. News ranking: Reg. Coll. (S), No. 19
Website: www.ucwv.edu
Admissions email: admissions@ucwv.edu
Private; founded 1888
Freshman admissions: selective; 2013-2014: 1,312 applied, 906 accepted. Either SAT or ACT required. ACT 25/75 percentile: 19-24. High school rank: N/A
Early decision deadline: N/A, notification date: N/A
Early action deadline: N/A, notification date: N/A
Application deadline (fall): rolling
Undergraduate student body: 1,250 full time, 136 part time; 42% male, 58% female; 1% American Indian, 1% Asian, 12% black, 2% Hispanic, 1% multiracial, 0% Pacific Islander, 64% white, 8% international; 72% from in state; 47% live on campus; N/A of students in fraternities, N/A in sororities
Most popular majors: 9% Biological and Biomedical Sciences, 40% Business, Management, Marketing, and Related Support Services, 6% Education, 6% Health Professions and Related Programs, 7% Social Sciences
Expenses: 2014-2015: $23,200; room/board: $9,100
Financial aid: (304) 357-4759; 81% of undergrads determined to have financial need; average aid package $17,500

West Liberty University

West Liberty WV
(304) 336-8076
U.S. News ranking: Reg. Coll. (S), No. 52
Website: www.westliberty.edu
Admissions email: admissions@westliberty.edu
Public; founded 1837
Freshman admissions: selective; 2013-2014: 2,175 applied, 1,549 accepted. Either SAT or ACT required. ACT 25/75 percentile: 18-24. High school rank: 11% in top tenth, 37% in top quarter, 72% in top half
Early decision deadline: N/A, notification date: N/A
Early action deadline: N/A, notification date: N/A
Application deadline (fall): rolling
Undergraduate student body: 2,197 full time, 463 part time; 40% male, 60% female; 0% American Indian, 1% Asian, 5% black, 1% Hispanic, 1% multiracial, 0% Pacific Islander, 89% white, 2% international; 68% from in state; 45% live on campus; 3% of students in fraternities, 4% in sororities
Most popular majors: 15% Business, Management, Marketing, and Related Support Services, 18% Education, 14% Health Professions and Related Programs, 7% Homeland Security, Law Enforcement, Firefighting and Related Protective Services, 17% Liberal Arts and Sciences, General Studies and Humanities
Expenses: 2013-2014: $6,226 in state, $13,540 out of state; room/board: $8,370
Financial aid: (304) 336-8016

West Virginia State University

Institute WV
(304) 766-3221
U.S. News ranking: Nat. Lib. Arts, second tier
Website: www.wvstateu.edu
Admissions email: admissions@wvstateu.edu
Public; founded 1891
Freshman admissions: selective; 2013-2014: 2,206 applied, 984 accepted. Either SAT or ACT required. ACT 25/75 percentile: 18-22. High school rank: N/A
Early decision deadline: N/A, notification date: N/A
Early action deadline: N/A, notification date: N/A
Application deadline (fall): 8/20
Undergraduate student body: 1,889 full time, 733 part time; 45% male, 55% female; 1% American Indian, 0% Asian, 12% black, 1% Hispanic, 0% multiracial, 0% Pacific Islander, 61% white, 1% international; 93% from in state; 10% live on campus; 1% of students in fraternities, 1% in sororities
Most popular majors: 13% Business, Management, Marketing, and Related Support Services, 13% Education, 9% Homeland Security, Law Enforcement, Firefighting and Related Protective Services, 22% Liberal Arts and Sciences, General Studies and Humanities, 9% Psychology
Expenses: 2014-2015: $6,228 in state, $14,558 out of state; room/board: $10,476
Financial aid: (304) 766-3131; 79% of undergrads determined to have financial need; average aid package $11,756

West Virginia University

Morgantown WV
(304) 442-3146
U.S. News ranking: Nat. U., No. 168
Website: www.wvu.edu
Admissions email: tech-admissions@mail.wvu.edu
Public; founded 1867
Freshman admissions: selective; 2013-2014: 16,079 applied, 13,713 accepted. Either SAT or ACT required. ACT 25/75 percentile: 21-26. High school rank: 20% in top tenth, 45% in top quarter, 79% in top half
Early decision deadline: N/A, notification date: N/A
Early action deadline: N/A, notification date: N/A
Application deadline (fall): 8/1
Undergraduate student body: 21,027 full time, 1,730 part time; 54% male, 46% female; 0% American Indian, 2% Asian, 4% black, 4% Hispanic, 3% multiracial, 0% Pacific Islander, 83% white, 4% international; 51% from in state; 24% live on campus; 6% of students in fraternities, 5% in sororities
Most popular majors: 12% Business, Management, Marketing, and Related Support Services, 8% Communication, Journalism, and Related Programs, 12% Engineering, 9% Health Professions and Related Programs, 9% Multi/Interdisciplinary Studies
Expenses: 2014-2015: $6,960 in state, $20,424 out of state; room/board: $9,582

Financial aid: (800) 344-9881; 55% of undergrads determined to have financial need; average aid package $7,271

West Virginia University–Parkersburg[1]

Parkersburg WV
(304) 424-8220
U.S. News ranking: Reg. Coll. (S), unranked
Website: www.wvup.edu
Admissions email: info@mail.wvup.edu
Public
Application deadline (fall): N/A
Undergraduate student body: N/A full time, N/A part time
Expenses: 2013-2014: $2,712 in state, $9,648 out of state; room/board: N/A
Financial aid: (304) 424-8210

West Virginia Wesleyan College

Buckhannon WV
(800) 722-9933
U.S. News ranking: Reg. Coll. (S), No. 12
Website: www.wvwc.edu
Admissions email: admissions@wvwc.edu
Private; founded 1890
Affiliation: United Methodist
Freshman admissions: selective; 2013-2014: 1,762 applied, 1,356 accepted. Either SAT or ACT required. ACT 25/75 percentile: 20-25. High school rank: 27% in top tenth, 56% in top quarter, 85% in top half
Early decision deadline: N/A, notification date: N/A
Early action deadline: N/A, notification date: N/A
Application deadline (fall): rolling
Undergraduate student body: 1,345 full time, 22 part time; 47% male, 53% female; 0% American Indian, 0% Asian, 9% black, 2% Hispanic, 3% multiracial, 0% Pacific Islander, 80% white, 5% international; 62% from in state; 79% live on campus; 25% of students in fraternities, 25% in sororities
Most popular majors: 13% Business, Management, Marketing, and Related Support Services, 10% Education, 11% Health Professions and Related Programs, 8% Homeland Security, Law Enforcement, Firefighting and Related Protective Services, 9% Parks, Recreation, Leisure, and Fitness Studies
Expenses: 2014-2015: $27,858; room/board: $7,890
Financial aid: (304) 473-8080; 80% of undergrads determined to have financial need; average aid package $28,234

Wheeling Jesuit University

Wheeling WV
(800) 624-6992
U.S. News ranking: Reg. Coll. (S), No. 11
Website: www.wju.edu
Admissions email: admiss@wju.edu
Private; founded 1954
Affiliation: Roman Catholic
Freshman admissions: selective; 2013-2014: 1,470 applied, 981

accepted. Either SAT or ACT required. ACT 25/75 percentile: 20-24. High school rank: 16% in top tenth, 43% in top quarter, 78% in top half
Early decision deadline: N/A, notification date: N/A
Early action deadline: N/A, notification date: N/A
Application deadline (fall): rolling
Undergraduate student body: 938 full time, 242 part time; 45% male, 55% female; 0% American Indian, 1% Asian, 5% black, 3% Hispanic, 0% multiracial, 0% Pacific Islander, 80% white, 3% international; 39% from in state; 59% live on campus; 0% of students in fraternities, 0% in sororities
Most popular majors: 23% Business, Management, Marketing, and Related Support Services, 5% English Language and Literature/Letters, 34% Health Professions and Related Programs, 6% Physical Sciences, 5% Psychology
Expenses: 2014-2015: $28,030; room/board: $6,827
Financial aid: (304) 243-2304; 75% of undergrads determined to have financial need; average aid package $23,406

WISCONSIN

Alverno College

Milwaukee WI
(414) 382-6100
U.S. News ranking: Reg. U. (Mid. W), No. 69
Website: www.alverno.edu
Admissions email: admissions@alverno.edu
Private; founded 1887
Affiliation: Roman Catholic
Freshman admissions: less selective; 2013-2014: 582 applied, 459 accepted. Either SAT or ACT required. ACT 25/75 percentile: 17-23. High school rank: 11% in top tenth, 35% in top quarter, 70% in top half
Early decision deadline: N/A, notification date: N/A
Early action deadline: N/A, notification date: N/A
Application deadline (fall): rolling
Undergraduate student body: 1,360 full time, 502 part time; 0% male, 100% female; 1% American Indian, 5% Asian, 18% black, 18% Hispanic, 3% multiracial, 0% Pacific Islander, 54% white, 1% international; 96% from in state; 11% live on campus; 1% of students in fraternities, 1% in sororities
Most popular majors: 13% Business, Management, Marketing, and Related Support Services, 6% Education, 44% Health Professions and Related Programs, 7% Liberal Arts and Sciences, General Studies and Humanities, 6% Psychology
Expenses: 2014-2015: $24,434; room/board: $7,500
Financial aid: (414) 382-6046; 92% of undergrads determined to have financial need; average aid package $17,004

Beloit College

Beloit WI
(608) 363-2500
U.S. News ranking: Nat. Lib. Arts, No. 61
Website: www.beloit.edu
Admissions email: admiss@beloit.edu
Private; founded 1846
Freshman admissions: more selective; 2013-2014: 2,253 applied, 1,525 accepted. Neither SAT nor ACT required. ACT 25/75 percentile: 24-30. High school rank: 29% in top tenth, 61% in top quarter, 89% in top half
Early decision deadline: 11/1, notification date: 11/30
Early action deadline: 12/1, notification date: 1/15
Application deadline (fall): rolling
Undergraduate student body: 1,254 full time, 52 part time; 41% male, 59% female; 0% American Indian, 2% Asian, 5% black, 8% Hispanic, 3% multiracial, 0% Pacific Islander, 71% white, 8% international; 19% from in state; 92% live on campus; 24% of students in fraternities, 22% in sororities
Most popular majors: 6% Anthropology, 5% Creative Writing, 6% Economics, Other, 5% History, General, 9% Psychology, General
Expenses: 2014-2015: $42,500; room/board: $7,470
Financial aid: (608) 363-2663; 69% of undergrads determined to have financial need; average aid package $31,215

Cardinal Stritch University[1]

Milwaukee WI
(414) 410-4040
U.S. News ranking: Nat. U., second tier
Website: www.stritch.edu
Admissions email: admityou@stritch.edu
Private; founded 1937
Affiliation: Roman Catholic
Application deadline (fall): rolling
Undergraduate student body: N/A full time, N/A part time
Expenses: 2014-2015: $26,570; room/board: $7,470
Financial aid: (414) 410-4048; 78% of undergrads determined to have financial need; average aid package $11,824

Carroll University

Waukesha WI
(262) 524-7220
U.S. News ranking: Reg. U. (Mid. W), No. 41
Website: www.carrollu.edu/
Admissions email: ccinfo@carrollu.edu
Private; founded 1846
Affiliation: Presbyterian Church (USA)
Freshman admissions: more selective; 2013-2014: 2,868 applied, 2,327 accepted. Either SAT or ACT required. ACT 25/75 percentile: 21-26. High school rank: 26% in top tenth, 58% in top quarter, 86% in top half
Early decision deadline: N/A, notification date: N/A
Early action deadline: N/A, notification date: N/A
Application deadline (fall): rolling

Undergraduate student body: 2,729 full time, 390 part time; 35% male, 65% female; 0% American Indian, 2% Asian, 1% black, 6% Hispanic, 2% multiracial, 0% Pacific Islander, 87% white, 1% international
Most popular majors: Information not available
Expenses: 2014-2015: $28,550; room/board: $8,550
Financial aid: (262) 524-7296; 82% of undergrads determined to have financial need; average aid package $19,011

Carthage College

Kenosha WI
(262) 551-6000
U.S. News ranking: Nat. Lib. Arts, No. 155
Website: www.carthage.edu
Admissions email: admissions@carthage.edu
Private; founded 1847
Affiliation: Evangelical Lutheran Church in America
Freshman admissions: selective; 2013-2014: 7,174 applied, 5,035 accepted. Either SAT or ACT required. ACT 25/75 percentile: 21-27. High school rank: 21% in top tenth, 44% in top quarter, 75% in top half
Early decision deadline: N/A, notification date: N/A
Early action deadline: N/A, notification date: N/A
Application deadline (fall): rolling
Undergraduate student body: 2,581 full time, 321 part time; 46% male, 54% female; 0% American Indian, 1% Asian, 5% black, 4% Hispanic, 2% multiracial, 0% Pacific Islander, 77% white, 0% international; 32% from in state; 67% live on campus; 11% of students in fraternities, 12% in sororities
Most popular majors: Information not available
Expenses: 2014-2015: $36,850; room/board: $9,970
Financial aid: (262) 551-6001; 79% of undergrads determined to have financial need; average aid package $24,219

Concordia University Wisconsin

Mequon WI
(262) 243-4300
U.S. News ranking: Reg. U. (Mid. W), No. 61
Website: www.cuw.edu
Admissions email: admissions@cuw.edu
Private; founded 1881
Affiliation: Lutheran Church-Missouri Synod
Freshman admissions: selective; 2013-2014: 2,510 applied, 1,755 accepted. ACT required. ACT 25/75 percentile: 20-25. High school rank: 21% in top tenth, 43% in top quarter, 72% in top half
Early decision deadline: N/A, notification date: N/A
Early action deadline: N/A, notification date: N/A
Application deadline (fall): 8/15
Undergraduate student body: 3,059 full time, 1,304 part time; 34% male, 66% female; 1% American Indian, 2% Asian, 18% black, 3% Hispanic, 3% multiracial, 0% Pacific Islander, 69% white, 1% international

Most popular majors: Information not available
Expenses: 2014-2015: $26,190; room/board: $9,780
Financial aid: (262) 243-4569; 83% of undergrads determined to have financial need; average aid package $19,230

Edgewood College
Madison WI
(608) 663-2294
U.S. News ranking: Nat. U., No. 181
Website: www.edgewood.edu
Admissions email: admissions@edgewood.edu
Private; founded 1927
Affiliation: Roman Catholic
Freshman admissions: selective; 2013-2014: 1,297 applied, 993 accepted. Either SAT or ACT required. ACT 25/75 percentile: 20-25. High school rank: 15% in top tenth, 37% in top quarter, 74% in top half
Early decision deadline: N/A, notification date: N/A
Early action deadline: N/A, notification date: N/A
Application deadline (fall): 8/14
Undergraduate student body: 1,681 full time, 317 part time; 31% male, 69% female; 0% American Indian, 2% Asian, 3% black, 5% Hispanic, 3% multiracial, 0% Pacific Islander, 80% white, 4% international; 93% from in state; 28% live on campus; N/A of students in fraternities, N/A in sororities
Most popular majors: 7% Business Administration and Management, General, 10% Business/Commerce, General, 4% Organizational Behavior Studies, 9% Psychology, General, 23% Registered Nursing/Registered Nurse
Expenses: 2014-2015: $25,590; room/board: $8,973
Financial aid: (608) 663-2305; 76% of undergrads determined to have financial need; average aid package $20,260

Herzing University[1]
Madison WI
(800) 596-0724
U.S. News ranking: Reg. Coll. (Mid. W), second tier
Website: www.herzing.edu/madison
Admissions email: info@msn.herzing.edu
For-profit
Application deadline (fall): N/A
Undergraduate student body: N/A full time, N/A part time
Expenses: 2013-2014: $11,150; room/board: N/A
Financial aid: N/A

Lakeland College[1]
Plymouth WI
(920) 565-1226
U.S. News ranking: Reg. U. (Mid. W), second tier
Website: www.lakeland.edu
Admissions email: admissions@lakeland.edu
Private; founded 1862
Affiliation: United Church of Christ
Application deadline (fall): rolling
Undergraduate student body: N/A full time, N/A part time
Expenses: 2013-2014: $22,950; room/board: $8,030
Financial aid: (920) 565-1298

Lawrence University
Appleton WI
(800) 227-0982
U.S. News ranking: Nat. Lib. Arts, No. 59
Website: www.lawrence.edu/
Admissions email: admissions@lawrence.edu
Private; founded 1847
Freshman admissions: more selective; 2013-2014: 2,710 applied, 1,970 accepted. Neither SAT nor ACT required. ACT 25/75 percentile: 26-31. High school rank: 42% in top tenth, 76% in top quarter, 97% in top half
Early decision deadline: 11/1, notification date: 11/15
Early action deadline: 11/15, notification date: 12/20
Application deadline (fall): 1/15
Undergraduate student body: 1,518 full time, 37 part time; 44% male, 56% female; 1% American Indian, 4% Asian, 3% black, 5% Hispanic, 4% multiracial, 0% Pacific Islander, 74% white, 9% international; 32% from in state; 92% live on campus; 20% of students in fraternities, 15% in sororities
Most popular majors: 10% Biological and Biomedical Sciences, 10% Foreign Languages, Literatures, and Linguistics, 9% Psychology, 18% Social Sciences, 23% Visual and Performing Arts
Expenses: 2014-2015: $42,657; room/board: $8,808
Financial aid: (920) 832-6583; 64% of undergrads determined to have financial need; average aid package $33,196

Maranatha Baptist University
Watertown WI
(920) 206-2327
U.S. News ranking: Reg. Coll. (Mid. W), No. 62
Website: www.mbbc.edu
Admissions email: admissions@mbbc.edu
Private; founded 1968
Affiliation: Baptist
Freshman admissions: selective; 2013-2014: 463 applied, 297 accepted. Either SAT or ACT required. ACT 25/75 percentile: 20-26. High school rank: N/A
Early decision deadline: N/A, notification date: N/A
Early action deadline: N/A, notification date: N/A
Application deadline (fall): rolling
Undergraduate student body: 692 full time, 249 part time; 45% male, 55% female; 0% American Indian, 1% Asian, 2% black, 2% Hispanic, 3% multiracial, 0% Pacific Islander, 82% white, 1% international; 29% from in state; 65% live on campus; N/A of students in fraternities, N/A in sororities
Most popular majors: 17% Business, Management, Marketing, and Related Support Services, 21% Education, 6% Health Professions and Related Programs, 31% Liberal Arts and Sciences, General Studies and Humanities, 16% Theology and Religious Vocations
Expenses: 2014-2015: $13,510; room/board: $6,480
Financial aid: (920) 206-2319; 85% of undergrads determined to have financial need; average aid package $9,918

Marian University
Fond du Lac WI
(920) 923-7650
U.S. News ranking: Reg. U. (Mid. W), No. 95
Website: www.marianuniversity.edu
Admissions email: admissions@marianuniversity.edu
Private; founded 1936
Affiliation: Roman Catholic
Freshman admissions: selective; 2013-2014: 1,021 applied, 772 accepted. Either SAT or ACT required. ACT 25/75 percentile: 18-22. High school rank: 7% in top tenth, 32% in top quarter, 69% in top half
Early decision deadline: N/A, notification date: N/A
Early action deadline: N/A, notification date: N/A
Application deadline (fall): rolling
Undergraduate student body: 1,339 full time, 349 part time; 29% male, 71% female; 1% American Indian, 1% Asian, 6% black, 4% Hispanic, 0% multiracial, 0% Pacific Islander, 84% white, 2% international; 88% from in state; 33% live on campus; 5% of students in fraternities, 5% in sororities
Most popular majors: 20% Business, Management, Marketing, and Related Support Services, 13% Homeland Security, Law Enforcement, Firefighting and Related Protective Services, 4% Psychology, 9% Radiologic Technology/Science - Radiographer, 28% Registered Nursing, Nursing Administration, Nursing Research and Clinical Nursing
Expenses: 2014-2015: $25,630; room/board: $6,490
Financial aid: (920) 923-7614; 86% of undergrads determined to have financial need; average aid package $22,412

Marquette University
Milwaukee WI
(800) 222-6544
U.S. News ranking: Nat. U., No. 76
Website: www.marquette.edu
Admissions email: admissions@marquette.edu
Private; founded 1881
Affiliation: Roman Catholic (Jesuit)
Freshman admissions: more selective; 2013-2014: 23,432 applied, 13,462 accepted. Either SAT or ACT required. ACT 25/75 percentile: 25-29. High school rank: 36% in top tenth, 69% in top quarter, 95% in top half
Early decision deadline: N/A, notification date: N/A
Early action deadline: N/A, notification date: N/A
Application deadline (fall): 12/1
Undergraduate student body: 8,046 full time, 319 part time; 48% male, 52% female; 0% American Indian, 5% Asian, 5% black, 9% Hispanic, 3% multiracial, 0% Pacific Islander, 74% white, 3% international; 35% from in state; 54% live on campus; 7% of students in fraternities, 15% in sororities
Most popular majors: 8% Biological and Biomedical Sciences, 25% Business, Management, Marketing, and Related Support Services, 11% Communication, Journalism, and Related Programs,

9% Engineering, 8% Health Professions and Related Programs
Expenses: 2014-2015: $35,930; room/board: $11,000
Financial aid: (414) 288-0200; 58% of undergrads determined to have financial need; average aid package $23,664

Milwaukee Institute of Art and Design
Milwaukee WI
(414) 291-8070
U.S. News ranking: Arts, unranked
Website: www.miad.edu
Admissions email: admissions@miad.edu
Private; founded 1974
Freshman admissions: N/A; 2013-2014: 583 applied, 369 accepted. Neither SAT nor ACT required. SAT 25/75 percentile: N/A. High school rank: 8% in top tenth, 26% in top quarter, 60% in top half
Early decision deadline: N/A, notification date: N/A
Early action deadline: 12/1, notification date: 12/15
Application deadline (fall): 8/1
Undergraduate student body: 653 full time, 15 part time; 34% male, 66% female; 0% American Indian, 4% Asian, 6% black, 11% Hispanic, 4% multiracial, 0% Pacific Islander, 71% white, 1% international; 64% from in state; 20% live on campus; 0% of students in fraternities, 0% in sororities
Most popular majors: 10% Animation, Interactive Technology, Video Graphics and Special Effects, 20% Graphic Design, 14% Illustration, 13% Industrial and Product Design, 10% Photography
Expenses: 2014-2015: $32,050; room/board: $9,000
Financial aid: (414) 291-3272; 83% of undergrads determined to have financial need; average aid package $22,040

Milwaukee School of Engineering
Milwaukee WI
(800) 332-6763
U.S. News ranking: Reg. U. (Mid. W), No. 14
Website: www.msoe.edu
Admissions email: explore@msoe.edu
Private; founded 1903
Freshman admissions: selective; 2013-2014: 2,167 applied, 1,482 accepted. Either SAT or ACT required. ACT 25/75 percentile: 25-30. High school rank: N/A
Early decision deadline: N/A, notification date: N/A
Early action deadline: N/A, notification date: N/A
Application deadline (fall): rolling
Undergraduate student body: 2,284 full time, 175 part time; 77% male, 23% female; 0% American Indian, 3% Asian, 3% black, 5% Hispanic, 1% multiracial, 0% Pacific Islander, 74% white, 8% international; 70% from in state; 37% live on campus; 4% of students in fraternities, 15% in sororities
Most popular majors: 18% Business, Management, Marketing, and Related Support Services, 1% Communication, Journalism, and Related Programs,

69% Engineering, 7% Engineering Technologies and Engineering-Related Fields, 5% Health Professions and Related Programs
Expenses: 2014-2015: $35,520; room/board: $8,520
Financial aid: (414) 277-7511; 83% of undergrads determined to have financial need; average aid package $23,055

Mount Mary University
Milwaukee WI
(800) 321-6265
U.S. News ranking: Reg. U. (Mid. W), No. 91
Website: www.mtmary.edu
Admissions email: mmc-admiss@mtmary.edu
Private; founded 1913
Affiliation: Roman Catholic
Freshman admissions: selective; 2013-2014: 478 applied, 258 accepted. Either SAT or ACT required. ACT 25/75 percentile: 17-23. High school rank: 26% in top tenth, 53% in top quarter, 78% in top half
Early decision deadline: N/A, notification date: N/A
Early action deadline: N/A, notification date: N/A
Application deadline (fall): rolling
Undergraduate student body: 685 full time, 241 part time; 2% male, 98% female; 0% American Indian, 7% Asian, 22% black, 14% Hispanic, 3% multiracial, 0% Pacific Islander, 52% white, 0% international; 96% from in state; 18% live on campus; N/A of students in fraternities, N/A in sororities
Most popular majors: 23% Business, Management, Marketing, and Related Support Services, 13% Health Professions and Related Programs, 8% Psychology, 9% Public Administration and Social Service Professions, 17% Visual and Performing Arts
Expenses: 2014-2015: $25,852; room/board: $7,738
Financial aid: (414) 256-1258; 91% of undergrads determined to have financial need; average aid package $19,944

Northland College
Ashland WI
(715) 682-1224
U.S. News ranking: Nat. Lib. Arts, No. 172
Website: www.northland.edu
Admissions email: admit@northland.edu
Private; founded 1892
Affiliation: United Church of Christ
Freshman admissions: selective; 2013-2014: 1,058 applied, 625 accepted. Either SAT or ACT required. ACT 25/75 percentile: 21-27. High school rank: 18% in top tenth, 36% in top quarter, 75% in top half
Early decision deadline: N/A, notification date: N/A
Early action deadline: N/A, notification date: N/A
Application deadline (fall): rolling
Undergraduate student body: 539 full time, 14 part time; 48% male, 52% female; 2% American Indian, 1% Asian, 1% black, 5% Hispanic, 3% multiracial, 0% Pacific Islander, 77% white, 1% international; 50% from in state; 77% live on campus;

More at usnews.com/college

0% of students in fraternities, 0% in sororities
Most popular majors: 16% Biological and Biomedical Sciences, 9% Business, Management, Marketing, and Related Support Services, 11% Education, 25% Natural Resources and Conservation, 8% Physical Sciences
Expenses: 2014-2015: $31,480; room/board: $7,858
Financial aid: (715) 682-1255; 89% of undergrads determined to have financial need; average aid package $35,251

Ripon College

Ripon WI
(920) 748-8337
U.S. News ranking: Nat. Lib. Arts, No. 113
Website: www.ripon.edu
Admissions email: adminfo@ripon.edu
Private; founded 1851
Freshman admissions: selective; 2013-2014: 1,320 applied, 992 accepted. Either SAT or ACT required. ACT 25/75 percentile: 21-28. High school rank: 23% in top tenth, 53% in top quarter, 84% in top half
Early decision deadline: N/A, notification date: N/A
Early action deadline: N/A, notification date: N/A
Application deadline (fall): rolling
Undergraduate student body: 888 full time, 16 part time; 47% male, 53% female; 0% American Indian, 2% Asian, 2% black, 6% Hispanic, 1% multiracial, 0% Pacific Islander, 83% white, 4% international; 62% from in state; 88% live on campus; 40% of students in fraternities, 27% in sororities
Most popular majors: 12% Business/Commerce, General, 11% English Language and Literature, General, 11% Health and Physical Education/Fitness, General, 13% History, 11% Psychology, General
Expenses: 2014-2015: $33,482; room/board: $9,085
Financial aid: (920) 748-8101; 84% of undergrads determined to have financial need; average aid package $27,134

Silver Lake College[1]

Manitowoc WI
(920) 686-6175
U.S. News ranking: Reg. Coll. (Mid. W), second tier
Website: www.sl.edu
Admissions email: admslc@silver.sl.edu
Private
Application deadline (fall): N/A
Undergraduate student body: N/A full time, N/A part time
Expenses: 2013-2014: $23,180; room/board: $8,298
Financial aid: (920) 686-6122

St. Norbert College

De Pere WI
(800) 236-4878
U.S. News ranking: Nat. Lib. Arts, No. 123
Website: www.snc.edu
Admissions email: admit@snc.edu
Private; founded 1898
Affiliation: Roman Catholic
Freshman admissions: more selective; 2013-2014: 2,088

applied, 1,711 accepted. Either SAT or ACT required. ACT 25/75 percentile: 22-27. High school rank: 27% in top tenth, 56% in top quarter, 87% in top half
Early decision deadline: N/A, notification date: N/A
Early action deadline: N/A, notification date: N/A
Application deadline (fall): rolling
Undergraduate student body: 2,118 full time, 42 part time; 41% male, 59% female; 1% American Indian, 1% Asian, 1% black, 3% Hispanic, 2% multiracial, 0% Pacific Islander, 90% white, 3% international; 76% from in state; 75% live on campus; 13% of students in fraternities, 10% in sororities
Most popular majors: 16% Business/Commerce, General, 15% Elementary Education and Teaching, 6% Psychology, General, 9% Sociology, 10% Speech Communication and Rhetoric
Expenses: 2014-2015: $33,023; room/board: $8,455
Financial aid: (920) 403-3071; 72% of undergrads determined to have financial need; average aid package $23,644

University of Wisconsin–Eau Claire

Eau Claire WI
(715) 836-5415
U.S. News ranking: Reg. U. (Mid. W), No. 33
Website: www.uwec.edu
Admissions email: admissions@uwec.edu
Public; founded 1916
Freshman admissions: selective; 2013-2014: 5,885 applied, 4,724 accepted. Either SAT or ACT required. ACT 25/75 percentile: 22-26. High school rank: 18% in top tenth, 51% in top quarter, 95% in top half
Early decision deadline: N/A, notification date: N/A
Early action deadline: N/A, notification date: N/A
Application deadline (fall): rolling
Undergraduate student body: 9,447 full time, 936 part time; 41% male, 59% female; 0% American Indian, 3% Asian, 1% black, 2% Hispanic, 2% multiracial, 0% Pacific Islander, 89% white, 2% international; 76% from in state; 26% live on campus; N/A of students in fraternities, N/A in sororities
Most popular majors: 21% Business, Management, Marketing, and Related Support Services, 8% Education, 16% Health Professions and Related Programs, 6% Psychology, 6% Visual and Performing Arts
Expenses: 2014-2015: $8,744 in state, $16,317 out of state; room/board: $6,986
Financial aid: (715) 836-3373; 57% of undergrads determined to have financial need; average aid package $9,772

University of Wisconsin–Green Bay

Green Bay WI
(920) 465-2111
U.S. News ranking: Reg. U. (Mid. W), No. 77
Website: www.uwgb.edu
Admissions email: uwgb@uwgb.edu
Public; founded 1965

Freshman admissions: selective; 2013-2014: 2,920 applied, 1,929 accepted. Either SAT or ACT required. ACT 25/75 percentile: 21-25. High school rank: N/A
Early decision deadline: N/A, notification date: N/A
Early action deadline: N/A, notification date: N/A
Application deadline (fall): rolling
Undergraduate student body: 4,314 full time, 2,130 part time; 35% male, 65% female; 1% American Indian, 3% Asian, 1% black, 4% Hispanic, 2% multiracial, 0% Pacific Islander, 87% white, 2% international; 93% from in state; 35% live on campus; 1% of students in fraternities, 1% in sororities
Most popular majors: 8% Behavioral Sciences, 12% Business Administration and Management, General, 9% Human Biology, 11% Liberal Arts and Sciences/Liberal Studies, 9% Psychology, General
Expenses: 2014-2015: $7,676 in state, $15,249 out of state; room/board: $7,224
Financial aid: (920) 465-2075; 72% of undergrads determined to have financial need; average aid package $10,728

University of Wisconsin–La Crosse

La Crosse WI
(608) 785-8939
U.S. News ranking: Reg. U. (Mid. W), No. 31
Website: www.uwlax.edu
Admissions email: admissions@uwlax.edu
Public; founded 1909
Freshman admissions: more selective; 2013-2014: 6,135 applied, 4,693 accepted. Either SAT or ACT required. ACT 25/75 percentile: 23-27. High school rank: 24% in top tenth, 69% in top quarter, 98% in top half
Early decision deadline: N/A, notification date: N/A
Early action deadline: N/A, notification date: N/A
Application deadline (fall): rolling
Undergraduate student body: 9,142 full time, 488 part time; 44% male, 56% female; 0% American Indian, 2% Asian, 1% black, 3% Hispanic, 3% multiracial, 0% Pacific Islander, 89% white, 2% international; 83% from in state; 36% live on campus; 1% of students in fraternities, 1% in sororities
Most popular majors: 13% Biological and Biomedical Sciences, 20% Business, Management, Marketing, and Related Support Services, 11% Education, 8% Health Professions and Related Programs, 9% Social Sciences
Expenses: 2014-2015: $8,795 in state, $16,368 out of state; room/board: $5,910
Financial aid: (608) 785-8604; 55% of undergrads determined to have financial need; average aid package $7,350

University of Wisconsin–Madison

Madison WI
(608) 262-3961
U.S. News ranking: Nat. U., No. 47
Website: www.wisc.edu
Admissions email: onwisconsin@admissions.wisc.edu
Public; founded 1848
Freshman admissions: more selective; 2013-2014: 29,675 applied, 15,161 accepted. Either SAT or ACT required. ACT 25/75 percentile: 26-30. High school rank: 51% in top tenth, 89% in top quarter, 99% in top half
Early decision deadline: N/A, notification date: N/A
Early action deadline: N/A, notification date: N/A
Application deadline (fall): 2/1
Undergraduate student body: 28,593 full time, 2,726 part time; 49% male, 51% female; 0% American Indian, 6% Asian, 2% black, 5% Hispanic, 3% multiracial, 0% Pacific Islander, 77% white, 7% international; 67% from in state; 25% live on campus; 9% of students in fraternities, 8% in sororities
Most popular majors: 8% Biology/Biological Sciences, General, 8% Economics, General, 4% History, General, 7% Political Science and Government, General, 6% Psychology, General
Expenses: 2014-2015: $10,410 in state, $26,660 out of state; room/board: $8,600
Financial aid: (608) 262-3060; 41% of undergrads determined to have financial need; average aid package $12,718

University of Wisconsin–Milwaukee

Milwaukee WI
(414) 229-2222
U.S. News ranking: Nat. U., second tier
Website: www.uwm.edu
Admissions email: uwmlook@uwm.edu
Public; founded 1956
Freshman admissions: selective; 2013-2014: 8,311 applied, 7,347 accepted. Either SAT or ACT required. ACT 25/75 percentile: 19-24. High school rank: 9% in top tenth, 28% in top quarter, 63% in top half
Early decision deadline: N/A, notification date: N/A
Early action deadline: N/A, notification date: N/A
Application deadline (fall): rolling
Undergraduate student body: 18,929 full time, 4,075 part time; 49% male, 51% female; 0% American Indian, 6% Asian, 8% black, 8% Hispanic, 3% multiracial, 0% Pacific Islander, 72% white, 3% international; 93% from in state; 16% live on campus; N/A of students in fraternities, N/A in sororities
Most popular majors: 24% Business, Management, Marketing, and Related Support Services, 7% Education, 11% Health Professions and Related Programs, 6% Social Sciences, 7% Visual and Performing Arts
Expenses: 2014-2015: $9,882 in state, $19,610 out of state; room/board: $9,136

Financial aid: (414) 229-6300; 81% of undergrads determined to have financial need; average aid package $7,635

University of Wisconsin–Oshkosh

Oshkosh WI
(920) 424-0202
U.S. News ranking: Reg. U. (Mid. W), No. 69
Website: www.uwosh.edu
Admissions email: oshadmuw@uwosh.edu
Public; founded 1871
Freshman admissions: selective; 2013-2014: 6,076 applied, 4,053 accepted. Either SAT or ACT required. ACT 25/75 percentile: 20-24. High school rank: 10% in top tenth, 33% in top quarter, 82% in top half
Early decision deadline: N/A, notification date: N/A
Early action deadline: N/A, notification date: N/A
Application deadline (fall): rolling
Undergraduate student body: 9,223 full time, 3,241 part time; 41% male, 59% female; 1% American Indian, 4% Asian, 2% black, 3% Hispanic, 2% multiracial, 0% Pacific Islander, 88% white, 1% international; 96% from in state; 32% live on campus; 3% of students in fraternities, 3% in sororities
Most popular majors: 18% Business, Management, and Related Support Services, 6% Communication, Journalism, and Related Programs, 13% Education, 14% Health Professions and Related Programs, 7% Public Administration and Social Service Professions
Expenses: 2014-2015: $7,442 in state, $15,016 out of state; room/board: $7,386
Financial aid: (920) 424-3377; 72% of undergrads determined to have financial need; average aid package $7,800

University of Wisconsin–Parkside

Kenosha WI
(262) 595-2355
U.S. News ranking: Nat. Lib. Arts, second tier
Website: www.uwp.edu
Admissions email: admissions@uwp.edu
Public; founded 1968
Freshman admissions: selective; 2013-2014: 1,740 applied, 1,197 accepted. Neither SAT nor ACT required. ACT 25/75 percentile: 19-23. High school rank: 10% in top tenth, 34% in top quarter, 71% in top half
Early decision deadline: N/A, notification date: N/A
Early action deadline: N/A, notification date: N/A
Application deadline (fall): 7/15
Undergraduate student body: 3,332 full time, 1,157 part time; 50% male, 50% female; 0% American Indian, 3% Asian, 9% black, 12% Hispanic, 4% multiracial, 0% Pacific Islander, 70% white, 2% international; 87% from in state; 19% live on campus; 1% of students in fraternities, 1% in sororities

Most popular majors: 9% Business, Management, Marketing, and Related Support Services, 11% Homeland Security, Law Enforcement, Firefighting and Related Protective Services, 8% Psychology, 11% Social Sciences, 9% Visual and Performing Arts
Expenses: 2014-2015: $7,316 in state, $14,889 out of state; room/board: $6,572
Financial aid: (262) 595-2004; 66% of undergrads determined to have financial need

University of Wisconsin–Platteville

Platteville WI
(715) 608-1125
U.S. News ranking: Reg. U. (Mid. W), No. 80
Website: www.uwplatt.edu
Admissions email: admit@uwplatt.edu
Public; founded 1866
Freshman admissions: selective; 2013-2014: 4,030 applied, 3,194 accepted. Either SAT or ACT required. ACT 25/75 percentile: 21-26. High school rank: 11% in top tenth, 36% in top quarter, 74% in top half
Early decision deadline: N/A, notification date: N/A
Early action deadline: N/A, notification date: N/A
Application deadline (fall): rolling
Undergraduate student body: 7,000 full time, 682 part time; 66% male, 34% female; 1% American Indian, 1% Asian, 2% black, 3% Hispanic, 0% multiracial, 0% Pacific Islander, 92% white, 1% international; 77% from in state; N/A live on campus; N/A of students in fraternities, N/A in sororities
Most popular majors: 9% Agriculture, Agriculture Operations, and Related Sciences, 10% Business, Management, Marketing, and Related Support Services, 23% Engineering, 9% Engineering Technologies and Engineering-Related Fields, 12% Homeland Security, Law Enforcement, Firefighting and Related Protective Services
Expenses: 2014-2015: $7,491 in state, $15,064 out of state; room/board: $7,036
Financial aid: (608) 342-1836; 61% of undergrads determined to have financial need

University of Wisconsin–River Falls

River Falls WI
(715) 425-3500
U.S. News ranking: Reg. U. (Mid. W), No. 69
Website: www.uwrf.edu
Admissions email: admit@uwrf.edu
Public; founded 1874
Freshman admissions: selective; 2013-2014: 2,946 applied, 2,138 accepted. Either SAT or ACT required. ACT 25/75 percentile: 20-24. High school rank: 11% in top tenth, 32% in top quarter, 71% in top half
Early decision deadline: N/A, notification date: N/A
Early action deadline: N/A, notification date: N/A
Application deadline (fall): rolling

Undergraduate student body: 5,210 full time, 584 part time; 39% male, 61% female; 0% American Indian, 3% Asian, 1% black, 2% Hispanic, 2% multiracial, 0% Pacific Islander, 90% white, 1% international; 49% from in state; 41% live on campus; 5% of students in fraternities, 4% in sororities
Most popular majors: 18% Agriculture, Agriculture Operations, and Related Sciences, 9% Biological and Biomedical Sciences, 13% Business, Management, Marketing, and Related Support Services, 9% Communication, Journalism, and Related Programs, 15% Education
Expenses: 2014-2015: $7,751 in state, $15,324 out of state; room/board: $6,435
Financial aid: (715) 425-3141; 68% of undergrads determined to have financial need; average aid package $6,855

University of Wisconsin–Stevens Point

Stevens Point WI
(715) 346-2441
U.S. News ranking: Reg. U. (Mid. W), No. 54
Website: www.uwsp.edu
Admissions email: admiss@uwsp.edu
Public; founded 1894
Freshman admissions: selective; 2013-2014: 4,598 applied, 3,690 accepted. Either SAT or ACT required. ACT 25/75 percentile: 21-25. High school rank: 18% in top tenth, 45% in top quarter, 88% in top half
Early decision deadline: N/A, notification date: N/A
Early action deadline: N/A, notification date: N/A
Application deadline (fall): rolling
Undergraduate student body: 8,746 full time, 546 part time; 48% male, 52% female; 0% American Indian, 2% Asian, 1% black, 3% Hispanic, 2% multiracial, 0% Pacific Islander, 89% white, 2% international; N/A from in state; 38% live on campus; 2% of students in fraternities, 2% in sororities
Most popular majors: 9% Biology/Biological Sciences, General, 9% Business Administration and Management, General, 10% Education, General, 13% Natural Resources/Conservation, General, 10% Social Sciences, General
Expenses: 2014-2015: $7,642 in state, $15,215 out of state; room/board: $6,794
Financial aid: (715) 346-4771; 61% of undergrads determined to have financial need; average aid package $8,759

University of Wisconsin–Stout

Menomonie WI
(715) 232-1411
U.S. News ranking: Reg. U. (Mid. W), No. 65
Website: www.uwstout.edu
Admissions email: admissions@uwstout.edu
Public; founded 1891

Freshman admissions: selective; 2013-2014: 3,355 applied, 2,766 accepted. Either SAT or ACT required. ACT 25/75 percentile: 20-24. High school rank: 9% in top tenth, 28% in top quarter, 65% in top half
Early decision deadline: N/A, notification date: N/A
Early action deadline: N/A, notification date: N/A
Application deadline (fall): rolling
Undergraduate student body: 6,779 full time, 1,401 part time; 53% male, 47% female; 0% American Indian, 3% Asian, 1% black, 1% Hispanic, 3% multiracial, 0% Pacific Islander, 88% white, 2% international; 68% from in state; 40% live on campus; 2% of students in fraternities, 3% in sororities
Most popular majors: 41% Business, Management, Marketing, and Related Support Services, 9% Education, 7% Engineering Technologies and Engineering-Related Fields, 6% Health Professions and Related Programs, 10% Visual and Performing Arts
Expenses: 2014-2015: $9,025 in state, $16,771 out of state; room/board: $6,434
Financial aid: (715) 232-1363; 61% of undergrads determined to have financial need; average aid package $10,818

University of Wisconsin–Superior

Superior WI
(715) 394-8230
U.S. News ranking: Reg. U. (Mid. W), No. 99
Website: www.uwsuper.edu
Admissions email: admissions@uwsuper.edu
Public; founded 1893
Freshman admissions: selective; 2013-2014: 910 applied, 605 accepted. Either SAT or ACT required. ACT 25/75 percentile: 19-24. High school rank: 10% in top tenth, 17% in top quarter, 73% in top half
Early decision deadline: N/A, notification date: N/A
Early action deadline: N/A, notification date: N/A
Application deadline (fall): 8/1
Undergraduate student body: 2,018 full time, 504 part time; 40% male, 60% female; 3% American Indian, 1% Asian, 2% black, 2% Hispanic, 3% multiracial, 0% Pacific Islander, 84% white, 6% international; 55% from in state; 28% live on campus; N/A of students in fraternities, N/A in sororities
Most popular majors: 21% Business, Management, Marketing, and Related Support Services, 12% Communication, Journalism, and Related Programs, 15% Education, 10% Multi/Interdisciplinary Studies, 8% Visual and Performing Arts
Expenses: 2014-2015: $7,240 in state, $14,813 out of state; room/board: $6,320
Financial aid: (715) 394-8200; 70% of undergrads determined to have financial need; average aid package $11,604

University of Wisconsin–Whitewater

Whitewater WI
(262) 472-1440
U.S. News ranking: Reg. U. (Mid. W), No. 48
Website: www.uww.edu
Admissions email: uwwadmit@mail.uww.edu
Public; founded 1868
Freshman admissions: selective; 2013-2014: 6,879 applied, 4,809 accepted. Either SAT or ACT required. ACT 25/75 percentile: 20-24. High school rank: 7% in top tenth, 30% in top quarter, 72% in top half
Early decision deadline: N/A, notification date: N/A
Early action deadline: N/A, notification date: N/A
Application deadline (fall): rolling
Undergraduate student body: 9,889 full time, 975 part time; 49% male, 51% female; 0% American Indian, 2% Asian, 5% black, 4% Hispanic, 2% multiracial, 0% Pacific Islander, 86% white, 1% international; 85% from in state; 43% live on campus; 49% of students in fraternities, 51% in sororities
Most popular majors: Information not available
Expenses: 2014-2015: $7,578 in state, $15,151 out of state; room/board: $6,050
Financial aid: (262) 472-1130; 63% of undergrads determined to have financial need; average aid package $8,045

Viterbo University[1]

La Crosse WI
(608) 796-3010
U.S. News ranking: Reg. U. (Mid. W), No. 109
Website: www.viterbo.edu
Admissions email: admission@viterbo.edu
Private
Application deadline (fall): N/A
Undergraduate student body: N/A full time, N/A part time
Expenses: 2013-2014: $23,330; room/board: $7,710
Financial aid: (608) 796-3900

Wisconsin Lutheran College

Milwaukee WI
(414) 443-8811
U.S. News ranking: Nat. Lib. Arts, No. 178
Website: www.wlc.edu
Admissions email: admissions@wlc.edu
Private; founded 1973
Affiliation: Wisconsin Evangelical Lutheran Synod
Freshman admissions: selective; 2013-2014: 870 applied, 553 accepted. Either SAT or ACT required. ACT 25/75 percentile: 21-27. High school rank: 19% in top tenth, 44% in top quarter, 75% in top half
Early decision deadline: N/A, notification date: N/A
Early action deadline: N/A, notification date: N/A
Application deadline (fall): rolling

Undergraduate student body: 1,002 full time, 68 part time; 47% male, 53% female; 1% American Indian, 1% Asian, 6% black, 5% Hispanic, 2% multiracial, 0% Pacific Islander, 83% white, 3% international; 78% from in state; 60% live on campus; 0% of students in fraternities, 0% in sororities
Most popular majors: 25% Business, Management, Marketing, and Related Support Services, 14% Communication, Journalism, and Related Programs, 9% Health Professions and Related Programs, 8% Psychology, 9% Visual and Performing Arts
Expenses: 2014-2015: $25,960; room/board: $8,900
Financial aid: (414) 443-8856; 81% of undergrads determined to have financial need; average aid package $19,114

WYOMING

University of Wyoming

Laramie WY
(307) 766-5160
U.S. News ranking: Nat. U., No. 161
Website: www.uwyo.edu
Admissions email: Why-wyo@uwyo.edu
Public; founded 1886
Freshman admissions: selective; 2013-2014: 4,348 applied, 4,154 accepted. Either SAT or ACT required. ACT 25/75 percentile: 22-27. High school rank: 23% in top tenth, 50% in top quarter, 82% in top half
Early decision deadline: N/A, notification date: N/A
Early action deadline: N/A, notification date: N/A
Application deadline (fall): 8/10
Undergraduate student body: 8,255 full time, 1,862 part time; 47% male, 53% female; 1% American Indian, 1% Asian, 1% black, 6% Hispanic, 2% multiracial, 0% Pacific Islander, 81% white, 4% international; 69% from in state; 23% live on campus; 5% of students in fraternities, 5% in sororities
Most popular majors: 4% Business Administration and Management, General, 4% Criminal Justice/Safety Studies, 8% Elementary Education and Teaching, 5% Psychology, General, 10% Registered Nursing/Registered Nurse
Expenses: 2014-2015: $4,646 in state, $14,876 out of state; room/board: $9,755
Financial aid: (307) 766-2116; 48% of undergrads determined to have financial need; average aid package $9,119

Webster University, MO
27, 101, 145, D-77
Welch
College, TN   110, D-131
Wellesley College, MA
82, 178, 183, D-64
Wells
College, NY   87, 182, D-97
Wentworth Institute
of Technology, MA
108, 145, D-64
Wesleyan College, GA   86, D-32
Wesleyan
University, CT   82, 178, D-21
Wesley College, DE   109, D-22
West Chester University of
Pennsylvania   94, 144, D-122
Western Carolina University, NC
99, 106, 128, 133, D-102
Western Colorado
State University   96, D-21
Western Governors
University, UT   D-139
Western Illinois University
101, 106, 130, 133, D-39
Western International
University, AZ   D-6
Western Kentucky University
99, 106, 132, 133, D-51
Western Michigan
University   76, D-69

Western Nevada College   D-80
Western New England
University, MA   94, D-64
Western New Mexico
University   D-85
Western Oregon
University   105, D-113
Western State Colorado
University   89, D-19
Western Washington University
104, 106, 145, D-147
Westfield State
University, MA   96, 128, D-64
West Liberty
University, WV   110, D-148
Westminster
College, MO   87, 142, D-77
Westminster
College, PA   86, D-122
Westminster College, UT
104, 145, 180, D-140
Westmont
College, CA   86, 142, D-17
West Texas A&M
University   105, D-138
West Virginia State
University   89, 117, D-149
West Virginia
University   76, 140, D-149
West Virginia
University–Parkersburg   D-149

West Virginia Wesleyan
College   109, 180, D-149
Wheaton
College, IL   84, D-39
Wheaton
College, MA   84, 142, D-64
Wheeling Jesuit University, WV
109, 132, D-149
Wheelock
College, MA   94, D-64
Whitman College, WA
82, 183, D-147
Whittier
College, CA   86, D-17
Whitworth University, WA
104, 180, D-147
Wichita State
University, KS   80, D-49
Widener
University, PA   78, D-122
Wilberforce University, OH
113, 117, D-108
Wiley
College, TX   114, 117, D-139
Wilkes
University, PA   94, D-122
Willamette University, OR
84, 142, D-113
William Carey
University, MS   99, 145
180, 183, D-73

William Jewell
College, MO   87, 142, D-77
William Paterson University
of New Jersey   96, D-84
William Peace
University, NC   89, D-102
William Penn
University, IA   113, D-46
Williams Baptist
College, AR   110, D-8
Williams College, MA
27, 82, 178, 183, D-64
William Woods University, MO
102, 133, 183, D-77
Wilmington
College, OH   112, D-108
Wilmington
University, DE   130, D-22
Wilson
College, PA   108, 180, D-123
Wingate
University, NC   99, 180, D-102
Winona State
University, MN   101, D-72
Winston-Salem
State University, NC
99, 116, D-102
Winthrop
University, SC   98, 106, D-127
Wisconsin Lutheran
College   88, 142, D-152

Wittenberg
University, OH   87, 142, D-108
Wofford College, SC
86, 142, 178, D-127
Woodbury
University, CA   104, D-17
Worcester Polytechnic
Institute, MA   74, 122, D-64
Worcester State
University, MA   96, D-65
Wright State
University, OH   80, 130, D-108

X, Y

Xavier University, OH
100, 145, D-108
Xavier University of
Louisiana   88, 116, D-53
Yale University, CT   26, 27, 72
122, 178, 183, D-22
Yeshiva
University, NY   72, 178, D-97
York
College, NE   113, D-79
York College of
Pennsylvania   94, D-123
Youngstown State
University, OH   103, D-109